Herndon's Informants

HERNDON'S INFORMANTS

Letters, Interviews, and Statements

about Abraham Lincoln

Edited by Douglas L. Wilson
and Rodney O. Davis

With the assistance of Terry Wilson

University of Illinois Press
Urbana and Chicago

Publication of this book was supported by grants from the
Abraham Lincoln Association; from the New Salem Lincoln League;
and from the Illinois State Historical Society, in memory of
King V. Hostick, a student of Lincoln and benefactor of the Society.

This book is printed on acid-free paper.

The portrait of William H. Herndon on p. ii appears courtesy of the
Illinois State Historical Society. The map on p. 428 appears courtesy of
the Huntington Library.

Library of Congress Cataloging-in-Publication Data

Herndon's informants : letters, interviews, and statements about
Abraham Lincoln / edited by Douglas L. Wilson and Rodney O. Davis
with the assistance of Terry Wilson.
    p.   cm.
    Letters, interviews, and statements collected by William H. Herndon
and Jesse W. Weik.
    Includes bibliographical references and index.
    ISBN 0-252-02328-5 (cloth : alk. paper)
    1. Lincoln, Abraham, 1809–1865—Archives. 2. Herndon, William
Henry, 1818–1891—Archives. 3. Weik, Jesse William, 1857–1930—
Archives.   I. Wilson, Douglas L.   II. Davis, Rodney O.   III. Wilson,
Terry, 1956– .   IV. Herndon, William Henry, 1818–1891.   V. Weik,
Jesse William, 1857–1930.   VI. Title: Informants.
E457.H59   1998
973.7'092—dc21   97-1448
                                                          CIP

Contents

Preface

This work makes available for the first time all the known letters, interviews, and statements about Abraham Lincoln collected by his law partner, William H. Herndon. It includes those items collected by Jesse W. Weik while working as Herndon's collaborator, but it does not include the very extensive array of documents that contain Herndon's own personal recollections of Lincoln, a body of material that would probably be at least as large as the present one.

Herndon's purpose in making this collection was to gather material for a biography of Lincoln, but a very substantial portion thereof could not be accommodated in the book that was finally published in 1889. Some of the material was thought to be inappropriate for a Victorian biography; some of it was deemed to be in error or doubtful or otherwise at odds with the portrait presented; and some was doubtless considered redundant, superfluous, or of little importance. But the passage of time inevitably alters the basis of such judgments, so that questions of what is appropriate, doubtful, or unimportant must always recur. Weik drew heavily on the unused material in his own book *The Real Lincoln* (1922), and Albert J. Beveridge made massive use of Herndon's informant material, before it became available to scholars in general, in his authoritative biography *Abraham Lincoln, 1809–1858* (1928). Yet in spite of its recognized standing as "the basic source for Abraham Lincoln's early years,"[1] Herndon's collection has never been presented in its entirety—until now.

The nature and extent of Herndon's project and the character of the testimony contained in the documents he collected have been the subject of considerable discussion and controversy. While the editors have their own views on these disputed issues, some of which are touched on in the introduction, the present work is not offered as a brief for a particular assessment of Herndon and his informants but rather is concerned with solving the problem of access. Full access to the documents in Herndon's archive has proved so problematic as to preclude wide exposure to the documents and a thorough exploitation of their contents. Not only are the collections difficult to navigate and the documents hard to read, but the original collection has been scattered and part of it lost. To maximize access and to enhance the reader's ability to understand and evaluate the testimony are therefore the major aims of this edition. Accordingly, this work includes, in addition to all the known texts, editorial annotation of certain matters that may cause readers

---

1. David Herbert Donald, *Lincoln* (New York: Simon and Schuster, 1995), 603.

difficulty. It includes a register of informants, consisting of brief biographical sketches of the people whose testimony about Lincoln came into Herndon's hands. The work also contains an appendix by Paul H. Verduin that presents, in outline form, a brief genealogy of the Hanks family.

The editors have enjoyed very extensive assistance over the course of this project, much of which is detailed in the acknowledgments, but some debts are in a special category, and we wish to acknowledge those here. It has been our good fortune to be fellow members of the faculty at Knox College when this project was conceived and carried out. A firm commitment to faculty research and a willingness to support it have been the rule at Knox during our long tenure, and we remain grateful to the institution and to the deans who faithfully supported us, John Strassburger and Stephen Bailey. Timely and generous support also came from the fund provided by John E. and Elaine Fellowes to sustain the professional activities of the Knox College English department. We have also had the benefit of outstanding work from committed student research assistants: Matt Norman, Dawn Campbell, Frank Doane, Chris Stratton, and Susan Han. Finally, we have attempted, by listing his name on the title page, to indicate the very extensive support and collaboration in research that we have received from our colleague in the Knox College Library, Terry Wilson.

It remains only to acknowledge the indispensable contribution of our wives, Sharon E. Wilson and Norma G. Davis, who shared the burdens and kept the faith.

Acknowledgments

The obligations that we have incurred defy a full accounting, for the scope and duration of this project have been such that our indebtedness has multiplied beyond our ability to properly record it. While we recognize this delinquency, we nonetheless take pleasure in acknowledging those obligations of which we are most keenly aware.

By far the largest portion of the letters and interviews gathered by William H. Herndon are in the Herndon-Weik Collection at the Library of Congress, and we pay tribute to the steadfast support and assistance of the staff of the Manuscript Division during our numerous visits. Oliver Orr helped launch the project by providing valuable assistance at the earliest stages, and John R. Sellers has faithfully aided us at every step along the way. To Mary Wolfskill and her helpful staff in the Manuscript Reading Room we owe a special debt of gratitude. James Gilreath, of the Rare Book Division, lent his considerable expertise and support, and for welcome hospitality during our sojourns in Washington we add thanks to Emily Gilreath.

The Huntington Library generously provided fellowships for our study of the important Herndon and Lincoln-related materials in the Ward Hill Lamon Papers and elsewhere. Martin Ridge, John Rhodehamel, Paul M. Zall, Virginia Renner, Robert Skotheim, and the late William Moffitt were all very supportive of our project and helped in various ways to make our visits to that great institution extraordinarily productive.

Some Herndon materials are in the Weik Papers at the Illinois State Historical Library, whose former director, Janice Petterchak, cheerfully and promptly responded to many queries and where Cheryl Schnirring in the Manuscript Department obliged us when our schedules were tight. Thomas F. Schwartz, curator of the Library's Henry Horner Lincoln Collection, State Historian of Illinois, and coordinator of the Abraham Lincoln Symposium, offered us early opportunities to speak about this project and its progress and kindly made some of his own unpublished work on Lincoln available to us. For these and many other valuable services we stand greatly in his debt.

At the Filson Club in Louisville, the splendid repository of Kentuckiana, we are under obligation to James Holmberg, Mark Wetherington, and Dorothy Rush. At the Willard Library in Evansville, where many of the records of the Southern Indiana Lincoln Inquiry are kept, we owe much to Lynn Martin, Susy Kiefer and Carol M. Bartelt.

The Knox College Library was an indispensable resource for us, particularly its special collections on the Civil War and the Old Northwest. The library was our major workplace as we brought this project to completion, and we are especially grateful to Jeffrey Douglas, Sharon Clayton, Carley Robison, Bonnie Niehus, Irene Ponce, and Kay Vander Meulen. The collection of Illinois local history materials at the Galesburg Public Library proved a rich resource, and Enid Hanks was untiring in aiding us in our numerous visits there.

Other libraries and librarians that offered aid and earned our gratitude include the Charleston, Illinois, Public Library: Barbara Krehbiel; the Illinois Historical Survey at the library of the University of Illinois at Urbana-Champaign: John Hoffmann; the Lincoln Library at Springfield, Illinois: Ed Russo; the Peoria Public Library: Elaine Pichaske; the River Bluffs Regional Library, St. Joseph, Missouri: Sue Horvath; the Thomas Balch Library, Leesburg, Virginia; and the Petersburg, Illinois, Public Library.

Lincoln's memory is perpetuated at a number of historic sites and commemorative institutions across the country. We found cordial assistance to be the rule at the Lincoln Boyhood National Memorial in Indiana, where Jerry Sanders and William Bartelt were our hosts. Mr. Bartelt has continued to serve us in a variety of ways. The same welcome has always been forthcoming at the Lincoln Home National Historic Site in Springfield, where the late George Painter and Linda Norbut Suits were especially helpful. At the Historic Sites Division of the Illinois Historic Preservation Agency and at Lincoln's New Salem State Park, Mark Johnson, James Patton, and Richard Taylor have answered our queries and shared their own research and other resources on Lincoln's early years in Illinois. The assistance of Cullom Davis and William Beard of the Lincoln Legals Project has been indispensable in attempting to make sense of the allusions to Lincoln's legal career. Leo Landis at the Conner Prairie Museum in Indiana answered an important question about plows used during Lincoln's lifetime.

Numerous historical and genealogical society officers have responded to our inquiries since the early 1990s, as we have sought information about some of Herndon's over 260 informants. They include the Cass County, Illinois, Historical Society: Mary Ann Bell; the Cincinnati Historical Society: Anne B. Shepherd; the Clackamas County, Oregon, Family History Society: Sandy McGuire; the Clinton County, Illinois, Historical Society; the Historical Society of Quincy and Adams County, Illinois: Philip Germann; the McLean County, Illinois, Genealogical Society: Joy Craig; the Madison County, Illinois, Historical Society: Deanna Kohlburn; the Madison County, Iowa, Historical Society: Lorraine Kile; the Maryland Historical Society: Mrs. I. W. Athey; the Rock County, Wisconsin, Historical Society: Maurice Montgomery; the St. Clair County, Illinois, Historical Society: Diane Kenner Walsh; the Sangamon County, Illinois, Genealogical Society: Wayne Temple and Jacqueline Stites; the Spencer County, Indiana, Historical Society: Becky Middleton; and the Tazewell County, Illinois, Genealogical Society: Lorie Bergerhouse. We also acknowledge the assistance of the University Archives at the University of Illinois: Robert T. Chapel; the Oberlin College Archives:

Brian A. Williams; the Central Illinois Conference, United Methodist Church: Richard Chrisman; and the Office of Congressman Lane Evans, 17th District of Illinois.

Some of our Knox College colleagues kindly answered our calls for help and provided much-needed expertise: Lance Factor, Mikiso Hane, Edward Niehus, Jorge Prats, Dennis Schneider, and Ross Vander Meulen. Such interdisciplinary collaboration is routine at Knox College, and it is one of the reasons why we have found it such a rewarding place to teach and work.

Paul Verduin has spent several years working through the maze of Hanks family genealogy, and he has generously shared his findings with us. We are especially grateful that he agreed to permit a brief outline of the Hanks genealogy to appear as an appendix in this work. James Harvey Young helped us with some nineteenth-century medical and pharmacological terminology. Michael Burlingame unselfishly shared important materials that were of great benefit and supported the project in many ways. We are especially grateful to him and to our friends and fellow scholars Robert Bray, Robert Johannsen, Mark Plummer, and Terence A. Tanner for the advice and encouragement that they have provided.

Three organizations have provided financial support in the form of subventions toward the costs of publication: the Abraham Lincoln Association, the Illinois State Historical Society, and the New Salem Lincoln League. We are honored that the officers and members of these organizations chose to endorse our efforts in this unequivocal form, and we thank them for their vote of confidence.

We must acknowledge the genealogical help that has been tendered by diligent and generous family historians across the country: Marilyn G. Ames, Champaign, Illinois; Janet H. Anderson, Houston, Texas; David Braswell, Belleville, Illinois; Lola G. Clark, Kilbourne, Illinois; Marie T. Eberle, Edwardsville, Illinois; Anna J. Foley, Greensburg, Indiana; Genevieve Goodpasture, Victoria, Texas; Phyllis Hodgen Hansen, Springfield, Illinois; Barbara Hevron, Newburg, Indiana; Margaret Hohimer, Springfield, Illinois; Mark D. Irwin, Belleville, Illinois; James P. Jones, Raleigh, North Carolina; Eileen R. Keithley, Bath, Illinois; James Steven Miles, Chicago, Illinois; James E. Remer, Leawood, Kansas; Rosella H. Rogers, Petersburg, Illinois; George E. Ross, Sandoval, Illinois; Star W. Rowland, Sterling, Virginia; Mary McMillion Sauerhage, Mascoutah, Illinois; Wendy Saul, Baltimore, Maryland; Ora E. Strom, Medford, Oregon; Debbie Walker, Omaha, Nebraska; William Reese Walker, Hot Springs Village, Arkansas; Judith L. Weber, Greenfield, Iowa; Jean Stevens Wiggin, Palm Coast, Florida; Frances M. Winston, Las Vegas, Nevada; and Elfred W. Worms, Belleville, Illinois.

Finally, we are grateful to the staff of the University of Illinois Press and in particular to Richard L. Wentworth, director of the Press, and Theresa L. Sears, managing editor.

Introduction

Facts are said to be the building blocks of history. For those living in an age where virtually everyone leaves a paper trail through government agencies, public schools, and local newspapers, documentation of the rudimentary facts of life is taken for granted, and the challenge of reconstructing the past is presumed to lie principally, if not exclusively, in the selection and interpretation of factual evidence. But for Abraham Lincoln's early life, documentary records and verifiable facts are difficult to come by, and the serious student is forced to come to terms with something more challenging and mercurial: the personal testimony and recollections of those who knew him. The present work brings to publication the richest and most extensive collection of such material.

How this collection came into being, what it contains, and why it is only now being published in a scholarly edition is a complicated story that began soon after the assassination of President Lincoln in mid-April 1865. It involves the character and career of what has been called "one of the first extensive oral history projects in American history,"[1] an effort which began as part of an attempt to write a more personal and revealing kind of biography but which succeeded in raising a cloud of controversy that has never receded. The motives of the persons involved, the competence of the witnesses, and the reliability of the testimony are issues that still swirl in the winds of debate. There is no disagreement, however, that at the center of the story—and the controversy—stands William H. Herndon.

Within a few weeks of the assassination of President Lincoln in April 1865, Herndon conceived the idea to write something about his old friend. The two men had been closely associated as partners in the Springfield firm of Lincoln and Herndon since 1843 and had known each other for several years before that. When Herndon tried out his literary aspirations on certain knowledgeable friends, they encouraged him to capitalize on his intimate personal knowledge of Lincoln's career.[2] But Herndon seems to have decided very early that what he wanted to offer to the world was something other than a memoir. On May 26 he wrote to the prospective biographer Josiah G. Holland: "When you were in my office I casual-

---

1. Charles B. Strozier, *Lincoln's Quest for Union: Public and Private Meanings* (New York: Basic Books, 1981), xvi.
2. See the letters of John L. Scripps (§1) and Horace White (§32).

ly informed you that it was my intention to write & publish the *subjective* Mr
Lincoln — 'The inner life' of Mr L." What he meant by this Herndon went on to
explain in his inimitable style: "I am writing Mr L's life — a short little thing —
giving him in his passions — appetites — & affections — perceptions — memories — judgements — understanding — will, acting under & by motions, just as
he lived, breathed — ate & laughed in this world, clothed in flesh & sinew — bone
& nerve."[3]

This sounds ambitious, if not grandly presumptuous, but Herndon thought
his close association with the fallen president in the practice of law had given him
an opportunity to observe Lincoln's mind and personality that was afforded no one
else. Nor was he alone in his thinking, for his correspondents frequently pointed
this out. What may have been the first letter he received on the subject of his proposed biography began: "I am glad you design giving us something about Lincoln.
Your long acquaintance and close association with him must have given you a clearer insight into his character than other men obtained."[4] The remark of a lawyer
and congressman from Menard County, and the son of one of Lincoln's former
New Salem neighbors, is fairly typical: "Your long association with Mr Lincoln in
business — in the same office, your knowledge of his opinions expressed on the
various subjects political religious social &c which came up in his daily conversation with you during that time & your personal acquaintance with his early associates enables you above all others to give a true & faithful story of his life."[5]

But Herndon was apparently not content to retail his own impressions where
Lincoln's early life was concerned. He seems to have had a passion for getting at
what he called "the facts," which is presumably what led him to embark at once
upon a series of inquiries, not just in Illinois, but in Kentucky, where Lincoln had
been born, and southwestern Indiana, where he grew up. When Herndon set out
at the end of May on his first fact-finding trip to Menard County, his announced
object was to search "for *the facts & truths* of Lincoln's life — not fictions — not
fables — not floating rumors, but *facts — solid facts & well attested truths.*"[6]

It is distinctly ironic that many of the "facts" that Herndon found so "solid"
and "well attested" would one day be regarded as the "fictions" and "fables" he was
trying to supplant, for Herndon was already reacting to the public's growing tendency to mythologize his former partner. He began purposefully and energetically to compile information for an account that would expose to the world not a
sainted martyr but the real man. The excited letter he wrote to Holland upon his
return suggests that he was unprepared for what he had found: "I have 'been down'
to Menard County where Mr L first landed and where he first made his home in
old Sangamon. . . . From such an investigation — from records — from friends
— old deeds & surveys &c &c I am satisfied, in Connection with my own Knowledg of Mr L. for 30 years, that Mr Ls whole Early life *remains to be written.*"[7]

3. WHH to Josiah G. Holland, May 26, 1865, Holland Papers, NYPL.
4. John L. Scripps to WHH, May 9, 1865 (§1).
5. T. W. McNeely to WHH, Nov. 28, 1866 (§313).
6. WHH to Josiah G. Holland, June 8, 1865, Holland Papers, NYPL.
7. Ibid.

Herndon's astonishment was undoubtedly genuine. He thought he had known his law partner well, so well that he was prepared to write his subjective, inner life. And since he also knew personally many of the Menard County residents he had interviewed, he was apparently amazed to discover from their stories of Lincoln in New Salem that he had actually known very little about his great partner's formative years. This seems to have intensified his zeal for discovery, for he proceeded to generate a whirlwind of investigative activity. In the early summer of 1865, he sent out scores of letters to people who had known Lincoln, he interviewed knowledgeable friends and associates who were closer at hand, and he systematically established contacts for the purpose of gathering information in far-off places such as Kentucky, Indiana, and even Virginia. Within a few months, in addition to his prolific correspondence and local interviewing in the Springfield area, Herndon had traveled to Chicago to interview Lincoln's cousins, John and Dennis Hanks; to Coles County, Illinois, to interview Lincoln's stepmother and other relatives; and to southwest Indiana, where he interviewed many of Lincoln's boyhood friends and neighbors.

Neglecting his law practice and other responsibilities, Herndon kept up this strenuous pace of investigation for nearly two years. When he was unable to go himself, he sent others to secure testimony.[8] To help track down witnesses and check out leads in Menard County, his most productive venue, he enlisted the aid of his father-in-law, G. U. Miles. In one letter Herndon wrote: "It is said in one of Mr Lincolns biographies that he attended a debating society in New Salem? Was there such a society & did Lincoln ever speak in it? Get all the facts & write to me. It is said that Mr Lincoln when elected to the Legislature in 1834–36 — & 1838 walked to Vandalia afoot? Is this true? Get all the facts — See Carman — Bails and others."[9] Miles performed many such errands, though he apparently had reservations about Herndon's prying so deeply into private matters. Reporting on his efforts in Herndon's behalf in the investigation of Lincoln's love affair with Ann Rutledge, Miles wrote: "the above statements I think you may rely on but if you Should undertake to write a history of my life after I am dead I dont want you to inquire So close into my Early courtships as you do of Mr Lincolns."[10]

The more Herndon corresponded and interviewed, the more surprising things he learned; and the more he learned, the more he became convinced that he had uncovered important information about Lincoln's early life that bore significantly on the formation of his character, and thus on his later accomplishments. If what his informants were telling him was true, the man whom a grieving nation was rapidly raising to sainthood had actually been born of doubtful parentage; he had been subject to deep and even tragic disappointments in love; he had been subject to bouts of mental derangement and had been suicidal on more than one occasion; he had been a rank unbeliever in religion and had openly ridiculed the

---

8. See, for example, the testimony solicited by John Miles (§3), Erastus Wright (§16), and J. W. Wartmann (§62).

9. WHH to G. U. Miles, Dec. 1, 1865, HW.

10. G. U. Miles to WHH, Mar. 23, 1866 (§178).

tenets of Christianity; he had proposed marriage to several women, and after becoming engaged to his future wife, Mary Todd, had fallen in love with someone
else; and after a long period of guilt and indecision, he had finally given himself
up to a loveless marriage to satisfy his sense of honor.

Nearly all of this was news to Herndon, who soon realized that the picture he
was in the process of putting together was scandalously at odds with what other
biographers had presented and with what the worshiping public had come to expect. When he tried out some of his findings on the public in November 1866—
in a lecture on Lincoln's tragic courtship of Ann Rutledge—he tactlessly gave offense by urging his own hypothesis that Ann's untimely death was a principal source
of Lincoln's lifelong melancholy and that Ann herself was the only woman Lincoln had ever loved.[11] When critics and friends alike objected that he was treating
subjects that should be left alone, he justified his approach with a doctrine of "necessary truth." It held that private and inappropriate to published biography as
certain facts or conditions might ordinarily be considered, they were *necessary* to
the understanding of Lincoln's character, which in turn was the key to what the
man had ultimately accomplished. Defending himself to a friend, Herndon wrote:
"All truths are necessary that show, explain, or throw light on Mr. Lincoln's mind,
nature, quality, characteristics, thoughts, acts and deeds, because he [suppressed]
the Rebellion . . . and guided the grandest of Revolutions through its grand con-
sumation."[12]

Knowing that he had additional revelations to make, even more unwelcome
and potentially disruptive than the Ann Rutledge story, gave Herndon serious
pause. Especially the ambiguous and inconsistent nature of the testimony he collected about Lincoln's paternity, from Kentucky informants he did not know and
whom he had never questioned face-to-face, seems to have contributed to his inability to complete a draft of his biography.[13] Herndon knew only too well the
traditional fate of the messenger bringing unwelcome news. "Would to God the
world Knew what I do," he wrote to his young correspondent Charles H. Hart,
"and save me the necessity of being the man to open and Explain all."[14] A short
time later he complained to Hart: "Mr Lincoln is hard to get at — ie it will take
so much talk — Explanation &c to get him properly before the world, that I almost despair."[15]

Herndon's plan was to draft his biography in 1867, but with the death of his
father in that year and his subsequent inheritance of a substantial farm, Herndon
let his biographical project languish. In 1869, under serious financial pressure, he

11. Herndon's lecture, "ABRAHAM LINCOLN. MISS ANN RUTLEDGE. NEW SALEM. PIONEER-
ING AND *THE* POEM" was delivered on November 16, 1866, and distributed as a broadside. It has been
reprinted in William H. Herndon, *Lincoln and Ann Rutledge and the Pioneers of New Salem* (Herrin, Ill.:
Trovillion Private Press, 1945).

12. WHH to Isaac N. Arnold, Nov. 20, 1866, in Hertz, 38–39. For a fuller treatment of Herndon's
doctrine of "necessary truth," see Wilson, 37–52.

13. See Wilson, 40–41, 46–47.

14. WHH to Charles H. Hart, Dec. 12, 1866, Lamon Papers, HL.

15. WHH to Charles H. Hart, Dec. 28, 1866, Lamon Papers, HL.

sold transcriptions of his collected materials, which he referred to as his "Lincoln Record," to Lincoln's friend Ward Hill Lamon and deferred his biography indefinitely.[16]

Although he continued, in the years that followed, to supply information about Abraham Lincoln to a great variety of correspondents, occasionally being drawn into public controversy, Herndon did not seriously resume his own biographical investigations until the mid-1880s, when he entered into a collaboration with one of his correspondents, Jesse W. Weik. Weik was a native of Greencastle, Indiana, who had boldly written Herndon for a Lincoln autograph in 1875, the year he graduated from college. The two met in 1882 when Weik was assigned to Springfield as a government pension agent, and a friendship developed between the aging law partner of Lincoln and the aspiring young writer, who was an admirer of both. Just before Weik returned to Indiana in 1885, the two men began a collaboration to produce a biography for which Herndon would supply most of the documentation and opinion and Weik would do most of the writing.[17]

Herndon began sending Weik a torrent of letters in late 1885, putting down on an almost daily basis incidents and anecdotes about Lincoln as they came to mind. To fill out his picture and clarify some issues, he went back to interviewing some of his old informants and located some new ones as well. Weik also conducted interviews and corresponded with people who had known Lincoln, even traveling to Kentucky for this purpose, something Herndon had never managed to do. From the surviving originals of the letters and interviews Herndon had assembled in the 1860s (some had been lost), from dozens of additional letters and draft material on Lincoln sent by Herndon, and from new letters and interviews, Weik crafted the text of the biography that was published in 1889 as *Herndon's Lincoln: The True Story of a Great Life*. Herndon died in 1891, but not before helping to prepare a revised edition of the biography, with new material, that appeared in 1892.

Most of the testimony assembled in this process by Herndon and Weik relates to Lincoln's life before he became president. They collected accounts of Lincoln's boyhood in Kentucky, his growing to manhood in Indiana, his six years in and around the village of New Salem, his domestic life in Springfield, his career as a practicing politician and officeholder, and his professional life as a successful circuit and state supreme court lawyer. This testimony came not just from a handful of like-minded people but from more than 250 widely differing informants: political allies and adversaries, fellow lawyers and judges, relatives and in-laws, clients and cronies, women to whom he proposed marriage, longtime comrades and erstwhile friends. As this listing suggests, the information imparted is not confined to political and public affairs but relates to the whole spectrum of his pre-presidential life and character.

---

16. See Donald, 250–53.
17. The story of the Herndon-Weik collaboration is told in detail in ibid., 296–321.

The importance of these documents is beyond dispute. Though many biographers wrote about Abraham Lincoln before and in the years immediately following his death, none carried their investigations to the lengths that Herndon did. Indeed, Albert J. Beveridge wrote that he could not recall "another case in history where, immediately after the death of a great personage, the facts of his personal life were collected so carefully, thoroughly and impartially by a lifelong friend and intimate professional associate, as the facts about Lincoln were gathered by William H. Herndon."[18] Even Herndon's biographer, David Donald, who had serious reservations about the testimony Herndon collected, acknowledged its special value: "It is doubtful whether any other biographer of his day had equal opportunities to gather these invaluable reminiscences; certainly no one else collected anything of comparable significance. Without the statements of Dennis Hanks, Mrs. Thomas Lincoln, David Davis, Joseph Gillespie, James Gurley, and a score of others—all given at Herndon's urgent solicitation—our knowledge of Lincoln would be incomparably poorer."[19]

From the time it was first assembled, Herndon's informant archive has been recognized as valuable. Ward Hill Lamon contracted with Herndon in 1869 to pay $4,000 for the transcriptions made by John G. Springer.[20] These materials, which were used as the basis for Lamon's ghostwritten life of Lincoln, published in 1872, are now part of the extensive Lincoln holdings in the Huntington Library in San Marino, California, and consist of transcriptions of virtually everything Herndon had collected up to the end of November 1866. The letters, interviews, and statements on Lincoln obtained from people who knew him constitute the heart of the archive, but what is not usually recognized is that the collection contains much more. Working in Herndon's office during the fall of 1866, Springer transcribed the welter of material that Herndon had amassed, including census data, population figures, resolutions in the legislature, reports on banks and internal improvements, information on early newspapers, court records, and legal documents. From old newspapers Herndon had Springer copy into his "Lincoln Record" articles and editorials, texts of Lincoln's early speeches, accounts of legislative sessions, articles relating to Lincoln's near duel with James Shields, items on his political activities and his debates with Stephen A. Douglas, and reports of his nomination for the presidency. The transcription of a speech Lincoln made in January 1841 resulted in the preservation of a primary source that would otherwise have been lost, since all issues of the newspaper from which Springer copied it have disappeared.[21]

The Springer transcriptions are eloquent testimony to the diligence and magnitude of Herndon's labors, and, though copies, they are useful in many ways to

---

18. Albert J. Beveridge, "Lincoln as His Partner Knew Him," *Literary Digest International Review* 1:33 (Sept. 1923), cited in Donald, 193.

19. Donald, 195.

20. Ibid., 252.

21. See *CW* 1:227–28. Had other rare issues of early Illinois newspapers suffered a similar fate, such things as Lincoln's speech to the Young Men's Lyceum, his temperance address, his Clay eulogy, and his speech before the Scott Club would still survive in Springer's transcripts.

the student of Lincoln's life. For one thing, they are legible, which many of the originals are not. Having been copied in Herndon's office under his supervision, they have considerable authority, as well as great utility, when it comes to deciphering the many passages in the originals that are difficult to read. Another consideration is that a substantial number of originals are no longer to be found. Herndon gives part of the reason when he reports that some were lost in an office fire, some were brazenly stolen by people he allowed to examine them, and some, when stored at his farm, were eaten by mice.[22] Other originals Herndon agreed to return to their owners, such as the detailed records provided him by Allan Pinkerton, soon after to be destroyed in the Great Chicago Fire, relating the discovery and circumvention of the Baltimore plot on President-elect Lincoln's life in February 1861. For such material and for originals that escaped the collection after November 1866, the Springer transcriptions at the Huntington Library represent the only known manuscript version still extant.

After Herndon's death, his collection of Lincoln documents became the property of his collaborator, Jesse W. Weik, who drew on them for his own biographical study, *The Real Lincoln,* published in 1922. Though Weik permitted a few trusted researchers to consult Herndon's materials—Horace White, for his life of Lyman Trumbull, and Joseph Fort Newton, for his book *Lincoln and Herndon,* to name two—he allowed them little exposure and resisted all attempts by others to purchase them.[23] After *The Real Lincoln* was published, Weik conferred the ultimate privilege on his old friend, Albert J. Beveridge, by allowing him not only to take possession of the documents but to photostat and transcribe them at will. Beveridge's access to the testimony of Herndon's informants and the careful and detailed use he made of them are the principal reasons his biography, though unfinished and written nearly seventy years ago, remains the most thorough and authoritative treatment of Lincoln's pre-presidential life.

Many other students of Lincoln were eager to examine Herndon's Lincoln archive during Weik's lifetime, but none of the notable Lincoln biographers of the time, such as Ida M. Tarbell, William E. Barton, or Carl Sandburg, was granted access. When Weik died in 1929, the bulk of the collection was bought by a combine of dealers as a speculation, and after changing hands and remaining on the market for a number of years, the documents were acquired by the Library of Congress in 1941.[24] Sorted and arranged and committed to microfilm in the 1940s, the preponderance of Herndon's informant testimony at long last became available to Lincoln scholars and the public at large.

---

22. See the memorandum appended to an interview with James H. Matheny (§472).

23. For Oliver R. Barrett's unsuccessful attempt at purchase, see Sandburg, 28–29; Joseph Fort Newton, *Lincoln and Herndon* (Cedar Rapids: Torch Press, 1910); Horace White, *The Life of Lyman Trumbull* (Boston and New York: Houghton Mifflin Co., 1913).

24. A portion of Weik's papers, including some of his Herndon material, ended up in the Illinois State Historical Library.

But the microfilm availability of this material has not been a satisfactory solution to the problem of access. When the microfilming of historical documents first came into general use in the 1930s, the historian Julian P. Boyd published an essay declaring that the need for printed editions of such material was henceforth at an end, that the availability of the document itself on microfilm would remove all future need for printed editions.[25] But, as he admitted later, he had badly miscalculated the situation, and within a few years of making this prediction, he himself became the principal editor of the most ambitious of all documentary editions, *The Papers of Thomas Jefferson.*

The Herndon-Weik Collection at the Library of Congress shows the value of documentary editions. For one thing, these handwritten documents are sometimes very hard to locate on the microfilm, the effort often necessitating the scanning of hundreds of documents to locate one. And once located, the documents are frequently very hard to read. The omnipresent hand of Herndon himself, especially when employed in taking down a statement at white heat, can be stubbornly illegible, so that someone unfamiliar with Herndon's hand might spend hours deciphering a single document and still not be sure that the text thus retrieved is accurate. A further difficulty is the uneven visual quality of the microfilm, for not all of the images are sufficiently in focus to be read with confidence.

As countless Lincoln researchers have discovered, there are other problems. The card index prepared by the Library of Congress, for example, is limited to names of letter writers or interviewees and is neither entirely accurate nor complete. The chronological arrangement is unreliable and subject to strange, unaccountable lapses. The individual leaves of letters and interviews are sometimes maddeningly out of order, while leaves of other documents have become widely separated and appear as fugitives or fragments. Some letters and interviews that were collected by Herndon have ended up in the part of the collection given over to the personal papers of Weik. All these difficulties plague the use of a collection that sprawls over several long reels of microfilm. And to crown the confusion, the collection itself has been reorganized, so that the researcher who needs to examine the originals soon discovers that they are currently arranged in a somewhat different order from that on the microfilm. Readers of the present edition are therefore warned that the foliation numbers assigned to the documents by the Library of Congress and duly recorded here do not appear in the microfilm currently available, as they were added to the documents after the film was made.

Another barrier to full and effective use of these documents has been the pall of suspicion that was cast over Herndon and his informant testimony even before the material became generally available. Disturbed by the uncertainties that attend reminiscence as historical evidence and by the way such things as the Ann Rutledge story had taken on too much importance and "usurped the spotlight," the leading Lincoln scholars of the second quarter of the twentieth century, led by Paul

---

25. See Julian P. Boyd, "Some Animadversions on Being Struck by Lightning," *Daedalus* 86 (May 1955): 49–56.

M. Angle and James G. Randall, forcefully called into question the reliability of both Herndon and the evidence given by his informants.[26] Because Herndon's evidence is highly subjective and typically was taken down many years after the events in question, nearly all of this testimony, these critics insisted, is sufficiently susceptible to the fallibility of human memory and other contingencies as to be unreliable as historical evidence.

Taking up the critique of Herndon's efforts, his biographer, David Donald, outlined some of the practical difficulties: "To collect historical data through oral interviews, though sometimes necessary, is always hazardous. The reminiscences of a graybearded grandfather have to be guided or they are likely to become incoherent rambling. Yet in controlling an interview, it is very difficult not to influence the informant. To ask some questions is to suggest the answers desired."[27] These caveats were reinforced by evidence that Herndon did not always write down what was offered to him and that he often had to put down later what he was told. "I did not take down in writing 100th part of what I heard men and women say," Herndon told Weik, "they talked too fast for me, not being a stenographer — Some I conversed with on the roads and other places and had no chance. Things which I did not deem of importance I paid not much attention to, but now I regret it, as I have often wanted the very things that I rejected."[28]

Such considerations seriously dampened confidence in Herndon's informant testimony for succeeding generations of Lincoln scholars. Some went so far as to regard Herndon as hopelessly biased and unscrupulous in his handling of evidence, but the principal concern was the quality and reliability of testimony so heavily based on memory. Randall's judgment of the Ann Rutledge testimony in 1945 would prove the prevailing sentiment:

> The historian must use reminiscence, but he must do so critically. Even close-up evidence is fallible. When it comes through the mists of many years some of it may be true, but a careful writer will check it with known facts. Contradictory reminiscences leave doubt as to what is to be believed; unsupported memories are in themselves insufficient as proof; statements induced under suggestion, or psychological stimulus, as were some of the stories about Lincoln and Ann, call especially for careful appraisal. . . . When faulty memories are admitted the resulting product becomes something other than history; it is no longer to be presented as a genuine record.[29]

The import for Herndon's evidence was clear: testimony that cannot be confirmed by known facts and reminiscence that is in conflict with other testimony need not be admitted to the historical record. Such a judgment, as intended, effectively

---

26. See Paul M. Angle, "Lincoln's First Love?" *Lincoln Centennial Association Bulletin* 9 (Dec. 1, 1927): 1–8; J. G. Randall, "Appendix: Sifting the Ann Rutledge Evidence," *Lincoln the President: Springfield to Gettysburg*, 2 vols. (New York: Dodd, Mead and Co., 1945), 2:321–42.

27. Donald, 195.

28. WHH to JWW, Dec. 13, 1888, HW.

29. Randall, "Appendix: Sifting the Ann Rutledge Evidence," 325.

placed much of what Herndon had collected in historiographical limbo. So successful was this critique among historians and biographers that even though much
of what is known about Lincoln's pre-presidential years comes directly through
Herndon, his name as a biographer has been seriously tarnished, and the evidence
he assembled has for many decades been widely regarded with suspicion.[30]

While the prejudice against Herndon and his informant testimony still pre-
vails, historians and biographers generally are much more open to the type of evidence he collected, and reminiscence no longer needs an elaborate defense as a
historical source. While its liabilities continue to be well understood, its special
importance is more widely recognized, so that reminiscence is nowadays considered essential by the most discerning historians and biographers. In the intervening years, oral history has become a respected subdiscipline of the historical profession, with a canon of its own.[31] From the outset, its practitioners have been
careful to identify the unique character of memory when used as an adjunct to
traditional sources. Oral history has been hailed from its beginnings as an enterprise that has empowered the subliterate or the underdocumented by providing
them a historical voice.[32] Professional practicioners are well apprised of informants'
frequent tendency to confuse events chronologically, or to telescope them, and of
the need to seek corroboration from a number of oral accounts of the same event.[33]
Though they acknowledge the vagaries of memory and emphasize the need to
develop interrogation techniques that will ensure the fullest and most accurate
interviews possible, oral historians have succeeded in demonstrating the value of
reminiscence as an important historical source.[34]

There are, in fact, many indications in the material presented in this edition
and elsewhere that Herndon himself was far from naïve about reminiscence or its
pitfalls. As the readers of this work will soon discover, he frequently questioned
his informants on what he heard from others, checked up on conflicting accounts,
and with certain informants made a point of revisiting their testimony.[35] After
selling copies of his "Lincoln Record" to Ward Hill Lamon, he counseled: "Human memory is uncertain and it is possible that somewhat of my ideas and opinions is made up of rumor and rumor alone. I state this to you to put you on your

30. See Wilson, 21–36.

31. The substance of oral history may be defined as testimony about events and situations that occurred
during the lifetime of the informants. See Jan Vansina, *Oral Tradition as History* (Madison: University of
Wisconsin Press, 1985), 12.

32. Michael Frisch, *A Shared Authority: Essays on the Craft and Meaning of Oral and Public History* (Albany: State University of New York Press, 1990), xviii–xx; Barbara Allen and Linwood Montell, *From Memory to History: Using Oral Sources in Local History Research* (Nashville: American Association for State and
Local History, 1981), 19–22; Cullom Davis, Kathryn Back, and Kay MacLean, *Oral History: From Tape to
Type* (Chicago: American Library Association, 1977), 2–3.

33. Allen and Montell, *From Memory to History,* 26–29, 35–36, 76–77; Vansina, *Oral Tradition as History,* 158–59.

34. Ronald Grele, "Can Anyone over Thirty Be Trusted? A Friendly Critique of Oral History," in *Enve-
lopes of Sound: The Art of Oral History,* ed. Ronald Grele and Studs Terkel (Chicago: Precedent Publishing,
1975), 206; Grele, "Private Memories and Public Presentation: The Art of Oral History," in ibid., 244, 260–
63.

35. See, for example, WHH's queries reflected in letters from Dennis F. Hanks: §§143, 160, 161, 165.

guard as to what I say, and what all men say. Much of the matter is ten years old, and watch all men, weigh well what is said, search for opportunities, casts of mind, education, and veracities. Follow no man simply because he says *so and so*. Follow your records, sharply criticizing as you go."[36]

As this passage suggests, Herndon knew from his own experience how memories can fade and become elusive. When his biography was finally in proofs, for example, he developed a concern about his own first glimpse of Abraham Lincoln and wrote to his collaborator: "Be sure that Lincoln Came all the way up to Bogue's Mill. It *seems* to me that he did and that, I at that time, saw Lincoln, but be sure that I am right. The records [i.e., his letters and interviews, then in Weik's possession] will fix it — it has now been 56 years since I saw what now *Seems* to be the truth to me. Try and get me right. If L Came up to Bogues mill I saw Lincoln & if he did not then I did not see him at Bogues mill."[37] While this dramatizes the precarious qualities of memory, it also demonstrates that Herndon was, to the last, deeply concerned about historical accuracy and more than willing, if the evidence warranted, to have his own memory corrected.

The letters, interviews, and statements included in this edition all relate to William H. Herndon's biographical project, but they are limited, with few exceptions, to those that purport to provide information or informed opinion about Abraham Lincoln. The great majority of these documents were received or taken down by Herndon himself, but his own personal recollections of Lincoln are outside the scope of this work. A respectable number of documents containing informant testimony resulted from the work of his collaborator, Jesse W. Weik. Weik continued his Lincoln inquiries after completion of the collaborative biography, but letters and interviews that he collected are restricted in this work to those acquired in the service of Herndon's overall project, which began in 1865 and ended with publication of the revised edition of their biography in 1892. The materials on Lincoln collected by Weik after that date for other projects are therefore not included. Correspondents who merely supplied copies of Lincoln's letters are ignored. These selection criteria effectively exclude from the present work a very substantial portion of Herndon's and Weik's papers, so that students interested in the progress and details of Herndon's biographical project, in Herndon's own writing on Lincoln, or in the material on Lincoln that Weik acquired after the appearance of the revised edition will need to supplement this edition with a wider array of documents.

Readers of the material presented here will readily perceive that the pertinence and quality of the testimony offered by Herndon's informants vary widely. Not surprisingly, witnesses are often demonstrably wrong in their recollections of fact. Particularly in such unforgiving matters as dates, informants are often in error (though perhaps a more remarkable circumstance is how often they are right). It

---

36. WHH to Ward Hill Lamon, Mar. 6, 1870, Lamon Papers, HL.
37. WHH to JWW, Nov. 10, 1888, HW.

is precisely this known degree of error, together with the notoriously treacherous character of human memory, that makes the assessment and evaluation of such evidence so problematic. Some, but by no means all, of the errors of fact have been noted by the editors. While it is widely agreed among historians and biographers of Lincoln that Herndon's materials must be used carefully and selectively, no clear consensus has emerged on the criteria that should be employed. Don E. Fehrenbacher, a noted Lincoln scholar who has dealt critically with one aspect of this problem—"judging the authenticity of recollected utterances"—has concluded that "there is no simple formula" in such matters and that "every recollection of spoken words is a separate problem in historical method."[38]

The editors' aim has not been to pass judgment on the merits of the evidence but rather to put the students of Lincoln's life into possession of the documents and, where possible, to provide information needed for better understanding and evaluating their content. In addition to annotating certain matters in the text that seem to call for explanation or comment, the editors have attempted to provide, to the extent that it could be located, pertinent biographical information for each informant. This information is in the "Register of Informants" that follows the documents. While the biographical data is often of necessity quite meager, it is offered to aid the reader in gauging the informant's relationship to Lincoln and to the people and events reported on. It goes without saying that, in many instances, much more information is needed to accurately judge the character of the testimony.

In his second lecture on discoveries and inventions, Abraham Lincoln observed that the invention of writing made possible the preservation of information and ideas whose value or usefulness, even if not fully understood at the time, might thereby be realized and exploited by others far into the future. The invention of printing, Lincoln went on to note, vastly extended this benefit to society, for "consequently a thousand minds were brought into the field where there was but one before."[39] Lincoln's insight helps to illustrate the basic purpose and potential value of printing Herndon's informant testimony. Well known and familiar as some of it is, there is much that is unfamiliar or known only through excerpts and inaccurate texts. Making it all available in printed form should dramatically expand its audience, and this, by Lincoln's formula, should make for a wider exposure to whatever clues and indications it might contain for future enhancements of our knowledge and understanding of Abraham Lincoln.

---

38. Don E. Fehrenbacher, *Lincoln in Text and Context: Collected Essays* (Stanford, Calif.: Stanford University Press, 1987), 281.
39. *CW* 3:362.

Editorial Note

Text

The editors have attempted to reproduce the texts of these documents exactly as found—word for word and letter for letter. But the reader is warned that this is not always the straightforward process that it appears. As Roy P. Basler, the most notable Lincoln editor of the twentieth century, wrote: "To record what the eye could see seemed simple enough. With Lincoln's handwriting being what it was, however, the trouble was to know what one saw."[1] And Lincoln's is a reasonably legible hand. Because writers frequently form words without forming discrete and discernible letters, handwritten text is often difficult to transcribe into print. Where this does not pose a problem as to what word was intended, there may still be a question regarding the intended spelling. The difference between a capital and a lowercase letter, though clear and potentially meaningful in print, may be very difficult to discern in a handwritten text. Another consideration is that Herndon's manuscripts contain the expected anomalies of unrevised composition, such as inadvertently dropped or repeated words. In accordance with the editorial plan followed here, even in the cases where the errors are clearly inadvertent—as with misspellings and dropped or repeated words—the document is always rendered as found, errors and all.

The resulting text makes demands on readers that a regularized or modernized text does not. Certain peculiarities of nineteenth-century spelling and punctuation present difficulties. Some of the writers represented here used scarcely any punctuation at all, while others used commas and dashes in profusion and in ways that seem to the modern eye whimsical or strange. Although some writers appear to have had their own fairly consistent system of punctuation—the most obvious being those who used none at all—most simply refused to restrict the comma or the dash or even the period to a fixed use.

Marks clearly intended as punctuation are sometimes ambiguous and might be, for example, taken as representing either a period or a comma. In such cases, the mark is here given a conventional interpretation, so that a mark at the end of a sentence that might be either a comma or a period is rendered in the text as a period. Certain other familiar aspects of nineteenth-century handwriting have been dispensed with.

---

1. Roy P. Basler, ed., *Abraham Lincoln: His Speeches and Writing* (Cleveland and New York: World Publishing Co., 1946), xxv.

The doubled dash, which resembles an equal sign, is rendered as a regular dash; the double underline is treated the same as a single underline and rendered in italic type. Raised letters are lowered to the normal position. Words that have been stricken by the writer are not usually shown, but where considered significant they are either shown as stricken in the text or commented on in the notes.

Square brackets are used to present material absent from the text or unable to be transcribed. When enclosing matter in roman type, square brackets indicate words or letters that the editors believe were originally in the document but have since been obliterated through stain or mutilation. To aid in the deciphering of mutilated documents, bracketed asterisks are used to indicate an estimated number of missing words, so that *[*]* indicates a single missing word, *[*/**]* indicates an estimate of one or two missing words, and *[*/?]* indicates an indeterminate number of missing words. Doubtful readings are given in square brackets in roman type, followed by a question mark. Bracketed material in italic type (such as *[illegible]* for illegible matter) represents editorial insertions.

FORMAT

In the interest of a consistent format, certain elements of the documents are always treated in the same way. In letters, the place and date of the document, where present, are given at the beginning of the text, regardless of where they appear in the document itself. Place and date are given exactly as written, except that the county, when added to the city, is usually ignored. Thus place and date for a letter headed "Charleston, Coles Co. Ills." with the date given at the end of the letter as "Friday, Oct. 25th 1865" is rendered at the beginning of the text as "Charleston, Ills. Oct. 25th 1865." The salutation is always given on the next line. The closing line, such as "Yours truly," and the signature are always printed at the end of the text. The inside address, if any, is omitted, as is the docketing, unless it is the source of the date or is cited in the notes.

SOURCES

The majority of documents presented here are reproduced from originals in the Herndon-Weik Collection at the Library of Congress. These are marked at the end of the entry by the designation *LC,* followed by *HW* and the foliation numbers: for example, *LC: HW2991–94.* The texts of considerably more than half of these originals exist in transcriptions made for William H. Herndon in the fall of 1866 by John G. Springer, now in the Ward Hill Lamon Papers in the Huntington Library. These are indicated by the designation *HL,* followed usually by *LN* and the volume and foliation numbers. Thus the designation *LC: HW2105; HL: LN2408, 2:361–64* signifies that the text is taken from an original document at the Library of Congress *(HW2105)* and that a transcription of this document is found in the Huntington Library *(LN2408, 2:361–64)*, where *LN2408* is the designation for the three bound volumes containing the Springer transcriptions and *2:361–64* indicates that the transcription of *HW2105* is found in the second volume on leaves *361–64*. In cases where no original is known and the text is taken from the Springer transcription, as with the first item in this work, the Huntington Library designation is listed by itself: *HL: LN2408, 2:340–41*. Originals are also found in the Jesse W. Weik Collection in the Illinois State Historical Library, and these are listed as *ISHL: Weik Papers,* followed by the appropriate box number. A very small number of documents come from other sources, which are duly identified following the text.

Dating

For undated documents, a conjectural date is usually printed in italic type within square brackets. Undated documents for which there is a Springer transcription may be presumed to have been written between May 1865 and the end of November 1866; where no more precise indication can be given, the date for these is given as *[1865–66]* and they are ranked alphabetically by informant between November 30 and December 1. Other conjectural dates have been based on evidence such as the paper on which the document was written, the general content, or indicative references in the text. The presence of a question mark indicates a degree of uncertainty about the dating; its absence implies the contrary. In some cases, the date for undated documents has been taken from that given in Herndon and Weik's biography, but as the dates given there are often demonstrably wrong, the editors have exercised restraint in adopting them and urge caution in their use.

Order

The general order of the entries in each of parts 1–4 is chronological. For dated material, the placement is straightforward, but undated documents present a separate problem. Where there is no indication of when the document was written, it is marked *[undated]* and ranked at the end of the category to which it belongs. Documents for which there is evidence only of the year (as when an informant's age is given) are ranked after dated documents from that year. Where there is evidence of the chronological range of the document, it is ranked after the dated documents in the latest year. In the sequencing of undated interviews with the same informant, Herndon's numbering on the back of the manuscript, where present, has usually been followed, with exceptions noted.

CATEGORIES

This work is divided into four parts, each arranged chronologically. Part 1, "Letters, Interviews, and Statements Collected by William H. Herndon and Jesse W. Weik, 1865–92," constitutes the main body of material, either in original documents or transcriptions.

Part 2, "Informant Testimony Reported in *Herndon's Lincoln: The True Story of a Great Life* (1889)," consists of testimony presumed authentic but for which no original document or transcription could be located. The reader is advised that Weik, who is presumed to have adapted the informant testimony to the narrative, did not always follow the exact wording of known informant material.

Part 3, "Informant Testimony Reported in William H. Herndon's Letters to Jesse W. Weik," consists of two kinds of material: testimony gathered recently by Herndon and testimony recollected from an earlier period. The reader is cautioned that some of the latter seems to represent testimony offered at a much earlier time. Only testimony about Lincoln that Herndon specifies as coming from others is included.

Part 4, "Informant Testimony Reported in Jesse W. Weik's *The Real Lincoln* (1922)," contains the text of a letter and the substance of several interviews that appear to have been collected as part of Herndon's biographical project but for which no original documents have been located. Given the liberties that Weik felt justified in taking with Herndon's informant material in composing the biography, it seems probable that the interviews are retrospective adaptations of notes or memories, rather than faithful transcriptions of contemporary documents.

The documents have been numbered in one sequence across parts 1–4, and documents are referred to in the notes by the section sign (§) followed by the document number.

Short Citations and Abbreviations

Adams
Will Adams. "Biographical Sketch of Josiah and Elizabeth (Anderson) Crawford." Ms. Public Library Genealogical File. Rockport, Ind.

AL
Abraham Lincoln

ALE
Mark E. Neely, Jr., ed. *The Abraham Lincoln Encyclopedia.* New York, 1982.

Angle
Paul M. Angle. "The Peoria Truce." *Journal of the Illinois State Historical Society* 21 (1929): 500–505.

Barrett
Joseph H. Barrett. *Life of Abraham Lincoln.* New York, 1865.

BDAC
Biographical Directory of the American Congress. Washington, D.C., 1971.

BDATG
Thomas A. McMullin and David Walker. *Biographical Directory of American Territorial Governors.* Westport, Conn., 1984.

BEI
Biographical Encyclopedia of Illinois of the Nineteenth Century. Philadelphia, 1875.

BEK
Biographical Encyclopedia of Kentucky. Cincinnati, 1878.

Benningfield
Edward Benningfield. *Lincoln's Birth County in the Civil War.* Utica, Ky., 1990.

Beveridge
Albert J. Beveridge. *Abraham Lincoln, 1809–1858.* 2 vols. Boston and New York, 1928.

Burlingame
Michael Burlingame, ed. *An Oral History of Abraham Lincoln: John G. Nicolay's Interviews and Essays.* Carbondale, Ill., 1996.

Carpenter
Francis B. Carpenter. *Six Months at the White House with Abraham Lincoln: The Story of a Picture.* New York, 1866.

CG
Ralph Shearer Rowland and Star Wilson Rowland. *Clary Genealogy: Four Early American Lines and Related Families.* Fairfax, Va., 1980.

CHS
Chicago Historical Society

Coleman
Charles Coleman. *Abraham Lincoln and Coles County, Illinois.* New Brunswick, N.J., 1955.

Cuthbert
Norma Cuthbert. *Lincoln and the Baltimore Plot.* San Marino, Calif., 1949.

CW
Roy P. Basler et al., eds. *The Collected Works of Abraham Lincoln.* 8 vols. New Brunswick, N.J., 1953.

CWTC	Charlotte Bergevin, Daisy Sundberg, and Evelyn Berg. *Camerons: Westward They Came.* N.p., 1983.
DAB	Allen Johnson and Dumas Malone, eds. *Dictionary of American Biography,* 20 vols. New York, 1928–46.
Donald	David Donald. *Lincoln's Herndon: A Biography.* 1948. Rpt., New York, 1989.
H&W (1889)	William H. Herndon and Jesse William Weik. *Herndon's Lincoln: The True Story of a Great Life.* 3 vols. Chicago, New York, and San Francisco, [1889].
H&W (1892)	William H. Herndon and Jesse W. Weik. *Abraham Lincoln: The True Story of a Great Life.* 2 vols. New York, 1892.
HCC	*History of Coles County.* Chicago, 1879.
HEI	Newton Bateman and Paul Selby, comps. *Historical Encyclopedia of Illinois.* Chicago, 1894.
HEI/Cass	Newton Bateman and Paul Selby, eds. *Historical Encyclopedia of Illinois and History of Cass County.* Chicago, 1915.
HEI/Coles	Newton Bateman and Paul Selby, eds. *Historical Encyclopedia of Illinois and History of Coles County.* Chicago, 1906.
HEI/Sangamon	Newton Bateman and Paul Selby, eds. *Historical Encyclopedia of Illinois and History of Sangamon County.* Chicago, 1912.
Hertz	Emanuel Hertz, ed. *The Hidden Lincoln: From the Letters and Papers of William H. Herndon.* New York, 1938.
HL	Huntington Library
HMMC	[R. D. Miller]. *History of Menard and Mason Counties, Illinois.* Chicago, 1879.
Holland	Josiah G. Holland. *The Life of Abraham Lincoln.* Springfield, Mass., 1866.
Howard	Robert P. Howard. *Mostly Good and Competent Men: Illinois Governors, 1818–1988.* Springfield, Ill., 1988.
HSC	*History of Sangamon County.* Chicago, 1881.
Hurdle	Judy Hurdle. *Hardin Bale's Indomitable Spirit.* Bath, Ill., 1989.
HW	Herndon-Weik Collection. Manuscript Division. Library of Congress. Washington, D.C.
HWSP	*History of Warrick, Spencer, and Perry Counties, Indiana.* Chicago, 1885.
IAMM	*Illustrated Atlas Map of Menard County, Illinois.* Chicago, 1874.
IDRPC	*Index to Death Record, Putnam County, 1880–1920.* Greencastle, Ind., 1940.
IPW	*Indiana Pocket Weekly.* Rockport, Ind.
ISHL	Illinois State Historical Library
ISJ	*Illinois State Journal.* Springfield.
JISHS	*Journal of the Illinois State Historical Society*
JWW	Jesse W. Weik

Lair	John Lair. *Songs Lincoln Loved*. New York and Boston, 1954.
Lamon	Ward H. Lamon. *The Life of Abraham Lincoln from His Birth to His Inauguration as President*. Boston, 1872.
LBNM	Lincoln Boyhood National Memorial. Lincoln City, Ind.
LC	Library of Congress
Lincoln Legals	Lincoln Legal Papers Project. Cullom Davis, ed. Springfield, Ill.
McKenzie	Molly McKenzie. *A Demographic Study of Select New Salem Precincts*. Springfield, Ill., 1979.
Miller	R. D. Miller. *Past and Present of Menard County*. Chicago, 1905.
MTL	Mary Todd Lincoln
NCAB	*National Cyclopedia of American Biography*. 60 vols. New York, 1893–1976.
NMB	*Nance Memorial Book*. ISHL. N.p., 1904.
NYPL	New York Public Library
NYT	*New York Times*
Oldroyd	Osborn H. Oldroyd, *The Lincoln Memorial: Album-Immortelles*. New York, 1882.
Onstot	T. G. Onstot. *Pioneers of Menard and Mason Counties*. 1902. Rpt., Havana, Ill., 1986.
PBRCC	*Portrait and Biographical Record of Coles County, Illinois*. Chicago, 1887.
Perrin	W. H. Perrin. *Kentucky: A History of the State*. Louisville and Chicago, 1885.
Pinkerton	Allan Pinkerton. *A Spy of the Rebellion*. Hartford, Conn., 1883.
Power	John Carroll Power. *History of the Early Settlers of Sangamon County, Illinois*. 1876. Rpt., Mount Vernon, Ind., 1991.
Quincy	*Quincy City Directory for 1871 and 1872*. Quincy, Ill., 1871.
Raymond	Henry J. Raymond. *The Life and Public Service of Abraham Lincoln*. New York, 1865.
Reep	Thomas P. Reep. *Lincoln at New Salem*. [Petersburg, Ill.], 1927.
Rice	Allen T. Rice, ed. *Reminiscences of Abraham Lincoln by Distinguished Men of His Time*. New York, 1886.
Sandburg	Carl Sandburg. *Lincoln Collector: The Story of Oliver R. Barrett's Great Private Collection*. New York, 1960.
Spgfld 55–56	*Springfield City Directory and Sangamon County Advertiser for 1855–56*. Springfield, Ill., 1855.
TISHS	*Transactions of the Illinois State Historical Society*
USBD	*United States Biographical Dictionary*. Cincinnati and New York, 1877.
Wallace	Joseph Wallace. *Past and Present of the City of Springfield and Sangamon County, Illinois*. Chicago, 1904.

Walsh   John E. Walsh. *The Shadows Rise: Abraham Lincoln and the Ann Rutledge Legend.* Urbana, Ill., 1993.

Weed   Thurlow Weed. *Life of Thurlow Weed, Including His Autobiography and a Memoir.* 2 vols. Boston, 1883–84.

Weik   Jesse W. Weik. *The Real Lincoln: A Portrait.* Boston and New York, 1922.

WHH   William H. Herndon

Whitney   Ellen Whitney, comp. *The Black Hawk War.* Vol. 1. Collections of the ISHL. Nos. 35–37. 1970.

Wilson   Douglas L. Wilson. *Lincoln before Washington: New Perspectives on the Illinois Years.* Urbana, Ill., 1997.

WWWHC   Hardin County Historical Society. *Who Was Who in Hardin County.* Elizabethtown, Ky., 1946.

HERNDON'S INFORMANTS: THE TEXTS

Letters, Interviews, and Statements Collected by William H. Herndon and Jesse W. Weik, 1865–92

1. John L. Scripps to WHH

Chicago, May 9th 1865.

My Dear Herndon:

I am glad you design giving us something about Lincoln. Your long acquaintance and close association with him must have given you a clearer insight into his character than other men obtained. I appreciate your compliment to the poor effort I made in 1860.[1] I do not think it a great stretch of modesty to say that if it were to be done over, I could improve upon it. It is gratifying to me, however, to see that the same qualities in Lincoln to which I then gave greatest prominence, are those on which his fame now chiefly rests. Is it not true that this is the leading lesson of Lincoln's life — that true and ending greatness, the greatness that will survive the corrosion and abrasion of time, change and progress, must rest upon character? In certain showy, and, what is said to be, most desirable endowments, how many Americans have surpassed him! Yet how he looms above them now! Not eloquence, nor logic, nor grasp of thought — nor statesmanship, nor power of command, nor courage — not any nor all of these have made him what he is — but these, in the degree in which he possessed them, conjoined to those certain qualities composed in the term *character,* have given him his fame — have made him for all time to come the great American Man — the grand central figure in American (perhaps the World's) History.

Send me whatever you may publish on the subject.

The plates on which the campaign life was printed were not preserved, and I have not been able to get a copy of it for you.

Very Truly Your
J. L. Scripps.

HL: LN2408, 2:340–41

---

1. A reference to Scripps's campaign biography, *Life of Abraham Lincoln* (Chicago, 1860).

2. Horace White to WHH

Chicago, May 17. 1865.

Dear Sir:

Your letter of the 15th instant is received. The apostrophe to the Declaration of Independence, to which you refer, was written by myself from a vivid recollection of Mr Lincoln's speech at Beardstown, August 12th 1858. On the day following the delivery of the speech, as Mr Lincoln & myself were proceeding by steamer from Beardstown to Havana I said to him that I had been greatly impressed by his concluding remarks of the day previous, & that if he would write them out for me I felt confident their publication would be highly beneficial to our cause as well as honorable to his own fame. He replied that he had but a faint recollection of any portion of the speech — that, like all his campaign speeches, it was necessarily extemporaneous, & that its good or bad effect depended upon the inspiration of the moment. He added that I had probably overestimated the value of the remarks referred to. In reply to my question whether he had any objection to my writing them out from memory and putting them in the form of a verbatim report, he said "none at all". I accordingly did so. I felt confident then, & I feel equally assured now, that I transcribed the peroration with absolute fidelity as to ideas, and with commendable fidelity as to language. I certainly aimed to reproduce his exact words, and my recollection of the passage as spoken was very clear. After I had finished writing I read it to Mr Lincoln. When I had finished the reading he said: "Well, those are my views, & if I said anything on the subject I must have said substantially that, but not nearly so well as that is said." I remember this remark quite distinctly, and if the old steamer *Editor* is still in existence I could show the place where we were sitting. Having secured his assent to the publication I forwarded it to our paper, but inasmuch as my report of the Beardstown meeting had been already mailed, I incorporated the remarks on the Declaration of Independence in my letter from Lewistown two or three days subsequently.[1]

Although a matter of little moment I have given you the facts thus in detail because you seem specially interested in it. Looking at the passage now I discover that it is not exactly in Mr Lincoln's style, which I deem unfortunate as it fails to convey the tremendous *directness* which he always gave to his utterances on those occasions when he rose to impassioned eloquence. And I will say here that, in such moments, I have never heard his equal, & I believe I have listened at times to nearly all the public speakers of considerable reputation in this country. I cannot conceive that Patrick Henry, Mirabeau, or Vergniaud ever surpassed him on those occasions when his great soul was inspired with the thought of human rights and Divine justice. I presume that your suspicions in regard to the passage on the Declaration of Independence have been aroused by noticing a slight aberration from his style, as I do not remember ever having related these facts before, although they have often recurred to me as I have seen the peroration resuscitated again &

---

1. For Lincoln's apostrophe on the Declaration of Independence, as printed in White's paper, the *Press and Tribune*, see *CW* 2:545–47. This account suggests that the apostrophe was delivered in Lewistown on August 17, 1858, rather than at Beardstown on August 12, as White indicates, and is signed "G.P."

again, and published (with good effect I trust) in the newspapers of this country & England.

In regard to the other topic in your letter I can only say that I accompanied Mr Lincoln almost constantly during the memorable campaign of 1858 — that I had the pleasure of hearing nearly all his speeches, those which were published & those which were not — & I am sure that I never heard him say anything of the sort attributed to him by Bishop Simpson.[2] I might add that it seems totally unlike him. My acquaintance with Mr Lincoln commenced in 1854, and continued, with frequent meeting, until his death, & I certainly should not hesitate to pronounce Bishop Simpson's citation an entire mistake.

Very sincerely your friend & obedient servant
Horace White

LC: HW2105; HL: LN2408, 2:361–64

3. John Hanks (John Miles interview)[1]

Decatur Ills. May 25 1865

Thomas Lincoln, Father of Abraham Lincoln was born in Virgina, moved to Hardin County Kentucky, when three years old, when he was, six years old his Father Mortica Lincoln was killed by the Igians, in Kentucky Thos. Lincoln mared, Nancy Sparow in Murser County Ky. and when Abraham Lincoln was nine years old, moved to spencer county Indiana, and move to Macon County Ill in March 1830. some years after he moved to Coles County Ill where he died in 1854 was bured 8 miles south of Charleston in said County.[2] He had Black Hare, Dark Eyes, was 5 feet 9 inches high, hevy set, fleshy and weighed about 180 pounds, he was a good quiet citizen, moral habits, had a good sound judgement, a kind Husband and Father Even and good disposition was lively and cherfull.

Nancy Sparow the mother of Abraham Lincoln was borne in Murser County Kentucky,[3] (her Mothers maiden name was Lucy Hanks and was borne in Virgina) She died in Spencer County Indianna, when her only child living, Abraham Lincoln, was twelve years old, she had dark, Hare, Hazle, Eyes, was 5 feet 7 inches high a spare delicate frame, weighed about 120 pounds, had a clear intilectual mind, was amible, kind, charitable and affectionate. and was loved and revered by all that knew her.

LC: HW2112; HL: LN2408, 2:342

---

2. Methodist bishop who delivered the eulogy when Lincoln was buried at Springfield on May 4, 1865. Simpson quoted from the peroration of Lincoln's December 1839 speech on the subtreasury (*CW* 1:159–79) but mistakenly attributed it to another context in 1859, which is why White did not recognize it.

---

1. Marginal note in WHH's hand: *This letter was written to me by John Miles. I desired him to go down and see Jno Hanks: he did so and wrote me this letter.*

2. Thomas Lincoln moved to Indiana in 1816, when AL was seven, and died in 1851.

3. AL's mother was born Nancy Hanks in Virginia and died in 1818. See the appendix.

4. John G. Nicolay to WHH[1]

Washington, May 27, 1865.

Friend Herndon:

I have this morning received your note of the 23d inst., and with great pleasure answer it at once.

Mr. Lincoln did not, to my knowledge, in any way change his religious ideas,
opinions or beliefs from the time he left Springfield to the day of his death. I do
not know just what they were, never having heard him explain them in detail; but
I am very sure he gave no outward indication of his mind having undergone any
change in that regard while here.

Yours truly

Jno. G. Nicolay

LC: HW2113; HL: LN2408, 2:282

5. J. Rowan Herndon to WHH

Quincy May the 28*th* 1865

Sir

you wrote to James some time Back for a histry of Mr A Lincoln whilst he Lived
at Salom Sangamon County   By his Requst i ancer it as i was the one that Lived
there and Knot James[1] — i first Became acquainted with him about the first of
January 1832 soon after he Returned from a trip to Neworleans on Bord of A Flat
Boat   he went down to Neworleens in the Spring or fall of 31 with the intention of staying there through the winter to Cut Cord wood But his Comrades took
sick and Caused his Return i think his half Brother was with him During the trip.
i am told By Captin Joseph Artis[2] the Comander of the Boat that he Came up the
River on that he was very modest and Kind to all the sick which made him very
Popular Both with Deck and Cabin Pasingers he Being a Deck pasinger him
self   he spent the winter after his Return to salim in Building Boats for a spring
trip in 32 But the Black halk ware Broke out and he volenterd to serve his Country with the Ballance of the Patriock Boys to Defend the frontier setters of this State
from the Savages tomihock and skelping Knife   he was Elected Captin of his
Company By a unamis vote against all oposition   after the Ware Closed and all
Returned home his friends urged him to Run for the Legislator Claming that they
had a wright to a member from that Part of the County he was urged By Both
Political Partys to Run and finely Consented   he Became very Poupelar whilst
in the army he Could throw Down any man that took hold of him he Could out

---

1. In top margin: *Private.*

---

1. James A. Herndon and John Rowan Herndon were brothers and also cousins of WHH.

2. Capt. Joseph Artus sent WHH four letters (June 13 and 21, 1865, Oct. 31, 1865, Nov. 3, 1866) about
this alleged contact with Lincoln on the Mississippi River in 1832. The editors consider this a clear case of
mistaken identity, and Artus's letters have not been included in this edition.

jump the Best of of them he Could out Box the Best of them he Could Beat all of
them on anictdote and he was the favorite of all of them and he Loved all of
then as they Loved him he was the favorite of all at home Men & women &
Childern   he was very fond of Childern he Come to my house to Board soon
after his Return from the army he most always had one of my Childern around
with him During his stay at my house   my family Became much atached to
him   he was always at home wherever he went very Kind to the Widoes & olfins
Chop there wood   he Read the News for all the County once a week as we had
only a weekly male   During the Summer Campain for the Legislate i herd him
speak frequntly and he was a full mach for any man that was on the track   in
one of his speaches he said   fellow Citersons   i have Been told that some of my
opponents have said that it was a disgrase to the County of sangamon to have such
a Looking man as i am stuck up for the Legislator now i thought this was a free
Cuntry that is the Reason that i adress you to Day had i have Known to the Contrary i should Knot have Consented to Run But i will say one thing Let the shue
pinch whoe it may when i have Been a Canidate Before you some 5 or 6 times
and have Bee Beaten every time i will Consider it a disgrase and will Be shure never
to try it again and i am Bound to Beat that man if i am Beat my self — mark
that   and shure enough he was Beat together with some of the Ballance of his
opponents Lincoln was Beat By some 9 votes i think But a majority of his ticket
was elected   Mr John T Sturt was one of them elected — the others i Canot Now
Remember   During the Campain at Paps town[3] one of his Best friends got into
a fight with a set of Ruffings and they atempted to shoe foul play he piched in and
Piched them out Like they ware Boys and told them his friend Could whp the
whole of them one at a time   that ended the fus[4]   the fall or winter of 32 or 33
i sold him my Stock of Goods or Lincoln & Berry on Credit and some time after
i Canot Recolect as I left there for a while they sold to two Brothers By the Name
of Trent   they failed and Bery dide and Lincoln had the Dt to Pay   the Last
Payment he made was after he went to Congress   he Comensed Reading Law
whilst he Borded at my house i bored such Book as he wished to Read from J T
Sturt he Beeing a particklar friend of mine as well as of Lincolns   he was much
Devoted to Reading and had the Best memory of any man i Ever Knew he Never
forgot any thing he Read Nor any friends   he Never used Bad Langag Nor seldom if ever Drank any sperits Never Quareled or fought But always was the Pease
maker infact all loved him and feared him   he was By fare the stoutest man that
i ever took hold of i was a mear Child in his hands and i Considered my self as
good a man as there was in the Cuntry untill he Come about   i saw him Lift
Betwen 1000 and 1300 lbs of Rock waid in a Boxx   Some time of the sumer of
33 he was appointed Debety survayor By J C Calhoon[5] and in 34 he again was a
Canidate for the Legislator on the whig ticket   he was one of the most Devoted

---

3. Papstown or Papsville was located west of Springfield, on Richland Creek.
4. See this writer's letter to WHH of June 21, 1865, where he identifies himself as the man attacked.
5. John Calhoun was surveyor of Sangamon County after March 2, 1833. The date of AL's appointment
as Calhoun's deputy is not known; his earliest known survey was recorded on January 14, 1834.

Clay whigs in all the State   Henry Clay was his favorite of all the great men of
the Nation he allbut worshiped his name as well as my self therefore we agread
Perfectly in Politics   he Came to my house near iland Grove[6] During harvest there
was some 30 men in the field he got his Diner and went out to the field where the
men ware at wort   i gave him & entroduction and the Boys said that they Could
Not vote for a man unless he Could make a hand   well Said he Boys if that is all
i am shure of your votes   he took hold of the Cradle Led the way all the Round
with Perfect ease   the Boys was satisfide and i dont think he Lost a vote in the
Croud —   the next Day was speaking at Burlin[7] he went from my house with
Doct Barrett the man that had asked me whoe this man Lincoln was; i told him
that he was a Canidate for the Legislator   he lafed and said Cant the party Raise
No Beter Materials than that   i said goe tomorrow and here all Before you pronounce judgement   when he Come Back i said Dock what say you Now   why
sir he is a perfect take in he Knows more than all of them Put to gether   he was
elected By a Large Majority over all the ticket and his whole ticket was Elected
Composed of A G Herndon W F Elkin J T Sturt N W Edwards   Jobe Fletcher
Dan Stone Andrew MCormack A Lincoln the other men i Doe Not Remenber
the Name of the Ballance of his Carear you know yourself   you Can take this &
Remade it to suit your self   i may Be mistaken in Dates But Not in the man or
his history for the Most of it is from Personal Knoledge and facts
                            Yours truly
                            J. R. Herndon

        LC: HW2116–18; HL: LN2408, 1:526–32

6. Mentor Graham to WHH (interview)[1]

                                              Petersburg Ills My 29th 1865
Dear Sir:
        In answer to your various Enquiries let me say — I came to Illinois in the year
AD 1829 and settled in Sangamon County — near the Sangamon River close to
the Village of New Salem & was at that time 26 years of age. My business has been
school teaching for forty-five years. In the month of August 1830 I first saw Mr
Lincoln. He came down the Sangamon River from Decatur Macon County Illinois to New Salem in Old Sangamon — Menard now being part of Old Sangamon. The first time I saw him was on Election day — we were deficient a clerk
for the Polls. Mr Lincoln was about the street looking around, and was asked by
some of us if could write he said "yes — a little." "Will you act as clerk of Elections to-day —" said one of the judges: "I will try and do the best I can, if you so

---

6. The Island Grove neighborhood is roughly twelve miles west of Springfield in Sangamon County.
7. Berlin is a village in Island Grove Township, west of Springfield.

---

1. This is one of several early interviews written out by WHH in the form of a letter addressed to himself
and signed by the interviewee.

request." He was then sworn in & acted as clerk of the August Election.[2] There were 49 Candidates, it being a general State election: He performed the duties with great facility — much fairness and honesty & impartially. This was the first public official act in his life. I clerked with him on that day and at the same polls. The Election books are now in the city of Springfield Ills, where they can be seen & inspected any day.

The next work he did was clerking in a store for Denton Offut, which was in the fall and winter of 1830 & 1831.[3] He was among the best clerks I ever saw: he was attentive to his business — was kind and considerate to his customers & friends and always treated them with great tenderness — kindness & honesty. He in fact superintended & managed Offuts whole business. Offut was an unsteady — noisy — fussy — rattle brained man, wild & unprovidential. Offut rented the water mill at the foot of the Salem hill of Cameron & Rutledge. Mr Lincoln frequently had to attend to store & mill. Offut broke up in the Spring or Summer of 1831, leaving Lincoln out of business again. Just before Mr Lincoln came to New Salem he had gone down the River with Offut & got off at Beardstown in Cass County & walked afoot to New Salem.[4] Then it was that he commenced clerking for Offut. After clerking for Offut & now being out of business he turned his attention to the law. He read Blackstone in the fall & winter of 1831 & 2. One word here: During the time he was working for Offut & hands being scarce Lincoln turned in and cut down trees and split enough rails for Offut to a pen sufficiently large to contain one thousand hogs; The pen was built under New Salem hill — close to the mill. Offut had purchased a great deal of Corn and had it at — in and about the mill. The hogs were purchased to Eat the corn — so that would become good — well fed & fatted hogs for Market. I know where those rails are now — are sound to-dy.

He went in 1832, about the month of May or June, to the Black Hawk war: He vlunteered as private and was without his knowledge Elected Captain of it. He went through the war and was spoken by all in his Company & Regiment — Especially his own Company as being a gentleman — a kind hearted & noble man who did his duty well without fear — gold, favor or Affection. He had a somewhat good Eye for Military affairs, as said by Competentt judges. I have no doubt of this. His heart & head were large & Comprehensive enough to Command a Company — regiment or other Core of men at any time or under any Circumstances.

When he returned from the Black Hawk war he became a candidate for the legislature and in his first or among his first political speeches in that Canvass which was in 1832, he addressed the People in Petersburg — the old town.[5] From the

---

2. Poll books show that AL voted in New Salem at the August 1, 1831, election and that the clerks were Mentor Graham and Abram Bergen.

3. Lincoln clerked for Offutt in the fall of 1831 and winter of 1832.

4. AL traveled to New Orleans for Offutt but, according to his own account, returned via St. Louis. For AL walking to New Salem from Beardstown, see §§9, 14, 15, 25, 56.

5. Petersburg was first laid out in 1832 or 1833 by its original promoters, Peter Lukins and George Warburton. The townsite was purchased by Hezekiah King and John Taylor and resurveyed by AL in 1836. See Miller, 293.

time of this speech & during that Canvass he read attentively the Louisville Journal — the Missouri Republican and other papers. His text book was the Louisville Journal. He was a regular subscribe to the Journal. Mr Lincoln was defeated
in the Election of 1832. He was a whig. After the Canvass of 1832 Mr Lincoln
turned his attention Exclusively to the law — surveying — History — Biography
& general newspaper reading. Mr Lincoln drew up deeds, Contracts & other papers for the People, never charging them for it — not a cent. In the month of Feby
AD 1833 Mr Lincoln Came & lived with me. and Continued with me about Six
months. It was here that he Commenced to study the English grammer with me,
I then was teaching School. I taught him the rules of surveying. I do not think
that Mr Lincoln was any thing of arithmetic — Especially so of geometry & trige-
monetry before he came to my house, and I think I may say he was my schollar &
I was his teacher. His deputyship under Calhoun was long after this — say 1 or 2
years. Mr Lincoln spoke to me one day and Said "I had a notion of studing grammar." "I replied to him thus   If you Ever Expect to go before the public in any
Capacity I think it the best thing you can do." He said to me "If I had a grammar
I would Commence now." There was none in the village & I said to him — "I
know of a grammar at one Vances[6] about 6 miles" which I thought he could
get —. He was then at breakfast — ate — got up and went on foot to Vances & got
the Book. He soon Came back & told me he had it. He then turned his immediate & almost undivided attention to English grammar. The book was Kirkham's
grammar[7] — an old volume, which I suppose — have so heard — is in the Rutledge family to-day. During this Spring — Summer & fall he read law — studied
& practiced Surveying and the Grammar & would recite to me in the Evening. I
have taught in my life four or six thousand people as School Master and no one
ever surpassed him in rapidly — quickly & well acquiring the rudiments & rules
of English grammar. This I repeat was in the Spring — Summer & fall of 1833
— As before stated he was writing deeds — Contracts & other papers for the
People. His playful hours for these years was pitching quoits[8] — jumping — hopping — Swimming — Shooting — telling Stories — anecdotes — and not un-
frequently as we in the west say — "[Setting?] up to the fine girls of Illinois —".

In the Summer of 1834 he was again a Candidate for the legislature and was
Elected. He went to Vandalia — the Capital of Illinois and there became a good
legislature — became then & there as I am informed with the great men in Illinois — probably with Douglas & others —   In 1836 he was again a candidate
for the legislature and was Elected; and was one of what is called the long nine —
2 tall Senators and 7 tall representatives from Sangamon County who moved the
Capital of the State of Illinois from Vandalia to Springfield. The members comprising the long nine were

---

6. John Vance's name was mistakenly rendered "Vaner" in H&W (1889).

7. Samuel Kirkham, *A Compendium of English Grammar, Accompanied by an Appendix of Familiar Lectures; Containing a New Systematic Mode of Parsing; Likewise Exercises in False Syntax and a Key to the Exercises: Designed for the Use of Private Learners and Schools* (1823). The edition in the Rutledge family that
Lincoln was said to have used, now in the Library of Congress, was published at Cincinnati in 1826.

8. Flattened rings of iron or circles of rope thrown at a pin, as in the game of horseshoes.

Senators and

Representatives.

He then moved to the City of Springfield in 1836 or 1837 since which time I have only seen him occasionally. I wish to say one or two words about his Character. It was this — he was a very simple open souled man: he was a sincere man — a man of purpous — was frank — ingenuous: he was kind, humerous and deeply honest — never deviating from the Exact truth: he was studious — so much so that he somewhat injured his health and Constitution. The Continued thought & study of the man Caused — with the death of one whom he dearly & sincerely loved, a momentary — only partial & momentary derangement. Mr Lincoln's character at once seized observation and that only led to a respect — love & confidence in Abraham Lincoln.

Your Friend
Mentor Graham

LC: HW2119–23; HL: LN2408, 1:351–57

7. *William G. Greene to WHH*

Tallula Ills May 29th 1865

Yours of the 20th inst. & I now respond to your Interogatories to the best of my recollection   1   Mr Lincolns Mothers Maiden name was Lucy Hanks   she was a native of State Va   I have understood that she was rather above the average size for women but know nothing further of her   2   Mr Lincoln weighed when he & I Clk for Denton Offutt 214 lbs   I have weighed him often   my impression now is that he was PO. M. in 1833   & — 34   his first Stump Speech ever made I have heard him say was in Macon Co in reply to two Men by the Names of a Mr Posey & Ewing[1] this was no Political Speech but an *Experementer* in 1830 or 31 that was before I knew him   all I know of that effort I learned from Mr Lincoln   I have often heard him regret that he had no copy of it as it was Extempo he has often shown & read to me his first Composition he prized it highly   it was full of witt & I pronounced a good thing   I will explain it more fully when I see you   it was personal an old Lady who lived & died in Sangamon but was written long before he came to Ills I think he   informed me that he was about fourteen years ould when he wrote it   3 he came to Sangamon in the fall preceeding the Winter of the *Deep Snow*[2] and assisted in building a Flat Boat (John Rool)[3] of your City worked with him on the Boat   Mr Lincoln last June told me how to guide myself as to the date

---

1. John F. Posey and William L. D. Ewing, who were campaigning for the Illinois House of Representatives in the summer of 1830. See Edwin Davis, "Lincoln and Macon County, Illinois, 1830–31," *Journal of the Illinois State Historical Society* 25 (1932): 97–99. For another account, see the WHH interview with John Hanks, §344.
2. The long-remembered "Winter of the Deep Snow" was in 1830–31.
3. John E. Roll.

of his coming to our part of *then* Sangamon Co which was this that he came down the Sangamon River as a sort of floting Drift wood on the great freshit produced in the thawing of that snow. he was a candidate for the Legislature & made his *first Political* Speech in Petersburg 1832   he was beaten althoug his precinct then which now comprises nearly all of Menard voted him or for him unanimus save and except *Three* Votes   in 1834 he was elected   4th he was elected Captain of a Militia Co in the Black Hawk War   his Men Idolized him   he was the finest Wrestler that belonged to that Army except a man by the name of Thompson who hailed from Union Co Ills[4] (I have many little Incidents of their Wrestle)   5th   he Studied Grammar & Surveying while he & I clerked in Offutts store which was in 1832 & — 33   6th   he at the same time *Devoured* all the Law Books he could get hold of   I left Ills in the Spring of 1836 at that time he was a Dep. Surveyor not of Calhoons as many have it but of T. M. Neal of your City   I now have in my possesion many Feald Notes signed T. M. Neal by A Lincoln Dep &C   I have spent a few nights with his Father   he then lived in Coles Co Ills. & was tending a small Water Mill the proffits of which nearly supported him & his second wife whose name was Johnson before she was married to Mr Thomas Lincoln Abrahams father   I believe I have answered your interogatories as well I can at this time   I will call and see you as I can give much better satisfaction verbal than written

Verry truly Your friend
W G Greene

P.S. will you say to J. K. Dubois & Jacob Bunn that the Citizens generally of Menard & myself especially think verry *strang* that this Co has not been honored with a Member as the "Lincoln association to raise funds" &c for a Monument   as the ould Poll-Book *now*   go & see it apart of the Archieves of Sang., will demonstrate that we people then before his greatness voted him with a uninimity that the wide World has no paralell

W G Greene

LC: HW2124–25; HL: LN2408, 1:474–77

8. Hardin Bale to WHH (interview)[1]

Petersburg Il My 29th 1865

Dear Sir:

I came to Sangamon County — in 1829 and Settled in New Salem then in Sangamon County; & now Menard County: it having been Cut off Sangamon in

---

4. AL won most of his wrestling matches but was bested by Lorenzo Dow Thompson of St. Clair County. For a version of AL's own account of this match, see Col. Risdon M. Moore, "Mr. Lincoln as a Wrestler," *TISHS* (1904), 433–34.

---

1. Written out by WHH in the form of a letter and signed by Hardin Bale.

1839 —: Lincoln Came to the County of Sangamon to New Salem — in 1830. When I became acquainted with Lincoln he was Keeping store for Offut or Nuf-fet — a gassy — windy — brain rattling man. Offut kept a kind of dry good store — probably some liquors in it. This was in 1830 & 31. The winter of the deep snow was in 1829 & 30. Lincoln kept the store in 1830 & 1831. He went into the Black Hawk war in 1832 — was Elected Captain of the Company. He then returned from the Black Hawk war. He Commenced reading law in 1832 & 3 — read in the mornings & Evenings — would play at varis games — jumping — running — hopping telling stories & cracking jokes. When his associates would return in the Evening to their various homes he would go to his reading & in the morning he would read till his associates would Come back the next day —: He Commenced Surveying in before 1834 —. Wm Berry & Mr Lincoln bought a kind of grocery store of Wm. G. Green, as said, and it is my impression he, L., kept it some time. This was in 1834 or 1835. It is said that Berry & Lincoln broke up by the improvidence of Berry in their business — Executions were had against the firm — & Lincoln Law Books — Compas — flag staff — Jacob Staff &c were sold to pay the debt. Jas Short became the purchaser of them and gave them back to Lincoln. Lincoln still read law and surveyed, In the Spring of 1834 or 35 Mr Lincoln invented a wheel — a water wheel — which ran under water: it promised at the time of some value. I do not know what became of it. He at this time fell in love with a Miss Ann Rutledge — a pretty & much accomplished girl of Menard County, living in New Salem. It was said that after the death of Miss Rutledge & because of it, Lincoln was locked up by his friends — Saml Hill and others, to prevent derangement or suicide — so hard did he take her death. He surveyed off — laid off the old town of Petersburg the County Seat of Menard County in the years of 1835 or 6 —. He surveyed and laid off the town of Huron[2] on the Sanga-mon River about 10 miles North of Petersburg. This was about the year 1835   At the time he invented or made his wheel he made a box in the mill — put stones in it and raised one thousand, by throwing straps across his shoulders — he get-ting on some logs. I saw the box — rocks & straps & it is said by good men & true that he lifted the thousand pouns. I helped him with his [illegible] wheel; his invention. He borded at Nelson Alley's who kept tavern in the village — There is now only one house in the village of S the balance of the houses having been moved to Petersburg. About the year 1834 A Lincoln wrote a work on infidelity, denying the divinity of the Scriptures and was persuaded by his friends — particularly by Saml to burn it which was done —

Truly Yours
Hardin Bale

LC: HW2126–27; HL: LN2408, 1:336–38

---

2. Located at Miller's Ferry on the Sangamon, a widely used crossing between Petersburg and Havana, the projected town of Huron was surveyed by AL and its plat recorded on May 21, 1836. See *CW* 1:48ff. and Harry E. Pratt, *The Personal Finances of Abraham Lincoln* (Springfield, Ill., 1943), 58–59.

9. Henry McHenry to WHH (interview)[1]

Petersburg Ills, My 29 1865

Mr. Lincoln came into Sangamon County — now Menard Co in the fall of 1830 —: he came down the Sangamon River in a flat boat with Offut in the summer of 1830[2] — went down the Sangamon to Beardstown on the Illinois and from this last he Came to the little town of New Salem: Offut brought some goods wares & merchandise up from Beardstown and Lincoln put them up — unboxed them & put them up on shelves —, he being then 21 ys of age & some few months — He attended — clerked for Offut, attending store and a mill at the foot of the Hill on the Sangamon River. He stayed with Offut from the fall of 1830 to about August 1831 — this was during the winter of the deep snow: He was a good — obliging clerk & an honest one: he increased Offuts business much by his simplicity — open — Candid — obliging & honest — Evry body loved him —. Soon after this and during the same year 1831 — he was deputy P. M under Saml Hill in New Salem —   At this time he borrowed law books of Jno. T. Stuart: he read He read law sometimes — always during good weather — in the open air: he sat on a goods box under a large white oak tree in Salem, barefooted as he came into the world —: Lincoln would come out & stay with me a week or two at a time, reading law — hunting squirrels with a gun. In the Spring or Summer of 1832 I had a horse race with Geo Warburton. I got Lincoln, who was at the race to be a judge of the race much against his will and after hard persuasion. Lincoln decided correctly and the other judge said — "Lincoln is the fairest man I ever had to deal with If Lincoln is in this County when I die I want him to be my admr., for he is the only man I ever met with that was wholy & purely and unselfishly honest". Soon after this and during the latter part of the year 1832 — or first part of 1833 he studied surveying and went at surveying practically during the same year. He studied surveying under Mentor Graham who now lives not more than two hundred yars from my residence in Petersburg Menard Co: he is a good, truthful & honest: he did not learn surveying of Calhoun, but became Calhoun's deputy surveyor. He still Continued reading law at the same time: he read so much — was so studious — took so little physical exercise — was so laborious in his studies that he became Emaciated & his best friends were afraid that he would craze himself — make himself derange from his habits of study which were incessant. I then moved to Cass and did see him only occasionally till 1836. We — the neighbors — had a disputed Corner in Town 18 N. of 8 R west.[3] We agreed to send for Lincoln & to abide by his decision as surveyor & judge: he came down with Compass — flag staff — Chain &c and stopped with me 3 or 4 days and surveyed the whole section. When the disputed corner arrived at by actual survey, Lincoln then stuck down his staff and said — "Gentlemen — here *is* the Corner." We then went to

---

1. Written out by WHH in the form of a letter and signed by McHenry.
2. AL's flatboat trip (to New Orleans) with Denton Offutt took place between April and July 1831.
3. Township 18 North, Range 8 West of the 3d Principal Meridian lies west of Petersburg on the line between present-day Menard and Cass Counties.

work and dug down in the ground — & found about 6 or 8 inches of the original stake, sharpened & cut with an axe and at the bottom a piece of charcoal, put there by Rector — who surveyed the whole County —.[4] When the supposed Corner was struck and when Lincoln's survey was demonstrated by figures & well as Material Evidences — namely the original stake & charcoal, all parties without a jar were Completely satisfied & that corner stands there this day a monument of all mens titles in the whole section of the County round about. The Black Hawk war was in 1831 & 2.[5] Lincoln went into army — Volunteers — as a private and was Elected by the Company Captain of that Company: All the men in the Company — as well as the Regiment to which he & they belonged loved him well — almost worshipped him. I heard him making his first speech after returning from the Black Hawk war. He brushed up his hair from his tall dark forhead and said: "Gentlemen I have just returned from the Campaign   My personal appearance is rather shabby & dark. I am almost as red as those men I have been chasing through the prairies & forests on the Rivers of Illinois —"

Lincoln in Politics was a whig: he became a candidate for the Legislature in 1832: he was defeated: he was a candidate in 1834, & was Elected. In 1836 he was Elected again & Elected and about the years 1835 or 6 he went from New Salem to the City of Springfield.

During all this time — during all these years — I never knew Mr Lincoln to run a horse race — it then being Common, if not universal over the whole County. I never knew him to drink a drop of liquor — or get drunk — or gamble or play Cards — nor fool nor seduce Women. I wish to say that he never sold liquor — nor dealt in it, he being opposed in his New Salem nor other places whilst in Menard County — or Sangamon. When he was a candidate for small or large offices I always voted for him — his Presidential terms both included and his virtues & honesty &c were the main reasons for so doing.

In 1859 I again renewed an intimate acquaintance in Sangamon. I there Employed him together with W H Herndon to attend to a suit for me involving many serious & knotty questions of law in relation to land — I had put up a house on the disputed land and I was then in possession of the land and living in the house —. Under false impressions — wrong views of my lines of my land; he told me to move out and give my opponent the possession of the land. I remarked somewhat angrily — I will be —d—d if I do: Mr. Lincoln then in the same spirit of momentary anger said — "I will be d—d if I attend to your suit, if you don't — I then remarked to him — "I will employ & other man then — You are not all the Lawyers in Springfield". Mr Lincoln — "Well — Henry, let us have a fair understanding of these things — we never differed before". I then sketched to him on what precise part of the land this house stood on, by a drawing on a piece of paper, he drawing it in sections. When he found out the precise facts of the Case, he

4. Elias and Wharton Rector contracted to survey this area in 1822.

5. Although a brief campaign against Black Hawk took place in 1831, AL's involvement was in the decisive engagement in the spring and early summer of 1832.

then said: "Henry — you are right," and then took a good hearty laugh over the mistake. He further remarked to me in the End — "Henry hold the possession of the land — you will beat the Enemy in the End —"   After 3 years struggle Lincoln's prophecy was fulfilled.[6] soon as the Suit was finally decided Mr Lincoln hitched up old bob and brought out with him his son Robert; they remained with me all day — Mr Lincoln said to me there: "Henry I want to see that old line of peach trees talked about so much in the Suit —" which I showed him, and which he looked over. From this time I saw Mr Lincoln as a friend frequently. During the whole of my acquaintance he always acted toward me as a brother — a christian and a gentleman & in my humble judgment no man living or dead was a better man. God bless him.

Henry McHenry

     LC: HW2128–34; HL: LN2408, 1:345–50

10. James A. Herndon to WHH

Quincy May 29th 1865.

Der friend

I resivd your letter som since reusting mee to give you all the information consirning A Lincolns Eirley life so far as I new which I wood have done bee fore this if it had not bin on account of Sickness in my famly   well in the firste place I took your letter to Rowen Herndon nooing hee cood give a mutch better histry of Mr Lincoln than I cood. Mr Lincoln borded with hin som time in Salam   I Saw J. R. H yesterday   hee told Mee hee Sirtnly wood attend to It rite of & give the names of All the canadats   I bee came acqanted with Mr Lincoln in 1832   Somtine in the Spring during Durin that Summer J R H & My Self moove A Stock of Goods to Salam   after Mr Lincoln was beeting for office him & Wm Barry bought out our Stock   I new but littel a bout him after that untell hee came to Springfiled tha Speach he made was at Paps Vill on Ritchland creek at Mr Smiths[1]   thar was a large gethering thar on account of a Sale of goods   hee was the only canadate thar & was call on to make a Speach

hee commence by Saying Fellow Sitisens I have bin Solisated by many frends to bee come a canadate for the ledeslator   I have So concluded to do   I prosume you all no ho i am   My Name is Abraham Lincoln   My politcks is Short & Sweet Like and old womans dance   I am in favor of nashonal Bank high & protectif Tarrif & the internal improvement System

if Ellected I will bee thankful if beeting I can do as I have bin doing worke for

---

6. For another account of this case, see §104.

---

1. Presumably David Smith, who sold the land on which Papsville and the store having the sale (Knapp and Pogue) were located.

a living[2]   this is a bout all I now plees excuse this   My love to all and your wif
in pertickler   let mee her from you a pon the resite of this
yours in haste
James A H

LC: HW2135–36; HL: LN2408, 1:547–49

11. *William G. Greene to WHH (interview)*[1]

Elm Wood May 30th 1865

My Dear Sir:

I came to Illinois in the year AD 1820 and settled on the Sangamon River above
Petersburg and near the town of New Salem, then in Sangamon County — Now
Menard County, this last County having been cut off Sangamon County in the
year AD 1838 & 9. Abraham Lincoln Came to Sangamon Town in the fall of 1829[2]
and to New Salem in the Spring of 1831. Mr Lincoln built a flat boat on the Sangamon River for Denton Offutt at Sangamon Town, about 7 miles north west of
the City of Springfield. Before landing at New Salem: He then Came down the
River on the flat boat with Dennis Hanks — Jno Johnson a step brother of Lincoln, & Offutt. The boat in coming down the Sangamon River grounded & lodged
on the New Salem Mill dam at the foot of the hill on which Salem was built. I
Saw the boat soon after it landed — on the same hour or day. and then and there
for the first time I saw Abraham Lincoln. He had on a pair of mixed blue jeans
pants — a hickory shirt and a Common Chip hat. He was at that time well and
firmly built: his thigs were as perfect as a human being Could be. and weighed
214: his height was six feet four inches. When I first saw him he was endeavring
to pry the boat over the dam. Whilst straining every nerve to push the boat off
the dam Mr Lincoln having noticed by his quick river eye that the River was falling remarked to Offut — "We will have to get the boat to the shore and unload it
or it will sink". Offutt submitted — the boat was got off the dam and brought to
the shore and unloaded. It was loaded with wheat — dry goods —.[3] Offutt then
rented the grist mill at the foot of Salem hill, owned by Cameron & Rutledge. Here
he ground his wheat and put up his goods in the store. Lincoln was made Offutts,
Chief and head Clerk. Within a few days after the goods were put up in the store
at New Salem   I went down there and was Employed by Offutt as clerk to keep
the store. Mr Lincoln & I clerked together for Offutt about 18 months & slept

---

2. WHH got this speech from James A. Herndon several months earlier and had it printed in the Springfield paper. See WHH to JWW, Nov. 22, 1888, HW, and *ISJ*, Nov. 5, 1864, p. 2, col. 3.

---

1. Written out by WHH in the form of a letter and signed by Greene.

2. AL came to Sangamon Town, northwest of Springfield on the Sangamon River, in the early spring of
1831.

3. Greene mistakenly believed that Offutt started his store with the goods on the boat, which were actually taken to New Orleans.

on the same cott & when one turned over the other had to do likewise. He was an attentive — Kind — generous & accommodating Clerk and was then as much a Centre of attraction as he was when President of the U.S. though not quite so grand a one. Whilst Mr Lincoln & I were clerk together he often Stated to me that his mothers name was — Hanks. Lincoln told me he was born in Hardin County in Kentuck — moved to Indiana in about 1817 & to Illinois in 1830. & then came down the Sangamon River as stated before. Soon after he landed and Commenced clerking he took a notion to study grammar & surveying. I told him I had a grammar & surveying books at home. This remark was in the summer & fall of 1830. He went down with me and got them and instantly Commenced his studies. Mr. Lincoln studied the grammar & surveying privately in his store — worked it out by himself alone as I recollect it, though others may have explained special problems — rules & such like things which he could not Easily Master. Mr Lincoln soon mastered his grammar & the general practical rules of surveying. He mastered them rapidly — like reading — so quick and Comprehensive was his mind. He generally mastered a book quickly — as one who was simply reading — so comprehensive was his mind. This studying & reading was whilst he was clerk for Offutt. Offutt was a wild — recless — careless man, — a kind of wandering horse tamer. He was somewhat Enthusiastic — intuitive and prophetic. He said — By God — Lincoln will yet be President of these U.S." Mr Lincoln after he had mastered the grammar & the practical rules of surveying Commenced the studying the fall & winter & Spring of 1832 & 33. He borrowed his books — his books — Blackstone — Kent and other law books of Jno. T. Stuart of Springfield, who was somewhat older than Lincoln. Mr Lincoln first commenced surveying in 1833 & 4 and Continued to do so till about the close of 1836. I hold in my hands his field notes made on the 16 & 17th 1836: he was then deputy of Thomas. M. Neal surveyor of Sangamon County.

Let me go back a little. The Black Hawk war broke out in the year 1832. Lincoln volunteered as a private and was soon Elected Captain of the Company over Wm Kirkpatrick. He went through the Black Hawk war & was idolized by his men & generally by all the Regiment & Core to which he belonged. I want to tell you a fact about Mr Lincoln discretion true valor & mercy. An old Indian Came to Camp[4] & delivered himself up, showing us an old paper written by Lewis Cass, Stating that the Indian was a good & true man   Many of the men of the Army said "we have come out to fight the Indians and by God we intend to do so". Mr Lincoln in the goodness & kindness and humanity & justice of his nature stood — got between the Indian and the outraged men — saying — "Men this must not be done — he must not be shot and killed by us". Some of the men remarked — "The Indian is a damned Spy"   Still Lincoln stood between the Indian & the vengeance of the outraged soldiers — brave, good & true. Some of the men said to Mr Lincoln — "This is cowardly on your part Lincoln". Lincoln remarked if

---

4. For other references to this episode, see §§269, 284.

any man thinks I am a coward let him test it," rising to an unusual height. One of
the Regiment made this reply to Mr Lincoln's last remarks — "Lincoln — you are
larger & heavier than we are". "This you can guard against — Choose your weapons", replied Mr Lincoln somewhat sourly. This soon put to silence quickly all
Charges of the Cowardice Cowardice of Lincoln. This is the first time or amongst
the first times I ever saw Mr Lincoln aroused. He was unusually kind, pleasant —
good humored, taking any & all things. But this was too much for Lincoln. This
hushed up at once all disputes about Lincolns courage. I was through the Black
Hawk war with Lincoln and can say no man was more Courageous, truly & manly so. No man had more moral courage. He would do justice to all though the
heavens fell. He had a considerible Eye for military affairs. By the by he was the
strongest man in our regiment and one of the very best wrestlers. One man in the
army alone could throw him and that man's name was Thompson. Speaking of
Lincoln physical Strength let me say I saw him lift one thousand & twenty four
pounds. He was harnessed with straps in the New Salem Mills. One other instance
of his honor — his moral Courage. The Company to which I belonged knew that
Mr Lincoln was physically powerful and artful & skilled in wrestling. The Company bet their Knives — blankets — tomahaks &c. on Mr Lincolns wrestling. The
man Thompson was his opponent. The men Lincoln & Thompson walked out
& fixed for the match. Thompson threw Lincoln fairly the first fall. Lincoln remarked to his friends "This man is the most powerful man I ever had hold of: he
will throw me and you will loose your all unless I act on the defensive   Mr Lincoln caugh Mr Thompson and held him off sometime. At last the man got the
crotch lock on Mr Lincoln. Lincoln slid off, but the man Caught him and partially threw Mr Lincoln. We were taken by surprise at the result & being unwilling to give up our property & lose our bets got up a kind of an Excuse as to the
result in order to avoid giving up our bets. We declared that the fall was a kind of
a Dog. fall.[5] We so asserted — did so apparently angrily to avoid the result. A fuss
was about to be a fight in the Companies generally. Lincoln rose up and said —
"Boys the man actually threw me once fair — broadly so. & the second time —
this very fall he threw me fairly, though not so apparently so. One other word in
reference to Mr Lincolns Care for the health — welfare & justice to his men. Some
officer of the US had claimed that the Regular Army had a preference in the rations & pay. Mr Lincoln was ordered to do some act, which he decreed unautho-
rized: he however obeyed, but went to the officer and said to him — "Sir — you
forget that we are not under the rules and regulations of the war department at
Washington — are only volunteers under the orders & Regulations of Illinois. Keep
in your own speere & and there will be no difficulty, but resistance will hereafter
be made to your injust orders. & further my men must be Equal in all particulars
in rations — arms — camps &c to the regular Army." The man saw that Mr L
was right and determined to have justice done. Always after this we were treated

---

5. An indecisive fall that counts for neither contestant.

Equally well & just as the regular Army was in evry particular. This brave — just and humane act in behalf of the volunteers at once firmly attached officers & rank to him as with hooks of Steel.

Lincoln returned from the black Hawk war and became in 1832 a Candidate — for the Legislature. He address the People in the town of Petersburg on the Election and the Causes which he advocated. It was what the world would call an awkward speech, but it was a powerful one, cutting the centre Evry shot. He was defeated at this Election, though the People in and around New Salem precinct voted him 275 — out of the 278 voters — so popular was he. After this he read law — studied surveying — read the newspapers, wrote deeds — Contracts and general business & official man for the whole Community, never charging one cent for his time & trouble —

In the year 1832 about the month of May or June I sold to Wm Berry & A. Lincoln my grocery store — I gave $400 — for it and they gave me $750 — (Here tell the Radford story — the Clary grove story of the men who got drunk — broke up Radfords store &c. My father was a babtist — came home told my father &c — he said Lizzie get up — [dollars?] — [blaze?] &c —).[6] Lincoln & Berry kept the grocery store, containing dry good — groceries — liquors — such a one as was kept Evry where in the Country at that time —. Offutt had broke up before the Black Hawk war and there was no other house of the kind was kept in town beside Lincoln's & Berrys. Hill & McNamar kept a dry good store at that time. Lincoln & Berry kept store about 6 or 9 months and through Berry's negligence & bad management — though not through dishonesty the store was broken up. A judgement was received against Lincoln & Myself on the old Radford note. Lincoln & Berry were to pay this note: it was now Lincolns & Berrys debt. At last I paid it. Lincoln however paid me, writing to me in Tennessee to come out and get my money. For some of the other debts of Lincoln & Berry execution were had against Lincoln & Berry   Lincolns law books were sold — his Compas — flag staff — Jacob Staff &c were sold to pay the debts. James Short bought them and gave them back to Lincoln. After this & being out of business Mr Lincoln read law with renewed Energy — studied surveying & practiced it — read the Sangamon Journal — the Louisville Journal & Mo Republican & other papers — in fact he read all he could touch his hands to. This was during the summer & fall of 1832. He now Commenced surveying in fact. through the Country: he surveyed a race track for Thos Wadkins — or the Wadkins track. He likewise at this time would and frequently did, as we say Pettifog before Justice of the Peace in and about the County. This was studiously & energetically Continued up to 1834. when he became a Candidate for the legislature. He was Elected in 1834 and I think him the foremost man, the People all over Sangamon were beginning to fully appreciate him as did his neighbors here in 1832. He went to Vandalia in Decm 1834 and became a leading member at once. It was at the subsequent legislature that

---

6. A fuller account of this story is in Reep. When Greene came home after this transaction, he woke his sleeping father, who was irate at Greene's having purchased Radford's store, until hearing how well Greene had done in reselling it. At that point, the father ordered his wife, Lizzie, to get up and fix Greene "a *fust rate* supper" (47).

Lincoln became with S. A Douglas. Mr Lincoln was a short time before this Dep. for Saml Hill and was now himself   P.M himself. He continued to practice law, survey & read history — Shakespear — Burns. By the by Shakespear — Burns & Byron were his favorite books. He nearly knew Shakespear by heart. Mr Lincoln was a very gentle — kind & humane man. His mind was skeptical and hence his deep humanity & skeptical tinge of mind made him love Burns — as well as Shakespear. He read Rollin — Gibbons histories. I loaned them to him.

In the summer of 1836 Lincoln was elected again to the Legislature and about this time I left the State of Ills & went to South. Here it was that Mr Lincoln wrote to me that he was happy to inform me that he had my money — the money he owed me which I came up and got. in 1838–9–40.

The boreing the hole in the boat is a story made out of whole cloth — Offutt suggested it and Lincoln said he couldnt see it. I know of no personal difficulties made or had between Lincoln & any one. —

Lincoln's physical Exercise running — jumping — pitching quoits — hopping swimming — shooting — he never played cards for money — never bet a cent in my life. He played for Sport — to pass time & purely for fun — just as gentlemen & ladies do now and with no other intent. He was a virtuous man — as much any man the sons of Adam. He, in the years year 1833 & 4 was in love with a young lady in New Salem by the name of Mis Ann Rutledge. She accepted the overtures of Lincoln and they were engaged to be be married. This young lady was a woman of Exquisite beauty, but her intellect was quick — Sharp — deep & philosophic as well as brilliant. She had a gentle & kind a heart as an angl — full of love — kindless — sympathy. She was beloved by evry body and evry boody respected and lovd her — so sweet & angelic was she. Her Character was more than good: it was positively noted throughout the County. She was a woman worthy of Lincoln's love & she was most worthy of his. She was suddenly — a short time before the marriage was to be she took sick with the brain-fever and died in 4 or 5 days. Lincoln went & saw her during her sickness — just before her death. Mr Lincolns friends after this sudden death of one whom his soul & heart dearly & lovd were Compelled to keep watch and ward over Mr Lincoln, he being from the sudden shock somewhat temporarily deranged. We watched during storms — fogs — damp gloomy weather Mr Lincoln for fear of an accident. He said "I can never be reconcile to have the snow — rains & storms to beat on her grave."

Mr Lincoln, in Conclusion, was a man of kindness — Courtesy — sincerity & honor, having a mind of great force & depth. and was as much a centre of attraction in that Early day as he was while President. He grasped the Peoples affections through simplicity of his good nature — his honesty — his integrity — his virtue — his high moral &noble qualities and when he once had a man's or a woman's love he never willingly let go its hold. He was a greatly manly man in Evry particular and will go down to history the greatest & foremost man of the world —

Verry Truly your friend
W G Greene

LC: HW2137–49; HL: LN2408, 1:324–35

12. William Walker to WHH

Havana, June 3d 1865

Friend Herndon

Your favor duly recieved. I am Glad you have undertaken the task of Writing the life of President Lincol for Publication   I did once know all about the Case as Armstrong but no doubt many things occured that have been forgotten. In the Summer of 1857 — at a Camp Meeting in the South East portion of Mason County a man by the name of Metzker was Murdered.[1] Two men were charge with the offence. James H Norris, & W*m*. D. Armstrong both of whom were Indicted at the Fall Term of our Court of that Year. Norris was tried & convicted of Man-Slaughter   Sent to the Penitentiary for Eight years. Armstrong took a Change of venue to Cass County and up to this time I had Conducted the defence —   In the Spring of 1858 — Armstrong at the Cass Court was put on his trial   Then Mr Lincoln first appeared in the Case. I had preserved the Evidence adduced on the trial of Norris. this Mr. Lincoln Scrutinised Closely and verry Soon was fully posted in regard to the Case. The testimony Showed that the *Decd* together with a large number of others were off Some distance Say half mile from the place of worship, where some wagons with provisions & Liquors, were stationed At one of these waggons, The difficulty occurred. The main witness Swore that he saw Norris Strike Metzker across the back of the head with Some large Stick, resembling a neck yoke of a waggon, and that Armstrong Struck *Decd* with what appeared to be a Slung-shot,[2] about the face, and that the parties clinched & fell to the ground, — Metzker lived one or two days. The witness who testified to this Stood off 10 or 15 paces, from the parties in the night about Eleven O clock. On Examination *Decd* Showed fracture of the Skul at the back & base of the Brain, and also an other fracture at or near the inner Corner of one Eye, which fracture occasion the most irritation, Either of which was shown would produce death. I Examined the witness & when through Mr.Lincoln, would tel me what to ask, having refference to the testimony of some witness on the Norris trial. we made or Showed numerous Contradictions. Thus we showed by an other witness that the man, who pretended to have Seen all the dificulty had not been on the ground at all that night. Mr Lincoln made the closing argument for the defence. He Spoke Slow, and Carefully reviewed the whole testimony, picked it all to pieces, and Showed, that the man though kiled had not recived his wounds at the place or time named by the witness, but afterwards and from the hands of Some one Els. He told of his kind feelings toward the Mother of the Prisoner, a widow, That she had been kind to him when *he* was young, lone, & without friends. The last 15 minutes of his Speech, was as eloquent as I Ever heard, and Such the power, & earnestness with which he Spoke, that jury & all, Sat as if Entranced, & when he was through found relief in a gush of tears   I have never Seen, Such mastery

---

1. On August 29, 1857, Metzker, Norris, and Armstrong were involved in a fight; Metzker was injured and died on September 1.

2. Armstrong's slung-shot was a lead weight wrapped in a leather pouch and attached to thongs.

Exhibited over the feelings and Emotions of men, as on that occasion. The Boy was acquitted — none of that sickning thing occured on his acquittal that Some writer has mentioned   the old Lady came to the Parlor, where Mr L — & the Judge & Some others were Sitting & took Mr L — by the hand and with Stream-ing Eyes Said God would bless him & his Children, because he had been kind to the widow & orphan. The work he done was the result of his large kind hort, his reward the Consciousness that he had done his duty — Should these facts be of any assistance — use them as you please.

Yours
W Walker

LC: HW2150–51; HL: LN2408, 2:334–36

13. John Hill to WHH[1]

Petersburg Ill June 6th 65

Dear Sir:

Yours of yesterday is at hand. I will be more prompt this time.

Miss Ann Rutledge died within a few days of September 1st 1835. *Certain.* Lincoln bore up under it very well until some days afterwards a heavy rain fell, which unnerved him and — (the balance you know)   As to the Lincoln & Smoot[2] story I know it to be true as it was told me by Mr Lincoln himself, and I after-wards told Mr Smoot of it and he remembered it. I remember Lincoln's words, but will see Smoot, & then give it to you. Whatever he says is as true as the word of man   Enclosed I send the printed slip   I published it in 1862. Every item in it I believe to have been true except in relation to keeping a stallion   I made good enquiry before writing & think I arrived at the truth. The order of succes-sion may not be technically true.

As to keeping a Stallion the origin of this was that Old Joe Watkins (now dead) kept a horse at Salem, and Lincoln requested him that when ever a mare come he would be sure to let him know it, as he wanted to *see it.* Watkins did so, and Lin-coln always attended, &c. — I have this from W. G. Greene & others as the truth.

Mother informs me that when Jas Short arrives that he will be able to give you more information than any or all the men in the county, if his memory serves him well.

Should I learn anything of interest I will advise you. I will hunt up the books Lincoln kept for Father, &c. He (L) *was* Post Master at Salem a short time

Yours truly
John Hill

---

1. Marginal note: *Don't destroy this slip of printed paper. J.H.* This refers to the newspaper clipping, the text of which follows the letter.
2. See §§102, 197.

[Enclosure]

14. *Clipping from* Menard Axis

[Feb. 15, 1862]

A Romance of Reality

About thirty years ago, on an inclement day of winter, there was seen a rough uncouth youth of twenty one years of age plodding with awkward step his way from Beardstown to this place. His appearance was far from prepossessing; and his dress was of the most ludicrous character. His long arms protruded through the sleeves of a coat which scarcely reached beyond the elbow in one direction, or below the waist in the other. He wore a pair of pants far better adapted for a man of much less height, and which left exposed a pair of socks which, although they had long been in use, had never received the attentions of any kind washerwoman. His large long foot partially enveloped in a well worn pair of shoes, presented a singular contrast with his very small head surmounted by a sealskin cap. Thus clad this youth reached the town of New Salem, situated two miles from this place. Without money or friends, he necessarily betook himself to manual labor that he might earn a livelihood. His frugality, and genial temper soon gained him friends. — His honest frankness and native shrewdness recommended him to the only merchant of the place, the father of the writer, who gave him employment as a clerk and bookkeeper in his dry goods store. — Soon the Black Hawk war broke out; and this youth, full of adventure and enthusiasm, left his situation to enlist as a soldier. This he did, but the war was over before he reached the field of action, so he returned home again.

Buying a second hand surveyor's compass, he announced that he would "do surveying." Under the pupilage of a present citizen of the county, he studied the elements of English grammar, and occasionally "read law." As a regular means of support during this time, he "stood" a stallion for a farmer living near to New Salem, and is said to have attended to the business pretty well.

Another season came, and the youth having accumulated a few dollars, resolved to go into business for himself. Selecting a partner, he struck up a trade for a grocery in town. In this business he with his partner continued for some time, but without success. An opposition liquor shop attracted the custom, while liabilities were accumulating to this firm. At length a constable entered the premises, and seized upon all of personal effects of the firm, as well as those of the individuals composing it. They were sold at constable's, sale under execution to the highest bidder. Our youth now found himself without money or credit. Every article which he owned in the world had been sold, save the clothes which he wore; and he was still in debt!

Again necessity forced him to manual labor. This he very much disliked to perform, but his honest pride would not allow him to eat the bread which he had not earned. Here, it is stated, he employed his intellectual faculties in writing a dissertation against the doctrine of the divinity of the scriptures. Of this he soon repented, and consigned his production to the flames. He had designed it for publication, but his senior friends, pointing him to Paine and Voltaire, wrought a change in his intentions, and perhaps his destiny.

At the constable's sale, a sympathizing friend had bought his surveyor's compass and given it back to him. A new town was to be surveyed two miles from New Salem, and he was employed to do the surveying. The present town of Petersburg is the first and last town in which he ever practiced this scientific profession.

He now became an actor in a new scene. He chanced to meet with a lady, who to him seemed lovely, angelic, and the height of perfection. Forgetful of all things else, he could think or dream of naught but her. His feelings he soon made her acquainted with, and was delighted with a reciprocation. This to him was perfect happiness and with uneasy anxiety he awaited the arrival of the day when the twain would be made one flesh. — But that day was doomed never to arrive. Disease came upon this lovely beauty, and she sickened and died. The youth had wrapped his heart with her's, and this was more than he could bear. He saw her to her grave, and as the cold clods fell upon the coffin, he sincerely wished that he too had been enclosed within it. Melancholy came upon him; he was changed and sad. His friends detected strange conduct and a flighty imagination. — They placed him under guard for fear of his committing suicide. — New circumstances changed his thoughts, and at length he partially forgot that which had for a time consumed his mind.

He now demanded active exercise, that both his mind and body might recuperate. A pork merchant gave him employment as a drover; and, in this business he continued for some months. At this time a local political question agitated the portion of the county in which he resided. A division of the county was anxiously desired by both political parties about New Salem; but was bitterly opposed by the people of another portion of the county. It was to be tested in the legislature the next winter. Those who wished for the division of the county, in looking around, could find no one more suitable for a representative of their interests than this youth. — He was nominated as their candidate, and elected without regard to party politics.

Who now would the reader suppose is this awkward youth — this dry goods clerk — this soldier — this keeper of a stallion — this grocery keeper — this bankrupt liquor merchant — this day laborer, infidel writer, surveyor, love-sick swain, hog drover and legislator? He is none other than ABRAHAM LINCOLN, the President of the United States and Commander-in-Chief of the largest army which has ever been assembled in modern times. Engaged in the great work of preserving a distracted Union, the eyes of all mankind are now turned toward h— the most conspicious, and the man having the greatest responsibility resting upon him, of any man now living in the world. 1832 and 1862 what a contrast!

What an example of ambition is for the youths of the land who now toil in the modest walks of unobserved secluded life! It should arouse them all to a higher appreciation of their importance in the great drama of the world. Ambition should awaken them — they should learn to labor in patience, do right to all mankind, and await the occasions which shall rule their destinies.

LC: HW2152 (letter), HW2153 (clipping); HL: LN2408, 1:513–14 (letter only)

15. William G. Greene to WHH

Home June 7th 1865

Dear Sir

Yours of June 1st recd. You will correct my statement as regards the Flat boat remaining at New Salem   upon consultation with friends I am satisfied that the boat was reloaded & pased down the sang. River as far as Beardstown Mr Lincoln footed it back to N. Salem   Then Commenced his clk. ship &c. The Trip to New Orleans that Rowan Herandon has referance to[1] was prior to Mr Lincoln coming to Ills   it was the Load of Hoop poles & was carried down the Wabash River the time he & the Negroes had such fight &c

Berry & Lincoln did *replenish* their stock of goods by purchasing the *remnant* of Rowan Herandon &c. Store. I still persist in the assertion that Mr Lincoln had no Teacher after he came to New Salem that he was self Taught it may be true that & I suppose it is *true* that Mentor Graham a verry kind & communicative man, did give Mr Lincoln many explanations & elucidations both in English Grammar & Surveying just as John T. Stuart did in the Law   I have seen Graham since I recd. your letter   he still persists that he taught him but when I questioned him wher when & what school house he had to admit that it was on the street behind the Counter when at Diner &c &c Just as you continually teach Law to inquiring friends   friend Graham has always been remarkable for his willingness to instruct the Youth of the community in which he lived & I agin repeat that he has many a time *bored* M Lincoln for hours as he a *hundred* times has your humble servant giving explanations for which I now am thankful

You will now make such alterations in my letter as will be necisary &c

Verry Truly

W. G. Greene.

P.S. Mr Lincoln *prior* to being Post-master acted as Dep PO. Master under Sam Hill   I do not know how long or any thing further of his Deputy PO. master ship

W. G. G.

You will of course write my letter over & make it *a modl* for *consistency* & *simplicity*

W. G. G.

LC: HW2154–55; HL: LN2408, 1:477–78

---

1. See §5. Although AL made two flatboat trips to New Orleans (1828 and 1831), Greene believed he made only one.

16. Dennis F. Hanks (Erastus Wright interview)[1]

Chicago Illinois 8th June 1865

Dennis F. Hanks at Chicago Illinois on 8th June 1865 makes the following statements in relation to the Genealogy of Abraham Lincoln Late President of the United States — at the request of Erastus Wright of Springfield Ills.

Abraham Lincoln was the Son of Thomas Lincoln who was the Son of Mordecai Lincoln. His Grand Father Mordecai was killed by the Indians near Boone Station in Kentucky when his Son Thomas was six years old. His Grand Mother whose maiden name was Lucy Hanks, *was my own Aunt.*[2]

The Grand Parents Mordecai and Lucy Lincoln were both born in old Virginia and lived on the Roanoke River the County not recollected. After they moved out into Kentucky near the year 1790 with their family   The Indians being irritated by the encroachments of the whites   Mordecai the Grand Father of Abraham was killed near Boone Station (suppose the renowned Indian Fighter Daniel Boone)

Thomas Lincoln, his Son and the Father of Abraham was born in Virginia on the Roanoke River. after he came to Kentucky was married in Hardin Co. Ky I think in the year 1806 to Miss Nancy Sparrow They lived in Ky near ___ years and had 3 children viz. Sally Thomas and Abraham   They moved from Kentucky to Indiana about the year _____   Nancy the wife of Thomas and Mother of Abraham was one of the best of women Meek quiet and amiable   She died in Spencer Co Indiana in September 1818. Sally their Eldest child married to Aaron Griggsby of Spencer Co Indiana and lived only about 12 months and died at the birth of her first child —

Thomas the 2d child named after his Father did not live 3 days

After living in Indiana by Farming and some mechanical work about 13 years, Thomas Lincoln hearing of the rich Prairies of Illinois already cleared up and prepared for the plow decided to go, and moved to Macon County Illinois on the 20th March 1829, where he lived until the time of the Black Hawk War in 1832 when he moved to Coles County Illinois about 8 miles South of Charleston and lived there until he died near 1851 in December just before Christmas

I think Abraham Lincoln was 9 years old when they moved from Ky to Spencer Co Indiana

Thomas Lincoln the Father of Abraham was a Pioneer in Kentucky and Also a Pioneer in Indiana and like most Pioneers delighted in having a good hunt   The Deer, the Turkeys the Bear the wild cats and occasionally a big Panther afforded him no small amusement and pleasure — and was a great Source of Subsistence as the wild Turkeys and Deer were very abundant — The Honey Bee Luxuriated

---

1. Erastus Wright interviewed AL's cousins, Dennis and John Hanks, at Chicago, providing an account of both interviews to Josiah Holland (Holland Papers, NYPL). The notes on Dennis supplied to WHH are more detailed, but if Wright also provided WHH with notes on his interview with John, they are not known.

2. Hanks is mistaken about AL's paternal grandfather, whose name was Abraham Lincoln, but Wright compounds the error by placing Lucy Hanks, AL's maternal grandmother, on the wrong side of the family tree.

on the Prairie flowers and afforded in the Groves a large supply of wild honey Thomas Lincoln could with propriety be classed with the "Hunters of Kentucky" he seldom failed of success   He was a large man of great muscular power his usual weight 196 pounds I have weighed him many a time   he was 5 feet 10½ inches high and well proportioned

His Religious belief coincided with the "Separate Baptists" often now called the "Free willd Baptists" to which church he belonged was good humoured sociable and never appeared to be offended

He was Singular in one point though not a fleshy man he was built so compact that it was difficult to find or feel a rib in his body — A muscular man, his equal I never saw

At a gathering in Hardinsburg Ky. a certain Wm Breckenridge was reputed and cracked up as the best man in Breckenridge county and Lincolns friends and neighbors disputed it and Said that with a fair chance Lincoln could whip him. It was agreed to and they both consented for a fair fight they soon stript and went at it, and Thomas Lincoln whipd him in less than two minutes without getting a scratch —[3]

Said Thomas Lincoln and Nancy Sparrow were married in Hardin Co Ky I think in 1806   Nancy Sparrow was born in Mercer Co Ky in 1792 near Elizabethtown, her Parents _____

Thomas Lincoln learnt his trade as a Carpenter in Hardin Co Ky with my Uncle Joseph Hanks and married Joseph Hanks Niece which was my own cousin — Lincoln was a farmer and mechanic and worked at either that was most profetable

Abraham Lincoln the late President was born on the 12th Feby 1809 in Hardin Co Ky on Knobb Creek, so called, which run into the Rollingfork which emptied into the Beach Fork and then into the Ohio River

His Father like most Pioneers lived in log houses most of the time was comfortable and happy and realized that *"the Sleep of the laboring man was sweet"*.

The first house shelter he had in Indiana was a half faced camp[4] such as is now often seen in Sugar Camps   Their Tables were broad Puncheons or slabs, split with mawl and wedges out of large logs and dressed off with the broad axe and auger holes put in to receive the legs   This was no uncommon thing then with all the new settlements   Yea! I made one of those tables myself in ___ for Thomas Lincoln the Father of Abraham as we both settled there near together in Spencer Co Indiana   Abraham went to school with his Sister Sally on Knobb Cr in Hardin Co Ky some 3 or 4 weeks when he was 6 or 7 years old — to a man by the name of Hazel and he got about Six months Schooling while he lived in Indiana the teachers name not now recollected.

Thomas Lincoln the Father of Abraham after his first wife died in Sept 1818 married again on _____ to one Mrs Sarah Johnston a Daughter of Christopher Bush in Hardin Co Ky he had no children by the second woman. She is supposed to be living now near Charleston Coles County Illinois —

---

3. Cf. §24.

4. A makeshift shelter closed on three sides but open on the front.

To all of the foregoing I cheerfully subscribe as written down by Erastus Wright of Springfield Illinois

(Signed) D F Hanks

LC: HW2156–57; HL: LN2408, 1:477–78

---

17. *J. W. Wartmann to WHH*

Rockport Indiana Thursday, June 8. 1865.

Dear Sir:

Your letter bearing date June 5th, and addressed to "Some good *Union* Lawyer," was, by our post-master placed in Judge DeBruler's box, and by the Judge handed to me. Judge L. Q. DeBruler, was a *personal* and political friend of our lamented Chief Magistrate. I will, as far as I am enabled to do so, obtain the information you desire.

Mr Lincoln, when a resident of our State resided near *Gentryville*, in this Co': The place is some 20 miles from here. There has been a singular fatality among his (L's) old friends within the last year. Col William Jones, for whom Mr Lincoln *clerked,* was *killed* last Summer near Atlanta. Josiah Crawford Senr., for whom Mr Lincoln split rails and pulled fodder[1] in payment of a "Weemes' life of Washington," died only a few weeks ago.

I will visit the neighborhood of Mr L's Early life here soon and report.

I need hardly say that I was an ardent "Lincoln Man," and Esteemed him for his personal worth as well as political principles.

Very Respectfully
Your Obt Servt
J. W. Wartmann

LC: HW2158; HL: LN2408, 1:170–71

---

18. *John Rowbotham to WHH*

Cincinnatti. June 9/65 —

Dear Sir:

Thanks for your letter, which came to hand this morning.

I quite understand your position, in respect to the contemplated work — and wish you every success.

Should you visit those scenes connected with Mr. Lincoln's early career in Indiana and Kentucky, I can give you some useful information, having been over the entire ground on a sketching tour.[1]

---

1. Probably stripping the leaves from corn stocks, to be fed to livestock.

---

1. Rowbotham had been commissioned to produce sketches for Joseph Barrett's biography. See Barrett.

I may tell you that the work I am connected with (not as author) *will not* be published in this country — but will be issued in London, Paris and probably Leipsic, simultaneously, so that there is no fear of our clashing.

The information I ventured to ask you for, was just an outline of Mr. Lincoln's career in Springfield with the dates. Should you find leisure to write me a line during your researches, I shall be glad to reciprocate the favor.

I will anticipate with pleasure the appearance of your book feeling sure from the many advantages you posess it will be reliable and instructed; and I quite endorse your opinion that the life of Lincoln has yet to be written.

Hoping your efforts will be rewarded as they deserve.

Believe me to remain,

> Yours Truly
> John Rowbotham.

HL: LN2408, 1:69–70

19. Joshua F. Speed (WHH interview)

[by June 10, 1865[1]]

Speed (Speed)   Joshua F. Speeds' *Statement to me*[2]
    Lincoln on Suicide — about 1840 — See journal 1840   Lincoln loved The Bride of Abydos — Devils drive
        Piece Put in was Inez —[3] Spanish maid[4] — Lincoln [said?] it was a mistake[5]
        Forsook Byron — never Shakespear — & Burns   Went into partnership with Stuart — Jno. T. Stuart.

> Judge Henry Puertle
> Louisville
> Ky

1. On June 10, WHH sent letters to Henry Pirtle and Samuel Haycraft, both of whose names and addresses appear in this memorandum. This suggests that Herndon was prompted to write these two Kentucky informants at Speed's suggestion on or before June 10, 1865.

2. The first word in this heading, and all of the text, is in pencil; the balance of the heading is in pen and was surely added later. The next item (§20), which is also in pencil and on the same distinctive paper, may have been part of this one.

3. The word "Byron" is interlineated directly above the dash, with a caret directly below.

4. Interlineated above: *& p. 758.*

5. This passage refers to AL's fondness for Lord Byron. "The Bride of Abydos" and "The Devil's Drive" are both poems by Byron. The reference to the piece that was put in apparently refers to the lyric "To Inez," which Byron inserted in the narrative of another AL favorite, *Childe Harold's Pilgrimage* (canto 1, following stanza 84). Editions of Byron's poems appearing in the 1830s revealed that Byron's first draft of *Childe Harold* originally had another lyric at this point, which was first printed in 1832 as "The Girl of Cadiz." WHH's reference to "p. 758" would appear to refer to the location of "The Girl of Cadiz" and an explanation of Byron's substitution in a then-current edition, *The Works of Lord Byron, Including the Suppressed Poems* (Philadelphia: J. B. Lippincott and Co., 1859).

Mordica Lincoln — Abes Brother[6] — went to Legislature of Ky — was somewhat Military man — great good Common Sense — Was Entitled to genius — inherited it — fairly —

Sam Haycraft
Elizabethtown
Ky

Logan } Lamborn
Lincoln   } Douglas
Baker } Calhoun[7]
   All dead[8]

   LC: HW3976; HL: LN2408, 2:249–50

20. Joshua F. Speed (WHH interview)[1]

[by June 10, 1865?]

2 Pennsylvania Women — Speed — Gen Dana — 2 weeks before hed died — Snatched out a thorn — planted a rose — one women Kneelded — L. took her up Saying dont pry to me. The other Lady — a modest one — a real dignified lady walked up to L. in a lady like way & Said Mr L taking one of his hands in both hers & Said — Mr L I thank you I never shall see you again— I hope to meet you in heaven — L then took her hands in his — walked with them to the door — & said — I dont know that I will eve get to heaven.

Lincoln was Simple and never above acknowleging his ignorance &c — machinery — words — Customs — Etiquette &c —

Don Quixott — The Bable — Esops Fables — Shakespear — Burns — Byron —

Speed says Lincon came here in 1835–6 Winter

Forquer

Did not wish to kill Shields[2] — Sometimes thought others — the very thought was agony —

---

6. Mordecai Lincoln was AL's uncle.

7. Probably refers to the opposing political debaters of Springfield in the late 1830s and early 1840s: Stephen T. Logan, AL, Edward D. Baker—all Whigs; Josiah Lamborn, Stephen A. Douglas, John Calhoun—all Democrats.

8. This line was apparently entered later.

---

1. This document may have been written at the same time as the previous item and may, indeed, belong to it. On similar paper and also in pencil, it was docketed separately and given the number 3.

2. Refers to Lincoln's near duel with James Shields in September 1842.

Lincoln was at Chicago after his Election — Saw Speed — &c. Jany or Feby. 1860.[3]

Speed heard Lincoln Speak her in 1836 Forquer attacked him & Lincoln replied —[4]

LC: HW3794–95; HL: LN2408, 2:392–93

21. William Engle to WHH[1]

Sweetwater Ills. June 10th 1865.

Dear Sir,

Yours of the 5th inst. came duly to hand and contents noted.

In regard to the questions asked, touching our once mutual friend Abraham Lincoln. It will take me some time to get up dates and get things in shape. But in regard to boreing a hole in the bottom of the flat boat, to let the water out, I am no witness in the case and know nothing about it. As for sewing up the hogs Eyes, I was not present but have seen them that were. I think I can get that up straight, and in a few weeks I will write you again, or come and see you. The President Mr. Lincoln has Eat and Drank and slept in my house, and I think I have some deeds of Surveys that he made me, that will assist me in dates. But should I never have the privilege of penning another line on the subject, I wish to say that through my long acquaintance with him, of near or quite forty years, his friendship was undying, it was eternal; always standing out in bold relief; it was truly friendship in marble and marble in Clay.

You will hear from me again, I think soon.

Give my love to your Father, those old acquaintance is dear to me.

Respectfully You[r]s
William Engles.

HL: LN2408, 1:552–53

22. William G. Greene to WHH

June 11th 1865

Friend Herandon

Yours of 5th inst recd. contents noted &c   Those Notes of Surveys are date respectively one the 16th & the other the 17th of November A.D. 1836 (I presume that that job was a bout the last of His surveying as he soon after went to Vandalia to take his seat in the Legislature & never permanantly Domiciled in this

3. WHH first wrote "Nov or Dec 1860" but later substituted "Jany or Feby."

4. For Speed's retelling of this incident, see §§370, 473.

1. Donald, 174, cites the original manuscript of this letter in the Weik Papers, ISHL, not located.

Co. afterwards)   If that ould Lady who you write lives "some 9 or 10. miles North West of your city who says Lincoln mad a Crop for her Husband some time in 1831–32 or –33"[1] was not a *woman* I would say she *Lied* like *Hell*   he never croped *for* or *with* any one in Sangamon Co. In reply to Interogitary No 3   Capt Lincoln Co Rendivoused at Beardston remained there 3 or 4 days then moved in a North Westerly direction & Camped the lst night at or near Rushville remained there 2 or 3 days untill all the Troops were fully organised the Colum struck the Missippie River at or near the *Yellow-Banks* General Sam Whiteside Comd the Volenteers General Gains & Gen. Adkinson were in comd. of the Regulars   I presume Gains was the senior

Capt Lincolns Co. was discharged at the mouth of Fox River on the West or North west bank of the Ills River   Lincoln reenlisted as a private and pursued the Indians untill they conqerd or drove them west of the Miss. River   My impression now is that his entire Coe. save & except our Noble *Captain* returned when we were mustered out at Now Otoway

The Whiskey Barrell story so help me god is true as Revelation & the statements made to Thayer are in the *main* True except I did not *cry* I was not Noble enough or *sensative* sufficient.[2] Though Lincoln's *Lecture* that Night after he & I were & a lone I now have no doubt was the nearest the Sublime that I shall ever *heare* I judge from the fact that what little success has smiled on me was from *resolves secretly* made to myself from his Lecture on the best or wisest course for wayward or penniless boys &c

The Rosting-Ear Story is a humbug and I would pay no regard to it the whole world knows Lincoln was a small feader.

I now think I shall be up next week & will Call & see you. your friend.

W G. Greene

LC: HW2159–60; HL: LN2408, 1:479–80

23. J. Rowan Herndon to WHH

Quincy June 11th 1865

Sir,

i recievd yours of the 5th inst — you say that Bill Grims[1] says that Lincoln Lest the Bote at salem and went to Clerking for Offet and others say that he went to neworlens   Now to Prove the fact that he went Down to New orleans i take Mr Lincolns own statement Greely or some other Person wrote Mr Lincoln from

---

1. The same story was collected for Josiah G. Holland by Erastus Wright. See Holland, 40.

2. This refers to an incident related in William M. Thayer, *The Pioneer Boy, and How He Became President* (Boston, 1863), 249–53. To help Greene win a bet, AL lifts and drinks out of a whiskey barrel, spits out the whiskey, and then lectures Greene on the evils of betting. In an interview with G. A. Pierce published in the Chicago *Weekly Inter Ocean,* May 5, 1881, Green identified the loser of the bet as a man named Eastep. Clippings in the Nicolay and Hay Collection, ISHL.

---

1. William G. Greene. See §§11, 15.

Newyork for a history of his Life he Writes Back and says i have Been one trip on
a flat Boat to Neworleans and Served as Capt in the Black Ware have Been a member of the Legislator several times and once a member of Congris and the Ballance
you Know there fore Mr Grimes is Mistaken Capt Josep Aartes[2] says that Mr Lincoln Came up on his Boat from Neworleans in January 1832 or very Early in the
spring of 32 that Mr Lincoln told him that he and his Company went Down with
the intention of Remaining through the winter But a Part of the Company got
Sick which Caused his and their Riturn Back again and During the trip he Became acquainted with him and Became much attached to him as Did the Pasen-
gers Both Cabin and Deck and that he was a very Plane and Modst young Man   it
is Not often that the Capt of a Steam Boat and the Cabin Pasingers make them
Selves farmilar with deck Paingers unless there is something atractive   i think Mr
Grimes must Be mistaken   and Reference to the Steem boat Talesmen that came
up the sagamon River in the spring of 32 very Early of that spring there was a
Company from springfield that chartered the Steamboat Talismen to Navigate the
Sangamon and she met the ice at the mouth of the River held there By Back Warter
from the illinois River   i think and shure that Mr Lincoln was one of the Company that Met hur at the mouth of the River and help Poilet hur up when she Came
to Salem the Mill Dam was in the way and they tore a part of it away and the Boat
was goten over and went as high as Boges Mill with the understanding that she
was to have $50-00 a Day for Every Day that She was Detained By Low water when
She Left Boges Mill the River was falling fast and the Boat only made about 3 or
4 Miles a Day on the acount of the high wind from the perary and the Capt was
in Know hury as he was to have the $50-00 a Day for Every Day that she was
Detained By Lowe warter. i was sent for Being & old Boatman and i met hur some
12 or 15 Miles above Salem   Mr Lincoln was eather on Bored when i Got to
hur or went with me we got to salem the Second Day after i went on bord when
we stuck the Dam she hung we then Backed off and threw the ankor over the Dam
and tore away a part of the Dam and and Raised steam and Run hur over the first
trial as soon as she was over the Company that chartered hur was Done with hur   i
think the captain Gave Mr Lincoln $40-00 to Run hur Down to Bairdstown i am
shure i Got $40.00 to Continue on hur untell we Landed hur at Bairdstown   we
that went Down with hur walked Back to Salem   the flat Boats that was Built at
Salem in the winter & Spring of 32 failed to Get over the Dam for there was But
the one Wrise that come that Spring to Let a Boat over and that one was when the
first Brakeup of snow & Raine During that winter & spring he was Mr Offetts
Clirk untell he volentered for the Blackhalk ware had he Been at home in the Spring
of 31 in Plase of Being Down to New orleans he would have sertainly have Benn
in the Campain of 31   that i am Shure of from what i have heard him say   Capt
Artis and myself agrees about the time and year that he Came up with him in Jany
1832 iff there is any thing more that i can explain i will willing Doe it   you must
Excuse me for not ancering you sooner as i Belong to the Quartermasters Depart-

---

2. See p. 6, note 2.

ment here and have Been Confined there During the Day intierly as thay are Preparing to Mustery out solders

Yours Truly
J R. Herndon

NB i will get the Capt to write you   the Boat the Cpt comande was Not the one
that went up the Sangamon.

LC: HW2161–62; HL: LN2408, 1:523–26

24. Dennis F. Hanks to WHH (interview)[1]

Chicago Ills — Sanitary fair June. 13th 1865

Dear Sir:

I received your letter dated the _____ asking 8 or 10 interrogations.
I take great pleasure in answering it, question by question as Each is put & in the order
asked. The ancestors of Mr Lincoln came from England about the year 1650 —: They
first settled in Rockingham County in the State of Virginia and not in Pennsylvania as stated in Abraham Lincolns Biographers —   The ancistors of the Lincoln
family were Scotch English. Two Men Came over from England about 1650 —
one of these brothers was namd Mordaci Lincoln and the other Thomas Lincoln
from whom the descendants derived their nature & their name. All died in
Virginia   These two men were ironside Babtists[2] —. There was one of the children of these men who was named Mordaci — the son of Thomas — I knew none
of the children of Mordaci. I think that this Mordaci was the great great grandfather of Presdt Lincoln. He was born in Virginia and died about 1700. Mordaci
Lincoln was the grandfather of Abraham Lincoln — Mordaci Lincoln was the
great grandfather of Abraham Lincoln Presdt. He was born in the State of
Virginia   Abraham Lincoln the son Mordaci, came his family from Virginia to
Ky in about 1780 among the Pioneers of Danl Boon.[3] He Mordaci died in Virginia. Mordaci was the father of Abrahams grandfather. Mordaci had 6 children
— 4 boys & 2 girls — The only one of his Mordaci's sons I now remember was
Abraham Lincoln born about 1755 — who was the grandfather of Abraham —
and the father of Thomas   He was killed by the Indian near Boonslick Ky no
County —. All these persons Abraham Lincoln the grandfather of Abraham the
presdt had 3 sons — Mordaci & Abraham — & Thomas Lincoln[4] the last being
the father of Abraham. All these sons & daughters scattered and went — some to
Ky — some to North Carolina — Tennessee — Indiana & Ills. The Hanks family
of which I am one was not Connected with the Lincoln family till about 1808 —.
Thomas Lincoln — Abrahams father was born in the State of Virginia on the

---

1. Written out by WHH in the form of a letter and signed by Hanks.
2. Baptist supporters of the Parliamentary cause and of Oliver Cromwell during the English Civil War.
3. Heavy corrections on the original document make meanings sometimes difficult to ascertain.
4. Cf. testimony on pp. 95–96.

Roanoke About 1775. Thomas Lincoln was 6 years old when his father was killed by the Indians —. I wish to state one fact here about the killing of Thomas Lincoln — Abraham's grandfather.[5] In Kentucky all men had to clear out their own field — cut down the trees — Split them into rails &c. and in putting on the last rail — the 8th on the fence one Indian who had secreted himself shot Thomas Lincoln. Then the Indian ran out from his hiding place and caught Thomas — the father of Abraham — Mordaci the oldest brother of Thomas — and uncle of Abraham jumped over the fence — ran to the fort — shot the Indian through the [port?] holes of the fort — the Indian dropt Thomas — ran and was followed by the blood the next day & found dead — In his flight he threw his gun in a tree top which was found. Mordaci said the Indian had a silver half moon trinket on his breast at the time he drew his "beed" on the Indian, that silver being the mark he shot at. He said it was the prettiest mark he held a rifle on —   So remains now of old Thomas Lincoln's children — boys — three — Mordaci, Thomas — & Silas.[6] — The children of Mordaci came to Sangamon — the children of Silas scattered — some in Ky — some in Tennessee — some in North Carolina — & Thomas Lincoln Came to Indiana. There is Thomas Lincoln Abraham father is a young man: he Thos at the age of 25 was married to Nancy Sparrow — not Hanks as stated in the Biographies of the day —. Nancy Sparrow — Abraham's mother was the child of Henry Sparrow. Henry Sparrow's wife was Lucy Hanks — Abrahams Mother. The stories going about, charging wrong or indecency prostitution in any of the above families is false — and only got up by base political Enemies & trattors to injure A. Lincolns reputation — name & fame —. Thomas Lincoln — Abrahams was married to Nancy Sparrow about the year 1808 in Hardin County & State of Kentucky. Nancy Sparrow — the child of Henry Sparrow married Thomas Lincoln when she was about 20 years of age: she was born in Mercer Co Ky. Thomas Lincoln was born in Virginia. Thomas Lincoln the father of Abraham owned about 30 acres in Hardin County on a little Creek called Knob Creek which Empties into the Roling Fork. He owned the land in fee simple. After the marriage of Thomas Lincoln and Nancy Sparrow — say in 3 or 4 years Abraham was born at that place. The cabin was a double one, with a passage or entry between. About the year 1813 or 14 as the volunteers of the War of 1812 were returning home they came by Lincolns house and he fed and Cared for them by Companies — by strings of them. I was a little boy at that time — Abraham was a little child and Sarah his sister and senior by 2 or 3 years was then likewise living and a little girl. They had no other children — Cause a private matter. It is said in the Biographies that Mr Lincoln left the State of Ky because and only because Slavery was there. This is untrue. He movd off to better his Condition — to a place where he could buy land for his Children & Thos. at $125 per acre[7] — Slavery did not operate on him. I know too well this whole matter. Mrs Lincoln — Abra-

---

5. The confusion about the name of Lincoln's grandfather in this instance is probably that of WHH.
6. Silas is a mistake for Josiah.
7. Meaning $1.25 per acre.

hams mother was 5-8 in high — Spare made — affectionate, the most affectionate I ever saw — never knew her to be out of temper — and thought strange of it.

He[8] seemed to be immovably Cam: she was keen — shrewd — smart & I do
say highly intellectual by nature. Her memory was strong — her [perception?] was
quick — her judgement was accute almost. She was Spiritually & ideally inclined
— not dull — not material — not heavy in thought — feeling or action. Her hair
was dark hair — Eyes bluish green — keen and loving. Her weight was one hun-
dred-thirty —. Thomas Lincoln Abrahams father — was 5 — 10½ high — very
stoutly built and weighed 196 pounds — His hair dark — his Eyes hazel. He was
a man of great streght & courage — not one bit of Cowardice about him —   He
could [illegible] fatigue for any length of time — was a man of uncommon En-
durance. Mr Lincoln's friends thought him the best man in Kentucky and others
thought that a man by the name of Hardin was a better man — so the two men
through the influence of their friends met at a tavern in Hardinsburg Ky. There
the two men had a long & tedious fight and Lincoln whipped Hardin without a
scratch.[9] They did not fight from anger or malice but to try who was the strongest
man — to try manhood. These two men were great good friends ever after. Thomas
Lincoln the father of Abraham could beat his son telling a story — cracking a joke
— Mr Thomas Lincoln was a good, clean, social, truthful & honest man, loving
like his wife Evry thing & every body. He was a man who took the world Easy —
did not possess much Envy. He never thought that gold was God and the same
idea runs through the family. One day when Lincolns mother was weaving in a
little shed Abe came in and quizzically asked his good mother who was the father
of Zebedee's Children: she saw the drift and laughed, saying get out of her you
nasty little pup, you: he saw he had got his mother and ran off laughing. About
Abs Early Education: and his sisters Education let me say this — Their mother
first learned their Abc's and then Ab's. She learned them this out of Websters old
spelling book: it belonged to me & cost in those days c75, it being Covered with
Calf skin — or suchlike Covering. I taught Abe his first lesson in spelling — reading
& writing —. I taught Abe to write with a buzzards quillen which I killed with a
rifle & having made a pen — put Abes hand in mind & moving his fingers by my
hand to to give him the idea of how to write —. We had no geese then — for the
Country was a forrest. I tried to kill an Eagle but it was too smart — wanted to
learn Abe to write with that. Lincolns mother learned him to read the Bible —
study it & the stories in it and all that was moraly & affectionate it it, repeating it
to Abe & his sister when very young. Lincoln was often & much moved by the
stories. This Bible was bought in Philadelphia about 1801 — by my Father &
Mother & was mine when Abe was taught to read in it. It is now burned together
with all property — deeds if any & other records — This fire took place in Charleston — Coles Co Ills Decr. 5th 1864 — lost all I have — my wife died December

---

8. Apparently a mistake for "she."

9. For another version of this story, see §16. Note that in the earlier account the name of Thomas Lincoln's antagonist is given as "Breckinridge" and the fight took place in Breckinridge County. Here the name
is given as "Hardin," the fight taking place in Hardinsburg, the Breckinridge County seat.

18th 1864. I was born in Hardin Co Ky in 1799 — May the 15 — on Nolan Creek near Elizabethtown —. I was ten years older than Abraham and knew him intimately and well from the day of his birth to 1830 — I was the second man who touched Lincoln after his birth — a custom then in Ky of running to greet the newborn babe. A man by the name of Hazel hellped to teach Abraham his letters Abc — spelling reading & writing &c —   Lincoln went to school about 3. mo — with his sister — all the Education he had in Ky — Parson Elkin a preacher of the old Babtist religion Came to Mr Thomas Lincoln's and frequently preached in that neighborhood.

At about the year 1818 Thomas Lincoln — the father of Abraham had a notion in his head — formed a determination to sell out his place and move to Indiana, then a new State where he could buy land as said before at $125[10] per. He sold out to _____   Mr Lincoln got $300 — and took it — the $300 — in whisky. The 30 acre farm in Ky was a knotty — knobby as a piece of land could be — with deep hollows — ravines — cedar trees Covering the parts — knobs — knobs as thick as trees could grow. Lincolns hous was in a hollow — high — tall & peaky hills & borded with cedar. Stood up against the sky all around — Mr Lincoln as stated before sold his farm for whisky. He cut down trees — made a kind of flat boat out of yellow poplar. He made the boat on the Rolling fork at the mouth of Knob Creek Hardin Co Ky — loaded his household furniture — his tools — whisky and other Effects, including pots — vessels — rifles. &c. &c on the boat. He took no dogs — chickens — cats — geese or other domestic animals. He floated on awhile down the Rolling Fork and upset — and lost the most of the tools &c and some of his Whisky. He went along by himself not taking his family. From the Rolling Fork he ran into the Beach fork and thence into the great Ohio. He landed at Thompsons Ferry at *Poseys*[11] — house or farm. He started out from this ferry in search of a place and found one and located it by making blazes — brush heaps &c to make a location, which he afterwards bought at $2.00 per acre — purchased it under the $2.00 act.[12] This was an 80 a tract, and Mr Lincoln not being able to pay for it, lost his $80 which he paid to the government and which the government kept and has to-day —. When he had Cornered the land — blazed it off — marked the boundaries he proceeded on horse back, with his own food & his horses fodder behind him to Vincennes where he paid the $200 per acre as stated before. Mr Lincoln never owned the land — more than a kind of preemption right & sold it when he moved to Ills. I fared like him in all these particulars. He then returned to the State of Kentucky from Spencer Co Indiana, then Perry Co — since divided — as Hardin Co Ky was — as Sangamon Co —. From the old homestead in Ky Hardin — now Lareau Co Thomas Lincoln —

----

10. $1.25.

11. A ferry connecting Kentucky with the Indiana side of the Ohio near the present town of Troy.

12. The Land Law of 1800 allowed the purchase of federal land on four years' credit at $2.00 per acre, and in 1804 the minimum allowable purchase was established at 160 acres. It appears that under the Act of March 2, 1821, Thomas Lincoln relinquished half of this original purchase, retaining 80 acres for which he was able to pay in full. See William E. Bartelt, "The Land Dealings of Spencer County, Indiana, Pioneer Thomas Lincoln," *Indiana Magazine of History* 87 (1991): 211–23.

Nancy father & mother of Sarah & Abe ther two children, & two feather beds —
clothing &c mounted 2 horses and went back to Spencer Co — then Perry Co
Indian where said land was located on a little Creek Called pigeon Creek — about
north of the Ohio — & about 70 miles north west of Hardin Co Ky — & across
& north of the Ohio —. They had no waggons — no dogs — cats — hogs —
cows — chickens or such like domestic animals. Abe was at this time 7 years of
age. — Abe read no books in Ky —   Abe was a good boy — an affectionate one
— a boy who loved his father & mother dearly & well always minding them
well —   Sometimes Abe was a little rude. When strangers would ride along & up
to his fathers fence Abe always, through pride & to tease his father, would be sure
to ask the stranger the first question, for which his father would sometimes knock
him a rod. Abe was then a rude and forward boy   Abe when whipped by his father
never bawled but dropt a kind of silent unwelcome tear, as evidence of his sensations — or other feelings. The family landed at Thompson's Ferry on the Ohio &
on the other side crossed the Ohio, and landed at Poseys Farm on the Indiana side.
Hence 17 miles northwest of the ferry. I went myself with them backwards &
forwards — to Indiana — & back to Ky & back to Ky & back to Indiana and
know the story & all the facts well. We all started from Ky in Septr 1818 & was
three or four days to the ferry & one day from the Ferry out to the place of location —   Here they stopt — Camped — erected a little two face Camp open in
front, serving a momentary purpose. Lincoln saw a wild turkey near the Camp
on the second day after landing and Mrs Lincoln — Abs good mother loaded the
gun —   Abe poked the gun through the crack of the camp and accidentally killed
one, which he brought to the Camp house. Thomas Lincoln then went to cutting
trees for the logs of his house — cutting down the brush and underwood — Indiana then being a wilderness and wholly a timbered Country. I assisted him to do
this — to cut timber — hawl logs. &c and helped him erect his log Cabin — &
Camp — one story high — just high Enough to stand under — no higher. This
took only one day. Abe Could do little jobs — such as Carry water — go to the
springs — branches &c, for water which was got by digging holes —   This was
a temporary affair. This was in 1818. We — Lincolns family, including Sally &
Abe & my self slept & lodged in this Cabin all winter & till next Spring. We in
the winter & spring cut down brush — under wood — trees — cleared ground
— made a field of about 6. acres on which we raised our crops —. We all hunted
pretty much all the time, Especially so when we got tired of work — which was
very often I will assure you. We did not have to go more than 4 or 5 hundred yards
to kill deer — turkeys & other wild game. We found bee trees all over the forests.
Wild game and were our [fir?] We ate no wild locust, like John The Babtist. We
had to go to the Ohio river 17 miles to mill and when we got there the mill was a
poor Concern: it was a little bit of a hand horse mill the ground meal of which a
hound could Eat as fast as it was ground. Yet this was a God Send. The mill was
close to Posey's. The Country was wild full of game — dense with vegetation —
swampy —. We could track a bear — deer — wolf or Indian for miles through
the wild matted pea vines. Indians — wild bears — wolves — deers were plenty.

We had no trouble with the Indians in Indiana, they soon left and westward. In the fall & winter of 1819 & 20 we Commenced to cut the trees — clear out the brush and underwoods & forest for our new grand old log cabin, which we Erected that winter: it was one Story — 18 by 20 feet — no passage — on window — no glass in it. The lights were made from the leaf Coming off from the hog's fat.[13] This was good mellow light & lasted well. The house was sufficiently high to make a kind of bedroom over head — a loft. This was approached by a kind of ladder made by boring holes in the logs, forming *[illegible]* one side of the house and this peg over peg we Climed aloft, the pegs creaking & screching as we went. Here were the beds — the floor of the loft was clap boards & the beds lay on this. Here I and Abe slept & I was married there to Abes stepsister — Miss Elizabeth Johnston — not Johnson. During this fall Mrs Lincoln was taken sick. with what is known with the Milk sick: she struggled on day day by day — a good Christian woman and died on the 7th day after she was taken sick.[14] Abe & his sister did some work — little jobs — Errand & light work. There was no physician near than 35 miles — She knew she was going to die & Called up the Children to her dying side and told them to be good & kind to their father — to one an other and to the world, Expressing a hope that they might live as they had been taught by her to love men — love — reverence and worship God. Here in this rude house, of the Milk Sick, died one of the very best women in the whole race, known for kindness — tenderness — charity & love to the world. Mrs Lincoln always taught Abe goodness — kindness — read the good Bible to him — taught him to read and to spell — taught him sweetness & benevolence as well. From this up to 1821 — Mr Lincoln lived single, Sarah cooking for us, she then being about 14 years of age. We still Keept up hunting — and farming it Mr Lincoln — Ab's father was a Cabinet maker & house joiner &c —: he worked at this trade in the winter at odd times, farming it — in The summer. We always hunted it made no difference what came for we more or less depended on it for a living — nay for life. We had not been long at the log Cabin before We got the usual domestic Animals, Known to Civilization. These were driven out from near the Ohio river or halled in a cart pulled by one yoke of oxen. Mrs Lincoln was buried about one fourth of a mile from the log cabin and the babtist Church, the Pastor was [Lamar?]. Abraham learned to write so that we could understand it in 1821 —. David Elkin of Hardin Co Ky — called Parson Elkin whose name has been mentioned before paid a visit —   I do not think Elkin Came at the solicitation & letter writing of Abe, but Came of his own accord or through the solicitation of the Church to which Mrs Lincoln belonged She being a hard shell Babtist Abe was now 12 years old. Elkin Came over to Indiana in about one year after the death of Mrs Elkin — and preach a funeral sermon on the death of Mrs Lincoln. Parson Elkin was a good — true — man and the best preacher & finest orator I Ever heard. I have heard his words distinctly & clearly one fourth of a mile. Some little time before this funeral ser-

---

13. Hanks seems here to be describing the homemade candles used for interior lighting.

14. Caret indicating interlineated note, "See 13," which seems to refer to further details on the death of Nancy Lincoln on page 13 of the manuscript.

vice he Thomas Lincoln went to Kentucky and married Johnson whose maiden name was Bush. When Thomas Lincoln married her she had 3 children — 2 daughters — & 1 son. The family Came to Indiana with their Step-father and their own mother. There was now 5 Children in the family — Sarah — & Abe. Lincoln — Elizabeth, John D — & Matilda Johnston —. I married the Elizabeth. I was just 21 — She was 15. Thos Lincoln now hurried his farming — his Calling & business, always remember hunting. Now at this time Abe was getting hungry for book, reading Evry thing he could lay his hands on. The marriage of Thomas Lincoln & the widow Johnson was in 1821 — Abraham being now 12 years old. Websters old Spelling Book — The life Henry Clay. Robinson Crusoe — Weems Life of Washington — Esops fables — Bunyan's Pilgrim's progress —. I do not Sy that Lincoln read thse books just then but he did between this time & 1825. He was a Constant and I my Say Stubborn reader, his father having Sometimes to slash him for neglecting his work by reading. Mr Lincoln — A bs father — often Said I had to pull the old sow up to the trough — when speaking of Abes reading & how he got to it, then and now he had to pull her away" From the time of the marriage Thos Lincoln & Mrs Johnson, Mrs Lincoln proved an Excellent Step mother: When she Came into Indiana Abe & his sister was wild — ragged & dirty. Mrs Lincoln had been raised in Elizabethtown in somewhat a high life: She Soaped — rubbed and washed the Children Clean so that they look pretty neat — well & clean. She sewed and mended their Clothes & the Children onc more looked human as thir own good mother left them. Thomas Lincoln and Mrs Lincoln never had any Children, accident & nature stopping things short. From 1820 to 1825. Mr Lincoln & Mrs Lincoln Each worked a head at their own business — Thomas at farming — Cabinet making — & hunting: She at Cooking — washing — sewing — weaving &c. &c — About the year 1825 or 1826, Abe borrowed of Josiah Crawford Ramseys life of Washington[15] — which got spoiled as specified generally in The Presidents life and paid as therein described —: he pulled fodder at 25c per dy to py for it. He worked 3 or 4 dys —. Abe was then growing to be a man and about 15 or 16 ys of age. He was then just the Same boy in Evry particular that he subsequently Exhibited to the world from 1831 — to the time of his death — at this Early age he was more humerous than in after life — full of fun — wit — humor and if he Ever got a new story — new book or new fact or ideia he never forgot it. He was honest — faithful — loving truth, Speaking it at all times — & never flinching therefrom. Physically he was a stout & powerful boy — fat round — plump & well made as well as proportioned. This Continued to be so up to the time he landed in Salem. Sangamon County. In 1825 or 1826 he then Exhibited a love for Poetry and wrote a piece of humorous Rhyme on his friend Josiah Crawford that made all the neighbors, Crawford included burst their sides with laughter. I had it was lost in the fire. He was humorous funny — witty & good humored in all times. Sarah[16] married a man (Aaron Grigsby): she married

---

15. David Pamsay, *The Life of George Washington, Commander in Chief of the Armies of the United States in the War Which Established Their Independence; and First President of the United States* (1807).

16. AL's sister.

him in 1822 and died in about 12 mo in childbed. About 1826 & 7 myself and
Abe went down to the Ohio & cut Cord wood at 25 c per Cord & bought stuff to
make Each a shirt. We were proud of this — It must have been about this time
that Abe got kicked by a horse in the mill and who did not Speak for several hours
and when he did speak — he ended the sentence which he Commenced to the
horse as I am well informed & blieve. From this last period 1825–6 & 7 Lincoln
was Constantly reading, writing — cipher a little in Pikes Arithmatic.[17] He Excelled any boy I ever saw, putting his opportunities into Conversation,. He then
Some had or got Barclay's English Dictionary[18] — a part of which I have now &
which can be seen now at my house — and which I am to give to W H Herndon
of the City of Springfield. During these years the ports of Mr Lincoln were hunting — shooting squirrels — jumping — wrstling — playing ball — throwing the
mall over head — The story about his Carrying home a drunken man is not
true as I think or re cellect. He was good Enough & tender Enough & Kind Enough
to have saved Any man from Evil — wrong — difficulties or damnation. Let his
claim nothing but what is true — Truth & Justice — & Mankind will make
him the *great* of the world: he needs no fictions to back him. Lincoln sometimes
attempted to sing but always failed, but while this is true he was harmony & time
— & sound. He loved such music as he knew the words of. He was a tricky man
and sometimes when he went to log house raising — Corn shucking & such like
things he would say to himself and sometimes to to others — I don't want thes
fellows to work any more and instantly he would Commence his pranks — tricks
— jokes — stories — and sure Enough all would stop — gather around Abe &
listen, sometimes Crying — and sometimes bursting their sides with laughter. He
sometimes would mount a stump — chair or box and make speeches — Speech
with stories — anecdotes & such like thing: he never failed here. At this time Abe
was Somewhat He was now and well as before a kind of forward boy & sometimes
forward too when he got stubborn: His nature went an Entire revolution. One
thing is true of him — always was up to 1830 when our intimacy ended, because
he went to Sangamon & I went to Coles Co.: he was ambitious & determined &
when he attempted to Excel by man or boy his whole soul & his Energies were
bent on doing it — and he in this generally — almost always accomplished his
Ends. From these years 1826 — & 7 what has been said of other years is applica-
ble up to 1830 — working — chopping — toiling — woman child & man —.
The plays & sports were the Same. In 1829 (March) Thomas Lincoln moved from
Spencer Co Indiana and landed in Macon Co Ills, ten miles west of Decatur. In
that spring & summer the log cabin which I now have on Exhibition at the
Sanitary fair in Chicago was Erected. Lincoln helped Cut the logs — so did John
Hanks — Abe halled them & I hewed them all in & raised it the next day we

---

17. Nicholas Pike, *A New and Complete System of Arithmetic, Composed for the Use of Citizens of the United States* (1788).

18. James Barclay, *A Complete and Universal Dictionary on a New Plan . . . to Which Are Prefixed a Free
Enquiry into the Origin and Antiquity of Letters . . . a New Compendious Grammar of the English Language;
and to the Whole Is Added an Outline of Antient and Modern History* (1774).

raised the Cabin. Abraham & his neighbors had a mall, [railing?] party 1830 and he
& they then split the rails to fence the ten acres of land which was done. In the
Spring & Summer of 1830 the ten acres of land were broken up with the place —.
This was on the north fork of Sangamon River in Macon Co Ills — Lincoln was
20 years of when he left Indiana, not 21 — as said in the Books. In the fall of 1830
he went down the Sangamon, he then being 21 years of age with John Hanks in a
boat of some kind.

I now have told you all I recollect & think worthy of being told. I hope this
will put history right, as I have taken time to reflect & to refresh my memory by
Conversations — times of well authenticated date — by records — friends &
papers. All of which I do hereby certify to be true in substance — time & fact —
knowing what is said to be true personally, as I was an actor pretty much all my
life in the scene —

Your Friend
D. F. Hanks

LC: HW2165–83

25. John Hanks to WHH (interview)[1]

Chicago — Sanitary fair — June 13th 1865 —
Dear Sir.

You have asked me some questions in your letter dated the ___ which I duly
received.

My Cousin Dennis Hanks has told you all he knew & I could but repeat the
same thing to you. What I shall say shall be short. I first became acquainted with
"Abe" Lincoln when he was 14 years of age his father — & his family were then
living in Indiana — Spencer Co about 17 miles from the Ohio river. I lived with
Thos Lincoln four years in Indiana working on the farm My Cousin has said
Abraham was farming — grubbing — hoeing — making fences &c.: he went to
school but little whilst I was there — say one or two months & his father has offten
told me he had not gone to school one year in all his life. He read the life of Washington — Histories — some poetry, — all he could get & learned the most of it
by heart quickly & well & alwys remembering it. He often for amusement for his
play fellows — neighbors & friends made quite good stump speeches when between the age of 15 & 20. I went to Indiana in 1823 and left ther after my four
years were out and went back to Kentucky & stayed there till 1828 — when I
moved to Macon Co Ills preseding Thomas Lincoln & his family. Thomas Lincoln moved to Macon Co in 1830. when the little Cabbin was built: it was built
in March 1830. This I am sure of. The ground was broken up 1830 — the same
year — the 10 acre tract has been Spoken of by my Cousin Dennis. I and Abe went
down the Sangamon River from Decatur to Springfield in a canoe. The spring we

---

1. Written out by WHH in the form of a letter and signed by Hanks.

went down the River was the spring after the deep snow. Lincoln went into Sangamon Co in 1831. We went from Springfield — to the mouth of Spring Creek
where it Empties into the Sangamon River and there we cut & cared — & hewed
timber to frame a flat boat — 80 feet long & 18 feet wide. The timbers were floated
down to Sangamon town on a raft. The timbers were taken out of the Sangamon
River — framed & put together at that place. The boat was then 1831. & there
built. We Camped in a Camp on the Sangamon River — done our own Cooking
— mending & washing. Lincoln boarded awhile with Carman. I don't think he
ever worked for Kirkpatrick at that time, for he was continually and busily Engaged on the boat. David Offutt was our Employer and it was for him we worked,
getting about $16 — or $20 pr mo. The boat was loaded, for I saw it loaded with
bacon — pork — Corn & live hogs. We proceeded on the lst of May down the
Sangamon River & landed for a short time at New Salem now in Menard Co. Ills.
The boat got on the mill dam and was fast. We got a small ferry boat & partly
unloaded — got over the dam — reloaded & proceeded down the river — Abe
— his step brother — Johnston & myself doing the navigating of the boat — feeding the hogs &c —   We got near the mouth of Salt Creek and it was there that
the pigs got their Eyes sewed up by Offutts men. Abe did not do this —   Abe
was fixing. Abe said I Can't sew the Eyes up, He held the head of hogs whilst Offutt did so up their Eyes —   Lincoln did bore a hole in the bottom of one End
of the boat, for the water to run out which it did — It did so in this way By putting out Pork — corn & one one of the boat sprang upwards — so that End did
not touch the water way below the dam — and a foot or two below the boat. When
the other End was lightened the heavy End Sank, but did not reach the water or
dam —   The water in the other End of the boat ran down hill according to him
and did run out at the hole bored by Abe this I saw — After the hogs a new &
additional lot were put in the at or near the mouth of Salt Creek where it Empties
into the Sangamon River   we then proceeded down the Sangamon — got into
the Ills — passed Beardstown — Alton St Louis &c. we landed in New Orleans
— in the year 1831. We both Came back to St Louis from New Orleans together,
Johnston being with us from Decatur to New Orleans, and back with us.[2] There
can be and is no mistake in these facts or the time when they took place. We walked
from St Louis out to Edwards afoot and there the Roads parted, he taking the
Charleston — Coles Co road & I the Decatur Road — both afoot all the way.
The next time I saw him he was at Dixon on Rock River — called Dixons ferry in
the year 1832 — month of May. He was the Capt of a Company from Menard
Co — then Sangamon. This was a few days before the Stillman defeat on Sycamore
Creek — about 30 miles from Dixons ferry — North east from there — Abe Lincoln footed it from Beardstown in 1832 coming from the Black Hawk war and
not as we went down the River to New Orleans. Thomas Lincoln moved to Coles

---

2. According to AL's account: "Hanks, having a family, and being likely to be detained from home longer than at first expected, had turned back from St. Louis" (*CW* 4:63–64).

Co in 1831. The next time I saw Abraham was in in the City of Springfield in the year about 1833 & 4; but was residing in Menard Co at that time — I never had a flat boat trip with Abe before nor since the one told you — have been often to New Orleans   I was down the River when Negroes tried to Rob Lincoln's boat — did not see it.[3] Abe Lincoln did Carry a drunken man home one night to keep him from freezing — but my Cousin did not know this & hence did not state it. The man I think his name was Carter told me Abe did — Abe told me — Abes father told me. and all this is good evidence enough. Carter told me Abe was right good & clever to pack him to the fire.

Abrm was after the black Hawk war a Candidate of the legislature — in 1832– 34–36–   I saw him some time after this pleading law at Decatur.

John Hanks (x) his mark

attest
W H Herndon

    LC: HW2184–88; HL: LN2408, 1:158–62

26. Dennis F. Hanks to WHH

Lincoln Cabin Chicago, June 15, 1865

Mr. Herndon:

I hasten to answer your interrogations, &c

1st. You are correct. Forefathers of Mr. L. I believe were born in Rockingham County, Roan Oak River, Va.

2d. Mr. Lincoln went to N.O in the fall of 36 or 37 with Gideon Romine, of Spencer County, Ind. Near Rockport. Went out of the Ohio river near Rockport. Mr. Lincoln's grandfather was named Abraham. Grandfat Name Abraham Lincoln — Great Grand father's name was Mordica Lincoln

Mr. L came back to Coles county — in the Spring following — remained with his father a few days and then went to Salem

A Lincoln father died 13 yrs ago 13th December[1] at Goose-nest, 8 miles South of Charleston

Yours &c
D F. Hanks

    LC: HW2189; HL: LN2408, 1:244

---

3. A reference to an incident on AL's 1828 flatboat trip to New Orleans from Indiana with Allen Gentry. See §78, 88.

---

1. Thomas Lincoln died on January 17, 1851.

27. *Edward R. Roe to WHH*[1]

Bloomington, Jun, 16th. 1865

Friend Herndon:

I take pleasure in answering your interogatories so far as I can. —
Mr. Lincoln's Praecipe vs. the I.C.R.R. was filed Jany. 3d. 1857
Declaration   "   " Same day,   "
Summons issued Same day   "
Served on S.W. Dodd, Station-agent, on Jany, 15th, 1857 and was returnable
to April term,   "
Judgement, June 23d. —   "
for $4,800.
Depositions of N.B. Judd, O.H. Browning S.T. Logan & Archy Williams in behalf of Pltff are on file.

Davis first Sat as judge at the April term, 1849, in the 8th dist. you must refer
to the current laws for counties composing district at that time, as I cannot learn
from the records.

He resigned a Short time previous to the December term of our court, 1862
— barely giving time for a Special election for his Successor, John M. Scott.

Respectfully yours
E. R. Roe, Clk

ISHL: Weik Papers, box 1

28. *William W. Thomas to WHH*

Jacksonville 16 June 1865.

D. Sr. — I answer your note of yesterday. —

I was Elected Circuit Judge of 1 Circuit in February 1839. my Commission
bears date 26 February 1839. up to 23 Feby 1839 the 1 circuit was composed the
counties of Sangamon, Morgan, Greene, Macoupin, Tazewell McLean, Macon,
see acts of 1837 p 112.[1] Logan was Judge until Spring of 1837. he resigned, &
Govr. Duncan appointed William Brown, — The Legislature met in June or July
'37 & Elected Jesse B Thomas. In 1838–9. Thomas was Elected comsr. of the Board
of public works, and I was Elected Judge as his Successor, — 23 Feby '39, the 8
Circuit was created (See acts of 1839[2] page 155.) composed of Sangamon, Macon, McLean, Tazewell, Menard, Logan, Dane & Livingston, & Logan was Elected Judge,   The first circuit was composed of Morgan, Cass, Pike, Calhoun, Green
Scott & Macoupin, Logan resigned shortly after his Election, and Judge Treat was

---

1. This letter is headed: *Cir: Clks's office.*

---

1. *Laws of Illinois, 1836–1837,* 111–13.
2. *Laws of Illinois, 1838–1839.*

appointed by Govr. Carlin. I held the court in March '39 in Sangamon, for Judge Logan, and again in the Summer, for Judge Treat, In the fall of 1839 I held the courts in Tazewell & McLean, — While Judge Treat held courts for me in Macoupin, Scott & I believe Cass, —

Mr Lincoln did not attend the courts in my circuit regularly. — he was at our court in Pike, — several Terms in Morgan, — he was at the courts in Tazewell & McLean, — and in the latter court, made one of the best speeches he ever made in defence of an old Indian Indicted for Burning a Steam Mill.

I ceased to be judge upon the passage of the Law of 1840 & 1 Abolishing circuit courts, & requiring Supreme Judges to hold cir Courts. — (See the Law — I became acquainted with Mr Lincoln first in the Spring of 1832 at Beardstown acting Capt. of a company going to the Black Hawk War of that year, —

Mr Lincoln was remarkable for liberality, fairness and honesty in his practice as Attorney. —

Your friend
W W Thomas.

LC: HW2190; HL: LN2408, 2:437–38

29. J. W. Wartmann to WHH

Rockport Indiana June 19, 1865

My Dear Sir:

Yours of 15th June, just at hand Silas Richardson, Nathaniel Grigsby — (Aaron Grigsby —, brother of Nathl, married Mr L's Step-sister), John W. Lamar and John Romine the post-office address of all whom is Gentryville, Spencer Co' Indiana, are reliable men and live near Thomas Lincoln's old home in this Co.' David Turnham, Dale P.O. Spencer Co.' Indiana, can also give you some valuable information.

What there is in "Raymonds Life of Mr Lincoln,"[1] is, so far as his history in this Co' is concerned, true and substantially correct.

It is *Weems'* — not Grahams' life of Washington[2]; at least, I never heard of any other than Weems' in connection with the story.

Mr L started from *here* (Rockport) *for* and *with Allen Gentry,* on his trip to N.O. in a flat-boat. Allen Gentry is dead, but his wife still lives, and remembers many anecdotes connected with Mr L. The trip was made about the year '29 or '30. Will send you some Mss in a few days. What I do send you can *rely on as true.*

Very truly Yours
J. W. Wartmann

It is extremely difficult to give *exact* times, dates & persons. *About* such a year, is as near as I can come to anything.

W —

LC: HW2192; HL: LN2408, 1:168–69

---

1. See Raymond.
2. Mason Locke Weems, *The Life of George Washington* (1800).

30. John B. Helm to WHH

Hannibal Missouri 20th June 1865

Dear Sir

In answer to yours requesting information of the early days of Hon A. Lincoln, I will say that I have written to three old friends for specific information and expect answers when these answers arive you shall hear from me again — Many persons knowing that I knew Mr Lincoln in his boyhood have verbally and by letter made enquiries Similar to yours and I have generally replied to them in about this stile

Let no man object to Abraham Lincoln because of his lowly birth — The Saviour of Mankind was born in a manger and his lineage miraculous and otherwise of lowly birth   So of A Lincoln the great man of destiny of these United States — He was born about *[blank space]* in Hardin County Kentucky, in an obscure back settlement of Cain brake society in a hunters hut not fit to be called a house, — descended from parents the most humble and obscure in this humble class of people — his father made his living by labour and hunting till game became scarce — he then settled at Elizabethtown the county seat of the county — His father being a day labourer and without education — looked upon bone and mussel sufficient to make the man and, that time spent in school as doubly wasted also his poverty would otherwise have prevented him from sending his boy to School And add to this A. Lincoln's father was not a thrifty man of his class. about 1816 he was living with a Miss *[blank space]* Bush who has been sometimes called his step mother. This Miss _____ Bush about that time sold an interest in a tract of land she had inherited to my uncle for whom I was keeping store for about thirteen hundred dollars her part, She being very poor and needing every thing she dealt much of it out but the remainder she drew in money and afterwards left the country   A. Lincoln was called A. Bush then it was during the time that his Step mother or adopted mother was dealing out this land contract in my uncles store I became acquainted with A. Lincoln then a small boy, that would come to the store with his mother.[1] He would take his seat on a keg of nails and I would give him a lump of sugar, he would sit and eat it like any other boy — but these little acts of kindness so impressed his mind that I made a steadfast friend in a man whose power and influence has since been felt throughout the world —   A. Lincolns father was not then called Lincoln — but Lincorn or Linckhorn as some say —   This was not an uncommon thing in those days where half the men that dealt in stores and gave notes, could neither write nor spell their own name — but upsets the stories of his ancient genealogy that some pretend for him.

A. Lincoln is emphatically a man of destiny — a self made man and — the founder of his family and name —   He was as you and every body else knows a good and great man notwithstanding his lowly origin —   This is I think enough to know of him in history —   His mother was a Miss _____ Hanks whether she was his fathers wife or not, or what became of her there are so many conflicting stories. — I can give no information — nor do I think they should go into history if I did know —   She was very obscure and was not of noble blood —   The

---

1. Helm's recollection cannot be reconciled with other accounts of AL's boyhood, including AL's own.

answers to the letters I shall receive will be clear on this point and will be communicated to you

He was about ten years younger than myself — I am 67 — I very much doubt whether any family record shows or ever did show his age —

Your friend

John B. Helm.

LC: HW2193–94; HL: LN2408, 1:29–32

31. James A. Herndon to WHH

Quincy June 20 1865

Dier friend

J, R, H[1] in forms mee that you wish to now moore difinet a bout the time that Mr A Lincoln made his speach   I will state to you as planing as I can   his speach was made at Paps Ville on Ritchland creek 1832   I think if you will Examon Close you will find in the letter I rote you that in place of my puting the date of the speach 1834 you will find 1832   now the Sale was the seling out of a stock of goods beelongen to Nape & Poge of Birds town[2]   well I am So bothard with peepel coming to the store that I have a poore chance to rite   one requste   Send Mee yours & your Wifes portigraf as I wood Value them Very high   Excuse this My Love to all your wife in per tickler   the Note that Mr Lincoln give was Sign over to E. C Blankinship

Pleas Ancer this as I like to her from you

James A Herndon

LC: HW2195; HL: LN2408, 1:546–47

32. Horace White to WHH

Chicago, June 20 1865.

My Dear Sir:

Yours of the 15th was duly received. I have not had time to attend to your request until this evening. I enclose you a list of Mr L's speaking appointments as I find them in the Tribune. I know that he made more speeches than are here mentioned as he sometimes found that he had time to do so, without interfering with the appointments previously advertised. The joint debates are marked thus X.

I was not aware until I received your letter that you were really preparing a biography having supposed before that you were merely preparing a lecture or memoir. I am very glad that you have taken the task in hand. I will see it has a good notice in the Tribune in a day or two.

Yours truly

Horace White

---

1. John Rowan Herndon.
2. Knapp and Pogue of Beardstown.

[Enclosure]

33. List of AL's Speaking Appointments in 1858

Beardstown	Aug 12	1858
Havana	14	
Lewistown	16	
Peoria	19	
X Ottawa	21	
Henry	23	
Augusta	25	
X Freeport	27	
Carlinville	31	
Clinton	Sept 2	
Bloomington	4	
Monticello	6	
Mattoon	7	
Paris	7	
Hillsboro	9	
Edwardsville	11	
Greenville	13	
X Jonesboro	15	
X Charleston	18	
Sullivan	20	
Danville	22	
Urbana	24	
Jacksonville	27	
Winchester	29	
Pittsfield	Oct 1	
Metamora	4	
Pekin	5	
X Galesburg	7	
Oquawka	9	
Monmouth	11	
X Quincy	13	
X Alton	15	
Mt Sterling	18	
Rushville	20	
Carthage	22	
Macomb	25	
Vermont	27	
Petersburg	29	

LC: HW2196 (letter), HW2110–11 (list of appointments); HL: LN2408, 2:449 (appointments only)

34. *J. Rowan Herndon to WHH*

Quincy June 21st 1865

Sir

i recieved you 3d Leter and will ancer it with the greatest of Pleasure   you
wish to Know about the Dets that Mr Lincoln Owed   the Dets that i aluded to
was Made for Goods that my Brother James and my self Sold to Lincoln and
Berry   those Goods was sold By them to another firm By the Name of Trent and
thay failed to Pay Lincoln and Berry and Berry Dide and Left Lincoln the Dets to
Pay   James and my self transferd the Notes to E C Blankinship as we oad him
for the same Goods and i have Bee told that he Lincoln Paid the Last Dollar of
that Det after he went to Congris and i have No Dout of the truth of the mater
Concerng that Det for the first time i saw him after his Return he told me that he
had Paid the Last of the old Det   those are the facts to the Best of my Memory
and that is very Good yet   you say that James Gave you a speach that Mr Lincoln Made at Paps town   that speach was at old Mr Smith some 12 miles from
Springfield on the old Rode to Bards town there was a store Kept there By the firm
of Poag & Knap and some time in the spring or sommer of 32 they made & auction of their Gods and all of the Canadates ware there at that sale[1]   Mr Lincoln
was there also and was the speach that aluded to so he says and it was on that Day
that i whiped Jessy Dodson   and his friends atempte to Sow foul Play and Mr
Lincoln Pachd in and threw them about Like Boys   i think he was abote to
Commence Speaking when the fight Commenced   i Know that it made him
many friends   as soon as Dodson hollowed Lincoln Puled me a way and to them
that if any moore of them wated to thased Jest fetch them on   But they was all
satisfide and all things went of Quiet the Ballance of the Day   the year that all
this took plas was 1832   this i know to Be the fact for my Book shoes the
Date   you must Excuse my Bad Speeling & Writing   there is one anctdote that
i must tell you that took plase when he was a Boy he told me him self   he said
that he used to Be very fond of Coon hunting and his farther youst to oppose their
hunting   But he would slipe out of a Knight after the old man had Gon to Bed
and take a hunt But thay had a sall fist Dog that would Detect them when thay
would Return so one Knight thay took the fist along thay Caut a Coon and skind
him and then streched it over the Litle Dog and soad him up and turned him Loos
and put the other Dogs on the track and they Ran him hone and Caught him in
the yard and the old man Jumped up and hised the Dogs on the fist thinking it
was a Coon and thay killed the fist thay Couldnt Come up to his Releaf   the Next
moning when the old man went to Examin the Coon it was the Litle Dog thay
ware Called up and ws both thrashd But the Litle Dog Never told on them any
moore when they went a Coon hunting   you can use this to suit your self   i

---

1. Cf. the account at §5.

will tak Pleasure in ancering any Note you wish to write and would Like to Be
Cone the agent for your Book when Complted

yours truly

J R Herndon

LC: HW2198–99; HL: LN2408, 1:532–35

35. Joshua F. Speed to WHH

Louisville 22 June 1865.

Dear Sir

Enclosed you have a copy of the letter you asked for —

I see by one of Lincolns letters that he made a temperance speech which was
published in the Sangamon Journal in 1842 or 3.[1] You can probably find it I wish
you would do so.

Your friend &c

J. F. Speed

[Enclosure]

36. AL to Joshua F. Speed[1]

Springfield, Aug. 24th 1855.

Dear Speed:

You know what a poor correspondent I am. Ever since I received your very
agreeable letter of the 22d of May — I have been intending to write you in answer
to it —   You suggest that in political action now, you and I would differ —   I
suppose we would; not quite as much, however, as you may think. You know I
dislike slavery; and you fully admit the abstract wrong of it. So far there is no
cause of difference. But you say that sooner than yield your legal right to the slave
— especially at the bidding of those who are not themselves interested, you would
see the union dissolved —   I am not aware that *any one* is bidding you yield that
right, very certainly *I* am not. I leave that matter entirely to yourself. I also acknowledge *your* rights and *my* obligations under the constitution, in regard to your slaves.
I confess I hate to see the poor creatures hunted down; and caught, and carried
back to their stripes, and unrenewed[2] toils; but I bite my lips, and keep quiet. In
1841, you and I had together a tedious low-water trip, on a steamboat from Louisville to St Louis —   You may remember, as I well do, that from Louisville to
the mouth of the Ohio, there were, on board, ten or a dozen slaves, shackled together with irons. That sight was a continual torment to me; and I see something

---

1. AL's Temperance Address was delivered before the Washington Temperance Society of Springfield on
February 22, 1842, and published in the *Sangamo Journal* on the following March 25 (*CW* 1:271–79).

---

1. *CW* 2:320–23.
2. AL's original reads "unrewarded."

like it every time I touch the Ohio, or any other slave border. It is not fair for you to assume, that I have no interest in a thing which has, and continually exercises the power of making me miserable. You ought rather to appreciate how much the great body of the Northern people do crucify their feelings, in order to maintain their loyalty to the constitution and the Union. I do oppose the extension of slavery, because my judgment and feelings so prompt me, and I am under no obligations to the contrary. If for this you and I must differ, differ we must — You say if you were president, you would send an army and hang the leaders of the Missouri outrages upon the Kansas elections; Still, if Kansas fairly votes herself a slave state, she must be admitted, or the Union must be dissolved — But how if she votes herself a slave state *unfairly*, that is, by the very means for which you say you would hang men? Must she still be admitted, or the Union dissolved? That will be the phase of the question when it first becomes a practical one. In your assuption that there may be a *fair* decision of the slavery question in Kansas, I plainly see you and I would differ about the Nebraska law — I look upon that enactment not as a *law*, but a *violence* from the beginning. It was conceived in violence, is maintained in violence and is being executed in violence — I say it was *conceived* in violence because the destruction of the Missouri Compromise, under the circumstances, was nothing less than violence. It was passed in violence, because it could not have passed at all but for the votes of many members, in violence of the known will of their constituents. It is *maintained* in violence, because the elections since, clearly demand its repeal, and the demand is openly disregarded.

You say men ought to be hung for the way they are executing that law; and *I* say the way it is being executed is quite as good as any of its antecedents. It is being executed in the precise way which was intended from the first; else why does no Nebraska man express astonishment or condemnation? Poor Reeder is the only public man who has been silly enough to believe that anything like fairness was ever intended; and he has been bravely undeceived.

That Kansas will form a slave constituion, and, with it, will ask to be admitted into the Union, I take to be an already settled question; and so settled by the very means you so pointedly condemn — By every principle of law, ever held by any court, North or South, every negro taken to Kansas is free; yet in utter disregard of this — in the spirit of violence merely — that beautiful Legislature gravely passes a law to hang any man who shall venture to inform a negro of his legal rights — This is the substance, and real object of the law — If, like Haman, they should hang upon the gallows of their own building, I shall not be among the mourners for their fate. In my humble sphere I shall advocate the restoration of the Missouri Compromise, so long as Kansas remains a territory, and when, by all these foul means, it seeks to come into the Union as a slave state, I shall oppose it — I am very loth, in any case, to withold my assent to the enjoyment of property *acquired,* or *located,* in good faith; but I do not admit that *good faith,* in taking a negro to Kansas, to be held in slavery, is a possibility with any man. Any man who has sense enough to be the controller of his own property, has too much sense to misunderstand the outrageous character of the whole

Nebrask business. But I digress —   In my opposition to the admission of Kansas I shall have some company; but we may be beaten. If we are, I shall not, on that account, attempt to dissolve the union. On the contrary, if we succeed, there will be enough of us to take care of the union. I think it probable, however, we shall be beaten. Standing as a unit among yourselves, you can, directly and indirectly, bribe enough of our men to carry the day — as you could on the open proposition to establish monarchy. Get hold of some man in the north whose position and ability is such, that he can make the support of your measure — whatever it may be — a *democratic party necessity,* and the thing is done. *Appropos* of this, let me tell you an anecdote —   Douglas introduced the Nebrask bill in January —   In February afterwards, there was a called session of the Illinois Legislature —   Of the one hundred members composing the two branches of that body, about seventy were democrats. These latter held a caucus, in which the Nebraska bill was talked of, if not formally discussed —   It was thereby discovered that just three and no more, were in favor of the measure —   In a day or two Douglas' orders came on to have resolutions passed approving the bill; and they were passed by large majorities!!! The truth of this is vouched for by a bolting democratic member —   The masses too, democratic as well as Whig, were even, nearer unanimous against it; but as soon as the party necessity of supporting it, became apparent, the way the democracy began to see the *wisdom* and *justice* of it, was perfectly astonishing.

You say if Kansas fairly votes herself a free state, as a christian you will rather rejoice at it. All decent slave-holders *talk* that way; and I do not doubt their candor —   But they never *vote* that way. Although in a private letter, or conversation, you will express your preference that Kansas shall be free, you would vote for no man for Congress who would say the same thing publicly. No such man could be elected from any district in any slave state. You think Stringfellow & Co., ought to be hung; and yet, at the next presidential election you will vote for the exact type and representative of Stringfellow. The Slave-breeders and slave-traders, are a small, odious and detested class, among you; and yet in politics, they dictate the course of all of you, and are as completely your masters, as your are the masters of your own negroes. You enquire where I now Stand —   That is a disputed point —   I think, I am a whig; but others say there are no whigs, and that I am an abolitionist. When I was at Washington I voted for the Wilmot-Proviso as good as forty times, and I never heard of any one attempting to unwhig me for that. I now do no more than oppose the extension of slavery. I am not a Know-Nothing —   That is certain —   How could I be? How can anyone who abhors the apprehension of negroes, be in favor of degrading classes of white people? Our progress in degeneracy appears to me to be pretty rapid. As a nation, we began by declaring that *"all men are created equal."* We now practically read it "all men are created equal, *except negroes.* When the Know-Nothings get control, it will read all men are created equal, except negroes, *and foreigners, and catholics."* When it comes to this I should prefer emigrating to some country where the make no pretense of loveing liberty —   To Russia, for instance, where despotism can be taken pure and without the base alloy of hypocrisy.

Mary will probably pass a day or two in Louisville in October — My kindest regards to Mrs. Speed — On the leading subject of this letter, I have more
of her sympathy, than I have of yours — and yet let say I am

Your friend forever

A. Lincoln

LC: HW2200; HL: LN2408, 3:493 (letter); HL: LN2408, 3:493–50 (enclosure)

37. George M. Brinkerhoff to WHH

Springfield, Ill., June 24th 1865 —

Dr. Sir —

I hand you all the statistics — I am able to; no others than these appear on my
books —

1840	population	2,579 —
1848	"	3,912 —
1850	"	5,106 —
1854	"	6,218 —
1855	"	7,250 —
1860	" U.S. census.	6,499
1862	"	10,709

Your friend

Geo. M. Brinkerhoff[1]

In 1837 about 1900 —

LC: HW2204; HL: LN2408, 2:230

38. John B. Rowbotham to WHH

Cincinnati June 24/65

Dear Sir,

Your letter not having the street & number did not reach me untill this mrng
— But I hasten to give what information I can to assist you in your researches —[1]

It will be better to begin with the birthplace (though I commenced at Springfield) & follow it out in chronological order — From Louisville take the cars to
Elizabeth Town old Thomas Lincoln worked there occasionally as carpenter & it
is probable there may be someone left who remembers him — but I did not stop
to inquire — From E.T. proceed to Hodgenville which is about ten miles south
east of there — & inquire the way to Rock Spring farm owned by Mr. R. A. Creal,
better known as "Old Dickey Creal" The farm is about 3 miles south east of
Hodgenville & a good straight road — The site of Mr. L's birthplace is on this

---

1. George Brinkerhoff was disbursing clerk in the office of the state auditor of Illinois.

---

1. Rowbotham had already traveled through Spencer County on a sketching tour. See §18, note 1.

farm about five hundred yards from Mr. Creals house — It is situated on a little knoll or rising ground & is now a barley field — Some rocks indicating the
site of the chimney are still there. At the edge of the field are two old pear trees
planted by Thomas Lincoln — between which — was a gateway leading to the
house — Mr Creal remembers him well — near the spot is a very romantic
spring from which the farm takes its name — & where no doubt Mr L as a child
often strayed — You will find Mr. Creele a truthful kind hearted man — It
appears Thomas Lincoln removed from here when his son was about four years
old — to a place called Nob Creek — Mr. Creal will direct you to the residence
of Mr Rapier, who is member for the county he lives on Nob creek which is four
miles S. West of New Haven — Mr Rapier will take pleasure in shewing
you the site of the house which was pulled down to make the Greensburg road in
1838 — The school house also is demolished —

From Louisville take the boat to Troy Ind which is close to Anderson Creek.
This is the place where the family first landed after leaving Kentucky — On this
creek which is about half a mile from Troy is a little place called Maxville inquire
for Mr Green Taylor — who remembers Mr. Lincoln well & is a reliable man —

From Troy to their first Indiana home is about sixteen miles & a mile & a half
from Gentryville — The road is very rough & I found it necessary to hire a
conveyance with a couple of mules — or rather three — as the driver was very
little better — his name is Frank Everhard & you may find it advisable to get
him as he knows the place — (Dont give him whiskey)

The house lies a little off the Gentryville road on rising ground & is the most
perfect reminiscence of Mr L's early life — A Mr John Heron occupies it now —
& it is still known as the 'Lincoln lot' they lived there 13 years Mrs Lincoln died
here & is buried on the summit of a thickly wooded hill about a quarter of a mile
& immediately opposite the house — Inquire for Siah Crawford, Jimmey
Romaine & also Mrs Richardson who was at the funeral of Mr Lincoln's mother — There is no stone to mark the spot, but it is well known — As you know
Johnney Hanks it will be unecessary to go into Illinois — Bye the way Mr L
does not appear *to have cared for home after the death of his mother,* perhaps you
may clear that up — It would take a series of letters to give minute descriptions,
but these are *the main facts* — I expect to leave here soon & shall be glad to hear
from you before going — You will understand that I was engaged by Moore —
Wilstack & Baldwin to illustrate their life of Lincoln by Barratt[2] — Wishing
you every sucess believe me to remain

Yours Truly
John B Rowbothem

P.S

Should I be unable to leave here as I want to — I will write you again on the
subject.

J.B.R.

LC: HW2205–6; HL: LN2408, 1:70–73

---

2. Barrett.

39. John L. Scripps to WHH

Chicago June 24*th* 1865

My Dear Herndon:

Yours of yesterday is at hand, and its tenor induces me to reply more specifically to your previous note of inquiry respecting my little campaign Life of Lincoln.[1] I believe I try to satisfy my conscience in whatever I do; and I assure you I never performed a work more conscientiously in my life than the production of that biographical sketch. I am also very sure that Mr. Lincoln was equally sincere and conscientious in furnishing me with the facts connected with his own and his family's history. The chief difficulty I had to encounter, was to induce him to communicate the homely facts and incidents of his early life. He seemed to be painfully impressed with the extreme poverty of his early surroundings — the utter absence of all romantic and heroic elements, and I know he thought poorly of the idea of attempting a biographical sketch for campaign purposes —   "Why Scripps" said he, on one occasion, "it is a great piece of folly to attempt to make anything out of my early life. It can all be condensed into a single sentence, and that sentence you will find in Gray's Elegy:

'The short and simple annals of the poor.'

That's my life, and that's all you or any one else can make of it."

Mr. Lincoln communicated some facts to me concerning his ancestry which he did not wish to have published, and which I have never spoken of or alluded to before. I do not think, however, that Dennis Hanks, if he knows anything about these matters, would be very likely to say anything about them. At all events, if his statements conflict with those of the biography, it is a question of veracity or of memory between him and Mr Lincoln.

To show you how careful I was in the matter let me relate an incident:

When the pamphlet was printed, I sent a few copies to Mr. Lincoln, and in an accompanying note, I said to him, I was in doubt only as to one statement I had made — and that was as to whether or not he had read "Plutarchs Lives". I had trusted somewhat to my memory on the subject of his early reading; and while I was not certain he had enumerated this book among them he had read in his boyhood, yet as I had grown up in about such a settlement of people as he had in Indiana, and as I had read Plutarch in my boy-hood, I presumed he had had access to it also. If I was mistaken in this supposition, I said to him, it was my wish that he should at once get a copy, and read it, *that I might be able to testify as to the perfect accuracy of the entire sketch.* Mr Lincoln did not reply to my note, but I heard of his frequent humorous allusions to it.

I have no copy of the campaign Life on hand, nor can I find one. Soon after the death of Lincoln, I succeeded in finding a copy, but I let Dr Holland have it. Can you find me a copy in Springfield? By the way, are you preparing a life of Lincoln? I am afraid neither Holland nor Dale Owen, will give the time and at-

---

1. John Locke Scripps, *Life of Abraham Lincoln* (Chicago, 1860); also published as *Tribune Tracts*, no. 6 (New York, 1860).

tention to the subject necessary for such a life of Lincoln as we want and ought to have.

Very Truly Yours

J. L. Scripps.

LC: HW2207–8; HL: LN2408, 2:289–92

40. Orlando B. Ficklin to WHH

Charleston Jun 25th 65

My dear Sir

I am in receipt of two letters from you touching your preparing to write the life of our mutual friend Lincoln, but courts & business have kept me going ever since the first was received.

Dennis Hanks is now at Chicago exhibiting log Cabin &c &c, will be at home in two or three weeks. On him & on Col Gus Chapman his son in law & John Hanks you will have to rely to a large extent. I spoke to Chapman yesterday in your behalf & he & Dennis could visit & stop with you long enough to furnish all the facts & fictions traditional or otherwise in their possession The Step Mother is too old & infirm to give much reliable information & her offspring & their descendants are not remarkable for their truth honesty or chastity, & it would be better to rely upon the Hanks who are blood relatives of Lincoln

By very close & direct reply, you can gain from Dennis Hanks much needful information & if you will say to him that I refered you to him for a truthful narrative he will talk freely to you.

It will be 30 years next Decr since Lincoln and myself met at Vandalia as members of the Legislature, a friendship then commenced which remained unbroken by political differences or personal interests or otherwise, up to his death.

I knew him well as a Lawyer a Statesman & citizen, valued him highly & deeply deplored his death. He was a case Lawyer but in a case where he felt that he had the right none could surpass him.

As a Statesman, he was deeply imbued with the Principles of Henry Clay, but was conscientously opposed to slavery all his life, & he expressed his views honestly & truly to the Ky delegation when he urged them so strongly to accept compensated emancipation. He had a nice & keen perception of right & wrong & did not wish to see rich men made poor by having their negroes freed without compensation

If I could be with you I could give many incidents which might be of interest & it would give me infinite pleasure no less on your own account than on account of a deceased friend to do all in my power to present fully & fairly a perfect life.

Very truly yours

O B Ficklin

LC: HW2209–10; HL: LN2408, 2:298

41. S. S. Brooks to WHH

Quincy, Ill., June 26th, 1865.

Dear Sir:

Yours of the 26th was received yesterday, and in reply to your inquiries I would say that, according to my recollection, Hooper Warren published the first newspaper ever printed in Springfield.[1] Politically it was opposed to the administration of Gen. Jackson, who was then President. It had but a brief career. I am unable to state in what year it was published, but it must have been in 1829 or 1830   I do not remember its title.

The second newspaper appeared soon after the discontinuance of Mr. Warren's paper, and was entitled the "Illinois Courier." It was published by a Mr. Meredith, and lived but a short time. It was published in 1831, but the date of its commencement or discontinuance I do not remember. I am not certain but that Warren and Meredith were in partnership in the publication of the "Courier." Your father, Elijah Iles, Esq. Col. John Williams, and others of the oldest citizens of Springfield, can probably give you more definite and correct information with regard to these papers than I can, as I did not remove to Springfield until after the "Courier" was discontinued

The third paper published in Springfield was issued by me in October 1831, Edward Jones, Esq. being for a short time a partner with me, and was discontinued in the fall of 1833. It sustained the administration of Gen. Jackson. It was called the "Illinois Herald".

The publication of the "Sangamo Journal" was commenced three or four weeks after the first issue of the "Herald." Simeon Francis, Esq., was the editor and publisher. With its subsequent history I presume you are familiar.

I am not certain whether the "State Register" was removed from Vandalia to Springfield in 1830 or in 1840, but think it was in '39, preparatory to the printing for the session of the winter of '39–'40. —   Mr. Weber or Mr. Lanphier can advise you correctly on that point.

I have thus given you all the information in reply to your inquiries that I can recollect. Should my memory hereafter recall any thing of importance to you connected with the publication of any of these papers, I will take pleasure in communicating it to you

Respectfully Yours &c
S. S. Brooks, Sen

LC: HW2211–12; HL: LN2408, 2:440–41

---

1. The *Sangamo Spectator*, edited by Hooper Warren, commenced publication in February 1827.

42. Tim G. Needham to WHH

Elizabethtown Ky June 26th 1865

Dear Sir.

By reference to the "*laws* and records" I find that Thos Lincoln held his farm in *fee*. He bought of *Dr* John Tom Slator. The Deed is dated 2*ond* Sept 1813 — Lincol's deed to Milton[1] is dated 27*th* October 1814 (instead of 1816 as you ask in your letter to me.)

Larue Co. was cut off this (Hardin) County in the spring of 1843 — as I wrote to you before.

I will assist Mr Wintersmith as far as I can.

Respectfully Yours
Tim G. Needham

LC: HW2213; HL: LN2408, 1:61–62

43. John B. Helm to WHH

Hannibal Mo 27th June 1865

Dear Sir

Yours of the 25th inst. is received.

In answer to it I will say, that you would have to apply to some one older than I am to tell when Stump Speaking and Camp Meetings were first introduced into Kentucky —   My understanding is that they were both institutions brought by the first emigrants from their Mother country Virginia   I have an old relative sitting by me ten years older than I am — who says you would have to apply to some one older than she is to tell when stump speaking and Camp Meetings were introduced into Ky.

You may safely say they were introduced immediately after or with the closing of the Indian Wars that attended the first settlement of Kentucky.

Very little change ever took place in the manner of Stump Speaking except at the two presidential elections, first When Harrison was elected and the next election when Polk was elected

The Whig party sung Harrison in — at the next election the Democrats beat the Whigs all hollow and sung Polk —   The manner of stump speaking in Kentucky has always been to pit the best speakers one on each side; and some times two or more on each side. The speakers generally lawyers were as respectfully to each other as if in a court Room at the bar

Camp Meetings with the Methodists has ever been an institution of the church and every neighborhood had its Camp Meeting regularly once a year after harvest and before the frosts of Winter —   No material change in the institution ever took place amongst the Methodists —   Other churches have from time to time had their Camp Meetings — but just like the Whigs in 1840 when they under-

---

1. Charles Melton, who purchased the Mill Creek farm of Thomas Lincoln.

took to beat the democrats and out sung them — so with other churches they have had all sorts of doings at their camp meetings

Candidates that could speak at all, generally spoke at all political meetings — Those who could not speak would go on the stand and announce themselves candidates — this took place almost invariably at county and Circuit court which is over in each month.

If you disire to know anything of the Bush family — I know them well

I shall get the information you asked for in relation to Lincoln very fully in a short time —[1]

J B Helm

LC: HW2215–16; HL: LN2408, 1:27–29

44. John Hill to WHH

Petersburg Ills   27th June 65

Dear Sir

Yours of 21st came duly to hand. Have awaited an opportunity to see Capt Wright in relation to Matheny's Speech before replying.[1]

The article in the Mo. Republican in relation to Mr. Matheny's speech at this place in 1856 was written by Capt Wright. Also, an article in the "Index" of corresponding date.[2] The articles excited considerable sensation at the time. They were not verbatim, but substantially correct. I think I remember that before the publication of the article in the Index it was submitted to Matheny and he endorsed the report of his remarks. The reports in the two papers very nearly correspond, and I think, aside from party coloring, are correct in every particular.

As to Mr Lincoln's book on Infidelity, I gave you all my knowledge verbally. Since my early childhood I remember to have heard it alluded to, hundreds of times by different old settlers. Of late years I have heard less of it, as these old men have many of them passed away. I have a better remembrance of it by my father's connection with it. You know that there are always some few things that strike into the minds of a child at early age which time will never eradicate. This is one of the circumstances from which I date my earliest remembrance. It could not have been on account of Lincoln's position, as that the time I knew no more as to who he was than I did of the inhabitants of the Fejee Islands. When I heard of my father having morally compelled Mr Lincoln to burn the book, on account of its infamy &c pointing to Voltaire, Paine &c, the circumstance struck me so forcibly that I

---

1. The last two sentences appear in the margin.

---

1. Probably James H. Matheny, an early friend and political associate of AL. The reference may be to a speech Matheny was said to have made alleging that "renegade Democrats" reneged on an agreement to elect AL to the Senate in 1855, a speech cited by Stephen A. Douglas at the Jonesboro debate with AL, September 15, 1858 (CW 3:108–9).

2. Only two issues of the *Menard Index* for 1856 survive.

have never heard the word infidelity, Paine or Voltaire, since, without thinking of it. My mother was strictly religious, and before hearing of this I had always thought my father to be averse to religion. I was so surprised that I suppose it made the deeper impression. As to date I do not know. It was in the winter time, as tradition says it was done in fathers store, while there was fire in the stove, & that there it was burned,   Your friend

John Hill

LC: HW2217; HL: LN2408, 1:514–16

45. Joseph S. Wilson to James Harlan[1]

June 27. 1865.

Sir:

In reply to the letter of Mr W. H. Herndon, who is writing the Biography of the late President, dated June 19. 1865, herewith returned, I have the honor to state, pursuant to the Secretary's reference, that on the 15th of Oct. 1817 Mr *Thomas* Lincoln, then of Perry County Indiana, entered under the old credit System;

1*st*   The South West Quarter of Section 32 in Township 4 South of Range 5 West, lying in Spencer County Indiana.

2nd   Afterwards the said Thomas relinquished to the United States the *East* half of Said South West Quarter; and the amount paid thereon was passed to his credit, to complete payment of the *West* half of Said South West Quarter of Section 32 in Township 4 South of Range 5 West; and accordingly a patent was issued to said Thomas Lincoln for the latter tract. The patent was dated June 6. 1827, and was signed by John Quincy Adams, then President of the United States, and countersigned by George Graham, then Commissioner of the General Land Office.

Thomas Lincoln was the father of Abraham Lincoln, late President of the United States, the latter having borne the christian name of his grandfather.

3d   In regard to the Bounty Land Warrants issued to *Abraham* Lincoln, for Military Services during the Black Hawk war as Captain of 4th Illinois Volunteers; the first warrant, No 52076 for forty acres, Act of 1850, was issued to Abraham Lincoln, Captain &c, on the 16th April 1852, and was located in his name by his duly appointed attorney, John P. Davies, at Dubuque Iowa, July 21. 1854, on the North West quarter of the South West quarter of Section 20 in Township 84 North of Range 15 West, Iowa.

A patent, as recorded in volume 280 page 21, was issued for this tract to Abraham Lincoln on the 1st of June 1855, and transmitted the 26th Oct. 1855 to the Register for delivery.

Under the act of 1855, another Land Warrant, No 68465, for 120 acres, was issued to Abraham Lincoln, Captain Illinois Militia, Black Hawk war, on the 22d

---

1. Joseph S. Wilson was acting commissioner of the General Land Office, and James Harlan was secretary of the Department of the Interior.

April 1856, and was located by himself at Springfield *Illinois,* Dec. 27, 1859, on the East half of the North — East quarter, and the North — West quarter of the North East quarter of Section 18 in Township 84 North of Range 39 West; for which a patent, as recorded in volume 468 page 53, was issued Sept. 10. 1860, and Sent Oct. 30. 1860 to the Register for delivery.

I am, Sir,

Very respectfully Your O'bt Servant

Jos. S. Wilson,

Acting Commissioner.

LC: HW4495; HL: LN2408, 2:120–21

46. John T. Stuart (WHH interview)

[*late June 1865[1]*]

Jno. T. Stuart

Says — that Lincoln Came to Springfield in 1836 or 1837 — Spring — or *fall & winter* — think the last — Stuart & L entered into partnership in 1837 — L. went to Congress in 1839[2]

— S & L then dissolved the legal firm — Logan & Lincoln then Entered into partnership. Lincoln went to the Legislature in 1834–6–8 & 1840 — again Elected in 1854 — refused to take his seat — became a candidate for U.S. Senate — beaten — Trumbull Elected U.S. S — S says he will write something for me, *but he won't* — give him any subject — topic he pleases in Lincoln's life. Logan & L dissolve partnership in 1844 —   Lincoln is a gloomy man — a sad man — His wife made him Presdt (?): She had the fire — will and ambition — Lincolns talent & his wifes Ambition did the deed — Lincoln Courted a Miss Short[3] in 1834 & 5: She refused him — probably in 1836 it was — Lincoln is — was a kind of vegetable — that the pores of his flesh acted as an appropriate organ for such Evacuations &c — differed with other men about this — Lincoln was a torpid man gloomy. That Speed said if Mr Lincoln had married an other woman — for instance Speeds wife he Lincoln would have been a devoted husband and a very — *very* domestic man: That Lincoln needed driving — (well he got that) That having his — L's peculiar constitution — this dormancy — this vegetable constitution — vitality — this tenacity — his want of passion — Emotion — imagination he was tough & Enduring & but for this Lincoln with all the strength at Washington would have died — been killed in 3 mos. L did forget his friends — That there was no part of his nature which drew him to do acts of gratitude to his friends —

---

1. Though WHH estimates that he first talked to Stuart five days previous to July 21 (see p. 77), the distinctive reference to a Miss Short, about which WHH queries James Short and which Short responds to on July 7, indicates that the interview must have been earlier. Note that G. U. Miles reports that Short received WHH's letter by June 30.

2. Marginal note in Springer transcription: *(a mistake) this means Stewart.*

3. Probably refers to AL's unsuccessful courtship of Mary Owens in 1836–37. See §56.

Says — That part of the Sangamon Volunteers in the Black Hawk war of 1832 — assembled at Springfield — went thence to Beardstown on the Ills — 45 m west of Springfield — all assembled — from thence all went to Rushville Schuyler Co — still westward — duly organized about 2 miles out of Rushville — went thence to Rock Island — called fort Armstrong. Stuart says he was in a Spy battallion — Lincoln was Captain, Stuart was under Dawson. Lincoln was in Command of his own Company — Gen — Col Henry was the Major of the Spy battallion. The time of Enlistment was 90 days: the time Expired — Lincoln re-entered — volunteered again. Stuart & Lincoln now became privates — went into Maj. Iles Company — Went from Rock Island to Dixon on the Ills River, East from Rock Island. We went from this place to the battle ground of Bad Axe[4] — thence up the Rock river near to fox River — thence between the Ills & Fox Rivers. we marched up to Ottowa — Lincoln & Stuart & Harrison came home together. Harrison lost his horse on the road — wrode and tied by turns among the boys — Each helped the one in want — so that all could walk awhile & wride awhile — Probably we were discharged before the 90 days by the State —   We did no could — could do no good — re-volunteered before the 90 days had Expired: It was at this time that Lincoln and my self went in as a private — we staid out our 30 days — came home.

Stuart Says — that about the year or between the years 1848 & 50 that Lincoln & himself were returning from court, homeward bound from Tazwell — rather Pekin or Tremont Court — near the little town of Dillon this side of Tremont[5] — he S said to Lincoln that the time would soon Come in which or when we must be Democrats or Abolitionists. "When that time comes my mind is made up," The Slavery question Can't be Compromised Said Lincoln in an Emphatic tone. "So is my mind made up too" Said Stuart just as Emphatically and so we now stand — did stand. Lincoln used to Carry around in the Circuit Court tramp with him say from 1846 — to 1855. Euclid's Geometry — Shakespear: he could well repeat much of Shakespear. Lincoln was an Educated Man in 1860 though he dug it out himself. Stuart further that while Lincoln as Presdt was promising — or giving by *implication* — giving the South to understand thatt, the Presdt, *was* preparing his Proc of Emancipation (I doubt this Herndon).

S— says further — he thinks that the marriage of Lincoln to Miss Todd was a policy Match all around — Lincoln was not a social man — was sad — gloomy: he couldn't Care for any man or any man's interests — attended to no public interest — those things that interest the unpolitical public — cared nothing for colleges — Assylums, Rail Roads — churches — Hospitals — and such like things & institutions — Attended no such meetings — Had no organizing abilities — felt no special interest in any man or thing —   Save & Except politics — loved

---

4. Stuart has confused the battle of Bad Axe, which was fought in Wisconsin at the conclusion of the war, with an Illinois battle, probably Stillman's Defeat.

5. Cf. §§377, 409.

principles and such like large political & national ones, Especially when it leads to his own Ends — paths — Ambitions — Success — honor &c. &c.

LC: HW2242–45; HL: LN2408, 2:200–204

47. *Henry Pirtle to WHH*

Louisville, 27 June 1865.

Dear Sir:

Yours of the 10th instant was received several days ago, and would have been answered at once, but I have been very unwell.

My father, when I was young, lived within a mile of Mordecai Lincoln, and a half mile, or less, from Josiah Lincoln, the older brothers of Thomas Lincoln, the father of the President. I knew them as intimately as a young person could know men of their age, and I went to school with their children. These Lincolns were excellent men, — plain, moderately educated, candid in their manners and intercourse, and looked upon as honorable as any men I have ever heard of. Mordecai Lincoln was the oldest son, and his father having been killed by the Indians before the law of primogeniture was repealed, (for the repealing act took effect on the first of Jan. 1787) he inherited a very competent estate — The others were poor.

The President was born some distance from the place where I lived in Washington County, and I did not know him until after he had arrived at manhood. He was born in Hardin County.

I have sent your letter to Hon. Samuel Haycraft of Elizabethtown, Hardin County, Ky.

Very Respectfully
Henry Pirtle.

LC: HW2218; HL: LN2408, 1:67–68

48. *John T. Jenkins to WHH*

Lincoln Ills. June 30, 65.

Dr Sir.

Yours of this date rec'd. The Town of Lincoln is situated on the N.W. ¼ Sec. 30 T. 20. R. 2 W. Said ¼ was entered May 21/39 by Isaac and Joseph Loose; Robert B. Latham purchased the same of Loose, and conveyed ⅔ interest to John D. Gillett and Virgil Hickox, who laid off a part of said tract into Lot, Blocks &c and called it "Lincoln". it was regularly platted, same acknowledged by said Latham, Gillett and Hickox August 26, 1853 and duly recorded. I believe this a *full answer* to your inquiry about Lincoln.

As your inquiry about when Matteson began to run the A.C.&St.L.R.R. and when his contract ended."

I can not give the desired information. I think however, it began in Summer or Fall of 1856 and ended perhaps in 1860 — I have no record date and cannot say positively —

You can get all the information in U.S. Court at Chicago — where there was a suit some years ago, in which the "Honest and virtuous Ex Governor" flourished "some".

Hoping the above may be satisfactory —

I am friend Bill
Yours Respectfully
John T. Jenkins.

HL: LN2408, 2:292–93

49. G. U. Miles to WHH

Petersburg Ill June 30th/65

Dear Sir

I have Examined your Block of lots   have not seen Mr Clark — they are worth more money   I will not Sell at that offer   I will be up last of next week and describe them to you

if you buy out Carey Chatterton I will furnish the money for Pet & Julia. but act on your own Judgment. This I forgot to Say to you when I was up

we are all well —

Yours Truly
G U Miles

your letter recd

I Saw Short found him in Bransons office Branson red him your letter   he took the letter home said he would make out an answer in in the course of a week

Kelso I was acquainted with for 4 or 5 years after I came here he mooved west to MO or Iowa 20 years ago & I have hurd nothing of him since   he was about the man you represent & if living must be 75 year old

G U M

[Notes on envelope in Herndon's hand:]
Kelso—*Miles Letter*
Kelso was an Educated as well as a well read Man — deeply & thoroughly read in Burns & Shakespeare

Lincoln & Kelso [Contested?] one another's [penchant?] for glory &c

LC: HW2220; HL: LN2408, 1:488

50. Samuel Haycraft to WHH

Elizabeth Town Kentucky [June 1865]

Dear Sir

Yours of 10. Ins Came to hand in due time. but it was at the Commencement of a 3 weeks term of the Hardin Circuit Court (of which I am Clerk) press of business has therefore prevented an earlier answer. I am really anxious to see a Correct History of the life of our late President, who was truly one of *natures* great men

In the years 1805. 1806. 1807. & 1808. I was intimately (though a boy) intimately acquainted with Thomas Lincoln father of Abraham Lincoln. Thomas Lincoln then called *Linkhorn* (but it was always spelled Lincoln) was a house Carpenter by trade done the joiners work on my fathers house — & the entire joiners work on the house of Hardin Thomas 2 miles out the work still exists to show for itself. He was an uneducated man. a plain unpretending plodding man attended to his work, peaceable good and good natured, He was a square stout built man of only ordinary height. He married a Miss Nancy Hanks in one of the years above named. say 1807   She was a woman of rather low stature but heavy & well set. and has many relatives now living in this County. of the Young family her mother was a *"Young"*[1] Some time in 1808. Thomas Lincoln moved to Nolin Creek at a place between Jos. Kirkpatricks & Hodgenville then Hodgens Mill (the house now gone)   on the 12th day of February 1809 Abraham Lincoln was born, (he had an older sister born in Elizabeth Town before removing to Nolin) — Shortly after Thomas Lincoln moved about   miles off to a cabin on the head of Knob Creek, Abraham Lincoln wrote to me that his first recollections were of Knob Creek residence.[2] He must have resided there several years, as it was from that place that young Abraham Commenced trugging his way to school to Caleb Hazle — with whom I was well acquainted & could perhaps teach spelling reading & indifferent writing & perhaps could Cipher to the rule of three — but had no other qualifications of a teacher except large size & bodily Strength to thrash any boy or youth that came to his School, and as Caleb lived in a hazle nut switch country, no doubt but that young Abraham received his due allowances —   The house in which Thomas Lincoln lived in Elizabeth Town is yet standing but has been removed three times — used twice as a slaughter house & now as a stable & within fifty yards of its original locality, about 14 feet square

I think that Thomas Lincoln moved to Grayson County Kentucky, before he went to Indiana & afterwards to Illinois. To all human appearance the early life of Abraham Lincoln was as unpromising for becoming a great man as you could imagine, indeed I would say it was forbidding, and proves to me that nature bestowed upon him an irrepressible will and innate greatness of mind, to enable to break through all those barriers & iron gates and reach the portion he did in life

---

1. Some members of the Hanks and Young families did intermarry, which probably formed the basis of Haycraft's recollection. See the appendix.
2. See AL to Haycraft, June 4, 1860, *CW* 4:70.

Thomas Lincoln the father lost his wife in Indiana, he came on a flying trip to Kentucky to see a widow lady named Sally Johnson (her maiden name was Bush) a poor woman but of spotless character her lst. husband Daniel Johnson died in April 1814 of the *cold plague,* as was called   I issued the license (being then Clerk) and they were married on the 2d day of December 1819. Abraham then was a little more than 10 years old and of course his early training was under this good woman, for I knew her well. she was scarce a half mile from myself & I know she was a good woman & when a girl her mother thought she was too proud, simply because the poor girl tried to make herself look decent & keep in the fashion of that early day —   As soon as Abraham began to prosper in the world. he remembered his father & Step Mother, bought & presented to them the farm on which Thomas Lincoln died. The widow now upwards of 80, lives with Isaac Hall her son in law in Effingham Co Illinois 8. miles from Charleston & 18 from Mattoon. These last facts I have from my Townsman Isaac Radly Esqr who saw her about 3 weeks ago —

Some of the facts I give are from my own knowledge & the balance from letters from Abraham Lincoln himself —   He wrote me five letters in 1860[3] — one of them after his election.

Although I have written a long letter. I feel conscious that it affords but a meagre account of that great & good man our late President.

I was opposed to his election, but before his death I was Convinced that he was the very man for the place. and look upon his assassination as wicked beyond description & one of the greatest calamities that could befall the nation & particularly the South. I always was a Union man. a proslavery man — & wanted all things restored as they were at the Commencement of the war, but the South made the abolition of slavery a necessity & I am now willing for the Constitutional Amendment —   It may be called fanaticism in me but it looks to me as if the Lord had raised up A Lincoln for the special purpose of blotting out Slavery, that God had permitted Slavery to exist too long. to Christianize Africans & then let them go free.

This letter is private & not to be used in publication, but the facts such as they are are at your disposal.

I fear my hand writing will puzzle you. I will be 70 years old 14. of Aug. if I live to see it, & age must account for this scrawl

Respectfully Yours
Samuel Haycraft

LC: HW2266–67; HL: LN2408, 1:33–37

---

3. See *CW* 4:56–57, 69–70, 97, 99, 139.

51. J. Rowan Herndon to WHH

Quincy July 3d 1865

friend William

i Recievd yours of the 26 June and have failed to ancer it untell this Moment for the Reason that we are Mustering out soldiers and i have Kept Buisy untell this Day   you say the Litle Dog story is too good to Be Left out and you want Some moore of his indana storys   you want to No some more about his Reading   well he used to Read By fire light of Knigh in the Coopers shop and Read Every thing he got hold of that would improve his Mind   as to his indanna storys he has told me many of them   there is one that he told me about & old Babtist Preacher — the Meeting house was way off in the woods from any other house and was olly used once a month   this Preacher was Dessed in Coars Linen Pants and shirt of the same Material   the Pants was made after the old fashion with Bigg Bag Legs and But one Buton to the wastbone and 2 flap Butons No suspenders and the shirt had Comp Sleaves and one Buton on the Collar   he Raised up in the Pulpit and took his tex thus   i am the Crist whom i shall Represent to Day   about this time one of these blu Lizerds or Scorpins Ran up his Legs   the old man Began to slap away on his Legs But Missed the Lizerd and Kept Geting higher up   he onbutend his Pants at one snach and Kicked off his pants But the thing keped onn up his Back   the next Motion was for the Collar Buton of his shirt and off it went   in the house was & old Lady took a good Look at him and said well iff you Represent Crist i am Done Beleaving in the Bible   this aictdote he told some-where in his speach in Reply to some of the opisit Canidtes whom had Represent-ed them selves as something Extry   there is many others that i could Mention But thay on the vulger order such as Pranks he used to Play off when going to mill   he was once whilst Living in salem Clled on By one peter Lukins to Prove his Carector and standing as to the velidity of his oath   the Atturny said Please state what you know as to the Carector of Mr Lukins as for truth & varasity   well said Lincoln he is Called Lying Peat Lukins   But said the Lawer would you Be-leave him on oath   he turned Round and said ask Esquirer Geen   he has tak-en his testimony under oath Many times   Green was asked the Qustion and ancerd i Never Beleave any thing he say unless some Body elce Swares the same thing   Lincoln was a Canidte at the time his habis Customs and Manners was of a Drole Singular Pleasant Manner   he applide himself Reding a greateal fond of Company and all that Knew him saut his Company for he was all Life and umor full of anect dotes would start one to get someone elce to follow But he was al-ways Ready to Mach any that was told in fact he Comanded all the Respet from all Both Men and women   you ask about him as Regard women   thay all Liked him and liked then as well   there was a Miss Rutlage i have Know Dout he would have Maried iff she had of Lived But Deth Prevented after i left there i am told that he Borded with Benett able the farthering Law of Nult Green   i think that Mrs able Could aid you Considerabe   she has a dauter that is thought to Be Lincolns Child thay favor very much   Mrs able is a very smart woman Well ed-

ucated and was of a Bigg & Welthy family in Ky   i think thay Live at this time
in Mason County   there was a man that use to come to salem and get tight and
stay untell dark he was fraid of Gosts and some one had to goe home with
him   well Lincoln Perswaded a fellow to take a Sheet and goe in the Rod and
Perform Gost   he then Sent an other gost and the man and Lincoln started
home   the Gost made his appearence and the man Became much fritend But the
Second gost made hs appear[ance] and frightend the first Gost half to Deth that
Broke the fellow from staying untell Dark anymore[1]

I must Close

Yours truly

J. R. Herndon.

LC: HW2221–22; HL: LN2408, 1:520–23

52. Nathaniel Grigsby to WHH

Gentryville Ind. July the 4th. 1865.

Dear Sir:

Yours of June 25. 1865, is just received; it finds me in bad health at the present
time, but I shall attend to your request as soon as possible. I am truly glad to know
that you are writing the history of that good and great man; for [you] alone can
do him justice. I will now say to you that I am an old acquaintence and personal
and political friend of his; himself and I being [at] school in the same room, also
his only Sister married my oldest brother Aaron Grigsby, but that good woman
died January 15th. 1826, being nineteen years of age, leaving no heir. I received a
note from your Attorney at Rockport some days since, informing me of your object, I immediately went to see him, and told him to come out to Gentryville, and
I would go the round with him, and see all of Abraham Lincoln's old friends, and
obtain all of the history of the Lincoln family. He said that his business would not
permit of his attending to it immediately. As you appear anxious to get all of the
history of the Lincoln's; and true history. I would suggest the idea of getting some
history in Hardin Co. Ky., where he was born. Any thing that I can do for the
history of that good and great man, I shall be happy to do it. Having lately returned from the Army, where I was in the service, in poor health, I am now out of
employment at the present time.

With these remarks I shall subscribe myself,

Your friend

N. Griggsby.

P.S.

Excuse bad writing and spelling, as my health is poor. I cannot collect my ideas
to-day. I hope to hear from you soon.

HL: LN2408, 1:295–97

---

1. Marginal note: *i Lived in salem about 18 months James Never Lived there.*

53. Henry Pirtle to WHH

Louisville, 4 July, 1865.

Dear Sir:

Yours of the 2nd. instant is at hand.

The Act repealing the Law of primogeniture was passed in Virginia in 1785, to take effect on the 1st. day of January, 1787.

I do not know that any of the Lincolns were ever members of our legislature.

I think the anecdote of Mordecai killing the Indian is true. He was then about sixteen years of age; Josiah two or three years younger, and Thomas younger than he. I always understood they were born in Virginia.

The Lincolns were modest people; but Mordecai was celebrated for his bravery, and had been in the early campaigns of the west.

very respectfully
Henry Pirtle.

LC: HW2223; HL: LN2408, 1:68

54. Tim G. Needham to WHH

Elizabethtown Ky   July 5th 1865

My Dear Sir,

Your very kind note of 29 June was duly recd — I thank you for the advice — good and true — contained therein, and will strive to profit by it.

The information I give — Thos Lincoln bot of *Dr* John T. Slator, 238 Acres of Land, and sold 200 Acres of same to Chas. Milton — He paid Slator 118 *Pounds* for the land, and sold the 200 Acres for 100 Pounds — Leaving *38 Acres unsold*, and which I suppose still belongs to the Lincoln's, as I can see no deed of conveyance recorded here —

If this is not *definite enough* — or is not *all* you wish to Know. write *again*, and as *often as necessary.* I will reply with pleasure —

I am Very Respectfully
Your Obt & humble Servt
Tim G. Needham

LC: HW2224–25; HL: LN2408, 1:60–61

55. A. D. Wright to WHH

Petersburg, July 6, 1865

Dear Sir:

Your note of 30 ult. is before me, and in relation to the speech of J. H. Matheny Esq., I believe I can say that it is substantially correct. I made out from recollection the next day the article as published.

J.H.M. spoke to me some days after about the report of his remarks as published in the Rep. and thought I had colored it too highly — But I think not.

As to my *"name"* being used or made public, I care nothing about that, I do not write anything, but what I believe to be true, and do not intend to do injustice to any one.

In relation to Mrs. A.[1] I have not seen her since your letter was received — will make the inquiry on first sight, but I think and *believe* it true, that her first application to Mr. L. was a letter written to him, for her, by me at my store. I have written for her several letters to Mr. L. on that subject of her sons misfortune and also since the war, to obtain a discharge from the Army.

Yours truly

A. D. Wright.

HL: LN2408, 1:555–56

56. James Short to WHH[1]

Petersburg Ill July 7, 1865

Dear Sir

In answer to your inquiries in reference to my knowledge of the early history of the late lamented President, Abraham Lincoln   I give you herein all the information which is now fresh in my memory.

My first acquaintance with Mr Lincoln was in May or June 1831 at New Salem. At that time I lived in Coxe's Grove, on the line between Morgan and Sangamon, and on coming into New Salem at that time, Mr Lincoln was pointed out to me by my sister, now Mrs Elias Hohimer, whom Mr L. had before that time employed to make him a pair of pantaloons. Mr L. at this time was about 22 years of age; appeared to be as tall as he ever became, and slimmer than of late years. He had on at the time a blue cotton round about coat, stoga shoes, and pale blue casinet pantaloons[2] which failed to make the connection with either coat or socks, coming about three inches below the former and an inch or two above the latter. Without the necessity of a formal introduction we fell in together and struck up a conversation, the purport of which I have now forgotten. He made a favorable impression upon me by his conversation on first acquaintance through his intelligence & sprightliness, which impression was deepened from time to time as I became better acquainted with him.

At this time I was engaged in farming and was about 25 years old. Mr L. just at this time was doing nothing, having just returned from New Orleans. This same year — 1831, — was the first year Mr L. ever came to New Salem. He went to New Orleans with Denton Offut in a flat boat, in 1831, & had just returned when

---

1. Probably Mrs. Hannah Armstrong.

---

1. This letter is in the hand of N. W. Branson, who seems to have functioned as Short's interviewer and amanuensis.

2. Stoga shoes are stout, coarse shoes, or brogans; casinet (or cassinette) is a lightweight twill trouser fabric, usually with cotton warp and wool filling.

I first saw him. When Offut came back from N.O. in 1831 he started a store in N.S. and Employed Lincoln as clerk or assistant; but what wages he paid Mr. L I do not know. Mr. L clerked for him about six months. Offut was a wild, harum-scarum kind of a man, and I think not much of a business man. After Mr L's return from N.O. he piloted a little boat to Beardstown for Dr Nelson, who was then removing from New Salem, on this boat. Do not know what became of Dr N. This was in 1833 I think. Mr L. did once foot it from Beardstown to N.S. but whether on his return from N.O. or from piloting this boat to Beardstown, I have forgotten.

The Black Hawk war first broke out in 1831. I enlisted in April 1831, & was gone about a month. Mr L. did not go out this year. The next year, 1832, Mr L. raised a company, of which he was elected Captain. The Company rendesvoused in Beardstown. I did not go out this year. I did go to B. to volunteer, but Majir — afterwards Col — E D Baker, having lost his horse, I sold mine to him, and before I could get another one & return, the Company had gone.

I don't know whether Mr L was Deputy Post Master under Hill or not. He was P.M. himself in New Salem two or three years, I think, commencing in 1833. He resigned his office.[3]

Mr L. boarded with the parents of Miss Ann Rutledge, from the time he went to New Salem up to 1833. In 1833 her mother moved to the Sandridge & kept house for me, until I got married. Miss R. staid at N.S. for a few months after her mother left, keeping house for her father & brothers, & boarding Mr L. She then came over to her mother. After my marriage, the Rutledges lived about half a mile from me. Mr L. came over to see me & them every day or two. I did not know of any engagement or tender passages between Mr L and Miss R at the time But after her death, which happened in 34 or 35, he seemed to be so much affected and grieved so hardly that I then supposed there must have been something of the kind. Miss R was a good looking, smart, lively girl, a good house keeper, with a moderate education, and without any of the so called accomplishments. She was about 20 years old when she died. I knew nothing of Miss Owens,[4] or her footing with Mr L. There was no Miss Short in this part of the country from 1832 to 1837, that Mr L went to see.[5]

Mr L. was very fond of out door recreations & sports, and excelled in them. He lifted 1000 pounds of shot by main strength. He never played cards, nor drank, nor hunted. New Salem & the surrounding country was settled by roughs and bullies, who were in the habit of winning all the money of strangers at cards, & then whipping them in the bargain. Offut in '31 made bet of 5$ that L could throw Jack Armstrong. Armstrong was a regular bully, was very stout, & tricky in wrestling. Lincoln was a scientific wrestler. They wrestled for a long time, withough either being able to throw the other, until Armstrong broke holds, caught L by

---

3. Here an entire paragraph is stricken, the subject (the judgment against AL for debt) being treated more fully later in the letter.

4. Mary Owens.

5. WHH appears to be following up on the testimony of John T. Stuart. See §46.

the leg & floored him. L. took the matter in such good part, and laughed the matter off so pleasantly that he gained the good will of the roughs and was never disturbed by them.

L, I think, first studied law in fall of '32 or winter of 32–3.

He first boarded with the Rutledges. Afterwards first with Nelson Alley and then with Caleb Carman, These were all the parties with whom he boarded at New Salem.

Wm. G. Greene's father's name was William. Think he had no books or surveyor's instruments. He was a drinking & illiterate man. If Mr L got any books it was from Bowling Greene, who was a reading man. L. was Denton Offut's first clerk. I don't know of Offut's having any other clerk. I have understood W G Greene & Charles Maltby afterwards clerked for him. Offut broke in latter part of 1831. I think L. never had any instuctor in surveying — if he rec'd instructions, it was from John Calhoun, whose deputy he was. Know nothing about his books — he had but few of them. If any one instructed him in grammar it was Mentor Graham.

Offut left New Salem in the latter part of 1831. Don't know where he went to nor where he is living now. I have understood that he has been at Washington since the inauguration of Mr L.

The stories about Armstrong & others cooking live pig &c may be true but I know nothing of it. Armstrong & others rolled a man named Jordan down hill at New Salem. Lincoln had nothing to do with any of these wild frolics. I know but little about them.

I have no recollection of the stories Mr L used to tell me about his history, habits &c while in Indiana.

Kelso was a great fisherman, very lazy, and I think not much of a literary man.

Radford sold out his stock of goods to W G Greene and Greene sold out to Lincoln & Berry. Lincoln & Berry gave their note for 400$ to Greene, and Greene assigned it to Radford. Radford assigned it to Peter Van Bergen. Berry in the meantime had died, and Lincoln lifted the note and gave him in lieu of it another signed by himself and Greene. Van Bergen brought suit in Sangamon Circuit Court and obtained judgment against Lincoln & Greene. An Execution was issued and levied upon Lincoln's horse, saddle, bridle, compass, chain & other surveyor's instruments. Mr L. was then very much discouraged and said he would let the whole thing go by the board. I was then living on the Sandridge, now in Menard Co, and Mr L was at my house very much — half the time. I did all I could to put him in better spirits. I went on the delivery bond with him, and when the sale came off — which Mr L did not attend — I bid in the above property at $120.00, and immediately gave it up again to Mr L. This was in 1833 or 1834. Mr L afterwards repaid me when he had moved to Springfield. Greene also turned in on this judgement his horse, saddle and bridle at 125$, and L afterwards repaid him.

Frequently when Mr L was at my house he would help me gather corn. He was the best hand at husking corn on the stalk I ever saw. I used to consider myself very good, but he would gather two loads to my one.

I think I have now answered all your inquiries so far as I am able.

Wishing you success in your enterprise I am

Yours Truly

James Short

LC: HW2226–34; HL: LN2408, 1:363–69

57. Charles Sumner to WHH

Boston 12th July '65

My dear Sir,

I have sent you at different times two copies of the Eulogy[1] in pamphlet, also one in the Newspaper, which is less complete than the pamphlet.

I have also sent Govr Andrew's Address[2] which contains an answer to your inquiry about the Mass. Soldiers killed at Baltimore.

I am not aware that in New England candidates have ever met each other before the people.

I look forward with interest to the biography which you are writing Let it speak as much as possible for the good cause.

Faithfully Yours,

Charles Sumner

LC: HW2235; HL: LN2408, 2:307

58. Mentor Graham to WHH

Petersburg July 15th 1865

Dear Sir,

In reply to your inquiries in regard to our much lamented Lincoln, he was good, and great as he was *good*, as he was good, Great not like Caesar staind in blood But only great as he was *good*.

I said to you in your first inquiries the first time I saw him was at the election in New Salem in 1830 I saw him frequently when a lad about 12 years of age though was not personally acquainted with him this was at his residence at his place of birth in the winter of 1819 & 20[1]   I went to school in the County of Hardin Ky, adjoing Green Co where I was raised, during my attendance at this school I

---

1. Charles Sumner, *The Promise of the Declaration of Independence: Eulogy on Abraham Lincoln, Delivered before the Municipal Authorities of the City of Boston, June 1, 1865, by Charles Sumner* (Boston, 1865).

2. John Albion Andrew, *An Address on the Occasion of Dedicating the Monument to Ladd and Whitney, Members of the Sixth Regiment, M.V.M., Killed at Baltimore, Maryland, April 19, 1861. Delivered at Lowell, Mass., June 17, 1865* (Boston, 1865).

---

1. Graham is clearly mistaken, as the Lincolns left the Nolin area ca. 1811 and Kentucky itself in 1816.

often past by old Mr. Lincoln's house & often saw his son Abraham out about the premises with his father, this was near No Linn river on the little stream Barren run, it was then a barren though picturesque country. the house was a rude cabin   I never had any conversation with either of them during my stay in that section   I remember thinking as I would pass by the place and see them out that they had the appearance of a dignified man & boy as they truly were. In regard to what he read & studied in Ky & Indiana it was principally the bible, he has spoken to me often of his employment in Indiania   after his Father moved over the Ohio river he devoted his time principally in assisting to clear a little farm and make a subsistence for the family and that every leisure moment was employed in writing for some of the neighbors back to Ky or in reading such books as he could obtain but they were limited except the bible   In New Salem he devoted more time to reading the scripture, books on science and comments on law and to the acquisition of Knowledge of men & things than any man I ever knew and it has been my task to teach in the primary school Forty five years and I must say that Abraham Lincoln was the most studious, diligent strait forward young man in the pursuit of a knowledge of literature than any among the five thousand I have taught in the scho   The time I allude to in his studies was in Salem from 1830 to 36

He was regular in his habits punctual in doing anything that he promised or agreed to do his method of doing *any* thing was very systematic he discharged all his obligations and duties to his God his fellow men himself and his country with more fidelity than is common to humanity

You ask what gave him the title of honest Abe, That is answered in these few words, he was strictly *honest truthful* & *industrious* & in addition to this he was one of the most *companionable* persons you will ever see in this world.

He was well calculated to be President of such a nation as ours and it may be a *long, long* time before we have another to be his equal   I have no idea that this or any other country has ever had his superior, he is now and always will be first in the hearts of his countrymen, how much, how deep how feelingly we have grieved his loss.

I have been harvesting two weeks & it is difficult for me to write

Yours respectfully

M Graham

LC: HW2236–37; HL: LN2408, 1:549–52

59. N. W. Branson to WHH

Petersburg Ills., July 19, 1865.

Dear Sir:

I am in receipt of your favor of yesterday's date. I rec'd no letter from you, telling me to express Mr Shorts' letter, nor did Mr. Miles give me such instructions.

Old settlers tell me Mr. Lincoln was elected Captain of a Military Company before the breaking out of the Black Hawk War; being another company than the one he commanded in that War.

Yours Truly

N. W. Branson

HL: LN2408, 1:362

60. John T. Stuart (WHH interview)

July 21st 1865

The first time Stuart talked was about 5 days before this — SEE Little Book[1]

Stuart further says that in 1834 & 6 Mr Lincoln was a Whig — supported Whig measures — Lincoln a mystery — Stuart was a candidate for Congress in '38 & took his seat '39 — Lincoln had no good — accute critical judgement or organizing power — had no idea of human nature — generally no will — when he put his foot down it was down. Stuart says he has been at L's house a hundred times, never was asked to dinner. In Washington L never asked about to any body — Says Judge Davis[2] says so too — never asked Davis to dine — never asked Davis how the People were about Bloomington — When I was a candidate in 1838 went to Chicago — spoke there — the people applauded — hissed — *this never pleased me* — had never seen the like — heard the like —. The Yankees at that time didn't like Stump Speaking or Stump orators — they have changed now —

The Convention System was adopted in all America about 1836 it was a Van Buren Democratic measure. The Republicans adopted it in 1856 — so did the Democracy. In old times there was no such thing — Evry man became a candidate who wanted to — run on his own hook — spoke for himself &c — All met and discussed questions together — dys at it — People Came 30–40 mi to hear it &c — acted like People at church. — The real questions at issue in 1860– to 65 — was really Federalism and State Sovreignty — Lincolns thinking was Federalism &c Johnson's[3] is different.

LC: HW2240–41; HL: LN2408, 2:194–96

61. David M. Pantier to WHH[1]

Petersburg Ill July 21. 1865.

Dear Sir

Understanding that you are engaged in procuring materials for a life of Mr Lincoln, I take pleasure in giving you all the information in my power.

---

1. This was probably one of the small memorandum books in which Herndon recorded private information about AL and which he loaned to Ward Hill Lamon in December 1869. The books were never returned, and their whereabouts is unknown.

2. David Davis.

3. President Andrew Johnson.

---

1. This letter was signed by Pantier but appears to be in the hand of N. W. Branson.

I was a private in Captain Lincoln's Company, which rendesvoused at Beards-town, Early in April 1832. Our forces, then under Gen Whitesides, reached the mouth of Henderson river, on the Mississippi, about the 10th of April. While in camp there a general order was issued, prohibiting the discharge of fire arms within 50 steps of the camp. Capt L. disobeyed the order by firing his pistol within ten steps of camp, and for this violation of orders was put under arrest for that day, and his sword taken from him: but the next day his sword was restored, & nothing more was done in the matter.

About the 15th of April we reached the mouth of Rock River. Three or four nights afterwards a man named Rial P. Greene, commonly called Pot Greene, belonging to a Greene County Company, came to our Company, and waked up the men, and proposed to them that if they would furnish him with a tomahawk and four buckets, he would get into the officers liquors, & supply the men with wines & brandies. The desired articles were furnished him, and with the assistance of one of our Company, he procured the liquors. All this was entirely unknown to Capt. Lincoln. In the morning, Capt L. ordered his orderly to form the company for parade. But when the orderly called the men to parade, they called "parade" too, but wouldn't fall into line. The most of the men were unmistakably drunk. The rest of the forces marched off & left Capt L's company behind. The Company didn't make a start till about 10 o'clock, and then after marching about two miles, the drunken ones laid down & slept their drunk off. They overtook the forces that night. Capt L. was again put under arrest, and was obliged to carry a wooden sword for two days. And this, although Capt L. was entirely blameless in the matter.

Wishing you success in your enterprise, I am

Yours Truly

David Pantier

LC: HW2253–55; HL: LN2408, 1:338–40

62. J. W. Wartmann to WHH

Rockport Indiana   July 21st 1865.

My Dear Sir,

Since writing you last, it has pleased God to sadly bereave me by taking from me a dear Son — aged over four years. If you are a parent you can readily sympathize with me.

The Court House with *all* our County records, has been totally destroyed by fire *twice* within a Space of thirty years. I have taken great pains to get *exact* dates, but cannot do so. *"About"* such a time, is as near as I can come at anything.

Before Indiana was admitted into the Union as a State, all this section of our state called the *"pocket"*— embracing now *10* counties — (the 1st Cong dist), was called *Knox* Co. and Vincennes was the County seat of the Knox district — or county. Subsequently, this district was divided into Knox & Perry counties. *"About"* the year 1819 or '20, Spencer Co' was cut off from Perry Co'. "Thompson's Ferry,"[1] is, or was, in Spencer Co', and is the point where Thos Lincoln and family reached Indiana. It is about 16 miles from the land Mr L. settled on. Thos Lincoln owned the land in *fee,* and located or Settled upon an "Entry" of 80 acres. Upon his removal to Ills, he (L) sold the land & improvements to his son-in-law *Chas Grigsby.*[2]

The land lies about 1½ miles South East of Gentryville. The present owner of the land is James Gentry Senior. The present occupant is Boone Morgan.

Thomas Lincoln was, in addition to being a farmer, a Cabinet Maker and Carpenter. At least, he worked at both these trades while here. Abraham Lincoln, as far as he was able, assisted him.

'Squire John W. Lamar, one of our county Comrs, has a small book case made by Abraham; The "Squire" prizes it highly and says it is a "first rate job."

The 'Squire tells this of "Abe". Old Mr Lamar ('Squires father) was one day going to election — and I (Squire L) was on the horse behind him. We fell in company with an old man named James Larkin —. This man Larkin was a great brag —, always relating some miraculous story or other. While riding along we overtook Abe Lincoln — going to the polls on foot. Old Man Larkin commenced telling Lincoln about the great speed & "bottom" of the mare he was riding.

Why, said Larkin, "Yesterday I run her *five* miles in *four* minutes — and She never drew a *long* breath." I guess — quietly replied Lincoln, She drew a great many *Short ones.*

Lincoln, is universally spoken of as scrupulously honest, truthful, moral, and industrious. His ready wit and quick retort are generally spoken of.

Before Abraham Lincoln left here —, smarting under an insult offered him by the Grigsby family, he wrote, and placed where the Grigsby's would find them —, *"The Chronicles,"* a poetic effusion abounding in wit and ready "hits." These hits were so palpable and cutting that the Grigsby's suppressed them —, though a few persons saw and read them. They were written in scriptural style and evinced decided talent. Abraham was studious and proverbially industrious. He is said to have litterally never lost a moment from study when he could devote himself to it. Having no slate, pens or pencils handy, he figured all over the smooth parts of some clap-boards in an old barn he used to use, with a pencil made of *clay.*

There is no doubt but that Abraham Lincoln did make rails for Josiah Crawford. Indeed, there are some yet remaining —, being known by forming the *floor* of an old barn and "notched" to fit the logs. The two days work pulling fodder for the "Weems' Life of Washington" is also, doubtless true.

Mr N. Grigsby informs me that he received your letter and will do all he can for you. You might get some valuable facts from William Woods, Dale P.O. Spencer Co.'

I will still continue to make inquiries and report any facts of importance.

It is now about 35 years since Mr L left here, and a new generation is come.

---

1. See p. 38.
2. Thomas Lincoln's son-in-law was Aaron Grigsby, a brother of Charles.

The "stories" concerning him are not of record —, but family traditions, and consequently it is almost impossible to fix dates. The grave of Mr L's mother is still unmarked by a head-board —, though known to a certainty.

Mr Lincoln told one of our citizens last winter that he intended visiting Spencer Co' once more before he died —, when his duties would allow it, and of putting a tomb-stone to his mother's grave.

Respectfully
Your Obt Serv't
J.W. Wartmann

LC: HW2256–59; HL: LN2408, 1:171–75

63. Lynn McNulty Greene to WHH

Avon Fulton Co Ills July 30th/65

Dear sir

Your letters in relation to Mr Lincoln's mode of Life at old Salem are both before me. I regret very much that I am unable to give you the information you desire   But when you reflect that I was only 16 years old when Mr Lincoln came to New Salem & that for 4 years of the 6 he lived there I was away from home at school Excepting vacations you will not be surprised at the paucity of the information I can give you however tenacious my memory may be. The first I knew of Mr Lincoln was the Spring after the deep Snow. He was then selling goods for Denton Offutt the man for whom he had built the flat Boat. He used to say to the boys & young men that they "might always know when he came to New Salem by the high water the Spring after the deep Snow that he came down with it as a kind "drift wood." It was while selling goods for Offutt & soon after he had come there that Lincoln and Jack Armstrong had a wrestle for $1000   Offutt & Bill Clary bet the money   Armstrong after Struggling a while with but a prospect of throwing Mr Lincoln broke his holts & caught Mr Lincoln by the legs & they came to the ground. Clary claimed the money & said he would hav it or whip Offutt & Lincoln both   Offutt was inclined to yield as there was a score or more of the Clarys Grove Boys against him & Mr Lincoln & my brother W. G. Greene But Lincoln said they had not won the money & they should not have it & although he was opposed to fighting if nothing else would do them he would fight Armstrong, Clary or any of the set   So the money was drawn and from that day forward the Clary Grove Boys Were always his firm friends

In the summer after he came home from the Black Hawk War he got possession of one of Kirkham's Grammars & began studying it on the hill sides of old Salem   I spent several days giving him instruction in this manner. In fact all the instruction he ever had in Grammar he rec'd from me as above indicated. In the summer of 1833 he engaged to be married to Miss Ann Rutledge of New Salem a beautiful and very amiable young woman   But before the match was consummated she took fever & died. Lincoln took it very hard indeed. At this time & perhaps a year before he was quite fond of Reading Burns & Campbell's Poetry

Some two years after the death of Miss Rutledge he paid considerable attention to Miss Mary S. Owens of Ky who was on a visit to her sister residing near
Salem   They talked the matter of Marriage over quite freely but as I understand
it never made a contract or agreement to marry   I think I have the right understanding of this matter I have talked with Miss Owens after her marriage on the
subject & she showed some of Lincolns letters to her on the subject. She was a
very superior woman but like some other pretty women (God bless them) she loved
Power & conquest —

The first Law Book Lincoln read was a Copy of Blackstone belonging to Vincent A. Bogue (who once packed Pork at Beardstown & died soon after.

While at Salem Lincoln never drank or played cards for *money* though he frequently played euchre and seven up & played them well.

But friend Herndon I will close & refer you to W. G. Greene who sold Lincoln and Berry the Grocery & who can give you more details of Lincoln's New
Salem life than any one I know.

I am with much respect

Yours &

L M Greene

LC: HW2260–65; HL: LN2408, 1:493–96

64. *John B. Helm to WHH*

1st Aug 1865

Dear Sir —

You with this will receive two Letters one from Hon S. Haycraft, The other
from Revd. Presly Nevil[1] — both addressed to me and in reply to letters written
to them by your request and under the strongest assurances of confidence on my
part that their names should not hereafter be alluded to —   Indeed all this would
not have sattisfied any of us to make unpleasant disclosures about the dead that
are gone unless some good might grow out of it   I also send you clipt from a Ky
paper an obituary of Jack Thomas written by the same Hon. S. Haycraft — simply to show an idea Haycraft admires Lincoln and cannot even write an obituary
notice of his dearest friend without bring in something if it occurs to his mind to
Strengthen and confirm his position that old Thomas Lincoln was somebody and
an honest man. Thus he says old Tom Lincoln the Presidents father did the Joiners work upon the house of old Hardin Thomas &c —   This amused me because when a boy going to school I boarded at old Hardin Thomas and in this same
house and did not remember any joining work on the house a rough log house
with two or three glass windows — plenty of rough room good cheer and honest
friendship was all they had and joiners work was scarce

Likewise the story got up on speculation about the veritable log cabin in which
Abe Lincoln was born near Hodgenville — that was hunted up taken to a saw mill

---

1. Presly Nevil Haycraft.

— sawed into slats and worked up into Cains and sold for gain Also the mirricle as one might call it that any living person should know on what day he was born is all mistery

After a careful reading of the letters of Haycraft and Nevil — you will find two or three points settled beyond dispute   Nancy Hanks was his mother. That Nancy Hanks was of low character but that Thomas Lincoln married her — and the presumption is before Abe birth —   Now outside of these letters I have other sources of information from a friend by the name of Wm Van Metre and others — who tell me that after Abe's birth a man by the name of Abraham Enlows claimed him as his son that Lincoln and Enlow had a regularly set to fight about the matter — In which fight Enlow lost the end of his nose —   Lincoln held the mother and child. But Enlow ever after claimed that he was the father of Abe Lincoln and the name his mother gave the boy was evidence old Enlow would contend of the fact and I heard Wm Van Metre say that he had heard old Abe Enlow claim Abe Lincoln as his son since Mr Lincoln was president of the US.

Now this Abe Enlow was as low a fellow as you could find — you need not try to find any thing under his circle

Hon S. Haycraft and others like him who cannot for their lives see how so great and good a man as Abe Lincoln could have sprung from such an origin have been trying to trace back his ancestral line to the Lincolns of Lincoln Shire &c — But lo! they fail they could trace him back to old Abe better

It is also plain that old Tom Lincoln had courted Sally Bush before she married Johnson and failed to get her — that Sally Bush and Johnson had had a number of children. And Tom Lincoln to get clear of Abe Enlow had removed to Indiana that in the winter 1813 & 1814 — The year of that dreadful plague that past over our country and left 13 dead bodies in our little village in 24 hours   I find myself then a school boy boarding in the house of Hardin Thomas the joining of which had been executed by old Tom Lincoln some years before — When I with others assisted to bury the dead — amongst them was Johnson Sally Bush's husband —

It also appears that not long after this Sally Bush then the widdow Johnson was lawfully married to Tom Lincoln and Abe was received into her family as a step son —   This is a new era in Abe Lincolns life —   The Bushes were rough, uncouth, uneducated beyond any thing that would seem credible now to speak of but the Hanks — Enlows &c — were along way below the Bushes again

A few years pass over our heads and I am clerk in my uncle Ben Helm's store when he my uncle purchased the old Bush farm and Sally being one of the heirs got her part of the purchase money and then for the first time the Great Man of destiny springs into my view. He was then a slender well behaved quiet boy — that was all attention to the wishes of his step mother — and well he should feel it so — for she was doubtless the first person that ever treated him like a human being — He was then by her aid trying to find out the truth as to who and what he was   He was with a lot of boys and girls by the name of Bush — Johnson &c — and he was one of them   By the aid of his Step Mother a matter of fact sort of a woman she gave him information. He retained the name of Abe, corrected the spelling of his fathers name and by name became Abe — Lincoln, as to the time of his birth he has it no doubt from Sally Bush who in all human probability gave it to him correctly

In one of your letters you inquired about the Camp Meetings of that day — before and after Abe's birth — the Hanks girls were great at Camp meetings after I could remember say 1816   I will give you one scene and if you will then read the books written on the subject you may find some appology for some of the superstition that was said to be in Abes character.

I was at a Camp Meeting as before said about 1816 when a general shout was about to Commence — preperations were being made a young lady invited me to stand on a bench by her side where we could all see over the altar. To the right a strong athletic young man about 25 years of age was being put in trim for the occasion — which was done by divesting him of all apparal except shirt and pants   On the left a young lady was also being put in trim in some what the same way so that her clothes would not be in her way and so that when her combs flew out her hair would go into graceful braids — She too was young not more than 20 per haps less   The performance commenced about the same time By the young man on the right and the young lady on the left — slowly and gracefully they worked towards the centre — Singing shouting hugging and kissing generally their own sex until at last nearer and and nearer they came — The centre of the Alter was reached and the two closed with their arms around each other — The man Singing and Shouting at the top of his voice — I have my Jesus in my arms — Sweet as Honey comb and Strong as baccon ham, just at this moment the young lady holding to my arm said they are to be married next week. her name is Miss Hanks — It was in the part of the country where Abe was born and possibly some of that family.

There were very few who did not believe this true religion inspired by the holy spirit and the man that could not believe it had better keep it to himself or be off for we had our bullies to keep order at such places — The Hanks' were the finest singers and finest shouters in our country — the only draw back on them was that some nine months after these interesting meetings some of them were likely to have baby's

A few words more as to the Enlow family and I am done with this subject — As far back as I can recollect there lived in Hardin County Three families of Enlow's all said to be cousins — I think from N.C. but not certain — Isham Enlow married a widdow Larue had a family of some distinction — Gov Helm is of Mrs Enlows descendants by her first husband Larue — and several other persons of distinction by her Larue and Enlow husband — Abe Enlow another cousin a tall dignified looking man of fine personal appearance very neat — silent and reserved — more of a book worm than for action — married a Vernon one of our best families — raised a respectable family

Then comes our veritable Abe Enlow who claims to be father of the President   This Abe was a man over six feet — pretty much in appearance as if he might have been of the same family of the president. He had a sister Polly that lived with him on a small farm a few miles from our town — His sister Polly was a notorious prostitute — had some half a dozen pretty daughters all raised up in the same way — like others of that stripe they had their broils — fights and fusses —

I remember old Abe — with part of his nose bit off as one of the institutions of our country for some thirty years — very silent — very unobtrusive — never drunk nor boistrous seemed not to suffer in reputation by the conduct of his Sister & her daughters — dont expect I ever had a dozen words with him except to sell him some article for his farm. He may have been a man of destiny also — and patiently filled the place assigned him by Providence

For over ten days I have been prostrated on a bed of sickness — Calomel Quinine Blue mass — these papers took possession of my mind when I had any mind —   I am determined this morning to place them beyond my reach — I hope you will burn them

Jn. Helm,

[Enclosure A]

65. Samuel Haycraft to John B. Helm

Elizabeth Town   July 5 1865

Dear Sir

I received yours of 22d June some time since, and being half sick & run to death with office & Court business, has delayed my answer   In reference to my recollections of Abraham Lincolns father & Mother &c you have been laboring under a mistake, My own recollection of the Matter assures me that you were Mistaken & a letter I have from Abraham Lincoln himself Confirms all, The old man Lincoln — "Thomas Lincoln" but when here he was always called *Linkhorn*   The old Gentleman was a young unmarried man when I first knew him in 1805 or 1806, he was a very illiterate man a tolerable Country house Carpenter worked some on my fathers house — in 1805 and afterward done all the Carpenter work on Hardin Thomas' house, the work is yet to be seen tolerably sound, He married Nancy Hanks whose Mother was a wife of old Sammy Youngs,[1] the same old man that married Sousana Sawyer — Thomas Lincoln as the name was always spelld but pronounced Linkhorn was a low heavy built clumsy honest man, his wife was rather a heavy built Squatty woman, (the Lord only knows except Abe Enlow did where Abraham Lincoln got his length & his sense)[2]

Abraham Lincoln was born Feby 12 1809. near Hodgens Mill then in Hardin County now Larue & the Hodgen Mill is now Hodgenville, the County seat of Larue County.

How old Abraham Lincoln was when the old man left Hardin County I can not tell, However Abraham before he left went to school to Caleb Hazle who lived beyond Hodgens Mill   After old man Lincoln moved to Grayson & then to

---

1. See Hanks genealogy in the appendix.
2. Most testimony describes Nancy Hanks as taller than average.

Indiana he lost his Hanks wife and then he came to Kentucky to get another wife — Do you remember Sally Bush who married Danl Johnson the Jailor who lived on the alley below me. Johnson died of the cold plague[3] about the 4th or 5 day of April 1814 — and if I mistake not you & Rhodes Vanmetre, Wal. Whitaker & myself laid Johnson out he left one or two children one named John Johnson. She lived an honest poor widow until 2d December 1819 & she lived in a round log Cabin just below me about that time old Mr Thomas Lincoln came to Kentucky for the express purpose of Marrying the widow —   When he called to see her about the following Conversation took place

---

T. Lincoln — Well *Miss* Johnson, I have no wife & you have no husband   I came *a* purpose to mary you   I *knowed* you from a *gal* & you *knowed* me from a boy — I have no time to loose and if you are willing, let it be done Straight off

---

Mrs Johnson. Tommy I know you well & have no objection to marrying you, but I cannot do it straight off as I owe some debts that must first be paid"

He asked her for a list of them which was given, he went & paid them off that same day next Morning I issued his license & they were Married *Straight off* on that day & left & I never saw her nor Tom Lincoln since

Abraham Lincoln just before the Presidential election in answer to a letter from me, informed that his father was long since dead that his step Mother was living with her son John Johnson and was comfortably off — Lincoln had no half brother or step brother named Bush, but if any they were named Johnson — or if any children followed — and after Abrahams election & before left for Washington he called on his step Mother   It is to me matter of Astonishment about Lincolns rise from such obscurity to the first office of the Nation — He was certainly a favorite of providence and I am thoroughly Convinced that he was not only a good man, but one of Natures great men.

A yarn is told of him that on one occasion he was splitting rails with only shirt & breeches on — Collar open & in that plight was not very likely to look at, a man happened to be passing with a gun, Called to Lincoln to look up — which he did, the man raised his gun in an attitude to shoot.

Says Lincoln   What do you mean,   the man replied that he had promised to shoot the first man he met who was uglier than himself —   Lincoln asked to see the mans face & after taking a look remarked — If I am uglier then you, then blaze away — opening his shirt bosom.

I have received a letter from Mr Herndon himself & have not yet replied, You may send this letter —

Some body in Iowa, has been beseeching me for one of Lincolns original letters. I have five, the only one I felt willing to spare was marked, *private & Confidential.*

---

3. Presumably influenza.

July 16 — 1865

Absolute press of business and illness has made this delay. but it has enabled me to speak more accurately — By searching the old Marriage Register — I find that Sally Bush was married to Daniel Johnson 13 March 1806 by Ben Ogden ME. preacher — I know from personal knowledge that Johnson died early in April 1814   The Marriage Register was badly kept indeed was not kept at all, previous to my being clerk. I made out the Register from Ministers returns on licenses in the office up to 1813 — and in doing so I overlooked or did not find the record of the Mariage of Thomas Lincoln & Nancy Hanks —

Thomas Lincoln died near 10 years before the date of A. Lincolns letter to me May 1860[4] so the old gentleman died about 1850. on a farm bought by Abraham Lincoln & presented to his father & Step Mother — She the Step Mother is still living & near about 80 years old — lives with her son in law John Hall in Effingham Co Illinois 8 Miles from Charleston & 18 miles from Mattoon — these last facts I have from our Townsman Isaac Radly who saw the widow about 16 days ago — She had no child by Tho Lincoln.

Yours truly
Saml Haycraft

[Enclosure B]

66. Presley Nevil Haycraft to John B. Helm

July 19th 1865 —

Judge Helm,

After my respects to yourself and family I will acknowledge the receipt of your letter to _____ requesting my sister and myself to answer certain questions relating to Abraham Lincoln and his father & wives &c to which I hasten to answer according to my recollection Question 1st.   What was the name of Abraham Lincoln's father? Ans: That is hard for me to answer, but his reputed father was called Thomas Linkhorn, but I presume it is properly spelled Lincoln, 2nd   The name of his mother, Ans: Nancy Hanks. 3d.   Were they ever married? Ans: They were; I was a boy and remember very well of hearing of their marriage. and hearing it said at the time "that there could be found a match for any one"   She was a woman that did not bear a very virtuous name, and it was hard to tell who was the father of Abe. I Knew her brother Jo Hanks, who had a red head and associated with the lowest class, Old Tom Linkhorn and his wife lived, or rather breathed awhile near Hodges Mill on Nolin Creek then Hardin County Now Larue   He then moved to Elizabethtown and settled in an old Cabin on a mill race. Abe was then a babe. I was twelve years of age when Abe was born and knew his reputed father. He was a perfect greenhorn but stout and able but of no respectability   When Abe was about seven years of age Tom Linkhorn moved to

---

4. See *CW* 4:56.

Indiana from that time until I was a young man, writing in the clerks office occassionally I heard nothing of the old man until he Came to the clerks office to procure license to Mary Sarah Johnson, stating that his wife was dead and that he had Courted Sarah Johnson before his first marriage but she had preferred Johnson, but that now he was dead and they were at liberty to marry — He secured liscence and was lawfully married, Her name was Bush before her first marriage, She came of a family that did not stand above mediocrity, but so far as her personal character was concerned nothing could be said against her individually. She had several children by Johnson. He had been a jailor for several years and was such when he died, He took her to Indiana where his first wife died and as for Linkhorn living with a Miss Bush there was nothing of it, As for why any of their children retained the name of Bush I know not, but it likely that some of them might have had their grand father's Bush's name as a double name and he might have been called by that   As for his reputed son I know nothing since he was a little shirt tail boy — I wrote to _____[1] about the time this was was commencing if it was possible that Abraham Lincoln the President of the United States, was old Linkhorn's Son   he answered that it was even so, or his reputed son as he had written to Abe Lincoln about the matter and he answered him stating the whole fact relating to his birth   It is very doubtful whether he was Linkhorns son or not. A Bush might have been his father for aught I know   But for that this deponent saith not   There must be a mistake about any of their children being called Bush, as he was lawfully married to both women, and his last wife had no illigitimate children while I Knew them, I dont Know whether Tom's last wife is still living or not — but while I Knew her she was considered honest and industrious and I now Know individuals who were acquainted with the family in Indiana who say they passed for honest people there but very poor[2]

Here our correspondent stops short — And says he knows some things he does not wish to tell not even under the seal of Confidence. It amounts to this old Tom Linkhorn was not an honest man and never should have been called such by any boddy having regard for truth. His wife and wifes [money?] and family saved him from public prosecution

Here again it is Stated that Abe Enlow always claimed Abe Lincoln as his son from the birth of Abe Lincoln to the death of Abe Enlow

Here again is a discription of Nancy Hanks — not very perfect — she had several red haired relations — was of good size comely and was old Abe Enlows first and only love Married Tom Linkhorn when she was encient with Abe Lincoln the man of destiny yet unborn.

LC: HW2268–70; HL: LN2408, 1:10–17 (Helm letter); LC: HW4498–4501; HL: LN2408, 1:22–26 (enclosure A); LC: HW4502–3; HL: LN2408, 1:18–21 (enclosure B)

1. Probably his brother, Samuel Haycraft, who corresponded with AL about his family after his nomination for the presidency.

2. The rest of the letter appears to be in Helm's hand.

67. *Lawrence Weldon (drafts for speech)*[1]

Aug 1st 1865

Yea hope and despondence — Pleasure

x   x   x   x   x   x   x   x   x   x

What a Just resemblance the above bears to his fortune —

Mr. Lincoln, at the time of his assination was encircled by a halo of glory such as never before graced the brow of Mortal. he had driven treason from its Capital slept in the palace of its proud. defiat but now vanquished leader saved his Country and its history from distruction and disgrace. rode not with the haughty and imperious brow of an ancient conqueror — But with the placid complacy of a pure patriot through the streets of the political Babalon of his country and his age — he had ridden over battle fields immortal in history when in power — at least he was the leader — having assured the misguided citizens of the South that he meant them no harm — he returns buoyant with hope to executive Mansion — where for four long years he had been held as it were a prisoner —   Weary with the storms of state he goes to the theatre sees the gay crowd as he passes, is cheered and graciously smiled upon by fair women and brave men — beholds the gorgeous paraperperalia of the stage the rich cushion. the brilliantly lighted stage. the grotesque and magnificently blazoned arched ceiling and polished wall. the audience cheers — the players — illuminate the genius of the author the inimitable play — Mr Lincoln is moved by the. *[illegible]* of the play —

Lawrence Weldon's — Notes &c —

The weird and melancholy association of eloquence and poetry had a strong fascination for Mr L. minds —

Tasteful composition either of prose or poetry which faithfully contrasted the realities of eternity with the unstable and fickle fortunes of time made a strong impression on his mind —   In the indulgence of this melancholy task it is related of him that the poem entitled "Mortality" he knew by rote and appreciated it very highly — Various newspapers have attributed the paternity of this touching and beautiful poem to Mr. Lincoln — this is a mistake it was written as all lovers of verse know by Mr Knox and committed to Memory by Mr Lincoln —   At a bar-meeting held in the United States Court in Spgfield in June 1865 it was related by Mr W. that Mr Lincoln had a strange liking for this poetry —

In travelling on the circuit he was in the habit owing to his regular hours of rising earlier in than his brothers of the bar. on such occasions he was wont to sit by the fire having uncovered the coals. and muse ponder and soliliquize wisper no doubt by that strange psychological influence which is so poetically described by Poe in the raven —   On one of these occasions at the town of Lincoln the year

---

1. Lawrence Weldon seems to have sent WHH two versions of a speech he gave eulogizing AL at a bar meeting: a preliminary draft (HW3995) and an expanded draft (HW3990–94) that he refers to in a note as "a rough outline of what I said in relation to Mr. L. — at the Bar-meeting." The preliminary draft is given first, followed by the "rough outline."

of his nomination sitting in the posture described he quoted aloud and at length the poem entitled Mortality — When he had finished he was questioned as to the authorship and where it could be found —   He has forgotten when he learned it but not the Author[2] — and said that to him it sounded as much like true poetry as any thing he had ever heard — he was particlaly pleased with the last two line verseses — which are as follows

> Yea! hope and despondence. Pleasure and pain —
> Are mingled together like sunshine and rain —
> The smile and the tear the song and the dirge.
> Still follow each other like Surge upon Surge. —

> Tis the the wink of an eye tis the draught of a breath.
> From the blossom of youth to the paleness of death —
> From the gilded Saloon, the bier and the Shroud
> Oh why should the spirit of mortal be proud —

What a just resemblance the above bears to his fortune —

Mr Lincoln at the time of his was encircled by a halo of glory. such as before never graced the brow of mortal man — he had driven treason from its capital   slept in the palace of its once proud defiant but now vanquished leader   saved his country and its accum- glories of three quarters of a century from destruction   rode not with the haughty and imperious brow of an ancient conqueror but with the placid complacency of a pure patriot through the streets of the political Babylon of modern times — he had ridden over battle fields immortal in history when in power at least he was the leader. having assured the misguided citizens of the South that he meant them no harm — beyond a determination to maintain the government — he return'd buoyant with hope to the Executive Mansion where for four long years — he had been held as it were a prisoner. Weary with the storms of State, he goes to seek the relaxation of amusement at the theatre   Sees the gay crowd as he passes in is cheered and graciously smiled upon by fair women and brave men. beholds the gorgeous paraphernalia of the stage the brilliantly lighted Scene — the arched ceiling with its grotesque and inimitable figuring to heighten the effect and make the occasion one of unalloyed pleasure the crowd heart beat in unison with his over a redeemed and ransomed land — A pause in the play — A faint pistol shot is heard   No one knows it significance save the hellish few who are in the plot. A wild shriek such as murder rings from the heart of woman is follows   the proud form of Mr Lincoln has sunk in death, The Scene is Charged with a wild confusion such as no poet can describe or painter deleneate. Well might he have said and oft repeated

---

2. "Mortality" is by William Knox.

Tis the twink of an eye tis the draught of a breath
From the blossom of youth to the paleness of death —
From the gilded saloon the bier and the Shroud
Oh Why should the spirit of Mortal be proud —

Dear Billy   The above is a rough outline of what I said in relation to Mr L at
the bar Meeting —

LC: HW3995, HW3990–94; HL: LN 2408, 2:115–18

68. N. W. Branson to WHH

Petersburg Ill Aug 3. 1865.

Dear Sir

On conversing with Mr Short I have elicited the following additional facts in
reference to Mr Lincoln

Mr L. used to tell Mr S. the following anecdote of himself. Once, when Mr L
was surveying, he was put to bed in the same room with two girls, the head of his
bed being next to the foot of the girls' bed. In the night he commenced tickling
the feet of one of the girls with his fingers. As she seemed to enjoy it as much as he
did he then tickled a little higher up; and as he would tickle higher the girl would
shove down lower and the higher he tickled the lower she moved. Mr L would tell
the story with evident enjoyment. He never told how the thing ended.

You can have the benefit of the above, even if your readers cannot.

Mr S. says Mr L was, in Salem times, an habitual reader of the St Louis Republican & the Sangamo Journal. He used to read a great deal, improving every
opportunity, by day and by night. S. never knew of his reading a novel. History
and poetry & the newspapers constituted the most of his reading. Burns seemed
to be his favorite. S. had a copy of "The American Military Biography"[1] which he
read a great deal. He read aloud very often; and frequently assumed a lounging
position when reading. He read very thoroughly, and had a most wonderful memory. Would distinctly remember almost every thing he read. Used to sit up late of
nights reading, & would recommence in the morning when he got up. He was
not an unusually early riser — at least it was not considered early for country habits,
though for the City it would be very early.

Mr L was very fond of honey. Whenever he went to S's house he invariably
asked his wife for some bread & honey. And he liked a great deal of bee bead in it.
He never touched liquor of any kind.

There was nothing of the poke about him. Whenever he went at any thing he
went at it to do it. Whenever he walked with me, he would keep me in a trot all
the time. Always put things through in a hurry. Was a fast eater, though not a very
hearty one. Didnt sleep very much as he always sat up late.

---

1. Amos Blanchard, *American Military Biography* ([Cincinnati], 1825).

He didn't go to see the girls much. He didn't appear bashful, but it seemed as if he cared but little for them. Wasn't apt to take liberties with them, but would sometimes. He always liked lively, jovial company, where there was plenty of fun & no drunkenness, and would just as lieve the company were all men as to have it a mixture of the sexes. He was very agreeable in company and every body liked him. Was always full of life & of fun — always cheerful — always had a story to tell. Was very sociable & fond of visiting. Knew every man, woman & child for miles around. Was very fond of children. Was fond of cats — would take one & turn it on its back & talk to it for half an hour at a time. I never in my life saw him out of humor. He never got angry. Once when major Hill[2] was wrongly informed that Mr L had said something against his — H's — wife, the Major abused him a great deal for it — talking to Mr L very roughly & insultingly. Mr L kept his temper, — denied having said any thing against her. — told the Major that he had a very high opinion of her, and that if he knew any thing in the world against her it was the fact of her being his wife.

Mr L. was fond of wrestling, in which he excelled.

Renewing the offer of my poor services

Yours Truly

N W Branson

LC: HW2272–73; HL: LN2408, 1:540–43

69. *J. Rowan Herndon to WHH*

Quincy August 16 1865

Friend Will

i Recieved yours of the 31st some Days since But have Been so Buisy Shiping Government Property to Stlouis that i have failed to Ancer untell this Date so you must excuse me for Delying   in ancer to your first Qustion his habits was very study and as to the Books & Papers he Rad thay ware of such as he Could Borrow   he had the use of such as i had shuch as the Life of Jeferson Washington Clay & Webster   he Read all of histry that he Could Get hold of   he had axcess to any Books that was in and arond the town of Salem for all Knew that he was fond of Reading   Mr Benet able had a goold Lot of history   Es.Quar Green Hill & Mackneel Merchats Mr Crisman Merchat all had a fare Lot of history and he had full axcess to any and all and Made Good use of them   he also studed English Grammar and Read Some Law Such as Blaxton[1] and other Works on Contracts with the State Statu   as to the News Papers he Read all that Came to the Plase   the Congreshinal Globe Acts of Congress Legislator and the Louis-

---

2. Samuel Hill, a New Salem merchant, married Parthena Nance in 1835.

---

1. Sir William Blackstone, *Commentaries on the Laws of England* (1765).

ville Journal Sangamon Journal Stlouis Republickin and papers that Came to the offisce as he had full axcess to the offisce   as to his Readng he spent the time Mostly of Knights in Readng history and Day tim News Papers for he generly Read for the By standers when the male Come which was weekly   he was the Great admier of Henry Clay   he Set up Late & Rose Early   when Nothing else ocipide his time he was Readng some work or paper   he Rote Conciderable But whether it went to the paper or Knot i Cant say But i think it Did as i am shure i Red som of his Writing   he scearsly ever went to Bed Befor 12 and was up By Day Light and often set up Later   as to the 3 Qustin he was some times seting some times stading and some times on his Back and very would walk Down to the River Reading when he would Return the same way iff Commenced Reading any thing very intrusting he generly Put it through and he allways Remembered what he Red   He frequntly wusd the Bible   as to the 5 Qustion he was very fond of Eating and fond of the Good things But only & ordinary Eator Reagular to his Meals But was fond of fruit Nuts & allway Reacd for his sheer of such things as thay ware frequtly Brought to him by his friends   he often took a strole to the Cuntry as he said for Refresh ment   he generly took a Book with him or Brough one Back   i think his object was to study and Be By himself   and as to his to his Dress he was Rather Slouchy iff his Close ware whole & Clean he seemed to Be satisfied   as he was only able to Dress in Common Cloths   as to his habits and ways of Life he was fond of Company of Both sects fond of anectdotes always Geting some body to start one and then he was shure to Beet it shure   he was fond of Exercise such as Jumping Rasling Paying Ball and all Kinds of funn   But if there was any fiting about to Commence he would try to stop the furs   But if fight thay must there must Be fareplay shone   he was very fond of Childern and always willing to help the widow and orfats and atentive to the sick in fact he was a friend to all and all a friend to him   i Believe that i have ancerd all of your Qustions to the Best of my ability   yours truly

                                J. R. Herndon

NB Capt Josef Artis[2] Desiers that you should Write to him again to Know whether you have Got the Crrect date that Lincoln Came up the River with him   Lincoln is a great favorite of his and he would Like to have his Name in the history   you must Write to him   i see Nat[3] Evry Day or so he very well thought of here By his friend he qute Study   all sends ther Best   Love to you and family

    LC: HW2274–75; HL: LN2408, 1:516–19

---

    2. See §5, note 1.
    3. Not identified.

70. Nathaniel Grigsby to WHH

Gentryville this 4 of Sept 1865

Sir

   i have Just seated myself to try to answer your request relating to the history of that great and good man Abraham Lincoln   in so doing i take pleasure, but i regret that i am not competent to do him Justice   i shall not offer any further apoligy as you wil see befor i am done my lack of ability   i shall give you facts to the best of my recollection,

   Thomas Lincoln the father of Abraham Lincoln emigrated to the State of Ind in yeare of 1817 from Hardin Co Kentucky crossing the ohio river at Ephraim Thompson ferry[1] twelve miles from where he settled himself in what is Spencer Co Ind 1 and a half miles east of gentryvill   this contry at that time was a perfect wilderness with out roads or bridges so that Thomas Lincoln and his little family had to cut a road throu the heavy forrests of timber which was unbroken by the hand of man also briging the small streams that ly betwn the river and the place where he maide his settlement on congress land, he afterwards purchace from government, his family then consisted of himself and wife and two children a daughter and son the daughter being the oldest her name was Sary or Sally as she was commonly called   the sons name was Abraham Lincoln who is the object of our history who at that time was eight or nine years old   his father and himself cut away the timber from where they built what is now called a squaters cabin the material was round logs or poles cut from the forist and clapboards foure feet long to cover the bilding with the flore consisted of what was then caled punchens the chimney being made of sticks and clay   in this huble cottage the family was happy and contented but did not remain so long for in the fall of 1818 the mothe of Abraham and wife of Thomas Lincoln was taken sick with a desease called the Milk Sickness or puken a desease commin at that time in the western contry her sickness was short but fatal as she deseas this life Oct 1818 leving Abraham and the rest of the family to morne the loss of a kind mother   Thomas Lincoln remaind on his litle farm doing the best he could with his two childre for a year or two he then went to Ky and married a second wife who was a widow Johnson,[2] about this time there was a scool house built two miles south of Thomas Lincoln farm that was the the first school house that was built in this part of the state the house was built of round logs Just high enough for a man to stand erect under the ruff, the floore was split logs or what we called punchens   the chimney was maid of poles and clay the window was constructed by by chopping out a part of tow logs and plasing peases of split bords at proper distence and then we would take our old coppy books and grease them and paste them over the windows this give us lite, in this shool room Abraham Lincoln and my self entered school the scool was taught bye a man by the name of Andy Crofford   After that Abraham went

---

1. See §24, note 11.
2. Sarah Bush Johnston.

to a man by the name of Hazel Dansey also another bye the name of Swany these were all of the scool teachers that Abraham was taught buy in this State   he was always at school early and atentive to his studies he aways was at the head of his cllass he progessed rapedly in all of his studies he lost no time at hom when he was not at work he was learning his books he pursued his studies on the Sabeth day he also packed books when at work to read when he rested from laber   his habit of life he was kind and clever to all indeed he apeared to cultivate it as a prinsipal alway being wel stored witty sayings giving no offence to any one he al so rit while very young   essays on bein cind to animals and crawling insects he was always temperet in all of his habits he was truthf and onest and industrious always working with his one hands when not at scool or studying at home   Thomas Lincoln the father of Abraham was a man of limited means so that it became nessessary for Abraham to work from home he ocaisially took Jobs of claring or making fense rails   Sometimes he worked on the ohio river at one tim he hired to Allen Gentry and went dow the River on aflat boat to new orleans as a bow hand reseving $8 per mont   Gentry paying his passage back on the deck of the boat but the most of his time wile at laber was at hom on his fathers farm   he sometime worked at the cabinet business his father being a carpente and cabinet maker, Sally Lincoln the sister of Abraham Lincoln grew up and made a smart intiligent lady and a devoted christian belonging to the baptist per swasion   She was married to Aaron Grigsby in August 182[6] after living with Grigsby about two years and being the mother of one son who died wile an infant   She Deceas this life february 1828 being nine teen years of age, the wife of Thomas Lincol and mother of Abraham Lincoln her maiden name was Hanks a lady of medium size lite complection and dark hair being a lady of intiligence and a cristian woman of the baptist per swasion   Thomas Lincoln the father of Abraham Lincoln was a good citizen and a worthy intiligent farmer and a devout Christian of the baptist order but like most of the western pioneers he emigrated to Ind from Ky with but little of this worlds goods he settled on a track of government land and made a farm of a bout forty acers and baught it of government i think there was 80 acers in the entry   his business chiely was farming but he was a cabinet maker and a carpenter there is yet in this contry furniture that he maid also houses standing that he done the carpenters work   there was nothing on commin a bout him only his onisty and industy   he left this state about the year 29 or thirty for Ill   With this history i wil cease riting for this time if you wish any more history that i can give you let me now what it is and i wil try to give it   i have done the best i can for you   so you must excuse bad riting and spelling   i wish you to rivise this history and comment on it so as to not alter the meaning of the instrument   hoping to hear from you soon

N Grigsby

PS i am sorry that i my narritive is so short but it is the best i can do for you so you must excuse me

LC: HW2276–78; HL: LN2408, 1:287–93

71. A. H. Chapman (written statement)[1]

[Ante Sept 8. 1865]

Mordica[2] Lincoln the Grand Father of the Late President was born in Halifax Co — Va on the Head Waters of the Roanoke River about the year 1744, his parents emigrated to this country from Lincolnshire Eng, settled in Halifax Co — Va & there thy died. His Father was a farmer & in affluent circumstances at the time of his death. Mordica Lincoln was married to a Miss Crume. Nothing is known of her parentage only that her Father was a Farmer & a poor man. after there marriage but before thy Had any heirs thy moved from Va to Ky coming through with several other families on pack Horses camping out of nights during their entire trip. They had several Fights with the Indians during their journey by which thy lost several of their party. Thy Settled on a peice of land near Boones Lick & Here three Children were all Born. The 1st Named Mordica, the 2n Josiah, the 3d Sarah & the 4th named Thomas, who was the Father of the late President & the 5th a Daughter named _____.[3] Lincoln commenced openning a farm when he was settled on a peice of Gov't land & was Killed while at work on this farm during the spring 1784. he was at work putting up a fence to a new field, his son Thos then only a little over 6 years old was with him. his other 2 sons Mordica & Josiah were at Work in some Fields. Mordica Lincoln Succeeded in escaping to the House, barricades the door, seizes His Rifle & repairs to the loft of the house, on taking a Survey through a port Hole he discovered His Father lying Dead where he had been at work, his Bro Josiah he could not see at all but he discovered his Bro Thos in the Hands of a very large Indian who had him by the nap of the neck and seat of the breeches & was a runing Down a lane with him   Just at this time the Indian stoped & faced towards the House. Young Thos Lincoln had Just remarked to the Indian dont kill me take me prisoner. the Indian looked down at him & smiled Just at this time the crack of a Rifle was heard the Indian bounded high into the air and fell dead. Young Thos Lincoln sprang to his feet & escaped to the House his Mother unbared the Door admitted him into the house & he was saved. The Indian had been shot from the loft of the House by Mordica Lincolns a distance of 160 steps. This Indian had on his Breast a Silver ornament or medal in the shape of a Half Moon & this was the mark at which young Lincoln aimed when he shot him.

Young Josiah on being attacked & seeing all chance of getting to the house cut of made his way to a Stockad Fort Some 2 to 4 miles Distant procured Help & returned to the assistance of the Family, but upon his arrivall the Indians had left & although thy were pursed could not be overtaken except one that was wounded & found in a top of a fallen tree near Lincolns place just outside of the

---

1. Docketing in WHH's hand: *Col. A. H. Chapman of Charleston wrote this. He is a relative of Mr Lincoln and handed me this paper — Sept 8th 1865 at the Union Hotel Charleston Ills — Cash $43.00.* Chapman was married to Harriet Hanks, the daughter of AL's second cousin, Dennis F. Hanks, and AL's stepsister, Elizabeth Johnston.

2. AL's paternal grandfather's name was Abraham.

3. Nancy Lincoln (1780–1845), who married William Brumfield in 1801.

[farm]   young Mord Lincoln Swore eternal vengance on all Indians an oath which he faithfully kept as he afterwards during times of profound peace with the Indians killed several of them in fact he invariably done so when he could without it being known that he was the person that done the deed. Some time after the death of Abram Lincoln his widdo[w] removed to Washington Co Ky & settled near the town of Springfield. Here Thos Lincoln the father of the President arrived at the age of maturity & here his mother died. After the death of his mother he Thos Lincoln went to Hardin Co now Larue Co Ky & setled on No Lin Creek on a piece of Gov't land near the Town of Hoginsville   Here he was married to Nancy Sparrow[4] a Daughter of Henry and Lucy Sparrow. Lucy Sparrows Maiden Name was Hanks. Henry Sparrow was born & raised in Rockingham Co. Va. from there he imigrated to Mercer Co. Ky & Setled near a Baptist church called Liberty Meeting House here he was married to Lucy ~~Sparrow~~ or Hanks, about the year 1787, Henry Sparrows Father was named Thos Sparrow & with his Family imigrated to Va from England. Lucy Hanks the wife of Henry Sparrow & Grand Mother of a Lincoln was also born & raised in Rockingham Co Va. Her Father Joshua Hanks also emigrated to this Co from England with his family,[5] The Hanks & Sparrow Families Emigrated to this country from the same part of England about the same time, Setled in the same part of Va then emigrated to Ky at the Same time and Setled in the same neighborhood in Ky   Thy came from Va to Ky on Pack Horses camping out of nights during there Trip. Henry Sparrow & his wife Lucy died in Mercer Co Ky   after there death there Daughter Nancy went to Hardin Co Ky to reside with her Fathers Brother Thos Sparrow & Here She & Thos Lincoln wer[e] married June 12th 1804[6] & at once commenced life together on there settle place on No-Linn Creek. Thos Lincoln was at this time in poor circumstances. Having but very little to commence keeping House with. Thos Lincoln the Father of a Lincoln was a Stout athletic man. 5 feet 10 inches High & weighed when in the prime of his life 196 lbs. he had the Reputation of being one of the Stoutest men in Ky. At one time while on a visit to some friends at Hardinsburgh Ky he had a Desperate fight with a man named Hardin, said Hardin was a Noted Bully & Desperado & Said to be the Stoutest man in Breckenridge County.[7] Thos. Lincoln whiped Hardin easily without he Lincoln receang a Scratch or Bruse. This is the only fight he ever had, after his encounter with Hardin no one else ever tried his manhood in a personal combat. he was a remarkable peacable man. He was rather Dark complected, Dark Hair, Dark Grey Eyes, Careless in his personal appearance, very industrious, remarkable good Natured, very fond of a Joke or story & of telling them, fond of Hunting & a fine Hunter, always Kept a fine Rifle but never neglected his labors on his farm to Hunt, Never cared for

---

4. AL knew his mother's maiden name as Nancy Hanks.

5. The true family line of Nancy Hanks is much disputed. See the appendix for the genealogy established by Paul Verduin, which the editors believe is the best available.

6. The existing record of the wedding gives the date as June 12, 1806.

7. Cf. §16.

Fishing, was temperate in his Habits, never was intoxicated in his life, was vy careless about his business, a poor Manager, at time[s] accumulated considerable property which he always managed to make way with about as fast as he made it, had but Little Education, Learning to read & write a Little after his Marriage, tooke the world easy & was what is generally called an unlucky Man in business. Was very unfortunate in most of his attempts to accumulate property or money, was a very Hearty eater but cared but Little what kind of food he had, was satisfied if he had plenty corn Brod & Milk, Was strictly a moral man, never used profane or vulgar language. Joined the Free will Baptist Church in Hardin Co Ky in 1816 was imersed by a preacher named Wm Downs, in Knob creek H Co Ky on his removal to Ind united with the Old Predestinarian Baptist & on his removall to Coles Co Ills united with same church but afterwards left them & joined the Christian Church in Charleston Ills & lived a Member of that Church in good Standing untill his death, was Strictly Honest in all of his dealings with his fellow men. He died 8 miles south of Charleston Coles Co Ills Jany 9th 1851 — his features were coarse & he had a remarkable large roman Nose. His first wife the Mother of the Late President was a Medium Sized Woman, rather spar[e] in her person, fair complexion, Light Hair, Blue Eyes, neat in her person & Habits, industrious, of a Kind disposition   Vy affectionate in her family never opposed her Husband in any thing, was satisfied with what suited him, was a Member of the Same Church as her Husband, & died in good Standing in her Church. She died in Spencer Co Ind Oct 5th 1818 — her Funeral was preached by the Rev David Elkins an old Ky friend who was then on a visit at the time of her death. She was buried about ½ a mile north of Little Pidgeon Baptist Church in a grove of Persimon Trees on a high eminence. The Rev Young Lamar was pastar of the Church at that time   The Disease of Which She died was Milk Sick. her & her uncle & aunt Thos & Elizabeth Sparrow Levi Hall & his wife all died about the same time & were all buried side by side. after the Marriage of Thos Lincoln to Nancy Sparrow thy resided on there little place on NoLinn, for a short time when thy moved to a place on Knob Creek ½ a mile above its Mouth which Lincoln bought for 2 Dollars per acre on this piece of land there 2 Children Sarah & Abraham Lincoln Late President were Born. The first Born Feb 20th 1807 the Last Feb 12th 1809, Thy also had another chi[ld] while thy resided here a son which died when only 3 days old. These ar[e] all the children thy ever had. Thos Lincoln continued to reside on Knob Creek untill the fall of 1816 accumulating quite a Little Stock of Hogs, Horses & Cattle, During the Sumer of 1816 he traded his Little place, for 400 Gallons of Whisky. he then built him self a Little Flat or Fery Boat Loaded on it his Whisky Farming utensils, a Chest of Cabinet & Carpenters Tools, Most of there House hold goods, in fact nearly there all except — clothing Bed Clothes & Stock. he then embarked & started down Rooling Fork & when near the Mouth of Brock Fork his Boat as capsized & all he had in it was thrown into the river. he succeeded in Saving Most of his Whisky a few Tools & a few other goods. he then got his Boat righted & Loading what he had saved from the wreck. he again started on his journey in quest of a new home, he finally Landed at Thompson Fery on the Ind Sid of the ohio River at a Mans Named Posey,[8] Storing his property with Posey & Selling him his boat he at once Started back to Ky for his family walking the entire   Distance 80 Mils packing amongs other things his clothing & Bedding & a fe[w] cooking utensils (viz 1 oven & lid, 1 Skillitt [&] Lid & some tin ware) on 2 Horses [&] then he with his wife & 2 Children starte[d] for there new home in Ind in Nov. 1816. thy camped out of Nights cooking there own vict-uals, Dennis F. Hanks & Ralph Croom drove Lincoln's stock of Hogs & Cattle from Ky to Ind[9]   arriving at Poseys he hired teams & loading on them his whis-ky & other goods which he had left at Poseys he Started out to an old acquainet-anes Thos Carters 17 Miles in the interior of Ind here he arrived all safe & Setled on a peace of Govt land (80 acres). this land he afterwards bought under the two Dollar act was to pay for it in installments, one Half he paid the other Half he never paid & finally lost the whole of the land. here he erected a cabin or camp of poles one side on the face of it being open & here he commenced life in Ind. he lived in this camp one year. in the Mean time he cleared some land & raised a small crop of corn & vegetables. the watter thy uised thy obtained by digging a Hole in the ground & was a miserable article had to be Stained in warm weather before uising it. as soon as he had raised a Little crop he built a Log House, into which he moved & in it he lived during the rest of the time he resided in Ind. In the fall of 1817 Mrs Lincolns Uncle[10] with his wife & a Nephew Dennis F Hanks Moved out to Ind from Ky & Moved into Lincolns old camp which he had just vacated. Here Sparrow & his Wife booth Deid in 8 Month with the Milk Sick. Mrs Lin-coln also Sickened and Deid with Same Disease about *the Same time,* She deid Oct 5th [1818]   The Milk Sick was very prevalent among the Setlers this year, near-ly all that were attacked with it deid. There was no Phisician in the county at that time the nearest one was at Yellow Banks Ky[11] 30 Miles distant. Thos Lincoln made all the coffins for those that deid in that neighborhood about that time. the Lum-ber was green & cut with a Whip Saw. There was scarcely enough will in the neigh-borhood that fall to Bury those that deid. Thos Lincoln continued to reside here with his Son & Dr & Nephew Dennis F Hanks untill the fall of 1819 working on his farm & at his trade Making rough Tables & such other articles as was most Needed in that community. During the fall of 1819 He returned to his old home in Ky & while there he was Married to a Widdow, named Sarah Johnston her Maiden Name was Bush. She was the Daughter of Christopher and Hannah Bush of Elizabethtown Ky. Thy were Married Dec 2 — 1819. Lincoln had been acquaint-ed with her & proposed marriage to her before either of them had ever Married but had been rejected by Her. on his return to Ky finding her a widdow he renewd his proposals of Marriage to her & at the urgent solicitation of her Friends who all liked Lincoln She accepted his proposals. as soon as Married Lincoln hired his

8. Francis Posey. For Thompson's ferry, see §24, note 11.

9. The sentence appears as a marginal note; Springer places it here.

10. Thomas Sparrow, who was married to Nancy Hanks Lincoln's aunt Elizabeth, or Betsey.

11. Yellow Banks is the site of present Owensboro, Kentucky.

Brother in Law Ralph Croom to take his Waggons & Ho[rses] there, to Ind with there House Hol[d] Goods. Mrs Johnston having a large supp[ly] of House Hold goods for [a] family in those days. Mrs Johnston Had 3 children all young a Son & 2 Daughter.[12] these thy took with them to Ind & thy constituted a part of Lincolns family untill grown & Married. Mrs Johnston now Mrs Lincoln took with her to Ind one 1 fine Bureau, 1 Table, 1 sett Chairs, 1 large Cloth Chest, cooking utensils, Dishes, Knives, Forks, Spoons, 1 Spining wheel, clothing, 2 Beds & Bedding & other articles. Mrs Lincoln is still Living with her Grand Children in Coles Co Ills & has this same Bureau still in her possession, it was made by a man named W*m* Parcells, in Elizabethtown Ky & cost when new 40 Dollars & was considered in those days a very fine peace of furniture & Still bears evidence of unusual fine workmanship. on there arrival at the residence of Thos Lincoln in Ind Mrs Lincoln was astonished to find that there was no floor or Door to the House of her Husband, no furniture of any Kind, no Beds or Bedding or scarcely any. thy used rough stools for chairs. had a Table Made by putt 4 Legs in a Hewed puncheon their bed was made by Boring holes in the wall & then resing a post at one corner inserting in them poles & on these poles were Boards & on these the family made there rude Beds. thy had no Dishes except a few Pewter & Tin ones. no cooking utensils except a Dut[ch] oven & Lid & 1 skellet & Lid. The Chil[dren] were Sufring greatly for clothes, thy [had] but one Suit each & these vy poo[r] the boys being Dressed mostly in Buck Skins. The Large Supply of goods brought by Mrs Lincoln came in good time. She at once had a floor Laid in the House Doors & Windows put in the Same Dressed the children up out of the Large supply she had brought with her in fact in a few week all had changed & where evry thing was wanting now all was snug & comfortable. Lincoln insisted on his Wife selling part of her furniture especially the Bureau, saying it was too fine for them to keep but this she refused to Do. She was a woman of great energy, of remarkable good sense, very industrious, & saving & also very neat & tidy in her person & Manners & Knew exactly how to Manage children. She took a an espical liking to young Abe, her love for him was warmly returned & continued to the day of his death. But few children loved there parents as he loved this Step Mother. She soon dressed him up in entire new clothes & from that time on he appeared to lead a new life. he was encouraged by her to Study & any wish on his part was gratified when it could be don[e]   The 2 Setts of Children got along finely together as if thy had al[l] have been the children of the same parents. Mrs Lincoln soon Discovered that young Abe was a Boy of uncommon natural Talents & if rightly trained that a bright future was before him & She done all in her power to Develope those Talents, Lincolns Little Farm was well Stocked with Hogs, Horses & cattle & that year he had raised a fine crop of Wheat corn & Vegetables. a Little Town named Gentryville had sprung up near them & from there thy obtained many necessaries in life that up to this time thy had Done without. Thy taned there own Leather & Young Hanks made them Shoes out of their rude Leather. There

---

12. John, Matilda, and Elizabeth.

clothing was all made at home & the Material from which it was made was also
made at home. Coff & Tea thy did not uise nor did thy dare to uise milk a great
portion of the year on act of Milk Sick. Thy first traded at Gentryville with one
Gid Romine & afterwards with one W*m* Jones, young Abe was warmly attached
to Jones also to one John Baldwin a Black Smith. Baldwin was a great hand at telling
stories & Abe took a great[13] spent Many of his Leisure hours wit[h] him. Mr Lincoln continued to reside here untill 1829 livi[ng all] the time on the peace of Lan[d
on] which he first Setled part of [the] time working at his trade & at other times
on his farm. His wife done all the trading for the family & had the entire management of the Children. in Aug 1826 Sarah the sister of a Lincoln was Married to
Aaron Grigsby & She deid Jay 20th 1828 in giving birth to her first and only child.
The child was Dead when born. Thos Lincoln Made Several trips down the River
while he lived in Ind taking flat Boats Loaded with Produce, principally Pork, from
these trips he realized but little profit simply turning what he raised on his Farm
into cash, he sold one entire load on a credit & never realized a cent for the same,
he also tooke 2 trips Down the river with flat Boats while he lived in Ky walking
all the way from New Orleans to his home in Ky   Young Abe continued to reside with his parent as long as they lived in Ind & emigrated to Ills with them in
March 1829. he helped his Father build his first cabin in Ills he also helped to Make
the rails & fence his first 10 acres of ground which the old man put in cultivation
in Ills. This was 8 Miles west of Decatur Macon Co — Ills on the north Bank of
the Sangamon River & in the spring of 1829 — The Rails to enclo[se] this firt 10
acres of Land were principally made by the neighbors, collecting in & making a
frolic of [it] & were nearly all made in 1 Day, it is not true that Abe Lincoln made
all of those Rails as he worked at them but a few days, John Hanks cut the logs to
build the Cabin. Abe Lincoln Hauled them out with a Dry Sled & 2 yoke of cattle & Dennis F Hanks Hewed them or Scotched them on 2 Sides the Neighbors
then collected in & helped them raise the House. The family being all the time in
a Camp made of Waggon Sheets. Thos Lincoln Moved from Ind to Ills with a 4
Horse Waggon Drawn by 2 yoke of oxen, The families of Dennis F Hanks & es-
quire Hall Came with him. Hanks & Hall had Married his Lincolns 2 Step Daughters,[14] In Aug 1822 A Lincoln D F Hanks, Squire Hall all went to Poseys Landing
on the ohio River to cut cord Wood supposing that they could get the Money for
the same but arriving there thy found thy would have to take the pay for any wood
they might cut in Store goods, thy cut 9 cord & recd for it 9 yds White Domestic
at 25 cts a cord of this Abe had a Shirt Made & this is posatively the first white
shirt he ever had in his life. Lincoln was then between 13 & 14 years old & this
[was] the first time he ever hired out [or] worked away from Home   In the year
1827 A Lincoln & h[is] Step Brother John D Johnston went together to Louisvill
Ky to try & get work & earn some money, thy obtained work on their arrivall there
on the Louisvill & Portland Canall & when through working there were paid off

---

13. Inserted with a caret: *took a great.*
14. Dennis F. Hanks married Elizabeth Johnston; Squire Hall, a half-brother of Dennis F. Hanks, married Matilda Johnston.

in silver Dollars. This is the first silver dollar Lincoln ever had or owned of his own & of it he was very proud.

The Stories that Lincoln worked at Andersons Ferry in Ind for 9 Month are all untrue. he never worked there or at any other Ferry in Ind.[15] This is true beyond a Doubt. his Step Mother Mrs Lincoln his Step Sister Mrs Moore & his cousin Dennis F Hanks all concur in this asertion. The only work he ever done on the Crawford Farm in Ind was as follows. He borrowed of Josiah Crawfo[rd] the Life of Washington.[16] while this Book [was] in his Lincolns possession it got dam[aged] by being Wet & on his returning it to [Crawford] he Crawford refused to receave it [but] insisted on Lincoln paying him for the Same which Lincoln agreed to do and as he had not the money to pay for the same he worked for Crawford a puling Corn Blades at 25 cts a Day & thus paid for the Damaged Book, & this is posatively the only work he ever done on the Crawford place. he Lincoln felt that Crawford had treated him unkindly in regard to this Book & wrote some rude verses on the subject in which he ridiculed Crawford in a Most unmerciful Manner. he Lincoln was not in the habit of Working out from home while thy resided in Ind only occasionly changing work with the Neighbors which was costomary in those days,[17] Lincoln when very young & while thy still resided in Ky went to School about 3 Months to a Man named Caleb Hazell. he was sent more as Company for his Sister than with the expectation that he would learn Much, he then & there Learned his Letters & to Spell a Little. While Living in Ind his cousin D F Hanks learned him to spell, Read & Write. he afterward went to schoo[l] in Ind about 5 Months during one f[all] and winter & Learned very fast Ma[king] rapid progress in his studies. after [this] he studied very hard during his [leisure] hours, he procured a copy of Pikes Arithmatic[18] & Mastered its entire contents with but Little help from others he also borrowed all the Books he could in the Neighborhood where thy lived & read the same. The damaged life of Washington was a great favorite with him. he also obtained a coppy of Barclays Dictionary[19] which aided him Much in his Studies, This Dictionary is still in the hands of his Step Mother in Charleston Ills as is also the old Family Bible of Thos Lincoln A Lincolns Father   he also wrote Much at home writing rude verses of his own composition in his coppy Books also working out Mathematical problims in his coppy Books, one of these coppy Books is Still in existance & in the possession of Thos Johnston a son of his Step Brother Johnston & bears date 1826 & 1827, the 3 mothes that Lincoln went to school in Ky & 5 Months in Ind is all the Schooling he ever received. The family never had newspapers whi[le] thy resided in Ind. He Lincoln first became a reader of news papers af[ter] he came to Ills. The first News pa[per] which he took & read regular [was] the National Inteligencer published

---

15. Cf. §§79, 86.

16. Most likely one of many expanded editions of the *Life of Washington,* by Mason Locke Weems, first published in 1800.

17. Exchange work is a reciprocal arrangement between neighbors for performing comparable work on each other's farms.

18. See §24, note 16.

19. See §24, note 17.

at Washington City. of this paper he was a warm admirer. When about 10 years old Lincoln first showed his talent as a speaker & from that forward would gather the children together Mount a stump or Log & harang his juvenile audience. he done this so often that it interfered with their labors when at work on the farm & caused him Many reproofs from his father, He would often after returning from church repeat correctly nearly all of the sermon which he had heard mimacing the Style & tone of the old Baptist Preachers, he was also in the habit of attending Law Suits before a neighboring Justice, This both amused & interested him very much 17 to 18 years of age. he attended to several suits before this Squire for his Neighbors & in most of which he was Successfull. the Justices Name was Griffitt.[20] Lincoln was not industrious as a worker on the farm or at any other Kind of Manu[al] Labor, he only Showed industry in attainment of Knowledge. he [was] from childhood very lively & qui[ck] in his disposition. at all times [full] of fun fond of a Joke and of te[lling] one. when a Boy a great Love at playing pranks on his companions, Never cared very much for hunting or Fishing yet when a youth was very Successfull as a hunter when he followed & a fine Shot with a Rifle. did not when a youth Show Much Diseir or inclination in acquiring this worlds goods. Sarah the sister of A Lincoln was married to Aaron Grigsby in Spencer Co Ind August 1826 and died January 20th 1828 in giving Birth to her first child. the child was still Born. Thos Lincoln A Lincolns Father was a Cabinet Maker by trade. Learned the trade or what he Knew about it with Josiah Hanks in Elizabeth Town Ky, after his Marriage he always lived on a farm working on his Farm during crop time & at other times at his trade also Making Doors & Door & Window caseings for the Setlers. while he resided in Ky he made two trips down the Ohio & Miss Rivers to New Orleans with one Isaac Bush. thy wa[lked] the entire distance across t[he] country from New Orleans b[ack] to their homes in Ky. The clothin[g for] the family while thy resided in [Ind] was all Manufactured at Home by them selves from cotton & Flax of there own raising. The Cotton thy picked carded & Spun with there own hands. there winter pants for the Men & boys was Made of Buckskin for Several years after there arrivall in Ind afterward from wool taken from some sheep which thy had procured but thy had no woollen clothing in the family untill about the year 1824. Cant ascertain the name of the Teacher that Lincoln went to School to in Ind. all agree Most posatively that Lincoln Made his first Money a working at the Louisville & Portland canall.[21] Thos Lincoln Moved from Ind to Macon Co — Ills in March 1830. Moved from there to Buck grove Coles Co Ills in the fall of 1831, Resided there one year & then moved to Muddy Point in coles co Ills & built the hose now owned as a residence by C. J. Dexter, resided there but a few Months then moved to & setled near goose Nest Prairie in Coles [Co] Ills where he continued to reside un[til] his death, with exception of one y[ear] one Season he rented Slows Mil[ls on] Embarass River. while there his [son] Abe visited him & spent some [10 days] with him. he never resided in Coles Co but

20. Not identified.
21. Canal around the falls on the Ohio River at Louisville, constructed in 1825–30.

called it home from the fact that his parents resided there, Thos Lincoln Moved from Ind to Ills in a Large 4 Horse Waggon drawn by 2 yoke of oxen & this is posatively the first waggon he ever owned. he brought to Ills with him some stock cattle. one Horse, 3 Beds & Bedding, 1 Bureau, 1 Table, 1 Clothes Chest, 1 sett of Chairs, cooking utensils, Clothing & So forth, three families came together, Lincolns, Esqr Halls & Dennis F Hanks. Hall & Hanks had Married Lincoln's two Step Daughters. Abe Lincoln drove his Fathers ox team from Ind to Ills. The watters were very high at that time & thy came near Loosing their team, waggon & its contents in crossing the Okaw or Kaskaskia River. Lincoln came to his Fathers in coles co after the Black Hawk war, also after his return from New Orleans. afterward while practicing law on this circuit he visited his Father twice a year & after that he visited him while he was sick & but a short time before he T[hos] Lincoln died. Thos Lincoln di[ed] from a disease of the kidneys, [His] A Lincolns Mother from Milk Sickness & his [sister] in giving birth to her first & only child, Lincolns Father bought 40 acres of Land in Coles Co Ills but he A Lincoln had to advance the Money 200 Dollars to pay for it & prevent his Father from Loosing it.

LC: HW2279–2300; HL: LN2408, 1:222–43

72. Dennis Hanks (WHH interview)

Charleston Ills   Sept 8th 1865 —
(Hon. O. B. Ficklin — and others told me to be careful about what Hanks said)
Dennis Hanks says he is *[blank space]* years old — Knew Thos Lincoln — Abe & Sister in Ky — think Miss Lincoln went to school in Ky — says that the Lincoln family came from England about 1650 — Two Lincoln's came to Virginia — think on the head waters of the Roanoke — probably in Halifax Co — were not Puritans — were not Quakers — never were in Penn. I opposed Abe in Politics when he became whig — was till 20 years of age a Jackson Democrat — turned whig — or whiggish about 1828–9 — think Col Jones[1] made him a whig — dont know it — The two original Lincolns had *[blank space]* children — (Here I closely & critically Examined Hanks and he confessed he knew nothing — Except as above stated — backed down from his Chicago letter to me.[2] Dennis gets gloriously tight — drinks to hard — is not to be relied on always —) — think Abe Lincoln's grandfathers name was Mordacai[3]   He was born in Virginia about 1740 — Mordecai the grandfather of Abe, had 3 sons — Mordecai — Thos — & Josias — & 2 daughters — Krume married one of them — Abe was born in 1809 on the farm his father sold to *[blank space]* —   the farm is about 4½ SE of Hodgensville Ky — Hardin Co — or now La Rue. The farm is on Knob Creek — Abe used to go with me down the branch to shoot fish in puddles & holes washed by the water — killed a fawn — Abe was tickled to death — Abe Exhibited no spe-

1. William Jones, the Indiana storekeeper for whom AL worked.
2. Probably the interview dated June 13, 1865. See §24.
3. AL's grandfather's name was Abraham.

cial traits in Ky, Except a good kind — somewhat wild nature — Thos Lincoln moved to Indiana about 1816 in what was Called Perry Co — now Spencer Co Indiana — moved on 2 horses — not a waggon — Abe rode with his mother & Sally with her father — Lincolns farm in Indiana is about 15 north of the Ohio River — and about 80 miles NW of Hodgensville. The Illinois farm of Thos Lincoln is worth about $1200 — Knew all these farms well — the Ky farm when Thos Lincoln left it contained in cultivated land only six acres running up & down the branch — about 40 feet wide on either side — Hills 300 or 400 feet high — Covered once with heavy timber — some ceder on the Knobs — Shrubs — &c. up the hills sides — Vallys narrow and deep —

When we landed in Indiana in 1817 I think there were lots of bears — deer — turkeys — ate them as meat — water & bread — the Country was full of chestnuts — Pawpaws — wild pea vines — or wild [lusty?] peas &c — Could track bears — wolves — horses — cattle & men for miles through and by the pea vine — would direct People by the tracks thus made when they wanted to find a place to go — got hogs in Ky — took them to Indiana — bears got among them — scared them — swam the Ohio went back to old homes in Ky — Saw them — knew them —: Abe could when 15 years of age or in the year 1824, could hear a Sermon — Speech or remark and repeat it accurately — He would go home from the church say to the boys & girls that he could repeat the Sermon — got on Stumps — logs — fences and do it well and accurately — Old People have heard him do it o'er & o'er again — have told me so — Could do the Same in what he heard and read. Lincoln would frequently make political and other Speeches to the boys — he was calm — logical & clear alwys — He attended trials — went to Court — read the Rev. Statutes of Indiana dated 1824 — Heard law Speeches & listened to law trials &c &c —   Lincoln was lazy — a very lazy man — He was always reading — scribbling — writing — Ciphering — writing Poetry &c.&c — He was a head & shoulders above us all — would learn us — set our Copies — The school only taught reading — writing and Ciphering — Ciphered up to single rule of three, never got up to the double rule of three[4] —. Thomas Lincoln Entered the farm in Ills in 1834 — Mortaded it to the School Comms — Abe paid the debt $200 — Thos Lincoln conveyed the farm to Abe reserving in the land a life Estate for him & his wife — and at their death the fee goes to Abe — Abe gave a bond to — Jno D Johnson — saying that if Johnson & his heirs woud on the death of Thos Lincoln & wife and in one year thereafter pay said $200 — that he Lincoln would convey to them — if they would pay interest to L at the rate of 6 per ct from the death of Thos L & wife — deed dated Octr 25th 1841 — Bond or agreement of Abe to Johnson about same date — (see Records in Charleston Ills — Book C.E.G — &c).[5]

---

4. The rule of three is a means of determining the fourth term in a proportion when three terms are given; confusingly, the double rule of three refers to calculation of the missing term when more than three are given.

5. Dennis later sent WHH a copy of this agreement in his letter of March 7, 1866. See §166; cf. *CW* 1:262–63.

To the question put by me to Hanks — "How did Lincoln & yourself learn so much in Indiana under such disadvantages" he replied — "We learned by sight — scent & hearing — We heard all that was said & talked over & over the questions heard — wore them slick — greasy & threadbare — Went to political & other speeches & gathering as you do now — we would hear all sides & opinions — talk them over — discuss them agreeing or disagreeing — Abe as I said before was originally a Democrat after the order of Jackson — so was his father — so we all were — Abe turned whig in 1827-8. — He preached Made Speeches — read for us — Explained to us &c — sang from Watts hymns — from Dupay's[6] —. Abe was a cheerful boy — a witty boy — was humorous always — sometimes would get sad — not very often — He would Joke — tell stories — run rigs — &c on the boys — Didn't love the Company of girls — didn't love crowds as a general rule — was *a retired* boy — & a good listener to his Superiors — bad to his inferiors — that is he Couldn't Endure Jabber — Could good [sense?] while he was learning —

One day a Yankee came round and said to Thomas Lincoln that he could find water on his farm — would do so by a divining rod &c. for the sum of five dollars — Old Man Lincoln couldnt beleive such stuff — Thos Lincoln had dug his hill to find water with a honey Comb as it were — wanted water badly — but said to the Yankee this — "Do you suppose I am going to give you $5 — for a pig in the polk". In Gentryvill about 1 m west of Thomas L's farm Lincoln would go and tell his jokes — stories &c. and he was so odd — original and humorous & witty that all the People in town would gather around him — He would keep them there till midnight or longer telling stories — cracking jokes — & running rigs[7] — &c —. I would get tired — want to go home — cuss Abe — &c. most hearty Lincoln was a great talker — a good reader & was a kind of news boy — Hanks went to Indiana about the time of the 2 marriage in 1819 of Thos Lincoln. Abe was so attatched to reading that we had to buy him — hire him to work — bought him, I think the Columbian Orator or American Preceptor.[8] We were Excellent bow shots — a squirrel couldnt Escape unless he got in his hole and then if Abe took the notion he would pull him or it out of his hole — Abe was born on Knob Creek[9] which runs into the rolling fork — thence into & then into the Ohio River —. Abe made no mark in Ky worthy of being Known: when he left there he was only 7 ys old — The date of the Copy book which you have got or a leaf of which &c — is dated 1824 — one part & the 2d pt 1826 — This book he made in Indiana — I bought the paper — gave it to Abe — Barclay's dictionary is dated 1799[10] —

---

6. Isaac Watts, *Hymns and Spiritual Songs* (15th ed., Philadelphia, 1741); Rev. Starke Dupuy, *Hymns and Spiritual Songs, Original and Selected* (Louisville, 1818).

7. "Running rigs" is to tease, banter, or ridicule.

8. Caleb Bingham, comp., *The American Preceptor; Being a New Selection of Lessons for Reading and Speaking* (1794); idem, *The Columbian Orator; Containing a Variety of Original and Selected Pieces; Together with Rules Calculated to Improve Youth and Others in the Ornamental and Useful Art of Eloquence* (1797).

9. AL was born on Nolin Creek and moved with his family to the Knob Creek farm at about the age of two.

10. See §24, note 17.

& the family Bible 1818 — Abe used both — his hand writing is in both — in a rough School boy's hand — Hall brought the Dictionary to Indiana in *[blank space]* & Thos Lincoln brought the Bible in 1818 — or 19 —   Lincoln didnt read the Bible half as much as said: he did read it — I thought he never believed it and think so still —

This I copied from notes taken on the Spot nearly in Hanks own words — copied this the 20th dy of Sept 1865 — in my office in presence of Zane & our Student Johnson read it to him — I say it is correct[11]

On the Copy book of Mr Lincoln — a part of which is given me is this Expression

"Abraham Lincoln is my name
I'll be a good boy — God knows when"

This is in his hand writing and I think I give the Exact words.
W H Herndon

LC: HW2301–8; HL: LN2408, 1:104–10

73. Sarah Bush Lincoln (WHH interview)

Septr 8th 1865
Friday — Old Mrs Lincolns Home — 8 m South of Charleston — Septr 8th 1865

Mrs Thomas Lincoln Says —
I Knew Mr Lincoln in Ky — I married Mr Johnson — he died about 1817 or 18 — Mr Lincoln came back to Ky, having lost his wife — Mr Thos Lincoln & Myself were married in 1819 — left Ky — went to Indiana — moved there in a team — think Krume movd us. Her is our old bible dated 1819[1]: it has Abes name in it. Here is Barclay's dictionary dated 1799[2] —: it has Abe's name in it, though in a better hand writing — both are boyish scrawls —   When we landed in Indiana Mr Lincoln had erected a good log cabin — tolerably Comfortable. This is the bureau I took to Indiana in 1819 — cost $45 in Ky   Abe was then young — so was his Sister. I dressed Abe & his sister up — looked more human. Abe slept up stairs — went up on pins stuck in the logs — like a ladder — Our bed steds were original creations — none such now — made of poles & Clapboards — Abe was about 9 ys of age when I landed in Indiana —   The country was wild — and desolate. Abe was a good boy: he didn't like physical labor — was diligent for

---

11. An explicit acknowledgment of what was apparently a common practice with WHH, that is, making notes when taking an interview and writing them up sometime later.

---

1. See §75.
2. See §24, note 17.

Knowledge — wished to Know & if pains & Labor would get it he was sure to get it. He was the best boy I ever saw. He read all the books he could lay his hands on — I can't remember dates nor names — am about 75 ys of age — Abe read the bible some, though not as much as said: he sought more congenial books — suitable for his age. I think newspapers were had in Indiana as Early as 1824 & up to 1830 when we moved to Ills — Abe was a Constant reader of them — I am sure of this for the years of 1827–28–29–30. The name of the Louisville Journal[3] seems to sound like one. Abe read histories, papers — & other books — cant name any one — have forgotten. Abe had no particular religion — didnt think of that question at that time, if he ever did — He never talked about it. He read diligently — studied in the day time — didnt after night much — went to bed Early — got up Early & then read — Eat his breakfast — go to work in the field with the men. Abe read all the books he could lay his hands on — and when he came across a passage that Struck him he would write it down on boards if he had no paper & keep it there till he did get paper — then he would re-write it — look at it repeat it — He had a copy book — a kind of scrap book in which he put down all things and this preserved them. He ciphered on boards when he had no paper or no slate and when the board would get too black he would shave it off with a drawing knife and go on again: When he had paper he put his sums down on it.[4] His copy book is here now or was lately (Here it was shown me by Mr Thos Johnson)   Abe, when old folks were at our house, was a silent & attentive observer — never speaking or asking questions till they were gone and then he must understand Every thing — even to the smallest thing — Minutely & Exactly —: he would then repeat it over to himself again & again — sometimes in one form and then in another & when it was fixed in his mind to suit him he became Easy and he never lost that fact or his understanding of it. Sometimes he seemed pestered to give Expression to his ideas and got mad almost at one who couldn't Explain plainly what he wanted to convey. He would hear sermons preached — come home — take the children out — get on a stump or log and almost repeat it word for word —   He made other Speeches — Such as interested him and the children. His father had to make him quit sometimes as he quit his own work to speak & made the other children as well as the men quit their work. As a usual thing Mr Lincoln never made Abe quit reading to do anything if he could avoid it. He would do it himself first. Mr. Lincoln could read a little & could scarcely write his name: hence he wanted, as he himself felt the uses & necessities of Education his boy Abraham to learn & he Encouraged him to do it in all ways he could — Abe was a poor boy, & I can say what scarcely one woman — a mother — can say in a thousand and it is this — Abe never gave me a cross word or look and never refused in fact, or Even in appearance, to do any thing I requested him. I never gave him a cross word in all my life. He was Kind to Every body and to Every thing and always accommodate others if he could — would do so willingly if he could.

---

3. The *Louisville Journal* began publication on November 23, 1830.
4. See *CW* 1:xxix–xlviii.

His mind & mine — what little I had seemed to run together — move in the same channel — Abe could Easily learn & long remember and when he did learn anything he learned it well and thoroughly. What he thus learned he stowed away in his memory which was Extremely good — What he learned and Stowed away was well defined in his own mind — repeated over & over again & again till it was so defined and fixed firmly & permanently in his Memory. He rose Early — went to bed Early, not reading much after night. Abe was a moderate Eater and I now have no remembrance of his Special dish: he Sat down & ate what was set before him, making no complaint: he seemd Careless about this. I cooked his meals for nearly 15 years —. He always had good health — never was sick — was very careful of his person — was tolerably neat and clean only — Cared nothing for clothes — so that they were clean & neat — fashion cut no figure with him — nor Color — nor Stuff nor material — was Careless about these things. He was more fleshy in Indiana than Ever in Ills —. I saw him Every year or two — He was here — after he was Elected President of the US. (Here the old lady stopped — turned around & cried — wiped her Eyes — and proceeded)   As Company would Come to our house Abe was a silent listener — wouldn't speak — would sometimes take a book and retire aloft — go to the stable or field or woods — and read —. Abe was always fond of fun — sport — wit & jokes — He was sometimes very witty indeed. He never drank whiskey or other strong drink — was temperate in all things — too much so I thought sometimes — He never told me a lie in his life — never Evaded — never Equivocated never dodged — nor turned a Corner to avoid any chastisement or other responsibility. He never swore or used profane language in my presence nor in others that I now remember of — He duly reverenced old age — loved those best about his own age — played with those under his age — he listened to the aged — argued with his Equals — but played with the children —. He loved animals genery and treated them Kindly: he loved children well very well —. There seemed to be nothing unusual in his love for animals or his own Kind — though he treated Every body & Every thing Kindly — humanely — Abe didnt Care much for crowds of people: he choose his own Company which was always good. He was not very fond of girls as he seemed to me. He sometimes attended Church. He would repeat the sermon over again to the children. The sight of such a thing amused all and did Especially tickle the Children. When Abe was reading My husband took particular Care not to disturb him — would let him read on and on till Abe quit of his own accord. He was dutiful to me always — he loved me truly I think. I had a son John who was raised with Abe Both were good boys, but I must Say — both now being dead that Abe was the best boy I Ever Saw or Ever Expect to see. I wish I had died when my husband died. I did not want Abe to run for Presdt — did not want him Elected — was afraid Somehow or other — felt it in my heart that Something would happen him and when he came down to see me after he was Elected Presdt I still felt that Something told me that Something would befall Abe and that I should see him no more. Abe & his father are in Heaven I have no doubt, and I want to go there — go where they are — God bless Abm

When I first reachd the House of Mrs Lincoln and was introduced to her by Col A H. Chapman her grandson by marriage — I did not Expect to get much out of her — She seemed to old & feeble —: She asked me my name 2 or 3 times and where I lived as often — and woud say — "Where Mr Lincoln lived once his friend too"　She breathed badly at first but She seemed to be struggling at last to arouse her self— or to fix her mind on the subject. Gradually by introducing simple questions to her — about her age — marriage — Kentucky — Thomas Lincoln — her former husband Johnston her children — grand children She awoke — as it were a new being — her Eyes were clear & calm: her flesh is white & pure — not Coarse or material — is tall — has bluish large gray Eyes: Ate dinner with her — sat on my west side — left arm — ate a good hearty dinner she did —

When I was about to leave she arose — took me by the hand — wept — and bade me goodby — Saying I shall never see you again — and if you see Mrs Abm Lincoln & family tell them I send them my best & tenderest love — Goodby my good son's friend — farewell.

Then went to Thos Lincoln's grave (describe it &c)

LC: HW2309–16; HL: LN2408, 1:78–84

74. Matilda Johnston Moore (WHH interview)

Sept 8th 1865 — at Mrs Lincolns House Mrs More — once Mrs Hall[1] — once Miss Johnson —

I am the youngest Step Sister of A Lincoln — remember Coming from Ky — remember Ohio River — My Earliest recollection of Abe is playing — Carrying water about one mile — had a pet cat that would follow him to the spring — went to school about 2 miles or more — Abe was not Energetic Except in one thing — he was active & persistant in learning — read Everything he Could — Ciphered on boards — on the walls — read Robinson Crusoe[2] — the bible — Watts hymns[3] —. When father & Mother woud go to Church, they walked about 1½ miles — Sometimes rode — When they were gone — Abe would take down the bible, read a verse — give out a hymn — and we would sing — were good singers. Abe was about 15 years of age —: he would preach & we would do the Crying — sometimes he would join in the Chorus of Tears — One day my bro John Johnston caught a land terrapin — brought it to the place where Abe was preaching — threw it against the tree — crushed the shell and it Suffered much — quivered all over — Abe preached against Cruelty to animals, Contending that an ants life was to it, as sweet as ours to us — Abe read I think Grimshaws History of the U.S[4] —

1. Matilda Johnston first married Squire Hall; after his death, she married Reuben Moore.
2. Daniel Defoe, *The Life and Surprising Adventures of Robinson Crusoe, of York, Mariner, Written by Himself* (1719).
3. See §72, note 6.
4. William Grimshaw, *History of the United States, from Their First Settlement as Colonies, to the Peace of Ghent: Comprising, Every Important Political Event* (1820).

and other books — Cant now remember what — Abe would go out to work in the field — get up on a stump and repeat almost word for word the sermon he had heard the Sunday before — Call the Children and friends around him — His father would come and make him quit — send him to work — Often Abe would make political speeches such as he had heard spoken or seen written &c —. He never forgot anything — was truthful, good to me — good to all — Once when he was going to the field to work I ran — jumped on his back — cut my foot on the axe — we said — "What will we tell Mother as to how this happened: I said I would tell her "I cut my foot on the axe" that will be no lie — said Lincoln, but it won't be all the truth — the whole truth — will it Tilda —   Tell the whole truth and risk your Mother Abe seemed to love Every body and Every thing: he loved us all and Especially Mother — My Mother, I think has given Abes character well —   I am about 50 years of age —

This was taken down by me from the lips of Mrs Moore at Mrs Lincoln's House as she Spoke it at the time —   Done in the Presence of Mrs Lincoln and the family — including Col Chapman who took me out —

W H Herndon

LC: HW2317; HL: LN2408, 1:156–57

75. WHH Notes from Lincoln Family Bible

Septr. 9th 1865

The following births — deaths & Marriages were taken from Mrs Lincoln's Bible, by me Septr. 9th 1865 — which record is in A Lincoln's hand writing and now in the possession of Col Chapman

Nancy Lincoln[1] was born February 10th 1807
Abraham Lincoln — son of Thos & Nancy Lincoln was born Feb 12th 1809
Sarah Bush first married to Daniel Johnson and afterwards the second wife of Thos Lincoln
Thomas Lincoln was born Decr 13th 1788 —
John D Johnson — son of Daniel & Sarah Johnson was born May the 11th — married to Mary Bar Octr 13th 1834 — who was born July 22d 1816
Thomas L. D. Johnston — son of John & Mary Johnston was born January 11th 1837
Abram L. D. Johnston — son of same parents was born March the 27th 1838.
Marietta Sarah Jane Johnston daughter of same parents was born January 21st 1840 —
Squire H. Johnston son of same parents was born December 15th 1841 —
Richard M Johnson son of same parents was born October the 26th 1845
Dennis F Johnson son of same parents was born December 13th 1847

---

1. This is AL's sister, whose name is usually given as Sarah.

Nancy. J. William was born March the 18th 1836

Abraham Lincoln — son of Thomas Lincoln was married to Mary Todd Nov 4th 1842

John D. Johnson was married to his 2d Wife, Nancy Jane Williams March the 5th 1851 —

Thomas Lincoln died January 17th 1851 — aged 73 years & 11 days —

Daniel. W. Johnston — son of John D & Mary Johnston died July 15th 1846 —

Nancy Lincoln wife of Thomas Lincoln died October the 5th 1818.

Sarah daughter of Thomas Lincoln, wife of Aaron Grigsby died January 20th 1828.

Thomas Lincoln Married to Sarah Johnston Decr 2d 1819.

Nancy or Sarah Lincoln daughter of Thomas Lincoln was married to Aaron Grigsby Aug. — 1826

This I copied from the bible of Lincoln — made in his own hand writing — now in the possession of Col Chapman — ie the leaf of the Bible — now in fragments Causing me trouble to make out — pieces small — worn it in some man's pockett.

Sept 1865

W H Herndon

LC: HW2318; HL: LN2408, 2:482–83

76. Nathaniel Grigsby (WHH interview)

Gentryville Ind. Septr 12th 1865

My name is N. Grigsby — am 54 years of age — Knew Abm Lincoln well — My father Came from Ky in the fall of 1815 and settled in what is called now Spencer Co — once a part and portion of Perry — Thomas Lincoln moved to this State in the year 1816 — or 1817 — He came in the fall of the year and Crossed the Ohio River at what is Called Ephraim Thompson's Ferry about 2½ miles west of Troy — The Country was a wilderness and there were no roads from Troy to the place he settled which place is about 1½ miles East of Gentryville — the town in which I now live and you are writing. Thomas Lincoln Lincoln was a large man — Say 6 feet or a little up — strong & Muscular — not nervous —. Thomas Lincoln was a man of good morals — good habits and Exceedingly good humored — he could read and sign his name — write but little. Mrs. Lincoln the mother of Abraham was a woman about 5 ft — 7 inches high — She had dark hair — light hazel Eye — complexion light or Exceedingly fair —. Thomas Lincoln & his wife had 2 children — one Sally and one Abraham — Sally was about 10 ys when she landed in Indiana — Abe was about 8 or 9 years of age. Thomas Lincoln when he landed in Indiana Cut his way to his farm with the Axe felling the forest as he went which was thick & dense — no prairies from the Ohio to his place —. I am informed that he came in a horse waggon to his farm — don't know but have heard this said in the family —: Abm Lincoln & Sally & myself all went to school — we 1st went to school to Andy Crawford in the year 1818, in the winter — the same year that Mrs Lincoln died she having died in Octr — Abe went to school nearly a year say — 9 mo — I was going to school all this time and saw Lincoln there most, if not all the time —   The 2d School Master we went to was a Mr Hazel Dorsy —   Abe Lincoln went to school to Hazel about 6 months — I went to school all the time — saw Lincoln there all or at least most of the time. We had to go about 2 miles to school — The 3*d* time we went to School was to a Mr Swaney who taught 6 mo. Lincoln did not go to school to him all the time Lincoln had to walk about 4 miles — Lincoln was, about, the 1st school 9 or 10 ys of age — The 2d school, he was about 14 or 15 and the 3d School he was about 16 or 18. Lincoln was Large of his age — Say at 17 — he was 6 & 2 inches tall — weighed about 160 pounds or a little more — he was Stout — withy-wirey —. When we started to School we had Dilworths' Spelling book[1] and the American Spelling book[2] — not Websters[3] I think — Lincoln ciphered at Crawfords school — Dorsys & Swanys — He used Pikes arithmetic —.[4] Ray's[5] was sometimes used —. We only wrote — spelled & ciphered —. We had Spelling Matches frequently — Abe always ahead of all the classes he Ever was in — When we went to Crawford he tried to learn us manners. &c. He would ask one of the schollars to retire from the School room — Come in and then some schollar would go around and introduce him to all the Schollars — male & female. Lincoln was a Studious. Lincoln while going to School to Crawford would write short sentences against cruelty to animals. We were in the habit of catching Turrapins — a Kind of turtle and put fire on their back and Lincoln would Chide us — tell us it was wrong — would write against it — Lincoln wrote Poetry while he was going to School to Dorsy —. Essays & Poetry were not taught in the school — Abe took it up of his own accord. He wrote a good Composition against Cruelty to animals whilst going to Dorsy and Swany. He wrote Poetry when going to these men. These things I remember & Know —. Cannot remember of his reading — any book — or books Excepting Esops fables — Bunyan's Pilgrim's Progress — the Bible — Robinson Crusoe Life of Washington — Dupee's Hymn book[6] — Our libraries consisted of Spelling books — Bibles — Arithmetics — Song books. Lincoln was Kindly disposed toward Every body and Every thing — He scarcely Ever quarreled — was prompt & honorable — He never was an intemperate lad: he did drink his dram as well as all others did, preachers & Christians included — *Lincoln was a temperate drinker.* When

---

1. Thomas Dilworth, *A New Guide to the English Tongue: In Five Parts* (1747).

2. Probably Asa Rhoads, comp., *An American Spelling Book, Designed for the Use of Our Common Schools* (1802).

3. Noah Webster, *The American Spelling Book: Containing an Easy Standard of Pronunciation* (1783).

4. See §24, note 16.

5. Probably Joseph Ray, *The Little Arithmetic: Elementary Lessons in Intellectual Arithmetic, on the Analytic and Inductive Method of Instruction* . . . (1834), published too late for use by AL in Indiana.

6. See §80, note 3 *(Pilgrim's Progress);* §74, note 2 *(Robinson Crusoe);* §24, note 15, and §71, note 16 *(Life of Washington);* and §72, note 6 (Dupuy).

he went out to work any where would Carry his books with and would always read whilst resting —

We wore buckskin pants — and linsey wolsey hunting coat to school. This was our school dress — our Sunday dress and Every day dress. Mr Lincoln was long & tall and like the balance of us he wore low shoes — short socks, wool being Scarce — between the shoe and Sock & his britches — made of buckskin there was bare & naked 6 or more inches of Abe Lincoln shin bone. He would always come to school thus — good humoredly and laughing — He was always in good health — never was sick — had an Excellent Constitution — & took Care of it —

Lincoln did not do much hunting — sometimes went Coon hunting & turkey hunting of nights — Whilst other boys were idling away their time Lincoln was at home studdying hard — would cipher on the boards — wooden fire shovels — &c — by the light of the fire — that burnt on the hearth — had a slate sometimes — but if not handy would use boards — He would shave boards bright and cipher on them — dirty them — re-shave them   Abe would set up late reading & rise Early doing the Same

Mrs Lincoln Abes Mother was born _____ and died in the fall — Octr 1818 — leaving her 2 children — Sally Lincoln was older than Abe — and Abraham — Sally married Aaron Grigsby — my brother — in Aug. 1826 — she died in about 2 years, &c — in 1828 —

Mrs Lincoln the mother of Abe Lincoln — was a woman Know for the Extraordinary Strength of her mind among the family and all who knew her: she was superior to her husband in Every way. She was a brilliant woman — a woman of great good sense and Modesty. Those who Knew her best — with whom I have talked say she was a woman of pale Complexion — dark hair — sharp features — high forehead — bright Keen gray — or hazle Eyes —. Thos Lincoln & his wife were really happy in Each others presence — loved one an other. Thomas Lincoln was not a lazy man — but a [tinker?] — a piddler — always doing but doing nothing great — was happy — lived Easy — & contented. had but few wants and Supplied these. He wanted few things and Supplied them Easily —   His wants were limited by wanting few things. Sally was a quick minded woman & of extraordinary Mind — She was industrious — more so than Abraham — Abe worked almost alone from the head — whilst she labored both. Her good humored laugh I can see now — is as fresh in my mind as if it were yesterday. She could like her brother Abe meet & greet a person with the very Kindest greeting in the world — make you Easy at the touch & word — He mind, though my brothers wife — was an intellectual & intelligent woman — However not so much as her mother —

My brother Wm Grigsby and John D Johnston a step brother of Abe had a severe fight — it was [attended?] from all around the neighborhood — Coming 18 Miles — strong men Came — bullies Came — Abe was there — Abe & my brother first had the quarrel — Abe being large & stronger than my brother turned over his Step brother to do his fighting — so they met — fought — fought ½ mile from Gentryville. There was a store here & probably a grocery — and a blacksmith Shop —   This was the town then, of Gentryville — Johnson was badly hurt, but not whipt — My brother was unhurt seriously so — Johnson & my bro were brave Strong men.

A. Lincoln came here in 1844 and made a speech for Clay: He was a Clay Elector in Ills for the race between Polk & Clay. Lincoln Spoke here — once — once at Rockport — and onc Carlin township about ¾ of a mile from the home farm. Lincoln in Early years — say from 1820 to 25 was tending towards Democracy — He afterwards Changed — Parties at this time ran Jackson — Adams and others. What changed Lincoln I dont remember — we were all Jackson boys & men at this time in Indiana —

Lincoln did go to New Orleans: he went to NO about 1828 with a man by the name of Allen Gentry who took — as well as owned the supercargo to New Orleans — The good were sold down on the river — Abe went as a bow hand — working the foremost oars — getting $8.00 per month — from the time of starting to his returning home. Gentry paid his way back on a boat. This I Know. He made rails for Crawford[7] — take jobs of work sometimes — would go to the river — the Ohio — 13 or 16 miles distant and there work. It is 60 miles to the Wabash — he did work on the Wabash[8] — but on the Ohio — Lincoln did not work on the Louisvill Can, but he may have done it nevertheless —

Lincoln did write what is called "The book of Chronicles"[9] — a Satire on the Grigsby's & Josiah Crawford — not the School Master, but the man who loaned Lincoln the Life of Washington —. The Satire was good — sharp —cutting and showed the Genius of the boy: it hurt us then, but its all over now. There is now no family in the broad land who after this loved Lincoln so well and who now look upon him as so great a man. We all voted for him — all that could — children and grand children — I was for Lincoln & Hamlin, first, last, & always — 2d Election I was at Decatur Alabama in the service of the US —

We had political discussions from 1825 to 1830 the year Lincoln left for Ills. We attended them — heard questions discussed — talked Evry thing over & over and in fact wore it out — We learned much in this way.

I said heretofore that Abe made his mark of manhood Even while in Indiana. His mind & the Ambition of the man soared above us. He naturally assumed the leadership of the boys —   He read & thoroughly read his books whilst we played —. Hence he was above us and became our guide and leader & in this position he never failed to be the leader. He was Kind — jocular — witty — wise — honest — just — human full of integrity — Energy — & acting. When he appeared in Company the boys would gather & cluster around him to hear him talk. He made fun & cracked his jokes making all happy, but the jokes & fun were at no mans Expense — He wounded no mans feelings

Mr Lincoln was figurative in his Speeches — talks & conversations. He argued much from Analogy and Explained things hard for us to understand by stories —

---

7. Probably Josiah Crawford.
8. WHH probably meant to write "he did *not* work on the Wabash."
9. See §113.

maxims — tales and figures. He would almost always point his lesson or idea by some story that was plain and near as that we might instantly see the force & bearing of what he said —

Never heard in the family or out of it that the Lincolns were quakers coming from Pennsylvania —. The History is that they came from Virginia[10]

LC: HW2320–28; HL: LN2408, 1:85–93

77. S. T. Johnson (WHH interview)[1]

Indiana — Septr 14th 1865

S. T. Johnson — say — I am aged 34 years — resided in this County 25 ys — from the year 1821. to 1830.[2] the County seat of Warrick Co was Boonville about 15 m from Gentryville N.W — Lincoln used to attend Court in that place. He became acquainted with a Jno. Brackenridge there — heard in which Brackenridge was Counsel. He was a fine lawyer. Lincoln attended a murder Case — trial & proceedings — was young — aged about 18. or 19 years. B. noticed the calm intelligent attention that L. paid to the trial. B moved to Texas in 1852 — Lincoln had not seen B from 1828 to 1862. B went to Washington. L. saw B. L. instantly recognized B. — L told Brackenridge that he at that time, the trial, formed a fixed determination to study the law and make that his profession. Lincoln referred to the trial — said to Brackenridge that he had listened to his, Bs, Speech at the trial and said Brackenridge — "It was the best speech that I, up to that time, Ever heard. If I could, as I then thought make as good a speech as that, that my Soul would be satisfied"

Summers[3] used to attend court there and frequently saw Mr Lincoln there — Knew he always attended Court and paid strict attention to what was said and done. The murder Case took place in 1828. L complimented Brackenridge at that trial, saying it was a clear, logical and powerful Effort. &c — Brackenridge looked at the Shabby boy —[4]

LC: HW2329; HL: LN2408, 1:124–25

---

10. The last paragraph is actually a marginal note.

---

1. Marginal note: *(First written in pencil and then Copied word for word — Herndon).*

2. These dates apparently refer to the tenure of the county seat rather than Johnson's residence in Spencer County.

3. Possibly Thomas Summer, a neighbor and contemporary of AL. See Francis Marion Van Natter, *Lincoln's Boyhood: A Chronicle of His Indiana Years* (Washington, D.C., 1963), 62.

4. Marginal note: *From Gentryville to Elizabeth 4 m. N.E a little Population of Each 300.*

78. Nathaniel Grigsby, Silas Richardson, Nancy Richardson, John Romine (WHH interview)

Lincoln Farm   Septr 14th 1865

I started from Nat Grigsby's house, with him as my guide & friend throughout the trip, Except at Rockport on the Ohio R. Grigsby lives in Gentryville — population about 300 — laid off in 1824 — runs North & South Mostly — Mainly — Started at 8 o'c M. Went to the Lincoln farm about 1½ m East of Gentryville and a little North. The house is a one Story hewed log one — porch in front: it is not the house that L lived in — though he built it. The old houses — the 1st & 2d are gone — fronts South — chimney at East End — has 2 rooms, the East one & west one — Stands on a Knowl or Knob about 50 feet above the road & about 150 yards north of the road. On the Gentryville road leading to the Hoffman Mills. The Country is a heavy timbered one — farms are cleared and cut out of the forests. The woods — the timber is hickory — white oak, called buck-eye and buck lands. The old farm now belongs to Jas Gentry — Son of Jas Gentry for whom, the old man the brother of Allen — Lincoln went to N. Orleans in 1828 or 29. John Heaven or Heavener now lives as tenant on the land: it an orchard on it part of Which Abm Lincoln planted with his own hands —   Allen Gentry got drunk and fell off the boat going to Louisville and was drowned — Abe Lincoln hewed the logs of this new house for his father — one door north & one South — 2 rooms — plank partition — one window — 2 rooms: it has been moved from its original position — placed further south than the old ones: it is not as Lincoln left it: it was not completed by Thomas Lincoln. The farm was sold to _____ by Thomas Lincoln in 1829 — went to the place of the old Spring N.W of the house — about 300 yards —: it was dry — Saw the place — Saw various old well all Caved in — it is Said water Could not be had on that hill — pity — Saw 5 or 6 old — old apple trees: the old house and Shelter are gone   I say again and again — Started to find Mrs Lincoln's grave — it is on a Knob — hill or Knowl about ½ m S.E of the Lincoln house — passed out of the lane going East — landed at the grave — tied my horse: the grave was — is on the very top or crown of the hill. The Know or Knowl is a heavy timbered one. A Space is cut out of the forest by felling the trees Somewhat circularly. In the centre of this Small cleared place about 15 feet from a large white oak tree — rather Somewhat between 2 of them, lies buried Mrs Lincoln. God bless her if I could breathe life into her again I would do it. Could I only whisper in her Ear — "Your Son was Presdt — of the U.S from 1861 to 1866," I would be satisfied. I have heard much of this blessed, good woman. I stood bare headed in reverence at her grave. I can't Say why — yet I felt in the presence of the living woman translated to another world. "God bless her," said her Son to me once and I repeat that which Echoes audibly in my Soul — "God bless her". The grave is almost undistinguishable: it has Sunk down, leaving a Kind of hollow. There is no fence around the grave yard and no tomb — no head board to mark where She lies. At her head — close to it I peeled a dog wood bush and cut or marked my name on it. Mrs

Lincoln is buried between two or more persons — Said to be Hall & his wife[1] on the one hand and Some Children on her left hand — There are two hollows or sinks. Nat Grigsby & Richardson were with me at the time — they said this was *the* grave. Mrs Richardson Saw Mrs. Lincoln buried and says it is not the grave — one of these sinks — graves crumbled in lies a few feet — 10 feet — South of the other: Mrs is the southern one as I think from Dennis Hanks & A. Lincoln told me. Mrs Lincolns body — her ashes lie just 15 feet west of a hollow hickory Stump & just 18 feet from — NE — from a large white oak tree. After looking at the grave and Contemplating in Silence the mutations of things — death — immortality — God, I left, I hope, the grave, a better man — at least if but for one moment

Went to Dennis Hanks old place — N.E from the grave yard about ¾ of a mile — just East of the old Lincoln farm about the Same distance. Got Silas Richardson — an old friend of Abes: he came to Indiana in 1816 — so did Lincoln. His mother Saw Mrs Lincoln buried; he went to the grave yard with us — Nat & myself and made certain what was before doubtful: he agrees with Dennis Hanks & A Lincoln. Richardson Says old man & Mrs Sparrow — Abes Grand Father & Mother lie on one Side of Mrs Lincoln. 2 Bruners[2] — probably children lie on the other side — or an old Lady and a child. Mrs Lincoln lies in the middle The grave is 6 feet from Said Shaved dogwood bush. Mrs Richardson is 83 years of age. Says that Mrs Lincolns grave lies 4½ feet South of the one I say is the Correct one. Dennis Hanks — A Lincoln — Silas Richardson — the old lady's Son and myself agree to the place. I only go by recollection & what others say — Mrs Richardson & her son go by what they saw — and Know. One Jno Richardson was the husband of old Mrs Richardson — & father of Silas Richardson. — There is no fence around the grave — no palings — Enclosures of any Kind — no headboard — no footboard to mark the Spot where Abm Lincoln's Mother lies — Curious — and unaccountable is it not? All is a dense forest — wild and grand.

I then proceeded to old Saml Howells House — South of the grave yard about ½ m — drank out of a good Spring near the little pigeon meeting house out of which Abe had Kneeled and drank a thousand times. Spring close to the Corner of the old Howell farm — part of which is turned out wild again. I passed the Spring — a little East — S.E — up a small rise or swell in the ground and landed at the famous Meeting house, called the little Pigeon Meeting House. It is a Babtist Church now and probably was then, but was free to all Comers of all & Every distinction. The House is a two is a two Storie one entrance, but one inside: it was intended to let the Choir and people set up there when crowded, but remains unfinished. This House is about 1½ m from Lincolns house — South & East. Went

---

1. Levi Hall and Nancy Hanks Hall, the sister of AL's grandmother. This Nancy Hanks was the aunt of AL's mother and gave birth out of wedlock to Dennis Hanks (by Charles Friend) before marrying Hall. See the appendix.

2. Apparently members of the family of Peter Brooner. See J. T. Hobson, *Footprints of Abraham Lincoln* (Dayton, Ohio, 1909), 17–19.

through the church, stealing in at the windows — The pulpit was made by Thomas Lincoln. I cut a small piece therefrom as memento. Passed East about 50 yds into the large grave yard — Saw the grave of Sarah Lincoln — Mrs Grigsby — Abe's Sister — God bless her ashes — Mrs Grigsby & her husband Aaron lie side by side — God bless 'Em. They lie 10 ft South of Nat Grigsby's wife — 1st & mother. Grave yard Slopes East & North — is in the forest — fenced in — quite a pretty place. Crawfords School House lies East of the church — East of the grave yard about 200 yds.: it is about 2 M from the Lincoln farm S.E: is now — the place Enclosed in a field — School house long since rotted away & gone.

I then Started for John Romines — SW — met Romine in the road meeting us. his age is 60 ys. Says — I Saw Mr Lincoln hundreds of times — have been in Spencer Co since 1815. Lincoln went to N.O. about '28 or '29 — halled some of the bacon to the River — not for Lincoln but for Gentry — Thomas Lincoln was a carpenter by trade — relied on it for a living — not on farming. Abe didn't like to work it — didn't raise more than was Enough for family & stock. Boat Started out of the Ohio in the Spring — Abe about 20 years of age — Started from Rockport — a Short distance below rather — at the Gentry landing — Give about 2 m. Lincoln was attacked by the Negroes — no doubt of this —   Abe told me so — Saw the scar myself. — Suppose at the Wade Hampton farm or near by — probably below at a widows farm. Abe was awful lazy: he worked for me — was always reading & thinking — used to get mad at him — He worked for me in 1829 pulling fodder. I Say Abe was awful lazy: he would laugh & talk and crack jokes & tell stories all the time, didn't love work but did dearly love his pay. He worked for me frequently — a few days only at a time. His breeches didn't & socks didn't meet by 12 inches — Shin bones Sharp — blue & narrow Lincoln said to me one day that his father taught him to work but never learned him to love it.

Saw old Man Gordons[3] Mill — rather the near ruins of it. This is the Mill where Abe got Kicked by a horse — hunted for Lincolns name written in tar & black lead & grease on a shaft of the mill — couldn't find it — got a cog or two of the mill — Romine tells me one verse of the Book of Chronicles — it runs thus —

Reuben & Charley have married 2 girls —
But Billy has married a boy
Billy & Natty agree very well
Mamma is pleased with the match.
The Egg is laid but won't hatch.

LC: HW2345, HW2344, HW2349, HW2347–48, HW2350–52; HL: LN2408, 1:140–46

---

3. Noah Gordon.

79. Joseph C. Richardson (WHH interview)[1]

[Sept. 14?, 1865]

My father Came to Spencer Co Indiana in 1828. Lincoln was tall and raw boned at 18. When 16 years of age he was 6 feet high — he was somewhat bony & raw — dark Skinned: he was quick and moved with Energy: he never idled away his time. When out of regular work, he would help & assist the neighbors: he was Exceedingly Studious. I Knew him well — he wrote me a copy in my writing Copy book which runs thus

Good boys who to their books apply
Will make great men by & by.

This Copy was written in 1829. The Weems Washington — the book Story took place in 1829. — one year before Abe went to Ills. Crawford[2] was a close penurious man — probably did not treat Lincoln generously, but Lincoln did not object to what Crawford required. The book Story is correct.

Onc Lincoln & Squire Hall raised some water melons — Some of us boys lit into the melon patch accidentally. We got the melons — went through the Corn to the fence — got over — All at onc to our Surprise and mortification Lincoln Came among us — on us — good naturedly said boys "now I've got you — sat down with us — cracked jokes, told stories & helped to eat the melons.

One day Abe's grand Mother wanted him to read some chapters in the Bible for her. L. did-not want to do it. At last he took up the Bible and read & rattled away so fast that his poor old grand Mother Could not understand it. She good naturedly ran him out of the house with the broom Stick — who being out, the thing he wanted he Kept shy that day — all done in sport & fun.

Lincoln did Keep ferry for Jas Taylor for about 9 mo — at the mouth of Anderson River on the ohio, between Troy & Maxville. The Lincoln & Grigsby family had a Kind of quarrel and hence for some time did not like Each other. Aaron Grigsby had some years before this married Miss Sarah Lincoln — the good & Kind Sister of Abe — Two other Grigsby boys — men rather — got married on the same night at the Same house — though they did-not marry Sisters — they had an infair at old man Grigsbys[3] and all the neighbors, Excepting the Lincoln family were invited — Josiah Crawford the book man helped to get up the infair: he had a long huge blue nose. Abe Lincoln undoubtedly felt miffed — insulted, pride wounded. &c. Lincoln I Know felt wronged about the book transaction. After the infair was Ended the two women were put to bed. The Candles were blown out — up Stairs — The gentlemen — the 2 husbands were invited & shown to bed. Chas Grigsby got into bed with, *by accident* as it were, with Reuben Grigsbys wife

---

1. Two marginal notes: *School House Pigeon 11/4 m SE of Lincolns* and *First School H1/4 E of the Pigeon meeting H.*
2. Josiah Crawford.
3. Reuben Grigsby, Sr.

& Reuben got into bed with Charles' wife, by accident as it were. Lincoln, I say was mortified & he declared that he would have revenge. Lincoln was by nature witty & here was his Chance. So he got up a witty *poem* — called the Book of Chronicles, in which the Infair — the mistake in partners — Crawford & his blue nose Came in Each for its Share — and this poem is remembered here in Indiana in scraps better than the Bible — better than Watts hymns.[4] This was in 1829, and the first production that I know of that made us feel that Abe was truly & realy *some*. This called the attention of the People to Abe intellectually. Abe dropt the Poem in the road Carelessly — lost it as it were: it was found by one of the Grigsby boys Satirised who had the good manly Sense to read it — Keep it — preserve it for years — if it is *not in Existence now.*

Grigsby challenged Lincoln to fight. Abe refused. Said he was too big — Johnson — Abe's step brother took Abes part — Shoes — met at the old School house — Johnson got whipt — worsted rather — Richardson Says that Lincoln was a powerful man in 1830 — Could Carry what 3. ordinary men would grunt & sweat at — Saw him Carry a chicken house made of poles pinned together & Covered that weighed at least 600 if not much more. Abe was notoriously good natured — Kind and honest. Men would Swear on his Simple word — had a high & manly sense of honor — was tender — gentle — &c — &c — never seemed to care for the girls — was witty & Sad and thoughtful by turns — as it Seemed to me.

God bless Abe's Memory forever

LC: *HW2330–31, HW2333–34; HL: LN2408, 1:125–28*

80. David Turnham (WHH interview)[1]

Septr 15 1865

I went to David Turnhams after leaving the town of Gentryville — T — lives in Elizabeth — a town about 4½ M North East — Elizabeth has a population of about 300 hundred people — same size as Gentryvill — Mr Turnham Commenced —

I came to Ind in the year 1819. Mch — settled in Spencer Co — settled about 3 M south of this and about 1 M North East of Thomas Lincolns — am now 62 years. I Knew Abm Lincoln wel! — Knew his father — didn't Know his Mother — immediately on landing in Ind I became acquainted with Mr Lincon. My father and his were acquainted in Ky — Abe was then about ten years of age. — I being 16 ys of age — Abe was a long tall dangling award drowl looking boy — went hunting and fishing together — Abe was a boy of Extraordinay mind I think

---

4. See §72, note 6.

---

1. In top margin in pencil: *Came by Aaron Grigsby's where abe's sister [died?] & then on next day went to Elizabeth 4 M from Gentryv.*

— went to School to-gether — Hazel Dorsy & Andw Crawford — Dorzey Kept first, I think: he kept school near the Pigeon Meeting house — about 1¼ miles from Thos Lincolns and south or SE of his his. Crawford (Andw) taught school next: he taught about ¼ East of the Pigeon School Meeting house. Dorsey Keept School before the Marriage of Aaron Grigsby — So did Crawford — Crawford Kept soon after Dorsey — say the next year. Our School were Kept in the fall and winter, working in the Summer. Lincoln went to school to these 2 men about four winters — didn't go steady — I didn't go to school to Swany — Lincoln had a strong mind. I was older than he was by 6 years and further advanced — but he soon outstript me. We Studied lst in Dilworths Spelling book —   2d in Websters[2] — Lincoln Studied arithmetic — no geography — nor grammar — Lincoln read the life of Washington — the Pilgrims Progress Robinson Crusoe — the Bible — the new Testament — hymn Books — Watts hymns & Dupuy's.[3] — think that news papers as Early as 1828–30 — Saw Sarah Lincoln many times — she was a woman of ordinary size — Have seen Mordecai Lincoln — he came to Indiana on a visit about 1822 or 3 — he was the oldest brother —   Sarah Lincoln had a good mind, but I did not Know her so well as I did Abe: She married Aaron Grigsby —. We had but few books at that time and our opportunities were poor —

Abe Lincoln was a moral boy — was temperate — Sometimes he took his dram as Every body did at that time: he was honest: he was an industrious boy — he didn't love physical work — wouldn't do it if was agreeable to all — always was reading, studying, & thinking — Taking all in all he was not a lazy man. Lincoln Sometimes hunted on Sundays — What Lincoln read he read and re-read — read & Studied thoroughly —. He was generally at the head of all his classes whilst at school — in fact was nearly always so — He loved fishing & hunted Some — not a great deal — He was naturally Cheerful and good natured while in Indiana: Abe was a long tall raw boned boy. — odd and gawky — He had hardly attained 6 ft - 4 in when he left Indiana — weighed about 160 —   I bought the hogs & corn of Thomas Lincoln when he was leaving for Ills — Bought about 100 and about 400 or 5 hundred bushes of corn — paid 10 c per bushel for the Corn — hogs lumped — Lincoln when a boy wore buckskin — for pants — wore Coon skin Caps — Sometimes fox Skin & possum Skin Caps — Buckskin was a Common dress at that time. When Lincoln was going about he read Everything that he could lay his hands on and it is more than probable that he read the Louisville Journal[4] as well as other papers before he left Indiana and as before remarked what he read he read well and thoroughly —   Never forgetting what he read —

Mr. N. Grigsby — says he now remembers that L. read newspapers — That they were Introduced about the time Col Jones came to Gentryville[5] The Lincoln's

2. For Dilworth, see §76, note 1; for Webster, see §76, note 3.

3. For *Life of Washington,* see §24, note 15, and §71, note 16; John Bunyan, *The Pilgrim's Progress from This World to That Which Is to Come* (1678); for *Robinson Crusoe,* see §74, note 2; for Watts's *Hymns* and Dupuy, see §72, note 6.

4. The *Louisville Journal* began publication after the Lincolns had left Indiana. See §231.

5. This sentence is in the margin.

moved to Ills in an oxe waggon — 2 yoke of oxen — waggon Ironed — Lincoln sold his farm to Gentry — Jas Gentry Sen   — the old man — Mr Lincoln wrote a book of Chronicles — Satirizing the Grigsby and Josiah Crawford — The production was witty & showed talent — it marked the boy — as a man. Grigsby & Johnson[6] had a fight — Grigsby would have whipt Johnson, had no foul play been used —   Bill Boland showed foul play — the fight took place after the marriage of Chas & Reuben Grigsby were married —   Thomas Lincoln had about 40 acres of land under cultivation when he left for Ills —   he planted a young orchard on his old farm —   Mr Thos Lincoln was a Carpenter & Cabinet Make. I have a Cupboard now in my house which Mr Thomas Lincoln made for me about 21. (1821 or 1822) Abe Lincoln has worked for my father some — worked at farming work —

To show Lincolns — Abes Humanity let me tell you a short story — One night when Lincoln & I were returning home fromg Gentryville we were passing along the road in the night. We saw something laying near or in a mud hole and Saw that it was a man: we rolled him over and over — waked up the man — he was dead drunk — night was cold — nearly frozen — we took him up — rather Abe did — Carried him to Dennis Hanks — built up a fire and got him warm — I left — Abe staid all night — we had been threshing wheat wheat — had passed Lincolns house — Lincoln stopt & took Care of the poor fellow — Smith — This was in the year 1825   There was one Store in Gentryville. Don't publish the mans name: he was an honorable man having now near us Excellent, dear & near relatives —

Went and took dinner with Mr Turnham — good dinner, good man. Abe Lincoln — was not fond of the Girls. Lincoln went to Gordons mills to grind We had hand Mills here[7]

I knew Thomas Lincoln very well — have Studied his make & his form: he was not tall — was dark skinned — was Stout — muscular — not nervous — nor Sinewy — He weighed about 165. *lbs.:* he was Somewhat raw boned —   Abe favored him in many particulars. Both were humerous — good natured — Slow in action Somewhat. Sarah Lincoln favored Abe: she dark Skinned — heavy built — favored Abe very much — looked alike —

I Knew Dennis Hanks: he was not the truest man in the world — would dodge — Equivocate and Exagerate: the idea that he taught Lincoln to read and write is to me preposterous —. The Hanks were a peculiar people — not chaste — Dennis Hanks was a bastard — was the son of _____   His mother married Levi Hall — Dennis Hanks married Miss Johnson Abe Lincoln's Step Sister — Squire Hall married Matilda Johnson — Squire Hall Hall was ½ brother to Hanks. Squire Hall was the Son   Levi Hall. These people were all good clever people I assure you, but they were peculiar —

---

6. William Grigsby and John D. Johnston, AL's stepbrother.

7. Marginal note: *Mallory built the Gordon Mill — Abe ground his corn there so say Nat Grigsby — Abe wrote his name on the Arms.* Note at bottom of page: *Sarah Lincoln — / Dennis Hanks — / Abe Lincoln — Sermon.*

Abe Lincoln preached the Sermon Jerimiah Cash. Cash had preached a sermon and Abe Said he could repeat it and we boys got him at it Abe mounted a log and proceeded to give the text and at it he went. He did preach almost the identical Sermon. It was done with wonderful accuracy — This was in 1827. Abe did not much like the girls — didn't appear to —

We had here in Early days hand mills on which — rather with which we ground our corn into meal

LC: HW2353–56; HL: LN2408, 1:97–103

81. *William Wood (WHH interview)*

Septr 15th 1865

Wm Wood

My Name is Wm Wood — Came from Ky in 1809., March, and settled in Indiana — now Spencer Co — Settled on the hill "yonder" — about 1½ m north of the Lincoln farm — am now 82 ys of age. Knew Thomas and Abm Lincoln & family well. Thomas Lincoln & family Came from Ky Hardin Co, in 1816 according to my recollection. Mrs Thomas Lincoln — Abes mother was sick about 1½ years after she came. I sat up with her all one night. Mrs Lincoln, her mother & father were sick with what is called the milk Sickness. Sparrow & wife[1] — Mrs Lincoln's father & Mother as well as Mrs L all died with that sickness — the Milk Sickness. Thomas Lincoln often and at various times worked for me — made cupboards &c other household furniture for me — he built my house — made floors — run up the stairs — did all the inside work for my house. Abe would Come to my house with his father and play and romp with my children

Abe wrote a piece Entitled the Book of Chronicles — a satire on a marriage —, Infair and putting the pairs to bed &c —: it showed the boy — this was in 1829. A wrote a piece on National politics — Saying that the American government was the best form of Government in the world for an intelligent people — that it ought to be Kept sound & preserved forever: that general Education Should   fostered and Carried all over the Country: that the Constitution — should be saved — the Union perpetuated & the laws revered — respected & Enforced &c (Mr Wood Said much more which I can recollect)   This was in 1827 — or 8. Abe once drank as all people did here at that time. I took news papers — some from Ohio — Cincinnatie — the names of which I have now forgotten — One of these papers was a temperance paper. Abe used to borrow it — take it home and read it & talk it over with me: he was an intelligent boy — a Sensible lad I assure you. One day Abe wrote a piece on Temperance and brought it to my house. I read it Carefully over and over and the piece Excelled for sound sense anything that my paper Contained. I gave the article to one Aaron Farmer, a Babtist Preacher:

---

1. Thomas Sparrow and his wife, Elizabeth Hanks Sparrow, who was AL's mother's sister. Nancy Hanks Lincoln was raised by these Sparrows; Woods and others regarded them as her parents.

he read it — it Struck him: he said he wanted it to send to a Temperance paper in Ohio for publication: it was sent and published   I saw the printed piece — read it with pleasure over and over again. This was in 1827 — or 8. The political article I Showed to John Pitcher an attorney of Posey Co Indiana who was travelling on the circuit — on law business — and stopt at my house over night: he read it carefully and asked me where I got it. I told him that one of my neighbor boys wrote it: he couldn't believe it till I told him that Abe did write it. Pitcher lived in Mt Vernon Indiana. Pitcher in fact was struck with the article and Said to me this — "The world can't beat it." He begged for it — I gave it to him and it was published — can't say what paper it got into — Know it was published. Abe was always a man though a boy. I never knew him to swear: he would say to his play fellows and other boys — Leave off your boyish ways and be more like men. Abe got his mind and fixd morals from his good mother. Mrs Lincoln was a very smart — intelligent and intellectual woman: She was naturally Strong minded — was a gentle, Kind and tender woman — a Christian of the Babtist persuasion — She was a remarkable woman truly and indeed. I do not think she absolutely died of the Milk Sickness Entirely. Probably this helped to seal her fate.

Abe came to my house one day and stood around about timid & Shy. I Knew he wanted Something. I said to him — Abe what is your Case. Abe replied — "Uncle I want you to go to the River — (the Ohio) and give me Some recommendation to some boat." I remarked — "Abe — your age is against you — you are not 21. yet." "I Know that, but I want a start said Abe". I concluded not to go for the boys good — did not go. I saw merchants in Rock-Port and mentioned the Subject to them. In 1829 — this was

Abe read the news papers of the day — at least such as I took. I took the Telescope.[2] Abe frequently borrowed it. I remember the paper now. I took it from about 1825. to 1830 — if not longer. Abe worked for me on this rigde — (on this road leading from Gentryville to Elizabeth — Dale P. Office place.). Abe whip sawed — Saw him cutting down a large tree one day: I asked him what he was going to do with it: he said he was going to saw it into plank for his fathers new house The year was 1828 or 9. Abe could sink an axe deeper in wood than any man I Ever Saw. Abe cut the tree down and he and one Levi Mills whip sawed it into plank. As I Said the plank was for Lincoln's new house: the house was not Completed till after Lincoln left for Ills. The house that Lincoln lived in is gone. Abe sold his plank to Crawford, the book man.[3] The book story is substantially Correct. Josiah Crawford put the lumber in his house where it is now to be seen in the South East room (I Sat on this plank myself — ate a good dinner at Mrs. Crawford's: Mrs C is a lady — is a good woman — quite intelligent)   Abe wrote Poetry. a good deal, but I can't recollect what about Except one piece which was Entitled the "Neighborhood broil"   Abe always brought his pieces — prose or Poetry to me straight. I thought more of Abe than any boy I Ever Saw: he was a strong man — physical-

---

2. *The Telescope* was published in New York (1824–30).

3. Josiah Crawford, who loaned AL a *Life of Washington,* as distinguished from Andrew Crawford, one of AL's schoolteachers.

ly powerful: he could strike with a mall a heavier blow than any man: he was long, tall and strong.

Mr Woods told me an axe story about Abe's bravery — which I can recollect '*Tell it.*

LC: HW2332, HW2337, HW2336, HW2335, HW2339; HL: LN2408, 1:129–33

82. Elizabeth Crawford (WHH interview)

Sept 16th 1865

I went to Josiah Crawfords — the book man — not the School teacher as represented. The School teacher was a different man[1] — landed there about 11. o'c AM — hitched my horse — Nat Grigsby with me, as he went all the rounds with me & to all places and was present at all interviews & conversations. Mrs Crawford was absent — at a sons house, distant about ¾ m attending to her sick grand child. I called for dinner. Mrs Crawfords daughter got us a good dinner — Sent for Mrs Crawford — her daughter rather would send for her. Before Mrs Crawford Came I looked over the "Library" — counted the Vols. There were 2 Bibles, 4 Hymn books — Grahams History of the U.S. abridged —, "Great events of America" — "Pioneers: of the New world" — a Testament — "Grace Truman" "Websters Dictionary"[2] — a small one — Some News papers — mostly Religious. There was 12 or 15 books in all — Mrs Crawford Came — is aged about 59 ys — She is good looking — is a lady at first blush — is Easily approached quite talkative — free — and generous. She Knew Abm Lincoln well. "My husband is dead — died May 1865. Abm was nearly grown when he left Indiana. Abe worked for my husband — daubed our Cabin in 1824 or 5 in which we lived — The second work he did for us was work done for the injured book — Weems life of Washington[3] — Lincoln in 1829 borrowed this book and by accident got it wet. L came & told honestly & Exactly how it was done — the story of which is often told. My husband said "Abe — as long as it is you — you may finish the book and keep it". Abe pulled fodder a day or two for it. We brought the book from Ky. Abe worked in the field yonder — north of the house. Our house was there the same little log cabin which Abe had *"daubed":* it was made of round logs "unhewn & unbarked" The old Cabin, which Stood here by this Cotton wood tree, was pulled down and this new one Erected there. We had cleared about 18 acres of land when Abe first worked for us. Abe made rails for us. Our first house was about 15 square — one room — low Thomas Lincoln made my furniture — Some of it was sold at my husbands admr Sale. Thomas Lincoln was at my house fre-

1. Andrew Crawford.
2. James Grahame, *The History of the United States of North America, from the Plantation of the British Colonies Till Their Revolt and Declaration of Independence* (1836); probably Francis Lieber, comp., *Great Events, Described by Distinguished Historians, Chroniclers and Other Writers* (1840); possibly Joseph Banvard, *Novelties of the New World, or the Adventures and Discoveries of the First Explorers of North America* (1850); Sallie Rochester Ford, *Grace Truman* (1857); Noah Webster, *An American Dictionary of the English Language* (1828).
3. See §71, note 16.

quently — almost Every week — Sarah Lincoln Abe's Sister worked for me: She was a good, kind, amiable girl, resembling Abe. The Lincoln family were good people — good neighbors —: they were honest & hospitable and very — very sociable. We moved to Indiana in 1824 — Came from Ky. I Knew as a matter of Course Sarah & Sally Lincoln very well. and I say to you that she was a gentle, Kind, smart — shrewd — social, intelligent woman — She was quick & strong minded: She had no Education, Except what She gathered up herself. I Speak more of what she was by nature than by culture. I never was a politician in all my life, but when such men ran as Abe Lincoln — as in 1860 I as it were took the Stump: he was the noblest specimen of man I Ever saw. Gentryville lies 4 m from here NW. Abe worked for us at various times at 25c per day — worked hard & faithful and when he missed time would not charge for it. I took some of the rails which Abe cut and Split for us and had Canes made from them. They were white oak — cut from this Stump here — some one got into my house and Stole *my* cane.

Can't say what books Abe read, but I have a book called "The Kentucky Preceptor"[4], which we brought from Ky and in which & from which Abe learned his school orations, Speeches & pieces to recite. School Exhibitions used to be the order of the day — not as now however. Abe attended them — Spoke & acted his part — always well free from rant & swell: he was a modest and Sensitive lad — never coming where he was not wanted: he was gentle, tender and Kind. Abe was a moral & a model boy, and while other boys were out hooking water melons & trifling away their time, he was studying his books — thinking and reflecting. Abe used to visit the sick boys & girls of his acquaintance. When he worked for us he read all our books — would sit up late in the night — kindle up the fire — read by it — cipher by it. We had a broad wooden shovel on which Abe would work out his sums — wipe off and repeat till it got too black for more: then he would scrape and wash off. and repeat again and again — rose Early. went to work — Come to Dinner — Sit down and read — joke — tell Stories &c. &c — Here is my husbands likeness — you need not look at mine. My husband was a substantial Man (and I say a cruel hard husband, Judging from his looks —). Sarah Lincoln was a strong healthy woman[5] — was Cool — not Excitable — truthful — do to tie to — Shy Shrinking. Thomas Lincoln was blind in one Eye and the other was weak — so he felt his way in the work much of the time: his sense of touch was Keen — Abe did wear buck Skin pants — Coon Skin — opossum skin Caps. Abe ciphered with a coal or with red Keel[6] got from the branches: he smoothed and planed boards — wrote on them — ciphered on them. I have seen this over and over again. Abe was Sometimes Sad — not often — he was reflective — was witty & humorous.

Abe Lincoln was one day bothering the girls — his sister & others playing yonder and his Sister Scolded him — Saying Abe you ought to be ashamed of

---

4. *The Kentucky Preceptor, Containing a Number of Useful Lessons for Reading and Speaking* (1812).
5. Probably AL's stepmother rather than his sister.
6. Red ochre, used for marking purposes.

yourself — what do you Expect will become of you "Be Presdt of the U.S," prompt-ly responded Abe. Abe wrote a good Composition — wrote prose and poetry. He wrote 3 or 4 Satires — one was Called the Book of Chronicles. He said that he would be Presdt of the US told my husband so often — Said it jokingly — yet with a Smack of deep Earnestness in his Eye & tone: he Evidently had an idea — a feeling in 1828 that he was bound to be a great man — No doubt that in his boyish days he dreamed it would be so. Abe was ambitious — sought to outstrip and override others. This I Confess.

One of Abes pieces — the Book of Chronicles — ran about thus —

"I will tell you a joke about [Josiah?] & Mary
Tis neither a joke nor a story
For Reuben & Charles have married 2 Girls
But Billy has married a boy
He tried ——— (Mrs Crawford blushed)
The girls on Every Side
He had well tried
None could he get to agree
All was in vain
He went home again
And since that he's married to Natty

I don't pretend to give the Exact words — nor its rhyme — nor metre now — will think it over — recall it and write to you in Ills. The Poem is Smutty and I can't tell it to you — will tell it to my daughter in law: she will tell her husband and he shall send it to you.

I left Mrs Crawford about 3 o'cl. P.M. Before leaving She gave me the Amer-ican Preceptor and a cane made from one of Abes rails — for both of which I thanked her: I really felt proud of the gift and felt a gratitude for them —   Mrs Crawford is a Lady of the Ky Stamp —

LC: HW2338, HW2340–41, HW2343, HW2342, HW2346; HL: LN2408, 1:134–39

83. *Nathaniel Grigsby (WHH interview)*

Gentryville Ind   Septr 16th 1865 —

After taking the rounds in Spencer Co Indiana I went with my old guide and Companion Nat Grigsby down to Wm Thompson who lived where Col Jones[1] had resided — ½ M west of Gentryville. Col Jones was Lincoln guide & teacher in Politics — Col J was Killed at Atlanta — Grigsby showed me where Lincoln Spoke in 1844 — When Lincoln was Speaking Grigsby went into the House where the Speech was being made — Lincoln Saw G Enter — He stopt Short — said there

---

1. William Jones.

is Nat. Lincoln then walked over the benches and over the heads of his hearers —
Came rolling — took G by the hand Shook it most Cordially — Said a few words
— went back — commenced his remarks where he had Stopt — finished his
Speech — told G that he must stay with him all night — Slept at Col Jones' —
When we had gone to bed and way in the night a Cat Commenced mewing and
scratching — making a fuss generally — Lincoln got up in the dark and Said —
Kitty — Kitty — Pussy — Pussy. The cat Knew the voice & manner Kind — went
to Lincoln — L rubbed it down — Saw the Sparkling —   L took up the Cat —
Carried it to the door & gently rubbed it again and again Saying Kitty — Kitty
&c — then gently put it down closed the doors — Commenced telling Stories &
talking over old times —

    As we were going down to Thompsons G told me this Story — which I had
heard before. A man by the name of Chas Harper was going to mill — had an
Extremely long wheat bag on the horse and was met by sister Gordon — who said
to Bro Harper — Bro H your bag is too long — No said Bro Harper — it is only
too long in the summer. They were Bro and Sister in the church — Mrs Gordon
told her husband of the vulgar — Gordon[2] made a fuss — had a church trial —
Lincoln got the Secret — wrote a witty piece of Poetry on the scenes & Conversations — The Poetry of Abe was good — witty — &c as said by all who read it.

    LC: HW2357–58; HL: LN2408, 1:94

84. John Oskins (WHH interview)

Septr 16th 1865

    Went to see Jno Oscans — or Hoskins — who lives about 1½ M South of
Gentryville — Saw him — is about 48 ys of age — went to School with Abe in
this Co —   The School House is situated yonder — down there by the Spring
— You see that big oak tree which is Scratched & burnt — The School House
was there — The fire & Smoke Coming out of the Chimney partially Killed the
tree — the School House was a Kind of hewed log house — had two Chimneys
— one door — holes for windows — greasy paper was pasted over the holes in
winter time to admit light &c —   Swany — or Sweeny[1] Kept school here — 2
M south of Gentryville & 4 M from Abes home —   Swany Kept school here in
1826 — Lincoln & myself were Schollars — Our books were Websters Spelling
books — Introduction to the English reader — We would Choose up and spell as
in old times Every friday night —   Here is a piece of the log of the old School
House —   I Know that it is a piece because I tore down the old School house
— removed the logs to this place — put them up in the Stable — &c —   say to
you that this piece of wood is a part of the old School house —   Yonder is the

---

2. Possibly Noah Gordon, the miller. For a reference to AL's poetry about Mrs. Gordon, see §128.

---

1. James Swaney.

Spring that Abe drank out of a thousand times — There it is (we went down to it) walled up with brick — here is the old burnt oak t.ee — here Stood the School house — here were the Chimneys.

Hoskins farm is on the road leading from Rockport to Gentryville — about 14 M north of Gentryville[2] — 1½ M South of Gentryvill — House Stands on the right hand of the road as you go from Rockport to Gentryville &c —[3]

LC: HW2359–60; HL: LN2408, 1:95–96

85. David Turnham to WHH[1]

Elizabeth Ind. Sept. 16 1865.

Sir:

After you left my house, I found a law Book, I suppose the first law book that Lincoln ever saw.[2] I was acting constable at that time, is the way I got the book in my possession. The way I happened to find it was hunting for two books that Lincoln used to read a great deal while at my house; "Sinabad the Sailor" and "Scotts lessons,"[3] they were entitled; those two I could not find.

Very Respectfully, Yours
David Turnham.

HL: LN2408, 1:180

86. Green B. Taylor (WHH interview)

Septr 16th 1865

My name is Green B. Taylor — aged 46 — am the son of James Taylor — I Knew Abe Lincoln well — He worked for my father 6 or 9 Months worked on the farm — run the ferry for my father from the Ky shore to the Indiana shore — The ferry crossed the Ohio — & crossed the Anderson River — Abe would ferry from one side to the other and land in Perry or cross the Ohio and Anderson and land in Spencer Co — Abe lived with my father in the year 1825 and worked about 6 or 9 mo — he plowed — ferried, ground Corn on the hand mill — grated Corn — My mother was Kind to Abe and Abe to her — he Abe went after the Doctress when my sister was born [illegible] my sister was born in

---

2. Presumably a mistake for Rockport.
3. Marginal note: *Whiskey Story was told me by Hoskins.*

---

1. A photostat of the original manuscript of this letter is in the files of the Abraham Lincoln Association, ISHL, but the location of the original is unknown. The Springer transcription given here appears to differ slightly from the original in accidentals and word order but not in substance.
2. *Revised Laws of Indiana, Adopted and Enacted by the General Assembly at Their Eighth Session* (Corydon: Carpenter and Douglass, 1824).
3. "Sinbad the Sailor" is one of the tales in *The Arabian Nights;* William Scott, *Lessons in Elocution, or a Selection of Pieces in Prose and Verse* (1779).

1825 — so it is no guess — Abe helped to Kill hogs for — John Woods — Jno Duthan & Stephen McDaniel — Barrells of hot water — blankets — clubs — were used in the process. Abe Lincoln was honest — industrious — social — Kind & courteous — I hit him with an Ear of Corn once — cut him over the Eye — he got mad — My mother whipt me severely as she should have done — Abe Lincoln got $6 per mo — and 31 c per day for Killing hogs as this was rough work — He and I slept up stairs — He usually read till near midnight reading — rose Early — would make a fire for my mother — put on the water & fix around generally— John Johnson & Wm Grigsby had a pitched fight — at or near Hoskins Near the Spring or close to Gentryville — My father was the second for John Johnson — Wm Whitten was the second for Wm Grigsby — They met and had a terrible fight — Wm Grigsby was too much for Lincoln's man — Johnson. After they had fought a long time — and it having been agreed not to break the ring, Abe burst through, caught Grigsby — threw him off some feet — stood up and swore he was the big buck at the lick — (It was here, says Hoskins, says that Abe waived a bottle of whiskey over his head and said as above[1]). After Abe did this — it being a general invitation for a general fight they all pitched in and had quite a general fight.

¼ M below Troy.

LC: HW2361; HL: LN2408, 1:162–64

87. John S. Hougland (WHH interview)

Septr 17th 1865

Doct Hougland — Rockport — aged about 40 ys — says he heard Col Jones Say over & over again that Mr Lincoln laid the foundation of his Character in Spencer Co Indiana — That Lincoln read Every book he could lay his hands on — Mastered it

Lincoln clerked for Jones — worked at packing pork — selling good — chopping wood &c — Thinks Jones took papers at a very Early day — say as Early as 1826 and on to 1830 — and down to his death —

About this News Paper business there is much dispute, but think it true — Old Mrs. Lincoln says it is so — so does old Man Wood — so does Grigsby & others — Lincolns Speeches here in 1832[1] Convince me that he was thoroughly posted in Politics — He left Indiana in 1830 — and during these 2 ys he was down the River — in the Black Hawk war & clerking and Could not have under these

---

1. See Oskins interview, §84.

---

1. That is, "here in Illinois."

Circumstances have read & learned so much &c. Dennis Hanks says the way they learned was to go to speech making gatherings &c. &c. and not by reading —[2]

LC: HW2360, HW2367; HL: LN2408, 1:97

88. *Anna Caroline Gentry (WHH interview)*

Rockport Ind Septr 17th 1865

My name is Mrs. Gentry — wife of Allen Gentry with whom Mr Lincoln went to NO for Jas Gentry Sen in April 1828 —   I knew Mr L well — he and I went to school together — I was 15 ys old — Lincoln about the same age — we went to school to Crawford in 1822 or 3   I think — I used Websters Spelling book[1] — Lincoln the same — One day Crawford put a word to us to Spell: the word to Spell was *defied*. Crawford said if we did not spell it he would keep us in school all day & night — we all missed the word — Couldn't Spell it. We spelled the word Every way but the right way —. I saw Lincoln at the window: he had his finger On his *Eye* and a smile on his face. I instantly took the hint that I must change the letter y into an I. Hence I Spelled the word — the class let out. I felt grateful to Lincoln for this Simple thing. Abe was a good — an Excellent boy. Speaking about the boat & the trip let me say to you that I saw the boat — was on it — saw it start and L with it. It started from yonder landing — Gentrys Landing — My husband was Allen Gentry —   They went down the Ohio & Mississippi for Jas Gentry Sen —   they Came back in June 1828. — flat boat started from Gentrys landing yonder — say ½ a mile from this house due South & ¾ of a M below Rockport. Abe read many books — cant say what they were — regret it — he worked and bought his books generally — fought his own way — When my husband & L went down the river they were attacked by Negroes — Some Say Wade Hamptons Negroes, but I think not: the place was below that called *Mdme Bushams Plantation* 6 M below Baton Rouche — Abe fought the Negroes — got them off the boat — pretended to have guns — had none — the Negroes had hickory Clubs — my husband said "Lincoln get the guns and Shoot — the Negroes took alarm and left. Abe did not go much with the girls — didn't like crowds — didn't like girls much — too frivalous &c. The Schools we went to taught Spelling — reading — writing and Ciphering to single rule of 3 — no further —. Lincoln got ahead of his masters — Could do him no further good: he went to school no more — Abe was an honest boy — a good boy — all liked him — was friendly — somewhat Sociable — not so much so as we wanted him — Abe was a long — thin — leggy — gawky boy dried up & Shriveled

---

2. The last paragraph of the interview and WHH's note both appear on a separate sheet. This sheet was treated by Springer as the end of the Dougherty interview, but the editors believe it more likely belongs to the Hougland interview.

---

1. Cf. §76.

One Evening Abe & myself were Sitting on the banks of the Ohio or on the boat Spoken of. I Said to Abe that the Moon was going down. He said "Thats not so — it don't really go down: it Seems So. The Earth turns from west to East and the revolution of the Earth Carries us under, as it were: we do the sinking as you call it. The moon as to us is Comparatively still. The moons sinking is only an appearance". I said to Abe — "Abe — what a fool you are." I Know now that I was the fool — not Lincoln. I am now thoroughly Satisfied that Abe Knew the general laws of Astronomy and the movements of the heavenly bodies — He was better read then than the world knows or is likely to Know Exactly —. No man could talk to me that night as he did unless he had Known something of geography as well as astronomy. He often & often Commented or talked to me about what he read — seemed to read it out of the book as he went along — did so to others — he was the learned boy among us unlearned folks — He took great pains to Explain — Could do it so Simply He was diffident then too — only 17 ys of age —

   LC: HW2362–64; HL: LN2408, 1:147–49

89. Absolom Roby (WHH interview)

Sept 17th 1865

My name is Absolom Roby — father of Mrs Allen Gentry — am 83 ys of age — Knew Lincoln well — forget — don't now remeber much about what he did and said — Knew Abe at Gentryville — Abe lived with & worked for Allen Gentry a mo or more — He and Gentry did go to N.O in April 1828. as Said by my daughter —. I was often at the landing from which Gentry & Abe started to N.O — Abe was a good, friendly, Sociable & honest boy — a long tall bony lad — strong and good natured —   He made a Speech in Rockport in 1844. I heard him —   when he was done he hunted me up — Caught hold of my hand and Shook it Cordially — Abe was always an industrious lad — worked at Something or was reading — not loitering away his time. Abe was in his 16 year an intelligent boy — as I took it — though not the best judge in the world. I predicted in 1827, if not sooner that Abe would cut a figure in this world — Chance or no chance. I thought this, taking what he was — what he said & did &c. as my guide. He understood a thing thoroughly & could Explain so clearly that I thought he had a good mind: he had good habits. and I have not much doubt but that Abe read the news papers of the day — think I remember Louisville Journal — can Say positively[1] — my memory is gone & I myself am fast going.

   LC: HW2365–66; HL: LN2408, 1:149–50

---

1. WHH probably meant to write "can't say positively," which is the way Springer transcribed it.

90. John R. Dougherty (WHH interview)

Sept 17th 1865

My name is Jno R Dougherty — am 40 ys old. Knew Allen Gentry well — didn't Know Lincoln. Gentry has Shown me the place where the niggers attacked him and Lincoln. The place is not Wade Hamptons — but was at Mdme Bushans Plantation about 6 M below Baton Rouche —   I was born in Spencer Co Ind. Lincoln worked & Clerked for Col Jones at Gentryville 15 M north of this place (Rockport) — L drove a team — cut up Pork & sold good for Jones — Col Jones told me that Lincoln read all his books and I remember _____ History of the U.S. as one — have forgotten all others and Even the name of that —   Jones often said to me that Lincoln would make a great man one of these days — Had said so long before & to other people — Said so as far back as 1828–9 —

LC: HW2366; HL: LN2408, 1:151–52

91. Ninian W. Edwards (WHH interview)

Septr 22d 1865

N W Edwards

Says — Septr 22d 1865 — That during Lincoln's Courtship with Miss Todd — afterwards Lincoln's wife — that he, Lincoln, fell in Love with a Miss Edwards — daughter of Cyrus Edwards, who was Brother of Govr N. W. Edwards — Matilda Edwards was her name: she subsequently became the wife of Mr Strong[1] of Alton.

Lincoln did not Ever by act or deed directly or indirectly hint or speak of it to Miss Edwards.: She became aware of this — Lincoln's affections — The Lincoln & Todd Engagement was broken off in Consequence of it — Miss Todd released Lincoln from the Contract, leaving Lincoln the privilege of renewing it (Poor fellow   H) if he wished — Lincoln in his Conflicts of duty — honor & his love went as Crazy as a *Loon* — was taken to Kentucky — by Speed — or went to Speed's — was Kept there till he recovered finally — (unfortunate man!   H)   He was cured — Edwards Admits that he wanted Speed to marry Miss Edwards & Lincoln Miss Todd: he gave me policy reasons for it — the substance of which I give in an other place[2] —   Matilda Edwards refused Speed — (J. F. Speed of Louisville Ky) as she S. A. Douglas   she refused Douglas on the grounds of his bad morals —

Lincoln did not attend the Legislature in in 1841 & 2 for this reason —   So is Mrs Wm Butler Correct as to her suspicions

LC: HW2368; HL: LN2408, 2:215–16

---

1. Newton D. Strong married Matilda Edwards on September 24, 1844.
2. Not located.

92. A. H. Chapman to WHH

Charleston Ills Sept 28th 1865

Dr Sir.

Yours dated the 26th containing 20 Dollars come to hand Last eve for which please accept my thanks. In answer to your enquiries I beg leave to state that Thos Lincoln never showed by his actions that he thought much of his son Abraham when a Boy. he treated him rather unkind than otherwise. always appeared to think much more of his stepson John D Johnston than he did of his own Son Abraham but after Abe was grown up and had made his Mark in the world the old man appeared to be very proud of him, Esq. Hall[1] Moved from Ky to Ind in 1820 & married Matilda Johnston in 1823 —

Extract from Lincolns coppy Books.

Abraham Lincoln is my name
And with my pen   I write the same
I will be a good Boy but God Knows when.

Enclosed is a Bond the Sufficiency of which I wish certified to by a Judge or District Attorney of a Dist Court of the US. will you please have it attended to for me & return it to me by first mail if possible. The securities are worth at Least 400.000 — the Least Worthy one of the 5 is worth at Least 40.000. Dollars. I enclose Letters from attays here to the Judge which I presume will be satisfactory to him or the Dist atty. I desighn Starting to Idaho about the 1st of Nov. This is a Bully place for Me & I can Make a heap of money out of it. Dick Yates Damn his Soul fought me at Washington & for another man.[2] This I did not expect of him. I reckon that he has not forgotten that I was a Judd Man in 1860. Yates by his opposition to me & by sustaining Reeves who is odious to the Republicans of this Dist has Made him Self very bitter enemies in this Dist among the Leading Republicans & his opposition to me will yet be paid with D D big int,[3] for my part I am content as I triumphed over all opposition & got just what I wanted. Will furnish you any information you may want before I leave. Please attend to the bond & have it approved & returned to me by first Mail. As ever

Your Friend
A. H. Chapman.

[Postcript on verso:] It makes no Diference which certifies to the sufficiency of the Bond Treat or Weldon

Chapman

LC: HW2372–73; HL: LN2408, 1:285–87

---

1. Squire Hall, half-brother of Dennis Hanks, married Matilda Johnston on September 14, 1826.
2. Chapman had just been appointed agent to the Flathead Indians in Montana. Richard Yates (1815–73), the junior U.S. senator from Illinois, had favored another candidate.
3. Damned big interest.

93. *J. W. Wartmann to WHH*

Rockport Indiana   Sept 28. 1865.

My Dear Sir:

Your favor of the 23d ult. enclosing draft on New York for Twenty Dollars, came to hand last Evening. Feel yourself under no obligations for the attentions shown you by myself.

Am glad to know you succeeded in paying yourself by coming to this state. Let me Know when your book goes to press, and remember the Suggestion about sending a prospectus to this Co.'

Very truly
Your friend
J. W. Wartman

LC: HW2374; HL: LN2408, 1:166–67

94. *Augustus H. Chapman to WHH*

Charleston Ills. Oct 8th 1865.

Dear Herndon,

Yours dated the 1st came to Hand two days since. I did not coppy the Quotation from Mr Lincolns Coppy Book but got it from Johnston[1] who said it was word for word as in coppy Book. I succeeded in getting hold of the coppy Book last evening & find that Johnston Lied to me. I find the extract in question in three places in the coppy Book all exactly alike & read as follows word for word — Abraham Lincoln his hand and Pen, He will be good but god Knows when.

In one place the following lines follow word for word,

Time what an empty vapor tis
And days how swift they are
Swift as an Indian arrow
Fly on like a Shooting star
The present Moment Just is here
Then Slides away in haste
That we can never say theyre ours

But only say they are past.[2] word for word & spelled exactly as in coppy Book. Farmington is the name of the Little town we passed through. It is 7 Miles South of Charleston, one Mile north of the Lincoln farm & one & a ½ miles East of the

---

1. Thomas L. D. Johnston, son of AL's stepbrother, John D. Johnston.
2. These lines are from the first two stanzas of a hymn by Isaac Watts, "The Shortness of Life, and the Goodness of God," which appears as no. 58 in book 2 of Watts's *Hymns and Spritual Songs* (1707). The first two stanzas are as follows: "Time! What an empty Vapour 'tis! / And Days how swift they are! / Swift as an *Indian* Arrow flies, / Or like a shooting Star. // The present Moments just appear, / Then slide away in haste, / That we can never say, *They're here,* / But only say, *They're past.*" See Isaac Watts, *Hymns and Spiritual Songs, 1707–1748*, ed. Selma L. Bishop (London, 1962), 220–21.

Grave Yard where Thos Lincoln is buried. Farmington, The Lincoln Farm & the Grave yard are all in Coles Co. I hardly Know how to write you a description of Mr Lincolns visit to his Mother before he Started to Washington in 1861 as there was so much excitement here & such a crowd around him all the time but I will give you the facts as near I can recollect them & you can write out to Suit yourself. Mr Lincoln Left Springfield about the lst day of February 1861 on Monday Morning to visit his relations & Friend here. He was accompanied by the Hon Thos. A. Marshall State Senator for this senatorial District & a resident of this place. (The Legislature was in Session at that time)   The weather was very cold & they failed to make Rail Road connections with passenger Train at Mattoon but came from that place to Charleston on a Frt Train arriving [here] about 9 o clock PM. They went to the residence of Mr Marshall. It soon became Know in town that Mr Lincoln had arrived & hundreds, called to See him. He was also serenaded by the Brass & Strings Band of the Town but declined making a Speech. The next morning early, he went up to His Coz. Dennis F Hanks. Again the House was crowded by those that were anxious to see him. After breakfast Mr Lincoln and my self got into a two Horse Buggy and started down to the Southern part of the County to see his Step Mother who was at that time at the residence of her Daughter Mrs Moore who resided at that time in Farmington. We had much difficulty in crossing Kickapoo a Little Stream 3 Miles South of Charleston on act of the Ice in the stream. We finaly succeeded in crossing it all safe & in a Short time arrived at Farmington. The Meeting between Mr Lincoln and his Step Mother was very affectionate. After resting there a short time we proceeded to the residence of John Hall on the old Lincoln Farm & from there to the grave of his Father. Mr Lincoln said he intended to have the grave enclosed and suitable Tomb Stones erected over his Fathers grave & requested me to acertain what the cost would be & he would furnish Dennis Hanks the money to have it done. Said he would furnish an inscription for the Tomb-[stone, such] as he wished inscribed on it, Said he would do it as soon as he got time for me then to see the marble dealer & write him the cost & he would furnish Dennis the Mony to have it all done just as he wished. We then returned to Farmington where we found a Large crowd of citizens nearly all old acquaintances waiting to see him. his reception was very enthusiastic and appeared to gratify him very much. after taking Dinner at his Step Sisters Mrs Moores[3] we returned to Charleston   His Step Mother coming with us. Our conversation during the Trip was Mostly concerning family affairs. Mr Lincoln spoke to me on the way down to Farmington of his Step Mother in the most affectionate manner. Said she had been his best Friend in this world & that no Son could love a Mother more than he loved her. He also told me of the condition of his Fathers Family at the time he married his Step Mother & the change she made in the Family & of the encouragement he Abe received from his Step Mother. he Spoke on the road of the various men that had supported him during

---

3. AL's stepsister Matilda Johnston (Hall) Moore.

the canvass & said he thought Caleb B Smith had done him More Service than any public speaker. Spoke of his Father & related Some amusing incidents of the old mans life. of the Bull Dog biting the Old Man on his return from New Orleans, of the old mans escape when a boy from an Indian who [was shot] by his Uncle Mordecai. Spoke of his Uncle Mordecai, being a man of very great Natural gifts, spoke of his step Brother, John D Johnston who had died a Short time previous in the Most affectionate Manner. Arriving at Charleston on our return from Farmington we proceeded to my residence   Again the House was crowded by persons wishing to see him. The crowd finally became so great that he authorized me to announce that he would hold a public reception at the Town Hall that eve at 7 Oclock but untill that time he wished to be left with his relatives & Friends, After supper he proceeded to the Town Hall where Large Nos from the Town and the surrounding country irrespective of party, called to See Him. He left this place Wednesday Morning at 4 Oclock to return to Springfield. Hon Thos A Marshall again accompanied him. (Marshall was a very intimate personal friend of Lincolns)   Mr Lincoln appeared to enjoy his visit here remarkable well. His reception by his old acquaintances appeared to be very gratifying to him. They all appeared so glad to See him irrespective of party & all appeared so anxious that his administration might be a success & that he might have a pleasant & honorable career as Prest. The parting between him & his Mother was very affectionate. She embraced him when they parted & Said she would never be permitted to see him again that she felt that his enemies would assassinate. he replied   No No Mama (he always caled her Moma) they will not do that trust in the Lord and all will be well. We will See each other — again   While at Farmington they tried to induce him to make them a Speech. he also declined speaking at Charleston. He never furnished me the inscription for his Fathers Tomb Stone & none has ever been erected on his grave. This as I understand it is all you request in your Letter. If any thing else is wanted before I leave write me & it will be furnished promptly & with pleasure   was offered 100 Dollars last week for facts & incidents of Mr Lincolns early life but Declined in fact have not time & if I had would not do so for less than 250 or 300. Dollars. Hope to get of by the 1st of Nov. *will follow your advice if it ruins me.* As Ever

your Friend

A H Chapman

Will be D D Hard up about the time I start, If you can remit the bal due on act of expenses in getting up facts for you please do so. It is about 30 Dollars. If I was not a going to be so hard up would not mention it.

C

LC: HW2375–77; HL: LN2408, 1:210–15

95. *David Turnham to WHH*[1]

Dale Ind. Oct. 12th 1865.

Dear friend:

I received your favor and was glad to hear of your good health. After you left my house I remmembered having brought with me to this county two books which Mr. Lincoln read frequently, one was entitled "Sinabad the Sailor", the other was entitled "Scotts lessons".[2] I thought I could find a part of the latter, and in search-ing for that, I found an old Law book, that I had, when Abe and I were associates, and he would come to my house and set and read it, and I think it was the first law book he ever saw. Thinking it might be of some interest to you, I got my son to write a few lines and take it and the book to you, expecting he would find you at Gentryville, but when he got there, Mr. Grigsby told him you had started home sick, but he (Mr. Grigsby) would send them to you by express, and I suppose you will get it.

I have no other information that you wish, but if I should come in possession of any I will forward it.

Respectfully Yours
D. Turnham.

N.B.

Please, if you get that book write me word.

D.T.

HL: LN2408, 1:177–78

96. *John J. Hall to WHH*

Farmington Ills. Oct. 14th 1865.

Dear Sir:

Yours of Sept. 22d. came to Charleston while I was bedfast, with a broken leg, and I did not receive it until yesterday.

In answer to your interrogations, I would say, that my father Squire Hall and my mother Matilda Johnston were married September 5th 1826; at the house of Thomas Lincoln, Spencer Co. Ind.

To your 2d interrogation respecting Mr. Lincoln's writing in his copy book, I would state that it is in Charleston, and I cannot answer this now, but suppose that you have received this from A. H. Chapman, if not let me know on the re-ception of this, and I will obtain the information and forward to you. The town that you passed through between here and Charleston is Farmington, should you desire any other or farther information you can obtain any that may be in my power

---

1. A photostat of the original manuscript of this letter is in the files of the Abraham Lincoln Association, ISHL, but the location of the original is unknown. The Springer transcription given here appears to differ slightly from the original in accidentals and word order but not in substance.

2. See §85, note 3.

to give, by addressing me, directing your letters to Campbell P.O. Coles, instead of sending them to Charleston.

Very Truly

John J. Hall.

HL: LN2408, 1:302

97. *A. H. Chapman to WHH*

Charleston Ills. Oct 18/.65.

Friend Herndon.

Yours dated the 16th is just at hand. I think it extremely doubtful about my succeeding in borrowing that Coppy Book of Johnston[1] for you but I will see him the latter part of the week & will do the best I can for you & if I succeed will Express it to you. I dont think I can get that Coppy of Barclays Dictionary[2] as Mr Hanks tried once to get it for myself but could not do So. I will try it & do my best. If I dont succeed in getting those Books for you before I leave I will leave the job in the hands of my Eldest Son who is as Sharp as Lightning & May Succeed in getting them for you. When Mr Lincoln was here in 1858 he Stayed at my House. His Mother Mrs Lincoln was Living with me at that time & was at home. I dont remember any thing that took place between them at that time only that Mr Lincoln left on the 4 am Train & that the Old Lady got up to see him before he Started & that he gave her 50 Dollars that morning although the Old Lady assured him that she did not need it. The quotation from Mr Lincolns Coppy Book is word for word & Letter for Letter as in the Coppy Book, you can rely on this as correct. If any other information I have is wanted I will send it to you cheerfully & rest assured no one else shall have the information I have already given you   In Haste

your friend

A. H. Chapman.

PS

Mr Lincoln was always a great favorite with the citizens of this Co. even his political opponents here rejoiced over his success Saying that they had every confidence in his honesty & patriotism & if thy had to be beaten by the Republican party that thy would rather be beaten by Mr Lincoln than any one else & many of Mr Douglases friends Said if we cant elect Douglass we want Lincoln to succeed. Mr Lincoln was a long ways More popular (personally) in this Co than any man in the Nation

AHC —

LC: HW2378–79; HL: LN2408, 1:283–85

---

1. See §94.
2. See §24, note 17; §71; and the index.

98. A. H. Chapman to WHH

Charleston Ills   Oct 25th 1865

Dear Herndon

I have not yet succeeded in getting the Coppy Book and the Dictionary for you. I leave tomorrow but my Eldest Son (Bob) will get them if possible & express to you. I want a coppy of your life of Lincoln as soon as published. When ready please remit to my wife Mrs A. H. Chapman at this place the Amt due me. (30 dollars).

Good By and May God bless you and yours,   In Haste
                    your Friend
                    A H Chapman.

LC: HW2380; HL: LN2408, 1:283

99. Nathaniel Grigsby to WHH

Gentrysville Oct 25th 1865

Deare Sir

After respect to you i have seated myself to answer your request of the 17th of Oct which has Just come to hand Chrles and Reuben Grigsby was married April 16th 1830[1]   I have obtained and wil express to you in a few days the Statute laws of Ind Published in the yeare of 1824 which was read by Mr Lincoln while in this Co and i think it was the first law book he ever red, my old brother Wm Grigsby tells me some things that past between himself and Abraham Lincoln which i wil rite and you can publish if you wish to, after the fite between Wm Grigsby and John D Johnson Abraham told Wm Grigsby that he had whiped Johnson but i can whip you but Wm told him that he did not dispute that but if he Lincoln would give he Grigsby a fair cance he would fite him he Lincoln wish to now how he wish to fite, Grigsby told Lincoln he would fite him a duel Lincoln told Grigsby that he Lincoln was not a going to fool his life away with one Shot, So the mater stoped

Permit me to troubl you a minit or two on political maters   wel old Ind always true to the government and true to her self has gaind another victory over our commin inimy this part of the State is called the pocket has turned in side out by carring nearly every Co for the union ticket bu large majority, i have seen Mrs Crawford a bout the plank which Abraham whipsawed for his fathers house and sold it to Josiah Crawford when Thomas lincoln left the State for Ill the plank remains in one of Crofford houses in perfect State where old man Wood laid it down   the old lady Crawford has a perfect recollection of the whole matter, i can obtain the plank and get sertifices to prove the i denty of it from Wm Wood and Mrs Crawford and have them sworn to if nessessary. if you think it of interest let me know and i wil do so   So nomore at pesant
                    N Grigsby

---

1. Charles Grigsby married Matilda Hawkins in Dubois County, Indiana; Reuben Grigsby, Jr., married Elizabeth Ray in Spencer County, Indiana, on April 16, 1829.

PS

pleas let me here from you as often as you can also let me know when youre history wil be published

LC: HW2381; HL: LN2408, 1:293–95

100. John T. Harris to WHH

Harrisonburg, Va.   Nov. 1st 1865.

Dear Sir:

After recovery from a long spell of illness I find your letter of the 25 Sept. & hasten to say so soon as I can learn accurately the facts desired by you from the "Oldest inhabitant" I will write you in full.

I Know all the Lincolns in this Country now living and I must rely on those much older than myself for correct information. I hope Mr. Shutt did not advise you to write to me on *account* of my *age* as being *a cotemporary* of the *elder* Lincolns (or as formerly pronounced here) *Link-horns.* Those I Know in this country are highly respectable & exceedingly stubborn people or such as are popularly denominated "bull-headed."

I think our records or those of Augusta will give the Wills & deeds of his Ancestors & might be of interest in your Book —   I will make the examination, tho' *a* Gen'l by the *name* Hunter[1] burnt most of our records & I fear those with the rest.

Regards to Shutt

Yours Resfully

John T. Harris

LC: HW2385; HL: LN2408, 1:1–2

101. William G. Greene to WHH

Tallula Ills Nov 27th 1865

Dear Sir

Yours of 22nd inst at hand Contents noted &c

(1st) Mr Lincoln read Shakespear Byron & Burns all extensively while he lived at Salem I should say that Burns was his favourite

(2) I have no idea that Mr Lincoln ever participated by *eating* or *otherwise* in the Pig Story I suppose that Armstrong[1] & others cooked or roasted a Pig and may have eaten it by way of winding up a Drunken frolick but Mr Lincoln had to much *Natal* refinement to not have been disgusted with it

---

1. Maj. Gen. David Hunter (1802–86) led Union forces in the Shenandoah Valley in 1864.

---

1. Presumably Jack Armstrong.

(3) Mr Lincoln while he lived in New Salem was entirely *free* from the vices mentioned in your 3rd Interrogatory viz running after Women Drinking whiskey or playing Cards for Money

(4) Lincolns customs or habits were not peculiar or striking while he lived in New Salem further than he was fond of company & reading especially in warm weather by Laying down & putting his *Feet* a gainst a wall or if in the woods up a *Tree*

Verry Truly your friend
W G Greene

LC: HW2392; HL: LN2408, 1:481

102. William G. Greene to WHH

Tallula Ills Dec 3rd 1865

Dear Sir

Yours 1st Inst at hand. We never had any *Debating* Society at New Salem it may be possible that once and a while the community may have had publick Discussions in which Mr Lincoln participated

It is *False* sofar as to his *walking* to Vandaly   if you will recollect or reflect for a minute you will Know better we had a regular *Stage* line from your place to Vandaly   Lincoln *borrowed* $100. of Colman Smoot who now lives in this Co to get a suit of Clothes which cost him $60. leaving forty for Stage Fare &c &c   I Know that I am correct. You are mistaken as to seeing any thing in Hollands book as coming from me   I Know nothing of Holland or his book[1]   I would like to see one I would carefully read it & note all Errors that I knew to be so

Verry Truly
William G. Greene

LC: HW2394; HL: LN2408, 1:482

103. David Turnham to WHH

Dale Ind Dec 6th 1865

Dear Sir

yours of the 22nd ult is received and Contents noted. I will answer your questions as well as I Can. Mr Lincoln was born in Kentucky, he was raised a baptist, Thomas Lincoln was a rather long faced man, dark hair, eyes, and scin, by no means hansome,

I never saw Mrs Lincoln

verry respectfully
D Turnham

LC: HW2395; HL: LN2408, 1:281

---

1. Holland was apparently able to cite Greene as a source because he had access to the notes of interviews taken by James Q. Howard in 1860.

104. *George U. Miles to WHH*

Petersburg Ill Decr 8th — 1865

Dear Sir —

Yours of the first inst is before me   we are all well Except my Self my Eyes are more dim than usual & have been so for two or three weeks & besides that Some ten days ago I was attacked with the piles So that I have not ben abel to get about much though I think they are a little better —   (Dick Spears was married this day a week ago)

I have made inquiry & find to a certenty that there never was a debating Society in New Salem during Lincoln time nor at any other time

McHenry[1] & others Say it is also false as to his walking to vandalia when Elected to the legislature

McHenry Sais it is also untrue as to Lincoln not attending to his law Suit —   that he never had but one Suit in Springfield & that was with Hiram Penny which you & Lincoln attended to & gained the case. it was in the circuit court before Judge Treat the papers in the case will Show you all about it

McHenry Sais he gave you a full history of the Case[2] w you were here which is as follows

Pennys wife was McHenrys oldest Sister. Penny[3] owned 242 acres of land in Sangamo Co on whiche lived had give Bob & John Erwin a deed of trust on it   Penny failed to pay the deed of trust Erwin Sold the land on his deed of trust held it two or three offering Penny the chance to redeem it   Penny failed to redeem & failed to pay rent as he had repetedly promised   Erwin refused any longer time to Penny — Penny then went to McHenry to get him to See Erwin & get further indulgence —   McHenry went to See Erwin & Erwin refused saying he had had more trouble with Penny than all the other Customers he had — but Said he would let he McHenry have the land at cost interest & rent   McHenry closed a contract for the land paying Erwin So mutch down the balance in three instalments   McHenry returned told Penny what he had done & Penny was well pleased and then agreed with McHenry that if he McHenry would pay the next instalment he McHenry Should have the 160 acres & he would pay the two last instalments & McHenry Should let him have the 82 acres on which he penny lived   thus it was agreed between the two —   McHenry had to pay all three of the instalments & then Suid for possession you & Lincoln his attorneys — Stewart & Edwards attys for Penny

There was a cabin on the 160 acres which McHenry mooved a family into & which Penny did not claim prior to the Suit — Some time after the commencement of the Suit Lincoln got it in his head that the cabin was on the 82 acres on which Penny lived and told McHenry he must moove that family out of there   McHenry said he Should not do it   well Said Lincoln if you do not I

---

1. Henry McHenry.

2. See §6.

3. Hiram Penny (1790–1852), a farmer in Cartwright Township in Sangamon County. He married Catharine McHenry in Kentucky.

Shall not attend to the Suit   McHenry told him he did not care a dam whather he did or not that he Lincoln was not all the Lawyer there was in Town   Lincoln Studied awhile & asked about the location of the cabin   McHenry told him it was on the 160 acres to which Lincoln replied   Mc you are right I will attend to the suit & did attend to it and gained it — & that was all the harsh words that past & that the only Suit McHenry ever had in Springfield[4]

Yours Truly

G. U. Miles

LC: HW2396–97; HL: LN2408, 1:485–87

105. Dennis F. Hanks to WHH

December 12, 65

Der Sir

I have in my posesion A Little Book the private Life of A Lincoln Comprising a full Life of his Erly years and a Succinct Record of his Career as Statesman and President By O. J Victor author of Lives of Garibaldi winfield Scott John Paul Jones Ect —   Newyork Beadle and Company publishers No 118 williams Street[1]   Now Sir I find a great Many things pertaining to Abe Lincolns Life that is Not trew   if you would Like to have the Book I will Mail it to you   I will Say this Much to you if you Dont have My Name very frecantly in you Book it wont Gow of at all for I have Ben East for 2 months have Seen a great Many persons in that tim — Stateting to them that thare would Be a Book the Life of A. Lincoln published giving a full a Count of the family from ingland to this cuntry   Now william if thare is any thing you want to No Let Me No   I will give you all the information I can   I have Seen a Letter that you Rote to My Daughter Hariet Chapman of Enquire Bout Sum things   I thought you was Iformed all a Bout them I Dont No what She has Stated to you a Bout your Questions But you had Better Cunsult Me a Bout them   yours Respecfuly

D. F. Hanks

LC: HW2398; HL: LN2408, 1:275–76

106. Harriet A. Chapman to WHH

Charleston Ills Dec the 17th 65

Sir

Your favor of the 2nd was duly received. I will now endeavor to answer the Same. Mrs Lincoln the 2d wife of Thomas Lincoln had 2 daughters and one Son   The Daughters were both married before they Come to Ills. My Father D F

---

4. Marginal note: *Mrs Armstrong or rather Mrs Wilcox lives in Mason Co & I may not see her this winter.*

---

1. Orville J. Victor, *The Private and Public Life of Abraham Lincoln* (New York, [1864]).

Hanks married the Eldest, and Squire Hall the Youngest Daughter.[1] S. Hall died in this County. Mr Moore[2] Married Mrs Hall Where She now resides on the old Lincoln Farm. Mr Thomas Lincolns height was about 5 feet 10 Inches, weighed one hundred and 96 pounds. Walked rather Slow never seemed to be in a hurry his Face rather round, Grey Eyes or Hazel as Some People call them, never the less they was about the Color of his Son Abrams High Cheek bones and very large nose which was his most prominent feature   had dark Course hair,

his Wife my Grand Mother Is a vary tall Woman Streight as an Indian, fair Complection and was when I first remember her vary handsome, Sprightly talkative and proud wore her Hair Curled till Gray is kind hearted and vary Charitable and also vary industrious. In Closed I will send you one of her Photographs taken about one year ago. If thare is ennything in the above which is not Satisfactory please let me know and I will correct the Same. When a Cild I Spent a great deal of my time with Grand Pa and Grand Ma Lincoln and loved them both dearly and enny information that I Can give in regard to *them* will be given freely although My discriptive powers are vary poor. The remitence you Spoke of in your letter will be thankfully received.

Respectfully Yours

H. A. Chapman

LC: HW2399; HL: LN2408, 1:281–82

107. William G. Greene to WHH

Tallula Ills Dec 20th 1865

Dear Sir

Yours of 16th inst. recd & contents noted. In Apl. 1836 I saw Thos. Lincoln A. Lincoln's Father I stayed over night with him   he was rather a square built man a bout six ft. high   I would suppose when young & full fleshed that his weight would have been about 185 lbs if my memory serves correctly his Eyes were Gray or Rather Bluish something of the colour of S. T. Logan of your City   while his Manors wer what might be termined Backoodsish yet they were easy so much so that I allmost would say they were polished   He was passionately fond of humerous jokes & stories it was my judgment at the time I saw him & still is that he had no superior in "Story telling" especially when we take in to account that he was destitute of an education   I regret that I cant give you a more minute description but it has been almost a *Third* of a Century since I saw the good old man and then only for one short night as it appeared to me as his wit humor a stories charmed me.

Truly

W G Greene

LC: HW2400; HL: LN2408, 1:482–83

---

1. For marriage dates, see p. 134, note 1.
2. Reuben Moore.

108. Dennis F. Hanks to WHH

December 24th 65

you Speake of My Letter writen with a pencil   the Reason of this was My Ink was frose

part first   we ust to play 4 corner Bull pen and what we Cald Cat.[1] I No that you No what it is and throwing a Mall over our Sholders Backwards hoping and halfhamen Resling and So on

2d   what Religious Songs

The onely Song Book was Dupees old Song Book[2] I Recollect Very well 2 Songs that we ust to Sing that was

O when Shall I Se Jesus and Rain with him a Bove[3]   The Next was

How teageos and Tastless the hour when Jesus No Longer I See[4]   I have tried find one of those Books But Cant find it it was a Book used By the old predestenarin Baptist in 1820   this is My Recollection a Bout it at this time we Never had any other

the Next was in the fields   Hail Collumbis Hap Land[5] if you aint Broke I will be Damned

and the turpen turk that Scorns the world and Struts a Bout whith his whiskers Curld for No other Man But him Self to See[6]

and all Such as this

Abe youst to try to Sing pore Old Ned[7] But he Never Could Sing Much

LC: HW2403; HL: LN2408, 1:277

109. Dennis F. Hanks to WHH

December 27th 65

Friend Billy

I think I have a few More Itims for you   that is this you No thare has Ben Conciderable in quire a Bout how did A Lincoln Rise to Eminance So fast   what Bookes Did he Read   I have Studed out this Much   The first Book that his farther Baught him was the united States Speaker the Life of Washington and henry

---

1. Bull-pen was a ball game in which a group of players threw a ball at other players within a designated "bull-pen." Cat (short for "catapult") was played by a group of boys forming a small circle. A stick (the "cat") was thrown out of the circle, and the person who was "it" chased after the stick while the other players scattered.

2. Dupuy's *Hymns and Spiritual Songs,* §72, note 6.

3. By John Leland.

4. By John Newton.

5. "Hail Columbia, Happy Land," by Joseph Hopkinson.

6. According to Lair, 19, the title is "None Can Love Like an Irishman." The first verse is: "The turban'd Turk, who scorns the world, / May strut about with his whiskers curled, / Keep a hundred wives under lock and key / For nobody else but himself to see; / Yet long may he pray with his Alcoran / Before he can love like an Irishman."

7. Lair, 82, suggests this may refer to an old Kentucky song with the following verse: "Pore old Ned, pore old Ned; / Slept all winter on a corn shuck bed. / Two at the foot, two at the head / And the one in the middle was pore old Ned."

Clay and the Bible and Websers Spillang Book whitch was Mine and an other one
Cald Robisons Cruso[1]   those are the principle Books that I think of at this time
But as Soon as any thin a cures too Me I will Let you No I cant find a volum of
the old Song Book Dupee[2]   if could I could tell you Every Song that we Sung   I
Recolect Sum More Cum thou fount of Every Blesing tune My hart to Sing thy
praise — when I can Read My title Clair to Mansions in the Sky How tedious and
tastless the hour when Jesus Now Longe I See O to grace how great a Detter[3] ower
Little Smuty Songs I wont Say any thing a Bout would Not Look well in print
But I could give it   I had Like to for got   how Did Abe get his Knowledge of
Law   this is the fact a Bout it   I Bought the Statute of Indiana and from that
he Lerned the principles of Law and allso My Self

Every Man Should Be Cum aquainted of the principle Law you will See in that
Little Book the word Demonstrate   what Does it Mean   I Never Could tell to
my Satisfaction what it Ment   Abe allways was trubled Bout words what they
Ment   I was allways in that fix My Self   webster Dont No any thing you want
to No   If it is in My power to Do it I will   Cherefuly

Be Careful and Note Down what you want

I Dont No whether you will understand My Markes in that Little Book or
Not   one thing is Shore a Bout it they Stole it all from the pionere Boy[4]

The Most of it is Not correct Sum is   Now all the Story a Bout the first Cabin
is fals

plese take Care of My Letters Not Loose them   Mite Be of use to us
                    Yours Respectfully
                        D. F. Hanks.

LC: HW2405–6; HL: LN2408, 1:246–47

110. David Turnham to WHH[1]

Dale Ind. Dec. 30 -'65.

Dear Sir:

Yours of the 16th inst. is received. I will cheerfully comply with your request
so far as I can.

---

1. Probably *The American Speaker; A Selection of Popular, Parliamentary and Forensic Eloquence; Particularly Calculated for the Seminaries in the United States* (Philadelphia, 1811); for *Life of Washington*, see §24, note 15, and §71, note 16; George Denison Prentice, *Biography of Henry Clay* (1831); for Webster, see §76, note 3; for *Robinson Crusoe*, see §74, note 2.

2. See §72, note 6.

3. These songs are from Dupuy's *Hymns and Spiritual Songs*, except for "Oh to grace how great a debtor?"

4. Possibly Raymond, borrowing from William Makepeace Thayer, *The Pioneer Boy, and How He Became President* (Boston, 1863).

---

1. A photostat of the original manuscript of this letter is in the files of the Abraham Lincoln Association, ISHL, but the location of the original is unknown. The Springer transcription given here appears to differ slightly from the original in accidentals and word order but not in substance. For a facsimile of the original, see Lair, 6–7.

As to the songs sung in those days, by the young folks; I have forgotten all except pious songs. Of these I will give you a few, and I will commence with one which Abe asked me to sing for his father, I complied, and the old gentleman would have me sing it often afterward. It commences thus:

I — There was a romish lady
    Brought up in popery.[2]

The Hymns used were Dr. Watts' and Dupuy's Hymns.[3]
    I will name a few of the hymns sung in church:

"Am I soldier of the Cross,
A follower of the lamb;"

"How tedious and tasteless the hour,
When Jesus no longer I see;"

"There is a fountain filled with blood,
Drawn from Immanuels veins;"

"Jesus my all, to Heaven is gone;
He, whom I fixed my hopes upon."

"Alas: and did my Savior bleed,
And did my Sovereign die:"[4]

Dear friend: I have tried to answer your questions as well as I can. If there is any thing more that I can be of any service to you, I will gladly serve you.
    I would like to know if you ever got that old law book, it is the revised statute of 1824. If you have not, and wish it, I will try to get it and send it to you.
    I wish you success with your book.
                        Yours Respectfully
                        D. Turnham.

HL: LN2408, 1:178–79

2. "The Romish Lady," a blatantly anti–Roman Catholic narrative, depicts a woman burned at the stake by the Church for secretly reading the Bible and renouncing the worship of idols. See Lair, 9.

3. See p. 105, note 6.

4. "Am I a Soldier of the Cross" and "Alas! and Did My Saviour Bleed" are by Isaac Watts; "How Tedious and Tasteless the Hour" is by John Newton; "There Is a Fountain Filled with Blood" is by William Cowper. All four appear in Dupuy's *Hymns and Spiritual Songs.* "Jesus My All to Heaven Is Gone" is not identified.

111. Dennis F. Hanks to WHH

[Dec. 1865?]

on The 24 page[1]   This is all Rong he never went to New oreleans. at that time   It Says he hired to a person who Lived nere By at the Rate of 10 Dollars per Month   this is false   those places that I mark is Rong   on the 18 page   Speaking of the first cabin that was Bilt is a Mistake it was not a cabin at all it was one of those half face camps a Bout 14 feet open in frunt fire place in the Back part

Now in answer to Requst   Thomas Lincoln was a man five feet 10 Inches high Darke hair Rather Corse — Hazel Eye weighing 196 lbs   Very Much Like Abe his Sun   he had a Broder face than abe   Walked Slow and Shore a Mity Staught Man   his Mother Spare Made thin visage Remarkable Keen perseption lite hare and Blew Eyes   I will Send the Bok   if I have for got any thing Let me No   you ask what Sort of plais   what we cald them at that was Bull pen & Corner and Cat hoping and half hamin   plaing at Nite old Sister feby[2]   this I No for I took a hand My Self   and Restling we Could throw Down any Body

Now William Be Sure and have My Name very Conspikus in the work and it gaw of well wright it Dennis. F. Hanks I Can Sell that work when it is published fast for I now what the people Say for I have told them that thare would Be Such a Bok out The Therow History Signed By Me

Yours Respetfully

D. F. Hanks

LC: HW3898; HL: LN2408, 1:244–45

112. Zebina Eastman to WHH

Bristol, Jan 2 1866

Dear Sir —

Seeing your name in a Chicago paper a few days ago, in connection with a lecture on the character of Mr Lincoln,[1] reminds me of old times. It is many years since I saw you at Springfield, when I came their with Cassius M. Clay.[2] I then learned that Mr. Lincoln's law partner was a thorough abolitionist, and that was yourself. Perhaps you were not aware at the time what my particular desire was in visiting Springfield, and particularly in my inquiry of you. It was to learn from some thing nearer than public report, and public life, what were Mr. Lincolns particular feelings and scruples in regard to the colored people of the United States.

---

1. Possibly refers to Raymond, 18–24. See p. 147, note 4.
2. Old Sister Phoebe, a play-party game. See Lair, 23.

---

1. Probably WHH's two-part lecture on AL's character, delivered on December 12 and 26, 1865, in Springfield.
2. Cassius M. Clay (1810–1903), a Kentucky lawyer and abolitionist.

I wanted to know if he was their friend — if he was their friend, we knew he was a a politician that could be trusted. You Satisfied me. You told me what Mr. Lincoln's private views were, and led me in to a sight of his heart. You remember that after that, as long as I printed the Western Citizen or Free West[3] it was sent to your office. I supposed Mr Lincoln read it some times.

You may perhaps remember that after that time there was no opposition to Mr Lincoln from the abolitionists proper. They were in a party of their own, and from repeated betrayals, had learned to distrust all professions of mere politicians. They gave their confidence to men that were worthy of it, — as they gave it to Washburne and Morton.[4]

After that visit I told all my Liberty Party friends to stand by Abraham Lincoln. These were times when he could hardly have expected to have received any office in Illinois. Dr. Dyer[5] was particularly in unison with me in these views. The abolitionists soon learned that we were all to be in harmony with Abraham Lincoln.

Dr. Dyer received the appointment by Mr Lincoln as Judge of the African Slave Trade Court. He sent me to this place[6] — after he had had a confidential interview with me at 7 o'clock in the morning. It is a pleasant thing to remember, as Mr. Lincoln told Dyer, — it was a great pleasure to him to appoint old abolitionists to office. Surely he was the Negro's friend. Therefore he became that eminently successful man. How different from those who preach the doctrine, that "Black men had no rights which white men were bound to respect."

Very truly yours,
Z. Eastman

LC: HW2409–10

113. Elizabeth Crawford to WHH

January the 4th 1866

Dear Sir

i received your letter of September the 28 and also another of December the 15   i beg to excused for not ancern your first letter as i was very buissy ageting ready to Sart to nelson County ky to See about my fathers estate and as you did not Say eny thing about us riting to you we neglected as we Concluded t[hat] you had got all the information that you wanted   thair was one thing th[at] i did not think of teling you   when you was here that was the flore you was Setting on when you was here was   plank that abraham lincoln whip Sawed about the year 1830

---

3. Eastman edited the *Western Citizen* in Chicago, 1842–53. In 1853 its name was changed to *Free West*, and two years later it was merged with the Chicago *Tribune*.

4. Elihu B. Washburne (1816–87), Republican congressman from Galena, Illinois; and Oliver H. P. Morton (1823–77), Civil War governor of Indiana.

5. Charles V. Dyer (1808–78), Chicago physician and an avowed opponent of slavery.

6. AL appointed Eastman consul at Bristol, England, where he served until 1869.

We moved to this Country in 1824 and Soon after become aquainted with the lincoln famly   when abraham was a strap of a boy and his play mats would fall out with him he would laugh and make rimes and Sing them and tell the boys that he intended to be presedent yet   while other boys would quarl he would apper to be a pese maker and while others would romp and lafe he would be engaged in the arithmetic or asking questions about Som history heard or red of

first Chronicles of ruben now thair was a man in those days whose name was ruben and the Same was very grate in substance in horses and Cattle and Swine and avery grate house hold and it Came to pass that when the Sons of ruben grew up that thay ware desirus of taking to them Selves wives and being too well known as to onor in ther own Country So thay took to them Selves a Journy in to a far Country and procured to them Selves wives   and it Came to pass that when thay ware about to make the return home that thay Sent a messenger before them to bare the tidines to there parents So thay inquired of the mesengers what time there Sones and there wives wood Come   So thay made a grate feast and Cald all ther kinsmen and neighbors in and maid grate preperations   So when the time drew near thay sent out two men to meet the grooms and ther brids with a treet to welcom them and to acompny them So when thay Came near to the house of ruben there father the mesengers Came on before them and gave a Shout and the whole multitude ran out with Sho[uts of] Joy and musick playing on all kinds of instruments of musick Some playing on harps and Some on vials and Some blowing on rams hornes Some Casten dust and ashes tourd heaven and amongst the rest Josiah bloing his buble making Sound So grate that it maid the neighborin hills and valys eco with the resonding aclamation So when thay had played and harped Sounded tell the grooms and brides approched the gate the father ruben met them and welcomed them in to his house and the weding dinner being now ready thay ware all invited to Set down to dinner placing the bridegroomes and ther wives at each end of the table waters ware then apointed to Carve and wate on the guests So when thay had all eaten and ware ful and mary thay went out and Sang and played tell evening and when thay had made an end of feasting and rejoising the multitude dispersed each to his one home the family then took Seat with

ther waters to Converse awhile which time preperations ware being maid in an upper Chamber for the brids to be first Convayed by the waters to ther beds this being done the waters took the two brids up stares to ther beds placing one in a bed at the rite hand of the Stares and the other on the left   the waters Come down and nancy the mther inquired of the waters which of the brids was paced on the rite hand and thay told her   So She gave directions to the waters of the bridegrooms and thair thay took the bridegrooms and placed them in the rong beds and Came down Stares but the mother being fearful that thair mite be a mistake inquired again of the waters and learning the fact took the light and Sprang up tares and runing to one of the beds exclaimed ruben   you are in bed with Charleses wife   the young men both being alarmed Sprang out of bed and ran with such violance against each other that thay Came very near nocking each other down which gave evidence to those below that the mistake was Ceartain   thay

all Came down and had a Conversation about who had maid the mistake but it
Could not be decided
    So ended the Chapter

i will tell you a Joke about Jouel and mary
it is neither a Joke nor a tory
for rubin and Charles has maried two girles
but biley has maried a boy
the girles he had tried on every Side
but none could he get to agree
all was in vain he went home again
and sens that he is maried to natty

so biley and naty agreed very well
and mamas well pleased at the matc[h]
the egg it is laid but Natys afraid
the Shell is So Soft that it never will hatc[h]
but betsy She Said you Cursed ball head
my Suiter you never Can be
besids your low Croch proclaimes you a botch
and that never Can anser for me

    this is memorised by Mrs elizeabeth Crawford an oald blind lady that Can
hardly See
        ritten by her Son and farweded
                                S A Crawford

    LC: HW2411–14; HL: LN2408, 1:186–90

114. Richard J. Oglesby to WHH

                                            Springfield Ills Jany 5d 1866
Dear friend
    I have just read the Synopsis of your lecture "on the Life and character of Abra-
ham Lincoln[1]   I regret I did not hear you deliver it. Your discriptions and delin-
eations of the great man — are true hapy and most complete — given with more
Effect than I have ever before heard. You constantly reproduce him to his old
friends, The discription of his Journey to the market house and return is vigorous
and full of Spirit. The closing Sentence struck me with such force I almost felt his
presence again this sentence ought not to be forgotten *"Sometimes* it *appeared* to
me *that* Lincolns *Soul was* Just *fresh from the presence of its creator"* Do you know
that at times I have been similarly impressed by that good man,

---

1. Oglesby refers to WHH's first lecture on AL, delivered on December 12, 1865.

What you say about what his *"Perception"* was is truthfully faultless and impartially correct. The remarks you have put together under the head of *"Sugges-
tiveness"* Show that you have studied the man and his mysterious character carefully —   you went through the bark into the heart of this giant of the intellectual
forest, I think your estimate of his Judgement is very nearly fair   It would have
been Entirely so had you — may I suggest —   made some distinction between
his Judgement of men and Things. Of men in detail he was not a good Judge of
Mankind as a class I think he was a good Judge. He knew how to estimate Society
or more correctly Societies, well; I think Mr. Lincoln at all times possessed strong
common sense but not upon all subjects. I mean to say he sometimes Seemed weak
in his Estimate of men — but he had an instinctive aversion to a Mean Man —
despised a knave pitied a fool and Laughed heartily at an ass There were however
classes who could and did impose upon him —   What you say of *"his grand
Elements"* no man who knew him can gainsay   you Struck the key note of his
whole nature and let his character out as God put it in him. I endorse Every word
you say under the head of His *"Heart and humanity"* a most truthful and correct
Statement it is of Just what he was. Mr Lincoln was not a man of strong attachments. He was the warm friend of few men but he was the true friend of Mankind. He loved Man as he loved his God Logically. I am sure you have weighed
and if I may say so dissected him most fairly and with Thorough correctness. As
an old and constant friend you have been Just to him, I hope your lecture may be
preserved in an Enduring form   I should be much pleased to have it in such shape
as to refer to it conveniently. do you remember that Mr Lincoln was never given
to praise much — of any living man. and was not good at Eulogy upon the Dead.
he never seemed to me to be an ardent admirer of any living being. He was as you
say pretty much his own model, — he even spoke spareingly of men he did not
like. and I believe was never a grumbler. he submited to adversity and injustice
with as much real patience as any Man I Ever knew — because he had an abiding
belief that all would yet come out right or that the right would appear and Justice
finally be awarded to him
    I enclose and return herewith the printed copy as requested
very respectfully   your friend
R. J. Oglesby

LC: HW2415–16

115. Dennis F. Hanks to WHH

January the 6th 1866

Friend Billy
    I Received your Letter January the 3d
    The first question that you ask is this   what has Be Cum of John Hall   he
was in town to Day   You Say that have writen 3 or 4 Letters to him and got No
answer   what was it Billy that you wanted to No of him   I can answer all that

he can he cant write very well   he Does Not No Much a Bout the Old Man Lincoln for he was a Boy at his Death   he has Nothing to Do with writing to any
one a Bout the Life of Lincoln it Dependes on Me to Do all this   I have writen
a Letter to Josiah Crofford in Spencer County Indiana Concerning Books that Abe
Read   I have No answer yet

Next question   how many people was at Mrs Lincoln furnel at hir
Beriel   Thare was a Bout 20 persons the hole Nabour hood   Do you Mean hir
funerl preaced or hir interment in the grown   I have jest Seen John Hall   he
Says that he got your Letters But Could Not answer any of them   ask Me the
questions   I will Answer them Satisfacttory   at Mrs Lincoln furnel preched was
By David Elkins of Hardin County Ky   Cum to pay us a Visit and preacht hir
furnel   the Customs of the people at time was very Ruff Drinking a Little whisky Corn Shuckings Log Rolings &c —   No Dancing as Sum Did —   Shooting Maches throwing the Mall over head.

Size of the fields from. 10. 12 16 20 acors Raised Corn Mostly Sum wheat a
Nuf for a Cake a Sundy Morning

Hogs and Venison hams was a Legal tender and Coon Skins all so

we Raised Sheep and Cattle But they Did not fecth Much Cows and Calfes
was onely worth 6 Dollars Corn 10 cts wheat 25 at that time

I think I will Be able to tell you all a Bout these things   I take plesure in Doing
so

Yours Respectfuly
D. F. Hanks

Not well at this time

Now a Bout the timber   it was Black walnut and Black oake hickory and Jack
oake Elm and white oake under grooth Dogwood in a Bundance grape vines and
Shewmake Bushes and Milk Sick plenty   all of My Relitives Died with that Disease on Little pigeon Creek Spencer County

this all at this time

LC: HW2418; HL: LN2408, 1:248–49

116. S. A. Crawford to WHH

January the 8th 1866

Dear Sir

i hav done as you requested me to do   i hav ritten all of the Cronicals of rubens
and poetry that my oald mother Could memorise of mr lincoln riting at the time he
worked with with her and father   at the time mr lincoln rote this it apiers that thare
was a little Coolness exising between the two famlys   mr lincoln not being invited
to the grate weding feast maid use of a little of his novelty in Stating facts that did
accour   rubin did go to bed with Charleses wife and Charles to bed with rubens
wife   i took the rubens Cronicals to gentryvill and red them in public   R. D.

grigsby being present got veary mad over it but naty who maried biley being present affirmed the Saim to be facts

i am very ancious for one of the Books of your grate intended work

yours truly

S. A. Crawford

LC: HW2419; HL: LN2408, 1:190

117. Robert T. Lincoln to WHH

Chicago Jan 8/66

My dear Mr Herndon

Both of your letters have been received. I should have answered the first one immediately, but I have been very much pressed.

I was not aware that my mother had written you & so of course I did not compose the letter you have received. I had seen a synopsis of your lecture & I assure you I saw nothing in it at which to take umbrage. In the first place, I would not judge a discourse by an abstract of it — but more than all, even when I differ with anyone in his views of my father's character &c. unless it were something flagrantly wrong, I would not discuss the subject.

While it is true that the details of the private life of a public man have always a great interest in the minds of some — it is after all his works which make him live — & the rest is but secondary.

I am extremely sorry to perceive that you seem to think that I bear ill-will towards you, from the correspondence which arose out of a misunderstanding —   I beg you to believe that nothing is further from the truth —   My feelings towards are of the kindest & I wish I had some means of proving them —

Sincerely Yours

Robert T. Lincoln

LC: HW2420–21

118. Henry McHenry to WHH

Petersburg Ill Jan 8th 1866.

Dear sir

Yours of the 10th ult came to hand in due time   I should have answered it before this but I confidently expected to have seen you face to face before this, & now, I promise you I will be up in a few days. I will say however some thing about the Points of which you spoke, 1st   As to the condition of Lincoln's Mind after the death of Miss R. after that Event he seemed quite *changed,* he seemed *Retired,* & loved *Solitude,* he seemed wraped in *profound thought, indifferent,* to transpiring Events, had but Little to say, but would take his gun and wander off in the woods by him self, away from the association of even those he most esteemed, this gloom seemed to deepen for some time, so as to give anxiety to his friends in regard to his Mind, But various opinions obtained as to the Cause of his change, some thought it was an increased application to his *Law studies,* Others that it was deep anguish of *Soul* (as he was all soul) over the Loss of Miss R, My opinion is, & was, that it was from the Latter cause, As to the Book, or Pamphlet, I do not recollect about what it "did Say" or "tried to Say" but it was I am sure Written after the death of Miss R, & I never heard any Scoundrel *"orthodox"* or Hetrodox, or any body Else bring the charge of Infidelity against his production until they found that they Might Make Political Capital out of base and groundless charges against Gods Noblest Work, *The honest Man,*

I think the two points are all you asked about, the Answer Is true, I think, I am willing to contribute My Mite to perpetuate unsullied the Memory of *Our* Lincoln,

I am not able to be out soon, but will be up as soon as I get over the awful cold.

Respectfully Your friend
Henry McHenry

by B. F. Farley Ams. —

LC: HW2422–23

119. Joshua F. Speed to WHH

Louisville 12 Jany 1866.

Dear Sir

Yours of the 9 propounding certain questions is at hand.

If Mr Lincoln ever went to Ky to see Mr Clay, I knew nothing of it —   He never alluded to any such visit, in any of his conversations with me —

I do not think he had ever read much of Byron previous to my accquaintance with him — He was a great admirer of some of Byrons poetry — Childe Harolde the Bride of Abydos Mazppa & some of his fugitive pieces.

I think that when I first knew Mr L he was skeptical as to the great truths of the Christian Religion. I think that after he was elected President, he sought to become a believer — and to make the Bible a preceptor to his faith and a guide for his conduct.

The last interview but one I had with him — was about ten days previous to his last inauguration. Congress was drawing its legislation to a close — it had been an important session — much attention had to be given to the important bills he was signing — a great was was upon him — visitors were coming & going to the President with their various complaints and grievances from morning till night with almost as much regularty as the ebb & flow of the tide. He was worn down in health & spirits — On this occasion I was sent for to come & see him — instructions were given that when I came I should be admitted — When I entered his office it was quite full and many more Senators & Members waiting —

As soon as I entered the room the President remarked that he desired to see me after he was through giving audiences and that if I had nothing to do I could take the Papers and amuse myself till he was ready.

In the room when I entered I observed two ladies in humble attire — sitting across the fire place from where the President sat — modestly waiting their turn — One after another came & went, each and all of them bent on their own business — Some satisfied, and others grumbling — The hour had now come to close the door to all visitors. No one was left in the room except myself the two women & the President —

With rather a peevish & fretful air he turned to them and said "Well ladies what can I do for you?

They both commenced to speak at once From what they said he soon learned that one was the wife and the other Mother of two men imprisoned for resisting the draft in Western Pensylvania —

Stop said he — dont say any more — Give me your petition — The old lady responded — Mr Lincoln — weve got no petition — we couldnt write one, and had no money to pay for writing one — I thought it best to come & see you — Oh said he — Dont say any thing more   I understand your cases — He rang his bell & ordered one of the Messengirs to tell Genl Dana[1] to bring him the names of all the men in prison for resisting the Draft in Western Pensylvania — The Genl soon came with the list — He inquired if there was any [difference?] in the charges or degrees of guilt   The General replied that he knew of none.

"Well said he these fellows have suffered long enough and I have thought so for some time and now that mind is on it, I believe I will turn out the *flock*" — So draw up the order General and let me sign it — It was done & the General left the room — Turning then to these women he said "now ladies you can go —"

The young woman ran forward & was about to kneel in thankfulness — Get up he said dont kneel to me — thank God & go.

The old woman came forward with tears in her eyes to say Good bye — good bye said she Mr Lincoln — I shall never see you again till we meet in Heaven —

She had the Presidents hand in hers — He instantly took her right hand in both of his and following her to the door & said I am afraid with all my troubles I shall never get there — But if I do I will find you — That you wish me to get there is the best wish you could make for me — good bye —

We were alone — I said to him — Lincoln with my knowledge of your nervous sesibility it is a wonder that such scenes as this dont kill you — I am said he very unwell — my feet & hands are always cold — I suppose I ought to be in bed —

But things of that sort dont hurt me — For to tell you the truth — that scene which you witnessed is the only thing I have done to day which has given me any pleasure — I have in that made two people happy — That old lady was no counterfeit — The Mother spoke out in all the features of her face — It is more than we can often say that in doing right we have made two people happy in one day —

"Speed die when I may I want it said of me by those who know me best to say

---

1. Assistant Secretary of War Charles A. Dana (1819–97).

that I always plucked a thistle and planted a flower where I thought a flower would grow —

Such is the recital of the interview you ask — The finishing touch to a portrait by Wilson[2] was given just after this interview — John Williams[3] has a copy of it —

There are some traits of character for which Lincoln was peculiar above all men I have ever known — He never forgot any thing espically any personal kindness — As an instance of this When he was in Ky in 1841 he was moody & hypochondriac — He was staying at the house of my Mother — She observed him and one morning when they were alone presented him with a Bible — Years rolled round & he was President — The old lady sent him word that she wanted his Photograph

He sent it with this sentence

"To my very good friend Mrs Lucy G Speed who gave me an Oxford Bible Twenty years ago
                    A. Lincoln"

It had faded from my Mothers memory — Till she was thus reminded of it —
He was not a selfish man — But upon this point you understand him as well as I do —
                    Your friend &c
                    J. F. Speed

LC: HW2424–26; HL: LN2408, 2:188–93

120. David Davis to WHH

Washington D.C. Jany. 14. 1866.

My Dear Friend.

It pains me to refuse you any reasonable request but I have been written to over and over again to furnish my views about Mr Lincoln, & have uniformly declined to give them — I could not give them to you & be consistent. I have no objections in person to talk the whole matter over with you, & hope to do so when I see you. — I have always understood that Mr. Lincoln's Emancipation proclamation, was his own conception; that he announced to his Cabinet, that he intended to issue it, and that he would hear suggestions, about verbal criticism &c — It is mean to try to deprive him of the glory of that —
                    Your friend
                    D Davis

LC: HW2429; HL: LN2408, 2:318

---

2. Matthew Wilson (1814–92). According to the artist, AL gave him one sitting just two weeks before the assassination.

3. Speed probably refers to John Williams (1808–90), a Springfield merchant and political associate of AL.

121. *Leonard Swett to WHH*

Chicago, Jan. 15. 1866.

Dear Sir.

I unexpectedly got through with my case at Springfield, so as to let me off on the next train of the day I saw you   I therefore failed to have another interview with you as I anticipated. I shall not fail to give you the letter as I suggested, but want to wait until I have time to read over your lecture again.

This afternoon, a banker at Richmond, who formerly lived in Washington & with whom I was intimate, sent me the two letters, which I enclose to you. He made no comment & did not state why he sent them to me, He only remarked that he had seen the originals in the hands of Robert Todd of St Louis, and knew them to be genuine.

I never knew Mr Lincoln had a brother   It is perhaps a little singular, but I never heard him speak of any relative, except as connected with his boy history.

The letters which I send sound like Lincoln   From the City from which they are sent, and from Mr Todd, if he is the man I think he is the construction put upon them may have been an unfavorable one to Mr Lincoln, as showing, in reference to his brother, a penurious disposition.[1]   To people who have been accustomed to look upon him *only* as President, with the supposed wealth & exalted ideas that station suggest the letter might bear that construction, but to you & I it would look different. Without knowing exactly I dont suppose in 1848. if that was the time the letter to the brother was written Mr Lincoln was worth $500. I do know generally that he was poor, with a professional practice suspended by his term in Congress as his only means of support   Besides his ideas of money were always far from lavish. I never knew him to refuse to spend for anything he needed   Yet he was always rigidly frugal and in no way indulged, in himself or others idleness or wastefulness   I think he always gave to meritorious objects but I dont think he would in anyone, continence thoughtlessness   I can therefore see how he would make it condition even with his brother, if he thought it necessary for his good that while he helped him that he should do something for himself   This would be austerely right, it was seeing the thing just as it was   It is another proof of your estimate of him. that he always rigidly saw the truth

To understand this letter, which I assume to be genuine, we must have two facts before us, one Mr Lincoln's estimate of amounts, the other the true character of that brother, The first I know, The second I do not.

I remember, not certainly to exceed three years before he was elected President, Mr Lincoln was, by agreement, holding Court, at Clinton, for Judge Davis. A case was pending of a merchant against the Father of a minor, for payment for a suit of clothes sold, without authority from the Father, by the merchant, to the son The question was whether they were necessaries & suited to his condition in life. The Father was a fair farmer living near Mt Pleasant & if I remember right owned a good farm. The bill for the entire suit was $28. I happened in Court, just as Lin-

---

1. Probably letters to his stepbrother, John D. Johnston, dated December 24, 1848, and November 4, 1851. See *CW* 2:15–16, 111–12.

coln was giving his decision   The substance of it was that the bill was too much   Said he "I have very rarely in my life worn a suit of Clothes costing $28.

The character of the brother I know nothing about   If he was simply poor & struggling in an humbler sphere in life, the letter would be unpardonable by the man who received it If the case was as strong as from the terms of the letter it may be supposed it may be justifiable

I cannot disguise that I have some curiosity to know whether there is any truth in this letter and if so to know what the real facts are.

There has been for a long time, among Mr Lincoln's Enemies, an effort to produce an impression that he was inhumane to his poor relatives   I was in General Grants tent once at City Point when he read me, from [Harrisburg?], I think, a detailed Statement of the destitute condition of his brother's family there, I think it was his brother, The Statement was that applications had been made to Mr L. at Washington in their behalf which was inhumanly refused & Gen'l Grant was asked why he was fighting to uphold such a monster. The Gen'l said he showed it to me, not to enquire seriously for its probable truth but as a specimen of what he sometimes received   I may get these details wrong but substantially I am correct. I assured Genl Grant, as I supposed, that he never had a brother.

If you know any facts in reference to this letter to the brother, or about the brother I would like to know them

Yours Truly
Leonard Swett

LC: HW2430–33

122. George E. Baker to WHH

Washington, Jan, 16, 1866.

My Dear Sir:

I have not by any means forgotten you and cannot consider you an "entire Stranger".

I doubt if it is proper or even possible for me to give you very intelligent replies to your inquiries, as to my views of Mr. Lincoln.

I have always said that his greatest lack was experience as an Executive and as a Statesman — and it was in my judgment a most serious deficiency. But his originality unaffected simplicity and devotion to duty impressed me with a great love and veneration for him.

After three years in the Presidency a marked improvement in his executive ability was apparent and six years I believe would have shown still greater improvement.

I think it is idle for any intelligent man to say he was peculiarly fitted or well fitted for an Executive. Under the circumstances he may have been *the* man for President, But it cannot be truly said that he displayed any ability except we bring all the extraordinary circumstances into the view with him.

His success it seems to me consisted very much in the confidence and respect he won from the people. Other wiser, greater and as good men might not have won this and then all would have been lost in some of our great crises.

So no one can overestimate Abraham Lincoln's services to the country.

In some haste

I am yours truly

Geo. E. Baker.

HL: LN2408, 2:299–300

123. Abner Y. Ellis to WHH[1]

[ca. Jan. 1866]

With the assistance of Such Men as Bolin Green, James Short and Denton Offutt Mr Lincoln Commenced his Carear first as Post Master & Surveyor & Captain in the Black Hawk War.

afterward in the State Legislatur after that he paddled his own Canoe With a good Supply of Good humor & affability He was a Man you Know, that was allways Susceptible of improvements in his own homespun way he Would Use acquirements He Made No display only as in imitation in telling in Story He was a good Mimic in Words & Jestures do you remember his Personating J. B. Thomas how he Made Thomas Cry

Mr Lincoln took great delight in in amusing others at times. His Way of Laughing two was rearly funney and Such awakard Jestures belonged to No other Man they actracted Universal attention from the old Sedate down to the School Boy then in a few Minnets he was as Calm & thoughtful as a Judge on the Bench and Was ready to give advice on the Most Serious and important Matters — fun and gravity both grew on him alike   See how Much Such Men as Judge Davis, N. B. Judd & Smith of Indiana resected his opinions in Political and Judical Matters   I herd Joseph Galaspie Not Long Since Say he used to differ with Lincoln in some points but finally foun Mr. *L.* was right and He Galaspie was rong

I, was once in Peoria and Douglas was to Speak their Next day as he Mr. D thought alone and of course had his Speach Studded out

But the Night before the day appointed Mr Lincoln Sliped in about 2 *oc* in the Morning unbeknown to any one but the Land Lord Mr King & his Night Clerks

Mr Douglass friends Called Erly in the Morning to see him and were having a good time in his Company, & thinking what a clear field he was to have that day all to himself, but all attone in Comes Mr King & informs them that Mr Lincoln was in No 84 having Come in that Morning from Indiana (I think)

---

1. Fragment of a letter. The paper, handwriting, and subject matter would indicate that these leaves were among those sent to WHH in January and February 1866 and that it may have been part of Ellis's first letter in the sequence.

Mr Douglas went imedately to Mr L. Room Shook hands with him & Mr L. Says and observed to him I am Sory Very Sory that you have Come as I well Know you business, however Mr D Went on with his Speach I did Not hear him but Mr L said it was the poores speach that Douglas ever Made & he himslf did Not Speak More than ¾ of an hour

Oh I forgot to say that I recived a Letter the other day from Geo. W. Glass-cock Now a Member of the Texas Legislator and in Speaking of Mr Lincoln he Says he used to Boat with him and he Mr L in his younger days was a Man of good habits   he Says Mr L Never Drank a drop of Liquor to his Knowledge — Never Swore an oath had No desire for strange Woman and allway Spoke the trouth   You May rember Mr Glasscock he Was My first Wifes Brother. he Say Mr Lincoln Pardoned him before he was assassinated

Mr G's Crime was he lived in Texas and while a Member Voted with the Ma-jority he was allways Easy to be convenced of allmost any thing.

He is Now a very rich Man So Tom Iles says of him

LC: HW5286–87

124. Leonard Swett to WHH[1]

Chicago. Jan'y 17*th* 1866.

Dear Sir:

I received your letter today, asking me to write you by Freaday. Fearing if I delay, you will not get done it in time, I will give you such hasty thoughts as may occour to me to night. I have mislaid your second lecture, so that I have not read it at all, and have not read your first one since about the time it was published. What I shall say therefore, will be based upon my own ideas, rather than a review of the lec-tures.

Lincoln's whole life was a calculation of the law of forces, and ultimate results. The world to him was a question of cause and effect. He believed the results to which certain causes tended, would surely follow; he did not believe that those results could be materially hastened, or impeded. His whole political history, es-pecially since the agitation of the Slavery question, has been based upon this the-ory. He believed from the first, I think, that the agitation of Slavery would pro-duce its overthrow, and he acted upon the result as though it was present from the beginning. His tactics were, to get himself in the right place and remain there still, until events would find him in that place. His course of action led him to say and do things which could not be understood, when considered in reference to the immediate surroundings in which they were done, or said. + + +[2] You will remember in his campaign against Douglas in 1858, the first ten lines of the first speech he made defeated him. The sentiments of the "house divided against itself," seemed

---

1. Swett revised this letter in 1887, and it appeared in that form in WHH's biography. See H&W (1889), 528–38.

2. Probably intended by Springer, the copyist, as an elision.

wholly inappropriate. It was a speech made at the commencement of a campaign, and apparently made for the campaign, and apparently made for the campaign. Viewing it in this light alone, nothing could have been more unfortunate, or unappropriate; it was saying first the wrong thing, yet he saw it was an abstract truth, but standing by the speech would ultimately find him in the right place. I was inclined at the time to believe these words were hastily and inconsiderately uttered, but subsequent facts have convinced me they were deliberate and had been matured. Judge T. L Dickey says that at Bloomington at the first Republican Convention, in 1856, he uttered the same sentences in a Speech delivered there, and that after the meeting was over, he (Dickey) called his attention to these remarks. Lincoln justified himself in making them, by stating they were true; but finally at Dickey's urgent request, he pronounced that for his sake, or upon his advice, he would not repeat them. In the Summer of 1859 when he was dining with a party of his intimate friends at Bloomington the subject of his Springfield speech was discussed. We all insisted it was a great mistake, but he justified himself, and finally said, "Well Gentlemen, you may think that Speech was a mistake, but I never have believed it was, and you will see the day when you will consider it was the wisest thing I ever said." + + +[3]

He never believed in political combinations; he never believed any Class of men could accomplish in politics any particular given purpose and consequently whether an individual man, or class of men supported or opposed him, never made any difference in his feelings, or his opinions of his own success. If he was elected, he seemed to believe that no person, or class of persons could ever have defeated him; and if defeated, he believed nothing could ever have elected him. Hence, when he was a candidate, he never wanted any thing done for him. He seemed to want to let the whole question alone, and for everybody else to do the same. I remember after the Chicago Convention when a great portion of the East were known to be dissatisfied at his nomination —. When fierce conflicts were going on in New York and Pennsylvania and when great exertions seemed requisite to harmonize and mold in concert the action of our friends. Lincoln always seemed to oppose all efforts made in that direction. I arranged with Mr. Thurlow Weed afther the Chicago Convention to meet him at Springfield. (I was present at the interview, but he said nothing. It was proposed that Judge Davis should go to New York and Pennsylvania to survey the field, and see what was necessary to be done.) Lincoln consented, but it was always my opinion that he consented reluctantly. He saw that the pressure of a campaign was an external force, coercing the party into unity. If it failed to produce that result, he believed any individual effort would also fail. If the desired result followed, he considered it attributable to the great cause, and not aided by the lesser ones. He sat down in his chair at Springfield and made himself the Mecca to which all politicians made pilgrimages. He told them all a story, said nothing, and sent them away. All his efforts to procure a second nomination were in the same direction. I believe he earnestly desired that nomination.

---

3. Probably intended by the copyist as an elision.

He was much more eager for it, than he was for the first one, and yet from the first he discouraged all efforts on the part of his friends to obtain it. From the middle of his first term, all his adversaries were busily at work for themselves. Chase had three, or four secret societies, and an immense patronage extending all over the country; Fremont was constantly at work; yet Lincoln would never do anything either to hinder them, or to help himself.

He was considered too conservative, and his adversaries were trying to outstrip him in satisfying the radical element. I had a conversation with him upon this subject in October in 1863, and tried to induce him to recommend in his annual message, the consitutional amendment abolishing slavery. I told him was not very radical, but I believed the result of this war would be the extermination of slavery; that Congress would pass the resolution; and that it was proper at that time to be done. I told him if he took that stand, it was an outside position and no one could maintain himself upon any measure more radical, and if he failed to take the position, his rivals would. Turning to me suddenly he said, "Is not that question doing well enough now?" I replied that it was. "Well", said he, "I have never done an official act with a view to promote my own personal aggrandizement, and I don't like to begin now, I can see that time coming; whoever can wait for it, will see it — whoever stands in its way, will be run over by it."

His rivals were using money profusely; Journals and influences were being subsidized against him. I accidentally learned that a Washington newspaper through a purchase of the establishment was to be turned against him, and consulted him about taking steps to prevent it. The only thing I could get him to say, was, that he would regret to see the paper turned against him. Whatever was done had to be done without his knowledge. Bennett with his paper you know is a power.[4] The old fellow wanted to be noticed by Lincoln, and he wanted to support him. A friend of his who was certainly in his secrets (it came out through a woman when a Frenchman would say, "Who is she?")[5] came over to Washington and intimated if Lincoln would invite Bennett to come over and chat with him, his paper would be all right. Bennett wanted nothing, He simply wanted to be noticed. Lincoln in talking about N. said, "I understand N. Bennett has made a great deal of money, some say not very properly; now he wants me to make him respectable. I have never invited Mr. Bennett or Mr. Greely here — I shall not therefore, especially Mr. Bennett."

All Lincoln would say was, that he was receiving everybody and he should receive Mr. Bennett if he came. Notwithstanding his entire inaction, he never for a moment doubted his second nomination. One time in his room disputing with him as to who his real friends were; he told me if I would not show it, he would make a list of how the Senate stood. When he got through, I pointed out some five, or six that I told him I knew he was mistaken in. Said he, "You may think so, but you keep that until the Convention and tell me then whether I was right." He

---

4. James Gordon Bennett (1795–1872), editor of the New York *Herald*.
5. This parenthetical remark was omitted in the 1887 version.

was right to a man. He kept a kind of account book of how things were progressing for three, or four months, and whenever I would get nervous and think things were going wrong, he would get out his estimates and show how everything on the great scale of action — the resolutions of Legislatures, the instructions of delegates, and things of that character, was going exactly — as he expected. These facts with many others of a kindred nature have convinced me that he managed his politics upon a plan entirely different from any other man the country has ever produced. It was by ignoring men, and ignoring all small causes, but by closely calculating the tendencies of events and the great forces which were producing logical results.

In his conduct of the war he acted upon the theory that but one thing was necessary, and that was a united North. He had all shades of sentiments and opinions to deal with, and the consideration was always presented to his mind, How can I hold these discordant elements together?[6] Hence in dealing with men he was a trimmer, and such a trimmer the world has never seen. Halifax who was great in his day as a trimmer, would blush by the side of Lincoln. Yet Lincoln never trimmed in principles — it was only in his conduct with men. He used the patronage of his office to feed the hunger of these various factions. Weed always declared that he kept a regular account book of his appointments in New York, dividing the various tit-bits of favor so as to give each faction more than it could get from any other source; yet never enough to satisfy its appetite. They all had access to him; they all received favors from him; and they all complained of ill-treatment; but while unsatisfied, they all had "large expectations," and saw in him the chance of getting more than from any one else — they were sure of getting in his place. He used every force to the best possible advantages. He never wasted anything, and would always give more to his enemies than he would to his friends, and the reason was, because he never had anything to spare, and in the close calculation of attaching the factions to him; he counted upon the abstract affection of his friends as an element to be offset against some gift with which he must appease his enemies. Hence, there was always some truth in the charge of his friends that he failed to reciprocate their devotion with his favors. The reason was that he had only just so much to give away — "He always had more horses than oats." An adhesion of all forces was indispensable to his success and the success of the country; hence, he husbanded his means with a nicety of calculation. Adhesion was what he wanted; if he got it gratuitously, he never wasted his substance paying for it.

His love of the ludicrous was not the least peculiar of his characteristics. His love of fun made him overlook everything else but the point of the joke sought after. If he told a good story that was refined and had a sharp point, he did not like it any the better because it was refined. If it was outrageously low and dirty,

---

6. In revising this letter in 1887, Swett at this point added: "It was here that he located his own greatness as a President. One time, about the middle of the war, I left his house about eleven o'clock at night, at the Soldiers' Home. We had been discussing the discords in the country, and particularly the States of Missouri and Kentucky. As we separated at the door he said, 'I may not have made as great a President as some other men, but I believe I have kept these discordant elements together as well as anyone could.'"

he never seemed to see that part of it. If it had the sharp ring of wit, nothing ever reached him but the wit. Almost any man that will tell a very vulgar story, has got in a degree a vulgar mind, but it was not so with him. With all his purity of character and exalted morality and sensibilty, which no man can doubt, when hunting for wit, he had no ability to discriminate between the vulgar and the refined — substances from which he extricated it. It was the wit he was after — the pure jewel, and he would pick it up out of the mud, or dirt just as readily as he would from a parlor table.

He had very great kindness of heart. His mind was full of tender sensibilities; he was extremely humane, yet while these attributes were fully developed in his character and unless intercepted by his judgement controlled him, they never did control him contrary to his judgment. He would strain a point to be kind, but he never strained to breaking. Most of men of much kindly feeling are controlled by this sentiment against their judgment, or rather that sentiment beclouds their Judgment. It was never so with him. He would be just as kind and generous as his judgment would let him be — no more. If he ever deviated from this rule, it was to save life. He would sometimes I think, do things he knew to be impolitic and wrong to save some poor fellow's neck. I remember one day being in his room when he was sitting at his table with a large pile of papers before him. After a pleasant talk, he turned quite abruptly and said, "Get out of the way, Swett; to morrow is butcher-day, and I must go through these papers and see if I cannot find *some excuse* to let these poor fellows off."

The pile of papers he had were the records of Courts Martial of men who on the following day were to be shot. He was not examining the Records to see whether the evidence sustained the findings. He was purposely in search of occasions to evade the law in favor of life. I was one time begging for the life of a poor devil.[7] It was an outrageously bad case — I confessed I was simply begging. After sitting with his head down while I was talking, he interrupted me saying — "Grant never executed a man did he?" "I have been watching that thing."[8] Some of Mr. Lincoln's friends insisted that he lacked the strong attributes of personal affection which he ought to have exhibited. I think this is a mistake. Lincoln had too much justice to run a great government for a few favorites, and the complaints against him in this regard when properly digested amount to this, and no more: that he would not abuse the privileges of his situation.

He was certainly a very poor hater. He never judged men by his like, or dislike for them. If any given act was to be performed, he could understand that his enemy could do it just as well as any one. If a man had maligned him, or been guilty of personal ill-treatment and abuse, and was the fittest man for the place, he would put him in his Cabinet just as soon as he would his friend. I do not think he ever removed a man because he was his enemy, or because he disliked him.

The great secret of his power as an orator, in my judgment, lay in the clearness and perspicuity of his statements. When Lincoln had stated a case, it was al-

---

7. In the margin: *devil.*
8. Omitted from the 1887 version: "I was one time . . . watching that thing."

ways more than half argued and the point more than half won.[9] The first impression he generally conveyed was, that he had stated the case of his adversary better and more forcibly, than his opponent could state it himself. He then answered that state of facts fairly and fully, never passing by, or skipping over a bad point. When this was done, he presented his own case. There was a feeling when he argued a case, in the mind of any man who listened to him, that nothing had been passed over; yet if he could not answer the objections he argued in his own mind and himself arrived at the conclusion to which he was leading others; he had very little power of argumentation. The force of his logic was in conveying to the minds of others the same clear and thorough analysis he had in his own, and if his own mind failed to be satisfied, he had no power to satisfy any body else. His mode and force of argument was in stating how he had reasoned upon the subject and how he had come to his conclusion, rather than original reasoning to the hearer, and as the mind of listener, followed in the groove of his mind, his conclusions were adopted.[10] He never made sophistical argument in his life, and never could make one. I think he was of less real aid in trying a thoroughly bad cause, than any man I was ever associated with. If he could not grasp the whole case and master it; he was never inclined to touch it.

From the commencement of his life to its close, I have sometimes doubted whether he ever asked anybody's advice about anything. He would listen to everybody; he would hear everybody, but he never asked for opinions. I never knew him in trying a law-suit to ask the advice of any lawyer he was associated with. As a politican and as President he arrived at all his conclusions from his own reflections, and when his opinion was once formed he never had any doubt but what it was right.

You ask me whether he changed his religious opinions towards the close of his life. I think not. As he became involved in matters of the gravest importance, full of great responsibility and great doubt, a feeling of religious reverence, and belief in God — his justice and overruling power — increased upon him. He was full of natural religion; he believed in God as much as the most approved Church member; Yet he judged of Providence by the same system of great generalization as of everything else. He had in my judgment very little faith in ceremonials and forms. Whether he went to Church once a month or once a year troubled him but very little. He failed to observe the Sabbath very scrupulously. I think he read "Petroleum V. Nasby" as much as he did the Bible. He would ridicule the Puritans, or swear in a moment of vexation;[11] but yet his heart was full of natural and cultivated religion. He believed in the great laws of truth, the rigid discharge of duty, his

---

9. In 1887 Swett inserted at this point: "It is said that some one of the crowned heads of Europe proposed to marry when he had a wife living. A gentleman, hearing of this proposition, replied, how could he? 'Oh,' replied his friend, 'he could marry and then he could get Mr. Gladstone to make an explanation about it.' This was said to illustrate the convincing power of Mr. Gladstone's statement.

"Mr. Lincoln had this power greater than any man I have ever known."

10. This sentence was omitted in the 1887 version.

11. For "Whether he went . . . moment of vexation;" Swett in 1887 substituted "In fact he cared nothing for the form of anything."

accountability to God, the ultimate triumph of right, and the overthrow of wrong. If his religion were to be judged by the line and rule of Church Creeds and unexceptionable language, he would fall far short of the standard; but if by the higher rule of purity of conduct, of honesty of motive, of unyielding fidelity to the right and acknowledging God as the Supreme Ruler, then he filled all the requirements of true devotion and love of his neighbor as himself.

One great public mistake of his character is generally received and acquiesced in: — he is considered by the people of this country as a frank, guileless, unsophisticated man. There never was a greater mistake. Beneath a smooth surface of candor and an apparent declaration of all his thoughts and feelings, he exercised the most exalted tact and the wisest discrimination. He handled and moved man *remotely* as we do pieces upon a chessboard. He retained through life, all the friends he ever had, and he made the wrath of his enemies to praise him. This was not by cunning, or intrigue in the low acceptation of the term, but by far seeing, reason and discernment. He always told enough only, of his plans and purposes, to induce the belief that he had communicated all; yet he reserved enough, in fact, to have communicated nothing. He told all that was unimportant with a gushing frankness; yet no man ever kept his real purposes more closely, or penetrated the future further with his deep designs. + + +[12]

I wish I had time to add some things and on the whole to make this shorter and better, but I have not.

I shall try, if desirable, to give you points from time to time, but you will please remember they are confidential.

Yours Truly
Leonard Swett

HL: LN2408, 2:90–105

125. Nathaniel Grigsby to WHH

Gentryville, Jan. 21st. 1866

Sir:

I am seated this good evening to try to answe some questions you wish to now which i sall do to the bes of my recollection. you wish to now what songs the commin people sung   we sung what is called carnel songs and love songs i cannot repeat any of them at this time   We sung a song called Barbra allen also we sung the Silk Merchant daughter and others i do not recollect   the religious people sung   Am i a solder of the Cross, a folier of the lamb and O When shall i se Jesus and reign with him above and Come thou fount of every blessing and Jesus my all to heaven is gone he whom i fix my hopes upon,[1] they were the most commin songs

---

12. Probably intended by the copyist as an elision.

---

1. "Am I a Soldier of the Cross" is by Isaac Watts; "Come Thou Fount" is by Robert Robinson; "Barbara Allen" and "The Silk Merchant's Daughter" are traditional English songs.

sung amongst the cristion people in the yeares you allude to, these songs is in Dupees Hims[2] which was mainly use at that time, i cannot tel you what his notions of the bible he a was great tallker on the scriptures and read it a great deal, he talked about religion as other persons did but i donot now his view on religion   he never made any profession while in Ind that i now of, Mr Lincoln while in Ind always apered Cheerful and not gloomy he also tried to make all a round him Cheerful also wile in Ind he alway attended hous raisings log rolling corn shucking and workings of all kinds he also atended plases of amusements but not plases of vice and crime i was rong in the date of the marriges of Charles and Reuben Grigsby   they were maried the 16 of April 1829   the Cronicals of Reuben was in the same yeare only a few months after   i supose you have got them i think they are correctly writen   i sent by express the lawbook that Mr Lincoln read in Ind,[3] i heare that *[illegible]* Masterson has the book that Mr Lincoln pulled foder for that is the life of Washington with his owne name in it riten by himsef if so i shall get it and send it to you   mr Mastison lives some dictance from here you must excuse my not riting more promply is not because i am dis pleased with you it has partly   neglect and pat for time, i do not think of any thing more at presant

I yet remain youre cincere friend and fellow servent
N Grigsby

PS

pleas let me here from you soon

LC: HW2434; HL: LN2408, 1:297–99

126. Abner Y. Ellis to WHH

Moro, Ill January 23rd 1866

Freind Herndon

I blocked out those remissences with the intention to coppy them but I do not feel able at present to do so I therefore send them as they are as I Know you are acquainted with my way of talking and Expessing Myself   Excuse bad spelling and *blots* and after you have gethered what you May think assenshal please burn them.

Oh I am allmost tempted to burn those pages up for I am fearfull that you will not be able to Make any Sence out of them do not let any person Except yourself see them

Yours Truly
A. Y. Ellis

---

2. See §72, note 6.

3. Presumably *Revised Laws of Indiana* (1824). See §85, note 2.

[Enclosure]

127. Abner Y. Ellis (statement for WHH)

I, Abner Y. Ellis,

First became acquainted with Capt. Abraham Lincoln in New Salem then Sangamon County, shortly after his return from the Black Hawk war — but not intimately untill the Summer and fall of 1833, in that year I went to New Salem with a stock of goods belonging to Mr N A Garland now of Springfield I then became I may say intimately acquainted with him We boarded at the Same log Tavern Kept by Henry Onstott and afterwards by Mr Nelson Ally   During my stay their he was not engaged in any partcular business, but I think he was preparing himself of Surveying   I remember he had an old form Book from which he used in writing Deeds, Wills & Letters when desired to do so by his freinds and neighbours, he also used a Small Size Dictionary when engaged in Writing. He also used to assist Me in the Store on busy days, but he allways disliked to wait on the Ladies he prefered trading with the Men & Boys as he used to Say

I also remember that he Used to sleep in the store on the Counter when they had two Much Company at the Tavern.

I also remember that Mr Lincoln was in those days a Verry shy Man of Ladies — On one occasion while we boarded at this Tavern there came a family Containing an old Lady her Son and Three stilish Daughters from the State of Virginia and stoped their for 2 or 3 weeks and during theer stay I do not remember of Mr Lincoln Ever eating at the Same table when they did. I then thought it was on account of his awkward appearance and his wareing apparel.

I well remember how he was dressed he wore flax & tow linnen pantaloons[1] — I thought about 5 inches too short in the legs and frequently he had but one Suspender — no vest or Coat   he Wore a Calico Shert Such as he had in the black Hawk War   he wore coarse Brogans Tan Couler   Blue Yarn Socks & straw Hat — old style and without a band

Salem in those days was a hard place for a temperate young Man like Mr Lincoln was and I have often wondered how he could be so exremely popular and and not drink and Carouse with them   he Used to run footraces & jump with the boys and also play ball   I am certain he Never Drank any intoxicating liquors he did not in those days even smoke or chew Tobacco. He was Great at Telling storys and anecdotes & I think that was one great reason of his beaing So popular with   It has been Said by Some that Mr Lincoln used to Keep a Dogery in New Salem, I think I Can tell how that story originated during Mr Lincolns resedence ther a young Man by the Name of Wm Bery Kept a store there and he had Liquors to sell and he became so fond of it himself that his freinds got Mr Lincoln to take an interest in the busines Which lasted only a few Months — to get red of the liquor trade — Berry however died and his freinds took charge Concern   Berry & Lincoln I understand Make No debts — & Berrys freinds paid

---

1. A coarse, heavy linen used in making clothes.

Mr Lincoln for his Servces by the Month   In the year of 1834 Mr Lincoln was persuaded by his old freind Bowling Green to become a candidate for the State Legislator   He was then in intire stranger to the people of Springfield in fact I am of the opinion that he New Very few persons except Myself and Blankenship[2]   when he came their he in those days put his horse in My old Jail stable that now stands Just back of Mesrs Withers & Bros shop —   I Had a room Just whare Concert Hall Now stands[3] and he staid with me Nights. I introduced him to the Leading Men of the old Whig party and they Elected him — and he afterwards removed to Springfield and read Law with J T Stuart I think

I Must tell you of Mr Lincolns appearance and Costums when he first Made his debut before the Sangamon audience

He wore a mixt Jeans Coat Claw hammer stile, short in the sleaves and bob tail in fact it was so short in the tail he could Not sit on it, Flax & Tow linnen Pantaloons and a Straw Hat I think he wore a vest but I do not remember how it looked he then wore Potmetal Boots[4] — I accompanied him on one of his electionarying trips to the Island Grove and he Make a Speach which pleased his party friends Very Well indeed — though some of the Jackson Men tried to Make sport of him, He told several anecdotes in his Speach and applyed them as I thought Verry Well   He also told the Boys Several Storys which drew them after him   I remember them but Modesty and my Veneration for his Memory forbids me to relate   I have a coppy of his first speach hear it is

Gentlemen and fellow citizens   I presume you all Know who I am   I am humble Abraham Lincoln   I have been Solicited by Many freinds to become a candidate for the Legislature   My politicks are short and sweet like the old Womans dance. I am in favor of a National bank. I am in favor of the internal improvement system and a high protective Tariff — These are my sentiments and politicle principles   if Elected I shall be thankful if not it will be all the Same[5]

As to the questions you ask concerning his habitts &c &c. I shall endeavor to do so the best I can

I think Mr Lincoln Was Not as high minded as a man of his honor and Integrity ought to have been for instance Just think of his low flung, black guard story   Many of them was redicilus as we both Know

Mr. L.— I think had no desire for strange woman I never heard him speak of any *particular Woman* with disresect though he had Many opportunities for doing so while in Company with J.F.S. and W*m* B two old rats in that way.

As to the books he read I do Not Know Much. I recollect of one Novel he read and recommended to Me it was George Balcomb[6] your Brother Elliot procured it for me and I read it   The plot commenced in and about St Louis and ended in Virginia I was interesting and exciting —   I think he read some of Tom Pains

2. Presumably Eli C. Blankenship (1800–1865), a Springfield merchant.
3. The Concert Hall was on the north side of Washington Street, between Fifth and Sixth Streets.
4. Work shoes made of hard, coarse black leather.
5. Ellis probably copied this from the *Illinois State Journal.* See §10, note 2.
6. Nathaniel Beverly Tucker, *George Balcombe: A Novel* (New York, 1836).

Works as he frequently spoke of Pains Book Common Since[7]   he once asked Me
if I had ever Read Volneys ruins[8] he Said he had and supposed that I had by My
calling my oldest son Volney, though I had never read them and never wished to

He never recommended me to read them Neither he speak in favor of them.

I rember too of his reading Some of Mrs C. L. Hentys[9] beautiful storys; one
in particular the prize story the Mob Cap[10] he said he wished he Could See the
Play

He was verry fond of short storys one & two columns long, like

Cousin Sally Dillard —
Becky Wilsons Courtship
The down Easter & the Bull,[11]

How a bashful Young man became a Marrid man with 5 little bashful Boys,
& How he and his read headed Wife became Millerits[12] and before they were to
ascend they agreed to Make a clean breast of it to each other   The old Man insisted that the Wife Should own up first as she had primsed in her Marriage Vow
to first obay her husband   Well Dear said she our little Sammy is Not your
child   well Said the husband whoes is he   Oh Dear Said She, he is the one Eyed
Shoe Maker he came to see Me once when you was away and in an vil hour I Gave
way   Well said the husband is the rest mine   No said she they belong to the
Neighbourhood

Well Said the old Man I am ready to leave; *Gabarial blow your horn.*

I have thought that Mr. L. had something to do with its getting up he used to
tell it with Embellishments. I suppose you have heard him telling it   he Said he
Never saw a Millerite but what he thought of the story

I remember once of Seeing Mr L out of temper & Laughing at the Same time.
it was at New Salem the boys were having a Jollification after an Election They
had a large fire Made of shavings & hemp [herds?], and Some of the Boys Made a
bet with a fellow that I shall call Ike that he could not run his little bob tail Poney
through the fire. Ike took them up — and trotted his Poney back about one hundred Yards, to give him a good start as he said. The boys all formed a line on Either side to Make Way for Ike & his poney presently hear he came full tilt With
he hat off & Just as he reached the blazing fire raised in his saddle for the Jump
Strait ahead but Poney was not of the Same opinion So he flew the track and
pitched poor Ike into the devouring Ellement   Mr L. Saw it and run to his as-

---

7. Thomas Paine, *Common Sense* (1776).

8. Constantin F. Volney, *The Ruins; or, A Survey of the Revolutions of Empires* (New York, 1796 [first American translation]).

9. Caroline Lee Whiting Hentz (1800–1856).

10. Caroline Lee Hentz, *The Mob Cap: And Other Tales* (Philadelphia, 1850?).

11. "Cousin Sally Dilliard" is by Hamilton C. Jones (1798–1868); the others are not identified.

12. Followers of William Miller (1782–1849), a New York farmer, who predicted that the world would end between March 21, 1843, and March 21, 1844.

sistance saying You have Carried this thing far enough   I could see that he Was Mad though he Could Not help laughing himself   the poor fellow Was Concderably scorched about the head & face   Jack Armstrong took him to the Dr who shaved his head to fix him up & put salve on the burn &c &c   I think M L Was a little Mad at Armstrong & Jack himself was Verry Sorry for it   Jack gave Ike Next Morning a Dram his brakefast & a seal skin Cap & sent him home

At another time I Saw Mr L cry, it was at his old freind Bowling Greens Masonic funural[13]   Mr L Was to deliver and address on the occasion he Was on the stand but When he arose he only uttered a few Words & commenced choaking & sobing he told he listenes that he Was un Maned & could Not precede he got down and Went to Mrs Greens old family Carriage, and I Saw him No More that day   I supposed he Went home with Mrs Green & our lodge took Dinner in Petersburgh   I do not remember Who took the stand after M L. got down   Mr L Loved Mr Green as he did his Farther & Mr Green looked on him with pride and pleasur. I have heard Mr Green Say that there Was good Material in Abe and he only Wanted Education   Mr Green had some little acquaintance with Mr Lincolns Mothers family the Hanks and he thought he inherited his good Sence from the old Stock of his Mothers relations. I Myself New Old Billy Hanks his Mothers Brother — and he was a Verry sesible old Man — He Was farther to Mrs Dillon[14] on Spring creek & Charly Billy Jr & John was his Sons   They We all low flung Could Neither read or Write   Some of them Used to live in the Island Grove in Sangamon Co

allthough Mr L. Was Verry fond of fun he Never played any pranks on any body & he took few libertys with any one and I do Not think he wanted any one to take them With him but if they had he would not have complained. I have been reading Some of your Lectures & I am Glad that you have Studded him so well and I think you Know him Well Enough, without My Saying any thing of him after he Came to Springfield   I Never saw or heard of his playing Cards or gambing in any Way for money

It is Not Strange to Me that Mr L. Should have Such a Great passion For dirty Stories it was his Early training by the Hanks Boys his Cousins and after he left them he commenced a different train of thought and Studdie, Honesty Was bread in the Bone with him and Nothing could induce him to Swerve from the true path   He did Not reguard the Right of Petitions Much; provided he New the partys himself   This I Know to My Cost but I Suppose he was right in Not appointing Me P.M. in 1861 he Was I am Now Certin he opposed to Me from the begginning   I blamed Butler[15] and Old Duboice[16] for Making him think that Was Not for him in 1858

---

13. Bowling Green's Masonic funeral took place in Petersburg on September 3, 1842, several months after his death in February. For other references, see the index.
14. Elizabeth Hanks, who married Reason Ray and, after his death, married Samuel Dillon in 1837.
15. William Butler.
16. Jesse K. Dubois.

I once heard Mr. Lincoln tell an anecdote on Col Ethan Allen of Revolutionary notoriety which I have never heard from any one besides him and for your amusement I will try and tell it as well as I Can[17]

It appears that Shortly after we had pease with England Mr Allen had occasion to visit England, and while their the English took Great pleasure in teasing him, and trying to Make fun of the Americans and General Washington in particular and one day they got a picture of General Washington, and hung it up the Back House whare Mr Allen Could see it

and they finally asked Mr A if he saw that picture of his freind in the Back House.

Mr Allen said no. but said he thought that it was a very appropriate for an Englishman to Keep it   Why they asked, for said Mr Allen their is Nothing that Will Make an Englishman Shit So quick as the Sight of Genl Washington   And after that they let Mr Allens Washington alone

He Tell another on page 11[18]

Once upon a time but Not so long as to be forgotten

Mr Allen Went With a party of Young Men in Vermont to an apple pealing

And they Knowing that Mr Allen was rather inclined to beleave in ghost story they concluded they Would Slip away from him so he would have to return home alone. and it appears that their was a long covered Bridge through which they had to pass, & they concluded to wrap themselves up in White Sheets and station themselves at the further End of the Bridge and about the time that Mr Allen should reach the Meddle they Would apper to him but it appeard that Mr Allen Caught a glimpse of them on Comeing down the hill and he picked up a hand full of good Sized stones and carried them with him, and as soon as they made their appearanc   Mr Allen as follows. — Be Ye Men or Be. Ye Be. Ye. Men. I fear Ye Not And if Ye. Be. Ghosts these stones will not hurt Ye   It is Supposed that they vanished in a way better imagined than described[19]

You ask me if reccollect the first time I Saw Mr L. Yes I do

It was shortly after his flat Boat disater at or Near Salem dam, time corn planting time I was out Collecting back Tax for Genl James D. Henry.[20] I went from the Tavern down to Jacob Bales old Mill and their I first Saw Mr L he was Setting on a Saw log taking to Jack and Rial Armstrong and a Man by the Hohammer. I shook hands with the Armstrongs & Hohamer and was conversing with them a few Moments when we was Joined by My old freind and former townsman George Warberton pritty tight as Usual and he Soon asked Me to tell the old story about Ben Johnson and Mrs Dales Blue Dye &c &c which I did. and then Jack Armstrong Said Lincoln tell Ellis the story about Govenor Tickner his city bread son & his Negro Bob   Which he did with several others by Jacks Calling for them.

---

17. See also §326.
18. The next page of the document.
19. Cf. §51.
20. James Dougherty Henry (1797?–1834), sheriff of Sangamon County at this time.

I found out then that Mr L. was a Cousin to Charley Hanks of Island Grove I told him I New 3 of the Boys. Jo. Charley & John and his Uncle old Billey H who lived up on the North fork of Sangamon River afterwards Near Decature

The Hankes were most of them Red headed & freckel fased and verry unshosible Except Charley he Was funny to the Extreame. By the bye Mrs Samuel Dillon in springfield was a Hanks, and was once Mrs Rezin Ray[21]   I think she is still living —

— I do not think I am Making this Scribble of Much interest to you, for My Early acquaintance with Mr Lincoln is so Much associated With anecdotes & storys & If Ever any one should wish to publish his Joke Book I Could do Much better though Many of them would Never do to go to print, evin if they Could be so Shaped into Manuscript form

I onc heard him say in speaking religious denominations that he thought Baptism by imertion Was the true Meaning of the Word for said he John Baptised the Saviour in the river Jorden because their was Much Warter & they Went down into it and Came up out of it.[22]

He Was at one time Verry much taken with Josephus Hewetts preaching   Hewett was a Campbellite preacher[23]

LC: HW2435 (letter), HW5273–85; HL: LN2408, 1:399–411 (enclosure)

128. William G. Greene to WHH

Tallula Ills Jany 23rd 1866

Friend Herndon

Yours 16th Inst at hand   Mr Lincoln was considered an Intelligent well Read young man when he first Located at New Salem especially for those *Times*. I am not positive as to the year he wrote Potery in relation to Mrs. Noah *Gordon* & her *Geese*,[1] my impression is that it was 1825   I have seen the Poetry it was charmingly good I thought   he was well pleased with his effort himself. It is all *Bosh* that Mrs any body ever made Buckskin Breeches for Lincoln after he came to New Salem[2]   Mr Lincoln never Courted to my Knowledge but Two Girls in this Co the 1st a Miss Ann Rutledge he would have married her but she sickened & died the 2nd one was a Miss Owens of Greene Co. Ky she was a verry Talented Lady as much or more so than any Lady I ever Knew she and Lincoln disagreed a bout carrying a Neighbors child when on some ramble (or in other words what was true potiteness) neither would *yield* a hairs breadth   great God Herndon is not strange

---

21. See p. 173, note 14.
22. Cf. §310.
23. A Protestant sect (also known as Disciples of Christ), founded in Pennsylvania in 1809 by Thomas Campbell (1763–1854) and his son, Alexander Campbell (1788–1866).

---

1. Cf. §83.
2. See the index for references to this dispute.

that it takes this peculiar Freaks or trates to make great Men & women too   Miss Owens succeeded well in life too. Lincoln never thought of learning any Trade to my Knowledge after he came to New Salem

Verry Truly,

W G Greene

LC: HW2436; HL: LN2408, 1:483–84

129. Dennis F. Hanks to WHH

January 26 1866

Dere William

I am jest in Receipt of your Letter of Enquire   I haston to Answer

question 1st   how, Many Acres Corn wheat   I No Exactly for I helped Do it   They had a Bout — 10 — acres of Corn and a Bout 5 Acres of wheat 2. acres of oates one acre of medow   This is in Indiana in 1824 Very Little Change to 1830

2d   was Lincoln warme harted   this is Abes farther   I Say he was   he loved his Relitives Do any thing for them he could   No Better Man then old Tom Lincoln Abes farther   I have Known him Neare 50 years

Very quiet Not hasty temper treted Me well

3d   Did Abrham Lincoln treat John. D. Johnston   I will Say this Much a Bout it   I think Abe Dun more for John than he desved   John thought that Abe did not Do a Nuff for the old people they Be Cum Enimes for awhile on this ground   I Dont want to tell all the thing that I No it would Not Look well in history   I Say this Abe treated John well

4th   What kind of a Man was Johnston   I Say this much   a Kinder harted Man Never was in Coles County Ill   Nor an honester man   I Dont Say this Because he was My Brother in Law I Say it Noing it   John Did Not Love to work any of the Best   I plaged him for Not working

5th   Did Ever Thomas Lincoln Send any produce to Neworeleans   Not from Indiana   he Did Not Jest Raised a Nuf for his own use he Did Not Send any produce to any other place Mor than Bought his Shugar and Coffee and Such Like   he was a Very pore man —

6th   Did Thos Lincoln trate Abe cruly   He loved him   I Never Could tell whether Abe Loved his farther Very well or Not   I Dont think he Did for Abe was one of those forward Boys   I have Seen his farther Nock him Down of the fence when a Stranger would Call for Information to neighbour house   Abe allways would have the first word

the Old Man Loved his Childern

7th   Did any of the Johnston family ask for office   No Thomas Johnston[1]

---

1. Thomas L. D. Johnston, son of Lincoln's stepbrother, John Johnston.

went to Abe he got this permit to take degarytipes in the army   this is all for they ar all Ded Except Johns Boys   they Did Not ask for any

8th   Did you or John Hanks Lincoln for any office   I Say this that John Hanks of Decatur Did Solisit him for an Indian Agency and John told Me that Abe Did as good as told him he Should have one But John Could Not Read or write   I think this was the Reason that Abe Did Not give John the place

As for My Self I Did Not aske Abe rite out for an office onely this I would Like to have the post office in Charleston   This was My wife that asked him   He told hir that Much was understood as much as to Say that I would get it   I Did Not Care Much a Bout it

9th   Do you think Lincoln Card for his Relations   I will Say this Much when he was with us he Seemed to think a great Deal of us but I thought Sum times it was hipocritical But I am Not Shore

As for his ant in Coles County he Never had any Nor I Dont No any person that he called ant if it was So I would have Known Sumthing a Bout it

William ask all questions you want   I am Very cirtin I Can answer them[2]

Yours Respectffully

D. F. Hanks.

LC: HW2437–38; HL: LN2408, 1:260–63

130. Charles Friend to Dennis Hanks

Hodgenville Jan 27th 1866

Dear Sir

yours of the 18 Inst was handed me a day or two since by the Post Master of this place. And would say in answer that I am a Grandson of Charles Friend who lived on the Greensburg Road 3 miles S.E of this place. Grandpa has been Dead 21 years last Aug. My Father (Fielding) whom you seem to have forgotten, is also Dead he Died in Oct /'52 at West Point Ky. Leaving My Mother & Six Children. I'll give you the mames agreeable to age: Harriet. M. Charles, John C, Robt C, James E, and Richard C. The oldes My Sister is married to a Mr A. H. Redman and Has two Children Chas. & James   Grandpa at his death left a widow and 9 Children three of whom are dead, Harriet Fielding & Elizy.

Uncles Richd & Robt live on the old place Uncle Jno Aunts Lydia Kitty & Matilda all Live in this county   Aunt Harriet Mayfield died in Missouri last August   Grandma is still living on the old place with uncle Robt the old Lady is Eighty Three years Old   I carried your letter out to Uncle Rob's but grandma was not at home. Uncle Richard said he remembered you well. Grandma remembers you for she has often told me of you and said that she would like to see you and would would write if she knew where to direct to. I passed through your town

2. WHH note on docketing: *Hank's Sober this time.*

last Sept and had I have known that you lived there I would have given you a
Call   Wer you in Indianapolis Ind. last Winter when the corpse of A Lincoln was
in state there. If you was we was clost to gather   I was there and seen the President.

The old Man Geo Brownfield[1] is dead but some of the Children live on the
old place. Jacob Elliott lives on the old Homestead, and Jno lives in Mo. Thomas
Creal is dead & Rich'd lives 3 miles from this place on the place of A Lincoln Birth.
You say in your letter that you are a Cousin of the late President.

The old settlers of this place was under the impression that you was half Brothers you Mother being same. Old Uncle Wm Cessna[2] is still living. Some 87 or 8
year of age   J. F. Cessna his son lives in this place was Judge of the County before the War. he remembers you.

Nothing More only I Remain

Yours Truly

Charles Friend.

LC: HW2439–40; HL: LN2408, 1:58–60

131. Abner Y. Ellis to WHH

Moro, Illinois   Jany 30th 1866

Freind Herndon

I am in recipt of your favor of the 28th and its Contents flatters me verry much
for I was fearful that you Could not make sense out of it —   I did intend to
Coppy it but laziness was my only Excuse and since I have wished a dozen time
that I had. but their is No Use talking Now You have it as it is up to the time he
Moved to your city Since then I have Said but little

I Shall Now endeavour to answer the questions proposed by you

Mr Lincoln I do not think belonged to any Secret Society Neither Masonic or
Oddfellows   I once heard Judge Denney[1] ask him if he was Not a Mason And
his answer Was I do Not belong to any society except it be for the Good of my
Country

The Judge asked him if he Was Not a Member of any Church his answer was
No   This Conversation was in the Store of Messrs Condell Jones &c[2] in the year
of — 1844

I lived in New Salem in the Summer & fall of 1833 I left Mr Lincoln their.
Rowen or James Herndon Was Not there at the time I Was

---

1. Candidate for Lincoln's father. See the index.
2. Another candiate for Lincoln's father. See the index.

---

1. Possibly William A. Denning (ca. 1817–56), a supreme court justice (1847–48) and judge of the Third
Circuit (1848–54).
2. Condell, Jones and Co., a Springfield mercantile firm, where Ellis was once employed.

I Cant remember the Year that Bowling Green died it Was after the year 1840.
Mr L used to read at Nights Wen in New Salem

he used to Read Shakespear & Burns in Springfield   He read this Novel
George Balcomb[3] in New Salem also Tom Pain & Volney.[4] As to the News papers
I Cant think of any he used to read Except the old Sangamo Journal   as to what
he Used to Eat I do not know but I think he was Not Verry particular in what he
Eaten   he Was fond of Pop Corn I remember

His speach in 1834 Was Verry — clear & Logical but he was Not verry self
possesed   he was a timid I thought

I do Not rember of Ever hearing him talk politicks in 1833   Neither do I
remember of his reading any thing More than I have Named and Whether he read
them through or Not I do Not Know

Oh Yes   I once loned him Some Play Book to read   I have them yet   They
wer as follows

The Wept of the Wishton Wish
" Lady or Lyons
" Illustorus Strange
" The Hypocrite
" Poor Pillicoddy[5]

William I think that Mr Lanning or Mr Lukins of Petersburgh could give you
conciderable information concerning his early history in Sangamon Count as they
were then his early associates also James Short I beleave I have answ all that you
desired but if you think of anything More Just Command Me

& I am You Obd Sevt
A. Y. Ellis

P.S. I should be delighted to have a Coppy of the Life of Abraham Lincoln by My
old freind Wm. H. Herndon

Extra

W*m* do you remember of Mr. Lincolns having a political — set to — Withe
Judge Jesse B Thomas in or on the old Court room steps in what Was Called
Hoffman Row —   When Mr L Made the Judge Cry by Mimicing him — I do

and at another time how he got Judge Logan once in the Cour room   By
informing the Jury that the Judge Was a Verry Knowing Lawyer but Said M L as
Smart as he is he dose Not Know that he has his shirt on with the pleated Bosom

3. See §127, note 6.
4. See §127, notes 7–8.
5. *The Wept of Wish Ton Wish: A Drama, in Two Acts* (1856) was based on James Fenimore Cooper's novel (1829) of the same name; Edward Bulwer-Lytton, *The Lady of Lyons: or, Love and Pride. A Play, in Five Acts* (first American edition, 1838); James Kenney, *The Illustrious Stranger; or, Married and Buried, an Operatic Farce in Two Acts* (1827?); *The Hypocrite* is the name of a play by Molière and also by Colley Cibber; John M. Morton, *Poor Pillicoddy: A Farce, in One Act* (Philadelphia, ca. 1845).

behind it Was a New Shirt that the Judge had Not Noticed very particular When he put it on   They Were Made to button the Collar band behind in those days

do you remember anything about his Mechanical jenious He in the year 1849 Mad a Model for a steam ship   I think he took it to Washington   I have Seen it   He Worked at it in Walter Davis' Shop   He liked Walter for Some Cause I never knew   he also liked James Short & Bowling Green and also Joshua F Speed & he allways thanked Josh for his Mary   I Know Many things about that *Match*

If I am Not Mistaken Mr Lincoln was Nomenated for the Legislater in the Year 1834 but Was Defeated

He Must have Studyed Law before he Came to Springfield but With Whomb I do Not Know

I think he had read Conciderable before he Came to New Salem but Not Law Books

When he first Came to New Salem he had Something to do With a Man Named Offut   I think he Was a Merchant in fact I Know he Was. (Whare is Offut   do You Know if he is living he is the Man that Could tell all about his first Coming to Salem &c &c

Lincoln Was Onc Post Master at New Salem under M Adams or Jackson. I guess it was Jackson

Felix Green is anothe Man that New him in his younger days. Bill & Nult was too Young then

LC: HW2443–45, HW2460–61; HL: LN2408, 1:411–15

132. Joseph Gillespie to WHH

Edwardsville 31st Jany 1866

Dr Sir

Yours enclosing a sketch of your lecture on the character of Mr Lincoln[1] is recd and I must say that I think you have delineated him with great truth & force   You wish me to give you my views & recollections respecting him   Ever since his death I have been endeavoring to recall to mind his prominent traits of character and I must confess that the task is no easy one   Mr Lincoln had but few peculiarities & hardly an eccentricity   His mind was made up of the traits which belong to mankind generally   He was a remarkably temperate man; eschewing every indulgence not so much as it seemed to me, from principle as from a want of appetites   I never heard him declaim against the use of tobacco or other stimulants although he never indulged in them   He was genial but not very sociable   He did not seek company but when he was in it he was the most entertaining person I ever knew   He was once pressed into service to entertain Mr Van Buren at Rochester in your County & he succeeded to admiration[2]   Mr

---

1. Probably WHH's long lecture delivered in two parts on December 12 and 26, 1865.
2. Former President Van Buren visited Rochester, Illinois, and then Springfield, June 16–19, 1842.

Lincoln was ambitious but not very aspiring   He was anxious to be in Congress but I think he never aspired to any thing higher untill the prospect for the Presidency burst upon him   I am very sure that Mr Lincoln was not aware of his own abilities or standing & that he never expected to attain a very marked distinction   In 1858 he made a speech in this place & had an appointment for one next day at Greenville   I took him out in my buggy   On the way the principal subject of conversation was the canvass he was conducting with Mr Douglass   Knowing Lincolns power of using anecdotes I asked why he did not employ them in the discussion   He replied that he thought the occasion was too grave & serious   He said that the principal complaint he had to make against Mr Douglass was his continual assumption of superiority on account of his elevated position   Mr Lincolns idea was that in the discussion of great questions nothing adventious should be lugged in as a make weight   That was contrary to his notions of *fairness*   His love of wealth was very weak   I asked him on the trip above spoken of how much land he owned   He said that the house & lot he lived on and one forty acre tract was all the real estate he owned and that he got the Forty for his services in the Black Hawk war[3]   I inquired why he never speculated in land and pointed to a tract that I had located with a land warrant which cost me ninety cents an acre   He said he had no capacity whatever for speculation and never attempted it   All the use Mr Lincoln had for wealth was to enable him to appear respectable   He never hoarded nor wasted but used money as he needed it and gave himself little or no concern about laying up   He was the most indulgent parent I ever knew   His children litterally ran over him and he was powerless to withstand their importunities   He was remarkably tender of the feelings of others & never wantonly offended even the most despicable although he was a man of great nerve when aroused   I have seen him on several occasions display great heroism when the circumstances seemed to demand it   He was very sensitive where he thought he had failed to come up to the expectations of his friends   I remember a case   He was pitted by the Whigs in 1840 to debate with Mr Douglass the Democratic champion   Lincoln did not come up to the requirements of the occasion   He was conscious of his failure and I never saw any man so much distressed   He begged to be permitted to try it again and was reluctantly indulged and in the next effort he transcended our highest expectations   I never heard & never expect to hear such a triumphant vindication as he then gave of Whig measures or policy   He never after to my knowledge fell below himself

In religious matters Mr Lincoln was *theoretically* a predestinarian   His stem logic & perhaps early bias led him to that result   He was never ashamed of the poverty and obscurity of his early life   He was thoroughly master of all the phases of frontier life and woods craft and his most amusing stories consisted of incidents

---

3. AL was entitled to a forty-acre military bounty by virtue of the Act of September 28, 1850, and to 120 acres more by the Act of March 3, 1855. The smaller tract was located in Tama County, Iowa; the larger tract, which Lincoln did not locate until 1859, was in Crawford County, Iowa.

in his boyish days amongst his country play fellows   He had a marvelous relish for every thing of that sort and the happiest faculty of turning his numerous reminiscences to good account in illustration in after life   No man could tell a story as well as he could   He never missed the nib of an anecdote   He always maintained stoutly that the best stories originated with Country boys & in the rural districts   He had great faith in the strong sense of Country People and he gave them credit for greater intelligence than most men do   If he found an idea prevailing generally amongst them he believed there was something in it although it might not harmonize with science   He had great faith in the virtues of the *mad stone*[4] although he could give no reason for it and confessed that it looked like superstition but he said he found the People in the neighborhood of these stones fully impressed with a belief in their virtues from actual experiment and that was about as much as we could ever know of the properties of medicines   Mr Lincoln had more respect for & confidence in the masses than any statesman this Country has ever produced   He told me in the spring of 1864 that the People were greatly ahead of the politicians in their efforts for and confidence in putting down the rebellion   He said the government had been driven by the public voice into the employment of means & the adoption of measures for carrying on the war which they would not have dared to put into practise without such backing   He prized the suggestions of the unsophisticated People more than what was called State craft or political wisdom   He really believed that the voice of the People in our emergency was next thing to the voice of God He said he had no doubt whatever of our success in overthrowing the rebellion at the right time   God he said was with us and the People were behaving so nobly that all doubt had been removed from his mind as to our ultimate success   The Army & the Navy he said were in the right trim & the right hands   He firmly believed that no People in ancient or modern times had evinced as much patriotism or such a self sacrificing spirit as the loyal People of the United States   But Mr Lincolns love of justice & fair play was his predominating trait   I have often listened to him when I thought he would certainly state his case out of court   It was not in his nature to assume or attempt to bolster up a false position   He would abandon his case first   He did so in the case of Buckmaster for the use of Denhom vs Beems & Arthur[5] in our Supreme Court in which I happened to be opposed to him   Another gentleman less fastidious took Mr Lincolns place and gained the case   In 1856, Mr. Lincoln had set his heart upon the U.S Senate   There was a majority for the first time in the history of Illinois against the Democratic party in the Legislature   This result was mainly attributed to his efforts and he was the first choice of all but five of the opposition members   I was a member & enthusiastically for Lincoln[6]   We (his friends) regarded this as perhaps his last chance for that high position   There was danger if we did not succeed in electing our

4. Usually calcium deposits from the guts of animals, madstones were thought to possess curative powers in cases of hydrophobia.
5. This case was argued before the Illinois Supreme Court on February 4, 1846.
6. Cf. §356.

man soon that some of the members who had been elected as free soilers would go over to Matteson & elect him   When the voting commenced to our amazement five of our men steadily refused to vote for Mr Lincoln & threw their votes upon judge Trumbull   After several ballots I went to Mr Lincoln and asked him what he thought we ought to do   He said unhesitatingly   "You ought to drop me and go for Trumbull   That is the only way you can defeat Matteson"   Judge Logan came up about that time and insisted on running Lincoln still   But the latter said if you do you will lose both Trumbull and myself and I think the cause in this case is to be preferred to men   We adopted his suggestion & turned upon Trumbull and elected him although it grieved us to the heart to give up Mr Lincoln   This I think shews that Mr Lincoln was capable of sinking himself for the cause in which he was engaged   Mr Lincolns sense of justice was intensely strong   It was to this mainly that his hatred of slavery may be attributed   He abhorred the institution   It was about the only public question on which he would become excited   I recollect meeting with him once at Shelbyville when he remarked that something must be done or slavery would overrun the whole country   He said there were about 600,000 non slave holding whites in Kentucky to about 33,000 slave holders   That in the convention then recently held it was expected that the delegates would represent these classes about in proportion to their respective numbers but when the convention assembled there was not a single representative of the non slaveholding class   Every one was in the interest of the slaveholders and said he this thing is spreading like wild fire over the Country   In a few years we will be ready to accept the institution in Illinois and the whole country will adopt it   I asked him to what he attributed the change that was going on in public opinion   He said he had put that question to a Kentuckian shortly before who answered by saying — you might have any amount of land, money in your pocket or bank stock and while travelling around no body would be any the wiser but if you had a darkey trudging at your heels every body would see him & know that you owned slaves — It is the most glittering ostentatious & displaying property in the world and now says he if a young man goes courting the only inquiry is how many negroes he or she owns and not what other property they may have   The love for Slave property was swallowing up every other mercenary passion   Its ownership betokened not only the possession of wealth but indicated the gentleman of leisure who was above and scorned labour   These things Mr Lincoln regarded as highly seductive to the thoughtless and giddy headed young men who looked upon work as vulgar and ungentlemanly   Mr Lincoln was really excited and said with great earnestness that this spirit ought to be met and if possible checked   That slavery was a great & crying injustice an enormous national crime and that we could not expect to escape punishment for it   I asked him how he would proceed in his efforts to check the spread of slavery   He confessed that he did not see his way clearly   I think he made up his mind from that time that he would oppose slavery actively   I know that Mr Lincoln always contended that no man had any right (other than mere brute force gave him) to a slave   He used to say that it was singular that the courts would hold that a man never lost his right to his property that had been stolen from him but that he instantly lost his right to himself if he was stolen   Mr Lincoln always contended that the cheapest way of getting rid of slavery was for the nation to buy the slaves & set them free   As you say Mr Lincoln could hardly be considered a genius, a poet, or an inventor but he had the qualities of a reformer   He endeavored to bring back things to the old land marks but he never would have attempted to invent and compose new systems   He had boldness enough when he found the building racked and going to decay to restore it to its original design but not to contrive a new & distinct edifice   He believed that the framers of our government expected slavery to die out and adapted the system to that and but that their views were being frustrated by adventitious circumstances and his aim was to restric[t i]t to its original design   Mr Lincoln had the appearance of being a slow thinker   My impression is that he was not so slow as he was careful   He never liked to put forth a proposition without revolving it over in his own mind but when he was compelled to act promptly as in debate he was quick enough   Douglass who was a very skilful controversialist never obtained any advantage over him   I never could discover any thing in Mr Lincolns mental composition remarkably singular   His qualities were those ordenarily given to mankind but he had them in remarkable degree   He was wonderfully kind, careful & just   He had an immense stock of common sense and he had faith enough in it to trust it in every emergency   He had passed through all the grades of society when he reached the Presidency and he had found common sense a sure reliance and he put it into practice   He acted all through his career upon just such principles as every man of good common sense would approve & say "that is just as I would have done myself"   There was nothing of the Napoleonic in his style of doing things   If he had been in Napoleons place he never would have gone off to Egypt to strike a blow at England & he would have been equally careful not to send an army to Moscow   Lincoln had no super human qualities (which we call genius) but he had those which belong to mankind generally in an astonishing degree   If I may be allowed the expression   Mr Lincoln was a great common man   He was a giant but formed & fashioned like other men   He only differed from most men in degree   He had only their qualities but then he had them in larger measure than any man of modern times   He loved the masses but was not strikingly partial to any particular individual   Mr Lincoln cared but little for minor elections but entered very zealously into important & general ones   Hence he was not generally successful at home & was not considered a good political organizer because he allowed the subordinate offices to be filled by those opposed to him   When he had a larger theatre to operate upon however it cannot be denied that he acted with great boldness & skill   He succeeded in breaking down the best organized party that ever existed in this, or any other Country and that under the lead of the most consummate chiefton we have ever had   Douglass was bold original & energetic   Polotics with him was a trade   It was only an episode in Mr Lincolns life   Douglass was idolized by his followers   Lincoln was loved by his   Douglass was the representative of his

partizans   Lincoln was the representative man of the unsophistocated People   Douglass was great in the estimation of his followers   Lincoln was good
in the opinion of his supporters   Douglass headed a party   Lincoln stood upon
a principle   Lincoln did not begin his operations for the Presidency at the head
of a party   He had the tact and good fortune to combine so much of the old Whig
& Democratic parties as rebelled against southern dictation, with the Free Soilers
proper, and thus secured a majority of the free States   At the time of his death
he had however succeeded in organizing a party   He had gained the confidence
of a majority of the whole People in his fitness for the place   All but the old
political hacks had settled down in the belief that he was master of the situation
& was the right man in the right place   The amazing popularity he obtained was
attributable to two things   He had been successful under the most trying circumstances and then he was most emphatically one of the People   He said and did
things in a way that commended itself to the public taste and so that all could
understand it   The masses are naturally delighted at seeing one of their own class
elevated if he proves competent and particularly if he succeeds by doing things in
their way   The idea that the affairs of State cannot be carried on in a plain common sense way is as old as the time of the Egyptian priesthood   Statesmen have
generally given countenance to this absurdity and inculcated the idea that state
craft was beyond the comprehension of ordinary mortals   When we found Mr
Lincoln administering the affairs of government with so much vigor & success we
felt proud of him   There was a strong tinge of sadness in Mr Lincolns composition   He was not naturaly disposed to look on the bright side of the
picture   He felt very strongly that there was more of discomfort than real happiness in human existence under the most favorable circumstances and the general current of his reflections was in that channel   He never obtruded these views
upon others but on the contrary strove as much as possible to be gay &
lively   There was a slight dash of what is generally called superstition in Mr Lincolns mind   He evidently believed that the perceptions were sometimes more
unerring than reason and outstripped it   I cant say that he fully believed in presentiments but he undoubtedly had gloomy forebodings as to himself. He told me
after his election that he did not count confidentially, on living to get through with
the task set before him; and I did not think that he apprehended death in the natural
way, still I do not believe that he took any precautions to guard against danger. I
met him once, coming alone from the war office to the White house, and remarked
to him that I thought he was exposing himself to danger of assassination. He replied that no precautions he could take would be availing if they were determined
to kill him. I rode out with him that evening to the soldiers home, when he was
accompanied by an escort of cavalry, on the way he said that the escort was rather
forced upon him by the military men, that he could see no certain protection
against assassination if it was determined to take away his life. He said it seemed
to him like putting up the gap in only one place when the fence was down all along

    Mr Lincoln was pre-eminently humane   He said to me once that Ould the
rebel commissioner for exchanges had just notified them that he had put 16000

of the men paroled at Vicksburg into the field without exchanging.[7] "Now" said he, "these men are liable to be put to death when recaptured for breach of parole   If we do not do something of that sort this outrage will be repeated on every occasion   What would you do under such circumstances? "Well" said I "that is too big a question for me"   "It is indeed a serious question"! Said Mr Lincoln, "and I have been more sorely tried by it than any other that has occurred during the war   It will be an act of great injustice to our soldiers to allow the paroled rebels to be put into the field without exchange   Such a practice would demoralize almost any army in the world if played off upon them   It would be nearly impossible to induce them to spare the lives of prisoners they might capture   On the other hand" said he, "these men were no doubt told by their superiors that they had been exchanged and it would be hard to put them to death under such circumstances, on the whole" said he "my impression is that mercy bears richer fruits than any other attribute"   Mr Lincoln was capable of immense physical & mental labor   His mind and body were in perfect harmony   He was verry powerful physically   He was reputed to be one of the best wrestlers in the country   The first time I saw him was in 1832 in the campaign against Black Hawk   He was engaged in wrestling with a man named Dow Thompson from St Clair Co[8]   The latter was the Champion of the Southern part of the State while Lincoln was put up as the champion from the North   I never heard Mr Lincoln complain of being fatigued   I think he was an utter stranger (in the early part of his life at least) to the feeling   I have heard him regret while he was President that it was impossible for him to give audience to all who wished to see him and I do not think he was disengaged for an instant from the time he assumed the Presidential office untill his death from the consideration of public affairs except when he was asleep   He was not in the habit of idolizing particular men and you would seldom hear him sounding the praises of any one   He admired Mr Clay & Mr Webster & had great respect for Gen Taylor   Of all men in the South (of those who differed from him on the slavery question I mean   Mr Stephens of Georgia was his favorite   I have frequently heard him speak in very respectful terms of Stephens   On the other hand he never manifested any bitter hatred towards his enemies   It was enough for him in a controversy to get the better of his adversary in argument without descending to personal abuse   He had not a particle of envy in his nature   I recollect his telling me once that he went to Cincinnatti to attend to a patent case[9]   He was expected to take the lead in the management of the suit but to be assisted by a young lawyer of that city   He said he prepared himself as he thought thoroughly and flattered himself that he knew something of mechanics but said when I came to compare notes with my young associate I found that I knew nothing, said he; I told my client that my associate could lose all I knew and

---

7. Robert C. Ould, a Confederate agent of exchange. A breakdown in exchange negotiations followed the great battles of 1863, as thousands from both sides filled prison camps.

8. For an account of this match, see the index.

9. A reference to AL's appearance in *McCormick v. Manny, et al.,* at Cincinnati in 1855.

not miss it and I insisted that he should take the lead   It required no effort on his part to admit another man's superiority and his admission that Gen Grant was right & he was wrong about operations at Vicksburg was not intended for effect as some suppose but was perfectly in character   I am unable to call to mind any expression from Mr Lincoln of a preference for one article of diet over an another   I should judge that he was totally indifferent on that head   Mr. Lincoln had an astonishing memory   I never found it at fault   He could recall every incident of his life particularly if any thing amusing was connected with it   Mr Lincoln used anecdotes as labour saving contrivances   He could convey his ideas on any subject through the form of a simple story or homely illustration with better effect than any man I ever knew   To illustrate   I was talking with him once about State sovereignty   He said the advocates of that theory always reminded him of the fellow who contended that the proper place for the big kettle was inside of the little one   There is one little incident in the political life of Mr Lincoln which perhaps ought to be explained, as it has been charged by some against him, as an act of dereliction of duty; and that was his jumping out of a window, to avoid voting as a member of the Legislature. The facts were these   Gov Carlin convened the Legislature of 1840–41, by proclamation: two weeks earlier than it would have met under the constitution. At the previous session an Act had been passed legalizing the suspension of specie payments by the Bank untill the end of the next session of the general assembly. On the morning of the last day of the first two weeks of the session, as we supposed, it was ascertained that the Democrats had determined to adjourn *sine die* & make those two weeks a distinct session, at the end of which the Bank would be compelled to resume specie payments or forfeit its charter. The Whigs believed that this step would be not only unfair to the Bank which had had no notice of or made any preperation for such a proceeding and that it would benefit only the Banks of other states which held the paper of our Bank by enabling them to draw its specie for its bills which they held while it could get nothing from them on their bills which it held and that the loss of the deprecetion of our Bank circulation would fall principally upon our citizens who were holders of small sums   The Whigs determined if possible to prevent the *sine die* adjournment knowing that the Constitution would convene the Legislature on the following monday   It required a quorum to adjourn *sine die*   Less than a quorum could adjourn from day to day   As the Constitution then stood it was necessary to have two members to call the ayes & nays to shew that a quorum was not voting   If the Whigs absented themselves there would not be a quorum left even with the two who should be deputed to call the ayes & nays   The Whigs immediately held a meeting & resolved that they would all stay out except Lincoln & me who were to call the ayes & nays   We appeared in the afternoon   motion to adjourn *sine die* was made & we called the ayes & nays   The Democrats discovered the game and the sergeant at arms was sent out to gather up the absentees   There was great excitement in the House which was then held in a church in Springfield   We soon discovered that several Whigs had been caught and brought in and that the plan had been spoiled and we (Lincoln & I) determined to leave the Hall and going to the door found it locked and then raised a window & jumped out but not untill the democrats had succeeded in adjourning   Mr Gridley of McLean accompanied us in our exit   The result of this operation was just as we anticipated the Bank resumed & paid out nearly all of its specie to Banks & Brokers in other states while not a cent could be obtained from them as the Banks every where had been authorized to suspend specie payment   In a few weeks the folly of the course of the majority became apparent and they themselves introduced a bill again legalizing a suspension but it was too late   Our Bank had been too much weakened & it went under at the general resumption of specie payments   I think Mr Lincoln always regretted that he entered into the arrangement as he deprecated everything that Savored of the revolutionary   In politics Mr Lincoln was before all things in favor of perfect equality   He consequently detested aristocracy in all its forms and loved our government and its founders almost to idolatry   He was for a National Currency Internal improvements by the general government and the encouragement of home manufacturies   On this latter subject I have heard him make arguments greatly more powerful and convincing than anything I have ever heard or read

This is a hasty sketch of what I remember concerning Mr Lincoln   If my attention should be directed to any particulars I might be able to recall other things and shall take great pleasure in answering any calls you may make on me   Let me hear from you often   If I can be the means of imparting any information touching the life of a truly good & great man I shall be supremely gratified   I feel proud of his fame as I have ever regarded him as the genuine product of American institutions

Yours truly
J. Gillespie

LC: HW2446–55; HL: LN2408, 2:20–40

133. Robert Mosely to WHH

[Jan. 1866?]

I handed the article to Jacob Harding Editor[1] — he refused to publish it or return it to me

It was about the time the Editor of the Prairie Beacon, was making arrangements to enter the copperhead ranks where he now is

Yours truly
Robt Mosely

---

1. Jacob Harding (1802–83) of Paris, Illinois, founder and editor of the *Prairie Beacon*. See §429.

[Enclosure]

134. AL to Robert Mosely

Springfield July 2, 1858

Robert Moseley Esq
My dear Sir
    Your letter of the 29*th* is received, and for which I thank you, —   Herewith
I send a little article which I wish you would have published in the "Prairie Bea-
con" Next Week.
    Besides my own recollection I have carefully examined the journals Since I saw
You, and I Know the Editor Will be enteerly safe in publishing the article —   Get
it into the first paper.
                            Yours very truly
                              A. Lincoln
Copy

    LC: HW5322 (letter), HW1994 (enclosure)

135. Abner Y. Ellis to WHH

Moro, Ills   Febr 1st 1866

Freind Herndon
    Your 3rd letter dated Jany 30th is before me and Contents Noticed and I am
Much pleased to hear from you that My humble efforts are of Some assistance to
you
    On Yesterday I Mailed to you address a package Containing 6 pages of the Same
Subject
    You ask Me in the one just recevd to relate Some of the Storys & anecdotes as
told by Mr Lincoln *whether smutty or chast*   this is hard to do as there is but few
if any who can tell them so well as he Could. however as You have promised that
No one Shall ever see them but Your Self I will endeavor do so though Many of
them you have heard before
    First; Bap McNabbs Red Rooster
I early times the Boys in and about old Sangamon Town Got up a Free chicken
fight or free to all to Enter his rooster   by payin 25 *cts* entrance fee
    Well Bap had a verry Splendid Red Rooster and he with others was entered
    Well the eventful day arrived and Bap with his little Beauty was their in all his
splendere.
    The time arrives and into the ring they toss their chickens Baps with the rest
but no sooner had the little beauty discovered what was to be done he droped his
tale and run
    Bap being very much disappointed picked him up and went home   loosing
his quarter & dishonored chicken

and as soon as he got home he tossed his pet down in the yard on his own dung hill — The little fellow then stood up & flirted out his beautiful feathers & Crowed as brave as a Lion. Bap Viewed closely & remarked

Yes you dam little cuss   you are Great on a parade but you are not worth a Dam in a fight

it is said that Mr L remarked to a freind soon after McClellands fizzle before Richmond That Little McClelland reminded him of Bap McNabbs Little Red Rooster.

Do you remember his Ground Squirl Story. for fear you May Not I will try and tell it as best I Can

Well an American an Irishman and dutchm was to Gether and the American proposed that one of them should ask a question each for the others to anser and if they failed to anser it they wer to Stand treat and it was agreed to   Well ask the American "how is it the little Ground Squirl digs his hole in the ground without leaving any dirt at its Mouth

I can tell that Shure it is because the squirel begings his digging at the Bottom   all right said the American

Ah Said the dutchman but how dose the little fellow get down there   Oh said Paddy that is a question of your own asking and for you only to answer

Well lets have the Lager said the good natured dutchman

I am fearful that My Selection of Storys are Not good and will be rather tiresome so I will colse with

Daddy Can Hold me

Yes, daddy Can hold Me

Two brave young Men was going to fight and were both stripping for the Contest and both Equally Eager by all outward apearances to get to gether but their freinds interfered and was holding the Most Noisey one back when he discoved his antagonist coming towards him he Said to his freinds Why dont Some of you hold the other Man Daddy Can hold Me, Yes Daddy hold Me daddy For You Know My temper

I Suppose you have heard about the young Democrat that was Willing to Swar that he ought to have a vote but he Wanted to Explain

He Said he Was honestly 21 but he had been cheated out of one Year by his Mothers having a miscarriage the first time and he blamed the Black republicans with it

they had Made his Father drunk and he frightened his Mother

Here is a little Irish Song I once heard him repeat he said he wished he could sing it   It tells how St Patrick came to be Born on the 17th of March and as Near as I can recollect it run in this Way

The first factional fight in old Ireland they say
Was all on account of St Pattericks birth day
its somewhare 'bout Midnight, without any doubt
And certin it is that it made a great rout

On the 8th day of March as some people Say
St Patrick at Midnight he first saw the day
While others assert 'twas the 9*th* he was born
Twas all a Mistake between Midnight and Morn

Some blamed the baby and some blamed the clock
Some blamed the doctor and some blamed crowing Cock
With all these cross questions Sure no one could Know
Whether the babe was too fast or the clock was, too slow

Some fought for the 8th for the 9th More would die
He who would not see right, should have a back Eye
At length those two factions so positive grew
They both had two birth days so Pat he had two

Till father *Mulcha* who shewed them their sins
he said None could have two birth days but as twins
and boys dont be fighting for the 8 or for 9
dont be allways but sometimes combine

Combine 8 with 9 — 17 is the Mark
let that be the birth day, Amen said the Clock
So they all got blind drunk which completed their bliss
And they have Kept up the practice from that day to [this]

Dont Speak to Me

Josh Beasley and Sam Meeks had been at logger heads for a long time but on day they met in a lane

And Beasley spoke to Meeks and M. indignantly replyed dont speak to Me Sam Beasley for I consider Myself intirely beneath your Notice

Store Tea & Baughton Sugar

Old Mrs Pattengill a selfpossessed old Lady in the Back woods in Indiana went to Town for the first time & stoped at a Tavern for Supper   The Land Lady politely ask her Which she Would have Tea or Coffee   her reply Was Store Tea & Baughton Sugar in it if you please Mam

Their Was once an old toper in Salem (I have for gotten his Name) complaining to Lincoln and Jack Armstrong — that he had out lived all of his freind But said he I have one yet that is in this old Jug pulling out a quart Jug & taking a horn at the same time

Jack Said to him Look hear old feller if you dont quit drinking you will Not Live to see — Christmas   I bet you Said he 50 Bushells of Corn I will Live to see Christmas   it is a bet said Jack   and Lincoln was the Witness   The old chap Wun the Corn and went & gethered it in Armstrongs Corn field   this was in the fall of 1833 the bet was made

Bob. once Sold John Burnap   he asked John how it was that the Sailors New that their was a Man in the Moon   John Said No   he could not tell — but how did they   Well said Bob they had been to *Sea.*

He told John that he got cured of the Cross Eye by peaping through the Key hole of the door

Do you recollect Mr Lincolns favorite pece of Poetry "oh why Should the Spirit of Mortal be proud"

LC: HW2457, HW2459 v/r, HW2458 v/r, HW5288; HL: LN2408, 1:418–24

136. Dennis F. Hanks to WHH[1]

February the 1st 66

Der Bille

I Received your Letter of Enquier to-day   I will postpone answering this Letter for Sume Days for I have written a Letter to Haginsville to the post master of that place and have found Sume of My relations is still Living and Lives on A Lincolns Birth place   I wrote Back to them for they no that is his Birth place   I want to No all they No a Bout it   when I get an answer from them I will give you a Rich Letter Bill Sopose you Rite a Letter to Richard Creal Haginsville Kentucky   this is the man that is said to live on A Lincolns birthplace   asks him whare it is   Name Sum old Settler that I may No   was it on Knob creek   or was it nere Buckharts old farm or close to Silas Inyards   get them to tell all this and Let me No a Bout it   we will make something out of this   thare is two persons Still a Living one is My Step Mother which is 83 years old and another Man that is still a Living By the Name of William Cissna which is 89 years old   Rite whare he was Born write to these persons   I think we will get it all at Last   I No these persons well   I thought they was all Ded   I entend to Se them Next Spring   So do as I tell you Billy we will find it all out yet   It has Ben 45 years sence I have Seen any of them

I am not Very well at this time So fare well

D F. Hanks.

LC: HW2462; HL: LN2408, 1:250–51

---

1. Note in top margin, possibly in JWW's hand: *Copy.*

137. John M. Scott to WHH

Bloomington Feby 2nd 1866

Dr Sir

Your letter was received during the session of Court and I had no time to give it any attention —

If I were in possession of any incidents in the life of Mr Lincoln It would give me great pleasure to communicate the same to you. But I remmenber nothing that is worthy to be recorded in history. And there is a reason for this. Mr Lincoln in the ordinary walks of life did not appear the "great man", that he really was — We all remember him well, and yet it is difficult to tell the peculiarities of his character — The ground work of his social nature was Sad — but from the fact that he studiously cultivated the humorous it would have been very sad indeed — His mirth to me always seemed to be put on and did not properly belong there Like a plant produced in the hot-bed it had an unnatural and luxuriant growth — In all the points of his character with which I was ever familiar, I think you have very justly and Elegantly set them forth in your lectures which I have read with great interest and I shall look to the publication of your work with all the more interest for having read them — It is not possible to select any one essential of character and say that it was that which constituted Mr Lincoln *great* — for *great* he surely was — When you come to analize his character, the elements that entered into it, you will find that he possessed no one element of character in any higher degree than many of his cotemporaries. His greatness sprang from a strange combination of all the essentials of character entering into and forming a grand and heroic character, independent of any one great essential — And such a character is always Self-reliant — He would gather up difficulties, though they were mountainous, in their proportions and would toss them out of his way as lightly as a boy would his Shuttle-cock —

Lincoln was a bold and courageous man — I don't mean that mere physical courage that meets death in its most awful forms undaunted, nor yet that higher form of courage that inspires noble action in times of public or private danger — nor yet that still higher form of courage that invests the countenance of the hero with that strange and flashing light in the hour of battle amidst the shock and conflict of armies, leading on to deeds of valor that startle and dazzle the world. All this he may have had I know not — But that highest of all forms of courage, that is only ambitious to do good, that rising far above the selfish prejudices of men strikes out boldly and grandly for liberty and humanity — that lofty courage that is inspired of Heaven — that dares to do *right* whatever may be the opinion of the world and *fears* only to do wrong. In this regard the history of Earths *great men*, will present few — if any, — more prominent characters —

I can add nothing to what you have already said — and so wel said — of Mr Lincoln — and need not perhaps have written the little that I have written —

I regret that I have not power to pen a thought that would be worthy of the great and good man whose life and public Services you propose to record —

Yours truly

John M Scott

LC: HW2463; HL: LN2408, 2:337–39

138. John Wentworth to WHH[1]

Washington, D.C. Feby 4 1866

Dr Sir:

From your letter I infer that you intend delivering some more lectures about Mr Lincoln. Personally I knew but little of Mr Lincoln. I served with him during his only term in Congress. Afterwards, I met him occasionally at Conventions & at Hotels. I have no remembrance of ever being in any room alone with him or of ever conversing with him upon any subject except politics.

I have heard private comparisons of him & Douglass that I have never seen in print. I came to Illinois 25th Oct 1836. He & Douglass were both in the Legislature, you know better than I whether for the first time or not. During that session Douglass made himself known all over the State & got himself made a Land officer against the wishes of our democratic delegation in Congress. As soon as the democrats could hold a convention, he was placed on the track for Congress against the influence of Col May[2] & his friends.

Lincoln at that time was scarcely known though having the same chance as Douglass. John T Stewart was the great man.

Though defeated for Congress, his friends did not give him up, but made him Supreme Judge. Where was Lincoln all this time?

Again, Douglass was sent to Congress in 1843 & I entered at the same time. In 30 days, Douglass had made his great speech & his fame was national. Lincoln lived then in a whig District, but was not thought of for Congress. Hardin was elected.

Then came Baker. Baker went to the war, & John Henry was sent to succeed him. Where was Lincoln all this while?

After Douglass had been elected to the Senate, in the 2nd Congress of Polk's administration, Lincoln was elected to the House. See Congressional Globe! What did he say? What did he do? Who knew him?

When nominated for President, few of his old colleagues remembered him Speaker Winthrop, of his own party, is said to have asserted of his nomination at Chicago that he would not recognize if he should meet him in the street. Mrs L was with him & created no sensation.

---

1. Note in top margin: *private.*

2. William L. May was elected to Congress in 1834 and 1836, but Douglas won the Democratic nomination away from May in 1838 in one of the earliest nominating conventions to be held in Illinois.

His whig friends did not renominate him. Logan was put on the track.

He tried to be Commissioner of the General Land office, & I suppose his recommendations are now on file. Justin Butterfield of Chicago beat him, although Lincoln was here on the ground & was acquainted with Prest Taylor, Vice Prest Fillmore & the most of his Cabinet, as well as members of the Senate & House. Butterfield was never in Congress.

Now, Herndon, look at all this carefully! Look at his official acts in the Legislature & then read the Globe very carefully. His motions were few & his speeches very few. This brings you to the free soil era.[3] Born & educated a whig, a notoriously conservative party, called a fossil or old fogy party, wherein did he show himself radical? What new measure did he start? Where did he show progress? Where did he become restless in the party harness?

See what Douglass was doing all that time? Minorities give the best chance to develope talent, & how did Lincoln improve his chance?

I write in great haste & merely to oblige you.

When I have more leizure & after I believe you have had time to examine this matter thoroughly, I will commence at the Free soil epoch, where under different associates he progressed & became one of the most successful & some say cunningest of politicians

Resply Yrs
Jno Wentworth

LC: HW2466–68

139. Richard G. Oglesby to WHH

Springfield Feb 5th 1866

My Dear Sir

I have gone patiently I may say critically over your last Lecture. It does not seem so good as the first only I suppose — I am able to give no better reason — because it was not first read. It seems to me beyond Question that in your anxiety to do Justice to the character the Life and fame of Mr Lincoln you divest yourself of all partiality and prejudice and enter into the very Sinews Nerves and raines of all there was of him and unravel hold up and expose. Each so faithfully and faultlessly all must confess you have done a good work for history and mankind. I could never discover why Mr Lincolns views of religion or on Christianity were so sedulously kept to himself. I Expected when I begun your last Lecture to find something on this subject. I discovered however that what you said about it had been purposely omited I do not see how it could hurt the world to know the truth about it. I Earnestly congratulate you upon the three best Efforts perhaps of your life. I would be hapy to honestly deserve the Just credit these honorable creations must bring to you — and I shall thank you If at any time you should reduce them to

---

3. Approximately 1846–52.

some enduring form to favor me with a copy of them — for there is nothing in them which I cannot and ought not to frankly and cordially approve.

truly your friend —
R. G. Oglesby

LC: HW2469

140. H. C. Wortham to WHH

Charleston Ills Feby 6th 1866

Dear Sir

In compliance with your request of 1st inst I have examined the Records of My Office, And find a Deed from Thomas Lincoln & wife to Abraham Lincoln for the following to-wit: NE ¼ SE ¼ Sec 21 T 11. R 7 E. reserving however the entire control of the same to the first parties or the survivor of them as long as they or the survivor should live dated Oct 25th 1841, consideration $200. Recorded in Book G. Page 5

I also find a Deed from Abraham Lincoln & wife to John D Johnston for the following, the NW ¼ SE ¼ & NE ¼ SW ¼ Sec 21 T. 11 R 9 E the interest here conveyed is that of sole heir of Thomas Lincoln Decd. subject to the dower of Sarah Lincoln his widow, in the premises dated August 12th 1851. Consideration $1. Recorded in Book O Page 215

With the exceptions above stated the deeds are similar to the generality of conveyances, from which I think you can form a much better opinion of the intentions of the parties than I, you being more familiar with the circumstances of the parties at that time. My opinion however, as to the first deed, is that A Lincoln was making a generous provission for his parents in old age &c, as to the second I see nothing remarkable but the small consideration

Hoping the above may prove satisfactory. I remain Sir very

Truly Yours &c
H. C. Wortham
Recorder Coles Co By Curtis L Davis

LC: HW2470; HL: LN2408, 2:311–12

141. Joshua F. Speed to WHH

Louisville 7 Feby 1866.

Dr Sir

I have delayed answering yours of the 30th which I found here on my return from a short visit to Washington, till I could find time to answer it properly —

It is certainly not true that I went to Ills or any other place North, South East or west to conciliate Radicals or Conservatives — or to do or say any thing in behalf of Mr Lincoln —

During his whole administration he never requested me to do any thing except in my own State — and never much in that — except to advise him as to what measures and policy would be most conducive to the growth of a healthy Union Sentiment in the State —

My own opinion of the history of the emancipation proclamation is, that Mr Lincoln forsaw the necessity for it — long before he issued it —   He was anxious to avoid it — and came to it only when he saw that the measure would subtract from their labor and add to our army quite a number of good fighting men —

I have heard of the charge of the duplicity against him by certain western Members of Congress. —   I never believed the charge — because he has told me from his own lips that the charge was false —   I who knew him so well could never after that credit the report —   At first I was opposed to the proclamation and so told him —

I remember well our conversation on the subject —   He seemed to treat it as certain that I would recognize the wisdom of the act when I should see the harvest of good which we would erelong glean from it — In that conversation he alluded to an incident in his life, long passed, when he was so much deppressed that he almost contemplated suicide —   At the time of his deep deppression —   He said to me that he had done nothing to make any human being remember that he had lived — and that to connect his name with the events transpiring in his day & generation and so impress himself upon them as to link his name with something that would redound to the interest of his fellow man was what he desired to live for —   He reminded me of the conversation — and said with earnest emphasis — I believe that in this measure (meaning his proclamation) my fondest hopes will be realized —

Your friend &c
J. F. Speed

Over 20 years had passed between these two conversations between us —   You may use my name in this connection if you choose.

LC: HW2473–74; HL: LN2408, 2:324–26

142. Benjamin F. Irwin to WHH

Pleasant Plain Feb 8 1866

Friend William

the Conversation to which you allude in yours of yesterday took place in the office of Lincoln & Herndon in the fall of 1854   in the presence of P L Harrison[1] and yourself the Conversation was at the time between Lincoln and myself   whether Just Before or after the Election   I am not altogether positive But I quite certain about 2 days after the Election   If I am right Harrison and

---

1. Probably Peyton L. Harrison of Pleasant Plains.

me was there to get returns of the Election   Mr Lincoln as I recollect said that the Next Morning after the Peoria Debate Douglas came to him and flattered him that he knew more on the question of the Territorial organization in this gover-ment from its organization than all the senate of the US and called his mind to the Trouble they had given him and replied that Lincoln had given him More trou-ble than all the opposition in the senate and then Proposed to Lincoln that if he Lincoln would go home and make no more speeches During the campaign that he Douglas would go to no more of his appointments and remain silent and I think if you will run your Mind Back Lincoln Did not make another speech until after Election[2]

NB   If you find that Lincoln spoke after the Peoria Debate you are write and if he did not then I am sure I am right   If you run your Mind Back to that con-versation   It originated in this way   after the Debate at Springfield on the 4th & 5th of October 1854 William Jane Myself John Cassady & Pascal Enos these names I remember filled out and signed a Written request to Lincoln to follow Douglas untill he run him into his hole or made him holler Enough and that day he was giving his report   I dont remember how many names was on the Peti-tion but the ones given I remember   I will see P L Harrison and in 10 days I will see you in Person

your
B F Irwin

I write this with a pencil the girls has Misplaced the Ink

LC: HW2471–72; HL: LN2408, 2:319–21

143. Dennis F. Hanks to WHH

Charleston Ill Febur 10th 1866

friend Billy

yours Rec[e]ived Febuary 9th for which I Hasin to answer those questions that you propond to Me is the Easest for Me to answer of All the Rest   I give it in full Noing what I Say

1st   what is the Name of A Lincoln Mother   I.this hir name was Nancy Sparow hir farther Name was Henory Sparow hir Mother Name was Lucy Spa-row hir Madin Name was Hanks Sister to My Mother[1]

2d   you Say why was She Cald Hanks   all I can Say is this She was Deep in Stalk of the Hanks family   Calling hir Hanks probily is My falt   I allways

---

2. For an account of the "Peoria Truce," see Angle.

---

1. Though Lincoln had told Herndon and others that his mother's maiden name was Hanks, Dennis F. Hanks maintained that AL's mother's maiden name was Sparrow, the surname of her mother's husband. See the appendix.

told hir She Looked More Like the Hankes than Sparrow — I think this is the way   if you Call hir hanks you Make hir a Baseborn Child which is not trew[2]

3d   Now Billy this question is all gaman[3]   I have herd a great Many things a Bout abe   those things Bout Abes Being a Basterd is false   the Man that Sayes So to Me Be well posted a Bout it shore those things I No what I Say   You Jus Say that Thomas Lincoln of Hardin County Ky was his farther and Nancy Sparrow was his Mother Now *Nancy* Lincoln thare is No gronds for for all this Shure while I Live I will Conterdict it for Billy I No this   I am all the Man that Can tell all a Bout it   I want this Richard Creal to tell you How he noes he Lives on A Lincolns Birth place

Billy I th[i]nk this will Do to Stop the Mouths of those fellows that is trying to Make Abe out a Base Borne child and his Mother if Call hir Hanks you Make hir a Base Born Child hir mother was a Hanks Billy you No this Much a Bout familys they will allways have Nick Names for one or an other   we Beat all people for this u Ever have Seen[4]

you will See that I have not answerd your other Letter wating for Information from my friends in Kentucky   if you wish I Should answer it I will plese in form
Yours Respectffuly
D. F. Hanks[5]

LC: HW2475; HL: LN2408, 1:251–53

144. E. N. Powell to WHH

Peoria Feby 10/66
Dear Sir

On my return home from Pekin Court yesterday I found your kind letter of the 7th inst

I hope you will make diligent search for the note as I do not wish to get into trouble about it

In regard to the matter you enquire about as to the debate here between Mr Lincoln & Douglas I presume I know as much or more about it than any other person I do not at this moment remember the exact time it occurred but I know it was after the passage of the Kansas and Nebraska Bill and before the joint debate between them in 1858 which I suppose is the one you allude to   The facts are as follows. Mr — Douglas was invited here by his friends to speak on a certain day   Mr Lincoln was attending court at Pekin   Myself and other friends induced Mr Lincoln to come here and make a reply   He did so. As the meeting

---

2. WHH note: *(Foolish answer to evade a truth — Mrs Lincoln was born 20 ys before Hanks — Herndon).*
3. Gammon: "misleading or nonsensical talk."
4. WHH note: *(Lincoln knew what his Mothers Name was, I guess — Herndon).*
5. WHH added two notes at the end of this letter: *I don't believe that Lincoln was a bastard — though it is a fact that doubts May be raised, I think Caused by a misunderstanding of the identity of persons & times* and *As to Mrs Lincoln her own Son A. Lincoln told me the truth.* Both are signed "Herndon."

was called for Mr Douglas alone we had no right to claim to have Mr Lincoln to participate in the discussion of the questions which then agitated the country but at all events it was so arranged, that Mr Douglas should open the debate and speak as long as he desired when Mr Lincoln should reply as long as he might wish when Mr Douglas was to have 40 Minutes to reply. Mr Douglas commenced and spoke for near three hours   As it was late in the afternoon when Mr D commenced he did not get through until about tea time when it was by universal consent of the audience the meeting was adjourned till after supper when Mr Lincoln made his reply and Douglas closed the debate. I need only say that the friends of Mr L were well satisfied with the result   It had been also previously arranged that Mr Douglas was to speak the next day at Lacon. Dr Boal[1] & Silas Ramsey came here with a carriage and induced Mr Lincoln to go up with them to Lacon to speak there

At that time the Rail Road from here to connect with the Rock Island Rail Road was only running from the Bureau Junction to Chillicothe a distance of 20 Miles from Peoria and a Boat ran from here in connection. Court was in session at Lacon and I was going to attend the same. On getting on to the Boat early in the morning I found Mr Douglas a board   As Mr Douglas and myself were ever personal friends although opposed in politics we had quite an interesting conversation about his visit to Russia but nothing in regard to politics

The cars ran to Chicago from Chillicothe   The Boat had been running in connection before with the rail road to Henry above Lacon and that morning was going for the last time to Henry and of course to Lacon. Some short time before we arrived at Chillicothe Mr Douglas enquired of me if I knew whether Mr Lincoln was to be at Lacon   I informed him that Dr Boal & Mr Ramsey had told me to inform their friends that they would be up about noon with Mr Lincoln

When the Boat arrived at Chillicothe I was surprised to see Mr Douglas get off the Boat and I then enquired of a special friend of Mr Douglas why he did not go to Lacon on the Boat   And he replied that he was going direct to Chicago and would not speak in Lacon that day   The Boat arrived at Lacon about the time the cars got to the Depot on the opposite side of the river about a mile or more distant and soon after Mr Douglas come over   If what I was informed was true I suppose he had changed his mind   Mr Lincoln was on hand   Mr Douglas was in a poor condition to speak being hoarse and not otherwise very well and did not wish to speak

Mr Lincoln ever generous to friend or foe proposed to Mr Douglas that if he Douglas did not wish to speak that he Lincoln would not   Mr Douglas thanked Mr L and said he would consult with his friends and advise him of what course he would take   He did so — and in a few moments it was publicly announced on the steps of the Hotel that there would be no speaking in Lacon that day. This was all there was of that matter all the rest was left to conjecture   I well remember what an impression it left upon my mind. Having heard them the day before at Peoria and thinking Douglas had the worse of the debate — and was not anxious

---

1. Robert Boal was a Peoria Republican.

at that time to speak when Lincoln was to reply — and as Douglas the next day spoke at Hennepin twenty miles further up the river where Mr L did not go.

Upon subsequent reflection I think this was in Oct 1854 from the fact that the day of the debate at Peoria we had received returns of the Elections in Iowa — Ohio Penn. & Maine all giving Squatter Sovereignty the go by

If this is intended for publication I would rather have the opportunity of putting it in better form   There other facts in regard to debates between Lincoln & Douglas within my knowledge which would be interesting to the public in a true life written of Mr L

Yours &c

E N Powell

LC: HW2476–79; HL: LN2408, 2:343–46

145. Robert L. Wilson to WHH

Sterling, Feb 10th 1866.

Dear Sir;

I became acquainted with Mr Lincoln in May 1834. He then was living at New Salem. Sangamon County, Illinois. he assisted Sam Hill, a merchant doing business in Salem, part of his time; Part of his time he was engaged in Surveying land — holding an appointment as Deputy County Surveyor, under John Calhoun, then County Surveyor. Mr Lincoln was well known all through that part of the County (Now Menard County) as a Surveyor.

At that early period the Settlers made it a point to Secure choice lots of timber land, to go with their prarie land, often not entering the prarie part of the farm until it had been under cultivation long enough to make the money of the land to enter it. But the timber lots had to be Surveyed for the purpose of entering them, but also to protect from trespass by cutting, To accomplish this, lines must be run and clearly marked.

Mr Lincoln had the monoply of finding the lines, and when any dispute arose among the Settlers, Mr Lincolns Compass and chain always settled the matter satisfactorily. He was a good woods man. at home in the dense forest   He was a geniel, fun loveing, young man. was always the centre of the circle where ever he was. Every one knew him; and he knew every one. His Stories and [fun] were fresh and Sparkling. never tinctured with malevolence; he never told a Story about or an acquaintance with a view to hurt or hold up to ridacule; but purely for fun. The victim always enjoyed it as much as any one else. esteeming it rather a compliment; than a Sarcasm, being. entirely destitute of malice.

Mr Lincoln, a[t] this time, was about twenty four or five years old. Six feet and four inches high in his Stockings. Some Stoop Shouldered. his legs were long, feet large; arms long, longer than any man I ever knew, when standing Straiht, and letting his arms fall down his Sides, the points of his fingers would touch a point lower on his legs by nearly three inches than was usual with other persons. I was present when a number of persons measured the length of thire arms on thire legs, as here Stated, with that result. his arms were unusually long for his hight, and the droop of his Shoulders also producd that result. His hands were large and bony, caused no doubt by hard labor when young. he was a good chopper. the axe then in use was a great clumsy tool, usually made by the country blacksmith, weighing about Six pounds, the handle being round and Strait, which made it very difficult to hold when chopping requiring a gripe as Strong as was necessary to wield a Blacksmiths Sledge hammer. This and running barefoot when young among Stones, and Stumps, accounts for his large hands and feet.

His eyes were a bluish brown, his face was long and very angular, when at ease had nothing in his appearance that was marked or Striking, but when enlivened in conversation or engaged in telling, or hearing some mirth-inspiring Story, his countenance would brighten up the expression woul[d] light up not in a flash. but rapidly the mucles of his face would begin to contract. Several wrinkles would diverge from the inner corners of his eyes, and extend down and diagonally across his nose, his eyes would Sparkle, all terminating in an unrestrained Laugh in which every one present willing or unwilling were compelled to take part.

In the Spring of 1836, the Citizens of New Salem and vicinity brought out Mr Lincoln as their Candidate for the Legislature. About the same time the People of the neighboring town Athens presented my name also as a candidate on the Same ticket. The different portions of the county brought their candidates until the ticket was full.

Sangamon County then was about as large as the State of Rhode Island. The county under the apportionment law then, was entitled to Seven Representatives, and two Senators. The Whig ticket for that election were, Abraham Lincoln John Dawson, Wm F Elkin, N. W. Edwards, Andrew McCormack, Dan Stone, and R. L. Wilson. The Sanators A G. Herndon and Job Fletcher.

The Democratic party had a full ticket in the field, prominant among them was John Calhoun who became conspicuous in the Kansas embroglio; a man of first class ability but too indolent to be a leader. hence he occupied a Subordinate position in his party.

The campaign commenced about six weeks before the election, which under the old Constitution was held on the first monday of August. Appointments being made and published in the Sangamo Journal and the State Register, the organs of the Parties then. We traveled on horseback from one grove to another — the praries then were entirely unoccupied — The Speaking would begin in the forenoon, the candidates Speaking alternately until all who could Speak had his turn, generally consuming the whole afternoon. The discussions were upon National and State questions, prominant among which were the Subject of a National Bank, and the Tariff, and a general System of internal improvement, by the State and the finishing the Illinois and Michigan Canal, then in progress of constuction —

Mr Lincoln took a leading part, espouseing the Whig side of all those questions, manifesting Skill and tact in offensive and defensive debates, presenting his arguments with great force and ability, and boldly attacking the questions and positions taken by opposing Candidates.

The Saturday preceding the election, the Candidates were addressing the People in the Court House in Springfield. Dr Earley one of the Candidates on the Democratic Side made some charge that N. W. Edwards one of the Whig Candidates deemed untrue, climbed on a table so as to be seen by Dr Early and evey one in the house, and at the top of his voice told Early that the charge was false. The excitement that followed was intense, so much so, that fighting men that a duel must Settle the difficulty, Mr Lincoln by the programme followed Earley, he took up the subject in dispute and handled fairly, and with such ability, that every one was astonished, and pleased. So that difficulty ended there, Then first time develloped by the excitement of the occasion he spooke in that tenor intonation of voice that ultimately settled down into that clear Shrill monotone Style of Speaking, that enabled his audience, however large, to hear distictly the lowest Sound of his voice.

This election was on the first monday of August 1836. and resulted in the election of the whole whig ticket. Sangamon County had been up to this election *uniformly* Democratic. The whigs carrying the County by about four hundred majority. Just before the meeting of the Legislature, which was on the first monday of December, 1836. A mass Convention of the People of the county met at Springfield, and passed resolutions instructing the members from that County to vote for a general system of internal improvement. In the evening after the temporary organization of the house, a convention of Delegates from nearly all the Counties in the State Convened in the hall of the House and organized with Col Thomas Mather of the State Bank as President, and after two days debate and deliberation, passed resolutions instructing the Legislature to pass a general system of internal improvements by authorizing the making of Rail Roads passing through nearly every county of the State, and also to improve the navigation of all Streams declared, and to be declared navigable; and to accomplish all this, to authorize the making of a loan of ten millions of dollars; issue bonds; Sell them; and pledge the faith of the State for thire redemption. The House organized, by electing Gen James Semple, by a Strict party vote, David Pricket, Clerk. The Senate, after a long contest organized by the election of Mr Davidson over Gen Whiteside.

Mr Lincoln Served on the Committee of Internal Improvements in the House, was an industrious, active, working member. The Internal Improvement bill, and a bill to permanently locate the Seat of Government of the State, were the great measures of the Session of 1836 & 7. Vandalia was then the Seat of Government, had been for a number of years, A new State House had been just built, Alton, Decatu, Peoria, Jacksonville Illioppolis and Springfield were the points seeking the location if removed from Vandalia. The Delegation from Sangamon were a unit, acting in concert in favor of the permenent location at Springfield. The Bill was introduced at an early day in the Session, to locate it by a joint vote of both Houses of the Legislature. The friends of all the other points united to defeat the Bill.

as each point a postponement of the location to some future period would give Strength to their location, The contest on this Bill was long, and severe; its enemies laid it on the table twice, once on the table till the fourth day of July and once indefinitely postponed it. To take a Bill from the table is always attended with difficulty; but when laid on the table to a day beyond the Session, or when indefinitely postponed, requires a vote of reconsideration, which always in an intense Struggle. In these dark hours, when our Bill to all appearance was beyond recussitation, and all our opponents were jubilant over our defeat, and when friends could see no hope, Mr Lincoln never for one moment despaired, but collect his Colleagues to his room for consultation, his practical common Sense, his thorough knowledge of human nature then, made him an overmatch for his compeers and for any man that I have ever known.

We surmounted all obstacles. passed the bill, and by a joint vote of both houses, located the Seat of Government of the State of Illinois, at Springfield, just before the adjournment of the Legislature which took place on the 4th day of March 1837. The Delegation acting during the whole Session upon all questions as a unit, gave them a Strength and influence that enabled them to carry through their measures, and give efficient aid to their friends. The Delegation was not only remarkable for their *number,* but for their *length,* most of them measuring six feet, and over. it was Said at the time that Delegation measured fifty four feet high, hence they were known as the *"long nine",* So that during that session and for a number of years afterwards, all the bad laws passed at that Session of the Legislature were Chargable to the management and influence of the "Long Nine."

I have often during my connection with Mr Lincoln in the Social circle alone, or as a member of the Legislature, Sat for hours and listened to his delineation of character; he appeared to possess but little malice or ill feeling against others; he had no animosities as other men have, although wary and vigilant in guarding his own rights, and the rights of his constituents, and personall, He was verry slow to believe that men prominant in life, would Stoop to do a dishonest or dishonorable act.

He was, on the stump, and in the Halls of Legislation a ready Debater, manifesting extraordinary ability in his peculiar manner of presenting his subject. He did not follow the beaten track of other Speakers, and Thinkers, but appeared to comprehend the whole situation of the Subject, and take hold of its first principles; He had a remarkable faculty for concentration, enabling him to present his subject in such a manner as nothing but conclusions were presented.

He did not follow a system of ratiocination deducing conclusions from premises, laid down, and eliminated; but his mode of reasoning was purely analytical; his reasons and conclusions were always drawn from analogy. his memory was a great Store house in which was Stored away all the facts. acquired by reading but principally by observation; and intercourse with men Woman and children, in their Social, and business relations; learning and weighing the motives that prompt each act in life. Supplying him with an inexhaustible fund of facts, from which he would draw conclusions, and illustrating every Subject however complicated with annecdotes drawn from all classes of Society, accomplishing the double purpose, of not only proving his Subject by the annecdote, But the annecdote itself possessing so much point and force, that no one ever forgets, after hearing Mr Lincoln tell a Story, either the argument of the Story, the Story itself, or the author.

In 1838, many of the Long Nine were candidates for reelection to the Legislature. A question of the division of the County was one of the local issues. Mr Lincoln and myself among others, residing in the portion of the county sought to be organized into a new County, and opposing the division, It became necessary that I should make a special canvass, through the North West part of the County, then known as Sand ridge. I made the canvass. Mr Lincoln accompanied me, being personally acquainted with every one, We called at nearly every house. At that time it was the universal custom to keep Some whiskey in the house, for private use and treat friends. The Subject was always mentioned as a matter of etiquutte, but with the remark to Mr. Lincoln, "You never drink" but may be your friend would like to take a little". I never Saw Mr Lincoln drink. he often told me he never drank, had no desire for the drink, nor the companionship of drinking men. Candidates never treated any body in those times unless they wanted to do so,

Mr Lincoln remained in New Salem until the Spring of 1837. He went to Springfield, and went into the Law office of John T. Stewart as a partner in the practice of Law, and boarded with William Butler.

During his Stay in New Salem, he had no property other than what was necessary to do his business, until after he Stopped in Springfield. He was not avaricious, to accumulate property, neither was he a Spendthrift, he was almost always during these times hard up. He never owned land.

The first trip he made around the circuit after he commenced the practice of law, I had a horse, Saddle, and bridle, and he had none. I let him have mine. I think he must have been careless as the Saddle skinned the horses back.

While he lived in New Salem he visited me often, he would Stay a day or two at a time. we generally spent the time at the Stores in Athens. he was very fond of company, telling or hearing Stories told, was a Source of great amusement to him, He was not in the habit of reading much. never read Novels. Whitling pine boards and shingles, talking and laughing constituted the entertainment of the days and eveings,

In a conversation with him about that time, he told me that although he appeared to enjoy life rapturously, Still he was the victim of terrible melancholly. He Sought company, and indulged in fun and hilarity without restraint, or Stint as to time   Still when by himself, he told me that he was so overcome with mental depression, that he never dare carry a knife in his pocket, And as long as I was intimately acquainted with him, previous to his commencement of the practice of the law, he never carried a pocket knife, Still he was not misanthropic. he was kind and tender in his treatment to others,

In the Summer of 1837, The Citizens of Athens and vicinity gave the Delegation, then called the "Long Nine," a public dinner, at which Mr Lincoln, and all the other members were present. He was called out by the toast "Abraham Lincoln one of Natures Noblemen" I have often thought that if any man was entitled to that compliment it was he.

In the Spring of 1840, I emigrated to Sterling, and did not see much of Mr Lincoln, until he was elected President of the United States. I went to Washington City in Feb 1861 and remained there nearly all the time, until October following; during that time I saw much of him.

He was a new man, comparitively among Politicians. as a matter of course, each faction of his own party intended to control his administration, and under ordinary circumstances would have succeeded. His predecessor had entered the Presidential Chair as the head of a Party; that was not true as to Mr Lincoln he was comparitively unknown. Old Politicians looked upon him with the same distrust, and want of Confidence, that Regular Army officer look upon officers in the Volunteer Arm of the Service, and they Supposed they would control his administration, not only as a matter of right, but they thought that he would be compelled to lean upon them for support; but he was not the man they bargained for. Many men who had made up their minds to serve their country were disappointed

The Army of officers to be appointed at the Commencement of each Presidental term is a bitter pill. First the Cabinate appointments, then begins the Scramble, each member of the Cabinet, Member of Congress, Governors of States, and all leading Politicians, each have a budget of appointments, and the rush on the President is alarming, he is beset to appoint some one of the family or some Political Pimp to whom they were under obligations, that could not be disreguarded

I was with the President one day, when Mr Grow, from Wilmot district Pa. came in, and in an excited manner demanded of the President the reason why he did not appoint his Brother-in-law as one of the Judges seat in one of the new Teritories. Mr Lincoln excused himself by saying that he had forgotten his Brother-in-law, at the time the appointment was made, but assured him that his friend Should have an appointment at an early day. Mr Grow was very angry, and talked, as it looked to me, impertinently, Mr Seward came in, and took part defending Mr Lincoln. Mr Grow used threats that surprised me. After Mr Grow and Mr Seward had retired, and we were alone, he was troubled. Said he had then been President five months, and was Surprised any body would want the office. he went on to speak about the duties; he said he was inaugurated, he supposed that although he realized that the labor of administering the affairs of the Nation would be arduous, and Severe, and that he had made up his mind, that he could, and would do it, all the duties were rather pleasant, and agreeable except making the appointments. He had Started out with the determination, to make no improper appointments, and to accomplish that result he imposed upon himself the labor of an examination into the qualifications of each Applicant. He found to his Surprise, that members of his Cabinate, who were equally interested with himself, in the sucess of his administration. had been recommending parties to be appointed to responsable positions who were often physically, morally, and intellecully unfit for the place. He said that it did appear that most of the Cabinate officers, and members of Congress, had a list of appointments to be made, and many of them were such as ought not to be made, and they knew, and their importunities were urgent in proportion to the unfitness for the appointee: he said he was so badgered with applications for appointments that he thought sometimes that the only way that he could escape from them would be to take a rope and hang himself, on one of the trees in the lawn south of the Presidents House,[1] looking out at the trees through the window at the same time.

I was with him one day in his office; parties were coming in, and doing business with him; he would send a card to the Department with which the business was being transacted. I remarked to him this reminds me of the office of the Justice of the Peace. Yes, says he, but it is hardly as respectable; he then went on to say that when he first commenced doing the duties, he was entirely ignorant not only of the duties, but of the manner of doing the business, he said he was like the Justice of the Peace, who would often speak of the first case he had ever tried, and called it, his "great first case least understood."

The night after the first Bull Run Battle, accompanied by Mr. Hanchett, M.P. from Wisconsin, and Mr McInder now a member, and the Successor of Mr Hanchett, now deceased, called at the White House to get the news from Manassass — as it was called. After having failed to obtain any information at Mr Seward's, and other places where we had sought it. The excitement was intense. Stragglers were coming in; but knew nothing except there had been a great fight, and they had made their escape, but did not know that any one else was so lucky. Messengers were coming in, bearing dispatches to the President, and Secretary of War, but outsiders knew nothing, but rumors, and no two agreed. We having arrived there, were told that Mr Lincoln was at the Secretary of War's office. We started for that place, but met parties who had just come from there, and said there was a great crowd around the building, but outsiders knew nothing. We sat down to rest, and while we were sitting. Mr Lincoln accompanied by Mr Nickolay, his private Secretary came along: and being the only one acquainted with Mr Lincoln, it was proposed that I should join the party, and ask of him the news. I did so. He said, it was contrary to Army Regulations to give military information to parties not in military service. I said to him then, I don't ask for the news, but you tell me the quality of the news, — is it good, or is it bad. Placing his mouth near my ear he said in a sharp, shrill voice, *"damned bad"*. This is the only time I ever heard Mr Lincoln use profane language — if indeed it was in that connection profane. When I became fully acquainted with the details of the fight, I became satisfied that, used at that time, and in qualification of the nature of the news, that no other word would have conveyed the true meaning of the word bad.

The labor caused by the breaking out of the war at the commencement of his Administration, imposed on him more work than one man could do. He adopted no hours for business, but did business at all hours, rising early in the morning, and retiring late at night, making appointments at very early, and very late hours. He never had any time for rest and recuperation.

---

1. A different hand begins here and continues to the end of the text.

The ante-rooms were crowded all the time from morning till night, with men, women and children all anxious to see Mr Lincoln to ask some appointment, or to see, and talk to him; and some to ask his advice about their private matters. That crowd swayed, and jostled against each other every day.

Members of the Cabinet, and Gen. McClellan, were admitted, whenever they came. and it did appear that they had to get his common opinion about anything they did, as they would call on him sometimes two or three times each day, and remain a long time in consultation about the duties of the several Departments.

In 1862, after Gen McClellan fell back on the Potomac, and the prospects were very dark, and uncertain; and Mr Lincoln's letters urging McClellan to strike and advance and take Richmond. I was that Summer with the Army under Buell and Halleck. The matter of placing Mr Lincoln at the head of the Army in the field, was generally advocated outside the Regular Army influence. It was conceded that he was not a military man. But he had proved to the world that he was equal to the exigencies of the times, and no man in the army appeared to be. That was the great trait of his character, all through his life. Whatever the exigency might be, he was equal to it, not only disappointing his friends, but also, I have no doubt, himself often —

> I am very respectfully[2]
> Your Ob't Servant
> Robert L Wilson

LC: HW2480–87; HL: LN2408, 2:1–19

146. Charles H. Ray to WHH

Chicago, Feby 11th 1866

My Dear Foolish old Fellow,

— Foolish because you suppose that I have any cause to "cut" you — most foolish in the assigning of a reason for that cutting which never happened. Your letter came to me in Canada when I was digging oil. I had, before its receipt, read your admirable lecture on Lincoln;[1] and if I did not immediately answer, it was because I had nothing to add to your able and comprehensive estimate of that great man's character.

There, now are you satisfied that all your old friends have not deserted you?

I do not see how I can aid you. You knew Mr. L. far better than I did though I knew him well; and you have summed up his leading characteristics in a way that I should despair of doing if I should try. I have only one thing to ask — that you do not give Calvinistic theology a chance to claim him as one of its saints and

---

2. In Wilson's hand.

---

1. Probably WHH's third lecture, "The Patriotism and Statesmanship of Abraham Lincoln," delivered in Springfield on January 23, 1866.

martyrs. He went to the old school church; but in spite of that outward sign of assent to the horrible dogmas of the sect, I have reason from himself to know that his "vital piety," if that means belief in the impossible, was of the negative sort. I think that orthodoxy, if that means the Presbyterian doxy, was regarded by him as a huge joke; but he was far too kindly and cautious to challenge any man's faith without cause.

I have really nothing to add to what you have said. Volumes, it is true, would not exhaust the subject; but you have given the heads of chapters and have the fullness of knowledge to fil in the details.

It is another Ray who is a college Professor here. I am an oil miner and general speculator.

With many kind wishes for your success, I am as of old

Yours very sincerely

C. H. Ray,

ISHL: Weik Papers, box 1; HL: LN2408, 2:282–83

147. Charles Friend to WHH

Hodgenville Feb. 12th 1866.

Dear Sir:

Yours of the 6th came to hand and contents noted.

Before I can get all the information required, you will have to answer one question. Who was D. F. Hanks Mother? and the names of all her sisters, also A. Lincoln's Mother and Aunts.

Yours Truly

Charles Friend.

HL: LN2408, 1:58

148. Nathaniel Grigsby to WHH

Gentryville Feb the 12th, 1866

Friend Herndon

i recd youre kind letter of Jan the 29 and was truly glad to here from you onse more, I have nothing of great importince to rite at this time, you wish to now if the letter that Mr Crawford sent you contained the whole of the book of Croni- cles,[1] it containd all of the Cronicles that Abraham Lincoln wrote on the ocasion of the weding, but he rit other Cronicles conserning other people, i have ben con- versing with some of Mr Lincoln old friends they say he rit manny Cronicles but i cannot learn the particular a bout them, i wish to now as neare as you can in- form me when youre history of the life of our friend Lincoln wil be published as

1. See §113.

manny persons is inquiring abut it of me they say that they are wating for youre history   any information you wil give me conserning youre book i wil have it pulished in the County papers, i can not think of any thing more at this time that would do you any good so i wil cease riting for this time hoping to here from you soon I yet remain youre friend and fellow servent

N Grigsby

PS

this leaves muse all wel hoping when it comes to hand it wil find you and friends all injoying alike blessing

LC: HW2488; HL: LN2408, 1:299–300

149. Abner Y. Ellis to WHH

Moro, Illinois   14th Feb 1866

Freind Wm.

I will endeavor to answer the questions proposed by you as well as I can

1st.   I do not *remember the year* that, Messrs Lincoln & Thomas had their — set-to — on the Steps of the old Court room in Hoffmans Row[1] prehaps it was in 1840 ask Noah Matheny, Amos Camp, or C. C. Phelps they May rember   I did not hear either Lincoln & Thomas speach   I was their about the time the laughing part Came on and Some one told Me that Mr L. had been Mimicing Mr T & had Made him cry

I remember I was selling goods in then in a room 2nd door north of Melvins Corner

2nd   he borrowed those plays of Me while I was PM prehaps in 185[2]   the Novel he Must of read before he came to Springfield

3nd   Mr L had this conversasion with Judge Wm A Denning in Condells store in the Year 1845 (concerning secret societys)

4th   it was in 1834 I think he wore the Blue Janes Claw hammer & Swallow tail Coat — You Must Certinally Know something about the old fashion Dress Coat some of them are worn at the present time by Gentlemen Who are Not hard on Coats —

5th   it was in the Year 1841 the told me that he had been reading — Volney & Tom Pain but when he had read them I do not know the reason   I remember the time it was at My House and he Wrote a Deed for me and I have it Now before Me

6th   Mr L never said any thing in My presents that I remember about which Side of his family he inherited his *Ways, Looks* or *thought*   he dose Not look like the Hanks family they are Sandy Complection Red Hair & Freckel all but John Hanks   I think & have allways thought he sound Judgment was from his Mothers side of the House

---

1. For other versions of the Jesse B. Thomas, Jr., affair, the "skinning of Thomas," see the index.

7th   I never heard him say any thing about this old stock in Virgina &
Kentucky

A. Y. Ellis.

I remember the time that Lincoln & E D Baker run in Convention to deside
Who Should run for Congress in old Sangamon destrict — that Some of Bakers
freinds accused Mr Lincoln of belonging to a proud and an erestricatic family
Meaning the Edwds & Todds I suppose and when it came to Mr Lincolns ears —
he laughed Verry hartially and remarked — Well that sounds strange to me for
said he I do not remember of but *one that ever came to See Me and While he Was in
town he Was accused of Stealing a Jews Harp*
    Josh Spead remembers his saying this I think you ought to remember
this   Beverly Powell & Myself live with Bell & Speed and I think he said so in
ther store — after *that* a Miss Hanks Came to spend the winter with Mrs.
Lincoln   I Never saw her that I remember

LC: HW2489–91; HL: LN2408, 1:416–18

150. Benjamin F. Irwin to WHH[1]

Pleasant Plain Ills Feb 14 1866

Sir
    yours of the 12 Inst is Recd requesting me to put in writing what I heard Mr
Lincoln say about an agreement made Between himself and Judge Douglas after
the Peoria Debate in 1854[2] where he said [it what he] did say and who was [present
Wha]t I heard him say wa[s in the office of] Lincoln and Herndon in [Springfield
Ills] *about 2 days*   W H Herndon Myself P [L Harrison an]d Isaac Cogdal was
present   what Lincoln said was about this   that the day after the peoria Debate in 1854 Douglas came to him (Lincoln) and flattered him that he Lincoln
understood the Territorial Question from the organization of the Government
Better than all the opposition in the Senate of the U.S. and he did not see that he
could make any thing by debating it with him and then reminded him Lincoln of
the trouble they had given him and remarked that Lincoln had given him More
trouble than all the opposition in t[he Senate co]mbined and followed up w[ith
the propos]ition that he would [go home and] Speak no more [during the] campaign if Lincoln would [do the sam]e to which proposition Lincoln acceded. If
you will run your mind Back you cant fail to Remember that in the Debate Between Douglas and Lincoln in Springfield on the 4th and 5th of October 1854
the friends of Lincoln thought that he proved himself equal to the task and really
that he was more than a Match for Douglas on that occasion as an evidence of
our Belief a written request was filled out By Wm Butler ex Treasurer and Signed
as I Remember by Myself Wm Jayne P [P Enos] John Cassady and a Number of

---

1. Text missing because of a rent in the original document supplied from the Springer transcription.
2. See §142.

[others now forg]otten and handed to L[incoln urging] him to follow Douglas [up until the ele]ction   On the day this Co[nversation too]k place he was giving t[he re]sult I Believe this fully answers your Interrogatories

Your Obt Servt

B. F Irwin

NB   I interline a word I have forgotten

I do believe the foregoing Statements to be true to the Best of My Recollection [as made] in my presence at the time by Lincoln —

P. L. [Harrison]

I was present at [the time referred] to and heard the above stat[ements made] by Mr Lincoln   Feb 1866

[Isaac] Cogdal

LC: HW2492–93; HL: LN2408, 2:457–58

151. Joshua F. Speed to WHH

Louisville 14 Feby 1866.

Dear Sir —

I am glad to learn that Mr Lincoln made sustantially the same remark to you that he did to me. This connected with his allusion to me after his emancipation proclamation, as that being the fulfilment of his long cherished hope should I think be incorporated in his life —   It was the fulfilment a day dream long indulged in — which few men live to realize —

Mr Lincoln was thought by many of his friends to have been a selfish man —

I propose giving you some evidence of his generosity and want of selfishness —

While Mr L was a member of Congress — and in Washington I was a member of the Kentucky Legislature in Frankfort —

Mr Crittenden was Governor. Gen'l Taylor was President — Governor Crittendens influence with Genl Taylor was thought to be very great — I received a letter from Lincoln stating that Baker was in Washington and desired to apply for a first class foreign Mission and that he wished me to try and get Governor Crittendens recommendation of Baker for such an appointment. I was requested not to apply for a recommendation but to see Gov Crittenden and in my own way ascertain what could be done — I have no copy of my reply to Lincolns letter — But I remember its substance and have his reply — to mine — I informed him that I had sought a private interview Mr C. and urged that in view of the great importance of securing the growing State of Illinois to the Whig party — I thought it would be well for Genl Taylor to confer upon some leading man of the party in the State a foreign Mission — adding that on general principles a man who was a Whig in Ills was a better Whig than one in Kentucky — In Ills a man had to fight against a majority — whereas in Ky he fought with a majority — "Mr C. denied that there could be in the world a better Whig than a Kentucky whig — But said he we wont dispute on that point —   I see that the great North west is to be a power in the land & that Illinois will be the first State among them — and that as a tactician — if (we the Whigs) could gain strength there by giving a foreign mission to some of our own friends, he thought that it would be well to do so —"

I then ventured to speak of Baker — in very flattering terms — Mr Crittenden replied that he knew Baker & as was not very favorably impressed from his limited acquaintance — There said he is Lincoln, whom I regard as a rising man   if he were an applicant I would go for him —

I wrote to Lincoln advising of all that was said — and have his reply — He expresses himself as very much obliged to Mr C for his favorable opinion of him —

I had intimated to him in my letter that if Mr Cs recommendation was of such value as he & Baker both supposed it was — Why not apply himself —?

In his reply he says I have pledged myself to Baker & can not under any circumstances consent to the use of my name so long as his is urged for the same place —.[1] Would a selfish have thus written? especially when we remember that both the place & its emoluments were such as was courted by many of the first men in the Nation —

I am
Your friend
J. F. Speed

LC: HW2494–96; HL: LN2408, 2:327–29

152. Leonard Swett to WHH

Chicago Feb 14. 1866.

Dear Sir.

Returning from Washington I found my wife very sick, so much so as to give me great concern for her recovery   Since then I have been with a council of Physicians and giving my attention to her.

I cannot probably in less than a week write you what came under my observation at Washington and particularly in reference to the Emancipation Proclamation. I may be able to do so before, some night at my house, if so I will.

One thing you must remember in writing history. That is no man is great to his "Valet de chambre"   There is but one true history in the world — that is the Bible. It is often said those old characters were bad men   They are contrasted with other characters in history & much to the detriment of some of the old worthies. The reason is the historian of the worthies told the whole truth, the inner

---

1. See AL to J. F. Speed, Feb. 20, 1849, in *CW* 2:28–29.

life   The heart and secret acts are brought to life & photographed   In other history virtues are perpetuated & vices concealed

If the history of King David had been written by an ordinary historian, the affair of Uriah would at most have been a quashed indictment with a denial of all the substantial facts. Sombody asked another what history was. He began to trace the word   Says he history comes from Histoire. L'Histoire means a story & a story means a lie   Now while I would have your history true. I would not have it too rigid   There's a skeleton in Every house. The finest character dug out thoroughly & faithfully Photographed & judged by that morality or excellence which we exact as a standard for *other* men is spoiled   Some men are cold some lewd, some dishonest some cruel   The trail of the serpent touches all characters   Excellence consists not in the absence of these unworthy attributes but in the degree to which they are redeemed by the graces and virtues of life

Lincoln's Character will bear a close scrutiny but even with him you must not let your Efforts run in the line of develloping his weaknesses. Now I am not afraid of you in this direction   Dont let anything deter you from diging to the bottom but in diging these & drawing the portrait dont forget if Lincoln had some faults Washington had more — few men have less.

I would like to have you write me what the skeleton was with Lincoln. What gave him that peculiar melancholy? What cancer had he inside? You may send it by express and as soon as I read it, *I will express it back to you.* I always thought there was something but never knew what. Must stop

Yours Truly
Leonard Swett

LC: HW2497–98; HL: LN2408, 2:287–89

153. R. A. Creal to WHH

Lincoln farm Larue Co. Ky Feb 18th 66.

The Lincoln farm the birth birth place of A B. Lincoln is situated three miles south of Hodgenville and one mile west of Inyards old farm   Thomas Lincoln married in this neighborhood bought this farm lived on it six or seven years failed to pay for it and moved to knob creek 10 miles north of this farm to a farm now owned by [Mr?] Rapier   I do not know whether he bought that farm (he built a house there) on the farm.

I new Thomas Lincoln he was called Linkhorn but know nothing about the History of him or his family Therefore I can write nothing only what I have been told by early settlers here   I do not know why he left this stat   he was an honorable respectable man here.

R. A Creal

LC: HW2500; HL: LN2804, 1:48

154. John T. Harris to WHH

Harrisonburg Va. Feby 19 1866

Dear Sir

Your last letter is to hand.

I have found much difficulty in getting the facts you desire in such form that I would be willing to see them go into history — Every *fellow* has his *tale* and all just exactly correct, but I have not been able to sift them so as to justify me in giving them to you — Our Court sits to day & will continue for 2 weeks after which I will write you the best I can on the subject —

My regards to Mr. Shutt —

Yrs Truly
John T. Harris

LC: HW2501

155. Elizabeth Crawford to WHH

feb the 21 1866

dear Ser

your letter of the 5th Came to hand in due time and we Should have Ancerd it Sooner but our buisness bin so that we could not conveniently have time   you wished me to tell you whether Abraham lincoln ever made Any pretensions of religeon during his Stay in this country   I never heard of his ever making any such pretensions   I dont think he ever did though he Seemed to be A well wisher   he went to meeting Some times and was well behaved   you also wished to know what Songes he used to Sing   I cant remember many of them   he use to Sing one that was cauld John adconsons lementation and one that was cauld william riley and one that was made about gineral Jackson and John adams at the time thay ware anominated for the presidency[1] though I cant memorise but verry little of any of them   he Sang but verry little when he was about the house   he was not noisy   as to his Jesturs or Jokes I cant recolect though he had A good many   I will give you as much of his favorite Songs as I can memorise as follows

John Adconsons Lementation
O Sinners poor sinners take warning by me
the fruits of transgressing behold now and See
my Sole is tormented my body confined
my friends and dear children left weeping behind

---

1. Cf. "John Adkin's Farewell" in Carl Sandburg, *New American Songbag* (New York, 1950), 52–53. For "William Riley," see Lair, 5. The setting of political lyrics to the tune of "Auld Lang Syne" was common in the nineteenth century. For the version that AL sang, see p. 216.

much in toxication my ruin has bin
and my dear companion have barberly slain
in yanders cold grave yard her body doth lay
whilest I am condemed and Shortly must die

remember John adconsons death and reform
before death overtakes you and vengeance comes on
my griefs overwhelming in god I must trust
I am Justly condemned my Sentance is Just

I am waiting the Summons in eternity to be herled
whilest my poore little orphans is cast on the world
I hope my kind neighbors ther gardeens will be
and heaven kind heaven protect them and me

---

    mr herndon   I have given you as much of the above Song as I could memorise   this was A favorite Song of Abraham lincolns   now I will give you A line or two of the Jackson Song that he used to sing and then I will have to close as my eyes is so weak that I cant see the lines on the paper

    let ould aquaintance be forgot
    and never brout to mind
    and Jackson be our president
    and adams left behind

---

excuse bad riting
                    elizabeth crawford

LC: HW2502–3; HL: LN2408, 1:193–95

156. David Turnham to WHH

                                         Dale Ind Feb 21st 66
Dear Sir.
    Yours of the 5th inst is at hand. as you wish me to answer several questions, I will give you a few items of the early settlment of Ind. when my father Came here in the spring of 1819 he settled in spencer County with in one mile of Thomas Lincoln then a Widdower. the Chance for schooling was poor, but such as it was   Abraham and myself attended the same schools, we first had to go seven miles to mill and then it was a hand mill that would Grind from ten to fifteen bushels of Corn in a day. there was but little wheat Grown at that time and when we did have wheat we had to grind it on the mill described and use it without

bolting[1] as there was no bolts in the Country. in the Course of two or three years a man by the name of Hufman built a mill on Anderson River about 12 miles distant   Abe and I had to do the milling on horse back, frequently going twice to get one grist. then they Commenced building horse mills of a little bitter quality than the hand mill

the Country was verry rough especiely in the low lands, so thick with brush that a man Could scarcely git through on foot, these places were Called Roughs, the Country abounded in game such as bears deers turkies and the smaller game. about the time Huffman built his mill there was a Road laid out from Corydon to Evansville, runing by Mr Lincolns farm and through what is now Gentryville. Corydon was then the state Capitat

About the year '23 there was another Road laid from Rockport to Blooming-ton Crossing the aforesaid at right angles where Gentryville now stands   James Gentry Entered the land and in about a year Gidian Romine brought Goods there and shortly after succeded in geting a post ofice by the name of Gintryville post office. then followed the laying of lots and selling — and a few were improved but from some Cause the lots all fell back to the original owner. the lots were Sold in 24 or 25. Romine kept goods there a short time and sold out to Gentry. but the place kept on increasing slowly. Wm Jones came in with a store, that made it improve a little faster but Gentry bought him out. Jones bought a track of land ½ mile from Gentryville moved to it went into buisness and drew the po and nearly all the Custom. Gentry saw that it was ruining his town he Compromised with Jones and Got him back to Gentryville, and about the year 47 or 48 there was another survey and sale of lots, which remains

This is as good a history of the rise of Gentryville as I Can give after Consulting several of the old setlers, at that time there was a great many dear licks and Abe and myself would go to those licks sometimes and wach of nights to kill deer, though Abe was not so fond of a gun as I was, there was 10 or 12 of those licks in a small Prarie on the Creak lying between Mr Lincolns and Mr Woods the man you Call More. This gave it the name of the Prarie fork of Pigeon Creak, the people in the first settling of this County was verry socieble. kind and accomidating, more so than now, but there was more drunkenness and stealing on a small scale, more immorality, less Religeon, less well placed Confidence.

you wish me to inform you if Abraham Lincoln was ever arested in Indiana. I was well and intimately acquainted with Mr Lincoln, from March 1819 until he left for Illinois having lived in one mile of him all that time and went to school with him, hunted game with him. worked on the farm with him, worked on the River fiting up a flat boat with him where the surrounding influance was verry bad. I believe I knew as much of Abraham Lincoln until he left Indiana as any other man living, and I never knew any thing disonerable of him, nor was he ever arested to my knowladge or belief, nor did I ever hear of such a Charge until lately, the source of such a falshood Can well be immagined.

---

1. The sifting process that separates flour from bran.

I believe I have answered your questions substansielly, if there if there remains any thing in which I Can be of service to you all you have to do is to drop me a few lines, and when you are ready, my son, T R Turnham wishes an Agency for Spencer County, I want a Coppy of your book an I know several that is wating and will buy no other til yours is out. Thomas had Just got home when you was at my house his is impared by being in the army he is not able to work and if he Can git an agency I think he Can sel a good many books, and as soon as he Can git a Canvasing book he will go to work

yours respectfully
D. Turnham

LC: HW2504–7; HL: LN2408, 1:180–84

157. David Davis to WHH

Washington Feb. 22. [1866]

Dear Herndon

Mr Bancroft totally misconceived Mr Lincoln's character, in applying, "unsteadiness" & confusion to it[1] — Mr Lincoln grew more steady & resolute, & his ideas were never confused —   If there were any changes in him after he got here, they were for the better —   I thought him always master of his subject —   He was a much more self possessed man than I thought — *He thought* for himself, which is a rare quality nowadays. How could Bancroft Know anything about Lincoln, except as he judged of him as the public do —   He never Saw him, & is himself as cold as an *icicle* — I should never have selected an old Democratic politician, & that one from Mass &c to deliver an eulogy on Lincoln —

Bancrofts strictures on France & England were in wretched taste, yea, cowardly, because the Foreign ministers had been especially invited — I guess Lord Palmerston Snubbed Bancroft when he was in England —

The effect of Bancrofts Eulogy was felt to day, because the foreign ministers were invited to attend the memorial services in honor of Henry Winter Davis, & some of them replied that the treatment recd on the 12th forbid the acceptance of the invitation.

In haste

Yr Frd
D. Davis

LC: HW2508–9; HL: LN2408, 2:318

---

1. George Bancroft, an eminent contemporary historian of the United States, delivered a eulogy before Congress on AL's birthday, February 12, 1866.

158. Charles Friend to WHH

Hodgenville Feb 22d 1866

Dear Sir

Yours of the 15th Inst was handed me yesterday.

You don't make the matter clear enough, yet as you seem to be in doubt your-self.

The impression here among the old Pe[ople] is that Hanks and Abe wer half Brothers, for the say, Jess Friend married Pollie Thomas Sparrow Betsie Levi Hall Scytha. Now there was only on to have been the Mother of H. & L. if they are Correct in these recollections.[1]

Thomas Sparrow had no Children, And therefor he took Hank to raise. My Grand Father, Charles, is said to be the Father of DFH   The Old Man blieved it himself for he took him and kept him 6 year, and would hardly be peswaded to let Sparrow have his Hanks also sayes in his Letter that he was half Brother to the Friend Family

Yours
Chas Friend

I send you what Mr Clagett sayes of the Lincoln Family he wrot it himself and I though I'd Just sen it, and if is worth any thin I'm glad he is a truthful man.

C F

[Enclosure]

159. William Clagett (statement)

Mr. Charles Friend

In forms me he is collecting all the information he can get about the ancesters of Abraham Lincoln late president of the United States. I will relate what little I have gathered from people much older than myself   I was raised in Grayson County Kentucky   about 40 years ago there lived a man there by the Name of Mordicai Lincoln who was said to be the brother of Thomas Lincoln the farther of Abraham Lincoln it was said the Indians Killed the farther of Thomas Lincoln and Mordicai Lincoln in early times in Bullett County Ky near shepherds-ville   Thomas Lincoln moved to Hardin County and Mordicai Lincoln to Gray-son County. the history of Thomas Lincoln will be furnished more Correctly than I Can give it but I will give the history of Mordicai Lincoln and his family as I have received it and know it myself   Mordicai Lincoln lived 40 odd years ago as I have stated in Grayson County on what was called Clay Lick fork of Bear Creek he had Two sons on Named James and the other Mordecai, and Two daughters one of the daughters married a man by the name of Washington Neighbours the other a man by the Name of Nicely

---

1. For Dennis Hanks's more accurate description of the relationship of his mother to Nancy Hanks Lincoln, see §143.

James Lincoln and Nicely moved to the State of Illinois over 40 years ago   I will give you and ancdote of James Lincoln he married Some Where about Shepherdsville his farther in Law give him a Negro man he brought him to Grayson County there Not being many Negroes there he be Came dissatisfied and Run away the Neighbors of Lincoln tried to pirsuade him to sell his Negro   James Lincoln said he would Not for he was mortal flish and he never would not sell mortal flish and took him and give him Back to his farther in Law and moved to the Illinois and said he would not Live where slavery existed   I will give you a history of old Mordicai Lincoln the Brother of Thomas Lincoln   While Mordecai lived in Grayson County there came a few Indians through there and old Mordicai heard of them passing through mounted on his horse and took his Rifle gun on his Shoulder and followed on after the Indians and was gone Two days when he returned he said he left one Lying in a sink hole for the Indians had killed his farther and he was determined to have satisfaction   I will Now give an annicdote of old Mordecia Lincoln   him and an old man by the Name of Putt met at a tavern in Litchfield and spent 2 or 3 days in drinking to gether   Putt was from the state of Georgie and was always call a tory   Putt cemmenced to tell Lincoln when the Revlutinry war was he Putt woul kill Infant children in the cradle that was moore than Lincoln could bear he raise up and says   God Damn you   and I will Kill you   and by the Interferance of the citzens saved Putts life but Lincoln let him know he had to Leave Town

William T. Clagett

Mr Wm McLure says Mordecai Lincoln killed Simon Girty the "Renagade"
W. T. C

LC: HW2510; HL: LN2408, 1:51 (letter); LC: HW3860–61; HL: LN2408, 1:52–54 (enclosure)

160. Dennis F. Hanks to WHH

Febuary — 22d — 66

well William

I have jest Received your Last Letter askin More questions   those is Very Easy to answer   But Billy thare is Sum words hard to Make out plese take pains to write plain if I Make a Mistake it will because I Dont understand your words

1st question   How Cumes it that Lincoln him Self Calls his Mother Nancy Hanks[1]   I Say this   I Dont Believe he Ever Said So for his Mother was Nancy Lincoln hir Madin Name Nancy Sparrow So what is the use of all this

2d   When Did first here it Said in the family or any where that — Abram — Enloe was Lincoln farther   I No Enloe Very well   Thare Never was any Such talk in the family a Bout Such a thing   it false I No it is   That Man is Ben Ded 55 years

---

1. See *CW* 3:511–12 and 4:60–67.

you Say that you have Received a Letter from Charles Friend — he wishes to
No Sum of your ants and unkels   I will say this Billy a Bout it   I am a Base
Born Child   My Mother was Nancy Hanks the ant of A Lincoln Mother   My
first ant Lucy Sparow Next polly Friend Next Elizabeth Sparow   These is on My
Mothers Side and — Abes — one ant on My farthers Side Maried Zary Willcox
hir name was Sally Friend   I Dont Recollect any More at this time for it has Ben
50 years Sence See them

tell Charles Friend that I was Raised By a Man By the Name of Thomas Sparrow the Brother of A Lincoln grandfarther this Charles Friend is My Brothers
Sun   write to Old William Cissne he Noes all a Bout us if he has Not forgot   he
is 89 years old   and Richard Creal this Man is My School Mate.

Billy Write to Robert Friend   he is Charles uncle   his postoffice is Buffalo
Larue County

Billy Write plain So that I will Make No Mistake

If I have Missed any thing Let Me No

When you get all the information from those friends of Mine Let Me No
                                                            D. F. Hanks

4.o.clock Eve

LC: HW2511; HL: LN2408, 1:253–55

161. Dennis F. Hanks to WHH

Febuary the 28th 66

Friend William

those questions is mity Easy to answer

1st who was the Mother of Nancy Sparow   Now this is Abes Mothers you
asking a Bout   it Was Lucy Hanks first and Next Lucy Sparow — My ant

2d   what was Miss Nancy Sparrows farthers Name   it Was Henry
Sparrow   Lucy Hanks was his wife the Mother of Abes Mother and My ant

Did Mister Sparrow and his wife have any Childern Except Nancy Sparow   I
answer yes they Had 8 Childern 4 Suns and 4 Daughters   James Thomas Henry George girls Sally Ellizabeth Nancy Lucy all Born in Murcer County Kentucky

3d   Who Did Jesse friend Mary   he Married My ant polly Hanks Abes
Mothers ant   Thomas Sparow Maried Elizabeth Hanks A Lincolns ant Sister to
Henry Sparrows wife Lucy Hanks   This is their first Name   who Did Levi Hall
Mary   he Maried My Mother Nancy Hanks which was Lucy Hanks
Sister   Henry Sparows wife Abes grand Mother   I Dont Recollect their farthers
Name   My grand farther and ther farther   I think old John Hanks Can tell who
was his grand farther all a Bout it   write to him if it is Importent   4   was you
Raised By Charles friend or Thomas Sparrow   I was Raised By Thom Sparrow

on the Little South fork of Nolin Ky   was Thomas Sparrow Mr Lincoln Mothers farther   I answer No   No Kin at all
                            Yours truly
                            D. F. Hanks

LC: HW2512; HL: LN2408, 1:255–56

162. Charles H. Hart to WHH

Phila Mar 3d. 1866

My dear Sir/

I owe you an apology for not having written before, but to tell you the truth,
I have had a great deal of mental excitement during the last three week which has
almost totally unfitted me for any thing. This must be my excuse.

I will now give you a recitation of the conversation I wrote about, and you can
take it for what it's worth.

In February '63 my father accompanied by mother and sister being in Washington, called one evening on Mr. Lincoln. after a little delay they were ushered
very unceremoniously into his library where he sat with no other companionship
than his books and public documents   He received them most cordially and
thanked them with great apparent sincerity for their *disinterested* visit "saying" it
was of no ordinary occurrence for it had not happened for months that a friendly
visit was paid to him   The conversation naturally turned upon the war, he spoke
with much sympathy of the slain and wounded and seemed wonderfully interested in many civilians who had entered upon a martial career. My father said his
position had been and still was a very anxious one, he replied; "My dear sir never
aspire to the Presidential chair I have neither rest by day nor sleep by night   I
am surrounded by people of such clashing ideas. For instance in regard to Grant.
I have testimony from men who *I am told* are most worthy honorable men, that
Grant is a drunkard, very immoral and every thing that is bad; on the other hand
I have the same amount of testimony, from men of the same station, saying he is
every thing that can be wanted, of a high moral character &c; now I have to weigh
each in my own mind and pass my judgment upon it; I have decided in his favor,
and time will show who is right. So it is with every appointment I make, after every
small victory I am crowded by men of every rank from a Colonel down to a cor-
poral, each one claiming the honor to themselves, they stating their superior officer
being absent &c &c and of course demanding promotion. My father then remarked
there were too many who wanted to be officers who are not suited to it, &c. Mr
L. replied "Yes, it is so. That reminds me of a story I heard in a small town in Illinois where I once lived. Every man in town owned a fast horse, each one considering his own the fastest, so to decide the matter there was to be a trial of all the
horses to take place at the same time. One old man living in the town known as
"Uncle" was selected as umpire, when it was over and each one anxious for his
decision, the old man putting his hands behind his back "said" I have come to one

conclusion, that when there are so many fast horses in one little town, none of them are any great shakes."

There was a particularly honest open manner in his conversation. He spoke most freely upon his election, saying he did not feel suited to the position, that he filled it because it had been thrown upon him for when he was informed of his nomination he was as much surprised as many others must have been. he said I only accepted it as I considered it was my duty, for I know very little of public life. I have only been [twice] in the state legislature and once in Congress   I was then so disgusted, I made up my mind to retire to private life and practice my profession.

As they were leaving he asked them if they had seen Mrs Lincoln, on their replying in the negative he said "just wait a minute and I will go and see where she is," leaving them alone in his library with all his papers loose about. He returned in a few moments out of breath and said "Mrs L was in the first parlor and would be most happy to see them.

Upon their departure he shook each one separately by the hand and thanked them most warmly for the pleasure he had received from their visit, remarking it was the first one in six months he had had of a purely disinterested nature, for many called with that appearance but before they left, it invariably wound up with seeking for a position for themselves or some friend and hoped if they ever came to Washington again during his stay, he might have the pleasure of seeing them again.

The above will I suppose be of very little use to you, except personally and even in that sense not as much to you who knew him so well as to those who knew him but passing.

How would you like to have an appendix to your volume in the shape of a "Bibliography of Lincolniana," containing the full title and size of every Eulogy, Sermon &c, which has appeared since his death. I think I could prepare a pretty full one if I had any time   I have now over 200, and by the by must thank you for sending for Nelson's sermon which was new to me. Who is to be your publisher?

Very truly yours
Chas. H. Hart

I have just thought of a very good *[illegible]* Mr L.s which may not have reached your ears, it had just a run in this city. After the Great Sanitary Fair which was held in June '64 and which Mr L. visited; a man by the name of [Orne?] who had been very officious to Mr L. during his visit to the Fair, and who keeps a Carpet store, applied to the President for a foreign Mission. which was needless to say refused. He afterwards in speaking of it to a Philadelphian said he supposed, when he returned he wanted to have a new sign painted as *Aixmunster* from *Bruxelles*. (Exminister from Brussels). This I think worthy the wit of a Sidney Smith or a Jeffrey.[1]

ISHL: Weik Papers, box 1; HL: LN2408, 2:293–97

---

1. Sydney Smith and Francis Jeffrey were two prominent British writers renowned for their wit.

163. Robert Boal to WHH

Peoria March 5th 1866

Dear Sir

Hon E. N. Powell of this City Called on me a few days since and requested me to Communicate to you, all the facts within My Knowledge, with regard to the discussions between Mr Lincoln and Judge Douglas in 1854.[1]

I then resided at Lacon in Marshall County, — Mr Douglas had an appointment to speak there and Mr Lincoln's friends having heard that he was to meet the Judge at Peoria the day previous, were anxious that he should also meet him at Lacon — accordingly Silas Ramsey Esqr and myself came to Peoria to see Mr Lincoln and obtain his Consent to Meet Judge Douglas, the following day — He agreed to accompany us to Lacon — Mr Lincoln Mr Ramsay and Myself, went up in a Carriage, while Judge Douglas went by way of the River —

When we arrived at Lacon, we found Judge D, already there, and a large portion of the people of the County assembled to hear him and Mr Lincoln — The Circuit Court then in Session adjourned for the same purpose — Soon after our Arrival, Mr Lincoln saw Judge Douglas — who informed him that he was very hoarse and felt unable to speak — Mr Lincoln then informed his friends that he would not take advantage of the Judge's indisposition, and would not address the people. His friends insisted upon a speech, but he refused to yield to their solicitations, and with his accumstomed magnanimity declared that it would be unfair and ungenerous in him to present his views to the people, unless Judge Douglas was able to reply — Consequently no discussion took place at Lacon. Mr Lincoln left that evening for Bloomington — On the following morning, Judge Douglas started with a gentleman in a Buggy, and went to Princeton, where he made a speech, to which either Mr. (now Chief Justice) Chase or Mr Lovejoy replied —

No agreement to my knowledge was ever entered into between Mr Lincoln and Judge Douglas with respect to any other discussion, than the one at Lacon — It is true, they did not meet afterwards in Public debate during that Canvass, but it was owing to the near approach of the election more than to any formal agreement to abandon the discussion of the Nebraska bill and its Kindred issues, I conversed freely with Mr Lincoln during our ride from Peoria to Lacon and subsequently, and I do not remember to have heard him allude to any agreement with Judge Douglas on that point — Had any such been made at that time I think I should have Known it —

It may not be improper to state that Judge Douglas was not aware that Mr Lincoln was to meet him at Lacon untill he was informed of the fact by a gentleman of Peoria (Hon E N. Powell) who was on the boat with him on the trip from Peoria to Lacon — Judge Douglas did not then allude to any agreement between Mr Lincoln and himself, to abandon the Canvass when he heard that Mr Lincoln

---

1. See Angle. For other testimony relating to the "Peoria Truce," see the index.

would meet him at Lacon — Had it existed, he Certainly would have spoken of it
to Judge Powell —

Yours truly

Robert Boal

LC: HW2513–14; HL: LN2408, 2:321–23

164. E. R. Burba to WHH

Hodgenville Ky — March the 5th 1866

Dear Sir

 I am in receipt of of note from you T. G. Needham of Elizabeth Town Ky —
in which I learn that you are engaged in writing the Biography of Abraham Lincon and desire all the informa you can get and from this (Larue) County in particular the County of his birth — I have lived within two miles of the place where
it is said he was Born. And any assistance I can render you in collecting information for the purpose you Speak of I will do it cheerfully I am aware that you
have already a correspondent in this place and there is but few persons in or near
here but Know it also —

 I presume Mr Needham will write you & let you Know how near I came in
filling the bill of the Kind of a Man whose services you wish to secure in this Matter — If you should write to me for certain reasons I would request you to write
to "*E.R. Burba clk* then it will pass off as a business letter unfortunately our post
office is not Kept as privately as some are — I have been Clerk of the County
& Circuit Courts here for some years & Most of the letters I receive are addressed
in that way and no notice in particular is taken of them

 Hoping you may meet with Success in your undertaking I am Very

Respectfully yours

E R Burba

LC: HW2515; HL: LN2408, 1:43–44

165. Dennis F. Hanks to WHH

March the 7th 66

Friend William

 I jest Received your Letter I was Down to John halls have Jest got home
walked thAre and Back Old fogy Like I got a Copy of that Egreement that you
wanted and Sent it to you this Day[1] Billy it Seemes to Me from the Letters that
you write to Me askin questions that you ask the Same questions over Several times
how is this do you forget or are you Like the Lawyer trying to Make Me cross
My path or Not — Now I will

---

1. See §166. See also §140.

Look Below for the answer

St   How Thomas Lincoln first Cum to Indiana on Horse Back   I Say on Horse Back 2 Horses as well as I Recollect packed threw to Little pigeon Creek and Struck his tent in the Brush in Spencer County Ia

this the Last trip

I have told you that the first time he Came Down the Rowling fork in a flat Boat Made By his own hands Landing at Poseys on the Indiana Side[2]   Thare Left his goods went out and Located him a place and went Back afoot on Knobb Creek whare he Started from and then packed up and Started on his Last trip to his Lowcation Rite in the Brush Raised a half faced camp whare abe Killed the turkey

2d   What Made Thomas Lincoln Leave   The reson is this We war perplext By a Disese Cald Milk Sick I My Self Being the oldest I was Determed to Leve and hunt a cuntry whare the Milk was not   I Maried his oldest Step Daughter[3]   I Sold out and they Concluded to gow With Me   Billey I was tolerably popular at that time for I had Sum Mony   My wifs Mother Could not think of parting with hir and we Riped up Stakes and Started to Illinois and Landed at Decatur   this this is the Reason for Leving Indiana   I am to Blame for it if any   as for get More Land this Not the case for we Could have Enterd Ten thousand acres of the Bist of Land   when we Left it was on a count of the Milk   Billy I Had 4 Good Milch Cows to with it in one week and Leve young Calfs   this was a Noug to Run Me Be Sides Liked toose My with it this Reason Nugh aint it for Leving Indiana

as to Thomas Lincoln Deed in Kentucky   I Say No   we Left Kentucky for the purpose of Hunting a New Cuntry whare we could get Land for 125 cts per acre and have the pick and choys   which we did

3d#   When Did Lincoln first Cum to Indiana   in the fall of 1818   I tell from My age when we Started to Indiana   Did he have have to Cut his own Road   the trew Statement of the Case is this   the Road had Ben Blazed out part of the way By a Man By the of Jesse Hoskins the Ballance of the way Lincoln had to Cut his way and part of the other for 5 Miles So that a Wagon Could pass   Was he on horse Back or in a wagon   this from poseys 18 Miles to his Location he was in a wagon   got threw Safe

was there any older Settlers than Thomas Lincoln   Yes Jesse Hoskins young Lamare Brewner Kitchen Jentry Thomas Carter John Carter T Turnham & Jones & woods[4]

you Seam to think if thare were older Settlers they Must cut a Road   I tell you this Much a Bout it is this   We Did Not Cum from the Same Cuntry Did Not Cross the Ohio at the Same place   this will Do wont it Billy

---

2. The town of Troy, Indiana, near the mouth of Anderson River, had been laid out for Francis Posey in 1815.

3. Elizabeth Johnston.

4. Jesse Hoskins was a neighbor of Thomas Lincoln. Rev. Young Lamar presided at the burial of Nancy Hanks Lincoln. Numerous Brooners and Gentrys lived in the area. Thomas and John Carter, Thomas Turnham, John and Lawrence Jones, and William Wood also lived nearby.

Billy I intend Starting to Kentucky whare I was Born   I want to Be thear on the 15th of May whare I was Born on the Very Spot which will Be 67 years a gow   I Have Not Ben there Sence the Battle of New Orleans or the Shaking of Earth[5]

So Billy if thare is any qustions Let them Cum for I think I Can answer them all

Yours Respectffuly

D. F. Hanks

[Enclosure][1]

166. Copy of Agreement

25th of October A.D. 1841.

Whereas: I have purchased of Thomas Lincoln and his wife, the North East, fourth of the South East quarter of Section Twenty one, in Township Eleven, North of Range nine East, for which I have paid them the sum of two hundred dollars, and have taken their deed of conveyance for the same with a reservation of a Life Estate therein, to them and the survivor of them. Now I bind myself my heirs and assigns to convey said tract of Land to John D. Johnston or his, at any time after the death of the survivor of the said Thomas Lincoln and wife, provided, he shall pay me my heirs or assignees, the said sum of two hundred dollars, at any time within one year after the death of the survivor of the said Thomas Lincoln and wife, and the same may be paid without interest, except after the death of the survivor as aforesaid.

Witness my hand and seal, this
25th of October A.D. 1841.
A. Lincoln.   (seal)

For value received I assinged the within title bond to John J. Hall, for the sum of fifty to me paid in hand, the rest of which is hereby acknowledged.

J. D. Johnson.

A. Lincoln's tittle bond, filed December 1st 1851, N. Ellington Clk. Recorded, Examined, December 3d. 1851 in Book No. 1. on page 43.

This is a true copy

D. F. Hanks.

LC: HW2516–17 (letter only); HL: LN2408, 1:256–60 (letter and agreement)

---

5. Hanks doubtless refers to the New Madrid earthquake of December 1811, which was widely felt in the Ohio and lower Mississippi valleys.

---

1. This may have been sent separately (see Dennis F. Hanks's remark in §165). The manuscript of the agreement is not in HW; the text is supplied from the Springer transcription.

167. R. A. Creal to WHH

Larue Co. Ky. March 12 1866

Mr. Herndon

I suppose the name was never changed it was only the People called it wrong. Abraham Lincoln the grand father of the President I have been told setled in the eastern Part of Bulitt Co. Ky. and was killed there by Indians. My farm is broken baren land but can all be cultivated with the Plow it is divided into basins hills and hillsides   the basins occupy about one third of the land and are very Rich the hills and hillside are less productive and are about ten or twelve feet higher land than the basins. Anciently this land was nearly destitute of timber being covered with barren grass weeds and shrubs and occasionally a little grove of timber consisting of Post Oake Black Oak and Hickory   a description of this farm is a very good description of all the country around except on the little creeks and branches the land is more level and heavy timbered

R. A Creal

LC: HW2518; HL: LN2408, 1:50

168. Dennis F. Hanks to WHH

Charleston the 12th of March, 1866

Friend Blly

it Seams that you Cant get Strait on those questions   I will try My Best this time

1st   how did Thomas Lincoln & his wife & family cum to Indiana the Last time   the time Mrs Johnston Came Did he Cum in a wagon   I Say he Cum in a wagon a 4 horse team Belonging to his Brother in law Ralph Crumes of Brackinridge County Ky

2nd   Did Hall & his wife[1] Cum at that time   I Say No not for 6 years after

3d   Did Mrs & Mr Sparow Cum at that time   I Say No   But the Next fall they Did But at the Same time he Drove his Stalk Hoggs to poseys and thar left them in the Beach Mast[2] and I and Sparrow Started home and we had Not Ben at home Not More than a week tell here Cum all the Hoggs   A Bare had got a Mung them Killed one this was a Bout 80 Miles they cum   we Started the Next fall My wifes farther was Daniel Johnston and Sally Johnston is heir Mother   A Lincolns Step Mother of Elizabeth town Ky thomas Sparrow & wife & my Self lived on Thomas Lincoln place and Died Shortly after My uncle and ant   uncle & ant to Abes Mother in Spencer County indiana   Died in 1819 as I Recall

4th   what is thompsons Now Called   it is Still the Same Name it is Bout one Mile and a half Below Troy   Troy is /2 Mile Bove Anderson River the oldest vilage in that County perry Laid out in 1816

---

1. Levi and Nancy Hanks Hall, the mother of Dennis Hanks and the aunt of Lincoln's mother.
2. For the location of Posey's, see §165, note 2. Beech mast is the accumulation of beech nuts on the forest floor, much fancied by hogs.

5th   Did Mr Sparrow with wife Moved 1819 from Hardin County Ky to Ia
Lived on thomas Lincoln place in that Darne Little half face Camp that Abe Killed
the Turkey No flooer in it   Lincoln had Bilt an other Cabin By this time and
got in it a Bout 40 Rods a part Died in Six Months after we got there

6th   what year Did A Lincoln Turn whig   After He Cum to Illinois a Bout
1830 for he was allways a Jacson Man tell He went to Springfield[3]   So you Can
tell your Self a Bout that he Never Voted for Jackson for he was two yung in Ia   he
allways Loved Hen Clays Speeches I think was the Cause Mostly Sum of the whigs
a Bout Springfield Judge Logan and others he was a great Reader of the united States
Speaker the Life of H Clay Shakespear Rollins works[4]

No Doubts a Bout the A Lincoln Killing the turky   he Dun it with his farthers Riffle Made By William Lutes of Bullit County Ky the Sise Ball was 120 to
the pound   I have Killed a 100 Dere with hir My Self turkies two Numer to
Mention

8th   what is the Name of the Creek &c   It was the South fork of Pigeon
Called Little Pigeon a Bout one Mile North of Lincolns a Bout the Same Distance
from Woodes [illegible]   this Creek is North of the Church a Bout 2 Miles or
Meeting house on one of its tributerys

William Lit in Dont Keep any thing Back for I am in for the hole hog Shore
for I No nobody can Do any for you Much for all they No is from Me at
Last   Every thing you See writen is from My Notes this you can tell your Self

I have got No answer yet from My Relatives in Kentucky I am fereful they have
Not got My Letters   I will Rite a gain Shortly

William write to William Hall in Frankford — Mo —   I think he can tell
Sumthing that will Be Interesting

D. F. Hanks

LC: HW2519r, HW2520r, HW2519v; HL: LN2408, 1:264–67

169. Edward McPherson to WHH

Washington, D.C., Mch 13, 1866

My dear Sir —

On inquiry yesterday, I ascertained that Mr Bancroft's oration on Mr Lincoln[1]
will not be issued under 6 weeks or two months. He is adding notes, & a steel
Engraving of Mr. L. is being prepared. The manuscript is still in Mr. B's hands.
— We have, this week, the criticism of the London *Times*,[2] which you anticipated
in yr. last. —

---

3. See §72 for a different view from the same informant.
4. "United States Speaker" probably refers to *The American Speaker*. See §109, note 1. "Rollin's works"
probably refers to Charles Rollin, *The Ancient History of the Egyptians, Carthaginians, Assyrians, Babylonians,
Medes and Persians, Macedonians and Grecians,* available in many editions.

---

1. "A Memorial Address on the Life and Character of Abraham Lincoln . . ." (Washington, D.C., 1866).
2. *The Times* (London), Feb. 27, 1866.

In the sentence you quote from Mr B's oration as to Mr Lincoln's unsteady supervision of affairs, &c., sometimes confusing things by sudden interferences, &c. I supposed Mr. B referred to occasional practice of Mr L. issuing a *direct* order on a given subject to the executing officer, & not *through* the dept to which the officer was immediatedly responsible; &, as a result, an officer sometimes found himself addressed by contradictory orders, & the *history* of the case became confused, as well as the action of the officer unsettled. Sometimes — in special cases — Mr L. set aside rules established by himself or with his approval, & without notice to the dept; &, occasionally, on being remonstrated with, revoked his action, when satisfied of its irregularity, or dangerous tendency. I think, his personal feelings sometimes swerved him from a necessary adherence to rule; & I believe it is true that, on points on which the Prest was weak, the admn of affairs was thereby made unsteady. — I have so understood. Of course, these were mere details, & never struck a principle. — On a great principle, he was immovable; yet on details affecting it, he was capable of being reasoned with & of taking reverse steps. A striking illustration was, in his consent given when at Richmond for the reassembling of the rebel Va legislature, subsequently revoked, on coming to Washn, & being satisfied that it was a mistaken privilege which cd be abused to the injury of the Govt.[3] — I know, he held back many hours, but at last revoked the consent. Mr Lincoln *grew* prodigiously during his term, in intellect, skill, & general administrative ability. — Yet I do not believe he ever became a first class executive officer. — He was rather too cautiously deliberate to succeed in that special line. I have reports of *two* of yr Addresses — not the *third*.[4] Can you send it? I hope you are pressing on with yr book — I will send a copy of Mr Bancroft's Oration as soon as printed.

Very truly Yrs
Ewd. McPherson

LC: HW2521–22

170. Dennis F. Hanks to WHH

[March 14, 1866[1]]

Friend Billy after Looking over your Letter I found that I Did Not answer your questions proponded to Me Correttly that is the word Buriel I Did Not under Stand But But Now I under Stand

was Mr Sparrow and wife[2] Beried on the Same Mond Close to gether   I Say yes the Woman was Side By Side. Abes Mother in the midle first first My ant which

---

3. See §§293, 303–6.
4. WHH's third lecture on AL was delivered on January 23, 1866.

---

1. This letter clearly belongs to the series written to WHH in 1866, and the Springer transcription notes: "The envelope dated Mch 14."
2. Thomas Sparrow and Elizabeth Hanks Sparrow, AL's mother's aunt.

was Thomas Sparrows wife on one Side of Abes Mother and my Mother on the othe Side   Levy Hall on the Side of his wife[3] whih was My Mother and Thomas Sparrow was on the Side of his wife which was My ant the 5 to geather   Abes Mother Died first   Close to geather in 1819 fall of September

September 1819 if I have forgot any thing More Let Me No if you want the Stump of the Sapling that Abe trimed up I will get it for you   I Seen it the other Day when I was Down thare I Stud By him when he Dun it   Dun it with My Knife if you want it I get it for you   I will have to Steal it they Said it was not thare   I Did Not Dispute with them a Bout it I No it is the Same it is a Bout 3 feet High

D. F. Hanks

LC: HW3896; HL: LN2408, 1:263–64

171. Nathaniel Grigsby to WHH

Gentryville, March, 15, /66

Sir,

yours of 22 of Feb last is before me   i was glad to here from you and wil try to give you the information you desier, Misses Bruner and child[1] on one side and Mr and Mrs Sparrow[2] on the other side   when we come to Ind there was but few bushes the contry was open under the imense forrest   trees that spred all over the Contry, the town lieing betwen gentrysville and Rockport is Centersville Spencer Co Ind, the Crek liing between wm woods old farm and Thomas Lin Colns old farm or the place where Abraham got the ox that creek is little pigeon Creek   i have answered all of youre questions as wel as i can. i yet remain youre friend and felow citizen

N Grigsby

PS

i hall send the book i spke of if i can find it   i have not seen the man that says he has got it

LC: HW2524; HL: LN2408, 1:301

---

3. Nancy Hanks, AL's mother's aunt, who gave birth to Dennis F. Hanks out of wedlock and later married Levi Hall.

---

1. Mrs. Peter Brooner was buried in the same lot as Nancy Hanks. The name of the Brooner child is not known.

2. Thomas and Elizabeth Sparrow.

172. Robert Boal to WHH

Peoria March 17th 1866

Dear Sir

I have delayed an answer to your letter of the 7th inst, that I might send you the result of my inquiries as to the fact of Douglas speaking at Princeton on the 17 or 18th oct 1854.[1] —   I received to day a letter from Hon John H. Bryant, which places the matter beyond doubt, and fixes the time with accuracy — I enclose you the letter, which speaks for itself, and shows Conclusively that the agreement between Mr Lincoln & Judge Douglas to abandon the Canvass (of which your letter leaves me no doubt) was violated immediately afterward by Judge Douglas. I am glad to find my statements confirmed by so reliable an authority as Mr Bryant.

Yours truly
Robert Boal

[Enclosure]

173. John H. Bryant to Robert Boal

Princeton, March 15 1866.

My Dear Sir

After some delay which I regret I have succeeded in finding an old file of our Princeton paper, from which I learn that Mr Douglas spoke here on Wednesday Oct 18th 1854. This fixes the date — I recollect that he staid at Tiskilwa six miles South of this the night before and a number of our Democrats went down the next morning and escorted him to this place

Douglas spoke first one half hour and was answered by Lovejoy one haff hour when Douglas talked till dark against time, Giving no opportunity for reply

Yours truly
John H. Bryant.

LC: HW2525 (Boal's letter); HL: LN2408, 2:119; LC: HW4518 (Bryant's letter)

174. Dennis F. Hanks to WHH

[Mch. 19 — 66[1]]

Frend Billy I have Jest Received your 2 Letters 16–17 Calling for a Letter from a man in Baltimore a Bout Sum Land of Abes grandfarther as Said in the Letter[2]   I Dont understand his Name to Be Abram I think his Name was Mordica   But this cuts No figer in the Case   I Send the Letter and you can Juge for your Self

---

1. For other testimony relating to the "Peoria Truce," see the index.

---

1. Date given in Springer transcription.

2. Springer copied this letter from W. W. Gitt as an enclosure to §153, but it seems to belong here and is given as §175.

1st   how Did Thomas Lincoln and Abes Mother Abe & Sarah Cum to Indiana   They Cum on horse Back   This I No Very well a Bout the year of 1817 — or 1816   I Dont Lecolect which they Came a little while Before I Came you will have to fix this thing up the Best way you Can for I Cant tell Exactly Bouts Dates

2d   Did go to School to Crawford[3] Before you came to Indiana   I Dont think that Abe went to School to Crawford at all for Cawford was Not in the Cuntry for Severl years after we Moved there   I Came thare a Bout the year 17 or 18   I Dont Recolect which there abouts

3d   She Died in 1833 as well as I Recollect Not positive.[4] In the County of Murcer Kentucky   Nere Perryville on the old Road Leding to Danvil Nere the Old Baptist Curch Liberty Meeting house in Murcer Co —

4th   was there Ever any Religeas tales in Ia among the Boys what Did Abe Say   I will Say this for Abe when he went to Church he allways Could tell te tex   as to his particlur Views in Religion   I Cant tell But I Dont Think he held any Views Very Strong   Raised under the predesternarin School his farther was a free will Baptist   Free Communion for all Christians

5th   what year Did Col Jones Cum India   William Jones was Raised in Vincenes in the State of — Ia — I think a Bout the year of 1826 He came to Gentry Vill with a Little Store Aand thare we got a quainted he was a fine fellow he was Killed in the army

6th   where was Thomas Lincoln Boat Lanched it was at the Mouth of Knobb Creek one half Mile from his place where he Lived the Last time Before he Moved to Indiana the Roling fork Emteing in to the Beach fork then into the Ohio to tompsons fery how far was it from Thomas Lincoln Hous I Say one half Mile

Yours Respectfully

D. F. Hanks

Abes Teacher

1818

[Enclosure]

175. W. W. Gitt to Dennis F. Hanks

Baltimore Md. Aug. 5th 1865.

Dear Sir:

I have in my possession the original patent or grant to Abram Lincoln, the Grand father of our lamented President, for 800 acres of land in Lincoln County Virginia, subsequently Kentucky.

It issued to him on a warrant dated 1780, survey 1784, and was patented to him in 1787; lying on Green River. I have a regular chain of title for this tract,

---

3. Dennis Hanks apparently has confused Andrew Crawford, the schoolteacher, with Josiah Crawford, who came to the neighborhood in 1824.

4. Possibly Lucy Hanks Sparrow, AL's maternal grandmother.

but know nothing of the land or validity of the title, as it has been long neglected for tax &c —. If you will pay me $2000.00 you can have all papers.
Answer to W. W. Gitt / Baltimore / Md.
Or address
    W. W. Gitt / Box 5739 New York, City

LC: HW3897; HL: LN2408, 1:269–71 (Hanks letter); HL: LN2804, 1:49 (Gitt letter)

176. *Charles Friend to WHH*

Hodgenville Mar 19th 1866

Dear Sir
    yours of the 28th ult. was received.
    Abh. Lincoln was born 3 Miles South of this place on a farm now owned by Richard Creal, Though there are others that say he was born on there   Land (Mr Jno B Cates & Mr Wm Cisell,) it seems that there was Small houses or Cabins on each of ther Lands, Close to the spring that is on Mr Creal's farm, but the old People all are of the opinion that Mr Creal has the best Claim. Mr Cates Promised to give me a plat of this District, or as you would say Township, and as soon as he Complies, I will send it forward,
    Thomas Lincoln came from Bullit County to this then Hardin, now Larue and bought the farm above spoken of (Mr C's) and there remained until after the birth of the President some 4 or 6 years, he then moved to Knob Creek. Not being able to pay for the farm on which he then lived and Settled on a Small farm now owned by Hon N A Rapier, our ex reps. to the Legislature of Ky. He moved from Knob Creek to Ind. though be fore he took his family he wet to look for his new Home, he left this country in a flat Boat, Launched at or near the mouth of knob Creek, wher the Litle Town of New Haven now stands. don't know how long he was gon, he then Came back for his family Consisting of his wife 3 Children, a girl & Two boys, this time he went by Land Through Elizabeth town, in a Small Wagon, don't know whi he crossed the Ohio.
    Mr A L went to Two School Masters Calib Hazle and one Riney. Hazle taught on my Grand Fathers C. Friend Farm, and to get to the school house he had to go some 3½ Miles. don't know Whr Riney Taught. but will *see Further.*
    I donot knot how they Spelt their Mames (but supose they Spelt same as Now,) but they wer called Linkhorn. that proves nothing as the old settlers had a way of pronouncing names as the pleasd   They Called Meedcalf, Cass, Kastor, they pronounced Custurd &c   Thomas Lincoln and wife was Baptist, and belonged to the Little Mount Church. he (Thomas) was Baptized in the Rolling fork by _____,
    Sallie Friend sayes the Hank Family Came from Penv. near Friends Cove, and the Lincolns came from Va.
    Rev. Jno Duncan says when he was quite small he recolets to have gone hunting with the President on Nolin and to have run a ground hog in a Clift of Rock

on the side of the creek with there dogs. he says Abl Seemed determined to not give up the chase until the hog was caught and proposed to go for tools to try and prize him out,

Mr B. A. Gollaher sayes once when he and the President was playing on the bank of Knob Creek, They Concluded to Cross to the other side of the stream and to accomplish there objact they wer Compelled to either "Coon" a small Sycamore Pole or waide. they prefered the first   he (Gollaher) trided it first and landed safe on the other side of "Jordan" but as the Presiden was about the Center of the stream he lost his balance and went headlong into the creek where the water was som 5 or 6 feet deep, Gollaher saye he Cralled out on the Pole again and by giving him his hand he so assisted him as to enable him to get to shore. Gollaher sayes they had no settled games. that he recolects of and it was their custom to climb up the high Knobs and Trees, Lincoln he say took a delite in excelling in each and evry sport the Might engage in.

Yours Truly
Chas Friend

LC: HW2526–27; HL: LN2408, 1:54–57

177. Dennis F. Hanks to WHH

Charleston Ill March 22 — 66

Friend Billey

I just Received your Last Letter Making Enquires   William you Ned not write to John Hall a Bout any thing for he wont answer any thing he cant write to give any Sattis to any one   I will try and get a Coppy of that Insterment   If I can get it from John he may think thare is Sumthing Rong a Bout it and I cant get Holt of it I will Do the Best I can for you

1st   when you Landed in Indiana was thare Much under Bruch   I will jest Say to you that it was the Brushes Cuntry that I have Ever Seen in any New Cuntry Spencer County — Ia — all Kinds of undergroth Spice wod Wild privy Shewmake Dogwood grape vines matted to Geather So that as the old Saying gowes you could Drive a Butcher Knife up to the Handle in it   Bares and wile Cats Deer turkyes Squirls Rabits &c

[2]d   what year Did Gentry off Gentry Vile   I think in 22 for I hewed the first Loggs in it to Raise the first Store House for Gideon Romine to Sell goods in   the first Backsmith was John Baldin Abes pertickler friend   Sum times we spent a Little time at grog picking waits and Resling telling tales

3d   Did Ever the Childern in Indiana Ever have Exibitions   Not in our time   the Manner Spilling in School was this   all Stand up the teacher gave out a word it Cept on tell was Spelt and the one that Spelt it went up hed if he was foot   No Speaches wa Mad   Not any of those things you aske   Spelt By hart Noon and Nite this is all

you Say what was Sum of the customs   I Sopose you Mean take us all to geather   one thing I can tell you a Bout we had to work very hard clair ground for to Keep Sole and Body to geather and Every Spare time that We had we picked up our Rifle and feched in a fine Deer or turkey and in the winter time we went a Coon Hunting for Coon Skins was at that time Consderd Legal tender and Der Skins and their Hams   I tell you Billy I Enjoyed My Self Better Then Than I have Ever Since

Charles Friend Says Abe Lincoln was Born on the old farm 3 Miles South of hoggins Vile   this is Not answering the Qustion that I want   he Says so   this Charles Friend is young Man and his uncles Dont No   thare is one Man that I think Can tell   it is William Cisna   he is 89 years old he must No Sumthing a Bout it for we was all Born and Raised Close thair abots   Richard Creal is a Bout My age I think he Can give Sum Information   what Noted place was that old farm Nere to   I Can tell in a Minite if the will tell what old was Nereist to him   was it on Nolin or Nob creek

I cant get any answer from My Brother Robert   I have Ben Expecting one for Sum time   in My Last Letter I Sent them 2 of my picturs   I would Like to No if they got them

I will gow Down in a few Days and get a Coppy for you

D. F. Hanks

LC: HW2528; HL: LN2408, 1:271–73

178. George U. Miles to WHH

Petersburg Ill March 23d — 1866

Dear Sir

in answer to yours of the 19th I have to Say that the references you gave me knew little or nothing of what you wanted to know So I called on the old women whoes heads are always clear & recolection good Especially on matters of courtship in Early life —

Mrs Bolin Green Says that Mr Lincoln was a regular suitor of Miss Ann Rutledge for between two & 3 years next up to August 1835 in which month Miss Rutledge died after a short ilness   that Lincoln took her death verry hard so much so that some thought his mind would become impared & in fear of it (her husband Bolin Green went to Salem after Lincoln brought him to his house and kept him a week or two & succeeded in cheering him Lincoln up though he was quite molencoly for months   She Misses Nancy Green thinks they would have ben married had She Miss Rutledge not have died & probably would have been married long before her death had it not have ben that She had a nother Bow by the name of John McNamer who She thought as much of as She did of Lincoln to appearances   McNamer had ben the partner of Maj Samuel Hill in the dry goods buisiness but they had desolved Hill buying him out   he McNamer had a farm Seven miles north of New Salem on which Col James Rutledge the father of Miss

Ann Rutledge resided & had for 9 or 10 months   previous to that time he Col
Rutledge had resided in New Salem for a number of years — Mrs Wm Rutledge
who resides in Petersburg and did reside in the neighbourhood at the time of Said
courtship and who is an Aunt to Said Ann Rutledge & acquainted with the parties & all the circumstances of the prolonged courtship coroberates all the above
Except She thinks that Ann if She had lived would have married McNamer or rather
She thinks Ann liked him a little the best though McNamer had ben absent in Ohio
for Near two years at the time of her death though they corrospanded by letter

Mrs Parthena W Hill coroberates all the above Except She thinks as Mrs Green
that Lincoln would have got her had she lived & it was so generally believed

As to Miss Mary Owens Mrs Hill Seamed unwilling to Say any thing, & Said
Miss Owens was yet living & a widow & she thought would not like to have her
name used — but Mrs Bolin Green Said She Miss Owens was here at Bennet Abells
on a visit for about one year next preceding the death of Miss Rutledge — that
Lincoln went to See her frequently during that time She living handy to Salem
that near the End of the year & a Short time before the death of Miss Rutledge
(perhapse Some months)   Lincoln went down into the neighborhood of Col
Rutledges to do a job of Surveying and Remained there about 3 weeks — that Miss
Owens got miffed at his long stay there & left Abells & went to Minter Grahams
& that Lincoln never went to See her any more

As to Lincoln going to See a Miss Berry or a Miss Short it Seams to be a mis-
tak those woman Say he did not & I can find no one that does know of it

Bolin Green died February 13 — 1842 — His Masonick funeral was that
Summer[1] at which Lincoln delivered the finest address and Euligy I Ever hurd on
such occasion — by calling on Lavely who was master of lodge numbe 4 in Springfield at that time you can get the date of the funeral as that lodge has it on record

The above statements I think you may rely on but if you Should undertake to
write a history of my life after I am dead I dont want you to inquire So close into
my Early courtships as you do of Mr Lincolns

All well — Nomore Yours Truly G. U. Miles.

NB   in 1835 when Miss Rutledge died & when Lincoln was going to See Miss
Owens this was Sangamo County —   Menard being formed at the Session of
1838 & 9

LC: HW2529–30; HL: LN2408, 1:489–92

---

1. See §127, note 13. For other versions of this event, see the index.

179. Abner Y. Ellis to WHH[1]

Spgfd Ills Mch. 24th 1866

Friend Abner

In one of your letters you say you Know much about *"Abes"* Lincoln's court-ship — marriage &c. and will tell me. I want to know all about it from beginning to end — from top to bottom — *in side* and outside. Come tell me

Your Friend

W H Herndon

I had it from good authority that after Mr L. was engaged to be Married to his wife Mary. That She a Short time before they were Married backed out from her engagement with him; He was at the time a Member of the Legeslator *then in Session* in your City and hur refusal to Comply actually Made Mr L. Sick and Con-sequently went to bed and no one was allowed to see him but his freind Josh Speed & his frend the *Doctor* I think Henry.[2] And that strong Brandy was administered to him freely for about one Week   and I was also informed that his freind Speed brought about a reconcliation between them   I was at that time in business with *Bell* & *Speed* under the name of A Y Ellis &c &c I could only See Mr Speed occa-tionally. Wm Keep as much of this to your self as possible

Yours Truly

A Y L 'S

LC: HW2531; HL: LN2408, 1:425–26

180. Samuel C. Parks to WHH

Lincoln, Ills. March 25,th 1866.

My old Friend

You have a right to think hardly of me for not writing you sooner but the fact is I did not & do not now know what to say   The trouble is you know more about Mr Lincoln than I do & any thing I could write would seem to you like a thrice told tale

After all the great feature in Mr Lincoln's character was his *integrity* in the long-est sense of that term — his devotion to truth justice & freedom in every depart-ment of human life & under every temptation   I have often said that for a man who was for the quarter of a century *both a lawyer & a politician* he was the most honest man I ever knew   He was not only morally honest but intellectually so — he could not reason falsely — if he attempted it he failed   In politics he nev-er would try to mislead — at the bar when he thought he was wrong he was the weakest lawyer I ever saw you know this better than I do but I will give you an example or two which occurred in this County & which you mat not re-member   A man was indicted for larceny   Lincoln Young & Myself defended

1. Written at the bottom of WHH's March 24, 1866, letter to Ellis, the text of which is also given here.
2. Dr. Anson G. Henry.

him   Lincoln was satisfied by the evidence that he was guilty & ought to be convicted. He called Young & myself aside & Said "If you can say any thing for the man do it — I cant — if I attempt it the Jury will see that I think he is guilty & convict him of course"   The case was submitted by us to the Jury without a word — the Jury could not agree & before the next term the man died   Lincoln's honesty undoubtedly saved him from the Penitentiary   In a closely contested civil case Lincoln had proved an account for his client who was though he did not know it at the time a very slippery fellow   "The opposing Atty then proved a receipt clearly covering the entire cause of action   By the time he was through Lincoln was missing — the Court sent for him to the Hotel   "Tell the Judge said he "that I can't come — *my hands are dirty & I came over to clean them*"

In the case of Harris & Jones vs Buckles, Harris wanted Lincoln to assist you & myself   His answer was characteristic   "Tell Harris it's no use to *wase Money on me* in that case he'll get beat"

In politics Mr Lincoln told the truth when he said he had "always hated slavery as much as any Abolitionist" but I do not know that he deserved a great deal of credit for that for his hatred of oppression & wrong in all its forms was constitutional — he could not help it   "The occasion of his becoming a great antislavery leader was the agitation of the Repeal of the Missouri Compromise   His first great speech in opposition to that measure & in reply to Mr Douglas in Spring field was one of the ablest & most effective of his life   It was probably made at the instance of Mr Josiah Francis of Springfield who had been for twenty years an intimate personal & political friend of Mr Lincoln   Pending the Repeal I was in Springfield & urged upon Mr Francis the necessity of the leaders of the Whig Party coming out at once against it   I remember well his reply "I will see Lincoln & get him to make a speech" against it   And Lincoln did make a speech & rallied the Whig Party of Central Illinois almost to a man against *"Nebraska Bill"*

Mr Lincoln's temper both as lawyer & politician was admirable But when thoroughly roused & provoked he was capable of terrible passion & invective   His *"skinning"* of one of his political opponents before the people (Judge Thomas) twenty years ago is still spoken of by those who heard it as awfully severe   And his denunciation of a defendant (before a Jury in Petersburg) who had slandered an almost friendless school mistress was probably as bitter a Philippic as was ever uttered[1]

I think it is a mistake to suppose that Mr Lincoln was a poor judge of men   He certainly knew those he associated with well

But my sheet is full — I dont think what I have said will be of any use to you but if it should you of course will not use the name of as *modest* a man as I am

Truly Yr Frd

S. C. Parks.

LC: HW2532–33; HL: LN2408, 2:312–15

---

1. *Cabot v. Regnier* originated in Menard County in June 1843, was retried in Morgan County, and then carried to the Illinois Supreme Court (Lincoln Legals).

181. E. R. Burba to WHH

Hodgenville Ky March 31st 1866

Dear Sir

After some delay I will give you what information I can concerning the late A. Lincoln — All the in formation I have is from some of the old settlers and it appears that they are at a considerable loss on that subject — As to Thomas Lincoln it is conceded that he married Nancy Hanks and they lived within about three miles (south) of this Village at the time Abram was born. they were quite poor. the old man was a Kind of rough Carpenter & quite use full in that way in those days the Country was Sparsely Settled. there is a roof on a barn in sight of this place now standing that he helped put on   It is a settled belief here that Abrams true name is not Lincoln — Some have thought it to be *Enlows*   this I doubt for I have conversed with the old man Enlows in a Manner that satisfied me to Contrary[1] — Others give it to *Cessa;*[2] the old man is still living and had some reputation in Earlier days of living rather inclined to the company of Women — In fact I have heard him say that he Knew Nancy as well as he ever Knew any woman. And he further says that Thomas Lincoln was not considered all right in Consequence of having the Mumps or something else, that he has been with him often in baithing together in the water — Mr Cessna is Considered a very reliable man. I Know him well   Still another comes in by the name of Brownfield[3] and after Sifting the matter the best I can my opinion is inclined to the latter name provided it is Not Lincoln   My reasons in part is from the Resemblance, true I never had the pleasure of Seeing the late Abram L — yet I never Saw more striking resemblance than his picture & some of the Brownfield family — I doubt whether this matter will ever be better understood than it now is —

2d — Thomas Lincoln was conceeded to be a Strictly honest hard working Man — He bought the tract of land that A — was born on but unable to pay for it gave it up, it is rather poor and at that day suppose not worth over (1$ per acre — I have never heard that Slavery was any Cause of his leaving Ky — and think quite likely it was Not — for there were very few Slaves in the whole Country round here then perhaps not 50 in what is now this County   My own opinion is that if it was true that the Hanks family were a little unfortunate that he had no desire to remain where it was so well known and being of a Stout hearty robust Constitution broke out to try some unknown parts, this is only My own Conjectures. So far as I can learn aught cannot be Said against any of the family save what I have noticed — I am told they were Baptist by profession

A Citizen of our County by the name of Creal Says he went to school with Abram a short time to a man by the name of Reno[4] — and that Abrm went to another by the name of Calip Hazle the latter I think was Some eight miles from here where his father mooved to Near the Rolling fork of Salt River Near what is

---

1. For other testimony on Enlow and AL's paternity, see the index.
2. William Cessna.
3. George Brownfield, a Lincoln neighbor in Hardin County. For other testimony about Brownfield and AL's paternity, see the index.
4. Possibly Zachariah Riney.

Known as Athertons ferry[5]   I cannot learn of any particular trait that was no-
ticeable more than he alwas appeard to be very quiet during play time Never
Seemed to be rude Seemed to have a liking for Solitude. was the one to adjust
difficulties between boys of his size when appealed to his decision was the end of
the trouble — was rather noted for Keeping his clothes cleaner longer than any
others — was considered brave but had few if any difficulties although quite young,
had a fondness for fishing and hunting with his dog & Axe when his dog would
run a Rabbit in a hollow tree he would chop it out —   In Regard to the Second
Marriage of Thos. Lincoln I Know but little about & would refer you to Samuel
Haycraft of Elizabeth Town Hardin County Ky —   I presume that had not the
Boy turned out to be what he did that his family Record would Scarce ever been
thought here any More —   Although Ky — was a Slave State yet I can assure
you that many of us here are proud of the name of Lincolnites   Many differ with
his political policy but few can refute it and I verily believe all things considered
he was the greates Man Since the Days of Washington   I have his life written by
Jos H Barrett[6] which is Mainly Correct so far as I Know. save the very nice points
of character of some of his ancestors —

    There is a man by the name of Dennis Hanks who lives in your State who ought
to be able to give more in formation on these points than any one here —   It
May be rather a delicate Matter with him However — as his real name should be
or is Frind —   I regret that I cannot be more positive or certain in regard to information yet this is about the whole gist of the information that can be obtained
here —   I Hope you will be able to Collect sufficient facts to enable you to give
a true history. I think it would be one of best things published for the rising generation. so clearly establishing the fact that the most humble can rise to the highest positions in life —   If I can be of any further Service to you at any time it
would afford me great pleasure to be notified by you —   The matters I have
spoken of here I Mearly wrote for your own satisfaction that you might know what
was the best settled opinion about his parents &c   Consequently you can use
them as you see fit —   Wishing you success in your undertaking
                              I am Very Respectfully yours
                              E R Burba

        LC: HW2534–35; HL: LN2408, 1:38–43

182. Dennis F. Hanks to WHH[1]

                                                  Aprail the 2nd 1866
    Dennis F. Hanks was Born in Hardin County on the Tributary Branch of the
South fork of Nolin on the old Richard Creal farm in the old peach orchard in a
Log cabin 3 miles from Hagans Ville   thence we moved to Murcer County and

---

5. Northeast of Hodgenville on Rolling Fork.
6. Barrett.

---

1. This is a copy of the original letter provided by F. M. Bristol, who bought the original from WHH.

Staid there a Bout 3 years and moved Back a gain to the Same place and there Remained until we moved to Spencer County Indiana This was I think in the year 1816 if my Memory Serves Me rite. My Mother and Abe's Mothers Mother war Sisters My Mothers Name was Nancy Hanks Abes Grand Mother was Lucy Hanks which was my Mothers Sister   the woman that Raised me was Elizabeth Sparrow the Sister of Lucy and Nancy   The other Sister hir name was polly Friend so you See that there was four Sisters that was Hankses

I have No Letter from my friends yet — I dont No the Reason   Billy Did you write to William Hall in Missouri Frankford   I think he could tell you Sumthing that would Be Rite. He is my half Brother try him

William I have Seen a Book which States that Lincolns ware a quakers   I Say this is Mistake they war Baptist, all this talk about their Riligious talk is a humbug   they try to Make them out Puritins This is Not the case

you asked Me what Sort of Songs or Intrest Abe took part in   I will say this any thing that was Lively   He Never would Sing any Religious Songs it apered to Me that it Did Not souit him   But for a Man to preach a Sermond he would Listin to with great Attention

Did you find out from Richard Creal if He Lived on the place whare A. Lincoln was Born or Not   I am gowing there in May to Visit my Birth place the 15th of May this is my Birth Day 1799 it has been 48 years Since

Any thing you want to No Let it cum

your friend

D. F. Hanks

My first School master was By the Name Warden taught School at the old Baptist church on Nolin Nere Brunks farm at the Big Spring Down in a Deepe hollow Close By the House

LC: HW2536–37; HL: LN2408, 1:267–69

183. Mentor Graham (WHH interview)

April 2d 1866[1]

Mentor Graham

I Knew Miss Ann Rutledge — took sick while going to School — Lincoln & her both were stayting at My house. They Rutleges came from White Co Ills. Rutelege & Cameron built the Salem Mill, about 1828 —   I saw the dam Commenced. Miss Rutledge died about 183. or 4 — She was about 20 ys — Eyes blue large, & Expressive — fair complexion — Sandy, or light auburn hair — dark flaxen hair — about 5-4 in — face rather round — outlines beautiful — nervous vital Element predominated — good teeth — Mouth well Made bautiful — medium Chin — weigh about 120–130 — hearty & vigorous — Amiable — Kind — [il-

---

1. Dated from docketing on verso of HW2540.

legible] — tolerably good Schollar in all the Common branchs including grammar &c. She was beloved by Every body — She loved Evry body. Lincoln and she was Engaged — Lincoln told Me So — She intimated to me the Same. He Lincoln told Me that he felt like Committing Suicide often, but I told him God higher purpose — He told me he thought so somehow — couldn't tell how — He said that my remarks and others had often done him good

She dressed plainly, but Exceedingly neat, was poor and Could not afford rich Clothing.

LC: HW2539; HL: LN2408, 2:252–53

184. Mentor Graham (WHH interview)[1]

April 2d 1866

Mr Graham

Knew Miss Owens always — my Cousin — Kew her in Illinois about 1834 & 36 — Knew her from a child in Ky — Abe Lincoln & Miss Owens: she was about 28 in Ills — black Eye over medium size — hair black — symmetrical face — features roundish — tolerably fresh — good natured, Excellent disposition — about 150 &c — 5-4 inches — 6 — She was a very intellectual woman — well educated — and well raised — free and social — beautiful & Even teeth — gay and lively — mirthfullness predominant — billious temperament. She came to Ills *I think* after Miss Rutledge: She was here twice: She has Some of Lincoln's letters now. Her Mind was better cultivated than Miss Rutledge: She now says that though opposed to Abe & his ads, Still he was one of the best and Most honest men she Ever Knew — She dressed neatly — gaudily never, though she Could well have afforded it.

LC: HW2540; HL: LN2408, 1:63–64

185. James Short (WHH interview)

Menard Co Co. Aprl 3d 1866 —

James Short

Knew Lincoln Ever since he Came to Ills — Knew Mrs Armstrong well — She never made Lincoln buckskin breeches,[1] he never wore them in Ills: She nor Jack Armstrong Ever had book to loan to Lincoln — Mrs Armstrong could not read — She is a good woman — loved Abe and Abe liked her — no doubt of this —

LC: HW2543; HL: LN2408, 2:194

---

1. In top margin: *(Mary Vineyard — / Weston / Mo)*. Dated from docketing, which also says: *In Court House.*

---

1. For the "foxing" of Lincoln's breeches—sewing a protective animal skin onto the front of them—see the index.

186. Tim G. Needham to WHH

Elizabethtown Ky April 11th 1866

Dear Sir

You will please pardon my delay, as I was unable to find the marriage of Thomas Lincoln and Miss Hanks — and the delay has been occasioned by my writing to Grayson & Washington Counties, to find if they were Married there, I have heard from Grayson Co. and they were not married there, Have not heard from Washington, but suppose they were not married there, or I should have heard from the clerk[1] — I am now unable to tell you any thing definite as to the said Marriage. He, (Thomas Lincoln). was Married in this County to Sarah Johnston — on the 2d day of December 1819. (This was his *second* marriage)

If the Knowledge of his *first* marriage ever comes to me I will communicate it to you *at once.*

Write me at any time, as to any matter you have any reason to believe I can furnish any information — I will be happy to serve you at any time —

Respectfully Yours

Tim G. Needham

LC: HW2544–45; HL: LN2408, 1:63–64

187. Dennis F. Hanks to WHH

Charleston Apreel 18. 66

Dere William

I am in posesion of your Letter the 14th

1s   whare and what County was Thomas Lincoln Maried   I Say in Hardin County Elizabeth Town in 1806 this I am not positive

2d   Is there a north fork and South fork Pigeon Creek   I think there was   Gentry Vile was on the South Side of the South fork Sumtimes Called the prary fork there was a Little prairy on it where we ust to Muster[1]

Who is Beried Nancy Lincoln   first Elizabeth Sparow Next Thomas Sparow Next Nancy Hall Next Levi Hall   Elizabeth Sparow is on the Side of Abes mother   Nancy Hall on the other which is My Mother the other is My ant Elizbeth Sparow

4th   who came out to Illinois with thomas Lincoln   Nobody But his Relitives 2 Sun an laws two Dauteran Laws Squier Hall D. F. Hanks

Matilda & Elizabeth Johnston   you Should have Said they Came with Me to Illinois   there was 13 in the three familys Thos Lincoln wife Abe J D Johnston Squir Hall wife Sun Dennis F Hanks wife 3 Daughters one Sun John Han Sarah

---

1. That Thomas and Nancy Hanks Lincoln were married in Washington County on June 12, 1806, did not become known until several years later.

---

1. In the late 1820s, every able-bodied man eighteen to forty-five years of age, unless exempted by law, was a member of the Indiana Militia, which mustered at least twice a year (*Laws of Indiana* [1828], 59–60).

J Hanks Nancy M Hanks Hariet A Hanks John Talbott Hanks   if there is any
thing Rong Name it gain   I am Not well at this time
                           your friend as yousal
                           D. F. Hanks

        I wrote this in My Lap —

        LC: HW2546; HL: LN2408, 1:273–74

188. *Elizabeth Crawford to WHH*

                                   gentryville indiana April the 19th 1866
dear Sir
        your letter of march the 1 Came duly to hand and I intended to ancer it ame-
diately but on account of Sickness and other trubbles I neglected it. I hope you
will excuse me for my neglect   you wished me to tell you whether children about
the year 18 and 26 and 28 have exibisions   I have bin Studying about it, but I
cant remember whether thay had exibitions or Speaking meetings   I think thay
had I recolect some of the questions thay spoke on the bee and ant water and
fire another wus which had the most rite to complain the negroes or the
indians   another which was the Strongest wind or water   I cant recolect the
School teachers name at this time   you wish me to tell you how the people use
to go to meeting how far thay went   about that time thought it nothing to go 8
or 10 miles   the oald ldys did not Stop for the want of A Shawl or cloak or riding
dress or two horses in the winter time but thay would put on ther husbands oald
over coats and rap up ther little ones and take one or two of them up on ther one
beast and ther husbands would walk and thay and thay would go to church and
Stay in the neighborhood tell tell the next day and then go home   the oald men
would Start of out of ther fields from ther work or out of the woods from hunting
with ther guns on ther Sholders and go to church   some of them drest in deer
Scin pants and mockisons hunting Shirts with A rope and lether Strap buckled
around them come in laughing Shake hands all round and Set down and talk about
ther game thay had killed or Some other worke thay had done Smoke ther pipes
together with the oald ladys   if in warm wether would kindle up A little fire out
in the meeting house yard to lite ther pipes if in winter time thay would hold church
in some of the neighbors houses at Such times thay ware allways thay ware allways
treated with the utmost of kindness A bottle of whiskey picher of water Shugar
and glass or A basket of apples or turips or Some pies or cakes   apples war verry
scarce them times   Sometimes potatoes war used as A treat   I must tell you that
the first treat that I ever received in oald mr linkerns house that was our presidents
fathers house was A plate of potatoes washed and pared verry nicely and handed
round it was something new to me for I never had Seen A Raw potato ate before   I
looked to see how thay made use of them   thay took of A potato and ate them
like apples   thus thay spent the time tell time for preaching to commence then

thay would all take ther seats the preacher would then take his stand draw his coat open his shirt collar and commence Service by Singing and prayer take his tex and preach tell the sweat wood role off in great drops   Shakeing hands and Singing then ended the Service   the people seamed to ingoy religeon more in them days than thay do now   they ware glad to See each other and ingoyed them Selves better than thay do now   well Mr herndon I recon I have I have ritten anough excuse bad riting and mistakes as I am so blind that I cant scearcely See the lines on the paper.

Elizabeth crawford

LC: HW2547–48; HL: LN2408, 1:191–93

189. Joseph J. Kelly & C. H. Moore to WHH

Clinton, April 24 1866

Dear Sir,

Your letter of 18th Inst. asking for certain information, relative to Mr. Lincoln's first appearance in this court &c. just received, and with pleasure I furnish you the information asked for, and have also referred your letter to C. H. Moore Esqr, who will add such incidents in relation to Mr. Lincoln as may occur to him, and which doubtless will be interesting.

1st   There was no court held in this county in 1838 — the County was not organized until 1839. — Mr. Lincoln first appeared (as of record) at May Term 1840.

2d   Mr. Lincoln last appeared at Oct. Term 1859.

3d   Two Terms holden in 1840

4th   ”   ”   ”   ” 1859.

5   No resident Atty in 1840. C. H. Moore Esqr became a resident Atty, here in 1841.

6th   In 1859 there were the following resident Attys C. H. Moore — L. Weldon — E. H. Palmer — S. F. Lewis — H. S. Greene — H. G. Wismer.[1]

7th.   When Mr. Lincoln first appeared there were on the docket 8 crim. causes — 18 common Law causes — and *one* chancery cause.

When he last appeared (1859) there were 57 crim. 407 Com. Law & 88 chy causes on docket.

Yours Respectfully
Joseph J. Kelly Clerk
Circuit Court.

His first Case was the people vs Turner for Murder, S A Douglas A Lincoln & K Benedict for the defense, Campbell & Colton[2] for the people

---

1. Clifton H. Moore, Lawrence Weldon, Solomon F. Lewis, and Henry S. Greene.

2. *People v. Turner* was tried in Dewitt County in May 1840. Lawyers named here: Stephen A. Douglas, Kirby Benedict, David B. Campbell, and Wells Colton (Lincoln Legals).

The defendant was acquitted
I cannot tell you any thing but what you know
                          Moore

LC: HW2549; HL: LN2408, 2:284–85

190. *Jackson Grimshaw to WHH*

                          Quincy Illinois   April 28th 1866
Dear Sir

Yours of 27 inst is recd. Your former letter was received — the incident does not seem to me of much important and I do not wish to figure in print. It looks like a desire to acquire reflected publicity my name must not be used.

In the winter of 1860 while at Springfield attending the Courts I spoke to Mr. Lincoln about the propriety of allowing his name to be used as a Candidate for the Presidency — after one or two conversations in the library of the Supreme Court several of us with Mr. Lincoln went up into what has since been used as the office of Superintendant of Public Instruction then used as a Committee Room at times and sometimes used as private room of Mr. O. M. Hatch the Secretary of State.

Mr. N. Bushnell of Quincy Mr. Hatch Secretary of State, Mr. N. B. Judd then Chairman of Republican State Central Committee were present perhaps one or two others but all of us intimate friends —   I think Mr. Peck then Reporter was present.

We all expressed our personal preference for Mr. Lincoln as the Candidate for the Presidency and asked him if his name might be used at once in Connection with the Coming Nomination and election.

Mr. Lincoln with his characteristic modesty doubted whether he could get the Nomination even if he wished it and asked until the next morning to answer us whether his name might be announced as one who was to be a candidate for the office of President before the Republican [Con]vention.

The next day he authorized us to consider him and work for him if we pleased as a Candidate for the Presidency.

I passed through Springfield on my way to the Chicago Convention in 1860 — I saw Mr. Lincoln in the Secretary of States office and Called him out, the train was Coming we sat a moment on the North Steps of the State House (I was not a delegate but as a member of Republican State Central Committee expected to take an active part)   I asked him whether in the event that he could not be nominated for President he would take the Nomination for Vice President. He said he would not — I asked him if I might say so for him he gave me full authority to say for him [*] that his name having been used for the Office of President he would not permit it to be used for the other office however honorable it might be.

You may use this for your book if you choose it will come better in a narrative form without the use of names than with the parade of obscure men over our *dead* friend.

Yours truly

Jackson Grimshaw

LC: HW2550–53; HL: LN2408, 2:65–67

191. Mary Owens Vineyard to WHH

Weston Mo. May the 1st 1866.

Dear Sir:

After quite a struggle with my feelings, I have at last decided to send you the letters in my possession, written by Mr. Lincoln, believing, as I do, that you are a gentleman of honor, and will faithfully abide by all that you have said.

My associations with your lamented friend were in Menard County, whilest visiting a sister, who then resided near Petersburg. I have learned that my maiden name is now in your possession, and you have ere this (no doubt) been informed that I am a native Kentuckian.

As it regards Miss Rutlidge: I cannot tell you anything. She having *died* pervious to my acquaintance with Mr. Lincoln, and I do not now recollect of ever hearing him mention her name. Please return the letters[1] at your earliest convenience.

Very Respectfully Yours

Mary S. Vineyard.

HL: LN2408, 1:539–40

192. Elizabeth Crawford to WHH

may the 3 1866

dear Sir

your letter of Aprile the 19 has came to hand and I was glad to hear that you was well pleased with what I had ritten you wish me to tell you the names of some of our wild woods flowers   thare is the wild Sweet william wild pink lady slipper wild roses butter fly weed wild huny Succle blue flag yellow flag and thare is A grate many other kinds that I cant recolect the names of at this time   now I will give you the names of Some of the garden flowers that was cultivated in this country by the first setlers or nearly So Say in 1824 26 and on for several years and Some of them tell this time   the sweet pink the popy the marygold the larkspur the techmenot the pritty by night the lady in the green the sord lilly the flower been the holly hock the batchlers buttens those buttens the girls use to string and hang them up in their houses for an ornament thay ware verry pritty as thay war white

---

1. Presumably AL to Mary Owens, Dec. 13, 1836, May 7, 1837, and Aug. 16, 1837, in *CW* 1:54–55, 78–79, 94–95.

ones and red ones the roses the Sweet or *[illegible]* rose the infant rose the pin-
ny the ould maids eyes the velvet pink the mullen pink the garden Sweet williams
the carolina pink you wis me to tell you the names of Some of the trees that grew
in Spencer county the black oak the white oak the popler the dogwood the hick-
ery the Sweet gum the maple the redbud ash and many other kinds I will give
you A few more of the names the willow box elder the plum the crab apple the
elam the patalpa this is A beautiful tree when in full bloom the wild plum is plen-
tyful in places in this country well now I will give you A part or all of A Song
that abraham lincoln use to Sing cauld it Adam and Eaves wedding Song this Song
was Sung at abrahams sisters wedding I do not know A Linkern composed this
song or not the first that I ever heard of it was the Linkern family sung it I
rather think that A l composed it him Self but I am not certain I know that he
was in the habit of makeing Songs and Singing of them I do not wish to rite
any thing but the truth I have amed at that all the time I wish he A true history
and hope to read A true one when yours is done

Adam and eaves wedding Song[1] as follows

when Adam was created
he dwelt in edons Shade
as Moses has recorded
and soone A bride was made

ten thousand times ten thousand
of creatures swarmed around
before A bride was formed
and yet no mate was found

the lord then was not willing
the man Should be alone
but caused A sleep Apon him
and took from him A bone

and closed the flesh in sted thare of
and then he took the Same
and of it made A woman
and braut her to the man

then Adam he rejoiced
to See his loving bride
A part of his one body
the product of his Side

---

1. The existence of similar texts, including Geoffrey Chaucer's fourteenth-century narrative "The Parson's Tale," argues against AL's authorship. See Lair, 23–25.

this woman was not taken
from Adams feet we See
So he must not abuse her
the meaning Seemes to be

this woman was not taken
from Adams head we know
to Show She must not rule him
tis evidently So

this woman She was taken
from under Adams arm
So she must be protected
from injures and harm

    mr Herndon   please excuse bad riting and mistakes as I am so blind that I
cant See the lines on the paper
Elizabeth Crawford

LC: HW2554–55; HL: LN2408, 1:198–201

193. *L. M. Greene to WHH*

Avon Fulton Co Ills   May 3rd 1866

Dr Sir
    yours of March 25th came to hand in due time.

    Miss Owens came to Ills in Oct 1833 on a visit of about 4 weeks   During
this visit Mr Lincoln became acquainted with her but not intimately as I think.
Then she came to Ills again on the day of the Presidential 1836   I was at the
Election & saw her pass through New Salem She remained in the neighborhood
till April 1838 —   She was *tall* & portly weighed in 1836 about 180 lbs at this
time she was 29 or 30 years of age — had large blue eyes with the finest trimings
I ever saw   She was jovial social loved wit & humor — had a liberal English
education & was considered wealthy   She was from the State of Ky   Bill I am
getting old & have seen too much *trouble* to attempt to give a life like picture of
this woman I won't try it, None of the Poets or Romance writers hav ever given to
us a picture of a heroine so beautiful as a good description of Miss Owens in 1836.
would be

    Miss Rutledge was from the State of Kentucky   Her Father moved to what
is now Menard Co in 1827 or 1828   She was of medium height plump & round
in form weighed 150 lbs Eyes blue not large & Hair a golden yellow Modest &
unassuming in bearing about 22 years old without property
Yours truly
L. M Greene.

LC: HW2556–58; HL: LN2408, 1:492–93

194. James H. Matheny (WHH interview)

(May 3d. 1866)

James H. Matheny

Says —

That Lincoln and himself in 1842 were very friendly — That Lincoln came to him one evening and Said — Jim — "I shall have to marry that girl." Matheny Says that on the Same Evening Mr & Mrs Lincoln were married —   That Lincoln looked and acted as if he was going to the Slaughter —: That Lincoln often told him directly & indirectly that he was driven into the marriage — Said it was Concocted & planned by the Edwards family —: That Miss Todd — afterwards Mr's Lincoln told L. that he was in honor bound to marry her —: That Lincoln was crazy for a week or so — not knowing what to do —: That he loved Miss Matilda Edwards and went to see her and not Mrs Lincoln — Miss Todd.

Matheny further Says that soon after the race — the political friendly race between Baker[1] & Lincoln — which was in 1846 or 7 and after Lincoln was Married that Lincoln took him — Matheny to the woods and there and then Said in reference to L's marriage *in the Aristocracy* — "Jim — I am now and always shall be the same Abe Lincoln that I always was —" Lincoln Said this with great Emphasis —   The cause of this was that in the Baker & Lincoln race it had been charged that L had married in the aristocracy — had marrid in the Edwards — Todd & Stuart family —

Matheny further says — he remembers L in 1837–8.9 &c often quote Burns — quoted Holy Willies prayer with great pleasure: That it was L religion: That during 1842 he though that L would Commit Suicide. Mr remembers L's old office up stairs above the Court Room — a small dirty bed — one buffalo robe — a chair and a bench — L would lounge in it all day reading — *"abstracting"* — "glooming" &&c — Curious Man — good Man — Mind Equal to any occasion — always rose So — Seemed Equal to the occasion —

L wrote out and published the Tailor Trial Case of circumstantial evidence about 1857.[2]

Mrs Lincoln often gave L Hell in general — Says the Baker[3] girls have seen it & heard it and told him So. *Ferocity* — describes Mrs L's conduct to L.

LC: HW2559–60; HL: LN2408, 1:492–93

195. Dennis F. Hanks to WHH

May the 4th 66

Friend William   I Received your Leter
    Plese answer
    1st   No Indians there when I first went to Indiana   I Say No Nun

---

1. Edward Dickinson Baker.

2. AL's account was published anonymously in the Quincy *Whig*, Apr. 15, 1846, in *CW* 1:371–76. See also AL to Joshua F. Speed, June 19, 1841, *CW* 1:254–58.

3. Presumably Julia Edwards and Mary Wallace, two cousins who were nieces of MTL and who married Edward L. and John P. Baker, brothers who became proprietors of the *Illinois State Journal.*

2d   I Say this Bar Deer Turkyes and Coon wilecats and other things and frogs
3d   frute trees
plum Crabaples Black Haws Red Haws &c and grapes Both fall and winter
grapes Dog wood and Shoemake Berys
what Kind of wild fruit
This I have Named a Bove
what Kind of flowers
Swomp Lilly Sentury and Sweet William and wild Roses and and Camamile
or Basal
those State Ments is Rite.
W— M—[1] Brian Lives Close to Me his farthers Name was Larsan   He gives
his Love to you
Now Billy if I Have Mist any thing let Me No
yours as yousal
D. F. Hanks

LC: HW2571; HL: LN2408, 1:274–75

196. John McNamar to G. U. Miles

May 5th 1866

My Dear Sir
    I have Seated myself in order to answer Some of the Enquiries made by Mr
Herndon Esq Respecting Mr Lincoln My Self and other persons, My answers must
necessarily be unsatisfactory for the reason that I was absent from here when the
affairs transpired in which he Seems Most interested
    I left here in 32[1] and came to the State of Newyork for the purpose of assist-
ing My Father's family my coming west being principally to obtain the means I
did not go by steamboat nor Stage if that has any thing to do with the Matter, but
rode old Charley a hero of the Black Hawk war, who had one Grievous — fault
he would go to Sleep accasionally fall on his nose and pich me over his his head
which occasioned some profanity no Doubt, about it, Circumstances beyond my
controll detained me Much longe away than I intended
    Mr Lincoln was not to my knowledge paying any particular attention to any
of the Young Ladies of my acquaintanc when I left there was no rivalry between
him and myself on that score on the contrary I had every reson to consider him
my Personal friend untill like Andy Johnson's Tailor Partner in Tennessee[2] I was
left so far behind on his rapid and upward strides to that imperishable fame which

---

1. Possibly William Bryan.

---

1. McNamar first wrote "or 33" then crossed it out. The date of his departure for New York is problem-
atical, but it was probably in the late summer or early fall of 1832.
2. President Andrew Johnson once had a tailor partner in Greeneville, Tennessee, named Hentle W.
Adkinson.

Justly fills a world that I did not deem myself to further notice, I corrected at his request Some of the Grammatical Errors in his first address to the voters of Sangamon Co[3]   his principal Hoby being the Navigation of the Sangamon river, the first time he presented him seff as a candidate for the Legislature, this production is no Doubt to be found in some of the old files of the Journal

I never heard and person say that Mr Lincon addressed Miss Ann Rutledge in terms of courtship neither her own family nor my acquaintances otherwise

I heard simply this Expression from two prominent Gentlemen of my acquaintance and Personal Friends that Lincoln was Grieved very much at her Death

I arived here only a few weeks after her Death   I saw and conversed with Mr Lincon   I thought he had lost some of his former vivacity he was at the Post office and propably Post master he wrote a deed for me which I still hold and prize not only for the Land it conveyed but as a valued Memento

Miss Ann was a gentle Amiable Maiden without any of the airs of your city Belles but winsome and Comly withal a blond in complection with golden hair, "cherry red Lips & a bonny Blue Eye"

I know nothing of Miss Owens nor of Mr Lincons intercourse with her   I would Refer you to Bennet Abel her Brother in Law with whom She resided at that time I know of nothing more to add that would be of any Benefit to any one

Very Respectfully Yours &c
John McNamar.

[Postscript by Miles to WHH:]

I went to See Mr McNamer as you requested he Said he Knew nothing of the matters you wished to know   after he read your letter I prevailed on him to take his time and write what he Knew of the Several questions you asked which he agreed to & to day he sent me the above which I inclose to you —   all well

Yours Truly
G. U. Miles.

LC: HW2572; HL: LN2408, 1:502–4

197. Coleman Smoot to WHH

Petersburg Ills May 7th 1866

Dear Sir

Yours of May 3d is at hand and contents noted   in answer to Inquiries will Say to You I became acquainted with Abraham Lincoln in the Spring of 1832 I believe. I had heard Abe Lincoln Spoken of very frequently and was very anxious to See him and I presume he had often heard my name Spoken and had expressed a desire to See me also. one day when I was at New Salem I went into the Store in

---

3. "Communication to the People of Sangamon County," published in the *Sangamo Journal*, Mar. 15, 1832, in *CW* 1:5–9.

which he was then acting as Clerk and some one Calling me by name Lincoln Came forward and Says is that Smoot   I remarked to him that was my name he then remarked that he was very much disappointed as he had Expected to See an old Propst of a fellow   I told him I was Equally disappointed with himself for I Expected to See a good looking Man

(Now you probably Know what he meant by a Propst of a fellow he had become acquainted with old Nick Propst of Sugar Grove who was a man of very Singular looks — Shape and actions hence the name Propst of a fellow)

In Regard to his Clothing I do not Remember anything of Interest any more than his Pantaloons were very Short Causing him to look very awkward —   I know nothing objectionable in his manners or habits during my acquaintance with him

Now Sir for the hogs Eye affair   Offitt had Bought hogs of Onstott who then owned a distillery on the farm on which I now Reside   the hogs were to be driven to the flat boat on Sangamon River and being very wild it was proposed to Sow up their Eyes in order to drive them   Robert Bracken then proposed to Lincoln if he would plow in his place he would help Offitt in the Sowing operation   it proved to be of no benefit for the hogs scattered in Every direction Causing Much trouble   Lincoln has Stayed with me many nights while Surveying in this Country he was always Sociable and agreeable making hosts of friends wherever he went

After he was Elected to the legislature he came to my house one day in Company with Hugh Armstrong   Says he Smoot did you vote for me   I told him I did   Well Says he You must loan me money to buy Suitable Clothing for I want to make a decent appearance in the Legislature   I then loaned him two hundred Dollars which he Returned to me according to promise. Now for an Anecdote in Regard to Offitt[1] Lincoln & Co navigating the Sangamon River   I presume it is true but will not vouch for its truth

Offitt Seemed to think that with Lincoln as Pilot or Captain there was no such thing as fail in the navigation of the Sangamon   While building his flat Boat he determined on their Return from down the River to build a Steam boat for the Sangamon   his friends Remonstrated with him on account of the lowness of the River for a large part of the Season and frozen over for months   Offitt Said he intended to build it with Rollers underneath so that when it come to a Sand Bar it would Roll Right over and Runners underneath for to Run on the ice   for when Lincoln Was Captain By thunder She would have to go   if there is any thing in these few lines that will be of any Service to You then you are welcome to it

Yours Truly

Coleman Smoot

LC: HW2573–74; HL: LN2408, 1:543–46

---

1. Denton Offutt, AL's employer.

198. Joshua F. Speed to WHH

Louisville, 8 May 1866.

Dear Sir:

Yours of the 6*th* is at hand — You propound certain enquiries as to Mr. Lincoln's habits during his occupation of the White House.

I was never an inmate of the house and consequently can know nothing definite in answer to your queries.

I would say however, from my knowledge of him and of his habits, that he worked by no rule — Saw people at all hours — eat his meals irregularly — and did things as no other man than he ever or over could.[1]

He was irregular in his habits of eating and Sleeping.

I remember asking him on one occasion, when he slept — his answer was — "just when every body else is tired out."

A minute answer to your enquiries could perhaps be better furnish by Nicolay than by any living man —

Your friend &c
J. F. Speed

HL: LN2408, 2:324

199. George E. Baker to WHH

Washington, May 23, 1866.

My Dear Sir:

I always take pleasure in answering a letter from you.

Mr. Seward announced the irrepressible conflict Oct. 25 1858, at Rochester. See works of W.H.S. Vol. IV p. 289. Although in the great Senatorial debate of 1850 he expressed the *idea* several times it cannot be said that he *distinctly* avowed it until Oct. 25 1858. See works Vol I pp 88. &c — Also in his Cleveland speech Oct. 26 — 1848 — Vol. III p. 291. I trust you have Mr. Sewards "Works" in your State Library —

Yours ever
Geo. E. Baker.

HL: LN2408, 2:333

200. Mary Owens Vineyard to WHH

Weston Mo. May 23d. 1866.

My Dear Sir:

Really you catechise me in true lawyer style, but I feel that you will have the goodness to excuse me if I decline answering all your questions in detail, being well

---

1. The last phrase is probably a copying error by WHH's scribe, John G. Springer.

assured that few women would have ceded as much as I have, under all the circumstances.

You say that you have heard why our acquaintence terminated as it did. I too, have heard the same bit of gossip, but I never used the remark which Madame Rumor says I did to Mr. Lincoln.[1] I think I did on one occasion say to my sister, who was very anxious for us to be married, that I thought Mr. Lincoln was deficient in those little links which make up the great chain of womans happiness, at least it was so in my case; not that I believed it proceeded from a lack of goodness of heart, but his training had been different from mine, hence there was not that congeniality which would have otherwise existed. From his own showing you perceive that his heart and hand were at my disposal, and I suppose my feelings were not sufficiently enlisted to have the matter consumated. About the beginning of the year thirty eight, I left Illinois, at which time our acquaintance and correspondence ceased, without ever again being renewed. My father, who resided in Green Co. Ky, was a gentleman of considerable means, and I am persuaded that few persons placed a higher estimation on education than he did.

Respectfully Yours
Mary S. Vineyard.

Mr. W. H. Herndon:

From the date of this letter you will perceived that I thought it was in your possession weeks ago, but through some mismanagement it was sent to Washington, and has just been returned to me.

Respectfully Yours
Mary S. Vineyard.

HL: LN2408, 1:537–39

201. E. R. Burba to WHH

Hodginville Ky May 25th 1866

Dear Sir

Your very Kind letter of the 2d. inst was duly Recd and after Some delay I reply by Saying that I am unable to give you much more information than I did before — As to your first inquiry in regard to Thos Lincoln not being able to get a "Baby" from his first Marriage, that seems to be the impression from the best information I can get — He was married it appears in this County but when no one Seems to recollect — At that day this part of the country was Sparsly settled & from what I have heard old men Say there was very little attention given to Books papers or records and as the Lincoln Family at that day Cut no Considerable figure all of these mior incidents are lost Sight of — In Most of Cases they

---

1. Probably a reference to her reported remark to AL that he would not make a good husband. See the interview (§421) with her cousin, Johnson Gaines Greene.

Settleled all their difficulties out of the Court House at some public gathering or old fashioned Ky — Knock down was the order of the day get up drink make Friends & all went on well — the man that came off second best must find Some one that he Could whip — unless a Man Could boast of whipping some body he was not taken up in the best of Society — yet if he was game he could pass. I never heard of any of the Lincoln family thus ingaged their history seems to be quiet & for peace this with some other things Might be the Cause of Lincolns mooving away this is only my guess as before stated I doubt whether the Negro cut much figure here at that time

Hodgenville is rather an old place of about 5 or 600 hundred inhabitants, rather a pretty country round about it land about rolling enough to be healthy — a beautiful little creek running through it (Nolin) large enough to Carry a Mill all the year — Some very good land as much so as river bottom — then Some as poor as Need be — in Some Cases it changes within a few rods. I might say from 1st to 4th rate — The country is pretty well Supplied with Small young timber. at the birth of Lincoln it was a barran waste So to Speak, Save Some little patches on the creek bottom — the place on which Abe was Born is rather poor yet it would sell for say 20$ per acre but it would take a Man a long time to get his Money out of it — the country round about is rather level, that is no hills of note but in many places Small Basins (as they are called here) which renders the face of the country uneven & disagreeable to work for farming, in these little Sinks or basins, ponds from which in many cases answer valuable purposes to the famer for Stock   It takes very little trouble to make a pond Just tramp one of these sinks & it has a red clay bottom & will hold water like a tub — Altogether the place is rather pretty all things taken together — It lies about 3½ miles near due south from this place near a creek called the South fork of Nolin (Say from one to two miles   Wheat, Corn Oats & Tobacco grow very well on it, the latter Stands very high in market as does all Tobacco raised on that Kind of Soil — Knob Creek runs out of the gorges of Muldrews hill which skirts this County East & S East it is only a few Miles in lenth, but one of the prettiest Streams I ever Saw you can See a pebble in 10 feet Water — it empties into the Rolling fork about two miles above New Haven — The Rolling fork is a tributary of Salt River — & Salt River empties into the Ohio about 24 miles below Louisville, at the mouth there is a little village called West point quite a romantic Country round about it — get a late Map of Ky — & you will see at a glance the localities   You Spoke of Coming out in June. I have no doubt that you could make your trip quite interesting, as to the danger I apprehend none whatever more than travelling in any other quarter and I think you may be enabled to geather many little items that would be of interest to you   After you arrive at Louisville you can then come here by way of Elizabeth Town or New Haven which are about equal distances from here say 12 miles   You come to these points by the Cars & we have a Daily Stage running to N Haven & Connects with the train — I Hope you may Come out if so I will take great pleasure in rendering you all assistance I can & you will find many others who will take an interest in giving you all in formation they Can

I Regret writing so much & Saying so litle — yet perhaps you May cull out Some thing of interest

Very Respectfully Yours
E. R. Burba

LC: HW2575–76; HL: LN2408, 1:44–48

202. John McNamar to WHH

Menard County Illinos June 4th 1866

My Dear Sir

I Received your very flattering Letter Some Times Since,

you Entirely Overrate My ability to give you any furthur information concerning M. Lincoln's intercourse with the young Ladies, I was absent from 32 to 35, During which time the Sayings or doings, of Mr Lincoln have not been reported to me further than I have already Informed you, I would remark that at that time I think Neither Mr Lincon nor my self were in a Situation to Enter into what Mr Seward would Call "Entangling Alliances,"

My aquintance with Mr Lincoln commenced at Old or as it was fancifully Called New salem whether those who named it had any Referance to the place where the Priesthood forever after the order of Mulchisedick was declared, I am not prepared to say   the founders and builders of the Old Mill there were John M Cameron, who was a preacher and Mr James Rutlege both belonging to Cuberland Presbyterian Pursuasion Mr Cameron is or was Early this Spring alive he lives in california and came from Georgia   I have forgotten what State the Rutleges Came from I believe the claimed Some Connection with the rutledges of the corolinas

Miss Ann Rutlege and her Father Both died on the farm where I now reside and then owned it formerly belonged to Mr Cameron, the Rutledge farm Joining it South   Some of Mr Lincolns corners as Surveyor are Still visible on Lines traced by him on both farms, the Deaths of both Mr Rutlege and Ann occurred in 35

I however Claim to be the first Explorer and discoverer of Salem as a business point, Mr Hill (Now Dead) and myself — purchased Some Goods at cincinnatti and Shipped them to Saint Louis whence I set out on a voyage of Discovery on the praries of Illinois and finally came across John Taylor out on the prarie Near Lick or Sugar Creek Hunting Horses or fillies who Piloted me to Springfield where I put up at the Famous Hotel of Mrs Johnson; at or in front your Father's Store I was met by a tall and Slender Stripling with a countenance of somewhat a southern aspect if the term is appropriate, and whom I took for a student, who very cordially accosted me and Kindly invited me to become a citizen of Springfield, that was all there was of J. T. Stuart in those days, I however soon came across a Noted Character who Lives in this vicinity by the name of Thos. Watkins. who set forth the beauties and other advantages of Camerons Mill as it was then called

I accordingly came home with him visited the Locality contracted for the Erection of a Magnificent Store house for the Sum of fifteen Dollars, and after passing a night in the Prarie reached Saint Louis in safety   Others soon followed   Geo Warburton was sent out by his Brother John (head of the house of Warburton & Ring — with Goods Probably through the influence of the amount of Business done with their house by us, The House they Erected was afterwards occupied by Offet, and Mr Lincoln who came to the place probably in 29 or 30 or about a year after I came there   My impression is that he came down the river on a boat Loaded with corn and stoped there while offet went on to New Orleans others however Say he went on to New Orleans with offet be that is it may Offet Came back and Lincoln if he went with him Came also   Offet rented the old Mill and Exchanged some Goods Principally Sugar & Coffee for Wheat, he may have however purchased Some of Warburtons Goods, who soon Closed out, the country not having improved his morels in the Estimation of his Friends, Offet and Lincoln occupied the House as soon as vacated, I have Entirely forgotten what amount of Goods they had or Business they Done, Dr John Allen Came to the place about Same time or Shortly before (through the recommendation of Mr Proctor of Lewiston) he resided there constantly until 37. he died as you are probably aware two or three years ago he could if alive give more information concerning Mr Lincon as he was there all the time Lincoln was in this part of the country, than probably any other Person   there was a Dr Nelson[1] came to the place with a Roman Catholic wife whom he married in Cincinnati whether whether from Religion or the want of it they did not live very hapily together   Nelson built a small flat Boat and Started for Texas Lincoln piloted them out of the Sangamon the river was very full overflowing its Banks   They Lost the river as I heard Mr Lincoln relate and ran about three miles out in the Prairie. of Mr Lincolns Religious Sentiments — I think they were Protesant unless Nelsons Catholic wife converted him, I never recolect hearing Mr Lincon Swear believe he was perfectly temperate in his habits he possessed a fund of Good Humour which often found vent in anecdote, I dont recolect at this distant Day however any of his Jokes, though they were as I Remember as "plenty as Blackberries" at the time

I do not think there was any party Politics hereabout in those days candidats for Election basing their Claims upon Local Hobeys. — Lincoln I think had not returned from the Black Hawk war when I left I cant recolect seeing him for some considerable time previous more over I recolect meeting Several Cadets at Columbus O on their way to the scene of that remarable Campaign,

the Last time I ever Saw Mr Lincoln was at Petersburg. at the time of the Great Senatorial Campain between him and Mr Douglas   After he was done speaking he pass among his old acquaintance   an gave Each a Cordial Shake of the hand me among the rest calling me by name, I fear this will nont be very satisfac-

---

1. For other references to this story, see the index.

tory   the rise and fall of old Salem Cannot interest you much. As I was the Pioneer I thought proper to advert to it

Verry Respectfully yours &c

John McNamar

LC: HW2579–80; HL: LN2408, 1:497–501

203. *J. W. Wartmann to WHH*

Rockport Indiana June 19th 1866.

My Dear Sir:

I handed your letter making inquiry as to trees, fruits flowers &c &c, in this co. to Gen'l Veatch —, an old friend and political friend of Mr Lincoln's, with a request that he would answer it *at once,* and give You the desired information.

I am reminded this morning that he has mislaid the letter and also, that he had never answered it. I am sorry for this, but will endeavor to answer some of your questions as best I can. I hope you will pardon the neglect in me, and trust the little information herein contained may be of some benefit to you.

Very truly

Your friend

J. W. Wartmann

Spring flowers
    Blood Root —
    Wild Rose   Do not Know the
    Spring Beauty   Botanical Names.
    Dog Wood
    Anemone or wind flower
Spring fruits —
    Wild Straw berries
    May Apples — (a wild fruit)
    Mulberries —
Summer fruits —
    Black berries
    Wild Plums
Fall & Winter "
    Persimmons
    Fox, or wild, Grapes
    Acorns
    Hickory Nuts
    Walnuts
    Hazel Nuts
    Paw-paws
    Red Haws
    Black "

There were but few orchards in this Co' in Mr Lincoln's day here. The leading timber & forest trees, are Hickory, Beech, Yellow & White poplar, Gum, Maple, Sugar tree, Black Walnut, White Walnut, Elm, Sycamores, (in the low lands & near creeks. Dog Wood. Hack-berry (grows only on the richest soil). Oak (Black & White), used mainly in making Rails.

LC: HW2581; HL: LN2408, 1:164–66

204. John T. Harris to WHH[1]

Harrisburg Va. July 19, 1866.

Dear Sir:

Your last letter is to hand.

I have found much difficulty in getting the facts you desire, in such form that I would be willing to see them go into history. Every *fellow* has his *tale,* and all just exactly correct, but I have not been able to sift them so as to justify me in giving them to you. Our court sits today and will continue for two weeks; after which I will write you the best I can on the subject.

My regards to Mr. Shutt.

Yours Truly
John T. Harris.

HL: LN2408, 2:402

205. Elizabeth Crawford to WHH

July the 22 1866

dear Sir

your god letter of may the 8 came duly to hand and I intended to ancer it amediately and when I Set down to rite I had no ink and before had time to get any I was cauld away to See the Sick and was gone Some weeks Since that time my eyes has bin So weak that I have not attempted to rite tell now and I dont know whether I can rite So that you can read it or not but I will try   I am So blind that I cant See the lines on the paper half my time and cant read what I am now riting   you wish me to tell you some of the wild fruits of Spencer in 1826   there was the wild farel grape winter grape fox grape wild plums wild cherry black haw red haw crab apple black berry rase berry goose berry plumbs dew berry straw berry you also wished me to give you A gineral discription of the lincoln Section of country   I dont know that I can give you A compleet one though I will tell you as much as I can recolect the country at that time was verry thinly Settled but very few houses and the most of them small cabins round logs roofs put on with wait poles   It has bin so long since that I have forgoten whether the Linkern house

---

1. In all likelihood, this is a misdated transcription of §154.

was round logs[1] or not I think it was I think the house Stood east and west the chimney in the east the door in the South with a log cut out in the north Side for A window   the garden in front of the door the ground was A littlee descending from the door   the lincoln house was about two miles north of the crawford farm whare I Still live   I dont know that I can tell any thing than I have told you be- for in former letters   if it is not too late and I think of any thing that I have not ritten I will rite   you wished me to tell you whether charles grigsby and grigsby maried Sisters   tha did not charles grigsby maried m matilda hockins and ruben maried miss betsy ray

   please excuse me for not riting Sooner
Elizabeth Crawford

   LC: HW2582; HL: LN2408, 1:196–97

206. Mary Owens Vineyard to WHH

Weston Mo. July 22d. 1866.

Dear Sir:

   I do not think you pertinacious in asking the question, relative to old Mrs. Bowling Green, because I wish to set you right on that subject. Your information, no doubt, came through my cousin Mr. Gaines Green, who visited us last winter. Whilest here he was laughing at me about Mr. Lincoln, and among other things, spoke of the circumstance, in connection with Mrs. Green and child. My impres- sion is now, that I tacitly admitted it, (for it was a season of *trouble* with me,) and I gave but little heed to the whole matter. We never had any hard feelings towards each other that I knew of. On one occasion did I say to Mr. L__ that I did not believe he would make a kind husband, because he did not tender his services to Mrs. Green in helping of her carry her babe. As I said to you in a former letter, I thought him lacking in smaller atentions. One circumstance presents itself just now to my minds eye. There was a company of us going to Uncle Billy Greens, Mr. L. was riding with me, and we had a very bad branch to cross, the other gentlemen were very officious in seeing that their partners got over safely; we were behind, he riding in never looking back to see how I got along; when I rode up beside him, I remarked, you are a nice fellow; I suppose you did not care whether my neck was broken or not. He laughingly replied, (I suppose by way of compliment) that he knew I was plenty smart to take care of myself. In many things he was sensitive almost to a fault. He told me of an incident; that he was crossing a prairie one day, and saw before him a hog mired down, to use his own language; he was rather fixed up and he resolved that he would pass on without looking towards the shoat, af- ter he had gone by, he said, the feeling was eresistable and he had to look back, and the poor thing seemed to say so wistfully — *There now! my last hope is gone;* that he deliberately got down and relieved it from its difficulty.

---

   1. Cabins built of round logs were considered less finished and more primitive than those built of hewn logs.

In many things we were congenial spirits. In politics we saw eye to eye, though since then we have differed as widely as the South is from the North. But me thinks I hear you say, save me from a *political woman! So say I.* The last message I ever received from him was about a year after we parted in Illinois. Mrs. Able visited Ky. and he said to her in Springfield, Tell your Sister, that I think she was a great fool, because she did not stay here and marry me.

Characteristic of the man.

Respectfully Yours
Mary S. Vineyard.

HL: LN2408, 1:535–37

207. *John Bennett to WHH*

Petersburg 3rd Augt 1866

Dr Sr

Yours of the 28th July came to our office in my absence, and consequently has not been earlier ansd. In reply I can say that I was present at the funeral of Bolling Green, and at the request of Mrs Green made through me to Mr. Lincoln, he made or delerd. his Eulogy. When I delivered Mrs Greens request to him, he remarked to me that he did not know what to say, that he had not thought upon the subject — I replied to him that it would gratify the old Lady, if he would make some remarks on the occasion — he then said he would try and do so — walked off out of the crowd, and in a short time mounted the stand, and made a few remarks in relation to the old mans manners, customs, habits of life &c and closed, and I must say, that I agree with Mr. Ellis,[1] that it was a failure so far as I was qualified to judge — But after all I don't know that it could be considered a failure, when we reflect that he had but little material to make a speach out of — This funeral was held in a Grove near the residence of the decd, and I think it was in the fall of 1842 — I know he died in Feb — of that year. He was buried by Springfield Lodge No 4. and by applying to the Sec of that Lodge, I presume you can get the exact time — it was before our Lodge here was organized

My first acquaintance with Mr. Lincoln was in March 1836 — he came to this place from New Salem, where he then lived, in company with Bowling Green, by whom he was introduced to me as a Whig and one of the Representatives to the Legislature which had adjd. but a few days before — I recollect the first thing he said after the introduction, was to call my attention to a pair of delicate *[illegible]* mitts that he was wearing — this he did in his peculiar way — I was struck with his appearance and manners, and an intimacy grew up between us, that lasted until the formation of the Republican party, when we took diffirent roads, or rather he switched off and I continued in the old track — I always found

---

1. In the sharp differences reported about AL's performance on this occasion, there may be a confusion of the funeral service in February 1842 with the Masonic memorial service, which took place several months later.

him a very kind, humane Gentlemanly man, always ready and willing to do a kind act — he commenced the Survey of our Town in the fall of 1835, and in the following spring completed it — he was several weeks about it and I was a good deal in his company, and the opinions I formed of him there as a man has remained unchanged

If any thing that I have said here will be of any use to you in making up his history, you are welcome to use it, provided my name is not used —

Yrs Resp
Jno. Bennett

LC: HW2587–88; HL: LN2408, 1:557–59

208. Allan Pinkerton to WHH

Phila., Aug 5th 1866.

Dear Sir:

Your favor of the 1st Inst. is duly received. Some days since I received a letter from Hon. Leonard Swett in reference to the Records containing an account of Mr. Lincoln's passage to Washington through Baltimore on his way to be inaugurated in the Spring of '61; to which I replied granting yourself and Mr. Swett their use with the pledge from you both that you would consider as strictly confidential all matter contained therein relating to the affairs of the Phila. Wil, & Balt. R.R., also that the name of the Broker who occupied rooms adjoining mine in Baltimore should be omitted as although he was undoubtedly a rebel at heart, yet he is a man of not much means; he has lost considerable during the war, and the publication of his name might tend to his serious injury in business. I deprecate this in any publications coming from my records. Aso, that you would consider as confidential any remarks which are found therein concerning Mark H. Lamon Esq.[1] I shall be very glad to correspond with you or assist you in anyway in which I can in compiling of your valuable history. If your letters are addressed to me at Chicago they will be sure to be forwarded to me wherever I may be, which will probably be the best for you to do, as I am travelling a great deal.

Yours Truly
Allan Pinkerton
— Bartlett — x^2

LC: HW2589

---

1. WHH apparently forgot about his obligation to keep this material confidential, for he sold copies of it to none other than Ward Hill Lamon, the man referred to here by Pinkerton.

2. Apparently Bartlett was the secretary who wrote out and signed this letter.

209. Robert B. Rutledge to WHH

Burlington Aug, 5th 1866

I have the honor to acknowledge the Receipt of your letter of 30th Ult, Making inquiry as to my knowledge of the early history of our *Martered President*, which will require some time to answer intelligably, As I will have to consult our Family Record, *My Mother* and elder Brother,[1] who are in Van Buren Co Iowa, Any information I can give you, I will take great pleasure in doing, I see some pretended histories of Mr. Lincols life, which are Manifestly in error in detail,

I Recollect all the men named in your letter, If Row Herendon Wm Green, Minter Graham & John — McNamar are living they will Recollect me as the 3d Son of the family,

I am dear sir Very Respectfully

your humble Servant

R, B, Rutledge

LC: HW2590; HL: LN2408, 1:553–54

210. Mary Owens Vineyard to WHH

Weston Mo. August 6th 1866.

Born in the year eight, fair skin, deep blue eyes, with dark curling hair; height, five feet, five inches, weighing about one hundred and fifty pounds.[1]

HL: LN2408, 1:537

211. Thomas L. D. Johnston to WHH

Decature Ills. Aug 10th/66

Dear sir

I dop you a not to let you know that I will be in your city in short time 5 or six dayes if not sooner. if it is not to late for you to make use of that copy Book, I will bring it with me you must parden me for not leting you here from me sooner for I have ben travling for a month or more & I didnot git your letter untill the other day. Nothing more untill I here from you if you need the Book I will be over

Yours & ct.

Thos., L, D. Johnston

LC: HW2595

---

1. Mary Rutledge and John M. Rutledge.

---

1. This brief passage, known only from Springer's transcriptions, represents either an extract from a longer Vineyard letter or a brief response by Vineyard to queries put by WHH.

212. Robert B. Rutledge to WHH

Burlington Aug 12th 1866.

Dear Sir

your two letters of the 8th & 9th inst. is before me and contents noted. I have to say in reply that notwithstanding I am very much engrossed with business, I will put forth my best efforts to comply with your wishes, in having my answer ready the 1st of Oct, about which time I expect to move to Oskaloosa in this State, which will in all probability be my permanent residence, having been sent to this place at an early stage of the War as Provost Marshal of 1st Congressional Dist of Iowa, my residence here is temporary,

When I get my answer prepaired, I will if at all practicable visit you, as I would like a personal intervew as there are some things involved in a full answer to your Interrogatories, of a delicate characture   No charge for time service or expense will be made, as I will be more than compensated, if I can contribute any thing to the history of that *Great good Man,* whose name and fame will ever live green in the Memory of a greatful American people

I Am Dear Sir

Very truly your Friend
R B Rutledge

LC: HW2597; HL: LN2408, 1:554–55

213. William Jayne (WHH interview)

August 15th 1866[1]

Wm Jayne —

I took the names of Judge Logan & Abrm Lincoln to the Sangamon Journal Office and had them published as candidates for the H.R of the Ills Legislature —   This was in the Mo of _____ 1854. Mrs Lincoln saw Francis the Editor and had Lincolns name taken out. Lincoln was absent. When L. came home I went to see him in order to get him to consent to run. This was at *his* house: he was then the saddest man I Ever Saw — the gloomiest: he walked up and down the floor — almost crying and to all my persuasions to let his name stand in the papers — he said "No — I can't — you don't Know all — I Say you don't begin to Know one half and that's Enough". I did however go and have his name re-instated and there it stood. He and Logan were Elected by about 600 majority — see Journal

Lincoln resigned his seat, finding out that the Republicans — the Anti Nebraska men had Carried the Legislature. N M. Broadwell ran as whig — Anti Nebraska man — was badly beaten —. The People of Sangamon County was down on Lincoln — hated him — Had Lincoln Kept his seat he would have been the Senator at that time. McDaniel, who beat Broadwell was a Democrat of the Douglas School.

---

1. The date is given at the end of the manuscript, followed by: *in Doct. Jaynes office —.*

Butler Hon Wm Butler — Secry of the Treasurer of this State — who clothed and boarded Lincoln for years — paid his debts — L's — debts & obligations, because L would not give him Butler in 1848 the land office swore he would be revenged on Lincoln. Butler pretended however to be L's friend. He was for Trumbull — got into Lincolns good graces — in Lincolns camp — heard all and revealed to Trumbull & his camp. Judd & Palmer in the Legislature heard all and Stuck to Trumbull, Knowing what L's plans were &c. Trumbull was Elected —   they were good friends — had no fuss — no words or misunderstanding — Matheny to the Contrary notwithstanding — his whole story was a lie — Judge Logan *pretended* as I think to be a friend of Lincoln but I have a notion that he was not, but was for Trumbull, my brother in Law —

When I was a boy *Mrs* Lincoln and *Mrs* Trumbull, both girls at that time got me to drop the Satiracle poetry against Shields[2] — Gen Jas Shields — which in part caused the challeng by Shields —

I saw Judd at the late Republican Convention (Aug 1866) and he and I got to speaking about Lincoln's Speech in 1858. After the Speech was delivered & printed Judd met Lincoln one day and said to Lincoln — "Well Lincoln had I seen that Speech I would have made you Strike out that house divided part" — "You would — would you Judd —" I guess you wouldn't — replied Lincoln

LC: HW2599–2600; HL: LN2408, 2:179–81

214. Allan Pinkerton Agency (report furnished to WHH)[1]

[1861?]

Opperations on Baltimore Conspirators.
(for the assassination of President Lincoln.)

Sunday 27*th*, February 1861

A letter was written of which the following is a copy —

Chicago 27*th*. January 1861

S. M. Felton Esq.
Prest. P.W.&B.R.R.[2]
Philadelphia.
Sir.

Should the suspicions of danger still exist, as was the case at our interview on the 19*th* Inst. I would suggest in view of the brief time we now have to operate in

---

2. Jayne presumably refers to delivering the satirical poem on James Shields written by his sister, Julia Jayne (later Trumbull), and Mary Todd (later Lincoln) to the *Sangamo Journal*, where it was published on September 16, 1842. See MTL's reference to this poem in §§252, 254.

---

1. Pinkerton told WHH in a letter dated August 11, 1866, that he had asked that copies of his agency's records of the Baltimore conspiracy of 1861 be sent on to WHH; by August 18, WHH had written to ask about them. See Pinkerton's reply at §218. The copies were apparently returned to Pinkerton.

2. Philadelphia, Wilmington, and Baltimore Railroad.

— that I should myself with from four to six operatives, immediately repair to the seat of danger and first endeavor to ascertain if any organization is in existence which might directly or indirectly have for its object the commission of the offence you alluded to, and if so, then to become acquainted with some of the members of such body, and, if practible, some of my operatives should join the same, and so soon as we learn positively who the leading spirits are that would be likely to do *The Active Labor* on the project you alluded to, an *unceasing Shadow* should be kept upon them every moment and, if, possible, a Shadow should even be located in the dwelling or boarding house occupied by the parties above alluded to. By some such an effort, I believe (If any organization exists — or any body of men are preparing for the service suspected), I could be able to learn their secrets and proposed plans of operations in sufficient time to be able to communicate them to you.

The only danger which I percieve to our operating is in the short time we have to work in. Basing all my operations upon the attaining a controlling power over the mind of the suspected parties — Our operations are necessarily tedious — Nay frequently very slow — Our strength lays in the secrecy of our movements, and thus we are frequently enabled to penetrate into the abodes of crime in all classes of society.

The shortness of time I design to make up for in part by the number of operatives detailed for this business — Had I plenty of time to work in, I might probably be able to ascertain all that you require with two or three operatives who could make their observations on one class of individuals, or individuals of a class and after applying the necessary test to these parties if it was demonstrated that they were not connected with any such matters as we sought information regarding, my operatives could quit their observations upon them and commence to apply the tests to other suspicious characters. But allowing we were to be already at work the time is too brief for me to work safely in this manner — If any good is to be realized from a movement of the kind contemplated by you it can only be by an attack on every point we can find accessible — and on account of the great importance of the business I should think it best and safest to be under my own personal supervision.

As I have before remarked Secrecy is the Lever of any success which may attend my operations and as the nature of this service may prove of a character which might to some extent be dangerous to the persons of myself, or any operatives I should expect that the Fact of my operating should only be known to myself or such discreet persons connected with your Company as it might be absolutely necessary should be entrusted with the same. But on no conditions would I consider it safe for myself or my operatives were the fact of my operating known to any Politician — no matter of what school, or what position.

As I have other matters which are pressing on me just at present you would confer a favor by letting me hear from you at your earliest convenience — By letter or Telegraph.

Respectfully Yours.
Allan Pinkerton.

Tuesday 12*th,* February 1861.

at 8.00. a.m. a Letter was received from A.P. —[3] enclosing one for N. B. Judd.
at 9.10. a.m. a Dispatch was sent of which the following is a copy.

Chicago 12*th* Feby 1861.

"N. B. Judd
"in company with Abraham Lincoln
"Indianapolis
"Ind.

"I have a message of importance for you — where can it reach you by Special
Messenger.

Allan Pinkerton."

at 12.20. p.m. a Dispatch was received of which the following is a copy —

"Indianapolis 12*th,* Feb'y 1861.

"A. Pinkerton
"At Columbus the thirteenth — Pittsburg the Fourteenth.
N. B. Judd."

at 12.30. p.m. a Dispatch was sent of which the following is a copy —

"Chicago 12*th* Feb'y 1861.

"W. H. Scott[4]
"Lafayette
"Ind.

"J— says will be at Columbus Thirteenth — Pittsburg Fourteenth — form
your own estimate by enquiring at Indianapolis.
G. H. Bang's"[5]

Tuesday 12*th* February 1861 —[6]

*   *   *

We then returned to the Fountain Hotel, and from there went to my room on
Holliday Street.

I will here mention that while I was in the parlor at Mr. Halls, waiting for my
room to be got ready — I was introduced by Hilliard[7] to a man by the name of
Hughe's, a Daguerreau Artist, who said that he had lived in New Orleans, and New

---

3. Allan Pinkerton.

4. Scott was Pinkerton's operative who was chosen to carry the warning of the assassination plot to Judd.
See Cuthbert, 20. For information on the people and events in Pinkerton's account of the Baltimore plot,
the editors are greatly indebted to Cuthbert's work.

5. Superintendent of Pinkerton's agency and his chief of staff at Chicago. See Cuthbert, 20.

6. According to Cuthbert, 20, what follows is a report from a Pinkerton agent in Baltimore, Harry W.
Davies.

7. O. K. Hillard, a Baltimore "soldier of fortune and secessionist." See Cuthbert, 135.

York, and that New Orleans was the Paradise of the United States. Hughes asked me how times were in New Orleans — I replied that times were hard — Hughes remarked "Well — times are hard here — I presume there is some excitement in New Orleans — they are all secession there — here we are about half and half — I understand *that they have men watching the Rail Road Bridge between here and Philadelphia: the Rail Roads are afraid that they will be destroyed — but I do not know if it will do any good —*" winking at the same time. I then left him to go to my room, inviting him to call at my room when he had leisure — He replied that he would be happy to extend the acquaintance.

When Hilliard and I left Mr. Hall's to go up the Street, he introduced me to a Mr. Starr, a Reporter for one of the Baltimore papers — about 30 years of age — and Hilliard asked him to join us in a drink which invitation he readily accepted. On leaving Starr, Hilliard and I went to supper at Mann's Restaurant, after which we went to Harry Hemlings Billiard Room, when I asked the latter to go with us to the Theatre — but he said it was now 8 o'clock, and too late for him to dress: that he would be pleased to go at any other time.

There was a man at Hemling's who had just arrived from South Carolina — and who was very much in favor of Southern Confederacy.

Hilliard and I left Hembling's and went to the "Pagoda" Concert Saloon and remained there until about 10.00. p.m., when Hilliard proposed to go to Annette Travis, No. 70. Davis Street, which we did. Hilliard and his woman seemed very much pleased at meeting, and hugged and kissed each other for about an hour, when I proposed to go. Hilliard's woman wished him to remain, and finally after asking him several times to come, I started for the door, went out on to the sidewalk and shortly Hilliard came out and we went to my room at Mr. Halls, where we sat and talked until about 1.00 a.m. Hilliard said that Company No. 4. National Volunteers[8] drilled to-night: that the Company which he did belong to would drill to-morrow night, and that he must go to the drill then. He then asked me if I had seen *a statement of Lincolns route to Washington City* — I replied that I had — Hilliard said *"By the By, that reminds me that I must go and see a certain party in the morning the first thing."* I asked him what about — He replied *"about Lincoln's route, I want to see about the Telegraph in Philadelphia and New York and have some arrangements made about Telegraphing —"* I remarked *"how do you mean?"* Hilliard said *"Suppose that some of Lincoln's friends would arrange so that the Telegraph messages should be mis-carried, we would have some signs to telegraph by: for instance supposing, that we should Telegraph to a certain point "all up at 7," that would mean that Lincoln would be at such a point at 7 o'clock.*

I would here state that in the evening we went to Farridina's Barber shop, under Barnums Hotel, but he was not in. Hilliard inquired for Captain Farridina.[9]

---

8. A Baltimore paramilitary political club, dedicated in 1860 to the Breckinridge-Lane ticket and in 1861 to resisting the passage of Federal troops through Maryland. See Cuthbert, 136.

9. Cypriano Ferrandini had long been connected with Baltimore military organizations and was a leader in the National Volunteers. See Cuthbert, 138.

In the conversation with Hilliard soon after going to my room, and after the Telegraph had been introduced in regard to Mr. Lincoln — I said to him "It is very singular that some plan of action, and mature arrangement by which you will know how to proceed, had not been proposed". Hilliard replied that there was a plan, and I asked him what it was — He said "My friend, that is what I would like to tell you, but I dare not — I wish I could — anything almost I would be willing to do for you, but to tell you that I dare not."

On Hilliard and I parting with Starr — the former said to me "anything that I have said to you be careful not to mention." He cautioned me in the same manner on leaving Harry Hemlings Billiard Room — as "Be careful not to say anything around here" — From his remarks I inferred that he desired me to be more careful about saying anything around Mrs. Hall's boarding House, and also around Hemling's Saloon.

In the course of the conversation during the evening, Hilliard remarked that there was something the matter with him. I remarked that it might be the _____ at this he seemed horrified.

Hilliard left me at 1. oclock in the morning and went to stay all night, or the balance of it with his woman at Annette Travis' house of prostitution No. 70 Davis Street, as he had promised, her to come, so he said — He promised to meet me again at 12.00. m.

During the day Hilliard did not drink as much liquor as usual. He appeared melancholy *most of the time that* he was with me.

C.D.C.W.[10] — Reports

Tuesday 12*th* February 1861.

At about 9.00. a.m. I went to the Office and wrote my Reports. I also saw Mr. P—, and told him that I was afraid I could not play my part, as I had come across a Mississippi man who knew every place. A. P— said there was no danger, and all I wanted was self confidence.

I soon after left, and returned to my Hotel, where I got into conversation with Howell Sherwood, who superintends the Bar, and is brother to the Landlord. He told me he was for peace, but would go with the South, although he hated to give up the Stars and Stripes, but if it must be, he would go to Texas; that he was for the union if it could be preserved, but if not he was for the South, although he did not belong to the Seces — crowd in the City: that there was a gentleman here (Baltimore) last week from South Carolina, and he met with an old friend who took him to one of their Secession Meetings, and the next morning he came and told himself, that if any one had said there was such a conspiracy in this or any other City, amongst Christians, he would not have believed it; that last night he heard the vilest proposition proposed, by men, calling themselves men that ever was heard of: that they proposed to blow up the Capitol on the day that the Votes

---

10. Charles D. C. Williams, the alias of an unidentified Pinkerton agent. See Cuthbert, 20.

were counted, and then blow up the Custom House, and Post Office (Baltimore), and what else he dare not tell.

I said to Sherwood that it was all nonsense, and that the man was humbuging him. "Oh my God, it is so", said Howell, the man had to leave that afternoon by the boat or they would have killed him: that there is a d—d white headed son of a b—, a Lawyer, named Mc— somthing, who goes every day to Washington, and brings the news to this crowd, and that they hold secret meetings every night; that there was another blagard, Tom Smith, the Oyster-man, who would blow h— out of everything: that he was one of the principal leaders for a time: that he did not care what become of the town, so long as he and his party gained their point"

I said there were black sheep in every flock, but that I could not believe that they were so bad as he represented, because if they were why did not the authorities put them down. "Why d— it" said Howell, they hold their meetings secretly at the Eutaw House, or some such place: that at first they held their meeting at Reuben Hall, on Fayette street, but when they found honest men would not join them, they commenced holding the meetings privately: that Tom Smith is a d—d black-hearted villian, and ruined the Democratic ticket in this City, and that he (Howell) voted for Bell and Everett.

*   *

*   *

Wednesday 13th February 1861.

W.H.S[11] — Reports,

At about 2.00. A.M. I arrived at Cincinnatti, and put up at the Burnett House, and learned that N. B. Judd had been in bed since about 11. o'clock, but that they would not disturb him: that I could see him in the morning as he did not leave until 9. o'clock.

They gave me a room, and I went to bed. I got up at 7.00. a.m. and waited until 8 o'clock when I saw "Judd" and gave him A. P—s letter.

After reading A. P—s letter, "Judd" said that he had been looking for this, and was going on to say more, when I said to him, that from information received from A. P—, I was satisfied that he (A.P.) desired this letter to him to be strictly confidential. Judd replied "that is true, and I am very much obliged to you and A. P— for the information." I asked him if he desired to Telegraph to A. P—, and after a moments reflection said "I think not," but would write to A. P— and that he had his address. I told him that I had a Cipher with me if he desired to Telegraph A.P. Judd said that he would like to take it with him in case he should conclude to do so. I replied that we had but in the Office and I could not spare it. the matter then dropped.

Judd repeated that he was very glad that he had got A. P—s letter, and asked me if I had just come through from Chicago. I replied that I had. He said that he had Telegraphed to us in Chicago that he would be in Columbus, Ohio, to-day. I replied that I left before this Dispatch was received. He spoke very feelingly of A.P. and said they had trained in the same school to-gether.

I then shook hands with Judd, and left for the Rail Road Depot, as I had been told a train left for Chicago at 9.00. a.m. On arriving at the Depot I learned that the morning train had left at 5.40. a.m. and that the next train left at 7.35. P.m. so I remained in town and saw the train leave with the President-Elect, and suite on board.

In buying my ticket I had to use some Eight Dollars of Illinois bills,[12] for which I had to allow fifteen per cent before I could get my ticket. I left at 7.35. p.m. for Chicago —

Friday 15th February 1861.

A. P— Reports
*   *   *   *

These opinions pleased Luckett[13] very highly, and he d—d Governor Hicks for the course he had taken, and alluded to the fact that the Legislature of Maryland had called a Convention in despite of the opposition of the Governor.[14] Mr. Luckett said that he was elected a member of that Convention which meets in Baltimore next Monday, that he was elected by the whole vote of his county but two, and that after a full and[15] expression of his views for immediate secession, Mr. Luckett said that he told the meeting which elected him, that this was not a time for men to be elected who would falter in doing their duty; that the responsibility attending on the members of the convention were of such a nature as required men only to be elected who would not hesitate if necessary to peril their lives for the rights of Maryland and the Southern Confederacy — and said that the *time was now come for us to act;* talking was now at an end — it was action which was necessary, and that action must be soon — No Hesitancy — If people or Governors, or Presidents, called it Treason — which they would after Lincoln is inaugerated — let them call it Treason, but let us act; Mr. Luckett said that the Maryland Convention would appoint a Committee to confer with the convention at Richmond Virginia, and that when Virginia Seceded Maryland would, and that then the District of Columbia having originally been *[blank space]* to the United States of America specially as a Capitol so long as the United States existed — and now as that Union had ceased to exist, the District *[blank space]* to the original owners, and that then Maryland and Virginia would take it, let the consequences be what they may; that those two States could concentrate a Hundred Thousand men around the Capitol in a very short time, and then see where General Scott would be.

---

12. Under the Illinois banking system, banks had no capital other than bonds they had placed with the state auditor.

13. Baltimore stockbroker and secessionist. See Cuthbert, 2, 5.

14. A convention to consider Maryland's stance during the secession crisis.

15. Marginal note: *word left out.*

Mr. Luckett said that the Northern Rail Roads were using their Roads to transport Troops to Washington, but that this would soon be ended; that the Roads would be stopped by law, or act of the Convention, and by the Virginia and Maryland Troops; that this should, and would be done. Mr. Luckett said that to-day there was a number of Troops coming from the North — they would be here this afternoon, but not many more should be allowed to pass through: that there were Thousands of Mechanics who were at the present time with their families in a state of starvation — *We are enlisting* them daily — said Mr. Luckett, we can get as many as we want of them — just say to them "all your sufferings come from this Black Republican rule, and we will give you each Ten Dollars and bread for your family, and good pay every month — We do not want you to leave your families, or your houses, but to stay here and fight for them — How many will refuse this"? said Mr. Luckett.

"I tell you my friend" said Mr. Luckett, "it will be but a short time until you will find Governor Hicks will have to fly, or he will be hung — He (Gov. Hicks) is a traitor to his God and his Country."

Mr. Luckett in reply to a remark of mine about President Lincoln passing through Baltimore said — "He (Lincoln) *may pass through quietly but I doubt it* —" "There are a great many men in this City Mr. Hutcheson[16] — good men — aye — and good blood to." I remarked that Police Marshall Kane had promised Lincoln a safe transit through Baltimore. "Oh!" said Mr. Luckett "that is easily promised, but may not be so easily done — Marshall Kane don't know any more than any other man, and not so much as some others — but time will tell — time will tell."

Mr. Luckett said that probable when the Southern Congress met it would prohibit the importation of Slaves into the Confederate States from the States outside the Confederation, and that if they did so, then then the Border Slave States must join the confederation or become Free States.

I fully endorsed this view of Mr Lucketts, and took strong grounds for immediate secession, and the occupancy of the Capitol. Mr. Luckett said that I should soon see a move made in the right direction; that no more Northern troops should be allowed to pass Southwards through Maryland; that there was an organization here which was powerful enough to bid defiance to Lincoln and his Abolitionist Crew. I (Luckett) shall never so help me God, acknowledge it as a Government — never, Mr. Hutcheson — never. We are raising money and giving it to the organization to purchase Arms, and also getting Arms, and amunition on hand so we can arm the Mechanics who are out of employment and starving — "Those men", said Mr. Luckett "will fight, when they believe that Lincoln is the cause of all this misery, aye, and they will fight to the death." Look Mr. Hutcheson at our City — at what it is now, and what it has been, and tell me if we are not going to ruin — Mr Luckett here told me of several business firms who had become Bankrupt within a few days — Of course in all these things I cordially sympathized with

16. An alias used by Allan Pinkerton. See Cuthbert, 5, 19–20.

Mr. Lucketts views, and taking out my wallet said that I was but a stranger to him, but that I had no doubt but that money was necessary for the success of this patriotic cause, and as I fully agreed with them, I begged to lay my mite at their disposal, and handed Mr. Luckett Twenty five Dollars, telling him that I should be obliged if he would see that this was employed in the best manner possible for Southern rights, and that when more was required I hoped he would call on me, and then took occasion to caution Mr. Luckett to impress it upon the minds of his friends to cautious in talking with ousiders, for myself I did not desire to ought — I would trust Mr. Luckett, and such like patriotic minded men &c. &c.

Mr. Luckett said they were *exceedingly cautious,* as to who they, talked with; that they *knew* who they talked with: that some time ago they found that the Government had spies amongst them, and that since then they had been *very* careful; that none knew anything about the movement of the Southern rights men, but such as were sworn to keep it secret: that he (Mr. Luckett) was not a member of the secret organization, for there were but very few, who could be admitted, but he knew many who were, and that Captain Ferrandina an Italian was the leading man: that he (Ferrandina) was a true friend to the South and was ready to lose his life for their cause, and that he (Ferrandina) had a plan fixed to prevent Lincoln from passing through Baltimore, and would certainly see that Lincoln never should go to Washington: that every Southern Rights man had confidence in Ferrendina, and that before Lincoln should pass through Baltimore he (Ferrendina) would kill him: that Ferrendina had not many friends that knew his purpose, but was a particular friend of his (Lucketts), and that the money I had given him (Luckett) would be given to Ferrandina.

Mr. Luckett said that he was not going home this evening and if I would meet him at Barr's Saloon on South Street he would introduce me to Ferrandina. This was unexpected to me, but I determined to take the chances, and agreed to meet Mr. Luckett at the place named at 7.00. p.m. Mr. Luckett left about 2.30. p.m. and I went to dinner.

I was at the Office in the afternoon in hopes that Mr. Felton might call, but he did not, and at 6.15. p.m. I went to supper. After supper I went to Barr's Saloon, and found Mr. Luckett and several other gentlemen there. He asked me to drink and introduced me to Captain Ferrandina, and Captain Turner. He eulogised me very highly as a neighbor of his, and told Ferrandina that I was the gentleman who had given the Twenty five Dollars, he (Luckett) had given to Ferrandina.

The conversation at once got into Politics, and Ferrandina who is a fine looking, intelligent appearing person, became very excited. He shows the Italian in I think a very marked degree, and although excited, yet was cooler than what I had believed was the general characteristic of Italians. He has lived South for many years and is thoroughly imbued with the idea that the South must rule: that they (Southerners) have been outraged in their rights by the election of Lincoln, and freely justified resorting to any means to prevent Lincoln from taking his seat, and as he spoke his eyes fairly glared and glistened, and his whole frame quivered, but he was fully conscious of all he was doing. He is a man well calculated for controlling and directing the ardent minded — he is an enthusiast, and believes that, to use his own words, "Murder of any kind is justifiable and right to save the rights of the Southern people". In all his views he was ably seconded by Captain Turner.

Captain Turner is an American, but although, very much of a gentleman and posessing warm Southern feelings, he is not by any means so dangerous a man as Ferrandina, as his ability for exciting others is less powerfull — but that he is a bold and proud man, there is no doubt, as also that he is entirely under the control of Ferrandina. In fact it could not be otherwise, for even I myself felt the influence of this mans strange power, and wrong though I knew him to be, I felt strangely unable to keep my mind balanced against him.

Ferrandina said that never, never shall Lincoln be President — His life (Ferrandina) was of no consequence — he was willing to give it for Lincoln's — he would sell it for that Abolitionists, and as Orissini[17] had given his life for Italy, so was he (Ferrandina) ready to die for his country, and the rights of the South, and, said Ferrandina, turning to Captain Turner "we shall all die together. We shall show the North that we fear them not — every Captain, said he, will on that day prove himself a hero — The first shot fired, the main Traitor (Lincoln) dead, and all Maryland will be with us, and the South shall be free, and the North must then be ours. "Mr Huchins," said Ferrandina, *"If I alone must do it, I shall — Lincoln shall die in this City."*

Whilst we were thus talking we (Mr. Luckett, Turner, Ferrandina and Myself), were alone in one corner of the Bar Room, and while talking two strangers had got pretty near us. Mr Luckett called Ferrandina's attention to this, and intimated that they were listening, and we went up to the Bar — drinked again at my expense, and again retired to another part of the room, at Ferrandina's request to see if the strangers would again follow us — whether by accident or design, they again got near us, but of course we were not talking of any matter of consequence. Ferrandina said he suspected they were Spies, and suggested that he had to attend a secret meeting, and was apprehensive that the two strangers might follow him, and at Mr. Lucketts request I remained with him (Luckett) to watch the movements of the strangers. I assured Ferrandina that if they did attempt to follow him, that we would whip them.

Ferrandina and Turner, left to attend the meeting, and anxious as I was to follow them myself, I was oblige to remain with Mr. Luckett to watch the strangers — which we did for about fifteen minutes, when Mr. Luckett said that he should go to a friends to stay over night, and I left for my Hotel, arriving there about 9.00. p.m., and soon retired.

*   *   *   *

---

17. Felice Orsini, an Italian patriot who tried to assassinate Napoleon III in 1858.

Friday 15*th* February 1861 —

C.D.C.W. — Reports.

*　　　　　*　　　　　*　　　　　*　　　　　*

I then returned to Sherwoods,[18] as I had made an appointment with Sherrington[19] to go to see "Tom Smith". We first went to his (Tom Smiths) Oyster Establisment on Market Street, but not finding him there we returned by way of Market Street, and over-took him (Smith) on the corner of Second and Market Streets.

Sherrington introduced him to me, when we went into Saloon on Market Street and had quite a talk. Smith informed Sherrington that they had broken up their meetings as they could do nothing; that they had become disheartened, and he was disgusted with Maryland; that he was going to settle up his business Summer, and go to South Carolina in the Fall: that he was really ashamed to own that he was a native of Maryland; that he had talked and talked to them but all to no use: that in five years we would be able to cut a good crop of grass in the streets of Baltimore. Sherrington then asked Smith if Lincoln was not coming through on Saturday. Smith replied that he did not know whether he was or not: that he doubted if Lincoln would ever pass through Baltimore. Smith said this in a peculiar manner, and winked at me — "if he does", said I, "I'll be d—d if I don't leave here, and go to South America, for I wont live under him," "Nor will I," said Sherrington, "If he does," Said Tom., "Mark me — if he does, then this town is ruined and grass will grow in the Streets": (He spoke in a slow deliberate manner, seeming to weigh every word, but never once getting excited): that the Marylanders were too slow for him: that they "blow" to much, and don't act enough". I then asked him (Smith) what would have happened if Maryland, had acted like South Carolina. He replied that Washington would have belonged to the Southern Confederacy, and Lincoln shall never have taken his seat; that there was no use talking to the d—d fools any more (meaning the Marylanders): that we must be ready to act, for by God there was hot work ahead. I asked him what he thought of the "Force-Bill".[20] Tom, said that they must never try that, for they could never subjugate the South — they might exterminate them, but they would never surrender.

Sherrington then wanted to know where they held their meetings now. Tom replied that he did not know, for he had nothing to do with them, "Well," said I, "they say us Secessionists want to blow H—l out of everything, "If they won't let the South have what belongs to them, then I say "blow" up the property sooner that let the North have it," said Smith. "Do you know" said I, "that we have a lot of d—d spies in town — Dick Sherwood[21] told us so to-day; that they had been to him for information as he was a Union man". Smith replied to this that there was a S— of a B— who stopped at Bucks Saloon on Lafayette Street; that he pre-

---

18. Sherwood's Hotel.

19. Captain Sherrington, involved with the National Volunteers.

20. Bills introduced in Congress in January and February 1861 dealing with the collection of Federal revenue, the recovery of Federal property, and the use of the militia to suppress general insurrection.

21. Richard P. Sherwood, proprietor of Sherwood's Hotel. See Cuthbert, 160.

tended to be selling watch pockets, made of canton flannel, and pine-burs sewed on them: that they had watched him going to the Telegraph Office several times a day &c". I said if he would show him to me I would make it too hot for him here, Smith answered, that he wished to G—d I would for he (the spy) was watching their every movement, and then said he reckoned we were all right, and to be on hand to act when wanted. He then bade us goodby, and we parted.

*   *   *   *

Monday 18*th*, February 1861 —

M. B—[22] Reports —

I got up at 7.30. A.M. and breakfasted at 8.30. a.m. — During the forenoon Mr. P— called and said I must get ready to go to New York on the 5.16. p.m. train. He also gave me my instructions and some letter's for N. B. Judd, and E. S. Sanford,[23] and then left.

After dinner I made arrangements to leave, paying my Bill &c —, and told them I wanted to take the train for Philadelphia. At about 4.00 p.m. I left for the Depot where I saw Mr. P—, and at 5.16. p.m. I started for New York.

Tuesday 19*th* February 1861.

M.B. — Reports

I arrived in New York at 4.00. a.m. took a carriage, drove to the Astor House, where I got a room, after much trouble, and went to bed, but did not sleep. I got up at 7.30. a.m. and had breakfast, after which I sent a note to Adams Express Office for E. S. Sanford, I waited until 3. o'clock, when not receiving any answer, I sent a second note to him (E. S. Sanford)

At 3.30. p.m. Mr. Burn's[24] came to my room with a note for from Mr. Sanford. He acknowledged the receipt of my two notes, and said that anything I had for him, I could send by Mr. Burn's, also anything I had to say Mr. Burn's would hear for him. I gave Mr. B— the letter from A. P— to E. S. Sanford, but told Mr. Burns that I could not talk with him. Mr. Burns then left promising to call again in the evening with any message that Mr. Sanford would have.

At 4.00. p.m. the President and Suite arrived at the Astor House. Lincoln looked very pale, and fatigued. He was standing in his carriage bowing when I first saw him. From the carriage he went direct into the House, and soon after appeared on the Balcony, from where he made a short speech, but there was such a noise, it was impossible to hear what he said. Just about this time Mr. Burn's came again saying that Mr. Sanford would call to see me at 7.00. p.m.

I then wrote a note to N. B. Judd, and asked him to come to my room so soon as convenient. I gave the note to the bell-boy and told him to deliver immediately

---

22. Mrs. M. Barley was the alias of Pinkerton's lady superintendent, Kate Warne. See Cuthbert, 9.

23. Edward S. Sanford, president of the American Telegraph Co., and vice-president of the Adams Express Co.

24. George H. Burns, an "attache of the American Telegraph Co. and confidential agent of E. S. Sandford, Esq." See Pinkerton, 82.

— The boy soon returned, and said that Judd had been left in Albany, but would be in New York on the first train, and so soon as he arrived would get the Note.

It was now about 6.30. p.m., so I went down and had supper — from the supper table I went direct to my room, and had no more that got in, when Mr. Judd called. I gave him a letter from A. P—, which he sat down to read, first asking me if he could light his cigar.

After reading the letter, Mr. Judd asked me a great many questions, which I did not answer, I told him that I could not talk on the business, but if he had any message for A. P— I would take it. He asked me when I would leave for Baltimore — I told him I should leave early in the morning. He said he was much alarmed and would like to show the letter I had given him to some of the party, and also consult the New York Police about it. I advised him to do no such thing, but keep cool, and see Mr. P—. Judd asked me what he should do. I told him would go direct to Baltimore, and have Mr. P— advise him by letter, and by Telegraph. Judd said that he wanted to see A. P— and asked me if I did not think he would come to New York if he Telegraphed for him. I said I knew it would be impossible for him (A. P—) to leave in time to see him (Judd) in New York. Judd did not know what to do; said that he would see me again so soon as possible, and that he must consult with one of his party.

Just at this moment — E. S. Sanford came in, and I introduced him to N. B. Judd. Mr. Sanford then handed Mr. Judd a note, from Mr Pinkerton. Mr. Judd read it, and said it was all right, and that he was glad to meet Mr. Sanford. Mr. Sanford replied that anything he could do for him (Judd) would be done with pleasure. Mr Judd then left promising to see me again during the evening. After Mr. Judd had gone, Mr. Sanford excused himself for not coming directly to see me on receipt of my Notes: said the fact of the matter was he was keeping out of sight for a few days, and did not want to be seen by any one, for all supposed him to be in Philadelphia, and said "Now what is the trouble?" I replied that I had come to deliver letters to him and Mr. Judd, and was ready to take any message back to A. P—; that I would leave early in the morning, and that was all I had to say on business. Mr. Sanford said there was something more, and I could tell him, for Allan always told him anything and everything. I replied that that was no reason why I should tell him all I knew, and that I had no more to say. Mr. Sanford rejoined "Barley, there is something more, and if you will only tell me how you are situated, and what you are doing at Baltimore I can better judge how to act." I said again "Mr Sanford, I have nothing more to say." He appeared quite dissatisfied, and said he supposed I had "roped" so many, I thought I could not be "roped" myself. I replied that it was as easy to "rope" me as, any one else, but that just now I really had nothing to say, Mr. Sanford laughed at this, and said that I was a strange woman. He seemed good natured again, and asked my advice about writing a Dispatch to A. P—, and sending Burn's to Baltimore.

He (Sanford) then wrote a Dispatch, and read it to me, after which he went down to send it, but before going asked me if he could bring Mr. Henry Sanford[25]

---

25. Henry Sanford was associated with Adams Express Co. See Cuthbert, 73.

to my room, and introduce him to me. I said that if it was necessary I should see Henry Sanford in regard to any business matter, I would do so, but not otherwise.

Mr. Sanford sent the Dispatch, and saw Mr. Judd, when he returned to my room, and talked to me about sending Burn's to Baltimore: said that it would be a great assistance to Mr. P— for he would give Burn's the full controll of the Telegraph wires from Baltimore to any point A. P— would wish, and that Burns could help A. P— very much in case he needed him. Mr. Sanford then said that he thought we were frightened (meaning Mr. P—, and myself). I suppose he thought now that I would go on and tell him all I knew, but I said nothing, only that we were not frightened and what was more I had never known A. P— to be frightened.

We now conversed on different subjects, and Mr. Sanford told me that he was keeping out of sight, to keep from having some old papers served on him: that it was an old California matter of the Adams Express Company's, for a Hundred and Forty Thousand Dollars; that himself, Dinsmore, and Shoemaker had to keep out of sight until Friday next. He laughed about it, and said I should tell A. P— that the Officers were after him (Sanford). He was very friendly and staid until after 10. oclock, when he bade me good night and left.

Mr. Sanford had not gone long when I received a Dispatch from Mr. P—, saying "Tell Judd I meant all I said, and that to-day they offer Ten for one, and Twenty for two." I immediately sent for Judd, who came at once to my room. I gave the Dispatch, and he (Judd) wanted to show it to Vice President Hamlin, and also that I should have an interview with Hamlin. I said that it would never do: that I could not say anything more to Hamlin than I had said to him (Judd), and that in the morning I should return to Baltimore.

Mr Judd urged me to have Mr. P— come on to Philadelphia and meet them there, so as to advise what to do. I promised Mr. Judd I would tell Mr. P— all he had said, and would do what I could to get him (A.P.) to meet them at Philadelphia. Mr Judd then told me about having been left in Albany, and said that he never felt so mortified in all his life. I could not but laugh to see how bad he felt. He also spoke of Mrs. Lincoln and said that she was tickled to death with all she had seen since leaving home. Mr. Judd left my room at 11.30. p.m. I then sent word to be wakened in time to take the early train for Baltimore in the morning — I went to bed tired.

Tuesday 17th. February 1861 —

T. W—[26] Reports.

*   *   *   *

Captain Keen[27] and some four or five others then came in, and got up a game of Ten-pins. we played until 1.45. p.m., when Springer, Taylor, and I went in to

---

26. Timothy Webster, a Pinkerton agent who in 1862 would be hanged in Richmond as a Federal spy, had been ingratiating himself into the Perrymansville Rangers, a secessionist paramilitary unit at Perrymansville, Maryland. See Cuthbert, 21; Pinkerton, esp. 70–73.

27. Keen, Springer, and Taylor were associated with the secessionist Perrymansville Rangers.

dinner — They commenced talking about what route Lincoln would take to Washington. Springer said that he was going over the Philadelphia, Willmington, and Baltimore Rail Road, and Taylor said "No"; that Lincoln would go over the Central Road; that he (Lincoln) had better not come over this road with any Military — for if he did that Boat would never make another across the River. Springer replied that they had not better attempt to take any Military over this Road, for if they did Lincoln would never get to Washington.

Taylor got the Horse and Buggy ready, when Springer and I, left for Aberdeen. We had got about two miles on our way, when we had to turn back on account of the bad roads. On the Springer talked some about Lincoln, and said that when Lincoln arrived in Baltimore, they would try to get him out to speak, and if he did come out, he (Springer) would not be surprised if they killed him; that there was in Baltimore about One Thousand men well organized, and ready for anything. I asked if the leaders were good men. Springer said they had the very best men in Baltimore, and that nearly all the Custom House officers were in the organization. I could not learn from him any of their names.

*   *   *   *   *

Tuesday 19*th*. February 1861 —

A. F. C— Reports.

*   *   *   *   *

After leaving there about half an hour, Hillard came bringing me a pair of worked slippers as a present — At the time I was lying on the bed, and he said to me "You look sober — what is the matter with you?" I replied "I am thinking about what a d—d pretty tumult this country is in — I have had all kinds of bad thoughts shoot through my mind — you know you cannot prevent a man from thinking?" Hillard replied "Of course not — what have you been thinking about?" I told him that I was thinking of a man had the _____ how he could immortalize himself by taking a knife and plunging it to Lincoln's heart; but it is impossible to find a man with the pluck to do it — It is not as it was in the time of Brutus and Ceaser — there is not the courage now that was then." Hillard rejoined "There are men who would do it!" I said "I will give Five Hundred Dollars to see the man who will do it, although it is of no interest to me; that I was out of the Union — I had no claim on this Government, and did not belong here, nevertheless I would give Five Hundred Dollars to see a man do it." Hillard said to me "Give me an article of agreement that you will give my mother Five Hundred Dollars, and I will kill Lincoln between here and Havre-de-Grace" — and then exclaimed in the language of Brutus "Not that I love Lincoln less, but my Country more"! He added the "Five Hundred dollars would help my Mother, but it would do me no good, because I would expect to die — and I would say so soon as it was done —   Here gentlemen take me — I am the man who done the deed. Hillard also remarked "If our Company would draw lots to see who would kill Lincoln, and the lot should fall on me, I would do it willingly, even if my Captain should tell me to do it I would do it". I said to him "By the By, friend Hillard, talking about your Company, you remind me of one thing I wanted to say to you, which is this: "Yesterday you contradicted yourself in your statements to me in regard to your Company — now you know I am a frank man, and have no desire, for it is none of my business to ask you questions about your Company, and no desire to know anything about it only so far — that I of course feel an interest in the cause, that you know is natural, being a Southern Man." He replied, "Yes my friend — I have told you all I have a right to tell you — and I tell you all I dare without compromising myself, my friends, and my honor — I have unbounded confidence in you, and know you to be a gentleman — I am a judge of human nature — I have been asked by my friends who you was, what you was &c —, and I have replied, that you was a gentleman, and that was all I knew about it, and all I wanted to Know."

We had left my room while this conversation was going on, and on arriving at the corner of Baltimore and Holliday Streets, Hillard said to me "I will go to supper and from there to the National Volunteer room, and will return at 9.00. p.m. to your room. I persuaded him however to go to supper with me at Mann's Resteraunt, where we went up stairs to a private dining room and there resumed our conversation — He said to me "ever since I went to Washington I am very careful in what I say — there are Government spies here all the time, (in Baltimore) even now, do you see that old man at the other end of the Room?" "this is the first time I have noticed him — just as likely as not he is a government spy — there is no telling — and may be before this he has my name down, and what I have said — We are all more careful (meaning the National Volunteers) — twenty times more careful than we were previously. I never recognize any of the boys now in the Street when I see them — We have to be careful — Do not think my friend that it is a want of confidence in you that makes me so cautious — it is because I have to be — I do not remmember to have spoken to a person out of our Company, and the first thing I knew I was at Washington before that Committee[28] — *We have taken a solemn oath, which is to obey the orders of our Captain, without asking any questions, and in no case, or under any circumstances reveal any orders received by us, or entrusted to us, or anything that is confidential,* for instance I was called to Washington City before the Committee — I must not divulge *the object nor the nature of our organization, but evade and if necessary decline to answer their questions."*

I asked Hillard what was the first object of the organization. He replied *"It was first organized to prevent the passage of Lincoln with the troops through Baltimore, but our plans are changed every day, as matters change, and what its object will be from day to day, I do not know, nor can I tell — All we have to do is, to obey the orders of our Captain, whatever he commands we are required to do — Rest assured I have all confidence in you, and what I can and dare tell you I am willing to and like to do it — I cannot come out and tell you all — I cannot compromise my honor".*

28. A select committee of five congressmen was named to investigate allegations that a secret antigovernment organization existed in Washington, D.C. O. K. Hillard was one of those called to testify before the committee. See Cuthbert, 139–41.

Friday 22d February 1861 —

A. P.— Reports —

At 12.10. A.M. I again left the Continental Hotel in search of Mr. Franciscus,[29] having previously called on Mr. Judd and requested him to remain until I could return. Henry Sanford was with Mr. Judd. I drove to Mr. Franciscus' house but was informed that he was not at home, but sent word to his family that he had gone to his Office in West Philadelphia. I accordingly drove there and found him. I went with him to his Office, and told what was required — viz — a special train to bring Mr. Lincoln from Harrisburg to Philadelphia this evening. Superintendant Franciscus said that if this was necessary of course it should be done, but that they all ready had three special trains on the Road for this evening, wich would be fully loaded with Citizens and Soldiers. My request Mr Franciscus accompanied me to the Continental Hotel, and to Mr. Judd's room, where we found Mr. Sanford. It was fully arranged that as early after dark as possible Mr Lincoln was to leave Harrisburg and get out to the train which would be about half a mile from the Depot, and that Superintendant Franciscus would himself take charge of the train and have Mr. Lincoln in West Philadelphia to meet me at about 10.30. p.m. This being arranged, and it being now about ____.00. a.m., I left with Mr. Franciscus and took him home in the carriage, and from thence drove to Mr. Burn's house on Prune Street, rung the bell and waked him up, and told him of what arrangements had been made, requesting him to be ready early in the morning to go to the Telegraph Office and get a practical Telegraph Climber and make arrangements for the Climber and him (Burns) to go to Harrisburg on the Presidential Train this morning at nine o'clock and to inolate Harrisburg from Telegraphic communications with the world by six p.m. and to keep it so until 7.00. a.m. tomorrow.

After leaving Mr. Burn's I drove to the St Louis Hotel it being now, and settled with the Hack-driver. At this time the people were rapidly assembling in front of Independance Hall to witness the raising of a United States flag by Mr. Lincoln which was announced for sun-rise.

Having washed and put on some clean clothes at 6.00. a.m. I went to see Mr. Dunn, Agent for Harnden's Express Company to procure him to go to Baltimore to see A.F.C. and procure the Reports of Operations in Balimore since I left. Mr. Dunn consented to go on the 8.00. a.m. train. I did not explain what the nature of the business was, but gave him a key to the Office and a letter to "A.F.C." requesting "A.F.C." to give him the Reports of himself and C.D.C.W., which had been made since I left, and also to send by him any verbal Report he might deem necessary for me, and assurring him (A.F.C.) that the bearer (Dunn) was fully reliable. I also gave Mr Dunn, Fifteen Dollars to pay his expenses and directed him to return on the train leaving Baltimore for Philadelphia at 5.15. p.m. and that on arriving at the Depot at Philadelphia he would there find "M.B," and to procure for her such tickets as she might require and see to her getting seats in the

---

29. G. C. Franciscus, superintendent of the Pennsylvania Railroad's division between Harrisburg and Philadelphia.

sleeping car, as also to deliver to. M.B.— all reports, verbal and written he might receive in Baltimore and to keep a look out in the Depot for my arrival which would be a few minutes after the time for the departure of the trains.

After fully instructing Mr. Dunn I returned to the St Louis and had breakfast, after which I went to Mr. Burns house on Prune Street, and arranged with him, that he have some person in the Telegraph Office in this City all evening to supervise any or all Telegraph Messages which might be received or sent, to or from this office bearing on this affair, and if any such were received that they should not be delivered, and if any such were brought in to be sent, that they should not be sent until the next morning, Mr. Burns agreed to see to this, and then I went to the Girard House and met Mr. Sanford (Henry). I rather urged upon Mr. Sanford who was about to return to New York to remain and stay in the Telegraph Office and supervise the messages — but he declined, saying that he must Return to New York to day, but stated that he would aid Mr. Burns to get things in a shape so that this would be taken care of.

It being now about 8.10. a.m. I went to the Continental Hotel to see Mr. Judd prior to the Presidental Cortege leaving for Harrisburg, Mr. Judd was not in his room. I saw W. H. Lamon Esq. who said that he would find Mr. Judd and send him to his room, so I went there and waited. In a few moments Mr. Judd came in. He said that the arrangements I had made last night in regard to the conveyance of Mr. Lincoln to Washington was all satisfactory and that I might go on and make the balance of them, and rely upon meeting Mr. Lincoln at West Philadelphia this evening: that he (Mr Judd) had thought the whole subject over and that he still _____ the course I had suggested as the only feasible one under the circumstances: that it would doubtless create a great deal of excitement throughout the Country and with the Politicians, but that this could not be helped, and that he (Judd) would take the responsibility of it. I assured Mr. Judd that I full believed the course I had indicated was the only one to save the country from Bloodshed at the present time.

After leaving Mr. Judd I went to the La-Pierre House, where I met Mr Felton, and made a full report of what had transpired last night and the arrangements made with reference to Mr. Lincoln going to Washington on to-nights train. Mr. Felton approved of what I had done and desired that I should see Mr. Franciscus and urge him to have the special train with Mr. Lincoln in on time, so as not to delay the departure of other trains on the Philadelphia, Wilmington and Baltimore Rail Road, as if that Train was delayed too late, the train from Baltimore to Washington would start, and then Mr. Lincoln would be obliged either lay over in Baltimore or hire a special train to take him through.

I left Mr. Felton to endeavor to see Mr. Franciscus, but on going to the Office of the latter, I found he had gone to Harrisburg on special train on which was Mr. Lincoln. I then returned to Mr. Felton's Office and had a very long interview with him in regard to this business. Mr. Felton said that he thought it would be adviseable to have both the Messrs. Stearn's come into Philadelphia, so that we could take steps to have Wm Stearn's[30] go to Baltimore and see the Superintendant of the Baltimore and Ohio Rail Road and say to him that in the event of this afternoon train on the Philadelphia, Wilmington and Baltimore Rail Road, that the train on the Washington Branch Road should be delayed until the arrival of the train on the Philadelphia on account of important Government Dispatches being on said train. Mr. Felton said that he did not think it safe to entrust the Superintendant of the Baltimore and Ohio Rail Road of the fact that Mr. Lincoln was going through to-night, and that as the Telegraph Office of the Rail Road Company at Philadelphia, George Stearns could be instructed to Telegraph from Wilmington to Wm Stearns at Baltimore the time the train passed Wilmington, so that if the train was much behind time, Mr. Wm Stearns could go and see the Superintendant of the Baltimore and Ohio Rail Road any get an order to delay the train on the Washington Branch until the arrival of the Train on the Philadelphia, Wilmington and Baltimore Rail Road, and that if the train was likely to be on time nothing need be said to the Superintendant of the Baltimore, and Ohio Rail Road.

Mr Felton said that he should like to have me call again at his office at 1.00. p.m. and meet Mr. Kinsey,[31] Master of Transportation of the Philadelphia, Wilmington and Baltimore Rail Road who would arrange to take this evening's train until the arrival of Mr. Lincoln and Myself.

On leaving Mr. Felton I went to the St Louis Hotel and received the following Notes and Telegram.

"Office of Adams Express Company,
"320 Chesnut Street
"Philadelphia _____186.
"I opened this to Burn's and it interests you more than him. I leave it with you"
H.S.[32]
"Westvilt[33] has gone to Harrisburg and the tel wire from N.Y. thro, will be watched lest a message be sent around via Buffalo."
Boston x x 11. N.D.
"G. H. Burn's
"Phila
"Tell Plums I had all Sumac[34] messages explainded, there are none that appear irregular — none from points along the route to any one party or to any parties in Baltimore except from Hood who has charge of trains. Is it possible that Plums has fallen on parties who are operating for the same object as himself and they are pumping each other. E. S. Sanford."[35]

---

30. Stearns was master machinist on the Philadelphia, Wilmington, and Baltimore Railroad. See Cuthbert, 142.

31. Henry F. Kenney (sometimes "McKinsey" or "Kensey"), superintendent of the Philadelphia, Wilmington, and Baltimore Railroad. See Cuthbert, 73.

32. Henry Sanford.

33. W. P. Westervelt, superintendent of the American Telegraph Co. See Cuthbert, 73.

34. "Plums" and "sumac" were code words for "Pinkerton" and "telegraph." See Cuthbert, 73.

35. Note below apparently in WHH's hand: *See page 26.*

Saturday 23*d* February 1861 —

A. P— Reports —

We arrived at Baltimore on time about 3.30. a.m., when M. B— left the train, took a Carriage and went to the Hotel, I got up out of my Berth on arriving at the Depot of the Philadelphia, Wilmington and Baltimore Rail Road. Whilst at that Depot Mr. W*m*. Stearns came in and I learned from him in a whisper that all was right. We now proceeded on to the Depot of the Baltimore and Ohio Rail Road, where at 4.15. a.m. we left for Washington. Mr. Lincoln did not get up — while at the latter Depot we had considerable amusement by the repeated calls of the Night Watchman of the Company to rouse the Ticket Agent who appeared to be asleep in a wooden building close by the sleeping car. He repeatedly attempted to awaken the sleepy Official, by pounding on the side of the building with a club, and hallowing "Captain its Four O'clock", This he kept up for about twenty minutes without any change in the time, and many funny remarks were made by the passengers at the Watchmans time being always the same. Mr. Lincoln appeared to enjoy it very much and made several witty remarks showing that he was as full of fun as ever.

We arrived at Washington about 6.00. a.m. and being all ready we left the car amongst the first   In passing through the Depot I obsered Mr. W*m* Stearns close by us — A gentleman looked very sharp at Mr. Lincoln who was on my right, and as we passed him he caught hold of Mr. Lincoln saying "Abe you can't play that on me". I hit the gentleman a punch with my elbow as he was close to me, staggering him back, but he recovered himself, and again took hold of Mr. Lincoln remarking that he knew him. I was beginning to think that we were discovered, and that we *might* have to fight, and drew back clenching my fist, and raising it to take the gentleman a blow, when Mr. Lincoln took hold of my arm saying "Don't strike him Allan, don't strike him — that is my friend Washburne[36] — don't you know him?"

I at once told Mr. Washburne as we walked along not to do or say aught which would attract the attention of the passengers — and we walked out of the Depot and took a Hack — Mr. Lincoln, Messrs Washburne, and Lamon,[37] and Myself got in and drove to Willards Hotel.

Mr. Washburne said that he was at the Depott, expecting Mr. Lincoln on account of a Telegraph Dispatch received from the Son of Governor Seward, and that Gov. Seward was to have been at the Depot also, but that he (Washburne) did not see him. I apologized for "Punching" him at the Depot, on the ground that I did not know him, and he expressed himself satisfied saying that he ought to have been more cautious. Before arriving at the Hotel, Mr. Lincoln, Washburne, and Myself left the carriage and walked to-wards the ladies entrance, and Mr. Lamon drove to the Hotel to request Mr. Willard to meet us at the Ladys entrance.

---

36. Elihu B. Washburne, Republican congressman from Illinois.
37. Ward Hill Lamon, Lincoln's former law associate on the Eighth Circuit, soon to be appointed marshal of the District of Columbia.

He did so, and showed us up to a room, when he would get the suite of rooms designed for Mr. Lincoln ready. In a few minutes Governor Seward arrived and was introduced to Mr. Lincoln, Mr. Lamon, and Myself by Mr. Washburne.

Mr. Lincoln explained to the Governor the Nature of the information I had given him which occasioned him (Mr Lincoln) coming to Washington in this manner. Governor Seward said that he (Seward) and General Scott fully approved of the step and that it had their cordial endorsement — as he felt sure that as circumstances were at present it was the wisest and best course for him (Lincoln) to take: that he (Seward) had in his posession conclusive evidence showing that there was a large organization in Baltimore to prevent the passage of Mr. Lincoln through that City and he felt confident that Mr. Lincoln could not have come through in any other manner without blood-shed: that this knowledge was what induced him after consultation with General Scott to send his (Sewards') son to Philadelphia to meet Mr. Lincoln with these letters and to urge a change of route; that this change would doubtless create quite a "Furore", but that he (Seward) would defend it, and endorse it, and that had Mr. Lincoln not taken this step — Genl. Scott was so plainly convinced of the danger to Mr. Lincoln that in all probability he would have sent United States Troops to Baltimore to-day to receive and escort the President Elect.

I informed Governor Seward of the nature of the information I had, and that I had no information of any large organization in Baltimore, but the Governor reiterated that he had conclusive evidence of this.

Mr. Lincoln expressed himself rather tired, so we left him and at Govr Sewards request went with him to his house where we again talked over this danger of Mr Lincoln's coming through Baltimore according to the published programe. I soon left the Governor's and with W. H. Lamon, I returned to Willards Hotel, where I registered the name E. I. Allen, New York, had a bath and breakfast, and then went and sent the following Dispatches.

*   *   *   *

Friday 22d. February 1861 —

A. P— Reports.

*   *   *   *   *

"Friday 10. a.m. — I go to N.Y., at 11. o'clk. It is all arranged to have Telegraph cut at Harrisburg in all directions at 6.00 p.m. This is the better plan for I could not prevent operators talking after dispatches were rec'd here of the kind we apprehend would be. We found Mr. Westervilt in town — he coincides in this plan and will go to Harrisburg at 12. with a professional Climber to do the needful thing in the right place & at the right time. I think we may safely rely that Harrisburg will be isolated completely. For your sake I hope.

H. Sanford"

At 12.18. p.m. I went to the Express Office and wrote the following Dispatch which Mr. McCullough sent to the Telegraph office.

"I. C. Babcock.

Adams Express New. York.

Telegraph Sanford that Plums is here and says no mistake — no doubt — no question — It is positive and beyond all cavil — as sure as cotton ever had Ten — and that he shall as certainly ruin if his orders is as warmly backed as Lemons did then.[38]

Plums will Sumac Lemons from

(Signed) R. P. McCullough"

At 1.00. p.m. I went to Mr. Feltons Office and met him and Messrs Stevens[39] and McKinsey. We had a very long discussion on the programe for this evening, It was finally agreed that W*m* Stearns should go to Baltimore on the accomodation train this evening and be prepared to act as Mr. Felton had suggested in our previous interview, as also that George Stearns should Telegraph Mr. Sanford from Wilmington as greed upon. Mr. Felton put up a Package of old papers and addressed it to E. I. Allen Esq. Williams Hotel, Washington. D.C. sealed it and marked it valuable and gave it to Mr. Kensey and wrote a note to the Conductor of the evening train South — requesting him not to start his train until he would receive this package from Mr. Kinsey — as this package *must* go through to Washington on *to-nights train*. Mr. Felton directed Mr. Kinsey to meet at the west Philadelphia Station of the Philadelphia Rail Road at 9.45. p.m. and to come with Myself and Mr. Lincoln to near the Philadelphia, Wilmington and Baltimore Rail Road Depot and after seeing that Myself and Party were on board to run into the Depot and hand the Conductor the package and start the train.

Mr. Felton said that in order not appear *Privy to any of these arrangements* he would go to the Theatre with his family this evening.

At 3.30. p.m. I left Mr. Feltons and returned to the St Louis Hotel and after getting dinner went to M. B—s room and directed her to be ready to leave the St Louis about 9.20. p.m.: to get a private carriage and drive to the Philadelphia, Wilmington and Baltimore Rail Road Depot and meet Mr. Dunn who would arrive from Baltimore at 9.50. p.m. and have him procure Tickets for three from Philadelphia to Washington, and also to secure four double berths and also to receive from Dunn all written and verbal reports he might have for me from Baltimore, then to get in the sleeping car and *keep* possession of the Sleeping Car Berths until my arrival with Mr. Lincoln. I directed her to secure the Berths in the rear part of the rear part of the Car, which would be the last in the train, and to request Mr. Dunn to get the rear door in the car opened so I could enter by it.

I then went to the Telegraph and Express Offices to see if any dispatches had been received but found none. I remained around the St Louis in a State of suspence until about 8.30. p.m. when I telegraphed.

---

38. "Cotton" is a reference to the Baltimore and Ohio Railroad, but the equivalents of "Ten" and "Lemons" have not survived. See Cuthbert, 143.

39. William Stearns.

"Geo. H. Burn's
    Harrisburg.
        Where is Nuts.[40]
            I. H. Hutcheson."

At 9.15. p.m. I received the following Dispatch.

Harrisburg Feb'y 22d' — 1861

"I. H. Hutcheson
    St Louis Hotel Philadelphia.
        "Nuts left at six — Everything as you directed — all is right —
            (signed) Geo. H. Burns",

I then procured a carriage for M. B— and went with here to the corner of Tenth and Chesnut Streets, where I got out and she went on to the Depot.

I then hired a carriage near the Girard House and drove with it to West Philadelphia. I stood with the carriage a few rods west of the stairs leading from the Street to Mr. Franciscus Office, and was soon joined by Mr. Kinsey. About three minutes past ten, Mr. Lincoln accompanied by W. H. Lamon, Superintendant Lewis, and assistant Superintendant Franciscus arrived. I met them on the steps. Mr. Lincoln wore a brown Kossuth Hat, and an overcoat thrown loosely over his shoulders. The evening was chilly but not cold. We immediately proceeded to the carriage and Mesrs Lewis and Franciscus parted from Mr. Lincoln. Mr Lincoln thanked them for their kindness &c —, and I promised to Telegraph them in the Morning. As the train on the Philadelphia, Wilmington and Baltimore Rail Road did not start until 11.50. p.m. I suggested to Mr. Kinsey to get on the box with the Driver and consume the time by driving Northward in search of some imaginary person, so that we should not arrive at the Depot, until about 11.00. p.m.

Mr. Lincoln, W. H. Lamon and myself took seats in the carriage. Mr. Lincoln said that after I had left him last night at the Continental, and he had gone to bed, that a son of Governor Sewards[41] had called him up, and delivered him letters from his Father (Governor Seward) and General Scott, Stating substantially the same as I had, but much stronger: that about Fifteen Thousand men were organized to prevent his passage through Baltimore, and that arrangements were made by these parties to blow up the Rail Road track, fire the Train &c —, and urging upon him (Lincoln) to change his route. Mr. Lincoln said that he had received the letters, but merely told young Mr. Seward that he would give him an answer at Harrisburg; that he (Mr. Lincoln) had in the morning after leaving Philadelphia told Mr. Judd about this, and on Mr. Judd's advice he had finally told young Seward that "He would change his route;" that after pledging himself to me to secrecy he did not think he had the right to speak to any one on the subject, nor would not until Mr. Judd told him he (Judd) would take the responsibility of his (Lincoln's) telling Seward and make it all right with me.

---

40. "Nuts" refers to AL.
41. Frederick Seward, son of William H. Seward.

Mr. Lincoln also said that upon his telling Mrs. Lincoln of the step he was about to take that she insisted upon Mr. Lamon accompanying him, and that he (Lincoln) found it impossible to get away from the crowd without the aid of Governor Curtin and Col. Sumner,[42] whom he was finally obliged to inform of this movement to secure their co-operation in order to cover his absence; that all approved of the step he had taken, but the Military men were anxious to accompany him, expressing doubt but that I might be leading him into a trap and selling him (Lincoln) to the Secessionists — to all of which Mr. Lincoln said that he knew me, and had confidence in me and would trust himself and his life in my hands.

Mr. Lincoln said that from the great interest I had manifested in this matter he had every confidence in me.

Mr. Lamon offered Mr. Lincoln a Revolver and Bowie Knife and I at once protested saying that I would not for the world have it said that Mr. Lincoln had to enter the National Capitol Armed; that I anticipated no trouble; that if we went through at all we must do so by stratagem, but that if fighting had to be done, it must be done by others than Mr. Lincoln. Mr. Lincoln said that he wanted no arms; that he had no fears and that he felt satisfied that all my plans would work right.[43]

Mr. Lincoln was cool, calm, and self possessed — firm and determined in his bearing. He evinced no sign of fear or distrust, and throughout the entire night was quite self possessed.

On arriving at the vicinity of the Depot we left the carriage and I walked round the corner to the Depot. Mr. Lincoln, and Mr. Lamon followed. I met Mr. Dunn in the Depot who showed me to the sleeping car. I entered by the rear followed by Mr. Lincoln — no one appeared to notice us. I found M. B— and got into our Berths. Mr. Dunn soon left us and in about three minutes from the time we got aboard the train started.

I received from M. B— the reports written and verbal brought by Mr. Dunn. Mr. Lincoln soon laid down in his Berth, and when the Conductor came around for his Tickets, I handed him the Tickets for Mr. Lincoln. He did not look in the Berths at all — left and did not return again during the trip.

None of our party appeared to be sleepy, but we all lay quiet and nothing of importance transpired.

Friday 22*d.* February 1861 —

M. B— Reports.

At about 3.00. a.m. A. P— came to my room, sick, and tired out, and told me that he would not leave the city until evening. Mr. P— then went to his room and I went to bed tired out.

I got up at 6.00. a.m. and saw Lincoln raise a Flag on the State House. The

---

42. Andrew G. Curtin and Edwin V. Sumner.

43. Here the copyist apparently skipped a paragraph and began copying the first line of the succeeding paragraph, beginning "On arriving at the vicinity. . . ." The manuscript has been torn or cut to obliterate this false start.

streets were crowded with peope. After breakfast Mr. P— told me that Lincoln would go to Harrisburg, and at 6.00. p.m. would leave for Philadelphia; that I should leave the St Louis Hotel at 9.45. p.m for the Baltimore Depot, where I would meet Dunn and get a verbal report from him, and also any package he might have for Mr. P—. A. P— gave me all necessary instructions and then left.

Just as I was about leaving the St Louis Hotel, Mr. P— came with a carriage, and drove to the corner of Tenth and Chesnut Streets, where he got out and left me to go to the Depot.

On arriving at the Depot I met Mr. Dunn who gave me his verbal reports, and some written reports. He then bought three Tickets to Washington, and got me four double Berths in the sleeping car. I found it almost impossible to save the Berths to-gether. This sleeping car was conducted differantly from any I ever saw before — they gave no Tickets, and any person could take a Berth where they pleased. I gave the Conductor half a dollar to keep my berths, and by standing right by myself we manage to keep them.

Just before the train started Mr P— accompanied by Mr Lincoln and Col. Lamon came into the Car. I showed Mr. P— the berths and everything went off well. Mr. P— introduced me to Mr. Lincoln. He talked very friendly for some time — we all went to bed early — Mr P— did not sleep — nor did Mr. Lincoln. The excitement seemed to keep us all awake. Nothing of importance happened through the night.

Mr. Lincoln is very homely, and so very tall that he could not lay straight in his berth.

A. P— Reports —   Saturday 23*d*. February 1861 —
         *   *   *   *

"N. B. Judd
   "Harrisburg Pa.
      "Arrived here all right
         (Signed) E. I. Allen."

"C. G. Franciscus or E. Lewis
   "Superintendants, Penn R.R.
      "Philadelphia
      "All right.
        E. I. Allen".

"E. S. Sanford
   "Gen'l Superintendant, American Telegraph Co.
      "New York
        "Plums arrived here with Nuts this morning — all right.
        E. I. Allen".

"G. H. Bang's
  "80. Washington Street. Chicago.
      "Plums has Nuts — arri'd at Barley[44] — all right.
          E. I. Allen"

"S. M. Felton
  "President. P.W.&B.R.R.
      "Philadelphia.
          "Arrived here all Safe.
          E. I. Allen."

After sending the Dispatches I Met Mr. Lamon. He was very much excited about the passage of Mr. Lincoln, and was anxious to Telegraph C. S. Wilson of the Chicago Journal in relation to it, and that he (Lamon) had arrived with Lincoln.

I endeavored to impress upon him that the arrival of Mr. Lincoln was yet considered secret and that nothing should be done by any one to make it public until it had been desired by Mr Lincoln and his advisers what shape his sudden arrival should assume, urging upon Mr. Lamon that the shape first given to Mr Lincoln's secret passage through Baltimore would in all probability be the shape it would retain; that this question in the present excited state of the public mind was fraught with grave consequences and that great care should be taken by all to consider well what was the best light to place it in. I also[45] reminded Mr. Lamon that whatever light this movement might be placed in, he must remember that I held Mr. Lincoln's pledge that I should for ever remain unknown as having anything whatever to do with it, All I could say to Mr. Lamon however appeared to be futile — regardles of all consequences he was determined to make a "Splurge" and have his name figure largely in it. The movement had been endorsed by Gov. Seward, and *"it must be right"*, and Lamon would act upon no reasoning of mine. He talked so foolishly that I lost patience with him and set him down in my own mind as a brainless egotistical fool — and I still think so.

I left Lamon and walked up the Avenue and returned in about an hour, when I observed Lamon in conversation with the Reporter of the New York Herald, Mr. Hanscomb. They were in the Hall near the desk and I could plainly see that Lamon had been drinking — as I passed them without recognizing Lamon I observed Hanscomb look very hard at me and he kept his eye on me while I was around — pretty soon Hanscomb, Lamon went to the bar, and drinked — talked for a short time and drinked again — soon after repeating the dose — then Hanscomb went to the table accompanied by Lamon and commenced writing occasionally stopping to talk to Lamon. I saw that Hanscomb was "pumping" Lamon, and I motioned Lamon to me, and at once very angrily accused Lamon of telling Hanscomb

---

44. Decoded: "Pinkerton has President — arri'd at Washington — all right." See Cuthbert, 84.
45. The manuscript has been corrected and torn off at this point, apparently by the copyist to facilitate a correction.

about me, and who I was. Lamon said that Hanscomb Knew me, and all about me, and I replied "I suppose you have told him", He (Lamon) said yes, when Hanscomb assured him that he did not know me. I got quite angry and *swore some* and told Lamon that Hanscomb did not know me, but had taken that method to draw it out of him, and that I had already told him (Lamon) that I held Mr. Lincoln's pledge of secresy as regards me, I should at once see Mr. Lincoln and insist upon his (Lincoln) making Lamon hold his tongue. Mr. Lamon was very much excited at this and begged that I should not do this, and that he would at once see Hanscomb and have him keep my name out of the paper. Lamon left me and returned and took a seat by Hanscomb.[46]

I remained around the Hotel until about 2.00. p.m. when I sent a card signed E. I. Allen to Mr. Lincoln — saying that I was about to leave for Baltimore and requesting to see him for a moment. I received an immediate reply asking me to come to his room. There was a delegation of Members of Congress there — Governor Seward and several other gentlemen. Mr. Lincoln took me into an adjoining room and thanked me very kindly for the service I had rendered him, saying that fully appreciated them &c. &c —, and requesting me to call upon him every time I came to Washington, and let him know when he could be of any service to me. He asked me how long I thought I should be in Baltimore and I replied that I presumed I would be there until the Inaugeration, and he requested that if I had anything further to communicate I could do so either directly to himself or to Mr. Judd. He again assured me that my connection with the affair should be kept secret by him. I shook hands and retired to the Office where I paid my bill, and then left for the Depot, taking the 3.10. p.m. train for Baltimore.

At the Annapolis Junction we met the train with Mr. Lincoln's Suite on board. I had an oppertunity of seeing Mr. Judd for a moment and he said that there was some very tall swearing being done by the members of the party — but that this would soon be all done. that none of them could understand it, nor why they each were not taken into the secret. I informed Mr. Judd of the foolish conduct of Mr. Lamon and he promised to attend to the fool on his arrival in Washington.

I arrived in Baltimore about 5.00. p.m. and in the Depot met Mr. Luckett. He was very glad to see me, and took me one side and told me about the d—ble manner in which Lincoln passed through Baltimore. He said that he was collecting money for the *freinds* in Baltimore, and they would yet make the attempt to assassinate Lincoln; that if it had not been for d—d spies somwhere, Lincoln never could have passed through Baltimore; that the men were all ready to have done the job, and were in their places, and would have murdered the d—d Abolitionist had it not been that they were cheated. He said that Captain Ferrandina had had

---

46. A piece of paper one by three inches is included in the manuscript at this point with the inscription, apparently in Ward Hill Lamon's hand: *A falsehood of Allen Pinkerton the Detective — 161 — 3 —Book.*

Marginal note: <u>*This is an infamous lie from beginning to end.*</u> — *This Detective, Allen Pinkerton was angry with me because I would not take sides with him — and make a publication in his favor when he and Kenedy — the New York detective had the difficulty as to which of them the credit of saving Lincoln's life was due from the public — Ward H. Lamon.* In 1866, John A. Kennedy, superintendent of the New York Metropolitan Police, claimed credit for uncovering the Baltimore Plot. See Cuthbert, 114–16, 151.

about Twenty picked men with good revolvers and knives that their calculation was to get up a row in the crowd with rotten eggs, and brick-bats, and that while the Police (some of whom understood the game) would be attending to this, that Captain Ferrandina and his men should attack the carriage with Lincoln and shoot every one in it, and trust to mixing up in the crowd to make their escape — but that if any of the members were taken the others were to rescue him at all cost, and at all hazard.

Mr. Luckett was very much excited and swore very hard against the d—d spies who had betrayed them, remarking that they would yet find them out, and when found they should meet the fate which Lincoln had for the present escaped.

I said to Mr. Luckett that it was indeed highly important that the spies should be found out, and trusted that no Effort should be spared for this purpose, and as I understood that Mr. Luckett was collecting money for the friends of Southern rights, I begged he would allow me to contribute a little more to this, and I took out my purse and handed Mr. Luckett, Ten dollars, but he refused saying that I had already been liberal enough, and I finally allowed him to return me Five dollars.

On leaving Mr Luckett I went to the Hotel and left my satchel and went to the Office where I found the men and received their reports, after which I went to the Post Office and got my mail. The whole people were in an excited state. The Hall of the Post Office, was crowded full with gentlemen and all sorts of rumors were afloat — I mixed in with them and of all the excitement I ever did see it was there — every-body appeared to be swearing mad, and no end to the imprecations which were poured out on Lincoln and the unknown Spies. I staid there about an hour, when I returned to the Hotel and found the following Dispatch.

*   *   *   *

Saturday 23d February 1861 —

A. F. C— Reports.

Hillard and I got up at 7.00. a.m., and he started for his boarding house agreeing to return to my room at 11.00. a.m. I then went to Mann's Restaurant and got breafast, and from there went to the Office and wrote my reports. At 11.00. a.m. I returned to my room where I found Hillard. He was very much excited on account of a rumor that Lincoln had passed through Baltimore incog — early in the morning. Hillard said that he did not believe the report; that he had orders to be at the Depot at 12.30. p.m., and he had to go and wanted me to accompany him; that the council had ordered out the National Volunteers with instructions to be there (at the Depot).

We went to Mann's and had dinner, and from there to the Depot. On our way there he showed me large numbers of the Volunteers, some of whom he stopped and spoke with. To-day he (Hillard) wore his Palmetto Tree[47] on the outside of

---

47. Palmetto tree cockades were symbols of support for South Carolina's secession.

his vest and in full view, I would here mention that along the streets and around the Depot were congregated some ten or fifteen thousand people.

On arriving at the Depot, Hillard said to me that if Lincoln had passed through Baltimore as was rumored, there would be an attack upon the Capital (Washington): that the Ball had commenced now for certain; that he did not know how in H—l it leaked out that Lincoln was to be mobbed in Baltimore, but that it must have leaked out or he would not have gone through as he (Lincoln) did — I told him he (Hillard) belonged to a d—d nice set; that seven thousand men could not keep track of one man: He replied that they had men on the look out all the time and he did not see how Lincoln got away — but it must be that they could not have been with him all the time; that there would be an attack made on Washington sure; At a little after 1.00. p.m. I left Hillard at the Depot and came up Balimore Street. He was still under the impression that the rumor was a sell, and that Lincoln had not gone through. Before leaving the Depot I made an engagement with Hillard to meet him at my room at 4.00. p.m.

The Streets on each side of the hill from the top down was crowded with men, standing close side by side, probably two thousand or more, and were supposed to be members of the National Volunteers — there were also large numbers around Monument Square. Hillard afterwards told me that all those men standing there were National Volunteers, and that they stood in that position on the side of the hill so as that when the carriage containing Lincoln should come up the hill they could rush en-mass upon it, and around it. when Lincoln was to be slain — they reasoning that with such a dense crowd around the carriage, it would be impossible for any outsider to tell who did the deed. In connection with this Hillard said that from his position he would have the first shot, as the Members of the Volunteers forbid a line across the street; that the Men at Munument Square were put there for the like purpose, if by any mishap Lincoln should reach that point alive: that at the meeting of the Committee the night previous that was the course determined upon. Hillard added in a significant manner "You did not see any Police on the Street — they would not have interfered." He also stated that there had been five thousand dollars raised that day among the business classes with which to buy arms.

I went to my room at about 4.00. p.m. and Hillard not being there I returned again to Mann's Restaurant. At about 5. o'clock I again started for my room and on Fayette Street near Hemling's Billiard Room I met Hillard in conversation with a man who he introduced me to as a Mr. Bradford and who he subsequently told me was an officer in the National Volunteers. Hillard, and Bradford were both under the influence of liquor — the latter more so than Hillard. I asked Hillad if he was coming to my room with me. He replied "Hold on a minute", but I remarked that it was raining and I could not wait and I went to my room alone. Shortly after Hillard came there he began to pace up and down the room and was unusually noisy. I told him to sit down, or lay down, and keep quiet. I said to him "That man Bradford you introduce me to was pretty tight". He then said as I have above stated that Bradford was an officer of the National Volunteers, and continually cautioned me to be careful and not breathe a word of what he told me, because he had no right to tell me and it would be bad with him if it was known that he had said anything to me.

Bradford is a man about 45 or 50 years of age: about 6 feet high, and has the appearance of a gentleman.

Hillard said that it was so arranged, or was so understood by him, that the Police were not to interfere only sufficient to make it appear that they were endeavoring to do their duty. He added "All that heavy Police Force that went down there (to the Depot), they all went into the Station House, and even if they had interfered what could they have done? We had four thousand of the Volunteers at and about the Depot besides what were at Monument Square, and you did not see Marshall Kane around. He knows his business." This was said in significant manner, peculiar to Hillard. He then remarked "I should not be surprised if the National Volunteers marched to Washington, between this and the second day of March."

The National Volunteers, so Hillard said, have a meeting this evening, and showed me the place where the secret Committee met — which is on Fayette Street near Barnum's Hotel Democratic, Head Quarters, and as Hillard and I passed the building I stopped and listened a moment, but could distinguish nothing that was said. There seemed to be a great deal of bustle and noise in the room, which is in the third story, some one was speaking at the time and at intervals there was clapping of hands and stamping of feet.

Hillard said, "it is a good thing that Lincoln passed through here (Baltimore) as he did, because it will change the feeling of the Union men — they will think him a coward and it will help our cause — the fact of Lincoln passing through Baltimore in the Manner he did, shows that he is Sectional". He said that he would tell me in the morning what course the National Volunteers had determined on this evening.

Hillard left my room soon after 6.00. p.m. and said he was going to his boarding house. I then went to the Howard House to see Mr. P— and made a verbal report to him.

From the Howard House I went to Mann's Restaurant and had supper, then returned to my room a little before 8.00. p.m., and Hillard came at 9.00. p.m. He was not sufficiently under the influence of liquor to show it. I commenced questioning him to which he gave evasive answers. I then proposed we should do something to pass away the Evening, and we took a stroll up the Street, when he suggested that we should go to Annette Travis No. 70. Davis Street and see his woman, and we went. While there Hillard got to talking with his woman (Anna Hughes) in relation to some fights there had been near the house, at the Depot, originating out of expressions, like as, "they wished Lincoln would come through there — they would like to see him &c —," and for which some one would knocked them down. At Annette Travis we had some wine, and in the meantime a man by the name of Smith came into the house, who Hillard introduced me to as a friend of his — He and Hillard got conversing about Lincoln, when Smith said winking, "I don't think he would have been hurt if he had come through Baltimore Smith and Hillard appeared to be warm friends, and Smith also has a woman at Annett Travis (Smith was a Grocer in Baltimore).

I drank but very little during the evening, though Hillard was quite merry. Smith left Annette Travis at about 11.30. p.m., and at the proper time I took Hillard to my room, After we had got at the room Hillard remarked that there would be by Monday (25*th* Inst.) fifty men in Washington City to watch for a chance to kill Lincoln; that the National Volunteers are to have another meeting on Monday evening; that he had been told that there was a man in Baltimore who would give Five thousand dollars to the man who would Kill Lincoln. I asked him who the man was and he replied that he did not tell me.

Hillard also told that one Charles Meyers, a liquor dealor in Baltimore had to-day given Five thousand dollars to the National Volunteers. I asked him if Smith belonged to the National Volunteers. He said he did not. Hillard had repeatedly said, pointing to a group of men, while we were around the Streets "they are National Volunteers —" but he would not give me any names — and if I asked him if such and such a one, or Mr. So, and so belonged to the National Volunteers he invariably replied that he could not tell me.

Hillard and I continued our conversation in my room until about 1.00. a.m. which was chiefly a repetition of what he had already said in the course of the day, and from what I could gather from him Washington City appeared now to be the principal point for action by those in the plot to take Lincoln's life. Hillard felt merry from the effect of the wine he had drank during the evening, still he was not drunk — and he remarked to me "I feel good, but I am not drunk — I could go into a drawing room and entertain it full of ladies." He also remarked to me "You thought this afternoon that I was tight, but I was not — I did not feel the liquor — it was the excitement — we went to bed at a little after 1.00. a.m. —

Sunday 24*th* February 1861

A. F. C— Reports —

Hillard and I got up at about 8.00. a.m. and he went to his boarding house, I to Mann's Restaurant and got my breakfast. I then went to the Office and wrote my Report for Saturday, and remained there until noon, when I returned to my room where I found Hillard with a gentleman named Foster from Tennessee — Foster was a strong Secessionist — nothing of interest transpired and Foster left at about 1.00. p.m.

Soon after, Hillard and I went to danner at Mann's, and from there went to the Cathedral to vespers, At 5.00. p.m. we returned to my room and remained until 7.00. p.m., when we went for a walk, and to get supper, which we had at Mann's Restaurant.

During the day there was nothing of any importance said in relation to the present political crisis.

After returning to my room for the evening, I asked Hillard if the National Volunteers Committee had come to any understanding as to what course they were going to pursue. He said they had, and from what had been intimated to him they would make a descent on Washington City; that they had received three thousand Dollars more — making Eight thousand in all with which to purchase arms, and that they (the Volunteers) would make a pretty hard fight; that there were two thousand Federal Troops in Washington, but said he "we can easily clean them out." I asked him if the National Volunteer Committee would have another secret meeting on Monday night, to which he replied "no": that on Monday night they were going to drill, and on Wednesday night they would have another meeting; that he was satisfied before another three days had passed, they would swell up to Ten thousand men; that "some d—d Son-of-a-B— had published in a Harrisburg (Pa) paper all the plot and detail". Hillard gave me the names of two of the Captains of the National Volunteers — one a Captain Samuel McAleby, who was in the Custon House — the other one Captain Thomas _____, The latter has a Restaurant on Lexington Street. Hillard said the National Volunteer Committee was composed of Fifty-four members. He seems to have great faith in their success — appeared in good spirits.

Foster the man from Tennessee, who is a travelling Agent for some Baltimore Firm, belongs to a Military Company in this City called the Baltimore Guards, who he says are all Secessionists.

Hillard and I went to bed at about midnight.

Monday 25th February 1861 —

A. P.— Reports —

I arrived at the Office at 8.40. a.m. and found C.D.C.W. and A.F.C. and received verbal reports from them. From Williams report and description of Thompson and Davis who had been stopping at Sherwood's Hotel. I infered that they were Detectives from the Metropolitan Force, New York, and that Thompson was "Sampson", and Davis probably Captain Walling, but I was very positive that Thompson was Tom Sampson. Williams said the Sherrington and others suspected those men of being Government Spies, and that they would be anihilated in Washington if oppertunity offered.

*   *   *   *   *

At 4.00. p.m. Geo. H. Burns arrived from Philadelphia bringing the New York Herald of to-day, which gives my real name in connection with the "movement" of Mr Lincoln. I concluded to send Mr. Burns to Washington with a verbal report to Mr. Judd, and as it was but barely time to get to the Depot — I went with him and got a carriage and drove to the Depot, giving him the particulars to report to Judd.

We arrived at the Depot just in time for the Train starting at 4.20 p.m. I directed Mr Burns to say to Mr Judd that Lamon and Judge Davis of Illinois were surely playing the Devil, and unless they shut their heads about me I would be obliged to leave; that if I was kept secret I would remain — if I was made public I would certainly leave.

*   *   *   *   *

Tuesday 26th February 1861

A. P.— Reports —

*   *   *   *   *

At 10.30. a.m. T. W— returned from Washington D.C. and made a Verbal report in relation to Detectives Tom Sampson, and Ely DeVoe, who were the parties known as Thompson and Davis, late of Sherwood Hotel, They were both very much frightened at the receipt of the news by T. W— and left their Hotel without paying the bill or getting their baggage — in short they made a precipitate retreat, thanking "T.W. for his information.

T. W— had also called on N. B. Judd in his room at Willards Hotel. Judd was very much pleased to see T. W— and laughed very heartily at the New York Detectives being discovered.

*   *   *   *   *

Tuesday 26th, February 1861 —

T. W— Reports —

I had breakfast, after which I went to the Depot and took the 7.40. a.m. Train for Baltimore.

On arriving at Baltimore I went to the Office, saw A. P— and reported to him. We then walked up town, A. P— all the time giving me my instructions. He requested me to leave Perrymansville on Wednesday, or Thursday, and laid the plan by which I was to draw off. A. P.— also told me that I was to go with one of his men (Williams) in the afternoon and get acquainted with some of the leading men of the Military Company's that were recruiting for South Carolina service. Williams was to meet me at the White Beer Brewery, and introduce me to Sherrington, after which we would go to the Drill room and get an introduction to Col. Haskill. Williams then went to look for Sherrington, while Mr P— went and "spotted" the White Beer Brewery to me.

I then left A. P— and went to Springer's Store. I found Mr. Forward in, but Springer had gone out to collect some bills. Forward, and I had a glass of beer — whilst we were drinking he told me that the boys felt mighty sore about Lincoln's giving them the slip; that if Lincoln had gone through when he was expected, he would have been shot, and then Baltimore would have been the battle-field but now he thought Charleston would be, I said, that was just what I thought. I then bade him good bye and went to the White Beer Saloon, where I took a seat and called for a glass of beer.

In about half an hour Williams and Sherrington came in, Williams called for two glasses of beer, and whilst drinking started up quite suddenly, came to-wards me and said "my God, Webster when did you come up here &c —" He then introduced me to Sherrington, and told him that I was of the right stripe — we then had another glass of beer each, and began talking politics. I said I thought Baltimore was going to be the battlefield, but old Abe had got safe to Washington. Sherrington replied "By G—d, he would not if the boys had got their eyes on him, that they would have shot him for they had everything ready to do it with and that if we would go up the street he would show us the kind of tools the boys carried here.

We then went to a Store on Baltimore Street, where he got the Clerk to show us some pistols. Sherrington said they were the kind that he was telling me a bout, and was the best Pistol that was made. I went into the backroom and tried one, and found it very good. Sherrington said that those were the kind the boys carried, and that he was going to get one.

We then went to a Saloon and got a drink, and from the Saloon went to Sherwoods where we got some Oysters, and another drink. There were several persons in the place talking about shooting "Old Abe" — some said that they did not believe Lincoln would have been hurt, and others again said that they knew a d—d sight better, for they were acquainted with men who belonged to the Organization who were ready for anything, and would just as leave shoot Lincoln as they would a rat. We then went to the Drill room, but found very few men there, We waited there some time, when a few more came, with whom Sherrington and William's got into conversation. They learned from this last party that Col. Haskell would not be in Baltimore until Friday: that they expected him here to-day so as to make arrangement to go with him to Charleston. I said that that would just suit me. Sherrington replied that if I came there on Friday I could see him, and I promised that I would try to be there, so as to make arrangements to go with him to Charlston, We then took another drink and seperated.

I then went to the Office, and reported to Mr. P—, after which I left for the Howard House, where I met H. H. L.—,[48] and went with her to Mr. Springers Store He told us that he would be in Perrymansville in the morning.

We then went to the Depot and took the 5.11. p.m. train for Perrymans, arriving there at 6.30. p.m. had supper, after which I called to see Captain Keen, I found Mr. Ellis and five or six others at the Store, talking about Lincoln's passage through Baltimore. Mr. Ellis said that they talked pretty hard about it in Baltimore, and believed just as we did here, that the Rail-Road Company knew all about it several days before he passed through. James Micheal (Captain Keens — brother-in-law) said that when you come to look at it, it was plain enough to see that the Company must have known all about it, and, that was why they had so many men at the Bridges, and changing the Telegraph Operatives. Mr. Ellis a member of the Rangers proposed to pull up the Rail-Road track and stop the travel South: that it was the only thing left to bring them Northerners to their senses. James Micheal thought to make the work complete they should besides tearing up the Rail-Road track, sink, or burn the boat at Havre-de-Grace, so they could not cross the River. Captain Keen wanted to bet that before three weeks had passed, that Maryland would be out of the Union, and then he would like to see them run the

48. Hattie H. Lawton, an associate of Timothy Webster, stationed with him at Perrymansville, Maryland. See Cuthbert, 21.

trains over this Road, or any other in the State. They talked on in this strain for some time, after which we all went over to Taylors Saloon, At 10.00. p.m. I went to my room, wrote my report and then went to bed. —

Thursday 26*th*. February 1861[49] —

A. F. C— Reports —

I and Hillard, who occupied a room with me (at the National Hotel, Washington, D.C.) got up at 8.00 — a.m. and had breakfast, after which Hillard went in search of a room, and I remained at the Hotel, Hillard returned at 11.00. a.m. and said that he had succeeded in finding a room, and I then went with him to said room, which was at the "European Hotel," situated on Eleventh Street — From there we went to the Capitol and remained until 2.00. p.m. On our way thence to our room, Hillard spoke to a man on the Street, and after passing the salutations of the day said to him "I have come to see *Old Abe*." The man said "Well, Old Abe, had a quick trip through Baltimore" — Hillard remarked "yes, and it was well for him that he went through as quick as he did." This acquaintance of Hillard's then accompanied us down the Street, and on the way (the friend), remarked pointing to a man, "There stands Jim Burns, commander of the National Volunteers," upon which he left us, and I and Hillard continued our walk, Hillard afterwards told me that this James Burns was one of the principal men in the National Volunteers.

In the course of our walk, Hillard purchased a Baltimore paper, and seeing a notice in it for the Members of Company No. 9. of the National Volunteers to meet at their room (in Baltimore) for the purpose of electing Officers, gave me to understand that this notice was only a "blind"; that it was intended for all the members of the Volunteers, and that there was no necessity for an Election of Officers — that the notice in the paper was to call all the members to their respective quarters without giving the public a chance to speculate on the meaning and object of the meeting.

Before we had arrived at our Hotel, we had stopped into a Restaurant where we met a man by the name of Bement, who I had seen at Niles. Michigan, where he delivered a Lecture. He said to me "How are you — when did you leave South Bend?" I replied "I left some time since". Hillard in the mean time went into a little side room to see how the eating department looked. I called Bement outside of the Saloon and told him that I did not wish to be known there, as I was employed by the State Bank of Indiana to hunt up some Forgeries committed on the Branch at South Bend. This seemed to satisfy him. Hillard came out, and we left. He did not say anything in regard to what passed Bement and me, but my impression was that he heard the word "South" but not "Bend".

On the Street we met a man from Kalamazo, Michigan, by the name of S. Chadwick, who knew me, and on his coming up said, "How are you." I appeared not to know him, *but it was no* go. He Said "Don't you know me — Kalamazo

---

49. An error: the twenty-sixth was a Tuesday.

against all the world! You and I, used to play Billiards to-gether there." I then said to him "How are you — I recollect you now." I took his arm and leaving Hillard standing, stepped a few paces aside when I said to him. "I am very busy now — I will call over at your Hotel and see you", I then returned to Hillard, Chadwick having gone. Hillard wanted to know where I had known that man. I replied "in New Orleans": that he was a gambler; that one evening in New Orleans with a party of my friends, I went into a Gambling House, and this Chadwick was there; that a stranger came in a little tight who said "Kalamazo against the world!" and remarked that he could beat any man playing in the room: that Chadwick sat down and beat him out of his money — over Two thousand dollars, and ever since that time, whenever Chadwick met me, he would shout out "Kalamazoo aginst the world"! What Kalamazoo meant I did not know.

By this time we had arrived at our room. I asked Hillard if he had seen any of the National Volunteers. He replied that he had seen several on the Street. I asked him "How many have you seen — one or two?" He replied "I have and more."

Hillard and I after supper went to the Odd Fellow's Hall to hear the New Orleans Minstrels, and as we were going he saw a man at the door, who he knew and spoke to, but without looking at him, and almost in a whisper. we returned to our room from there at about 11.00. p.m., and went to bed.

Hillard to-day appeared cheerful in Spirits, but drank pretty heavy.

Thursday 28*th* February 1861

A. P.— Reports —

I arrived at the office at 8.30. a.m. and soon after went to the Post Office and received a letter from Superintendant Kennedy of which the following is a copy.

"N.Y. Feb. 26*th* 1861

"A. Pinkerton Esq.
"Dear Sir
"I regret I did not know you were in Balto. — Had I been apprised of it I could have seen you on my return. I left Washington yesterday afternoon at 3. o'clock and came through by the Owl; and find yours on my desk this morning."
"I shall at once have search made for the man and things you named; and inform you of the result."
"The field of operation is now transferred to the Capital. Whatever is done remote from there will be limited to raising funds and the collection of material, so that I have withdrawn my Corps Observation from your present vicinity — But for that reason I shall be happy to receive any suggestion from you that may require attention from my hands."
"Very Respectfully
Yours &c—
John A. Kennedy"

Friday 1*st*. March 1861 —

A. F. C.— Reports —

Hillard and I got up at 7.30. a.m., he going to get breakfast as he said, and I went to Mann's Restaurant and got mine — after which I went to the Office and wrote my report, and then returned to my room at 10.30. a.m.

At 11.30. a.m. Hillard came to my room, Nothing of note transpired, and at 12.30. p.m. we left the room, he starting for his boarding House, and I for Mann's Restaurant for dinner. At 1.30. p.m. Hilliard came to the room, I having returned from dinner.

In conversation Hillad said "Some Detectives have got in with the Naitional Volunteers," and he continued "Did you read where they (the Detectives), Said that every man of the National Volunteers had to take an oath to kill Lincoln if they could?" I replied that I did not read it, but could not believe it was so. He said that they (the Volunteers) *had taken such an oath,*" and added "I need not do it, because I have withdrawn, but I can exercise my own pleasure about it" — and that "the members are bound to Kill Lincoln yet, if the oppertunity presented itself," "I have not the right" said he, "to tell you this, but as the thing has leaked out, it is no harm to mention it to you — the Committee are to hold a meeting to-night.

We left my room to-gether at 4.30. p.m. and went up Holliday Street to the corner of Baltimore Street, where I excused myself saying to Hillard that I had some little matter to attend to, and then left him and went to the Office to fill an appointment with Mr. P—.

On arriving at the Office I received orders from Mr. P— to go to Washington on Monday the 4*th* instant. I then returned to my room at 6.00. p.m. and found Hillard there. He was very anxious for me to go in the evening with him and visit his sister, a married lady about 40 years old, whose name I do not recollect, but I excused myself on the plea of indisposition, for the reason that I did not consider that my business called me there.

Hillard remarked that the New York Herald said that May be Lincoln would not be inaugerated *yet*. We remained at my room during the evening, and went to bed at about midnight. Hillard said that he was determined to go to Washington with me on Monday; that he was bound to see Lincoln Inaugerated — He drinks as much as usual.

        Conspiracy — To assassinate[50]
              Police Pinkerton
        Head Quarters.
        National Volunteer's.

---

50. This heading and the inscription on the next line, *"Police Pinkerton,"* are in WHH's hand. In the left margin he wrote: *26 pages.* (apparently referring to this section of Pinkerton's report, which covers only twenty-five pages in the transcription). This is what his earlier notation (see p. 285, note 35) apparently refers to.

Baltimore Feb. 20, 1861.

This is to certify that Charles Williams
Is an enrolled Member of the National Volunteers,
Company "A" and entitled to all the privileges of the Same.
Robt. E. Hasletz. William Byrne,[51] President.

After getting our Certificates, Mr. Hack, Sherrington, and I went to Gerry's Saloon. I asked Mr. Hack what drill they used. He replied that they used no regular drill yet: that the trouble was there were too many "bosses": that he had been drilling Company "B," but had been ordered to attend "A", and also that there was some talk of sending Five Hundred men to Charleston next week. I told him I was some acquainted with Military Tactics, and would like to copy their drill so as to be ready to act when wanted. Mr. Hack, said that he had been through the Mexican War, and made me promise to attend next Monday, when they intended Organizing and electing their Officers, and that he intended running for first Lieutenant.

On our return to the Hotel I got into conversation with two gentlemen who were stopping at Sherwoods — one was an Englishman, but said that he came to this country when he was sixteen months old: that he had recently come from Alabama here (Baltimore), and was travelling with his friend, who had some business to transact.

In the evening we went to the Melodion Concert Hall to-gether. The Englishman said his name was "Thompson," and his friends name was "Davis". Thompson said that he owned a nice little farm in Lymer County, Iowa,[52] which he intended some day settling on. I asked him if he was not for the South, He said "Oh! Yes," but he was for peace, and hoped that the Union would be preserved. I replied that I too owned land in Iowa, but I would be d—d if I would live in a Northern State.

Thompson was very talkative about his farm, and in the middle of his conversation turned to Davis and said, "Don't forget — you must go after that money to-morrow." There was something peculiar about their movements that Sherrington did not like. He told me to be careful of them, for that he believed they were two d—d spies. Davis talked some about the Alabama River, where it seems he had run a Scow — this gave Sherrington a little more confidence in them but still he suspected that they were not "all right."

Mr. Thompson said that he would show me a splended Revolver, that had been sent him from London, if I would remind him of it to-morrow. On returning to the hotel they took a lamp and went to their room. Sherrington again remarked that he did not like those fellows.

---

51. Besides heading the National Volunteers, Byrne was the delegate chosen to carry Maryland's electoral vote to Washington, D.C., after the 1860 election. See Cuthbert, 141.

52. Possibly Lyon County, Iowa.

Wednesday 20*th* February 1861.

H. H. L— Reports

We had breakfast at 7.00. a.m. after which we conversed some but nothing was said worthy of note. Just before dinner a stranger came and asked if he could have something to eat. Mr. Taylor said that dinner would soon be ready and asked him to wait, which the stranger said he would do.

At 2.00. p.m. we all sat down to dinner, when the stranger told us that he was a Minister, and was going to preach at a place some six miles from Perrymansville — also that he had lost some money in Philadelphia. After he had finished eating his dinner he told Mr. Taylor that he could not pay him for he had no money, and asked if he (Mr. Taylor) would take a pledge, or wait until he (the stranger) got the money, when he would sent it — said that his name was "Jones," and that he was from Louisville, Kentucky: that he travelled from place to place preaching &*c.*

Mr. Taylor was very indignant at the way the stranger had managed to get his dinner, and said that was what he called sneaking mean: that the man had not better come to his place again, for he would not fare quite so well if he did. Mr Taylor went on to say that he believed this man had plenty of money, and reckoned that all he came in the country for, was to have the Slaves rise up against their Masters, and he hoped no more would come.

After the 6.30 p.m. Train had passed, Mrs. Taylors little boy picked up some cards which he brought into the house. Mrs. Taylor remarked that she thought it very strange that they should be thrown of here. I replied to this — that persons got tired playing sometimes, and would throw them out of the window when they did not want them any more.

We had two strangers at supper, and remarks were made about the Preacher who dined with us. During the evening Mr. Taylor came into the house and said that he was going to Havre-de-Grace in the morning to make arrangements about getting his Mother-in-Law to live with him the rest of her life. Nothing more transpired worthy of note — At 9:45. p.m. I went to bed.

Thursday 21st February 1861.

A. P— Reports

Thursday 21st February 1861.[53]

I went to breatfast at 7.00. a.m. and at 8.45. a.m. I called at No 413 Prune Street, and saw Mr Burn's. I requested him to telegraph Mr. Judd who was with the Presidential Party, and who could be reached at either Newark or Trenton, New Jersey, and say to him (Judd) that I was in Philadelphia and would see him this evening.

At 9.10 — a.m. I met Mr. Felton at the La Pierre House, and walked with him to the Depot of the Philadelphia, Willmington and Baltimore Rail Road. Whilst walking with Mr. Felton, and after arriving at his Office, I made a full Report of

---

53. The repetition is apparently an inadvertent copyist's error.

what had come to my knowledge, in regard to an attempt being likely to be made upon the President-Elect; and his Suite while passing through Baltimore on Saturday next, and said that judging from the Reports of my Detectives, and allowing that even they were probably imperfectly posted, that I had no doubt but that there would be an attempt mad to assasinate Mr. Lincoln and his Suite — not that I believed there was any large organization or body of men who would be willing to go so far, but that from all I could learn there was not probably over Fifteen or Twenty men who would be reckless enough to attempt anything of the kind, and instanced O. K. Hillard as a speciman of the recklessness of this class, and argued that a few determined men by uniting in their effort and taking advantage of the large crowd of people who would probably be turned out on the occasion of the passage of the President Elect: that these few determined persons could accomplish a great deal, and that from the excitibility of all Mobs, and more especially a Baltimore Mob — the first shot fired — the first blow struck, and the whole became a living mass of mad ungovernable people.

I also stated to Mr. Felton the substance of the conversation I had over-heard of Police Marshall Kane on Saturday afternoon last at Barnums Hotel, when Kane had discredited the idea of "giving a Police Escort" for same purpose, and I further said to Mr Felton that I knew of nothing liky to transpire in Baltimore which might require a Police Escort, except it was on the arrival of the President Elect, and assuming that Marshall Kane meant this arrival and could not see the necessity of a Police Escort, then I argued that there was more danger to Mr. Lincoln, for from the familiar manner of Marshall Kane and many of the rabid Secessionates there could be no doubt but that they were aware that Kane was not going to give an Escort. I also argued that it was impossible for Marshall Kane not to know that there would be a necessity for an Escort for Mr. Lincoln on his arrival in Baltimore, and, that if with this knowledge Marshall Kane failed to give a Police Escort, then I should from this time out doubt the loyalty of the Baltimore Police.

Mr. Felton approved of what I had said and of the view I had taken of the case, and said that after having seen Mr. W*m* Stearns on his return from Baltimore, and recieved the verbal report from me — he (Mr. Felton) had mentioned the existance of danger to Morton McMicheal Esq. Editor of the "Philadelphia North American," and that Mr. McMicheal had taken a deep interest in it, and had this morning left to meet the Presidential Party on the way from New York to Philadelphia, and that he (Mr. Felton) had instructed Mr. McMicheal not to mention the subject to any one in the "Cortege" except Mr. Judd — Not even to Mr. Lincoln himself, and that he (Mr Felton) should like very much to have me meet them (Judd and McMicheal) with himself this evening and suggest to them the absolute necessity for a change in the Presidential Programe. I agreed to meet the gentleman as Mr. Felton requested, and informed him of the presence of Mr. Burns in Philadelphia, and the power conferred on Mr. Burn's, by Mr. Sanford to be used in case of necessity.

I remained with Mr. Felton until 11.15. a.m., when Mr. Felton having some other business to attend to, agreed to meet me at 1.00. p.m. at his Office. On leaving Mr Felton I went to the St Louis Hotel and directed M. B— to remain in the Hotel as I might require her.

I next called at Mr. Burn's house but he was not at home, so I left word that I would endeavor to see him again at 3.00. p.m.. I then went to the Express Office to ascertain if Henry Sanford had arrived from New York, but found he had not, and it being now nearly 1.00. p.m., I went to the Depot of the Philadelphia, Willmington and Baltimore Rail Road to keep my appointment with Mr. Felton — I found him in his Office, but he being engaged I made an appointment with him to meet at the La Pierre House at 5.00. p.m..

At 2.30. p.m. I found Mr. Burns at his Mother's, No. 413 Prune Street. He informed me that he had Telegraphed to Mr. Judd as I had requested, and informed me that he (Burns) had received a Dispatch from E. S. Sanford Esq. saying that Henry Sanford would leave New York for Philadelphia at 2.00. p.m. if I thought it necessary. I said that as far as the safety of the Express was concerned from attack by a Mob, that I thought I should be able to receive information regarding such an attempt in season to notify the Express Company, but that I thought it would be advisable to have the Messengers between Philadelphia and Baltimore and Harrisburg doubled, and that none should go as Messengers but good, resolute, reliable men, and that they should be well armed, and that as these changes could be made by Mr. Burn's, through Col. Bingham the Philadelphia Superintendant of the Adams Express Company —   I did not think it necessary for Henry Sanford to come over, but as it was now to late to reply to this Dispatch I supposed that it was just as well to let the matter go. Shortly after Mr. Burn's received another Dispatch from E. S. Sanford Esq. saying that Henry Sanford had left at 2.00. p.m. and requesting Mr. Burns to arrange with Col. Bingham to meet Henry Sanford at the Girard House at 8.00. p.m..

I said to Mr. Burns that in making arrangements for putting on the extra Messenger's, I did not suggest it in view of any real danger of which I had information, but merely as a precautionary measure, and that I did not desire that either Col. Bingham or Mr. Shoemaker of Baltimore the manager of Adams Express Company at that point should know of my being the party who advised it or furnished the information.

I requested Mr. Burns to go to the Kensington Rail Road Depot, and await the arrival of the Presidential Party who was expected to arrive about 3.00. p.m., and watch for the first oppertunity to see Mr. McMicheal, and say to him that it was Mr. Felton's desire to meet him (McMicheal), and Mr. Judd, with myself at the earliest possible moment after the Cortege should reach the Continental Hotel, where Mr. Lincoln and Suite were going to put up, and that failing in seeing Mr. McMicheal, he (Mr Burns) was to endeavor to see Mr Judd, and arrange for a meeting with myself and Mr. Felton at the earliest possible moment — that in regard to the place for meeting there would be such a crowd at the Continental that I did not think it safe for me to go there for fear of being recognized. Neither did I think the Girard safe, nor the La Pierre House on account of the number of Southerners stopping at those Houses: that upon the whole I deemed my room at the St Louis the best and safest for the meeting, but that I should meet at any place which might be deemed most advisable and convenient for Mr Judd.

I told Mr. Burns that I had to meet Mr. Felton at the La Pierre House at 5.00. p.m., and I should inform Mr. Felton of what I had done in this respect and would expect Mr. Burn's there about 5.0.0. p.m. to let us know when the arrangement for the meeting was perfected

At 5.00 p.m. I met Mr. Felton at the La Pierre House and we talked over the probable chances of Mr. Lincoln changing his route. I said to Mr. Felton that I had some delicacy in recomending a change in the route, as it might hereafter be argued that it was a trick devised to encourage travel by a Mail Rail road Line, but that I felt satisfied that there was iminent danger in Mr. Lincoln taking the published route from Harrisburg to Baltimore, Via the Northern Central Rail Road and that I should not hesitate in saying so, leaving it for Mr. Lincoln and his advisers to change the route or not, just as he saw fit.

Mr. Felton approved of this, but said that if it was possible for Mr. Lincoln to leave his party to-night and take berths in the sleeping Car through to Baltimore and Washington it would be the best and safest thing which could be done, as he (Mr. Felton) felt assured from other sources of information besides what I had that there would be bloodshed in Mr. Lincoln's attempting to pass through Baltimore openly by the route proposed

Mr. Felton also said that he had just to-day received a Telegraph from Vice President Elect Hamlin asking for a special Car on the Noon Train, South from Philadelphia to-morrow for him (Hamlin) to go to Baltimore in. Mr. Felton feared that this dispatch would get into the Telegraph news of associated Press and might thus complicate any change of route which Mr. Lincoln might deem advisable.

I informed Mr. Felton that I expected Mr. Burns every moment to apprise me of when and where we would meet Mr. Judd, and that when Mr. Burns arrived I should have him Telegraph Mr. Sanford at New York to prevent the appearance of this Dispatch in the Telegraph News — but that in view of this move of Mr. Hamlin I thought it would be advisable for us to meet Mr. Judd as early as possible and lay the whole matter before him.

Just at this time I heard the sound of music, and concluded that the Presidential Procession was going down Walnut Street, and went out and found it to be so. Just as I reached Walnut Street, I saw Mr. Burns break through the ranks of the Police surrounding the carriage in which was the President Elect and Mr. Judd, and hand Mr. Judd a note — in a few minutes afterwards Mr. Burn's came through the crowd which was very dense, when I met him, and he told me that the meeting was arranged for to be in my room at the St Louis Hotel, at 7.30. p.m.. I requested Mr. Burn's to endeavor once more to see Mr. Judd and say to him that some circumstances had transpired which rendered it advisable to meet earlier and ask Mr. Judd if he could not name an earlier hour. How Mr. Burn's was to get through the crowd and overtake the carriage I could not see, nor how he would again break the ranks of the Police I could not tell — but he left me and with superhuman strength I saw him go through the crowd like nothing, and bursting through the ranks of the Police again reach the carriage — In a few minutes he returned and said that Mr. Judd would see me immediately at the St Louis.

Mr. Burn's and myself then went to the La Pierre House and informed Mr. Felton who agreed to come right down to the meeting. I also arranged with Mr. Burn's to telegraph Mr. Sanford in relation to suppressing the news of the intended departure of Vice President Hamlin from New York or the route chosen by him.

I left the La Pierre with Mr. Burn's who went to the Telegraph Office and I to the St Louis and had a fire made in my room No — 21 — Soon Mr. Felton arrived and about 6.45. p.m., Mr. Judd arrived. I introduced him to Mr. Felton and Mr. Felton explained his cause for fearing that the track of the Philadelphia, Willmington and Baltimore Rail Road was in danger, and consequently his employment of me, and how in my researches of this kind I had discovered the fact that some persons meditated the assasination of the President Elect. Mr. Felton also informed Mr. Judd that from all he had heard from other sources he had no doubt but that if Mr. Lincoln adhered to the published programe he (Felton) did not doubt but that there would be blood-shed in Baltimore, and that should blood be shed it would certainly precipitate War.

Mr. Judd said that he knew me well enough to know that I would not in any case exaggerate or speak of any thing without I felt assured that it was so, and told Mr. Felton how long he had known me, and paid me a very high compliment for Ability, honesty, integrity &c —.

At Mr. Judd's request I briefly detailed to him the circumstances which had come to my knowledge as detailed in the Reports of my operations. I dwelt at some length on the statement of Marshall Kane, which I had over-heard at Barnum's Hotel, assuming that Kane was at that time alluding to the Presidential Cortege not to recieve an escort of Police in passing through Baltimore.

I also informed Mr. Judd of the drilling and movements of the Rangers of Perrymansville and the Infantry troops at Bel-Air which was about midway between Cockeysville on the Northern Central Rail Road which was on the route published for the Presidential Cortege to take from Harrisburg to Baltimore, and Perrymansville on the Philadelphia, Willmington and Baltimore Rail Road. I communicated at some length on the character, Standing &c of O. K. Hillard, and assumed that there was iminent danger from this class of men, whose patriotism was influenced and who looked upon their Country as being entirely South of Mason and Dixons Line, whose every sympathy was with the South and would deem it an honor to become martyrs in their cause. In this respect I instanced the courage of John Brown who almost single handed threw himself into a fight against the Nation. I also told Mr. Judd that in my opinion a large body of men was not necessary to accomplish the object desired to be obtained: that a few resolute men could in a crowd do more than even a large body would; because they could act more united. I also spoke of the oath bound associations of National Volunteers spoken of by Hillard; and his statement that he "would do whatever his Captain called upon him to do, without asking a why or a wherefore." and to the avowed determination of those men that Lincoln should not pass through Baltimore alive.

I also spoke of the Privateer spoken of by Captain Sherrington, and the Fire Balls or Hand Grenades spoken of by the Baltimore Secessionists, and to the disloyalty of the Baltimore Police who it was even doubtful if they would make a decent show to preserve order, and instanced the difficulty experienced by the Presidential Party in Buffalo where with a Loyal Police the pressure was great as to seriously injure Major Hunter[54] one of the Party. I said to Mr. Judd that the danger was from a small number of men in the crowd acting in concert, and asked what would be the consequences where the Presidential Party was hemmed in a crowd unable to move and a few men bent on taking life — armed, prepared and determined on doing so even if they had to give a life, for a life — and argued that situated as the country was this was no time to go into War, which would be the result if the President Elect was assassinated in Baltimore: that at present we had no Government and could have none before the Inaugeration of Lincoln: that as things stood now Mr. Lincoln had no power: that nameless and unknown as I was, I could stand a better chance for my life, than did Mr. Lincoln as I at least had some of my own men with me who would die in their boots before I should be injured. I said that the danger was not so much to the President whilst upon the Train as it was from the time he landed at the Northern Central Depot until he could pass in an open carriage about a mile and a quarter to the Depot of the Washington Branch Rail Road, and said to Mr. Judd that I did not believe it was possible he (Lincoln) or his personal friends could pass through Baltimore in that style alive.

I enquired of Mr. Judd if he knew if any arrangements had been made in Baltimore by any parties with view to the friendly or patriotic reception of the President elect, and he replied that he did not know of any such arrangements. I then enquired of Mr. Judd who Mr. Wood[55] was, who was acting as manager for the Presidential Party, and Mr. Judd said he did not know, nor could not tell who he was: that he had asked Mr. Lincoln himself this same questions and could not learn that Mr Lincoln knew any thing about him further than that he came from New York and had been recommended by Erastus Corning, and Gov. Seward.

Mr. Judd said that all this was a very important subject, and that after what he had heard he believed there was great danger to Mr. Lincoln to attempt to pass through Baltimore according to the Programe: that he had not mentioned this to Mr. Lincoln, as in my letters to him at Cincinnati and New York, I had exacted strict secresy and that he should now have to see Mr. Lincoln in regard to it, and enquired of Mr. Felton and myself what we thought best to be done. Mr. Felton advised that if it could possibly be done, Mr. Lincoln should quietly leave the Party to-night and with me take a passage in the Sleeping Car and go on to Washington arriving there to-morrow morning.

I assured Mr. Judd that I thought this could be done in safety, and that from what Mr. Felton had told me of General Scott, I believed that if once the President Elect was in Washington that he would there be safe, and further said that I

---

54. Later Gen. David Hunter.
55. William S. Wood, an associate of William H. Seward from New York City.

was positive that if he (Lincoln) ever arrived at Washington at this time, he must pass through Baltimore by a Stratagem.

Mr. Judd expressed his thanks to Mr. Felton and myself for our interest in this affair and in accordance with our request promised that we should not be exposed or known in this matter whatever, the consequences might be, as also that he would mantain secrecy to all except with Mr. Lincoln as to the aid we had received or expected to receive from E. S. Sanford President of the American Telegraph Company.

Mr. Judd said that it was 9.00. p.m. he would like if I would go with him to the Continental Hotel and meet Mr. Lincoln and lay the subject before him and decide upon what course we had better pursue.   He (Judd) expressed himself very decided in reference to the necessity of a change of route from that which had been published and said he had no doubt but that Mr. Lincoln would upon the circumstances being laid before him, would see the necessity for action of this kind.

On leaving the St Louis we parted from Mr. Felton and I agreed that I would see Mr. Felton at the La Pierre House so soon as Mr. Lincoln had decided and let him (Mr. Felton) know what the decision was, — from the immense crowd in Chesnut Street and the Continental Hotel I afterwards found that it was impossible for me to fulfil this egagement.

On Mr. Judd and myself arriving within a block of the Continental Hotel the crowd was one dense mass of people. I accordingly took Mr Judd around to Samson Street where we obtained an entrance by the rear of the Hotel. On getting Mr. Judd in I told him that I would join him soon and went to the Girard House to meet Mr. Burns and Henry Sanford Esq., with whom I had made an engagement but found it utterly impossible to get into that house owing to the denseness of the crowd. It took me over Thirty minutes to again get out of the crowd, when I returned to Samson Street and entered the Continental. The interior of the house was as densely crowded as was the outside and I found that all were "getting up stairs," when I reached the last of the stairs I found that Mr. Lincoln was in a balcony at the head of the first landing, bowing to the people as they passed up the stairs. There was no way for me to get up but to go into the jam and go up with the human tide, so I went in — but such a jam. In due time however I reached the head of the stairs where I found the Halls about as much crowded as they were below. The people were kept moving in a steady stream around through a double file of Police to the stair-way on Tenth Street and thus out. I managed to get outside of the file of Police and soon found Mr Judd's room where I found him waiting for me. Judd said that as soon as Mr. Lincoln got through with recieving the people on the Balcony he (Judd) would send for him to come to his room.

I sent a note by a waiter to George H. Burns or Henry Sanford at the Girard House and soon after Mr. Sanford came to Mr. Judd's room. I introduced him to Mr. Judd and talked over with him in relation to the co-operation I might require from the Telegraph Company to secure the successful carrying out of my plans in reference to the change of route now deemed by the President Elect.

I also suggested to Mr. Sanford that as a precautionary measure I should think it advisable for the Express Company to double thier Messengers for the present on the runs between Philadelphia and Baltimore and between Harrisburg and Baltimore, not that I had any idea that any parties who might be contemplating an attack on the life of President Lincoln meditated an attack on the property of the Express Company, but that should anything of the kind occur professional theives seeing an oppertunity offer to operate successfully might with a view to plunder join the attacking party.

Mr. Sanford said he would see Col. Bingham and at once have this attended to, and at my request said that no explanations should be made to Mr. Shoemaker of Baltimore in relation to the reason for doubling the force of messengers. I made this request not that I doubted the Honesty or Loyalty of Mr Shoemaker but that I feared his discretion.

About 10.15. p.m. having learned that Mr. Lincoln had retired to his room, I carried a note from Mr. Judd to him saying that he (Judd) desired to see him (Lincoln) at his (Judd's) roon so soon as conveninent on Private business of importance. Col. Ellsworth[56] who was officiating as Equery in waiting refused to deliver the note, but accompanied me to Mr. Judd's room, who at once ordered Ellsworth to deliver the note, and in about ten minutes thereafter Mr Lincoln entered the room — of course a very large crowd followed him to the door which was at once guarded by Ellsworth. Mr. Judd introduced me to Mr. Lincoln who at once recollected me. I then introduced Henry Sanford Esq. who immediately retired.

Mr. Judd briefly detailed to Mr. Lincoln the circumstances under which I had gone to Baltimore to operate with a view the protection of the Philadelphia, Willmington, and Baltimore Rail Road, and that whilst so operating amongst the Secessionists that I had discovered a determination amongst certain parties to attempt taking the life of him (Mr. Lincoln) whilst passing through Baltimore.

Whilst Mr. Judd was talking Mr. Lincoln listened very attentively, but did not say a word, nor did his countenance which I watched very closely, show any emotion. He appeared thoughtful and serious, but decidedly firm.

When Mr. Judd had concluded he requested me to detail the circumstances connected with Ferrandina, Hillard and others, and what my opinion was of the probable attempt. I did so commenting at some length on the fact of overhearing Col. Kane, Marshall of Baltimore, state of last Saturday at Barnum's Hotel that he would give "no Police Escort" probably referring to the passage of Mr. Lincoln through Baltimore, I alluded to the expressions of Hillard and Ferrandina: that they were ready to give their lives for the welfare of their Country, as also that their country was South of Mason's and Dixon's line: that they were ready and willing to die to rid their Country of a tyrant as they considered Lincoln to be. I said that I did not desire to be understood as saying that there were any large number of men engaged in this attempt — but that on the contrary I thought there were very

---

56. Elmer Ellsworth had briefly studied law in the Lincoln-Herndon Office in 1860. In early 1861 he served as commander of a Zouave regiment and was killed while removing a Confederate flag in Alexandria, Virginia.

few — probably not exceeding from fifteen to twenty who would be really brave enough to make the attempt. — but that I thought Hillard was a fair sample of this class — a young man of good family, character and reputation — honorable, gallant and chivalrous, but thoroughly devoted to Southern rights, and who looked upon the North as being aggressors upon the rights of that section and upon every Northern man as an Abolitionist, and he (Mr. Lincoln) as the embodiment of all those evils, in whose death the South would be largely the gainers. I also told Mr. Lincoln that there would be a very large crowd in Baltimore on the occassion of his passing through that City: that he (Mr Lincoln) had had some experience of the danger in a large crowd from accident which met Col. Hunter at Buffalo where the Police were loyal, but that it would be infinitly worse in Baltimore, where owing to the depression in all kinds of business, there were very many people out of employment, and the crowd would in all probability be very large — this with "no Police Escort", or if there was an Escort it would be by a Disloyal Police, and the slightest sign of discontent would be sufficient to raise all the angry feeling of the Masses, and that then would be a favorable moment for the conspirators to operate: that again, as by the published route, he (Mr. Lincoln) in taking the Northern Central Rail Road from Harrisburg to Baltimore, would arrive at the Calvert Street Depot, and would have about one mile and a quarter to pass through the City in an open carriage, which would move but slowly through the dense crowd and that then it would be an easy matter for any assasin to mix in with the crowd and in the confusion of the moment shoot Mr. Lincoln if he felt so disposed: that I felt satisfied in my own mind that if Mr. Lincoln adhered to the published programe of his route to Washington that an assault of some kind would be made upon his person with a view to taking his life.

During the time I was speaking Mr. Lincoln listened with great attention only asking a question occasionally. We were interrupted once by the entrance of W. H. Lamon of Bloomington, Ills. who entered the room to give a note to Mr. Lincoln. Mr. Lamon recognized me, but I am positive he could not have known me had he not been informed by some one that I was with the President Elect.

After I had concluded Mr. Lincoln remained quiet for a few minutes apparently thinking, when Mr. Judd inquired. "If upon any kind of statement which might be made to him (Lincoln) would he (Lincoln) consent to leave for Washington on the train to-night." Mr. Lincoln said promptly "No, I cannot consent to this, I shall hoist the Flag on Independance Hall to-morrow morning (Washingtons birthday) and go to Harrisburg to-morrow, then I (Lincoln) have fulfilled all my engagements, and if you (addressing Mr. Judd), and you Allan (meaning me) think there is positive danger in my attempting to go through Baltimore openly according to the published programe — if you can arrange any way to carry out your views, I shall endeavor to get away quietly from the people at Harrisburgh to-morrow evening and shall place myself in your.[57]

---

57. The text is marked here and in the margin to indicate a word is missing.

The firmness of tone in which Mr. Lincoln spoke showed that there was no further use in arguing the proposition and Mr. Judd inquired of me what I thought best to do in the emergancy and I said that if Mr Lincoln could manage to get away unobserved, from the people at Harrisburg by about dusk to-morrow evening that I thought we could get a special Train on the Pennsylvania Rail Road to bring him from Harrisburg to Philadelphia in time for the train going South on the Philadelphia Willmington and Baltimore Rail Road when we could secure seats in the sleeping Car which goes directly through to Washington and thus save us from being observed at Baltimore, as we would not require to get out of the Car.

This was finally after some discussion agreed upon, and I promised to see the Superintendant of the Pennsylvania Rail Road in regard to procuring the special train, and making all the arrangements for the trip. I requested Mr. Lincoln that none but Mr. Judd and myself should know anything about this arrangement. He said that ere he could leave it would be necessary for him to tell Mrs. Lincoln and that he thought it likely that she would insist upon W. H. Lamon going with him (Lincoln); but aside from this no one should know. I said that secrecy was so necessary for our success that I deemed it best that as few as possible should know anything of our movements: that I knew all the men with whom it was necessary for me to instruct my movements and that my share of this secret should be safe, and that if it only was kept quiet I should answer for his safety with my life.

At 11.00. p.m. Mr. Lincoln left. The crowd was very dense around the door of the room all the time he was in.

I omitted to mention that I enquired of Mr. Lincoln if any arrangement had been made in Baltimore with the public Authorities for his reception in that City, and he said he did not know of any, nor had he heard from a single individual in that City: that he (Lincoln) had left that arrangement with Mr. Wood, but that Wood had not said anything to him in relation to any reception. I then enquired "who Mr. Wood was," and what he knew of him, and Mr. Lincoln said he knew "Nothing of him": that he (Wood) had been recomended to him (Lincoln) as being all right by Gov. Seward. Mr. Lincoln said that Mr. Wood should not know anything in regard to our movements.

When Mr. Lincoln left I told Mr Judd that I would now get a carriage and go to find T. A. Scott Esq. Vice President, Pensylvania Rail Road, and arrange for the special train to-morrow evening and that I should call back and see him. Henry Sanford came into Mr. Judd's room and agreed to wait until I should return.

I immediately took a carriage and drove to Mr. Scott's on Spruce Street, but found he was at Harrisburg, and I drove to Mr. Francisus, Division Superintendant, Pennsylvania Rail Road on Chesnut Street, but found that he was at the Continental Hotel to which place I returned and upon enquiry found that he had gone home shortly before my arrival. It being now about 12.00. p.m..

HL: LN2408, 3:258–376

215. John D. DeFrees to WHH

Washington, Aug 21st 1866.

My dear sir:

There is a *little* truth in the telegram to the Tribune[1] — but not much.

The State Convention at Indianapolis, Feby 22d 1864, was the first one held on the opening of the Presidential Campaign of 1864. There was a combination among some prominent men in our State (who ought to be ashamed of it) to prevent our indorement of Mr. Lincoln for a second term. This was well understood by Mr. Lincoln. *I did* go to Indianapolis a few days in advance of the meeting of that Convention, with Mr. L.' knowledge and approval to do all I could to get such an endorsement, — *but, I did not take* out an autograph letter from Mr. Lincoln appealing to his friends to take steps to make Mr. Johnson vice President — nor, did I ever hear Mr. Lincoln express a preference for Mr. J. or any one else — but, on the contrary, I heard him say that, on that question, he would say nothing.

I did think it was good policy to place some one living in a Southern State — who had been true — on the ticket and favored Johnson — for which the Lord forgive me.

Yours Truly
Jno. D. Defrees

P.S. When your book is out, I must have a copy. I have all the lives yet written. Dr. Holland's, I think the best yet published — but, you have advantages over any one else — and will write the best book.

J.D.D.

[Enclosure]

216. Newspaper Clipping

[undated]

Johnson and Hamlin.

————

The great crime and blunder of putting Johnson in Hamlin's place, has sometimes been supposed to be chargeable to Massachusetts men. If the following extract from the Washington telegraphic dispatch to the New York *Tribune* (July 28) be trustworthy, we may add this to the other blunders of Abraham Lincoln.

Noticing the appointment of Gen. Steedman as Superintendent of Public Printing, in place of Mr. Defrees, the dispatch goes on to say:

"Early in 1864 Mr. Defrees, who was a warm friend of Mr. Lincoln, was sent to Indianapolis with an autograph letter from Mr. Lincoln, appealing to his friends in the State Convention to inaugurate the movement to make Gov. Johnson Vice-

————

1. This is presumably a response to a query about the report in the enclosed newspaper clipping (§216).

President. Mr. Defrees succeeded admirably. The Convention led off in placing him in nomination, and backed it up at Baltimore.

LC: HW2601; HL: LN2408, 2:459 (letter); LC: HW2601A (clipping)

217. J. Henry Shaw to WHH

Beardstown Ills. Aug. 22. 1866

Dear Sir:

In the case of the People vs. Wm. Armstrong, I was assistant prosecuting counsel. The prevailing belief at that time, (& I may also say at the present) in Cass Co. was as follows. Mr. Lincoln, previous to trial, handed an almanac of the year previous to the murder, to an officer of court, stating that he might call for one during the trial, & if he did, to send him that one. An important witness for the People had fixed the time of the murder to be in the night, near a camp-meeting, that "the moon was about in the same place that the sun would be at ten o'clock in the morning & was nearly full," therefore he could see plainly &c. At the proper time Mr. Lincoln called to the officer for an Almanac, & the one prepared for the occasion was shown by Mr. Lincoln, he reading from it that at the time referred to by the witness the moon *had already set.* That in the roar of laughter following, the jury & opposing counsel neglected to look at the date. Mr. Carter, a lawyer of this city who was present at, but not engaged in the Armstrong case, says he is satisfied that the almanac was of the year previous, & thinks he examined it at the time. This was the general impression in the court-room. I have called on the Sheriff who officiated at that time, James A. Dick, who says that he saw a "Goudy's" Almanac laying upon Mr. Lincoln's table during the trial, & that Mr. Lincoln took it out of his own pocket. Mr. Dick does not know the date of it. I have seen several of the petit juryman who sat upon the case, who only reccollect that the almanac *floored* the witness; but one of the jury, the foreman, Mr. Milton Logan, says that the almanac was a "Jayne's Almanac," that it was the one for the year in which the murder was committed, & that there was no trick about it, that he is willing to make an affidavit that he examined it as to its date and that it was the almanac of the year of the murder. My own opinion is, that when an almanac was called for by Mr. Lincoln, *two* were brought, one of the year of the murder and the other of the year previous; that Mr. Lincoln was entirely innocent of any deception in the matter. I the more think this, from the fact that Armstrong was not cleared by any want of testimony against him, but by the irresistable appeal of Mr. Lincoln in his favor. He told the jury of his once being a poor, friendless boy; that Armstrong's father took him into his house, fed and clothed him & gave him a home &c. the particulars of which were told so pathetically that the jury forgot the guilt of the boy in their admiration of the father.

It was generally admitted that Lincon's speech and personal appeal to the jury saved Armstrong.

Mr. James Taylor (now a resident of Springfield) was Clerk of the Circuit Court of Cass County at that time. By calling upon him, you can probably get his description of the affair.

The murder occurred, I think, in 1857. He was indicted in Mason Co. & a change of venue to this county. At the Nov. Term 1857 of Cass Cir. Court, Mr. Lincoln labored hard to get Armstrong admitted to bail, but his motion was overuled. The trial & aquital occurred at the May term 1858.

Yours Respectfully

J. Henry Shaw.

LC: HW2602–3; HL: LN2408, 2:305–7

218. Allan Pinkerton to WHH

Philadelphia, August 23d 1866

Dear Sir:

Yours of the 18th Inst. is duly received, and I hasten to reply.

I see you are at a little loss to understand the manner in which the Records start. I will endeavor to give you hurriedly what I supposed my Chief Clerk had sent you from Chicago, an idea of how to attain all which is of interest in connection with Mr. Lincoln.

I cannot now recollect the Dates, My Record, however, will show an application from Mr. S. M. Felton, at that time President of the Phila, Wilmington and Baltimore R.R., requesting me to ascertain through my Detective Force if there was an attempt on the part of the Secessionists of Maryland to seize the large Steamer of the Company used in ferrying their trains across the Susquehanna River at Havre de Grace, as also to burn the Bridges of the Company between Havre de Grace and Baltimore. If I recollect aright I commenced Detective Operations for this purpose in January 1861. You will probably find this under the heading of Reports of A.P., or the time set when accompanied by several of my Operatives (Detectives) I left Chicago for Baltimore. Upon arriving at Baltimore I distributed my Operatives around the City for the purpose of acquiring the confidence of the Secessionists. One of those Detectives, named Timothy Webster, accompanied by a Lady, was stationed by me at Perryman'sville, a Station about 9 miles South of Havre de Grace on the P.W.&B.R.R., where a Rebel Company of Cavalry were organizing. Webster, as you will find from his Reports under the Heading of T.W., and those of the Lady who accompanied him, under the Heading of H.H.L., succeeded admirably well in cultivating an acquaintance with the Secessionists. You will find much of interest in Webster's Reports, showing the manner in which the first Military organization of Maryland Secessionists was formed, and the promises repeatedly made by Governor Hicks of arms being furnished to them; and, if my recollection serves me aright, of arms finally being furnished to that Company; their Drilling at Belle Air etc., Webster was afterwards exicuted in the Spring of 1862 by Order of Jefferson Davis at Richmond, Va., as a Union Spy, and was the first who paid the penalty of his life for such Service. If you wish to bring in this subjict I will furnish you all the Reports relating to it, or will write it out as soon as I can.

I located my own Head Quarters at Baltimore under the name of John H. Hutchinson, Stock Broker, renting Offices for that purpose. Here I formed the acquaintance of a Mr. Luckett (I think that was his name) a Stock Broker having Offices on the same floor with my own. From my Reports you will see how accidentally I discovered the plot to assassinate the President elect, at that time. If I mistake not the Initials of the Operatives who were upon this operation for the P.W.&B.R.R. Co. were, beside those already mentioned, A.T.C., C.D.C.W., and M.B. and their Reports show the state of feeling in Baltimore at that time, and how embittered and poisoned it was, showing that the Secessionists of that city were prepared to do anything which they deemed necessary in order to break up the Union. As you will observe by the Records the various circumstances connected with the attempt to assassinate Mr. Lincoln came gradually to light; but not until about the time Mr. Lincoln left Springfield on his tour to Washington, there to be inaugurated, did the plot culminate in very decisive information that he was to be assassinated upon his arrival and passage through Baltimore. At that time the Baltimore Police were entirely in the hands of the Secessionists; their Chief being George P. Kane, a rabid Rebel, who was subsequently a long time imprisoned in Ft. McHenry, and after being discharged from there made his escape into the lines of the Confederacy and became a Brigadeir General in the Rebel Army. He is a man with some fine feelings, but thoroughly Southern, and in that respect unscrupulous. Mr. Lincoln's published program was for him to leave Harrisburg via the Northern Central Railroad and land at Calvert Street Station, at which point he and his Suite were to take carriages to the Eataw House, and thence to Camden Street Station by carriage to take the Baltimore and Ohio Railroad train for Washington. The distance between the two Stations is a little over a mile. No provision for his reception had been made by any Public Committee in Baltimore. The few Union men there were there at the time were overawed by the Secessionists and dared not make any demonstration. Remember at that time that James Buchanan was filling the Presidential chair, and the whole Nation was without any protection while Rebels were arming in every direction. It was but a few days after the passage of Mr. Lincoln through Baltimore that the Mass. 6th was mobbed in passing through that city although they were an armed and organized troop. In order to show how easy it was to assassinate Mr. Lincoln at that time every attention should be called to the condition of the country, especially of Baltimore and Maryland, at that time. A sample of the feeling among these people at that date may be formed from the young man (whose name I do not recollect) whom you will find repeatedly spoken of in the Reports of my Operative A.T.C. and who was to be one of the Assassins, as frequently using the words of Brutus: "It is not that I love Caesar less, but Rome more", when his conscience roused him to a contemplation of the awful crime he was about to commit, which he seemed to think a justification of his course.

Everything was nearly in readiness about the time Mr. Lincoln started from

Springfield. The plan was skilfully laid and would have been an effective one had it not fortunately been discovered in season to prevent its exicution. Chief of Police Kane had intimated that he had not any special Police to spare for the occasion, and could not detail many to attend at the Calvert Street Station, but would send what he could of them. One of the leading Spirits in this murderous plot was a Barber, whose name I do not remember, but you will find it in the Reports. His place of business was under Barnum's Hotel, the Head Quarters of Secessionists from all parts of the country. There every night as I mingled among them I could hear the most outrageous sentiments ennunciated   No man's life was safe in the hands of those men. The whole Municipal power of Baltimore was Secession, as were also the courts at that time. Those Bullies were all armed, and would not hesitate on the slightest provocation to use these arms to shoot down a Union man. Ballots were drawn at a Secret meeting, in which those who drew a certain Kind of card were to consider themselves as bound to be the party to assassinate the President elect. None Knew that any more than one of those ballots were drawn, although I think there were some six or eight who made themselves thus incumbent to strike the fatal blow, neither Knowing that any one except himself was to strike it. The time when this was to be done was just as Mr. Lincoln would be passing through the narrow vestibule of the Depot at Calvert St. Station, to enter his carriage. A row or fight was to be got up by some outsiders to quell which the few policemen at the Depot would rush out, thus leaving Mr. Lincoln entirely unprotected and at the mercy of a mob of Secessionists who were to surround him at that time. A small Steamer had been chartered and was lying in one of the Bays or little streams running into the Chesapeake to which the Murderers were to flea and it was immediately to put off for Virginia. Excuse me for endeavoring to impress the plan upon you. It was a capital one, and much better conceived than the one which finally succeeded four years after in destroying Mr. Lincoln's life. I am proud that just at that time their plots and plans were discovered. True it was accidentally by me. I was looking for nothing of the Kind, and had certainly not the slightest idea of it. Had Mr. Lincoln fallen at that time it is frightful to think what the consequences might have been. Having tested the information and found it reliable, I deemed it my duty, in as much as all information acquired by me upon an Operation I consider the property of the parties who are paying me for my services, at that time to communicate the same to Mr. Felton, the President, as I have previously said, of the P.W.&B.R.R., who was and is now a thoroughly reliable Union man and one who has proved himself true during the worst hours of our Nation's trouble. I said to him that I Knew this information was theirs but I knew of no reason why it should not be imparted to Mr. Lincoln or his friends with a view to avoid'g the peril which threatened his passage through Baltimore according to the schedule which was then arranged and published in the Papers throughout the Country.

A Mr. Wood was at that time acting as Agent or manager for Mr. Lincoln and his Suite until their arrival in Washington. I asked Mr. Lincoln subsequent to the time I having been speaking of, as you will see by Reports, who this man was. He said that he did not Know the man, and that he had been sent to him by some friends to fill that position and he had allowed him to do so — an evidence of the confiding and innocent feeling of the man at that time upon whom the Nation's destinies rested. Mr. Felton at once assented to my proposition and directed me to inform Mr. Lincoln of what had been discovered. Accordingly upon the day Mr. Lincoln arrived in New York city, fearing to leave Baltimore myself in case of any thing vital taking place there which would need my immediate attention, I sent a lady, Mrs. Warn, who had been for many years in charge of my Female Detective Force, and upon whose discretion I Knew I could rely, with a letter to My friend the Honorable N. B. Judd who was at that time accompanying Mr. Lincoln and was with him in New York. Knowing the difficulty of getting an interview with Mr. Judd, I also gave her a letter to my friend E. S. Sanford Esq. of New York, Vice President of the Adams Ex. Co. and President of the American Telegraph Co., with a request for Mr. (now General) Sanford to arrange for an interview with Mrs. Warn: which was done, and Mr. Judd, having read my letter and obtained what additional verbal information he could from Mrs. Warn, arrived at the conclusion that he would not tell Mr. Lincoln until after the arrival of the party in Philadelphia. I was telegraphed from New York by Messrs. Sanford and Judd, as also by Mrs. Warn to say nothing to anyone and to meet Mr. Judd in Phila. upon the arrival of the President's party. I did so, and through the agency of Capt. Burnes met Mr. Judd at the St. Lewis Hotel on Chestnut Street, the President of the P.W.&B.R.R. accompanying me. At that time the Streets were crowded with people. All was excitement. The loyal mass were waiting to congratulate and welcome their future Ruler. As you will observe by my Report I communicated to Mr. Judd the particulars of the plot in my Room at the St. Louis Hotel only in the presence of Mr. Felton. Mr. Judd was deeply impressed with the danger which surrounded Mr. Lincoln, but he said that he feared very much if he would be able to get him to change his route, which was what I urged' my idea and that of Mr. Felton's being to have him leave Phila that night by the midnight train for Washington, thus passing through Baltimore thirty six hours before the time when he would be expected. Mr. Judd said that Mr. Lincoln's confidence in the people was unbounded, and that he did not fear any violent outbreak; that he hoped by his management and conciliatory measures to bring the secessionists back to their allegiance. There was no doubt whatever in Mr. Judd's mind of the correctness of the information, the manner in which it was obtained stamping it as reliable. After a long conversation and discussion Mr. Judd desired that I should go to the Continental Hotel with him and have an interview with Mr. Lincoln. We did so. A dense crowd of people filled Chestnut Street, every square inch of ground was occupied by them as Mr. Lincoln was holding a Reception at the Continental, and it was with the utmost difficulty that we were able to get into the building. I think somewhere about 11 O'clock in the evening that I met Mr. Lincoln at Mr. Judd's rooms. He was rather exhausted from the fatigues of travel and receptions. He met me as usual Kindly and I narrated as briefly as possible the information I had acquired as he expressed himself as in a hurry and much exhausted. He asked me several questions upon the subject, which I do not now recollect; but you will find them detailed in my Report. He then asked Mr. Judd and myself what course we thought he had better pursue, and I urged upon him that as the train would not leave Phila. for about an hour he had better take that train thus avoiding the Conspirators as his passage through would not be expected. This Mr. Lincoln firmly and positively refused to do, saying that he had an engagement for the next morning to raise a flag on Independence Hall in Philadelphia, and that he had also promised the citizens of Penna. to meet them at Harrisburg on the following day; that he had positively engaged this to Governor Curtin, and that he would fulfil those engagements under any and all circumstances, even if he met with death in doing so. Mr. Lincoln said, however, that after the meeting at Harrisburg on the following day if I could arrange matters he would make his programme as follows: He would hoist the Union Flag on Independence Hall about 6 A.M. the next morning, take Breakfast at the Continental at 7 and leave for Harrisburg by Special train about 8 or 9 O'clock; at Harrisburg meet Governor Curtin and the Pennsylvanians, and after his reception was over there, come back to Phila. by Special train in time to connect with the Regular Midnight train leaving for Washington, placing himself entirely in my hands: but that he would not forgo his engagements for the next day at Independence Hall and Harrisburg whatever his fate might be. During the interview Mr. Lincoln was cool, calm, and collected. During the years of the War I was pretty well acquainted with him. When he came to the Army of the Potomac to review the Troops I invariably met him. In fact my tent was more of a place of resort for him than even that of General McClellan's; and I never saw him more cool, collected and firm than he was on that evening at the Continental Hotel. In fact he did not appear to me to realize the great danger which was threatening him at that moment. He said that if once he reached Washington there was no danger; Mr. Buchanan would soon vacate, and he could rely upon General Scott until that time for protection.

You may recollect his speech on the following morning at the raising of the flag on Independence Hall. I cannot quote it correctly, but I think I have got an extract from it at my Office in Chicago. It was something like this: I will preserve the Union, even if the Assassin's Knife is at my heart. I do not Know as this is anything like the quotation, as it was much more eloquent, but such was the substance as it was impressed upon my mind. This speech at that time received marked attention, and you will probably be able to find it in the files of some of the Daily Newspapers. I have a complete file of the Chicago Newspapers in my Office there.

Finding Mr. Lincoln resolute I told him that I would endeavor to make the necessary arrangements for his passage from Harrisburg after dark on the following evening to Philadelphia and thence to Baltimore and Washington, being well acquainted with the Officers of the Penna. R.R. After leaving Mr. Lincoln and promising to call and see Mr. Judd again during the night (it was now about 1 A.M.), I started to find my friend Col. Thomas A. Scott, Vice President of the Penna RR. with a view to arrange with him for a Special train to bring Mr. Lincoln from Harrisburg to Phila. I found he was out of town, and consequently applied to my friend G. C. Fransiscus, at that time Supt. of the Division of the Penna R.R. between Harrisburg and Phila. The City being all excitement I had some difficulty in finding Mr. Fransiscus, and did not do so until about three A.M. Knowing him well as a true and loyal man, I had no hesitation in telling him what I desired. He at once said that he would make the arrangements for a Special train for Mr. Lincoln, saying, however, that there were many difficulties in the way as there were so many special trains leaving Phila. for Harrisburg which would return on the same evening which Mr. Lincoln proposed to go over the Road; but that he would arrange that Mr. Lincoln's train should be the last of those special trains which would leave Harrisburg on that evening, and would side track all the other trains leaving Harrisburg prior to Mr. Lincoln's so that they would not arrive until after Mr. Lincoln had left for Baltimore. This being satisfactorily arranged I then hunted up Mr. E. S. Sanford, President as I have previously said, of the American Tel. Co., who was then in town, and arranged with him to have the proper parties sent to Harrisburg in the morning with a view that at the time when Mr. Lincoln would leave Harrisburg all the telegraph wires leading out of that city in every direction should be cut, except that of the Railroad Co. which was necessary to be left on account of the running of the trains. I omitted to state that I had also arranged with Mr. Fransiscus for none but trusty Operators to be at the wires of the Company, and that no dispatch should be sent over the wires excepting such as related to the running of trains.

About 6 O'clock the next morning Mr. Lincoln addressed the people of Phila. at Independence Hall and raised the flag. About 7 A.M. I met Mr. Judd and told him of my arrangements, and it was agreed that Mr. Lincoln alone should leave Harrisburg of all his party so as to avid any suspicion, and that just before leaving he should withdraw to his room on the plea of indisposition. Mr. Lincoln had remarked that none should be acquainted with his secret but Mrs. Lincoln. This he said he could not avoid as otherwise she would be very much excited at his absence. I also learned that morning for the first time that General Scott and Mr Seward had discovered some evidence of a plot to assassinate Mr. Lincoln when he passed through Baltimore and had employed some New York Police Officers with a view of ferreting out the same; who had found evidences of it, though not as clearly as my own men; but yet at the same time sufficient to impress upon General Scott and Mr. Seward with the idea that there was danger to Mr. Lincoln if he followed the programme which had been published in passing through Baltimore. Mr. Seward had therefore sent a communication by his son Frederick to Mr. Lincoln to the effect that they had information of a plot to assassinate him in Baltimore, urging upon him to change his route; to which he replied to Mr. Seward that he might do so and would attend to his suggestion, but without giving any idea as to how soon he would arrive in Washington if he did change his programme.

Mr. Lincoln left for Harrisburg with his suite, and during the day I arranged with Mr. Felton the programme for the passage through Baltimore and to Washington. This was that Capt. Burnes, Mr. Sanford's Confidential Agent, Mr. H. E. Thayer, and Mr. Andrew Winn should proceed to Harrisburg to cut the wires, the same not to be again united until after Mr. Lincoln would have reached Washington; that in the evening shortly before the departure of the Regular train for Baltimore I was to send Mrs. Warn, accompanied by Mr. George Dunn of Newark, N.J. to engage two sections, the rear ones if possible, of the Sleeping car through to Washington, for a sick friend and party; while I myself in company with H. H. Kenney, Esq. now General Supt. of the Phila, Wilmington & Baltimore Road, was to meet Mr. Lincoln with a carriage at the West Phila. Depot of the Penna Central R.R., and convey him from there to the Depot of the P.W.&B.R.R., so that none of the employe's of that Road with the exception of Messrs. Felton and Sterns (the Genl. Supt.) and Mr. Kenney should Know aught of the important passenger who was to pass over their line. Mr. Felton arranged for the delay of the train a short time by instructing the Conductor that the train should not leave the Depot until he received a package from him (Mr. Felton) addressed to E. J. Allen (the name which I went under in Washington), at Willard's Hotel, Washington, which package he should hand to the Conductor of the Baltimore and Ohio Railroad to have delivered to its proper address. This package was bogus, put up for the occasion by myself and delivered to Mr. Kenney to deliver to the Conductor after Mr. Lincoln and myself were in the Sleeping car. I arranged my own Operatives along the line of the Road at certain points with instructions to be out displaying a particular signal, which I could see from the platform of the car, if all was right. Mr. Lincoln arrived in Phila. accompanied by Mr. Lewis, Gen. Supt. at that time of the Penna R.R., and Mr. Fransiscus the Division Supt, as also by Mr. Ward H. Lamon of Bloomington, Ills. Mr. Lincoln received me very Kindly, but was as cool, calm and collected as I ever have seen him. He wore an overcoat thrown loosely over his shoulders without his arms being in the sleeves, and a black Kossuth hat,[1] which he told me somebody had presented to him. The story of the Scotch cap I may as well at this time pronounce a falsehood made out of whole cloth. Mr. Lincoln took a seat in the carriage with Mr. Lamon and myself, Mr. Kenney taking the seat with the driver; and as it was too early for us to approach the Baltimore Depot Mr. Kenney had the Driver take us around the City, apparently as if he was looking for some one, until it was just about time to reach the Depot five minutes after the starting time of the train. We left the carriage at a dark spot a short distance from the Depot, and Mr. Lamon Keeping a little in the rear of Mr. Lincoln and myself, Mr. Lincoln leaning upon my arm and stooping a considerable for the purpose of disguising his hight, we passed through the Depot rapidly and entered the Sleeping car, and within two minutes from the time we had entered the Depot, Mr. Kenney having passed rapidly up to the Engine and delivered the package, the train was in motion, and we were whirling away towards Baltimore on our eventful Journey. None of the party slept any. At Havre de Grace Mr. Lincoln remarked to me upon my returning inside the car after having been out to see if the signals were all right: "We are at Havre de Grace. We are getting along very well. I think we are on time." Although Mr. Lincoln did not sleep, he was not by

---

1. Style of hat named for Lajos Kossuth (1802–94), a Hungarian revolutionary hero.

any means restless. I cannot realize how any man situated as he was could have shown more calmness or firmness than he did during the whole trip to Washington. Upon arriving at the Depot of the Baltimore and Ohio RR. in Baltimore we had to wait about half an hour. I was the only one of the party who went out of the car at that time. I recollect well of Mr. Lincoln telling me some jokes upon my return to the car, but in a quiet voice so that no one heard it but Mr. Lamon and myself. At Baltimore Mrs. Warn left the car and proceeded to the Hotel for the purpose of ascertaining what the feelings of the people were in the city, as I proposed to return there by the evening train. I think we arrived at Washington about 6 A.M. and were met by Mr. Washburn of Ills., and Mr. Seward. We proceeded at once to the Hotel (Willard's) by carriage where Mr. Lincoln registered his own name and those of Mr. Lamon and myself, and was assigned rooms, though not the ones which were expected he would have as he had arrived very unexpectedly.

During the morning after the news of Mr. Lincoln's arrival spread the wildest excitement prevailed in Washington. Few were willing to beleive that he had arrived, and many were the vile and bitter imprecations which I heard heaped upon his head while mixing among the excited secissionists of that, I think at that time, most rebellious city.

Mrs. Lincoln, accompanied by Mr. Judd and the rest of the cortege, left Harrisburg and went through to Baltimore. Before they left, however, the news had been telegraphed all over of the arrival of Mr. Lincoln in Washington. Upon the arrival of the party in Baltimore they met with anything but a cordial reception. These things, however, you can glean from the Newspapers of that day.

At Mr. Lincoln's request I returned to Baltimore that afternoon for the purpose of learning whether any attempt was to be made to assassinate him at the Inauguration, and remained there until after that ceremony had taken place.

I have thus endeavored to give you a brief account of this matter as it comes to my recollection, in which you will doubtless, upon referring to the Records, find many errors; but I think it will give you considerable assistance.

You will observe that many of my Operatives simply detail the feelings of the Secessionists at the time they were in Baltimore. This arises from the fact that they were seeking for the feelings of these people with regard to the danger to the Steamer and Bridges of the P.W.&B.R.R. and not for any plot to assassinate Mr. Lincoln.

I hope this will prove satisfactory to you If not, when I return to Chicago, which I expect will be in about two months, I will endeavor to take the Record and go over the thing more fully than I have here.

There are many matters of interest connected with Mr. Lincoln which appear from time to time in my Records of the Secret Service of the War Department, Army of the Potomac, etc., which I think would be useful and tend to show the man in his true light as a great man and true philanthropist. I cannot recall them now; but if I could sit down with you and talk there are many things which would come up in my mind without wading through the mass of my Records. After my return to Chicago (in about two months) I expect I will shortly have to leave again, and it will probably be about three months before I will have much time in Chicago. If that will not be too late for you I will truly enjoy to meet you there and talk over any matters which may be of use to you in compiling the life of the noblest statesman America has ever produced.

Yours truly
Allan Pinkerton

P.S. Please consider Mr. Luckitt's name as confidential

    LC: HW2604–19; HL: LN2408, 2:132–52

219. Benjamin F. Irwin to WHH

Pleasant Plains Ills Aug 27, 66

Friend William

    Yours of the 24 Recd   In Reply Peyton Harrisons Memory is not six Inches Long or he would no Better   I am quite certain Preacher Shorts[1] wife never saw Lincoln certain she never Lived In sangamon untill about 15 years ago and was Married Before she came to Ills   The facts of the case I think is about this   in 1832 or 3 Lincoln was wofully in Love with a Remarkable hansome young Lady by the Name of Rutledge   2 other men was in the same fix all three Paying their address to her   who was first in her estimation I know not   In the mean time she died and Lincoln took it so hard that some of his friends really thought he would go crazy, or was Partially so about it   Lincoln told Isaac Cogdal all about this in the Secretarys office in 1860 a portion of this I remember about and the Ballence I get from his old Personal and Political Friend Josiah Combs   I will make further Inquiry and if this is not substantially true I will correct the Error   I could give you the Names of the two opponents after the young Lady but that you dont wish or desire

B F Irwin

    LC: HW2623; HL: LN2408, 1:564–65

220. William Walker to WHH

Lexington Mo Aug 27th 1866

Dr Sir

    In regard to the tryal of Armstrong in Beardstown, It was testifyed by the witness that the deed was done bout Eleven at night, and that thare was a bright Moon, and I think an Almonic was brought in at My request for the Year propper, from Some one of the Clerk's offices below, The witness Said he was Some 30 Yds dis-

---

1. WHH is presumably following up on the testimony of John T. Stuart that Lincoln courted a woman named Short. See §46, note 3.

tant and that he Seen the blow Struck with a Slung-Shot   We Showed by the Almonic that at the hour of 11 — at night no Moon was visable And by other witnesses that at the time of the troubble it was quite dark, Mr L— in his Speach may have alluded to the absence of a Moon to Show that in as Much as the witness was Mistaken in regard to one thing, the Jury Should receive all his testimony with Caution, Mr Lincolns argument was that no Jury ought Ever to convict, upon Such testimony

The Jury acquitted, — Mr L Speach was in Evry Sence honorable, high-toned & professional   I think Judge Dummer was presant during the tryal and perhaps remembers the particulars of the tryal as fully as I do   I Se from a memorandum book brought with Me, that a Note to You Signed by Dan Roberts was paid to me Just before I left, $50.00 Just the principle — I do not recollect wither I Sent it or Not, If I did not You Must induldge Me Some til I Can Make Some Money here among the Rebels, Please write to me & let me Know how it Stands.

Are You Safe in Ills. on the questions of the day
                                        Truly yours &c
                                        W Walker

LC: HW2624; HL: LN2408, 2:332–33

221. Mary Todd Lincoln to WHH[1]

Chicago — Ill Aug 28th *[1866]*
My dear Sir:

Owing to Robert's absence, from Chicago, your last letter to *him,* was only shown me last evening. The recollection of my beloved husband's *truly* affectionate regard for *you* & the knowledge, of your great love & reverence for the best man, that ever lived, would of *itself,* cause you, to be cherished with the sincerest regard, by my sons & myself. In my overwhelming bereavement, those who loved my idolized husband — aside from *disinterested* motives — are very precious to me & mine — My grief has been so uncontrollable — that in consequence, I have been obliged, to bury myself in solitude — knowing, that many whom I would see, could not fully, enter into the state of my feelings — I have been thinking for some time past, that I would like to see you & have a long conversation — I write to [know?] if you will be in Springfield *next* Wednesday week — Sept — 4th[2] — if so — at 10 o'clock, in the morning, you will find me, at the St Nicolas Hotel — please — mention *this visit to S.* to *no one* — It is a most sacred one — as you may suppose to visit the tomb — which contains my All, in life — My husband. You will excuse me, enclosing you, this sentence, of yours & asking its meaning.[3] With

---

1. Note in top margin in MTL's hand: *Private — please burn —*. Though not given, the year of the interview is put beyond doubt by Robert T. Lincoln's letter to WHH of October 1 (§257).

2. MTL is confused about the date. This letter was written in 1866, but September 4 was a Tuesday.

3. This refers to a fragment in WHH's hand, presumably clipped by MTL from a note sent by WHH to Robert T. Lincoln: *Robt — I want to give a sketch — a short life of your mother in my biography up to her marriage to your father — or say up to 1846 — or 1858 —. I wish to do her justice fully — so that the world will understand things better. You understand me. Will she see me.* (HW3774)

the remembrance of years of *very very* great domestic happiness — with my dar-
ling husband & children — my sons & myself, fail to understand your meaning
— will you be pleased to explain —

If it will not be convenient — or if business — *at* the *time* specified should
require yr absence — should you visit Chicago — any day, this week, I will be
pleased to See you. I remain

Very truly

Mary Lincoln

LC: HW2625–26

222. George M. Harrison to WHH

[late summer 1866?¹]

Dear sir,

It would afford me much pleasure to be specific, without spoiling the sayings
of Lincoln

Mr Lincoln went into the Black hawk war many months before I did. He went,
I think, in command of a company; I went a private. During the war many companies went to the army and voluntarily offered their services, but were rejected
because they were not needed: they bore their own expenses to and from, but were
well supplied while there with Uncle Sam's bread and meat. The company I went
with found the army at Dixon's; remained there about a week, disbanded and returned home. But I had found a considerable number of my old acquaintance,
who were just disbanded by their own request, having been out from the commencement of the war, members of Cap. Elijah Iles' company, — who were just
then, or, as many of them as were not quite ready to return home, by permission
of the commanding general — Atkinson — forming a new company, by taking
to themselves such as they chose from the multitude of the disappointed. The new
company thus formed was called the Independent spy company; not being under
the control of any regiment or brigade, but receiving orders directly from the commander-in-chief; and always, when with the army, camping within the lines, and
having many other privileges, such as, never having camp duties to perform, drawing rations as often and as much as we pleased &c. &c. — Dr. Early dec'd, of
Springfield was elected Capt. Five members constituted a tent, or "messed" together,
our mess consisted of Mr. Lincoln, Johnson, — a half brother of his, — Fanchier,
Wyatt, and myself. The independent spy company was used chiefly to carry messages, to send an express, to spy the enemy, and to ascertain facts. I suppose the
nearest we were to doing battle was at Gratiot's grove, near Galena. The spy company of Posey's brigade was many miles in advance of the brigade when it stoped,
in this grove, at noon for refreshment. Some of the men had turned loose their
horses, and others still had theirs in hand, when five or six Sack & fox indians came
near to them. Many of the white men broke after them, some on horseback, some

---

1. Approximate dating from the contents of Harrison's next letter (§410).

on foot in great disorder and confusion; thinking to have much sport with their prisoners immediately: the indians thus decoyed them about two miles from the little cabins in the Grove, keeping just out of danger; when suddenly sprang up from the tall prairie grass, 250 painted wariors — with long spears in hand, and tomahawks & butcher knives in thir belts of deerskin and buffalo, and raised such a yell that our friends supposed them to be more numerous than Blackhawk's whole clan; and instantly, filled with consternation, commenced the retreat. But the savages soon began to spear them, making it necessary to halt in the flight, and give them a fire; at which time, they killed two indians, — one of them being a young chief— gayly appareled — Again, in the utmost horror, such as Savage yells alone can produce, they fled for the little fort in the grove: Having arrived, they found the balance of their Company, — terrified by the screams of the whites and the yells of the savages, — closely shut up in the double cabins: into which they quickly plunged, and found the much needed respite. The Indians then prowled around the grove shooting nearly all the companie's horses, and stealing the balance of them. Here, from cracks between the logs of the cabins, three of the Indians were shot and killed, in the act of reaching for the reins of bridles on horses. They endeavoured to conseal their bodies, by trees in an old field which surrounded the fort, but reaching with sticks for the bridles, they exposed their heads & necks, and all of them were shot with two balls each, through the neck. These three, and the two killed where our men wheeled and fired, make five Indians known to be killed; and on their retreat from the prairie to the grove five white men were cut into small pieces. The field of this action, is the greatest battle ground that we saw. The dead still lay unburied untill, after we arrived, at sunrise the next day: the forted men — 50 strong — had not ventured to go out until they saw us; when they rejoiced greatly that friends, and not their dreaded enemies had come. They looked like men just out of Cholera: having passed through the cramping stage. The only part we could then act, was to seek the lost men, and with hatchets and hands to bury them. We buried the white men, and trailed the dead young chief where he had been drawn on the grass a half mile and consealed in a thicket. Those who trailed this once noble warior and found him, were Lincoln, — I think — Wyatt, and myself. By order of Gen. Atkinson, our Company started on this expedition one evening, traveled all night, and reached Gratiots at sunrise. A few hours after, Gen. Posey came up to the fort, with his brigade — of nearly 1000 men — when he positively refused to pursue the indians, being strongly solicited by Capt. Early, Lincoln and others; Squads of indians still showing themselves in a menacing manner, one and a half miles distant. Our company was disbanded at Whitewater, Wisconsin, a short time before the Massacre at Bad Axe by Gen. Henry, and most of our men started for home on the following morning. But it so happened that the night previous to starting on this long trip, Lincoln's horse and mine were stolen, probably by soldiers of our own army — and we were thus compelled to start out side the cavalcade; but I laughed at our fate, and he joked at it, and we all started off merrily. But the generous men of our Company walked and rode by turns with us, and we fared about equal with the rest. But for this generosity, our legs would have had to do the better work; for in that day this then dreary route furnished no horses to buy or to steal. And whether on horse or afoot we always had company, for many of their backs were too sore for constant riding.

Thus we came to Peoria Here we bought a canoe in which we two paddled our way to Pekin; the other members of our company separating in various directions stimulated by the proximity of home, could never have consented to travel at our usual tardy mode. At Pekin, Lincoln made an oar with which to row our little boat, while I went through the town in order to buy provisions for the trip. One of us pulled away with our one oar, while the other sat astern to steer, or prevent circling. The river being very low was without current, so that we had to pull hard to make half the speed of legs and land: in fact we let her float all night, and in the next morning always found the objects still visible that were beside us the previous evening. The water was remarkably clear for this river of plants; and the fish appeared to be sporting with us as we moved on, near them. On the next day after we left Pekin, we overhauled a *raft* of saw logs, with two men afloat on it, to urge it along with poles, and to guide it in the channel; we immediately pulled up to them and went on the raft, where we were made welcome by various demonstrations; especially by that of an invitation to a feast on fish, corn bread, eggs, butter, and coffee: just prepared for our benefit. Of these good things we ate almost immoderately, for it was the only warm meal we had made for several days. While preparing it, and after the dinner, Lincoln entertained them, and they entertained us, for a couple of hours, very amusingly.

This slow mode of travel, was, at the time, a new mode, and the novelty made it for a short time agreeable. We descended the Illinois to Havanna; where we sold our boat, and again set out, the old way, over the Sand ridges, for Petersburg. As we drew near home, the impulse became stronger, and urged us on amazingly. The long strides of Lincoln, after slipping back in the burning Sand six inches every step, were just right for me; and he was greatly diverted when he noticed me behind him stepping along in his tracks to keep from slipping.

About the third day after leaving the Army at Whitewater, we saw a battle in full operation, about two miles in advance of us. Lincoln was riding a young horse the property of L. D. Matheny — I was riding a sprightly animal belonging to John T. Stewart: at the time we came in view of the Scene, our two voluntary footmen were about three fourths of a mile before us, and a half mile behind most of our company, and three or four afoot still behind us, leading their soreback horses; but the owners of our horses came running back, and meeting us, all in full speed, rightfully ordered us to dismount: We obeyed, they mounted, and all pressed on toward the conflict; they, on horseback, we, afoot. In a few moments, of hard walking and terribly close observation, Lincoln said to me "George, this can't be a very dangerous battle!" reply, "much shooting nothing falls." It was at once decided to be a sham battle for the purpose of training cavalry; instead of Indians having attacked a few white soldiers, and a few of our own men on their way home, for the purpose of killing them.

The first place I ever saw Mr. Lincoln was aboard a flat bottom boat, on the

Sangamon, about four miles North East from my house: — a hand on the boat, about 18 years of age. He then and there attracted the farmers engaged in hauling corn to load the boat, by his profusion of anecdotes & jokes.

I think, that I never saw Mr Lincoln angry or desponding; but always cheerful, and his spirit and temper such as would engender the like cheerfulness in all surrounding minds: in fact the whole company, even amid trouble and suffering, received Strength & fortitude, by his buoyancy & elasticity.

Yours truly
Geo. M. Harrison.

LC: HW3916–17; HL: LN2408, 1:504–12

223. *J. W. Wartmann to WHH*

Rockport Indiana Sept 4. 1866.

My Dear Sir

Your favor of a late date Enclosing a news-paper paragraph, and making inquiries in regard to a Miss Wood &c, came duly to hand. I have made diligent inquiry, *and find there is nothing in the story.* Old Mr Wood, at Elizabeth — (whom you saw when there) has a daughter named Elizabeth, who is near Mr Lincoln's age and who knew and associated somewhat with Mr L. There never was a proposition of marriage made to her by L. though Mr L occasionally visited her. This Elizabeth Wood (still living in this Co') first married Samuel Hammond. Hammond died some years ago, and she married one Michael Trumper —, who is still living and resides not far from Grandview in this Co.' Mrs Gentry —, whom you also saw when here, says there is nothing in the story.

I saw also Nathl and Redmond Grigsby, who state there is nothing in it.

Command me at any time when I can serve you.

We dont go "my policy"[1] *"much"* in these parts.

Judge DeBruler is our Union Candidate for Congress in this Dist.

This is Court week and I am quite hurried.

Very truly
Your friend
J.W. Wartmann

LC: HW2627; HL: LN2408, 1:167–68

224. *John Hay to WHH*

Paris, September 5. 1866.

My Dear Mr. Herndon

I am so constantly busy that I have had no quiet day in which I write you what you desired in your letter several months ago. I have been Chargé d'Affaires near-

---

1. "My policy" was a derisive Republican reference to the Reconstruction policies of President Andrew Johnson.

ly all summer, my day filled with official business and my night with social engagements equally imperative. Even now, I write because I am ashamed to wait any longer and have a few minutes disposable. I will answer your questions as you put them without any attempt at arrangement.

Lincoln used to go to bed ordinarily from ten to eleven o'clock unless he happened to be kept up by important news, in which case he would frequently Remain at the War Department until 1 or 2. He rose early. When he lived in the country at Soldiers Home, he would be up and dressed, eat his breakfast (which was extremely frugal an egg, a piece of toast Coffee &c) and ride into Washington, all before 8 o'clock. In the winter at the White House he was not quite so early. He did not sleep very well but spent a good while in bed. Tad usually slept with him. He would lie around the office until he fell asleep & Lincoln would shoulder him and take him off to bed.

He pretended to begin business at ten oclock in the morning, but in reality the anterooms and halls were full before that hour — people anxious to get the first axe ground. He was extremely unmethodical; it was a four-years struggle on Nicolays part and mine to get him to adopt some systematic rules. He would break through every Regulation as fast as it was made. Anything that kept the people themselves away from him he disapproved — although they nearly annoyed the life out of him by unreasonable complaints & requests.

He wrote very few letters. He did not read one in fifty that he received. At first we tried to bring them to his notice, but at last he gave the whole thing over to me, and signed without reading them the letters I wrote in his name. He wrote perhaps half-a-dozen a week himself — not more.

Nicolay received members of Congress, & other visitors who had business with the Executive Office, communicated to the Senate and House the messages of the President, & exercised a general supervision over the business.

I opened and read the letters, answered them, looked over the newspapers, supervised the clerks who kept the records and in Nicolay's absence did his work also. When the President had any rather delicate matter to manage at a distance from Washington, he very rarely wrote, but sent Nicolay or me.

The House remained full of people nearly all day. At noon the President took a little lunch — a biscuit, a glass of milk in winter, some fruit or grapes in summer. He dined at fr. 5 to 6. & we went off to our dinner also.

Before dinner was over members & Senators would come back & take up the whole evening. Sometimes, though rarely he shut himself up & would see no one. Sometimes he would run away to a lecture or concert or theatre for the sake of a little rest.

He was very abstemious — ate less than any one I know. Drank nothing but water — not from principle, but because he did not like wine or spirits. Once, in rather dark days early in the war, a Temperance Committee came to him & said the reason we did not win was because our army drank so much whiskey as to bring down the curse of the Lord upon them. He said dryly that it was rather unfair on the part of the aforesaid curse, as the other side drank more and worse whiskey than ours did.

He read very little. Scarcely ever looked into a newspaper unless I called his attention to an article on some special subject. He frequently said "I know more about that than any of them." It is absurd to call him a modest man. No great man was ever modest. It was his intellectual arrogance and unconscious assumption of superiority that men like Chase and Sumner never could forgive.

I cant write any more today. I may see you before long — I dont know — & so I wont waste time by telling you what you must know as well as I do.

I believe Lincoln is well understood by the people. Miss Nancy Bancroft[1] & the rest of that patent leather kid glove set know no more of him than an owl does of a comet, blazing into his blinking eyes.

Bancrofts address was a disgraceful exhibition of ignorance and prejudice. His effeminate nature shrinks instinctively from the contact of a great reality like Lincoln's character.

I consider Lincoln Republicanism incarnate — with all its faults and all its virtues. As in spite of some rudenesses, Republicanism is the sole hope of a sick world, so Lincoln with all his foibles, is the greatest character since Christ.

Yours

J. H.

LC: HW2628–33; HL: LN2408, 2:460–63

225. J. Henry Shaw to WHH

Beardstown Ills. Sept. 5, 1866.

Dear Sir,

Six of the seven interrogatories propounded by you in yours of the 1*st* inst. have relation to a motion for a writ of *Habeas Corpus* in the Armstrong case. In reply, I would say that I have no recollection of there having been an effort made for a *habeas corpus* in that case. I went to the record & also searchd *all the papers* in the case, but nothing can be found intimating that such a motion was made. It is not usual, or at least necessary, that the papers connected with such a motion be filed with the Indictment, and possibly by writing to Judge Harriott at Pekin you might find the facts in the case. My impression is, that no such motion was made. My recollections of that trial are rather good, from the fact that I was with Mr. Lincoln a great deal of the time during both of the terms in which the Armstrong case was pending. My connection with him during those terms was as follows,

Not knowing that he was intending to attend our Nov. Term 1857, I wrote to him that I wished his assistance for defendant in the case of Ruth A. Gill vs. Jonathan Gill at that term, which was a suit for divorce, custody of child & alimony. He came down, as I then supposed, exclusively to attend to that case. The question of divorce was left for a Jury, who bro't in a verdict for complainant, who also got the custody of the child; but the question of Alimony, the most important point in that case, was left open until the next term of court. At this term, Nov. 1857, Mr. Lincoln argued the motion in the Armstrong case to admit to bail,

1. A disparaging reference to the historian George Bancroft.

which was overuled. At the May term I expected Mr. Lincoln down to assist in the *Alimony* case again, & he came in due time, called at my office, & said I had "been sueing some of his clients, & he had come down to attend to it." He then had reference to a new Chancery case entitled "George Morre vs. Christina Moore & the heirs of Peter Moore" for a specific performance, the defendants all living near Springfield. I explained the case to him, & showed him my proofs. He seemed surprised that I should deal so frankly with him, & said he should be as frank with me, that my client was justly entitled to a decree, & he should so represent it to the court, that it was against his principle to contest a clear matter of right. So my client got a deed for a farm, which, had another Lawyer been in Mr. Lincoln's place, would have been litigated for years, with a big pile of costs, & the result probably the same. Mr. Lincoln's character for proffessional honor stood very high. He never vexed an opponent, but frequently threw him off his guard by his irresistable good humour. But I digress — I still thought that Mr. Lincoln had come to our court more particularly to attend to the Gill & Morre cases, and was very much surprised afterwards to see the immense interest he took in the Armstrong Case. He went into it like a Giant. The evidence bore heavily upon his client.

There were many witnesses, & each one seemed to add one more cord that seemed to bind him down, till Mr. Lincoln was something in the situation of Gulliver after his first sleep in Lilliput. But when he came to talk to the jury (that was always his forte) he resembled Gulliver again; he skillfuly untied here and there a knot & loosened here & there a peg, until, getting fairly warmed up, he raised himself in his full power & shook the arguments of his opponent from him as though they were cobwebs. He took the jury by storm. There were tears in Mr. Lincoln's eyes while he spoke. But they were genuine. His sympathies were fully enlisted in favor of the young man, and his terrible sincerity could not help but arouse the same passion in the jury. I have said it a hundred times, that it was Lincoln's *speech* that saved that criminal from the Gallows, and neither money or fame inspired that speech, but it was incited by gratitude to the young man's father, who, as Mr Lincoln said "was his only friend when he was a poor homeless boy." These are the only facts which I now recollect occurring at our Court worthy of your notice concerning that case. I might say however, as part of the previous history of the case, that the Indictment was found at the Oct. Term 1857 of the Mason Cir. Court, against James H. Norris & Wm. Armstrong. The indictment charges that on the 29*th* day of August 1857 they murdered James Preston Metzker — Norris striking him on the back of the head with a club & Armstrong striking him in the right eye with a *slung shot*.[1] Norris was tried at the Oct. Term 1857 Mason Cir. Court, found guilty of Man-Slaughter & sent up for 8 years. Dilworth & Campbell[2] were council for Norris.

At the Oct. term 1857 Mason Co Wm. Walker appeared as Counsel for Armstrong, and made two Motions, one to quash the indictment, which was overuled. The other to discharge the prisoner, which was withdrawn.

---

1. See p. 22.
2. Mason County attorneys George H. Campbell and Caleb J. Dilworth.

At the close of the trial of Armstrong in the Cass Cir. Ct. Mr. Lincoln had possession of the slung-shot with which it was shown Armstrong killed Metzker.

He, Mr. L. handed it to me, saying, "here, Henry, I'll give you this to remember me by."

I have that same Slung-shot now. It was made by Armstrong for the occasion. He took a common bar of pig lead, pounded it round, about the size of a large hickory nut, then cut a piece of leather out of the top of one of his boots, & with a thread & needle he sewed it into the shape of a slung-shot, & thus improvised in a few minutes a very fatal weapon. If I can be of any other assistance to you in your worthy undertaking, shall be at your service

Yours Respectfully
J. Henry Shaw.

LC: HW2634–35; HL: LN2408, 2:300–304

226. *David Turnham to WHH*

Dale Ind Sept 5th 1866

Dear Sir.

Yours of the 17th ult is at hand. I have taken time to find out the Circumstance about which you interrogate me Concerning Abraham Lincoln

This Miss Wood, is a Daughter of William Wood of Dale, or as you call him grand Pa Wood. She (Elizabeth Wood) first married a man by the name of Samuel Hammond   After his death She married Mr Michael Tremper with whom She is Still living. She and the Old man Wood Say that Lincoln was about their house a great deal and Jokes were frequently passed by him and Miss Wood but no such thing as Courting or proposing was ever thought of.

In her young days Miss Wood with her Father lived a mile South of our Town, and 3½ miles north of Gentryville. She was the Oldest Daughter   There can be no truth in the assertions made in the piece you refer to. With regard to his writings (Grand Pa Wood Says) The Piece on Temperance was written first and the one on National affairs[1] was written about two months after that time, both however in the year 1827.

The Johnson & Grigsby fight[2] took place in 1829, but I can not find out anything about the language used, If there is any thing else that I can do for you, let me know

Respectfully
David Turnham

Pr. Jno J. Turnham.

LC: HW2636; HL: LN2408, 1:184–85

---

1. See §81.
2. See §76.

227. Elizabeth Crawford to WHH

dear Sir

  your letter dated July the 2 came to hand A few days Since in which you requested me to give you A history of mr lincoln while he worked for my husband
how he acted and So fourth   I will tell you as much about him as I can recolect
when mr lincoln came to our house he would Stop at the door raise his hat make
A bow and Speak politely and when invited Step in and Set down if not in A hurry to go to work if So he would pass compliments in A plain but polite and friendly
way and go to his work   he was no hand to pitch in at work like killing Snakes
but he would take hold of his work as camely and pleasant as his maner was other
ways   it Seamed that his motto was to do his well and to please the man he was
at work for   as to the books he read and Studed I am not able tell you all of nor
the half of them   it has bin so long Since that I have forgot   he read the life of
washington and when ever he would get hold of A new book he he would examine it and if he thought it A good work and would be an advantage to him to read
it he would do So but if not he would close it up and Smile and Say I dont think
this would pay to read it or words to that amount and get something else and So
on   it seamed that he was after Something that would be an advantage to him
in after years he als Seemed to Study his oald fathers intrust and family as well as
his one   when he would come in from his work to his meals or any other time if
he would get to reading or talking and he thought it time to go to work he would
Say well this will never get the child A coat   Some times my husband would trip
him as he would walk out and then thay would have A Scuffle in the yard before thay would go to work and it was a tite Scuffle   Some times lincoln would
throw mr crawford and Some times crawford would get the best of him   thay
war allways Joking or playing Some prank on each other when thay war out
together   Lincoln was A plain [soclibel?] and kind young man and under A good
carrecter So far as I ever new   as to what all kinds of work he use to do I can not
tell

  he use to work in the Shop with his father and he us to make rails make fence
clear ground work in the fields cut pork and any other kind of work done on A
farm

  when I rote to you before in giveing you the names of the wild fruits I think I
forgot to name the Parcimon which is plentiful in places   well I dont know that
I can give you any more information at this time   excuse bad riting and mistakes
as my eyes is So Sore and blind that I cant See the lines on the paper half my time

  mr herndon   I wish to inform you that my husband Josiah crawford was A
union man and A lincoln friend   he departed this life on the 12 day of may 1865

  he was A man that allways kept his buisiness in A good position tell the last
two or three years before his death after that time that he thought that every man
was honest and left considerable of his money in peoples hands unsetled and I
believe that I am or will be wronged out of Some hundreds of dollars which will

leave me in verry limeted circumstance and it vexes and pesters me tell I cant think of as much as I would to rite to you concerning the lincoln family, and thar is other grate loses that I have had which keeps me confused tell my mind is allmost alltogether unprepard to sit down to rite at all   I dont rite this as A complaint but as an excuse for my neglect in ancerring your letters Sooner   I wish to get Some advice from you concerning my buisiness if it is convenient hearafter   I am so blind that I cant rite any more at this time

yours with respect
elizabeth crawford

    LC: HW2637–38; HL: LN2408, 1:207–9

228. Nathaniel Grigsby to WHH

Gentryville, Ind. Sept 8th 1866

Sir

    your note of resent date is recd, i shall answer youre questions to the best of my abilitys   the most popular church in Southern indiana was the united baptist of America   Mr Sparrow[1] was not the father of Msses Lincoln, the mother of Abraham Lincoln was a hanks   gentryvile is not on the head waters of litle pigeon creek   it lyes one mile south of said Stream   no other question recollected

i yet remain youre friend
N Grigsby

PS

    this leaves me all wel hoping the same to you, Ind wil give a good report of her self to morrow at the labet box as She did on the battle field as we have the same foe to meet Yours truly

N G

    LC: HW2639; HL: LN2408, 1:203–4

229. William Walker to WHH

Lexington Mo Sept 8th 1866

Dr Sir

    Yours of the 1th Inst Came to hand, in due time

    In answer to the first question, I was in the Case & So was *Col* Dilworth. 2d   Lincoln first appeared in the Case after the Case was taken to Cass. I wrote the affidavit for the Change   The Change was from Mason County to Cass and the application was made to Judge Harriott. Armstrong remained in the Jail at

---

1. Presumably Thomas Sparrow, the husband of Elizabeth Hanks, who was Nancy Hanks Lincoln's aunt.

Beardstown bout Six months   On the trial we denied that Armstrong Committed the deed. That if he did "he done it in Self defence

I feel obliged to You for the indulgence in the money Matters   When You
Complete Your work & have it published please Send Me Coppy —

Truly Yours
W Walker.

LC: HW2640; HL: LN2408, 2:355–56

230. Dennis F. Hanks to WHH[1]

Charleston Ills September 10. *[1866]*[2]

friend William
Dere Sir

I Received your of Inquire it Did you Ever know a man in Indiana By the name
of Jason Duncan I say No 2*d* Nancy Lincoln Abe's Mother moved to Indiana in
Spencer County there Died.

3*d* I am told that Abe Lincoln was always a Whig in Indiana this is not trew
he was a Jackson man or Boy as you please he was made a Whig in your town

the Copy Book that thomas Johnston has is not in my reach he lives in prary
City 18 miles from me you had Better write to him a Bout it — Prary City Cumberland County Ills

I have been sick very Nervous
D F. Hanks

William I have answered all them questions a Bout abe's Mother Be fore what is
the Matter. Do you loose the letters how do you cum on with the publication of
the Book.

LC: HW3899; HL: LN2408, 1:202–3

231. Joshua F. Speed to WHH

Louisville 13 Septr 1866.

Dear Sir.

Yours of the 9th is at hand. My recollection is that the Poem on Suicide was
written in the Spring of 1840. or Summer of 1841.[1]

It was published in the Sangamon Journal soon after it was written
The first No of the Louisville Journal issued 24 November 1830.

---

1. Note in top margin: *Copy of letter furnished W H Herndon Jan 2 1888 to be given S. B. Morrison of Chicago.*
2. The inquiry about Jason Duncan indicates the year.

---

1. This poem has not been located. WHH believed it had been removed from the *Journal's* backfile.

In about a year the Louisville Focus an Older paper on the same Side sold out to the Journal.

The new Constitution of Ky was adopted in 1850 — The Convention which framed it was held in in the winter of 1849 & 50.

I know nothing of where he learned the Poem alluded to.

Your friend

J. F. Speed

LC: HW2642; HL: LN2408, 2:193–94

232. John T. Harris to WHH

Harrisonburg Va. Sept 15th 1866

Dear Sir:

Yours red. on yesterday and I proceeded to answer at once. I hope I have answered satisfactorily. But in the Lincoln matter, I find it more difficult   Enclosed I send you a draft that an old and intelligent friend gave me, who Knew the Lincoln family intimately and lived adjoining them. It was our intention to fill the blanks, but I have almost despaired & send you the skeleton as it is.

How are parties getting on in your State? I presume the Radicals will carry it. Logan,[1] I see *out-Herods, Herod.* He has changed *slightly,* since he was going to Kill old Kellogg[2] for abusing the Democracy in the winter of 1860. How is [Tritt?]? which side does he take? McClearnand is right I see. I hope for the best.

By-the-by how much can *good* lawyers (I mean *good* lawyers!) make in Springfield and other cities of your State? *Answer* me on this —

I am Circuit Judge now, but would prefer a larger income.

Write me the political prospects as *they really are.*

Yours Truly

John T. Harris

not John *"G."*

As I am on the subject of names, is your first initial N. or W.? You so write it I cannot distinguish and am in superscription, driven to *Copy*

[Enclosure A]

233. Statement on ancestors of Lincoln

The ancestors of President Lincoln were among the earliest settlers of the County of Rockingham in the State of Virginia — the _____ grand-father of the President became the owner of a very valuable tract of land on the waters of Linville's Creek about eight miles North of Harrisonburg — the county Seat of Rockingham — the tract contained ___ acres is now divided into __ farms is well im-

---

1. John A. Logan.
2. Congressman William Kellogg (1814–72) of Canton, Illinois.

proved and highly fertile and productive (Mema — all barns and out building —
were destroyed by Sheridans army acting under orders we presume of the President) — was procured by purchase 176_   from Hite Green & McKay — grant-
ees from the r____ royal Governor of Va as shown by ____ 176_   now of record
in the County of Augusta — _____ the — grand father died in ____ and by
will conveyed his land to his sons — ___ the ____ grandfather of the President
emigrated to Kentucky in *[blank space]* _____ — There are numerous decendants,
family Still residing in the County and owning and occupying the land originally
belonging to _____ Lincoln the earliest progenitor of the family — they are in
general in easy and independant circumstances, Some of them may be Said to be
wealthy. they are respectable, and worthy citizens, In the late unfortunate controversy between the North & South, when the dreadful alternative, of taking sides
was was forced upon them, those who were liable to bear arms without a single
exception cast their fate with the land of their birth. and during the whole term of
the war, faithfully performed their duty as they believed, and bore themselves gallantly and bravely as confederate Soldiers, — Several were severely wounded in
the various battles —

Since, the surrender of Lee and the close of the War they have in common with
all our *people,* acquiesced in the decision, and are now Loyal and law-abiding Citizens of the *U.S.*

The family trace their descent from the Lincoln family of Massachusetts, and
still retain the same family names. To wit: Levi, Mordecai, Abraham, Jacob, John,
David &c — Dorcas, Abigal — Rebecca &c   Jacob Lincoln, who died in this
County in the year 18__ was a Lieuten at the Seige of Yorktown and after his death
the writer Knows, that his representatives — applied for pay for this services under the pension laws of the *U.S.* and that the late President then a member of
Congress from Illinois, as their Kinsman, kindly undertook to attend to the matter in Congress, The correspondence between the P. & the family on the subject
cannot now be found)

They always wrote and pronounced their name — "Lincoln" — as Shown by
all, deeds wills & of record in our courts — Yet the common pronnciation — by
the vulgar and illiterate was *Linkhorn* — which was often annoying & offensive
to them, The wills, deeds and other records of the Courts containing much valuable information in relation to the History of the Lincoln were burned by Gen
Hunter in _____ 1864 at the time of his famous raid up the Valley.

[Enclosure B]

234. Statement on Episcopal Church in Virginia
About the Episcopal Church[1]

The earliest history of the Episcopal Church in Virginia, dates back to October 1621, when Sir Francis Wyatt Governor, who brought over a new frame of

---

1. This material on the church and practice of religion in early Virginia was apparently compiled by either Harris or an anonymous informant in compliance with Herndon's requests. The text is taken from the
Springer transcription.

government for the colony dated July 24th 1621, establishing a Council of State and a General Assembly. Amongst his instructions was one, for the permanent guidance of the Govr. and Council. He was to provide for the Service of God in conformity with "the church of England as near as may be". Ministers were ordered in Session March 1630 to "conform themselves in all things according to the cannons of the Church of England". The first act of the Session 1632 provides "that there be a uniformity throughout this Colony both in substance and circumstance to the Cannons and Constitution of the Church of England as near as may be; and that every person yield ready obedience unto them upon penalty of the pains and penalties in that case appointed." Another act directs that "Ministers shall not give themselves to excess in drinking or riot, spending their time idly by day or night playing at dice, cards or any other unlawful game."

In 1661 laws were passed demanding strict conformity and required *all to contribute* to the established church. The Vestry was now invested with the power of perpetuating its own body by filling vacancies themselves.

By an Act of Assembly passed in 1662 a Salary of £80 was settled upon every minister "to be paid in the valuable commodities of the country, if in Tobacco, at 12 shillings the hundred, if in cord, at 10 shillings the barrel."

In 1696 the salary of the clergy was fixed at 16,000 lbs of tobacco worth at that time about £80. This continued to be the amount of their stipends, until 1731 when the value of Tobacco being raised, they increased to about £100 or £120. This was exclusive of their Gebes and other perquisites.

In 1779 former acts providing salaries for the ministers, which had been suspended from time to time, *were repealed.*

Whilst the right existed from *Oct. 1621* to tax for the ministry, yet I do not see that it was exercised until *1661.* Then to answer your question I assume that the tax *commenced* in *1661* and *ended with the act of 1779.* After this period the Episcopal Church continued to exercise peculiar privileges until the act of January 1799 put them on a footing with all other Churches and the Act of 1802 gave their Glebe lands to the State for certain uses.

An act to Establish Religious Freedom soon followed — a copy of which I send you. It was the work of Mr. Jeffersons great mind.

It only remains for me to answer your question "When was the law of Primogeniture repealed in Virginia?"

I answer in 1785 to take effect on the lst day of January 1787. This law was the production of the united labors of Mr. Jefferson, Mr. Pendleton and Mr. Wythe. As reported by them and passed by the Legislature, it made no difference in the *descents* of *infants* estates and those of adults. I send you a copy of this law as re-enacted in 1819 and somewhat changed, but not in its cardinal principles.

I think the foregoing answers your questions. I regard it reliable as it is *culled* from works of character and *copied* almost *verbatim.*

"The works of Jefferson" to which I *have not access* at this time, will furnish you fuller information on all these subjects than I can now give — See his *1st Vol.*, not his "Correspondence" or "Memoirs," but "The works of Jefferson."[2]

LC: HW2643 (letter), HW2644 (enclosure A); HL: LN2408, 1:2–8 (letter, enclosures A and B)

235. *William Walker to WHH*

Lexington Mo Sept 15th 1866

Friend Herndon

The truth is I did not understand the question, You repeat in Yours of the 10*th* inst, I thought You asked if the hurt was Confesed, I do not think a *writ* of Habes-Corpus was taken out at any time — My Recollection is that after Norris was tryed & Convicted of *Man slaughter* Judge Harrutt hearing the testimony decided on Motion to fix Armstrong Bail at $5000,

Mr Lincoln only appeared the one time, and that on the trial, Mr. Lincoln, Closed the argument for the defence, In a Speach of bout one hour, It was a Close and Searching annilessis of the testimony for bout three fourths of the time, the Remainder was an appeal to the Jury and was the Most Eloquent & impressive I have Ever heard, the feelings of the Jury Seamed to harmonise with the Speaker, and he Conveyed to them by his Earnestness the Conviction that Armstrong was innocent, not only to the Jury but Evry one Els, — The instructions Given to the Jury for the defence, will be found in Mr Lincolns own hand writing Carefully prepaired while the prosecution Closed the argument. I believe I have answered all Your questions if not Keep on, I have but little to do & love to think about the Greatest Man that Ever lived, and to *Curse* in my Soule the authors of his death

Truly Yours &c
W Walker.

P.S. I will be in Ills in a few days —

LC: HW2645; HL: LN2408, 2:354–55

236. *Joshua F. Speed to WHH*

Louisville 17 Septr 1866

Dear Sir

Yours of the 15th making enquiry about my recollection of Lincolns speech made in the Presbyterian Church in the winter of 1839[1] is at hand   I cheerfully comply with your request and all the more readily since I can correct an erroneous impression which seems to rest upon your mind

---

2. *The Writings of Thomas Jefferson,* ed. H. A. Washington, 9 vols. (Washington, D.C., 1853–54).

---

1. This is AL's speech on the subtreasury. See *CW* 1:159–79.

I had nothing whatever to do with the composition or arrangment of the speech — The thought, style Composition and arrangment were all his own. so far as I know — Certainly so far as I was concerned —

My recollection of the circumstances under which the speech was made was about this — An arrangement was made between the Whig & Democratic parties for a discussion of the principles then at issue before the country —

Logan Baker & Lincoln were the Champions of the whig party & Douglas Calhoun & Lamborn the chosen champions of the Democratic party — I remember the debate — The whigs were so much pleased with Lincolns speech that it was published by private subscription in pamphlet form[2] & circulated as a campaign document —

I remember also that you were living with me then and that you one evening expressed the opinion that I had had some hand in composing the speech — It certainly was not true — I remember also that Blankenship who was rooming in the house about that time was also under that impression — I may have read it in manuscript before it went to press. But do not now remember that I did — even so much as that — as to my having originated an idea or written a line in it I never did —

I sold out to Hurst 1 Jany 1841. and came to Ky in the spring —

Lincoln came to see me & staid sometime at my mothers in the Summer & fall of 1841. I returned with him to Ills and remained till the 1st of Jany 1842.

When he was in Ky he was at times very melancholy — My Mother observed it — and one morning when he was alone — she with a womans instinct being much pained at his deep depression — which she had obsirved — presented him a bible — advising him to read it — to adopt its precepts and pray for its promises —

It made a deep impression upon him — I often heard him allude to it — even after he was President — As an evidence of the impression made upon him — Soon after his election he sent her a photographic likeness of himself — with this inscription in his own handwriting

"To my very good friend Mrs Lucy G. Speed from whose pious hands I riceived an Oxford Bible Twenty years ago
A. Lincoln

How touching! to Christian a woman! How beautiful & how simple — The old lady now 80 years old prizes above all price
Your friend
J. F. Speed

LC: HW2646–47; HL: LN2408, 2:329–32

---

2. *Speech of Mr. Lincoln, at a Political Discussion, in the Hall of the House of Representatives, December, 1839. At Springfield, Illinois* ([Springfield, 1840]).

237. Abner Y. Ellis to WHH

Moro; Illinois 19th Sept 1866

Freind William

Yours of the 17th is recd and contents Noted

Mr Lincoln Says he was Shown this piece of Poetry when he was a young Man "by a freind."[1]

I have the Whole of it pasted in My Scrap Book   do you wish it   if you do I think I Can get it out for you, it is the the same —. "Oh Why Should the Sperit of Mortal be proud"[2] The Time and place he Committed this to Memmory I Never New

2nd Question   I Never Knew a Man in Sangamon or Menard by the Name of Jason Duncan.[3] I Know a Man in Salisbary Sangamon County by the Name of Jason Miller, and the Duncans and Millers are relativs

Morris Linsay is a Brother in Law to Jason Miller

From your freind

A. Y. Ellis.

I have Just read the peice of Poetry refered to and it Makes Me think of his old Uncles & Aunts   they we Jealous of Proud People

I can imagine how Old Mrs Reason Ray his Aunt Could say it — She was old Billy Hanks daughter   I Knew her Well

Your Father also Knew him —

PS   It has been raining and I could not go to the PO sooner.[4]

I think if I was you I would try and see his old aunt — the last I knew of her, she was living only 4 miles west of Springfield near John Simmes — remember near John Simmes; her first husband was Reason Ray and her last was Samuel Dillon. I think she can be of some assistance to you. I have to do this with my pencil as no pen is near just now.

By the by she may only be his old cousin instead of aunt

(A. Y. Ellis)

LC: HW2666; HL: LN2408, 2:348

---

1. Marginal note: *It was in Menard Co Ills about 1835 — when & where he learned it I am satisfied from what I Know & have heard <u>Herndon</u>.*

2. The first line of "Mortality" by the Scottish poet William Knox.

3. Because Francis B. Carpenter recently had written that AL told him he first learned of the poem named above from a man named Jason Duncan, WHH wrote to many of his informants about this time seeking information on Duncan.

4. The balance of the original letter is missing; the text is supplied from the Springer transcription.

238. Joseph Gillespie to WHH

Edwardsville, 19th Sept 1866

Dear Sir

yours of the 10th is recd in reply to which I have to say that I only remember the general run of the events connected with the Senatorial election in 1854 in which Mr Lincoln & Mr Trumbull were candidates and in which Trumbull succeeded   We held a caucus in which all but five of the opponents of the pro-slavery Democracy were present and at which Lincoln was selected as our Candidate   When the Houses met in joint convention Those five to wit   Judd of Cook, Cook of Lasalle Palmer of Macoupin and Allen & Baker of Madison voted for Trumbull while the rest of us voted for Mr Lincoln   The reason they gave according to my recollection for voting for Trumbull was that having been elect-ed as Democrats they could not vote for any one but a Democrat for US Senator   I tried hard to persuade them to go with us   They stated that they had no objection to Mr Lincoln except his political antecedents but that they could not sust[ain t]hemselves at home if they were to vote for him but expressed regret that they were so circumstanced   After a number of ballots I asked Mr Lincoln what he would advise us to do when he said promptly   "I would go for Trum-bull by all means"   We understood the case to be that Shields was to be run by the Democrats at first and was then to be dropped and Joel A Matteson put up and it was calculated that certain of our men who had been elected on the free soil issue would vote for him after they had voted with us long enough to satisfy their consciences & constitutents   Our object was to make an election before they got through with their *programme*   We were savagely opposed to Matteson and so was Mr Lincoln and he said that if we did not drop in & unite upon Trumbull those men would go for Matteson & elect him which would be an everlasting disgrace to the State   We reluctantly complied with Lincolns suggestions & went upon Trumbull & elected him   Mr Lincoln did not appear to have any hard feelings towards Trumbull although he was of course disappointed & mortified at his own want of success   This is the impression left on my memory of the event   I do not [rem]ember how many ballots we had but I should think we had five or six   I do not think there was much ill feeling felt or manifested amongst Lincolns friends although we looked upon it as a great misfortune to him person-ally that he could not succeed on that occasion but at home there was consider-able bitterness displayed by some of the old Whigs who regarded it as an affront put upon men who had belonged to that party   Trumbull was present when the election came off but I do not believe that he was charged with being instrumen-tal in bringing about the result — nor do I suppose that he took any pains to pre-vent it or any active part in the matter one way or another   I know that we — the opponents of the pro slavery party, harmonized during the rest of the session   I remember that judge S. T. Logan gave up Mr Lincoln with great reluctance   He begged hard to try him one or two ballots more but Mr Lincoln urged us not to risk it longer   I never saw Mr Lincoln more earnest and decided   He said he was satisfied that he could not get the support of those five men and it would be unwise to contend any more and incur the risk of electing Matteson   I know that the friends of Matteson were greveously disappointed at the result   They felt sure that he would be elected in due season and appeared to be taken by surprise when we united on and elected Trumbull. These are my impessions but owing to the length of time which has elapsed and the vagueness of my recollection I would not be answerable for any thing more than their correctness in general and not in detail   You are at liberty to make such use of them as you may deem proper if their publication can conduce in any way to vindicate the truth of history   If not necessary I should of course prefer not to have them made public

Your friend
J Gillespie

LC: HW2667–68; HL: LN2408, 2:434–36

239. Nathaniel Grigsby to WHH

Gentrysville, Ind Sept, 19,th 1866

Sir

After respects to you, i shall try to answe[r] youre requests, first   Abraham Lincoln never corted with intention of Maring a Miss Wood, or any othe Lady   while in this contry with intention of Mariage as none by myself, or any of his old friends, i think the nuse in the papers to that affect is in correct, the fite that took place betwen Wm Grigsby and John D Johnston took place on 16,th of July, 1829 neare Ggentryville Ind

N. Grigsby.

PS   this leaves me and family wel, Friend Herndon you wil excuse me for troubling you with, afew words on politicks   we are in the mdst of A heted canvass the ishue is now betwen the contending parties is whither the men and party that saved this goverment shall rule it, or those that tride to distroy it   i am with the loyal people that stood by the goverment i think presidet Johnson is head and front of the rebels, and there aiders and Abeters come ware come death or come what wil i shall stand by a loyal congress to the biterend, old Hosier will come out all rite   N, G

LC: HW2669; HL: LN2408, 1:204

240. David Davis (WHH interview)[1]

September 19th 1866.

Judge Davis —

I was Elected Judge Sept 48. Sat in Sangamon Co up to 1857 — 14 Counties, Sangamon, Tazwell, Woodford — McLain, Logan — De Witt — Piatt, Champaign Vermillion, Edgar — Shelby, Moultre — Macon, & Christian — are about 100 m square — see a Map. Lincoln was with me all around the circuit — Travelled around the Circuit twice per year; out 6 mo Each year —

Lincoln Commenced practicing in Bloomington in 1837 and never ceased to come here and attend the Court. He practiced under me — for the years of 48. to 1858 — went all around the Circuit.[2]

I met in 1861 in Indianapolis, Judd, Lamon — were with him all the way — Hunter & Sumner &c — got in Springfield — Browning went with Lincoln went as far as Indianapolis Ind. I went to Harrisburg. — Judd had Pinkerton to investigate the Conspiracy. Pinkerton reported I think reported at Philadelp, Lamon went throug; it was decided at Harrisburg. I never heard that a torpedo or other thing was put on the track or in the cars. We went to Washington through Baltimore the next day.

I was appointed Judge of Supm Court in 1862 was with Lincoln some. Lincoln was a peculiar man: he never asked my advice on any question — sometimes I would talk to him & advise him: he would listen — The idea that he told his religious views to any one is to me absurd, I asked him once about his Cabinet: he said he never Consulted his Cabinett. He said they all disagreed so much he would not ask them — he depended on himself — always. I may say that he did once or twice ask me some questions about money affairs and how to put out his money — &c &c   He wanted me to go to Baltimore Convention — didn't go. April 4th 1864 is the last time I saw him until he was dead and in his Coffin — He never would turn a man out off and hence his Cabinet clung together. He said He ran the Machine himself.

Bancroft knew nothing about Lincoln: He was an old democrat and never sympathized with. Lincoln was a remarkbl man: he said that as a Republican government all men & women & Children had a right to see the Presdt & State his grievances. I Know it was the general opinion in Washington that I knew all about

---

1. In a manuscript entitled "Lincoln as Lawyer — Politician & Statesman" (LC: HW4190–4219), WHH, in quoting from his interviews with Davis, wrote in a margin: "While passing I wish to say that I examined Judge Davis in '66 at Bloomington and he dictated while I wrote. That writing is in my hand now" (LC: HW4193). The contents of this manuscript were apparently based on §§240–42, §381, and §419 and were later adapted by JWW for their joint biography. Whether all these notes derive, like §§240–42, from the interviewing sessions of September 20 and 21, 1866, is not known.

2. AL and Davis became close friends and often traveled and roomed together on the circuit. As Davis attests, AL usually traveled the entire circuit with him twice a year during this period and was thus in his company a great deal. For an account of their experiences on the circuit that details some of the cases referred to in Davis's interviews with WHH, see Willard L. King, *Lincoln's Manager: David Davis* (Cambridge: Harvard University Press, 1960), 71–87.

Lincolns thoughs but I Kew nothing. Lincoln never confided to me anything. He never told me a word on reconstruction — Lincoln would never have split with Congress: he would have fought it out on his own fronts — Johnson was a low down — a demagogue &c. Seward was a Kind tender Man: he said to Johnson on this question of reconstruction — I'll Stand by you. Seward thought that the South had done Enough — namely repudiate the rebel debt — pass the amendment and repudiate the Southern debt. All looks dark now to me: hate hate. hate — &c —

I was at the City of Springfield about the time of Lincolns & Trumbulls Election. I got some Abolitionists to go for Lincoln. Told Lincoln to watch Jo Gillespie and Bill Butler. Lincoln earnestly urged his friends to go for Trumbull (see Sam Parks)

1840 —

Lincoln was around Every where discussing politics: he & Douglas around   Douglas & Lincoln went in 1840 all around the Circuit with Treat, & Spoke in the afternoon —

The Arch Williams Story.
The Orm & Dutch Story. — I wanted Orm appointed — Lincoln saw me Coming — Said — There's Davis he bothers one nearly to death — I applied for Orm. Lincoln said he would appoint him — said the list Contained Orms name — asked Lincoln to let me see it: he said Davis you have no *faith*. I said Lincoln I am a cautious man and want to see for my self. Let me see your list. I read it and and saw they were out They were out. Told Lincoln so — and Said By G—d I'd go and see who did it & Knife him — He sent it over and had it Corrected —

Conscienciousness great —
Great in court anywhere if he thought he was right. he Inquired more into cases than into the Philosophy: was a good Circuit Court Lawyer   Pride of success — not unscrupulous — Knowledge of human Nature — Knew the law of nature must catch it quickly.

Patterson trial[3] — fort Sumpter times — in Champaign — Patterson had killed a man: he had lots of friends & money — Lincoln & Sweat[4] defended him. Ficklin & Lamon for People — After hearing the testimony Lincoln said he — the man was guilty — Swett you defend him. I can't — They got a fee of five hundred or a thousand dollars —.

The Woman case — in Champaign — the Seduction case Lincoln got to believe that the witnesses were false — A young man was put on the Stand who re-

3. See pp. 632–33.
4. Leonard Swett.

fused to testify. Lincoln went the idea that the witnesses were all wrong — went at them, crushed them — Every Man in the Court house except Lincoln and Jury. Lincoln got a verdict of $800. or a thousand.

LC: HW2650–54; HL: LN2408, 2:41–45

241. David Davis (WHH interview)

20th Sept 1866

Mr Lincoln was not a social man by any means: his Stories — jokes &c. which were done to whistle off sadness are no evidences of sociality: he loved the struggling masses — all uprising towards a higher Civilization had his assent & his prayer. His was a peculiar nature

Lincoln had no spontaneity — nor Emotional Nature — no Strong Emotional feelings for any person — Mankind or thing. He never thanked me for any thing I did — never as I before said asked my advice about anything — never took my advice, Except as to the dollar: he asked no man advice — took no mans advice — listened patiently to all that had an idea —

I saw Browning at Chicago: he was 1st for Bates.[1] I told him there was no Earthly Chance for him — Bates. Browning turned in and went for Lincoln heartily. Logan[2] did nothing much — was not the kind of a man to go to men and order — Command or Coax Men to do what he wanted them to do — did not set up & toil — couldn't do so — was not in his nature.

Logan was beat for Congress by his own folly in connection with Lincolns momentary unpopularity. Logan told his friends at and around Delevan that his Election was sure — That they need not go to the polls. as they hated to vote for —

I don't Know anything about Lincoln's Religion — don't think anybody Knew. The idea that Lincoln talked to a stranger about his religion or religious views — or made such speeches, remarks &c about it as published is absurd to me. I Know the man so well: he was the most reticent — Secretive man I Ever Saw — or Expect to See. You know more about his religion than any man — you ought to Know it as a matter of Course.

Mr Lincoln was advised as Presdt that the various military trials in the Northern States — Even in the Southern border States where the Courts were open and untrammeled & free, were unconstitutional & wrong — and would not be sustained by the Supm Court — could not be — ought not to be. That such proceedings were dangerous to liberty — Mr Lincoln Said he was opposed to hanging — &c. That he did not love to Kill his fellow men — That if the world had no butchers but him he guessed the world would go bloodless. When _____[3] went to Lincoln about these military trials and asked him not to execute the men Convicted in Indiana, who had been Convicted by a military Commission   he

---

1. Edward Bates, who would become the attorney general in AL's first cabinet.
2. Stephen T. Logan.
3. Possibly in WHH's hand: *Joseph E. McDonald.* See §§242, 554.

said he wouldn't hang them — Execute them — but said — I guess I'll Keep them in prison awhile to prevent them from Killing the government. I am Satisfied that Lincoln was thoroughly opposed to these Military Commissions Especially in the free States, where the Courts were open — & free.

One word about Mr Lincoln as a lawyer &c. After he had returned from Congress and had lost his practice, Goodrich of Chicago proposed to him to open a law office in Chicago & go into partnership with him. Goodrich had an Extensive — a good practice there. Lincoln refused to accept — gave as a reason that he tended to Consumption — That if he went to Chicago that he would have to sit down and Study hard — That it would Kill him — That he would rather go around the Circuit — the 8 Judicial one than to sit down & die in Chicago. In my opinion I think Mr Lincoln was happy — as happy as *he* could be, when on this Circuit — and happy no other place. This was his place of Enjoyment. As a general rule when all the lawyers of a Saturday Evening would go home and see their families & friends at home Lincoln would refuse to go home —. It seemed to me that L was not domestically happy.

One time when I wanted to run for Circuit Judge of the 8th Judicial Circuit   Lincoln hadn't the manhood to come out for me in preference to Ben Edwards whom he despised — wouldn't do so because Ben was in the family — that is Ben Edwards bro Nin married Lincoln's wife's Sister. I had done Lincoln many, many favors — Electioneered for him — spent money for him — worked for him — toiled for him — still he wouldn't move. Lincoln I say again and again was a peculiar man. "None such."

LC: HW2655–58; HL: LN2408, 2:45–48

242. David Davis (WHH interview)

Sept 20th Contd.

The democrats name I spoke about was Joseph E. McDonald Indianapolis — Joseph E. McDonald — good man — is true —.

As to the Press I told Lincoln, telegraphed him that the suppression of the Times Chicago was an error. Lincoln was too good a lawyer to know that this proceeding was Constitutional. The Vanlandingham[1] was an Error — the decision an outrage — and I should have so decided. Lincoln told me in Connexion with this, that he verily believed that Some of his men and officers did things to get him into trouble & difficulty — &c. Schenck's[2] Conduct as well as others.

Lincolns Statesmanship adherence to principle: he studied where the truth of a thing lay and so acted on his conviction: bent his whole soul to that idea and End. He looked far into the future and was philosophical truly scintific in his inductions — wherein was his forte —

---

1. Clement L. Vallandigham, an Ohio congressman, was tried and convicted of treason by a military court in 1863.

2. Presumably the Ohio congressman and later general Robert C. Schenck.

I informed Lincoln that the [Military?] trials as above Spoken of Could not Stand the test of Law and Constitution as I thought — and Said.[3]

Lincoln was not a well read Man — read no histories — novels. — biographies &c — Studied Euclid — the Exact Sciences — His mind struggled to arrive at moral & physical — Mathematical demonstration. He Studied the Latin Grammar on the Circuit. He had a good mechanical mind and Knowledge. He never Complained of any food — nor beds — nor lodgings — He once Said at a table — "Well — in the absence of anything to Eat I will jump into this Cabbage. He hated drunkenness: Mr. Lincoln had unsurpassed reasoning powers — his Logical faculties were great: He reasoned from his own mind — his nature — and reflection rather than by. His analogy was great — his Comparison. When he believed his Client was oppressed — such as the Wright Case[4] he was terrific in denunciation — had no Mercy. Remember the *Jessie* B. Thomas Case[5] — Speech — Terrible — This was in 1840 —

Lincoln could bear no malice — nor could Thomas. Thos wrote to L. "Lincoln said I am sorry that I made that Thomas Speech."

Lincoln loved Clay — see Hollands life:[6] it is all false. He did not go for Clay because he Knew Clay Couldn't be Elected: he told me so: he loved & adored Clay — I Know this — all other Statements are unmittegated lie — Lincoln never visited Clay.

As a lawyer when he attacked Meanness & littleness — vice & fraud — he was most powerful — was merciless in his Catigation —

When Lincoln was Elected as Presdt he swore in his soul he would act justly: he said he intended to appoint democrats & Republicans alike — that the Republican payto[7] Composite — made up of all parties associations &c — Justice was Lincolns leading characteristic, modified by mercy — when possible.

Lincoln was a Man of strong passion for woman — his Conscience Kept him from seduction — this saved many — many a woman.

Lincoln was peculiar man. McWilliams[8] was a low vulgar man — yet Lincoln loved sharp — witty things — loved jokes &c and Lincoln atatched himself to this poor unfortunate Creature — This is how Lincoln happened to draw to him Some of his low vulgar & unscrupulous Men. It was wit & joke meeting & loving wit & Jokes — not the man for the men. Lincoln used these men merely to whistle off sadness — gloom & unhappiness. He loved their intellects. minds and felt sorry

---

3. This paragraph has a large "X" drawn through it, as though stricken, but it is not clear who drew it or why.

4. According to WHH, "a suit brought by Lincoln and myself to compel a pension agent to refund a portion of a fee which he had withheld from the widow of a revolutionary soldier" (H&W [1889], 340–42). WHH identifies Erastus Wright by name in his letter to JWW, Nov. 12, 1885, HW. AL's client seems to have been an acquaintance from his New Salem days, Rebecca Thomas, for whom he appeared in court on November 16, 1846. See Paul H. Verduin, "A New Lincoln Discovery: Rebecca Thomas, His 'Revolutionary War Widow,'" *Lincoln Herald* 98:1 (Spring 1996): 3–11.

5. Not a law suit but a verbal assault in a political speech that reduced Thomas to tears. For other references to this incident, see the index.

6. Holland.

7. WHH probably intended to write "party."

8. Amzi McWilliams, a Bloomington attorney.

for their failings — and sympathised with them — He used such men as a tool — a thing to satisfy him — to feed his desires &c. McWilliams came up to Lincoln one day, and Said — "By ging Lincoln I don't intend to belong to any party in which I do myself & friends any good and to do no harm to any one Else. Lincoln said Good McWilliams — good — good.

The meanest man in the bar would always pay great deference & respect to Lincoln —

He never took advantage of a mans low character to prejudice the Jury. Mr Lincoln though that his duty to his client Extended to what was honorable and high minded — just and noble — nothing further —

Lincoln shrank from Controversy as a general rule. — hated quarrell — hated to say hard & sharp thing of any man and never Stept beyond this Except that his duty — his honor or obligations — principles demanded it

Lincoln had no power of organization — thought he had no administrative ability till he went to Washington. A man when forced to do Can do more than he or his friends dream of. & had administrative and Executive ability — to a certain degree — more than any man dreamed of.

He was Slow to form his Opinions — he was deliberate — Cool & demanded the light of all the facts Surrounding the Case — When he formed his opinions he was firm, Especially about questions of justice — principle — &c.&c.&c —

LC: HW2660–63, HW2659; HL: LN2408, 2:48–52

243. Dennis F. Hanks to WHH[1]

Decatur, Ill., Sept. 20 1866

Dear Sir.

Yours of 17th received

Answer to first question: Mr. & Mrs. Sparrow[2] died in Mercer County, Ky. near Danville

Ans 2d. Yes, I knew Ben Romine. He was a a scholar and business man — don't know that he was ever a surveyor[3]

Relative to the Book you speak of as being in your office and coming from Indiana, I know nothing about.

I am now in Decatur — will remain a week or So. If you have business of importance, you had better Come down.

Yours &c
D F Hanks

LC: HW2672; HL: LN2408, 1:204

---

1. Marked *Copy* and written on the stationery of the *Decatur Magnet* in a hand other than that of Hanks.

2. Probably Henry Sparrow and Lucy Hanks Sparrow, AL's maternal grandmother.

3. A memorandum in WHH's hand (HW3745) describes a copy of Robert Gibson's *Theory and Practice of Surveying* dated 1814 that purports to carry several Lincoln signatures, plus that of Ben Romine, a former Indiana neighbor. This is probably the book Hanks has been asked about.

244. Barlow A. Ulrich to WHH

Chicago Sept 21 /66

Dr Sir

I see from an article in the Chicago paper you desire copies of letters written by the late president Abraham Lincoln of whatever nature. I send herewith a copy of one which you may insert if you wish. —

I gained an interview with the president on the 30th of January 1865. When he heard my name & that I was from Springfield on the introduction of Mr. Longyear M.C., of Michigan he said he knew my family well — told the gentlemen how my name was pronounced. He read over my letters to him from various gentlemen of Illinois in relation to my appointment to a foreign counselship in Germany and Said he would do all he could for me. Seeing a Copy of a German article I had written during the campaign he remarked that he had commenced learning that language but had not advanced any farther than to say "Sprechen Sie deutch mein herrn?" He then doubled up my papers & wrote the following on the back of them.

"Will the Secretary of State please see and hear the bearer Mr B. A. Ulrich and oblige him if he conveniently can. he is a young man raised in the place of my residence and of a most respectable family as he also is himself.

A Lincoln"

Jan 30th 1865.

There were nearly a dozen stories told while we were in his room and most of them by the president himself. —

Yours Truly

Barlow A. Ulrich

Atty

I will take one of your books when published —

LC: HW2674-75

245. Benjamin F. Irwin to WHH

Pleasant Plain, Sept 22 1866

Wm H Herndon

I am told by one of Lincoln's Company Robt Plunkett that Lincoln was in no Battle in the war at the time of the Badax fight he was Stationed at Dixon Some 14 Miles Distant   if you will examine Congressional globe 1st session 30th Congress 1848   you will see in a Congressional Speech Lincoln said he was in No Battle also you will see the same on page 46 of Barretts Life of Lincoln[1] stated by him

In regard to Miss Rutledge this I learn to be true Lincoln Samuel Hill (Now Dead) and one McNamer was all paying their Respects to her at the same

---

1. Barrett.

time   she did not seem to be very favorably Impressed with Lincoln at Least he so thought. Lincoln was then young poor and awkward the other two was up in the world   she Married Neither of the Men   in addition she was verry hansome so considered at the time Lincoln took his luck to heart as was thought to such a degree that he was thought to be partially crazy and did really seem strange at the time   my Informants differ as to her death one who pretends to know says she died but Cogdal says she was livng in Iowa in 1860 as Lincoln told him and Lincoln did say in 1860 that he really did love the woman in 1834 and loved her still in 1860 and Could not help it[2]   as regards lincolns Company they was a whole souled hard set of men all fighting stock after the Pugalistic Stile. Lincoln often expressed a desire to get into an engagement to see how they would meet Powder & Lead but failed to do so   Wm Miller who Belonged to another Company says that Lincolns Company was the hardest set of men he ever saw and no man but Lincoln Could do anything with them and that Lincoln was their Idol and there was not a Man but what was obedint to every word he spoke and would fight his death for Lincoln   he was with them all the while in Jumping or foot Racing and Lincoln done the wrestling for the Company against every Bully Brought up   he tells me that when any of his company got into a Muss or quarrel Lincoln could Stop it at a word he had such perfect control over them   he was always Lively in a good humor and full of Anecdotes.

NB   There is two of the Rutledges Still in or near Petersburg that is relation of the woman to Wit, Wm & McGrady Rutledge   they can tell if she is living still or died as combs[3] thinks in 1834 I do not know the men in Person but know they are there. McNamar I also learn still lives in Menard County   But the facts are as I state as near as you will ever get it with the exception her Death

I will see you soon soon as the road dries up till I can get to Town

Respectfully

Ben F Irwin

LC: HW2676–77; HL: LN2408, 1:565–67

246. A. D. Wright to WHH

Petersburg, Sept. 23d/ 66.

Friend Herndon:

I have made the enquiries you requested in your note of 11th, and find that Bowling Green died in 1842, Feby also —

I have seen Hannah Armstrong and she will meet you here at court.

Yours truly

A. D. Wright.

HL: LN2408, 1:431

---

2. Irwin is apparently confused. See Cogdal's testimony, §§328–29.

3. Probably Jonas Combs, an early settler in the Rock Creek neighborhood, south of New Salem, who was still living there in 1865.

247. Isaac Moore to WHH

Boonville Inda Sept. 27th 1866

Dear Sir

Our P.M. hands me your favor of the 23d inst, he also handed me your previous letter which I enclosed to Judge DeBruler of Spencer County for reply

There was an attorney practicing here in 25 & 30 named John A. Brackenridge, who afterwards say about 1850 moved to Texas and during Mr L's administration visited his old friends here, and also the city of Washington. Mr B. was a native of the city of W. and son of the Rev John Brackenridge a clergyman of the old school Presbyterian Church. He the lawyer came here when about 22 years of age, and was in active practice until about /48, when his health failed and was regared as at the head of the Bar, in this section of the State, I have no Knowledge of the matters refered to by you as I was not born until /31

Judge Pitcher a resident of Posey County who is judge of this common Pleas district came to this part of the State about the time Mr B. did. He will be here on the 15th of Oct next, when I will inquire if he recolects anything about the trial.

Rest assured that I will do what I can to assist you in the matter because I desire to accommodate you, and more especially because of my reverence for the great and good Mr Lincoln

I sent your other letter to Judge DeBruler because Mr L. was a resident of that County and the probabilities are that the trial took place at Rockport instead of Boonville

Very Respectfully
Isaac S. Moore

LC: HW2682

248. Rebecca Herndon (WHH interview)[1]

Septr: 28th 1866

Rebecca Herndon (My Mother — God bless her

Says — am from Virginia — am 76 years old — Came to Ky in _____ when I was 8 years of age —. We Sang old hundred in Va. and other Christian Songs of that day — about 1798. We cultivated tobacco — and sent it to Richmond — We came in a squad of 40 persons to Cumberland Mountains as we came to Ky — Sold our waggons — packed our horses — men generally walked — women and children rode — went through what is called the Crab apple orchard — Some — Most of the Settlers of Ky from Va Came down the Ohio — Some crossed the [border?] river called _____ We came by Stanford Ky a small village in _____ Co Ky — and thence to Green Co Ky —. I forgot — We Sang Songs against the Yankees *then*. Now all that prejudice is gone — gone long since — They are good people — good neighbors — good citizens. A Scotch lady gave me a copy of Burn's as Early as 1812 or 1815 — We — my sisters & myself learned Burns by heart — Sang his Songs — Such as "Bonny Doon —" "Highland Mary" "Soldiers return"[2] — I learned a song which I can now repeat — called the Indian Philosopher, a fine poem of some 10 or more verses — it is what may be called a sad — rather reflective Poem. — —

We danced Sang cheerful Songs — Christian ones too — am a Methodist — parents old school Presbyterian. I was a school mistress in Ky in 1812 or 15 — We visited — were Social, more so than now. We raised our own Cotton — carded Spun it — wove it — have picked Cotton Many Many a day —. Seeded it with my own fingers till Whitneys Cottin gin was invented about 1791. Am an abolitionist in sentiment — in feeling & ideas — run with my husband[3] who is democratic: Your grandfather Day[4] was through the Revolution — was a true & tried Patriott — Emancipated his Slaves about 1789 — as I now recollect. — You remember he used to tell you his Revlutionary Stories — his trials — Sufferings — his good old but Ever undaunted. You remember how you when a little lad used to [fire?] up & your Eyes run over with tears at the recitle — of American wrongs — and our hardships. &c. You ask me about Ills — We your father & myself, with my good old father & mother now dead & gone —, Came poor & friendless to Ills in 1821. My mother now lies buried in Menard Co & my father in DeWitt Co — Shall soon follow them.

LC: HW2683–84

249. Archer G. Herndon (WHH interview)

[September 28, 1866?[1]]

A. G. Herndon

Says — am from Virginia — The Customs & habits of Virginia we brought from England. — only partially So — We wanted — or found new uses adapted to our conditions &c — Our games were (5) fives — striking a ball up against a perpendicular wall — Say 30 feet high by 40 or 50 feet wide — We played long bullets[2] — We had an iron ball — weighing from 2 to 5 pounds and rolled it on the highway — in order to see who Could roll the limited distance in the least number of throws — We have raced it — Cock fought it. We played Cards — game Called all fours — ie Seven up[3] — We fox hunted it in the Mornings — fished — Sang Songs going to Corn Shucking[4] — niggers beat us — Sang of

1. The docketing, after the name, reads: *only as to customs — &c. of Va & Ky.*
2. Possibly "The Banks o' Doon," "Highland Mary," and "When Wild War's Deadly Blast Was Blawn."
3. Archer G. Herndon, WHH's father.
4. Edward Day (1760–1836), Rebecca Herndon's father.

1. Using Herndon's age (seventy) as a guide, this interview was given between February 13, 1865, and February 13, 1866, but the close similiarity of this document to the previous one suggests that husband and wife gave their testimony at the same time.
2. The game, long bullets, is described in what follows.
3. A popular card game for two players known variously as All Fours, Seven Up, or Old Sledge.
4. Communal gatherings that combined the work of husking corn with music and entertainment (supplied in Southern states by black musicians) and general festivity.

evening going to Corn shuckings — sung out — I have whip sawed[5] it in this City in 1823. — got one dollar per dy — Sawed 200 feet — got from 1.50 to 200 per hundred — 2 men to saw 200 feet. The virginians — of a good order or class read the best Brittish literature of the day and Studied Philosophy — &c — Old virginia boasted then as now of her integrity — honor — valor — power to rule [or] reign — Am too sick to talk more. 70 years of age —

LC: HW3920

250. O. H. Miner to WHH

Springfield, Sept. 29 — 1866.
Dear Sir:

I am unable to find the assessments in Illinois tabulated for the particular years (all of them) named in your request. I give you herewith all of the years except *1835.* with others Viz:

1839	$58,889,525	
1845	82,327,105	
1855	334,398,425	
1856	349,951,272	
1857	407,477,367	*largest ever made*
1861	330,823,479	

I have not had oppertunity to ascertain what I can find with regard to the State Debt, and shall be absent all next week — on my return I will investigate —
Yours Respectfully
O. H. Miner.[1]

HL: LN2408, 2:231

251. David Turnham to WHH

Dale Ind Sept 29th 1866
Mr Herndon.

Yours of the 10th Inst is at hand. I think when the Lincoln's left here, they were Jackson men. I think that Jackson's opposition to the U.S. Bank and the Crisis that followed Caused them to turn. As regards Lincolns Grand Mother & father, I know nothing about them   I do not think however, that they ever Came to Indiana. I think from my best recollection that whip Sawed Lumber in 1827 to 1830 was worth about 75 cts per hundred. But I am not positive about that.

5. Sawing plank from logs by hand.

1. Orlin H. Miner (1825–79) was the auditor of public accounts from 1864 to 1869.

The Jason Duncan you speak of I never knew, nor heard of, I believe your questions are answered to the best of my ability. I am still ready to render you any service in my power

Your friend
David Turnham
pr <i>Jno J Turnham</i>

LC: HW2685–86; HL: LN2408, 1:205

252. Mary Todd Lincoln (WHH interview)[1]

[September 1866]

Mrs. L. was born in 1823[2]   Lexington Fayette Co Ky — 13th day of Decr   Robt. S. Todd   Eliza S. Parker — Mrs. Todd — her mother died when very young — Educated by Mdme Mentelle[3] — French — opposite Mr Clays — She was well Educated — French — Spoke nothing Else — not allowed to — Finished a Mr Wards accademy[4] — People from the north visited — went to School —

Came to Illinois in 1837 — was in Ills 3 months — went school 2 years after   I came to Ills — returned to Ills in 1839 or 40 — This after Mrs Wallace[5] —

My husband intended when he was through with his Presdt time to take me & family to Europe — didnt in late days dream of death — was cheery — funny — in high Spirits. He intended to return and go to California — over the Rocy Mountains and see the prospect of the Soldiers &c digging out gold to pay national debt.

He & Sumner were like boys during his last days — down on the River after Richmond was taken — they acted like boys — were so glad the war was over. Mr L. wanted to live in Spgfd and be buried there up to 1865 — Changed his notion where to live — never settled on any place particularly — moving & travelling —

Mr L was the kindest — most tender and loving husband & father in the world — He gave us all unbounded liberty — Said to me always when I asked him for any thing — You know what you want — go and get it. He never asked me if it was necessary. He was very very indulgent tu his children — chided or praised for it he always said "It is my pleasure that my children are free — happy and unrestrained by paternal tyranny. Love is the chain whereby to lock a child to its parent."

I have none of my literary scraps — poems — compositions &c — Except I know of the <i>Shield's</i> poetry[6] —

---

1. This appears to be the earliest version of WHH's notes on his only interview with MTL, possibly set down at the time. Unlike the following two items, a copy of this text appears in the Springer transcriptions, which were made before December 1, 1866. This suggests that the next two items may have been written later.

2. MTL was born in 1818.

3. Victorie Charlotte Leclere Mentelle operated a boarding school in Lexington.

4. Dr. John Ward conducted a coeducational school in Lexington.

5. MTL's older sister, Frances Todd, who preceded MTL to Springfield and married Dr. William S. Wallace.

6. See §213.

Mr Lincoln had a dream when down the River City Point — after Richmond was taken   he dreamed that the white house burned up — sent me up the River — went — met Stanton — &c. Mr L. told me to get a party and come back — did so.

Mr L. had no hope — & no faith in the usual acceptation of those word.

He found out that N. W Edwards was stealing as he though: intended to turn him out. My husband placed great Confidence in my knowledge in human nature: he had not much knowledge of men

LC: HW3065–66; HL: LN2408, 2:227–28

253. Mary Todd Lincoln (WHH notes on interview)[1]

[September 1866]

Sumner & Mr Lincoln were great chums after they became acquainted with one an other. They watched Each other closely. Down at Ciy point once Johnson followed us — was drunk — Mr L said to me — "For God's Sake dont ask Johnson to dine with us —" "No do not," Said Sumner   I did not do so.

I often Said that "God would not let any harm Come of my husband — we had passed through 5 long — terrible — bloody years unscathed that I thought so — so did Mr L: he was happy over that idea. He was cheerful — almost joyous as he got gradually to see the End of the war.

I used to read News paper charges — news paper attacks on him — He said — "Dont do that, for I have enough to bear — yet I care nothing for them. If I am right I'll live and if wrong I'll die any how — So let them pass unnoticed. I would playfully say — That's the way to learn — read both sides —

Mr Lincolns maxim and philosophy was — "What is to be will be and no cares of ours can arrest the decree."[2]

I could tell when Mr. Lincoln had decided any thing: he was cheerful at first — then he pressed — or compressed his lips tightly — firmly When these thing showed themselves to me I fashioned myself and So all others had to do sooner or later — and the world found it out.

When we first went to Washington Many though Mr L weak. But he rose grandly with the circumstances and men soon learned that he was above them all. I never saw a man's mind develope so finely: his manners got quite polished.

He used to say to me when I talked to him about Chase & those who did him Evil — Do good to those who hate you and turn their ill will to friendship — Sometimes in Washington, being worn down he spoke crabbing to men — harshly so — Yet it seemed the People understood his Condition & forgave him —

LC: HW3067

---

1. These notes on WHH's interview with MTL are incorporated into the item that follows but do not appear in the previous item or in the Springer transcriptions.

2. Compare the version of this maxim in the following item, §254.

254. *Mary Todd Lincoln (WHH interview)*[1]

[September 1866]

Mrs Lincoln's Conversation in substance with me at the St Nicholas Hotel — She Said — "I [was] born in 1823[2] in Lexington Fayette Co Ky [on] the 13th day of Decr — daughter of Eliza. S. Todd Maiden name Eliza S. Parker *[two words illegible]* [My m]other died when I was very young — was [educ]ated by Mdme Mentelle — a French lady — opp[osite] Mr Clays: She was well Educated — was French, Spoke nothing Else — not allowed to — finished my Education at Mrs Wards accademy. People from the North visited Lexington — went to School here. I Came to Ills in 1837 — was in Illinois 3 Months — went to school two years after I Came to Illinois in Ky. I returned to Ills in 1839 or 40. This was after Mrs Wallace came out.

My husband intended when he was through with his Presidential terms to take me and family to Europe — didn't in late years dream of death — was cheery — funny — in high Spirits. He intended to return & go to California over the Rocky Mountains and see the prospects of the soldiers &c. &c digging [out] gold to pay the National debt. He and Sumner were like boys during his last days — They were down on the River after Richmond was taken: they acted like boys — were so glad the war was over. Mr Lincoln up to 1865 wanted to live in Springfield and be buried there — Changed his notion where to live — never settled on any place particularly — intended moving & travelling some

Mr Lincoln was the Kindest Man — Most tender Man & loving husband & father in the world: he gave us all unbounded liberty — Said to me always when I asked him for anything — "You Know what you want — go and get it": he [never] asked me if it was necessary: he was very — indulgent to his children — chided or prais[ed them] for it — their acts —: he always said "It [is my] pleasure that my children are free — happy & unrestrained by parental tyranny. Love is the chain whereby to Lock a child to its parents"

I have none of my literary scraps — poems — Compositions &c, Except I Know the Shields poetry

Mr Lincoln had a dream when down the River at City point after Richmond was taken: he dreamed that the white House burned up — Sent me up the River — went — Met Stanton &c. Mr Lincoln told me to get a party and Come back. I did so.

Mr Lincoln found out that Mr N W Edwards — his Bro-in-law was stealing, as he thought — intended to turn him out. My husband placed great Confidence in My Knowledge of human Nature: he had not much Knowledge of men

---

1. This is the latest of the three surviving manuscripts relating to WHH's sole interview with MTL, incorporating the texts of the two earlier manuscripts (HW3065–66 and HW3067) and some new material. The date refers to the time of the interview, not the composition of this text, which may postdate the last of the Springer transcriptions (Nov. 30, 1866). Illegible material in the original has been supplied in brackets from earlier texts and from the Springer transcription of the earliest version (HW3065–66). The docketing is difficult to read but appears to be: *Mrs Lincoln's Evidence Copied.* A nearly indecipherable note below this apparently relates to something WHH's law partner Alfred Orendorff told him about MTL in 1874.

2. MTL was born in 1818.

Our expenses at the White House were about [two] thousand dollars per month — breakfasted at [9] o'clock am — lunched at 2 o'cl PM — dined [at] 6 o'cl PM. Mr Lincoln got up irregularly — Saw the people — attended to the Hospital &c. [Woul]d turn Seward out when peace was declared — hated Andrew Johnson. Once Andy Johnson followed Mr Lincoln when he said — "Why is this man following me."

A Letter got out in the army from Mr Lincoln to me. Mr L was tender. I deny [D]inners Cost $500. for friends and diplomatic [corps &c] — twenty four Todd Connexion at frequently [illegible] table. Bakers wife[3] — bad Conduct

Mr Linc[oln] had a Kind of Poetry in his Nature: he was [a terribly] firm man when he set his foot down — none of us — no man nor woman Could rule him after he had made up his mind. I told him about Sewards intention to rule him —: he said — "I shall rule myself — shall obey my own Conscience and follow God in it. Mr Lincoln had no hope & no faith in the usual acceptation of those words: he never joined a Church: he was a religious man always, as I think: he first thought — to say think — about this subject was when Willie died — never before. he felt religious More than Ever about the time he went to Gettysburg: he was not a technical Christian: he read the bible a good deal about 1864

Mr Sumner & Mr Lincoln were great chums [after] they became acquainted with one and other: [they] watched Each other closely. Down at City Point once Johnson followed us — was drunk — Mr Lincoln said — "For God's Sake dont ask Johnson to dine with us" — "No do not" said Sumner [and] I did not ask Johnson.

I often said that [God] would not let any harm Come to my husband. We had passed through 5 long years — terrible — bloody years unscathed that I thought so — so did Mr Lincoln: he was happy over that idea: he was cheerful — almost joyous as he got gradually to see the End of the war.

I used to read News paper c[harges —] News paper attacks on him — He said ["Don't do] that for I have Enough to bear — yet I [care] nothing for them. If I am right I'll live & if wrong I'll die anyhow — so let them [pass by] unnoticed." I would playfully say "That's the way to learn — read both sides"

Mr [Lincoln's] maxim & philosophy were — "What is to be [will be] and no Cares (prayers) of ours Can [arrest] the decree[4]

I could tell when Mr Lincoln had decided anything: he was cheerful at first then he pressed or compressed his lips together — firmly When these things showed

---

3. Julia Baker, MTL's niece, the daughter of Ninian W. and Elizabeth Edwards and the wife of *Illinois State Journal* editor Edward L. Baker, was rumored to have kept too close company with gentlemen other than her husband during a White House visit in 1864. See Justin G. Turner and Linda Turner, eds., *Mary Todd Lincoln: Her Life and Letters* (New York, 1972), 187–88.

4. Quoting from this interview in a draft chapter for his biography, WHH glossed this passage thus: "Mrs. Lincoln told me in 1866 in Springfield in her Examination by me at the St Nicolas Hotel that Mr. Lincolns philosophy was 'what is to be will be and no cares (prayers of ours can arrest nor reverse the decree. I have heard him Say the Same thing Substantially and so have many others in and around Springfield Illinois his home and where he lies buried — Entomed" (HW4261). WHH's point seems to be that he had heard this maxim from Lincoln in a different form: "no prayers of ours can reverse the decree."

themselves to me I fashioned myself accordingly and so did all others have to do sooner or later, and the world found it out. When we first went to Washington Many thought that Mr Lincoln was weak, but he rose grandly with the Circumstances [and] Men soon learned that he was above [them all.] I never saw a man's mind develope so finely: his manners got quite polished. [He] used to say to me when I talked to him about Chase and those who did him Evil — "Do good to those who hate you and turn their ill will to friendship" Sometimes in Washington [being] worn down he spoke crabbedly to men — [Harshly so —] yet it seemed that the People underst[ood the] Conditions around him and forgave.

LC: HW3061–64

255. William Miller? (statement for WHH)[1]

[September 1866?]

In the Spring of 1832 Soldiers Beng called for in the Black Hawk war a company was organized in what was then Sangamon County But out of which Menard is since formed and among the privates was Abraham Lincoln they went as far as Beardstown and for some Reason was Dismissed or not Recd a New call was then made and at Rushville Schuyler Co Ills a company was organzed and abraham Lincoln was Unanimously elected Captain without even presenting himself as a candidate for the office upon his Beng elected he in a very plain unassuming manner thanked the Company for the Confidence they had expressed in Electing him to Command and promised very plainly that he would do the Best he could to prove himself worthy of that confidence so expressed, after the organization of the Company it remained at Rushville one day and two Nights   Company Attached itself to the Reg Commanded by Col Samuel Thompson   from Rushville the Reg went by land entire to a fort in what is now warren County this fort was Distant about 45 Miles and was made out of Posts set in the ground and 8 feet above ground   we there Remained one Night feeling perfectly secure in the fort with But few guards on duty and enemies close at hand from this fort We went to Henderson River in what is now Henderson County this River is a small Stream some 50 yds wide and Perhaps the water is 8 or 10 feet Deep   to cross this River we cut Down trees and pack and fill in with Brush so as to make a Bridge to get over on   our Baggage train was Drawn by cattle and Horses we took the waggons across by hand and the cattle and horses had to swim the stream we was one entire day and Night Building and filling in to Bridge so we could get over   in getting down the steep Banks to the river the Horses was compelled to slide down

---

1. WHH has written *Menard Co.* and *B. F. Irwin* in the top margin. The document is in Irwin's hand, but Irwin himself was only ten years old in 1832 and could not have given this firsthand account. It may represent the results of an interview with William Miller, whom he names in his letter to WHH of December 22, 1866, as an informant about Lincoln in the Black Hawk War. Unlike Robert Plunkett, Irwin's other Black Hawk War informant, Miller did not serve in AL's company, and while the interview suggests close observation of AL at several points, other details suggest less familiarity with the activities of AL's company.

in so doing several was killed   from this place we went to the Yellow Banks on the Mississippi River in what is now Henderson County we here remained one day and Night   while at this place a considerable Body of Indians of the cherokee tribe came across the River from the Iowa side with the white flag Hoisted   this was the first Indians we saw they was verry friendly and gave us a general war Dance we in return gave them a sucker Ho down all enjoyed the sport and It is safe to say no man enjoyed it better than Capt Lincoln   from this point we went to dixons ferry on Rock River where the City of Dixon Now stands and Remained two days and Nights waiting for Provisions whitch was to come up the river to this point   our supplies all came by water after two days waiting our supplies came and we drew a Bountiful supply of Beef and Beans with a small quantity of flour to mix with it. while we was here Stillman[2] passed us refusing for some reason to Join the Main army after he left taking the Direction of Rock isand Proceeded about twenty Miles that night found himself cut off by the Indians and Attacked he failed to hold his handful of men about 75 in number they fled in all directions   about 12 oclock that Night they commenced coming into our camp, and kept coming in all the remainder of that Night and Next day untill about twenty came in some on foot and some on horse back Leaving the killed and Missing about Sixty in number   on the second day after the Battle the army under Gen Whitesides was camped on the Battle ground gathering up the Dead and wounded the dead was all scalped some with the heads cut off Many with their throats cut and otherwise Barbourously Mutilated   of the wounded we founded few in number and they hid in the Brush as well as they could   among the wounded Joseph Young and Jessy Dickey I Rember that was Badly wounded and Recovered   after caring for the wounded and Burying the Dead the main army Struck for a Bend or outlet in Rock river where Black Hawks vessels called Perogues was said to be   This was thought to be a dangerous undertaking as we knew Indians was plenty and close at hand   To provide as well as might be against danger one man was started at a time in the direction of the point when he would get a certain distance Keeping in sight a second would Start and so on until a String of men extending five miles from the main army was made each to Look out for Indians and give the sign to Right Left or front by hanging a hat on the Bayonet erect for the front and Right or Left for enemies as the case might be. to raise men to go ahead was with difficulty done and some tried hard to Drop Back But we got through safe and found the place deserted leaving plenty of Indian sign a Dead Dog and several Scalps taken in Stillmans Defeat as we supposed they Beng fresh taken   finding no enemy to fight we returned to the Battle ground and remained one day & night and Started for Rock Island and then Joined the main army under Gen Atkins here we Drew Rations again   from this point we was sent to the Mouth of Fox River   at this place our time was up and we was Discharged from service after going to Peru and getting supplies for our men and horses which came up the River by Boat in Charge of Thomas Wilbourn of Beardstown   During

---

2. Maj. Isaiah Stillman, the officer in charge at the debacle described in what follows.

this short Indian campaign we had some hard times often hungry but we had a great deal of Sport Especially of Nights   foot Racing some horse Racing Jumping telling anecdotes in which Lincoln Beat all Keeping up a constant Laughter and good humor   among the soldiers some card playing and wrestling in which Lincoln took a prominent part   I think it safe to say he was never thrown in a wrestle   While in the army he Kept a handkerchif tied round him very near all the time for wrestling purposes and Loved the sport as well as any man could   he was seldom ever Beat Jumping   during the campaign Lincoln himself was always ready for any emergency he endured hardships Like a good Soldier   he never complained nor did he fear Danger   when fighting was expected or danger apprehended Lincoln was first to say less go he had the Confidence of every man in his company and they Strictly obeyed his orders at a word. his company was all young men and full of Sport while at Dixon some Six or Eight friendly Indians with white flags hoisted came to us from Paw Paw Grove and urged protection against other Indians some of our men suspected them for Spies and they had to be put under guard to Keep the soldiers from Killing them whtch was with some difficulty done and at their urgent request guards was sent to protect them clear to Chicago   they was Doubtless what they Professed to be friendly disposed. in all this campaign clear through from Rushville to the Mouth of Fox River, we had with us two to us Rather Strange characters James Wilson & Thomas Bristo from Morgan County they was old man full Sixty or Sixty five years old they went on their own hook furnished their own Blankets and guns and would have no pay they marched with Capt Smiths Company of Morgan County   Both Intelligent men every night they would go outside of our lines to camp and our officers for their safety had to go out and Bring them inside the lines they could not be Induced to Join a company or have any pay they would Draw Rations with our men and they was as anxious for a fight as any men I ever saw and they was grit   Bristo Died about 1846 and wilson about 1851   Both Died at Arcada in Cass Co Ills   while on our march from Dixon to Fox River one night while in camp whitch was formed in a Square enclosing about 40 Acres our horses outside grazing about Nine Oclock got Scared and a general stampede took place they Ran Right through our lines in Spite of us and ran over many of us   no Man Knows what noise a thousand horses Make running unless he had Been there it beats a young earthquake especially among Scared men and certain they was then   we expected the Indians to be on us that Night   fire was threw   Drums Beat   fifes played   whitch added additional fright to the horses   we saw no real enemy that night   A Line of Battle was formed   there was no eyes for sleep that night we stood to our post in line and what frightened the horses is yet unknown   But certain many of them we never saw though we spent two days in hunting them   our time of service was about forty days from the time we rendezvoused at Rushville to the Return   I neglected in the proper place another Singular and odd Soldier in the army   Uriah Wolverton, about 45 years old   from Sangamon County   that took it a foot and kept up with the army on horseback   he Like Wilson & Bristo went on his own hook and would not Join the army or have pay for his services   he was an old Bachelor and by the way a good soldier and a clever man generally if there was no wimen about while at camp   one night in warren County a white hog a young sow   came into our lines which showed more good sense to my mind than any hog I ever saw   This hog swam creeks and rivers and went with the us clear through to I think the Mouth of Fox River and there the Boys killed it or it would Doubtless have come home with us   If it got Behind in Day light as we was marching whitch it did sometimes   It would follow on the track and come to us at night   It was naturally the cleverest friendly Disposed hog any man ever saw and its untimely Death was by many of us greatly Deplored   for we all Liked the hog for its friendly Disposition and good manners for it never Molested any thing and Kept In its proper place

this is all

LC: HW3928–34; HL: LN 2408, 1:448–55

256. Joseph H. Barrett to WHH

Washington, D.C. October 1, 1866

Dear Sir:

Your letter of the 23d ult. was duly received. I can only reply to your inquiry that, with the exception of the authority specified in a foot note on page 14 (last edition) of my "Life" of Mr. Lincoln, my information was derived exclusively from Mr. L. himself (in relation to his ancestry.)[1] His statements were made to me orally, and I took notes as he went along.

Truly yours,
Jos. H. Barrett.

LC: HW2687

257. Robert T. Lincoln to WHH

Chicago Oct 1 /1866

My dear Mr Herndon

Yours of Sept 28 is received — I have not any letters which could be of any interest whatever to you or to anyone — You may remember that I did not leave home until my father became so busy in public affairs that it was next to impossible for him to write to me — Accordingly the few letters I have, ranging over a period of five years, are with one or two exceptions letters enclosing money — I was much too young for him to write to me on general matters — at least he never did so — I spoke to my Mother on the subject and she says she had a talk with you on the subject when at Springfield and that her letters are of too private a nature to go out of her hands.

---

1. Barrett.

You say also that my father used to write "short poems' — I never knew it before and if I came across any, I would willingly let you see them — I have never seen any thing of the kind —

Yours Sincerely

Robert T. Lincoln

LC: HW2688

258. J. W. Scroggs to WHH

Champaign, Ills. Oct. 3d, 1866.

Dear Sir.

Your favor dated Sept. 28th was duly rec'd. In reply allow me to say, that on the 27th *of April 1859,* Mr. Lincoln was in the *"Central Illinois Gazette"* office, where a conversation occurred upon the subject of the probable candidates for the Presidency in 1860. I suggested his name, but he — with characteristic modesty — declined. However his name was brought forward in the next issue, *May 4th 1859.* In the "Gazette" of *Dec. 7th 1859* another article appeared setting forth Mr Lincoln's claims. On the *21st of Dec. 1859* his name was placed at the head of the editorial columns where it remained until after his election. In the "Gazette" of Janurary 18th 1860 an editorial appeared setting forth the claims and fitness of Mr. Lincoln and arguing at some length the absolute policy of nominating a western man, and especially Mr. Lincoln. This article was copied throughout the northwest, and appeared in several eastern journals.

After his nomination, election, and inauguration the first time, I thought we could clearly see that the necessities of the country, — and the force of circumstances then existing, — would make Lincoln Pres't a second term. This belief was expressed in various editorials from time to time, and on the 8th of *May, 1861,* I placed the name of Abraham Lincoln for Prest in 1864 at the head of my columns.

Yours very Respy

J. W. Scroggs

LC: HW2689; HL: LN2408, 2:413

259. Johnson Gaines Greene (WHH interview)

Octr. 5th 1866

J. Gaines Green

Says he Knew Jason Duncan in or about New Salem about the year 1835–6: he was a physician — Knew Lincoln well ie Duncan did. D & Lincoln were great friends — Duncan married a Miss Burner — Jane: They live in Canton Fulton. Duncan's Wife had a child — father uncertain — supposed to be Duncan's — or Lincoln's L. advised Duncan to leave and Marry

Polly Owen — now Mrs Vinyard of Missouri is decidedly the most intellectual woman I Ever Knew. She was Abes "*Sweetheart* —" is now about 59 years of age —

I heard the Eulogy of A Lincoln on Bolin Green:[1] he made a failure — cause Emotion — a swelled heart & soul — &c — This was in 1842.

The People at New Salem rolled Scanlan & Sol Spear down Salem hill. The children at School had Made a wide Sliding walk from S to the River in which they slid down from the top of the hill to the river about 250 or 300 yards on sleds & boards — and it was down this [path?] Jack Armstrong and others Started the the men — in a hogshead — hogshead went wrong — leaped over an Embankment — came near Killing Scanlin —

Jack Armstrong & a man had a difficulty — Jack called him a liar — a son of a bitch — coward — &c. &c the man backed up to a wood pile — got a Stick — struck Jack a blow — felled him. Jack Armstrong was as strong as 2 men. Jack wanted to whip the man badly. At last they agreed to Compromise the Matter — Made Abe arbitrator — Abe said — "Well Jack what did you say to the man" Jack repeated what he had said — Lincoln then Said — Jack if you were a stranger in a strange place as this man is, and you were called a d—d liar &c — What would you do — Said "Jack hit by God." "Well then Jack." Said Lincoln "this man has done no more to you than you would have done to him. "Well Abes" — responded Jack "Its' all right." Jack took hold of the mans hand — shook it honestly — forgave the man — treated him &c —

Petersburg was laid of — Taylor's addition — Feby 17th 1836 — Surveyed by A Lincoln — Petersburg — Bennetts addition was laid off by A Lincoln — June 6th 1837 — Huron was surveyed by A Lincoln 6th July 1837.

(Petersburg Bennetts add was laid off by A Lincoln 6 June 1837
Huron d o   d o   do   6th July 1836)[2]
Petersburg was laid off Feby 17th 1836 — by A Lincoln
I. 397–321

LC: HW2690–92; HL: LN2408, 1:387–88

260. Stephen T. Logan (WHH interview)

Octr. 5th 1866

Judge Logan

Says that most of the original settlers that emigrated from Va to Ky crossed the Cumberland Mountain — sold waggons at foot of the Mountains — packed horses &c —

Crab Orchard is in Lincoln Co Ky —

Says further that Holland lies when he says that Clay snubbed Lincoln — was cold & aristocratic &c. and that L opposed Clay on that account.[1] The citizens of

---

1. See §127, note 13.
2. The matter in parentheses is on a separate slip attached to the document.

---

1. See Holland, 95–96.

Spgfd Ills had a meeting including the Members of the Legislature who wrote to Lincoln at Washington — or saw him in person & as it were instructed him to go for Taylor — The reason & only reason was that Clay could not be Elected and that Taylor could &c. Clay was in principal the only choice of the whigs of Ills. — That Taylor was their policy man

LC: HW2693; HL: LN2408, 2:208–9

261. John G. Kyle to WHH

Harrodsburg Ky., Oct — 8th 1866 —

Dear Sir:

Yours of inquiry in reference to the ancestors of President Lincoln was handed to me about a month ago by our post-master through whom it was Sent, and I have not replied Sooner because I have been endeavoring to get some information that might be of benefit to you —. I have not been able to learn any thing of the grand father of the late president, but I learn that President Lincoln's father lived at one time in what is now Boyle County Ky. which was formerly a part of our County, Mercer — I learn that Judge J. P. Mitchell of Danville Boyle Co. Ky — Knows more about President Lincoln ancestors than than any one in this section of the country — I have not been able to see him since the reception of yours, but I have this from those who have Conversed with him. I suggest that you write to him in reference to it, and say to him that I advised you to write to him and he will take pleasure in giving any information he may have — I learn that he frequently saw Pres. Lincoln while a boy. I think after the time that Pres. Lincoln's father lived in what is now Boyle Co. he lived in Hardin Co — K. the County Seat of which is Elizabethtown — I have frequently Seen this statement in the papers, and that the log house in which he lived still stands; though I believe I have seen some statement that it had been removed and was on exhibition somewhere — I will make further enquiry about the matter, and will write you any information I may gain —

Very truly,
John G. Kyle

ISHL: Weik Papers, box 1; HL: LN2408, 1:75–76

262. William G. Greene (WHH interview)

Octr 9th 1866

Wm Gren

I Know Jason Duncan well — Knew his wife — Miss Nancy Burner — well — was a good [clean?] girl — Duncan was quite a good physician — practiced in New Salem — This acquaintance with Duncan & wife in 1833 — possibly in 1832 — though not probable. Lincoln Knew the girl — Knew me — used to laugh at me — and at her — Lincoln never touched her in his life. This I Know — no man

Ever touched her —. Lincoln & I urged Duncan to Mary her & go off — They now live in MCComb Ills — or near their — are honest — virtuous & good — got rich by industry & Economy. Duncan was intellegent man — his wife was a clever girl — a handsome girl — not brilliant, but good. &c. &c

Lincoln beat Bill Kirkpatrick for Captain in the Black Hawk war —: it was not Thos. Kirkpatrick. Lincoln had halled logs for Bill K. K did not treat L well. when L beat K L said dam him, Ive beat him: he used me badly he [never?] settled for my toil —

   LC: HW3894; HL: LN2408, 1:389

263. George U. Miles (WHH interview)

Octr 9th 1866[1]

Maj G. U. Miles.

I Know all about the Lincoln Morris letter,[2] dated the 26th of March. 1843 —. Under its influence we in Menard got up a Convention of the People — had Lincoln's name before us — Morris & I were appointed delegates and were instructed to go for Lincoln and then for Hardin — Morris was taken Sick — Reigner was appointed in Morris' place. R belonged to me — would do as I wanted. Baker Kicked up at our first Convention — called the 2d & Lincoln was our choice & Hardin next as at first — I went up to Pekin — Lincoln was there — took me out & Said — "Other Counties have gone for me & are instructed for me if I'm a candidate — Ill be nominated the 1st ballot — My honor is out with Baker. I'd Suffer my right arm to be cut off before I'd violate it. It impossible for me to run. I, after the Nominations, will get up & decline and I want you to go for Baker. Menard — your two votes — will settle the question. Baker will be nominated. "But," I said, "I as well as Reigner am instructed to go for Hardin after you. and will suffer my right arm Cut off before I'll violate my instructions" So the matter Ended. Hardin was nominated. & Elected. Baker did not make a flaming speech[3]

   LC: HW2699; HL: LN2408, 1:392–93

   1. Date given in the docketing.
   2. AL to Martin S. Morris, *CW* 1:319–21.
   3. Written in the margin and then stricken: *after Hardin was nominated & Elected The Convention was struck — rose to its feet and Nominated Baker went to Galena — and this took Lincoln by surprise — and so it ended. Baker succeeded Hardin & Lincoln succeeded Baker —.* The phrase "went to Galena" is inserted with a caret and seems to have been intended as a parenthetical.

264. V. Hewitt to WHH[1]

Sarah Bush & Daniel Johnston were married on 13 Mar 1806   Would have written you before but have been *very* busy

V. Hewitt[2]

LC: HW2092; HL: LN2408, 1:76

265. Henry McHenry (WHH interview)

Octr 10th 1866

Henry McHenry

Says — I was present at the wrestle of Lincoln & Armstrong —: We tried to get Lincoln to tussel & scuffle with Armstrong. L refused — saying — I never tussled & scuffled & will not — don't like this wooling — & pulling —. Jack Armstrong was a powerful twister. At last we got them to wrestle: they took side holts — we bet Knives — whiskey — &c. L at last picked up Armstrong — swing him around — couldn't throw him — set him down — Saying — Jack let's quit — I can't throw you — you Can't throw me. Abe & Jack quit — were always good friends — Lincoln would have fought any or all of them if necessary.

You ought to see Rial Clary: he was with Lincoln out in the Black Hawk war —: he is a jolly good old fellow — is honest — truthful and has a wonderful Memory — I'll go out to night & bring him to town & then you can Examine him thoroughly

LC: HW2703; HL: LN2408, 1:391

266. Robert T. McNeely (WHH interview)

Oct. 10, 1866[1]

Robt. T. McNeely

Says — I Knew Lincoln in 1831 — Early. — Knew he was Elected to the Captaincy of a Company in Clary's Grove under the Malitia law of Ills — Know it was before the black Hawk war — was there & voted for Abe — Abe was absent in Spfgd when he was voted for — accepted the office as soon as informed of it.

LC: HW2704; HL: LN2408, 1:393

---

1. This note is at the bottom of a letter from WHH to "Mr. Clark" and dated October 4, 1866.
2. Hewitt was clerk of Hardin County, Kentucky.

---

1. Dated on the verso.

267. Mentor Graham (WHH interview)

Oct. 10, 1866[1]

Mentor Graham

Says that no foul or ill play was shown to Lincoln in his wrestle with Jack Armstrong — That it was an ordeal through which all Comers had to pass. Injustice has been done to the Clarry's Grove: that was settled up by a moral & intelligent set of people from East & South: they were gentlemen & ladies in Clary's Grove. The frolickers lived in little grove — about 1½ or 2 north of Clary's grove — ie — that is the Settlements were about that far apart —

LC: HW2704; HL: LN2408, 1:394

268. Johnson Gaines Greene (WHH interview)

Octr 10th 1866[1]

Gains Green

Says — I really do not Know who was the father of Miss _____ Child — Mrs. Jason Duncan:[2] Bill Green & Lincoln used to run the machine. They have Said in my presence that she was a handsome woman — had not much Sensse — had Strong passions — weak will — Strong desire to please & gratify friends — was a good woman. L & Green persuaded Jason Duncan to marry her and move off — did so — Duncan is a Yankee — good man — is respectable — So is his wife & Children — live in Illinois —

LC: HW3888; HL: LN2408, 1:390

269. Royal Clary (WHH interview)

[October 1866?]

Roil. A. Clary.

Aged 53 — Knew Abe Lincoln in June 1831.: he was clerking in the store for Offutt in New Salem — He was humorous — witty & good natured & that geniality drew him into our notice So quick — He liked to see sport going on — would wrestle — pitch iron bars — throw malls — sell goods —

it is about 2½ or 3 miles from Salem to the South East corner of Clary's Grove: it was settled up by good Moral men from south as Early as 1819 — the Eastern people came in 1830. Little grove was the place where all the devilment Came from. However all the grove was called Clary's grove. I Knew Jason Duncan: he was a doctor. He left in N. Salem in 1835 or 6 —: he married in Salem: he married Nancy Burner. I Knew Jack Kelso: he could could cach fish when no man could get a bite.

---

1. Dated on the verso.

---

1. Date given in the docketing.
2. Nancy Burner.

Lincoln boarded with Kelso: Knew Rowan Herndon & Jas. Herndon — were merchandising in N. Salem — They sold to Trent and Trent[1] to Lincoln — Jim Herndon sold to Trent & Row Herndon to Lincoln — sold out in 1832 & 1833. Lincoln & Berry sold goods — Green Kept grocery in the other end of the house — There were about 15 houses in N. Salem. Jack Armstrong and others did roll down a man or men down the hill at N.S. Old man Jourdon agreed to be rolled down the hill for a gallon of whiskey — Lincoln stopt it.

I went to the Black Hawk War: Lincoln was my Captain —: I joined at Beardstown — was drafted twice — escaped & still Volunteered — was 18 years old — They rendesvoused at Beardstown — Bill Kirkpatrick — he was our Quarter master. We were all mounted men — passed near Rushville — Encamped there 2 nights — Elected our officers — Col & Maj. Sam Thompson was our Col & Achilles Morris Major — passed near Macomb — thence in the north western direction to the Yellow Banks — Oquawgy is now near that place. Heare we drew provisions — it was on the Misssippi River — staid there 2 or 3 days. Whitesides was General. Buckmaster & Semple were his aids — We volunteered for 30 — I think: it may be 60 — The discharges, called for 48 days — We left the Yellow Banks — and went to Rock Island — Rock River & Island was all called one thing — Atchinson[2] took Command at Rock River. The Governor — Reynolds was with us & discharged when the time Expired. Atchchinson took Command at Rock Island. Rock Island — Fort Armstrong was 5 from Rock river. Atchinson belonged to the U.S. Army. We went from Rock Island for Dixon on the south side of Rock River — south side — on the Indian trail. This was about the 1st of May — I volunteered about 15 April. We stopt at Dixon about 5 days — waited for provisions to come up Rock River in boats — two boats — Here we met Stillman[3] with his squad a battalion. We had Captured 2 Indians, & it was Said we were within about 20 miles of Black Hawk: He — Stillman — went out reconnoitering — got scared — got badly whipt — for his rashness — Stillmans defeat took place about the 14th day of May in what the Indians Called "old mans creek" — The Indians were Encamped at Sycamore about 6 M north west of the old man creek — Stillmans men had Encamped on old mans creek — the advanced guard — spies or what not discovered Stillmans men — appeared on a hill — Stillman's men rushed on them — got frightened — Scared — and got badly whipt — Whites lost 12 Killed — found 11 — 25 were wounded —. They were horribly mangled — heads cut off — heart taken out — & disfigured in Every way. We went up to the battle ground the next day after the defeat of Stillman. We then left the battle ground and went back to Dixon — had no provisions — had had no provisions for 4 days — occasionally a Ear of Corn. Gen Henry was Maj. of the Spy battalion — an advanced guard — a look out as it were a spy — a good brave & noble man. We laid by after getting (3 or 4 day) provisions and proceeded on up to the

---

1. Martin S. and Alexander Trent apparently succeeded to the Berry-Lincoln store and its goods, rather than selling out to Lincoln as described here. See McKenzie.

2. Gen. Henry Atkinson.

3. Maj. Isaiah Stillman.

Stillman battle ground — the boats Came up to within 3 or 4 miles of the old man creek: the boats were discharged & went down to Rock River. We got provisions — packed our horse & having heard that the Indians had Committed depredations on *Fox* river — had killed some men women & Children we started for them — generally in a southerly direction — say south East — The Indians had gone — the Indians: they had Killed Davis & Pettigrews family — halls[4] 2 girls with them: they were young women. We Saw the Scalps they had taken — scalps of old women & children. This was near Pottowatomy village — farming place. The Indians Scalped an old Grand Mother — Scalped her — hung her scalp on a ram rod — that it might be seen & aggravate the whites — They cut one woman open — hung a child that they had murdered in the womans belly that they had gutted — strong men wept at this — hard hearted men Cried[5] — We staid here one night and proceed on for Ottowa on the Ills — went food & provisions — no roads — no bridges — no Conveniences — Bill Clary had 2 ox 2 yoke each teams — The ox teams did more good than a thousand horses: they could go through mud & mire — slosh & rain and do well — not so with horses. We couldn't follow the Indians for more than 3 or 4 days: it was impossible for our horses to carry man — gun — & his food — the horse — himself & his food through the muck & mire — swamp & brush. The horses gave out — wore litterally out — no grass — no nothing — too early for grass — in May — cold up there. The horses were jaded. The clothes of the men gave out — torn to pieces by briar & brush. We carried our tents on our horse — the poor horse carried everything: the baggage waggons Couldnt keep up — no roads — no bridges & no ways to travel — and hence the horses suffered all — and bore all. We were mustered out of Service at Ottowa about 28 or 29. The Govr Said "The mens times are up — horses jaded & worn out — men naked &c and they must be discharged & so wer were. He said he would send the Lieut Govr[6] for new men — He called on the men — all who could stay by possibility to stay 20 days more as a Kind of Guard — Abe re-enlisted for the 20 days — staid it out — Lincoln never got out of Ills — never got into the Wisconsin line — was in no battle — Demint[7] scoured the N. western part of Ills. Lincoln was with him —

In the Camps of the Evening we played Cards — sometimes — We were generally to tired & hungry to have sport & fun. An Indian came into Camp or was Caught by Doct Early's[8] Company and our boys thought he was a spy — sprang to our feet — was going to shoot the man — he had a line or Certificate from Cass. Lincoln jumped between our men & Indian and said we must not shed his blood — that it must not be on our Skirts — some one thought Lincoln was a coward because he was not savage: he said if any one doubts my Courage Let him try it.

---

4. Rachel and Sylvia Hall, two survivors of the massacre of the William Hall family, were kidnapped by the Indians and later released near Galena.

5. Neither Clary nor Lincoln saw the actual victims of this attack, but they apparently did see the scalps that Clary describes at an abandoned Pottawatomie village. See Whitney.

6. Lt. Gov. Zadoc Casey.

7. Maj. John Dement, in charge of a spy battalion. It appears doubtful that AL served with him.

8. Dr. Jacob M. Early of Springfield commanded the third Black Hawk War unit in which Lincoln served.

I saw the great wrestle between Lincoln & Dow Thompson from Sinclair Co. Ills. He threw Lincoln — Wrestled at Beardstown — wrestled thigh holds — first man that Ever[9]

LC: HW3850, HW3851, HW3854, HW3852, HW3853, HW3855; HL: LN2408, 1:370–75

270. Caleb Carman (WHH interview)

Petersburg Octr 12th 1866

Caleb Carman

— aged 62 — Knew Lincoln well — first knew him in Sangamon Town — 7 M North west of the city of Spgfd. Saw Abe work a flat boat — Broadwell sawed the lumber with an up right Saw — Steam Mill — There was no whip sawing of the boat plank —: it was sawed in a mill — Abe — long — tall & green — Cloathed in light blue Jeans — Coat & pants — round about Coat — Short one — trowsers short — not Strapt down. hat broad brim low wool hat. — Shoes. He was funny — joky — humorous — full of yarns — stories — rigs. &c —: he was frequently quoting poetry — reciting prose like orations —: had a Kind of Shantee — down on or near the river — Abe cooked — played seven up in the Camp after dark — Abe played a good game: he worked with the hands — Offutt — John Hanks & Jno Johnson were with Abe — they worked too — building the boat about Six weeks — Knew Abe in 1831 —. I was in the Indian war of 1828. or 9 — Abe was not out then — wasn't out in the Black Hawk war — Know no Evil — no wrong — no meanness — Am a democrat — opposed to Lincoln in politics, bitterly So — but loved the Man. Never saw him under the influence of liquor — took his dram with me when he felt like it — not often — His conduct to women & children was Kind and Condesending — I saw Abe at a show one night at Sangamon town — up stairs at my uncles — Jacob Carman: the Showman Cooked Eggs in Abes hat — Abe, when the man called for the hat Said — "Mr the reason why I didn't give you my hat before was out of respect to your Eggs — not care for my hat." Lincoln boarded with me one or two years at New Salem — Abe was boarding with me when he went to the Legislature in 1834: he was P.M — not deputy — went from Springfield in Carriage — don't think he ever walked to Spgfd to borrow Law Book: he lived at my house when he studied law first — as I understand it: he never intended to learn the black smith trade: this story I know to be a humbug: he surveyed in 1834 — surveyed Petersburg — boarded then with me —: he merchandised in N. Salem before I got there — He Kept grocery too before I got down from Sangamon town. I lived in the house in which Berry & Lincoln Kept grocery — New Salem laid off East & west — running on the back of the hill — about 25 — or 30 houses — all gone but one —: he bottomed — Lincoln did — some chairs for me in 1834 & 1831 — One Morning I Saw Abe up Early with an axe on his shoulder — I said to him — "Abe what in the devil are you going to do" "I'll tell you directly" said Abe he went in

---

9. Clary apparently means the first man that ever threw Lincoln.

the woods — cut down 2 hickory sapplings — peeled off the Course outer bark — peeled off the clean tender inner bark and with it bottomed my chairs. Abe ceased boarding with me in 1836 & 7. Abe was very good Kind & courteous to children & women — was sometimes sociable with men — Seen him Survey many times — he often to my own Knowledge attended law cases before Justices of the Peace in & near Salem from 1834 to 1837 — He loved Burns' poetry — Shakespear — and some few other books — read the News papers of the day — the Sangamon Journal & Mo Republican & Louisville Journal: He was always quoting Poetry — singing songs— "Old Suekey blue Skin"[1] — Quote Speeches — orations — Make good Speeches to — wrote deeds — contracts — agreements &c for the neighbors & Charged them nothing — He was a good reader rather than a "much reader" as the Indian would Say: what he read he read thoroughly & well & never forgot it. He frequently visited from 1833 — to 1837. young ladies — he Courted Miss Rutledge: she moved down the river a few miles before I got to Salem. He went to see & Courted Miss Owens about 1835 — or — 1836   She was frequently at my house & Abe would gallant her down to Abels[2] about 2 M down the River. It is said that she came all the way from Ky to get Lincoln. This I Know nothing about — but doubt. Miss Owen was a handsome woman — a fine looking woman — was Sharp — Shrewd and intellectual I assure you   Miss Rutledge was a pretty woman — good natured — kind — wasn't as smart as Miss Owens by a heap. Mentor Graham — and the Greens helped Abe in Grammar — Graham aided him exclusing in Surveying —. I don't remember any jokes about Abe — I Know he sat up late at night and studied hard — rose tolerably Early. Abe ate mechanically — very moderately — didn't seem to Care much what was Set before him — So it was clean. I Knew John A. Kelso: he was a School Master: well educated — loved Shakespear and fishing above all other thing. Abe loved Shakespear but not fishing — still Kelso would draw Abe: they used to sit on the bank of the river and quote Shakespear — criticise one an other. Kelso lives now as I understand in Mo. Kelso, if at himself is a good Shakesperian Schollar for a western man. — think he was a Kentuckian — I say to you that from 1832. or 3 to 1838 — that Lincoln studied law — Studied, Surveying and general politics — was member of the legislature 3 times from New Salem — probably twice and part of an other term. I think Abels frame house was built down under the hill — and not on the top of it: it was a log house on the hill that Lincoln used to see Miss Owens in according to my recollection — Lincoln was Sometimes Sad — was deeply reflective — Sometimes it seemed to me a mix'd State of abstraction & Sadness. His clothing in the winter was Jeans & linnen generally in the Summer. Lincoln never hunted much: he was no hunter — loved sports — threw malls — large pieces of iron — jump — pitch quoits — dollars — never gambled — probably attended horse races — I never saw him at one — played old sledge for fun, and drank his dram occasionally when he wanted it. His friends forced

---

1. A Negro minstrel song, also known as "Zip Coon." See Lair, 50–51.
2. Bennett and Elizabeth Abell.

him to drink Sometimes and possibly he never would have touched it but for his friends — He used to worry — tire himself down at Study & work at Salem — would retire to Armstrongs — Shorts — Grahams & other places to get recruited —

LC: HW2706–10; HL: LN2408, 1:357–62

271. John McNamar (WHH interview)

Oct. 16*th* 1866.

Mr. McNamar of Menard Co. tells me that Lincoln in 1832 to 1834 took the Louisville Journal, and the Sangamon Journal, and Hill & Bale took the Mo. Republican and Cincinnatti Gazette.

Herndon.

HL: LN2408, 2:403

272. George Spears to WHH

Tallula Ills Oct 17th 1866

Dear Sir

yours of the 17th inst came Safe to hand but I was absent from home in the State of Missouria at the time it came so that I now hasten to answer your enquiries   My first acquaintance with Mr Linken was whilst in a Dry goods Store with a man by the name of Offit[1] he was Clerk   the Nex thing he was engaged in for a short time he was Postmaster   Then him & Berry engaged in a Dry Goods Store & I think they got their Goods of Blankenship though I am not positive   Row & James Herndon wer in Buisiness a bout that time   whether he Bought them out or not I cant say   as for the Grocery that Greene Speaks of   I think it was so but I do not know whether Lincoln ever attended   I think not   he about that time he went into the Black Hawk war & whilst absent Berry Squandered evry thing & left Lincoln flat   it always was a mistory to me why a man of Mr Lincoln integrity would enter in to partnership with such a caractor   Poor Lincoln he was honest & manly   the next then in Lincolns Life he came home from the Black Hawk war & we Elected him County Surveyor   Served in that capacity 2 years & then Elected him to the Legislator   after that as yo know he went to Springfield & commenced the study of Law

Respectfully yours

George Spears

LC: HW2714; HL: LN2408, 1:428–29

---

1. Denton Offutt.

273. David Turnham to WHH

Dale Ind Oct 19th 1866

Friend Herndon

Yours of the 5th inst is at hand. Abe Lincoln was a Jackson man when he left here. turned whig in Illionoi. I wrote you this however in my last. The maiden name of Abe's Mother was Hanks. This Old Mr Sparrow married her Sister. Mr & Mrs Sparrow Died in Indiana and was buried on the Same ground that Mrs Lincoln (Abe's Mother) was buried on, Sometime afterward. Mr & Mrs Hanks the father & Mother of Mrs Lincoln never came to this State and of course did not die here.

Mr Hall & Wife[1] moved to Ill about the Same time that Lincoln did but what part of the State I do not know.

I was acquainted with Ben Romine. He was a farmer and lived on the River about Eighteen miles from Lincoln's   He was an intelligent man, but I do not think he knew anything about Surveying.[2] and he and Abe Lincoln were not together a great deal   I have no knowledge of Abe ever undertaking a Study with him. I do not think Abe ever Studied Surveying while he was here, but the Book you have may have been his.

Abe's Mother, Dennis Hanks' Mother & Mrs Sparrow were Sisters. This Hall married Dennis Hanks' Mother after he (Dennis) was born. They Surely moved away from here about the time the Lincolns did.

Yours Respectfully

David Turnham

LC: HW2715; HL: LN2408, 1:205–6

274. James W. Grimes to WHH

Burlington, Iowa, Oct. 20, 1866

My dear Sir

Mr. Lincoln did visit Burlington in the Autumn of 1858 and spoke to a very large assembly of our people much to their satisfaction & delight. No man ever addressed an audience here who was abler to make such an impression upon them as Mr. Lincoln did on that occasion. He remained over Sunday at my house & started on Monday morning towards Quincy where he was to meet Mr. Douglas in debate, speaking however, if I remember right at two or three intermediate places.

I have some letters of Mr. Lincolns but they are ordinary business letters and of no general interest to any one

I am very truly

Your Obdt. Servt,

James W. Grimes.

LC: HW2716; HL: LN2408, 2:448

---

1. Turnham seems to be confusing two Halls. Levi Hall and Nancy Hanks Hall, AL's aunt, died in Indiana. Their son, Squire Hall, married AL's stepsister, Matilda Johnston, and they moved to Illinois with the Lincolns in 1831.

2. See §243, note 3.

275. William G. Greene to WHH

Home Oct 24th 1866

Sir

yours of 17th Inst at hand   I am not able to positivly say whether James &
Rowan Herendon sold Lincoln & Berry any Goods or Groceries   my *Impression*
is that they did *not*   I think they sold their stock to Nelson Alley —

I *posiitively* did buy of R. Radford his stock of Groceries by the *lump* say $400,
on six months time & re sold them the same day to Lincoln & Berry for $650,
which *transaction* was Mr Lincolns first or maden effort in trade   it matters not
who may *tell* or *write* you to the *contrary* Jason Duncan lives at or near McComb
in McDonath Co. Ills

Truly
W. G. Greene.

LC: HW2718; HL: LN2408, 1:430

276. A. D. Wright to WHH

Petersburg, Oct. 26th 1866.

Mr. Neely has just shown me your letter to him — making some enquiry how
Lincoln carried sail early in his salem life. And Z. C. Inghram Esq. was here, who
was intimately acquainted with Lincoln nearly three years, ending Oct. 1834. Mr.
I. is a man on whose statement you may rely — Has a very retentive memory —
and has fund of amusing Lincolnia anecdotes. Inghram is the very man you want.
He lives in St Louis where you may write to him.

Yours
A. D. Wright.

Jack Kelso lives in the N.W. county in Mo.

Mr. Ingraham is now, and will be absent from St Louis until the middle or last of
next month.

HL: LN2408, 1:431–32

277. James W. Grimes to WHH

Burlington, Iowa. Oct. 28.th 1866

My dear Sir

Yours of the 23d inst is at hand. I have looked in vain for Mr. Lincolns old
letters. As they were of no special importance at the time they were written and
being upon subjects of no lasting importance *[*/?]* probable that I did not attempt
to preserve them, though I have always been in the habit of preserving my letters.

I have no knowledge that mr. Lincoln was ever in Iowa more than once. He
came here from Oquawka Ill. on the Saturday preceeding the 13th Oct. 1858 and

spoke in my [hall?] to an audience of not less than two thousand people. I need not say that he made a deep impression upon his audience for he always did that   No man ever addressed an Iowa audience who so won the hearts of those who listened to him. Mr. Lincoln remained at my house over Sunday which was a very *[*/?]* & left on Monday morning to resume his canvass in Ill. I had read his debates with Mr. Douglass up to that time & we frankly discussed & criticized the points made by each of the disputants. I insisted that he suffered Mr. Douglass to put him too much on the defensive, — that he should assume the aggressive & attack his adversary in turn, — that it was useless to defend himself against Mr. Douglass' charges, for, as one would be refuted another would be trumped up. During the afternoon he called for writing materials & said he would go to his room & to prepare his speech to be delivered at Quincy two or three days afterwa[rds. In] about an hour or an hour and a half he returned from his chamber with half a sheet of paper in his hand upon which he had noted down the heads of the speech he intended to make at that place & which upon reading his speech made there I was satisfied was the same prepared in my house.

I believe my dear sir, that this is all I know of Mr. Lincolns visit to Iowa worthy of comment

I am very truly

Your obdt — servt —

James W. Grimes

LC: HW2719–20; HL: LN2408, 2:356–57

278. J. Rowan Herndon to WHH

Quincy Oct 28th 66

Sir

i Recievd yours of the 16th Some time Since and Now ancer with peasur   1   i ancer By Saying that i was acquntd With all the Men that you Name Sincho Hill. Baile — Bill Gren E C Blankinship Rewben Radford & Jim Short

2   James Herndon Sold his intrust to Wm Berry and i Sold to A Lincoln Something Like Six weks or 2 moths after Bery Bought from James Herndon   the Goods Cosisted of a Small asortment of Dry Goods & Grcrys that Was Perchse of E C Blakinship By My Self & James Herndon and Sold as above Stated taken ther Notes Seperate James takin Berys and i Lincolns those Notes was asind to E C Blaknship — Lincoln & Bery Sold to two Brothers By the Name of Trent and they Rann off Leavng Lincoln the Burden to Bar as Berry Dide soon after

3   i think that Radford Sold to Green & Loid[1] — iff thay Sold to Berry & Lincoln i Never Knew it   Lincoln & Bery desolved When thay Sold to the 2 Trents

---

1. Possibly Tarleton Lloyd, a resident of nearby Rock Creek.

4th   Lincoln & Bery oned a small Dry gods Store in 1832 & 3 — 5th iff he Ever had any thing to Doe with a Whisky Shop i Never Knw it   i am shure he Did Knot own any With Bery — as to the Speach in 1832 i think it Was that it was Late and his first attempt and after the fight — ther was many speakers & he was Last

i have ancerd to the Best of Knowledge at Present
Yours Truly
J R Herndon.

NB Capt Josef Artus says had you of ancerd his Leter he Might have Given you many incidents that transprd on the Boat as they Came up the River   Pet Van-Burgin[2] was on Bord   You Mite See van and it may yet Be Worth Wile to Write him — your hand Writng is very hard to Read   Excuse my Not Writng Soner as my helth is vry Bad at Present
J, R, H

LC: HW2721–22; HL: LN2408, 1:441–43

279. Annie E. Jonas to WHH

Quincy Ills Oct 28th 1866.

Dear Sir

I am ashamed to confess the error I made in copying the letter I forwarded to you marked "Confidential"; of course the letter was dated, as the contents (for availability before the election) would indicate — 1860.[1] My apology for apparent careleness, is must also extenuate the seeming negligence of not having replied to your enquiry before — my time is not at my own command, and consequently I copied; as I now write in a room full of talkers — I shall be only too happy to do any-thing in my limited power to aid you, in your labor of love; but if your request was made in the principal papers, of the largest circulation, in the cities; unheard of letters might be brought to light — In our locality we have only seen your request once in the NY Tribune — I delayed sending you copies of the letters I had, in order to obtain a couple from New Orleans; having failed to obtain them, I will at least tell you the story of them; which you can make use of, if you like — E[i]ther in the winter of 1856, or the spring of /57 some colored man from Springfield, went to St Louis, and hired himself — (for what special service I forget —) as a hand on a lower Missisippi boat — arriving at New Orleans, without free papers; he having been born free — he was subjected to the tyranny of the black code — all the more stringently enforced, because of the late excitement

---

2. Peter Van Bergen.

---

1. *CW* 4:85–86.

attendant upon the Fremont campaign, and thrown into prison until the boat left; Then, as no one was especially interested in him, he was forgotten. After a certain length of time, established by law, he would inevitably have been sold into slavery to defray prison expenses had not Mr — [L]incoln heard of it, and written to a brother of mine, a young lawyer — to get him out, and charge the expense incurred to him; My brother did so, but he now writes me that the only person who accepted remuneration for his services, was the *now* "radical" Col — A. P. Field. My brother was a rebel, and upon my asking for Mr Lincoln's letters for you — answered that with other papers they were *stolen* from his office by some U.S. Quarter-master, whom he hoped to discover through his forwarding the letters to you. I too hope the letters will find their way to you, though as they were in the office of the Lt Gov — (Hyams) of the state, I should [s]ay both Office, and papers were [ta]ken *"possession of."* Pardon me, if I have been waarisome, but if the letters come to you, you will know their story, I am afraid they were destroyed. You are not kind in denying us letter forwarders the privalege of paying our own postage, Respectfully

Annie E. Jonas

ISHL: Weik Papers, box 1; HL: LN2408, 2:316–17

280. Mary Owens Vineyard to WHH

Weston Mo. October 29th 1866.

Mr. W. H. Herndon:

Please let me know what are your motives and intentions, for asking the questions you have, relative to my lamented Husband; because I could not for a moment entertain the idea, of my married name appearing in that history.

The House was a frame, and set upon the hill. My education was thoroughly english, and was received at Nazareth near Bardstown Ky.

Respectfully
(Mrs. Vinyard)

HL: LN2408, 1:443

281. Robert B. Rutledge to WHH

Burlington Iowa Oct 30th 1866

Dear Sir

your letter of 27th inst is Received, and in answer have to say that I cannot give dates, as to the arrival of Kelso, or his leaving N Salem, or his whereabouts, nor can I give the desired information of Dr. Duncan   Recollect both the men very well, but so long a time has intervened, that I cannot give dates, but they were in New Salem in the years of 1832 & 1833,

In answer to 3d question, My Father & John Cameron built the New Salem Mill in 1828 & 1829, he moved from N. Salem to Concord neighborhood in 1834,

Ann Rutledge died Aug 25th 1835, I will forward my answer to your letter of recent date in a few days as I have it ready, as soon as I can get it transcribed in a legible hand.

I fully appreciate the importance of the answers to your questions, Have compared notes with parties who were eye witnesses to the incidents related, Have Just returned from Madison Co, some 200, miles west of this place, & compared notes with John Jones formily of Menard Co Ill, who fully coroborates my statements.

would be very happy to visit you, but business engagements forbid at present, Hope to see you after I get moved to Oskaloosa, to which place I will move inside of ten days, and to which place you will address me in the future,

Will be highly gratified to Receive a copy of your lecture,

believe me Dear Sir very truly   your friend
R. B. Rutledge

LC: HW2723–24; HL: LN2408, 1:433–34

282. Robert B. Rutledge to WHH

[ca. November 1, 1866]

Dear Sir

Believing that any authentic statements connected with the early life and history of the beloved Abraham Lincoln should belong to the great American people, I submit the following replies to the interrogatories contained in your recent letter. I trust largely to your courtesy as a gentleman, to your honesty and integrity as a historian, and to your skill in writing for the public, to enlarge wherever my statements seem obscure, and to condense and remove whatever seems superfluous. Above all I trust to your honor and your sense of right and consistency, to exclude from print anything which in your judgment may injuriously affect the surviving actors in the great drama which you propose to re-enact once more.

Many of my statements are made from memory with the aid of association of events; and should you discover that the date, location and circumstances, of the events here named should be contradictory to those named from other sources, I beg you to consider well the testimony in each case, and make up your history from those statements, which may appear to you best fitted to remove all doubt as to their correctness.

You ask 1st When did you first become acquainted with Lincoln, where was it, and what was he doing?

I answer. In the year 1830 or 1831 in the town of New Salem Illinois. He was at that time a clerk in the store of Denton Offatt having just returned with Offatt from New Orleans with whom he had gone on a flat boat as a hand to that city. At that time he boarded with John Cameron, a partner of my father in laying out the town of New Salem, and in building a mill on the Sangamon river. At that period New Salem was a small village of not more than ten or fifteen families, who lived in log cabins, and who were as sociable and familiar as persons are, who find themselves thus isolated from the great world outside. The mill was a saw and grist mill — was the first one built on the Sangamon river, and supplied a large section of country with its meal, flour and lumber. At times when it was necessary to construct a dam to afford the proper water power, word would be sent through the neighborhood and the people would come ten and fifteen miles *en masse,* and assist gratuitously in the work.

On such occasions Mr Lincoln was ever ready to work with his stalwart hand, and to assist in constructing or repairing the dams or mill, raising houses in the village &c, and this too when he had no personal interest in the success of the enterprise.

This is mentioned here as an illustration of the generosity and nobleness of the settlers at that early day. It also shows an element of the character of the people among whom Mr. Lincoln received his first impressions and may assist in proving that he was then, and why he always appeared afterwards, one of the people, and an ardent sympathizer with the masses.

It has been stated that Mr Offatt owend or had an interest in the mill and that Mr Lincoln was employed to assist in taking care of the new enterprise. This is a mistake — James Rutledge and John Cameron partners, first commenced erecting a mill on Concord creek about six miles below New Salem, where they owned the land, but large inducements being offered and the proprietors fearing a scarcity of water removed to New Salem in 1828 and built the mill and laid out the town. Neither Mr Lincoln or Mr Offatt had any pecuniary interest in it. It belonged solely to Rutledge and Cameron and Mr Lincoln only assisted in repairing it as other neighbors did, gratuitously. He was at this time the clerk of Mr Offatt who Kept a general country store including dry-goods, groceries, and all the varieties which belong to such an establishment

You ask 2nd   Did he board with you — Your father and family — how long — when — and all about it.

On Mr Lincolns arrival at New Salem he boarded with John Cameron along with Offatt. He afterwards boarded with my father, during the years 1833 & 1834 as appears, from papers still in possession of the family. I am satisfied he boarded with us both prior and subsequent to the years named, but so long a time has intervened that I cannot fix the date with precise certainty.

You ask 3rd. In regard to my father and the family.

My father was born in South Carolina, removed to Kentucky and from thence to White Co Illinois in 1816. The first three children Jane, John and Ann were born in Kentucky, the later six were born in Illinois — David. Robert, Nancy and Margaret born in White Co, and William and Sarah in Sangamon Co. My father removed to Sangamon Co in 1825 and died in Menard Co which was formerly a part of Sangamon Co Decr 3rd 1835

4th   You make some pertinent inquiries concerning my sister and the relations which existed between herself and Mr Lincoln. My sister Ann was born January 7th 1813 and died August 25th 1835. She was born in Kentucky and died in Menard Co Ills. In 1830 my sister being then but 17 years of age a stranger calling himself John McNeil came to New Salem. He boarded with Mr Cameron and was keeping a store with a Samuel Hill. A friendship grew up between McNeil and Ann which ripened apace and resulted in an engagement to marry — McNeil's real name was McNamar. It seems that his father had failed in business and his son, a very young man had determined to make a fortune, pay off his father's debts and restore him to his former social and financial standing. With this view he left his home clandestinely, and in order to avoid pursuit by his parents changed his name. His conduct was strictly hightoned, honest and moral, and his object, whatever any may think of the deception which he practised in changing his name, entirely praiseworthy.

He prospered in business and pending his engagement with Ann, he revealed his true name, returned to Ohio to relieve his parents from their embarrassments, and to bring the family with him to Illinois. On his return to Ohio, several years having elapsed, he found his father in declining health or dead, and perhaps the circumstances of the family prevented his immediate return to New Salem. At all events he was absent two or three years.

In the mean time Mr Lincoln paid his addresses to Ann, continued his visits and attentions regularly and those resulted in an engagement to marry, conditional to an honorable release from the contract with McNamar. There is no kind of doubt as to the existence of this engagement David Rutledge urged Ann to consummate it, but she refused until such time as she could see McNamar — inform him of the change in her feelings, and seek an honorable release.

Mr Lincoln lived in the village, McNamar did not return and in August 1835 Ann sickened and died. The effect upon Mr Lincoln's mind was terrible; he became plunged in despair, and many of his friends feared that reason would desert her throne. His extraordinary emotions were regarded as strong evidence of the existence of the tenderest relations between himself and the deceased. McNamar however, returned to Illinois in the fall after Ann's death.

5th. Ann was as before stated 17 years old in 1830. My age at the same time was 12. She went to school to Minter Graham, who was a successful and popular teacher, in 1832 and 1833. My sister was esteemed the brightest mind of the family, was studious, devoted to her duties of whatever character, and possessed a remarkably amiable and lovable disposition. She had light hair and blue eyes.

6th *Question* — I have already written you in relation to my acquaintance with Samuel Hill, Offatt , Green & others. Perhaps too much credit is awarded William Green for Mr Lincoln's Knowledge of grammar. Mr Lincoln clerked for Offatt in 1831 & 1832. James Rutledge owend an interest in a grocery in New Salem — a remnant of a stock belonging to Rutledge and Sinco.[1] Sinco bought a lot of horses, took them south and broke up, Rutledge sold out to Lincoln and Wm

---

1. Henry Sinco.

Berry. Mr Lincoln only had possession a very short time and never gave it his personal attention. He soon sold out to Berry — who gave his note to Lincoln for
the amount, who paid Rutledge with Berry's note Soon after Berry failed and after awhile Lincoln came to Rutledge and Made him a tender to pay half the note.
This Rutledge utterly refused to accept from Mr L, alleging that he had taken
Berry's note for the debt and if he could not make it out of him, he would not
accept it at all. About this time Mr Lincoln was employed in surveying, he having
learned the science, and being engaged in a good business in the profession.

7th   My father moved to and laid out the town of New Salem in the sum-
mer of 1829. I moved in 1836 with my mother and elder brother from Menard
Co to Fulton Co Illinois, and from thence in the fall of 1837 to Van Buren Co
Iowa. My father was born in South Carolina May 11th 1781, and died in Menard
Co Illinois December 3rd 1835, being about 54 years of age.

8th   I cannot give you a satisfactory reply to many items embraced in this
inquiry for the lack of dates or circumstances corroborating them. Many things
said of him and done by him are indellibly fixed in my mind but the absence of
the proper surroundings impels me to withhold them.

Mr Lincoln studied Kirkham's Grammar — the valuable copy which he delighted to peruse is now in my possession.[2] He also studied Natural Philosophy,
Astronomy, Chemistry &c. He had no regular teacher, but perhaps received more
assistance from Minter Graham than any other person. He could be seen usually
when in pursuit of his ordinary avocations with his book under his arm; at a
moment of leisure he would open it, study, close it and recite to himself. When in
young company he has been Known to excite the most uproarious laughter by
singing the tune called "Legacy" in the "Missouri Harmony" substituting the words
"Old Gray" for "Red Grape". The effect is very ludicrous as any one can see by
reference to the lines quoted.[3]

His enjoyment of a joke was very intense; and all that has been said in truth of
his disposition is no exaggeration.

About the year 1832 or 1833 Mr Lincoln made his first effort at public speaking. A debating club of which James Rutledge was President was organized and
held regular meetings — as he arose to speak his tall form towered above the little
assembly. Both hands were thrust down deep in the pockets of his pantaloons. A
perceptible smile at once lit up the faces of the audience for all anticipated the
relation of some humorous story. But he opened up the discussion in splendid style
to the infinite astonishment of his friends. As he warmed with his subject his hands
would forsake his pockets and would enforce his ideas by awkward gestures; but
would very soon seek their easy resting place. He pursued the question with reason and argument so pithy and forcible that all were amazed. The President at his
fireside after the meeting remarked to his wife that there was more in Abe's head

---

2. See §6, note 7.
3. *The Missouri Harmony; or, A Choice Collection of Psalm Tunes, Hymns, and Anthems* (1820). The verse
in question: "Bid her not shed one tear of sorrow / To sully a heart so brilliant and light; / But balmy drops
of the red grape borrow / To bathe the relief from morn till night."

than wit and fun, that he was already a fine speaker; that all he lacked was culture to enable him to reach the high destiny which he Knew was in store for him. From that time Mr Rutledge took a deeper interest in him.

Soon after Mr Rutledge urged him to announce himself as a candidate for the Legislature. This he at first declined to do, averring that it was impossible to be elected. It was suggested that a canvass of the County would bring him prominently before the people and in time would do him good. He reluctantly yielded to the solicitations of his friends and made a partial canvass. The result, though he was defeated was highly gratifying to him and astonished even his most ardent admirers.

At the next election he was placed as a candidate for Assembly on the regular Whig ticket, and was triumphantly elected in a district profoundly Democratic.

In illustration of his goodness and nobleness of heart, the following incident is related:

"Ab Trout," a poor barefooted boy was engaged one cold winter day in chopping a pile of logs from an old house or stable which had been pulled down. The wood was dry and hard and the boy was hard at work, when Lincoln came up and asked what he got for the job, and what he would do with the money? "Ab" said $1.00 and pointing to his naked feet said, "A pair of shoes." Abe told him to go in and warm and he would chop a while for him. The boy delayed a little, but Lincoln finished the work, threw down his axe and told him to go and buy the shoes.[4] "Ab" remembered this act with the liveliest gratitude. Once, he, being a cast iron Democrat, determined to vote against his party and for Mr Lincoln; but the friends as he afterwards said with tears in eyes made him drunk and he had voted against Abe. Thus he did not even have an opportunity to return the noble conduct of Mr Lincoln by this small measure of thanks.

In the early times of which we write an appeal was often made to physical strength to settle controversies. To illustrate this feature of the society in which Mr Lincoln was mingling it may be well to relate an incident.

Two neighbors, Henry Clark and Ben Wilcox had had a lawsuit. The defeated declared that although he was beaten in the suit, he could whip his opponent. This was a formal challenge and was at once carried to the ears of the victor — Wilcox — and as promptly accepted. The time, place and seconds were chosen with due regularity — Mr Lincoln being Clark's and John Brewer Wilcox's second. The parties met, stripped themselves all but their breeches, went in and Mr Lincoln's principal was beautifully whipped. These combats were conducted with as much ceremony and punctiliousness as ever graced the duelling ground. After the conflict the seconds conducted their respective principals to the river washed off the blood, and assisted them to dress. During this performance, the second of the party opposed to Mr Lincoln remarked — "Well Abe, my man has whipped yours, and I can whip you." Now this challenge came from a man who was very small in size.

---

4. *Ab Trent* is written in the margin next to the name *Ab. Trout.* Cf. Reep, 67, where the boy is called Ab Trent. See also §378, where the boy's name is given as Wadkins.

Mr Lincoln agreed to fight provided he would "chalk out his size on Mr Lincoln's person, and every blow struck outside of that mark should be counted foul". After this sally there was the best possible humor and all parties were as orderly as if they had been engaged in the most harmless amusement.

In all matters of dispute about horse-racing or any of the popular pastimes of the day, Mr Lincoln's Judgement was final to all that region of country. People relied implicitly upon his honesty, integrity, and impartiality.

Very soon after Mr Lincolns coming to New Salem and while clerking for Offatt, Offatt made a bet with William Clary that Abe could throw down in a wrestle any man in the county. This bet was taken, and Jack Armstrong, a rough, and the best fighter in Sangamon, was pitted against him. The match took place in front of Offatt's store. All the men of the village and quite a number from the surrounding country were assembled Armstrong was a man in the prime of life, square built, muscular and strong as an ox. The contest began and Jack soon found so worthy an antagonist that he "broke his holt," caught Abe by the leg, and would have brought him to the ground, had not Mr Lincoln seized him by the throat and thrust him at arms length from him. Jack having played foul, there was every prospect of a general fight. At this time James Rutledge having heard of the difficulty, ran into the crowd and through the influence which he exerted over all parties, succeeded in quieting the disturbance and preventing a fight.

His physical strength proved of vast utility to him in his many arduous labors, up to the time he became President, and a man of less iron frame, would have sunk under the enormous burdens laid upon him during four years, marked by Executive cares that have no parallel in history.

After this wrestling match Jack Armstrong and his crowd became the warmest friends and staunchest supporters of Mr Lincoln.

This Jack Armstrong was father of the boy, who was some years afterwards arrested and tried for the murder of young Metzger,[5] and who was voluntarily defended and cleared by Mr Lincoln. The account of this remarkable trial is already before the public and it is not necessary that I should repeat it here —

Mr Lincoln never forgot the friends with whom he was associated in early life. Soon after his nomination for the Presidency, some grand-children of James Rutledge circulated the report that Mr Lincoln had left their grandfathers house without paying his board bill. These boys were reared under copperhead influences and continued in the faith during the war. This slanderous report reached the ears of Mrs Rutledge widow of James Rutledge and whom he always called "Aunt Polly". She took immediate steps to correct the infamous libel and caused a letter to be written Mr Lincoln. Mr Lincoln at once wrote Mrs Rutledge expressing his thanks for her Kindness and the interest manifested in his behalf, recurring with warm expressions of remembrance to the many happy days spent under her roof.

While Mr Lincoln was engaged in surveying he wore jeans pantaloons "foxed" or covered on the forepart and below the Knees behind with buckskin. This add-

5. For other testimony about this case, see the index.

ed to the warmth, protected against rain and rendered them more durable in performing the labor necessary to his calling. His other clothing was such as worn by all the inhabitants of the village.

Trials of strength were very common among the pioneers. Lifting weights, as heavy timbers piled one upon another was a favorite pastime, and no workman in the neighborhood could at all cope with Mr Lincoln in this direction. I have seen him frequently take a barrel of whiskey by the chimes and lift it up to his face as if to drink out of the bung-hole.

This feat he could accomplish with the greatest ease. I never saw him taste or drink a drop of any kind of spiritous liquors

I am Very Respectfully
Yours &c.
R. B. Rutledge

I have omitted an incident in the early life of Mr Lincoln which I will here relate

The only man who was ever successful in bringing Lincoln to the ground in a wrestle was Lorenzo D Thompson, a very large and powerful man. This match took place at Beardstown Ills, the general rendezvous while waiting for orders to march against Black Hawk and his warriors — In this match Lincoln was taken by surprise and in the first trial Thompson brought him to the ground but in two successive matches Lincoln came off victorious[6]

R. B. R.

(Copy)

Wintersett Iowa   Oct 22nd 1866.

Having seen the statements made by R B Rutledge in reference to the early life of Abraham Lincoln and having Known Mr Lincoln & been an eye-witness to the events as narrated, from my boyhood, I take pleasure in saying they are literally true.

As to the relation existing between Mr. Lincoln and Ann Rutledge, I have every reason to believe that it was of the tenderest character, as I Know of my own Knowledge that he made regular visits to her. — During her last illness he visited her sick chamber and on his return stopped at my house. It was very evident that he was much distressed. I was not surprised when it was rumored subsequently that his reason was in danger. It was generally understood that Mr Lincoln and Ann Rutledge were engaged to be married. She was a very amiable & lovable woman and it was deemed a very suitable match — one in which the parties were in every way worthy of each other

(Signed) John Jones

LC: HW2923–37; HL: LN2408, 1:306–23

---

6. For other versions of AL's wrestling match with Thompson, see the index.

283. John B. Weber (WHH interview)

Pawnee — Sangamon Co Ills. [ca. Nov. 1, 1866[1]]

Jno B. Webber — Aged 57

I was born in virginia in Shepherdstown Jefferson Co. Va on the Potomac   I Came to Ills in 1836 — april in my 27th year. I Knew Mr Lincoln in 1836 — heard him make a Speech against Doct Jacob Early Jno Calhoun — Martin Van Buren. I may or not have been a voter at that time — July or Aug, but voted in Nov. The Speech that Mr Lincoln made — in 1836 was made in the old Court House where the State house now Stands —. I think Van Buren — was a Candidate — so was Hugh L. White — Harrison &c. They in this section united under the *White* Ticket. The Democracy that day spoke through Doct Early — Jno Calhoun & others. I was a democrat at that time. Douglas was not yet among us. He was then in Jacksonville, but soon Came to the Capital: he favored the removal of the Capitol from Vandalia to Springfd. The Speech that Lincoln made was made on the current politics of the day and Especially against Doct Early. Lincoln was the best Speaker. that dy. I thought & felt that day that Lincoln was a young man of Superior intellect: he polite & courteous — debated the ability & honesty — more so than other politicians of the dy. His candor & fairness — his Courtesy gained my Confidence.

Soon after this Mr Lincoln & I became near neighbors & intimate friends. Mr Lincoln in 1836 and Came to Springfield in the Spring of 1837. As I understand it Mr Lincoln sat down to Study law in Earnest and soon went into partnership with Jno T. Stuart. I don't remember any political discussion in 1838, Sufficiently Certain to speak of any one man — I heard all the discussions as I Suppose, but do not remember them distinctly. I Couldn't stay away from Political discussions — Such was my temperament. Before I go further let me sy that my printing my bros press was mobbed by a gang of men in 1838 or 9. Douglas wrote the article that Caused the Mob. After the Capital was moved to Springfield *in fact* — which was in 1839 — Decr. the Senate Sat in the Methodist Church — and the House sat in the new — 2d presbyterian Church. Mr Douglas I think Came to Springfield permanently so in 1838 — Came as the Register of the land office. Mr Douglas & Lincoln frequently had debates — and I suppose I heard them all. Messr Lincoln and Douglas addressed the People of this County frequently in 1838 and 1840: the Tariff question — the Bank question, Van Buren — and other democratic & whig measures & men were discussed thoroughly & well. Personally I never had a hard feeling my life towards Mr Lincoln. I was attatched to Mr Douglas politically, very much. I was more attatched to Lincoln more than to Douglas Morrally. The discussion between Douglas & Lincoln were fairly & ably discussed: they were able speeches — truly so. Mr Lincoln used to stagger me with his tariff speeches: he so arranged his facts — his arguments — his logic that it approached me from such a peculiar angle that they struck me forcibly. Mr. Van Buren voted

---

1. The marginal note on this document (see p. 389, note 5) refers, in brief outline, to a story Weber related at WHH's request in a letter dated November 5, 1866. The conjectural date given here assumes that Weber wrote out the story soon after WHH outlined it here.

for the Negro $250 in the NY Convention of 1820: he was charge with this: there was a speech on this very question in the old Market house in 1840, but forget the names of the parties[2] —. These discussions frequently took place.

I rember the discussion — Bakers speech in the old Court House in the Hoffman row of buildings. This was in 1840 — or ~~1844~~.[3] Baker Said this — "Wherever there is a land office there is a paper to defend the Corruptions of office." This was a personal attack on my Bro Geo Webber.: I was in the Court House and in my anger I cried "Pull him down" —. I regret this now. — have always advocate free speech — & press — I do not recollect Lincoln being there that night but I do Know that some one made some soothing — Kind remarks and the difficulty Ended and Baker permitted to End his Speech.[4] This was done under great anger and as I thought at that time it was a personal attack on my bro. He as well as other of my friends interfered — held me till the Excitement ceased —: so it Soon Ended in quiet & peace. Baker and I was personal friends at that time: we belonged to the Military Company.

The temperance question in the Washintonian reformation. I remember Lincolns temperance Speeches well: he & I used to go to the Country together in his buggy: he had a horse & buggy & I had none: he and I were neighbors then — I lived across the street and a little South of me. I could see him better in this position than if I had been coser. The temperance question lasted some years. I can't say how long Mr Lincoln Continued the speeches. I went to California in 1849. Lincoln & I Continued the discussions — Speeches &c. from 1841 to 1849, according to my recollections. Remember I was a severe democrat during all these years.[5]

Let me give you an incident in Mr Lincoln's life. He was frequently away from home for a week or so at a time attending Court & on political discussions. One night he Came home late at night. I heard an axe: it rang out at Lincoln's — got up — Saw Mr Lincoln in his Shirt Sleeves Cutting wood — I suppose to cook his supper with: it was a cold night — the moon was up — and I looked at my clock — it was between 12 & 1 o'cl. This I remember well — used to tell it on the stump and in Conversation — told him so — when he was a candidate for Presdt — did so in the presence of several gentlemen — one from N.Y.. Mr L did not say aye or nay — yet he took it as intended — Complimentary.

Once I heard a scream of — Mr Webber — Mr Webber — it was the voice of apparent distress — I looked back — saw Mrs Lincoln — "She said — Keep this little dog from biting me". The dog was a little thing & was doing nothing — too small and good natured to do anything. — Again — one day I heard the scream — "Murder" — "Murder". "Murder" — turned round — Saw Mrs Lincoln up

---

2. See §364.

3. This incident is almost certainly the one described in the *Illinois State Register* for November 30, 1839, as having occurred the previous Saturday, November 23.

4. Cf. §451.

5. Marginal notes: *1 Washed Story — Bill — pump — &c — Ky* and *2 Temperance Meeting — Dunlap — Signers &c. Webber got near 50 — Lincoln none.* For "Washed Story," see §289.

on the fence — hands up — Screaming — went to her — she said a big ferocious man had Entered her house — Saw an umbrella man come out — I suppose he had Entered to ask for old umbrellas to mend. He Came out and Said — "Should be sorry to have such a wife". & passed on.

I distinctly remembr that Lincoln & Calhoun in 1844 had & held a joint discussion in the Court room which was in the Hoffman row — N.W. Corner of the public of the public Square: it lasted Several nights.[6] Calhoun was an able man. a very albe debater — & fair Courteous in debate. Lincoln was all this — the discussion was an able debate.

I rem — the Cartwright & Lincoln — don't remember any discussion at that time. Lincoln was Called by some an infidel and was charged with it in this race — don't remember whether it got in print or not — don't think he was an infidel — he used to talk to me on morals — Lincoln was a moral man.

LC: HW3984–89; HL: LN2408, 2:53–58

284. William G. Greene to WHH

Home Nov 1st 1866

Friend Herandon

Yrs. of Oct 28th recd. Dr Duncan came to Salem in 1829 (but he cut so small a figure while there that I failed to note the year of his exit)   he *is windy*   Kelso came to Salem in the year 1828 remained there some 8 or 9 years then moved Mo. he is an excellent *reliable* man   I can't say where his PO. or residence is. Lincoln & Thompson[1] Great Wrestle was at or near Rockisland. The Indian (*Jack*) who Lincoln protected came to our Camp at or near Henderson Creek or River

Verry Truly
W G Greene

LC: HW2725; HL: LN2408, 1:430

285. William W. Thomas to WHH

Jacksonville 1 Novr. 1866

D. Sr. —

to answer your Questions I make this statement. In 1826–7 the state was divided into four Judicial Circuits, the first was composed of the Counties of Greene, Morgan, Sangamon, Tazewell, Peoria Fulton, Schuyler, Adams, Pike Jo Daviess & Calhoun, and Judge Lockwood was assigned to it (Laws of 1826 — page 119. &

---

6. Lincoln and Calhoun engaged in a series of debates beginning on March 18 and continuing until at least March 27.

---

1. Lorenzo Dow Thompson of St. Clair County.

114. In 1828–9 the fifth Circuit was created, and Judge Young Elected Circuit Judge, composed of the Counties of Adams, Schuyler, Fulton, Peoria Jo Daviess and all the unorganized Counties North of the Illinois River. See Laws of 1828–9 38 & 51. In 1828–9. the Counties of Macoupin & Macon were created and attached to first Circuit, Laws of 1828–9 p 26 & 28.

In 1830–31 McLean County was created, and attached to first circuit, Laws of 1830–31, 57 & 46. In 1832–3. no new County was created, In 1834–5. Five circuit Judges were authorized to be, & were Elected to Hold circuit courts   Laws of 1835 p 150. Stephen T Logan was Elected Judge of first circuit, composed of Counties as before, except Pike, which was attached to 5 circuit, —

In 1836–7 the 7 Judicial circuit was Established not touching the first. —

In the Spring of 1837 S. T Logan resigned his office of Judge, & Govr. Duncan appointed William Brown of this place to fill the vacancy. In July thereafter at a called session of the Legislature, Jesse B Thomas was Elected Judge of 1 circuit,

In 1838–9. Jesse B Thomas resigned, and was Elected Commissioner of the Board of public Works, and I was Elected Judge of first circuit. At the same Session, the Counties of Cass, Scott, Pike & Calhoun were attached to this court, and the 8 circuit was created, composed of Sangamon, Tazewell, McLean, Livingston, Macon, — Dane (now Christian) Logan & Menard, and S. T. Logan was Elected Judge, Shortly after his Election Logan resigned and Judge Treat was appointed by Govr Carlin, the Successor, — remained Circuit Judge until he was Elected Judge of the Supreme court.

In 1840 — & 41. the Legislature abolished the circuit courts, added five Judges to the Supreme Bench, & required the 9 Judges to perform circuit duties, —[1]

1 circuit, Morgan, Cass, Scott, Pike, Calhoun, Green Jersey, & Macoupin, Lockwood Judge

2 circuit Breese, 3d. Scates, 4 Wilson, 5 Douglass. 6. Thos C Browne, 7 Theoppilus W Smith 8 S H Treat, 9 Thos Ford. the 8th circuit was composed of the Counties of Menard, Sangamon, Christian, Logan, Shelby, Macon, Dewitt, McLean, Champaign, Tazewell, Mason, Piatt & Livingston

In March 1839 I held the court in Sangamon, after the 2 or 3 day of the Term, Judge Ford held the first 2 or 3 days, until I reached Springfield from Vandalia, — I also held the court there in the Summer of 1839.

I held the courts for Treat in Tazewell & McLean in the Fall of 1839 or 1840   I do not remember which, & he held courts for me in Macoupin, Scott & Cass, —

Mr Lincoln practiced before me in Sangamon, Tazewell, McLean, Morgan, & Pike, — though he did not regularly attend the Courts in Pike or Morgan

From the Reorganization of the courts in 1840 & 41 but few, if any changes, were made until after the adoption of the Constitution in 1848. and you can trace the history by looking at the Laws. —

---

1. The judges of the Supreme Court in 1841: Samuel D. Lockwood, Sidney Breese, Walter B. Scates, William Wilson, Stephen A. Douglas, Thomas C. Browne, Theophilus W. Smith, Samuel H. Treat, and Thomas Ford.

From the beginning of his practice, Licoln was distinguished, for fairness and candor in conducting or defending Suits, as well as for clear, Logical, Statements & deductions, — It was next to impossible for a Judge to detect an error in any grounds that he assumed in argument. Admitting his premises his conclusions were irresistable, —

Yours &c

W. W. Thomas

LC: HW2726–27; HL: LN2408, 2:68–70

286. J. W. Wartmann to WHH

Rockport Indiana November 1 1866

My Dear Sir:

Your favor of Oct 24th ult, came duly to hand; and I send herewith such answers to your several interrogatories as I have been able to procure. I have named the kinds of birds, fish & game most common in our country: There are others of rare varieties which can hardly be said to belong here. I give the names as they are Known by here.

1st *Birds* —. Humming Bird, Blue Bird, Robins, Blue Jay: Wood-Pecker: Quail (a species of the Pheasant — usually hunted & bagged as *game*) Pheasants: Meadow Larks: Red Bird; Thrush: Owl: Night Hawk: Chicken Hawk: Whip-poor-will: Ground Robbins: English Snipe: Crane (water-fowl), Turkey Buzzard: Crows: Black Birds: Wild & Tame Pigeons: Wood-Cocks: Turtle Doves: Wren; Rain Crow; Swallows: Martins; Cat Birds. King Fishers (Water fowls).

2d Fish: Cat Fish —. 2 Kinds, Blue & Mud: Buffalo: Yellow White and Grey fin Perch: Carp: Bass (not many); Toothed Herring; Skip-Jacks: Black-fin Suckers. Pike (more in the *White* than Ohio River): Gar-fish; Shovel fish: Sturgeons, Minnows (very small —, usually used as bait for larger fish); Sun fish: Eels: *Soft-Shell Turtles*

3d *Game*   Deer: Squirrels: Rabbits: Coons: Wild Turkies: Wild Ducks: Oppossum: (Musk-rats, Otter, Panthers, Wild Cats Catamounts Red & grey foxes and a few Bear were in this Co, in Lincoln's day, and were hunted as *game*, but, with the exception of the Bear, were never eaten). Coon hunts at nights was, & still is, a favorite sport for boys & young men.

The game usually hunted for Eating purposes was, in L's day, & still is, Deer, Squirrels, Rabbits. Wild Turkies. Wild Ducks & Pheasants & Quails & *'Possums*   I, myself, have known persons to have little other meat to Eat during the fall & winter than, Deer, Squirrels, Wild Turkies & 'possum & rabbits:

The kinds of game I have named is common all through Southern Indiana.

I trust these imperfect answers may do you some good. I shall always take pleasure in answering any questions I can for you.

Very truly Your friend

J.W. Wartmann

P.S.

I spell my name thus *J. W. Wartmann*

P.S. No 2.

We beat in this Co' the "Cops"[1] by an *increased* majority over any previous Election.

LC: HW2728–29; HL: LN2408, 1:216–17

287. George Spears to WHH

Tallula Ills Nov 3d 1866

Dear Sir

in answer to yours of the 1st of Nov I hasten to answer your enquiries so fair as I can   as it regards the time that Doc Duncan came to New Salem I can not give the date   he left I think in the fall of 1833 & went to Knox Co, Ills is in Knoxville & is living there yet so fair as I know;[1] 1 Jack Kelso Left Salem in 1837 & moved to Missouria But I never knew the County[2]   an Old friend of mine in St Louis was at my hous this Somer past & told me that he was at Kelsoe's house in, *Mo* but I never asked him the County   the Mans name is Z. C. Inghram   I will write to him & assertain the County & inform you as Soon as posible   this man Inghram kept a Store in New Salem at the time that Lincoln & Bery Dunkin & Kelso all lived there and Can give you all the dates, there is no end to his recollections   he never for gets any thing that he sees or hears[3]   If you write to him tell him that I refered you to him for the information though he is a Strong Democrat yet he will answer your enquiries; I took my horse this morning & went over to the Neighbourhood of Newsalem among the Potters & Armstrongs & made all the enqirys I could but could learn nothing   the Old Ladys would begin to count up what had happened in Salem when such a one of their children was born & such a one had a Bastard but it all amounted to nothing   I could arrive at no dates only when those Children wer Born   Old Mrs Potter[4] affirms that Lincoln did sell Liquors in a grosery   I can't Say whether he did or not   at that time I had no idia of his ever being President therefore I did not notice his course as close as I should of had. there is a man in Mason County Ills by the name of Henry Sears who was always about Salem   he never for gets Dates & can tell you all

---

1. Copperheads, or Democrats.

---

1. This turned out to be a correct location for Duncan.

2. Jack Kelso seems to have moved from New Salem to Jasper County, Missouri, in 1841. He apparently moved again in 1846 to Macon County, Missouri, and again four years later to Atchison County, Missouri. See McKenzie, 185–88.

3. The editors could find no evidence that WHH communicated with Inghram.

4. Probably Elizabeth (Armstrong) Potter (1805–86), the wife of Edward (Ned) Potter and the sister of Jack Armstrong.

about Lincoln & Berry or any person else that ever lived there   If you write to him he could give you the information that you want

My bes respects to your Self & family

George Spears

PS

if you write to Henry Sears his Postoffice is Havanah

LC: HW2732; HL: LN2408, 1:427–28

288. *John M. Rutledge to WHH*

Birmingham Iowa November 4th 1866

Dear Sir

I received yours the 3 inst with pleasure   the information you ask of me I supose you have by this time   Brother Robert was here some time since and we hunted up Some papers and gave all the information we could So it would not be nessary for me to State them here, but from due respect I acknowledge your Kind letter   however I will answer one or two lest Robert might not have done   the disease my Sister died of if I remember was of the head or brain   I have the Life & Speeches of Lincoln by J. H. Barrett[1]   if I remember rite they never owned that mill at New Salem as the history States but I need not remark farther as you have all the facts thro Bro Robert that I am able to gave, I would not spare no pains in furnishing you with facts in my power,

I must state here that Lincoln was a man I always loved I was with him in the Black Hawk war   he was my Captain   a better man I think never lived on the earth   Surly God has Saved his Soul, ma God Bless you Mr Herndon in your work in getting up this history   I feel like I must have one

your humble Servent and friend

John M Rutledge

when I See Bro Robert if any thing is neglected we will Send it on

LC: HW2733; HL: LN2408, 1:432–33

289. *John B. Weber to WHH*

Pawnee Ills Novem 5th 1866,

Friend Herndon,

When I last saw you at your office in Springfield, I told you an anecdote of Mr. Lincoln which you requested me to put in writing, to be inserted in the life of Mr Lincoln, which you are now writing for publication.

---

1. Barrett.

In doing so, it is unecessary to say to persons who were intimate with Mr Lincoln, that his company was of the most agreable character, his conversation was simple, instructive, and amusing, and when he desired to impress his ideas upon the minds of those present, He would almost invariably illustrate his point by telling an anecdote which was always appropriate and well applied,

During the Washingtonian Temperance Reformation, Societies were organized in most of the School houses in Sangamon County, and were attended monthly by volunteer speakers, Mr Lincoln and I rendered a part of this volunteer service, I freequently succeeded in getting Mr Lincoln to fill my appointment, and on all such occasions we rode together in Mr Lincolns buggy, We were near neighbours living on the same Street nearly opposite each other.

Mr Lincoln was a deciple of Henry Clay, and the Champion of the Whig party in Central Illinois, and I was a member of the Democratic party until the repeal of the Missouri Compromise, Consequently, when together partisan politics were never aluded to by either of us.

On one occasion, I think in 1843, Mr Lincoln and I attended a Temperance Meeting on the north side of the Sangamon river, about 11 miles from Springfield. On our way home, the conversation between us turned upon Mr Lincolns early life,

He had been Captain of a Company in the Blackhawk war, and afterwards a candidate for a seat in the Illinois Legislature.

This was before Sangamon was divided, John Calhoun was then County surveyor, and Mr Lincoln was his Deputy for that part of the territory which is now Menard, and part of Mason Counties, Mr Lincolns home was in Salem, (now in Menard County) While living there, said he, a gentleman from Pensylvania who was said to have plenty money located down in the neck, as it was then called (now in Mason County)   The fact that he had plenty money induced the people at Salem to believe him to be an old Pensylvania Miser, and under such impression very little respect was entertained for him, Sometime afterwards, Mr Lincoln was called upon to go down to the neck to survey some land in which this Pensylvanian was interested, The day was agreed upon, and at the fixed time the interested parties were all on hand, and the work was pushed forward with energy, The evening was cold, and most of the persons engaged in the work went to the Pensylvanians house to Supper, and after an excellent supper was disposed of, the Company seated themselves around a big log fire in a big fire place, such as the people had in those days, All were in fine humor for amusement, Mr. Lincoln told them an anecdote which was received with applause, The Pensylvanian then told one in reply, which was approved by an uproar of laughter, One anecdote was told after another until midnight, at which time the Pensylvanian said it was now time to retire, Mr. Lincoln replied by saying in a moment Sir, Before retiring I wish to show how easy persons may be deluded by forming conclusions upon ideas not based upon facts, He the addressed himself to the Pensylvanian, saying, that when we folks up in Salem first heard of you, we heard you were a Pensylvanian and had considerable money, from which we concluded you were an old miserly Dutchman, but the facts show that we were very much mistaken, and I am happy to acknowledge that I have been very agreably disappointed, Well, said the Pensylvanian, as you have done me the honor to give me an account of the first opinion formed by you of me, it is no more than right that I should now report my first opinion of you, and then said when I first heard of you, I heard that you had been a Candidate for the Legislature, consequently I had come to the conclusion that on your arival here I would see a smart looking man. At the close of this statement Mr Lincoln laughed heartily, I felt indignant, and said to Mr Lincoln, The Pensylvanians reply was very ungenerous, inasmuch as your remarks concerning him were highly complimentory, but I added, probably it was only intended for the amusement of the moment, No, No, said Mr Lincoln, He meant all he said, for it was before I was washed, and then said I will have to tell you an anecdote to give you some idea of the fix I was in before I was washed, but said I dont vouch for the truth of the anecdote,

He then said, when I was a little boy, I lived in the state of Kentucky, where drunkeness was very comon on election days, At an election said he, in a village near where I lived, on a day when the weather was inclement and the roads exceedingly muddy, A toper named Bill got brutally drunk and staggered down a narrow alley where he layed himself down in the mud, and remained there until the dusk of the evening, at which time he recovered from his stupor, Finding himself very muddy, immediately started for a pump (a public watering place on the street) to wash himself. On his way to the pump another drunken man was leaning over a horse post, this, Bill mistook for the pump and at once took hold of the arm of the man for the handle, the use of which set the occupant of the post to throwing up, Bill believing all was right put both hands under and gave himself a thorough washing, He then made his way to the grocery for something to drink, On entering the door one of his comrades exclaimed in a tone of surprise, Why Bill what in the world is the matter   Bill said in reply, I G—d you ought to have seen me before I was washed,

This picture of Mr Lincolns early life drawn by himself I presume is highly colored. I have heard him tell other anecdotes relating to himself, in all of which (according to his own representation) he was made to cut but a small figure. He never blew his own trumpet, but his deeds of Patriotism, Heroism and Benevolence has introduced him to the world,

Yours very respectfully
Jno B Weber

Friend Herndon,

Please find on first page of accompanying letter, these words, And I was a member of the Democratic party until the repeal of the Missouri Compromise, These words I wish inserted as a matter of justice to myself, otherwise it may be inferred from your life of Lincoln that I was politically opposed to Mr Lincoln up to the time of his assassination, While it is known here that we were both candidates on the same tickett at the election in 1854, he for the Legislature, and I for Sherriff, In 1856 we were both members of the Bloomington Convention which organized the Republican party in Illinois, In 1860 I was an outsider at the Chicago convention doing all I could to secure the nomination of Mr Lincoln, and I am constrained to believe that the outside pressure on that occasion done the work, After his nomination I electioneered for him until elected When his call was made for men to suppress the rebelion, three of my sons, all under 21 years of age, left their plows in the furrow and entered the army of the U.S. two of which were lost in the service and when Lincoln fell by the hand of the assassin no man mourned more than I, Therefore, I intend that nothing shall be published with my consent, from which it may be inferred, that during the rebelion I was a member of a party composed of infamous traitors

Yours &c J B W

In relation to other anecdotes, I will see you when I visit Springfield, J B W

LC: HW2735–37; HL: LN2408, 2:165–72

290. Thompson Ware McNeely to WHH

Petersburg, Ills Nov 12th 1866

Friend Herndon

I have talked with Bennett[1] & other men who became acquainted with Mr Lincoln and lived near Salem shortly after the period of his reported *insanity* —

They say that they learned from the people — the immediate associates & friends of Mr Lincoln that he had been *insane* — that his Mind had been *shaken* — that disappointed *love* was the cause — Her name *Miss* Rutledge — It was then talked of as a part of the history of the *men of the town*. The extent of his insanity was such that men were *then* occasionally talking of it & *still* remembered by them.

Lincoln — Old Maj Hill & McNamer[2] were in love with the girl — She died and Lincoln for some time after *So acted* that every body who Knew & saw him pronounced him *crazy* — as they called it —

If you will write to Z C Ingram — St Louis, you can get much valuable information. He is the man of whom Ed L.[3] & I spoke to you when in Springfield.

Father[4] asks me to say that he never was in Lincoln's House — but then understood it to be a common grocery — *whiskey shop* — *by the drink* — He knows nothing of the present residence of Kelso — Doct Duncan or Jason Duncan — Radford & Sincho are dead — He thinks Doct Duncan lives in McDonough — He says write to Z C Ingram, St Louis —

Yours truly
T W McNeely

LC: HW2743; HL: LN2408, 1:435

---

1. Probably John Bennett (1805–85), a former legislator and Petersburg merchant.
2. Samuel Hill and John McNamar.
3. Possibly Ed Laning, referred to in Onstot.
4. Robert T. McNeely.

291. Henry C. Whitney to WHH

Lawrence Kas. 13*th* Nov. 1866.

Bro Herndon

Some of our friends (I forget who) told me that you were prepairing a life of our lamented best friend and that you were desirous to get copies of all documents of his production which might illustrate his singular character   an entry of his on the "Judges Docket" of Champaign Co. Circuit Ct. ought to be reproduced: — he was holding Court for Judge Davis in '59, I think & there was a writ on a suit in which some dozen of the leading men of Champaign were Defts. & one "Chaddon" or "Chase use of Chaddon" was plff. — the defts. really had no legal but a good moral defence but desired to *stav it off:* we bothered the Court about it until late on Saturday day of adjournment when he adjourned till after supper with nothing left but this Case to dispose of: — after Supper he heard our twaddle for nearly an hour & then made the Entry in the case which is so odd that your book will be imperfect without it: if you desire to get it write to "*Wm H. Somers* Esq." of Urbana (he was then Clerk): — As the debate with Douglas forms a leading incident of Lincolns life, I herewith send copy of letters to me which may prove useful   "Springfield Nov 30. 1858 H.C. Whitney Esq. My Dear Sir: Being desirous of preserving in some permanent form the late joint discussions between Douglas & myself. ten days ago I wrote to Dr Ray requesting him to forward to me by express two setts of the No*s* of the Tribune which contain the reports of the discussions — up to date I have no word from him on the subject — Will you if in your power procure them and forward them to me by Express? If you will I will pay all charges and be greatly obliged to boot — Hoping to meet you before long I remain as ever your Freind

A. Lincoln"

"Springfield Dec 25. 1858
H C Whitney Esq. My Dear Sir   I have just received yours of the 23*d* inquiring whether I received the newspapers you sent me by Express   I did receive them and am very much obliged. There is some probability that my scrap book will be reprinted and if it shall I will save you a copy — Your Friend as ever   A. Lincoln

under date of July 9. '56, he writes

It turned me blind when I first heard Swett was beaten and Lovejoy nominated but after much anxious reflection I really beleiv it is best to let it stand   This of course I wish to be Confidential.

Under date of Dec 18. 1857

Let me say to you confidentially that I do not entirely appreciate what the republican papers of Chicago are so constantly saying against Long John[1] — I consider those papers truly devoted to the republican cause & not unfriendly to me: but I *do* think that more of what they say against "Long John" is dictated by per-

---

1. John Wentworth (1815–88), congressman and mayor of Chicago (1857–63).

sonal malice them themselves are conscious of — We cannot afford to lose the services of "Long John" and I do believe the unrelenting warfare made upon him is injuring our cause — I mean this to be confidential. —

under date of June 24. 1858.

Give yourself no concern about my voting against the supplies unless you are without faith that a lie can be successfully contradicted — There is not a word of truth in the charge & I am just considering a little as to the best shape to put a contradiction in — Shew this to whom you please but do not publish it in the papers"

Shortly after Bull Run I spent a whole afternoon with him alone — he excluded every one & relaxed himself by telling me stories & giving me his whole theory of the rebellion & his plan for putting it down   if it was indeed possible to do so of which he had the gravest doubts: if your Book goes deeply into details you had better know in detail that interview.

It having been asserted & denied that McClellan declined once to see Lincoln when the latter called upon him — Lincoln desired once that I should see Mc-Clellan & wrote a note to him now in my possession asking him to see me a moment (not stating for what) & McClellan sent down word that he was busy & could not see me: it was Lincolns own desire that McClellan should see me: — I am glad that *you* are going to write Lincolns life as you can write a truthful one which is a thing not yet come to pass

Your Friend

H. C. Whitney

LC: HW2744–45; HL: LN2408, 2:348–52

292. *Mary Owens Vineyard to WHH*

Weston, Mo. November 16th 1866.

Dear Sir:

Yours of the second instant, has been received, and the explanation accepted. My husband was a native Kentuckian, a gentlemen of education, and superior intellect; his pursuits were agricultural. We were married in Green County Ky. March thirty-nine. In a former letter, I said something about a message Mr. Lincoln once sent me, by my Sister; Upon reflection, I was mistaken in the time, it was the fall after I left Illinois, which was in April thirty eight. Notwithstanding your flattering notice of my qualifications as a writer, you will have the goodness to excuse me, if I decline attempting such a letter as you request at my hands. Time was, when writing was both natural and easy, for me to accomplish, but within the past four years, there has been so much *trouble* and *care* pressed upon me, that it has become quite a task, to attempt, even an ordinary letter; besides it would require a more graphic pen than mine, to describe the manners, customs, Sayings and doings, in and around New Salem, at the time of which you speak. Since our correspondence, scenes, and circumstances (which have for years slumbered) came looming up in the distance, and stand out in bold relief. When you have done with Mr. L's letters, please return them, and as you are a *Kentuckian,* give me an assurance that all of mine are destroyed, and I will be content.

Respectfull

(Mrs. Vineyard)

HL: LN2408, 1:446–47

293. *J. M. Howard to WHH*[1]

Detroit Nov. 18. 66

Dear Sir:

I see by the papers you are engaged in writing a life of Mr Lincoln your former law partner

There is one incident in his life to which pardon me for calling your attention. I allude to his interview with John B. Baldwin of V*a* early in Apl. 1861, & beg you to peruse B's testimony before the Committee on Reconstruction, & also that of John M Botts & of a Mr Lewis of Va. Mr Botts asserts that a few days after the interview bet. Mr. Lincoln & Mr. Baldwin the former told him (Mr. Botts) that he had assured Baldwin that in case the Va. convention, then in session, would adjourn & go home he would [recal?] the troops from Ft. Sumter &c. Mr Baldwin denies that Mr Lincoln ever told him any such thing or that he (Bald.) ever said he did. When I exd. Bald. on the Com. I was careful to go into this subject fully in order that Mr. Botts who was to be examined might be fully informed of the former's views; and allowed him to read Baldwin's deposition before he testified. I did this because I thought it impossible Mr Lincoln could have given any such opinion, — in short because I thought Mr. Botts' statement — or rather the proposal of such terms by Mr. Lincoln, incredible, as it would have produced an outcry throughout the north. I must assure you I think so still, and that Mr. Botts must be mistaken — innocently of course.

Now, that conversation with Mr. Baldwin was of high importance and it would be strange if Mr. Lincoln, so careful, so truthful, so sensible how easy it was for Mr Baldwin to misstate or misrecollect it, should not have left some written memorandum of it. Such a memo. especially if in his handwriting would forever end the dispute bet. Botts & Baldwin, who have both written pamphlets on the subject.[2] It would also undoubtedly vindicate the reputation of Mr. Lincoln himself from what the world may call an act of timidity or at least irresolution. &, Is it not worth while to make a particular & thorough search among his private papers, for such a memo? I have written, once, to Mrs. L. about it, but she answered

---

1. In Howard's hand in the top margin: *(Private).*

2. John B. Baldwin, *Interview between President Lincoln and Col. John B. Baldwin, April 4th, 1861: Statements and Evidence* (Staunton, Va., 1866). No pamphlet by Botts on this incident has been discovered, but see John M. Botts, *The Great Rebellion: Its Secret History, Rise, Progress, and Disastrous Failure* (New York, 1866), 194–203.

that all such papers were in the possession of Judge Davis the Exr. & that she had none such. — The fact is — and you are entirely at liberty to smile — a *medium* of her own accord & without the slightest suggestion from me or any one, in answer to my question, What were the real facts about that interview, said, or rather Mr. Lincoln said through her — "Senator, I never offered a bribe to treason in my life"; and went on to say that he made a memo. of the conversation in his own hand writing at the time & placed it in a leather pocket or memorandum book & that it was in a trunk, and requested me to write his wife for it. This took place at Washington last spring.

But whatever may be the truth as to the memo. I have felt it a duty to call your attention to the conflicting stories of Messrs Botts & Baldwin.

Very respectfully Yours
J. M. Howard

LC: HW2748–49

294. John M. Rutledge to WHH

Birmingham Iowa Nov — 18th 1866

Dear Sir

yours is received & I much regret that I have such a poor memory, and you will see by these lines that I am neither a Scribe or a Schollar   in this you will Some what excuse me. I will just drop a word or two that you ma gave Some gess why I have not remembered no more, in the first plase I was allways at work and one of these still Say nothing boys   dident go out in company much, when in the Black Hawk war I was all ways at my post or in the tent didnt run round much   of corse would not See half what others would, now if thare is any thing in this that is worth any thing and is two awkward done I would be willing to get help and doe it over again

your humble J.M. Rutledge

question 1st   I dont remember the name of the plase whare Lincoln was elected, in my mind I can See the plase whare the men was mustered and volenteerd   I Suppose thare is Some old Letters that can tell, William Green was in the Black Hawk war   I think he lives in Menard Co —

2d   I dont remember about the restle after we had gone out. at Beardstown I saw Lincoln restle with a man I cant be certain about his name   he threw Lincoln twice with two new trips   afterwards they took holt and Lincoln threw him quite easy

3d   thare was Indians in camp while we lay at what was cald at that time Dixons ferry on Rock River   I was Sick at that time and did not See them   I herd them make the war hoop and men laughing

5th   I Knew Doctor Duncan and Kelso but the dates I dont remember   I think they ware Some what intelligent

7th   I believe thare was a debating Society but nothing remembered, Jokes nothing worth relating, however I will tell one if it is not worthy of any thing you need not Show it one day as Lincoln as walking up Street past the house of mr Ally a little girl I believe it was, about 2 or 3 years old ran out in the Street naked   Lincoln picked it up threw it under his arm and walked on, a parsel of men a bout a store door to laughing at the sean

9th   Jack armstrong & Lincoln had a restle in New Salem on the hill neare the mill   no one Shoed foul play as I remember, but I think Jack loosed his holts and caught Lincoln rather by the legs and partly threw him   I did not think it fairly done. thare was like to be a fuss but was Setled, I notised Lincoln standing with his back against a Store house neare by whare they wrestled and a crowd of men Standing around him he Seamed to be undanted & fearless. if I remember rite the bet was made by Offet though not Sure

LC: HW2751–52; HL: LN2408, 1:462–64

295. Robert B. Rutledge to WHH

Oskaloosa Nov. 18/66

My Dear friend,

I Sometime Since Recd. your very kind letter of 3d inst., and owe you an apology, for not answering sooner, but know you will pardon my seeming indifference, when I tell you, I have been moving from Burlington to this place, You suggest that the probable cause of Ann's sickness was her, conflicts — Emotions, &c, as to this I cannot Say, I however have my own private convictions, the character of her sickness was brain fever,

I am glad to know that you feel as I do, that injustice is done Minter Graham, and trust largely to your sense of, justice, to place him in his true light, before the Reading World, and award to him that meed of praise that is due the man, who assisted in laying the foundation of Mr. Lincoln's Greatness, I know of my own knowledge that Mr. Graham contributed more to Mr L. Education whilst in New Salem than any other man,

If Mr Graham is living & you should meet him, tell him, I remember my Old teacher with gratitude,

I received a copy of your lecture,[1] a day or two since, which is bold manly and substantially true, I will take the liberty to throw a little light on one point, for your future use, to wit, Samuel Hill first courted Ann, She declined his proposition to marry, after which, McNamar paid his addresses, Resulting in an engagement to marry, after McNamar left Menard Co. to visit his parents and during his prolonged absence, Mr Lincoln courted Ann, resulting in a second engagement, not conditional as my language would seem to indicate but absolute, She however in the conversation referred to by me, between her & David Rutledge urged

1. WHH's Ann Rutledge lecture, delivered on November 16, 1865.

the propriety of seeing McNamar, inform him of the change in her feelings & seek an honorable releas, before consumating the engagement with Mr L. by Marriage,

I hope to be able to visit you this winter, as I assure you nothing would give me more pleasure than to see & talk with the man who appreciates the virtues & character of *Abraham Lincoln*

I Am My Dear friend
Very truly yours
R B Rutledge

LC: HW2753–55; HL: LN2408, 1:444–45

296. David Turnham to WHH

Dale Ind Nov 19th 1866

Dear Sir

Yours of the 23 ult is at hand   Neither Mr Wood nor myself ever saw Mrs Lincoln Abe's Mother.[1] But I have been to See a man in Dubois County by the name of Brooner[2] who was living here and about (15) fifteen years old at the time She died. He Says She was rather above Mediate hight. More Spare Made than otherwise, weighing 120d   She was rather Coarse featured had the appearance of a laboring woman but nevertheless was a good looking woman. Her Hair was black, Her Eyes I think were blue. She was a Laboring woman and one of very good and moral habits. I do not know whether She belonged to any church or not   if she did she must have been Babtist   This Mr Brooner was living here at the time. He Seems to rember well these facts with the Exception of the Color of her Eys. He is a man who may be relied on for truth.

Yours &c
David Turnham.

LC: HW2756–57; HL: LN2408, 1:278

297. Henry C. Whitney to WHH

Lawrence Kas 20. Nov. 1866.

Bro Herndon

I am very sorry on your own account & mine that I cannot comply with your request as you expect — in the first place I did not Keep letters as a rule & 2dly after Lincoln got to be a great Man I was obliged to & did in fact give away his letters: I find Myself reduced to the very few unimportant ones of which I send Copies: they are not of a character to serve you but I send them as you request: — it is with diffidence that I attempt to furnish incidents in his life to you who Knew

---

1. See Wood's account, §81.
2. Henry Brooner.

him so thoroughly: — I have no faith that any thing will be of any use to you unless it be his views about the War just after Bull Run   My impressions are that he was usually reticent about this subject which will give more value to this Conversation: I am very much interested in your lecture:[1] Could You not send me a Copy of your other lecture of which I saw but an extract? — in the Matter of Poetry, our friend was likewise very fond of Holmes "last leaf" — I have heard him quote oftentimes from it — he likewise took from my library once a copy of "Byron" & read with much feeling several pages commencing with "There was a sound of revelry by night."[2] — A son of his foster brother was arrested in our County for stealing a watch   Lincoln came to a Mass Meeting while the boy was in Jail & got me to go with him at dusk to see the boy[3] — L. Knew he was guilty & was very deeply affected   more than I Ever saw him: at the next term of Court McWilliams & I went to the prosecution witnesses & got them to come into open Court & state that they did not care to prosecute. — to a stranger I could furnish many anecdotes illustrative of Lincolns Character but to you I can impart nothing   I am very glad you are getting up a "Life"   you ought to do it to vindicate his Character from the assaults of these Bohemians like Holland, Raymond &c. — if it will not tax you too much will you please procure from the Clerk of the Supreme Court an authenticated Copy of my authority to practice Law issued by Scates & Caton in '55. & forward me with statement of charge for making same: — also, as much emigration has come from your County to this State if you see any business please Send it along

Your Friend
H.C. Whitney

LC: HW2758; HL: LN2408, 2:424

298. Henry C. Whitney (statement for WHH)[1]

[November 1866?]

About one week after the 1st Bull Run I made a call upon Mr. Lincoln having no business except to give him some presents which the Nuns at the "Osage" Mission School had sent to him — A Cabinet meeting had just adjourned; Stackpole[2] told me to go right to his room. Lincoln was writing on a card — an old gentleman was with him; when he had concluded he read the writing aloud; it was something like this: "Sec'y Chase — the bearer Mr. _____ wants to be appointed _____ of Baltimore — if you find his recommendations to be suit-

---

1. WHH's lecture on Ann Rutledge.
2. *Childe Harold's Pilgrimage,* canto 3, stanza 21.
3. Thomas L. D. Johnston, son of Lincoln's stepbrother, John D. Johnston.

---

1. Possibly sent with the previous item. In H&W (1889) a footnote on this account states: "This interview with Lincoln was written out during the war, and contains many of his peculiarities of expression" (545).
2. Thomas Stackpole was at various times an engineer, watchman, and steward at the White House.

able and I believe them to have been very good the fact that he is a Methodist and is urged by them ought not to make against him as they complain of us some". Said I, "the Rebels do that" "Yes", Said he, "but not in that way, Whitney" — The old gentleman retired with the card and Sec. Seward came in — Says Lincoln (rather sportively) before he got seated, "Well *Governor,* what now? Seward stated his case, which related to New Mexico — Says Lincoln — "Oh! I see, they have not got either a Gover*nor* nor Gover*ment:* well you see Jim Lane — the Secretary is his man and he must hunt him up" — Seward then left, under the impression, as I thought, that Lincoln wanted to get rid of him and diplomacy. Several other parties were announced — Lincoln stated that he was busy and could not see them; he was as playful and sportive as a child — told me all sorts of anecdotes — dealt largely in anecdotes of Chas. Jas. Fox; — asked all about several odd characters that we both knew in Illinois. Gen. James was announced —: "Well as he is a feller what makes cannings" (cannon), (James sent word that he must leave town that P.M. and positively *must* see Lincoln before he went), "I must see him — tell him when I get through with Whitney I'll see him —". No more announcements were made and James left about 5 o'clock declaring that Lincoln was a fool and had got closeted with a damned old hoosier from Ills. and was telling dirty stories while the country was going to hell. Lincoln got his maps of the seat of war and gave me a full history of the preliminary talk and steps about the Battle of Bull Run — he, L., was opposed to the battle and explained to Gen. Scott by those very maps how the enemy could by the aid of the R.R.'s. reinforce their armies at Manassas Gap until they had brought every man there, keeping us at bay meanwhile — L. showed to him our *paucity* of R.R. advantages at that point, and their plentitude; but Scott was obstinate and would not hear of the possibility of defeat, and now "You see I was right, and Scott now knows it, I reckon." "My plan was and still is, to make a strong feint against Richmond and distract their forces before attacking Manasses." Said I — are you going to do it yet? Says he — That is the problem that Gen'l McCellan is now trying to work out. He then told me of the plan he had recommended to McC. — to send Gun Boats up one of the Rivers (not the James) in the direction of Richmond and divert them there while the main attack was made at Manassas. Said I, — I expect McClellan will be your successor —. Said he, "I am perfectly willing if he will only put an end to this war" —: he then gave me his theory of the rebellion by aid of the Map: "We must drive them away from here (Manassas Gap) and clean them out of this part of the State so as they can't threaten us here and get into Maryland; then we must keep up as good a blockade as we can, of their ports; then we must march an Army into East Tennessee and liberate the union sentiment there, and then let the thing work; we must then rely upon the people getting tired and saying to their leaders — 'we have had enough of this thing,' of course we can't conquer them if they are determined to hold out against us." In reply to a question about the blockade, he said — "The coast is so long that I can't keep up a very good blockade;" — then he said — "The great trouble about this whole thing is that *Union* men at the South won't fight for their rights." He told me of his last interview with Douglas; "He came rushing in one day and Said he had just got a telegraph dispatch from some friends in Ills. urging him to come out and help get things right in Egypt, and that he would go, or stay in Washington, just where I thought he could do the most good — I told him to do as he choose, but that he could probably do best in Ills., upon that he just shook hands with me and hurried away to catch the next train." I seized a good oppertunity to say of Judge Davis — "I expect you'll appoint him Supreme Judge — anyway" — he at once grew sad and said nothing until I changed the subject. I never saw Lincoln in so jolly a mood — he ought to have been busy too, as Congress was about to adjourn —: he said to me — "My business just now is to make Generals". At another time I wanted a line from him to the Pay Master General, asking a favor for me. I went to his house at breakfast time and found a crowd — hence I went into his room at once and found him just come in — I stated my business; he said, "let us go right over and get it done" — I said — I don't want you to go; "but I can do it better by going —" he said: he never was more radiant —. I took advantage of it to say "Mr Lincoln, Wm Houston — a brother of Sam Houston — is here wanting that little clerkship" — he frowned like a bear and said — "don't bother me about Bill Houstin he has been here sitting on his a—s all summer, waiting for me to give him the best office I've got —"; "but," said I, "if he will select a small clerkship" — "I hain't got it," roared Lincoln with more impatience and disgust than I ever saw manifested by him: Said I, "that ends it" — and he at once became cheerful and jolly and we started on. Lincoln and I were at Centralia Fair the day after the debate at Jonesboro — night came on and we were tired, having been on the fair ground all day — the train was due at mid-night — everything was full — I managed to get a chair for Lincoln in the Ills. Cen. R.R. Supt. office — but small politicians would intrude so that he could scarcely get a moments sleep — the train came and was filled instantly — I got a seat at the door for L. and myself; he was worn out and had to meet Douglas next day at Charleston; an empty car, called a "Saloon" car was hitched on to the rear of the train and locked up. I asked the Conductor, who knew Lincoln and myself well, (we were both Atty's of the Road) if Lincoln could not ride in that car as he was exhausted &c., and the conductor refused. I afterwards got in by stratagem. At this same time McClellan was in person taking Douglas around in a special car and Special Train, and that was the indignant treatment that Lincoln got from the Ills. Cen. R.R. — every interest of that Road and every employee was against Lincoln and for Douglas. During the sitting of the 1st Phila. Convention in '56, Lincoln was attending a special term of Court in our County —.[3] Davis, L., and my self roomed to-gether — at noon I would get the Chicago paper — one day the telegraph showed that Dayton was nominated Vice President — that "Lincoln" received ____ votes; Davis and I thought it was our Lincoln — but Lincoln said *he* thought it was the other *great man* of the same name from Mass. — Davis and I were impatient for next days news, and it showed that it was our Lincoln; but the main subject of the news was not apparently at all moved by the prominence given him — The next day after that, when I came to our room

---

3. Marginal note by Ward Hill Lamon: *This is not true L.*

with the mail L. looked *guiltily foolish* and also *amused;* it transpired that in coming through the parlor where the gong was, to get to our room, L. had hid it in a Centre Table and the Landlord was looking all around for it, and was then at the Stable hunting it. L. and I went to the parlor together and while I held the door shut he replaced it, and then went up the stairs to the room three steps at a time. He once told me of you — that "he had taken you in as a partner, supposing that you had system and would keep things in order, but that you would not make much of a lawyer, but that he found that you had no more system than he had, but that you were a fine lawyer, so that he was doubly disappointed." As late as '57, he once said to me while we were going together to a speech making, — "I wish it was over" — upon my expressing my surprise, he said — "when I have to make a speech, I always want it over" —

HL: LN2408, 2:426–33

299. Harriet A. Chapman to WHH

Charleston Ills Nov the 21st 66

Sir

Your favor of the 15th Came duly to hand. I will now endeavor to answer the Same. Enny information that I Can give you in regard to the loved and lamented Lincoln will be freely given, but would rather *Say nothing* about his Wife, as I Could Say but little in her *favor* I Conclude it best to Say nothing. and I persume it is not really nesessary that I Should. You ask me how Mr Lincoln acted at home. I Can Say and that truly he was all that a Husband Father and Neighbor Should be. Kind and affectionate to his wife and Child. Bob being the (only one they had when I was with them),[1] and vary pleasent to all around him never did I hear him utter an un kind word to enny one. for instance one day he undertook to correct his Child and his wife was determined that he Should not. and attempted to take it from him   but in this She failed   She then tried tongue lashing but met with the Same fate, for Mr Lincoln corrected his Child as a Father ought to do, in the face of his Wifes anger and that too without even Changing his Countenance, or making enny reply to his wife. His favorite way of reading when at home was lying down on the floor   I fancy I See him now lying full length in the *Hall of his old home* reading   When not engaged in reading law Books he would read literarry works, and was vary fond of reading Poetry and often when he would be or appeard to be in a deep Study — Commence and repeat aloud Some piece that he had taken a fancy to and Commited to Memory Such as the one you *have already* in print.[2] and the burrial of Sir Tom Moore,[3] and So on. he often told laughable Jokes and Strories when he thought we was looking gloomy.

---

1. Robert T. (Bob) was born on August 1, 1843; Edward B. (Eddie), the next child, was born on March 10, 1846.

2. A reference to William Knox's "Mortality," better known as "O why should the spirit of mortal be proud." This poem was prominently featured in WHH's lecture on Ann Rutledge, which was printed prior to its delivery on November 16, 1866.

3. Probably "The Burial of Sir John Moore," by Charles Wolfe (1791–1823), first published in 1817.

Your Lecture has been received and Carefully read   I found it vary interesting. please accept my thanks for the Same. Will write you again when I return from a visit to Grand Ma Lincoln

Yours with respect —

H A Chapman

LC: HW2760; HL: LN2408, 1:279–80

300. William G. Greene to WHH

Home Nov 21st 1866

Friend Herndon

Yours of the 19 Recd   I have carefully read your Lecture[1] on Mr Lincoln

You describe the state of his mind by the shock of Miss Rutedgs death to letter

I think you rather over draw the *Picturesk* of N— Salem still every surrounding is there that you mention

Your description of the People of that day is a master success not even our lamented oald friend E. D. Baker could have surpassed it I have no doubt your Lecture was well recd. I thank you for the Copy sent me

Truly

W. G. Greene

LC: HW2761

301. Robert B. Rutledge to WHH

Oskaloosa Nov 21st 1866

Dear Sir

I have just received your two letters, of 18 & 19th insts and hasten to answer,

you ask, first, Do I truthfully paint the Old pioneers, with classes — the Oldest Class, and our Fathers.[1]

I answer, you do, you ask, secondly do I get the condition of Mr Lincoln's mental Suffering and Condition truthfully? I cannot answer this question from personal knowledge, but from what I have learned from others at the time, you are substantially correct, you ask *thirdly* Do I truthfully describe New Salem her surroundings from 1825 to 1837.

I answer, your picture is well and truthfully drawn, as it appeared to me from 1828 to 1836, the time in which I was familiar with the place.

you ask Forthly Do I get the facts all correctly — and tell them truthfully, I answer, substantially you do, but probably a little in error in detail in one or two

---

1. WHH's lecture on Ann Rutledge, which was printed prior to its delivery on November 16, 1866.

---

1. That is, in WHH's lecture on Ann Rutledge.

particulars, to wit, In your lecture you say three men, fell in love with Ann Rutledge simultaneously, the facts are Wm Berry first courted Ann and was rejected afterwards Saml. Hill then John McNamar, which resulted in an engagement to marry at some future time, he McNamar left the Country on business, was gone some years, in the mean time and during McNamars absence, Mr Lincoln, Courted Ann and engaged to marry her, on the completion of the sudy of law, In this I am caroborated by James Mc Rutledge a cousin about her age & who was in her confidence, he say in a letter to me just received, "Ann told me once in coming from a Camp Meeting on Rock creek, that engagements made too far a hed sometimes failed, that one had failed, (meaning her engagement with McNamar) Ann gave me to understand, that as soon as certain studies were completed she and Lincoln would be married   He says you & Mr Cogsdell[2] talked with him on this subject, but he did not tell you as much, as he thot you had a design in it," you can correspond with him and say to him that this is no longer a delicate question, in as much as it must of necessity become a matter of history, that I desire the whole truth to be recorded.

I think you are in error as to the Cause of Ann's Sickness, You will pardon me for my frankness, as I wish to assist you in developing the truth the whole truth and nothing but the truth,

I have no dout but Ann had fully determined to break off the engagement with McNamar, but presume She had never notified him of the fact, as he did not return until after her death.

you are also in error in relating the conversation had with McNamar on 14th Oct 1866. you will bare in Mind, McNamar left the country in 1832 or 1833 to fetch his Fathers family to Menard Co, and did not Return with them until the fall of 1835 after Ann's death, his Mother died some years after he brot her to Menard Co and was buried in the same grave yard, McNamar had purchased the Farm on which we lived at the time of Ann's & Fathers death, prior to his leaving the country in 1832,

you aske me how I like your lecture, I answer, I like it very much, the great wonder with me is, how you have unearthed, developed, & brot to light & life So much dead matter, and made so few mistakes, I Am Dear Sir truly

your Friend,

R B Rutledge

(PS) In folding this Mrs Rutledge, suggests that she would be pleased to recive your Photograph for her new album, as she desires to fill it up, with new as well as Old friends

Yours

Rutledge

LC: HW2762–64; HL: LN2408, 1:466–68

---

2. Isaac Cogdal.

302. George Spears to WHH

Tallula Ills   Nov 21st 1866

Dear Sir

yours of 18th inst has jest came to hand & I hast to answer; your Lecture[1] came safe to hand & I read it carfully over & there is nothing in it but what is strictly true your description of New Salem is as corect as can be given as to Mr Lincolns Crazy Spell I do not recollect as it regards the Second Crop of Pioneers your discription is corect as to the flowers on those hills in thos days Spoken of it was like a flower garden; I am very Sorry that my recollection is so poor; for I have seen enough in the first Setling of New Salem & the early history of Mr Lincolns life if I had made Notes of it to have filled a large volum   I see things done & said in those days that looked very strang to me comeing out of a civilised cuntry in to this it loocked very Strange to me so much so that I thought I never could reconcile it to my feelings to rais a family in Such a comunity but things have changed & now I feel proud that I live in Such a comunity & Such a cuntry I must close my best respects to your Self & family

Respectfully yours
George Spears

LC: HW2765

303. Jacob M. Howard to WHH

Detroit. Nov. 22/66

Dear Sir —

I enclose to you 1st Copy of Mr Lincoln's memorandum made at Richmond early in April 1865 respecting *peace* &c.

2d, Judge J A Campbell's letter to Major General Ord of 14 April enclosing the same to Gen'l. O.

3d   Mr Lincoln's letter to Genl. Weitzel of April 6th 1865, permitting "the gentlemen who had acted as the Legislature of Virginia" to assemble &c.

These papers Come to me in a perfectly authentic & reliable form. Indeed I have not the least doubt of their authenticity as I have them from the proper official source. Supposing you might not have had access to them and knowing them to constitute an important item in Mr Lincoln's biography I take great pleasure in forwarding you the copies. I had not, I confess, supposed that Mr Lincoln's letter to General Weitzel Contained so distinct a recognition of the rebel legislature of Virginia; and yet it does not recognise the authority of "those gentlemen" to legislate. I was told by Mr Sumner that this letter to Weitzel was written hastily at City Point on board a steamer in the presence of himself & a few others but not shown

---

1. WHH's lecture on Ann Rutledge, which was printed prior to its delivery on November 16, 1866.

nor in any way Communicated to them. Atty Gen'l Speed[1] informed me in June 1865 that on seeing Gen'l Weitzel's order issued under this letter, he at once repaired to the President's house & remonstrated very plainly & earnestly with him against it and that Mr Lincoln with his usual patience and bonhommie said to him "Go ahead Speed." After Speed's explanation and argument Mr L. frankly admitted that the order would not do and must be revoked.

Very truly Yours
J. M. Howard

[Enclosure A]

304. Abraham Lincoln to Gen. E. O. C. Ord

The following is a Copy from the original in Mr Lincoln's hand-writing
> P. Ord U.S.A.
> A.D.C. to General Ord.

As to peace. I have said before and now repeat, that three things are indispensable.

1. The restoration of the National Authority throughout all the States.

2. No receding by the Executive of the United States on the slavery question, from the position assumed thereon, in the late annual message to Congress, and in preceding documents,

3. No cessation of hostilities short of an end of the War, and the disbanding of all force hostile to the Government.

That all propositions coming from those now in hostility to the Gov't. and not inconsistent with the foregoing, will be respectfully considered and passed upon in a spirit of sincere liberality. I now add that it seems useless for me to be more specific with those who will not say they are ready for the indispensable terms, even on conditions to be named by themselves. If there be any who are ready for those indispensable terms, on any Conditions whatever, let them say so, and state the conditions, so that such Conditions can be distinctly known & considered.

It is further added that the remission of confiscations being within the Executive power, if the war be now further persisted in, by those opposing the Government, the making of confiscated property at the least to bear the additional cost will be insisted on: but that confiscations (except in Cases of third party intervening interests) will be remitted to the people of any State which shall now promptly and in good faith withdraw its troops and other support from further resistance to the Gov't. What is now said as to remission of confiscations has no reference to supposed property in Slaves.

(The original of this paper was returned by Judge Campbell & turned over to the President, shortly after the death of Mr Lincoln)

---

1. James Speed.

[Enclosure B]

305. John A. Campbell to Gen. E. O. C. Ord

Richmond Va. April 14*th* 1865[1]

Maj. Gen'l E. O. C. Ord — Commanding General,

Your note of this morning requesting the withdrawal of the paper left by President Lincoln with me by his direction, has been received. I have taken a copy of the only paper left by him with me and now return the original to you, No further action will be taken with this paper. I addressed thro, General Grant a telegram to Gen. Taylor,[2] at Mobile yesterday acquainting the latter with the events that had occurred in Virginia, the Contents of this paper, and advised a cessation of hostilities, My letter was handed to Maj. Gen'l Weitzel to be sent to General Grant.

The communication of President Lincoln in respect to convening the legislature of Virginia in Richmond was addressed to General Weitzel. I read the communication by the authority of the writer and communicated its purpose to those who were interested in fulfilling its requirements. The object was to restore peace to Virginia on the terms mentioned in the enclosed paper, by the agency of the authorities that had sustained the war against the U.S. I still think that the plan was judiciously selected and that the issue would have been most favorable. The events that have since occurred have removed some impediments to the action sought for and preclude the possibility of its failure.

In that portion of the telegram of President Lincoln, that refers to my letter to Gen. Weitzel, there is some misapprehension as to the import & object of the letter. After reading the letter of the President to Gen. W. — I told him that if the same policy were pursued in North Carolina that the result would be beneficial; That the most prominent Citizens of that State were ready to act through the Legislature. He invited a communication in writing on the subject — My letter had special reference to the recommendation I had made, although there were suggestions of an important character which I supposed would facilitate the great end of obtaining a speedy pacification without further destruction of human life. I had no reference to the measures to be taken under the letter of the President and none as to the Conditions Contained in the paper enclosed. General W. has made no disposition of the letter that he was not justified in making, but if he had failed to send it to Washington, or to take any action upon it at all, he would not have violated any obligation or duty towards me.

This explanation I Conceive to be proper under the Circumstances.

I am General, Very Respectfully

Yours

(Signed)   J. A. Campbell

---

1. Headed: *Copy.*

2. Lt. Gen. Richard Taylor (1826–79), Confederate commander of the Department of East Louisiana, Mississippi, and Alabama.

(The foregoing is a true copy)
            P. Ord.
            A.D.C. to Gen. E. O. C. Ord

[Enclosure C]

306. Abraham Lincoln to Gen. Godfrey Weitzel
                            Copy
The following is a copy from the original in the hand writing of Mr. Lincoln —
                            P. Ord U.S.A.
                            A.D.C. to Gen'l Ord —
        Head Quarters of the Armies of the United States
            City Point, April 6, 1865.
Major General Weitzel
    Richmond Va.:
    It has been intimated to me that the gentlemen who have acted as the Legislature of Virginia, in support of the rebellion, may now desire to assemble at Richmond and take measures to withdraw the Virginia troops, and other support from resistance to the General Government. If they attempt it give them permission and protection until, if at all, they attempt some action hostile to the United States, in which case you will notify them and give them reasonable time to leave; and at the end of which time arrest any who may remain. Allow Judge Campbell to see this, but do not make it public —
                    Yours &c.
                    (signed) A. Lincoln

LC: HW2768 (Howard's letter), HW4493–94 (enclosure A), HW4491–92 (enclosure B); HL: LN2408, 2:405–11 (letter and all enclosures)

307. James M. Ashley to WHH
                            Toledo Ohio   Nov 23d 1866
Dr Sir.
    I send you copy of the last note I ever received from Mr Lincoln. It was written on the back of one which I sent him by the hands of John G Nicholly Esq his private Sec. The following is a copy of my note.

                            House Reps   January 31st, 1866.[1]
Dr Sir.
    The report is in circulation in the House that Peace Commissioners are on their

---

1. A mistake for 1865.

way or are in the city, and is being used against us. If it is true, I fear we shall loose the bill. Please authorize me to contradict it, if not true.

Respectfully

J M Ashley

To the President.

So far as I know, there are no peace Commissioners in the City, or likely to be in it. Jan. 31. 1865.   A. Lincoln

I send you this note because it is connected with a historical event, of great importance

I had given notice that at one oclock on the 31" of January I would call a vote on the proposed constitutional amendment abolishing Slavery in the United States.

The opposition caught up a report which had been put in circulation that evening that Peace Commissioners wer on the way to the City or were in the City   Had this been true I think the proposed amendment would have failed, as a number who voted for it could easily have been prevailed upon to vote against it, on the ground that the passage of such a proposition would be offencive to the Commissioners.

Mr Lincoln *knew* that the Commissioners were *then* on their way to Ft Monroe where he expected to meet them and afterwards did meet them. You see how admirably he answered my note for my purposes and yet how *truly.*

You know how he afterwards met the So called Commissioners, whom he determined, at the time he wrote this note, should not come to the City. One or two gentlemen who were present when Mr Lincoln wrote the note, & to whom he read it have spoken to me about it, as being so characteristic of Mr Lincoln. Genl Carl Schutz[2] spoke to me about it the other day when I was in Detroit & I thought if it was of sufficient importance for him to remember and refer to, that you might be pleased to get it.

Truly yours

J M Ashley

LC: HW2771–72; HL: LN2408, 2:418–20

308. Benjamin F. Irwin and Ira Emerson to WHH

Pleasant Plains Nov 24 1866

yours Requesting of me the Mannors modes of Living advantages Disadvantages Dress Fashions &c &c &c, &c In Ills at an early day I now answer   Beginning at say 1825 first as to advantages there was none but Disadvantages in Abundence and the first and one great Disadvantage to settlers to get was Milling done whitch was a horse Mill the only kind run by 2 or 4 horses each

---

2. Carl Schurz.

man generally having to furnish his own team often going ten Miles to Mills ridng one horse carrying a Sack of Corn or wheat and leading a horse Both harnessed ready to hitch to the Mill and to get the turn at the Mill the time of starting was about 12 at Night as by day light there was generally a days grinding on hand whitch would be about 20 or 25 Bushels of corn or wheat and the Bolting of Flour[1] was done by hand thus Mills was generally Built By Posts put in the ground 8 feet high and a Log Mill house on top such a Mill put on exhibtion in 1860 would be a Better show than Barnums Museum or Dan rices circus at that time Meal was often made by grating the corn on an oval piece of tin punched full of holes with a common nail and tacked on a Board another Method of getting meal was Sub-stituted by Burning a hole out of the end of a solid Log sawed off say 3 feet Long 18 Inches across Burn out the end untill it would hold ½ Bushel then get an Iron ring Put on the end of a Pole an drive in an Iron wedge to use as a Butt and in this Mortar pound the corn into Meal or hominy thus kind of a Mill hundreds used and Lived happy and fine on the Meal this substitute was called a Mortar   after a few years Inclined wheels and water Power took the place of the single Band Mills[2]   But a short time previous to these difficulties some of the first settlers of sangamon County actually went to Madison County to Mill   Distances of 80 Miles to get Meal or flour and the trip had to be made by crossing without any Bridges what would now seem to be Impassable streams at this time it was no uncommon thing to see men with Coon skin caps on for a covering of the head such sights would now frighten a Beholder But fashion had then no votaries the wimen Made all the clothing   old fashioned wheels cards[3] and yarn Cotton and wool could be found at every house the wimen made their own sunday ware of Clothing whitch was Checked Cotton or flannen Dresses the fashion was tight sleeve Dresses four widths of Cloth made a Large 3 widths Dress often these Dresses for a fine article was checked of various Colors made of grass walnut or oak Bark was used for Coloring also shoe make[4] Berries it was in these days a Common thing to see the trees Stripped of Bark as high up as a woman could reach and every man seeing a tree Barked new what it was done for, Mens Clothing was Generally plain white or But nut yellow[5] mad with walnut Bark either Cotton or wool goods the Children as a common thing from early in the Spring, until fall wore nothing But a Shirt and many never had a Shoe the year round in verry cold weather they sat in the house to keep Comfortable if a woman got a calico Dress of any kind she was Dressed so fine the whole Neighborhood would Know it and at this time it took at least 10 Miles square to constitute a Neighborhood and a woman would thnk nothing of picking up a child and walk 4 or 5 Miles to visit a Neighbor Calico was the finest article used for a Dress a sun bonnet made of Calico Blue or checked

---

1. See §156, note 1.

2. Probably horse-drawn mills using a rawhide belt.

3. Cotton or wool fibers were cleaned and disentangled by means of hand-held cards, then spun into yarn on spinning wheels.

4. Sumac.

5. Presumably "butternut" yellow.

was most common and a Gingham Bonnet was thought to be an extra fine article there was another stile of Bonnetts whitch was Super extra fine called Calash or Gig toped mad of yellow nankeen shaped Like a Buggy top hoops or Bows made of Ratan or cut out of hickory splits It would now Be amusing to see a yound Lady Rigged and start to church as they then did every thing was high and economy had to be used the women as Before said would walk 4 & 6 Miles to church carrying their Shoes and Stockings untill they got near the Meeting and then put them on and go into Company after Meeting they would get out the crowd and take off shoes and Stockings and go home Barefotted on Larger occasions the farmers would hitch a yoke of Steers to the wagon and the family would get in and ride to Meeting (I mean if the Distance was great say 8 or ten Miles) and have a good and happy time seeing old friends and forming new acquaintences for in those days friendship was genuine the churches was generally some school house say 18 by 20 feet Built out of round Logs a Board roof and the earth for a flooring the seats slabs 4 or 6 Inches wide with 4 Pins in them for Legs to support them the windows in these school houses was mad by cutting out one Log nearly the entire length of the house and hang a plank over it in time of a Storm the Preachers was generally plain homespun Men plain in every sence of the word always as plain Dressed as their Congregation they never attempted to make any display or show and then again their Manners and gestures was natural their Language was common and adapted always to the Intelligence of the hearers the Preachers of an early day Made human Nature their Study they understood man in all his relations and they adapted their discours or sermons to man as they found him in all his relations and surroundings the preacher would read his text and preach his sermon from it as a whole making generally no Divisions or subdivisions of the subject and still Bring out all its general Bearings and relations to the duties of man and close with an application or exortation which seldom failed of effect upon the congregation

There seemed to be a Divine agency or Power that attended the Ministry in these days that is not seen now they generally had the Confidence of all their Neighbors and as a Natural result had uncommon good order and Attention their Prayers were generally verry solem childlike and earnest no display of words or modulation of voice But the emenations of an earnest honest feeling heart such as truly Becomes an honest faithful embassador of Christ then prays and sermons were directly addressed to each person understanding so forcibly that they they could not shake it off and the result was many splendid revivals in every small congrations ministers in these days Did not generally take the stand to warn men or tell them of their wrongs but would go to them Individually and talk to them freely frankly and plainly and almost every one loved them for so doing if there was a Sick man woman or child ten Miles of a Preacher he made it his Business to visit them and see to there wants temperal as well as Spiritual and pray with them and objects of charity or Benovolent enterprises never failed of having their aid and Cooperation Preachers in these days were Industrious in every sense of the word and Bent all their energies to the encouragement of honest faithful Labor and rigid econimy they were faithful and Prompt at house raisings and in the harvest fields generally at Both of which some thing to Drink according to custom had to be on hand But they generally tried to Discourage the Idea of having whisky on such occasions and yet if the employer Did not furnish whisky he could not get his grain taken care of or a house raised and on such occasions all was willing to help and it was no uncommon thing for a man to go 8. or 10 miles to help a Neighbor harvest or raise a house all felt their Dependence in those days Corn huskins Rail Maulings wood Choppings and quiltings was a common thing in which all took a part at the work. the Closing scene of these tranactions of Course was a dance at Night in which the older ones took no Interest But the young made it up the manner of Dancing was entirely different from any thing seen Now there was no calling off 4 or 8 persons Boys and girls of Equal Numbers would take the floor and run the set off hand & at the sound of the fiddle each one would go to shuffling and kicking for Godsake they would keep it up all Night and in the Morning there was sore toes in earnest. each one would return home and go right to work the Women to carding and Spinning weaving &c which they all understood and the Boys to Ploughing hoeing Breaking flax or Picking Cotton   there was no Dodging Labor and none tryed to evade it all looked upon Labor as being honorable the Fathers taught it and they Controlled their children then there was then with Boys But verry little swearing or fighting this was Left to men of years and you would never hear of such a thing as a Boy Bing Drunk or seldom swearing or stealing or Idling away their time often a 12 year old boy would make a good hand in a harvest field and again they all had to be in the field at that time by sun rise and there Labor untill sun Down that was the rule and each one governed himself accordingly in relation to Dress in Ills in early day there is an incident or two I will relate as showing the curiosity felt or Manifested in regard to Dress About the year 1825 or 6 two young men from Sangamon County R S Plunkett & N C Irwin went to St Louis and Bought a Black or Blue Cloth Coat at a Cost of about $40 each and one a pair of common Buckskin gloves these Coats attracted general attention and was the Subject of Remarks for Miles around the Stile of these Coats was high Stiff quilted Collers Close Bodied Short waist and pidgeon tailed, Previous to this the wedding Coats for young men was Blue Jeans home made and it is a Matter of fact these Coats and gloves was Borrowed as a wedding garment on Many occasions for Miles around another Incident I have from J H Matheny as furnishes a good Illirations & some man at Springfield Ills about the same time got a Blue Cloth Coat the News spread about Town old and young heard of it and on a certain Sunday it was Supposed he would appear at Church in his New garment and children in the Neighborhood in groups assembled on the Road to Church to see the young man pass and get a Sight of a Black or Blue Cloth Coat a Menagarie or Caravan Passing would have Been no greater Curiosity to the children and in addition at that time Let a young gentleman or Lady come to church with an extra fine Rig the Minister was sure every time pay his Respects to pride for the opinion was general that pride and Industry was enemies and we was taught from the Pulpit that Laziness and Christianity did not go together I Neglected in its proper place to say we all Lived in Log Cabbins mad of Round Logs the cracks

filled with Mud and Straw Mixed, some floored with Puncheons or slabs and others floored with Mother earth   the chimblies was made of Lath or Split Strips
Laid in Common mud and Plastered with the hand in side to protect them from
the Sparks or fire and the Back and Jams was generally Laid with Rock. this Stile
of Chimblies Never fails to carry off the Smoke admirably

Amen

NB Sutch is my recollection of the Early history of Ills

Ira Emerson
Preacher in charge
Pleasant Plain Ills

Billy I could write a volume But I think this is enough   *Ben Irwin*[6]

LC: HW2775–84

309. Daniel W. Wilder to WHH

Rochester, N.Y. Nov. 24th 1866.

Dear Sir —

Having an item in regard to your book in the paper this morning it gives me
an excuse for writing to you.

You may have forgotten, but I most pleasurably remember meeting you at
Springfield in the summer of 1859. I was there to see Chas. B. Brown (since Killed
while most gallantly standing by our colors) and met you and Mr. Lincoln. — Well,
here is a little of my history since — I was then publishing the Elwood (Kan.) Free
Press. In the summer of '60 I went into the St. Joseph (Mo.) Free Democrat. We
managed it so spiritedly and Republicanly that we got 410 votes for Lincoln there
(where not one Repub. vote had ever been cast before) and, in Dec., got ourselves
indicted for publishing an "incendiary" sheet. That stopped the paper (for we were
guilty by Mo. law and should have been convicted if tried) — we had lost our cause,
time & money, and had to cross over into Kansas to escape the Sheriff's process.
Two of the Editors became Capts. in our Army, one printer, a Major (he is now in
the Mo. Legislature making another kind of laws) one printer a Capt. and I think
everybody in that little printing office served in our army in one way or another
before the war was over. Some of them made histories which it would be a delight
to write out & publish.

I went down to Leavenworth & became Editor of the *Conservative* (always
intensely Radical, saying in the first number that it was *Freedom* that we were to
conserve) started in Jan. '61 on the day that Kansas was admitted. Soon afterwards
I became proprietor, and remained with the paper about four years. In '63 Mr.
Lincoln (at the solicitation of Jim Lane) made me Surveyor General of Kan. &.

---

6. This note is written down the center of the page.

Nebraska. In March '65, at the same solicitation, he removed me. (Mark W. Delahay, of Leavenworth, my predecessor in office, ought to give you many facts in
regard to Mr. L., but he is a very diffuse writer & not famous for hard sense. He
corresponded much with Lincoln during the war.)

The cause of Lane's opposition and my removal was my going against his re-
election as U.S. Senator — a record with which I am well pleased — his vote on
the Civil Rights bill &c. showing just what he was.

Mr. Lincoln Knew Lane well even when I first saw him ('59) and it is one of
the most surprising of his many contradictions of character that he should have
taken into his confidence a man whom he Knew was utterly rotten, heartless and
corrupt. I believe Lane dispensed more patronage than any other western Senator, and some of it corruptly. Still, when the re-nomination came along, Lane was
for Chase (without Lincoln's Knowledge, I suppose) until about Feb'y '64 when
he wrote me a letter that it was time to come out openly (in the paper) for Lincoln. Lincoln was not my first choice; I preferred somebody more radical. Lane
simply wanted the man who was to win — and for the sake of the spoils.

Wm P. Dole of Indiana is another man (and a bad one too, I believe,) who had
much to do with Lincoln. For a long time he had an exclusive back-stairs entrance
to the White House and intrigued for himself (in thieving Indian contracts) and
for Lane. Cale Smith (dead) was another Indian contract jobber, yet Mr. Lincoln
made him U.S. Judge afterwards. Millions of money were dispensed in Kansas &
the story connected with it would be a strange one — could it ever come to light,
as it never will. The orthodox ministers who make Mr. Lincoln a part of the God-
head (you told me he was not Orthodox when I was in Springfield, but inclined
to our own Theodore Parker {in writing *his* life, as I wish you had, you would have
had no contradictions to reconcile} — a fact he bravely concealed while President)
would be terribly shocked could they Know that Mr. Lincoln was the most adroit
of the political schemers of his day. Thurlow Weed was not a fractional quarter
section to Lincoln's township.[1]

From all this don't understand (as I Know *you* will not understand) that I do
not appreciate that part of Mr. Lincoln's morality which sometimes made him an
Apostle and a Prophet. I remember all those words and acts and Know that no
other American President — not *Washington* — Ever approached them in sublimity.
When Lincoln wrote to the Copperheads he used to tell them that he was following, not leading, the people. There must have been a twinkle in his eye when he
wrote those things, for, though the Radicals led him, he was, by those very words,
converting and leading Copperheads. It was "strategy, my boy."

By the way, Lincoln's greatest speech, Gettysburg, has two ideas — self-conse-
cration and a "government of the people, for the people and by the people." This
last is word for word from Theodore Parker (unconsciously, of course, to Lincoln
at the time, his mind having assimilatied it) and you must give him the credit for

---

1. A quarter-section is 160 acres; a township is 36 sections, or 23,040 acres.

it.[2] I can find the Sermon where it occurs. — I am now (since April 1st) one of the Editors and publishers of the Rochester Express.

Your friend,

Daniel W. Wilder.

LC: HW2796–97; HL: LN2408, 2:414–17

310. John McNamar to WHH

Petersburg Ill Nov 25th 1866

My Dear Sir

Since receiving your rather Flattering request to write up some of the Ancient reminicences of this Locality the Great Political Battle has been fought and won   "Saved we the Gods" for the victory Let Andy[1] swing as Ben Butler would say the higher the Better, he might have been a great man had not the Tayler that made him up, cabbaged the proper Trimmings[2]   "There is a tide in the affairs of men" which Andy did not take at the Ebb" but which Mr Lincoln without having read Shakespear in Early life, triumhantly [flooded?] on to lasting fame; if not to fortune. I remember Mr Lincoln's first miscellaneous Reading he got possesion of a Copy of Burns and repeated with great Glee "Sic a wife as willy had I wudna Gie a button for her," others, yourself perhaps would have joined with Tam O Shanter, in admiration of the "Cutty Sark"[3]

There was not many Books in the region at that time   I had a copy of Shake-spear Popes Homer and essay on man and Don Quixotte[4] I dont remember whether Mr Lincoln ever read Either of them when I went away I locked up Shakespear in a trunk with some other articles among which was a few packs of cards. It was afterwards Broken open Shakespear was not disturbed and I have him yet, But the cards were among the missing, you can infer which was the most popular   but what I considered very remarkable at the time was seeing a copy of Homers Oddes-sy quite old and torn and printed with ancient type in the hands of Some of the old setters   I cant remember whom now   its history, the manners habits and customs of the People of those days was of that Primitive order that usually char-acterize New Settlements with an abundance of the necessaries of life, its Luxu-ries were unknown or uncared for Lavish hospitality and Brotherly love abound-ed and every where the Latch string hung out to all comers, The Majority of the Citizens were professing Christians or church members a second Class though not belonging to the churches associated with Church members in preference to the

---

2. AL's phraseology is not identical but apparently owes much to Parker's. See Garry Wills, *Lincoln at Gettysburg: The Words That Remade America* (New York, 1992), 107, 281n.

1. President Andrew Johnson (1808–75).

2. A reference to Johnson's former career as a tailor.

3. "Sic a wife as Willie had, / I wad na gie a button for her" is the refrain from the Robert Burns poem "Willie Wastle." "Weel done, Cutty Sark!" is the spontaneous cry that gives away the hero of Burns's "Tam O'Shanter."

4. Alexander Pope's translation of Homer and his long poem "An Essay on Man"; Miguel de Cervantes Saavedra's satiric novel *Don Quixote.*

3d Class which was Decidedly Rowdy, the first Class in their profession and faith were Earnest simple and childlike in their faith and practice, as the incident I related to you of stopping the effusion of blood by the Bible well prove,[5] in fact "the Cotters Saturday Night" By Lincolns favorite Author[6] would describe many a prarie Cabin here away in times past

Or as the homesick Englishman expressed it

The prayer of thanks giving in harmony swelling
All warm from the heart of the family Band
Half raised is from Earth to that rapturous dwelling
Described in the Bible that Lay on the Stand
    The old fashioned Bible the Dear Blessed Bible
    The family bible that Lay on the stand[7]

There were four Denominations of Christians represented here, when I came, the Methodists whose headquarters were at Ezekiel Harrison's the Father of our popular County Judge[8] he lived a little East of Jim Purkapiles where the Elder Matheny[9] used sometimes to hold forth there was a little incident occured of which Bill Green was the Hero which may be worth relating as Lincoln enjoyed it Hugely, we the youngsters had attended a night meeting in Mass at Harrisons   On starting home a young Doctor[10] who had Set up a shop in old salem not unlike perhaps "Romeo's Apothecary" and remarkable for the frequent use of the word "Modes opperandi," he cut out Bill that is took his gal from him   Bill Trudged along in Silence some time   Either meditating on his sins or "Nursing his wrath to keep it warm"[11] at length he came along side of his "Bright particular" who with the doctor was Leading the column and Began to plead his lost cause with the fair one   The Girls in the rear began to hurry up to hear, After many arguments that Seemed unavailing Bill finaly put in a clincher Saying you Know we have done things that we ought not if we are going to seperate, — The Girls wilted and fell Back in the rear.[12] while speaking of the Methodists I take Great pleasure in recording my hearty aproval of their Loyalty and Patriotism During the Late National strife. Nevertheless they have some peculiarities they as you are aware Believe in "Backsliding" some, my wife belongs to the Methodist Church consequently you will Leave the above paragraph out as not Germain to the Subject"   I forward you this much of what I have written at odd times as the rest of my manuscript is in an unfinish state

John McNamar

5. Probably refers to a conversation between WHH and McNamar.
6. Robert Burns.
7. These verses are not identified.
8. Milton B. Harrison.
9. Charles R. Matheny (1786–1839), a Methodist preacher and father of AL's friend James H. Matheny.
10. Probably Jason Duncan.
11. An allusion to Robert Burns's poem "Tam O'Shanter."
12. Marginal note in McNamar's hand, referring to the last several lines: *Pardon & correct Blunders.*

The most numerous Body of professing Christians However at that time here were the Cumberland presbyterians so called from the county in which they Originated they are as I presume you are well aware an offshoot from the Old Presbyterians at an Early day there was a Great revival in the Presbyterian Church in Cumberland and perhaps other Counties on comberland river   A great many of the Converts as is generally the Case wanted to preach "Dr Syntax[13] Said nay, they wanted Preachers such as Paul Brought up at the feet of Gamalial. to stand forth "the messenger of truth the Legate of the Skies" whose theme Divine" they considered too sacred to be commited to the hands of Uneducated Men, they held to the Maxim Expressed in the Old College Saw "Ne suter ultra crepidem Est"[14] while the young Convert Burning with Newborn Zeal considered himself abundently capable of Playing upon a harp with a thousand Strings "and he played"   there is but few of that class of Preachers now   they have a more educated if not a more able Ministry, the rev'd John Berry was the acknowleged Leader of the sect here

He was a large and powerfull Man had a powerful Voice and was altogether a powerfull Preacher but in Later years he became somewhat dogmatical on baptism and some other points, the People in Most Churches have adopted Douglas's "Popular Sovreignity" on the Mode of Baptism and their Pastors generally acquiesse except Perhaps the Baptist. Mr Berry however published a Book on Baptism[15] Denounced immersion as no baptism at all, stating as one reason that the river Jordon when our Saviour was baptized was not Shoe Mouth deep, which reminds me of a little story I heard Mr Lincoln relate he said he was talking with a virginian once an FFV[16] and while speaking of James river the Virginan said he knew it when it was only a little Brook, could step across it any where   But we had other preachers one of whom I have mentioned before he like Mr Lincoln obtained a Grammar I heard him attempt to parse a little in one of his Sermons soon after, My Brethren he Says is is a verb of the diminitive Mood and the present Tense emphatically; whether he ever went beyond is this deponent Saieth not yet he was a good soul and may be pardoned a little pious vanity

LC: HW2798–2800

---

13. A fictional clergyman created by the British satirist William Combe and the artist Thomas Rowlandson.

14. Presumably a reference to the Latin proverb "Ne sutor supra crepidam," translated as "Let the shoemaker stick to his last."

15. Possibly a reference to John M. Berry, *Lectures on the Covenants, and the Right to Church Membership, with Other Subjects: To Which Is Added an Appendix* (Louisville: By the author, 1849).

16. First Families of Virginia.

311. John M. Rutledge to WHH

Birmingham Iowa November 25th 1866

Dear Sir

I received your lecture[1] & a letter also thankfully. with much embarisment I attempt to answer from the fact I have no learning of any consequence   I Should have done this Some time ago but I have ben vary busy geting in my corn, and am not vary well at presant   hope you will excuse me if I am a little Short in writing. I believe I am not able to detect any error in your description   of New Salem & her Suroundings, all is rite as far as I know, thare is one thing in the Lecture that Seames to deviate a little that is if I understand the meaning   whare it Sais he purchased the farm on the account of the memories that cluster over it[2]   I think he purchased the farm before he left the country the first time, however he bought I think more to the farm after Annys death   the Lecture I am well pleased with, a part of it was read with a full heart to here the past seans brought fresh to memory   I often herd Mother Say the last time She herd Anny Sing was a few days before She was taken sick up Stairs in that old house of McNamers like this.

vain man thy fond persuits forbare
Repent thy en is nigh
Death at the fartherst cant be far
Oh think before thou dye, & so[3]

but I must close for I feel more like Saying to my Self,
O my Soul when shall I be delivered from this body of clay, if I have said any thing rong I hope to be corected.

your friend
John M. Rutledge

LC: HW2801; HL: LN2408, 1:464–65

312. J. D. Wickizer to WHH

Chicago. Illinois   25th Nov. 1866

My Dr Sir —

some time ago you asked me to relate any anecdote or incident, I might Know connected with the late lamented President Lincoln   The following "pig story" No. 2[1] is literally true

In 1855 Mr Lincoln and myself were traveling by buggy from Woodford Co. court to Bloomington Ills. — and in passing through a little grove, we suddenly

---

1. WHH's printed lecture on Ann Rutledge.
2. McNamar himself is the person referred to, though not named in the lecture.
3. A hymn written by Joseph Hart (1712–68).

---

1. The first pig story may have been related in conversation or included in undiscovered correspondence.

heard this terrific sqealing of a little pig near by us. Quick as thought Mr L. leaped out of the buggy, seized a club, and pounced upon an old sow, and beat her lustily, that was in the act of eating one of her young ones. and thus he saved the pig and then remarked "By jings! the unnatural old brute shall not devour her own progeny" This, I think was his *first* proclamation of Freedom The following, shows his ready wit In 1858 in this Court at Bloomington Ills. Mr. Lincoln was ingaged in a case, of no very great importance, but the atty on the other side, Mr S.[2] a young lawyer of fine abilities (now a judge) was always very sensitive about being beaten, and in this case manifested, unusual zeal and interest. The case lasted till late at night, when it was finally submitted to the jury — Mr. S. spent a sleepless night in anxiety, and early next morning, learned to his great chagrin, he had lost the case — Mr Lincoln met him at the Court House and asked him what had become of his case with lugubrious countenance and melancholy tone, Mr S. said "It's gone to h—l" "O well" said Mr L. "then you'll see it again"

When do you expect to finish the Life of Mr Lincoln? I opine it will be a very readible Book, from what I have seen of it

I think your portraiture of him is most excellent[3] But I think, take him all in all, we shall never look upon his like again

I have a letter writ in his own hand writing, he gave me at Washington 22 Aug. /64, the last time I ever saw him which I intend to Keep most suredly and hand down to "posterity *yet unborn*"

Let me hear from you

God and Liberty — Amen

J. D. Wickizer

LC: HW2802–3; HL: LN2408, 2:446–47

313. Thompson Ware McNeely to WHH

Petersburg Ills Nov 28th 1866

Friend Herndon

I have delayed answering yours of the 20th inst on account of illness and am not now able to leave my room to inquire into the facts suggested in your last but will do so in a few days with pleasure.

I have carefully read your lecture[1] and will briefly answer your questions as you have asked them —

I think you correctly describe Lincoln's condition except when you say that the "mental dethronement of his reason could only be detected by his closest friends." He may not have been "for a time totally insane" but he was so near that condition that every body who saw & knew him at once set him down as insane — Your

2. Marginal note: — *cott.* Probably John Scott.
3. Probably a reference to WHH's first four lectures on AL.

1. Presumably the Ann Rutledge lecture.

description of New Salem in its hopeful days is perfect. I have hunted over & around its hills & fished at its mill so often that I can see its log house, its long single street its branches bluffs flowers trees fruits birds &c just as you have discribed them. A correct discription of Mr Lincoln's town home & their surroundings at that period of his life where about to turn his steps into intellectual paths is very necessary to the student of his after life. The superficial reader may object to your discription on account of its minutness & extent but that is necessary in order to distinguish it from hundreds of other towns & spots of Earth —

I read your discription of the early people of New Salem with a great deal of interest as it is my idea of New Salem in its palmiest days ever before written which I had formed from hearing the early history of the Town reported for the last twenty years by those who then lived in & about it & helped to make its history.

I have so often heard these men and their doings of which you speak described & talked of by eye-witnesses that I endorse what you say but you will find it difficult to convince your readers who reside at a distance — say in the East, that you do not speak extravigantly — Such men did live then & there and made their kind of history all of which you correctly set down but many will not believe it.

I like your lecture as a whole and most if not all of its philosophy.

Your long association with Mr Lincoln in business — in the same office, your knowledge of his opinions expressed on the various subjects political religious social &c which came up in his daily conversation with you during that time & your personal acquaintance with his early associates enables you above all others to give a true & faithful story of his life. If Law-partners do not become acquainted with each other in hand & heart discussing with each other & with clients as they do every subject known to men in that free candor & sometimes confidential way peculiar to a lawyers office life then it is impossible for one man to know another —

The task you have Entered upon is a difficult one — He is a bold man who undertakes to write true biography of a public man especially of one called by the world — a Martyr —

Wishing you success in the undertaking and hoping that you may give the world at least one true picture of an eventful human life with all its lights & shades

I am very truly

Your Friend
T W McNeely

LC: HW2806–7; HL: LN2408, 1:303–5

314. B. B. Lloyd (WHH interview)

Nov. 29th 1866

Dr. Lloyd — Dentist

Says — Just before Lincoln left for Washington I met him on the Street, and Knowing that he had received many threatening letters of assassination &c, I suggested to him the propriety of care — caution — told him he had better take a cook from his own true & tried female acquaintances here: Mr Lincoln said — I will be cautious, but God's will be done. I am in His hands — & will be during my admr, and what he does I must bow to — God rules, and we should submit &c — This was Earnestly said

(This is correct H)

LC: HW2809; HL: LN2408, 2:404

315. Robert B. Rutledge to WHH

Oskaloosa Nov 30th 1866

Dear Friend

your letter of 29th inst, is received, and I take pleasure in answering your intarogatories, so far as my recollection Serves me,

you asked 1st What books did Mr Lincoln read & Study at New Salem,

He studied first Kirkhams Grammar[1] and the Arithmetic, then Natural philosophy, Astronomy & Chemistry, then Surveying, and Law, In the mean time read history & other books, the news papers of the day, in fact any and books from which he could derive information or knowledge, You asked 2d what month & year did he read each one in course, So long time has interveaned that I cannot give dates, but he studied Grammar, philosophy, Astronomy &c during his first years residence in New Salem and while clerking for Offatt,[2]

you asked 3d "What Method — way — manner &c, did he read," He had no regular teacher, but received more information from Minter Graham than any other person, While clerking for Offatt as Post Master or in the pursuit of any avocation, An opportunity would offer, he would apply himself to his studies, if it was but five minutes time, would open his book, which he always kept at hand, & study, close it recite to himself, then entertain company or wait on a Customer in the Store or post office apparently without any interuption, When passing from business to boarding house for meals, he could usually be seen with his book under his arm, or open in his hand reading as he walked, he frequently would seek young female company for entertainment & amusement, On such occasions he uniformly carried his book, Would alternately, entertain and amuse the company by witicisms jokes &c, and study his lesson, He never appeared to be a hard student as he seamed to Master his studies with little effort, until he commenced the study of Law, in that he became wholly engrossed,

I think he never avoided men until he he commenced the study of Law, further than to read & study at late hours after the business of the day was disposed of, in the Summer season he frequently retired to the woods to read & study, you asked did he read newspapers, More than he did books, he read papers incidentally for the news of the day, if there was any wit or good stories he was certain to

---

1. See §6, note 7.
2. Denton Offutt.

find them & to read to others, he took great pleasure in reading Jack Downings letters,

I have endeavored to condense this letter as much as posible, and the result is I have rendered it very unsatisfactory to me as it will no dout be to you, so I will close it, by promising you that at some other time when I feel in a better mood for writing, I will enlarge on this, Will be glad to receive two or three copies of your lecture[3] as also an other copy of your former lecture as the Editor of the Hawk Eye borrowed the one you sent me,

Pleas excuse all blunders as I find they are too numerous for me to correct at this hour

very truly yours
R B Rutledge

LC: HW2824; HL: LN2408, 1:568–70

316. *George Spears to WHH*

Tallula Ills No 30th 1866

Dear Sir

yours of Nov 27th came to hand & I hast to reply   I went to Petersburg yesterday and engaged the servises of Mr Hamilton the County clerk to draw a sketch of New Salem   he is a regular Railroad Enginear & practical Surveyor & this morning we went on to the spot & I pointid out the different old Locations & he Mr Hamilton skitched them as I pointed them out[1]   you may rely on them as being corect   the Offit house on the Top of the hill on the East end of the Plat is the Little store that Mr Lincoln first Clerked in when he came to New Salem & after that him & Berry sold goods in the first House East of Hill as you will see from the Plat   The old Bale House you will see marked on the Plat; North West of that some 60 or 80 feet stands the Rutledge Tavern   it was the first Store house of Hill & McNamer after that remodeled & made a dwelling or Tavern it being due south of Lincoln & Berys Store   now dear Sir I hope with this Explanation you may be able to understand this sketch   I offered to pay Mr Hamilton for his servises but he refused   too Strong Lincoln for that; hoping to hear from you soon I remain as ever your friend

George Spears

LC: HW2825

---

3. WHH's Ann Rutledge lecture.

---

1. This is probably the map now in the Lamon Papers at the Huntington Library. See the illustration on p. 428.

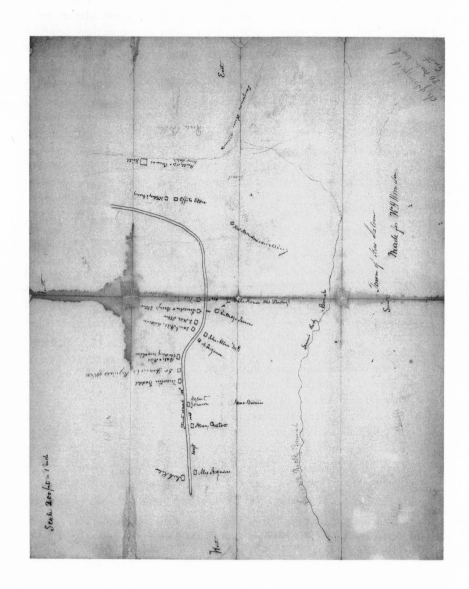

317. Caleb Carman to WHH

Petersburg Ills Nov 30th 1866

Friend Herndon

I Recd your letter of the 29th Reiuesting me to rite what I new Concerning Lincoln   I will Commens at the first of my Knowledg of him i Saw Lincoln in Sangamon Town about the year 1826   He Came Down from Decater with Denton Ofitt & Hankas & Johnson[1] said Ofitt imploied Lincoln Hanks & Johnson to build the Boat the Boat that is spoken of so often that Lincoln worked on Lincoln Hanks & Johnson Built the boat i think the boat went Down to New Salem & then was Loaded with Corn for New Orleans — I will now inform you what my opinion was of Mr Lincoln when i first him i thought him a Green horn tho after half hours Conversation with him i found Him no Green Horn   His Apperance was very od his dress was a short Roundabout of Blew Janes[2] Lite Blewe & pants of the same the pants very Short in the Leggs which Gave him a very curous Apperance with a corse pare of Stoga Shoes[3] on a Low Crownd Brod brimed Hat on this Completed his Dress after all this bad Apperance i Soon found to be a very inteligent young man His Conversation very often was a bout Books — such as Shakespear & other histories and Tale Books of all Discription in them Day   He Talked about policks Considerable He semed to have the Run of politicks very well he was a John Q Aadams man & went his Lenght on that Side of politicks   He was opposed to Slavery & said he thougt it a curse to the Land i liked to forgaten the Egg fried in Lincoln Low Crownd hat, at Sangamon Town one nigh at a Show it Caused a Great laff but Lincoln turned of the Joke very well as he Always did on any Occation   now Lincoln is Gon Down the River to New Salem I do not so mutch about him for Some Time

I do not know wether Lincoln went to New orleans or not whare he dide I Cannot Say but he Returnd again to New Salem & became a Candidate for the Legislator for the first time and was beatan this was before Sangamon Cty was Devided the next Time he was a Candidate for the Lagislature he was Elected & made a good member — Before was Elected i had moved Down to New Salem when i first moved to that place Lincoln Borded with one Mentor Graham after that he Boarded Nelson Alley for Some Time how long i Cant Say i Baught out Alley my Self & a one horse Tavren & Lincoln came to Live with Me Boarded with me Some Two years as near as i Can Reclect   Lincoln was post master & had it at my house the winter he went to Legislator i Kept the Office for him — the next time he was Elected was after he went to Springfield i think Lincolns Songs he Sang was a great many i do not think of all of them such as oald oald Suckey blew Skin & the woodpecker stoping on the hollow Beach tree[4] and a Great many others that was funny — he told a Geat many Jokes & yarns he was allways verry mery & full of fun — Lincoln once rote an Artical against Peter Cartwrgh which was a good

---

1. Denton Offutt, John Hanks, and John D. Johnston.
2. A short, close-fitting jacket, here made of the durable twilled cotton cloth called jeans.
3. A stout, coarse shoe or brogan.
4. For "Old Sukey Blue Skin," see §270, note 1.

one the name Sined to it was Diotrefus you may Bet it used the old man very Ruff it was a hard one it was Published in the Beardstown Cronicle by Francis Earns[5]   Simeon Francis would not publish in the Sangamon Journal — you wished to know what Lincoln used to Read he Read Shakespear & histories of all kinds news papers &c you wished to know something about the time Ann Rutledg died i cannot find out the time yet but i will try find out & let you know as Soon as i can   you wished to know about lincoln Reading he Read Setting Lying down & walking in the Streets he was allways Reading if he had Time, he was Some Time Surveying   Some Times tending the post office   Some times to law suits before a Justice of the peace you wished to know Something about Lincolns Love with Ann Rutleg this i cannot Tell mutch about   it is true he Loved Miss Rutledg i suppose this hapend before i moved to Salem i saw Mr James Short about this matter he says it is not so about Lincolns Refuseing to Eat on the account of the death of Miss Rutledg — I must Come to Close for i getting tired i will Rite again i will find out about the time of Miss Rutledgs death as Soon as i can — You must Excuse my bad hand Riteing — you Can fix it up to Your notion if you can read it —

Yours with Respect
Caleb Carman

LC: HW2811–15

318. Joshua F. Speed to WHH

Louisville 30 Nov 1866.

Dear Sir

I enclose you copies of all the letters of any interest from Mr Lincoln to me[1] —

Some explanation may be needed — that you may rightly understand their import —

In the winter of 40 & 41 — he was very unhappy about his engagement to his wife — Not being entirely satisfied that his *heart* was going with his hand — How much he suffered then on that account none Know so well as myself — He disclosed his whole heart to me —

In the summer of 1841. I became engaged to my wife — He was here on a visit when I courted her — and strange to say something of the same feeling which I regarded as so foolish in him — took possession of me — and kept me very unhappy from the time of my ingagement until I was married —

This will explain the deep interest he manifested in his letters, on my account —

---

5. Francis Arenz, editor of the *Beardstown Chronicle and Illinois Military Bounty Land Advertiser,* November 1, 1834. For the text of the letter, see Wilson, 63–66.

---

1. As Springer was probably not transcribing new material at this date and no such copies are known, it is unclear which letters Speed copied and sent to WHH.

If you use the letters (and some of them are perfect jems) & do it carefully, so as not to wound the feelings of Mrs Lincoln —

One thing is plainly discernable — If I had not been married & happy — far more happy than I ever expected to be — He would not have married —

I have erraced a name which I do not wish published — If I have failed to do it any where strike it out when you come to it — That is the word Sarah[2] —

I thank you for your last lecture[3] It is all new to me — But so true to my appreciation of Lincolns character that independant of my knowledge of you I would almost swear to it —

Lincoln wrote a letter (a long one which he read to me) to Dr Drake[4] of Cincinnatti discriptive of his case. Its date would be in Decer 40 or early in January 41. — I think that he must have informed Dr D of his early love for Miss Rutledge — as there was a part of the letter which he would not read.

It would be worth much to you if you could procure the original —

Chs D. Drake of St Louis may have his Fathers papers — The date which I give you — will aid in the search —

I remember Dr Drakes reply — which was that he would not undertake to priscribe for him without a personal interview —

I would advise you to make some effort to get the letter

Your friend &c

J. F. Speed

LC: HW2826–27

319. *James H. Matheny (WHH interview)*

Nov. 1866[1]

Col. Matheny

The first time I Ever Saw Lincoln was probably in 1832 — or 4. The first time I have any distinct recollection was when he came into our clerks office — in the Elkin brick House — South Side of the Square. I was deputy P.M under Mitchell from 1832 to 35 say. — got to Know Lincoln's hand writing as such P.M — He Lincoln used to write Editorials as far back as 1834 — or 5 for Francis — the Sangamon Journal — took hundreds of such Editorials from Lincoln to the Journal office — Lincoln was P.M at that time because his letters were *franked*. My opinion from what of Lincoln is that he Knew Shakespear as well — probably better in New Salem than he did in Spfgd.

1*st*   Lincoln was witty — humorous at 1832 & so down: the People would

---

2. Presumably Sarah Rickard (1824–1911).

3. WHH's Ann Rutledge lecture.

4. Daniel Drake.

---

1. Dated in the docketing. Springer's transcription seems to have been inadvertently omitted from the bound collection later sold to Lamon and filed with WHH's originals.

flock to hear him — loving jokes — humor &c —. This quality of his nature declined. When he first came among us his wit & humor boiled over

2d   My opinion is that Mr Lincoln's sadness — melancholy — despair, grew on him — He had 2 Sentiments — one to Stick his head in a hollow log, & see no one; & the other was to climb up — to win the [tithes?] of his ambition

3d   My own opinion is that Mr Lincoln's fancy — Emotion, & Imagination dwindled — ie — that is to Say his reason & his Logic — swallowed up all his being — ie became dominant

4th   Mr Lincoln grew more. more abstracted — Contemplative — &c. as he grew older.

I have often heard Mr Lincoln talk of the miraculous Conception, inspiration — Revelation — Virgin Mary say in 1837 — 8 — 9 &c   His was the language of of respect yet it was from the point of ridicule — not scoff— as I once loosely Said.

Mr Lincoln was a close Student in his way — he read Slowly — carefully and thought much — thought much more than he read —

I say I think Lincoln got more tender & humane as he got older — probably gentler would be a better word.

In 1834 & 5, my father[2] being a strong Methodist — a Kind of minister and loving Lincoln with all his soul hated to vote for him because he heard that Lincoln was an Infidel. Mr Lincoln did write a pamphlet attacking the divinity of christ — Special inspiration — Revelation &c —. All these things were talked about in 1835–6. & 7 — were talked of discussed &c in the Lincoln-Cartwright Congression rase in 1846 — Many Religious — Christian whigs hated to vote for Lincoln on that account — had to argue the question &c. with them. &c. &c — All this I distinctly well. In my for mer testimony[3] I used the word Scoff— Sneer &c — I think the better way of Expressing my [case?] is as follows — As it were he Seemed to do So — yet it was not a scoff— &c —: it was an argument of ridicule

The abve I Know in fact & sincerely believe all — do so from all my Knowledge of Mr Lincoln — facts from others. &c. Thse things & conclusions & correct

W H Herndon

LC: HW2566–67 (interview), HW2568–69 (Springer transcription)

320. Norman B. Judd (WHH interview)

[November 1866[1]]

N B Judd.

I Got on the cars with Lincoln at Spfgd and went the trip thru — never heard don't think that there is any truth in the Indiana or Ohio story about throwing

---

2. Charles R. Matheny.
3. See §365.

---

1. Pinkerton advised WHH, in a letter dated November 7, 1866, to see Judd about the Baltimore affair.

train off the track or in Killing Lincoln   Got Pinkertons letter At Cincinnati —
sent special messenger with letter their to me — One of Mr. Pinkerton's female
detectives met me at N.Y — Spy — laid all the facts before me —; I then arranged
that on my arrival at Philadellphia get a room and arranged to meet Pinkerton —
went to the Continent — quit it — went down to _____ hotel. Meet Pinker &
Felton Presd of Baltimore and Wilmington — There the Evidence was laid before
me — Pinkerton laid all the Evidence before me — was discussed — Pinkerton
was Exceedingly anxious that Lincoln Should go on to Washington that night (11
ocl) train — Felton & I agreed to it. The conclusion was that Pinkerton should
go to the Continental — see Lincoln and lay the whole facts before him — which
was done — went to my room — Lincoln was surrounded by the usual Crowd.
Lincoln was taken to a room —. Probally Nickoly   Lincoln liked Pinkerton —
had the utmost confidence in him as a gentleman — and a man of sagacity. All
the facts in detail were there given to Mr Lincoln — in detail. Go you must —
The world will laugh at you I know prepare to meet the charge of cowardice and
laughed at even by friends — and you must prepare yourself to be laughed at —
So will your friends — I am convinced that there is danger — Presdt Felton says
there is danger — Pinkerton says there is danger — There's danger, but you must
prepare to be laughed at by friends and foe. Lincoln Said — I can't go to-night —
Lincoln said, I can't go tonight"   I impress this idea on Mr Lincoln and you must
Enlarge on it. The Evidence was such as to Convince all honest minds — yet the
Evidence Could not be laid before the public because it would Endanger the very
agents of the Government — Pinkertons men and all. who were at that moment
playing their wise game among the Secessionists — in the Military Companies —
one was hung. I was hung —. I told Mr Lincoln all and tried to impress the danger on him — told him that friend & foe would laugh at him — yet he must stand
it — bear the sneers and scoffs — & scorn of men — friend & foe alike. — Evidence couldn't be got before the world — Mr Lincoln Said I have engaged to raise
the flag on to-morrow morning over Independence hall — I have engaged to go
to Harrisburg. Beyond these I have no engagements — after these engagements
are fulfilled you are at liberty to take such course as you please. I then said to Mr
Lincoln We don't to take any course that will endanger you or bring you into ridicule, because you are to bear the burthen of the thing." Lincoln then Said — Well
— I've Known Pinkerton for years and have Known and tested his truthfulness
and sagacity and my judgement co-incides with yours. I then Said to Lincoln —
We will then complete the arrangements and I I will tell you in detail to-morrow
[o]n the Cars between Philadelphia & Harrisburg. Mr. Nichol Knew of this interview — so did Lamon — neither Knew of what was doing or said — or being
said — Yet they Knew of the interview — Mr Lincoln then returned to the Par-
lors in the Continental and Mr. Felton Presdt — Mr Scott of Pa central and Mr
Sanford General Telegraph agent of the United States — were sent for and came
the room — the one we had the interview with Mr Lincoln then and there we made
the arrangements — engaged all — nearly all night in arranging & completing
the programme of next day. It was arranged that Special Car should leave Harrisburg at 6 o'c PM and reach Phila. on the 11 oc train — in season for the Train for

Baltimore & washington — (But one person of the party should accompany Mr Lincoln, that was talked over at the time.) That every train on the Penn. Central should be off the track from 6 — till that Lincoln Car had passed — Harrisburg to Pa — Come back — had passed and going or reached Philadelphia — That Pinkerton should meet Mr Lincoln with a Carriage at or on the outside of the City, and convey him — L to the Depot of the Baltimore & Wilmington depot, so as not to go through the heart of the city. Pinkerton did so — did his part well — artisticly so — Keenly shrewdly and well — Pinkerton was & is a good friend of Lincoln —: It was agreed that Felton should detain the 11 oc Baltimore train, on the Baltimore & to Baltimore until Mr L's arrival — That Mr Sanford should see to it the telegraph and take the Proper measures for the Execution of the plan — that no telegraphic message went over any of the wires until all this that evening was accomplished his Knowledge & skill being "equal to that task" — ie Sanford. Raised — L did — the flag. according to Programme — left for Harr — In the morning just before the train was ready to start for Harrisburg Mr Lincoln sent for me to Come to his room and there I Saw and met Fred Seward — Mr Lincoln said — Mr Seward has been sent by his father to inform me of the same Conspiracy. that you and Pinkerton Explained to me last night" (saw him Fred Seward at Philad) and advises that I proceed immediatly to Washington — You can Explain to him so far as you think fit what has been dne — I said to Mr Seward that arrangements had been made to pass Mr Lincoln Safely in Washington and you may so assure your father — that the mode — the manner in detail it is not necessary to detail." We left for Harrisburg and on the way I gave to Mr Lincoln a full and precise detail of all the arrangements that had been made — I said to him that the step to him was so important that I felt that it should be Communicated to the other gentlemen of the Party — Lincoln said — "You can do as you like about that"

As soon as the ceremonies are over at Harrisburg I will fix an interview between him and Col Sumner — Maj Hunter — Judge Davis — Capt Jno Pope — and Lamon; they being part of the Presdt party — I Changed my seat — Nickloly said to me, Judd there is something *up*. — What is it, if it is proper that I should Know — I said — Geo there is no necessity for your Knowing & one man can Keep a matter better than two — Arrived at Harrisburg — Ceremonies — got into the Parlor — Explained to Sumner & the Party the facts as well as I Could and the Plan and programe that should Carry Lincoln to Washington — Mr Sumner Spoke the first word — "That proceeding Said Sumner will be a d—d piece of cowardice" — I replied to this pointed hit — by Saying "that view of the Case has already been presented to Mr Lincoln" — A discussion of the matter, Pope favoring our arrangement — Sumner said — I'll get a Squad of Cavalry Sir, cut our way to Washington Sir." I said probably before that day comes the inauguration dy will have passed: it is important that Mr Lincoln Should be in Washington that day —" after Considerable discussion Judge Davis who had Expressed no opinion, but had put various questions to test the truthfulness of the story — turned to Mr Lincoln and said — You personally heard Mr Pinkertons Story — you heard this discussion — What is What is your judgement on the matter"? Mr Lincoln said I have listened to this discussion with interest — I See no reason — no good reason to change the Programme — and I am for Carrying it out as arranged by Judd —" This silenced all discussion and now the question was — Who should go with him (*all this* was at Harrisburg) to Washington? I stated that it had been deemed by those who had talked it over that but one man should accompany Mr Lincoln and Mr. Lamon's name had been named as that person — Sumner demurred Saying — I have undertaken to see Mr Lincoln to Washington. Mr Lincoln then went to his dinner — Lincoln heard all this Conversation — A Carriage to the door of the _____ hotel to take Mr Lincoln back to the Cars & thence to Philadelphia ~~where Pinkerton was to meet him as stated. Sumner was a fighting cock — If I had gone Sumner Pope & &c would have got mad, but Lamon's going could insult nor wound the feelings of any one — so it was Concluded. Lincoln agreed with me, or I should have been kicked out of court.~~ Lincoln was at the dinner table when the Carriage had arrived to take him to the track and thence to Phil. Lincoln was Called and went to his room, and Changed his Coat — Came down Stairs into the hall with his party — I said to Lamon hurry with him — he & Mr Lincoln quickly passed out of doors, followed by the others of the party. I put my hand on Col Sumners Shoulder who was going to get into the Carriage and Said — "One moment Col"   He turned to me — and while he turned to me — the Carriage drove off — and a madder man you never saw —. At 2 o'cl am I recd a dispatch from Mr Scott Stating that Mr Lincoln passed through Philadelphia —: Lincoln was in a dress coat — dinner Coat — Changed his coat — his shawl — a felt had &c that he carried with him — called by the world Scoth plaid —

LC: HW3951–58; HL: LN2408, 2:466–72

321. Edward L. Baker (WHH interview)

[1865–66[1]]

Baker Editor —

Says that Lincoln marked 3 passages in Mo — Democrat. that Lincoln marked the 3 passages — that he Baker took them up to Judge Davis — then he got here on the night train — the day before the nomination: that Lincoln & himself went to what is called the bull ring — a play at 5 vs — that the alley was full — was preengaged — that they went to a Excellent & neat Beer Saloon to play a game of Billiards — that the tables was full and took a glass of Beer — that they then went to the Journal office — there recd the first dispatch stating the result in the first ballot — & finally they parted — Each his own way — Baker to Dinner — Lincoln to his paper &c[2]

LC: HW3835; HL: LN2408, 2:81

---

1. In *The Real Lincoln* (1922), 264, JWW dates this interview July 1865.
2. Marginal note: *Baker will get Mo Democrat & see what the marks were — Logan had a letter in his pocket authorizing him to withdraw Lincolns name on Conditions.*

322. Rev. George J. Barrett (WHH interview)

[1865–66]

Revd _____ Barrett — (now in Paris Ills —)[1]

Says he Knew Mr Lincoln well — Knew him in Menard — Says that he was Coming from the South going North when he met Mr. Lincoln going in 18__   to his duel ground[2] — Several men were with him — just as we met we came to a man who had mired down in the mud — couldn't get out. Lincoln was about to stop when one of his Company — "Now Lincoln don't make a d—d fool of your-self — Come — Come along —" Lincoln didn't pay no attention to what the man said — got off his horse — L took my horse & his own & tied them to the strangers waggon by ropes — Straps & strings — pulled the man with his family — When we got through scarcely any man Could have told what or who we were. When it was over L got on his horse and simply rode on to Catch up with his Company. Didn't Know at that time where L was going nor on what business — Had I Known I should have tried my hands on peace.

LC: HW3841; HL: LN2408, 2:177–78

323. Newton Bateman (WHH interview)[1]

[1865–66]

Newton Bateman

Says that Mr. Lincoln moved his office or what not down to the State House in the Govorners room, just after he was nominated — long before he was elect-ed. The one I occupied was the reception room — just north of Mr. Lincoln's — a door between us — Lincoln came to his office about 9 or 10 o'clock A.M. — sometimes sooner — in the Governor's room about 7 months — Wood[2] was Gov'n.

Lincoln stayed in the office till January and part of it — then moved to Johnson's building No. 3 — in Jan'y 1861. The question of Religion discussed by Mr. L. and myself was in Oct. — late in Oct. 1860 — put it down in writing — a kind of general points — not precise — didn't write out in particular and full till after Mr. L. was assassinated. His attention was occupied all the time — run

---

1. Reverend Barrett, whose first name WHH neglected to write down, was the father of the Lincoln collector Oliver R. Barrett. See Sandburg, 28.
2. September 21 or 22, 1842.

---

1. This is the only known text deriving from WHH's interviews with Bateman. In a letter to Isaac M. Arnold, WHH wrote: "I took down notes of Bateman's conversation, and showed them to him, after they were written out, and he confessed to their substantial correctness: they are dated the 3d — 12 — & 28 Dec. 1866 (see Lamon's L 496. Read my whole letter in Lamon 492–97" (Dec. 27, 1882, CHS). The whereabouts of the originals of notes taken on these dates are not known. The text given here, because it is a Springer transcription, had to be based on earlier interviews.
2. Springer first wrote *Bissell*, then struck this out and wrote *Wood* above it. William Bissell died in office and was succeeded by John Wood.

to death — hardly had more visitors at Washington. — Rankin[3] a Mississippi *[blank space]* came to see Mr. Lincoln — heard this conversation — The Col. said — If the *[blank space]* could only hear your conversation &c — all would be right.

One of Mr. Lincoln's friends — said on seeing Mr. Lincoln — "Well — how do you do, Mr. President," "Not yet President — better not count the chickens till they are hatched," said Mr. Lincoln. "Well, but Mr. Pres'd't they are *[blank space]*" replied the man.

HL: LN2408, 2:175–76

324. George Brinkerhoff (WHH interview)

[1865–66]

Geo M Brinkerhoof —

Says on the 8th of august Meeting AD 1860 Lincoln made his appearance on the ground, Fair Grounds in a Carriage —. That the People Surrounded the Carriage — sunk it in the mud — stuck tight — broke in the top of the Carriage — Came near smothering Lincoln — Brinkerhoff & others backed up Crowders horse into the Crowd where Lincoln was — picked him up — slipped him over the horses tail on to the saddle — led the horse to town — Lincoln held on to the Knob of the Saddle — a little german man — a chicago wide awake[1] ran from the fair grounds — got to Ls house before L did — helped L off — L said who are you — belong to Chicago wide awake — "Tell 'em to come down to my house to-night — want to shake hands with 'em —" Wide Awakes did go down — and he did shake hands with them — &c

LC: HW3846; HL: LN2408, 2:176–77

325. Christopher C. Brown (WHH interview)

[1865–66]

Chris Brown says that on the day that Lincoln got nominated he L was very nervous — told vulgar Stories[1] &c vehemently — said that as the balloting was going on that Lincoln said in reference to the balloting & Seward — "I've got him" Lincoln never Enquired of Young Stuart[2] any thing about his old friends —

LC: HW2371; HL: LN2408, 2:217–18

---

3. Possibly W. J. Rankin, then U.S. senator from Mississippi.

---

1. Uniformed semimilitary units of Republican partisans in the 1860 campaign that participated in torchlight parades, sang songs, kept order at meetings, and served as poll-watchers.

---

1. See §326.
2. Possibly a reference to one of the three sons of Brown's father-in-law, John T. Stuart.

326. Christopher C. Brown (WHH interview)

[1865–66]

C. C. Brown

Says that he came down to Lincoln's office Early on the morning of the day when Lincoln was nominated.

Lincoln was lieing on the Sofa — said "Well Brown, have you heard any thing."— Lincoln said "Lets go to the telegraph office., Brown" They did go over about 10 o'cl am. Lincoln stopt awhile till the telegraph brought the intelligence of the first ballot — the 2d. ballot — the 3d &c. Lincoln then exclaimed — "I've got him."

Lincoln played ball with me on that day (so he did with P. P. Enos, Baker[1] &c) L was nervous, fidgety — intensely excited Lincoln told stories — one of which was Washingtons picture in a necessary — privy in England — make an English-man S—h—t.[2]

Lincoln came all the way from Coles Co., 80 or 90 M, to my wedding. Married Jno. T. Stuart — a relation to Lincoln[3] — In the morning after My Marriage Lincoln met me and Said — "Brown why is a woman like a barrel —" C.C.B. could not answer. Well Said Lincoln — You have to raise the hoops before you put the head in"

Lincoln was our relative — The Todd — Stuart — Edwards family — with preacher & priest — dogs servants &c — got mad at Mr L because he made the house-divided-against-itself Speech. We flinched — dodged — Lincoln said he would Explain: he did Explain — see his Speeches with Douglass —

Lincoln was a radical — fanatically so — & yet he never went beyond the People. Kept his views & thoughts to himself. — ie he never told all he felt. —

Brown Says further, that some Eastern Man — who had something to do in or with a news paper in N.Y — Came to our office (S.E & Brown[4]) on some business before L was generally spoken of as a candidate. The man Expressed a wish to see L. I took him to see Lincoln. The man said to Lincoln — I told our boys to put your name for Presd or Vice Pres on the banner. &c —

Mr Lincoln Said — Well my friend — I am much obliged to you — I guess either position is big & high Enough for me"
Brown Says

I never heard Lincoln say anything about his religious views — or religion in any aspect —

LC: HW3844–45; HL: LN2408, 2:159–61

---

1. Pascal P. Enos, a Springfield merchant and politician, and Edward L. Baker, editor of the *Illinois State Journal.*

2. Cf. §127.

3. Since John T. Stuart's mother, Hannah Todd, was the sister of Robert S. Todd, MTL's father, Stuart was MTL's first cousin and thus "a relation to Lincoln." Brown married (as WHH failed to record) Stuart's daughter Bettie.

4. Refers to the law firm of Stuart, (Benjamin) Edwards, and Brown.

327. Augustus H. Chapman (WHH interview)

[1865–6]

Col. A. H. Chapman —

Says that Abram Lincolns grand fathers name was Mordecai — & not Abraham — That Mordecai — the grand father was Killed by the indians in Mch 1784. Morecai had three sons —: Mordecai, Josiah & Thomas —. The grandfather was working in the field — laying up the last rails — when an Indian shot him — Mordecai ran to the house — Josiah ran to a stockade some four miles. Mordecai ran to the House got a rifle — ran up Stairs or aloft put his gun through the port hole — Saw the Indian with Thomas in hands or arms — took site — shot the Indian fell — Another Indian saw the port hole in the house — cautioned the other Indian but too late — the Indian in the field ran — threw away his gun which was found. Mordecai Killed 3 Indians — Kiled the Indian in the lane — one in the field and one that ran toward the fence — dropt his gun leaned up against the fence — got over — leaving his gun — crept into a tree top — In the mean time the party with Josiah came from the fort or Stockade & found what was done &c.

It is the opinion of the the Col that no man Knows that the original Lincoln's were Quakers — nor from Penn — nor were they born or raised in Rockingham Co Virginia — thinks from family reputation that they were born in Halifax Co. Virginia on the head waters of Roanoke — He gives this reason: he says Hanks tells him that it was the reputation in the family — including men & women — young & old that they the Grand father & Bros *rolled Tobacco* to Richmond —: there they rolled it — the Tobacco — about 60 or 70 miles — which rolling was putting the Tobacco in a hogshead — ran the pole through the tobacco to give the pole the power of guiding the Tobacco — use hand spikes &c — &c

Lincoln Came down to see his mother after Election — visited the grave of his father — as soon as I get time I want the grave fixed — wanted grave Enclosed —[1] Took a good parting from his Step Mother —

Bull dog story[2] — 3 Girls, 1 his daughter and 2 of his last wife & old lady ran — So did the dog — bit him — He said G—d d—n the dog — take him off — Lincoln's Step mother — money sent to her — by Abe — did her no good

Lincoln was a great wrestler — he returned home about 1831. from N.O from one of his trips, and his fame for this was wide Spread —. Danl Needham heard of it and Came to see Lincoln — Lincoln & Needham met at Wabash point in Coles Co —. and Needham challenged Lincoln — Lincoln accepted it, agreeing both to wrestle side holds. Lincoln threw Needham twice — Needham said — Lincoln "You have thrown me twice, but you can't whip me." Lincoln replied — Needham are you satisfied that I can throw you? If you are not and must be convinced through a thrashing I will do that too for Your Sake."

LC: HW3847–49; HL: LN2408, 1:153–55

---

1. Marginal note: *wanted his fathers grave to have a plain, neat Tombs Stone —.*

2. This story seems to be told on Thomas Lincoln, and it must date after 1819 when Sarah Lincoln and her family came to Indiana.

328. Isaac Cogdal (WHH interview)

[1865–6]

Isaac. Cogdale.

I Knew Abe Lincoln the first week he came to Salem in 1831 — June or July.
He Kept Store for Offutt in Salem in 1831 & 2. — Saw Offutts goods opened —
Lincoln boarded with Jas Rutledge at the time he was a Clk of Offutt. Rutledge
lived in Salem — Kept tavern — small frame one story house made of Clap boards
— fronting south and on the Main street — which East & west — but one Street
in town — house had 4 rooms. The house was on the north side of the Main Street
— fronting South[1]   The first book I ever Saw in L's hand was Blackstone — in
1832 — He surveyed for Calhoun & Neal — one in 1834 to 1836 — the other
from 1836 to 1838, I think — Salem was a great place for fighting and Lincoln
was called the Peace Maker: he always interfered. He became acquainted with Miss
Ann Rutledge in 1831 — 2, & 3: he courted her — and after he was Elected Presdt.
he said to me one day — "Ike Call at my office in the State house about an hour
by sun down. The Company will then all be gone" —

Cogdale went according to request & Sure Enough the Company dropt off
one by one — his, Ls, Clerk included.

"I want to enquire about old times and old acquaintances" Said Lincoln. He
then said — "When we lived in Salem there were the Greens, Potters Armstrongs
— & Rutledges. These folks have got scattered all over the world — some are dead.
Where are Rutledges — Greens — &c."

"After we had spoken over old times — persons — Circumstances — in which
he showed wonderful memory I then dare to ask him this question —

May I now in turn ask you one question Lincoln Said Cogdale Most assured-
ly. I will answer your question if a fair one with all my heart. then it was that he
answered — as follows[2]

Abe is it true that you fell in love with & courted Ann Rutledge" Said Cogdale.
Lincoln said, "it is true — true indeed I did. I have loved the name of Rutledge to
this day. I have Kept my mind on their movements ever since & love them dearly" — said L

Abe — Is it true — Said Cogdale, that you ran a little wild about the matter:

I did really — I run off the track: it was my first. I loved the woman dearly &
sacredly: she was a handsome girl — would have made a good loving wife — was
natural & quite intellectual, though not highly Educated — I did honestly — &
truly love the girl & think often — often of her now."

Bakers praire comes up — on the East side of the river just Even with Salem
— a little north — The forest on the hill eastward joins Bakers prairie and is East
& South of Salem —

---

1. This sentence is in the margin.

2. This paragraph is written in the margin and seems to represent the result of WHH's cross-examina-
tion of Cogdal on this point.

The Able[3] house was a frame house — it is the same house under the hill now: it was once on the top of the hill — fronted East — looked into Bakers Prairie —

LC: HW3856–57; HL: LN2408 1:469–71

329. Isaac Cogdal (WHH interview)

[1865–66[1]]

Cogdale

I Knew Lincoln — Knew him in 1832 — you ask about the Crazy spell. It is my opnion that if Mr Lincoln was craz it only technically so — and not radically & substantially so. We used to say — you were Crazy about Ann Rutledge. He was then reading Blackstone — read hard — day & night — terribly hard — did love Ann Rutledge for he told me so — was terribly melancholy — moody.

I have often talked to Mr Lincoln on the question of Religion in his own office & in your presence too (This is true Herndon). Mr Lincoln believed in God — and all the great substantial groundworks of Religion — Believed in the progress of man and of nations — He believed that nations like individuals were punished for their Sins — there violations of fundamental rights — &c —

He did not believe in Hell — Eternal punishment as the christians say — his idea was punishment as Educational. He was a Universalist tap root & all in faith and sentiment. I have talked this often and often with him Commencing as Early as 1834 and as late down as 1859 — (This is Correct Herndon). He did not believe in the orthodox Theologies of the day —

I do Know that Mr Lincoln did write a letter, pamphlet — book or what not on the faith as I understand he held — denying Special & miraculous Revelation — Inspiration & Conception — As I stated Lincoln thought that God predestined things — and governed the universe by Law — nothing going by accident. He could not believe that created[2] a world and that the result of that would be Eternal damnation &c — His mind was full of terrible Enquiry — and was skeptical in a good sense —[3]

LC: HW3858–59

330. Jesse Dubois (WHH interview)

[1865–66]

(Dubois)

One day — just before Lincoln delivered his house divided against Speech — Dubois Came into Lincolns office & found L writing — Dubois Said — L. what

---

3. The house of Bennett and Elizabeth Abell, where AL sometimes stayed.

---

1. This interview would appear to be later than the one given in §328.
2. The subject of "created" appears to have been inadvertently dropped.
3. On the docketing: *I think the with in about true   W H Herndon.*

are you writing. I am writing something which you may or may never see — Said Dubois — let me see it now — No Sir Said Mr Lincoln I have Said I will not. The conversation between L & Dubois then changed to a subject of business. In a few dys after this his house divided against itself speech Mr Dub & L met. Mr L said now Dubois I will tell you what I was doing when you Came into my office and why I would not show you what I was doing. You need not say what you were writing says Dubois — because I now Know. Mr Lincoln then said let me Explain why I would not read that Speech to you. This passage in the Speech about the house divided against itself I would not read it to you because I Knew you would make me Change it — modify & molify. & I was determined to read it — had willed it so. and was willing to perish with it, if nescessary. Mr Lincoln did this because he wanted to cut the winds out of *Seward* & *others*

Dubois Said Lincoln was selfish — was ambitious no administrative capabilities and was not in all things at all times perfectly honest — Wrote to me to go for him for Speaker. Where light was L was always there: he was a man of deep and profound [policy?], hiding &c. &c.

What Bill Jayne Said

LC: HW3862; HL: LN2408, 2:158–59

331. H. E. Dummer (WHH interview)

[1865–66]

Hon H. E. Dummer —

I Came up to Springfd Ills in March 1832 on the Talisman — about 120 Tons — Polluck[1] Capt.— Mrs Polluk a hoar — The citizens gave Poluk a good reception — got up a ball — danced in the old Court house — Coming up from mouth of Sangamon River one whole week — about 45 M Straight — about 150 — When I landed in the town of Spfgd the whipping stood on the public — Court house square — State House do —

Lincoln used to come to our office in Spfgd and borrow books — don't Know whether he walked or rode: he was an uncouth looking lad — did not say much — what he did say he said it strongly — Sharply.

In 1859 I was in the Supm Court room in the State house: Lincoln was or had been telling his yarns. A man — a Kind of lick spittle — a farmer Said — Lincoln why do you not write out your stories & put them in a book" Lincoln, drew himself up — fixed his face, as if a thousand dead carcusses — and a million of privies were Shooting all their Stench into his nostrils, and Said "Such a book would Stink like a thousand privies".

Lincoln had 2 characters — one of *purity* — & the other as it were an insane

---

1. J. M. Pollock, master of the *Talisman*.

love in telling dirty and Smutty Stories — A good story of that Kind has a point
with a sting to it.

I will give you my reminiscences of Mr L in broken doses —

LC: HW3868; HL: LN2408, 2:245–46

332. Elizabeth Todd Edwards (WHH interview)

[1865–66[1]]

Mrs N W. Edwards

I am the wife of the Hon N. W. Edwards.: Mr Lincoln married my Sister —
Mary. We Came to Springfield about 1835 — My sister Mrs Wallace now Came
to live with us about that time. Doct Wallace & her were married in 18___[2] We
had a vacancy in our family by that marriage — wrote to Mary to Come out and
make our home her home: She had a Step Mother with whom she did not agree.
Marry was born in 1818 — well Educated — taught at a private School in Lexington — Mrs _____[3] Keeping it.

Mary Came to Illinois about 1838 — Mr Lincoln Commenced Seeing Mary
about 1839 & 4 — the winter of 1839 & 40 — directly after Doct Wallace was
married   I Knew Mr L well — he was a cold Man — had no affection — was
not Social — was abstracted — thoughtful. I Knew he was a great man long years
Since — Knew he was a rising Man and nothing Else modifying this, desired Mary
at first to Marry L. L. Could not hold a lengthy Conversation with a lady — was
not sufficiently Educated & intelligent in the female line to do so — He was
charmed with Mary's wit and fascinated with her quick sagacity — her will — her
nature — and Culture — I have happened in the room where they were sitting
often & often and Mary led the Conversation — Lincoln would listen & gaze on
her as if drawn by some Superior power, irresistably So: he listened — never Scarcely
Said a word. I did not in a little time think that Mr L. & Mary were Suitable to
Each other & so Said to Mary. Mary was quick, lively, gay — frivalous it may be,
Social and loved glitter Show & pomp & power. She was an Extremely Ambitious
woman and in Ky often & often Contended that She was destined to be the wife
of some future President — Said it in my presence in Springfield and Said it in
Earnest. Mr Speed Came to See Miss Matilda Edwards — left & went to Ky —
Miss Edwards Staying. Mr Lincoln loved Mary — he went Crazy in my own opinion — not because he loved Miss Edwards as Said, but because he wanted to marry
and doubted his ability & Capacity to please and support a wife. Lincoln & Mary
were Engaged — Every thing was ready & prepared for the marriage — Even to
the Supper &c —. Mr L failed to meet his Engagement — Cause insanity. In his

1. H&W (1889), 227, gives the date as January 10, 1866.
2. Frances Todd and Dr. William Wallace were married in 1839.
3. Madame Victorie Charlotte LeClere Mentelle.

lunacy he declared he hated Mary and loved Miss Edwds. This is true, yet it was not his real feelings. A Crazy man hates those he loves when at himself — often — often is this the Case. The world had it that Mr L backed out. and this placed Mary in a peculiar Situation & to set herself right and to free Mr Lincoln's mind She wrote a letter to Mr L Stating that She would release him from his Engagements. Mr Edwards & myself after the first Crush of things told Mary & Lincoln that they had better not Ever marry — that their natures, mind — Education — raising &c were So different they Could not live happy as husband & wife — had better never think of the Subject again   However all at once we heard that Mr L & Mary had Secret meetings at Mr S. Francis' — Editor of the Spfgd Journal. Mary Said the reason this was So — the Cause why it was — that the world — woman & man were uncertain & slippery and that it was best to keep the secret Courtship from all Eyes & Ears. Mrs Mrs L told Mr L that though She had released him in the letter Spoken of — yet She Said that She would hold the question an open one — that is that She had not Changed her mind, but felt as always. The whole of the year year the Crazy Spell Miss Edwards was at our house[4] — Say for a year. I asked Miss Edwards — Subsequently Mrs Strong if Mr Lincoln Ever Mentioned the subject of his love to her. Miss Edwards Said — "On my word he never mentioned Such a Subject to me: he never even Stooped to pay me a Compliment."

Mr Douglas used to come to see Mary — probably: it is quite likely that his intentions were true & Sincere. Mary was asked one day by some of her friends which She intended to have — "Him who has the best prospects of being President Said Miss Todd. The marriage of Mr L & Mary was quick & sudden — one or two hours notice.

Miss Edwards one dy was asked why she married such an old dried up husband — such a withered up old Buck:[5] She replied: "He had lots of houses[6] & gold"   Mary was present at this question & answer and She then remarked — "Is that true — I would rather marry a good man — a man of mind — with a hope and bright prospects ahead for position — fame & power than to marry all the houses[7] — gold & bones in the world." Mary Lincoln has had much to bear, though she don't bear it well: she has acted foolishly — unwisely and made the world hate her: She opened a private letter of mine after I left Washington & because in that letter my Daughter gave me her opinion of Mrs L She became Enraged at me. I tried to Explain — She would Send back my letters with insulting remarks. Mr Lincoln Shed tears when I left Washington — had been Solicited to Come to Washington by Mr & Mrs Lincoln. Mr Lincoln Said to me — Mrs Edwards — "do Stay with me — you have Such a power & control Such an in-

---

4. WHH originally wrote: "In about one year from the Crazy Spell. . . ."

5. Matilda Edwards married Newton D. Strong in 1844 at the age of twenty-two; he was thirty-four. See J. Bennett Nolan, "Of a Tomb in the Reading Cemetery and the Long Shadow of Abraham Lincoln," *Pennsylvania History* 19:3 (July 1952).

6. Possibly "horses."

7. Possibly "horses."

fluence over Mary — Come do Stay and Console me." This was sometime after Willies death[8]

Once I took Mr L — to Calm his mind — to Cheer him — to inspire him, if you please, with hope & Confidence — to turn away his attention from business as well as grief — down to and through the rich Conservatory — hot house cold house &c. where the flowers are Kept & where the world is represented by flowers that Speak. and made the remark to Mr L. — "O — how beautiful this is — these roses — &c. are fine — these Exotics are grand." and to which Mr L. said — "I never was in here before: how Spring like it looks — I don't care for flowers — have no natural or Educated taste for Such things." I made him walk to the Park one day north of the White H. He hadn't been there for a year and Tad went with us: Tad locked the gate — hid the key — Mr L. told Tad to get the key. Tad laughed and L thought it Smart & Shrewd. I respect & love Mr Lincoln — think he was a great man — a good man & an honest one. He was a little ungrateful I think from the want of [illegible][9]

Mr Lincoln was Kind & good to his domestic & other Servants: one day the girl threatened to leave unless She Could get $1.50 per week. Mrs L. Could rather would not give the Extra 25 c: the girl Said he would leave. Mrs L. Said Leave. Mr L heard the Conversation — didnt want the girl to leave — told his wife so — asked — begged her to pay the $1.50. Mrs L remained incorrigible   Mr L slipt round to the backdoor and Said — Don't leave — Tell Mrs Lincoln you have Concluded to Stay at $1.25 and Ill pay the odd 25c to you. Mrs Lincoln overheard the Conversation and Said to the girl & Mr L — What are you doing — I heard Some Conversation — Couldn't understand it — I'm not going to be deceived — Miss you Can leave and as for you Mr L I'd be ashamed of myself."

Mr Lincoln's habits were like himself odd & wholy irregular. He loved nothing and ate mechanically. I have seen him Sit down at the table and never unless recalled to his Senses, would he think of food. He was a peculiar man

Mrs Lincoln insulted Seward one day. Mr Seward was the Power behind the Throne. Mrs L had heard of this often & often — One day She Said to Mr Seward. It is Said you are the Power behind the Throne — I'll Show you that Mr L is President yet.

Mr L and Mary Saw Each other in that parlor there. This house is about as it was, Excepting this Porch which has been added Since — Two Story brick — ceiling low — &c —

LC: HW3870–73; HL: LN2408, 2:220–26

---

8. William Wallace Lincoln died on February 20, 1862.

9. In his biography, WHH expanded considerably on these notes in his account of what Elizabeth Edwards told him about her visit to Washington. See H&W (1889), 508–10.

333. Ninian W. Edwards (WHH interview)

[1865–66[1]]

Lincoln went in[2] —
   1836. for Internal improvement and the Bank.
   1838. School Laws — Banks —
In *1834* — Canal Bills — Central Rail Road Bill — 1
In 1840 —
   Candidate Speaker — once or Twice
Called Session of 1835[3]
Lincoln drew up the law removing the Seat of *Government.*

The reason why Lincoln was so popular in 1834 was because the Democrats ran
him — They the Democracy went to Lincoln and made the bargain — he told
Stuart of it — Stuart told him to do: he did it and *[blank space]*[4] were Elected —

LC: HW2369; HL: LN2408, 2:215–16

334. Ninian W. Edwards (WHH interview)

[1865–66]

N W Edwards went to Washington in 1861 & 2 — says Lincoln read Shakespear Every Evening — not the Bible — Says he — Lincoln Enquired of no
friend —: asked no questions about old friends — Mrs Edwards says he has no
heart. Thinks Lincoln once told him he believed that the Bible &c was the Divine Revelation &c —
   When he first came to City Edwards says Lincoln was a mighty Rough man
— did much for Lincoln — was at Edwds house for 4 ys   Every Sunday.
   Edwards Says that he thinks that Lincoln was not a warm hearted man —
Seemed to be ungrateful — was not — did not think — if brought home to him
he would do what was right —
   In Washington I saw Lincoln made[1] twice — once at Wade & Sherman: they
said for certain they would not speak to him: he said this was too hard — had done
more for them than any two men in the nation —
   Edwards thinks that he always thought L would be great man. Edwards made
him promise that when he was Presdt he L would give him Edwds a good office.

---

1. On the basis of WHH's sequential numbering of his four interviews with Edwards, this and the following two items (which WHH numbered 1, 2, 3) may have been written earlier than §91, the interview
dated September 22, 1865 (which WHH numbered 4).
   2. Presumably refers to AL's legislative interests and activities in the Illinois House of Representatives (1834–
41). Edwards himself served in the House (1836–39 and 1848–52) and also in the Illinois Senate (1844–48).
   3. Refers to a special, as opposed to regular, session.
   4. WHH left room for the names of those elected.

---

1. Presumably "mad."

Had I been Lincoln and had been taken in as Butler[2] did Lincoln I certainly would have given him an office — *[illegible]* Butler got mad — Swore he would put L down — took up — B did to beat Lincoln — did it &c —

LC: HW2371; HL: LN2408, 2:216–17

335. Ninian W. Edwards (WHH interview)[1]

[1865–66]

Lincoln's Speech — Dick Taylor — N. W. Edwards

During his canvass for the Legislature in 1840 Col E. D. Taylor charged him Abe with belonging to the aristocracy. To which charge he replied that whilst Col. Taylor had his stores over the county, and was riding in a fine carriage, wore his kid cloves and had a gold headed cane, he was a poor boy hired on a flat boat at eight dollars a month, and had only one pair of breeches and they were of buckskin now said he if you know the nature of buckskin when wet and dried by the sun they would shrink and mine kept shrinking until they left for several inches my legs bare between the top of my Socks and the lower part of my breeches — and whilst I was growing taller they were becoming shorter: and so much tighter, that they left a blue streak around my leg which you can see to this day — If you call this aristocracy I plead guilty to the charge.

LC: HW2370; HL: LN2408, 2:218–19

336. Wesley Elliott (WHH interview)

[1865–66]

Wesly Elliott — aged about 46 years of age[1] —

Says my Father moved into the County 1 Mile north of the city on the Athens road in the Spring of 1831. He was the owner & Keeper of a two story log Cabin and for a tavern — had a passage between East & west room — was on the south side of Jefferson Street fronting north opposite Capps grocery — west of the Chicago and St Rail Road depot about 300 yards — The Tavern had a porch in front of it up & down — ie to each story — The Sign was a fine fat buck with fine horns pointed: he was painted proudly Standing & as it were Stamping: the deer looked north East — at as appeared at your fathers Indian Queen — a tavern Sign. The boys one night shot the deer full of bullet holes — he looked as if he ought to be dead yet he Stood on the Sign and Swung — My father about 1832 Sold the old

---

2. William Butler (1797–1876) boarded and lodged AL when he first lived in Springfield.

---

1. Marginal note (possibly in WHH's hand): *1840.*

---

1. The presence of this interview in the Springer transcriptions (1866) and Elliott's birth date (1822) indicate a discrepancy in the testimony about his age.

tavern to Morris — who lived out in the Country — Mrs. Abrams — Mrs Johnson
— sometimes Called Kept a Similar tavern during the Same years just west of my
fathers about 100, just opposite your present house where you live. It was in my
fathers Tavern that Lincoln Stopt in 1831 — if he Stopt at the Buck horn —
South Side of West Jefferson, between 1 & 2 Street

    LC: HW3874; HL: LN2408, 2:251–52

337. Hardin H. Elmore (WHH interview)

                [1865–66]

Hardin H. Elmore

    In 1834 — one man Could, with one horse & plow, plow in the Spring in or-
der to put the ground in operation to Seed from an acre & one half to 2 acres —

    Now in 1860 — Single plow 2½ to 3 acres — & Now with double plow 6
acres

    Could Cut ¾ acres of wheat with a Sickle — Could Cradle from 2 to 2½
acres —

    Cut now with a reaper from 10 to 12 acers —

    Could thresh & tramp about 15 Bushels — wheat —

    Now 300 bushels —

    Could fan & Clean about with a Sheet 20 Bushels — Could fan out with fan
Machines 100 Bushels —

    Now thresh & clean 300 —

    Carry Plow — wooden mould boards — ½ Iron & half wood — Jewett Plow
Iron mould board — Now [Pane and Prince?]

    Could plant Corn 3 acres per day — Now 20 for 2 hands —

    Travel 30 M in 1830 — in 1860 400 —

    Hall 28 hundred 2 horses 5000 with 4 or 6 horses — Now in cars —

    Travel intelligence 50 — per day — Now around the globe

    LC: HW3875; HL: LN2408, 2:242–43

338. P. P. Enos (WHH interview)[1]

                [1865–66]

P. P. Enos

    Tells this as a fact. A man was making Some improvements about Mr Lincolns
house: the thing to be done, Could not be fixed and Completed without Cutting

---

    1. In the top margin: *(Domestic Happiness —)* and *(Hell &c —.*

down a pretty & valuable Shade tree in front of the house. The workman told Mrs L that the tree would have to Come down or the plan altered. "Cut the tree down," Said Mrs L'. The man did not want to do it — went to See Mr L. and stated what would have to be done. Mr L Said — "Have you seen Mrs L." "Yes was the reply" of the man "— Then in God's name cut it down clean to the roots" Said Mr L'.

Again — (P.P.E. Says) — Once while A. Y. Ellis was P.M,[2] L Came off the Circuit — went to P.O after Eating his Supper — read the letters — Cracked jokes &c — till about 11oc (Night time.) Lincoln Said all at once "Well I hate to go home." Said Ellis "come down to my house and Stay all night — Know you hate to disturb your family — So Lincoln went and avided — well — well —

LC: HW3876; HL: LN2408, 2:173–74

339. William G. Greene (WHH interview)

[1865–66]

Wm Green
Says that in 1831. I went to a Show at new
LC: HW3879

340. Russell Godbey (WHH interview)[1]

[1865–66]

Squire Godbey
I first Knew Lincoln in 1832 — I Saw — the first time I ever Saw Abe with a law book in his hands he was Sitting astride of Jacob Bails wood pile in New Salem — says I "Abe what are you studying" "Law — replied" Abe — Great — God Almighty — responded Godbey —. He Surveyed the first piece of land I Ever had Surveyed — He staid with me all night and Sold him two buck skins — well dressed to fox his Surveyors pants. Mrs Armstrong did the foxing — I always loved to meet him and talk to him — I voted for Lincoln in opposition to my own creed & faith in Politics. Snodgrass told me not to vote for him because Abe was a deist. I did it. When a fight was on hand Abe would Sy to me — Lets go and break up the Row with a laugh & we generally did it — Voted for him in 1834 *[illegible]* — Martin gills — Abe [undid?]

LC: HW3879

---

2. 1849–53.

---

1. This appears to be an earlier draft of §341.

341. Russell Godbey (WHH interview)

[1865–66]

Squire Godbey

I first Knew Abe Lincoln in 1832 — I Saw him — the first time I Ever Saw him with a law book in his hands he was Sitting astraddle of Jake Bails wood pile in New Salem — Said to him — "Abe — what are you Studying" "Studying law" — replied Abe. "Great God Almighty —" Said Godbey. Lincoln surveyed the first piece of land I Ever owned or Ever had Surveyed. He Stopt with me all one night after Surveying. I Sold two Excellent well dressed buck skins. He — Abe wanted them to fox his Surveyer's pants. to prevent thorns — briars — bushes & vines from cutting them — &c —. Mrs Armstrong did the foxing and Sowing.[1] I always loved & respected Abe, though he and I radically differed in politics. I loved to meet — greet & talk to Abe. He was a witty — humorous & genial man — an honest man —. I voted for him in 1834 against my political Creed & principles   He was Elected. Snodgrass[2] told me not to vote for him — because Abe was a Deist — &c — I did vote for him nonetheless — and never regretted it.

When a fight was on hand Abe used to Say to me "Lets go and Stop it — tell a joke — a Story — Say Something humorous and End the fight in a good laugh". We never failed to accomplish the End.

One time Abe and I were on the North Side of the River and a man Came a long who got down & hitched his horse &c. It had martin gails[3] on it. The horse got these tangled — I tried to undo them — look at them — was surprised — was taken aback at their oddity — &c. and halloed to Abe — "Abe do come here and See these thing. A Philadelphia lawyer Can't undo them. You are an Ills one and may do it. Abe looked at them Some time — Studied them — &c. and undid them — & this Cut a Knot I Couldn't

LC: HW3877–78; HL: LN2408, 1:394–96

342. Mentor Graham (WHH interview)

[1865–66]

Mentor Graham

Says that Lincoln told him that the way he learned to write so well & so distinctly & precisely was that many people who Came with them from Ky & different sections after they moved to Indian says his perceptions were sharpened — he learnd to see other people thoughts and feelings and ideas by writing their friendly confidential letters —

LC: HW2541; HL: LN2408, 2:234

---

1. Hannah Armstrong. See her testimony at §415.
2. Isaac Snodgrass was a neighbor to and brother-in-law of Godbey.
3. A martingale is a strap to restrain a horse from throwing back its head.

343. James Gourley (WHH interview)

[1865–66¹]

Jas Gurley

I Knew Lincoln as Early as 1834: he used to Come from New Salem afoot & get books at Stuarts & Dummers² office: he was Post Master or D.P.M at that time: he used to Come to Stuart & Dummers office and tell his Stories: he once helped box a fellow up in a hogshead and roll him down — Jack Armstrong was the leader — I run a foot race in 1836 with H. B. Truett — now of California — got Lincoln to be my judge — Truett had a running Suit — Indian Style —. Lincoln felt good as I beat Truett — a boaster. Lincoln loved to see the wind out of the windy fool. Col E D Baker and I used to run foot races. I Know when Lincoln Came to this City — in 1837 — probably in May 1836. We played the old fashioned town ball — jumped — ran — fought & danced. Lincoln played town ball — he hopped well — in 3 hops he would go 40.2 on a dead level. He was a great wrestler — wrestled in the black Hawk war: his mode — method — or way — his Specialty was Side holds: he threw down all men. Lincoln was a good player — could catch a ball: he would Strip and go at it — do it well—

I heard Lincoln make a Speech in Mechanicsburg Sangamon Co in 1836. Jno Neal had a fight at the time — the roughs got on him and Lincoln jumped in and Saw fair play — We Staid for dinner at Greens close to M— drunk whiskey sweetened with honey. there — the questions discussed were internal improvements — whig principles —: he peeled _____³

I heard Mr Lincoln during the Same Canvass. Early was a candidate — Lincoln skinned Dick Quinton in the Court in July 1836, I think. It was at the Court house — where the State house now Stands —. The whigs & democrats had a general quarrel then & there. N. W. Edwards drew a pistol on Achilles Morris — During the Congressional race between Jno. T. Stuart & S A Douglas they had a fight in Herndons grocery — the brick layer: they fought in a grocery:⁴ they both fought till Exhausted — grocery floor Slippery with Slop. Stuart ordered out a barrel of whiskey and wine —. I became acquainted with Douglas in 1836 when he first Came here as Register of the Land office — Douglas & I wrestled many and many a time — When Harrison White & Co run their race I was a Har—n man — Lincoln was a Clay man — Heard Douglas & Lincoln Speak on the questions of the day many times: heard Lincoln & Calhoun in their great Tariff debate in the Court house⁵ — a rented room in Hoffman's row — N.W. Corner of public Square: This debate lasted 3 or 4 nights or more. Lincoln's arguments were profound — Calhoun was an able man — No mistake — one of the ablest men that ever made Stump Speeches in Ills — He came nearer of whipping Lincoln in debate than

1. H&W (1889) gives the date as February 9, 1866 (590).

2. John T. Stuart and Henry E. Dummer, law partners from 1833 to 1837.

3. Possibly a reference to someone Lincoln put down in debate.

4. Possibly Archer G. Herndon's tavern, the Indian Queen, or its successor; the bricklayer is not identified.

5. Probably the series of debates in March 1844.

Douglas did —. These men — Douglas — Calhoun & Lincoln I have often heard
from 1834 to 1840 —

Lincoln was a great temperance man during the time of the Washingtonians
— he would go a foot 5 or ten miles to talk. One of his Speeches was printed in
the Journal[6]   He was a good temperance man — he Scarcely Ever drank. I got
Lincoln to join the Sons of temperance about 1854. He joined & never appeared
in it again. If Lincoln Ever drank it was as a medicine I think. He took no part in
in the great temperance move in 18__[7] when an act of the Legislature was passed
and Submitted to the People.

In 1840 he Spoke frequently to Harrison Club: he advocated the Tarriff —
Bank — Internal improvements by the Gen Government — & the distribution
of the proceeds of the Sale of the public land and particularly & generally all whig
measures. Lincoln was for Clay up to the time of Gen Taylors race in 1848. He
was for Clay in the Harrison — Van Buren — White Webster & Co[8] — He and
I once went to Petersburg he to make a Speech against Peter Cartwright in his
Congression race — 1846 —. He skinned Peter & Erastus Wright — the abolition (Note this — remember the Wright law Suit[9])

One day Lincoln was gone to Chicago to attend to the Rock Island bridge
Case.[10] While he was gone — say in 1857 — Mrs Lincoln & myself formed a
conspiracy to take off the roff and raise the house.[11] Lincoln Came home — Saw
his house — and Said — Stranger do you Know where Lincoln lives: he used to
live here". He Scolded his wife for running him in debt. Again — when Lincoln
was gone once I chose her — Mrs L — a Carriage — a fine one — Lincoln Complained, but all to no purpose. Again when Lincoln was away from home Mrs
Lincoln had a bad girl living with her: the boys & men used to Come to her house
in Ls absence and scare her: She was crying & wailing one night — Called me and
said — "Mr Gourly — Come — do Come & Stay with me all night — you Can
Sleep in the bed with Bob and I. I don't want boys: they'd go to Sleep to Soon &
won't & can't watch — Come do — Sleep with Robt. & myself —

I lived next door neighbor to Lincoln 19 years: Knew him & his family relations well: he used to Come to our house with Slippers on — one Suspender &
and an old pair of pants — Come for milk — our room was low & he Said Jim
— you have to lift your loft a little higher: I Can't stand in it well". He used to say
to my wife that little people had Some advantages: it did not take quite So much
wood & wool to make their house & Clothes.

Lincoln never planted any any trees —: he did plant Some rose bushes once
in front of his house: he planted no apple trees, cherry trees — pear trees, grape

6. AL's temperance address was delivered on Washington's birthday, February 22, 1842, and printed in
the *Sangamo Journal* on March 25. *CW* 1:271–79.
7. The prohibitory liquor law was presented to the voters in 1855.
8. The 1836 Union ticket.
9. Erastus Wright is the pension agent AL "skinned" on the stand for withholding money from the widow of a revolutionary soldier. See §242, note 4.
10. *Hurd vs. Rock Island Bridge Co.*, the so-called *Effie Afton* case, in 1857.
11. The enlargement of AL's home began in the spring of 1856.

vines Shade trees and Such like things — he did not it seems Care for Such things

He once — for a year or So had a garden & worked in it: he Kept his own horse — fed & curried it — fed & milked his own Cow: he Sawed his own wood generally when at home. He loved his Horse well.

Lincoln & his wife got along tolerably well, unless Mrs L got the devil in her: Lincoln paid no attention — would pick up one of his Children & walked off — would laugh at her — pay no Earthly attention to her when in that wild furious Condition. I don't think that Mrs Lincon was as bad a woman as She is represented: She was a good friend of mine. She always Said that if her husband had Staid at home as he ought to, that She could love him better: She is no prostitute — a good woman, She dared me once or twice to Kiss her, as I thought — refused then — wouldn't now.

Lincoln would take his Children and would walk out on the Rail way out in the Country — would talk to them — Explain things Carefully — particularly. He was Kind — tender and affectionate to his children — very — very —. Lincoln I think had no dog — had Cats — Bob used to harness Cats — Bob & my boy and used to harness up my dog & they would take him & go into the woods and get nuts —

Mrs & Mr Lincoln were good neighbors. Lincoln was the best man I ever Knew: he gave my boy a position in the Navy. Lincoln was a great reader: he read the Bible.

As to Mr Lincoln I do not think he Ever had a Change of heart — belonged to no religious Sects — was religious in his way — not as others generally. Had he Ever had a Change of heart — religiously Speaking, he would have told me about it: he Couldn't have neglected: he Couldn't have avided it.

In 1844 I used to play ball with Abe Lincoln — E D Baker — &c others: the game was Called fives — Striking a ball with our hands against a wall that Served as alley. In 1860 Lincoln & myself played ball — this game —

Lincoln went home from the Journal Office directly after his nomination for Presdt: he was agitated — turned pale — trembled. We — a good many — Soon went up to See him at his house. Lincoln played ball the day before his nomination — probably he played Some in the morning — Early

LC: HW3880–87; HL: LN2408, 2:124–30

344. John Hanks (WHH interview)

[1865–66]

John Hanks[1]

I was born in Ky on the 9th day of Feby 1802 (1802) in Nelson Co in 4 M of Beardstown. My father moved to Hardin Co in 1806 — I Knew Abraham Lin-

---

1. Marginal note: *I can say that this testimony can be implicitly relied on. Mr Lincoln loved this man — thought him truthful — honest and noble. Lincoln has stated this to me over and over again. / Herndon.*

coln in Ky. Abrah was Known among the boys as a bashful — Somewhat dull, but peacable boy: he was not a brilliant boy — but *worked* his way by toil: to learn was hard for him, but he walked Slowly, but Surely. He went to School to a man by the name of Hazel: the School was but a Short distance. Lincoln lived on the Bank of Knob Creek — about ½ mile above the Rolling fork, which Empties into Salt River which Empties into Ohio R. Abraham Lincoln's mother and I were Cousins Abm & I are 2d Cousins. I Knew Mrs Nancy Lincoln — or Nancy Sparrow before marriage. She was a tall Slender woman — dark Skinned — black hair & Eyes — her face was Sharp & angular — forehead high — She was beyond all doubt an intellectual woman — rather Extraordinary if any thing. She was born in Mercer Co Ky about 1780 — her nature was Kindness — mildness — tenderness — Sadness — obedience to her husband. Abrm was like his mother very much. She was a babtist by profession

My recellection, in fact Abm's Father told me so that his great grandfather was an Englishman — Came from England and Settled in Virginia. This is the family reputation. When I was in Ky in 1864 I was Shown a house in Mercer Co which was Said to be the house that Abm's Grand had built. I doubt the House, but don't the farm — about 10 M from the mouth of Kentuck river — about 10 or 2 M from Harrisburg — South East from Harrodsburg.

I Knew Thomas Lincoln in Ky: Knew him well — He was Cabinet & House Carpenter — farmed after he got married — Still working at his trade. He was a man about 5 feet 10 in high — weigh about 180 — Eyes dark gray — hair black — a little Stupt Shouldered — good humored man — a Strong brave man — a very Stout man — loved fun — jokes and equalled Abe in teling Stories. Happiness was the End of life with him. He, Thos, was older than his wife — Say about 5 years — being born about 1775 —. Thomas was born in Virginia — So was his wife — Thos. was 6 years of age when he Came to Ky   His father was Killed by the Indians as Dennis Hanks has Said. The Indian Story of Dennis Hanks is generally Correct as told you by Dennis — So is Chapmans story generally Correct[2]   Thomas Told me So. My Father & Lincoln were born in Old Va in what is called the Rappahannock River — We Knew Each other in Virginia — that is the families did. Abm's Mother was my first Cousin. Abrm's grand mother was my father Sister. Abrms Grandfather & Mother on his Mothers Side lived in Mercer Co Ky — about 20 M South of Abrms grand father on his fathers Side — the one Killed by the Indians. Dennis Hanks & I are Cousins. Mr Sparrow & Mrs Sparrow never Came to Ills. They lived in Ky in Mercer Co. Sparrow married my fathers Sister — Henry Sparrow was his name — lived & died in Mercer Co — never Came to Indiana. They came from Old Va. All these families Came from about the same County — Can't say what Co.

Thomas Lincoln moved to Indiana in 1818 — probably 1816 and settled in Spencer Co near what is now Caled Gentryville Indiana. I staid in Ky — did not Come out when Dennis Hanks did — Dennis Hanks came out in about 1818 —

---

2. For Dennis Hanks's account, see §16; for A. G. Chapman's account, see §327.

Mrs Lincoln died say in 1818. I think and lies buried South East of the Lincoln farm about ½ m on a rise-Knowl or Knob. She was buried by the Side of Mr Hall & his wife,[3] as I understand it. I Came out to Indiana in 1822 after Thos Lincoln had married his 2d wife & Staid in Indiana near to & with Thomas Lincoln for 4 ys   I remember Abrm well in Indiana   He was then 10 ys of age then & 14 ys when I left Indiana & went back to Ky. I was in 1822 20 ys.

Abrm was farming when I got there & when I left & went to Ky. He went to School but little: he went to School to Dorsey or Swaney, I can't now Say which. Old man Lincolns house the was a rough-rough log one — not a hewed one — his 2d one was Sorter hewed but is gone — never standing in 1860. The 3d one was hewed, logs: that one never was occupied by Lincoln: it was up but not inhabited.: the House Stood East & west and faced the South — chimney in East End. it was — is about 4 M to Gentryville from the Lincoln farm — N. of East a little — The House stood on a round Hill — Knowl or Know — Lincoln's farm was on the forks of big pigeon & little Pigeon. The big pigeon is north and the little one South —

When Lincoln, Ab & I returned to the house from work, he would go to the Cupboard — Snatch a piece of Corn bread — take down a book — Sit down on a chair — Cock his legs up as high as his head and read — He and I worked bare footed — grubbed it — plowed — mowed & cradled together — plowed Corn — gathered it & shucked Corn — Abrm read Constantly when he had an opportunity — no news papers — then — had monthly meetings at church — Sometimes at private houses — Abe went to Church generally — not always — I Know he read weems washington[4] when I was there — got it wet — it was on a Kind of book shelf Close to the window — the book shelf was made by 2 pins in the wall & a clap board on them — books on that — Lincoln got it of Crawford[5] — told Crawford & paid it in pulling fodder by 2 or 3 days work. He frequently read the Bible. He read Robinson Crusoe — Bunyans Pilgrims progress —. Lincoln devoured all the books he could get or lay hands on: he was a Constant and voracious reader — I never Could get him in Company with women: he was not a timid man in this particular, but did not seek such Company. He was always full of his Stories — as much so in Indiana as Ills — He would go out in the woods & gather hickory bark — bring it home & Keep a light by it and read by it — when no lamp was to be had — grease lamp — handle to it which Stuck in the crack of the wall. Tallow was Scarce — Abrm was a good hearty Eater — loved good Eating. His own Mother & Step Mother were good Cook for them day & time. In the summer he wore tow linen pants & flax Shirt and in the winter he wore linsey wolsey — that is during the time I was there. I have Seen Lincoln — Abe — make Speeches to his Step brothers — Step Sisters — and youngsters that would Come to See the family.

---

3. Levi Hall and Nancy Hanks Hall, AL's aunt.
4. See §71, note 16.
5. Josiah Crawford.

I moved from Ky to Ills in the fall of 1828 and settled where I now live — 4 M north west of Decatur. and built the first house in Decatur. I wrote to Thos Lincoln what Kind of a Country it was: he Came to this State the 1 day of Mch 1830 — to my house. He then built 10 M west of Decatur — & about 100 Steps from the N. F of Sangamon River & on the North side of it on a Kind of bluff — The house — the logs of it, I cut myself in 1829 & gave them to old man Lincoln: The house set East & west — fronted South — chimney at west End — the Same House which was Shown in Chicago. Lincoln broke up 15 acres of land Abrm & myself Split the rails: he own 4 yoke of oxen — broke prairie in the Summer — broke 30 acres for my brother[6] — he broke prairie for others. 2 yoke belonged to Thomas Lincoln and 2 to my brother. Dennis Hanks Came out at the Same time — Mr & Mrs Hall[7] — Dennis Hanks married Abes Step Sister — So did Hall —. Abrm during the winter of 1830 & 1 walked 3 M and maul 1000 Rails for Maj. Warnick[8] —

I Knew Abs own Sister Sarah: She was a Short built woman — Eyes dark gray — hair dark brown: She was a good woman — Kind, tender, & good natured and is Said to have been a smart woman. That is my opinion.

After Abrm got to Decatur — rather to Macon — My Co — a man by the name of Posey[9] Came into our neighborhood and made a Speech: it was a bad one and I Said Abe could beat it. I turned down a box or Keg and Abe made his Speech. The other man was a Candidate — Abe wasn't. Abe beat him to death — his subject being the navigation of the Sangamon River. The man after the Speech was through took Abe aside and asked him where he had learned So much and what he did so well. Abe Explained, Stating his manner & method of reading and what he had read: the man Encouraged Lincoln to persevere.

Offutt Came to my house in Feb'y 1831, and wanted to hire me to run a flat boat for him — Saying that he had heard that I was quite a flat boatman in Ky: he wanted me to go badly. I went & saw Abe & Jno Johnson — Abes Step brother — introduced Offutt to them. We made an Engagement with Offutt at 50 per day and $60 to make the trip to N Orleans. Abe & I Came down the Sangamon River in a Canoe in March 1831. — landed at what is now Called and Known as Jamestown — 5 East of Springfield — once Called Judy's ferry. We left our Canoe in Charge of Mr Man[10] — walked afoot to Springfield and found Offutt. He was at a tavern in Old town — probably Elliotts: it was Elliotts.[11] He Offutt Expected to find his boat according to Contract at the mouth of Spring Creek 5 north of Springfield — got disappointed — Abe — Johnson & myself went down to the mouth of Spring Creek & there Cut the timbers to make the boat — we were

---

6. Probably Charles Hanks.

7. Squire Hall and Matilda Johnston Hall, AL's stepsister.

8. Capt. William Warnick of Macon County, a landholder and aspiring politician who commanded a company of mounted rangers during the Black Hawk War.

9. Probably John F. Posey. See §7, note 1.

10. Uriah Mann, a farmer who emigrated to Sangamon County in 1831, settling in what is now Clear Lake Township.

11. See §336.

about 2 weeks Cutting our timber — suppose it was on Congress land — Abe
walked afoot to Springfield — thence to Judy's ferry — got the Canoe and floated
it down to the mouth of Spring Creek where the timber was Cut: we then rafted
the logs down to Sangamon River to what is Called Sangamon town 7 miles N.W
of Springfield. We boarded when we were working at the mouth of Spring Creek
— walked 1. M — Eat 2 meals a dy. When we got to Sangamon town we made a
shantee-shed — Abe was Elected Cook. We sawed our lumber at Kirkpatricks Mill
on Prairie Creek about 1½ M S.W. of Sangamon Town. We hewed & scored the
timber at the mouth of Spring Creek. We finished making & launching the boat
in about 4 Weeks — we loaded the boat with barrell pork — Corn & live hogs —
and left Sangamon twn. I remember a jugglers show at Sangamon Town. Abe went
to it. Abe was full of jokes during all this time — Kept us alive. Offutt was a whig
— so was Lincoln but he Could not hear Jackson wrongfully abused — Especially where a lie & malace did the abuse. I can say that Abe never was a democrat: he
was always a whig — so was his father before him.

We landed at the New Salem mill about the 19th April and got fast on Rutledges Mill dam — now called Bales Mill dam. We unloaded the boat — that is
we Changed goods from one boat to a borrowed one — rolled the barrels forward
— bored a hole in the end of the boat over the dam — water ran out and thus we
got over — on the dam part of a day and one night. We then went on down to
the Yellow bank or blue banks on the Sangamon River near Squire Godbys[12] about
1 M above the mouth of Salt Creek. We purchased Some hogs of I think Squire
Godby — am not sure — tried to drive them, Couldnt — ran them back in the
pen — Caught them — Abe held the head of them — I the tail — and Offutt
sewed up their Eyes — wouldn't drive — couldn't — put them in a cart — Carried them to the boat about one mile to the river — Abe recd the hogs — Cut
open there[13] — Johnson & I halled them — to Abe —

We then proceeded — Offutt — John Johnson — Abe Lincoln & Myself,
down the Sangamon River — thence into Ills —. We Kept our victuals & in fact
Slept down in the boat — at one End — went down by a Kind of ladder through
a scuttle hole. We used plank as Sails — & Cloth — Sometimes — rushed through
Beardstown in a hurry — people Came out & laughed at us — passed Alton —
Cairo — and Stopt at Memphis — Vicksburg — Natches — &c. There is nothing worthy of being Known going down the river.

I Can say we soon — Say in May we landed in N.O.[14] There it was we Saw
Negroes Chained — maltreated — whipt & scourged. Lincoln Saw it — his heart
bled — Said nothing much — was silent from feeling — was Sad — looked bad
— felt bad — was thoughtful & abstracted — I Can say Knowingly that it was
on this trip that he formed his opinions of Slavery: it ran its iron in him then &
there — May 1831. I have heard him say — often & often — Offutt — Johnson

---

12. Russell Godbey.
13. Presumably cut open their eyes.
14. See AL's autobiographical statement, which asserts that John Hanks did not go all the way to New
Orleans. *CW* 4:64.

— Abe & myself left NO in June 1831. We Came to St. Louis on the Steam boat together walked to Edwardsville 25 N.E of St Louis — Abe, Johnson & Myself — Abe & Johnson went to Coles Co. & I to Springfield Sangamon Co. Thomas Lincoln had moved to Coles Co in 1831 in — say June.

I Came near forgetting some facts. I was in the Black Hawk war — was in Stillman's defeat, which was on the 14th day of May 1832. Lincoln was out in that war. I went in March 1832 — Lincoln Started as Captain of the N Salem Company about the same time — Lincoln was at Dixons fery at the time of Stillmans defeat —. I did not go to the battle of the Bad Axe. Lincoln I think was there, though not in the action, as I understand it. I was out about 4 or 6 mo — So was Lincoln — Lincoln went with Maj Henry[15] I Know. I was discharged at Ottowa & Lincoln at Rock Island or near that — Met at Dixon's ferry — after the Stillmans defeat. Lincoln went on with Henry. We were ordered to build a fort at Ottowa to protect the People. The Stillman defeat affair grew out of the drunkenness — folly — cowardice. The fight with Black Hawk was about Sundown — 1 h by Sun at or near Sycamore Creek about 700 Indians — and about 200 white —

Saw Abrm in Springfield in 1833 — Summer: he was in town on business & So was I. I Saw him frequently from this time — Every year from this time till he was Elected Presdt. He practiced Law in Decatur. He came out to my house frequently, leaving Court in the Evening & after court was over — Ended — I ate dinner with him after he was Elected Presdt. He wrote me a letter that he was going to See his mother — Came by Decatur — I went with him — Saw his fathers grave. He stayed with his Mother one. We ate dinner at in Farmington — Pretty woman there that took Abes Eyes — I assure you. We then went back to Charleston — & Came to Springfield. I saw him in Washington when he was inaugurated — was in his rooms Several times — Never Saw him again till I Saw his dead form in the City of Springfield —

I Served in the Army of the USA in 1861 — and toiled there 3 years to preserve and defend what he loved.

LC: HW3900–3913; HL: LN2408, 1:111–23

345. William H. Hannah (WHH interview)

[1865–66]

W. H. Hannah — of Bloomington

Says that Since 1856 Mr Lincoln told him he was a Kind of universalist — That he never Could bring himself to the belief in Eternal punishment — That men lived but a little while here & that if eternal punishment were man's doom that he should spend that little life in vigilant & ceaseless preperation — by never Ending prayer —

15. James D. Henry.

That on one occasion he Hannah — Supposing Lincoln poor — Lincoln then running for U.S. Senator Said to Lincoln — if you want money draw on me for $500. — Lincoln said I am not so poor as you suppose — don't want any money — don't know how to use money on such occasions — Can't do it & never will — though much obliged to you.

H Said Saw Lincoln about 1849 — Came to Court at Bloomington — went to See him — was Social agreeabel — & made me think I was forty years old — forgot my boyhood — Supposed I was a man — was so treated &c — loved him after that

LC: HW3914; HL: LN2408, 2:157–58

346. Elliott B. Herndon (statement for WHH)[1]

[1865–66]

E. B. Herndon

[I am] particularly requested to write down my [opinio]n of the mind of Abraham Lincoln late [Presi]dent of the United States. I concent do so [wi]thout any other motive than to Comply [with] the request of a brother. for if I Know [myse]lf no other motive would induce me [to do it] because I believe myself wholly [indif]ferent as to the future of his memory. [The o]pinion I now have was formed by an [usu]al personal and professional acquaint. with the man for a period of say ten years. and which opinion has not altered since he was elected President. I Know of no official act which in the least dist[urbs] that opinion. and on the other hand t[here] may have been many now and forev[er] resting in oblivion which might hav[e] confirmed my opinion. The adulation [of] base multitudes of a living and the peg[eantry] and hypocarcy surrounding a dea[d] President does not shake my w[ell] settled convictions of the mans ment[al calibre.]

The American people are about as well [qualified] to form a correct opinion of mental c[apacity] as an idolitor is to judge of the christ[ian] religion, and are just as Susceptabl[e to] imposition of their own credulity as [the] chinaman who believes in his go[d Josh] — Hence I am not under that sort [of] influence. So here we go. Physio[logically] and Phrenologically[2] the man was a [sort] of monstrosity. His frame was large lo[ng, bony] and muscular — his head disprop[ortionately] small and shaped. He had large [square jaws] — large heavy nose, small lacivious mouth and Soft tender bluish eyes. I would say he was a cross between Venus and Hercules. I believe it be inconsistent with the laws of [hum]an organization for any such creature [to p]ossess a mind capable of any thing [cal]led great. The mans mind partook [of] the incongruities of his body. His mind [was] incongruous. He had no mind [not] possessed by the most ordinary of [men]. It

---

1. The manuscript is badly torn, and the text is here partially reconstructed from the Springer transcription.

2. Phrenology, which had a considerable vogue in the nineteenth century, purported to explain character and mental capacity from the shape of the skull.

was simply the peculiarity of [his] mental, the odity of his physical and [qualit]ies of his heart that singled him out [from] the mass of men. His nature love of [truth] justice and humanity led his mind [a gre]at way in the accomplishment of his [object]s in life. That passion or sentiment [stead]ied and determined an otherwise [inde]cisive mind. According to the analysis [of men]tal philosophy his mind was not [unco]mmon in any part or division in [perce]ption, memory, reasoning. immagin[ation] &c. but all those qualities of the mind [in his] were irregular and confused. He had such an organized mind as was incapa[ble] of Comprehending thoroughly and co[mpletely] from foundation to Turret — By [reason of] its Confusion of ideas his min[d tended] to monamaniaism. I never [knew him to] thoroughly understand any [thing, in law] mathamatics, phylospy, [poetry, history,] mechanics, anatomy, chess, [billiards, checkers,] backgammon, cards, or wha[t not. He was] decidedly common in ev[ery thing he ever] undertook within [my observation.] His mind was visionary a[nd impractable.] He had a feverish and unsettled m[ind] incompatable with a brain of power. [He had] tenacity of purpose, but not of min[d. To] wind up what can be said of [that] mind which honestly and conf[idently] is capable of its own conv[iction] that it can equally comprehend the [law,] invent a patent right, compose [poetry,] write a tradegy, understand *[illegible]* and polotics, master logic an[d] mathamatics and demonstra[te a] geometrical absurdity, criticise [Milton an]d Shakespear, become dreamy[3] over [Volney] and yet cannot compose [or write] three good english sentances. [I say wha]t can be thought or said [of such a mind] except, that it is visionary, [irregular, we]ak and incongruous. [Those who admire] Webster for his mental greatness. May well [point to his reply to] Hayne. So it may be said of all great [minds, but let] the admirer of the mental greatness [of Lincoln point] out if they can one intellectual act [of his whole lif]e. Which stands out prominently [as a proof of a]ny great mental power. [He had the position,] the name, and favorable circumstances [in which to do some] intellectual act demonstrative of great intellect.

   LC: HW3921–22; HL: LN2408, 2:454–56

347. James A. Herndon (WHH interview)

[1865–66]

Jas. A. Herndon

   I Knew Mr Lincoln in 1832. Row Herndon — My brother & I took a Store down to N. Salem that year. I didn't like the place and sold out to Berry. Row Herndon in 1832 Sold to Lincoln his part. I Saw a general fight at the Sale of Knapp & Pogue in Papsville on the head of Richland. about 11 m west of Springfield — Saw Lincoln Catch a man by the Nape of the neck and a__ of the breeches and toss him 10 or 12 feet, Easily. I Saw Lincoln frequently in N.S. in an old open

_____

3. The writer first wrote, then struck out: *wild.*

Cooper's Shop gather up Shavens & Stick and feed the flame on an old Stove while he read books — Can't Say what they were — heard Lincoln make his Short Speech[1] — repeated it to him over and over and he Sanctioned every word & Sentence — Lincoln was an industrious Man — always seemed to be doing Something Coolly & Slowly so — Saw him many — many times after this —

LC: HW3923; HL: LN2408, 1:471–72

348. Virgil Hickox (WHH interview)

[1865–66]

Virgil Hickox

Says that the first regular train from Alton to Springfield on the Rail Road ran to Spfgd 10th day of Septbr 1852 — Completed to Bloomington Octr 18th 1853 — Central R.R took passengers to Rock Island Rail Road — This put us in Connection with the East partially. On the 4 day of august 1854 the Chicago & Alton Rail Road was completed for business to Joliett.

We then used the *[blank space]* that was built from thence to Chicago. This put us into Complete & perfect Connection with the East for the first time. We were Connected with St Louis by river on the 10th day of Septr 1852 — St Louis had Connexion with the East.

This was all done before we were put in Connection with the East through Indiana or other places by the Northern Cross R. Road.

LC: HW3924; HL: LN2408, 2:174–75

349. Elijah Iles (WHH interview)

[1865–66]

Maj. Iles

Says Lincoln surveyed and laid off Petersburg — Huron and New Boston on the Miss. in the North West part of Illinois.

HL: LN2408, 2:172

350. Benjamin F. Irwin (WHH interview)[1]

[1865–66]

Ben Irwin —

I came across a Pensylvanian in Pleasant Plain in Sangamon Co. in 1860. He wanted to see Lincoln: his name was Jackson. He & I came to Spfgd. to see Mr

1. See §10.

1. Though located among the Springer transcriptions, this is in the hand of WHH.

Lincoln — L's child was sick — I sent Jack Smith — the merchant up to see L. and had him state what I wanted — wanted Jackson to see L badly —. L sent word down that his child was too sick to leev it — that the man must come down to or up to his house — Jackson & I went up — Knocked at the door — were invited to come in — went in — Sat down. L's [manner?] was democratic — common — The man look'd at every thing — carpet — chairs — glasses — book cases &c. &c — and said do you think this man will ever be presdt of these U.S. Soon Mr L. came down in his Shirt Sleeves — in his Sock feet — was introduced — shook the Mans hand cordially — both about Penn familiarly — Staid there 1½ hours — The man was evidently struck — bewitched — we left — came down in town separated — The man called me and said — "I am an office holder under Buchanan — but I intend to vote for that man. I have been told he was a fool & an ugly man — He's a man a man of great good sense — familiar & honest. He's not an ugly man — but is a good looking man — What do you call him ugly? I don't." The man then went on to say —. Though Pen gave Buchanan _____ majority it will give an overwhelming vote for Lincoln —. Pen will turn the biggest summerset you ever heard of." and sure Enough when the news did come it was overwhelming &c —

HL: LN2408, 1:460–61

351. _____ Johnson to WHH[1]

[1865–66]

Wm H. Herndon Esq.

You ask me to put upon paper, what I saw of Mr Lincoln, while at the Decatur Republican Convention, early in the Spring of 1860. For some reason, to me now, and perhaps, then unknown, there was an intense interest felt in what was to be done by that Convention. And each County sent up large numbers of delegates even if they had only few votes to cast. There too was gathered most of the choice political spirits of Illinois of the Republican party. The meeting had been organized but a short time when a gentleman (Oglesby I think), rose to say that he "was informed that a distinguished citizen of Illinois — and one whom Illinois would ever delight to honor was present, at the meeting, and he wished to move that this body invite him to a seat on the Stand". Here as if knowing that an outburst would follow, the Speaker seemed purposely to delay mentioning any name, as if to tease expectation to the verge of desperation, At last he said he alluded to Mr Lincoln. The Storm of applause burst forth loud — long and deep As it subsided — the motion was seconded — and passed. I in the mean time, being near the door saw the then future President Sitting on his heels, just within the door of the Wigwam. Everybody in that vicinity, seemed inspired with a new born desire to get close to him — to take hold of him. I think he was seized and lifted to his

---

1. In the top margin, in an unknown hand: _Johnson._

feet, An effort was made to jam him through the crowd, towards the stage, This not succeeding as well as those immediately about him wished, he was "boosted" up until he found himself, kicking scrambling — crawling — upon the sea of heads between him and the Stand, The enthusiasm was at to high a pitch, for the ludirousness of the scene, to have been generally noticed, or laughed at if seen   As he neared the Stand, Some half dozen Gentlemen, Seemed to have him their arms — bundled up promiscuously, — and thus he was placed upon the Stage. The cheering was like the roar of the sea, Hats were thrown up by the Chicago delegation, as if hats were no longer useful,

Mr Lincoln rose bowing and blushing, I then thought him one of the most diffident and worst plagued men I ever saw. He was Smiling and as the applause subsided a little, he thanked the meeting for their Manifestations of Esteem   Whether it was right away or after the lapse of some hours I do not remember — that Oglesby again rose to his feet, and in another teasing speech — Said, there was an "Old Democrat had something he wished to present to this meeting" Here some hollowed "Receive it!" — "Receive it!" Myself and some other Egyptians who were innocent of "cut and dry" affairs, Cried out "What is it!" "What is it!" Suspecting the Old Democrat might wish to hoist us with some infernal machine The cry of "Receive it" prevailed. Mr John Hanks was ushered in, bearing something — which when exhibited proved to be two, Small triangular (I think) heart rails — bearing a banner with this inscription —

Two Rails
From A Lot made By Abraham Lincoln, And John Hanks, in the Sangamon Bottom, In the Year 183

Again the tempest of enthusiasm burst forth, wilder — Stronger and more furious than before The Chicago — and Central Illinois folks seemed perfectly beside themselves. Mr Lincoln — blushed but seemed to shake with inward laughter. The meeting became uproarious for a speech.

At last Mr Lincoln rose and said:

Gentlemen, I Suppose you want to know something about those things (pointing and laughing)   Well, the truth is John Hanks and I did make rails in the Sangamon Bottom. I dont know whether we made those rails or not. — Fact is dont think they are a Credit to the Makers (laughing). But I do know this. I made rails then — and I think I could make better ones than these now! So he sat down — to the utter, dismay of everybody — but the managers of things. After it was all over with I began to think I could smell a very large mouse — and this whole thing, was a cunningly devised thing of knowing ones, to make Mr Lincoln, President and that banner was to be the "Battle flag," in the coming contest between "labor free" and "labor slave," between democracy — and aristocracy. And all this was maneuvering between the East and West for a Standard bearer, Little did I think of mighty issues that that little ploy, would bring about. Little did I dream *that* rail splitter, bowing and blushing with awkward grace, was to be a greater man than

Washington, And that that name should echo in Chants of praise, along the Corridors of all coming time

LC: HW3944–50; HL: LN2408, 2:84–87

352. James W. Keyes (statement for WHH)

[1865–66]

In my intercours with Mr Lincoln I learned that he believed in a Creator of all things, who had neither beginning nor end, who possessing all power and wisdom, established a principal, in Obediance to which, Worlds move and are upheld, and animel and vegatable life came into existance.

A reason he gave for his belief was, that in view of the Order and harmony of all nature which all beheld, it would have been More miraculouis to have Come about by chance, than to have been created and arranged by some great thinking power —

As to the christian theory, that, Christ is God, or equal to the Creator he said had better be taken for granted — for by the test of reason all might become infidels on that subject, for evidence of Christs divinity Came to us in somewhat doubtful Shape — but that the Sistom of Christianity was an ingenious one at least — and perhaps was Calculated to do good —

As to the Ordanances adopted by the diferant denominations of christians, I never heard him express any preference for One over the other —

ISHL: Weik Papers, box 2; HL: LN2408, 2:439

353. Turner R. King (WHH interview)

McLain Station McL. Co [1865–66]

Turner R. King

I Came to Ills in Dec 1840 — Knew Lincoln as Early as 1840 — & 1841. In March 1841 I used to see Mr. Lincoln — hanging about — moody — silent & &c. The question in his mind was Have "I incurred any obligation to marry that woman". He wanted to dodge if he could. Douglass[1] was Secy of State when I came here —. Calhoun & Lincoln discussed the tariff: they were the best debaters — most Logical & finest debates on the Tariff question in the State[2] — Lincoln & Cartwright became candidates for Congress in 1846. The leading democrats gave up the Contest — Conceding Lincoln's Election —

Lincoln took his seat in Congress in 1847. Mr Lincoln had me appointed Register of the land office. I was then a resident of Tazewell Co — came to Springfield —

---

1. Stephen A. Douglas.
2. Presumably refers to AL's series of debates with John Calhoun in March 1844.

In his political Speeches he was candid — fair — honest — Courteous — and [manly?] to his opponent. He stated his propositions Candidly — Clearly — He required to be Kicked — roused to be at himself —

I don't think Mr Lincoln approved in toto the Compromis —

Once I hired him in a trial. The opposite Atty spoke sharply: Mr Lincoln looked at him Keenly sharply — for an instant — Crushed his anger and Inquired who that man was. Lincoln could not & would not bear insolence &c from no man.

Lincolns wife was a hellion — a she devil — vexed — & harrowed the soul out of that good man — wouldn't Cook for him — drove him from home &c — often & often —

LC: HW3959; HL: LN2408, 2:172–73

354. John Klein (WHH interview)

[1865–66]

Jno. Klein

Volunteered April 1832 — Capt. Goodan[1] 4. Reg. Lincoln in the 4. Reg. Moses K. Anderson   Col of Reg't[2] — Achilles Morris Major — Whitesides commander in chief of the whole army — Gen'l —

Rendesvoused at Rushville — on horses — all mounted men — went to Rock Island — at Fort Armstrong — went N.W. to Henderson Co, at Yellow Bank, no Oquaqay[3] — Miss River — crossed the Rock River — passing over various streams — burnt Sack Town (Saxe) — Recrossed the Rock River and went up to Dixon's Ferry — now Dixon — on the South side — Dixon is on Rock River. Stillman's defeat was in Ogle Co. in 1832–35 above Dixon — battle on Kishwakee Creek — Gen. Henry commandant of the Spy battalion. Thence we came S.E. to Fox River. This was about the month of June or last of May. Here our time expired and a new levy was ordered. 1st enlistment 60, and they during the war — Lincoln reinlisted, The Gen, now was Gen Henry — passed thence up the four Oaks — in Wisconsin — Here the battle of Bad axe was fought — south side of the river — Wisconsin then down to Bad Axe — and thence drove them west to the Miss. river — from thence we went to Prairie Du Chein (in Wisconsin) and there we were disbanded — Lincoln was with us all the day —

The fight as told to Klein by Jack Armstrong —
    (See Kleins again)[4]

---

1. Capt. Levi W. Goodan commanded a company in the same regiment in which AL served.

2. Klein must be confused as to the identity of his regimental commander, as there is no record of a Moses K. Anderson serving in the Black Hawk War. The colonel of the Fourth Regiment was Samuel M. Thompson; Achilles Morris was lieutenant colonel.

3. Meaning "now Oquawka."

4. Presumably another interview with Klein, which has not been located.

Gov'r Duncan was Gov'r in 1831
Gov'r Reynolds was   ″   ″ 1832
Oliphant a lawyer wrote the Poetry of the Illinois Sucker Young and Raw.[5]

HL: LN2408, 2:241–42

355. Ward Hill Lamon (WHH interview)

[1865–66]

Mr Lincoln would let in People indiscriminately — Members of Congress Could get to see him most any time — when possible. House opened from 7 o'cl am & 11 o'cl P.M.

He loved apples better than all Else — strong drink of Coffee — He loved oyesters —

He was passionately fond of fine Horses — He did love Tadds Catt — less Tadds goats —.

He was a hearty Eater — when hed had no passages he alwys had a sick head ache — Took Blue pills — blue Mass[1] —

He was as Sociable at Washington taking all things into Consideration as he was whilst in Springfield. — gloomy — uncheery at times — most of his life — The greater time of his life he was gloomy — but would in special times become Cheerful with Chums — and when they retired he would relaps —

Took but little physical Exercise

He was generally good humored but at some times he would burst out — Women would Come to him sometime — He woud Scold them — saying — "You would Kill me now if you Could — and still you are asking favors of me — The would get up — Cry — start away and the Presdt would Call them back saying — Now if you go back South you will do some mischief — You would overturn the Government if you Coud"   Still he would sit down — take up a little Square piece of Paper and write — To all Commanders — Let the bearer pass through our lines —

Lincoln wrote to but few persons — never wrote many letters.

Lincoln & Greely —
Greely had power over the Presdt.

5. The last three paragraphs may belong to the Klein interview or may be stray pieces of information Herndon noted and Springer duly copied.

1. Blue mass was a mercury preparation used as a laxative. See *The Dispensatory of the United States of America* (Philadelphia, 1883), 929–31. The editors are grateful to Professors James Harvey Young and David L. Cowen for this reference.

Mrs Lincoln struck Mr Lincoln in the face on a boat going to or at Richmond — Struck him hard — damned him — cursed him — Capt Stackpole[2] told this W. H. Lamon —

Rufus Andrews Surveyor of the Port of N.Y.[3]

LC: HW3760; HL: LN2408, 2:76–77

356. Stephen T. Logan (WHH interview)

[1865–66]

Logan[1]

Jud Cook Pamer Gullaspee & Baker held out.[2] Gullaspie voted for Cyrus Edwards. I had heard that Madisin[3] would be elected the next ballot   Some of Archibald Williams friends Came to me and wanted me to give Judge Williams a Complimentary vote — I could not do So, as it was certain that Lincoln would be defeated and Matteson would be elected. I went to Lincoln & said to him — "The next ballott — Matteson will be Elected if we stick to you: It is Matteson or Trubull —" Lincoln thought that his men could draw the minority in the Anti Nebrask party to him but he was mistaken. Lincoln said [however?] "I am for Trumbull." Lincoln did not like the turn thing had taken: he was cut and mortified. Some of our old whigs — 2 or 3 of them would have gone for Mattison on the next ballot. There was an agreement between Some of the democrats that at a certain ballot they should drop Matteson and run Shields — I had determined to beat Matteson

During that canvass — race, Mr Lincoln was in a fix — Lovejoy and others in the Legislature: they wanted Lincoln to say that he would go for the doctrine that there should be no Slavery in the Territories: Lincoln came to me and asked me about the matter, Saying to me Knowing my politics, will it tramp your toes — I Said "No — whatever you do, though I don't agree to the doctrine it won't tread on my toes. Lincoln made the pledge. Lincoln and I had supported the wilmot proviso, but this pledge was broader — more radical —

LC: HW2696–97; HL: LN2408, 2:205–6

2. See §298, note 2.

3. A Radical Republican sympathizer of Salmon P. Chase, appointed surveyor of the Port of New York in April 1861 and removed in September 1864.

1. Note in the top margin: *Jas Shields was a Candidid.*

2. Norman B. Judd, Burton C. Cook, and John M. Palmer were members of the Illinois Senate, and Henry S. Baker was a member of the Illinois House in the 19th General Assembly during the senatorial election of 1855.

3. Gov. Joel A. Matteson.

357. Stephen T. Logan (WHH interview)

[1865–66]

Judge Logan

Says — In the great debate in 1839 in the 2d Presbyterian Church — the time when Lincoln made his published Speech to be seen in the Sangamon Journal of Mch 1840. that he — Logan — Baker — Lincoln & Browning as whigs had a debate with — S. A. Douglas — Calhoun. Lamborn & J. B. Thomas, as democrats —

L. further Says — Lincoln & Calhoun — Logan & Campbell held an other debate in the Court House in Hoffman's row as whigs, in 1844, against Calhoun & Campbell as Democrats. The subject was the Tariff — Clay &c — The Speeches of 1839 were on Van Buren and the Sub Treasury — &c — all of which he thinks —

Judge Logan Says — I was Judge of the Cir Court of Sangamon Co. in 1855[1] — held to about 1838 — resigned — Elected again in 1839 & held the office about two Months — resigned (see 1st Scammon[2] at beginning of the vol where the dates Can be Seen   Herndon)[3]

LC: HW2695; HL: LN2408, 2:206–7

358. Stephen T. Logan (WHH interview)

[1865–66]

Judge Logan

Says there was no agreement — no understanding between Hardin — Baker — Lincoln & Logan about rotation in office — ie in Congress — That there was a bitter hostility between Hardin & Baker — a suspicion and dislike between Baker & Lincoln —: That Baker & Lincoln once run against Each other by friendly Convention. Baker beat Lincoln — Baker was Elected to Congress —, Afterwards — Baker went to Galena — Lincoln was a candidate — Elected — returned.[1] Logan became a Candidate — was beaten — Lincoln's unpopularity among other things helped to beat Logan. &c.

Logan says that Lincoln gave him a letter during the Chicago Convention in 1860 authorizing him to withdraw Lincoln's name if he thought prudent so to do according to the rules & regulations of the Conventions proceedings —

LC: HW2694; HL: LN2408, 2:207–8

---

1. A mistake for 1835.
2. A listing of all Illinois Supreme Court justices, circuit judges, and attorneys general from 1818 to 1840: J. Young Scammon, *Reports of Cases Argued and Determined by the Supreme Court of the State of Illinois* (1840).
3. On the back of the document: *(note — White says he was Elected 6th day of May 1857 — Judge Rices Curcuit made in 1857).*

---

1. Marginal note: *See Matheny's Statement of this matter.* See §363.

359. James Long (statement for WHH)[1]

[1865–66]

James Long —

Mr. Lincoln was appointed Postmaster at New Salem, Sangamon Co, Ills. May 7. 1833, and continued in office until May 30, 1836. when the office was discontinued.

Accounts as Postmaster were settled by the Post Office Dept. Sept. 30, 1836.

On the 1st of June 1855, a patent was issued to him for 40 Acres of land, which was located at Dubuque Iowa, No. of warrant — 52076.

On the 10th of Sept. 1860, a patent was issued to him for the East ½, N.E. ¼ and N.W. ¼ of N.E. ¼, 18, 84 N, 39 W, containing 160 acres, and located at Council Bluffs, warrant No. 68645.[2]

On the 6th June, 1827, a patent was issued to Thomas Linckern, alias Lincoln, for the W. ½, S.W. ¼, Sect. 32, T. 4 S. R. 5, W. in Indiana. This land was taken under the credit system of the Goverment, and as Mr. Linckern, alias Lincoln paid up on this a patent issued, and it did not revert to Government.[3]

On the 22d. of May 1849, a patent was issued by the U.S. Patent Office to A. Lincoln for an improved method of lifting vessels over shoals.

HL: LN2408, 2:155–56

360. A. F. Lord (WHH interview)

[1865–66]

A citizen of Springfield who visited our office on business, about one year before Mr Ls. nomination relates the following.

Mr Lincoln was Seated at his table listening very attentively to a man who was talking earnestly in a low tone. After the would be Client had stated the facts of his case, Mr Lincoln replied; Yes, there is no reasonable doubt but that I can gain your case for you; I can set a Whole neighborhood at loggerheads; I can distress a widowed Mother and her six fatherless children, and thereby get for you six hundred Dollars which you seem to have a legal claim to; but which rightfully belongs, it appears to me, as much to the woman and her children as it does to you. You must remember that some things that are legally right are not morally right. I shall not take your case — but I will give you a little advice for which I will charge you nothing. You seem to be a sprightly, energetic man, I would advise you to try your hand at making six hundred dollars in some other way.

LC: HW3962; HL: LN2408, 2:123

---

1. A former resident of Menard and Sangamon Counties, James G. Long had a clerkship in the pension office and was Herndon's contact in Washington for information in government records.

2. See §45.

3. See §45.

361. James H. Matheny (WHH interview)

[1865–66]

Jas. H. Matheny

  Says that about 1837–8 & 9 a parcel of young men in this City formed a Kind
of Poetical Society — association or what not. Lincoln once or twice wrote Short
Poems for the book None of the Poems are recllected in full. *One verse* of one, on
Seduction by Lincoln, runs thus —

  Whatever Spiteful fools may Say —.[1]
  Each jealous, ranting yelper —
  No woman ever *played* the *whore*
  Unless She had a man to help her.

  W. H. Herndon[2]
  Newton Francis   }
  Evan Butler   }   Some of the members
  Noah Rickord   }
  J. H. Matheny[3]   }

  LC: HW2561; HL: LN2408, 2:211

362. James H. Matheny (WHH interview)

[1865–66]

J. H. Matheny

  Says —

  Lincoln loved Burns generally — Shakespear — didn't care much if anything
for such thing as Campbells' pleasures of Hope — Akenside's imagination &c. &c
— Loved Byron's
  Don Juan —
  Darkness
  The Hosts of Sanacherib
  Last leaf by O. Holmes —
  Burns address to a young friend
  Burns' Cottre's Saturday Night
  Holy Wille's Prayer —
  Immortality —
  Child Harold —[1]

  LC: HW2562; HL: LN2408, 2:212

---

1. Verses and list of members are in another hand, presumably Matheny's.
2. WHH has written his own name in here; the other names are in the hand presumed to be Matheny's.
3. Under this list, WHH or JWW has written: *Mathy Clerk & enter pieces in a book.*

---

1. Titles referred to: Thomas Campbell, "The Pleasures of Hope"; Mark Akenside, "The Pleasures of the
Imagination"; Lord Byron, "Don Juan," "Darkness," "The Destruction of Sennacherib"; Oliver Wendell
Holmes, "The Last Leaf"; Robert Burns, "Epistle to a Young Friend," "The Cotter's Saturday Night," "Holy
Willie's Prayer"; William Knox, "Mortality"; Lord Byron, "Childe Harold's Pilgrimage."

363. James H. Matheny (WHH interview)

[1865–66]

J h Matheny

J. J Hardin went to Congress first — Say about 1844 — after this district had been organized —: Baker was the next candidate — Hardin beat Baker first and by a Kind of agreement — understanding implied, Baker was to run — rather the Convention that nominated Hardin "said it". Lincoln was the next caniddate: he was Elected in 1848 — Baker in 1846.[1] Baker resigned his seat & went to the war with Mxico. John Henry of Morgan was Elected to fill Bakers seat in Congress. Baker came back and wanted to run, but seeing Logan on the track he went to Galena. Originally there was a Kind of implied understanding that Hardin — Baker — Lincoln should rotate in Congress — Something broke it up — what it is or was I don't Know.

LC: HW2563; HL: LN2408, 2:212–13

364. James H. Matheny (WHH interview)

[1865–66]

J. H Matheny

Says he was present, he thinks in the Market house in 1840 and heard a debate between Douglas & Lincoln — the subject Martin Van Buren. Lincoln had asserted that Van had voted for Negro Suffrage under certain limitations. Douglas denied it. Lincoln then read from Hollands life of Van Buren.[1] Douglas said it was a forgery. Lincoln drew Fithians letter from Van Buren on Douglas.[2] Douglas got mad — Snatched up the book and Slung it into the crowd — saying d—n such a book.

Lincoln told me this Story too. (Herndon)[3]   Further — Lincoln told me that Douglas was always calling the Whigs Federalists — Tories — Aristocrats &c. That the whigs were opposed to freedom. Justice & progress. Lincoln told me that he said — "Douglas Says the Whigs are opposed to liberty — Justice & Progress. This is a loose assertion I suppose to Catch votes. I don't like to *catch votes by* cheating men out of their judgment, but in reference to the whigs being opposed to Liberty &c let me Say that that remains to be seen & demonstrated in the future. The brave don't boast. A barking dog don't bite.

LC: HW2564; HL: LN2408, 2:213–14

---

1. AL was elected to Congress in 1846, Edward D. Baker in 1844, and John J. Hardin in 1843.

---

1. William M. Holland, *The Life and Political Opinions of Martin Van Buren, Vice President of the United States* (Hartford, 1835).

2. William Fithian was a Vermillion County Whig politician. Van Buren's letter reportedly acknowledged that Holland's book "contains as far as it goes a substantially correct history of my political course." See *Sangamo Journal,* Sept. 18, 1840.

3. This interpolation by WHH probably refers to the story of Douglas slinging the book, rather than what follows.

365. James H. Matheny (WHH interview)

[1865–66]

J. H. Matheny

Says that in 1836 — probably in 1838 — that Col E.D. Taylor —, a finely dressed — an aristocratically dressed man — having ruffle shirts — gold Chain & watch &c —, was making a speech at _____ against the Whigs: he boasted of his Democracy — Called the whigs aristocrats &c — loomed up in his palaver — Lincoln saw it — felt develish — thought he could take the wind out of Taylor's Speech by a simple act — Lincoln nudged up — moved up to Taylor inch by inch — Lincoln raised slightly up — Caught Dick Taylors vest corner — gave it a quick jerk — it unbuttoned and out fell Dick ruffle shirt like a pile of Entrails — Swung out to the wind — gold chains — gold watches with large seals hung heavily & massively down. This was too much for the good People — Democrat & Whig alike — and they burst forth in a furious & uproarious laughter — Dick Saw the trick — Saw that it Killed him — was vexed & quit and never much afterwards said Even to himself *Aristocracy.*

Matheny further Says — as to Lincolns Religion — that when Lincoln first Came to Springfield in 1837 — Matheny being clerk — and Lincoln's office in the same building and Lincoln & Jim being friends, That Lincoln, when all were idle and nothing to do, would talk about Religion — pick up the Bible — read a passage — and then Comment on it — show its falsity — and its follies on the grounds of *Reason* — would then show its own self made & self uttered Contradictions and would in the End — finally ridicule it and as it were Scoff at it — (I guess he Scoffed — if he did scoff — at the fact of Contradictions to reason and to itself. Herndon)

LC: HW2570, HW2565; HL: LN2408, 2:214–15

366. George U. Miles (WHH interview)

[1865–66]

Jno G. Hardin & E D Baker were Candidates for Congress in the year of AD 1843: they mutually submitted their claims to the decision of a whig Convention held at Pekin. Hardin — Baker and Lincoln all lived in this Congressional district at that time & included in the district the Counties of Sangamon — Morgan — Menard — Tazwell & others Counties. These three men now have a wide reputation — Lincoln more than the other two —

The Convention met in Pekin in April, 1843.[1] Lincoln was not a Candidate — Baker & Hardin were. Hardin got all the Southern Counties in the District & Baker got all North of the District. This made a tie. Two County Conventions were held in Menard. Hardin was in Ky during both Conventions and beat Baker, Hardin getting Menard County. Before the final Ballot Many Counties were in-

---

1. WHH seems to have first written 1840, then 1842, before writing 1843.

structed for Lincoln & Could have beaten both Candidates. He was asked if he would not become a Cadidate. He said No — that he would rather Cut his arm off, rather than become a Candidate under the Circumstances, having as supposed made some kind to some one that he would not be   Hence he refuse   Hardin was nominated and went to Congress and took his seat in 1844. Baker went to the Mexican war — returned & went to Galena: Hardin went to the war and got Killed at Buena vsta. Baker went to Congress from the Galena District. Lincoln remained at home and went to Congress — was Elected to Congress in 1846 & took his seat in 1847 —

Postage — Miles — c25 — Lincoln not able to pay — 1849 —

LC: HW3789–90; HL: LN2408, 2:239–40

367. James Miles (WHH interview)[1]

[1865–66]

Jas Miles

Says — That Saml Hill told him of this story of Lincoln — One Johnson[2] — an ignorant, but ostentatious — proud man, used to go to Lincolns P.O. Every dy — sometimes 3 or 4 times a day — if in town, and Enquire — "Anything for me" — This bored Lincoln — yet it amused him: L. fixed a plan — wrote a letter to Johnson as coming from a negress in Ky — saying many good things about opposum, — dances — Corn shuckings — &c. and Ending — "Johns — Come & see me and old master won't Kick you out of the Kitchen any more." Elmore took it out — opened it — couldn't read a word — pretended to read it — went & got some friends to read it — read it correctly — thought the reader was fooling him — went to others — with the same result — At last Johnson said he would get Lincoln to read it — presented it to L: it was almost too much for him — read it. The man never asked afterwards — Any thing here for me.

LC: HW3964; HL: LN2408, 1:473

368. Joseph C. Richardson (statement for WHH)

[1865–66]

My Mother Settled Near Mr Thomas Lincoln, in 1828. it was Considered at that time that Abraham was the best penman in the Neighborhood. One day while he was on a visit at my Mothers house, I asked him him to write Some Copys for me. he very willingly Consented. he wrote Several. but one of them I have Never forgotten although a boy at the time   it was this. "Good boys who to their books apply; will all be great Men by and by."

---

1. In the docketing: *James Miles / Elmore.*
2. Probably Johnson Elmore, a New Salem area resident.

the year before the Lincoln family left the County. we had a Corn Crib put up, of large round logs the building was So arrainged that it required large posts Or forks, and they lay Some distance off.

and when we got ready for them Some of the men Commenced preparing Sticks to Carry them.

but young Lincoln told them that if they would assist him to get them On his Shoulder he would Carry them to the place. which he did to the astonishment of all present.

Young Lincoln was Considered One of the Most Studious boys in the Neighborhood and very Kind to all but always jovial and full of inocent jokes alwas had an answer for every body and every thing that was Said

when Abe was reading his father Made it a rule never to aske him to lay down his book. No difference what was to do, but let him reade Until he saw fit to lay it by himself

J C Richardson

LC: HW3966–67; HL: LN2408, 1:175–76

369. George Shutt (WHH interview)

[1865–66]

Geo. Shutt

Says —: The valley of the Shenandoah in Virginia is on an average about 30 or 40 miles wide and is about 100 miles long —: the Valley lies in West Virginia — ecept Jefferson and Berkley Counties: it is a rich beautiful valley, and lies between the Alleghanies and the Blue Ridge. The valley is one of the richest soils in the world — especially for small grain — corn grows well— well and handsomely improved. The soil is a redish lime stone soil. The better classes live in the Country. It is an agricultural country and the educated and high born and bred mostly live in the country: The people are a brave — generous — and hospitable people — and educated people.

The farmers have their Strawberries — Raspberries — pears — peaches — plums &c — &c — and every Luxury — Brick and Frame houses — fine style of architectcher — late —

HL: LN2408, 2:181–82

370. Joshua F. Speed (WHH interview)

[1865–66]

J. F. Speed

In 1840 Lincoln went into the Southern partt of the State as Elector Canvasser debator Speaker — Here first wrote his *Mary* — She darted after him — wrote him — Lincoln — seeing an other girl — & finding he did not love his wife wrote a leter saying he did not love her — ~~Speed Saw the letter~~[1] — tell the Conversation — between Lincoln & Speed — Went to see "Mary" — told her that he did not love her — She rose — and Said "The deciever shall be decieved wo is me."; alluding to a young man She fooled — Lincoln drew her down on his Knee — Kissed her — & parted — He going one way & She an other — Lincoln did Love Miss Edwards — "Mary" Saw it — told Lincoln the reason of his Change of mind — heart & soul — released him — Lincoln went Crazy — had to remove razors from his room — take away all Knives and other such dangerous things — &c — it was terrible — was during the Special session of the Ills Legislature in 1840[2]   Lincoln Married her for honor — feeling his honor bound to her —

Lincoln made a great Speech in 1837. or 8 — on internal improvements — Money — given him in 1837 or 8 — $200 — Spent 75c — paid back. $199.25 Saying I didnt Know how to Spend it. This money was given him to sustain & Maintain the Internal improvement policy as well as himself as its defender &c —

In 1840 Reuben Radford ran the Rail Road, East about 5 Miles[3] — the august Election Came off. & during the day of voting: it was rumored that Radford had taken the polls and was Excluding the whigs. Lincoln jumped up and went down to see what was the Matter and to see fair play. Radford was angry — Said much to Lincoln. Lincoln — said "Radford you will spoil & blow if you live much longer." Lincoln wanted to hit Radford, but Could get no chance to do so. Lincoln said "I intended to Knock him down & go away and leave him a-Kicking" —

When Lincoln was Elected Presdt he sent for me at Chicago whither he had gone — took Lincoln's letter — Couldn't get in till he Showed Lincolns letter — that let him in — Lincoln was much worn down & fatigued — After the Compliments — Lincoln Said — Speed have you got a room — "Yes" — Said Speed — "Name your hour Speed and I'll Come & see you, — will bring my wife. Lincoln went — took his wife — Said — "Mary & Fanny can Stay her — lets you and I go into your room — Lincoln threw himself on the bed — and Said — Speed what are your pecuniary Conditions — are you rich, or poor"   Speed Said — "Mr Presdt. I think I Know what you wish. I'll Speak Candidly to you — My pecuniary Conditions are good — I do not think you have any office within your gift that I can afford to take".

Lincoln wanted to make Guthry of Ky Secy of War — didn't want to write to him So that he could turn the refusal on me. You go and feel of Guthrie. Speed went — Guthrie refused. Guthrie Said the Union must be maintained. I am old and don't want the position anymore.

Lincoln said in reference to Fort Sumpter — My Mind was fixed on this Matter — Called my Cabinet — had just 1½ man — I was firm about its defence. &c. and my Cabinet was a unit when I was determined.

---

1. See below for another segment of this letter, beginning "Speed saw the letter," intended to be inserted here. For an explanation of why it is given separately, see p. 477, note 7.

2. *Lincoln went crazy . . . in 1840* is written in the margin, with the insertion point indicated by carets.

3. The Northern Cross Railroad began building at Meredosia, Morgan County, Illinois, in 1838 and did not reach Springfield until 1842.

Mr Lincoln in reference to Internal improvements & the best interest and advancement of this State, that his highest ambition was to become the De Witt Clinton of Ills.

Messr Douglas — Baker — Lincoln and others were in Speeds Store one Evening in Decr 1839 —. They got to talking politics — got warm — hot — angry. Douglas Sprang up and Said — Gentlemen, this is no place to talk politics — We will discuss the questions &c publicly with you — Then the banter came — see Journal. Decr. 1839.[4]

Religion — Beard of Ky was a Know nothing — went into a catholic Section of Ky to make Speeches against Foreigners — was making a Speech — Some one in the Crowd — a revered and gray haired leader — and Said — "Have you any Religion" — Beard Said it — the question was a poser — a Stumper — Yet gather himself Beard said — "Yes Stranger — thank God — I have got Some Religion — I had better be without money than with out Religion So far from home. From this time he swayed the crowd "for there was a great truth in this reply said" Lincoln. Speed you had better be without money than without Religion Said Lincoln. Speed is Satisfied that Mr Lincoln was a growing man in Religion — (this is true as to *Religion* though not so as to *Christianit*

Lee had surrendered — Davis had fled. and Lincoln joyous — Called his Cabinet togethe about the only one he Ever had. and asked Each one of his Cabinet what had better be done. Some were one way & Some an other — Speed[5] was Sharp & hard on the Traitors — Said they ought to be hung — Each one Expressed his own opinions. After all had Expressed their Opinions — Lincoln turned to Speed and Said — Speed you are hot after the Rebel. I Should have though that you would have been for mercy — Kindness — tenderness &c — Speed Said — Mr Presdt you asked me my opinion and I gave it honestly — Tut — Tut Said Lincoln patting Speed on the Shoulders I Know that and admire you the More for it, yet I say I am mistaken. Mr Lincoln made a Speech to his Cabinet: it was sublime for it was in spired. (I can't get this — H.) Lincoln Said I can describe my feelings by telling a story[6]   "I feel" said Lincoln jokingly — like a litte neighbor boy of mine in Indiana his father was a hunter: he was tender & chicken hearted: his father one night Caught an old Coon and her young — Killed the old one — and all the young Except one — tied a little rope around the neck of it and told the boy to watch it while he the father went & got a chain — the boy was afraid his father would treat it Cruelly — Lincoln went over to see the boy — the boy was apparently crying — was tender — never would throw at a bird — Said to Abe — "I wish this Coon would get away —, but if I let him go, dad will whip me — I do wish it would run off — So I feel by these leading rebels.

---

4. *Messr Douglas . . . Decr. 1839.* is written in the margin, with the insertion point indicated by carets.
5. James Speed (1812–87), the elder brother of Joshua F. Speed, served as attorney general under AL.
6. *Lincoln Said . . . a story* is written in the margin, with the insertion point indicated by carets.

— Davis — Lee &c — I wish they Could get away — yet if I let 'em loose — dad — the People would whip me — and yet I do wish they would run away out of the land — &c.

Speed Saw the letter to "Mary" written by Mr Lincoln. Speed tried to persuade Lincoln to burn it up. Lincoln Said — "Speed I always Knew you were an obstinate man. If you won't deliver it I will get Some one to do it. I Shall not deliver it nor give it to you to be delivered: Words are forgotten — Misunderstood — passed by — not noticed in a private Conversation — but once put your words in writing and they Stand as a living & eternal Monument against you. If you think you have *will* & Manhood Enough to go and see her and Speak to her what you say in that letter, you may do that. Lincoln did go and see her — did tell her &c — Speed said — Lincoln tell me what you said and did" — Lincoln told him — Speed Said — The last thing is a bad lick, but it cannot now be helped — Lincoln Kept his promises and did not go to see her for months — they got together somehow.[7]

LC: HW3968–73; HL: LN2408, 2:59–64

371. Joshua F. Speed (statement for WHH)

[1865–66]

In 1836[1] Mr Lincoln was a whig candidate for the Legislature in Sangamon County. At that time he resided in the lower part of the County near Petersburg — I was a merchant in Springfield had never seen him — but had heard of his power upon the stump from the young men in that part of the County — They were proud of him, and spoke of him in high terms of encomium — A short time before the election, he made a speech in Springfield, in the old Court house where the State house now stands — The crowd was large. His friends & admirers had Come in from the Country —

I remember that his speech was a very able one, using with great power and originality all the arguments then used to sustain the principles of the Whig party, as against its great rival the Democratic party of that day — The speech produced a profound impression — The Crowd was with him —

7. *Speed saw the letter . . . got together somehow.* This passage, written on a separate sheet, is WHH's attempt to expand on what, in writing out his interview with Speed, he had first put down about AL's engagement to Mary Todd. A caret at the point early in the narrative where WHH first wrote *Speed saw the letter* and the striking of these same words clearly indicate the point at which WHH intended that this passage be inserted. It is given separately here in the interest of chronological clarity. Because it inadvertently carries the story far beyond the conversation between Lincoln and Speed, inserting the entire passage at the place indicated (as the Springer transcription does) has the effect of seriously disrupting the chronology of events, particularly when the text reverts to the original version of Speed's testimony. For a reconstruction of this testimony in chronological order, see Wilson, 102–3.

1. The text is in Speed's hand. Written above the line by WHH: *1834—Speed now Says.* For another version of this story by Speed, see §474.

The Candidates in opposition and the party opposed to him felt it — Depression on one side & exultation on the other was evident —

Mr George Forquer an old Citizen, a man of recognized prominence & ability as a lawyer was present — Forquer had been a whig — one of the Champions of the party — But had then recently joined the Democratic party and Almost simultaneous with his change — had been appointed Register of the land office — which office he then held —

Just about that time Mr F had Completed a neat frame house — the best house then in the village of Springfield and upon it had erected a lightning rod — the only one in the place and the first one Mr Lincoln had evr observed — He afterwards told me that seeing Forquers lightning rod had led him to the study of the properties of electricity & the utility of the rod as a Conductor —

At the Conclusion of Lincolns speech the Crowd was about dispersing when Forquer rose and asked to be heard —

He commenced by saying that this young man would have to be taken down and was sorry that the task devolved upon him — He then proceeded to answer Linclns speech in a style which while it was able and fair — in his whole manner asserted & claimed superiority —

Lincoln stood near him and watched him during the whole of his Speech —

When Forquer Concluded he took the stand again — I have heard him often since — in Court and before the people — but never saw him appear so well as upon that occasion — He replied to Mr F with great dignity and force — But I shall never forget the conclusion of that speech —

Turning to Mr F. he said that he had Commenced his speech by announcing that this young man would have to be taken down —

Turning then to the Crowd he said it is for you, not for me to say whether I am up or down.

The gentleman has alluded to my being a young man — I am older in years than I am in the tricks and trades of politicians — I desire to live — and I disire place and distinction as a politician — but I would rather die now than like the gentleman live to see the day that I would have to erect a lightning rod to protect a guilty Concience from an offended God.

LC: HW3974–75; HL: LN2408, 2:392–93

372. John T. Stuart (WHH interview)

[1865–66¹]

Billey. Fagan —

In the year 1828–9 town of Sprgfd there lived a man by the name of Uncle Billy Fagan: he was a representative man — a gentleman *&* a wit. A Young lawyer

---

1. This and the four undated Stuart interviews that follow are ranked according to WHH's sequential numbering of the manuscripts.

has just Come from Ky a Mr _____.[2] After has having been here a few
days the gentleman dressed up in his rich broad cloth and walked up town to the
grocery — the usual and comunal place of business — of rest & fun to see the
new world in which he was about to settle & landing & leaning up against a post
looking on. Uncle Billy saw him — and edged his way up to him and after Shrewdly
& Eyeing — penetrating the young lawyer — Accosted the young lawyer thus —
"You are a stranger in these parts, I guess" and the lawyer said in reply — "Yes,
Sir, I am a stranger. Uncle Billey Eyed the lawyer again from head to foot, keenly
and shrewdly and thus again addressed the lawyer — "Stranger, where are you from"
and to which the Stranger replied — "From Kentucky" — "Kentucky—Eh! Kentucky Eh." responded Uncle Billy. The old gentleman Eyed the young lawyer again
and again — from head to foot — paused awhile — threw his keen grey Eye up
to the lawyers face and interrogated the lawyer again thus — "What — might your
business be stranger"   "My profession is that of a Lawyer, Sir" responded the Atty.
Uncle Billy now more particularly Scanned and Scrutinized the law — thought
— cocked his Eye up — put his finger on the side of his nose as if in meditation
&c — reflected — and thus again Said — Stranger — "May I tell you what I think
of you". The lawyer rose up in a dignified way, Expecting to get a compliment from
the old gentleman whom the lawyer had detected as more than an ordinary loafer
— "Said — Yes Sir, I Should like to have your opinion" — Uncle Billey then put
his finger on the soft part of his nose close to his cheek as if in study and meditation. Said — Stranger, I think you are — are — a damned Slim chance

Tom Edwards Story —
        Stuart
        Lincoln

Judge Davis
        Lincoln   { old fool Stories
        Stuart   { a Slander Case
[illegible]

    LC: HW2252; HL: LN2408, 2:196–97

373. John T. Stuart (WHH interview)

[1865–66]
        Lincoln was once a candidate under Filmore's admr for Comms of the Gen.
land office — got Beat. Cyrus Edwards was a candidate — so was Justin Butterfield
— Butterfield got it.
        Filmore then offered Lincoln the Governorship of Oregon Territory — Jno.
T. Stuart & Lincoln were at Tremont — or Bloomington — some one brought

---

2. Stuart told this story on himself, but WHH apparently agreed to withhold his name.

the news — Coaxed Lincoln to take it — Said he woud if his wife would consent. Refused to do So — Stuart told Lincoln he could soon return to the U.S. Senate from Oregon &c —

Mr Lovejoy went to Cooper institute in Feby 1862 or 3 — Lincoln was conservative — told the border States men So. (Write to Speed)   The Preachers saw him — Said he did not intend to go Radical — Story conversation — a Popes Bull — Wrote the Proclamation before — Issued it Soon after — Knowing it was written and would be issued — Why did Speed come out — Radicals beat Lincoln —

LC: HW2249; HL: LN2408, 2:198

374. John T. Stuart (WHH interview)

[1865–66]

Jno T Stuart
Says from 1830 up to 1837 the tendency in Illinois was for every man of ambition to turn Democrite — Ford Forquer — Cartwright.
There was a fear that the Yankees about 1832 to 1837 imigrating to Ills would be whig — but when they got here were no more than democrats — and this [illegible] and changed all.
That in 1834 at Danleys[1] Abe came to him and Said, Stuart the Democracy want to run me &c that Stuart Said — Run. That the Democracy did drop 2 of their men — and run   Abe & Dawson — came near beating Stuart.
That Sangamon Co was Democratic till 1834 and in 1836 & 7 it became Whig — Herndon[2] & others went for *White*[3] of Tennessee and this Settled Old Sangamon for nearly 20 ys —
Lincoln stood true to his ideas of Whiggery —
It was the custom to Stump it all over the Country.

LC: HW2251; HL: LN2408, 2:198–99

375. John T. Stuart (WHH interview)

[1865–66]

Stuart —
Says — that Lincoln & himself entered into partnership in 1837 — Keept office in a little room above the Court room — he slept — and lounged — talked — joked —

---

1. In describing this episode to John G. Nicolay, Stuart said: "I remember we were out at Danleys on Clear Lake. They had a shooting match there. The country people met to shoot for a beef (the candidates as was the custom were expected to pay for the beef.) and we were there electioneering" (Burlingame, 11). Clear Lake is about six miles east of Springfield.
2. Archer G. Herndon.
3. Hugh L. White.

Crossings — Chunks — Stick — bricks — no pavements —
Runsdells Kept Tavern 1837 — Population 1200. 1100. in 1834 — 1000 in
1832.

Mr Stuart   Says that Lincoln during the sessions of the Leg in 1834 — &
36 he frequently traded Lincoln off: he was the author of no special or general act
— had no organizing power — When he learned in 1838 & 40 more of the tricks
&c of men he refused to be Sold. *He never had a price*

LC: HW2248; HL: LN2408, 2:199–200

376. *John T. Stuart (WHH interview)*

[1865–66]

Jno. T. Stuart
    Says — We, in Sangamon Co. — volunteered on the *[blank space]* day of April
1832 — the day of our Cir Co — went to Beardstown & rendezvoused there a
few days — went to Rushville — and then organized into Companies and regiments — Lincoln was Elected Captain at N.S — We proceeded thence, packing
provisions on our horses to Rock Island — staid there a few days — and then
proceeded to Dixon — were out of provisions — bought some flour & whiskey
of Dixon[1] — when I got into camp the boys had a Spree — proceeded to Ottowa
— thence by Gratiots Grove — to Galena. The fight at Gratiots Grove Lincoln
was not in — Lincoln & myself were in Iles — Spy Battallion — Got to Galena
— went to the hoar houses — Gen Henry went — his magnetism drew all the
women to himself — All went purely for fun — devilment — nothing Else — At
Ottow we beat up for volunteers — Lincoln & I belonged to _____ 3. Companies Constituted a Spy battallion — I was a member of the Spy battallion before I landed at Dixon — Was in Dawson's Company Spy battallion called —
Henry Commanded the Spy battallion — At Ottow we we called for a regiment
for 20 days — joined Early's Company of the Spy battallion —: First under Iles as
Captain — Commanded by Henry — & 2dly under Dawson. Lincoln was in these
Spy Companies   Our provisions were brought to us at Beardstown by steam boat
— loaded our horses her — landed at Rock River — met boats — got provisions
struck for Dixon — Carried Some provisions on horse back — boats — perogues
&c — &c met up as often as possible —*SEE. Maj Iles* —

LC: HW2250; HL: LN2408, 2:204–5

---

1. John Dixon (1784–1876), proprietor of a ferry and store on the Rock River.

377. John T. Stuart (WHH interview)[1]

[1865–66?]

Lincoln & Stuart Coming down the hill
Delavan —
Stuart Said — Lincoln the time is Coming when you & I will have to be Democrats or Abolitionists — When that time Comes My mind is fixed — I cant Compromise the Slavery question
1848–50

_____

Lincoln was a vegetable — His skin performed what other organs did for the   He was sluggish — apathetic —

LC: HW4010v

378. James Taylor (WHH interview)

[1865–66]

I came up in the boat with Bogue[1] in 1831 — Knew Lincoln as Early as 1833   I saw him painting a sign in N.S. in 1837. He surveyed, laid off Petersburg — Jack Armstrong used to plague Abe a great deal a bout his — Abe's son, which he had by Mrs Armstrong; it was a joke — plagued Abe terribly —

About the year 1835 the roughs of N Salem and surrounding Country did Cook a live pig[2] in a tin plate stove — did barrel up — put in a hogshead a drunken man and roll him down the hill[3] — Lincoln surveyed land for me.

Rutledge kept a grocery in NS: he saw a fellow in town bare-foot — Wadkins[4] — and told Wadkins if he would cut up an old house that he would give him a pair of shoes: Wadkins started on his job — Abe Saw him — got his axe & helped him to cut up the thing — "Now go get your shoes" Said Abe

LC: HW2922; HL: LN2408, 1:472

_____

1. These notes by WHH on a conversation with Stuart appear on the back of HW4010, a statement in the hand of Zane (§347).

_____

1. Vincent Bogue of Springfield sponsored the trip of the *Talisman* up the Sangamon River in April 1832.
2. See §§56, 101.
3. For other versions of this story, see §§259, 343.
4. There were a number of Watkins families in the New Salem area. See §282, where R. B. Rutledge tells a similar story of AL and Ab Trout.

379. Judge Samuel Treat (statement for WHH)[1]

[1865–66]

Mr. Lincoln' fairness to his political opponents.

When Mr. Lincoln first ran for congress, the opposing Candidate was a Methodist preacher. During the Canvass, an aspiring Democrat said to Mr. Lincoln, "Such is my utter aversion to the meddling of preachers in politics, that I will vote for you Even at the risk of losing cast with my party, if you think the contest doubtful." Mr. Lincoln replied, "I would like your vote, but I fully appreciate your position, and will give you my honest opinion on the morning of Election day." On that morning he called on the Democrat and said, "I am now satisfied that I have got the preacher by the _____, and you had better keep out of the ring."

LC: HW3977; HL: LN2408, 2:182–83

380. Judge Samuel Treat (statement for WHH)[1]

[1865–66]

Mr. Lincoln' first appearance in the Supreme Court of Illinois.

A case being called for hearing in that court, Mr. Lincoln stated that he appeared for the Appellant, and was ready to proceed with the argument. He then said: "This is the first case I have ever had in this Court, and I have, therefore, examined it with great care. As the Court will percieve by looking at the abstract of the record, the only question in the case is one of authority. I have not been able to find any authority sustaining my side of the case, but I *have found* several cases directly in point on the other side. I will now give *these cases* to the Court, and then submit the case."[2]

LC: HW3978–79; HL: LN2408, 2:183

381. Judges Samuel Treat and David Davis (WHH notes)[1]

[1865–66]

Judge Treat
    Judge Treats Circuit was Called 8 Judicial curcuit —
    Was appointed District Court 1855

---

1. Presumably in Treat's hand. Docketed: *Lincoln in 1846, Judge Treat.*

---

1. Presumably in Treat's hand. Docketed: *Judge Treat.*
2. According to the Illinois Reports, *Scammon v. Cline* (3 Ill. 456) was the first case for which Lincoln is recorded as counsel. He is, however, named as counsel for the appellee, not for the appellant.

---

1. Docketed: *Judge Treats & Judge Davis Statement.* This document seems to incorporate notes from interviews with AL's two principal judges on the Eighth Circuit. The last two passages apparently reflect Davis's remarks; the earlier note, Treat's.

Appointed Cir Judge in 1838 — 14 Counties
Judge of Supm Court 1841 —
Supm Judge 1848

Judge Davis Succeeded Judge *Treat*
Lincolns 1s appearance
                          England vs. Clrk[2]

Judge Treats time actually on the Bench was 6 Mo — on an average — Each
year

Sometimes 5 Mondays in a Week — Lincoln didn't Come — we did

Want of will — want of Administrative ability; he did not fully foresee all —:
he did not organize by a solid plan: hence his Adm didn't run smooth — Had no
foresight — no Care for the future. He was frequently seen in the Street hunting
wood — Hay and when asked &c would say it is not my way

    LC: HW3980; HL: LN2408, 2:184

382. *William A. Turney (WHH interview)*

                                                              [1865–66]

(Wm. Turney)   Oneida Co—
                          Lincoln
   One Idea —
        Caton — Breese and Skinner — all from one Co. — yes, says, Lincoln, I
thought you from some one Idea County — Lincoln had lost some motion in
Court

    HL: LN2408, 2:178

383. *Peter Van Bergen (WHH interview)*

                                                              [1865–66]

Peter Van Bergen
        Says that Jas. Smith — the Preacher who once lived here is now in Dundee
Scotland. Smith was in 1850 preacher of the 1st Presbyterian Church here — Smith
once said to Lincoln — "Lincoln — you are a rising man. You will be Presdt yet."
"If I am Ever Presdt "I'll banish you to Scotland". replied Lincoln good naturedly.

---

2. *England v. Clark*, tried at the June term 1841 of the Menard Circuit Court, was appealed to the Illinois Supreme Court (5 Ill. 486), where AL and J. D. Urquhart represented the plaintiff in error. The case
was originally argued at the December term 1841 but was reargued in December 1843, with the court eventually deciding in favor of the defendant.

After L was Elected he recd a letter from Smith. Lincoln did appoint him Consul at Liverpool.

Speed tells Van Bergen that once he called his Cabinet together and requested their individual opinion as to the necessity & policy of hanging the Rebells. Each gave his opinion. Speed tarried after the meeting had ajdourned. Lincoln Said "Speed you are quite a har man." "Yes," Said Speed   I feel this way, said Lincoln — Once a man & his small son Caught several Coons — Killed all but one and the old man tied it with a String — Lincoln Came along and the boy told him the Story — Said let him go — The boy Said I wish I could he could get away — but if I let him go dad will whip me — "I feel as to hanging &c like the boy about the cool. "If I let them go I'll get whipt" Said Lincoln.[1]

Van B — Says Lincoln showed him Van B the war maps of Vicksburg. Explained &c. &c and finally said — "Grant here displayed about Vicksburg more generalship than Ever was shown by any general in America

LC: HW3981; HL: LN2408, 2:122

384. Frances Todd Wallace (WHH interview)

[1865–66]

Mrs. Doct Wm Wallace — (Mrs Lincoln Sister —

I Came to Ills in 1836 or 7 — was maried in 1838. — Sent for Mrs Lincoln at that time. My husband & myself boarded at an old tavern — opposite of the Episcopal church. Mary married in 1842 — Came to the same house — was Kept by Saunders — or Mrs _____ at that time — house now as then — no improvements that I Know of. I then moved to a house 3 doors South of Doct Helms[1] — nearly opposite (East) of Hickox's.[2] Mr L before he was married used to Come to our house — was attatched to my eldest girl[3] — very much so —. He was not attatched to Children generally as I think — was to his own — was to my oldest girl — one year older than Bob Lincoln — Don't think Mr L. was much attatched to Cats & dogs — one reason was that Bob once had a little dog — he bit Bob — Lincoln took him off to the Mad Stone in Terrehaute or other place in Indiana I think. Mr L's first private home was where he lived when Presdt. It looks better now than then — more care &c — are now bestowed on it. His — L's — back yard was used as a woodpile he used to Saw wood for Exercise —: he really loved to do it: he was the very best Kindest and father I ever saw: he was a domestic man I think by nature. I used to go over and see my sister and L was always at home if in town: he would read generally aloud — (Couldn't read otherwise   H): would read with great warmth all funny things — humorous things &c.: Read Shake-

---

1. See §370.

---

1. Dr. Meredith Helm.
2. Possibly Virgil Hickox, although it could also refer to one of his brothers, Horace or Addison.
3. Mary J. Wallace.

spear that way: he was a sad man — an abstracted man — have gone over to his house many times — talked with my sister — Lincoln would lean back — his head against the top of a rocking Chair — sit abstracted that way for moments — 20 — 30 minutes — and all at once burst out in a joke — though his thoughts were not on a joke — Mr nor Mrs Lincoln loved the beautiful — I have planted flowers in their front yard myself to hide nakedness — ugliness &c. &c. have done it often — and often — Mrs L never planted trees — Roses — never made a garden, at least not more than once or twice —

LC: HW3982–83; HL: LN2408, 2:88–89

385. Stephen Whitehurst (statement for WHH)[1]

[1865–66]

W.H.H. *Here is that thing* — the truth as near as I can tell it.

That Mr L was not above the feelings of other men and subject to the same anxieties and emotions is instanced by his great desire to have the respect of his friends and neighbors — and to see tokens of their confidence and esteem. He was very anxious, when a candidate for the Presidency the first time, that he might receive a majority of the votes of his own County and more particularly in the city of Springfield, and was much as the friends of Mr. Douglass' men working in every way to keep their majority in the city and County, & of which they were confident   Mr L. *sent* for one of the candidates for a County office on the Republican Ticket and the messenger failing to deliver his message *went* himself and inquired of the candidate what measures, if any, had been adopted to get out the full republican vote; and upon being told that every honorable effort had been made in the country precincts to have a full vote cast, and that the Republicans would probably wait until a few days before the election before any systematic effort would be made in the city, seemed very much dissatisfied, and was very energetic in his actions and Language, condemning such a course. He was requested to make any suggestions that might occur to him, with the assurance that the candidates and the Committees would make every effort in their power to carry out any plan he might offer. — He then detailed to the candidate his plan for procuring a full vote and securing to the Republican ticket such electors as were careless or doubtful. The suggestions were carried out and the result fully justified his expectations; and a majority of the votes of his own city were given him despite the efforts of his political opponents, and the Democratic majority in the County reduced to a few votes.

~~Probably no such political contest ever took place before in our county as~~
~~This contest on both sides was very warm and thorough~~

LC: HW3996; HL: LN2408, 2:163–64

---

1. Marginal note: *Whitehurst, Vote on Lincoln for Pres in Springfield 1860, what L said.*

386. *Charles S. Zane (statement for WHH)*[1]

[1865–66]

Analysis of Mr Lincolns Intellect, or the ability of his Intellect to act in particular ways; sometimes called powers, faculties or susceptibilities.

Mr Lincoln had a quick accurate perception of outward objects and of the acts
of the minds their agreements and disagreements or alike or unlike

His Conceptive power was accurate but not active and quick — By the conceptive power I mean the faculty of replacing in the minds eye (as Shakspear expresses it) Sensations and perceptions, in the absence of their causes or their objects and without any account of the period when the objects which laid the
foundation of them were present. Or to be more brief the susceptibility of reviv-
ing in the mind those impressions which have been previously received through
the medium of the senses

His capacity for analysis was remarkable viz. his minds susceptibility of indicating those separate and subordinate feelings to which the Complex mental State
is virtually equal. To illustrate what I mean suppose the Complex idea expressed
by the term government is presented for his Consideration he would indicate with
great clearness the subordinate ideas which Compose it, and are equal to it Such
as power, right, obligation, command and the relative notions of superior and
inferior.

His abstractive power was also remarcable that is to say he could not only indicate point out partic[ular] partes of a Complex notion, but could fix his attention upon it detain it, hold on to it, feel of it, handle it, and carry it about in his
mind (if the expressions are allowable) the other parts disappearing being forgotten for the time.

His capacity for generalization was also good viz. The susceptibility of the mind
when it has made a subordinate part of a complex notion a subject of attention to
extend that notion to other objects or to detect its presence in many subjects —
Not having had the time and opportunity for a thorough Study, of science and
the liberal arts, his field for generalization was not so broad and extended, as it
otherwise would have been; hence some men have said his mind was not remarcable for compass.

He had a mental Capacity for classifying and forming general abstract truths
or principles and for applying and using them; and for Contemplating the particular nature of things divested of all superfluous and specific circumstances.

His capacity of fixing his attention was remackable; viz. His perceptive faculy
grasped an object of Contemplation with power and held on with tenacity, while
his will when founded on Some Sentim of duty or feeling of desire directed, condensed, and Confined the perception.[2]

He had a great power of relative suggestions or judgment — what I mean to
say is this when his intellect perceived different objects together or had immedi-

---

1. Docketed: *C. S. Zane. — Estimation of* <u>Lincoln's Mind</u>.
2. Marginal note: *affections of the heart.*

ately Successive Conceptions of absent objects he had a great susceptibility of feeling that they were equal or unequal, like or unlike, the same or different in respect to place and time or that they had the same or different causes. He had such a clear perception of what belonged to an object and what did not that he could not be imposed upon by that Confusion of ideas which in so many Cases distorts the judgment of the multitude.

He had a philosophic memory or that Species of memory which is sustained chiefly by the relation of resemblance Contrast and cause and effect or which is based upon the above laws or principles of association. He had not a circumstantial memory or that species of memory based chiefly on the relation of contiguity in time and place or that principle or law of association   Having a philosophic memory he looked more deeply into the nature of things. He bestowed but slight attention on what is purely outward and incidental but detected with a discriminating eye the analogies and oppositions the causes and consequences of events. He helped his memory by the concious and strict observence of the truth. He may not have remembered so much as many others; but within the limits which for good reasons undoubtedly he set to his recolection he was very exact and reliable.

His reasoning power was remarcable viz. that susceptibility of the mind whereby Conclusions are deduced from two or more propositions premised. When he spoke or reasoned he had a Strong desire to arrive at the truth hence the great body of the propositions brought up were found to have a greater or less reference to the general subject, and by his quick accurate perception of their relations to the point to be proved, their Suitableness or want of suitableness their agreement or want of agreement — He made his selections from among them with great judgment. He is mind inclined to demonstrative reasoning; hence he made a liberal use of definitions and built upon first principles — he had great ability however for moral reasoning — hence he formed Correct opinions Concerning the duties and general Conduct of life. He loved the truth hence he always Stated the Subject of discussion and his propositions as well as those of his opponent with great farness and clearness.

He seldom exercised the power of imagination viz That power of the mind by means of which various Conceptions are combined together so as to form new wholes. However in his speech at Springfield June 17" 1858[3] he certainly brought this faculty of his minde into exercise in describing the house build by Stephen Franklin Roger and James. And again in his message of December 1st 1862. When he said "The occasion is piled high with difficulties and we must rise with the occasion; and when further along in the same message he "Says: "The fiery trial through which we pass will light us down in honor or dishonor to the latest generation"[4] now and then Similar passages found in his speaches leads me to believe that he had more imagination than it is generally supposed he had.

Mr Lincoln surpassed the average of man kind more in his power of Concep-

3. This is the "House Divided" speech (*CW* 2:461–69).
4. *CW* 5:537.

tion than Imagination more in generalization than Conception more in memory
than generalization more in perception than memory more in relative Suggestion
or judgment than perception than in in the power of reason than relative Suggestion more in Analysis than reason more in Abstraction than analysis[5]

Mr Lincoln had Strong Emotional sensibilities   here is where we find his
motives; for it   It is in the emotions that we find the Causes which render men
restless and inquisitive; which prompts them to deeds both good and evil; here is
the great field for human motives — here burns forever the hidden fire that lights
up the material Structure and sets the intellect in motion that drives it on to all its
achievements; here is where the instincts, the appetites, the propensities, the affections, the desires, the feelings of moral approval and disapproval, and the feelings of moral obligation, the heart and the Concience, fight their battels and strou-
gle for ascendency.

Mr Lincoln appreciated the beautiful he had emotions of beauty. His taste was
not cultivated in many directions viz. his power of judging of the beauty or defor-
mity of objects In his letter adressed to [*blank space*] bearing date [*blank space*] &
his last inaugural and other documents he displayed taste; hence I believe him a
man of great taste in some directions.

He relied upon reason at all times — placing but little confidence in his instincts

He had a Strong desire of knowledge or as it is otherwise called the propensity
for curiosity or knowledge. He had no propensity for imitation. He kept his desire of esteem within its due and appropriate limits. He had a desire of power, but
it was that he might in the use of it benefit his fellow men. never allowing it to
run inordinately into ambition

He loved the truth — the principle of veracity or the propensity to utter the
truth was possessed by him in a remarcable degree, his principle of Sociality or the
desire of Society was moderate.

He seemed to be almost destitute of that class of affection founded on resent-
ment — hence he was not envious, Jealous, revengeful, or fearful.

He possessed the benevolent affections or those founded, on love, in a remarcable degree; hence he was willing and ready to extend aid & help to the needy
and the week. he sympathized with pittied and encouraged the unfortunate and
the retched; he was forgiving and had much charity for the errors and follies of
his fellow men. He loved his family his Country the whole human family without
reference to races tongs creds or colors

He loved the Supreme Being.

His feelings of moral approval and disapproval were very Strong. Some men
have feelings of moral approval, but seem to be without any feelings of moral
obligation, he felt a perfect obligation, to do what his Conscience approved. He
believed in an immutable Standard of right and wrong by which to try every and
all questions; by reference to that great Sublime and glorious Standard, of recti-

5. Marginal note: *understanding includes Judgment, perception — Conception —*.

tude, he measured the morality of every action and every question upon which he was called to act:

Many men Consider objects chiefly as they have a relation to themselves   he Considered them as they related to all possible existences; Some look at things in the aspect of their desirableness   he fixed his eye on the sublime feature of their rectitude; Some ask what is good   he asked what was right.

Mr Lincoln instincts relatively speaking were Stronger than his appetites. his propensities were Stronger than his instincts; that Class of his affections founded on love were Stronger than his Propensities; his feelings of moral approval were Stronger than his affections his feelings of moral obligation were Stronger than his feelings of moral approval.

He never allowed his natural emotions or the emotions of the heart to become agitated excited broken up and thrown out of their proper action; from which it may have been inferred that his natural emotions were not strong   I believe the emotions of his heart were deep and Strong but they had the benefit of the light and wisdom of a great intellect, and the admonitions of a great Conscience. It is difficult for me to decide whether he Should be more distinguished on account of his intellect his heart or his Conscience. I incline to the opinion however, that he Surpassed other men more in the Strength of his intellect than in the depth of his natural Sensibilities or the strength of the emotions of his heart; and more in his moral Sensibilities or in his conscience than either.

(Zane)[6]

LC: HW4011–15; HL: LN2408, 2:106–14

387. Charles S. Zane (statement for WHH)

[1865–66]

About nine oclock on the morning of the Eighteenth of May 1860 I was sitting in the law office of Messers Lincoln and Herndon, Conversing with a Student in the office, when Mr Lincoln came in, On entering he said — Well boys what do you know? And Sat down in a chair on the North side of the office — I remarked (to him) Mr. Rosett[1] who came from Chicago on the morning train thinks your chances for the nomination are good. He asked me if I knew what Mr. Rosett's reasons for thinking so were. A short conversation then followed during which Mr E. L. Baker entered the office with a telegram which said the names of the Candidates for nomination had been announced to the Convention; that Mr Lincolns name was received with greater applause, than that of any other candidate — Soon after he Lincoln went to the telegraph office accompanied by those

---

6. Not in Zane's hand.

---

1. John E. Rosette (1824–81), a Springfield attorney.

present; After waiting there some time the telegraph of the first ballot first ballot Came over the wires. From the manner in which Mr Lincoln received this dispatch it was my impression that it was as favorable as he expected   His opinion was or had been that if Mr Seward did not get the nomination on the first ballot or come very near to it he would not be likely to get it at all   After waiting a short time the another telegram of the second ballot Came — This I thought from his manner he considered as virtually deciding the nomination. He then went to the Office of the Illinois State Journal. The local Editor with four others including myself returned to the telegraph office and remaind until the third dispatch came   Upon receiving it the operator threw down his pencil evidently excited then taking it up wrote out the dispatch and handed it to the local[2] who read it to himself. Those present asked how it looked he said very bad — which lengthened some of our faces considerably. on the way to the Journal Office he remarked that it looked bad for Mr Seward and the other defeated Candidates. Entering the Office where Mr Lincoln was seated the Local proposed three cheers for the next president, which were given then read the dispatch. Mr Lincoln being seated rose up took the telegram and read it then said when the second ballot came I knew this must Come". He received all with apparent coolness from the expressions playing upon his Countenance however a close observer Could detect Strong emotions within. When the result was made known on the Streets it was followed by Shouts for Lincoln

In the remarks which followed the last dispatch Some one said Mr Lincoln I suppose we will soon have a book containing your life now; To which he replied there is not much in my past life about which to write a book as it seems to me. He then came down out of the office (which was on the second floor) on to the sidewalk his neighbours and friends gathering around him Commenced shakeing his hand and Congratulating him; he then said jesting gentlemen you had better come up and shake my hand while you can honors elevate some men. After spending a few moments in receiving their Cordial Congratulations looking in the direction of his home he said well gentlemen there is a little woman at our house who is probably more interested in this dispatch than I am; if you will excuse me I will take the dispatch up and let her see it.

As he walked up the Street his friends and neighbors looked after him with a feeling of great satisfaction and as I thought mingled with Considerable of pride others Coming up the Streets would pint after him and say yonder goes Lincoln showing that he had grown in their interest that morning

LC: HW4009–10; HL: LN2408, 2:78–81

---

2. Probably Edward L. Baker, the local editor of the *Journal.*

388. Charles S. Zane (WHH interview)

[1865–66]

C. S. Zane

I was present in the Illinois State Journal on the day when Lincoln was nominated: he was present & when he received the news of the 3d Ballot. Lincoln Said I Knew it would Come to this when I Saw the 2d. Ballot. When _____ came in with the Ballot — the 3d one he cried out 3 cheers for the next Presdt. —. Lincoln was sitting down — rose up — the 3d dispatch was handed to him: he then Said I Knew it would Come to this — L. was cool, but you could see he felt well: Lincoln Said "I must go home: there is a little short woman there that is more interested in this Matter than I am". As Lincoln came down stairs to go home he was met by a number of Irish & American Citizens at the foot of the Stairs at the Journal office, who Congratulated him on the nomination. Mr L said — "Boys you had better come and shake hands with me now that you have an oppertunity — for you do not Know what influence this nomination may have on me. I am human, you Know.

As Mr Lincoln wended his way home, the People look at him and after him — watching his steps, saying to enquiring friends — There goes Lincoln —

Lincoln played ball pretty much all the dy before his nomination — played at what is called fives — Knocking a ball up against a wall that served as an alley — He loved this game — his only physical game — that I Knew of — Lincoln said — This game makes my shoulders feel well.

LC: HW4005–6; HL: LN2408, 2:162–63

389. John McNamar to WHH

Menard Co Ill Dec 1st 1866

My Der Sir

I do not wonder, at the Reproachfull Surprise, you manifest at my Neglect of Duty with regard to my mother's Grave after devoting the whole of my Early manhood in acquiring means and expending all was available of the same for the Benifeit of my Fathers family it certainly is very Strange that I Should lose all traces of my Mothers grave But "tis true tis pitty and pitty tis, tis true" if I may use the quibble of old Poloneas on such an occasion

You are mistaken however in the time of My Mothers Death Death[1]   the absence I alluded to was in holding some of the petty county offices and knocking about Petersburg some Eight or Ten years, never Dreaming of losing the Grave of my relatives by the rapid filling up of the grave yard and the rank growth of vegatation   Perhaps it was merely a Lawyers tact in alludeing to the Subject in order to get a speedy answer to other questions if so you have succeeded admirably.

---

1. Marginal note: *While on the Subject of graves I will mention that I cut the initials of Miss Ann Rutlege on a bord at the head of her Grave 30 years ago.*

With regard to the crazy Spell of Mr Lincoln, I had never heard of it Before, on application to My Brother in Law James Short who was quite intimate with Mr Lincoln in his younger Days and I think in Later years he frequently expressed a friendship for him   He informs me that there was such a report though not very publick and at a later period than you Supposed and from a different source   Namely a lovers disappointment with regard to the Lady whom he afterwards Married, he was in the Legislature at the time and resided in Spingfield   I am unabl to give dates or particulars he thinks   John T Stuart told him the circumstance   I thererefore refer you to him he can also Most probably inform concerning the Dockument you refer to[2]   I communicated with Mr Lincoln in the winter of 36 & 37 while in the Legislature at vandalia concerning a tract of Land which could not be found on the assessors Books. he with a good deal of Trouble ascertained that the assessor had Located it another Township some 7 miles off and located old Salem upon it, the same man having Entered both tracts, Mr Lincoln paid the tax however with his own funds and forwarded me the recept of the secretary of state the Hon James Shields I think,

Mr Lincoln wrote a first rate Notice of the Revd Peter Cartwright,[3] before he left here   Mr. Cartwright being a candidate for some office also a political Squib against Mr. Carpenter of Springfield the article alluding to Mr Cartwright obtained a good deal of notoriety from the fact that Mr Hill[4] rather inocently I should think, signed the article with his own name and published it and consequently Received the Skinning that old Peter administered in a public speech at Salem shortly after, I think Lincoln must have enjoyed the joke rather Hugely, I think you can find the article in the Journal somwhere from 33 to 36   I have never heard of any thing from the pen of Mr Lincoln of a sentimental Charactar, while here

Mr Short also informs me that Mr Lincoln and Berry[5] formed a partnership as you suggested when you were here and that at the Death of Berry the Firm was not in a very Solvent Condition as Mr Lincoln's horse and Surveying outfit was sold to pay the Debts   Mr Short Buying them in for the use of Mr Lincon, I am dotting down the Material for the other communication you refer to and will Shortly forward the Same

I have the Honor to be with the Greatest respect

yours truly

John McNamar

Note if you have any oil prospectors, in Springfield send them down I can show them oil floating on a small spring Branch for a quarter of a mile

JMcN

LC: HW2828–29

---

2. Marginal note by McNamar: *take out the K.* This refers to the "k" in "dockument."
3. For the text of this letter, see Wilson, 63–66.
4. Samuel Hill.
5. William F. Berry (ca. 1811–35).

390. George E. Eisenmeyer to WHH

Mascoutah, Dec. 3. 66.

Dear Sir!

I seen a notice in the Mo. Democrat a few days ago in regard to your request of letters from Mr. Lincoln. The following is from Memory of a conservation Mr. John Pearson of Alton Ill. had with Mr Lincoln A.D. 1860. Tom Corwin Esqr. made a Speech at Edwardsville during the fall Champaign of that year, in which he said, that if the Gulf States wanted or needed Slavery to till their land they might have it. To this sentence Mr Lincoln objected on the following ground. I doubt the propriety of making such assertions, I have before me the Census returns of the State of South Carolina in which I find that one half of the white population of that State are noneslaveholders, since it is not likely that so large a body of people can Support themselfs by theft and Crime we must conclude that they work for a living; now if one half of the inhabitants of a state can maintain & support themselves by labor, the other half can likewise. To Mr. Lincolns Credit and for the benefit of mankind in general the above ought to go on record, it shows Mr Lincolns fine sense of justice, he was not willing that his friends should[1] Speeches that would not stand the test of truth & justice. The reason that I have in writing to you is this, that every body so far as I know, will use what is called political expediencies to gain an election, yet Mr. Lincoln who was in that Champaign largely interested was not willing that his friends should make use of any arguments derogatory to his general expressed opinions, that mankind evry where could & might be free.

You will please excuse me by calling on you, a stranger to you, for a favor, but as Mr. Lincoln figures largely in both articles, which were printed by the Belleville Advocate, I thought it would be of interest and advantage to all concerned that both articles should appear in the State Journal with a recommendation of $100.000. for the L. Monument instead of fifty, I did not wish to propose so much to start with and expected our Editor to do it, but he is an ___.

Yours very Respectfully,

George C. Eisenmeyer.

NB. Please send me a copy of the Journal or the articles as they are

LC: HW2830-31

391. Francis B. Carpenter to WHH

New York   Dec. 4th 1866.

My dear Sir,

Yours of last week, mentioning that you had sent me a pamphlet, — "a lecture on the mind:" reached me on Saturday. I have delayed answering it, hoping

---

1. Verb omitted.

the lecture would come to hand also but it is behind for some unexplained reasons —

I am also indebted for your kind note of previous date, accompanying the lecture on Mr Lincoln's love for "Ann Rutledge," &c, You asked me in that note to write you frankly, my opinion of that lecture.

I should have done this before, for I read the whole of the lecture the evening it was received. The marvellous analytical power shown in your previous lecture, (which I found floating in the newspapers, and used, without knowing that it was one of a series.)[1] led me to expect *much* in anything coming from your lips or pen, I do not know as I can express precisely the effect produced upon me, by reading the lecture on that evening. I was a good deal *disturbed* by it, I will frankly confess. — It seemed to me an invasion of a sacred *chamber* — a tearing away of the veil which conceals the "holy of holies." I could see the reason for this, — the necessity the author felt of showing the secret springs of action in Mr Lincoln's life — feeling as he did, that this unrevealed history was the key to his character. — But it seemed to me that the *fact* of this experience might have been given without treading so far upon ground which all feel intuitively to be *sacred.*

The lecture seemed to me incoherent, in parts. — to dwell too long upon topography, etc. I know your object was to show the effect on Lincoln's mind of all these surroundings. You are decidedly a *pre-Raphaelite* in biography — the danger, I should say, is that *"pre-Raphaelitism"* may become morbid, and abnormal in your case, as it frequently has done with Art-students.

But I cannot *criticise you.* I will say — and I say it truthfully, when I finished reading the report of the first lecture (afterward incorporated in my little book) — I was as much impressed with the power and originality shown in *it,* as by any thing I ever read of *Lincoln's*   I could but wonder how two such remarkable men could have come together, in co-partnership.

I *should* have written you and asked your consent to embody the lecture in my book. — But I did not fall in with it until after the most of the book was prepared — and as I have mentioned above I had no idea it was to be followed by other lectures. — It was in my mind that artists and sculptors would be likely to refer to my book for a personal description of Lincoln, and I desired to make this as *full* as possible. — And what you had given was so immeasurably beyond any thing I could say or write, that I made very little attempt as you have doubtless remarked at any thing of my own beyond a record of incidents.

The truth is I had no idea of writing a book at the time of painting my picture, — I did not even keep a record of incidents, but simply a pocket diary of my work from day to day. By referring to this however various incidents would return to me, — When I wrote my first sketch in the Independent[2] I had no thought of writing a record. — The interest of the public, in every thing relating to *Lincoln* was the occasion of the continuation of the series.

---

1. WHH had delivered four widely reported public lectures on AL.

2. Carpenter's first article, "Personal Impressions of Mr. Lincoln," appeared in *The Independent* on April 27, 1865.

I send you a copy of the book, with my "autograph" in the frontispiece[3]. I am much mortified that I should have neglected this so long. For six weeks or two months after its publication however I was absent in the country, and since my return have been very busy, engaged with other matters.

You ask if my "study" portrait of Lincoln is being engraved?" — I am happy to say that it is, and nearly completed. — The engraver Mr Halpin[4] (the best engraver in the style Known as *stipple and line,* in this country) has had the original portrait in his hands for the last eighteen months and has spared no pains to reproduce it faithfully   As a piece of engraving it is exquisite. The original portrait was painted *by itself,* before I commenced my large painting   It was pronounced by Mr Lincoln himself at the conclusion of one of the sittings, the best ever made of him. I think these were his words, "I feel that there is more of *me* in this portrait than in any representation, ever made"

It is sad, thoughtful, care-worn, the far-away expression in those eyes which was so often seen by those who were near to him, and *loved* him. I aimed to make it the *standard* portrait, — throwing enough of the ideal into the expression to satisfy those who should come after us. Whether I succeeded or not or whether the engraver has faithfully translated my meaning is for others to say — Meanwhile Marshalls portrait[5] — (made up from *photographs,*) has come out, though he returned from Europe — painted and engraved his picture some time after Mr Halpin commenced upon mine. — Marshall's is the more imposing perhaps the *work* being largely on the *back-ground,* while Halpin's is almost wholly upon the *head.* —

I shall next week send you a proof impression of this portrait. Do not make up your mind about it until after several days study, of it upon your wall   *Then* write me what you think of it. — Of course I am sensitive as to its reception by the public. — I have aimed to represent the man in his most solemn moments — thoughtful, dignified, intently considering the problems of the age. — It is *Lincoln* the *Emancipator.* —

I hope it will *strike* you pleasantly, but I much prefer that it shall grow upon you by *study.* — However it must take its chances.

Pardon the freedom with which I have written to you. It seems almost as if you were a friend of years. Should you come to New York be sure nothing would give me more pleasure than to welcome you to my little house at "96 West 45th St."

Faithfully & truly yours

F. B. Carpenter

LC: HW2841–44

---

3. *Six Months at the White House* (New York, 1866).
4. Frederick Halpin (1805–80).
5. William Edgar Marshall (1837–1906).

392. John D. DeFrees to WHH

Washington, Decr. 4 1866.

My dear Sir:

Your letter of the 29th ult reached me a few days ago.

I cannot remember ever having heard Mr. Lincoln converse on the subjects about which you require.

A Convention of Preachers held, I think, at Philadelphia, passed a resolution asking him to recommend to Congress an amendment to the Constitution directly recognising the existence of God. The first draft his message prepared after their resolution was sent him, did contain a paragraph calling the attention of Congress to the subject. When I assisted him in reading the proof, he struck it out, remarking that he had not made up his mind as to its propriety — I think he had several conversations with the Rev. P. D. Gurley, Pastor of a Presbyterian Church of this city, on the subject of religion, about the time of the death of his son Willie. Mr. Gurley would, no doubt, give you an account of it.

I read the lecture[1] you Sent me with great interest. It presented Mr. Lincoln in a new light to me.

I am anxious for your book. — Have you read "Carpenter's 6 months in the White House?" There are some good things in it

Yours Truly,

Jno. D. Defrees.

LC: HW2845

393. Robert B. Rutledge to WHH

Oskaloosa Decr 4th 1866

Dear Sir

Your letter of 1st inst is before me,

And I answer, 1st I think Mr. Lincoln read Law in 1834 & 1835, read surveying probably in 1833 & 1834. 2d I cannot say whether Mr Lincoln was radically a changed man, after the event, of which you speak or not, as I saw little of him after the time, 3rd when he first came to N. Salem and up to the time of which we write, Mr Lincoln was all life and animation, seemed to see the bright side of every picture, 4th Cannot say as to his habit of learning eloquent pieces by heart, he was ever ready with an appropriate response, to any vein of humor or eloquence when occasion required, have frequently heard him repeat pieces of prose & poetry, his practise was, when He wished to indelibly fix any thing he was reading or studying on his mind, to write it down, have known him to write whole pages of books he was reading, 5th cannot tell you how he read in the woods, as I never intruded on his retirement, Simply know he read in the woods by seeing him re-

---

1. WHH's Ann Rutledge lecture.

turn & having heard him say he had been reading in the brush, have seen him reading, walking the streets, occasionally become absorbed with his book, would stop & stand for a few moments, then walk on, or pass from one house in the town to an other, or from one crowd or squad of men to an other, apparently seeking amusement with his book under his arm, when the company or amusement became dry or irksome, he would open his book & commune with it for a time, then return it to its usual resting place, and entertain his audience, 6th as well as I remember he was not what is usually termed a quick minded man, altho he usually would arrive at his conclusions very readily, seemed invariably to reflect & deliberate, never acted from impulse, so far as to arrive at a wrong conclusion on a subject of any moment,

I desire you to learn all you can from Jas Mc Rutledge as to the breaking of the engagement — between Ann & McNamar,

Very truly yours,
R B Rutledge

LC: HW2846–47

394. Joshua F. Speed to WHH[1]

Louisville 6 Decr 1866

Dear Sir

Yours of the 29 Nov. asking my recollections of Mr Lincolns habits — his reading Conversation thought &c &c is at hand —

The field is a wide one, embracing much more than I could find time to write & many things so trivial that they would not be worth recording — As my mind runs back to my long & intimate acquaintance with that great & good man — I endeavour to forget that which is not worth remembering and to treasure only that which is of value —

Mr Lincoln was so unlike all the men I had ever known before or seen or known since that there is no one to whom I can Compare him —

In all his habits of eating, sleeping — reading Conversation & study — he was If I may so express it regularly irregular —

That is he had no stated time for eating, no fixed time for going to bed or getting up —

No course of reading ever was chalked out — He read law History, Browns

---

1. The original of this letter is not in the Herndon-Weik Collection, and its location is unknown. Fortunately, the original was in the collection when consulted by Albert J. Beveridge in the 1920s, and the text given here is transcribed from a white on black photostat in the Beveridge Papers that lacks the final page of the letter. The text for this missing page, which appears within brackets, is taken from an accompanying transcript. Two typographical errors in the transcript—"pice" and "Douke"—are assumed to have been made by the typist and have been corrected.

Philosophy or Paley[2] — Burns Byron Milton or Shakespeare — The news papers of the day — and retained them all about as well as an ordinary man would any one of them — who made only one at a time his study —

I once remarked to him that his mind was a wonder to me — That impressions were easily made upon his mind and never effaced — "No said he you are mistaken — I am slow to learn and slow to forget that which I have learned — My mind is like a piece of steel, very hard to scratch any thing on it and almost impossible after you get it there to rub it out" — I give this as his own illustration of the character of his mind — it is as good as any I have seen from any one else —

The beauty of his character was its entire [symplicity?] — he had no afficta-tion in any thing — True to nature true to himself, he was true to every body and every thing about and around him — When he was ignorant on any subject no matter how simple it might make him appear he was always willing to acknowl-edge it — His whole aim in life was to be true to himself & being true to himself he could be false to no one.

He had no vices — even as a young man — Intense thought with him was the rule and not as with most of us the exception.

He often said that he could think better immediately after Breakfast — and better walking, than sitting, lying or standing —

His world wide reputation for telling anecdotes — and telling them so well — was in my judgement necessary to his very existence — Most men who have been great students such as he was in their hours of idleness have taken to the bottle, to cards or dice — He had no fondness for any of these — Hence he sought relax-ation in anecdotes —

So far as I now remember of his study for composition it was to make short sentences & a compact style — Illustrative of this — he was a great admirer of the style of John C Calhoun — I remember reading to him one of Mr Calhouns speeches in reply to Mr Clay in the Senate — in which Mr. Clay had quoted pre-cedent — (I quote from memory.) Mr. Calhoun replied "that to legislate upon precedent is but to make the error of yesterday the law of today"[3]   Lincoln thought that was a great truth greatly uttered —

Unlike all other men there was entire harmony between his public and private life — He must believe that he was right and that he had truth and justice with him or he was a weak man — But no man could be stronger if he thought that he was right —

His familiar conversations were like his speeches & letters — In this — That while no set speech [of Mr. Lincoln (save his Gettysburg speech) will be consid-

---

2. Presumably, Thomas Brown (1778–1820), a Scottish philosopher, whose *Lectures on the Philosophy of the Human Mind* (1820) had a considerable vogue in England and America in the 1830s; William Paley (1743–1805), an English divine, whose writings on the natural basis for Christian beliefs were widely read in the nineteenth century.

3. See Calhoun's Senate speech of January 13, 1834, in Robert E. Meriwether, W. Edwin Hemphill, and Clyde N. Wilson, eds., *The Papers of John C. Calhoun,* (1959–), 12:214.

ered as entirely artistic complete — Yet when gems of American literature come to be selected from great Authors as many will be selected from Lincolns speeches as from any American Author.

So of his conversation & so of his private correspondence — all abound in jems.

I gave you in a former letter a history of my Mothers presentation of a Bible to him — and of his acknowledgment of it after he was President. I made an error in copying his language which I send on a separate piece of paper.

I hope you will get the letter to Dr Drake.

Your friend

J. F. Speed]

Written on a photograph of Mr Lincoln.

For Mrs Lucy G. Speed from whose pious hands I accepted the present of an Oxford bible Twenty years ago

A. Lincoln

Washington D.C.
October 3, 1861.

   LC: Albert J. Beveridge Papers, box 411

395. Abner Y. Ellis to WHH

Moro, Illinois   Decr 6th 1866

Yours of the 5th is recived and I Shall endeavour to answer as best I Can

When I first Knew Mr Lincoln he was Sad at times — but It did Not grow on him. The More I became acquainted with him the More humorous I found him to be. I do not think he was Very Witty befor he Came to Springfield to reside.[1] Witt & humor bothe appeard to grow on him up to 1861

Soberness of thought Commenced Growing on Mr Lincoln I think When he was Elected to Congress in 1848 though He came home with a great Many New Storys some Was Very dirty. he used to give a Mr. Haskell[2] the credit of telling them. Mr H. was also a member of Congress at the same time — from La. I think

4th qustin That Star gazing thinking Look, as if Looking at vacancy, he also Contracted them in Washington or Soon after he Came home

5th I do not think he liked Solitude; he would Not be long without Company

Mr Lincoln in 1832, 33, 34, Was Not Very Jovial Though at times Some one could remind him of a Story that he once herd & he would tell it

I think he cheerfulness commenced growing on him a few years after he came to reside in Springfield and it Must have remained with him up to the time of his Nomination for President. He said in My presents a few day after that he Should

---

1. Marginal note: *at least he never tryed to be.*
2. Probably William T. Haskell, a Whig representative from Tennessee from 1847 to 1849.

have to shape his *Course* or *Was*[3] differently in future This I remember Very distinctly

6th qustin those fancy Storys he bord of me was I think While I was in the PO Except One and that Was I think in 1837 I remember it Was the Mob Cap by Mrs Hentz[4] and at another time I loned him one of Bullyer novels Now a Play Calld the Lady of Lyons[5]

Those that I loned him When I was PM. Was Plays, he returned them and I think he had read some of them   He Said he has Seen the Illustrious Stranger[6] Played in Washington

I Never New him to Write Poetry I have herd him repeat some Short Sentances and they Was of a funny Charactor

I Never Knew him to Write for any News Paper: or Write anything that Was intended for Publication

I allways thought that Mr Lincoln improved rapidly in Mind & Manners after his return from Vandalia his first Session in the Legislature but then he Commenced his Great Cariear, as Story Teller and he had a great Many Who liked to listen to them and See and hear him, Laugh and those Storys at that time first Made his Company desireable by a great Many Young Members of the Legislator as Well as the rising Young Lawyers and he became a favorite with them and as he improvd in His Law Studdies he used to apply Some of them in Some of his arguments, and his good Sencee told him Never to *over act* in telling or applying them these are only My opinions as to how he first brought him self in to Notice (*Not intentionally* by *any means*

But I think He him Self finally Made that discovery in a few years refined Ladies Could Never See Much of his humor

Wm You ask Me to review Mr Lincoln life & habits from My first recollection of him up to the time of his leaving Springfield for Washington, in 1861

When I first Saw him I thought Verry little about him. But I soon found he Was a Young Man that was relyable, He Never to My Knowledge told a Wilful falshoood. I Never herd him swear an oath or take goods Name in Vain   Hee did Not go to Church, and I think gave but little thought of religeuous Matters   Mr Lincoln, liked to have any person ask his opinion about Matters and things, and he was allways Very Candid in giving them

Mr. offutt[7] his first employer at New Salem Saw this. he Mr O was a good Judge of Men and human Nature & so was Boling Green his allmost Second Farther Mr Green Used to Say that Lincoln Was a Man after his own heart and I think Myself he was Mr Lincoln Used to say that he owed more to Mr Green for his advancement than any other Man and I think Well he May Say   Mr. James Short was

3. Probably *ways*.
4. See §127, note 10.
5. See §131, note 5.
6. See §131, note 5.
7. Denton Offutt.

another admir[?][8] Though at time, he would be as little Witty & humorous With his Personal aqquaintances, I have Said More prehaps, than desired if I have Not I Will try again — When Ever You wish. You Must Excuse My hurry as it is late and I am going to St Louis tomorrow Morning & after My return I May think of Something that I wanted to Say

Your Freind

A. Y. Ellis

I hope you will have time to Muddle out My bad Composition & Spelling

Yours Truly

A. Y. Ellis

LC: HW2853–58

396. Samuel Haycraft to WHH

Elizabeth Town Ky   7' December 1866

Dear Sir

I am in recept of your two letters in relation to the letters written to me by A Lincoln just preceding and immediately after his election[1]

They were written Confidentally to me But really Contain nothing of importance and as you are his personal friend and writing his life I will under stand and Mason's injunction against thier exposure will enclose the originals?[2] to you & to be returned again to me after you have gathered all you Can from them —

Altho they Contain nothing of importance yet I regard them highly for the Respect I entertain for the writer. I admired him for his kindness of heart as shown in granting my request in relation to some men who had been betrayed into the rebellion

In his cruel Murder the South lost the best friend they had. Had Mr Lincoln lived the South would ere this have been restored and Conciliated, He had the Confidence of the North, and the South were beginning to learn and acknowledge his sense and justice and he could have done for them what President Johnson Could not effect. Mr Lincoln was born in 1809, as you will see by his letter to me. It was the same year I went into the clerks office boy then 14 years old, and his father with whom I was intimately acquainted. leave the County at an early age of his son Abraham I Cannot answer the enquiries of your second letter ex-

---

8. The last part of the word is no longer on the page. The apparent break in continuity suggests a missing page.

---

1. AL to Haycraft, May 28, June 4, Aug. 16, [Aug. 23], Nov. 13, 1860, in *CW* 4:56–57, 69–70, 97, 99, 139.

2. Haycraft's meaning is probably "I will understand and, invoking the Mason's injunction against their exposure, will enclose."

cept that Abraham was a tall spindle of a boy — and had his due proportion of harmless mischief — After he left Ky I heard and knew nothing of him until I heard he was elected to Congress which was Matter of great surprise —

His father was a house Carpenter a plain unpretending and scrupulisly an honest man, there is a house two miles from Town with the Original work on it originally done by him, the house he lived in, has since been used for various purposes — It was pulled down & rebuilt as a Slaughter [house?] [*illegible*] and this removal has brought it back within 50 yards of where it originally stood and is now owned by an Irishman named Thomas Callahan & used as a Stables in the various removals some logs were lost or rotten & replaced by others. But I can point out all the original logs

Abrahams oldest sister was born [*illegible*] he removed to a place 11 miles from this Town where Abraham was born & if my recollection is not at fault Thomas Lincoln the father with his family returned to his old house for a time and then left the State, lost his wife and about 1819 returned & married a widow Mrs Sarah Johnson, who I am informed is still living

Yours very respectfully

Saml Haycraft

Since writing — I remember that I cut the name off of one of the letters & sent it to some person not now recollected who wanted his Autograph

I also find a memo I kept in these words

"Daniel Johnson & Sarah Bush 13 March 1806 / B Ogden / [married?]

Thomas Lincoln & Sarah Johnson   2d Dec 1819[3]

Widow lives with her son in law John Hull Effingham Co. Illinois 8 miles from Charleston 18 from Mattoon Ill

She raised A Lincoln, he bought a piece of land & gave it to his father & Step Mother,

PS. Old Mr. Lincoln, (whose name was generally pronound Linkhorn) made a very short Courtship, He came to see her on 1. Dec 1819 & in a plain Straight forward Manner told her that they knew each other from child hood, that he had no wife & she no husband and that he came all the way to Marry her & if she was willing he wanted it done right off   She replied that she Could not right off as She owed Some little debts which she wanted to pay first. He replied give me a list of them, he got the list, paid them off that evening next Morning I issued the license and they were married in 60 yards of my house & left *right off*—

S. Haycraft

LC: HW2863–64

---

3. Marginal note: *Marriage.*

397. Caleb Carman to WHH

Petersburg Ills Decb 8th 1866

Dear Sir

I Recd your letter of the 5th Decb whishing to know if Lincoln quotied Shakespear in Sangamon Town it was in Sangamon Town & Newsalem the words I Can not Recollect often in Conversation he would Refer to that Great man Shakespear allso Lord Byron as being a great man and Burns & of Burns Poems & Lord Nellson as being a Great Admarall & Naval Commander & Adams & Henry Clay Jackson George Washington was the Greatest of all of them & was his Great favorite in Conversation he would Refer to those Great men & would say thay was Great men now i will tell you about Lincoln and his two Cats i Had forgoten this till now — when Living with me in Salem we had two kittens Lincons favorite pets he would Take them up in his lap & play with them and Hold their heds together & say that Jane had a beter countanance than Susan Had that being their names Jane & Susan he would not alow them hurt the winter he went to Vandalia to the Legislator he Left very strict orders for the cats to be well taken care of not Bing well to day i will close this liter i will Rite you again if Required — yours &c

Caleb Carman

LC: HW2866

398. T. Lyle Dickey to WHH

Ottawa Illinois Dec — 8th 1866

Dear Sir

In reply to your letter I have to say — that I was present at a political Meeting held in a hall (I think Major's Hall) at Bloomington — one the evening of someday in September or October of 1856 at which Abraham Lincoln (late President) made a political speech to a large audience — the precise date of the meeting & the name of the hall can be found I doubt not in the old files of the Bloomington Newspapers of that day[1]

In that speech Mr Lincoln distinctly proclaimed it as his opinion that our Government Could not last — part slave & part free —: that either Slavery must be abolished every where — or made equally lawful in all the states or the Union would be dismembered. I Can not be mistaken about this — for I was very sorry to hear him express an opinion which I regarded as erroneous & very dangerous — After the Meeting was over — Mr Lincoln & I returned to Pike House — where we occupied the Same room — Immediately on reaching the room I said to Mr Lincoln — "What in God's name could induce you to promulgate such an opinion" Mr Lincoln replied familiarly — "Upon my soul Dickey I think it is true" — I reasoned to show it was not a correct opinion — He argued strenuously that the opinion was a sound one — At length I said to Mr Lincoln — "Sup-

1. This is AL's famous "Lost Speech," delivered at Bloomington on May 29, 1856.

pose you are right in this opinion, & that our Government Can not last part free
& part slave — What good is to be accomplished by inculcating that opinion (or
truth if you please) in the minds of the People? — After a moment of silence &
apparent reflection Mr Lincoln Said — "I do not see as there is any good to be
accomplished the dissemination of the doctrine." To which replied — "I can see
much harm which it may do" "You convince the whole people of this — & you
necessarily make Abolitionists of all the People of the North & Slavery proponents
of all South — & you precipitate a struggle which may end in disunion — The
teaching of the opinion it seems to me tends to hasten the calamity" After some
minutes reflection Mr Lincoln rose & approached me extending his right hand to
take mine & Said —

"I dont see any necessity for teaching this doctrine — & I dont Know but it
might do harm" — At all events from respect for your judgment, Dickey, Ill promise
you I wont say so again during this Campaign" — We shook hands upon it & the
subject was dropped — I heard no more of this time of thought[2] from Mr Lincoln until the year of 1858 — when he proclaimed it in his famous Speech at
Springfield — at the Opening of that years Canvass —

If these facts are thought of any importance in history — you & the world are
welcome to them —

Yours truly
T. Lyle Dickey

P.S. Thank you for copy of that fancy lecture[3] — Romance is not your forte —
The few grains of history stirred into that lecture — in a plain narrative would be
interesting — but I dont like the garnishments

T. L. D —

LC: HW2867–68

399. Joseph Gillespie to WHH

Edwardsville Dec 8th 1866

Dear Friend

yours of yesterday is recd in which you ask if I remember whether Mr. Lincoln was given to abstract speculation or not My impression is that he was less
given to pure abstraction than most of thoughful and investigating minds I
should say that he was contemplative rather than speculative He wanted something solid to rest upon and hence his bias for mathematics and the physical
sciences I think he bestowed more attention to them than upon metaphysical
speculations I have heard him descant upon the problem whether a ball discharged from a gun in a horizontal position would be longer in reaching the ground

---

2. Presumably, "I heard no more of this type of thought."
3. WHH's lecture on AL's love affair with Ann Rutledge, delivered on November 16, 1866.

than one dropped at the instant of discharge from the muzzle the gun and he said it always appeared to him that they would both reach the ground at the same time even before he had read the philosophical explanation   He was fond of astronomy but I cant call to mind any reference of his to geology   He doubtless had read and thought of the subject but it did not engage his attention to the degree that astronomy and mechanical science did   He invited me one day at Washington city to call upon him in the evening when he said we would go to the observatory and take a look at the moon through the large telescope   It proved to be cloudy and I did not go   I have no recollection of ever hearing Mr Lincoln express him self in reference to the infinities   sometimes his mind ranged beyond the solid grounds, on which it delighted to dwell. He exercised himself in endeavoring to trace out the source and developement of language and he told me that on one occasion he prepared (or perhaps) delivered a lecture[1] in Springfield on that subject and that he was surprised to find his investigations in that direction so interesting and instructive to himself He used to say that the attempt to ascertain wherein wit consisted baffled him more than any other undertaking of the kind That the first impression would be that the thing was of easy solution but the varieties of wit were so great that what would explain one case would be wholly inapplicable to another   I am of opinion that there was a slight tinge of fatalism in Mr Lincolns composition which would or might have led him to believe somewhat in destiny   Mr Lincoln told me once that he could not avoid believing in predestination although he considered it a very unprofitable field of speculation because it was hard to reconcile that belief with responsibility for ones act   After he became President he gave unmistakable indications of being a believer in destiny   I feel quite sure that there was not a moment when he despaired of success in putting down the rebellion and he trusted more in Divine power than in human instrumentality   Mr Lincoln had as strong a faith that it was in the purposes of the Almighty to save this Country as ever Moses had that God would deliver the Israelites from bondage and he came to believe that he himself was an instrument foreordained to aid in the accomplishment of this purpose as well as to emancipate the slaves   I do not think that he was (what I would term) a blind believer in fate or destiny but that he considered the means foreordained as well as the end and therefore he was extremely diligent in the use of the means   Mr Lincoln had a remarkably inquiring mind and I have no doubt he roamed over the whole field of knowledge   There were departments however upon which he fixed his attention with special interest   Those which were of a practical character and having a solid and indisputable basis he made himself master of so far as time & opportunity would allow and this will account for his bringing out certain branches in conversation and being silent in regard to others about which he must have read as much as persons ordinarily do   He did not seem to think that to be of much value which could not be proven or rather demonstrated   His love

---

1. Speech and writing were prominent topics in the second version of Lincoln's public lecture, "Discoveries and Inventions." See *CW* 3:356–63.

of and capacity for analysis was wonderful   He analysed every proposition with startling clearness and only discussed those branches of his case upon which it hinged leaving the others clear out of view   He was a marvel of fairness in debate both in the courts & the political arena and he never desired to obtain an unfair advantage   From this I should infer that the sense of right & wrong was extremely acute in his nature   Mr Lincoln was undemonstrative and consequently his character had to be studied to be understood   One would not comprehend his salient traits at first aquaintance and so he was sometimes misunderstood   He was by some considered cold hearted or at least indifferent towards his friends   This was the result of his extreme fairness   He would rather disoblige a friend than do an act of injustice to a political opponent   His strong sense of justice made him hate slavery intensely but he was so undemonstrative that he seldom gave utterance to his feelings even on that question   He never talked feelingly on the subject to me but once although he knew that I agreed with him about the wrongs of that institution   To sum up his character I should say that he had greater natural mental cabilre than any man I ever Knew   He was extremely just and fair minded   He was gentle as a girl and yet as firm for the right as adamant   He was tender hearted without much shew of sensibility   His manners were Kind without ostentation   He was unquestionably ambitious for official distinction but he only desired place to enable him to do good and serve his country & his kind   It was somewhat strange how Mr Lincoln constituted as he was could be a radical But radical he was so far as *ends* were concerned while he was conservative as to the *means* to be employed to bring about the ends   I think he had it in his mind for a long time to war upon slavery untill its destruction was effected but he always indicated a preference for getting rid of slavery by purchase rather than the war power   He was an artful man and yet his art had all the appearance of simple mindedness   For instance he would not begin the work of emancipation when proposed by Freemont nor would he proclaim the freedom of the slave untill he had given the masters one hundred days notice to lay down their arms   This was done to place them obviously in the wrong and strengthen his justification for the act   Mr Lincoln Knew that it was not in the power of the masters to lay down their arms but they being in the wrong he had no scruples about making that wrong appear monstrous   He was grave and gay alternately   He was the most rigidly logical in debate and yet he illustrated every point by a humerous anecdote

Study with Mr Lincoln was a business not a pleasure   He was extremely diligent when he had any thing to do in preparing himself but when his task was done he betook himself to recreation   The information he gathered up was in reference to special questions and not with a view of laying in a general store of knowledge expecting that he would have occasion to use it and yet his natural tastes and aptitudes led him to explore most of those departments of study which bore mainly on the practical affairs of life   He had not a particle of envy in his nature   He always admitted that Douglass was a wonderfully great political leader and with a good cause to advocate he thought he would be invincible   Mr Lincoln appeared to be either extremely mirthful or extremely sad although if he had griefs he never spoke of them in general conversation   It was as a humorist that he towered above all other men it was ever my lot to meet   In early times Illinois was conspicuous for the number of its story tellers   The prevailing taste at that time took that direction   When Mr Lincoln was about I never knew a man who would pretend to vie with him in entertaining a crowd   He had an unfailing budget of genuinely witty and humerous anecdotes with which he illustrated every topic which could arise   The application was always perfect and his manner of telling a story was inimitable   although there was no *acting* in his manner for he was not in the least degree histrionick   He never invented any of his stories but simply retailed them but how he could gather up such a boundless supply & have them ever ready at command was the wonder of all his accquaintences   It might seem that this faculty would detract from his dignity but it did not   No man ever commanded greater respect from or inspired more confidence in an audience than Mr. Lincoln did   He used his stories as much for producing conviction in the minds of his hearers as for creating merriment   If Mr Lincoln studied any one thing more than another and for effect it was to make himself understood by all classes   He had great natural clearness and simplicity of statement and this faculty he cultivated with marked assiduity   He despised everything like ornament or display & confined himself to a dry bold statement of his point and then worked away with sledge hammer logic at making out his case   I believe Mr Lincoln succeeded in his purpose for I think the great body of our People understood and appreciated him better than any man this Country has ever produced

In religious matters I think Mr Lincoln cared but little for tenets or sects but had strong & pervading ideas of the infinite power wisdom & goodness of Deity and of mans obligations to his Maker and to his fellow beings   He was economical without being parsimonious   He never attempted a speculation in his life but always displayed a commendable zeal & alacrity to obtain business   He was brave without being rash and never refrained from giving utterance to his views because they were unpopular or likely to bring him into danger at the same time he abstained from needlessly giving offence   Mr Lincoln never idolized particular men but had wonderful faith in in the honesty & good sense of the masses   In politics he was an old line whig a devout beleiver in a National currency, the developement of American industry, and internal improvements by the general government   He always deprecated the removal of men from office for opinion sake although Mr Lincoln was eminently national in his feelings he looked with disfavor upon the American party and contended that a love of liberty & free government was not confined to this country; he ascribed our beneficent institutions rather to circumstances by which we were surrounded and the political ideas which had began to take root just before the revolution than to any superior intelligence or liberality on our part   He contended that we were more indebted to our government than it was to us and that we were not entitled to greater credit for our liberality of sentiment on political questions than others equally liberal who were born and raised under less favorable auspices   Mr Lincoln never I think studied history except in connection with politics with the exception of the history of the Netherlands and of the revolutions of 1640 & 1688 in England and of our revolutionary struggle he regarded it as of triffling value as "teaching by example"   Indeed he thought that history as generally written was altogether to unreliable   In this connexion he alluded to the fact that Gen J. D. Henry the most prominent figure in the black Hawk war of 1832 was completely ignored by the historians   He also referred to the almost universal belief that a spirited passage at arms took place in Congress between Tristram Burgess & John Randolph when as Mr Lincoln said he never believed they had been in Congress together[2]

The above is about all I can scrape up relating to Mr Lincoln   If it is of any use to you you are welcome to it

your friend

J Gillespie

LC: HW2869–73

400. *Grant Goodrich to WHH*

Chicago Decr. 9/66

Dr Sir

Your favor of the 5th is received. In reply I have to say, Mr Lincoln was my associate first in the trial of the cases vs Grace [Lawrence?] in 1845, for fraud and misrepresentations, in the sale of land. The cases were severely contested, Mrss Butterfield & Collins & Ewd. Baker Esqr. being counsel for deft. Mr Lincoln in closing the case made the best Jury argument I ever heard him make. Judge Pope, said it was one of the best he ever heard.[1]

The Case of Parker vs Hoyt was for infringement of a patent water wheel.[2] My recollection is, it was commenced in 1846 or 7 — Mr Lincoln was employed for the defense   It was for trial in June 1848. There was some technical error in the notices of matters in dispute & on motion of the pliff. most of the defendants evidence was excluded and defeat seemed inevitable. At that time a term of the U.S. District Court was held at Chicago on the 1st Monday of July. The only way of saving the case was to get it over to the term at Chicago, by which time would be secured to correct the error in the notices. Motions were made on both sides, which involved numerous questions, new to the Counsel & Court, as very few patent cases had then been tried in that Court, The time occupied in this discussion, was so extended, that the case had to be transferred to Chicago for trial. The

---

2. Congressman Tristam Burges of Rhode Island did assail John Randolph in the House of Representatives in 1831, but Randolph was not serving in the House at the time.

---

1. This case was tried in federal court in 1845. Nathaniel Pope was sole U.S. district judge in Illinois, from the beginning of statehood until his death in 1850.

2. *Parker v. Hoyt* was tried in U.S. district court in Chicago between July 9 and July 24, 1850 (Lincoln Legals).

testimony was procured, but under the rulings of the Court, was excluded for the main purpose for which it was offered, but was admitted for an other purpose. We placed great reliance on an elder patent to establish the want of novelty in the invention of the plaintiff

The case was prosecuted with great zeal & ability, & the trial lasted for several days. Mr Lincoln took a great interest in the case. He had tended a saw-mill for some time, & was able in his arguments to explain the action of the water upon the wheel, in a manner so clear & inteligable, that the jury was enabled to comprehend the points and the line of defense. It was evident he had carried the jury with him, in a most Masterly argument, the force of which could not be broken by the reply of the opposing Counsel. But the Court was evidently infused with the Conviction that the plaintiff should recover, and charged on every material point for the plaintiff; & in effect told the jury that the prior patent on which we so much relied was no defense.

After the jury had retired Mr Lincoln became very anxious & uneasy. The jury was in another building, the windows of which opened on the Street. They had been out for some two hours — In passing along the Street, one of the jury, on whom we had very much relied, he being a very inteligent man & firm in his convictions, held up to him one finger — Mr Lincoln became very much excited, fearing it indicated that eleven of the jury were against him.

He was assured, that if this man was for him, he would never yield his opinion — He replied, if he was like a juryman he had in Tazwell County, the defendant was safe — That he was there employed to prosecute a suit for a divorce — His client was a very pretty refined & interesting woman in Court. The defendant was a rather gross, morose, querulous, fault finding, cross, & un comfortable person, entirely unfitted for the husband of such a woman. And though he was able to prove the use of very offensive & vulgar epithets applied by him to his wife, & all sorts of anoyances, but no such acts of personal violence assigned by the statute to justify a divorce. He did the best he could & appealed to the jury to have compassion on the woman & not bind her to a man & such a life as awaited her, as the wife of such a man. The jury took about this same view of it in their deliberations. They desired to find for her, but could find no evidence which would really justify a verdict for her; and drew up a verdict for the defendant and all signed but one, who when asked to do so, said, "gentlemen, I am going to lie down to sleep, & when you get ready to give a verdict for that woman, wake me up, for before I will give a verdict — against her, I will lie here until I rot, & the pis-mires carry me out of the Keyhole." Now said Mr. Lincoln, if that jury man will stick like that man, we are safe.

In a short time the jury came in with a verdict for the defendant. He always regarded this as one of the most gratifying triumphs of his professional life — He was afterward employed in one or two other patent suits, but they never came to a final trial. He had a great deal of Mechanical genius, could understand readily the principles & mechanical action of machinery, & had the power, in his clear, simple illustrations & Style to make the jury comprehend them.

The most important Case he ever had here, & the one in which his powers were exhibited to the most advantage, was the Rock Island Bridge Case.[3] Hon. N. B. Judd was attorney in that case

And now friend Herndon, I have complied with your request, imperfectly it is true, but as well as I could.

You will admit, that while I say, I have none but the tendrest feelings for you, you have never given me occasion to entertain any others. I therefore, as your friend, & the friend of Mr Lincoln, propose to say a few things, prompted by that friendship — but which I know the vanity of all men rebels against —

1st In my opinion, you are the last man who ought to attempt to write a life of Abraham Lincoln — Your long & intimate association with him, unfits you for the task. No one holding the intimate relations to another, which you did to him, ever has succeeded. There may be exceptions, but I cannot now remember one. They are mere eulogists — or having known him, in other conditions than on those fields, & in those departments where his fame was won, he regards, & exhibits him in those humble, & different, aspects, & characteristics, in which the public have no taste, & which bring him down from the high sphere of his tryumphs, to the hum drum everyday affairs of life, which are stale & incipid to the public. To enter into the private every day life of ordinary or extraordinary men, can only be made indurable to readers, or safe to the fame of the subject, without the most discriminating taste & art; & no one is safe to undertake it without much practice, & knowledge of the public taste. Again, contact with great men, always dispells something of the awe with which they are contemplated at a distance. In intimate association, we fix upon some characteristic or peculiarity, & fail to catch other liniaments, We can only regard them as the kind friend, amusing companion, & generous mind — In the distance, we see the bold outline of the mountain; its sumits wraped in sunshine, or swathed in cloud. When we approach it, we catch a view of, of the deep it may be dark gorges — the ragged cliffs, the lean rocks — & distorted outlines — So in the characters of our dearest friends. See how Boswell, with all his literary abilities failed in his life of Johnson — No blow so severe was ever struck at Johnson — Think of these things.

If I am to judge of what your production will be by the publication of a portion of your Salem lecture,[4] I am more solicitous still. I fear you did not realize what an injury & injustice you did to the memory of your dear friend, & mortification you caused his friends, but especially his widow & children. Ask yourself, if he was living, whether he would not have revolted at the uncovering to the public gaze that drama of his life? And shall his friends, exhibit what we know he would have preserved in sacred privacy. If the facts are truly stated, I should as soon thought of exposing his dead body, un coffined, to the vulgar gaze of the public eye — It should never have been dug up from the grave, where time had buried it —

Besides, your style is not well adapted to such an undertaking. The want of

---

3. *Hurd v. Rock Island Bridge Co.* was tried in U.S. district court in Chicago in September 1857.
4. WHH's lecture on Ann Rutledge.

practice is palpable — Your style is purely legal. Such an one as is acquired by drawing legal documents & pleadings, and is [*illegible*] different from one formed by familiarity with the best writers — It is rugged, abounding in adjectives & explications — full of climaxes — & hard, dry words — It reads as if it had been jerked out, word by word — it gives one the sense you have in riding in a lumber wagon over a frozen road — or the noise made in machinery when a cog has been broken.

Now my friend I have spoken plainly , but sincerely — I may do you injustice, but it is not intentional I may lose your friendship by it, but I have only done what I would wish one to do to me under the same circumstances. And I have observed in myself & others, that the very points in which Strength is supposed, are the very points of weakness

I am Yours &c
Grant Goodrich

LC: HW2876–79

401. Harriet A. Chapman to WHH

Charleston Ills Dec the 10th 66

Sir.

Please pardon my long delay in answering your letters received Some time Since. The Cares of my family prevented my doing So Sooner. The Scraps of paper taken from the Lincoln bible that my Husband[1] had in his posession when you was here, he gave to Father Hanks and he let Gen Black[2] have them. If you are really desirious of obtaining Said papers I will get Father to write to Mr Black for them.

You wish to know if Mr Lincoln read news papers. *He did* yes and often vary late at night. he was not a vary *early riser.* his usual way of reading was lying down in warm weather he Seemed to prefer the floor he would turn a Chair down on the floor and put a pillow on it and lie thare for hours and read. He was remarkably fond of Children one of his greatest pleasures when at home was that of nursing and playing with his little boy. Mr Lincoln was what I Call a hearty eater and enjoyed a good meal of victuals as much as enny one I ever knew. I have often heard him say that he could eat corn cakes as fast as two women could make them. although his table at home was usually set vary Sparingly. Mrs. Lincoln was vary *economical*   So much So that *by Some She* might have been pronounced Stingy   Mr Lincoln Seldom ever wore his Coat when in the house at home. and often went to the table in his Shirt Sleeves. which practice anoyed his wife vary much. who by the way loved to put on *Style*

I have often herd Grand Pa Lincoln tell what a jovial fun loving boy Abram was. when Small. I remember his telling of one time. In the early Settlement of

---

1. Augustus H. Chapman.

2. "Father Hanks" is Dennis F. Hanks, the writer's father. "Gen Black" may refer to John C. Black, a Lincoln associate who served in the Union army and was practicing law in Champaign.

Indiana that one day they had nothing for dinner but rosted potatoes. after Grand Pa L. got through returning thanks, which duty he never neglected. If he only had dry bread or potatoes he would ask the Same blessing when he Sat down to eat So this time uncle Abram put on a long face. and looked up at his father and papa I call these meaning the potatoes vary poor blessings.

I never knew him to make a garden, yet no one loved flowers better than he did. I have not been able to get down to See Grand Ma Lincoln yet, the roads have been So dreadful bad but I think I can get down in a few days. after which I will write you again

Yours with respect —
H A Chapman

LC: HW2883–84

402. Abner Y. Ellis to WHH[1]

Moro, Ill 11th Decr 1866

Yours o[f] Yestarday is recvd an[d] Conten[ts] Noticed

It is allmost [**/***] remember the [**/***] Lincoln — Bu[?] they [were?] Plays Mostly

Viz

Lady of Lyons by Bullyer

Mob Caps by Mrs C. L. Henty

Vilage Stranger a Play

Illustrious Stranger also a play

The Wept of the Wish Ton Wish[2]

Not Know Whether he read them Though   I Think he May has done

as to his own Books [I never?] Knew of his having any Excep [*?] Law Books

And as to What he [*?] read I Cant say for Certin [*?] I think He Said he had r[ead] George Balcom[3] (a Novel)   I [*/**] and He & I was Taking about s[ome] passages in it.

And I am almost ce[rtin] He read Tom Pains. Common Sen[se] and Volneys Ruins[4]

I Never Knew of h[is] Borrowing any Books & I do not th[ink] He Card Much for those he had of Mine. He Had also read Some Poetry [per]haps conciderable of Burns Poem[s] [I]s their Such a Book as Gilblass,[5] I think he Used to quote Some from it   I Never Saw it

---

1. This letter is badly mutilated, though a preponderance of the text survives. Wherever possible, the editors have inserted words and parts of words that would appear to have been present originally and have indicated the likely number of words that cannot be confidently interpolated.

2. See §127, note 10 (Mob Cap); §131, note 5 (Lady of Lyon, Illustrious Stranger and Wept of Wish Ton Wish).

3. See §127, note 6.

4. See §127, notes 7–8.

5. Alain René Le Sage, The History and Adventures of Gil Blas of Santillane, first published in English in 1716.

I think he onc quoted Something like This in one of his Speaches H[e] Said Some Man remind[ed] him [of] it

He The Man *[***/****]*

That Made *[***/****]*

Could Not tell *[*/**]*/[wheth]er he was going out or Com[ing] Back

after he had quoted it he Said Gilblass giving him the Credit as I thought

I am of the opinion that He used to take a Literary Paper Published in Philadelphia Called the Saturday Courer[6] & He read Mrs Caroline Lee Hentz[7] [s]torys this I am Not certn [tho]ugh I think He took 2 years [w]hile I was PM.[8] You yourself May remember whethr he did [o]r Not

I Must close as I have answrd all you asked for but if any thing More you have only to Command Me

You Frend

A. Y. Ellis

LC: HW2888

403. John H. Littlefield to WHH

Washington Dec. 11th 1866

Respected Friend:

I have been trying very hard to obtain a file of papers for you but I fear I shall have to give it up.* [*note at bottom of page:* I had hoped to get files owened by private individuals,] The Washington Star contains the fullest account of the entry of Mr Lincoln in the City of Washington in 1861   The Gentleman that reported for it is a friend of mine & is entirely reliable & he says that he had an interview with Mr. Lincoln when he first arrived here in 61   It will be necessary to employ a person to copy such parts of the Star and other papers as may Seem required for your work   I would copy them myself but I can not possibly find time besides Mrs L. is very sick with pneumonia. If it is your wish I will employ a person to copy such parts of the Star & other papers as you may require at once. I will State an anecdote that came under my observation   In 1862, there was considerable Said about the Yazoo River Expedition   Mr Lincoln one evening at the White House was Suffering with pain caused by the extraction of a "raging tooth"   "Pet Halsted"[1] several others and myself called on Mr Lincoln and found him out of the room which he generally occupied. We sat down in the Private Sec's

---

6. Possibly the *Saturday Chronicle and Mirror of the Times*, published in Philadelphia between 1836 and 1842.

7. See §127.

8. Ellis was postmaster of Springfield during the Whig administrations of Taylor and Fillmore (1849–53).

---

1. Oliver S. Halsted was one of the regular male visitors to MTL's Blue Room Salon at the White House and a lobbyist for munitions manufacturers.

room and remained there Some minutes when Mr Lincoln hearing our voices came in & Sat down (just as he used to in the office in Springfield) and notwithstanding the pain that afflicted him chatted humorously with here & there a flash of real logic that showed that he comprehended the Situation. The Yazoo River Expedition received his attention — he Said by the way of preamble that he found it necessary to Yield here a little & there a little in order to keep peace in the family & that if he interfered in a plan that was not essential, vital, the West Pointers, ie the regular officers who had the execution of all plans would in Some way or other obstruct or defeat the execution of his Scheme therefore in as much as they had to be depended upon at *last* he found it best to trust them at *first* & rely on events & the power of persuasion to rectify errors   In regard to the Yazoo River expedition he Said (pointing to the map*) [*note at the bottom of the page:* (This was a large map which hung in his room which he often referred to)] how can a force go dow a river that is only a few rods wide when it can not get down a river that is a mile wide? & if it could it would only wind about & come out into the the Same river that it is contended by the millitary officers you can not pursue — the Mississippi & for this reson you wish to leave the Mississippi above Vicksburg   This expedition proposes to follow the Yazo & come out in the Mississippi what have you accomplished? You have have gained nothing   I cant better make this clear that by relating an incident that came under my own observation. There was a man in Ill a good many years since that was troubled with an old sow & her pigs — again & again the old man & his Sons drove her out & repeatedly found her in the lot   One day he & his boys Searched about & found that She got in to the lot through a certain hollow log that had been placed in the fence; they took out this log and built up the fence by placing the log a little differently than before & the next day what was the astonishment of the "Old Lady" to find that she & her *litter* came out of the log *outside* of the field instead of *inside* — It is just so with the Yazoo River expedition Said Mr L. "it comes out of the Same Side of the log"[2]

This little story it seems to me illustrates the fact illustrates the fact that Mr L — comprehended millitary problems far better than was generally supposed   I will endeavor from time to time to arrange little incidents that I was an eye witness of or collect such anecdotes that have not yet been published as may seem to be of Some Service to you. If you should desire to have a faithful likeness engraved of Mr Lincoln I may be of some service   I am now painting Gen. Grant in oil & expect to publish his picture in *pure line engraving* the head of which will be 6 inches long   I expect also to paint a life Size head of Mr. Lincoln which I will have engraved if I can bring it about   It is quite doubtful if there is a living artist that has such varied & servicable remembrances of the *good man* as your humble servant. When Your book is ready for publication I may put you on track of good houses in New York or elsewhere   Please write me at your earliest convenience & if you desire it I will set a man to copying the points you require at once   I

2. The Yazoo Expedition was an abortive effort in December 1862 to ascend the Yazoo River and approach Vicksburg from the north.

should esteem it a great favor if you would favor me with a copy of your Lecture[3] on the *Courtship* &c of Mr Lincoln

Affectionately Yours

J H Littlefield

LC: HW2889–90

404. Robert T. Lincoln to WHH

Chicago Dec 13 /66

My dear Sir:

Your letter of Dec 10 is received and it contains just what I understood to be the result of our conversation at Springfield.

As I said then, I have never had any doubt of your good intentions but inasmuch as the construction put upon your language by everyone who has mentioned the subject to me was so entirely different from your own, I felt justified in asking you to change your expression. Beyond this, I do not wish, nor have I any right to go. Your opinion may not agree with mine but that is not my affair. All I ask is, that nothing may be published by you, which after *careful consideration* will seem apt to cause pain to my father's family, which I am sure you do not wish to do.

Very sincerely your friend

Robert T. Lincoln

LC: HW2894

405. John H. Wickizer to WHH

Chicago Ills 13 Dec 1866

My Dear Friend

I send copy of last note I rd from Mr Lincoln Its date was the last time I ever looked upon that benign countenance — the last grasp of his friendly hand —

You ask me to note his religious sentiments. I have no well defined indication of his religious sentiments I think he was *naturally* religious, but very liberal in his views, I think he believed in "Jesus Christ, and him crucified." — I will see you at Springfield during the session of Legislature.[1]

Yours Truly

J H Wickizer

LC: HW2898

---

3. WHH's lecture on Ann Rutledge.

---

1. Marginal note in WHH's hand that appears unrelated to this letter: *Mr. Short — Finney — Jacksons Judici* [torn] *— Tariff.*

406. *Grace Bedell to WHH*

Albion, Orleans Co. N.Y. Dec 14th. 1866

Hon. L. R. Herndon:

Hearing that you were preparing for press the Life of the noblest of men, and that you wished all unpublished letters of his composing sent to you, I concluded that I would ask if a letter which he once wrote me would prove acceptable. I do not know that it would answer your purpose or I would send a copy of it now. however, I will tell you its subject and you shall judge. Before Mr Lincoln's election in 1860, I, then a child of eleven years, was presented with his lithograph. Admiring him with my whole heart I thought, still, that his appearance would be much improved should he cultivate his whiskers. Childish thoughts must have utterance, so I proposed the idea to him, expressing, as well as I was able, the esteem in which he was held among honest men. A few days after I received an answer to my communication. a kind and friendly letter which is still in my possession. It appears that I was not forgotten, for, after his election to the presidency, while on his journey to Washington, the train stopped at Westfield, Chautauque Co, at which place I then resided. Mr Lincoln said "I have a correspondent in this place, a little girl, her name is Grace Bedell, and I would like to see her." I was conveyed to him, he stepped from the cars extending his hand and saying, "You see I have let these whiskers grow for you, Grace." kissed me shook me cordially by the hand and, was gone. Afterward I was frequently assured of his remembrance. If this letter would be of any service in completing your book, I should be pleased to send you a copy. Asking pardon for consuming so much of your valuable time. I remain

Grace. G. Bedell.

Springfield, Oct 19th, 1860.

Miss Grace Bedell,

My Dear Little Miss:

Your very agreeable letter of the 15th is received — I regret the necessity of saying that I have no daughter — I have three sons — one seventeen, one nine, and one seven. They, with their mother, constitute my whole family. As to the whiskers, as I have never worn any, do you not think that people would call it a piece of silly affectation, if I were to begin wearing them now?

I am, your fine friend
and sincere well-wisher
A. Lincoln.

LC: HW2899–2900

407. Robert T. Lincoln to WHH

Chicago Dec 14 /66

My dear Sir:

An old friend Dr. Smith,[1] now Consul at Dundee in Scotland, has written me asking me to give to him a certain book of Western History once owned by my father, — I wish very much to do so if I can find the book — I remember a year ago, a young man in your office showed me the book taking it from a case on the South side of the room — I think the name is "Western Annals"[2] — If still there will you be kind enough to have it well wrapped & sent by mail to my Mother mark "Free" — it needs no postage.

Very sincerely Yours
Robert T. Lincoln

LC: HW2901–2

408. David Turnham to WHH

Dale Ind Dec 17th 1866

Dear Sir

Yours of the 1st inst is at hand, Contents noted. I am as ever willing to give any assistance in my power. 1st Question, I would say that, While Abe was in Indiana he was or seemed to be always cheerful and happy. I never discovered any Sadness or Melancholy in his appearance. 2nd Question, So far as his being accustomed to deep thoughtfulness and lost in reflection. He never was but on the Contrary was always quickwitted and ready for an answer. 3rd Questions. He was apt to be talking about what he had read and would Sometimes quote nice pieces of Prose & Poetry to his associates 4th. In my first acquaintance with him in the year 1819 I discovered in him that wit and humor. He was then about ten years old. This lively and jesting disposition seemed to be natural with him and continually growing on him   5th   Abe was by no means lazy Saucy or insolent, neither was he forward but rather timid and not Sensitive. 6th   When in Company with Men & Women he was rather backward but with the Boys, he was always cheerful and talkative. He did not Seem to seek the Company of the girls and [when abou]t them was rather backward. His Conduct toward all Persons was kind, and modest. 7th   He was not a noisy nor fighting boy but always peaceable, and quiet. I Scarcely ever knew him out of humor. In regard to dates. This was his Conduct all the time he was in this state, I can think of nothing more of interest to write.

Your friend as ever
David Turnham
by Jno. J. Turnham

LC: HW2903–4

---

1. Rev. James Smith, former pastor of the Second Presbyterian Church in Springfield, which the Lincolns attended.

2. Probably James Handasyd Perkins, *Annals of the West: Embracing a Concise Account of Principal Events, Which Have Occurred in the Western States and Territories, from the Discovery of the Mississippi Valley to the Year Eighteen Hundred and Forty Five* (1847). After Perkins's death in 1849, several editions were published in St. Louis under the direction of John Mason Peck.

409. *John T. Stuart (WHH interview)*

Decr 20th 1866[1]

Jno T. Stuart

Says — Mr Lincoln Commenced Carrying around with him on the Circuit — to the various Courts, books such as Shakespear — Euclid as Early as 1844 and continued to do so down as late as 1853.: he loved Burns — Carried Poe around on the Circuit — read and loved the Raven — repeated it over & over — loved Hallecks Poem called[2] —

In the Evening Lincoln would strip off his coat and lay down on the bed — read — reflect and digest — After Supper he would Strip — go to bed — get a Candle — draw up a chair or table and read till late of night: he read hard works — was philosophical — logical — mathematical — never read generally — didn't know anything about history — had no faith in it nor biography — didnt know geography generally — knew it in spots. He had nothing Rhetorical in his nature — no belles letters — he read specially — dug out things — He never read poetry as a thing of pleasure, Except Shakespear — he read Poe because it was gloomy — So of Burns at *"Bottom"*. Lincoln was a schollar from 1835 — rather a hard student to 1845 — He was an Educated Man in 1860 — more than is generally known. It was in 1851 when he & I were coming down the hill the other side of Delavan that I said to him — "Lincoln the time is soon coming when we shall all have to be all abolitionists or all democrats" "My mind is fixed on that question — when it Comes, replied Lincoln" and I said — "So is mine."

We — L & my self always stopt at Hobbitts[3] on the Kickapoo: here we Enjoyed ourselves much — read — went fishing &c. The family were always glad to see us. Hobbitt was an ancient abolitionist —

Mr Lincolns Religion as I understand was of a low order — he was an infidel Especially when young — Say from 1834 to 1840 I know nothing of his book — or pamphlet — know nothing of his crazy spell — do know of the one in Springfield in 1841– or 2

LC: HW2246–47

410. *George M. Harrison to WHH*

Richland — Dec'r 20th 1866

Dear sir,

you will please excuse my long delay, when you are aware of the fact, that four months past, my family has been, and is yet much afflicted of that slow fever — the typhoid. Eleven of us, out of a family of Twelve, have been, and some are now sick: but all — without any mortality — are likely to fully recover. I desire sir that you make use of any facts that my letters contain, if any suit your purpose, in your

---

1. Dated in the docketing.

2. Possibly Fitz-Greene Halleck's "Burns." See AL to James G. Wilson, *CW* 4:48.

3. Probably Samuel Hoblit (1805–66), who settled on Kickapoo Creek near present Atlanta, Logan County, Illinois. In 1839 he built a two-story house on the State Road between Springfield and Bloomington, where he entertained travelers, including the itinerant circuit court lawyers.

own language; but not in the incoherent manner that you get them from me. Being so short a time in the army, about two months, — I am not able to give many interesting particulars.

I became a member of the Independant Spy Company when it was reorganized at fort Wilbourn, a few miles below Ottawa. Previous to this time, this company was commanded by Elijah Iles of Springfield, Ills after this time, it was commanded by Jacob M. Early of Springfield, Ills. Many of the officers & privates of our company were from Sangamon, i.e. A. Lincoln, J. M. Early, John T. Stewart, J. F. Reed, L. D. Matheny, Hugh Mc Gary, & others.

When the army lay at Fort Wilbourn, as then called, near La Salle, its supplies came by steam boats; also by boats when at Dixon on Rock river, at the two points much of the time was passed by the whole army, or by one or more of the four brigades, especially by Gen. Atkinson[1] and the Regulars, with whom we generally camped, in company with 95 Potawatomis a few Winnebagos & Menominees which indians usually accompanied our company, both in camp and on the move. Our supplies were carried by *horse teams usually, by pack horses occasionally,* when not at or very near navigable streams; and when our company was sent on express our supplies and some of the baggag was carried by a beautiful mare mule called Jim Crow —

Being midsummer, our Idle days were mostly spent under the forest trees in the sitting or horizontal posture. We had some plays & some songs; but not being apt to participate I shall have to refer to Hugh Mc. Gary and others for a statement of these. About the tenth of may, I think, Joined Doct. Early's company; and the whole company was disbanded at White Water in Wisconsin about the tenth or middle of July, and nearly all of the company then returned home. Mr. Lincoln & myself came afoot from Havanna on the Ills river to Petersburg on the Sangamon, we crossed the Sangamon river at Miller's Ferry; several miles northwest from Petersburg.

> Yours truly
> Geo. M. Harrison

LC: HW2905

411. Francis B. Carpenter to WHH

New York   Dec 24th 1866

My dear Sir,

Many thanks for your letters of the 11th. 13. 17. and 18th. — The longest letter that of the 11th interested me profoundly. I think you are *right*. The *truth* is what the world wants. Lincoln's love for Anne Rutledge, may yet loosen up the history like Dante's for Beatrice, or Petrarch for Laura, — We are too near to him. (& were the great public) to profoundly appreciate these revelations.

---

1. Gen. Henry Atkinson, commander of Regular army troops in the Black Hawk War.

At first, as I proudly wrote you, with Lincoln's family *before me,* your lecture while it intensely interested me, and explained much before mysterious about Mr Lincoln, seemed almost a rash drawing aside of the curtain which should enshroud some part of every man's life. It seemed to me that Mr Lincoln himself would have deprecated it — and yet after further reflection, I am satisfied the truth should be Known, — Suppose we should shut off John Milton's domestic experience how little comparatively would be Known of him? How imperfect the material upon which to form a correct judgement of the man? — Go ahead my dear sir, as Thomson says in "The Seasons"

xxxx"Be still as now discreet / the time may come" &c.[1] — You mention in the letter of the 18th the reception of my little book,[2] — Further on you say, "As to the orthodox christian deportment of it Good Heavn's!" —

Just here I feel bound to say one word. — What you say of Lincoln's, religious experience & beleif up to the time of his election I believe. — But during the last four years of his life he passed through what few men could have experienced without growth and change, You know whether the incident I extracted from Holland, given him by Bateman,[3] of Springfield is reliable or not. —

Dr. Vinton's account,[4] of what followed the death of Willie, — his interview with the President, is about word for word as he repeated it to me. — Do you know *Noah Brooks* who was to have been Nicolays[5] successor as private Sec.? — The article he published in Harper's Monthly, (June 1865) I think the most valuable of the "personal reminescences" I have seen. He was much with Mr Lincoln, and what Lincoln said to him about the "process of chrystalization." which he passed through (spiritually.) after his election, seems rational and truthful. — John Jay, of this city told me not three weeks ago, that going down to Norfolk, on the steamboat with Mr Lincoln, on one occasion Lincoln disappeared. Mr Jay said that subsequently he passed a corner in an out of the way place, and there he came upon Mr Lincoln, reading a dog eared *pocket* copy of the New Testament all by himself.

I can but think if you could have resumed your old intercourse with him at the end of his four years you would have found his religious sentiments more fixed, possibly more *christian* for "deism" is not Christianity

Your praise of my little book is very sweet to me. I have felt that I had no business to make a book, and indeed this was the last thing in my thought to do, while I was with Mr. Lincoln   But like Topsy, "it grew," I believe some incedents therein throw light on the character of the man. — I had little or no training for literary work   My schooling was all at a country district school, with one term of twelve weeks, at the village academy. — I know little of the classics, or in fact of *anything,*

1. James Thomson, *The Seasons* (1744).

2. *Six Months at the White House with Abraham Lincoln* (New York, 1866).

3. Bateman had related to Josiah Holland a purported conversation with AL in which the latter claimed to have experienced a religious change of heart. See Holland, 236–39. See also §§323, 457.

4. Francis L. Vinton was assistant rector of Trinity Church in New York City. His visit to the White House and his published sermons were reportedly of great consolation to the Lincolns. See Carpenter, 117–19.

5. John G. Nicolay.

— speak no language and know no language but English and poor at that. — But I *loved* Mr Lincoln, as I never loved but one or two men

He did not Know it. — Indeed I imagine he felt me a sort of nuisance, at times, but I kept on studying and loving him.

After the assassination, Tilton of the "Independent,"[6] (newspaper) wished me to give him a sketch for a *memorial* number of his newswpaper, — I wrote out hastily three or four little stories,

These were so widely copied that I was induced to repeat the articles; and the result was the *book* — When I sat down deliberately with the *book* before my mind I was *appalled.* did not know how to begin or how to do it. — Finally determined to tell my story in my own way. How I came to conceive of painting the picture, — and the *facts,* right straight through —

Of course I do not "falter:" as you say, all between the the covers. But I know the origin and *reliability* of most of the matter. — Some of the *stories,* attributed to him inserted may possibly not have been told by him, but these are *few,* if any   Most of them, which I did not hear myself, were told me by the parties, who heard them.

— So much for that. — The reception the book has received from the public is very pleasant to me. The publisher's have not been able to supply the demand so far. The 15th thousand now printing the first edition published (about) four months since

Since I commenced this your note informing me of your having sent to me Mr Lincoln's "Byron", has come — I do not know what I can say to express to you my *thanks.* It is the only thing I shall have of his excepting his *autograph,* which leads the subscribers to my picture, — this "letter" too, — I shall treasure the two book & letter as the most precious of any presents.

— Later   The *book* and the *letter,* have arrived, safely — a thousand blessings on you for thus remembering a *stranger.* I wish I could make you some adequate return, but I cannot.

still later   Since I commenced this letter I have been variously interrupted   Now I have also to acknowledge two letters about the *engraving,* of Lincoln, by Halpin,[7] which I sent you. The first, a note, was so good, so *satisfactory,* that I extracted the substance of it for an advertisement in Weekly Tribune. I hope I have not done wrong in this. But We have been put back by various things in getting the portrait before the public and the publisher of the portrait was so delighted with your note that he carried me with him in the matter of its publication.

Your last letter, the most perfect analysis of the portrait I have ever had, I shall reserve, for the present   It deserved to be *framed* in gold — think I will have it so framed and hang in my studio. When I publish it, will send you proofs, as you wish. I *trembled* for your *verdict.* My heart and soul were in my *work,* I did not know if another would appreciate this. *You* do certainly, — bless you for it.

---

6. Theodore Tilton was editor in chief of *The Independent.*

7. Frederick W. Halpin engraved a study of Lincoln made in preparation for Carpenter's painting "The Emancipation Proclamation."

Commendation under these circumstances is especially pleasant. Your opinion of the portrait is endorsed by Arnold,[8] also *Robert*[9] whose letter came to day. I hope it may be popular; for like all artist's, I have always been *poor*, — borrowed the money to paint the picture, which by the way, had not yet been paid.

I shall try to sell the large painting to Congress, think of going over to see about it in January.

I wish you could see it *now*   I went all over it last summer improving it greatly. — Every one says it should go to the Capitol. — One of the last talks I had with Mr Lincoln was about this, and he said "it would greatly please him to have Congress buy it, but it was a delicate subject for him to speak of" —

Do you know that Robert Dale Owen is writing a life of Lincoln, also! — He is a very able man, and will make a very valuable work. —

He was spending the evening with me, when your *present* arrived, ("Byron,")   Has read the Ann Rutledge lecture,[10] and is intensely interested of course in this new development of Lincoln's character. Will write to you, and is *coming to see you, sure.* His book will not interfere (in one sense) with yours. being from a very different stand point. — I want you to know him. He is good man to have for a friend.

Why will you not come to New York and see us all? Nothing would give me more pleasure than to have you at my house as long as you will stay — bring your good wife with you. — Come and *"smell* salt water," and see the *Knickerbocker's,* in their homes.

I am glad of one thing, I have helped many people to Know *you* as well as Lincoln; if I did *steal* your lecture for my book. This is one of the *compensations*   Seriously, one of the best things which have come of the *book* is the acquaintance with you. You are just the sort of man I should like to *paint.* — Would we not have great talks?

I am rattling on, as if I had Known you for years. Perhaps we *have* Known each other unconsciously, — perhaps consciously *somewhere* — if Edward Beecher's theory is true? — By the way your lecture on the *"Soul"* came at length. Have not yet read it carefully, Owen carried it off the other night. Shall read it when he returns it.

Do you Know anything of *Swedenborg?* Your idea of the law of the mind I think is *sound.*

I am greatly indebted for your careful examination, and translation of the portrait. — By the way I want a card photograph of *you.* Please send, — and I will exchange

Sincerely & gratefully yr's

F.B.Carpenter

LC: HW2909–14

---

8. Isaac N. Arnold.

9. Presumably Robert Todd Lincoln.

10. Herndon's fourth lecture, delivered on November 16, 1866.

412. Robert T. Lincoln to WHH

Chicago Dec 24 1866

My dear Mr Herndon

I should have acknowledged your letter sooner but I have been very much engaged. I am sorry about the book but only because our old friend Dr Smith will be disappointed.[1] In answer to your question I have to say that I do not know of Dr Smith's having "converted" my father from "Unitarian" to "Trinitarian" belief, nor do I know that he held any decided views on the subject as I never heard him speak of it.

I *infer* from your letter, but I hope it is not so, that it is your purpose to make some considerable mention of my mother in your work — I say I hope it is not so, because in the first place it would not be pleasant for her or for any woman, to be made public property of in that way — With a man it is very different, for he lives out in the world and is used to being talked of — One of the unpleasant consequences of political success is that however little it may have to do with that success, his whole private life is exposed to the public gaze — that is part of the price he pays. But I see no reason why his wife and children should be included — especially while they are alive — I think no sensible man would live in a glass house and I think he ought not to be compelled to do so against his will. I feel very keenly on this subject, for the annoyance I am subjected to sometimes is nearly intolerable   I hope you will consider this matter carefully, My dear Mr Herndon, for once done there is no undoing —

Sincerely your friend
Robert T. Lincoln

LC: HW2915

413. Robert T. Lincoln to WHH

Chicago Decr 27 /66

My dear Mr Herndon

Your letter of yesterday is at hand and I am very glad to find that I misunderstood your language and that you do understand my feelings on that subject. There is no need of saying anthing more about it.

Dr. Smith did not say the book was *his* — merely that my father had once loaned it to him and that he desired very much to possess it. You did all right about it of course — I can doubtless hunt up something that will please the Dr. quite as well.

Very sincerely yours
Robert T. Lincoln

LC: HW2916

---

1. See §407.

414. Henry C. Whitney to WHH

Lawrence Ks 30th Decr 1866.

Bro Herndon —

Dr Oliver Wendell Holmes of Boston is quite anxious that it should be incorporated in You life of Lincoln the high estimation he had for his poem "The Last Leaf"[1] :— of course you Know that it was a great favorite of Mr Lincolns — & Gov. Andrew[2] of Massachusetts says that in the darkest days of our history while being in consultation with Lincoln that the latter repeated to him the Entire poem: excuse me for mentioning this matter but it is so proper that it should find a place in your life of Lincoln & Dr Holmes is so justly anxious that it should do so that I could not avoid bringing it to your attention

Your Friend
Henry C Whitney

It will not pay you to send for copy of Lincolns entry on the docket in Champaign Co. here is a copy of it:—

"Plea in abatement by B. L. Green a Dft. not servd filed Saturday at 11 o' clock A.M. April 24th 1856. stricken from file by order of Court. Demr to Dec. if there ever was one overuled — Defendants who are servd now at 8 o'clock P.M. of the last day of the term ask to plead to the merits which is denied by the Court on the ground that the offer comes too late & therefore only nil dicit judgment is rendered for the Plff against the Defts who are servd in the process:[3]

LC: HW2921

415. Hannah Armstrong (WHH interview)

[1866]

Mrs. Jack Armstrong

Am the wife of Jack Armstrong — was so — Knew Abrm Lincoln in July or August 1831 — Know this by the birth of one of my children. Lincoln was clerking for Offutt at that time. I was living 4 M. from New Salem — Our acquaintance began then. Abe would Come out to our house — drink milk & mush — Corn bred — butter — bring the Children Candy — would rock the Cradle of my baby — the boy that was put on trial and the one Abe cleared[1] — while I got him Abe something to eat. Abe is one year older than I am — am now 55 years — My husband Jack Armstrong died — about 1857 — I foxed his pants — made his shirts — didn't made any buckskin pants — only foxed his surveyors pants[2]

---

1. Holmes's "The Last Leaf" was first published in 1831.
2. John Albion Andrew.
3. See §§489, 521.

---

1. For other references to the Duff Armstrong trial, see the index.
2. For other references to the foxing of AL's pants, see the index.

— He has gone with us to parties with us — he would tell stories — joke people — girls & boys at the parties — He would nurse babies — do any thing to accommodate any body — I never Saw him drink a drop of liquor. Jack Armstrong and Lincoln never had a word: they did wrestle — no foul play — all in a good humor — commenced in fun and ended in sport. I had no books about my house — loaned him none — we didn't think about books — papers — We worked — had to to live. Lincoln has staid at our house 2 or 3 weeks at a time.

In reference to the trial of my son I wrote to Lincoln first — he then wrote to me — have lost the letter — went to see Lincoln at Springfied — Saw him in his office: he promised to come down to defend my Son — did so — cleared him — told the stories about our first acquaintance — what I did for him and how I did it &c — was truly eloquent. After the trial was over L. came down to where I was, in Beardstown. I asked him what he charged me — told him I was poor —: he Said — "Why — Hannah I shant charge you a cent — never. Any thing I can do for you I will do for you willingly & freely. without charge." He wrote to me about some land which some men were trying to get frm me. Mr. Lincoln said — "Hannah they Cant get your land — let them try it in the Circuit Court and then you appeal it — bring it to Supm Court and I and Herndon will attend to it for nothing.

In 1863.: I wanted to get one of my Sons — Wm — the boy whom Lincoln cleared in Beardstown out of the Army — needed him — all I had — wrote to Lincoln at Washington: he telegraphed to me as follows —

Sept. 1863

"Mrs. Hannah Armstrong —

I have just ordered the discharge of your boy, William — as you say now at Louisville Ky

A. Lincoln.[3]

As to the trial — Lincoln said to me "Hannah Your son will be cleared before sun down". He and the other lawyers addressed the Jury, and closed the case. I went down at Thompsons pasture. Staton[4] Came and told me soon that my Son was cleared — and a free man. I went up to the Court house — the Jury shook hands with me — so did the Court — so did Lincoln. We were all affected and tears streamed down Lincoln's Eyes. He then remarked to me — "Hannah — What did I tell you." I pray to God that Wm may be a good boy hereafter — that this lesson may prove in the End a good lesson to him and to all.

Mr Lincoln lectured in the Evening after the trial on discoveries and inventions:[5] it was a funny production and if I can judge a very good — that is a solid & good one.

3. AL to Mrs. Hannah Armstrong, Sept. 18, 1863, *CW* 6:462.
4. Probably Daniel Staton.
5. Probably the first version of AL's lecture "Discoveries and Inventions." *CW* 2:437–42.

A few days before Mr Lincoln left for Washington I went to see him — was a widow — the boys got up a story on me that I went to get to sleep with Abe &c —. I replied to the Joke that it was not every woman who had the good fortune & high honor of sleeping with a President. This stopt the sport — cut it short. — Well I talked to him some time and was about to bid him good by — had told him that it was the last time that I should ever see him — something told me that I should never see him — that they would kill him — He smiled and said — jokingly — "Hannah — if they Kill me I shall never die an other death. I then bade him goodby.

I never was in Springfield till 1859. — The stories going the rounds about jumping. I was in Springfield after my Son was cleared — saw him — shook hands with him — Saw his wife. Abe never spoke to me about his wife — never introduced me to her — thought something was the matter with him & her — The first time I went to his house knocked at the door — heard no answer — went to the back door — roused the girl — Saw Lincoln Come up Stairs

Jno. T. Stuart &c — tell it.[6]

You understand the customs & habits of the People of Menard in 1831 to 1837 as well and better than I do and Can write them out — am sick — want to go home — will see you in Springfield sometime — will then tell you more — Goodby &c —

LC: HW3830–34; HL: LN2408, 1:377–81

416. Esther Summers Bale (WHH interview)

[1866]

Mrs Bale — wife of Hardin Bail
 Knew Mr. Lincoln well — Maiden name Summers — Cousin to Miss Owens — Knew her well — is blue Eyed — dark hair — handsome — not pretty — is rather large & tall — is handsome — truly handsome — matron looking — over ordinary size in height & weight of a standard woman — She is fair tolerably fair complexion — is smart. sharp — quick & strong minded — *Knew* Miss Rutledge well — had auburn hair — blue Eyes — fair Complexion — slim — pretty — Kind — tender good hearted woman — height about 5 feet 3 in — weighed about 120 pounds — was beloved by all who Knew her. McNamar — Hill & Lincoln all Courted her near the same time — died as it were of grief — Miss Rutledge was beautiful — Miss Owens was handsome — that is to say was noble looking — matronly seeming.

LC: HW3836–37; HL: LN2408, 1:383–84

---

6. Apparently Mrs. Armstrong's story reminded WHH of another involving (or told by) John T. Stuart.

417. *Hardin Bale (WHH interview)*

[1866]

Hardin Bale — aged 49.

I came to Ills in 1829 — setled — wintered in Petersburg — then a farm — went to Salem in the Spring of 1832 — Knew Lincoln. Row Herndon & Jim Herndon merchandised in N. Salem — mixd store — goods & groceries — Knew Radford: he Kept a Kind of a grocery — whiskey — pepper — Sugar Salt &c — Row & Jim Herndon sold their goods to Berry —. I don't think Lincoln ever owned a dry goods store — Don't think he ever Kept an exclusively whiskey shop — though it is said so — Lincoln Commenced studying Law 1833 — Commenced surveying in 1833 — or 4 — Knew Kelso — Knew Doct. Jason Duncan — Am a Democrat — never Knew anything Evil wrong or criminal. He was a great fellow to try projects — invented a wheel— fixd a box — strapt himself and weighed a thousand or more pounds —: it seems to me that Sincho[1] — bought out these various lots of goods — (Sincho). Kelso and Lincoln were great friends — always together — always talking and arguing. My Father was a Babtist preacher.

LC: HW3836; HL: LN2408, 1:382–83

418. *Henry Clark (WHH interview)*

[1866]

Henry Clark aged 61

I came here in 1825 — lived in Bakers Praire — Bakers Praire is opposite Salem — ie North East — Knew Lincoln in 1831 — Keeping Store for Offut. I had a fight in 1832 Lincoln my Second — I was Lincolns frend: he was my frind —: When he was Presdt. he Sent me his respects:[1] Jas & Rowan Herndon had a store — a kind of grocery store in Salem — probably Blankenship had something to do with the goods — Radford had some goods — groceries — whiskey. The Clary boys gutted the concern — It is Said Bill Green bought out Radford & Sold to Berry & Lincoln. I have got things now I bought of Lincoln who was clerk for Offutt. Offutt sold out his remnant of goods to Warburton — Lincoln was a good fellow — humorous — Saw Jack Armstrong & Lincoln once wrestle — Jack took the advantage of Lincoln — threw him — good humored. Never saw or knew any evil of Lincoln — Never heard a man say a word of wrong in my life. Politically he has been cursed — privately no man can utter a word against him — never heard a man whisper aught Evil of Lincoln — Couldn't if they told the truth —

LC: HW2585; HL: LN2408, 1:381–82

---

1. Henry Sinco.

---

1. AL reportedly asked William Greene during the 1864 presidential campaign to remind Clark, a critic of the war, that "when he had a hard fight on his hands I *stood by him,* and now that I have a hard fight on I want *him to stand by me*" (Reep, 29). See also §282.

419. David Davis (WHH interview)

[1866]

Judge Davis

Judge Davis was Judge of the 8th Judicial Circuit Elected in 1848 — Elected 3 times — 14 counties — Treat was elected Supm Judge. I Circuit Judge — Elected last time June 1861 — Appointed Supm US Judge in Oct 1862 — Lincoln went to all the Courts. Judge Davis in Time held his Court about 6 mo.: the first time he held Circuit Court was in 1849 —

Never was a Man of gushing feelings — Eminently just — felt for the Poor — was not a man of [strong?]— Yielding except in [corrections?] of *[illegible]*

Lincoln was conscentious — See Early life in Menard — see Abolitionism — in 1856 — was for Taylor over Clay —. He had this Kind of Faith — namely — He believed in the People — though that then Like 2d thought his would eventually prove successful — No man can be a man with out this faith — Purple practiced in the Circu and as a general rule asked nor granted favors — would give Lincoln what he wanted — Had no faith in the Christian sense of that term — Had faith in laws — principles — causes & Effects — Philosophy. He had scelf-relying power — in this — He had no faith in any mans judgment — Could not Absorb — could suck in — drink in memory, but Must Know by investigation — as it were by Experiment — had no faculty or organizing power: hence a child Could Conduct the Simple & technical rules — the means & the mode of getting at Justice better than L. The Law has its own rules & a student could get at them better than L — Sometimes Lincoln studied things, if he could not get the rubbish of a case removed. &c &c. He had no invention or organizing ability &c — no Admr. Ability

Patterson murder case[1] in Champaign — Davis — Lincoln — Sweat — Lincoln was on the wrong side — wanted to compromise — Sweat said no — L was so conscious that he did not do much good — but that Sweat did — that he proposed to give the whole fee to Sweat[2]

LC: HW2664–65; HL: LN2408, 2:185–86

420. James Davis (WHH interview)

[1866]

Jas Davis — aged 60

Came to Clary's grove in 1829. Knew Lincoln well — Knew Jim & Row Herndon — They sold out to Berry — one of them did — afterwards the other sold out to Lincoln — the Store was a mixd one — dry goods, a few, groceries such as Sugar Salt &c — and whiskey — solely Kept for their Customers — or to

---

1. For other references to this case, see the index.
2. This paragraph appears in the margin of the first sheet of the interview.

sell by the Gallon — quart or pint — not otherwise —. The Herndon's probably had the blankenship goods — Radford had a grocery Store — salt, pepper & such like things — with whiskey. It is said Green bought this out & instantly sold to Lincoln & Berry — Lincoln & Berry broke — Berry subsequently Kept a doggery — a whiskey saloon, as I do now or did — Am a democrat — never agreed in politics with Abe: he was an honest man. Give the devil his due: he never sold whiskey by the dram in New Salem. I was in town every week for years — Know I think, all about it — I always drank my drams & drank at Berry's often — ought to Know — Lincoln got involved, as I think in the first operation — Salem hill was *a Barren*[1] —

LC: HW3837, HW3839; HL: LN2408, 1:384–85

421. Johnson Gaines Greene (WHH interview)

[1866]

Johnson G. Green

I Came to Ills in 1821 — am now 46 — Know Mrs Mary Vineyard — once Mary Owens — I Knew her as Early as 1837 in Ills at Salem — She Staid with Mrs Able in Menard Co in Ills — Mrs Able was her Sister — Mr Owens was a Kentuckian — rich & well Educated — married the 2d time — his wife — the 2d one & Miss Owens didn't agree. Miss Owens Came to Ills as Early as 1836– or 7 — lived with her Sister, Mrs Able — It was at Mrs Ables that Miss Owens & Mr Lincoln Saw Each other — Miss Owens was about 24 or 5 ys of age in 1837 — She is 5 feet — 7 in high — Strong nervous & muscular woman — has dark blue Eyes — dark brown hair — flesh light colored and weighed 160 pounds — She is my Cousin — Saw her in 1866 in the winter and Spring at Weston Mo. — She & I had a Conversation about Lincoln when I Saw her at Weston Mo — She Said She remembered Lincoln well — had recd letters from him — is an intellectual woman — the most intellectual woman I Ever Saw — She had a fine Education — her forhead is massive & angular — Square, prominent & broad—. I had heard a great deal about Lincoln's & her Courtship — was determined to have it & dragged it out by degrees —

Lincoln had gone to Havana to Survey Some land — had been gone about 3 Weeks — One of Ables boys went up to get the mail — Lincoln had just got back: he asked the little boy if Miss Owens was at Mr Ables: the boy replied — yes: Tell her — Said Lincoln that I'll be down to see her in a few minutes". Able lived about 1 M north of Salem. The boy told Miss Owens this — Miss Owens had that Evening determined to go Mentor Graham's her Cousin: She thought a moment and Said to herself if I can draw Lincoln up there to Grahams it will all be right: they had had a difficulty about Mrs Bolin Greens boy before this — The difficulty arose in this way — Miss Owens & Mrs Bolin Green were going to Ables from Bolin Greens. Lincoln Came along just at that time — Mrs B. Green said they

---

1. Apparently a tract of treeless land.

were going to Ables, and asked Lincoln to go along. Mrs B.G's child was along —
it was a great big fat child — heavy & crossly disposed — Mrs. BG. had to Carry
her own child up — L & Miss Owens walking behind — Lincoln did not appear
to notice the old lady's struggles and when they all had got up to the house — Say
100 ft & pretty Steep. Miss Owens Said to Lincoln — laughingly — You would
not make a good husband Abe: they Sat on the fence & one word brought on an
other, till a Split or breach Ensued — It was with an Eye to this quarrel that Miss
Owens wished to test L love   That if he came to Grahams it was all right. She
wanted to make L bend. Lincoln according to promise went down to Ables and
asked if Miss Owens was in: Mrs Able replied that She had gone to Grahams, about
1½ M from Ables — due south west —: Lincoln Said — "Didn't She Know I was
Coming". Mrs Able Said — "No." One of the children Said — "Yes Ma — She
did for I heard one of the children — the boy Saml who went to the P.O told her
So." Lincoln Sat a Short time — went to Salem to his office — place of business
— bording house and didnt go to Graham's. The fat was now in the fire. Lincoln
thought that as he was Extremely poor and Miss Owens very rich that it was a fling
on him on that account. This was at that time Abes tender spot. Abe was mistak-
en in his guesses for wealth Cut no figure in Miss Owens Eyes — Miss Owens
regretted her Course — Abe would not bend and Miss Owens wouldn't: She Said
if She had it to do over again She would play her Cards differently. She went back
to Ky about 1838 — did not Court any one for Several years — married in Ky to
a man, about 1842, by the name of Jesse Vineyard: he was a good man — a man
of property. they Subsequently went to Mo where he died — Say about 1862. Mrs
Vineyard had 2 Sons in the Southern Army: She Said — Mrs Vineyard — that if
Either of her Sons had got into difficulty that she would willingly have gone to
Old Able for relief. She has got 3 children now — 2 boys & 1 girl. The oldest boy
is a lawyer & a good one   The other is a farmer.

The Able house was about 1838 or 9 moved from the top of the bluff to the
bottom of the hill: it is the Same house Except the Ell which has been put to it
Since — house 18 by 30.

Mrs Owens[1] herself told Green the above.

LC: HW3889–93; HL: LN2408, 1:341–44

422. Thomas L. D. Johnston (WHH interview)[1]

[1866]

Thomas L. D. Johnson — aged 29th
    Am the Son of John D. Johnson who helped Lincoln to make a flat boat near
Sangamon Town in Sangamon Co. in 1831. My father is — was the son of Mrs

1. *Vineyard* is written above *Owens*.

1. This is the Springer transcription, which somehow escaped inclusion in the bound volumes and is in
the Herndon-Weik Collection at the Library of Congress.

Lincoln by her first husband — My father is the brother of Mrs More,[2] who was the wife of Squire Hall. Mrs Moores 1st husband was Esqr Hall — her second husband was Reuben Moore — Both died in Coles Co. Hall married Miss Johnson — or Mrs Moore in Indiana. Moore married in Coles. My father and mother are both dead[3] — buried in the grave yard — one mile south west — of Farmington on the right hand side of the road, leading from Charleston Coles Co to Praire City Cumberland Co Ills. All the parties mentioned herein, including Thomas Lincoln are buried in this grave yard — Called Gordons grave yard — 9 miles from Charleston — South, bearing a little west of Charleston. Dennis Hanks married a Johnson[4] — who was the Child of old Mrs Lincoln by her first husband — Danl Johnson. My father died in 1852 — mother in 1849 — leaving 6 children. Hall died in 1851 — Mrs Hall is living: her name is Mrs Moore. She had 10 children by her 1st husband — one by her 2d husband. Dennis Hanks wife died in 1854 — had 6 children. My father in Coles Co in 1835. Hall was married in Indiana — Dennis Hanks was married in Indiana — Dennis Hanks — his wife & children — Hall his wife and Children — John D. Johnston, Thomas Lincoln — Sarah his wife and Abm all came to gether from Indiana to Ills in March 1831.[5]

Dennis Hanks is fast failing in body & *mind* — has quit his liquor — is more foolish than Grand Mother Lincoln. Grand Mother Lincoln is a little childish — yet she is much smarter than usually thought: she needs rousing: thats' all. and when roused she talks well for she remembers well. Dennis Hanks so his own children say is Crazy — nearly so — is decidedly foolish — has to my mind been so for 3 or 4 years.

I hand you Mr Lincolns old copy book to use in your history of Mr Lincoln It was a copy book as I and family Know it made up of Mr Lincoln's labor when he was — & was not going to school: he worked out his sums & problems at various times — & places. The latter years of the book is gone: It took 5 or 6 years to make the book as we understand it — Know it: I give you some of Mr Lincolns private letters to my father. One was printed in the Charleston Courier in the year 1865[6] — The one that has the poetry in is the Charleston paper — the Courier — The Decatur Gazette & Chronicle of Octr 17th 1866 publish the Poetry — swift as an arrow &c — The Poetry &c published as above in the Courier was "I'll be a good boy — God Knows when &c."[7]

Mr Lincoln took a fancy to one of my bros — Abraham — wanted him to come to Spfdgd — stay at L house — go to school — L saw his wife about it — refused furiously — caused hard feelings — L wrote to my bro that what he had proposed could not be filled on his part on account of domestic difficulty, but to go on and he L would give him money — books — pay schooling &c — &c my

---

2. Matilda Johnston Moore.

3. Mary Barker was his mother's maiden name. She married on October 16, 1834.

4. Elizabeth Johnston, stepsister of AL.

5. Marginal note: *Jefferson Adams* — / *Thomas Phipps* — / *Jas. Phipps* — (write to them) Campbell, PO Coles Co Ills.

6. No copies of the Charleston *Courier* for 1865 appear to have survived.

7. For the surviving remnants of AL's copybook, see *CW* 1:xxix–xlviii.

bro did not do as wished — got a good Common English Education — died in 1861 — aged 22 —

The Lincoln farm is 8½ miles South of Charleston — & ¾ mile from Farmington. It is called 8m from Charleston to Farmington.

I dont think that Thomas Lincoln was a witty man — a humorous man: he was a social man — loved Company — peeple & their Sports very much: he seemed to me to border on the serious — reflective — He read his bible — told Indian Stories — that thrilled my young nature — was about 16 years of age — he died in 1851. I was then in my 15th year. The Indian Story as told me by Thomas Lincoln — the Father of Abm is true as related to you by Dennis & Jno Hanks. I Know the story because I was young: it interested me much & is now vivid in my mind. Thomas Lincoln — my grand father told me in what Co in Ky it took place, but have forgotten it. Thos Lincoln was the boy that the Indian had and was running off — 2 or more Indians were Killed then & there.

LC: HW3936–39, HW3940–43 (Springer transcription)

423. Bunbry B. Lloyd (WHH interview)

[1866?]

B. B Lloyd

The plays of the People in Ky — generally ball — corner ball, called bull pen, cat & town ball. We had Corn Shuckings.[1] We would pile all one Crop of Corn in one pile or string about 5 feet high at the Centre, divided Equally — Chose Captains. A general wrestle — and Sometimes a fight would Ensue — generally good humored — had lots of whisky — had suppers — hoe downs — dances old fashion — old nigger would play — pat juba — Sing "Juba — you old dog Juba"   No nigger Could Stand Still at this — "Come down — "Juba, you old dog juba" and then the feet would Come down[2] — Shooting matches at Christmas/. for turkeys — beeves. &c — played marbles. — had swings — went to school in log cabins — &c — went to Church in log houses — sometimes frame and rough stone — went to Camp Meetings. — Elections — had 3 days — voted in Districts or Counties — fights — &c whisky — all voted at the Co Seat. — Songs. — Nathctes under the hill or sugar in the gourd. Christian Songs — old Hundred

When Shall I see Jesus. &c

How happy are they. &c.[3]

LC: HW3960

---

1. See §249, note 4.

2. Setting up complicated rhythms by patting the feet on dancing boards, along with patting other parts of the body, was called "patting Juba." Juba was an African name given generically to black entertainers. See Roger D. Abrahams, *Singing the Master: The Emergence of African American Culture in the Plantation South* (New York, 1992), 94.

3. For "When Shall I See Jesus," see §108, note 3. "Old Hundredth" was a musical setting for the 100th psalm composed by Louis Bourgeois for the Genevan psalter (1551). "How Happy Are They Who the Savior Obey" appeared in Charles Wesley, *Hymns and Sacred Poems* (1749).

424. Henry McHenry (WHH interview)

[1866]

Henry McHenry — aged 64 —

I Came to Salem or near it in 1823 — Knew Lincoln the 2d day he came to New Salem in 1831 — came in July or August — Berry and Lincoln owned a horse in partnership — Berry traded for Radfords Groceries — put the horse in as part pay with Lincoln's Consent. Berry bought the goods — don't think Lincoln had anything to do with it — the store — grocery. Berry owned the goods. Lincoln never had a dry good store in his life I think — He sold good for Offutt. Don't think Lincoln Ever had any dry goods — Lincoln surveyed in 1832 or 3 — studied law as Early and both together — Surveyed my land in 1836 — surveyed the Wadkins[1] race track in 1833 — Read law in 1832 or 3 — walked to Spgfd for books — borrow them of Jno. T. Stuart — This is true — first Lincoln Said So — others who saw him do it said so and I Know we plagued Lincoln for it and he never denied it. In his surveying jobs & trips he needed a horse — told him so — He said he didn't need one — was somewhat of a *"hoss"* himself. He used to read law in 1832 or 3 barefooted seated in the shade of a tree — would grind around with the shade — just opposite Berry's grocery store — a few feet south of the door — Bails[2] house is North of Berry's grocery — was so once — Hills store was west of it — town one straight gut of a street — 60 or 70 feet wide — about 20 houses — 100 people. Lincoln's grocery so called was North of Hills — across the Street 60 or 70 feet. — Salem once was Covered with large timber — trees scattered — cut down to make place for the town in 1829. I think — Salem gut ran East & west — Country barreny a little — I have seen Miss Rutledge a thousand times — had blue Eyes — fair skin — Sandy — rather, living Auburn hair — slender — nervous — quick — good — Kind, social — goodhearted & was really a beautiful — a pretty woman would express my ideas better — was an ordinary height — weighed about 120 pounds — Straight as an arrow, and as quick as a flash. Lincoln would have been happy with Miss Rutlege.

LC: HW3839, HW3838; HL: LN2408, 1:385–86

425. George U. Miles (statement for WHH)

[1866]

G. U. Miles

I came to Ills 1816 — St. Clair — then to Ky — then to Wayne Co — then to White — then [the?] 1825. to Peoria Co — now Logan — first camped — had a wife and 2 babies — made a house — cut the trees — built a fire in the centre of the house — dug down through the frozen ground to soft ground — made mortar — daubed the house — erected the chimney — built jamb & tuck with dirt — [laid?] up boards. & put dirt between the jamb and boards and pounded it hard took away the boards — put in a fire — broke prairie with a bar Shear plow — Carry plow soon followed about 1827–8 — Diamond plow after that about 1836

---

1. Thomas Watkins trained racehorses on his farm north of New Salem (Onstot, 142).
2. Jacob Bale.

— 2d Came in use about 1828. 3d came in about 1836 — *[illegible]*. Plowed corn with old fashioned bar shear plow — and shovel plow[1] — now riding plows, double &c — With 2 yoke oxen and a span of horses — 6 animals in all. Indians all around me — fanned wheat with a Sheet — tramped out the wheat with horses — girls & boys riding them — fanning mills[2] Came in use about 1834 or 5 — The second plow was the Carry plow — Break 2 acres a day — have seen hand mills of 2 Kinds — one with stones with a pole that worked in a socket over head — the rock at the End going close to an other rock — Corn between. The other was like a coffee mill. — Mills used about 1810–12–1816.1818 in Ills. — Went to mill 20 miles — ground about 20 Bushels per day — Blacksmith shop about 20 miles — Beat corn in a mortar — grated it on grater —

1820
to
1827, Rail Splitting 37½ per hundred 100-150-200 —

	per day —	150
Corn	per bushels —	6 to 8 c
Wheat		20. to 25
Eggs		3 to 4.c
Butter		6c 8
Chickens		6.
Cow & Calf		$6 to $8 —
Horses		$35. to 50
Beeswax —		14 to 16 ⅔ c
Labor		37½ to 50
Wagon		
Pork		$1,00 to 1,25

1866

Rail Splingting.	150 per hundred
Corn per bushel	25 to 30
Wheat	150 to 175
Eggs	10 to 15 pe doz.
Butter	25 to 30
Cow & Calf.	$35 — 50
Horse	$75. to $150.
Pork.	c7 pe pd. to c9
Labor	$150—200 $25 per mo
Wagon	$130. $175.
Chickens	$200 pe doz 16⅔ to 20c
Beeswax	c50

---

1. The widely used shovel plow was simply a piece of iron shaped like a pointed shovel and attached to a stick. The bar-share plow consisted of a primitive wooden moldboard with a lance-shaped iron point as a share. The moldboard of the Cary plow was plated with sheet iron; the share was of heavy wrought iron. The Diamond plow was a cast-iron plow whose advantage was in working with less resistance than wooden moldboard plows encountered, but on prairie soils it did not scour well.

2. Devices for blowing chaff out of threshed grain.

4 yards of wolsey Linsey 1 yd wide made a dress for any woman: the skirt was long & narrow — The waist was Short — just under the arms. There were no Crimps or puckering or frills Except at the back of the dress which were few and far between —

Girls used to Carry their shoes to within 50 or 100 yds of Church — then they would put them on and go into church as large as life & 2wice as natural — Boys went barefoot till 17 or 20 ys of age in Summer time

Mens coats were made at home & made out of Striped Cotton cloth — split up behind — narrow tails — Claw hammers — & Short waists — jeans in winter made do — in good families

Women wore Corn fied bonnets — Sun Bonnetts — for Every day — dress on Sunday Bonnetts were Scoop Shaped — being long and flaring before and a little long & contracted behind

Women danced bare footed on puncheon floors — all night — drank whiskey toddy —

Men Corn Shucked it — log rolled it — dance all night barefoot on puncheon floor — drink heap whiskey — and work or hunt & fish all day — fight — foot race or horse race it &c.

1st Superstition   horse breathing on a child would cause hooping Cough — Iles. Elijah did this —

2d Make fence in the light of the moon to prevent sinking —

3d Cut down the trees to make rails in the light of the moon & the Early part of the day —

4th Plant potatoes to plant in the dark of the moon — So with all roots

5th Things that grow up & out in the light of the moon —

6th If you want your mare to have a horse colt put her in the dark of the moon.

7th Begin Nothing on friday

8th Cut all animals by the signs in the Almanac & cut when in the feet of the legs —

9th Make Soap in the light of the moon — turn with a stick one way alone — no other person must touch it

10th Birds flying and Setting in window Some of the family would soon die —

11th If a dog ran across the path when you were hunting this was bad luck unless you instantly hooked your little fingers & pulled till the dog ran out of sight —

12th Ghosts — witches — Spirits — preventions — horse shoes nailed on the door steps — over doors — Hair balls in Cattle were made by witches — send for witch doctors —

13th Faith Doctors — all believed in nearly.

	a
old Sickle	1 —
now Reaper	15 — to 16 —
old Wheat fan out	20 — with cloth
now "Thrashing Machine	300 — to 400

old Wheat ground	20 — bushes — per day
now Wheat —	200 bush per day
old Plow ground	2 acers
now " "	5 acers
old Plant Corn	10 acers *4 hands 10 acers*
now Plant Corn	16 — 20 1 Man & boy —

LC: HW2700, HW2702, HW2701; HL: LN2408, 2:234–39

426. Samuel C. Parks (statement for WHH)

[1866[1]]

Senatorial Contest of 1854 and 5.

In the contest for the U.S. Senate in the winter of 1854 and 5 in the Illinois Legislature nearly all the Whigs and some of the *"Anti Nebraska Democrats"* preferred Mr. Lincoln to any other man; Some of them (and myself among the number) had been candidates, and had been elected by the People for the express purpose of doing all in their power for his election; and a great deal of their time during the sesion was taken up both in caucus and out of it in laboring to unite the Anti Nebraska Party on their favorite; but there was from the first as the result proved and inseperable obstacle to their success. Four (4) of the Anti Nebraska Democrats had been elected in part by Democrats and they not only personally preferred Mr. Trumbull, but considered his election necessary to consolidate the union between all those who were opposed to repeal of the Missouri Compromise and to the new policy upon the subject of slavery which Mr. Douglas and his friends were laboring so hard to inaugerate; they insisted that the election of Mr. Trumbull to the Senate would secure thousands of democratic votes to the Anti Nebraska Party who would be driven off by the election of Mr. Lincoln — that the Whig Party were nearly a unit in opposition to Mr. Douglas, so that the election of the favorite candidate of the majority would give no particular strength in that quarter; and they manifested a fixed purpose to vote steadily for Mr. Trumbull and not at all for Mr. Lincoln and thus compel the friends of Mr. Lincoln to vote for their man, to prevent the election of Gov. Matteson who it was ascertained could after the first few ballots carry enough Anti Nebraska men to elect him. These four men were Judd, of Cook, Palmer of Macoupin, Cook of Lasalle and Baker of Madison; Allen of Madison went with them, but was not inflexible and would have voted for Lincoln cheerfully, but did not want to seperate from his Democratic friends. These men kept aloff from the caucuses of both parties during the winter. They could not act with the Democrats from principle and would not act with the Whigs from policy.

---

1. WHH's note to himself in his David Davis interview of September 19, 1866, to "See Parks" about the election of Trumbull suggests that this statement was provided after that date and before December 1, 1866. The missing original was seen and is cited by Horace White in *The Life of Lyman Trumbull* (Boston and New York, 1913), 46n.

When the election came off, it was evident after the first two or three ballots, that Mr. Lincoln could not be elected, and it was feared that if the balloting continued long Gov. Matteson would be elected. Mr. Lincoln then preadvised his friends to vote for Mr. Trumbull. They did so and elected him.

Mr. Lincoln was very much disappointed, for I think that at that time it was the height of his ambition to get into the U.S. Senate. He manifested however no bitterness towards Mr. Judd or the other Anti Nebraska Democrats by whom practically he was beaten, but evidently thought that their motives were right. He told me several times afterwards that the election of Trumbull was the best thing that could have happened.

During the entire session Mr. Gillespie seemed *moderately* for Mr. Lincoln, but some of our men thought he was secretly for Trumbull all the time.

Judge Logan was devoted for Mr. Lincoln all winter and did all he could for him; he and some others of Mr. Lincoln's friends in the Legislature seemed to think that the conduct of Judd and Co. in compelling us to vote for Mr. Trumbull was ungenerous and selfish. Mr. Waters of McDonough was especially indignant and utterly refused to vote for Mr. Trumbull at all. On the last ballot he threw away his vote on Mr. Williams.

There was a great deal of dissatisfaction throughout the State at the result of the election. The whigs constituted a vast majority of the Anti Nebraska Party; they thought they were entitled to the Senate and that Mr. Lincoln by his contest with Mr. Douglas had earned it; Mr. Lincoln, however, generously exonorated Mr. Trumbull and his friends from all blame in the matter.

Trumbull's first encounter with Mr. Douglas in the Senate, filled the people of Illinois with admiration for his abilities and the ill feeling caused by his election gradually passed away.

(From S. C. Parks)

HL: LN2408, 2:443–46

427. A. D. Wright to WHH

[1866]

"Berry's Creek" and "Concord Creek" are the same and they empty into and form that beautiful Lake, called "Blue Lake", and then into the Sangamon River —

Carman came to N.S. before J. Duncan left —

Yours

A. D. Wright.

HL: LN2408, 1:431

428. Jason Duncan to WHH

[late 1866–early 1867¹]

I first went to reside in New Salem in August AD 1831 to practice my profession, procuring an office room in the public house of James Rutlege. I became acquainted with Abraham Lincoln late president of the United States shortly after my arrival in that place, his external apperance was not prepossessing, but on cultivating an acquaintance with him found some thing about the young man verry attractive evincing intellegence far beyond the generality of youth of his age and opportunities. he had the approachable air common to young men who like him grew up on the western frontiers entirely destitute of those conventional trammels, which are thrown around young men in the older States. the open frank manner of Mr Lincoln in his youthful days coupled with a flow of good humor and great witticism, always made him a welcome member of any group or Society of intellegent men. he was not obtrusive in his manners, but his genial nature seemed to invite any one to form his acquaintance. he was a verry obscure young man when I first became acquainted with him at New Salem. he had no influential friends to bring him into public notice or money to aid him in procuring an education: in fine I have thought that in all the range of my acquaintance never did I Know an individual who had the difficulties to Surmount to reach the pinicle of fame and usefulness that seemed to lie in the pathway of A. Lincoln, his disposition was of a concilliatory Stamp always seeking to avoid personal difficulties, hence he became popular with all classes. many men sought and made his acquaintance who were not of the most refined and quiet dispositions, yet he so managed with that ~~pugilistic~~ class as to obtain complete control over them. for there was a clan in that vicinity who prided themselves on their manhood and ready to measure steel with any one who could be induced to enter the Contest or trial of manhood.

his employment when I first became acquainted with him was rough clerk for a man by the name of Offit,² who had a lease on the Salem mill. he used to unload Sacks of wheat from farmers wagons, measure out and settle with them for the same, this I believe he followed as long as Offit continued proprietor of the Mill; the winter following Abraham requested me to assist him in the study of English Grammar, which I consented to do to the extent of my limited ability. his application through the winter was assiduous, and untiring, his intuitive faculties were Surprising. he seemed to master the construction of the english language and apply the rules for the same in a most astonishing manner, The first time I ever heard him attempt to Speak in public, was at a polemic Society meeting in an underground room of a rude log cabin which Stood on the South hillside to the right of main street looking toward the river from the west. that ancient cabin I believe has long since gone to ruins. I often bring up in my mind, the old log cabin in connection with the verry earnest and able manner in which the afterward

---

1. WHH pursued Duncan's whereabouts during the fall of 1866 and apparently did not learn his actual location (Knoxville, Ill.) until the Spears letter of November 3.

2. Denton Offutt.

great and pure statesman argued his side of the question. I am inclined to the belief that in that cabin he uttered his maiden Speech.[3] As there were no Attorneys
nearer than Springfield his services were sometimes sought in suits, at law. and he
frequently consented to appear before Esq Bowling Greens' court, to argue cases.
but never charged his clients any fees so far as I Knew, the only lawbook which
Mr Lincoln had in his possession was the first Old revised code of Illinois. from
this he drew all his legal knowledge, the manner in which he used to force his law
arguments upon Esqr Bowling Green was both amuseing and instructive, so laconic often as to produce a spasmatic shaking of the verry fat sides of the old law
functionary of New Salem — Bowling Green permitted him to speak at first more
for amusement than any thing else. but in a short time was led to pay great respect to his powers of mind in a forensic point of view. The first law books which
Lincoln owned were purchased by him at a sheriffs sale at Springfield consisting
of a copy of Blackstones Commentaries. after he purchased those books he determined to make the profession of law his pursuit. at this time he was greatly embarrassed in financial matters at times seemed rather dispondent at one time he
engaged in a Small way in dry goods and grocery business in company with a man
by the name of Berry — but was unsucessful and in a short time closed out with
some loss, commiserating his Condition I put forth an effort to procure the appointment of Mr Lincoln to the office of Postmaster. he objected to the move on
the ground that he did not want the then incumbant Supplanted. but considers-
ations connected with the public good, prompted me with others to prefer charges at the department against Hill, who on receiving notice from the department
to acquit himself of the charges prefered, or Steps would be taken to turn him out
as Post Mast. Shortly after receiving this notice he resigned the office in Mr Lincolns favor, which post he held until the office was discontinued at that place. While
Mr Lincoln was in the Black Hawk war his friends in the vicinity of Salem brought
his name before the public as a candidate for the State legislature the contest was
a Spirited one though he was beaten by a verry Small majority, it served to bring
his name prominently before the people and pave the way to a brilliant career in
the history of his native country. So Singular is it, and sometimes to my mind so
marvelous, that a man at the age of twenty one with so few advantages for prefer-
ment, should at last reach the goal and posterity place his name high up with those
of Washington Adams Webster and Clay upon the same page of history. Mr Lincoln was in favor of Henry Clay in 1832 voted for him during that memorable
campaign, though the New Salem precinct was largely for Jackson such was his
personal popularity that he obtained a majority, verry many Jackson men of the
most violent party feelings voting for him, on the grounds they believed him an
honest and worthy young man after Mr Cameron with whom he boarded moved
away Mr Lincoln took up his residence with the family of Mr James Rutlege,
though Mr Lincoln did not seem so ardent in his attachments to his friends as some
persons are yet he alwas evinced great respect for their opinions in all matters, his

---

3. See §282.

memmory was remarkably tenacious. hardly ever forgetting any thing which he read possessing any interest to his mind, he was proverbial for his benevolence, always giving something of what he possessed to charitable objects — I often thought he was too confiding, thereby laying himself liable to impositions, his goodness of heart often led him to make great allowances for men's foibles, I have often thought of the conditions and Surroundings of Mr Lincoln at Washington Compared with those at New Salem. just as much unlike as Could possibly be, I often imagine him Standing Six feet and upward pointing his long bony finger at Old Bowling Green who was presiding in his Court Capacity with great dignity, with [illegible] shirt and breeches on the latter supported by one tow linnen suspender over his shoulder, an enormously fat man weighing I should think not far from 300 lbs given to mirth as generally fat men are

If there was a trait of Mr Lincolns Character which stood out more conspicuously than an other it was his regard for truth and veracity, he had less prevarication than almost any man with whom I was ever acquainted. he always had a fund of Anecdotes, but rarely ever said a foolish thing, his anecdotes were always amuseing, and the occasion of this rehearsal timely, his comparisons were inimitable, I boarded with Bowling Green Esqr for some length of time, at that time Mr Lincoln frequented his house. many were the laconic remarks made by these gentlemen to the amusement of any neighbor or friend who might happen to be present. Although Green was a determined democrat of the Jackson school and the leader of the party in the vicinity of New Salem, and Mr Lincoln a firm Clay man, they never to my Knowedge had any difficulty politically or otherwise, and I think they always voted for each other when candidates, on public days it was customary among young men to try their skill in athletic exercises Mr Lincoln would wait till all who were disposed to try their muscles had made their best jumps, then come forward with a heavy weight in each hand with his long muscular legs raise himself from the ground and light far beyond the most successful champion, indeed so far generally, that the man who would under take to over reach it, would become the laughing stock of the crowd. there was a goodeal of humor in his composition sometimes bordering on innocent mischief especially among his lady acquaintances, though only with those he was well acquainted. he would prove to them a complete hectorer. he was verry reserved toward the opposite sex. while I lived and boarded in the same place with him, do not recollect of his ever paying his addresses to any young lady though I Know he had great partialities for Miss Ann Rutlege, but at that time there was an insurmountable barrier in the way of his ambition. for her hand I have reasons to Know was promised to a man by the name of McNamar, or as he called himself at that time McNeil   this man left that part of the country and remained away for the space of a year or two   I think without any one Knowing where he was most of the inhabitants supposed he never would return and never did till after I left that part of the country which was in the Autumn of 1834. So little was Known of Mr Lincoln by the inhabitants of Sangamon at the time he first became a candidate for the legislature that when a few miles out of town in my rides would be asked who Abraham was they had never

heard of such a man. then when I would tell them who he was some few responded and siad I believe that is the man who went to Orleans on a hog boat for Of-
fett. I replyed in the affirmative, and would recommend him to their consideration
not as a tried politician but a young man of extraordinary talents for one of his
opportunities. Some years after I left that part of the state Mr Lincoln wrote me
that he should be a candidate for U.S. Senator and wished me to see the Hon.
Samuel Brown who at that time was the Representative elect for Knox County and
procure his pledge if possible as a supporter of Mr Lincoln in his efforts for a seat
in the Senate — that pledge I suceeded in obtaining, and which was honorably
redeemed by Mr Brown

After Mr Lincoln was elected President he appointed Mr Brown collector of
the port of Vancouver on the pacific coast. —

Mr Herndon

Sir, it would seem proper in view of the general disere expressed by the people
for all the incidents in the life of Mr Lincoln that can be obtained should be given
to the public at as early a period as practicable — It is a subject of congratulation
to me that the work has been undertaken by yourself. as you certainly have had a
better opportunity, than perhaps any living man to acquire all the statistics necessary to a full and complete history of the life of that great Statesman — What I
have written to you is from the best of my recollection, and if you can draw any
facts from the same which will aid you in your enterprise I shall be glad

Verry Respectfully Yours
Jason Duncan

P.S There may be some slieght errors in my statements but I think in the main are
correct

J D

LC: HW3864–67

429. Jacob Harding to WHH

Paris, Ills. Jan. 7th, 1867.

My dear Sir :

In reply to your letter of the 31st ult., I send you copies of two letters from
Mr. Lincoln to myself — one written in 1854, the other in 1855. I submit them
both, entire, to your discretion. These are all I have been able, so far, to find. I
remember having received an article intended as editorial for my paper, to which
you allude, but I have not been able to find it — nor can I now recollect even the
substance of it. I did not use it because I had long before made it a rule to publish
nothing, on editorial; not written by myself, or by my co-editor, when I had an
assistant. Had I thought it expedient to suspend the rule for any one, it would have
been done for Mr. Lincoln, for he stood higher in my estimation than any other

man in the State. Indeed, I was among the first, if not the very first in the editorial corps of Illinois, who proposed him for the presidency in 1860. Should I find that article you desire a copy of, I will cheerfully comply with your request.

Respectfully, yours &c.

J. Harding,

[Enclosure A]

430. AL to Jacob Harding[1]

Danville, May 25, 1855

Friend Harding:

I have been reading your paper three or four years, and have paid you nothing for it — Herewith is a receipt of Sylvanus Sandford for two claims amounting to ten dollars: — If he has collected the money, get it from him, and put it into your pocket, saying nothing further about it —

And now, if you please, I should be glad for you to put in your paper of this week, the names of *Stephen T. Logan,* as a candidate for Judge of the Supreme Court; and of *Stephen* A. *Corneau,* for Clerk of the Supreme Court —

Please also print, and distribute a suitable number of tickets[2] for them; and we, at Springfield will pay the reasonable charge —

As the sir-name of our candidate for clerk is rather an uncommon one I try to write it very plainly — "Corneau" the last letter being, not an "N" but an "U"

Very truly yours

(Signed) A., Lincoln —

[Enclosure B]

431. AL to Jacob Harding

The following letter, of which this is a copy, you will see, was confidential. But I can see no good reason for with holding it from your discretion at this time. Do as you think best with it.

Clinton, De Witt Co. Nov. 11, 1854

Harding Esq.

My dear Sir

I have a suspicion that a whig has been elected to the Legislature from Edgar? — If this is not so, why then *"nix cum arous"* but if it is so, then could you not make a mark with him for me, for U.S. Senator? — I really have some chance —

---

1. Headed: *Copy of a letter from A. Lincoln to J. Harding.*
2. Ballots provided by the political parties.

Please write me at Springfield, giving me the names, post offices, and political positions, of your representative and senator, whoever they may be —

Let this be confidential —

Yours truly

(Signed)   A., Lincoln

LC: HW2941 (Harding to WHH), HW1972 (enclosure A), HW1973 (enclosure B)

432. Elizabeth Abell to WHH

January the 13th 67

Dear Sir

Some time back I received a very friendly letter from you asking me a great many questions with regard to our lamented President Abraham Lincoln. I am truly ashamed to say to you that your letter is misplaced and I do not recollect the questions you ask me only one and that was what broke of the engagement between Mr Lincoln and my Sister so suddenly when Mr Lincoln was paying his respects to my sister he lived in old Salem but in the mean time he remooved to Springfield after he had been there some little time he wrote my Sister a letter[1] and in it he told her the subject they had been talking uppon   he wanted her to consider and reconsider it that he was poore   and there was a great deal of splashing and dashing in Buggys here and she would have to be a silent looker on and not a percipitant   but he said I rather have you then any woman living it stoped at that, what man on earth would have done such a thing but Abraham Lincoln he was two honest a man for this world he run his race and finished his work and the Lord remooved him to himself if this much will do you any good make use of it as you please in the mean time if I come across your letter I will write you again give my best respects to your most estimable wife with
respect

I remain your friend

Mrs Elizabeth Abell

LC: HW2944

433. Isaac Cogdal to WHH

January the 18d 1867

Sir I received your Lectur & letter for which I thank you for on account of absesce yours was not answered until now as to the enquarys of your letter I advise you as I would any and all Men to Speak and wright the truth the truth good or Bad let all Come in full then you are left with a Clear Conscience before God and

---

1. AL to Mary S. Owens, May 7, 1837, *CW* 1:78–79.

the World then let the Devil and his Angels leave which is the Coperheads and you have no favors to ask

yours with Respect

Isaac Cogdal

ISHL: Weik Papers, box 1

434. *John McNamar to WHH*

Menard County Ill Jan 20th 1867

My Dear Sir,

I receved your Letter Some time since   The intervention of the Holidays and other causes have prevented me from answering sooner, I now proceed categorically to answer, the Questions you propound

1st My Mother Died in the month of Oct 1845   I was confined by Sickness Some time before and after My Mothers Death and scarcely realized it at the time

2d That portion of My farm where I reside and Some other tracts were purchased Dec 9th 1831   I will here mention that in Looking for dates I made some unexpected discoveries one was a letter from Mr Lincoln Dated Vandalia Dec 24th 1836[1] informing me of a Design of Some of the Setters East of here to have the State road changed from its original route advising a prompt and vigorous remonstrance and Saying moreover that he would write me a long letter on political Subjects but finally refered me to the News papers &c   My Next Discovery was that Mr Lincoln & Chas Maltby were witnesses to my Deed   Maltby the Last I heard of him was Superintendent of Some of the Indian Agencies in California. an other Discovery was a small Braid or Tress of Ann Rutleges Hair much worn and aparently moth eaten

3d with regard to the motive for purchasing the farm   I intended it for a home for my Fathers family intending Myself to pursue the Mercantile Business and in which I reentered in company with Dr Allen in the fall of 36 but the crash of 37. induced us to close out with considerable Loss. consequently all the association which have rendered it dear to me have attached since I owned it the Rutleges were induced to occupy and take care of the place by my Friend and agent Dr Allen

with regard to your Last question concerning Mr Lincoln's Religious writings and the summary manner in which they were disposed of by Major Hill[2] I can only answer in scotish prose "I dinna Ken"   about the time I received your Letter I saw a Notice of your Lecture[3] in the Chicago Republican from a Boston Paper and correspondent, The Scotchman[4] is good so is the "Aristocracy" and Literary attainments of Miss Ann, undoubtedly She was about as Classic a Schollar as

---

1. *CW* 1:60.
2. Samuel Hill.
3. WHH's lecture on Ann Rutledge.
4. McNamar refers to the way he is denominated in the Ann Rutledge lecture.

Mr Lincoln at that time I think she attended some Literary institution at Jacksonville a short time or was intending so to do in company with her Brother[5] who adopted the profession in which you have become so eminently distinguished the sickness of Sauny[6] was well put only it was not himself, but his Fathers family. One of those Long interminable fevers that Sometimes occur in the East came into My Fathers family and prostrated Every member thereof except myself and continued for Months making victims of three of them one of whom was my Father — so — you see. "There is a Providence that shapes our ends and aims rough hew them how we will"   There are several other equally veracious Statements which I have not Space to Mention.

Turn we now to our old Friend who we left Parsing,[7] one more anecdote concerning him and we will take Leave of him and his sect with the passing remark that they believe in election but ignore Forordination   our Friends' Father in law an inteligent old gent from Gorgia he questioned John somewhat Doubtingly in regard to his call to Preach   John answered promptly that it was all right no mistake the old man said it may be so but I think it was some other John

There were not many of the "Simon Pure" Presbyterians here my Friend Dr Allen was the respresentative man here of that persuasion, he introduced Sunday Schools and Temperence Societies at which our baptist bretheren turned-up their Pious Noses in disdain our old Friend Minter Graham became a member of the Temperance Society and he being a member, of the Baptist church they turned him out, a short time after Mentor got "Tight" and the Temperence Society expelled him then the Baptist brethren took him in again[8] however they expelled members some times for other causes than Temperance as an old gentleman informed me once that they turned him out because he would not own to a Lie not for lying but because he would not own up

You will perceive by the date that I prepared a paper some time ago in answer to your inquiries, but intending to add some thing more. I have neglected Sending it untill it is undoubtedly to Late have any significance if it ever had any it is with a great deal of reluctance that attempt writing at all on any subject   and more over I have been unwell since I commencd this communication you are[9] that I have not the facilities of a Lawyers office for writing that I seldom Leave home and often Lack the material for writing

You will see by some comments that I have a prety good Idea of your celebated Lecture, I received a Letter from my Son in California a Short time ago who verey inocently informed me that the scotchman is Identified very readily by several of the old acquainance of Mr Lincoln myself who reside there

he moreover thinks you Life of Mr Lincoln will sell rapidly in that region and wishes an agency for the sale of your Book

---

5. David Rutledge.

6. Apparently another reference to himself, the "Scotchman" of Herndon's lecture.

7. See his previous letter, §310.

8. Some predestinarian Baptists disapproved of temperance societies, whose activities were considered efforts to alter matters predestined by God.

9. Apparently a word was omitted.

You will confer a favour upon me by giving him as extencive an agency as your business arrangements will permit

his address is John B Mc Namar

Petaluma Sonoma County Cal

send me a copy of your Lecture by all means

Yours Truly

John Mc Namar

LC: HW2955–57

435. James Smith to WHH[1]

Dundee 24th Jany 1867

Sir.

Your letter of the 20th December was duly received. In it you ask me to answer several questions in relation to the late illustrious President, Abraham Lincoln. With regard to your second question, I beg leave to say, it is a very easy matter to prove that while I was Pastor of the 1st Presbyterian Church of Springfield, Mr. Lincoln did avow his belief in the Divine Authority and Inspiration the Scriptures; and I hold that it is a matter of the last importance, not only to the present, but to all future generations of the great Republic, and to all advocates of civil and religious liberty through out the world, that this avowal on his part and the circumstances attending it, together with other very interesting incidents, illustrative of the excellence of his character in my possession should be made Known to the public.

I am constrained however most respectfully to decline choosing you as the medium through which any such communications shall be made by me. My reasons are as follows: —

Early in December last an article went the round of the Papers in this Country purporting to be part of a lecture delivered by you on Mr. Lincoln and his past history which I read with feelings of mingled indignation and Sorrow, because coming as it did from his intimate friend and law partner, it was calculated to do the character of that great and good man an incalculable injury, deeply to wound the feelings of his heart broken widow and her orphan boys, and to place that whole family both the dead and living, in their family relations, in a most unenviable light before the public.

In the article referred to speaking of the death and grave of Miss Ann Ratledge   you represent Mr. Lincoln as having said "that his heart Sad and broken was buried there." You give it as your opinion "that he never addressed another Woman Yours affectionately". That he generally and Characteristically abstained from the use of the word love. That he never ended his letters "Yours affectionately" but signed them "Your friend Abraham Lincoln"

---

1. WHH note at the top of the page: *Foolish This man left a bad Character here. Herndon.* Marginal note: *Knows nothing of Lincoln. Smith gave Lincoln a book of his. Lincoln never condescended to write his name in it.*

Now Sir I maintain that every reflecting person who believes your Statements to be true is bound to reply to your third question that Abraham Lincoln was not an honest man; for he assiduously and perseveringly sued for the hand, the heart the love, and the devotion for life of a young lady, who was much admired for her intelligence, her fine conversational powers and capability of making herself agreable in any circle, and who could if so disposed have wedded with the first of the land. This he did when according to you, all he had to give in return was a dead heart buried in the grave of another woman, and he was in such a Mental Condition that he had to abstain from the use of the Word love. Therefore when that young lady accepted his suit and promised to become his wife, he could not go even so far as to Say "I am Yours affectionately"   Nay more when Abraham Lincoln led his Bride to the hymeneal Altar, immediately before that bond was tied which death alone can dissolve, he most Solemnly promised before God and man to be to that lady a faithful, loving and affectionate husband, until parted by death, when according to you he had neither love nor affection to bestow. Therefore your Statements being true Abraham Lincoln was worse than a dishonest man.

He was often absent from his family and no doubt wrote his wife many letters. According to you he never ended any of these letters "Yours affectionately" but always "Your friend" Abraham Lincoln"   An insult which every lady of any feeling and Spirit would resent, and I must Say, your Statements being true, to me it is strange, nay passing Strange! that the lady to whom these letters were addressed who you know as well as I do possesses exquisite Sensibility, Spirit, and high sense of honor not only did not resent the first insult of that Sort but patiently and Silently submitted to the repitition of it from month to month, and from year to year. And what a cold hearted man must he have been who for so many years thus treated the wife of his bosom whom he had Solemnly promised to love and Cherish.

Your statements also contain a most cruel and I fear malignant attack upon his heart stricken Widow, as one for whom her husband entertained no love, no affection.

Oh! Sir was it not enough that she should be overwhelmed and stricken to the earth by the dreadful by the dreadful blow which had fallen upon her, in the Cruel death of her husband, but you must Come on the Scene and mingle your poisoned chalice into that cup of woe which she must drink even to the dregs —

This is not all, but the necessary tendency of your Statements is to put a public brand upon the boys of that great and good man to whom you are under so many and great obligations, as the sons of a man who never loved their mother.

Such is the Character of the martyred president which must necessarily be drawn from the Statements made Concerning him and given to the public by his intimate friend and law partner for twenty years.

A law office is by no means the best field for judging the Characters of each other by those who are brought in Contact there. No Sir. It is in the family Circle the man exhibits himself as he really is. His bearing towards his Wife — his treatment of his Children and dependents his free and easy conversations with those who are admitted into that Circle. These are to be found the best tests by which a man's Character and feelings are to be determined, and no one enjoys better opportunities, to be enabled to put a proper estimate upon the members of it, than the pastor who is respected and esteemed by them: who has buried their dead and baptised their living: who in seasons of sorrows has administered to them, those Consolations which the Gospel of the Son of God can alone Communicate: Who is viewed by Certain of them as the honored instrument in bringing them from darkness to light, from the degredation of Sin and misery to faith in Jesus and the hope of Glory : who by them is held to have been "true to them ever in joy and sorrow," joying in their joy and Sorrowing in their Sorrow; and as a Consequence is admitted to their full Confidence, and even their Secular affairs, when thought necessary is asked for his advice and counsel. This is the man who provided he possesses understanding and judgement above all others is prepared to put a true estimate upon the Characters of each of the members of such a family.

All the surviving members of it, I am assured will testify that such was the position occupied by your humble Servant in the family of that truly great and good man Abraham Lincoln. To say nothing of his Calls upon myself and our pleasant Conversations in drives over the prairies. During seven years when he and myself were at home, scarcely two weeks ever passed during which I did not spend a pleasant evening in the midst of that family Circle and my intercourse with himself there convinced me that Abraham Lincoln was not only an honest but preeminently and upright man ever ready so far as in his power to render unto all their just dues, and that he was utterly incapable of witholding from the Bride he led to the Altar that which was her due, by giving her a heart dead and buried in the grave of Another; but that in the deep and honest sincerity of his Soul, he gave her a heart overflowing with love and affection; and my intercourse with him and his famly left the abiding impression upon my mind by his demeanour towards her, that he was to the Wife of his bosom a most faithful, loving and Affectionate husband who would on no occasion have insulted her by ending a letter with "Your friend Abraham Lincoln." I do most Solemnly testify that during my oft repeated Visits, I never saw a frown upon his brow or heard him utter a harsh or unkind word to his Lady or any of her Children, but seemed overflowing with geniality, good humour and Kindness, Clear proofs of his love and Affection

This then for the present is the Vindication of the Character of the Martyred president, from the foul aspersions, You Sir have Cast upon it, and by the person whose high honor it was to place before Mr. Lincoln arguments designed to prove the Divine authority of the Scriptures accompanied by the arguments of Infidel objectors in their own language. To the arguments on both sides Mr. Lincoln gave a most patient, impartial and Searching investigation. To use his own language "he examined the Arguments as a lawyer who is anxious to reach the truth investigates testimony." The result was the announcement by himself that the argument in favor of the Divine Authority and inspiration of the Scripture was unanswerable.

I Could say much on this Subject but as you are the person addressed for the present I decline. This much however: — the preparation of that work Cost me long and arduous mental labor, and if No other effect was ever produced by it, than the influence it exerted upon the mind of that man whose name thrills the heart of every patriotic American, I thank God that I was induced to undertake the work. Immediately after the above avowal Mr. Lincoln placed himself and family under my pastoral Care, and when at home he was a regular attendant upon my ministry. I was always treated by him with high Consideration, and he Conferred upon me and mine, disinterested acts of Kindness. To say nothing of higher motives, I would feel I was making a most unworthy return for his many Kindnesses did I remain silent on the present occasion. More especially as the statements already referred to, made by you in your Ann Ratledge romance followed by the letter from yourself — to which this is in reply — not only opened the way before me; but in my judgement rendered it my imperative duty to speak out as I have done, and thus to rebuke the false friend, who when their natural head and protector Could no longer defend them has entered into the sacred sanctuary of Mrs. Lincoln's family has dragged its sorrow stricken members from before its altar and held them up to the public gaze, as the Wife and Children of one who had No heart, no love, no affection to bestow upon them.

The assassin Booth by his diabolical act unwittingly sent the illustrious martyr to glory, honor and immortality, but his false friend has attempted to send him down to posterity with infamy branded on his forehead, as a man who notwithstanding all he did and all he suffered for his Country's good was destitute of those feelings and affections, without which there can be no real excellency of Character.

Sir

I am

With due respect

Your most obeat. Servant

Jas. Smith

LC: HW2966–77

436. John S. Bliss to WHH

West Milton Jan. 29*th* 1867

Yours was re*c* in due time — and herewith I send you brief notes relative to conversation with Abraham Lincoln in Springfield *July 18th 1860* — at his house — and at the State House — I hope you will find the whole, or any part of the M.S.S. of use to you, in your undertaking —

If it is suitable for your use as a letter publish it — or such part as you need

I hope you will let me know just what you think of the communication, and what you think you can do with it,

Also when will your book be issued Please let me hear from you When you rec this.

Certainly Yours

J. S. Bliss

Abraham Lincoln

One beautiful July morning eighteen hundred and Sixty — I awoke in the city of Springfield Illinois.

The sun arose clear and bright, and appeared to radiate peace, and tranquility, as his long Slanting beams Sped from the far east to the Western prairies

Beautiful indeed was this auspicious morning.

The rumbling of the wheels, and the clatter of hoofs on the pavements bespoke life and gladness, at the Capital of Illinois

After the luminary had gained so higher altitude, a favorable opportunity offered itself for a morning walk, and it was but a brief time before I presented myself to the door of our nominee, for the highest office in the gift of a great nation.

I say not this in *egotism,* or what may follow.

I was ushered into the sitting room — by the young man who answered the bell, and from that place, I Sent my *verbal card* to Mr Lincoln — I was prepared with no letter of introduction — but as unarmed as I was, I waited for Mr. Lincoln

I was sitting opposite the door and partly in sight of the Stairs.

After a short time, Mr L. came tripping down the Stairs, as lively as a young man of sixteen years of age — sliding his right hand on the bannister — He approached me and after shaking hands — we were soon immersed in a lively conversation on various topics.

As I was from near Madison Wisconsin, he was anxious *too,* and did inquire, as to the resources, and developments, to which I replied, to the best of my ability.

The Black Hawk War was talked of freely, for Mr Lincoln was Capt. at that eventful period and camped on the Same ground — of which we were then Speaking, and which had been overturned by the husbandman since that time —

He spoke of the press in Wisconsin, and gave readily the course they had pursued — (especially Some of the Milwaukee papers) as readily as a resident of that City.

A connected history of the Springfield press was also given, and when I asked how the matter was politically at that particular time, he replied, that, "a few weeks ago, the chances were somewhat against us, but at present is very evenly balanced"

He cared not how high the great democratic flagstaff was that floated over the Capital City, and appeared to frown down upon his head — He did not use such words however.

While sitting there, the Chimney Swallows came down behind the fire boards, and absolutely twittered, fluttered and Sung as to nearly drown our voices.

I remarked that the birds rarely decend so low, but Mr. L. replied, "that they usually came down once a day."

I decided it to be a Seranade to Mr. Lincoln and so it passed,

In answer to our interogative relatinng to the population of Springfield Mr. Lincoln Said —

"With those who want a *large city,* there are Sixteen and Seventeen thousand, but *I* suppose there is thirteen or fourteen thousand inhabitants".

This showed the character of the man — that he was emphatically *"honest Abe"*

On a section of the wall of his parlor, hung a picture of himself and Mr Hamlin; and he said he had not seen Mr Hamlin yet.

Whereupon, I took the liberty to remark, that they would meet in the City of Washington ere long to which he smiled in his then usual good natured Style

We stepped to the opposite side of the room, where was one of the best executed pictures of Mr Lincoln I had ever Seen and it was *this one,* I was paying rather more than ordinary attention.

He was immediately at my left, and pointing to it said — "T*ha*t picture, gives a very fair representation of my homely face"

This was in a *Slow plain* Style of Speech — I thought that Saying, under the circumstances was worth a trip to Springfield hence I called the debt cancelled.

A *what not* in the corner of the room was laden with various kinds of shells, I took one in my hand and said,

"*This* I suppose, is called a *Trocus* by the Geologist or Naturalist"

Mr Lincoln replied, "I do not Know for I never Studied it"

The time was nearing for my departure from the house of this good man and I manifested it — but Mr Lincoln said,

"You cannot get out of this town before befor a quarter past eleven" and solicited a longer Stay — but as my mission was nearly fulfilled — and being Satisfied with my visit — and putting it down as one of *the,* days of my life I decided to go —

"Well" said Mr Lincoln, suppose you come over to the State House before you go to Chicago".

After a moment of mental deliberation I promised to do so, and departed. Mr L. following without his hat — continuing conversation — shook hands across the gate — and Saying *"Now come over"*

I wended my way to my hotel, and after a brief period — was in his office at the State House, and resuming conversation, he said

"If the man comes with the key, before you go, I want to give you a book"

I certainly hoped the man *would* come with the key —

Some conversation had taken place at the house on which his book treated — but I had forgotten this — and soon Mr L. absented himself for perhaps *two* minutes and returned with a copy of the debates between him and Stephen A. Douglas[1] — placed it upon his knee — as he sat back on *two* legs of his chair, and wrote on the fly leaf — *"J. S. Bliss from A. Lincoln"*

This is written with a pencil, and is a *genuine* autograph,

Besides this, he marked a couple of paragraphs near the middle of the book,

This he presented me, which I still retain, and I would not part with it for all the Southern Gold, paid for assassinating him.

While Sitting in his office little *Willie* came in and said —

---

1. *Political Debates between Hon. Abraham Lincoln and Hon. Stephen A. Douglas, in the Celebrated Campaign of 1858, in Illinois* . . . (Columbus, 1860).

"Father I want twenty five cents"

"My son" said Mr Lincoln "What do you want of twenty five cents"?

"I *want* it *to buy candy with*"   "My son, I Shall not give you *twenty five* cents, but will give you *five* cents", at the Same time putting his thumb and finger into his vest pocket, taking therefrom five cents in *silver,* and placed it upon the desk before the boy —

But this did not reach *Willies'* expectations, and he Scorned the pile, by turning away — and clambering down Stairs — through the halls of the Capitol, leaving behind him his five cents, and a reverberation of Sound.

Mr L. turned to me and Said —

"He will be back after that in a few moments"

"*Why do you think* so" said I.

"Because, as soon as he finds I will give him no more he will come and get it."

After the matter had been nearly forgotten — and conversation on different subjects indulged in — *Willie* came cautiously behind my chair and that of his father — picked up the *Specie* and went away without saying a word,

I have mentioned these plain and simple facts, and incidents to add, if possible to the characteristic of this plain hearted — honest — unassuming man. a true representative man of the West. — his equal *rarely* if *ever* to be found, and whose name will live and be remembered with the name of Washington.

I departed from him for the train, and time will never be able to efface, the recollections of that warm grasp and also the utterance of the word *"Good By"*

I saw no more of Abraham Lincoln, until his lifeless corpse was brought to Chicago enroute to Oak Ridge.

Indeed, a *great* man had fallen — by the hand of a vile assassin, and that was a time when I could cry — "Vengence is mine"

This was a time when the sun had Set — in Sorrow to this afflicted country — When a dark pall fell heavily over the entire American nation — and the Nations of the World, when from every heart heaved an unfathomable Sigh which reaches to Heaven today.

Fraternally Yours

J. S. Bliss

LC: HW2978–90

437. George M. Harrison to WHH

Richland Jan'y 29th 1867 —

Mr. Herndon:

I will proceed to answer *some* of your questions, as well as I can. I would answer *all* if I could. Foot-racing when cool, and bathing swimming &c when warm, were favorite amusements or exercises. Our red boys and white, would frequently race against each other; and sometimes wrestle. In a short race, the white boys generally beat; but a very long race generally, if not always, resulted in favor of the

Indians: and so of wrestling, the whites could throw them, but in a very long continued effort the Indians were apt to be victors. Very few men in the army could
successfully compete with Mr Lincoln, either in wrestling or swimming; he well
understood both arts. But his good humor & Quaint sayings, always preserved
pleasant feeling Chess, Checkers, & Cards, were among the favorite plays or amusements, of both Indians and whites. But smoking is the great pleasure of the Indian. As to songs, I have nothing. Our foe was so insignificant as not to excite the
muse. Our food consisted wholy of raw material. Government furnished the army
four raw articles, from which we prepared our diet: *bacon hams* and *shoulders,* pick-
led *pork* — clear sides,[1] — *flour,* and beef *cattle* — So you see, we were expected
to live on bread & Meat alone. When we had coffee & sugar, we bought them;
and *[page torn]* chance for this, was not often. The bacon the pork, and the flour,
were of the very best quality; and the cattle were tolerably good. We drew pork
chiefly, when near the steamboats — at Fort Wilbourn and at Dixon's Ferry, — at
other times always bacon. of these, we always had plenty, unless failing to carry
with us enough: which happened two or three times. Once in particular, at an old
evacuated Winnebago town, called Turtle Village,[2] after stretching our rations
nearly four days, one of our mess, — an old acquaintance of Lincoln, G. B. Fanchier — shot a dove, and having a gill of flour left, we made a gallon and a half of
delicious soup, in an old tin bucket that had been lost by indians; this soup we
divided among several messes that were hungrier than we were, and our own mess,
by pouring in each man's cup a portion of the esculent. Once more, at another
time in the extreme northern part of Illinois, We had been very hungry for two
days, but suddenly came upon a new cabin — at the edge of a prairie — that the
pioneer sovereign squ[att]er family had vacated and skedadled for fear they would
lose their scalps, and there were plenty of chickens about said cabin, much hungrier than we were ourselves if poverty is to test the matter, and the boys heard a
voice saying "slay and eat" so they went to shooting, clubbing, & running them
as long as any could be found. Whilst the killing was going on, I climed to the
ridge pole of the smokehouse to distinctly see, what I saw obscurely from the
ground, and beheld the cleanest sweetest jole[3] of all I ever saw — alone — half
hid by boards and ridge pole, stuck up no doubt for future use. By this time many
of the chickens were broiling, for want of grease or gravy to fry them, among the
rest were a rooster & a hen belonging to our mess, and the jole belonged to us by
the right of discovery & possession, so after broiling the fowels some time, while
the bacon was frying, some interested one proposed to give the chickens all the
benefit of the grease, by completing the process by frying; the proposition was
adopted, and they were soon fried. We began to eat the tough dry chickens and
the bacon: and Mr Lincoln came to the repast when we were about finishing, with
the querries "eating chicken boys?" "not much sir." — We had ope[ned] princi-

1. Clear sides of pork do not include ribs.
2. Site of Beloit, Wisconsin.
3. Jowl, in this case probably a cured hog jowl.

pally upon the jole for it was sweet an[d] rich indeed — "They are much like eating saddle bags, but I think the stomach can accomplish much to day, but what have you got there with the skeletons, George,?" "We did have a sweet jole of a hog sir, but you are nearly too late for your share, at the same time making room for him to approach the elm *bark* dish. He ate bacon fat, a moment; then commenced dividing by mouthful to the boys who came to see what "Abe" was at, and saying to them funny remarks suited to the time and the jole. at the time of eating, as w[ell] as at other times, he was occasionally with his m[en] — but he always slept at home. He was acquainted with nearly every body, and he had determined as he told me, to become a candidate for the next legislature. The mess unanimously pitched upon him as our water bearer and he accepted the office; so immediately after pitching tent, he took the bucket and started for water. This always, by special agreement, — exculpated him from the onerous duties of getting fuel, cooking &c. Indeed he was the best water man in camp, for he always succeeded quickly no matter how difficult the task from the greatness of the crowd and scarcity of water, our Lincoln was so well known, so facetious, and so strong. Please excuse the digression. The flour and the meat furnished were always of so good a quality that without vegatables condiments &c. except common salt, which was bountifully furnished, we could easily prepare a palatable diet for any class of woodsman. Our only variety was found in the different modes of cooking. The meat, we could boil, — when we could get a pot, — broil, roast, or fry: the latter was generally practiced, in order to save all the grease for the bread; to shorten and to fry. The bread we could bake, or fry; the latter mode was generally practiced, for it was the less trouble, and the less time of the two modes: the former mode we usually practiced by wrapping the stiff shortened dough in a spiral manner around our ramrods, then sticking the rods in the ground before the fire, where it would nicely bake into a most esculent bread; the dough was coiled into a long snake like shape, the one end stuck upon the top of the rod, to keep it from slipping down on the ground, and then wraped closely and firmly roud and round and round and round the rod, then stuck before the fire. The beef cattle were used almost exclusively by the Indian part of our army. I think they got nothing to eat but fresh beef, that is beef cattle, which they killed when convenient, hung the quarters on trees and cut off hunks for boiling or roasting as they wanted: in this fix the quarters would sometimes remain for several days, in the months of June & July, & exposed to the action of sun and flies. Some of the Indians were very fond of bread, for they would stroll around camp and steal, beg, or buy every, morsel that they could get. The main object with them in becoming part of the army probably was to get plenty of beef, but the ostensible object was revenge on their enemies — the Sacs and Foxes. Having boiled a piece of beef, one of them would take the whole, and immediately the others would form a circle around him, when he would cut off each ones piece and toss it to him or on the ground by him, like feeding dogs. Our utensils for cooking &c. consisted of a frying pan with a short handle, a tin water bucket — furnished by Government — and pocket knives or bowie knives, hatchets, tin cups, a coffee pot & elm bark for dishes. kneading tray

— furnished by our selves — Our coffee we would parch in the frying pan, grind in a tin cup by placing the cup on the solid ground or a log and punching it with the end of a hatchet handle until it would do to boil in the coffee pot, and cool in our tin cups: and if a cup or cups should be pilfered or lost, we had to enter into partnership until another was procured. The noise throughout camp, early of a morning, made by this mode of grinding coffee, was striking in a high degree: the chuck, chuck, chuck, chuck; would make one think of a thousand wood chucks sitting all a round, on fences, on logs, on stumps, and on chunks, each one exerting himself to the utmost.

As to wet days, I have little to say, as there was but one rain during the whole time that I was out from home in the army; at that time there was also quite a storm of wind, and all of us *passed* the *time* trying to hold up the tents and keep off as much rain as posible; but in spite of our efforts we got a thorough drenching: this was at sycamore creek some 20 or 30 miles above Dicksons ferry; the very spot where stillman was encamped when the Indians attacked him and killed so many of his men, well known as Stillman's defeat. At this time our company was alone and overstayed the time, and our rations failed to hold out, and we hastened back to Dixon's[4] in a hurry: when we got there we found prepared for us, an abundant supply of boiled bacon and light bread of an excellent quality, cooked in vessels borrowed from Mr. Dixon, by the soldiers — Mrs Dixon also gave us Ten gallons of sweet fresh milk and several pounds of butter, with which to finish the repast. Several of our men ate so much, and ate so fast, no wonder they got sick At last — Were very near dying of colic. This is the way we passed the da[ys] We passed our evenings by jumping, playing checkers, chess, swimming our horses, which was a favorite sport when near Rock-river, to give them exercise and cool them, and telling tales, stories &c. &c.

Yours truly
Geo. M. Harrison

LC: HW2991–94

438. Elizabeth Abell to WHH

February the 15th 67

Dear Sir

as I told you in my short epistle I wrote you some time back if I come across your letter I would write you again and answer all your questions that I am capable of doing the first question what month and year did I first know Lincoln in October 1833 in my little log Cabbin on the hill South of Petersburg 2d was he a sad man I never considered him so he was always social and lively and had great aspirations for his friends always decided and good natured 3d the Courtship between him and Miss Rutledge I can say but little this much I do know he was stay-

---

4. Dixon's Ferry, a supply point on the Rock River during the Black Hawk War.

ing with us at the time of her death it was a great shock to him and I never seen a
man mourn for a companion more than he did for her he made a remark one day
when it was raining that he could not bare the idea of its raining on her Grave that
was the time the community said he was crazy he was not crazy but he was very
disponding a long time I Think that was in the year 34 or 35   Mc Namars &
Hills[1] I know nothing about. I lived on the hill on the bluff in 1836 & 37, in the
log Cabin. as for his Christian habits he was truly a Christian not in the common
term of Christianity now of days long face on Sunday and grind the poor on
Monday but he was always doing good the same to day and to morrow I never
heard him use a profain word drink a drop of spirits or chew tobacco in my life
and he was neither eccentric or visionary, he was very sensitive and backward nothing rash about him and certainly he was the best natured man I ever got acquainted with he stayed at our house on the bluff when he was surveying all those Hills
between us and Petersburg our oldest boy carryed the Chain for him when Lincoln would come in at night all ragged and scratch up with the Bryers he would
laugh over it and say that was a poore mans lot I told him to get me a Buck skin
and I would fix him so the Bryers would not scratch him he done so and I Foxd,
his pants for him, if I could see you I could tell you a great many things I can talk
better than I can write, your hand is a very difficult place for me to read all and
that I could make out I have answered to the best of my knowledge it is very poorely
done and I guess you will throw it by with a great many other letters,

your Friend
Mrs E Abell

LC: HW2999–3000

439. John Duncan to WHH

Larue County 'Ky Feb 21st 1867

My Dear Sir

I received yours of Nov 30th and intended to answer in a few days, but was
taken Sick and have been confined every since. I am now only able able to Set up
and write — The inquires you make of me respecting Mr "Lincon"   I am only
able to answer one of these. that is as to his hunting he was very determined in
pursuit of game as an instant him and my Self on one occasion ran a Groun hog
in a hole in the rocks — we worked Some 4 or 5 hours in trying to git him out —
I gave it out Lincoln then went off about a quarter of a mile to a black Smith Shop
and got the black Smith to make an iron hook and fasten it on a pole the black
Smith went with young Abe and hooked the Groun hog out of the rocks

I never went to School with Mr Lincoln   I was well acquainted with the family
when they lived in this Country — I am now preaching to Little Mount Church
the Church that Mr Linolns Farther Mother and Gran Mother belong to when

---

1. Probably refers to John McNamar and Samuel Hill, both suitors for the hand of Ann Rutledge.

they lived in this Country — the Church was then a Seperate Baptist Church it has Since changed to a United Baptist   "Old Abe" Grand mother and a little brother died and was buried at what is called Redmans Grave Yard on the top of Muldroghs hill in this County — my impression is that old Abs Sister Sally left this Country with the balance of the family these things you proble Know better than I can tell you

Mrs Silvester West William Redman and B. A. Galaher could let you know more about your inquires than I

Your Friend
John Duncan

NB I hope my excuse for not writing will be Satisfactory — I live about 14 miles from West Redman and Galaher

LC: HW3003

440. Robert B. Rutledge to WHH

Oskaloosa March 6th 1867

My dear Friend

pleas find enclosed, an artacle cut from Supplement St Louis Democrat of 28th Ult. from the pen of Some Scribling correspondent for N.Y. Tribune, which does great injustice to the memory of Ann Rutledge as well as Mr Lincoln, he treats the subject with that reckless disregard of truth.[1] I feel it due you to call your attention to it, believing however that he has got his impressions from a casual conversation inflicted upon you,

I am very truly your Friend
R. B. Rutledge

[Enclosure]

441. Newspaper Clipping

Lincoln's Early Love.

A Springfield, Illinois, correspondent of the New York Tribune, after some conversation with Mr. Herndon, writes:

The tenderness of his (Lincoln's) nature was not always manifest, yet he had his romance in early manhood, and as of this Mr. Herndon had spoken in public, I asked particularly about it.

At Sangamon, Illinois, a pretty and high spirited girl, without fortune, made havoc in many hearts, and Mr. Lincoln constituted one of three earnest suitors who wanted her in marriage. She preferred the addresses of a young merchant of the

---

1. George Alfred Townsend, who wrote under the pseudonym "Gath," was the *Scribling correspondent for N.Y. Tribune*. The original article appeared in the *Tribune* on February 15, 1867.

town, and gave the other two their conge.[1] Her affianced soon afterward went East to buy goods, but as he returned was taken with brain fever in some wayside town, and lay raving for three months unknown by name or residence to his entertainers. A rumor started that he had run away to avoid marrying his lady, and waiting some time in vain to hear from him, she received anew the attentions of Mr. Lincoln. About the time when they passed from courtesy to tenderness, and marriage between them was more than hinted at, the sick man returned like a ghost, gauged the condition of affairs, and upbraided the lady with fickleness. She had a delicate sense of honor, and felt keenly the shame of having seemed to trifle with two gentlemen at once; this preyed upon her mind till her body, not very strong, suffered by sympathy, and Mr. Herndon has oral and written testimony that the girl died out of regret at the equivocal position she had unwittingly assumed. The names of all the parties he has given me, but I do not care to print them.

On the dead woman's grave Mr. Lincoln promised himself never to marry. This vow he kept very long. His marriage was in every respect advantageous to him. It whetted his ambition, did not nurse too much a penchant for home indolence that he had, and taught him particularly that there was something called society, which observed one's boots as well as his principles. He was always a loyal and reverent husband, a gentle but not positive father, and his wife saw the presidency for him before the thought of it troubled him.

LC: HW3004 (letter), HW3004A (clipping)

442. John W. Lamar to WHH

Buffaloville Indiana May the 18/67[1]

Der Sir

After My Respects I will Informe you that your letter of Oct 28th/66 Came to hand the other Day the Reason of the Delay of the Letter is that it was sent to the Rong post office you will Derect your letters if you wish to me as heded on this letter Buffaloville

Well Sir you make Some Inquiry about the life of Mr Lincoln   I Do not no whither it is worth while to Rite as I supose you have got all the Information a bout the good man that I Can giv you long before this as I under stand you have ben in this part of the Contary and Visited Lincolns old nabors and I See your Corspondence with Mrs Crawford who has givven you more Information than I Can as She is older and abe worked for them you asked me how long I new abe before he left Indiana well I was about 10 yers old when Lincoln left her but I was but I was Boned and Rased in the Same Naborhood wher Lincoln lived in Indiana So you Can tel I Can Recolect abe a bout as far Back as aney boddy Else I

---

1. That is, dismissed them.

---

1. Dated in the margin.

Remember Verry Destinctley the first Time that I Remember Seeinge Lincoln I
was a Small bowey and went with my father to Some Kind of a lection and one of
our neer nabors by the name of James Larkins was thar and Larkins was a grate
hand to Brag on his horse and he Steped up before abe in the Croud and Comenced
talking to abe and Comenced Braging on his horse and Sed abe I have got the best
horse in the County hare you yes I Run him five miles this morning in 4 minets
and he never fetched a long breth I persume Sir he fetched a good maney Short
ones Sed abe[2]   Larkins Lerned to think that abe Did not appesiate his talk Verry
well and was a bout to go a bord of abe, Lincoln Looked as if he Did not Cear and
told Some Kind of a Joke that fit Larkinses Case and put the Croud in a uproar of
Laftar and Larkins Dride up from that time tel this I wold of new him if he was
liveing I have herd him Speake Some he lived in Springfield Ill   he looked Some
what Diferent in the way of Dress to what he Did when he left her but aney person that Ever was a quanted with him one wold Know him a gain thar was one
thing about the man that aney Boddy Cold See and that is he was Determied to
make Som thing of him Self tho pore and hard to liv Thar is one thing that I will
Speak of Rite her the old man Lincoln had a old Grey horse and he was not able
to plow as mutch as abe was and abe while the horse Rested had his paper pen
and ink out in the field and made use of the time while the horse Rested he all
ways put in the time to a good advantage I have a peace of furniture in My house
that abe and his father Sawed out by hand with a whip Saw the house Caut fire
and Burned one Corner off I have though Several times that I wold Send it out to
Springfield aney infermation I Can giv you if not to late I will be happey to Do
So free of Cost I will Send your Stampe back as I think it is my Duty to do So
yours Truley
John. W. Lamar[3]

LC: HW3008–9

443. Robert T. Lincoln to WHH

Chicago, May 24 1867

My dear Mr Herndon:

I am very much obliged to you for letting me know about the books — I certainly would like to have a chance for some of them at least, for I do not own a
single law book that ever belonged to my father. — I am so pressed by my business just now that I cannot go to Springfield as I would like to do about the matter and I would consider it a favor if you would have some one make a list of the
books & prices which you think right & send it to me —
Very truly yours
Robert T. Lincoln

LC: HW3010

2. Cf. §62.
3. Marginal note: *If I Can Do you any good I will be happy to Do so.*

444. Henry Wilson to WHH

Natick, Mass. May, 30th, 1867.

My Dear Sir,

In looking over my papers, I find a letter of yours of the 20th of August last requesting me to give you my ideas of Mr Lincoln's character as a man and a public officer. With this letter, I find another letter of Yours dated December 21st 1860 in answer to a letter of mine, asking you to give me your opinion of the President just elected. In this letter to me you say of Mr Lincoln, what more than four years of observation confirmed. After stating that you had been his Law partner for sixteen years, and his most intimate and bosom friend all that time you say, — "I know him better than he does himself. I know this seems a 'Lie', but I will risk the assertion. Mr Lincoln is a man of *heart* — aye as gentle as a woman's and as tender, — but he has a will as strong as iron. He therefore loves all mankind — hates Slavery — every form of Despotism. Put these together — Love for the Slave and a determination — a *will* that justice, strong and unyielding, shall be done, where he has got a right to act; and you can form your own conclusion. Lincoln will fail *here* — namely, if a question of political economy — if any question comes up, which is doubtful — questionable — which no man can demonstrate, then his friends can rule him; — but when on justice — right — Liberty the government and Constitution — Union — humanity, *then you may all stand aside;* he will rule them and no man can move him — no set of men can. There is no *fail here.* This is Lincoln, and you mark what I say. You and I must keep the people right: God will keep Lincoln right. Dont you fear, Mr Wilson. I have conversations with him but am not authorized to speak."

These words of yours made a deep impression upon my mind, and I came to Love and trust him even before I saw him. After an acquaintance of more than four years, I found that your idea of him was in all respects correct — that he was the Loving, tender, firm and just man you represented him to be, while upon some questions in which moral eliments did not so clearly enter he was perhaps, too easily influenced by others. As Chairman of the Military Committee, I had nearly fifteen thousand nominations of his to act upon, and was often consulted by him in regard to nominations, and, also, the Legislation for the army and I had the best opportunity to see him under all circumstances. I saw him often under the most trying circumstances at the War Department by day, and by night too. and I had the best possible opportunities to study and judge him, and I can truly say that your discription of this Loving, tender, true, Just man was a correct one.

Mr Lincoln was a genuine Democrat in feeling, sentiment and action. How patiently and considerately he listened, amid the terrible pressures of public affairs, to the people that thronged his Anti Room   I remember calling upon him one day during the war on pressing business. The Anti Room was crouded with men and women seeking admission. He seemed oppressed, care-worn, ueasy. I said to him, — "Mr President, you are too exhausted to see this throng waiting to see you; you will wear yourself out, and you ought not to see these people to-day". He replied with one of those smiles in which sadness seemed to mingle — "they dont want much and they dont get but Little, and I must see them."

During the war his heart was oppressed and his life burdened with the conflict between the tenderness of his nature and what seemed to be the imperitive demands of duty. In the darkest hours of the conflict disertions were frequent, and army officers urgently pressed the execution of the sentences of the Law, but it was with the greatest effort he would bring himself to consent to the execution of the judgements of the Military tribunals. I remember talking early one Sabbath morning with a wounded Irish officer who came to Washington to say that a soldier who had been sentenced to be shot in a day or two for desertion had fought bravely by his side in battle. I told him that we had come to ask him to pardon the poor soldier. After a few moments reflection he said, "My officers tell me the good of the service demands the enforcement of the Law, but it makes my heart ache to have the poor boys shot. I will pardon him, and then you will all join in blaming me for it. You all censure me for granting pardons, and yet you all ask me to do so." No man ever had a more loving and tender nature than Mr Lincoln.

He was as you say a firm man when he clearly saw duty. His most earnest, devoted and ablest friends in and out of Congress pressed him for months to issue a declaration of Emancipation, but he could not be coaxed nor driven into action till he saw the time had come to do it. His firmness was again tried after he wrote the letter to Mr Clay and other rebels in Canada, at the time of Mr Greeley's mission. Our timid politicians were alarmed. The Democratic Convention at Chicago was about to meet. Some of our most active men hurried on to Washington to induce him to write another letter modifying the other. Learning this, I hurried to Washington, saw these timid Leaders about the White House, and made an appointment in the [evening?] with Mr Lincoln. When the time came, I said to him that I had come to Washington to say to him, that I believed it would be fatal to us if he qualified his Letter, — that the Letter would be great strength in the canvass, that it had given great confidence to the Anti Slavery men and they would determine the result. He spoke of the pressure upon him, of the condition of the country, of the possible action of the coming Democratic Convention and of the uncertainty of the election in tones of sadness. After discussing for a long time these matters, he said with great calmness and firmness, — "I do not know what the result may be, we may be defeated, we may fail, but we will go down with our principles. I will not modify, qualify nor retract my proclimation, nor my Letter." I can never forget his manner, tones, nor words nor cease to feel that his firmness, amid the pressure of active friends, saved our cause in 1864.

Yours Truly
Henry Wilson

LC: HW3011–14

445. Edgar Conkling to WHH[1]

Cincinnati O. July 25 '67

Dr Sir:

Seeing reference to your gathering facts & history of Mr. Lincoln I have thought you might appreciate the information I give you without endorsing its correctness & furnish you the opportunity of treating the question as truth and justice requires. I am responsible for what I tell you, being well known here & in your town by my brothers J.C.C. & Wm J Conkling all mutual friends of Mr Lincoln. Some years since I was in a law office here + + + + a Kentuckyan who related to me as follows: Mr Lincoln is a bastard, the son of a farmer; that Mr. Lincoln greatly resembled[2] living at Muldraugh's Hill south of Louisville Ky. The child so resembled his real father as to induce him to get his reputed father to marry his mother and move to Indiana. While there he was taught by a young preacher that has since recognized him as Mr. Lincoln. This Kentucky lawyer while telling me the history of Lincoln was visited by one of the Todd's from Ky. a cousin of Mrs. Lincoln who confirmed the statements said he knew all about the locality & it was well known that Revd Dr Breckenridge[3] knows it to be true also. I forget the name of the farmer but can get it if you desire the details. The lawyer yet lives here & if I am kept out of view & no names used I can secure information from. I will take the trouble to get for you the particulars. You will fully understand me. I have no reason to endorse the report & if true think no less of Mr. Lincoln, nor do I write to prejudice his history but simply to advise you of the report *confidentially* thinking you will act wisely in the matter

It occurs to me before a reliable history is printed of Mr Lincoln a personal visit to Ky. & different people there will be essential *[blank space]* may leak out statements like the above which if not true should be set at rest, but if true so dealt with as to protect the memory of Mr L. as well as to do justice to history. I can put you on the track of information if you desire it.

Very Respy

Edgar Conkling.

LC: HW3016

---

1. Contains the notation: *Copied by Jesse W. Weik March 12 1919 Originals sent to Clinton L. Conkling Springfield Ills March 13 1919.* At the top: *Confidential, Positively —*

2. Some words apparently left out when copying.

3. Rev. Robert J. Breckinridge was an outspoken Kentucky Unionist during the Civil War and editor of the Danville *Quarterly Review.*

446. Edgar Conkling to WHH[1]

Cincinnati O. July 31 1867.

Dr Sir

Yours of the 29th just recd. & am glad to know you appreciate my suggestions. In order that you may secure reliable information I will refer you to the attorney I referred to. Richard H. Collins, P.O. Box 90 North West Corner 4th & Main St this city. This precise address will prevent any other similar name getting your letter. He will at your request put you on the trail of important facts names &c. He is an old friend of Rev Dr Breckenridge and connected with Danville Review & well known in Ky. I cannot do more that this. I have shown him your letter & he thinks by your personal visits where Mr. Lincoln was born and learning the character & history of his real father you will find a solution of interesting questions as to the traits of Mr. L and who he inherited them from, whether from father or mother &c. I think you will learn that Mr. L. went to *Ia near Richmond* & was taught there by a Rev. Dr Monfort[2] a Prebytn Preacher now here & who says Mr. Lincoln manifested great taste for arithmetic. You must see by following up the early history of Mr L. at different points. Your history of him will embrace more facts & philosophy that will be sought for than any other history.

Very Respy
Edgar Conkling

LC: HW3021

447. Edgar Conkling to WHH

Cincinnati O. August 3d 1867

Dr Sir.

I have just talked with Mr. Collins & he has just talked with Rev. Dr Montfort (Publisher of Presbyterian) who well remembers teaching Mr. Lincoln at Camden Preble Co. Ohio, near Richmond Ia. about 1827. He thinks valuable facts can be obtained there & incidents about Mr Lincoln some of which I learn but cannot now relate, Montfort will gladly aid you & go with you there. If you should show Mr. Lincoln's likeness there it might be seen how it resembles his reputed father. so his likeness compared with that of his real father in Ky. might lead to facts from old citizens there   Collins says the more he thinks of it the more he can post you up. He published Danville Review years since with Rev. Dr Breckenridge of Lexington Ky where the Todd family lived. He says Dr R. took Mrs. Lincoln into his church. That among the administration papers in the estate of Mrs. Lincoln's parents may be found letters from Mr. Lincoln ordering sale of slaves or a slave, his wife was interested in showing his views at that time; that he thinks

---

1. Copied by JWW and the original presumably returned to C. L. Conkling.
2. Rev. Joseph Glass Monfort of Cincinnati was the editor of *The Presbyter.*

Prentice[1] of Louisville Journal & others at that time thought of publishing Parentage of Lincoln but suppressed it fearing it would re-act on them. Doubtless one fact will lead to another not now thought of & which may make an unprecedented demand for such a history in this country & Europe & the track I am putting you on is reliable & gets down to the very core of the matter. I think you will be able to account for the long hesitancy of Mr Lincoln to hurt slavery from inheriting his real fathers instincts for it & customs as a slave holder. Mr Lincoln was divided in his nature on it. He felt for freedom inherited from his Mother less aristocratic & had to struggle against the instincts inherited from his real father as well as influenced by his wife and her family & Democratic party making him slow to strike down slavery the most I differed with him for.

Should you be able to identify a family likeness between Mr Lincoln & his real father either from discovering likenesses or portraits or opinions of other citizens you will have established an interesting fact; but which can only be done by your visiting several localities & carefully consulting with Mr. Lincoln's relatives on each side of his parents & their characters etc. This as yet has not been done nor likely to be as you can do it & while parties are living it should now be done. No man can do it as well as you can nor will you be willing to treat as facts as they should be done unless you yourself get them from sources that you can verify to the world as personally known to you. I look on it as important to get Mr. Lincoln's letters from the administrators estate in Lexington on the subject of selling slaves, his wife was interested in.[2] Did he seek to prevent it? or did he personally favor selling them for money, or for Mrs Lincoln. I doubt not Mrs Lincoln had notions not very agreeable to him and which so affected his domestic peace as to force him off in the circuit & thus prepared the way for him becoming a public man as well as tinged his course as President which if so if not creditable to her is due to the world to know. I doubt her affection as genuine for him as his for her from what I learn & her not as yet visiting his grave She had the opportunity of earning a world-wide reputation for sympathy for her country and the oppressed but rebellion & pride absorbed her powers & deprived her of national sympathy. Whatever may be the parentage of Mrs Lincoln if you suppress it others will yet publish it to your injury as a historian. If you could get likenesses of Mrs Lincoln's parents all the better. All of them I sent you some days since Mr. Collins address

Very Respy

Edgar Conkling

Bancrofts Memorial address p. 16 says Lincoln floated down the Ohio to Spencer Co. Ia. When 8 years old Mother could read not write, father do neither. But they sent him to school &c. Where is all this verified? Dr Montfort claims to have taught

1. George Dennison Prentice, an early biographer of Henry Clay, edited the *Louisville Journal* from 1830 to 1866.

2. Such letters are unknown.

him in Ohio in 1827 at age of 19. With which father reputed or real does the traits of Mr. Lincoln correspond with as well as his likeness agree?   E. C.

LC: HW3022–23

448. Joseph G. Monfort to WHH[1]

Cincinnati   Aug 10 1867

Dear Sir:

   After seeing Mr Lincoln on his way to the inauguration in 1861 I was reminded that I had taught a young man in Nov & Dec 1827 at Camden Preble County O. of his name and size who was about 19 years old & thought it might have been L — After seeing some biographical sketches of him I gave it up. Afterwards I mentioned it to Rev Dr R L. Breckenridge in presence of Rich. Collins Esq. He says that Dr B said the family lived in Ohio. This I do not remember. If he had said this I think I should have pursued the matter further. I have since asked a gentleman who has lived for fifty years at Camden who told me his impression was that the father of my pupil had moved a few miles north toward Richmond Ind & died there but he was not sure. As Mr Barrett,[2] one of Mr Lincolns biographers had confidential relations with Mr L. I took it for granted that my pupil must be some other person though age, name & personal appearance was in favor of his being the same. I can find out by a little effort something about the family over at Camden if it is probable that my former conjectures are worth pursuing further. As the Abram Lincoln who was my pupil was under my care three months I took it for granted that he would have let Mr Barrett know of it if he were the same. After these statements I leave it to you to say whether I shall inquire further

                         Yours truly
        (Signed)   J. G. Monfort

LC: HW3024

449. Richard N. Collins to WHH[1]

Cincinnati   Aug 19 '67

Dear Sir

   Yours of the 5th duly reced. I have deferred answering until I could have another interview with Rev. Dr Jno G. Montfort in reference to his probably having been a teacher of the late President Lincoln when the latter was 19.

---

1. This letter is a copy in JWW's hand. Though Monfort's personal encounter with AL turned out to be mistaken, his letters are included here by virtue of their interconnection with the Conkling and Collins sources.

2. Joseph H. Barrett.

---

1. This letter is a copy in JWW's hand.

In company with Mr Edgar Conkling I have just had an interesting conference with Dr Montfort. He had just received your letter in reply to his to you which was brought out by my first interview with him. He is now thoroughly interested and is very pardonably proud (in advance) of the pleasant notoriety your Book will give him as a teacher of the late President — if the strong belief can be made facts by proof He will write you again in a few days. If you will come to Cincinnati I have no doubt Dr Montfort will take special pleasure in going with you to Camden Preble county Ohio and searching up the needed confirmation. Perhaps he may go on and succeed without you.

Mr. Conkling has unintentionally misled you as to the extent of my *Knowledge* about Mr Lincolns parentage &c. The origin of my talk with him was this: In the summer of 1861 Rev. Dr Robert J. Breckenridge on returning from a visit to Baltimore via this city, to his home at Lexington and Danville Ky. called at my office for an hour — then a room adjoining the office of the "Presbyterian" of which Rev D*r* Montfort and Rev John M. Wampler are editors & proprietors. Seeing Dr Breckenridge pass their door towards mine they called on him in my office, and soon began to 'jump' him as to the private, political and war news he had learned in the East — supposing until Dr B. deneid it that he had been at the White House in confidential conference with Mr. Lincoln. Dr B. was nettled by their persistence in seeking to learn the secret history of *his* movements &c. &c — and failing to turn the conversation readily by other remarks asked if they knew that Mr Lincoln was a 'bastard'. Of course they were astonished, nay startled — and more 'curious' than ever. He proceeded to tell them that Mr Lincoln's parents were poor tenants in the edge of the largest home-farm of a wealthy & influential land holder (whose name I have forgotten), that in the absence of the tenant Lincoln, at work on the farm, the landlord frequently visited the log cabin for adulterous purposes with Mrs. L. — and thus became the actual father of Abraham L   This intimacy which was more than suspected by the neighbors, occasioned some talk; and as the infant boy grew apace and became well known for miles around the unlikeness to his nominal father and the remarkable resemblance to the landlord in build, appearance & manners increased the suspicions and pointed allusions to the intrigue to such an extent that the landlord arranged and provided means for their removal.

This is a rough outline of the conversation which I have only repeated two or three times in a private way   Of course *you will not repeat my name in this connection;* but search out the facts for yourself from the hints below

I think it likely that Dr Breckenridge would give you such names & other data as would enable you to search up & prove the facts in detail as fully & satisfactorily as is now possible. I heard it intimated not a year before Mr. Lincolns death that a full detail & in form that would carry conviction had been prepared for publication — probably for political purposes — but that it was suppressed through the influence of individuals who were politically unfriendly to Mr Lincoln's re-election to the Presidency who condemned such a mode of electioneering & besides believed it would recoil on those who had prepared it. If what I heard was true Geo. D. Prentice Esq., of the Louisville Journal was active in suppressing it & could give you a clew to the information you want. If approached by you in person I think he would aid you; or at least would put you on the track of the most definite information that is accessible at this late day.

If I can serve you further write me.

Yours very respectfully
Rich*d* N. Collins

LC: HW3025–26

450. Edgar Conkling to WHH

Cincinnati, O. August 19/67

Dr Sir

I have just seen Revd Dr Montfort, with whom you are in Correspondence. He is disposed to be at much labor in aiding you get at the facts. Is willing to go with you to Camden. O so soon as hears from there in answer to questions. Says he is now satisfied, Mr. Lincoln had some motive in withholding his having lived in Ohio. He & Collins both think your personal visits to several localities will be essential to compare likenesses, get recollections of old citizens of the appearances of real & reputed fathers & their mental characteristics &c &c   Many incidents may be secured of great value not to be got otherwise,

On reading Hollands life of Lincoln[1] I see defective history

Probing the real history will create a demand for at least one hundred thousand in this country & Europe giving it a preference over any other

If you fail to do so, others will do it,

Now, while you are on the track, with good aid, is your time to do it up.

You are at liberty to consult with my brother JCC,[2] if you see proper, as it respects my letters to you

Vr Resy
Edgar Conkling

LC: HW3027

451. Josiah G. Holland to WHH

Springfield, Aug 19, 1867

Dear Mr Herndon: —

In rummaging my drawers, this page comes to light. It answers a question you put to me some weeks since. It is in the hand writing of U. F. Linder of Chicago. There were other details of the matter that I obtained either from Mr Linder's lips,

---

1. Holland.
2. James C. Conkling.

for I had a long talk with him of which I took notes, or from some other source. How are you getting on with your work?

Yours Truly

J. G. Holland

"All I am or shall ever hope to be I owe to my loving angel mother, God bless her!"

(Concerning Niagara)

"Where did this vast body of water come from?"

(About Col Baker)

"Gentlemen let us not disgrace the age and country in which we live. This is a land where freedom of speech is guaranteed. Mr Baker has a right to speak and ought to be permitted to do so. None shall take him from the stand while I am here if I can prevent it"

"Oh how hard to die and not be able to leave the world any better for one's little life in it."

"By G__ I'll have that negro back soon, or I'll have a twenty years agitation in Illinois until the Governor does have a legal and constitutional right to do something in the premises."[1]

[Enclosure[1]]

452. Usher F. Linder (part of statement for J. G. Holland)

Mr. Lincoln — tho' a supporter of and a great admirer of Henry Clay had very little personal acquaintance with that gentleman. In 1847, I think, Mr. Clay started the emancipation movement in Kentucky — and gave notice that he would address the people at Lexington on the subject. Mr. Lincoln had then never seen Mr. Clay — but, went to Lexington to hear him make his speech. — Mr. Clay had written his speech and read it to his audience — a very unusual thing for him — and its delivery did not come up to Mr. Lincoln's expectations — but, he made the proper allowance. — Mr. Clay invited Mr. L. — to dine with him at Ashland, — which he did. — They never saw each other afterward

---

Mr. Lincoln seldom read newspaper attacks upon him — nor did he care to hear what was said about him.

I do not think he ever read the de-

LC: HW3029–30 (letter), HW5313 (enclosure)

---

1. WHH's note: *The Expression of* [illegible] [My?] *run who read — is not in this — write for it to Holland —*.

---

1. This fragment, not currently filed with Holland's letter, is marked by JWW "written by U.F. Linder for Dr. J.G. Holland." This single page was numbered "(3)" by Linder.

453. Joseph G. Monfort to WHH

Cincinnati Aug 21, 1867

Der Sir

The prefixed letter from James Barnet of Camden Preble Co O seems to settle the question that my pupil was not President Lincoln — I feel quite confident that my pupil was Abraham not John & that John was a youngr brother but if there was a John, Thomas & Anna was, though the fathers name was Thomas, it must have been another family, as President Lincoln had but one brother who died in infancy as Barretts life[1] tells us & Mr Barrett must have derived his information from President Lincoln   There is a possibility that the children of the second wife by her first husband may have assumed the patronimic Lincoln   Mr Barnet is about 65 years old & has been on the ground all the time since 1823. My impression was that old Thomas Lincoln had just come to Camden in 1827 but Mr Lincoln ought to know. I can find out certainly whether my pupils name was Abram or John as there are pupils still living there

Do you think the matter worth any further investigation?

My conjecture is that Old Thomas was a cousin of President Lincolns father being of the same name

Yours truly
J G. Monfort

[Enclosure][1]

454. James Barnet to Joseph G. Monfort

Camden O. Aug 19 /67

Dear Sir:

Your very kind favour of the 12th Inst came duly to hand in which you make enquirys about a family by the name of Lincoln commonly called Linkhorn. I knew the family well the old Gentleman's name was Thomas the young mans name that went to school to you was John and I suppose he was about 19 years old in 1827 he worked for me 2 or 3 years and died on my premises in 1840 he had two other Brothers Thomas and Ananias there was not any of the family named Abraham and I suppose they were not related to the great Abraham Lincoln if they were it was distant, Thomas Lincoln was an old Settler here he was living here in 1823 when we came to Camden

Yours Truly
(Signed)   James Barnet

P.S. Camden in 1823 was called Dover.
JB

LC: HW3031 (Monfort letter), HW4523 (enclosure)

---

1. Barrett.

---

1. This document is a copy, so labeled in the hand of JWW.

455. *Edgar Conkling to WHH[1]*

Cincinnati O. Sept. 27/67

Dr. Sir:

I see by the papers that a Dr. Eaton[2] of Ky. recently died suddenly a half brother of A. Lincoln   This may be another clue to information

Dr Montfort is writing for facts but I dont think it is practicable to get them by writing to parties too busy to get them or to remember them, while by personal visit to locations many may be seen who will remember what those written to know nothing of, but which facts after a while will leak out. Whatever the facts are I should like to see you get them reliable

Very Respy
Edgar Conkling

LC: HW3032

456. *Anonymous to WHH*

Parris, Ky *[ca. 1867]*

Sir,

I percieve you doubt as to the legitimacy of the birth of A Lincoln—

If you will consult old Mrs Thatcher, who lives on Turnpike ½ way from Paris to Winchester Ky, who was cousin of Abes mother, and Milton Bealle & an old coloured woman & her daughter living with Milton Bealle, they will prove these facts: Abraham Inloe while a millwright bulding Thatchers mill was intimate with _____ Hanks and got her with child — Inloe had a man working with him of name of Lincoln — Miss Hanks threatened a suit for seduction, & Inloe to hush the thing up, give Lincoln $200 to marry her & take her off, which he did to Green river country; where Abe was born, & he was called Abraham after his real father, and Lincoln after the man who agreed to marry her — The old Coloured woman who lives with Beall is alive, who, as well as Mrs. Thatcher, knows all about it.— Inloe got the old black woman with Child the same year, & the child now an old woman is living with the mother at Beall's —

If you will see Beall & Mrs. Thatcher & the old coloured woman & her daughter you will learn the truth about Abe's geneology —

Whether Lincoln carried out his promise to marry is unknown here — Yours —
One who has head parties tell all about it —

LC: HW4017

---

1. This document is a copy in JWW's hand.
2. Not identified.

457. Newton Bateman to WHH[1]

Springfield Mch. 8th 1869

My Dear Sir:

I have yours of 7th inst. I am too unwell & too busy to write or think to-day — will try to Speak of the Subect of your note when I can – – *Meantime please do not use or refer to our private Conversations or any part of them.* My aversion to publicity in such Matters is intense. The tone Manner &c of Mr Lincoln was deeply solemnly *religious* — it inspired me with awe. He was *applying* the *principles* of moral & *religious truth* to the duties of the hour — the Condition of the Country & the Conduct of public men — ministers of the Gospel &c. I had no thought of Orthodoxy or heterodoxy — unitarianism, trinitarianism or any other ism during the whole Conversation & I don't suppose or *believe he had.* The room was full of God & high truths & the awfulness of Coming Events — Sects & dogmas in Such a presence! He was alone with the Great God the problem of his Countrys future & his own & I but heard the Communings of his soul —

Truly yours
Newton Bateman

LC: *Jeremiah Black Papers,* 59644

458. Andrew H. Goodpasture (statement for WHH)

Petersburg, Illinois March 31. A.D. 1869

About the year A.D. 1855 in the town of Clinton Dewit County Illinois pending the investigation of a suit in the circuit cort: in which a Mr. George Tanner was plantiff and some 15 or 16 ladies of Marion Dewit County Ill. were defendent[1]

The atterney for the plantiff urged the tecnicalities of the Statute law in all caces of destruction of property (The ladies having been indited for knocking out the heads of some whiskey barels owned by Mr. Tanner who kept a grocery at Marion where they resided)   In defending the ladies the atterney evinced some want of tack to meet the case, and Mr. Lincoln became restless, placed his head forward and rubed his hair with his hands, and before the jury retired he addressed the Cort sayin he wished to make a few remark (before the jury retired.) And first, he would change the order of inditement and have it read The State against Mr. whiskey instead of the State against the *Ladies.* And tuching this case there were 3 laws, First the law of self protection. Second the law of the land or statute law: & Thirdly the Moral law or law of God.

---

1. Copy in WHH's hand.

---

1. On May 18, 1854, AL and John T. Stuart defended nine women in DeWitt Circuit Court who had been indicted on charges of riot for dumping a grocer's supply of liquor after he had refused to close his establishment. The women were tried by a jury and found guilty but were fined only $2.00 each (Earl Schenck Miers et al., eds., *Lincoln Day by Day: A Chronology, 1809–1865,* 3 vols. [Washington, D.C., 1960]).

And first the law of selfprotection was a law of necessity as evinced by our Fathers in casting the Tea over board, and aserting their rights to the persuit of *life liberty* & happiness. And that in this case it was the only defence the Ladies had: for Tanner, neither feared God nor regarded *man*.

Secondly, the law of the land or statute law: and that the Plantiff was recre-lient to both. Third the Moral law or law of God, and this was with out any efect in the case before the jury. Gave some of his own observations upon the effects of Whiskey: and its ruin in society and that it should be arested: his feelings became deeply inlisted and such was his power in presenting truth and carrying his audi-ance with him that before he closed his speach many were bathed in tears, the Judge not excepted. When he sat dow the judge said "*Ladies* go home and if there is any fine wanted of you we will let you know it: but no fine has ever yet been called for.

These statements are substancally the same as given to the undersigned By Rev. R. D. Taylor who was present at the time.

A. H. Goodpasture[2]

LC: HW3036–37

459. Andrew H. Goodpasture (statement for WHH)

Petersburg, Illinois March 31st. A.D. 1869

About the A.D. 1846 Mr. Lincoln visited Petersburg and as usual quite a num-ber of citizens gathered near to him; evinceing great pleasure in hearing him talk, and ever now and then he would tell some joke causing all to manifest pleasure in his society: after some time in his company I passed on giving attention to the business of the day, and after an hour or so I returned back along the street, and still there was quite croud with Mr. Lincoln, all in good glee, and as I was passing them, I thought I would say something, and remarked that Where the great ones are there will the peopel be. Mr. Lincoln replyed Ho! *Parson* a little more Scrip-tural; "Where the carces is there will the eagels be gathered togather:[1] There was quite a laugh, and so I passed on. I know this to be truth:

A. H. Goodpasture

LC: HW3038

---

2. WHH's note below the signature: *Herndon says, Judge David Davis presided — Archer Herndon's wife — his mother — was one of the defendants.*

---

1. Luke 17:37: "Wheresoever the body is, thither will the eagles be gathered together."

460. Andrew H. Goodpasture (statement for WHH)[1]

Petersburg, Illinois   Mar 31 A.D. 1869

At an early day General Ewing[2] was canvasing this state for office, and having an appointment to speak near Decature Mr Lincoln and Mr. Close,[3] as they were near the place fensing in a peace of ground; stoped to hear what was said: Mr. Ewing's speach was heared with interest by Mr. Lincoln, and after he was done an other gentelman addessed the peopel urging the propriety of Illinois beeing a slave state; before he was done Mr. Lincoln grew quite restless and whispered to his friends that if he had the stand he would tair that speech to peaces; so when the man closed; the cry was a speach from Lincoln; a spech from Lincoln! Mr. Ewing called for Mr. Lincoln to come on the stan not knowing who he was; and immediately Mr. Lincoln steped upon stage and began to addess the people his appearance was rather noval being in his shirt sleeves, and his pants some what woren out by the *Praire* grass, notwithstanding he soon gained the attention, answering each argument until he [sived?] the speach and before he closed his speach, he remarked that he was opposed to slavery and ever expected to be so long as the whip cracked over the yellow girl's back: Mr. Ewing was so pleased that he urged Mr. Lincoln to come to Springfield and give this attention to reading &c.

The above is about as related to me several times by Mr. Close, who was Lincoln's pardoner in fencing in a peace of land at that time:

A. H. Goodpasture

LC: HW3039

461. John Armstrong (WHH interview)[1]

[February 1870]

Jno Armstrong —

Says — that some few days before Lincoln delivered his house divided against itself Speech he called his friends together, in the Library Room in the State house in the city of Springfield, for the purpose of getting their opinion of the policy of delivering that Speech — the Speech delivered on the 17th day of June AD 1858. There were some Eight or twelve friends met. After seating them at the round table

---

1. Someone, possibly JWW, has written "Not Authentic" in blue pencil across the face of this statement.
2. William L. D. Ewing.
3. George Close.

---

1. Marginal note: *Send this back to me when you are done with it — Dont forget. WHH*

This interview seems to have been sent to Ward Hill Lamon in WHH's letter of February 19, 1870. On February 25, WHH wrote to Lamon: "I sent you some days since more at the request of Jno Armstrong than of myself a short account of what I had to say on Lincoln's house divided against itself speech — should not have sent it for the same reason that I have refused — failed to say more — write more to you — namely I do not wish to be considered a blow — boast — or fool who wishes to be noticed &c. &c." (Lamon Papers, HL).

he read that clause or section of his Speech which reads — a house divided against itself cannot stand. &c.: he read it slowly & cautiously so as to let Each man fully understand it. After he had finished the reading he asked the opinions of his friends as to its wisdom or polity. Every Man among them Condemned the speech in Substance & Spirit and Especially that Section quoted above: they unanimously declared that the whole Speech was too far in advance of the times and they all Condemned that Section or part of his Speech already quoted as unwise & impolitic, if not false. Wm H Herndon sat still while they were giving their respective opinions of its unwisdom & impolicy; he sprang to his feet & said Lincoln By — God — deliver it just as it reads. If it is in advance of the times let us — you & I if no one Else — lift the people to the level of this Speech now & higher hereafter. The Speech is true — wise & politic; and will succeed — now or in the future. Nay it will aid you — if it will not make you president of the United States."

Mr Lincoln sat still a short moment — rose from his chair — walked backwards & forwards in the Hall — stopt & said — "Friends: I have thought about this matter a great deal — have weighed the question well from all corners; and am thoroughly Convinced the time has come when it should be uttered & if it must be that I must go down because of this speech then let me go down linked to truth — die in the advocacy of what is right & just. This nation cannot live on injustice — a house divided against itself cannot stand &c I say again & again." This was Spoken with some degree of emotion — the effects of his love of truth & sorrow from the disagreement of his friends with himself.

W H Herndon heard this speech read some days before this in his & Lincoln's office. Mr Herndon then approved the speech & urged Mr Lincoln to deliver it — See Hollands life of Lincoln at page *[blank space]* where the facts are correctly stated — quote it — or State the facts as therein

In a few days after the speech had been delivered a gentleman — Doct Long, came into Lincoln's office and said — "well, Lincoln that foolish speech of yours will kill you — will defeat you in this Contest — and probably for all offices for all time to come — am sorry — very sorry. I wish it was wiped out of existence — Don't you now wish so." Mr Lincoln was intently writing while the Doct was loudly lamenting. Lincoln stopped — raised up his spectacles — put the pen down — looked at the Doct one Moment with a peculiar look of insulted dignity — sorrow for a timid soul, & contempt of his weakness — Said — "Well Doct —, If I had to draw a pen across and erase my whole life from Existence & all I did; and I had one poor gift or choice left, as to what I should Save from the wreck, I should choose that speech and leave it to the world unerased." Mr Lincoln met with many cold shoulders for some time — nay during the whole canvass with Douglas. In the times & hours & moments of debates — you could hear from all quarters in the crowd, Republicans say — "D__n that fool speech; it will be the cause of the death of Lincoln and the republican party — such folly — such non sense! Is Lincoln crazy,? D__n it."

HL: LN368

462. John T. Stuart (WHH interview)[1]

[by March 2, 1870]

Jno. T. Stuart says

I Knew Mr Lincoln when he first came here and for years afterwards — he was an avowed and open Infidel — Sometimes bordered on atheism. I have often and often heard Lincoln & one W. D Herndon who was a free thinker talk over this Subject. Lincoln went further against Christian beliefs — & doctrines & principles than any man I ever heard: he shocked me — don't remember the Exact line of his argument — Suppose it was against the inherent defects so-called of the Bible & on grounds of reason — Lincoln always denied that Jesus was the Christ of God. — denied that Jesus was the son of God as understood and maintained by the Christian world. The Revd Doct Smith who wrote you a letter tried to Convert Lincoln from Infidelity so late as 1858 and Couldn't do it

HL: LN2326

463. James H. Matheny (WHH interview)[1]

[by March 2, 1870]

Jas. H. Matheny — says

I Knew Mr Lincoln as Early as 1834–37 — Know he was an infidel — have heard Lincoln call Christ a bastard — He & Wm D. Herndon used to talk Infidelity in the Clerks office in this city about the years 1837–40. Lincoln attacked the Bible & new Testament on two grounds — 1st From the inherent or apparent contradiction under its lids & 2dly From the grounds of Reason — sometimes he ridiculed the Bible & New Testament — sometimes seemed to Scoff it, though I shall not use that word in its full & literal sense — never heard that Lincoln changed his views though his personal & political friend from 1834 to *1860*— Sometimes Lincoln bordered on absolute Atheism: he went far that way & often shocked me. I was then a young man & believed what my good Mother told me.

Stuart & Lincoln's office was in what is called *the Hoffman* row on North 5th Street near the public Square. Stuart & Lincoln's office was in the same building as the Clerk's office & *on the same floor*. Lincoln would Come into the clerk's office where I and some young men — Evan Butler — Newton Francis — & others were writing or staying; & would bring the Bible with him — read a Chapter —argue against it: Lincoln then had a smattering of Geology if I recollect it. Lincoln often if not wholy was an atheist —: at least bordered on it. Lincoln was Enthusiastic in his infidelity. As he grew older he grew more discrete — didn't talk much before Strangers about his religion, but to friends — close and bosom ones he was always open & avowed — fair & honest, but to Strangers he held them off from Policy.

---

1. Appended to the letter from WHH to Ward Hill Lamon, Mar. 2, 1870.

---

1. Appended to the letter from WHH to Ward Hill Lamon, Mar. 2, 1870.

Lincoln used to quote Burns. Burns helped Lincoln to be an infidel as I think —
at least he found in Burns a like thinker & feeler. Lincoln quoted Tam O'Shanter
— "What send one to Heaven and him to Hell all &c.[2]

From what I Know of Mr Lincoln, and his views of Christianity: and from what
I Know as honest & well founded rumor — from what I have heard his best friends
say & regret for years — from what he never denied when accused & from what
Lincoln has hinted & intimated to say no more he did write a little Book on Infidelity at or near New Salem in Menard Co about the year 1834 or 1835 —. I
have stated these things to you often Judge Logan — Jno. T. Stuart — yourself
Know what I Know and some of you more.

Mr. Herndon you insist on Knowing something which you Know I possess &
got as a secret and that is about Lincoln's little book on Infidelity. Mr Lincoln did
tell me *that he did write* a little Book on Infidelity. This Statement I have avoided
heretofore, but as you strongly insist on it — probably to defend yourself against
charges of misrepresentation I give it to you as I got it from Lincoln's own mouth.
(Mr Matheny after strong & repeated solicitation from me, as it were under pro-
test told it to me — evidently hating to do it — Herndon)

HL: LN2326

464. James H. Matheny (WHH interview)[1]

Springfield Ills. Mch. 6th 1870

Jas H. Matheny tells me that from about 1854 to 1860. that Lincoln played a
sharp game here on the Religious world — that Lincoln Knew that he was to be a
great man — was a rising man — was looking to the Presidency &c. and well
Knowing that the old infidel, if not Atheistic charge would be made & proved
against him and to avoid the disgrace — odium and unpopularity of it tramped
on the Christian toes saying — "Come and Convert me": the Elders — lower &
higher members of the churches, including Ministers &c flocked around him &
that he appeared openly to the world as a seeker — that it was noised about that
Lincoln was a seeker after Salvation &c in the Lord — that letters were written
more or less all over the land that Lincoln was soon to be a changed man &c and
thus it was he used the Revd Jas Smith of Scotland — old man Bergen and others.
I have often thought that there was something in this, but cant affirm it to be so.
This is Matheny's honest opinion and no man is superior to Matheny's judgments
&c of human nature — actions & motives &c: he knew Lincoln as well as I did I
think.

HL: LN366

---

2. Matheny is referring to another Burns poem, "Holy Willie's Prayer," containing the lines: "O Thou
that in the Heavens does dwell, / Wha, as it pleases best Thysel, / Sends ane to Heaven an' ten to Hell / A'
for Thy glory, / And no for onie guid or ill / They've done before Thee!"

---

1. WHH to Ward Hill Lamon, Mar. 6, 1870.

465. Jesse W. Fell to WHH

Normal Sept. 20/70

Dr Sir

In complyance with your request years ago, I intended writing you a Statement of my recollections of Lincoln's religious views. — Last winter I learned you had sold out your Ms. to Wa Lamon — who renewed the request. Lately he has done so again, & in response thereto I have written the enclosed, which I will thank you to examine and Send it back to me, telling me, briefly, how it compares with your own recollections. Hoping you will find time to do so at an as early a day as possible I am

Truly yours
Jesse W. Fell

P.S. Of course I did not Know Mr. L. half as well as you, but have written from my Stand-point. Am I not correct in my Statement as to his views being pretty well represented by Parker? — I so understood him in *substance* tho' not in *terms* — or words. —

[Enclosure]

466. Jesse W. Fell to Ward Hill Lamon

Normal Sept. 22/70

Dr Sir —

Yours of the ___ Ult. Soliciting a Statement of My recollections of the religious opinions of the late President, — Mr Lincoln — as derived from repeated Conversations with him on that Subject — came duly to hand and would have been Sooner answered but for the pressure of business. Though everything relating to the character & history of this extraordinary personage is of interest, & should be fairly Stated to the world, I enter upon the performance of this Duty — for So I regard it — with some reluctance, arising from the fact that in Stating my Convictions on the Subject I must necessarily place myself in opposition to quite a number who have written on this topic — before me, & whose views largely preoccupd the public mind. This latter fact, whilst contributing to my embarrassment on this Subject, is perhaps the Strongest reason however why the truth in this Matter Should be fully disclosed, & I therefore yield to your request. —

If there were any traits of character that Stood out in bold relief, in the person of Mr Lincoln, it was that of Truth, and Candor. He was utterly incapable of incincerity, or of professing views of this or any other Subjects, he did not entertain. Knowing Such to be his true character, that incincerity, much more implicitly these traits wholly foreign to his nature, many of his old friends were not a little Surprised at finding in some of the biographies of this great man, Statements concerning his religious opinions So utterly at variance with his Known sentiments. True, he may have changed or modified those views, after his removal from among us, though this is hardly reconcilable with the history of the man, & his entire devotion to public matters during his four years residence at the National Capitol. It is *possible* however that this may be the proper Solution of this conflict of views; or it may be, that with no intention on the part of any one to Mislead the public Mind, those who have represented him as Religious in the popular theological views of the times, may have Misapprehended him, as experiance has shown to be quite Common, where no special effort has been made to obtain critical accuracy on a Subject of this nature. This is the more probable from the well Known fact that Mr Lincoln Seldom communicated to any one his views on this Subject. But, be this as it may, I have no hesitation whatever in Saying, that whilst he held many opinions in common with the great mass of Christian believers, *he did not* believe in what are regarded as the orthodox or evangelical views of Christianity.

On the inate depravity of Man, the character & office of the great head of the Church, the atonement, the infallibilty of the written revelation, the performance of myricles, the nature & design of present & future rewards & punishments, (as they are popularly called) and many other Subjects, he held opinions not only unsustained, but utterly at variance with what are usually taught in the Churches. Whilst he was practically, as I certainly think, one of the best of Christians, his views on these & Kindred topics were such as to place him, in the estimation of most believers, entirely without the pale of the Christian Church; tho' to my mind Such was not his true position, tho' he never attached himself to any religious Society whatever.

His religious views were eminantly practical, and are Sumed up in these two propositions, "the Fatherhood of God, and the Brotherhood of Man." He fully believed in a Superintending & overruling Providence, that guides & controls the operations of the world; but Maintained that Law and Order, & not their violation or suspension; are the appointed means by which this providence is exercised —

I will not attempt any Specification of either his belief or disbelief on vareous religious topics, as derived from conversations with him at different times during a period of about 20 years, but as conveying a general view of his religious or theological opinions will State the following facts. Some eight or Ten years prior to his death, in conversing with him on the Subject, the writer took occasion to refer, in terms of approbation, to the Sermons, & writings generally, of Dr. W. E. Channing; and finding he was considerably interrested in the Statement I made of the opinions held by that author, I proposed to present him (Mr L.) a copy of Channing's entire works,[1] which, I soon after did. Subsequently, the Contents of these volumes, togeather with the writings of Theodore Parker, furnished him, as he informed me, by his friend, and Law Partner Mr Herndon, became very Naturally topics of Conversation with us, although far from believing there was an entire harmony of views on his part with either of those authors, yet they were generally much admired and approved by him.

No religious views with him Seemed to find any favor except of the practical

---

1. William E. Channing, *The Works of William E. Channing* (1843).

& rationalistic order; & if from my recollections on this subject I were called upon to designate an author whose views most nearly represented Mr Lincoln's, on this Subject, I would say that author was Theodore Parker. —

As you have requested from me a candid Statement of my recollections on this topic, I have thus briefly given them, with the hope that they may be of Some Service in rightly Settling a question about which — as I have good reason to believe — the public mind has been greatly misled. —

Not doubting that they will accord Substantially with your own recollections, & that of his other intimate & confidential friends [illegible] with the popular verdict, after this matter shall have been properly canvassed, I am with great Respect

Yours truly

Jesse W Fell

LC: HW3052 (Fell to WHH), HW3048–51 (Fell to Lamon)

467. James Hall to WHH

St Denis P.O. Md. Sept 17th/73

Sir.

I am Sure some apology *should* preface the infliction of a letter from a Stranger upon you on the biographer of Mr Lincoln, Mr Lamon: but I have none to offer except as you may infer from the page or two enclosed.

On page 145 of "Life of Lincoln" in speaking of Denton Offutt,[1] "The most cunning & searching enquiries have failed to discover a spot where he lingered" &c — Of what consequence to know or learn more of Offutt I cannot imagine, but be assured he turned up after leaving New Salem. On meeting the name, it seemed familiar, but I could not at once *locate* him. Finally I fished up from memory, that some 20 or 25 years since, one "Denton Offutt" appeared in Baltimore, hailing from Kentucky, advertising himself in the city papers, as a veterinary Surgeon, & *horse tamer*, proposing to have a secret to whisper in the horse's ear, or a secret manner of whispering in his ear, which he could communicate to others, & by which the most refractory & vicious horses could be gentled & controlled. For this secret, he charged five dollars, binding the recipient by oath not to divulge it. I knew several persons, young fancy horsemen, who paid for the trick. Offutt advertised himself not only through the press, but he appeared in the streets on horse back & on foot in plain citizens dress of black, but with a broad sash across his his right shoulder of various colored ribbon, crossed on his left hip under a large rosetta of like material, rendering his appearance most ludicrously conspicuous — Having occasion to purchase a horse at this time, I encountered him at several of our Sale Stables & was strongly urged to avail myself of his secret — So much for Offutt — Therefore if Mr Lamon sees fit, he can add a note to relieve the anxiety of any who may have made such

---

1. Lamon.

cunning searches for him, in any future edition. But, were he living in /61 I doubt not Mr Lincoln would have heard of him[2] — I met a gentleman, Lawyer, resident of Vicksburg or Natchez last year, who claimed to have loaned Lincoln his first law book[3] — & in this wise. He & his partner were sitting one afternoon in their office, unemployed, door open, when Lincoln appeared with compass & staff. "Well how now Abe, whats up?" "I'm dead broke — enough surveying, but all on tick no pay —" "Well, better study law — you see how busy we are." "If you'll lend me books I will." Thus commenced the law — The gentleman professed to have for years ridden the circuit with *Abe* — & told many anecdotes of him, rehearsing his *bon mot* — if they could be called *bon*. Will you be kind enough to drop a line to my address, advising me if a Springfield Lawyer of about that time afterwards moved to Miss. & if so, what name —?

Now after this opening trespass I beg you to permit me to say a word as to the way the assassination story is treated by Mr Lamon. Without going into details or attempting to prove which was intended allow me to express my conviction that mischief *was meant,* and might or might not have been executed — Mr Lamon bases his disbelief of it on three grounds. 1st The character of the parties Suspected. 2d This open manner of speaking of it — 3d That the parties were not afterward [restricted?] — Two of the parties were well known to me, & more fit men for such a purpose could not be found: but the agents were merely agents, men & women of the highest standing in Balto. could have [schemed?] the assassins of Lincoln then, as did Dr Mudd afterwards— & tis not absurd, or does not appear so to those on the spot to believe that the agents had high support — [Lucket?][4] was not a common man or *common* drunkard — He was from the lowest origin in Charles Co. M'd, but made his way up. married into one of the most aristocratic families of Md. a daughter of Gov. Thomas   He became a merchant in Balto. of high standing at one time. was a state director in the Bank of Balto. a vestryman in Christs Church &c — However, he failed just before the war & became addicted to drink — He lived in good style at a Country Seat near the Relay H. on the ? R.R — & was elected Capt of a Company of horse to be raised to reject the Yankees in Nov./60. He was a most rabid secessionist — Capt Ferrondina[5] is an Italian, & a man of energy & pluck. headed a company of volunteers under the Com. of Safety after 19th Apl. & although a Barber by trade ambitious of distinction — & quite as likely, "poor knight of the Soap Pot," as he is styled by Mr Lamon, as was the Knights of the Buskin & sock, Booth, to do the damning & damn'd deed — True, he might have cowed, as did Asterolt,[6] in doing the assigned duty, but most who know him, believe, he would have rather Come to time, like Brother. As to the public manner in which the subject talked — noth-

2. See Denton Offutt to AL, Feb. 11, 1861, Abraham Lincoln Papers, LC.

3. Probably Josephus Hewitt, who came to Springfield about 1830 and read law with Stephen T. Logan.

4. See p. 273, note 13.

5. See p. 270, note 9.

6. George Atzerodt, one of Booth's co-conspirators, was assigned the task of assassinating Vice President Johnson but lost his nerve at the last moment.

ing else was talked in public. Such a thing as a black Republican was unknown in Balto. at that time, or if known as such, dared not speak out in public — The very air was lurid with rebellion — equalling Charleston S.C. — Long before that period in the Freemont & Buchanan Canvass a very highly respectable Episcopal Clergyman, Harry B. Goodwin of Charles County, & by the way, Lucket's Pastor when a boy, declared to me, that if Freemont was elected, he should never live to reach Washington, that if the South did not rise to act, he, individually, would put a bullet through his heart, that he would consider it his duty as a Christian to save his Country from *nigger* rule — And Goodwin too, was a Northern Man, married a Chs. Co. Lady, & even freed some fifty Slaves & sent them, under my care, to Liberia — Nor was he more crazy than Mr Calhoun with whom he was somewhat intimate — "Why was Ferrandina & others not molested?" Simply because, they had only *talked* as most others talked & as there was no chance for action, their talk subsided, & there was nothing to apprehend from them. It might as well & better be asked why were not the Southern Editors, who urged the "assassination of the Tyrant" punished, or the fellow who offered to do it for a certain sum? or Mr Southern[7] of St. Marys Co. who shot down a sergeant for coming on his place for his Negroes? I cannot but think Mr Lamon has treated this matter too lightly, considering how the Mass. troops were treated by our *people* not *rabble,* soon after. Not knowing Mr Lamon's address, I pitched this at you — & you may pitch it at him, or into the fire, as you see fit — but I must express my obligation to you & him for a pattern biography, scarcely second to Boswells Johnson —

very respectfully —
James Hall.

LC: HW3094–95

468. James H. Matheny (WHH interview)[1]

Springfield Decr 9. 1873.

Mr Matheny told me that he said that he understood that up to the time Lincoln left Springfield Ills in 1860 that he was a confirmed infidel, but that after he got to Washington and associating with religious People that he believes that Mr Lincoln [thought?] became a Christian — Knows nothing of Mr Lincolns investigations into the Subject of Christianity — He — M — says he told Reed & Melvin[2] the histories of this — Reed — Melvin & Matheney were talking about the home of the *[illegible]* — Reed wrote the letter which I signed[3] — Matheny

---

7. Probably John H. Sothoron, who killed a white army lieutenant who was recruiting blacks along the Patuxent River in Maryland.

---

1. Marginal note: *Mr Matheny told me in this conversation that he told Mr _____ ?* This is apparently an unfinished version of the marginal inscription given in p. 583, note 4.

2. Rev. James A. Reed and Samuel H. Melvin. Reed engaged in a public controversy in 1873 with WHH over AL's religion. See Donald, 272–82.

3. Refers to a statement Matheny gave Reed, recanting some of the testimony he had given WHH on AL's religious beliefs. See §472.

told me he thought Lincoln played a sharp game on the Christians in 1858 to 1860, and I somewhat coincide with him —[4]

LC: HW3108

469. *William Jayne to WHH*

Springfield Ill   Dec 19th 1873

Dear Friend

I received your letter yesterday. I have heard your lecture commented on a good deal — The religious or rather those who claim to be, the pious ones; say why does Herndon drag this matter before the Public why not let Mr Lincoln's religious views stand as the Church & orthodox world have declared his views to be — A majority of the people I have heard talk believe you have told the truth as to his views, but even some of those who believe you are right in your views, think it might be well enough not to tell the whole truth   The orthodox world is determined to claim Abraham, & are not willingly going to give up one of their idols.

I have been to the Journal Office & looked over the papers, but do not find many notices either good or bad —

I dont think the Chicago papers published your lecture, if they did I failed to see them & I have noticed pretty close.

The Times published part of it. I do not see the Chicago Sunday papers — The Globe, St Louis in their Sunday issue published it entire — [Olney?] furnished them a copy   The New York Herald is very bitter on you

Any man who strikes any blows at the orthodox faith of this country must expect some bitter assaults. Orthodoxy pays, but in this country — Editors know which side of their bread is buttered.

Saturday

I have this morning seen an editorial in the Inter Ocean,[1] which I think is the fairest & most impartial of any thing on the Lincoln Herndon & Reed controversy. I send you the paper by mail also a Globe

I had a talk with Ninian Edwards to day in the barber shop —

I find that he is not so good an orthodox witness in private as in the public prints —

So I guess with all if they would tell the *whole* truth —

Yours truly

W Jayne

LC: HW3114

---

4. Marginal note: *Mr Matheny told me in this conversation that he took Mr — Doct Smith to be a* [pirate?]. For the "sharp game," see §464.

---

1. A Chicago newspaper.

470. Chauncey F. Black to WHH[1]

York Apl 30. 1874

My dear Sir.

I send you herewith [a clip?] sent me by Mr Dana of the *New York Sun*. The writer is evidently on the wrong scent, or else given to much lying.

I met the other day in Washington Col Dick Wintersmith,[2] born and raised down there — His theory is that *Ben Hardin* was Mr Lincoln's father and gave facts and incidents which go far to support it. He says he will come here to see me and I shall then write down what he says. In the meantime I hope you will find out that fellow you heard about in Kentucky.

But have you heard nothing from Lamon or anybody else? Have you consulted with any publisher?[3] Or making any progress? This letter of inquiry has been on my mind a long while, but I have been so very busy that I couldn't get it done. Mr. Dana offered me a large salary to go to New York and take charge of the *Sun* — I declined chiefly because I have some prospect of going to Congress from this District[4] — and at all events can't abide the thought of living in a city — He then offered me a smaller salary for six articles a week & to remain at home — I have accepted that and it keeps me as busy as a [nailor?] But I shall never die happy unless we get something done about the *Life of Lincoln*. Do you see that John Hay and Nicolay are said to be preparing a *Life*.?

Most truly / as ever
Chauncey F Black

[Enclosure]

471. Newspaper Clipping

The Question as to the Marriage of Abraham Lincoln's Father and Mother.

The following letter from an octogenarian to one of our citizens upon a mooted question as to the paternity and birth of the late President Lincoln, is not without interest:

DEAR SIR: In the Louisville Courier-Journal of February 20, 1874, is a communication about Mr. Lincoln's family, copied from the Indianapolis Journal. which bears the impress of truth. I knew Mordecai Lincoln, Thomas Lincoln and the Berry's. I will try to copy it for you:

To the editor of the Indianapolis Journal:

Some time since, by chance, there fell into my hands an Evening Journal containing a letter from the Louisville Commercial, in which it was hinted that there

1. Marginal note: *C.S.H.V. is Mr. C. S. Hobart Vawter of Indianapolis.*
2. Presumably Richard M. Wintersmith.
3. Black and WHH were contemplating collaborating on a revision of Ward H. Lamon's *Life of Lincoln*, which Black had ghostwritten.
4. Marginal note: *Confidential.*

had existed doubts in the public mind as to the marriage of Mr. Lincoln's father and mother. In the year 1859 I went to Springfield, Kentucky, to teach and was in that neighborhood when he received the nomination for President. On the announcement of the name of the candidate all were on the *qui vive* to know who the stranger was, so unexpectedly launched upon a perilous sea. A farmer remarked that he should not be surprised if this was a son of Thomas Lincoln and Nancy Hanks, who were married at the house of Uncle Frank Berry (the old house is still standing). In a short time this supposition of the farmer was confirmed by the announcement of the father's name.

A few days after I visited an aged lady by the name Litsay, who interested me much by giving me a description of the wedding of the father and mother of the new candidate, she having been a friend of the bride and present at the marriage. In 1866, after the liberation of 4,000,000 slaves had made the name of Abraham Lincoln memorable, I was again in the neighborhood and visited the old house in which was celebrated the nuptial rites above referred to. Its surroundings are among the most picturesque in Kentucky. The Beach Fork, a small river of wonderful meanderings, flows near and is lost to view in a semi-circular amphitheatre of hills. While surveying the surrounding landscape, I thought it not strange that inspiration had fallen on the mother of him who should be known as the liberator of the Nineteenth Century.

The official record of this marriage will probably be found at Springfield. The newly married pair soon after left the county.

As I remember the story of Nancy Hanks, it ran thus: Her father and mother were Virginians, and died when she was very young. Her mother's name before marriage was Shipley, and she was known to have two sisters, one of whom was married to man by the name of Berry and the other to Robert Mitchell, who came to Kentucky about the year 1780; while on the journey the family was set upon by the Indians and Mrs. M was fatally wounded, and their only daughter, Sarah, a child of eleven years old, was captured and borne away by the Modocs of the Wilderness. Mr. Mitchell bore the dying wife to a crab orchard and, like Abraham of old, purchased the renowned spot for the burial of his wife. After the last sad rites he mounted his horse, accompanied by his friend, Gen. Adair, and went in search of his daughter, but was drowned in Dip river while attempting to cross. The sons of this father and mother were scattered to different parts of the State. One of them, Daniel, settled in Washington county on the Beach Fork, a few miles from Springfield, and near two cousins, Frank and Ned Berry. To these cousins came Nancy Hanks, whom they welcomed to their homes, for legend is "her cheerful disposition and active habits were a dower to these pioneers." Soon after Mad Anthony Wayne's treaty with the Indians in 1794 or 1795, the lost cousin was returned to her friends. The returned captive lived at the house of her brother, and Nancy Hanks at the house of her cousin, Frank Berry. These girls were soon as intimate as sisters. Sarah Mitchell was the pupil of Nancy in learning to spin flax — the latter being an adept in that now lost art. It was the custom in those days to have spinning parties, on which occasions the wheels of the ladies were carried to the house designated, to which the competitors, distaff in hand, came ready for the work of the day. At a given hour the wheels were put in motion, and the filmy fibre took the form of firmly lengthened strand in their mystic hands. Tradition says Nancy bore the palm, her spools yielding the longest and finest thread.

Mr. Lincoln was not an exception to the rule for great men, which requires that their mother shall be talented. Thomas Lincoln came, it is believed, into this neighborhood to visit his uncle Mordecai Lincoln, who lived near Major Berry, and there learned of the skill of Nancy. As Ulysses, he was ambitious, and became the husband of Nancy, whose threads of gold has been worked by the hand and pen of Abraham into the warp and woof of the national constitution. Sarah Mitchell became the wife of a Virginian, and the mother of an interesting family. She was a woman of high order of talent, and retained until death the greatest veneration for the memory of her cousin, whose name she gave to one of her daughters.

Modesty has laid the impress of silence upon the relatives of a noble woman, but when the voice of calumny has presumed to sully her name, they hurl the accusation to the ground and proclaim her the beautiful character they had learned to love long before they knew to her had been given an honored son.

One who learned from sainted lips to admire her grandmother's cousin.

C.S.H.V.[1]

I have no idea who was the author, only the initials being given. But I have no doubt that it is substantially the true history. After the marriage of Thomas Lincoln and Nancy Hanks he brought her to Elizabeth Town, where he lived and worked at the carpenter trade. A house is still standing in this neighborhood, the inside work of which he did. I knew him well, he had one daughter in Elizabeth Town, and she died, after which he removed to a place called Buffalo, about 14 miles from Elizabeth Town, in the same county — Harden — now Laura. At this point Abraham was born; then they moved about four miles to the head of Knob Creek, in the same county. After which he removed to Indiana, when I lost sight of him until Nancy was dead. He then came back to Elizabeth Town and in short order married a widow Johnson, whose maiden name was Sally Burt. I was then clerk and issued the license and know all about it.

April 18, 1874.

SAM'L HAYCRAFT (in 79th year),
Elizabeth Town, Ky.

Mr. Byron M. Hanks,[2] Rochester, N.Y.

LC: HW3155 (letter), HW3155A–55B (clipping)

---

1. Charlotte S. Hobart Vawter, an Indianapolis woman who maintained that her grandmother, Sarah Mitchell, was a first cousin of Nancy Hanks Lincoln.

2. Byron M. Hanks wrote WHH a series of letters about a family named Hanks that would appear to be entirely unrelated to AL.

472. James H. Matheny (WHH interview)

Octr 6th '81

I went into Mr. Matheny's office Octr 5th '81 and he and I had a conversation — Mr. Matheny said, substantially — "I do not know whether Lamon's life of Lincoln was before me when I wrote the Reed letter[1] or not — do not rember one way or the other whether I told Mr Reed that Lincoln investigated Christianity — Reed wrote the Letter and I signed it, telling him before he wrote the letter facts as I now remember it — I signed the note in Lamon's life of Lincol[2] — never supposing that it would be published — sorry it is published — don't blame you — I think he said it was private —

I then told him that I was in the act of financially breaking — and was compelled to sell — I expressed regret about the matter.[3] I said that the book was an unfortunate book for writer and publisher & c.

I took these notes on the morning of the 6th day of Octr. '81

W H Herndon

Further — I showed My my notes of Decr. 9th 1873[4] — he said they were correct. down to — sharp game — he repeated to me however that the saying in his opinion was true so I say — I remarked. — I told him something about Yates — Lincoln — Ellis & myself — which I never will make public

Herndon[5]

Many of my papers have been lost — Some have been Eaten up by Mice — My office was once gutted by fire & by the People during the fire — Zane & I were then in partnership — up stairs above Miller's hard ware store — kept my papers there — I am surprised that many of my papers have been stolen — let every man see & read them — didnt watch them — Took Some papers with Me when I lectured in reply to Reed[6] — to the capital city where I had them [from] the one lost probably I can find Em. Think I had Stuarts & Mathenys & Mrs Lincolns notes at the Lecture — to Show — Read & Exhibit if I was contradicted — Cant lay my hand on them now —

LC: HW3170

---

1. See §468.

2. See Lamon, 487–88.

3. WHH refers to selling Ward Hill Lamon copies of his letters and interviews about AL, on which Lamon's biography is based.

4. §468.

5. Marginal note: *I wrote to Mr Arnold of Chicago — before I sold my materials to Lamon, telling him I wanted to sell — wrote to some people in Boston & &c the same — got no buyers — sold to Lamon under financial troubles. H.*

6. WHH exchanged public lectures with Rev. James A. Reed in Springfield in 1873 on the subject of AL's religion.

473. Isaac N. Arnold to WHH

Chicago Dec. 18. 1882

My Dear Sir

Thanks for Your letter of the 16th.

In regard to Mr Bateman he does not stand up very squarely. I wrote to him once to ask him if Holland had repeated him correctly & he replied — as I recollect *"substantially".* His letter was burned in the great fire.

My idea of Mr Lincoln's settled Views of christianity is about this. He believed in the great fundamental principals of Christianity — but as to creeds & dogma, he was not strictly *orthadox.* I shall send you in a day or two — my paper on *"A Layman's Faith,"* Which will give You my ideas of What the fundamental principles of christianity are. — I say nothing about trinity — eternal punishment &c — I refer You to this paper for *my* faith. Which is not of any importance to the world. What do you say to Lincoln's letter to John Johnston — dated Jany 12. 1852?[1] — Lamon p. 336. I dont know, but if You & I were to sit down & compare our opinions about Mr Lincoln's religion I think we should not be so far apart as we seem — can you spare a copy of Your reply to Reed?

If we differ — it will be an *honest* difference — & we shall not cease to believe — each means to be truthful —

Very truly Yours
Isaac N. Arnold

LC: HW3183

474. Joshua F. Speed (statement for WHH)[1]

[by 1882]

Incidents in the early life of A. Lincoln;
by Joshua Speed — Louisville, Kentucky.

In 1834, I was a citizen of Springfield, Sangamon Co, Ill. Mr Lincoln lived in the country, fourteen miles from the town. He was a laborer, and a deputy surveyor, and at the same time a member of the legislature, elected the year previously. In 1835, he was a candidate for reelection. I had not seen him for the first six months of my residence there, but had heard him spoken of as a man of wonderful ability on the stump. He was a long, gawky, ugly, shapeless, man. He had never spoken as far as I know of, at the county seat, during his first candidacy. The second time he was a candidate, he had already made in the legislature, considerable reputation, and on his renomination to the legislature, advertised to meet his opponents, and speak in Springfield, on a given day. I believe, that that was the first public speech, he ever made at the court-house.

---

1. See AL to John D. Johnston, Jan. 12, 1851, *CW* 2:96–97.

---

1. This statement is in an unknown hand and seems to have been sent to WHH by Speed before his death in 1882. It first appeared in Oldroyd, 143–47.

He was never ashamed so far as I know, to admit his ignorance upon any subject, or of the meaning of any word no matter how ridiculous it might make him appear. As he was riding into town the evening before the speech he passed the handsomest house in the village which had just been built by Geo. Forquer. Upon it he had placed a lightning rod. The first one in the town or county. Some ten or twelve young men were riding with Lincoln. He asked them what that rod was for. They told him it was to keep off the lightning. "How does it do it"? he asked. None of them could tell. He rode into town, bought a book on the properties of lightning, and before morning knew all about it. When he was ignorant upon any subject, he addressed himself to the task of being ignorant no longer. On this occasion a large number of citizens came from a distance to hear him speak. He had very able opponents. I stood near him and heard the speech. I was fresh from Kentucky then, and had heard most of her great orators. It struck me then, as it seems to me now, that I never heard a more effective speaker. All the party weapons of offense, and defense, seemed to be entirely under his control. The large crowd, seemed to be swayed by him as he pleased. He was a whig, and quite a number of candidates were associated with him on the whig ticket; seven I think in number; there were seven democrats opposed to them. The debate was a joint one, and Lincoln was appointed to close it, which he did as I have heretofore described in a most masterly style.

The people commenced leaving the court-house, when Geo, Forquer, a man of much celebrity in the state, rose, and asked the people to hear him. He was not a candidate, but was a man of talents, and of great state notoriety, as a speaker. He commenced his speech by turning to Lincoln and saying, "This young man will have to be taken down, and I am truly sorry that the task devolves upon me". He then proceeded in a vein of irony, sarcasm, and wit, to ridicule Lincoln in every way that he could. Lincoln stood, not more than ten feet from him, with folded arms, and an eye flashing fire, and listened attentively to him, without ever interrupting him. Lincoln then took the stand for reply. He was pale and his spirits seemed deeply moved. His opponent was one worthy of his steel. He answered him fully, and completely. The conclusion of his speech I remember even now, so deep an impression did it make on me then. He said, "The gentleman commenced his speech by saying that this young man would have to be taken down, alluding to me; I am not so young in years as I am in the tricks and trades of a politician; but live long, or die young, I would rather die now, than, like the gentleman change my politics, and simultaneous with the change, receive an office worth three thousand dollars per year, and then have to erect a lightning-rod over my house, to protect a guilty conscience from an offended God"

He used the lightning-rod against Forquer as he did everything in after life.

In 1837, after his return from the legislature, Mr Lincoln obtained a license to practice law. He lived fourteen miles in the country, and had ridden into town on a borrowed horse, with no earthly goods but a pair of saddle-bags, two or three law books, and some clothing which he had in the saddle-bags. He took an office and engaged from the only cabinet-maker then in the village, a single bedstead.

He came into my store (I was a merchant then), set his saddle-bags on the counter, and asked me "what the furniture for a single bedstead would cost." I took slate and pencil, and made calculation, and found the sum for furniture complete, would amount to seventeen dollars in all. Said he, "It is probably cheap enough; but I want to say that cheap as it is I have not the money to pay. But if you will credit me until Christmas, and my experiment here as a lawyer is a success, I will pay you then. If I fail in that I will probably never be able to pay you at all." The tone of his voice was so melancholy that I felt for him. I looked up at him, and I thought then as I think now, that I never saw so gloomy, and melancholy a face. I said to him; "The contraction of so small a debt, seems to affect you so deeply, I think I can suggest a plan by which you will be able to attain your end, without incurring any debt. I have a very large room, and a very large double-bed in it; which you are perfectly welcome to share with me if you choose". "Where is your room"? asked he. "Upstairs" said I, pointing to the stairs leading from the store to my room. Without saying a word, he took his saddle-bags on his arm, went up stairs, set them down on the floor, came down again, and with a face beaming with pleasure and smiles exclaimed "Well Speed I'm moved". Mr Lincoln was then twenty-seven years old, almost without friends, and with no property except the saddle-bags with clothes mentioned within.

Now for me to have lived to see such a man rise from point to point, and from place to place, filling all the places to which he was called, with honor and distinction, until he reached the presidency, filling the presidential chair in the most trying times that any ruler ever had, seems to me more like fiction than fact. None but a genius like his could have accomplished so much, and none but a government like ours could produce such a man. It gave the young eagle scope for his wing. He tried it and soared to the top!

In 1839 Mr Lincoln, being then a lawyer in full practice, attended all the courts adjacent to Springfield. He was then attending court at Christiansburg, about thirty miles distant. I was there when the court broke up. Quite a number of lawyers were coming from court, to Springfield. We were riding along a country road, two and two together, some distance apart, Lincoln and Jno. J. Hardin being behind. (Hardin was afterward made Colonel and was killed at Buena Vista). We were passing through a thicket of wild plum, and crab-apple trees, where we stopped to water our horses. After waiting some time Hardin came up and we asked him where Lincoln was. "Oh," said he, "when I saw him last" (there had been a severe wind storm), "he had caught two little birds in his hand, which the wind had blown from their nest, and he was hunting for the nest". Hardin left him before he found it. He finally found the nest, and placed the birds, to use his own words, "in the home provided for them by their mother". When he came up with the party they laughed at him. Said he, earnestly, "I could not have slept tonight if I had not given those two little birds to their mother".

This was the the flower that bloomed so beautifully in his nature, on his native prairies. He never lost the nobility of his nature, nor the kindness of his heart, by being removed to a higher sphere of action. On the contrary both were increased. The enlarged sphere of his action, developed the natural promptings of his heart.[2]

I enclose these incidents in the early life of Mr Lincoln — I do hope that you may prize them —

With kind regards to Stuart & Judge Gillespie when you see them I am
Your friend
Joshua F. Speed

ISHL: Speed Papers

475. *Elizabeth Herndon Bell (JWW interview)*

Petersburg Menard Co Ills. Aug 24 1883

Mentor Graham — Lincoln's teacher now 80 years old and living in Dakota — daughter Mrs Lizzie H. Bell 50 years old lives in Petersburg — father kept hotel at N. Salem — Mother went away, one day to see friends who had just come from Kentucky leaving Lincoln and a large girl Polly — who was ugly & awkward to Keep house while she was gone — They broke so many dishes & spoiled so much food — L. made a hoe cake & put handful of salaratus instead of salt in it — when Mrs G. returned L ran down the road in the mud without hat to announce his bad luck — L. went to Graham's school with Ann Rutledge who died an old maid in Iowa yrs afterward — Ms. B. attended quilting when Ann helped quilt. Ann was beautiful girl and skillful with the needle   At this quilting L. sat beside her and whispered words of love into her ear   She was so much excited or worked up over it that she overlooked her work and made long irregular stitches and the quilt now in possession of person at Petersburg shows by the long stitches today when L. talked love to her — L. offered Mrs B. brother Simpson Graham a new jack Knife if he would Kiss a certain pretty girl as she went to school. Simpson agreed to do it. So L. and some other boys hid behind a clump of trees along the road to see the work done. Simp. met the girl — stepped up put both hands on her cheeks and made the attempt to kiss her — but the girl was equal to the occasion — they carried with their dinner to school in those days a jug of milk — this the girl broke on Simpson's head the milk bespattering his jeans clothes. L. & the boys enjoyed the fun and Simp was given the Knife by L. for his attempt.

When L first came to N Salem he wore a suit of grey jeans clothes and a stove pipe hat — a long shaft for a hat with a narrow brim — a very fashionable style in those days. for a time worked in a hotel

ISHL: Weik Papers

---

2. The portion of the manuscript ending here, pages numbered [1]–6, is in an unknown hand. The remaining portion, on a separate page, is in Speed's hand.

476. Isaac N. Arnold to WHH

Chicago   Nov. 27. 1883

My Dear Sir

I have Your letters of Nov. 24 & 26th.

The expression in the P.S. of Your letter of 24th is "I dont think Mr Lincoln had a broad & *Universal* affection for men." I will change the word *"universal"* to *generous.*

The story of *"Tilda"* is very interesting.[1] I had never seen it before. I think I shall use it —. *Truth,* integrity — *honesty,* these were indeed the basis of his charactar — The story of the P. Office money, which Dr Henry[2] told me — & other new-Salem anecdotes — shew his sterling honesty, as the story of Tilda does his truthfulness.

I never asked about Lincolns virtue, because I never had any reason to doubt it, & I thought on this point I knew him, but Your knowledge is far greater & I am glad You confirme my impressions.

I rather agree with You — about Lincoln's affection for men — if you mean *personal* attachments. He had warm friends though.

But take men as a whole I think he thought better of them than they deserve. He had more *faith* in mankind, the masses than any other man I ever knew. He was never directly acquainted with the vice, corruption of our great cities — man as he knew him best on the frontier — was as Lincoln believed — disposed to do right — but in these great corrupt cities — there is always a large class far below Lincoln's general Estimate of humanity.

With many thanks / I am

Very truly Yours
Isaac N. Arnold

LC: HW3191–92

477. Elizabeth and Ninian W. Edwards (JWW interview)[1]

December. Thursday 20. 1883.

In the afternoon called at the home of N. W. Edwards & wife. Asked the latter as to marriage with Lincoln of her sister Mary Todd. She said arrangements for wedding had been made — even cakes had been baked — but L. failed to appear. At this point Mr Edwards cautioned his wife that she was talking to newspaper man and she declined to say more. She had said that Mary was greatly mortified by Ls strange conduct. Later they were reunited and finally married

LC: Beveridge Papers, box 412

---

1. See §74.
2. Dr. Anson G. Henry.

---

1. This is an entry from JWW's diary. The text is taken from a photostat of the page on which it is entered.

478. *Travis Elmore (JWW interview)*

[1883?¹]

Nelson Alley Kept hotel when L. first came to Salem. Plug Hat — blue jeans swallow tail coat — worked for his board — next year went to work for Saml Hill goods brought from St Louis — even after became surveyor made Hill's house headquarters —

Travis Elmore — says while L. was surveyor he stopped at Ms Rhoda Clearys — had her to mend his breeches while he sat in bed — his surveying instruments were sold also his pony by constable to satisfy debt — Bid in by Jim Short and given by him to L.

ISHL: Weik Papers, box 2

479. *George B. Balch (statement for JWW)*

4 10 '85

Lincoln's Memory.

In the early settleing of Illinois it frequently happened that farmers turned their young stock on the range in early Spring and never saw them again until "Chill Novembers surly blast" warned them that winter was approaching. As young horses were seldom branded, it sometimes happened that two men, both being perfectly honest, would claim the same animal; in all such cases the dispute would end in a lawsuit.

In the Spring of 1837 John Rodgers, who resided in the south part of Coles Co. and near where Abraham Lincoln's father resided turned his yearling and two year old colts out on the boundless pasture. Late in the fall of the same year they were found about fifteen miles away and brought home. One yearling mare colt in the lot was claimed by another man who brought suit for the recovery of his property. The suit was before a justice of the peace, and Abraham Lincoln was employed by Mr. Rodgers to defend his case.

After a full hearing the justice decided that the colt belonged to Mr Rodgers. The plaintiff appealed the case to the circuit court of Coles County.

Mr Lincoln again appeared for Mr Rodgers and showed by preponderance of evidence and the most convinceing argument that the animal rightfully belonged to his client. The court so decided and Mr R took possession of the property.

The years rolled by: the colt grew to be a splendid animal, and soon became the favorite family nag. Still the years swept by. Lincoln had been in Congress, the war with Mexico had been fought, Lincoln and Douglas had stirred the political caldron of Illinois to the bottom, the wild expanse of prairie had been changed to fruitful fields. Illinois was rapidly wheeling into line as the fourth State in the union, and Lincoln had been elected President of the United States, but the mare still lived and was known throughout the surrounding country as "Old Trim."

---

1. On a facing page is a notation dated October 23, 1883.

Early in February 1861 Lincoln came into the same neighborhood to visit his aged Step Mother and take a last look at the grave of his humble Sire. These sad duties discharged he stoped in the viliage of Farmington near by to get dinner. A knowledge of his presence spread like wild fire, the school was dismissed and teachers, scholars and villiagers hastened to the house where he had stoped to see the nations chief.

Among those who heard of his presence was his old friend and client John Rodgers who lived, about one mile away. He at once saddled "Old Trim" and galloped to the villiage. Lincoln met and greeted him in the most cordial manner. After the first salutations Mr Rodgers addressed him as follows:

"Well Abe, I still own the mare you gained for me in the lawsuit a long time ago; I rode her to the election to vote for you and have rode her here, Do you remember that lawsuit."

Lincoln promptly replyed "O yes John, I remember it well, it took place in 1837"!!

Twenty three years had passed by and yet without any apparant effort to grasp it he gave the exact date.

Geo B. Balch

Friend Weik my hand is sore therefor my writing is very poor — no one but an expert can read it.

If references are needed on my part I refer you to Hon. J S Canon of Danville. Gov Oglesby, or any prominent man in Coles Co.

Geo B. Balch

LC: HW4576–80

480. Paul Selby to JWW

Springfield, Ill., Aug. 16 1885.

Dear Sir.

Hon. N. W. Edwards has referred to me your letter of the 10th inst., in reference to the letter written by Abraham Lincoln in 1836 to Col. Robert Allen,[1] of this city. Mr. Edwards being himself too unwell to reply, has asked me to do so for him.

He states the letter was written as stated by you, being called out by Col. Allen's statement that he was aware of certain facts which if known would insure the defeat of both Lincoln and Edwards, who were candidates on the Whig ticket for the State Legislature. Lincoln's letter challenged Allen to produce his alleged facts, but no response was made to the Challenge and the conclusion was that he had nothing to produce.

Allen was a prominent "Jackson Democrat" who died many years ago.

Respectfully Yours,
Paul Selby

LC: HW4587–88

---

1. *CW* 1:48–49.

481. George B. Balch (statement for JWW)

[Janesville, Ill., 1885?]

"Honor thy father and thy mother."
Abraham Lincoln's
first attorneys fee, and how
he used the money.

When Abraham Lincoln was granted license to plead law in the courts of Illinois he put the precious document in his pocket and immediately set out to visit his father who lived in Pleasant Grove, Coles County.

Just at that time James Gill, a man of considerable wealth who lived near Thomas Lincoln brought suit against another man who had allowed his stock to destroy the growing crops of the plaintiff.

The suit was for trespass, and before a justice of the peace. Mr Gill learning that the young attorney was in the neighborhood secured his services.

Mr Lincoln conducted the case to the entire satisfaction of his client, and secured a judgment for ten dollars and cost against the defendent. As soon as the case was decided Mr Gill took out his pocket book and taking a ten dollar bill therefrom presented it to Mr Lincoln saying "here Abe is your fee." Lincoln replyed "No Mr Gill, this is my first case, and besides you are a neighbor of my father and I had no thought of charging you anything." Mr Gill insisted and Mr Lincoln continued to to refuse, saying that the amount was too great for the service rendered. Gill was a proud-spirited impulsive man, and Lincoln, seeing that resistance was useless, addressed him as follows: "Well Mr Gill as you insist upon it I will take the money and give it to father, for he is poor and needs it." So saying he took the bill, and turning to his father, who was present, gave it to him.

This is the beginning of the professional career of a man whose name is known and whose praise is sung wherever Liberty has found a home.

This incident was related to the writer by Mr Gill a short time before he died. He was one of the pioneers of Eastern Illinois, and was a man of undoubted veracity. He died in 1884 at the age of 87 years.

Geo. B. Balch,

LC: HW4581–83

482. George B. Balch (statement for JWW)

[1885?]

The Grave of the
Father of Abraham Lincoln
By Geo. B. Balch.

The grave described in the following lines is situated in a quiet Country church yard near the south line of Coles Co Illinois. Until the year 1876 a small boulder and a little mound of earth was all that marked the last resting place of Thomas Lincoln, the "Amram"[1] of America.

In February 1861 Abraham Lincoln visited the last resting place of his humble Sire, and with his pen-knife cut the initials "T.L." on a bit of oak board and placed it at the head of the grave; this was afterwards carried away by some curiosity hunter and the grave was only distinguished from others by the few remaining persons who were present at the burial.

In 1876 as before alluded to the writer, fearing that the grave would be entirely lost, pened the annexed lines and had them published in some of the local papers; this called attention to the matter, and about four years thereafter a suitable stone was placed over the grave.[2]

LC: HW4584–86

483. Alexander C. Campbell to JWW

La Salle Sep 29 1886

Dear Sir

Yours of 27th received   In reply would say that I have but one of Mr Lincolns letters which I special reasons for retaining in my possession.[1] Believing that when Good public men die much of their private correspondence in relation to Men and Measures might be wrongly Construed I Consigned to the flames all his letters Except the one refered to. And I would not give it to the public were it that he after many years after it was written Communicated to the Contents to parties some of whom were personal friends of he and I. and some that were otherwise   Having several applications similar to yours particularly in reference to the letter in question I have Concluded to have it photographed and if the artist is successful in producing a perfect Copy I will mail one to you with a brief history of the Cercumstances under which it was written which is the best I Can do for you and other inquering friends of the great and good man so univerally admired by Men of all parties

Yours Very truly
A. Campbell

LC: HW4590

484. Margaret Ryan (JWW interview)

Oct. 27 1886

Margaret Ryan — 47 year. Lived at Lincoln House till Feby 1860 — Mrs L was cranky — told M before L. was nominated that she would go to the White House

---

1. Father of Moses.
2. A six-stanza poem by Balch is omitted.

---

1. Probably AL to Campbell, June 25, 1858, CW 2:473.

yet. L hired M. and told her he would pay M. 75¢ More than Ms L. to stay there — not to fuss with Mrs. L. often would put hand on Ms — head and tell her to Keep courage. Ms L would whip Bob a good deal. She was half crazy — black women Jane Jenkins colored woman did not live there — in next block. M went to Washington — saw L at White House — he gave her a pass back home — told her to call next day and get some money &c for clothes for her children — but that night he was assassinated — while in Sp L. went to Taylorville hired M. to stay while his wife was confined — gave birth to boy. Dr Wallace attended her. Ms L. often struck other girls but never struck M. — When L. was leaving for Taylorville his wife ran him out half dressed — as she followed him with broom — he told to Meg not to get scared — that Ms L. would get over it — M had to go and bring him out his clothes — he dressed and went up town through wood-house & alley — when he returned in evening would come in through kitchen and find out from M. if ML. was all right before going in front of house — At another time saw Mrs L. strike L. on head with piece of wood while reading pa-per in South Parlor — cut his nose — lawyers saw his face in Court next day but asked no questions

ISHL: Weik Papers, box 2, Memorandum Book 1

485. George B. Balch (JWW interview)

[1886?]

Geo B Balch born in Tenn. came to Coles Co. in 1830 — Thos Lincoln came in 1830 frm Spen Co Ind in a rude wagon with oxen — wagon all wood not a bit of iron in — moved to Macon Co & Thos L & family returned to Coles Co in 1833 — Abraham did not come   After A Lincoln became law student he walked all way from Springfield to see his father and Balch recollects of seeing Thos Ls son — the young lawyer from Springfield. At another visit Abraham conducted lawsuit for one of his fathers old neighbors Richard Gill for trespass — obtained judg. for $10. Gill offered fee of $10 which Abe refused but gave to his father. Balch says Thos L. could write because Squire Grimes has mortgage signed by Thos L. & he could read Bi-ble. an excellent spec. of poor white trash — *[illegible]* with large nose not so tall as Abraham. Abe visited his grave shortly before going to Washington to be inaugurat-ed to see his fathers grave & visit his stepmother who was living — made arrange-ments to have stone placed over fathers grave & iron fence but was not done

Thos L had [long?] face & rough man — never drank but lazy & worthless — had few sheep — poked around behind them talked an walked slow —

Lincolns step mother said when her own boy was away at dances Abraham was at home with head at fire place reading or studying.

In 1837 during visit Abrah L. represented neighbor Rogers in Coles Co be-fore Justice and got possession of mare. 1860 during visit to step mother before going to Wash. *[illegible]* John Rogers came over and brought same mare — said he rode her to polls to vote for L & later remembered mare.

ISHL: Weik Papers, box 2, Memorandum Book 1

486. Dennis F. Hanks (JWW interview)

[1886?]

Nancy H Lincoln — was a spare made woman — little above ordinary height — sandy complexion — hair dark brown — eyes hazel — chistian woman — could read the Bible — easy temperament never Mad — Abe ran in room while old lady was weaving at window and asked Mother who was father of Zebidie's children — this fretted old lady — She was Baptists by religion — Abraham took his disposition and Mental qualities from his Mother — his father was stout heavy man — very stout and solid built — Mrs. L. was sympathetic woman conscientious and of good intelligence — Old Mr L. had one trait that Abraham inherited story telling. All of them had good memories — All the family disputes were referred to Abraham

Nancy Hanks was really the daughter of Lucy Hanks and Henry Sparrow but she resembled the Hanks so much they called her Hanks — The Hanks and Sparrows moved from Va to Mercer Co Ky.

ISHL: Weik Papers, box 2, Memorandum Book 1

487. John W. Lamar to J. W. Wartmann[1]

Buffaloville Ind   Jany 3rd /87

My Dear friend

yours of the 29 at hand, allways glad to hear from you, inclosed you will find the Herndon letter I think you can get all the facts you want in the matter of the Lincoln-Grigsby affair, from what I have allways understood the thing happened about as Mr Herndon heard it. My father-in-law told the story to me and my wife often.

My wifes father was a brother to the old lady Grigsby,[2] and was at the infair when the thing happened, and Lincoln wrote a piece about nearly all the people present, and a piece about my father-in-law that he never got over until after Lincoln was a candidate for President

Old John Swaney, who was a carpenter, was working about the old Grigsby house, and found the paper, that Lincoln wrote about the Grigsby affair, and called it the "Cronicals of Reuben as Reuben was the old man Grigsby's given name. My wife was at the Grigsby infair, but too young to recollect much about only what her parents talked about the matter. Red Grigsby[3] could tell a good deal about it, if he would. Red told me that his brother Bill and Johnson had fight over the Cronicals of Reuben.

---

1. This is a copy, so labeled. Marginal note: *This letter was written to J.W Wartmann and sent to me by Wartmann — I wrote to Wartmann for the facts & got 'em.   H*

2. Lamar's wife, Milley (1825–1913), was the daughter of William Barker, whose sister, Nancy (1780–1848), was the wife of Reuben Grigsby, Sr.

3. Redmond Grigsby (1818–1907) was the tenth of twelve children born to Reuben and Nancy (Barker) Grigsby.

Mr Swaney worked for me after he found those papers and told me, that he gave them to some of the Grigsby as well as I recollect.

One of the Grigsby widows is living yet. she being one of the parties, could tell all about it, if she would. she lives near Corn island in this County.

I think I will go down and see her, and see if she is yet old enough to talk about it. I understand that she refused to talk about it. Please excuse me for so much

Yours Truly

John W. Lamar

I will tell you what Swaney told me about the papers that he found in the Grigsby house, that Lincoln wrote Tim Swaney the old man Swaney's son found them first and spent too much time reading them as the old man thought and the old man ordered the younger to go to work when the young man said, hold on father here is part of the Holy Bible, that never has been revealed yet, so that settled the matter, and the father went to reading

J.W.L.

LC: HW4593–94

488. Benjamin R. Vineyard to JWW

St. Joseph, Mo., Jany 13 — 1887

Dear Sir,

Your letter of 10*th* inst. has been received. I have no picture of my mother (who died July 4*th* 1877) except a photograph taken a few years before her death and about the time she was sixty-five years of age. This picture is reasonably true to life, and if you desire, I will have a reprint taken of this photograph and send you. I wish I had a picture of her when young, as I have often heard her spoken of by those who then Knew her as being very handsome. Most biographers of Mr. Lincoln, so far as I have seen their references to my Mother, whose Maiden name was Mary S. Owens, have been very Kind and fair. Once only, and that in a newspaper article wherein language was attributed to my mother insinuating that she was an uneducated woman, have *I* thought myself called on to say anything in her defense. What I then said was published in a local paper here (The Gazette) in its issue dated June 12*th,* 1881, and a clipping therefrom I send you inclosed, with a request that you return it to me again. I Knew my mother to be a woman of good education, reared in good society by a wealthy father, and that she could not have made use of the illiterate language attributed to her; and so I wrote and had published the article inclosed, and which, I believe, was quite largely copied into other papers.

If you will tell me in reply all (in detail) that you wish from me, I will as far as I can comply with your request, simply bespeaking for my mother, whose memory is dear to me such reference as a good woman who in all things, I am sure, acted honorably with Mr. Lincoln deserves. I do not mean by this the suppression of truth, but such fair treatment as a young lady of good standing, who had the honor, after a courtship in which she took no unladylike course, to reject the offered hand of Mr. Lincoln.

I think most of the letters to my mother from the ex-president, except those published in Lamon's work, were destroyed. I will, however write my sister, who has Mother's old papers and learn. Hoping to hear from you again, I subscribe myself, Yours truly,

B.R. Vineyard.

LC: HW4595–96

489. J. W. Porter to JWW

Urbana, Jany. 14th 1887

Dear Sir:

In reply to your letter of 2nd inst. addressed to the County Clerk of this Co., who referred it to me I herewith send you a Copy from the Judges docket of 1858 of this Court showing an entry made therein by the great Martyr to American Liberty Mr Lincoln. At the time he made this entry as I have been informed he was one of the leading lawyers practicing in the Courts of this part of Illinois. And Hon. David Davis was then sitting as Judge in the Circuit of which this Co was a part. — It was the habit of Judge Davis to frequently leave the bench when attacked with headache or indisposition and Call one of the principal attorneys to sit in his place for an hour or two, And he Called upon Mr Lincoln more than any one else to take his place, they being very warm and Close friends, It was on such an occasion that the case here designated came up and was heard by him and he made the rulings as designated on the docket.

Very respectfully yours
J.W. Porter
Clerk

Extract from Page 24 of Judge's docket, April term 1858
Circuit Court of Champaign County Illinois
Names of Parties
L. D. Chaddon vs J. D. Beasley, Albert Gere L. Lancaster, John H. Thomas, S. Dean, Jas. H. Smith, Charles T. Dox, James N Boutwell, B. Z. Green M.L. Dunlap, Lewellen Powell, Peterson McNutt, J. J. Sutton, N. M. Clark, Wm Stokes James Curtiss, C.M. Sherfy, Jonathan Bacon, John H. Angle C.W. Angle, and Robert Smith.

Kind of Action.
Assumpsit.

Judge's Remarks
Plea in abatement by B. Z. Green a defendant not Served filed Saturday at 11

o'clock A.M. April 24*th* 1856. Stricken from the files by order of the Court. Dem. to the declaration if there ever was one overruled,

Defendants who are served, now at 8 o'clock P.M. of the last day of the term ask to plead to the merits which is denied by the Court on the ground that the offer comes too late, and therefore as by Nil Dicet judgement is rendered for the Plff. against the defendants who are served with process. Clerk assess damages.

(The above entry Commencing with word plea, was cut out (it being in hand writing of Hon. A. Lincoln) and sent to North Western Sanitary Fair at Chicago May 23d 1865.

O. O. Alexander Clerk.)

LC: HW4597–98

490. Nancy G. Vineyard to JWW

Victoria Texas Feb 4th 1887

Dear Sir

Your letter of inquiry regarding the courtship of my sister Mary S Vineyard and Abram Lincoln was received, and in reply, I am sorry to say I know very little about the matter farther than this, that she spoke of his asking her to marry him and he not being the style of man she wished to marry rejected him. She viewed him as a man of fine intellect and (although crude) energetic and aspiring and thought he would some day rise far above his then humble and modest position in society. My sister then Mary S Owens of Green County KY where she was born and married, was a young lady of beauty and intelligence and much vivacity, and had many admirers especially gentlemen. She had many offers of marriage from the best young men of her acquaintance, who, strange to say, always parted with her in friendship, and continued friendly towards her afterwards. This was the case with Mr Lincoln, who wrote to her some time after they agreed to disagree. Of course these letters were mostly letters of friendship. At the time she met Mr Lincoln she was visiting her sister[1] in Sangamon county Illinois, where I think Mr Lincoln then resided. At the time this took place I was living in Missouri and knew but little of the happenings of my family and was not associated but little with my sister until she married my husbands brother and moved near me several years after her visit to Illinois. Her son B R Vineyard of St Joseph Mo had many letters some time ago written by Mr Lincoln to his mother and her daughter Mrs Kate Cunningham of Weston Platte county Mo (not far from St Joseph) had a very good Ambrotype taken of her mother when she was much younger than in the picture you have. I am sorry I cannot give you any farther information

Respectfully

Mrs Nancy G Vineyard

LC: HW4601–2

---

1. Elizabeth Abell.

491. Dillard C. Donnohue (JWW interview)

Feb 13 '87

was with Lincoln at War Dept. when news of Ft Donelson battle rec'd. As news grew brighter some fellow being jubilant cried out "lets have a drink." Lincoln said "All right bring in some water."

L. said on the Subject of religion that he once happened in at a class meeting in Ills. and an old man named Glenn testified that when he did good he felt good, when he did bad he felt bad. That, says, L. is my religion — deeds done in the body &c.

During the very darkest hour of the rebellion — after the blowing up of mines & men — utter failures to the Union Army on Aug 1st 1862 day of fasting & prayer. Donnohue went down one day to the White House — negroes assembled for prayer meeting in park between White House & Jackson Monument. One old chap with voice like a gong prayed with hands uplifted 'O Lord command the sun & moon to stand still while your Joshua Abraham Lincoln fights the battle of freedom." Then an old woman with handkerchief tied over head and a magnificent voice "Aunt Kitty Burton sang this song

> Believers in that day
> They will rise and fly away
> Glad to hear the trumpet sound
>   In that Morning
> Crying O Lord See How I long
> Glad to hear the trumpet sound
>   In that morning

Donnohue was at Charleston when Lincoln & Douglas made speeches, L had open & close. L. was dissatisfied with result & action of Douglas day before — Said if Douglas angered him he would state "that he (L) did not have to have his wife along to keep him sober." Donnohue had induced Greencastle Ind drum corps Conkling boys to accompany L & D on the trip. At Charleston Lincoln told story of loafer stealing butter & putting it under hat   Proprietor of store saw stealing and made loafer stay while he prepared stew at stove. Latter had to sit by stove while making stew and melted butter ran down his head while owner of store inquired of him why he was sweating so.

ISHL: Weik Papers, box 2, Memorandum Book 1

492. Andrew S. Kirk (WHH interview)

Petrsburg March 7th '87

Mr A. S. Kirk tells me this story —: In 1840 Mr Lincoln was a Candidate for the legislature. He went out to Mr Kyles[1] store in Sangamon Co. to make a speech and did so. After he was done making the Speech the boys — some of his old acquaintances — democrats, Said to Lincoln — "See here Lincoln, if you can throw

---

1. West of Springfield.

this Cannon ball further than we Can, We'll vote for you"   Lincoln picked up the large Cannon ball — felt it — swung it around — and around and said "Well, boys if thats all I have to do I'll get your votes" and then he swung it, the Cannon ball, around and around and gave it a good pitch or throw: the Cannon ball thrown by Lincoln went Some four or Six feet further than any one Could throw it.[2]

Some of the customs — habits — plays & the like of the people in 1840 and before are as follows — Marbles — pitching or throwing mauls — quoits — foot races — horse races — town ball — cat — bull pen — dancing — quiltings — social gatherings — Corn huskings; 9 Saturday was the universal day to go to Springfield & other villages to do business — get drunk and to fight

    LC: HW3843

493. H. H. Hoagland (WHH interview)

[March 7, 1887[1]]

H. H. Hoagland — Judge of the Co Court Menard James Murray — of Irish grove — William Engle Sugar grove both in Menard Co & A Lincoln of Springfield sat up all night at Bennetts Tavern[2] and vied with others in telling stories till broad day light — Treat was Judge — Menard was cut off from Sangamon in 1839. This was in 1840–1   This was continued with more or less Energy — &c during years — say from 1837 to 1842 — All of these men were splendid Story tellers — jokers &c[3]

    LC: HW3842

494. Augustus K. Riggin (WHH interview)

[March 7, 1887[1]]

Gustavus Riggin — once Clk of Menard Cir Co
    Said that during a Court in 1842 of Menard Co Lamborn — Douglas — Logan — Stuart[2] &c many of the big lawyers of the State attended Court — and that his father[3] attended Court during that Session — Father Said to me — "I wish I could raise a Son as big as Lincoln is bound to be if he lives — I have heard all three men speak at the bar and on the stump for some years and Lincoln is the greatest of them all. I say this to you, my son, though I am a democrat"[4]

    LC: HW3842

---

2. Marginal note: *Jo. Plunket / Shade Willum / Henry Perry / Robt Perkins — all were present / Col E. D. Baker / Col E. D. Taylor et. all were there —.*

---

1. This belongs to the same set of notes as §492, dated March 7, 1887.
2. Probably the hotel kept by Dr. Richard Bennett (see Onstot, 178).
3. Marginal note: *Lincoln of Sangamon Murray and Engle of Menard.*

---

1. This belongs to the same set of notes as §492, dated March 7, 1887.
2. Josiah Lamborn, Stephen A. Douglas, Stephen T. Logan, and John T. Stuart.
3. Harry Riggin, a founder of the village of Athens.
4. Marginal note: *T B Turner certificate (survey) Athens Ills.*

495. Henry Hohimer (WHH interview)

[March 7, 1887[1]]

Henry Hohimer aged 81 —

    Knew Lincoln well — Knew Ann Rutledge well — handsome woman — It is my opinion that they were engaged — would been married had he lived —. I came here in 1824 — am 81 years of age Lincoln Cut out McNamar — I was in New Salem when the boys rolled old man Jordan[2] down the hill — Lincoln tried to Stop it — The boys used to tie the horses tails together. Lincoln picked up od peices of paper and read it over and over & then threw it down: he was a great man[3]

    LC: HW3843

496. William Bennett (WHH interview)

[March 7, 1887[1]]

Wm Bennett — son of the clerk

    Heard a Conversation among the old Settlers — such as Squire Short — Godby[2] & others and it was their opinion that Lincoln & Ann Rutledge were engaged to be married —

    LC: HW3843

497. Parthena Nance Hill (WHH interview)

[March 1887?]

    Mrs. Samuel Hill[1] — am 70 years old — was married in 1835 — 28th July — My Husbands name was Saml Hill — Knew Mr Lincoln well — McNamar and Ann Rutledge. Mr Hill & McNamar were partners in the Store business — dissolved in 1832–3. McNamar was called McNeil — went to New York — stayed 2 years — Never got back till Anns death — I was married to Mr Hill in the Country — moved to N. Salem in the fall 1835 — Ann Rutledge had a brown hair — heavy set — Ann Rutledge Came out to my fathers house saw her frequently — Knew her well — Mr. Lincoln staid at our store — Saw him frequently — almost daily — heard him Spin his funny yarns — Mr Hill told me that Anns Sickness was Caused by her Complications — 2 Engagements — She — Ann did not hear of McNamar for a year or more — at last got a letter from McNamar telling

    1. This belongs to the same set of notes as §492, dated March 7, 1887.

    2. Probably James Jordan (see Onstot, 83).

    3. Marginal note: *Jasper Rutledge / J. M Rutledge.*

    1. This belongs to the same set of notes as §492, dated March 7, 1887.

    2. James Short and Russell Godbey.

    1. Marginal note: *Mrs. Hill is the wife of Saml Hill the man who Courted Ann Rutledge & burned Lincolns treatus on Infidelity.*

her to be ready they having been engaged &c to be married — Lincoln took advantage of McNamars absence — Courted Ann — got her Confidence &c and were in Mr Hills & my opinion — as well as the Opinion of others that they were Engaged — Ann well thought that McNamar was playing off on her.[2]

The women had plays — quiltings — social gatherings — went to Church &c

I think that if McNamar had got back from NY before Anns death that she would have married McNamar — I saw McNamar unload his furniture on arriving from N.Y. This is my honest opinion —

I have heard Lincoln tell his Stories — Our Store was a kind of meeting — Social gathering place — roof over the front Shed or porch — back floor — Shingle roof — men met here and talked politics — told stories &c

Board was about $100 — $150 — washing about $100 — $125[3] per month — didn't cost much to live, I assure you.

LC: HW3925

498. Elizabeth Herndon Bell (WHH interview)[1]

[March 1887[2]]

Lizzie Herndon Bell

I am the daughter of Mentor Graham — am 55 years old — Born near New Salem 1833 — Knew Mr Lincoln well — he was frequently at my fathers house — lived about ½ mile from New Salem —. Fanny Bails had a quilting at the request of Lincoln in New Salem — Ann Rutlidge was there — An Rutledge I think had her Eye on Hill — more than on Lincoln — don't think that Ann Rutledge was absolutely Engaged to Lincoln though She sent for him during the last sickness — At the quilting Fanny Bailes had her eye on Lincoln and Lincoln had his Eye on Ann — To make Ann a little more attentive to Lincoln he L seemed to go for Miss Bails —. Miss B stuck a neadle in her finger — Lincoln pulled it out. Lincoln quilted on the quilt a line or two The quilt is wore out. Lincolns acts nettled Ann to a kind of jeolesy. Ann paid him back in his own Coin — Lincoln would ask my mother if he should marry this or that woman. Lincoln & Ann had a fly up, but on her deathbed she sent for Lincon & all things were reconciled. McNamar returned before the death of Ann — McNamar would not marry Ann because she flirted with Lincoln — I was simple a child in 1835–6 and don't Know much of my own knowledge only heard people talk

LC: HW3842

---

2. The next two paragraphs were written in the margin.

3. These figures, given without decimal points, represent amounts of from $1.00 to $1.50.

---

1. WHH marginal note: *Daughter of Mentor Graham, both father & daughter — cranky — flighty — at times nearly non copus mentis — but good & honest.*

2. Even though her age should place this interview in 1888, the year of her death, it seems more likely that it belongs to the cluster of Petersburg interviews WHH did in March 1887.

499. Elizabeth Herndon Bell (WHH interview)[1]

[March 1887?]

Mrs Bell — continued[2]

Mr. Lincoln Knew nothing much originally about Surveying. After he had surveyed a piece of land — getting Corners — distances — directions &c he would Call at our house and get my father to calculate the figures &c and get the number of acres — &c My father & Lincoln would sit till midnight Calculating, unless mother would drive them out to get wood for Cooking or for Sunday. Lincoln would say to mother — "Its too hard Mrs. Graham to disturb you so — but never mind, Mentor and myself will go out and get you wood." Father would hitch up the oxen and father and Lincoln would go out and soon return with great tree tops — the tops of trees — only the rail Cut, Cut Cut off at the Stump End, rails having been made out of the Stump End or the first Cut. When the wood was got in and Cut up then Lincoln & father would sit up till midnight or later calculating the figures &c. We lived about ½ mile from New. Salem. Lincoln loved my mother and would frequently ask her for her advice on different questions — Such as love — prudence of movements &c — girls — &c. &c. Fanny Bails at Lincoln's request had a quilting in New. Salem. Ann Rutledge was there — Lincoln seemed to pay his attention to Miss Bails — did so to Nettle Ann — Ann flirted with Hill and paid Lincoln back in his own Coin — had a Kind of a flair up — Settled on Anns death bed — in 1835–6 — I was only about 3 ys old, but heard people talk much

LC: HW3926

500. Jasper Rutledge (WHH interview)

Petersburg Mch. 9th '87

Jasper Rutledge — Treasurer of Menard Co — I am 50 years of age — am related to Ann Rutledge: She died before I was born — have heard much. My brother J. M. Rutledge[1] knows all about the story of Ann Rutledge — McNamar & Lincoln. Ann Rutledge and McNamar were engaged to be married. In making out some deeds McNamar signed the deed as McNamar — when McNamar called himself *McNeil*. This opened Anns Eyes — McNeil — ie McNamar went to New York about 1834 — did not write much to Ann if any. Ann found out that McNeils' name — his real name, was McNamar and not McNeil — quit correspondend, if they ever corresponded. Ann dropt McNamar — saying that she would have nothing to do with a man with two names — Lincoln in 1834–5 seeing the

---

1. In the top margin: *Mentor Graham and Mrs Bell his daughter flighty — cranky.*

2. The previous item, §498, is presumably the first part of the interview that was continued. It is possible that the "continued" indicates that WHH is here adding to his notes, after the fact, of an earlier interview.

---

1. James McGrady Rutledge.

way things were tending went to see Ann — he boarded at Rutledges and Ann & Lincoln were engaged to be married. My brother knows this as well as he knows anything — he has told me this substantially. Ann sent for Lincoln in her last sickness. I am the double cousin to Ann[2] — see my brother James McGrady Rutledge and he will tell you all about it: he lives north west from this place 3½ miles. Ann dropt McNamar entirely — McNamar did not get back from New York till after Ann's death.[3]

LC: HW3365

501. Caleb Carman (WHH interview)

[March 1887[1]]

Caleb Carman — am 84 years — first new Lincoln in Sangamon Town in Sangamon Co in 1831. I used to go down to the river and play cards with Lincoln — he and Jno Johnston & Jno Hanks built a boat at Sangamon Town — lived in [shanty?] about 90 feet from the River — Sawed his [lumber?] at Broadwells mill in Sangamon Town — Mill up on the town — I next knew Lincoln in New Salem: he boarded with me in N Salem — He was engaged to Ann Rutledge — Lincoln was PM and kept it at my house — was Elected PM & kept it for him while in the legislature — Played cards — went to horse races — thru mauls — pitch quoits — wedges — & — All in 1831

LC: HW3366

502. James McGrady Rutledge (WHH interview)[1]

[March 1887[2]]

What is your Name, Age and Occupation
James M Rutledge, Age 72 years Occupation Farmer
Was you well acquainted with Ann Rutledge, and If related to her You may state what relationship Existed
I am. We were first Cousins

2. Ann's father, James, and Jasper's father, William, were brothers, and Jasper's mother was also related to the Rutledges.

3. Marginal note: *The universal reputation of the old people here and about here is that Lincoln & Ann Rutledge were engaged to be married. have examined many persons and all agree &c. Herndon.* Also in the margin: 1837 shown subtracted from 1887 with a result of 50.

1. Carman's stated age would put this interview in 1889, but the distinctive paper used for the interview, which is identical to that of the dated interview with Jasper Rutledge, assures that this is one of the interviews WHH conducted in Menard County in early March 1887.

1. This may or may not be in WHH's hand.

2. The distinctive paper on which this interview is written, identical to that of the interview with Jasper Rutledge dated March 9, 1887, fixes the date within a few days.

Do You Know any thing Concerning the Courtship and Engagement of Abraham Lincoln and Ann Rutledge   If so state fully Concerning the same

Well I had an Oppertunity to Know and I do Know the facts. Abraham Lincoln and Ann Rutledge were Engaged to be married. He came down and was with her during her last sickness and burial. Lincoln was Studying Law at Springfield Ill. Ann Rutledge Concented to wait a year for their Marriage after their Engagement until Abraham Lincoln was Admitted to the bar. and Ann Rutledge died within the year.

J. M. Rutledge

LC: HW3369

503. *Michael Marion Cassidy to JWW*

Mt. Sterling, Ky. March 10th 188[7]

Dear Sir

Your two letters are before me, and I hasten therefore to briefly respond.

I am a busy man of my age — being Sixty Years Old, and am from home at Least half my time at present. — As you will See from the heading of My paper I am engaged in Mineing Sixty Six Miles from the City of Mt Sterling Ky — Where I reside. Should You come to Ky. I would be pleased to have you come to My house in the City after Thursday in the Week, for I am at My Mines generally the first three days in each week.

I will give you Such information as has come down to Me from Many Sources in the way of tradition. Of Course I know Nothing personally. I have conversed with Many old persons within the past thirty five Years that assumed to know from personal knolledge all about his Paternal & Maternal Ancestors. The facts Concerning his paternity has been Spoken of by Many of the old people of Bourbon County as — undoubted facts thirty years ago.

I will be able to give you Som information as to where and who to call on for information. I have heard about all the traditions. I Suppose that were Surely believed in this country thirty years ago by hundreds of persons. — There could as far back as 1856 have been quite a No of certificates obtained from Men that they Saw him the day after his birth in the County of his birth. and as to his Mother it is possible you can trace her family — I have known many of those Said to belong to the Same relationship or family of Hornbacks.

Just come to my house and keep your mission to yoursel. — and I will be pleased to give you all the information privately — I am a Modest & humble Man — and My Maternal ancestor connects Somewhat with Mr Lincolns unwritten history — on his paternal Side. — If tradition is true My Sainted Mother and Mr Lincoln were very near Kin. Hence I Say to keep your mission — quietly to yoursel. as My family have always refused to be intervided — which I think was just and proper — as the record of our family — both paternal & maternal have been Spotless & pure.

I have been requested by many authors to give them what has long been believed as to the begetting & birth of this Great man in the family — but have thus far not done so for the reason of family pride and objections — on the part of my Mothers Kinsmen. I Shall be pleased to See you at my house in Mt Sterling Ky. Write Me as to time—and I will try to be at home.

Yours very Truly.
M. M. Cassidy.

LC: HW5269

504. Benjamin R. Vineyard to JWW

St. Joseph, Mo., March 14 — 1887

Dear Sir,

I have just returned from My sisters near Weston and gotten from her to send you the ambrotype of my Mother taken Many years before the photograph a copy of which I sent you. The photograph was taken when she was about sixty-five, — the ambrotype was taken perhaps twenty-five or thirty years earlier. I had forgotten that this old picture existed, until seeing my sister it was brought to my recollection. We do not know the date when the ambrotype was taken but think it was probably taken when she was about the age of thirty-five. I run the risk of sending you this ambrotype of my Mother by this day's express. Please let me know as soon as you get it, and return it to me as soon as through using it. By taking in a reprint the face and bust only for the benefit of your readers I am sure that it will be much more satisfactory than the photograph I sent you before.[1] I send you also inclosed the original letter of Mr. Lincoln to my mother dated August 16th, 1837, which I got from my sister. Please take the best of care of it, and return to me by Mail just as soon as you can get through using it. You see I am trusting you (a stranger) considerably. I trust my confidence will not be misplaced.

I have written (also inclosed) a short account of my Mother and Mr. Lincoln's courtship of her. I do not wish it published over my signature, but send it to you as my idea of what is probably true, that it may serve you as the basis of what you may wish to write on the subject.

Please acknowledge receipt of this, as soon as it reaches you.

I received your last with contents as stated.

Yours truly,
B. R. Vineyard.

Mary S. Owens, daughter of Nathaniel Owens, was born in Green County Kentucky, on the 29th day of September, 1808. She was married to Jesse Vineyard on the 27th day of March, 1841. Of this union there were born five children

---

1. In the margin: *I see the fashion was for the ladies to wear caps those days and by suggesting the reprint of the face and bust only, I do not mean that you should exclude the cap if you think it should appear as is probably the case.*

of whom only two survive. Jesse Vineyard died December 27*th,* 1862, and Mary, his widow, on July 4*th,* 1877.

Mary received a good education, her father being a leading and wealthy citizen of his time and locality. A part of her schooling was obtained in a Catholic Convent, though in religious faith she was a Baptist —, and in after years united with that denomination, and continued a Member thereof until the time of her death. She was good looking when a girl, by many esteemed handsome, but growing fleshier as she grew older. She was polished in her Manners, pleasing in her address and attractive in society. She had a little dash of coquetry in her intercourse with that class of young men, who arrogated to themselves claims of superiority. But she never yielded to this disposition to an extent that would willingly lend encouragement to an honest suitor, sincerely desirous of securing her hand, where she felt she could not in the end yield to a proposal of marriage if he should make the offer. She was a good conversationalist and a splendid reader, but very few persons being found to equal her in this accomplishment. She was light-hearted and cheery in her disposition. She was kind and considerate for those, with whom she was thrown in contact.

She first became acquainted with Mr. Lincoln while visiting a sister of hers who had married Bennett Able, and who was an early settler of the Country about New Salem. Young Lincoln was a frequent visitor at the house of Able and a warm friend of the family, and during the first visit of Mary Owens, which did not continue a great while, he learned to admire her very much. Later she made a second visit to her sister, Mrs Able, returning with her from Kentucky. Lincoln had boasted, so it has been said, that he would marry Miss Owens if she came a second time to Illinois, a report of which had come to her hearing. She left her Kentucky home with a predetermination to show him, if she met him, that she was not to be caught simply by the asking. On this second visit Lincoln paid her more marked attention than ever before, and his affections became more and more enlisted in her behalf. During the early part of their acquaintance following the natural bent of her temperament, she was pleasing and entertaining to him. Later on he discovered himself seriously interested in the blue-eyed Kentuckian, whom he had really underestimated in his preconceived opinions of her. In the mean time, Mary, too, had discovered the sterling qualities of the young man who was paying her such devoted attention. But while she admired, she did not love him. He was ungainly and angular in his physical make-up, and to her seemed deficient in the nicer and more delicate attentions, which she felt to be due from the man whom she had pictured as an ideal husband. He had given her to understand that she had greatly charmed him. But he was not himself certain that he Could make her the husband he thought she would be most happy with. Later on, by word and in letter he told her so.[2] His honesty of purpose showed itself in all his efforts to win her hand. He told her of his poverty and while advising her that life with him meant

---

2. See AL to Mary Owens, Aug. 16, 1837, *CW* 1:94–95.

to her, who had been reared in comfort and plenty, great privation and sacrifice, yet he wished to secure her as a wife. But she felt that she did not entertain for him the same feeling that he professed for her, and that she ought to entertain before accepting him, and so declined his offer. Judging alone from some of his letters it has been supposed by some that she, remembering the rumor she had heard of his determination to marry her, and not being fully certain of the sincerity of his purposes, may have purposely left him, in the earlier stages of his courtship somewhat in uncertainty. But later on, when, by his manner and his repeated announcement to her that his hand and heart were at her disposal, he demonstrated the honesty and sincerity of his purposes, she declined his offer kindly but with no uncertain meaning. In speaking of him in after years she always referred to him as a man with a heart full of human kindness and a head full of Common sense.

LC: HW4604–10

505. Michael Marion Cassidy to J. G. Craddock

Mt Sterling Ky. March 21*st* 1887

My dear friend.

The Bearer of this letter Mr Jesse W. Weik of Greencastle Indiana who is engaged in Seeking and collecting data and Matter for the purpose of getting at the exact truth as to who was the Father & Mother of the Late Abraham Lincoln and he would Should know the true facts as to these things of the past

I want you to go out to the place of Lincolns *Birth* Thachers Old Mill on the Pike Road to wincher. on Strodes Creek and if you know who of the decendants of the Old families of that Neighborhood know the traditions of his begetting and birth take Mr Weik to them and let him have a Short interview with them   Squire John Thomas & Ed Thomas now Own the Old "Inlow" place   Abraham Inlow the real Father of A Lincoln. You doubtless know many in the County who know this Tradition   This will Introduce to you Mr J.W. Wick.

If you cannot go out with him get Some one to go who know the peopl out in the Neighborhood.

And Oblige Your friend &c

M M Cassidy.

Perhaps Frank Kennedy may be able to detail these matters as they have come down from the Fathers   Yours &c M.M.C.

LC: HW4613

506. Emilie T. Helm (JWW interview)

March 22, 1887.[1]

Ms Emma Helm

half sister of Mrs L. — say Mrs. L. had two bros — Dr Grott and Levi Todd in Confed. Service — both died after war. Say Mrs L. was raised like lady whereas her husband was raised otherwise — she complained because L. would open front door instead of having servant do so and because L. would eat butter with his knife she raised "merry war."

ISHL: Weik Papers, box 2, Memorandum Book 2

507. Judge Alfred M. Brown (JWW interview)

Elztn Mch 23 87

Judge A M Brown —

raised at Hodgenville — knew Abe Enlow well — lived & died at H.

Geo Bromfield[1] — real father — was kind of heart & resembled him — characteristics — Abe Enloe may have been but being asked denied it. Geo Bromfield was intellectual looked like L in face — Brom died before L. attaind any prominence — both Enloe & Bromfield had chance to be father but Enloe to have been must have ben only 18 years old Bromfield was older. N. Hanks was rather loose woman — Gen Helm was cousin of half blood of Ab Enlow.

Nancy Hanks was loose woman and either Enlow or Brownfield might have been the father of AL. Brownfield had the kindness of Lincoln and was good natured   Was of clear reasoning faculties and a man of real intellect. It is said that show coming to Hodgville had picture of Abe L. and an old man said before he knew who it was that it looked like Bromfield. Men from Hodgenville were at Elizabeth town good deal — Enlow died during war but Bromfield died long before L became prominent

ISHL: Weik Papers, box 2, Memorandum Book 2

508. Robert L. Wintersmith (JWW interview)

Elizabethtown Ky. March 23 1887

Robert L. Wintersmith

Thos L. lived on Cedar Creek 10 Mi N of Elizabethtown till after first dau. was born then moved to Elizbeth — tended mill till Dec 10 1808 when pair moved to 3 mi S. of Hodgenville — remembers date because my Aunt Polly Walters moved on the day before to the same neighborhood and was present when L. was born.

---

1. The previous entry in the Memorandum Book indicates the date.

---

1. George Brownfield. JWW writes it both ways: "Bromfield" and "Brownfield."

Sammy Young bro. of Nancy Hanks[1] and his descendants were all very tall and slender. Mrs L. was a good singer and used to sing with Rev. Isaac Hodgen — Wintersmiths uncle a great Baptist divine

Only 6 persons in Hardin Co. voted for Lincoln — of these R. L. Wintersmith who was a Lincoln elector in 60 & 64 — Peter Stader an old German another — John Humphries —

ISHL: Weik Papers, box 2, Memorandum Book 2

509. Lizzie Murphy (JWW interview)

[March 1887]

Lizzie Murphy 55 years old dau Sarah Letcher dau of Polly Enloe sister of Abe Enloe   Abe Enloe buried at West Point — opp the Ind Shore — in Hardin Co — been dead. Heard Mother & Grandmother say Abe Enloe was real father of L.

Abe Enloe was tall — had large nose — long ears — long arms — was a great hunter — wore moccasins and fur cap — was big — had big brown eyes and the very largest feet possible

Abe Enloe lived — Most of time at Elizabethtown — died at residence of Malvida Hackley in Indiana was brought across river and buried at West Point on Ky Shore — Abe Enloes nose was large and slightly bent to one side

ISHL: Weik Papers, box 2, Memorandum Book 2

510. Michael Marion Cassidy (statement for JWW)

Mt Sterling Ky March 28 87

Michael Marion Cassidy son of Francis Cassidy. Jane Inlow who was dau. of James Inlow. latter was bro. of Abraham Inlow who was born in Frederick Co. Md. — removed to Bourbon Co Ky early in history. Abraham's brothers were named Elliott, James, Isham, Three children of James Inloe reside in Rush Co. Indiana, Isham, Isaac and Jemima McCorkle. Abraham Inlow resided at time of trouble with Nancy Hornbeck afterward Hanks at Strode's Creek in Bourbon Co Ky. — five miles fr. N. Middletown. He & his brother Elliot were building mill for Abraham Hornback. The latter's niece Nancy Hornback carried dinners to the men at work and Abraham Inlow got her in family way. There being threats to prosecute him for seduction & bastardy he hired old Thomas Linkhorn for 160 dollars in silver to marry the girl. This man Linkhorn was a shiftless worthless man who worked here and there — a sort of vagabond — worked for the Hutchcroft, Thatcher, Hornback and Cunningham & Talbut families in Bourbon Co Ky. — without character and feeble of mind. Inlow took the newly wedded pair to the edge of

1. For a possible basis of confusion regarding the Young and Hanks families, see §50, note 1.

Madison Co and placed them on a piece of land but within a month they returned to Strodes Creek where the mill was building and the very night of their return Nancy the wife was delivered of a child in the little cabin which stood on the banks of the creek and which Inlow being a bachlelor had been occupying while working at the mill. Old Mrs Hornback, Mrs Talburt and other women of the neighborhood attended her. Elliott bro. of Abraham Inlow afterwards moved to Putnam Co. Ind. raised family. This Nancy lived in family of uncle Abraham as domestic. After child was 4 weeks old, Inlow took the pair into Lincoln Co. Ky — with wagon of meat and provisions & bought piece of land for them. Land was deeded to Mother during Marriage & widowhood with remainder to son Abraham. It is said that Mr. Lincoln afterwards brought suit to obtain possession of land and sold same but the records of Lincoln County have been destroyed and there is no further evidence of it — said so by Judge Breck in 1850 — Thomas Linkhorn returned alone to Bourbon Co — leaving the woman and child back — and was shortly afterwards killed by a falling tree. Nancy his wife became a notoriously bad woman now and her house was burned down more than once. A man named Hanks living there took up with her and she bore his name after that. They ran off into Hardin, Larue & sometimes into Washington County. Occasionally she would return to Lincoln Co. but the people would force her back to Hardin Co. until finally when the boy Abraham was 10 or 12 years old she moved to Indiana & was lost sight of.[1] Meanwhile Abraham left his Mother on account of her dissolute habits and took a trip or two on keel boats to New Orleans walking most of the way both times. Went in company of man named Lee who was a boatman and lived in Fleming County. He then came to farm of James Inloe — his real uncle —. This man being religious man refused to permit boy who was rude and profane to stay longer. Boy went off again down towards Salt River — returning again to Fleming Co. and worked with Edward & John Inlow sons of James one summer, After this he turns up at Springfield Ills where he tends bar for this same John Inlow who was keeping hotel in Springfield. This latter John Inlow afterwards moved to American Bottoms near East St Louis where he died 10 years ago. No further knowledge of Lincoln in Kentucky. Shortly after the birth of the child of Abraham Inlow and Nancy Hornbeck, Inlow being a respectable and discreet man, was goaded by mortification of the affair until he moved to Springfield Ohio selling his land in Bourbon Co Ky. where he grew wealthy, raised a family and died. One of Abraham Inlow's sons — a Judge — received an appointment by Lincoln within a month of his inauguration. he lived in North Eastern Ohio. The whole Inlow family was of more than ordinary respectability and of strong mental qualities, tall angular, bony men. The writer M. M. Cassidy never saw Lincoln more than once. It was while attending U.S. Court at Indianapolis about 1854 or 55. In conversation with the writer (M.M.C) he asked if he knew they were kinsmen. My answer was that I had so learned from the traditions of

---

1. Marginal note: *Thomas Hanks was said to have been killed in personal encounter in Garrard or Lincoln County after which Nancy bore the name of Hanks.*

the family. "Its probable Mr. Cassidy" he responded. "You may have some relatives that are handsomer than I am" and no more was said about the relationship. The Inlow family were slow spoken rather drawling in their manner of conversation. Lincoln had the voice of the Inlows.

LC: HW4611–12

511. John Hanks to JWW

Linkville Klamath Co. Oregon June 12, /87

Dear Sir

I was at Fort Klamath when your came and I did not get untill the other day. Thomas Lincoln Was 5 ft — 10 in in hight Dark completion Dark Eye ank Black hair And he hevy sque built man he Weigh about 180 lbs. I did not see him drink any thing that were intoxicated. he could read little; he could not right. He was religion   he and his Wife Belong to the Baptis Church

Abraham L__ he was rether dark complextion

he was tall like his mother A__ Was 6 ft — 4 in in hight. His mother 5 ft. 10 in in hight she had Black haire Dark Eye and Dark complextion I got first acquaited with him in Kentucky Harden Co. he was a carpenter By trade he lirn trade of Jo. Hanks. I saw him last in Cold County Ill. in 1850   he never vist A__ after got marriage to my Knowledge do not Know Why

2

Nancy the mother of Abraham L__ she was a shrowd woman she was not much of talkative   Dark complextion   Dark Eye Black haire she weigh about 130 or 140 her hight were 6 ft Abraham he was tall like his mother and dark skin. I did Know in Kentucky as well Ind — Her mother and my father or William Hank were Brother and sister her mother marriage Henry Sparrow. in Hardon County Kentucky. She was very religious her dispstion was very quiet

(3)

I was well acquainted with her   she wa short hevey built woman gooddeal like here Father in every way. she had Dark complextion Dark Eye Black haire she was smart and shrowd Woman

4

It was his step Brother he mad that remark to. his name was John Johson I was not at the sail at the time[1]

A__ Lincoln Was Born in 1809 — Feb 12

I was 1802 9 day of Feb

---

1. Possibly a reference to the remark, supposed to have been made by Lincoln after seeing a slave auction in New Orleans, about hitting slavery hard if he ever got the chance.

I think you can under this you can can correct all errors in this letter
You mite send me one of your Book

> Your Truly
> John Hanks,

ISHL: Weik Papers, box 1

512. Henry C. Whitney to WHH

June 23*d* 1887

Friend Herndon:

I much regret that while you was here for so long last winter I did not see more of you:[1] but a great city is the most unsocial place in the world. As I have heretofore informed you I have written a considerable about Lincoln to take the form either of a Lecture or of a series of Essays: and on some matters about which I am not certain I [want?] your kind assistance to help me out. You may take as little trouble as you can but I will esteem anything that emenates from you as a favor. The fact is that some of Lincoln's pranks were so *bizarre* that they would not be beleived and a lecture or essayist should be very sure of his facts. I will state my points methodically.

Lincoln used to tell me of driving up his cow: he once said, "I went out to the commons (or outskirts) to drive up my cow: she was a *new* cow and I didn't know her thoroughly but I did know her calf. I could not pick out my cow from other cows who resembled each other but I knew my calf & so I waited a little while & my calf went to a cow & sucked her & in that way I knew it was my cow." — Up to how late a day did he habitually drive up his cow? Did he milk her? did he clean out his own stable? & how late did he do this. I thought this "cow" story, flimsy reasoning for Lincoln but I have known him to go off "half cocked" at other times. For instance in case of "Dean v. Kelley"[2] an important land case in Champaign I once met him at Champaign *en route* to Chicago (because his hat was chalked[3] that way & not the other) and I said to him "our case is ruined: Kelley has taken the deposition of old Henry Dickenson who swore" — so & so. Lincoln said promptly: "we'll beat that easy enough for Henry Dickenson has served a term in the Penitentiary". Now, Dickenson was one of our highest citizens: never heard of the Penitientiary. Again when Tom Johnston[4] stole the watch in our town & it was a clear case & I got it *rolled* for Lincoln: we were speaking of the case & Lincoln said: "it all amounts to this: the watch was where he could have stolen it; and it was found where he might have left it." But that was a very superficial view to take of it: because he surely stole it & admitted it.

I can't recollect exactly how Lincoln used to travel when I first knew him in

---

1. WHH served briefly as curator of the Lincoln Memorial Collection in Chicago.
2. Law case litigated in 1857.
3. Presumably the destination was indicated on a marker stuck in the hatband.
4. Thomas L. D. Johnston, the son of AL's stepbrother.

1854. & from that time to 1858. when he changed some: His hat was brown & faded & had no *nap* — nap worn off. — a faded green umbrella with "A. Lincoln" in large white letters on the inside: knob gone: a literal *carpet* bag. I think he wore a short cloak: his trousers were always too short. I forget what sort of a coat — or shirt he wore: or collar or neckercheif: you can supply this. I think he wore boots. But I recollect distinctly at some times when we slept together on the circuit he slept in a short home made yellow flannel undershirt & had nothing else on. I don't *know* certain if that was a constant habit or not. *Help* me out on these.

Jim Matheney informed me in March that Lincoln was *not* melalcholy: that he was light-hearted & jovial always: I know better — both from you & Stuart & from my own observation: but I am surprised exceedingly that a man of the opportunity to observe that Matheney had should say this I will give you my version of Lincolns melancholy, not to tell *out* but it is my *belief.* This is private. 1st Nancy Hanks Lincoln — was in a constant trepidation and frequent affrights from reasons we have talked together about while she was pregnant & these affrights & trepidations made a maternal *ante natal* impression on our hero: that was the most of it. This melancholy was stamped on him while in the period of gestation: it was part of his nature and could no more be shaken off than he could part with his brains. Stuart told me his liver did not secrete bile — that he had no natural evacuation of bowels &c. That was also a cause but I beleive the former to be the principal one.

My opinion is (somewhat unlike yours) that Lincoln would have greatly enjoyed married life if he had go either Ann Rutledge or Miss Edwards. I think he would have been very fond of a wife had he had one to suit. But I also doubt if he would have been as *great* a man as he was. I have heard him say over & over again about sexual contact: "It is the harp of a thousand strings." Oliver Davis thought his mind run on sexual [matters?][5]

Jim Matheny thinks that Lincoln's mind ran to filthy stories — that a story had no fun in it unless it was dirty and I must admit it looks very plausible. I can't think he gloated over filth however. I think he was some like Linder in this that he had great ideality and also a view of grossness which displaced the ideality.

I am very anxious to get hold of your lectures in some way. Were they not published anywhere? in a newspaper or a book? Who has any which I could borrow? You seem to have sent them to me and I seem to have sent them to Senator Fowler of Tennessee. I find a synopsis of one in Carpenters "6 months in the White House."[6] Later. I read the synopsis of your lecture in Carpenters Book last evening and I consider it as a marvelous analysis of his character and probably in the main correct. I think you should have required fame and money by virtue of your inti=

---

5. The passage between rules has been canceled with cross-hatched lines; the last sentence also has a line drawn through it.

6. Carpenter.

~~macy with Lincoln. You knew much more about him than any one else originally~~
~~& then your great research made you a complete master of the subject. What do~~
~~you say to a lecture tour yet? Have you any idea where the most fruitful field is to~~
~~dissemanate ideas about Lincoln. I have recently imbibed a strong desire to get up~~
~~an excellent lecture on Lincoln. but after reading your exhausting analysis, I am~~
~~rather in dispair. yet a miscellaneous audience might be attracted by a generality.~~
~~my memory is good and I recollect a great many incidents while we were on the~~
~~circuit together which I found greatly in demand in the 2 or 3 times I either lec-~~
~~tures or entertained a crowd in an informal way. Of course I have not 1/100 the~~
~~advantage you would have as a lecturer & that is what discourages me. I found~~
~~that a man having the capital you have could make an overwhelming success. but~~
~~whether one with a little rush light like myself could do anything satisfactory ==~~
~~Quaere? However I already have letters on that subject from Davis & some Sena-~~
~~tors. and I presume I could obtain some endorsements from Swett and yourself.~~
~~If I get up a manuscript lecture I shall want to trespass on your kindness sufficiently~~
~~to read it == make some corrections if desired and give me a letter == somewhat~~
~~of endorsement. If I do anything in that line I shall do as you did in "Lamon's"~~
~~book.~~ [7] ~~I shall not say anything discreditable of either Bob or the Madam. Con-~~
~~trawise, I should praise Bob if I had to say anything for his Fathers sake. and I should~~
~~really like to see Bob president for his Fathers sake. I must this A.M. to Hesler~~ [8] ~~the~~
~~photographer to get a picture of Uncle Abe   He has one taken in Washington~~
~~which makes him look very respectable == unlike *any* Lincoln. thus he has one~~
~~taken by him in 1857, somewhat faded but like our Uncle Abe. then he has the~~
~~one which he took in Springfield in 1860, and which was furnished to the Centu-~~
~~ry Co. which he is going to print for me. By the bye. Who is going to print your~~
~~book? and when do you expect to get it out. Do you know anything of Lamons~~
~~vol. 2?~~ [9] ~~There was a report in the papers that he was going to have it published. I~~
~~hope you will take time to read this long letter & note down answers to the vari-~~
~~ous topics suggested as you go along. I feel that it is trespassing on your patience.~~
Your Friend

H C Whitney

appropos of the suggestion in Lamons life and also in Dubois' letter[10] i.e. that
Lincoln neglected his friends — let me give you this incident from real life which
lies peculiarly in my own knowledge and from which you may draw inferences.

In the summer of 1861. — There came to Washington from Illinois the following persons — all desiring to be appointed Paymasters as U.S.A. Victor B. Bell
— formerly member of Legislature from Wabash Co. Whig. Ninian W. Edwards
— with his wife & [others?] they lived at White House {Dr Wariner?} [11] ~~an utter-~~
~~ly worthless nobody from Bloomington~~

---

7. Lamon.
8. Alexander Hesler (1823–95).
9. Ward H. Lamon had projected a second volume of his biography of AL.
10. See §513.
11. Dr. R. O. Warinner was an early member of the Republican party in Bloomington.

Robert L. Wilson — one of the long nine
and two or three utter nonentities from interior counties in Illinois.
~~Geo Phelps = an utter nobody from Fulton Co.~~

I was in Washington in the Indian service for a few days before August and I
merely said to Lincoln one day — "Everything is drifting into the war & I guess
you will have to put me in the army." He said "I'm making Generals now & in a
few days I will be making Quartermasters & I'll then fix you." — That was all that
was ever said between Lincoln & me or anyone else on that subject. Wilson went
to Lincoln and frankly said "Lincoln I have come on to secure the office of Paymaster in the Army: you know its in the line of business as Clerk and my son is
excellent at accounts & I wish to make him my clerk." — Lincoln made no reply
but cast his eyes down to the floor as if in the greatest mental distress & was silent
for about 2 minutes. Wilson told me he was almost on the point of leaving the
room & going home: but Lincoln turned the conversation on other matters &
made no reply at all.

Edwards was assured tacitly at least that he should have the office. Now — on
August 6th 1861. I got a N. Y. Herald & in it read the appointments of myself
and all the above except Bell ~~& my own appointment~~   To Victor Bell he simply
gave a letter to Yates[12] asking him to Commission Bell as Captain of a volunteer
regiment: and you doubtless know that Lincoln went to the Adj. Regts. office and
struck off Edwards name after he had made it. The reason he gave Edwards was
that he had already appointed Dr Wallace[13] & fault would be found with him if
should appoint — brothers in law. But before Edwards found it out he had given
a paymaster bond with Dickey & Mc Clernand[14] on it.

Think of this. Two of the appointees were utterly worthless & I could just as
well have been given & satisfied with a lesser place. & What meant his performance
with Wilson.

Again. Ben. James (then of Chicago & formerly of Tremont) & W. O. Stod-
dard of Champaign — both wrote Lincoln stating they wanted to be Private Secretary. They both told me that Lincoln entertained with favor the idea of appointing
one but not wishing to offend the other, he concluded to keep Nicolay: This may
or may not be so: but how do you account for his failure to insist on *your* filling
that closely confidential relation instead of the nobody he did take?

And how do you Explain his earnest desire to take into his Cabinet Judd a
comparative stranger to him instead of his earnest friend Davis.

On the subject of Davis: let me give you two points.
1st. on March 5th 1861. I saw Lincoln & requested him to appoint Jim Somess
(of Champaign) to a small clerkship. Lincoln was very impatient & said abruptly

12. Governor Richard Yates of Illinois.
13. Dr. William S. Wallace, husband of MTL's older sister Frances.
14. T. Lyle Dickey and John McClernand.

— "There's *Davis,* with that way of making a man do a thing whether he wants to or not, has forced me to appoint Archy Williams Judge in Kansas right off and Jno. Jones to a place in the State department: and I have got a bushel of dispatches from Kansas wanting to know if I'm going to fill up *all* the offices from Illinois." ~~(2.) In June 1862, I informed Lincoln that Davis said that when he Lincoln returned to Ill~~ I think I will not tell that. Suppose you prepare a lecture on Lincoln in your best vein & commence in Sept. a regular lecture tour: have 1*st* class advertisements &c. Don't do it unless you do it in *first class* style. Your management here last winter was not what I mean.

Your Friend

H C Whitney

[Enclosure?[1]]

513. Jesse K. Dubois to Henry C. Whitney[2]

Springfield 6th April 1865.

Dear Whitney

Your favor is before me. I have Known the Hon. M.W. Delahay for a good many years and always favorably: and indeed he is one of those sort of men who improves wonderfully on acquaintance. I should say without fear of successful contradiction upon all correct rules as applied to any other man than the President that he D. had his whole Confidence for Mr Delahay was Lincolns friend long ago: and to my certain Knowledge he L. trusted in 1860. his destiny so far as Kansas was Concerned to his hands and since being made President has made him 1st Surveyor General and upon the death of Hon. A. Williams District Judge and I should hope he is still his friend. I Know of no gentleman of all my acquaintance who I think is more trustworthy and reliable and who never in adversity or prosperity stands more steadfast to his friends than *Delahay.* And if by my going on my hands and Knees to Kansas would secure him the position I would as cheerfully do it as I ever went to my meals. I have seen him tried and Know him to be true —

Lincoln is a singular man and I must Confess I never Knew him: he has for 30 years past just used me as a plaything to accomplish his own ends: but the moment he was elevated to his proud position he seemed all at once to have entirely changed his whole nature and become altogether a new being — Knows no one and the road to favor is always open to his Enemies whilst the door is hymetically sealed to his old friends. I was not as much disappointed as my friends were at my late defeat as I never did believe Lincoln would appoint me although he time and again urged I had more talent than any of them. But I was his old friend and I could afford to be disappointed

Yours Truly

(signed by)   Jesse K. Dubois.

LC: HW3376–78 (Whitney letter), HW4490 (Dubois letter)

---

1. Whitney's reference to Dubois's letter above suggests that it may have been sent with this letter.
2. In H. C. Whitney's hand. Headed: *(Copy).*

514. Henry C. Whitney to WHH

Chicago   July 4. 1887.

My Friend

You must allow me to thank you for your recent letter which is certainly very full and very correct. I guess the fact is that so great & peculiar a man as Lincoln could not make any woman happy. I guess he was too much allied to his intellect to get down to the plane of domestic relations.

I hav had "Six months in the White House"[1] for some days and have read & re read your lecture on Lincoln. No one certainly knew him except you and you knew him thoroughly. When you get out your book you ought to resurrect the lectures — in fact all of them & include them in your Book. A man who held the relations that you did with Lincoln ought to impress his views on the world. I will trouble you no more but if you do get time give me what points you can. You knew Lincoln so very much better than any one else that it seems nonsense for any one else (unless it is Matheny) to try to delineate him.

Your Friend
H C Whitney

Hesler[2] has 3 photos. of Lincoln. One was taken here by him in 1857. Another was taken by him in Springfield just after he was nominated, in 1860.

That is the one Which the Century folks got for their magazine.

It is good.

Then he has the Washington one with whiskers. I can send you either one.

LC: HW3379

515. Henry C. Whitney to WHH

Chicago   July 18*th* 1887.

Friend Herndon

I enclose to you herewith the 2 photos of Lincoln asked for. The 1857 one was taken under these circumstances. He used when in Chicago as you know to make the office of Dickey & Wallace his headquarters as a law office & Hesler[1] the photographer was right opposite in the same hall: so one afternoon he stepped in & had his photo taken I suppose in the regular course of business. After he was nominated for President, Hesler (Who was then Chicago's best artist) wrote him he would like to have his photo' again. Lincoln replied, inviting him to come to Springfield & take it, if he chose — and he did so.

The 1860. one was that from which the "Century" magazine picture was taken: you will observe that the wrinkles are considerably smoothed out of it, but I think they are the best that are obtainable. If you want a cut for your Book from

---

1. Carpenter.
2. See p. 618, note 8.

---

1. See p. 618, note 8.

either of these I can get it for you here very low by the *"Levytype"* process.[2] You can see the great interest that the public takes in Lincoln by the fact that "Bob" is desired all over the country by the Republicans for President or Vice President: the Tribune (Which is for Blaine) had quite an Article on that subject the other day. The paper said that Bob was the 3*d* choice universally: probably if Blaine was to die Bob would be nominated: it is very probable he will be run for Vice P. anyway. In view of what he really is, this shows the firm & enthusiastic hold Uncle Abe had on the affections of the people: and I must confess that it takes with me: I know that Uncle Abe would rejoice to see Bob, president: that is enough for me: I hope that he will be a president o[n] that account: of course there is no other reason. If I only had your capital to go on, I certainly should lecture on *Lincoln:* In the first place you had every opportunity possible to know all about him after that part of his life that was worth knowing commenced: i.e. from the date of his arrival in Springfield: 2*d* you have the acuteness of vision that we attribute to Lincoln: you saw him as he was & knew him far better than all other living men combined (not excepting Matheny & Speed) and know how to delineate him. 3*d* you acquired much of his analytical power from Lincoln himself by attrition: you thought deep as he did: and veiwed matters as he did: your mind & mental processes were much like his: you was more like him in mental view & grasp than any other man. 4*th*   He had unbounded confidence in your adhesion to him & in your intuitions: he said to me on the day Douglas was elected to the U. S. Senate — & bitterly too — "I expect everyone to desert me except Billy." In the normal order of things, he should have had you at his elbow through his troubles: — he should have insisted on you as his private secretary & mentor in the same sense as Sidney Webster was Pierces private secretary — an *alter Ego:* it is astonishing that he took Nicolay — a mere clerk — and did not have a confidential friend of astuteness & affection like you: Who could have eased him of half his burdens. so it seems to me that if you would get up an excellent lecture as you could that it would take immensely. I do indeed design to try my hand; but when I contemplate my inferiority of advantage to you I feel very discouraged: but I am going to reproduce my lecture and forward it to you for your criticism and secure your opinion on it.

LC: HW3382

516. Elizabeth and Ninian W. Edwards (WHH interview)

July, 27th 87[1]

Mrs N. W. Edwards

Said — Mr Herndon I have no phos of myself — have had some — unwillingly taken — don't know where any of these are now — have a likeness — a

---

2. Popular in the 1880s as a process by which photographs could be copied for reproduction, the Levytype process still required augmentation by artists.

---

1. Herndon first wrote, then struck out, *Septr.*

portrait of myself here which you can have photographed, if you must have it. When you go to Indiana I will answer your letters asking questions. I have no phos of Mrs. Lincoln: she too was opposed to having her face scattered abroad. Mrs. Lincoln was an ambitious woman — the most ambitious woman I ever saw — spurred up Mr. Lincoln, pushed him along and upward — made him struggle and seize his opportunities. Lincoln's & Mary's engagement &c were broken off by her flirtations with Douglas — Mr Edwards & myself told Lincoln & Mary not to marry — said so more or less directly: they were raised differently and had no [congruity?] — no feelings &c — alike. We never opposed Lincoln's marriage with Mary. It is said that Miss Edwards[2] had something to do in breaking Mary's engagement with Lincoln — its not true. Miss Edwards told me that Lincoln never condescended to pay her even a poor compliment: it was the flirtation with Douglas that did the business. Mr. Lincoln and Mr Speed were frequently at our house — seemed to enjoy themselves in their conversation beneath the dense shade of our forest trees. After the match was broken off between Mary and Lincoln Mrs Francis[3] shrewdly got them together. Doct. Henry[4] who admired and loved Mr. Lincoln had much to do in getting Mary and Lincoln together again. — Speaking about phos, Mr Herndon, I am too old now to have one taken. At one time in my life I should not have been ashamed to Show my face — (She once was a very — very pretty woman H).

Mr Edwards was present during this conversation — said that when Lincoln first came to Springfield I assisted Lincoln — offered to buy him a good law library and send him to some law school and these offers he refused — said that he was too poor and did not wish to involve himself — said that Lincoln was, during part of the time, in the legislature of 1841 — called Session —

Both Mr Edwards and Mrs Edwards have been willing at all times to answer all proper questions and to make things plain to me. This memorandum was taken down by me quickly after the Conversation was had and is in every particular Correct substantially.

W H H

It seems to me — infer it that Mary Todd flirted with Douglas in order to spur up Lincoln to a greater love. Lincoln was undemonstrative. Miss Todd didn't know her man. Lincoln was somewhat cold and yet exacting — blew up to quickly — From various conversations with Mr & Mrs Edwards I infer as above.[5] Mary Todd wanted Lincoln to manifest a tender and a deep love, but poor woman, she did not know that Lincoln was an undemonstrative man in this line. The devil was to play and did play his part in Mr. Lincoln's and Miss Todd's affairs — nay during their lives —

H

LC: HW3384–85

2. Matilda Edwards.

3. Mrs. Simeon Francis.

4. Dr. Anson G. Henry.

5. WHH marginal note: *Miss Todd used Douglas as a mere tool — refused his hand.*

517. Mrs. Simeon Francis to WHH

Portland Aug 10*th* /87

Miss Herndon,

Your communication received; in reply would state that my intimacy with Mr & Mrs Lincoln was of so sacred a nature, that on no consideration could I be induced to open to the public gaze, that which has been buried these many years. To me it would look like a breach of trust. Excuse me for thus refusing your request I cannot do otherwise in justice to myself and deceased friends

Mrs Simeon Francis

[illegible] —

LC: HW3387

518. Russell Godbey to WHH

Curtis Ills August 17 87

Mr Herndon

Your letter came to hand to day. and I will answer amediately   In Regard to the Receipt you spoke of. I have it and i will send it to you If it will be of any. benefit to you. you May keep it. yes. he done serveying for Me and I gave him too Buckskins for pay and Hannah Armstrong sewed them on the front of his Pants so that the briers would not wear his clothes out   If there is any other Favors I can d please Inform Me and I will answer I am in my 87 year

Yours

Russell Godbey

ISHL: Weik Papers, box 1

519. William Jayne to WHH

Springfield, Ill., August 17th 1887

Dear Friend

Your letter received — I should have replied at an earlier date but delayed to give you the information asked — James H Matheney & Beverly Powell were the gentlemen who stood up at the Lincoln & Mary Todd wedding — My sister Julia M Jayne was one of the Bridesmaid — but the other lady was I cannot say — Jim Matheny does not remember. I have seen Ninian Edwards — neither he or his wife, Mrs Lincoln's sister — can remember.

Mr and Mrs Edwards, knew nothing of the wedding until the morning of the day of the wedding. Only meager preperations could be made on so — short notice & only a few friends were present — the company present was quite limited in numbers.

Mrs Lincoln at the time of her marriage was a bright, lively, plump little woman — a good talker, & capable of making herself quite attractive to young gentlemen

— Fifteen & twenty years after marriage she became fleshy & stout in personal appearance —

The last year of her life — she was in poor health & lost flesh — when I last looked upon her upturned face when she was laid out in her coffin, I thought she looked, (save the difference of years) much as she did when I knew her so well in her girlhood days.

In her size, color & general look — she bore my memory back 35 years.

Mrs Lincoln was a woman of quick intellect & strong passions — decided in her friendships & intense in her dislikes — my own acquantance with her was pleasant & is kindly impressed on my memory

In her young days my Sister & She were very close friends — their intimacy continued until the election of my Sisters husband to the US Senate,[1] when Mr Lincoln was also a candidate for Senator After Trumbulls election to the Senate Mrs Lincoln was no longer intimate with his wife. Disappointmt over the result of that election may have caused this.

Yours truly

W Jayne

I have no photograph of my sister at the time of the wedding.

I have a very good Small Sized photograph taken about 1860 or 1862 My Sister died in 1868 at the age of 44. If a photograph of that day would be of service to you — I could Send that one — but if Sent — it must be taken care of & returned to me without fail as it is the only one I have.

LC: HW3388, HW3935

520. Henry C. Whitney to WHH

August 23*d* 1887.

Friend Herndon

Your three letters are all at hand to day on my return from a three weeks trip East. on my return last night I passed through Greencastle at midnight but had no idea you was there.[1] You should hav recd the last photo long since: I sent it and it is an admirable likeness: the best I have seen. I am going in for a "Lecture on Lincoln" and I need your endorsement: I will see you about it later. If the mail has lost the photo: I can replace it — but I presume it is not lost. I mailed it to Springfield.

As to the *cause* of Lincolns melancholy I have *no* facts whatever of my own: and my judgement & opinion are founded on matters that have been mentioned between us privately & which cannot be printed. From Lamon's life[2] & what was

---

1. Lyman Trumbull, elected U.S. senator in 1855.

---

1. WHH was at JWW's home in Greencastle, Indiana, during the month of August 1887, working on their biography of AL.

2. Lamon.

then stated I based my inference mainly: then my reasoning was that Lincolns melancholy was illogical & unexplainable by any course of observation or reasoning — it was ingrained & being ingrained could not be reduced to rule or the cause arrayed: and was necessarily hereditary — but whether it came from a long line and far back or was simply formed during the period of gestation cannot be determined. Stuart said it all arose from abnormal digestion — from the failure of his liver to work while Matheny said he wasnt melancholy at all. I can't help you on this & *please don't mention me in connection with it.* The thumps kicks[3] &c. I know nothing about: really my ideas on the whole subject I got from Lamons life which really on that subject is not very clear: You owe an apology to the world for not having written that book after doing so excellent service in gathering such a world of material. I think if you had written such a work it would have been the most *graphic American* Biography of anyone.

You touch me on a tender chord when you ask about *Lincoln & Davis.* The latter is now dead: he had many virtues & some defects & I can never forget his kindness to me in the first years of my acquaintance: but I dont think Lincoln held *Davis* very close to his heart: he was too loquacious — too vain — too vacillating in his friendships: look at Davis' array of posthumous friends & where are they? & who are they? we tried to raise $1000.# to pay for a bust of Davis & I will tell you of the success so far as I pursued it: and I pursued it through all his friends that I knew.

Weldon cheerfully subscribed $100.# Bishop ditto: Frank Orme $50.*00:* Swett $100.# & then the thing stuck: altho' the widow Davis expressed some desire to pay for the whole thing. Clifton H. Moore refused: Jno. G. Nicolay refused: George Perrin Davis refused: Mrs Swayne refused: Jesse Fell refused to try to do anything: so you see that when Davis' autocratic force was withdrawn, all love must also. I think Davis had no influence on Lincoln: he believed in you — Swett — Williams — Browning — Judd — Logan — Stuart: but he despised O. L. Davis — & only barely tolerated D. Davis Weldon — C. H. Moore: he liked Cullom & Lamon — both: this he told me himself in 1856. when both wanted to run for Pros Atty. Look at Thurlow Weeds autobiography[4] & you will there see Lincolns feeling of contempt for *Davis* portrayed. I think Lincoln meant just what he said & what might be implied from what he did say. I can give you some further facts about *Lincoln & Davis* (not very significant) from my own knowledge: and will do so if you desire when I get a moments leisure. I have forgotten what office Dubois wanted: but it was no secret in Springfield & elsewhere that he did want a specifically named office. It seems to me it was 5*th* Auditor: but I am not clear: but any one in Springfield will recollect. He made a strong effort for it & was greatly chagrined when he got defeated. I don't recollect what the office was or who got it. Nicolay can inform you on both points:[5] I think Lincoln never had any intention

---

3. Possibly a reference to AL's being kicked by a horse as a boy. See §§24, 78. The story is told in greater detail in H&W (1889), 59.

4. Weed, 1:607.

5. See §530.

of appointing Davis to any office at all & was disgusted at Davis' hoggishness after office for himself — for H. Winter Davis his cousin & for all his personal friends: In this very short time after Lincoln took the Presidential oath; Davis sought him out & *forced* him to appoint Archy Williams District Judge of Kansas & Jno A. Jones, Supt. of statistics in the State dept. Lincoln felt very sore over this to *my certain knowledge*. I can repeat nearly verbatim what Lincoln said to me about it on March 5*th* 1861. Davis undoubtedly had Williams appointed to get him out of the way of filling Mc Leans vacancy:[6] & he had Jones appointed from pure love. When Davis was appointed with Holt & Campbell to adjust the Freemont claims[7] his rage at Lincoln knew no bounds: he sent for me to meet him at St Louis at the Planters House and he kept me there for 2 days discussing *Lincoln & Davis* &c. he substantially sent a message to Lincoln by me — but I never delivered it: but I did say to Lincoln in 1861. (July) "Davis thinks you ought to make him a Supreme Judge & it looks as if you ought to do it." Lincoln didn't make the least reply. I feel satisfied he had not the slightest idea of doing so then. But if you want these matters more fully developed I will do so at greater length.

~~I can't help you on the ante-natal influences: it is a mere theory which I will run out at some length as soon as I can get a little time if it will avail you any~~

In haste / as ever Your Friend

H C Whitney

LC: HW3391–92

521. Henry C. Whitney to WHH

Chicago August 27*th* 1887.

Friend H.

I rec*d* your letter of August 25*th* this A.M. and in reply to your side question answer that you may use my information if you please in your book of course. I have just mailed you todays "Chicago News" which has the first of Lamons copyright article on "Lincoln"[1] in which he rehashes the old stories about his dreams: if you fail to get the paper advise me as you will want to see it: He is going to publish a series of articles on Lincoln. I think they will be interesting but Hill will be sensational at the expense of truth probably. I cannot exactly say now what grave errors I saw in Lamons life of L.[2] I took no note of them at the time: but they are

---

6. Justice John McLean of the U.S. Supreme Court died on April 4, 1861.

7. The commission (consisting of David Davis, Joseph Holt, and Hugh Campbell) was appointed by the president in October 1861 to dispose of unsettled claims arising from the troubled administration of Maj. Gen. John C. Frémont.

---

1. Ward Hill Lamon, "Abraham Lincoln's Strange Dreams: His Singular Philosophy in Regard to Dreams and Presentiments," *Chicago Daily News* (morning edition), Aug. 27, 1887. Lamon is referred to a few sentences later as Hill.

2. Whitney enumerates some of these "grave errors" at the end of this letter. See also his undated statement, §536.

chiefly such errors as a biographer unacquainted with his subject would be apt to commit. a successful biographer must know his subject as Boswell knew Johnson or you knew Lincoln. appropos of that I refer you to Jno P. Ushers article on "Lincoln" in Allen G. Rices book[3] in which he says that Lincoln never had a doubt but that he would conquer the Rebellion at any time: now I happen to know from L. himself that he had the gravest doubts about it in 1861, and did not expect to do it. Mr Swett[4] in his article in the same Book says that L. told him that when he emigrated from Indiana he came direct to Coles County: I told Swett that Lincoln at Decatur showed me exactly *where* they went through Decatur on that trip: but Swett persisted that Lincoln told him it was Coles Co. of course he is wrong: then one of his biographers speaks of the historic rails split in Coles Co. I spent ½ day with Lincoln at the White House all alone with Lincoln just after Bull Run. Lincoln then said to me "I am going to enforce the blockade as rigidly as I can — its mighty hard to do as the line is so long but will do the best I can about it: I am then going to push an Army into East Tennessee and liberate the Union sentiment there: I am going to cut them off from supplies from the outer world and make them feel the privations of war in the hope that the people will arise and say to the politicians, 'this thing has got to stop': for there is no use, Whitney, in trying to conquer so many people so long as they are united on the proposition that they wont be conquered".

Those are almost his exact words. So Usher is wrong. — Now as to Davis: The old man justly felt as if he should have been rewarded: and Lincoln couldn't see the exact place for him: I have no idea he intended to make him Supreme Judge: When Swayne[5] was appointed D. was mad but he thought possibly that L. felt a necessity of naming a man from McLeans[6] state: but when he passed over Illinois to appoint Miller,[7] he felt that his chances were getting desperate: so I supose: he went to work with extraordinary vigor. Among the men whom he doubtless relied on to punch Lincoln up were Lamon — W. P. Dole Comr of Indian affairs: Caleb Smith Secy of the Interior & Swett. I will go to Swett tonight and ask him as I see you want to know and advise you what he says. I have no doubt he has been sent to Washington often by Davis at his own expense about this matter. Davis had very few cordial friends. He complained to me that Lamon wouldn't do anything for him: Dole and Swett were doubtless the most active. No doubt L. heard of Davis' indignation as the latter was very loud & noisy and would send for every body he knew to come to him at their expense & pour out his sorrows: at Washington in March, as he left, he told me he had no doubt Lincoln would give him an office if he would ask him for it but he never would do that — *no sir:* he wasn't that kind of a man. But he set others on the hunt. Dole is still living & could tell. I know him well but have forgotten his address. I will get it if you wish.

---

3. Rice, 77–100.
4. Rice, 455–68.
5. Noah H. Swayne (1804–84) of Ohio was appointed to the U.S. Supreme Court by AL in 1862.
6. Justice John McLean of Ohio.
7. Samuel F. Miller (1816–90) of Iowa was appointed to the U.S. Supreme Court by AL in 1862.

You are in error in supposing that I attribute any errors to *you* in Lamons life: *not so:* any errors are those of Chauncey F. Black who wrote it: and arose from not knowing Lincoln and from misconceiving you. I will get Lamons life soon and inform you of what I consider errors. If I knew the plan and scope of your Book I might help you more. My memory is good and I took to Lincoln on the Circuit from the start and happened to have rather more intimacies with him than ordinary. Davis and Swett were more intimate — Lamon, Weldon, Parks, Moore, Hogg, Voorhees & McWilliams[8] less so. ~~Oliver L. Davis at Danville he despised and Oliver hated him. Lincoln had no love for Voorhees: but you are in Indiana and must look out. One reason I think likely, for his not liking D. Davis[9] & C. H. Moore better was their sordidness and avarice.~~ I could narrate incidents of Lincoln by the hour which occurred on the Circuit as my memory is good, but I don't know the scope or design of your work. I understand it is a social, & not a political history: The idea that Allen G. Rice should publish a Book of Remeniscences of Lincoln[10] & go to such codfish as Ben Perley Poore Dan Voorhees Walt Whitman: and not seek you John T. Stuart & Jim Matheny shows how humbug rules the world. The mode of getting out your book — who publishes it and how extensively it is advertised will largely determine how great a run it will have. I have not been able to do anything with my lecture of late: I have been away and have also been busy and shall be for some little time but I want to get at it and get into the lecture field this winter and I rely on you to aid me. I don't think L. considered Davis a suitable kind of a lawyer for the supreme bench.

Swett says that the reason why Lincoln did not act in the matter of the appointment of a Supreme Judge when Davis was appointed sooner was that it got the goby &c. and that he vacillated between Browning & Davis and that he intended to appoint Browning all along: and that in Bloomington they heard definitely that Lincoln said: "If I had made the appointment before this time, there was no single day in all the time that I would not have appointed Browning": upon hearing this a consultation was had in Bloomington & Swett said "I am going to Washington": Davis said "don't go: its of no use": (that was shrewd way he had of not paying his expenses.) Swett went however & talked with Lincoln ½ a day about it: they went over the whole subject of his former relations with Davis & covered the whole ground & the result was that Lincoln at once made the appointment. I think you may safely say that Davis[11] fully intended to appoint Browning and simply did not do it from not having fully made up his mind about it's effect on Davis; or rather had nothing at the time to offer Davis as a counterpoise and while in this condition Swett came along with his wonderful persuasiv powers & converted Lincoln over and thus Swett rescued Davis from utter oblivion and made him

---

8. Ward H. Lamon, Lawrence Weldon, Samuel C. Parks, Clifton H. Moore, Harvey Hogg (1833–62), Daniel W. Voorhees (1827–97), and Amzi McWilliams (d. 1862). All were from Illinois except Voorhees, who was from Terre Haute, Indiana. All practiced with AL in the courts of the Eighth Circuit.

9. Possibly intended as a reference to Oliver L. Davis.

10. Rice.

11. Clearly a mistake for "Lincoln."

a great man. Swett has always been poor except for about a year during the war:
and Davis was always rich and always a hog: would it not have been well for Davis
to give Swett a present of $10,000.#? But he wouldn't have given him a cent to
save his life: nor would his heirs do so. But you must not mention this: Swett did
not: but I can't help thinking. Had Davis not been appointed Sup. Judge he would
have died, an obscure hog financially: and left no reputation behind him beyond
that of a circuit Judge. still I think Lincoln did right to appoint him but awfully
wrong to not give Swett anything.

Davis used to get Lincoln to hold court for him and Lincoln was always ready
& willing: Davis liked to get out in town & meet the people. Lincoln held court
a great deal for Davis. Lincoln was very bashful when women were called on. I
once went with him to Mayor Boydens[12] at Urbana to tea: — he got on so-so while
I was in the room but I was called to the gate by a client and on my return was as
bashful as a school boy. Lincoln was so good natured & so willing to give advice
that young lawyers went to him a great deal. He was at Urbana once prosecuting
a man named A. G. Carle in Urbana for seduction & one S. H. Busey an adverse
witness tried to create the impression that he was a great ladies man. Lincoln went
for him in his speech thus, "there is Busey — he pretends to be a great heart smasher
— does wonderful things with the girls — but I'll venture that he never entered
his flesh but once & that is when he fell down & stuck his finger in his ———";
right out in open Court. Things were free & easy in Urbana & Danville: There
was a hard crowd used to meet us in the latter town.

Lincoln was not as gloomy in that end of the Circuit as in yours. I was Atty
for the Ill. Cen. R.R. & we had a contract that Lincoln was to take no case against
us & I could call on him to help me when he was there: & when my clients wanted help I always got Lincoln. The most noted cases in which Lincoln & I were
together were "People v. Patterson" manslaughter   "Spink v. Chiniquy" Slander
from Kankakee Co. "Harvey v. Campbell" chancery case about part of Champaign
City: "Dean v. ~~Campbell~~ Kelley: chy. case about the most valuable farm in Champaign. "People v. Barrett" murder, "Van Onum v. ——— sheep rot case. Brock v.
I.C.R.R. — Cunningham v. Phifer — partnership[13]   When he struck one end
of the Circuit I was with him continuously till he left it: after I moved to Chicago
& went in with Gen. Wallace[14] he made our office his head quarters. He carried
on the circuit a shirt cloak — a striped carpet bag & a faded green umbrella with
cloth letters "A. Lincoln" sewed on the inside as baggage. He slept in a home made
— yellow flannel undershirt. He got the inspiration for his lecture; from Bancrofts

---

12. Ezekiel Boyden was mayor of Urbana, 1856–57 and 1858–59.

13. Some of these cases and dates have been identified as follows: *People v. Patterson* (manslaughter), April
term 1859; *Spink v. Chiniquy* (slander), October term 1856; *Harvey v. Campbell et al.* (bill for relief), October term 1859; *Dean v. Kelly et al.* (injunction), April term 1858; *People v. Barrett* (murder), October term
1856; *Brock, Hays & Co. v. Illinois Central R.R.* (assumpsit), April term 1857 (appealed to the Illinois Supreme Court, December term 1857).

14. Probably Martin R. M. Wallace (1829–1902), who served during the war as colonel of the Fourth
Illinois Cavalry and was awarded the brevet rank of brigadier general of volunteers.

lecture of Nov. '54,[15] which I read to him on the route from Urbana to Danville. Lincoln & George Lawrence — a [noteless?] drunken lawyer used to play billiards together: one played about as well as the other / Lincoln used to always attend the circuits of the *Marshall* family of Jacksonville when they sang: Mrs Hilliss one of them he said was the only woman who liked him. Davis said "I thought you was an universal beau." He bought his first pair of spectacles at a little shop in Bloomington in May '56. — gave 37½ for them; we were stopping together at Davis': — Dickey — Williams,[16] Lincoln & myself — at the great convention. During the setting of the Philadelphia convention in 1856, Lincoln was attending a special term of court in Urbana & Davis Lincoln & myself roomed together at the American House: I read him the accounts of the convention each noon from the Chicago paper: he paid but little attention to it & was not gloomy as Lamons life has it: he was very gloomy one day after all the news was in. I showed him Fremonts head in the paper, "says I What a head!", Lincoln looked at it & said "I don't see anything wrong about that head." said I; "a man who will part his hair in the middle like a woman aint fit to be President": He looked at it again a moment & gave me the paper without any more comment. He was very gloomy on that day but on no other day then. Have I written enough Billy?

W.

Lamons life.[17]
on p. 481. he does not depict L. correctly: he did not make boon companions of the coarsest men: he did praise rivals — as A Williams — Judge Logan — Browning — Dickey — Swett. his encomiums were not incinsere.
p. 480. Lincoln drank temporately &c. — he did not drink at all. p. 468. "Few men believed that L. possessed a single qualification for his great office" x x "he was a very common ordinary man" &c. *This is a lie.*
p. 471. Herndon locked the front office & Lincoln returned to the back office &c. — You know this aint so.[18]

The whole talk about Mrs Lincoln is not true: she belonged to the pro slavery crowd as the Blacks[19] did: and they want to ennoble her at Lincolns expense.
p. 475. What Stuart said was this "Lincoln's digestion was organically defective so that the excreta escaped through the skin pores instead of the bowels": and I "advised him to take Blue Mass and he did take it before he went to Washington & for five months while he was President but when I went to Congress he told me

15. George Bancroft, "The Necessity, the Reality, and the Promise of the Progress of the Human Race," delivered November 20, 1854. See Bancroft, *Literary and Historical Miscellanies,* 2 vols. (New York, 1855), 2:481–517.

16. Archibald Williams (1801–63).

17. Lamon.

18. The passage Whitney refers to describes AL coming to the law office too distraught by domestic affairs to talk or do business.

19. Chauncey F. Black (1839–1904), Lamon's ghostwriter, and his father, Jeremiah S. Black, former attorney general and secretary of state.

he had quit because it made him cross." Black has no such statement on p. 475.[20] in 478. stated that he read "Childe Harold". In my office in 1854. he picked up "Byron" and read commencing "They mourned but smiled at length" &c. to "He who ascends to mountain heights shall find. &c.[21] out loud; as impressively as it ever was read in the world. D. Davis: Swett: Lamon Alex Harrison & myself were present. "The mossy marbles rest"[22] &c. was a great favorite: but his greatest favorite, Alas!, was "Mortal man with face of clay

"Here tomorrow: gone to day."

What Davis & Scott say on p. 479. is substantially my idea of his frivolity[23]
p. 481. I don't believe he "damned with faint praise" at all: this is not true at all. I do think however that the next sentence commencing "fully alive" is correct. in fact all the succeeding lot of short sentences is correct.[24]

I don't think he forgot the devotion of his warmest partizans (482.) that is a clear mistake: take Lamons case: or mine: or Judds. He was eccentric in this matter. His secretiveness we will all agree on alike. I never heard him mention religion at all.
P. 83. Jno. Hanks came to Washington in a new suit of blue jeans — wanted an Indian agency: Lincoln really wanted him to have it but he couldnt read or write. Lincoln talked with me about its propriety — said Hank's son could be his clerk &c. wanted to appoint him but did not.

---

about Henry Clay: Lincoln admired him greatly while I knew him: spoke of him in the warmest terms.
P. 312. "At the 1st opportunity he commissioned Davis" &c This is not true as I have shown.
p. 322. The "Patterson" case was thus: Tom Patterson was a worthless doggery keeper at Sadorus: an old good natured drunkard who had then got drunk & talked rambling drunken talk in the crowd & picked up a spade & spoke of hitting some one &c — He was too drunk to hold the spade steady: Tom was several feet away

---

20. The biography associates Stuart with the view that certain physical conditions contributed to AL's famous melancholy and that "in some respects he was totally unlike other people." It adds that "blue pills were the medicinal remedy which he affected most" (Lamon, 475).

21. Canto 3, lines 280–397.

22. From Oliver Wendell Holmes's "The Last Leaf."

23. David Davis is quoted as saying that AL's humor was simulated and that his jokes and stories were meant to "whistle off sadness." John M. Scott states that Lincoln's humor seemed to be "put on" and that it "did not properly belong there" (Lamon, 479).

24. "Fully alive to the fact that no qualities of a public man are so charming to the people as simplicity and candor, he made simplicity and candor the mask of deep feelings carefully concealed, and subtle plans studiously veiled from all eyes but one. He had no reverence for great men, followed no leader with blind devotion, and yielded no opinion to mere authority. He felt that he was as great as anybody, and could do what another did. It was, however, the supreme desire of his heart to be right, and to do justice in all the relations of life." Whitney probably meant to include the balance of this paragraph, which runs over to the following page.

with a two pound flat lead weight in his hand concealed: he seized a time when the drunkards head was turned away & threw the weight with such force that his own coat tail flew over his head & the weight hit him just back of his ear & penetrated the scull & the victim fell at once & when picked up the weight (whose edge struck first) was imbedded in the scull so that it stayed in as he was lifted up. Lincoln Swett & myself were employed by Pattersons wifes relations (who were rich Quakers) to defend   we each got $200.# & each took & kept it: Patterson was indicted for manslaughter (through an influence) and the next term we tried him: Ficklin did not help Lamon but Jno. C. Moses did: and they insisted that the real crime was murder (as it was): Swett made a first rate speech: & Lincoln who closed our case a very poor one for us: and he got 3 years: & Lincoln got Wood to pardon him out after one year so you can see how little reliable biography is. Turn to your books in Spring of 1858. You will find that L. got $200.# for Patterson's case.[25]

Lamons life. P. 331. "Lincoln v. I.C.R.R." — L. claimed $5000.# and took judgement by default: but Jno: M. Douglass solr went to Bloomington after the default and asked L. to set it aside which L. did: then Douglass had a talk with me & Davis (I was Atty for the Company in our county) and we concluded that it was very poor policy to make an enemy of Lincoln so Douglas settled it for the full amt. as I remember: there was no contested trial.[26] It was not Douglass our Solicitor, but Jas. F. Joy advisory counsel who treated Lincoln rudely. (P. 332.) Reaping machine case. Lincoln formed a poor opinion of Judge Mc Lean[27] at that time: thought him an old Granny & with no discrimination.

P. 358. Lincoln told me the reason he didnt speak any more with Douglas in 1854. was that D. claimed to be sick & unable to speak but that he also didnt want L. to speak to which he agreed.[28]

P. 359. On Oct. 24, 1854. L. made the Springfield speech at Urbana. I heard it myself: he was then at court. P. 421. Lincoln got the inspiration for his lecture from a lecture by Bancroft in Nov. '54.[29] This I read to him in 1855. as we were going to Danville court: it was on the wonderful progress of man: Lincoln then told us — Swett, Mrs. Swett & I, that he had thought much of the subject & believed he would write a lecture on Man and his progress. Afterward I read in a paper that he had come to either Bloomington or Clinton to lecture & no one turned out.[30] the paper added "that don't look much like his being President". I joked him about it: he said good naturedly "don't: that plagues me".

---

25. Lamon's biography states that AL refused to participate in Patterson's defense or accept his share of the fee.

26. There was, in fact, a jury trial at the April term 1857 of the McLean Circuit Court. See John J. Duff, *A. Lincoln: Prairie Lawyer* (New York, 1960), 316–17.

27. U.S. Supreme Court Justice John McLean presided at the trial of *McCormick v. Manny et al.* in Cincinnati in September 1855.

28. For other testimony on the "Peoria truce," see the index.

29. See p. 631, note 15.

30. AL delivered the first version of his lecture on "Discoveries and Inventions" in Bloomington on April 6, 1858.

I may remark that I have not had time to go carefully through the "Lamons" life: but I make the above suggestions as they occur to me. I shall be busy for a few weeks but I hope to be able to write out my lecture as I wish to have it done.

Now as to a publisher: You want Harper or J. R. Osgood & Co. or some publisher who will have great facilities for advertising it.

Lew Wallace (my intimate friend) got Harper Bros & his book (Ben Hur) has had 185,000 circulation. He is at Atlantic City now but lives at Crawfordsville near Greencastle: & if a letter to him will do you any good I will send it to you. I don't know how he got the Harpers for a publisher but he can tell you.

I will want to see you after a while and I will stay with you 2 or 3 days   I might come to Greencastle or Springfield

The proper way for you to write a book is to have a clerk by the month who is a stenographer and type writer both: you can get up a book in that way in ¼ the time you can do it by old fashioned methods.

Swett says you sent him a letter which he wrote some years since with a request to know if you might publish it and that he is going to answer soon. Of course you will know what is proper to publish of what I tell you & what not. I don't want any reflection on any body living or dead but what Lincoln told me is all right & now belongs to history & can do no harm. Swett corroborates what I say about Ls view of success in the war Lincoln had no faith in success in '61. & '62.

Your Friend as ever
H. C. Whitney

Speaking of Lincoln holding Court for Davis, several of us lawyers annoyed him very much in attempting to defend against a note to which there were many makers. We had no genuine defence but wanted to [stay?] it over the term by one expedient & another

Here is the order as Lincoln entered it: the original was cut out of the docket and sent to a Sanitary Fair.

"Plea in abatement by B. Z. Greene, a defendant not served filed Saturday at 11 o'clock am April 24*th* 1856; stricken from the files by order of Court. Demurrer to declaration if there ever was one, overruled. Defts. — who are served now at 8 o'clock pm. of the last day of the term ask to plead to the merits, which is denied by the Court on the ground that the offer comes too late: and therefore, as by nil dicet judgement is rendered for the Plaintiff against the Defendants who are served with process. Clerk assess damages."

Said I "How can we get this up: He looked at me quizzically & said: "You have all been so mighty smart about this case that you can find out how to take it up".

This was in Champaign Co.[31]

LC: *HW3393, HW3395, HW3394, HW3396–97, HW4001*

---

31. On the verso in Whitney's hand: *I will consider the question of a publisher and write you further about it   The picture could not have been lost unless some one took it as directions to return it to me on the outside of the envelope.*

522. Henry C. Whitney to WHH

Chicago August 29*th* 1887.

Friend Herndon —

Replying to Mr Weiks note recd yesterday I may say that Lew Wallace is still in the East — I dont just Know where — and that a letter will not reach him at home at present.

I may likewise say that Harpers Bros do not have the reputation of being very liberal with authors: — in fact, to not put too fine a point on it, they are mean and as you have the whole world before you where to choose I think you had better canvass the subject somewhat before you decide — because a publisher is quite [as] important as the author. Among publishers, I may mention Charles L. Webster of New York and New Haven who publish Mark Twains works and James R. Osgood & Co. of Boston. Had I Known of this one month since I could have been quite serviceable to you inasmuch as I was at Boston and New York with plenty of leisure. I doubt [whether?] Harpers are what you want, after all.

---

you and I could only hav a common object [how]ever with regard to our great friend who [ca]n no longer speak for himself I hope you will not deem it essential to your purpose [to] go behind the marriage certificate which Hay & Nicolay found shewing that Thomas Lincon & Nancy Hanks were man and [wife]. That makes it presumptive in law [that] Thom Lincoln was Abraham Lincolns father and Lincoln has always said so in public; and of course wants [it to] go so in history. I therefore think that his friends ought not to try to cast any suspicion on it. It is one thing for you and I to talk among ourselves [&] another thing to proclaim to the world even an authentic fact if it was so distasteful to Lincoln or to his friends & I as one friend should very much dislik[e] to see any doubt cast upon Lincolns legitimacy for the public eye; and I hav[e] no doubt his friends generally would do so you are aware what a great deal of trouble Davis Swett & Fell had to induce Hill Lamon to suppress or change one Chapter [of] his book. That affords an example of how Lincolns average friends regard the matter I will tonight write you quite a chapter about Lincoln & his habits on the Circuit and life on the Circuit generally & Enclose in this. I am sorry accurate picture of him is lost. I will get another as soon as I can & forward. When and where shall I meet you to read you my Lecture?

Your friend
H C Whitney

This is Swetts description of Lincoln as a lawyer.[1]

As he Entered the Trial, where most lawyers object, he would say he "reckoned" it would be fair to let this in or that and sometimes, where his adversary could not quite prove what Lincoln Knew to be the truth he would say he "reckoned" it would be fair to admit the truth to be so & so   When he did object to the Court after

---

1. Written by Whitney on the back of the enclosed description (also in Whitney's hand) that follows.

it heard his objection answered he would [then] say "Well I reckon I must be wrong. Now about the time he had practised this ¾ through the case if his adversary didnt understand him he would wake up in a few minutes finding that he had [secured] the Greeks too late and wake up to find himself beat. He was wise as a serpent in the trial of a cause but I have got too many scars from his blows to certify that he was harmless as a dove. When the whole thing is unravelled, the adversary begins to see that what he was so blanly giving away was simply what he couldnt get & Keep. By giving away 6 points and carrying the 7th he carried his case and the whole case hanging on the 7th he traded away every thing which would give him the least and in carrying that. Any man who took Lincoln for a simple minded man would very soon wake [up] with his back in a ditch

LC: HW3398 (letter), HW3399 (Swett's description)

523. *Leonard Swett to WHH*

Chicago, Aug 30 1887

My dear Sir,

Mr Henry Whitney, of this city, called upon me saturday Evening, Either to ascertain what I know of the circumstances of the appointment of David Davis, as one of the associate Justices of the Supreme Court, or to settle a law suit, we have in hand & I do not know which. Of course he put the Davis matter ahead & talked it over & over, and it seemed as though he never would come to the suit, but when I mentioned it, he tumbled to it so kindly that I still am in doubt which was his real object.

I have concluded, however to write out the Davis matter, which I have done. I sent it herewith for such use as you may cho[o]se.

I reread my letter, of twenty one years ago.[1] It comes back to me like one from the dead. I cannot remember of writing it at all   I have a shadowy [&c?] remembrance of dictating something to a reporter. and as this is in some person's hand writing other than my own. I presume I did dictate it. Even the corrections are so hastily made that they, in some instances destroy, rather than correct the sense.

Notwithstanding these facts it is, in my judgement, a better analysis of Mr Lincoln than I could make without it, and I return it with some slight alterations for such use by you, as you chose to make of it.

You will note that I have striken out all allusion to Mr Lincoln's swearing, and reading the Bible, & the reason is that I am satisfied the public does not want to hear them   Lamon's book fell flat, every body connected with it lost money & the public have not yet forgiven him for making it, because it stated things which the public did not want to hear of its hero. There is after all some sense in this. History is made to perpetuate a man virtues or hold up his vices to be shuned. The heroes of the world are its standards, and in time, all faults and all bad or

---

1. See §124. For a letter on the Davis appointment, see §607.

common humanities are eliminated and they become clothed with imaginary virtues. Thus, for instance, the hatchet story of George Washington

A man in making a history of General Grant, should entirely omit to state that he used to get drunk & that when in the army and on the plains he got so bad that in a craze, he "did his business" in the mess pan of his companions   His historian should rather dwell on the glories of Appomatox, & leave to oblivion this little episode.

It is said a publishing house, in our day, got on to the story of George Washington & his mistress — his illegitimate son, in Philadelphia. The fruit of his winters stay there, during the Revolutionary war, but when the facts were obtained they were so real & so human that the publisher, although he had obtained them at great expense, destroyed them, because it was believed that the public had made such a hero of George Washington & he had become so much of what Bob Ingersoll calls *a steel plate engraving* that these facts would not be acceptable reading to the public.

If I should say Mr Lincoln ever swore & you were to publish it, the public would believe I lied about it. It would damage your book, and if the book were otherwise acceptable, the next edition would leave out that fact, in the publication.

I will be glad to assist you in any way in my power. This letter is also confidential.

Yours Truly
Leonard Swett

Philadelphia is an old city & is full of curious things & I am informed in a way I believe it to be true that there is an original autograph letter in existence there, from George Washington from Mount Vernon that he (George) is saving up a very fine yellow girl, which he proposes when ripe to send to his friend in Philadelphia   How would this story go to ornament the Steel plate Engraving[2]

LC: HW3400–3403

524. John Palmer, Alfred Orendorff, Shelby Cullom, William Jayne, James H. Matheny, Richard Oglesby (WHH interviews)[1]

Tuesday Septr 6th, 1887.

(Let all this be private as to names)[2]

I saw Govr. Palmer at his office privately and talked to him freely about Mr Lincoln — his mother — and Thomas Lincoln, and their ancestry — and origen.

---

2. This postscript appears as a marginal note.

---

1. This document records the substance of a series of WHH interviews on the same date. Above the date, WHH has written: *Opinions of Men—file them.*

2. Marginal note: *All these various conversations were noted down by me within 10 minutes after they were made — each in succession — did it before I saw others — and had conversations with them. The replies were watched closely — more closey than anything else. / W. H Herndon.*

This was at 9 o'c am. I asked him his advice — asked him to give me his opinion as best how to proceed — in writing the life of Lincoln, whether to state all the facts or to state none or only so much as history and the nations, world demand-ed. I carefully and cautiously related the facts — told him all I knew as well for Thomas — Nancy & Abraham as against them. Govr Palmer thought one mo-ment and said — "This is too delicate a question and I do now[3] wish to give any advice on the matter — will think more about it and then if I think proper I will tell you my opinion — will see you again however, nothing happening &c". I left the office. [Zimri?] A. Enos came into the room about the time the Govers & my conversation ended. Don't think he heard a word

I saw A. Orendorff[4] — stated substantially what I did to Govr. Palmer and in reply he said — "The People wished and greatly wished to have the story of Lin-coln's legitimacy well settled and forever fixed: he thought that on the whole and for the best, to tell the whole story and clear up Lincoln's legitimacy". This was about 9–10 ock am at or near the Bank just below Orendorff office.

I saw at Senator Cullom's[5] office — Sen Cullom and Doct Wm Jayne — had a private conversation with both of these men — told them the whole story as I had it on my fingers end and the same as I told to Govr Palmer & Orendorff — and to all other persons — told them the story of Lincoln's supposed illegitimacy — went over all the facts, stating to them that I wished to make it appear that Lincoln was the legitimate child of Thomas & Nancy — that that was my inten-tion. Cullom seemed surprised and said "The public believed that you want to make him Lincoln illegitimate". I said, in this you are mistaken — I want 1st to tell the truth and 2dly I want by that truth to make Lincoln appear — nay to be the law-ful child and legitimate heir of Thomas Lincoln & Nancy Lincoln — once Nan-cy Hanks. Cullom thanked me for this declaration of intentions on my part. I further said to him that in so doing I should have to touch up old Thomas Lin-coln[6] and immediately after this running conversation I asked these gentlemen for their opinion and advice &c &c as to the best way in which to write the Life of Lincoln. These gentlemen said "That if you say anything about the matter you had better tell it out, giving all the facts so as to put Lincoln in his proper place or attitude in history — Glad that you expressed your opinion of intentions about Lincolns legitimacy, it being favorable to him." This Conversation was the long-est which I had with any person or persons, knowing that Cullom misunderstood my purposes. &c. &c. I got up the meeting on purpose to hear Cullom & Jayne's opinion. This was about 9-20 m AM — Conversations all private.

I saw Judge Matheny at his office 11.30 am and had a private conversation with him — told him all the facts just as I did to all others — Palmer — Orendorff — Cullom & Jayne, — and when I had stated over all the facts I then asked him to give me his opinion — give me his advice as to the best method of dealing with

---

3. Herndon probably intended to write "not."
4. Alfred Orendorff, former law partner of WHH.
5. Shelby Moore Cullom (1829–1914), then senior U.S. senator from Illinois.
6. By this WHH apparently meant glossing over the troubling reports of Thomas Lincoln's impotence.

the matter and to which question he said — "If you can clearly make Lincoln out to be a legitimate —, a lawful child of Thomas & Nancy and make it out that Nancy Lincoln, Thomas Lincolns wife was chaste &c &c I would do it by all means, not thereby injuring others &c   The whole story is new to me, but by all means clear Lincoln & his mother, if you treat the subject". I said this cannot be done without touching up Thomas Lincoln. The judge said — "That's bad but put Lincoln & his mother in their proper place." All persons Examined — advice & opinions asked for all seemed to talk honesty and fairly, though I kept my eyes open. — wide open.

I had a long and a good conversation with Govr. Oglesby — told him over & over all the facts of the case just as I did to all others and said to him that I had the materials out of which, by a lawyer's argument, that I could make it appear that Lincoln was the lawful child of Thomas & Nancy — told him that Thomas was castrated but that no time was fixed by the witnesses of the said event. The Govr. then said — "The very idea that old Thomas Lincoln would fool Mrs Johnson was foolish — (Here he gave his reasons). That Theory won't do — better go upon the Theory — proposition that Nancy Hanks was the illegitimate child of the Virginia planter and that the people had mixed things up. This is the best explanation, but it would be better for your book to say nothing about it at all. That the People's good sense had settled the whole matter long ago — That the People don't care about such things anyway. They go upon merit — the man and his own genius & character." This Conversation with the Govr was private as in all other cases and it took place in the Govr's room at 11½ o'c AM — possibly 12

W H Herndon

LC: HW3411–13

525. John Lightfoot (WHH interview)

Septr 13th '87

Saw John Lightfoot to day: he says that Oliphant[1] wrote the poetry about the Talisman — the Steam Boat of '32 — Says that Pollock was the Commander — remembers one verse of the poem — the same one that Matheny does — remembers the ball given in honor of the occasion — Mrs. Pollock — the mistress of Polic got tipsy & played the devil — so report said at the time in '32. The Elite and Cultured ladies of the city were in high dudgeon — highly offended. &c. &c.

Lightfoot further Says that it was currently reported in 38–40 that Lincoln Courted *Sarah* Rickard — that she flung him high & dry (Rember Speeds letter[2] about the word *Sarah*   H) Don Matheny and *Susan* Rickard were Engaged to be married — Don died about '34–5 — Susan in subsequent years married Dav Talbott, whose wife went deranged because of the loss of any only daughter —

1. Ethelbert P. Oliphant.
2. See §318. Marginal note: *See Speeds letter wherein he says scratched out a certain word & that word is Sarah.*

She is too bad to be Examined now as to the fact of Lincoln's Courtship with *Sarah* — now Mrs Barrett of Kansas — will See John Rickard — Miss Butler & others.[3]

LC: HW3417

526. Anna Miles Herndon (WHH interview)[1]

[September 13, 1887]

My wife's mother, step mother, was a *Rickard* and my wife says — on further Examination that she understood her mother to Say *Susan,* but that it may have been *Sarah:* She says that she has heard Mrs *Butler* — a *Rickard* as well as her step mother a Rickard say that Lincoln did Court *Sarah* and that She would not have him — Lincoln. Sarah married badly and Mrs Butler & my wifes mother both, Rickards have often Said — both of them *Rickards* & now dead, that Sarah ought to have taken Lincoln as she did so badly with Barrett. (I guess there is no doubt of all this   H) Lightfoot's Evidence I read to my wife and that suggested to her the whole story. I then referred her to the word *Sarah* and Speeds letter to me. She now says that she guesses that it was Sarah. — probably not *Susan.* She Says see Miss Butler and write to Mrs Barrett all of which I shall do. My wife further Says that the question formerly put to her was a special one — namely the one about *Susan,* She supposing that I well Knew Lincoln's courtship for *Sarah* or that she would have told it as She understood it.

LC: HW3417

527. Thomas H. Nelson to JWW

Terre Haute, Ind. Sept. 16th. 1887

My Dear Sir,

My version of the amusing incident to which you refer, is substantially told in the enclosed slip[1] from the T.H. Express of several years ago.

Mr. Lincoln used to tell the story with many ludicrous variations.

Very Truly Yours

Thomas H. Nelson

---

3. Three lines of text were stricken.

---

1. This interview is a continuation of WHH's notes (see §525) on his interview with John Lightfoot.

---

1. Nelson's clipping from the Terre Haute, Indiana, *Express* is missing, but the text was printed in Herndon's biography and is included below. Nelson confirmed in a January 29, 1890, letter to JWW (LC: HW4690–91) that the story told in the biography was accurate.

[Enclosure]

528. *Clipping from the* Terre Haute *Express*

[undated]

"In the spring of 1849," relates Nelson, "Judge Abram Hammond, who was afterwards Governor of Indiana, and I arranged to go from Terre Haute to Indianapolis in the stage coach. An entire day was usually consumed in the journey. By daybreak the stage had arrived from the West, and as we stepped in we discovered that the entire back seat was occupied by a long, lank individual, whose head seemed to protrude from one end of the coach and his feet from the other. He was the sole occupant, and was sleeping soundly. Hammond slapped him familiarly on the shoulder, and asked him if he had chartered the stage for the day. The stranger, now wide awake, responded, 'Certainly not,' and at once took the front seat, politely surrendering to us the place of honor and comfort. We took in our travelling companion at a glance. A queer, odd-looking fellow he was, dressed in a well-worn and ill-fitting suit of bombazine, without vest or cravat, and a twenty-five-cent palm hat on the back of his head. His very prominent features in repose seemed dull and expressionless. Regarding him as a good subject for merriment we perpetrated several jokes. He took them all with the utmost innocence and good-nature, and joined in the laugh, although at his own expense. At noon we stopped at a wayside hostelry for dinner. We invited him to eat with us, and he approached the table as if he considered it a great honor. He sat with about half his person on a small chair, and held his hat under his arm during the meal. Resuming our journey after dinner, conversation drifted into a discussion of the comet, a subject that was then agitating the scientific world, in which the stranger took the deepest interest. He made many startling suggestions and asked many questions. We amazed him with words of learned length and thundering sound. After an astounding display of wordy pyrotechnics the dazed and bewildered stranger asked: 'What is going to be the upshot of this comet business?' I replied that I was not certain, in fact I differed from most scientists and philosophers, and was inclined to the opinion that the world would follow the darned thing off! Late in the evening we reached Indianapolis, and hurried to Browning's hotel, losing sight of the stranger altogether. We retired to our room to brush and wash away the dust of the journey. In a few minutes I descended to the portico, and there descried our long, gloomy fellow-traveller in the center of an admiring group of lawyers, among whom were Judges McLean and Huntington, Edward Hannigan, Albert S. White, and Richard W. Thompson, who seemed to be amused and interesting in a story he was telling. I enquired of Browning, the landlord, who he was. 'Abraham Lincoln, of Illinois, a member of Congress,' was the response. I was thunderstruck at the announcement. I hastened upstairs and told Hammond the startling news, and together we emerged from the hotel by a back door and went down an alley to another house, thus avoiding further contact with our now distinguished fellow-traveller. Curiously enough, years after this, Hammond had vacated the office of Governor of Indiana a few days before Lincoln arrived in Indianapolis, on his way to Washington to be inaugurated President. I had many opportunities after the stage ride to cultivate Mr. Lincoln's acquaintance, and was a zealous advocate of his nomination and election to the Presidency. Before leaving his home for Washington, Mr. Lincoln caused John P. Usher and myself to be invited to accompany him. We agreed to join him in Indianapolis. On reaching that city the Presdiential party had already arrived, and upon inquiry we were informed that the President-elect was in the dining-room of the hotel, at supper. Passing through, we saw that every seat at the numerous tables was occupied, but failed to find Mr. Lincoln. As we were nearing the door to the office of the hotel, a long arm reached to my shoulder and a shrill voice exclaimed, 'Hello, Nelson! do you think, after all, the world is going to follow the darned thing off?' It was Mr. Lincoln."

LC: HW4614 (letter); H&W (1889), 303–6 (text of clipping)

529. Henry C. Whitney to JWW

Chicago September 17th 1887

My Dear Sir

I recd your note of inquiry of Septr 15 also a note from Herndon dated at Springfield to which I replied. 1st. as to your inquiry about a publisher. I should not consider it amiss for you to come here with your MSS. when you get it ready and consult with the several publishers who are here. There are several subscription book publishers and a few trade book publishers. Of the former I may mention "L. W. Yaggy" as the most prominent and of the latter "S. C. Griggs" — and "Jas. Cockroft" as the most prominent.

I talked with Yaggy Whom I Know very well about your Book. It is probably too small to be published as a subscription book: such books have to have a large profit in order to pay the various parties — canvassers &c. their share. A book has to pay at least $3.00 to answer at all as a subscription book. Then you must have a trade book publisher such as Harper Bros or Appleton. The reason you need such a publisher is to be advertised: they not only advertise the book but they likewise send out instalments of it to the trade: and in no other way can you succeed. Yaggy told me you would have to go to the East & leave your mss. with the proposed publisher & they must inspect it and determine if or not they desired to publish it: and you would probably receive 10 per cent of gross receipts if they should publish it. I think it will be well for you to come here and get all the ideas you can about publishing and you can then determine if or not you want to go East. It will be well for you to have your MSS. in good shape as considerable may depend on that. I intend to have my book type written in good clear style: but if yours is written in clear hand writing it will doubtless answer the purpose.

Am quite sorry & much surprised that my letter to Mr Herndon containing the picture of Lincoln should have been lost inasmuch as directions were on the back of the letter to have it returned to me after a certain number of days: still it is lost and I can get another after Octr 1st when Hesler will have got into his new gallery. I think I will be here all through this & next month & Swett likewise. of course I will aid you in any way with your book: and properly published it ought to have a run: but the number of trashy Lives of Lincoln is somewhat prodigious. on reflection it seems to me that you had better consult the publishers here first: then: you can determine if or not you should go East for one. I think you had better meet Herndon here when you come to see a publisher.

As to anecdotes &c. — probably the only way I could do that effectively would be to have a stenographer take down whatever was needed: and then a type writer reproduce it: but it would be better for Herndon to be present in order to determine what he wants to preserve & what reject: as it would not [be w]ell to write a lot of stuff in vain. of course I Know a great deal about Lincoln & remember much of it — and I suppose even such gossip as I could narrate would be quite acceptable to the public. I notice that often men with quite as good a capacity as I had to acquire information cannot narrate it either from treacherous memories inattention or some other cause. I remember a great deal about Lincoln and shall never forget it: and I have an idea (altho' others have the same) that Lincoln confided his opinions about men to me more fully than he did to most of his friends: and I Know that he had more faith in Herndon as a friend & adviser than in any other man in Illinois if not in the world. other men that he beleived in strongly were T. Lyle Dickey — Archie Williams — O. H. Browning Leonard Swett Ward H. Lamon.[1]

of course when Dickey abandoned our political faith in 1858, Lincoln no longer had any faith in him. But Lincoln felt very much grieved when I informed him that Dickey was about to leave us. I Knew it beforehand from one occupying the same office together. *(I don't want anything said about my opinion of Lincolns feelings for Davis)* Lincoln despised Douglas. All that I ever heard him say about John A. Logan was to tell an anecdote thus: — "When John was in the Legislature a Committee was raised to meet some one or body to discuss the subject of Dram Shop license: some member proposed to pass a Resolution to the effect that the Committee had no right to adopt or propose any ultra temperance policy &c: but John squelched it by saying Oh! that is needless: the noses of the Committee are an emphatic declaration of their anti temperance principles."

The first story I ever heard Lincoln tell was in Court. Court stopped to hear — "its like the lazy preacher who used to read very long sermons: When asked how so lazy a man used to write such long sermons, one of his deacons said; "Oh! he gets to writing & is too lazy to stop."

Lincoln & I were once puzzled in a case to Know how the Court would hold: so Lincoln solved it thus: in the Judge's room that evening Lincoln said to the crowd: "Fellers hows so & so? — Davis promptly answered as Lincoln had hoped: and we then found out how the man who was going to decide the point would decide it. When Lincoln returned from Cincinnati after appearing before Judge McLean in a Patent Case he said to me "Judge McLean is a man of considerable

---

1. At this point Whitney wrote, then struck out *but I think not David Davis.*

vigor of mind but no perception at all: if you was to point your finger at him and also a darning needle he would not Know which was the sharpest.

Lincoln was very adroit in managing a case: I once had the case of "Peggs. vs. Scott"[2] to try in Champaign County and was all alone in it. Lincoln & O. L. Davis were on the other side. O.L. was a dirty fellow & he informed me that they were going to bea[t] me *awfully* and I got alarmed & went to Lincoln about it, he reassured me — said it was like any other lawsuit — they might be beat or I might but not to worry &c. But when the trial came Lincoln bore down on me harder than any one. The great majority of Lincolns stories were very nasty indeed. I remember many of them but they do us no good. Now as to my matter. I want to lecture about Lincoln and I think of limiting myself to Ohio for this Ensuing winter for the following reasons, viz: 1*st* It is said by lecture men to be the best lecture state in the Union. 2*d* I was a Paymaster there for 2 years & paid many Ohio troops & my reputation for that reason whould be of some value. 3*d* I have got to organize my own campaign and need a circumscribed area to do it effectually in. I might slop over into Indiana some. I should get good literature & advertise intensively & use the Grand Army of the Republic for all it might be worth.

I don't commence in Illinois for the reason that I would fear that Herndon or Matheny or Moore or someone else would be present & would know more of Lincoln than I did. I want to help Herndon all I can and will be glad to do it in any way

Your Freind

H C Whitney

LC: HW4615–16

530. John G. Nicolay to JWW

Washington, Sept 22, 1887

My dear Sir:

My absence has delayed an answer to your letter of the 16th. My recollection is that it was the office of Secretary of the Interior which Hon. J.K. Dubois desired. But my Knowledge of the matter is all mere hearsay, as I never had any conversation either with Mr. Dubois or Mr. Lincoln on the subject.

Yours truly

Jno. G. Nicolay

LC: HW4617

---

2. Not identified.

531. Samuel E. Kercheval to JWW

Rockport Ind Dec 2/87

Dear Sir:

Yours of the 23d ult to R.T. Kercheval at hand. My father R.T.K died Sept last one year ago, but the information desired I send you herewith with some additional facts about the marriage of the parties and the Lincoln family as furnished me by Joseph C. Richardson a resident of our town born in this County in 1816 and Knew Mr Lincolns family and the Grigsbys and Knew all about the marriage of Charles & Ruben Grigsby —

The marriage record shows license issued to Ruben Grigsby and Elizabeth Ray April 16th 1829 but can find no record of license to Chas Grigsby & Matilda Hankins,[1] but Mr Richardson says both weddings occured on the same day and as was the custom in those days an infair was given by the parents of the grooms to the young married couples at the residence of the said parents and all the people for miles around in the County — (the County being sparsely settled) were invited to the infair except the Lincoln family — Augt 2d 1826 Aaron Grigsby, brother to Chas & Ruben, married Sarah Lincoln sister of Abe. His cruel treatment of his wife caused trouble between the Lincoln & Grigsby families and on account of that family feud the Lincolns were not invited to the infair and further the difficulty between Lincolns & Grigsbys was to be settled in the accustomed way of settleing differences between parties in those days, (a fist fight) the day arranged and the men of the country came out to witness the settlement of bad blood — Wm Grigsby said he would not fight Abe Lincoln, he was too large for him — Then Lincoln pitted his step brother John Johnson against Wm G. seconds were chosen. — Lincoln being second to Johnson and Wm Bolen second to Grigsby. The result was a draw fight between Grigsby & Johnson they being seperated and Wm Bolen got a shoulder dislocated by a blow from Lincoln — Sarah Grigsby lived but a short time and her husband married again soon after her death — Mr Richardson who gave me this information knew Lincoln personally and well — What Magazine are you furnishing this article for and what number?

Yours respy

Sam E. Kercheval

LC: HW4621–22

532. Ella A. Thompson to JWW

Portland Dec 16th/87

Dear Sir

Mrs Francis[1] desire me to say, that so many years have Elapsed since her connection with Mr Lincoln and Wife, that if she ever knew anything concerning

---

1. See §125.

---

1. Eliza (Rumsey) Francis, wife of Simeon Francis, editor of the *Sangamo Journal.*

them, which would have been worthy of a place in your History, it has passed from her remembrance. She is in very feeble health, and it is very unwise to trouble her further about the matter. In regard to the Photographs while she feels honored at your desire thus to immortalize her, and her Husband, she must decline the honor, as she would rather not have her Husband, and self thus brought prominently before the public in connection with anything which might have transpired at their Home. Hoping this may be satisfactory and final.

I remain your truly
Miss E. J. Thompson

LC: HW4624

533. Harriet A. Chapman (JWW interview)

[1886–87]

Harriett Chapman — aged 60

Ms L. had 3 children by Johns[1] John D. Elizabeth & Matilda   MC dau of Eliz

Thos L. about 6 feet high — heavy build — hair dark eyes grey — weight about 180 — not profane — always asked grace at table — read the bible — he could write — not a good reader or scholar — would take a dram not a hab. drinker — never drunk on Christmas had one or two hot apple toddy. Abraham L. inherited his fathers features rather than his mothers — Ms C has seen first Mrs L. but cannot recollect much of her appear   she was intelligent [& keen?] [withal?] delicate spare made woman.[2]

No education — Mr L. was proud of Abraham while in Congress — MC. lived at Springfield frm 42 to 44. — Robert was then boy — never was there after 44 — Abraham wife high strung — lying in hall one day with pillow on floor ladies called Mr L. in shirt sleeves invited visitors in and stated that he would "trot women folks out" — this made Mrs L. mad —

Mrs L. was engaged to Sen Douglas but she broke off engagement — she became sick — Douglas did not want to release her but her bro in law Dr Wallace who was treating her told Douglas he must give her up. Ms L. told Ms C. that she was engaged to D.

Story of leaving out her cousin dau of Dr. Todd when inviting guests to a party because cousin had intimated that Robert L. who was baby was a sweet child but not good looking.

ISHL: Weik Papers, box 2, Memorandum Book 1

---

1. Refers to Sarah Bush Lincoln and her first husband, Daniel Johnston.
2. Either JWW misunderstood or Harriet Chapman misspoke, for she was not born until after the death of Nancy Lincoln. She may have been recalling Nancy's mother, Lucey Hanks Sparrow.

534. Henry C. Whitney (statement for WHH)

[1887?]

When Thurlow Weed opposed Montgomery Blair for the Cabinet, Lincoln asked him whom he s[hould] appoint. He replied, "Henry Winter Davis."[1] Linco[ln] replied (David) "Davis has been posting you up on this question. He came from Maryland and has got Davis on the brain. Maryland must, I think, be a good State to move from."

And he then told a story of a witness in a neighboring County, who, on being asked his age, replied "Sixty." Being satisfied that he was much older, the Judge repeated the question; and on receiving the same answer, admonished the witness, saying the Court Knew him to be much older than sixty: "Oh!" said he; "Your'e thinking about that fifteen years that I lived down on the Eastern Shore of Maryland: that was so much lost time and don't count."

Billy — you will find the above in Thurlow Weeds autobiography:[2] and I think expressed Lincolns opinion of old Davis' pertinacity in trying to force appointees on him

LC: HW4003

535. Henry C. Whitney (statement for WHH)

[1887?]

I first saw Lincoln on June 3d 1854. He — Davis — Swett — & D. B. Campbell were in a light wagon in front of Baileys tavern in Champaign Co. returning from Danville Court. I was just coming to Champaign to settle as a lawyer. On Oct. 24. '54. Lincoln drove into our town Urbana to attend Court — Davis & Swett had just preceded him. That night after rest he made his "Springfield" speech once again. It was masterly. Next morning he went north via I.C.R.R. and as he went in an old 'bus. he played on a boys harp[1] all the way to the deppot   I used to attend the Danville Court regularly as well as our own, of course. At Urbana I used to room with Lincoln & Davis frequently — same at Danville: Davis found me to be useful in doing errands. At Danville we used to stop at McCormicks hotel an old fashioned frame country hotel & jurors counsel prisoners & everybody all ate at a long table: After Judge [D?] Lincoln & I had the ladies parlor fitted up with 2 beds. at Danville Lincoln — Swett & McWilliams of Bloomington — Whitney of Urbana — Voorhees of Covington Indiana — O.L. Davis, Drake Lamon, Lawrence, Beckwith, O.F. Harmon of Danville — Chandler of Williamsport Indiana and Whiteman of Iroquois were the lawyers. It was quite a big court.

---

1. Henry Winter Davis (1817–65), a cousin of Judge David Davis.
2. See Weed, 1:607.

---

1. Probably a jew's harp, or harmonica.

The way we travelled was thus: Lincoln, Davis, Swett, O.L. Davis, Lamon, Drake & myself would ride from Urbana in livery rigs to Danville — take a day — 36 miles: sing & tell stories all the way: stop at a farm house & wait for them to kill & cook chickens for our dinner: get to Danville at dark. Lamon would have whiskey in his office for the drinking ones: those who indulged in petty gambling would get by themselves & play till late in the night. Lincoln and Davis & a few local wits would spend the evening in Davis room talking politics, wisdom & fun. Lincoln & Swett were the great lawyers. O. L. Davis was an irascible but good lawyer. Lincoln always wanted Swett in jury cases: regarded him as first rate before a jury — We who stopped at the hotel would all breakfast together — then all go out in the woods: hold Court and sometimes go to a ball or a party or to take tea with some one. We were of more consequence then than a Court & bar is now. sometimes we would be invited out in the Country to tea or to eat fruit. The feelings were those of great fraternity in the bar: Davis would freeze out of the charmed circle any disagreeable persons: no lawyer came to Urbana or Danville in my day from the West except Lincoln Swett & McWilliams. I attended Court once at Bloomington. In addition to the local bar there was Stuart & Moore & Weldon from Clinton besides Lincoln. Lincoln was fond of going all by himself to any little show or concert: I have known of his going to a small show of magic lanterns &c. really for children

He was in one town two days once holding Court all alone for Davis — a special term. on Sunday he & I went into the big grove after breakfast & neither of us had a watch & when we got back it was ½ past 3. He would tell stories in Court: Davis was always willing to stop business to hear Lincolns stories. Davis was somewhat particular what he ate or where he slept: Lincoln didnt care what he ate — who he ate with or where he slept or who he slept with. Just before Lincoln was nominated for President he was in Chicago trying the "Johnson" sand bar case: (I lived at Chicago then) he made our office his head quarters & I spent the evenings with him: one night I said to him: "Mr. Lincoln I have got 3 complimentary tickets to a high toned nigger show won't you go"? "Of all things in the world I should like that": and I never saw Lincoln happier than at that show which really was first rate: "Dixie" was played & sung & he was especially fond of that. It was entirely new.

I came to Covington Indiana in a canal boat on June 3d 1854. and took stage for Urbana — passed through Danville about 10 o'clock a.m. and at 12 o'clock m. overhauled a 2 seated carriage on the road at Baileys tavern with 4 gentlemen in it: and an hour later we drove up to Jo. Kelleys log hotel and overtook the same party who had just dined. this party consisted of Judge Davis: Leonard Swett David B. Campbell & Abraham Lincoln just going home from Danville court: singular to say I noted well & have always recollected the three former on account of some peculiarity — but have no especial recollection of Lincoln except as he made up the four persons: I saw them in fact only for about two minutes as they were just in the act of leaving as we drove up.

On October 24th 1854. Abraham Lincoln came to Urbana where I then lived to attend court: he had the appearance of a rough intelligent farmer: and his rough, homemade buggy & rawboned horse enforced this belief. This Court was a very small & not very dignified one: and Lincoln had scarcely any business but was in fine spirits & full of stories which he told in and out of court: and Kept it lively for us: on Oct. 25*th* he delivered in a dingy, dirty court house: lit with a few tallow candles the famous "Peoria" speech: and I marked him then — and correctly as it seems — as one of the greatest men on Earth: He towered way up majestically above all other men I ever saw: I have never heard that speech equalled before or since except by Lincoln himself.

On March 5*th* or immediately thereafter (I think it was after 5th) 1861. I called at the White House with a young friend of both of us to procure for him a small clerkship. It was about noon, and we were soon admitted, altho' a large crowd was waiting for admission. The President was sitting before a fire in the fire place, very gloomy and dejected. He received us cordially, but abstractedly: and in reply to my request, said wearily: "Just let Jim wait a little: don't press anything now: I am much annoyed about something that has just happened: Davis, with that way of making a man do a thing whether he wants to or not made me appoint Williams[2] Judge in Kansas and John Jones in the State department: and I've got a hat full of dispatches already from Kansas cheifly: protesting against it, and asking if I was going to fill up all the offices from Illinois."

Not long after the inauguration Davis went with Lawrence Weldon to the White House: and demanded that he should be appointed District Attorney for Southern Illinois, and it was done. It was largely at Davis' importunity that Caleb Smith was appointed to a cabinet position and William P. Dole as Commissioner of Indian affairs: he failed, however, to get either himself or his cousin, Henry Winter Davis, in the cabinet. In appointing Judge Davis on the Supreme bench; he did no more than common gratitude demanded: for to Davis more than to any other man, he owed his nomination. I think Lincoln rather too hard on the "Davis" family in his interview with Thurlow Weed, as appears in the autobiography of the latter.[3]

I don't Know whether or not you want to correct errors in your book: but a great many creep into biography: I note some I think of: Father Chiniquy (the recusant Catholic Priest) recently writes[4] that he was a great friend of Lincoln — that Lincoln was his lawyer — & that Lincoln told him a lot of sickly sentimality about his destiny &c. that was not like Lincoln and I doubt if it ever happened: but it is true Lincoln was his lawyer in one case in Champaign "Spink v. Chiniquy for slander:[5] We tried the case twice & got a jury to try it a third time when

2. Archibald Williams, a Quincy attorney, was appointed judge of the U.S. district court for Kansas in 1861.

3. Weed, 1:607.

4. Rev. Charles Chiniquy (1809–99), a Roman Catholic priest responsible for bringing colonists from Canada, France, and other European nations. His break with the church and the criminal prosecution in which he was represented by AL are portrayed in his autobiography, *Fifty Years in the Church of Rome*, 3d ed. (Montreal, 1886), which also recounts a visit to Washington during which AL purportedly spoke of his destiny (688–96).

5. *Spink v. Chiniquy*, tried in 1856. After the jury failed to reach a verdict, AL arranged an out-of-court settlement.

by Lincolns earnest efforts it was settled & by virtue of admissions made by Chiniquy of record as I recollect Chiniquy in some was got out of the Catholic church.

Leonard Swett in every speech he makes says that Lincoln & his father migrated from South. Indiana to *Coles* Co. Ill. and two years later Lincoln left home & emigrated to Macon Co. Now I Know this is not true: Lincoln & his Father emigrated directly to Macon County from Southern Indiana for Lincoln has not only told me so but has showed me all the landmarks of his arrival at Decatur on the spots themselves.

In Lamons life it is stated that in the "Tom Patterson" murder case in Champaign,[6] Lincoln beleived Patterson to be guilty & declined to take any fee & would not argue the case: this is not true. Patterson was guilty & we all thought so but Lincoln Swett & myself each got the same amt of fee $200.# each & each Kept his & Lincoln made the closing speech & I can to this day repeat almost verbatim a part of his speech[7]

LC: HW3997–4000

536. Henry C. Whitney (statement for WHH)

[1887?]

In looking over the Life of Lincoln by Chauncey F. Black. I can see that he has given a false coloring to many of the assumed facts. It would have been a much more readable book had *you* written it out in full. Fell[1] told me at great length of the mode he adopted to induce Lamon to change the statements shewing the connection between our friend & Abe Enlow. Under the circumstances, suppositions & possibilities I don't see how Lincoln received the name of "Abraham"? Do you know?

LC: HW4002

537. Ella A. Thompson to JWW

Portland Feb 9th/88

Sir

The answer given to your first communication to Mrs S. Francis, is the only answer she can return to you. Her high sense of honor forbids her to reveal to the public gaze, anything which she may know of the private life of her Friends. As

---

6. Lamon, 322.
7. See pp. 529, 632–33.

---

1. Jesse W. Fell (1808–87).

before written this is final, and she hopes you will receive it as such. No amount of persuasion, threats, or *[illegible]* can change her.

E.J.T.

For Mrs S. Francis

LC: HW4625

538. James K. Rardin to JWW[1]

Chicago, March 9, 1888.

Dear Sir —

I really have no time at present to enter upon the merits or generalities of this Lincoln affair. I do not know anything about Thomas Lincoln's loss of manhood if such was the case — I studied the Lincoln history from a calm cynical view, regarding Abraham Lincoln as rather a sharp politician and rather a "smart" jury lawyer, who was elected president and the war coming on he performed his part honestly enough, but in rather a weak dilly-dallying manner — You perhaps regard him as a saint; I do not — His mind was rather of the low order — reveling in vulgar, smutty anecdotes etc., and yet when we remember that his father, or *reputed* father was an ignorant and improvident ass, who traded his farm for some whisky, We ought to accord Abraham praise for pulling away from home and going into Secretary of State Field's office where he learnt his cunning in politics and changed with Field from a Jackson Democrat to a Whig[2] — As to his mother, she was a bastard; so was Dennis Hanks' mother. The mother of Dennis and the mother of Nancy (Lincoln) Hanks were sisters. Mrs Lincoln's mother was the Elder — Her name was Hanks — her daughter's name was Hanks — Dennis' mother was a younger girl; brought forth Dennis without marriage — His name is Hanks — The more you dig into the Lincoln or Hanks families the more disgusting immorality you find — The Lincoln and Hanks families Know this and they discourage all efforts to get at it — But I got at it — I have a long article written on the Lincolns, which your letter reminds me to trim up and publish — The Century article[3] is mostly bosh — Dennis Hanks is not only old but he is also noted for years as being a pretty big liar even in his pristine days. Now, write to me Exactly what you want to know and why and I will inform you and much quicker if you want to write a historical article — Many people do not believe Thomas Lincoln was Abraham's father — If he isn't, that honor belongs to a dutchman who owned the farm that the worthless Thomas Lincoln dwelt upon at the proper moment — I rather incline that way if it was so — but I guess he was Thomas Lincoln's

---

1. Headed: *Confidential.*

2. Alexander P. Field (1800–1876), Illinois secretary of state from 1829 to 1840. AL is not known to have worked in his office.

3. Presumably the account of AL's early history by John G. Nicolay and John Hay, whose biography first ran serially in *Century* magazine, beginning in 1886.

son — Mrs Lincoln was not of dark complexion as the Century has it — She was very fair — almost sandy blue eyes freckled face and had two very large "butter teeth", She could not read or write or sing — She was a Missionary Baptist although she died a hard-shell because there were no missionaries in Indiana — I have Thomas Lincolns signature; my recollection is that it runs like this[4]

Very truly Yours

J. K. Rardin

Editor Chicago Democrat[5]

LC: HW4626–28

539. Frank Marshall Eddy to WHH

Shawneetown, Ills   March 21st 1888

Dear Sir:

I see from an edition in a late paper that you are revising your life of Abraham Lincoln and thinking that I can put you in remembrance or on the track of an old case decided in the Supreme Court, that will assist you if necessary in proving to mankind the noble nature of the great Martyr of Liberty.

The case I refer to was brought up in this — Gallatin Co by Major Samuel D. Marshall for an orphan girl by the name of Rebecca Daimwood, against Ex Sheriff John Lane her Guardian, to receive certain, lands sold by him for her maintenance.[1] Marshall gained the case in the circuit court, Lane appealed it. Marshall from some cause could not go to Springfield to attend to it, and wrote Abraham Lincoln to do so for him. Lane was full handed and employed 4 or 5 of the best Lawyers in the state — among them my father Henry Eddy a brother in law to Major Samuel D. Marshall. Lincoln *alone* beat them as the Record on the Supreme Court Docket will show.

Miss Daimwood in the mean time had married William Dorman a worthy but very poor young man. Neither he nor her ever expected to recover any of the land and the suit was brought by Marshall and finished by Lincoln, almost against their will. Marshall wrote Lincoln that Dorman wanted to pay him for his services. Lincoln wrote back that he made it a present to the young couple. Marshall did the same.

Dorman was a very strong Democrat but always voted for Marshall and named his youngest boy by Rebecca for him, and I have often heard him say that had his wife lived to have borne him another son he would have named it Abraham Lincoln. When Mr Lincoln ran for president in 1860 Dorman voted for him inspite of all his fellow democrats could say or do. It seemed odd to them, but he would

---

4. Signature traced.

5. On the verso: *I had intended to have this copied on the type writer and corrected but as my time is precious just now I am obliged to send now or delay 2 wks — Write me again. / JKR.*

---

1. *Dorman et ux vs. Lane* (1842–45).

say; "Lincoln & Marshall recovered my wifes Land and made me what I am and would not charge me a cent and I will vote and fight for them to show gratitude". I have heard about this from his lips many times, especialy in 1860 when Mr Lincoln first ran for president.

I merely mention the above that you may be enabled to find a record of the case on the Supreme Court Docket and from it get the *date* of the same as I have forgotten it — but think it was between 1840 and 49. *not later* than the latter, however.

I do not think there has been a greater man than Lincoln born since the star of Bethlehem piloted the shepherds to the manger.

Very Respectfully
Frank Marshall Eddy

P.S.

The first lecture I ever heard on Mr L. was by you in Rutledges Commercial College Spfld. in the winter of 1865–66. You admitted your inability to do him justice, but said enough to keep me awake all night — I know,

LC: HW3442–44

540. Dennis Hanks (JWW interview)[1]

Paris Ills Mch 26 1888

Dennis Hanks born in Elizabethtwn Ky May 15 1799 — moved to Spencer Co Ind in 1817 — cousin of Lincoln's mother — Lincolns mother born of a Hanks woman who had come from Va and in Ky married a Sparrow — had 8 children — 2d child was Nancy — but she bore name of Hanks although Sparrow was right name — was not illegitimate   Describes visit to Wash D.C. to see about Charleston rioters who were confined at Fort Donelson[2] — L gave H. lots of papers directing him to go to Secrty but H. didn't know who Sec was. Sec Stanton came in while H. was in rom and asked L why in Hell he didn't hang rioters — L. directed then that pris. be sent frm Fort Donelson to Charleston to be tried which was done. Ficklin was lawyer and defended them — venue to Effingham Co. but no one appeared against them —

Thomas L & his 2d wife buried near Janesville Coles Co Ills — Tombstone placed there by Rob L. 2 years ago. —

H. has watch given him — plain silver one — given him by Lincoln when he made his first visit to Washington

---

1. In the top margin: *Interview with Dennis Hanks at Paris Ills.*

2. As a result of a gun battle on March 28, 1864, in Charleston, Illinois, between antiwar "Copperheads" and furloughed Union soldiers, several persons on both sides were killed. Fifteen Copperheads were arrested and sent to Fort Delaware at Newcastle, Delaware. On AL's order they were returned to Coles County. Only two were ever tried, and they were found not guilty. The notes for this interview are apparently the basis of the account of Hanks's visit to Washington given in more detail in H&W (1889), 518–20.

One Beautiful wm at visit to W House — to see Lincoln — *[three words illeg-ible]* in Rebe Army — Wrote endorsement on woman application to Secty "This woman is a leetle smarter than she lets on to be". Hanks saw L write this. H & L laughed over it. — Another poorly dressed woman came — smarter than other one. She had Son & husband in prison — wanted them out — L. turned in and wrote discharge.

Stanton says Hanks was a little bit tainted Yankee — when said Charles men should be hung Lincoln "responded if these men become good citizens whose hurt —" H asked L why he didn't spank Stanton — L told H. that he had more trouble with cabinet than all else[3]

ISHL: Weik Papers, box 1

541. Stephen M. Warner to WHH[1]

Centralia, Ills. April 5" 1888

Dear Sir.

I understand that you are writing the "Life of Lincoln". A little instance hap-pened at the State fair, held in Central City (one & a half miles north of this place) in 1858 to which I was an Eye witness.

I was attending the fair, & when I learned that Lincoln was on the ground, I had a great desire to see him, & hear him talk. So for some time, I kept close enough to him, to hear him talk: after spending some time, I left to take in the other at-tractions. Had gone but a short distance when I met James McKee[2] (father of Gen. G. C. McKee [now?] of Jackson Miss. & who for two terms was a representative to Congress from that state. & P.M. when Cleveland came into office.) James McKee was a *noted* abolitionist, and when I met him, I said to him, did you know that Lincoln was on the ground: "No, where can I find him". I said, come with me, & I will show you. In a short time I came where he was, surrounded by a group of gentlemen. We stood a short distance from them, looking up to Lincoln. When Lincoln spied, or saw Mr McKee (We always called him "Uncle Jimmy") he at once, stepped out from those about him, & reached out his hand, grasping McKees hand so earnestly, & said, "Why is this you, You that founded Joliet. what are you do-ing down in Southern Illinois"

This may be of no use to you, but I trust you will excuse me for troubling you, but I could not suppress my desire I had to add my testimony, to the many others showing how from the goodness of his heart, he never forgot his old friends, Even

---

3. This paragraph was written in the margin. At the top of the page: *Abrahm Endloe was only 16 years old at time of Thos Ls marriage.*

---

1. Marginal note: *Weik look over this W.HH.*

2. James McKee, a native of Kentucky, lived in Jacksonville, Ill., before moving to Joliet in Will County in 1834. He was the first justice of the peace in Joliet Township.

though in the lower walks of life. Should you wish to know more of James Mc-Kee, or myself, I refer you, to Hon. G. A. Sanders of your City.

Respectfully
S. M. Warner

LC: HW3445–47

542. William M. Dickson to JWW

Cincinnati, Ohio, Apl 17 1888

Dear Sir,

Your letter of 13th inst rec'd — What I Know in reference to your inquiry may be found in a letter of mine published in the Cin: Com'l of date April 17, 1876. The substance of this letter I again published in Harper's Monthly Mag. of date June 1884, or 1885 or 1886 — I forget wh.[1] Under this heading — "Abraham Lincoln at Cincinnati." or words to that effect, the fuller statement is in the Com'l — I have not time now to repeat the incidents. I was not in the case; but Mr Lincoln staid at my house during the trial — He had been of council — original — in the case in Ill. To suit the Convenience of Judge McLean the argument of the Case had been adjourned to Cin, the judge residing here. Mr Lincoln expected to make his law argument in this case & had a pride to measure swords with Reverdy Johnson, Counsel for McCormick, Mr Harding was associated with Mr Lincoln & was Expected to make the mechanical argument. To Mr L's surprise on reeching here he found that Mr Stanton had been brought into the case; also R. M. Corwin[2] — when the time came for assignment of duty between the lawyers — Mr C. moved that only 2 counsel shd argue the Case — wh. was carried — when Mr Stanton said "then Mr L — you will make the law argument —" no said Mr L. you make it. Very well said Stanton — This is the statement given me at my house by Mr L. on the day when it occurred. Mr L. felt that he had been "tricked" out of the case & the transaction deeply affected him. He said McLean was not friendly to him & he felt he had been shabbily treated all round — But never heard nor do I believe Stanton used unseemly language towards Mr L.

Sincerely Yours
W. M. Dickson

LC: HW4629–30

---

1. "Abraham Lincoln at Cincinnati," *Harper's New Monthly Magazine* 69 (June 1884): 62–66.

2. Reverdy Johnson (1796–1876), an eminent constitutional lawyer and former U.S. attorney general; Edwin M. Stanton (1814–69), a prominent attorney from Pittsburgh who served as AL's secretary of war; Richard M. Corwine, a Cincinnati attorney and later a political correspondent of AL.

543. John Hanks to JWW

Linkville Klamath *Co* Oregon Apr 19*th* 1888

Dear Sir

I wil Try to answer your questions   I and Abe Lincolen ware in New orleans several times together but I Dont Now whether he got his fortune told or Not[1]   Abe Lincolens Mothers Name was Nancy Hanks and was Bornd in virginia and was Maried to Thomas Lincolen in Washington County kentucky June 12*th* 1806 her Fathers Name was Joseph. Hanks Lincolns his step Mothers Name was Sarah Bush

I would send you my Picture if had one here you can get one by sending to A. T. Mettler at Decatur Ill

yours Respectfulley
John. Hanks

LC: HW4631

544. Alexander Campbell to JWW

La Salle May 18th 1888

My dear sir

I was greatly pleased to receive your letter of 8th inst as it afforded me the opportunity of Explaining what you had reason for regarding as gross negligence if not some thing worse on part which I assure you was not the Case as I regard promises of that Kind as binding as business Engagements

Besides I was more particularly diserous of Complying with your request believing you to be a friend and admirers of the great and good Lincoln. It was not for some time after receiving your first letter that I Could procure a photograph of Mr L's letter and in the mean time your letter got mislaid or lost and I had forgotten your address so it was out of my power to fulfil my my promise   Again I had the misfortune to have my right wrist broken some 10 or 12 weeks ago which prevented me using my pen until some three weeks past. soon thereafter the miserable weather we are still having set in, This brought on a severe attack of rheumatism which has rendered my hand nearly as helpless as the fracture in the first instance. It is with great difficulty that I can use my pen now. I have delayed answering your last letter for some days hoping for a Change in the weather that would relieve my rheumatism and enable me explain how and why the letter was made public   The understanding between between Mr Lincoln and myself at the time was that the matter was to be considered strictly private and it so remained until the National Banking System was brought forward to supercede the legal-tenders (or Greenback) which I then believed and still believe would prove highly detrimental if not fatal to the interest of the government and people and so told the President. It was at this time that that Mr Lincoln told of this matter. You will notice

---

1. It is doubtful that AL and Hanks made more than one trip down the Mississippi together. According to AL, Hanks did not go all the way to New Orleans in 1831 but turned back at St. Louis. See *CW* 4:64.

that the letter of which the enclosed photograph is a copy is dated June 25th 1858.[1] When the debates between Mr Lincoln and Senator Douglas. took place, but it was in Fremont Campaign that I authorized him to draw on me for the five hundred dollars. But as an a clear and inteligent Explanation of the Circumstances Connected with the affair would require more labor than would be possible for to bestow upon it at this time I have concluded to send you the letter and to give you the Explanation when I have recovered the use of my hand

I have taken the liberty of sending you a photograph of myself with some of my of my views on finance and Currency Hoping that what I have been able to say in reference may be satisfactory for the present

I am very truly yours
A Campbell

LC: HW4633–34

545. Samuel H. Melvin to WHH

East Oakland, Cal., June 16th 1888

My dear Sir:

A good many months ago, I recd a letter from you which I laid aside until I cd take time to reply *in extenso.* The old adage. — "out of sight out of mind". — holds good in this instance, for, I regret to say, I had entirely forgotten the matter, until reminded, a few days ago, by receipt of a letter from one Jesse. W. Weik, of Greencastle Ind, in wh he states "I have been requested by Mr W H Herndon of Springfield Ills," etc. By the way, who is Mr Weik, and why was it necessary to go to Ind. to find a party to remind me of my short comings? Now in regard to the subject matter of yr letter: Yes, I have the manuscript of a lecture[1] del by Lincoln in Cooks Hall on night of 22nd Feby 1860, for the benefit of the Spg'f'd Library Ass'n I heard him deliver it. You ask me to let you have this manuscript or a copy of it. Now friend Herndon there is no man in Spr'gf'd I w'd rather oblige than y'rself, but in this case I do not see my way clearly to comply with yr request.

The manuscript has a money value, and a large one too. and if I were to furnish you a *copy* for publication, such publication would render the original valueless except as a specimen of Lincoln chirography.

Under the circumstances I will let *you* have the document for $500 but I will not part with it to any one else for that sum

Henry J. Raymond offered me double the amt for it, but I *then* had plenty of money and declined the offer.

Yrs truly
S. H. Melvin.

LC: HW3454–55

1. *CW* 2:473.

1. AL's lecture on "Discoveries and Inventions," of which there were two versions. See *CW* 2:437–42, 3:356–63.

546. Oliver C. Terry to JWW

Mt. Vernon, Ind., July 14, 1888.

Dear Sir

Your letter of inquiry, regarding the whereabouts of one "Pritchard," "a law-yey of 1828, who rode this Juditial district about that time, and an associate of Abraham Lincolns," is received, and in answer will say, that I cannot assertain from any of our old citizens any thing that would throw any light upon "Pritchard," I will say however, that the party you refer to is no doubt the Hon Judge John Pitcher of this City. I have Known this Gentleman for the last thirty five years, and will without further preamble Give you a condensed history of this Gentlemans career in this state, as give me by him, on more than one occation. Judge John Pitcher was born in the State of Connecticut, in August 1795.

The Judge informs me that he was born in the "Old Nut Meg State," about ½ mile from the old Cider Mill, where our Puritin fathers would whip the cider barrels for working on Sunday. And in the year 1819 married there, and in the year 1820, removed to Rockport Spencer County Ind. where he began the practice of law.

In 1819, Thos Lincoln father of Abraham Lincoln had settled in Spencer County on a farm not far from Rockport. Judge Pitcher soon became acquainted with the Lincoln family Abraham being yet a boy, or verry young man, would fre-quently call at Pitchers office at Rockport, and was very desirous to read law with Pitcher, but his family being verry poor he could not give his time off the farm, but would borrow books from Judge Pitcher and read at home during leasure hours. After the death of Lincolns mother the family moved to Ills. and Judge Pitcher left Rockport and went to Princeton Gibson Co. where he lived and practiced law until 1835, when he came to Mt Vernon Posey Co. where he has lived ever since.

Pitcher received letters occationally from his friend Lincoln, after they had left spencer County, but did not meet him again until the summer or fall of 1840, when Lincoln came to Rockport and delivered a whig Speech during the Harrison Cam-paign of that year.[1] Lincoln wrote Pitcher he would be at Rockport and the Judge went up and met him and heard (using the Judge's own language) "hered one of the best political speaches he ever listened to."

Pitcher and Lincoln did not meet again until 1862, when Pitcher called on him at the White House in Washington, and at that time informed Lincoln that he only called to shake hands with him and to Congratulate him upon his success in life, and upon the policy of his administration, that he was asking nothing, wanted nothing and would not accept any thing. Lincoln has written the Judge prior to this, to Know what he could do for him?

Judge Pitcher, like Lincoln, was a Whig. And in 1836 received the nomina-tion for Congress in this (the 1st) district by his party. The Democracy nominat-ed Ratliff Boon, who defeated Pitcher by 21 majority in the District. In 1840 the Whigs nominated Pitcher for state senator to represent Posey and Vanderburgh Cos to which office he was elected and served until 1844.

---

1. AL spoke in Indiana during the Polk-Clay campaign of 1844.

Genl Thos G Pitcher of the Regular Army is a Son of Judge John Pitcher.

Genl Pitcher was born at Rockport Ind in 1824, entered West point in 1840 entered the Army as a 2d Lt in Inft, and served through the Mexican War — was promoted to Capt. and was under Genl Twig when the war broke out in 1861, but had wisely taken a 6 months furlough, and was here in Mt Vernon when Twig transferred his Command to the Confederacy.

Genl Pitcher did good service during the rebellion, was promoted to Col of regulars and Brigadier of Vols. Wounded in 1863 which has maimed him for life. And is now on the retired list with the rank of Col in the regular Army.

Genl Pitcher has two Sons, both 1st Lieutenants of Cavalry in the reg, Army. One an Aid on Genl Schofields Staff.

The subject of this letter, Judge John Pitcher, (as already indicated) will be 93 years of Age next month. he tells me he feels as well as he ever did in his life, does not suffer an ake or a pain. Apetite good, sleeps sound, And, if it were not for a broken hip, received 8 years ago by a fall, he could get round as well as he had for 80 ys prior,

The Judge as stated had been a life long whig. voted for Lincoln in 1860 & 64 — but on account of family relations, in 1868 he drifted into the Democratic ranks where he has remained until now. And after 20 years of Rip Van Winkle sleep, the old Judge is awakened, and returns to his first love, and will vote for Harrison this fall.

He does not wish to be quoted, as he is dependent on his family and as he says all are "locofocos"

As to the Rev Aaron Farmer, of whom you inquire, I can assertain nothing & do not think he figured in this neck of the woods. Judge Pitcher says he has no recollection of such person.

You ask how I like Harrison & Morton nomination! It could not have been improved upon. *Its thee very best could have been made and will win* — We are going to return Hovey to Congress from this Dist.

Pitcher informs me, that neither he, nor Lincoln ever wrote any thing upon the subject of temperance at any time, they both had mor sense than to meddle with something they knew nothing about as the question was not agitated at that time

You must excuse this miserable written letter. I have been sick five weeks and am so nervous I can scarcely write Am a poor hand at best.

Let me hear from you at your convenience—

We have a candidate here for Supreme Judge, or will be before the republican Convention on the 8th. its Judge William P. Edson. he has made two races for it and with the rest of his ticket should defeat. Can you help us on him in the Convention?

Very respectfully
O. C. Terry

LC: HW4636–40

547. J. W. Wartmann to JWW

My Dear Mr Weik

I send herewith an installment of Mss which I hope you can use. I have prepared it under peculiar circumstances of especial mental trouble, but am now about well again and hope to send more soon.

I will see Mrs Stapleton soon & write with especial reference to the "Chronicles".

Please, be candid, & let me Know just how this matter suits you. Is it in the style you wish?

Your friend

J. W. Wartmann.

The town of Lincoln is located on what is called the "Rock Port branch" of the Louisville, Evansville and St Louis Railway, and is distant from Rockport, — the County Seat of Spencer County, Indiana, about nineteen miles. Gentryville is only about two miles away, and, by the "old road," — as the Early settlers call it —, is hardly as far as that.

The town of Lincoln is situated on the old Lincoln farm and the depot is within a stones throw of the old homestead.

The mother of Abraham Lincoln lies buried on a hill in sight of the town and the monument marking the grave is visible from the cars when the foliage is off the trees.

Mrs Lincoln died of what is commonly called "milk sickness," a disease communicated by the eating of the flesh or using the milk of cows poisoned by eating some herb or shrub which grows in certain localities in the West.

Some two miles south of the town of Lincoln is located the old "Si" Crawford" farm.

Josiah Crawford was born in Nelson County Kentucky, September 23d 1802, and moved to Spencer County in 1825 and settled on the farm on which he died May 12. 1865. The former widow of Mr Crawford is still living. Her present name is Elizabeth Stapleton, she having married a man by that name after Mr Crawford's death. Mrs Stapleton is again a widow

Mrs Stapleton makes her home with her daughters Mrs Adams and Mrs Huff, dividing her time at their respective homes.

Mrs Adams resides on part of the "old home place" and her house is within sight of the late dwelling (now burned down), the lumber for the floors of which Thomas Lincoln and his son Abraham "whip-sawed" out of timber grown on the place. Abraham Lincoln worked for Mr Crawford a great deal and the Customary compensation for his labor was twenty five cents per day and board!

On one occasion Mr Lincoln borrowed of Mr Crawford a book called "Weems' Life of Washington"   This book Abraham Lincoln read by "spells" as he could snatch from his daily toil. During the time Abraham had the book, by accident it got wet and the back came off. Great was Mr Lincoln's sorrow at the dilemma in which he was placed by having to return the book in its damaged condition.

True to the promptings of his inborn honesty he took the book back to Mr Crawford and said to the owner "here Uncle Si is this book I borrowed of you, it got wet by accident and the back came off; "I can't repair it and there are no book-binders in this section All I can do is to pay for it."

"Well Abe, said Mr Crawford, "You pull blades for two days and you may keep the book."

Abe did pull corn blades for two days for Mr Crawford and thus became the possessor of the first book perhaps he ever owned.

Mr Crawford was a wheelwright and Shoemaker by trade and it was under Mr Crawford's instructions that Abe made the rude wagon with wooden tires in which the Lincoln family moved from Spencer County, Indiana, to Illinois.

Abraham Lincoln liked to be at the Crawford home. For both Mr and Mrs Crawford he entertained the sincerest respect, and the affection he had for Mrs Crawford was manifested in countless ways

Mrs Crawford is a woman of strong intellectual parts and, in her youth was quick of apprehension, witty and fond of jokes.

She was a congenial companion for Abe and readily and quickly appreciated the dry humor of the "farm hand." As she talks of the days when Abraham Lincoln was a common laborer on her husbands farm her eyes will fill with tears often, and the love she bore the future president is expressed in her homely but honest way of saying, "Abraham Lincoln, Sir, was a good and true young man": he was honest and upright always and we were always glad to have him at our house."

Mr Crawford was delighted to hear of Mr Lincoln's success in Illinois, and when he was nominated for the presidency in 1860, he was overjoyed, and voted for him at the election of that year.

It is a singular fact that among those who knew Abraham Lincoln while he was a resident of Spencer County Indiana, not a single person ever says a harmful word of him, on the contrary, everyone speaks in terms of praise of the boy and man who once lived among them.

About twelve miles from the Lincoln farm is situated the town of Maxville, on the Ohio river at the mouth of Anderson Creek, or river as it is sometimes called.

Near this town lived a man named Taylor for whom Abraham Lincoln worked as a "hand" for some time. It was while Abraham was working for Mr Taylor that he did the ferrying that is so often spoken of. After Mr Lincoln was nominated for the presidency the second time, and while the war was still going on, he expressed his opinion of the wisdom of the Convention in renominating him by saying "it is a bad time to swap horses while crossing a stream"

His experience as a ferryman impressed him with the force of the adage.

LC: HW4645–60

548. Oliver C. Terry to JWW

Mt. Vernon, Ind., July 1888

Yours of the 16th received, and would have answered earlier, but for my health. I have been confined to my room for several days since my first letter to you —

In answer to yours of the 16th will say, I have had a long interview with the venerable Judge John Pitcher, and read your letter to him — He says the passage you quote from Lamons life of Lincoll where it referred to "Abes trial on National Politics."[1] mus have been written after Lincoln left Indiana — and that he (Pitcher) never knew any one at that time by the name of *"Pritchard"* —

The Judge says Thos Lincoln — the father of Abraham — settled in spencer Co Ind in 1816 — Pitcher settled at Rockport in 1820   Thos Lincoln left Indiana for Ills about 1829 or 1830 — Pitcher left Rockport about the same time, and settled at Princeton Gibson Co Ind — Judge Pitcher is verry clear in his recollections of Lincoln —

His distinct recollection of Mr Lincoln's borrowing books from his (Pitchers) library is assigned as follows.

1st Lincoln lived about 16 miles from Rockport at or near a place now called Gentryville — A man by the name of Crawford, a well to do farmer lived in the same neighborhood. Crawford was noted for his littleness in all his dealings with his neighbors. This man Crawford owned Weems Life of Washington in one volume — Mr Lincoln borrowed this from Mr Crawford, and before he had finished reading the book, he left it in an open window, when a rain storm wet the book, causing the covers to warp, and otherwise damage the book.

Mr Lincoln felt verry much hurt over this misfortune, took the book to Mr Crawford and said to him — "I have no money with which to pay you for the damage the book has sustained, but will work it out if you have any work I can do —" When Mr Crawford told Mr Lincoln to "pull fodder two days, and they would call it even."

This story Mr Lincoln told to Judge Pitcher in Pitchers office in Rockport — Judge Pitcher says, "Lincoln said to me, you see I am tall and long armed, well I went to work, and there was not a corn blade left on a stalk, where I worked during the two days I were paying the damage sustained by the little wetting that book received. I made a clean sweep."

It was then that Judge Pitcher told young Abe, to help him self to any thing he wished to read — that he (Pitcher) had in his library, which he did — and frequently afterwards — The Judge does not Know now just what books it was he lent to Mr Lincoln — but Says they were all standrd works of that day, and some may have been law books, as to this he will not be positive — says the Judge, Abe wanted to read law with me, but his father was too poor to spare him away from the farm and mill —" I asked the Judge about the mill — when he said — "Tom Lincoln built a horse mill for grinding corn — It would not be called a mill now, but it answered then, and the people were glad to have it. I have ate many corn dodgers made from

---

1. Lamon, 69.

the meal from that old mill — It would make good chicken feed now — but we were glad to get it then. Abe use to bring me my meal regularly."

This man Crawford (above referred to, had a verry large nose, And was Known by the name of Nosey Crawford —

Judge Pitcher says Mr Lincoln would frequently refer to his friend "Nosey," and laugh about stripping all the corn blade off of 6 or 8 acres of Corn to pay about a 25c damage to a "book —"

The last time the Judge met Mr Lincoln was in 1862. He tells me now it was upon a letter from Mr Lincoln — and in the interest of the Judges Son, Genl Thomas G Pitcher —

At that time Thos G. Pitcher was a Capt in the regular army, and the old Judge visited the President in the interest of his son, who was at once promoted from a Capt. to a Colonel in the Regular army, and a brigadier Genl of volunteers. At that time Mr Lincoln asked about his friend "Nosey." I have had a good deal of trouble to secure a photgraph of the old Judge, and had to half way steel it.

This is the only picture ever taken of him that was one and a half years ago — Its good —

Pardon bad breaks — in speling — grammer and poor witing — a sick man cant work you Know — I write a while then rest. my health is verry poor, and not improving — hoping you can read my writing I will close. Will not attend the Sate Convention health will not permit.

Very respectfully
O. C. Terry

You[2] must arrange this data — if it can be called such — I am in no condition to write — sorry for it.

I was in no condition to interview the Judge when I did — I being so weak, and he so deaf, made it quite a task —

The old gentleman said he was a younger man now than I am — his genl health is as good now as it ever was, and he has always been a healthy man

I will here say — the Judge has lost or given away all of Lincolns letters. He remembers of about four, but just the contents — he is unable to state

Terry.

LC: HW4661–65

549. Sarah Rickard Barret to WHH

Connors Kan. Augt 3d 1888.

Dear Sir

Yours of the 20th ultimo is before me and as an old friend I will answer the question Propounded to me.

---

2. The remaining text appears as a postscript on the verso.

Mr. Lincoln did Propose marriage to me in the winter of 1840 and 41, as was his costom he brings quotations from the Bible how [know?] but Sarah will become Abrahams wife. My reasons for refusing his Proposal was that I was young only 16 years old and had not thought much about matrimony. I had the highest Regard for Mr Lincoln and he seemed allmost like an older Brother being as It were one of my Sisters family

Yours in friendship
Sarah A Barret

P.S.

In April last I wrote you about this matter through my Brother John Rickard and supposed you had Recieved It.

You can make any use of this letter you wish.

Will be willing to furnish You any Information in my Possession in regard to Mr Lincoln life.

S. A B.

LC: HW3465–66

550. Richard F. Barret to WHH[1]

Connors Kan Augt 12.th 1888.

Dear Sir

Yours of the 12th inst to my wife is before me, as you request her to send you her photograph I herewith Enclose one Taken in 1870. when she was 46 years of age. we have not one taken when she was younger. when this picture was taken she had passed the turn of life and was fleshey and was unlike her younger days, when Young her hair was brown, her Eyes Brown her flesh fair between a brunett and a Blonde.

like most women she thinks this is not a good picture and did not want to send It but I perswaided her to let me Send It.

when you get a copy pleas return this picture as I have *only* the *one*.[2]

Yours Respectfully
R. F. Barret.

LC: HW3469

---

1. Marginal note: *Weik Mrs Barret is an excellent and a very reliable woman — have known her since 1830 — Excellent family   H*

2. Note at the bottom: *Weik — I have promised Sarah to keep the person who gives the information and who sent the pho private — told her that I would tell the story & publish her first letter to me but not tell who gave the other information. W.HH.* Marginal note: *Take a copy and send back to me the original / H.*

551. Sarah Rickard Barret to WHH[1]

[August 12, 1888]

Sir

With a soar finger on my right hand I Get my Husband to do my writing. When I first met Mr Lincoln at Mr Butlers I was ten or twelve years of age. as I grew up he used to take me to little Entertainments the first was the Babes in the woods. he tooke me to the first Theater that ever played in Springfield. when I arrived at the age of 16 he became more attentive to me. I allway liked him as a friend but you know his pecular manner and his General deportment would not be likely to fasinate a young girl just entering the society world.

Mr Lincoln in after years used to say when I first met Sarah she was a little Girl wearing these Pantletts.

I agree with You that Mr Lincoln was very unfortunate in Marrage.

I remember very distinctly Thos[e] little Instances of our Young days.

Give my Respects to Your wife and accept the same to Your self

Sarah A Barret

LC: HW3840

552. James H. Matheny to JWW

Springfield Ill., August 21 1888

Dear Sir

I filled up the blank that you Sent to my Son and gave to him to Send you.

The Wedding incident, refered to was one of the funiest things to have witnessed imaginable — No description on paper can possibly do it justice — I never Saw the Book you refer to and therefore do not Know how it was given.

Old Judge Brown was a rough "old timer" and always said just what he thought without regard to place or Surroundings — There was of course a perfect hush in the room as the ceremony progressed. Old Parson Dresser in clerical robes — Brown Standing just behind Lincoln — the Parson handed Lincoln the ring, and as he put it on the brides finger, went through the church formula. "With this ring I thee endow with all my goods and chattles, lands and tenements" — Brown who had never witnessed Such a proceeding, was Struck with its utter absurdity and spoke out So everybody could hear, in an expression, used by him on all occasions by way emphasis, "Lord Jesus Christ, God Almighty, Lincoln, the Statute fixes all that" — This was too much for the Old Parson — he broke down under it — an almost irresistable desire to laugh out, checked his proceeding for a minute or so — but finally recovered and pronounced them Husband & wife.

I saw Mr. Herndon to day and he explained to me about the likeness — As it is Simply to represent the "Sangamon Bar" I will have my son Send you one — I

---

1. This letter was apparently written out by her husband and included with his letter to WHH of this date.

have always had a distaste to perading pictures unless they illustrated Some special purpose — For my old friend Herndons Sake I do hope that you have got up a good Book and that it will Sell Well

Very Respectfully

Jas H Matheny

I have written out the Marriage incident, not for publication but that you might, in your imagination enjoy the Scene.

LC: HW4666

553. James H. Matheny (JWW interview)[1]

Aug 21 88

1. *How long before his marriage did Mr. Lincoln give you notice of it? Was it not on the morning of the wedding-day?*

It was about noon of Wedding day

2. *Who else besides yourself attended him? Did Beverly Powell do so? What lady other than Miss Jayne attended the bride?*

Beverly Powell attended him besides myself. I have forgotten the name of the other brides maid

3. *How many guests were present? Name if you can some of them. Was a feast or supper served?*

There was present a goodly number of persons — Mr Lincolns personal friends. Cannot now remember whether supper was Served or not.

4. *Was the marriage celebrated with ring and book?*

It was.

5. *Is the incident related in the "Every Day Life of Lincoln" by F. F. Browne, of the comical observation by Judge Brown of the Supreme Court of Illinois correct? I refer to the suggestion by Judge B. when in the marriage ceremony the groom is made to say to the bride: "I endow thee with all my goods and chattels", "Why Lincoln the Statute fixes all that".*

It is correct so far as the incident taken place   I never Saw the publication

6. *If any further incidents occur to your recollection please relate them.*

I do not now recollect anything further of importance[2]

LC: HW4668

---

1. JWW's questions are typed, and Matheny has filled in the answers by hand.
2. On a slip laid over the interview form: *Written by J.H. Matheny.*

554. Joseph E. McDonald (JWW interview)

Aug 28 88.

Met L. first in 1856 — was in Cong. 49 to 50 wth [Indiana congressman?]   In 56 was elec Atty Gen   In 56 — Met L at Danville — In Jan '65 consulted L. as to military trials — L — told about record —

In 1858 met at Danv. with Swett L. & others who had returned from adj. Co. & were discussing murder trial when L pros & Swett def — & def was insanity. They were telling it in MCormacks hotel when McD asked for name of def. — Isaac Wyant — McD saw he had def — in Ind for evry crime in calender. Next day L. asked MD on way to Court House if "Wyant was possuming" L. said "I wasnt certain W. was possuming — Said if he thought he was W was insane he didnt want to push him — if he didnt realize crime he didn't want to punish him

Int as Consp trials — McD & H. spent an entire evening till 11 PM. with L[1] 1864 — [Mort?] [T?] McDonald —

ISHL: Weik Papers, box 2, Memorandum Book 2

555. James H. Matheny (JWW interview)

Sep 12 88

Matheney
In 1839–40 Shoemaker who whipped his wife and lived back of Hoffman's row. Lincoln Evan Butler Noah Rickard & Matheney Notifed him if he ever did so again they would whip him. He did so and L & the others tied him to a post near a well back of Court House stripped his shirt — sent for his wife — who whaled him tremendously   L. wanted to do it himself a few days before.

Sep 12 '88

Matheney says has heard Tiger tell the story of Mrs L. and his niece dozens of times.[1] T. said Ls answer took the starch out of him

---

1. There is a much-expanded version of this interview in H&W (1889), 556–57n.

---

1. This relates to the story told earlier by Matheny to WHH (see §604). A note in JWW's memorandum book identifies "Tiger" as Jacob Taggart:

Jacob Taggarts daughter — Miller. moved from Ohio

Lost Story of Lincoln.
Miller whose niece had trouble with M Lincoln — latter put truck out on [pavement?] — Ms L. hit Taggart in face with broom — T. asked L for satisfaction Lincoln said to him "Cant you stand this 1 lick whe I have stood it 20 years". When Taggart hunted Lincoln up for satisfaction L. was in Laverty's store telling yarn.

The sentence "Ms L. hit . . . for satisfaction" was added later. See Weik Papers, inside cover of Memorandum Book 1, ISHL.

Matheny also says young men serenaded Mary Todd few days after arrival with flute fiddle and old time instruments. Next night she was at party. Met one Peck one of the players. On being introduced to him she made such sneering allusions to the music. Said she had met him (Peck) before, referring to the serenade. "That music" responded Peck who was a wild frolicsome fellow was intended for Susan" the servant at Edwards's.[2]

ISHL: Weik Papers, box 2, Memorandum Book 2

556. Alexander Campbell to JWW

La Salle Dec 5th 1888

My dear sir

Yours of 2nd inst is received   The only apology I have to offer for what must seem to unpardonable neglect in replying to your requests months ago is that a severe attack of rheumatism unfitted me for any business. and rendered a change of Climate and of treatment absolutely necessary. I visited the White Sulphur Springs in Pa where I remained for about two months without material benifit. In the hurry before leaving my papers got mislaid and supposing that you had got your book out before the time of my return it would be useless to write you. After thinking the matter over I find that in order to make the matter of my relations with Mr Lincoln inteligble to you and others will require a brief history of the Circumstances, Connected with the Case which I had purposed writing out to day but the death of a particular friend whose funeral I am invited to attend will prevent. I will however immediately on my return give attention to the Subject and mail it to you the Early part of the Coming week: Probably what I have to say would cover a page or two of your book but you will only publish what you May proper. As you have been at the Expense of Engraving my photograph and may be subjected to further Expense of publishing what you may think proper of the Communication I shall send you I will Cheerfuly recompense you therefor with sincere thanks for your Kindness

I am in haste

Very truly yours
A Campbell

ISHL: Weik Papers, box 1

---

2. JWW expands on this story in *The Real Lincoln,* where he gives the date of the interview as March 1883 and Sally as the name of "the colored servant at the Edwards mansion" (98).

557. Alexander Campbell to JWW

La Salle Dec 12 1888

My dear Sir

I regret Exceedingly that I Could not Comply with your request sooner and in better Shape   As I stated to you I attended the funeral of my friend and took a severe Cold which with rheumatism has quite unfitted me for Either thinking or writing   Besides I spent too much time in thinking and writing over what I could not Condense and get in the space & shape I intended   I hope what I have sent will be a satisfactory answer to your Main question but if you print you must look it over and Correct Mistakes for in my present state of health to think or write   Thinking that having my photograph Engraved it may have been destroyed I send you another. One thing I wish to state is that it Occurs to My Mind that Mr Herndon stated some two or three years ago that I gave Mr Lincoln Either One hundred and seventy five or two hundred and seventy five dollars in their office in Springfield   I remember give him some money in their office in 1856, but do not remember the Amount. But have no recollection of giving him any there in 1858 if I did the Amount must have been small.

My arrangement with Mr Lincoln 1856 was that it was to be strictly private and it was after many years that he told of it. As the publicity has given a great deal of annoyace I intended giving a brief history of the personal relations between Mr Lincoln and myself but Could not get it in as Consise and Clear form as I wished   If my health gets better in the Course of a few days some thing in reference but do not delay the publication of your book on that uncertainty

I am in haste yours sincerely

A. Campbell

LC: HW4675–77

558. Alexander Campbell to JWW

La Salle Dec 12th 1888

My dear Sir

Your letter of 2nd inst has been received   In answer to your interogotories in reference to money I gave Mr Lincoln for Campaign Expenses in 1856 and 1858   To the first. Did Mr Lincoln receive from you the Sum asked for in the letter which you have? I answer No.

I was present at the discussion between him and Douglass at Ottawa which I think was their first meeting in that Memorable and Ever to be remembered discussion and had short interview with him after the Close of the debate when I gave him I think thirty or forty dollars. I recollect give him Some more at two or three times thereafter during that Canvass but do not remember the amounts. I do however remember well that they were not as large as I Could have wished. For "times were "tighter" with me than they were 1856

After Careful refection I do not think My Contributions to him during the dissions between him and Douglass were much of any over One hundred dollars.

2nd As to Mr Lincoln's reference in a published letter to N B Judd[1] of a note for Five hundred dollars for Expenses incurred in the debates with Mr Douglass. I have to Say that the first and only and Knowledge I ever had of any such note is the mention of it in your letter   I will add that I never had Mr Lincoln's note or other obligation for the payment of money. and that I never Kept any account of or even Charged my Memory with any money I gave him. It was given to defray his personal Expenses and other wise promoting the interest of a Cause — which Scincerly believed was for the public good — without any expectation or thought of a dollar of it Ever being returned   And from What I Knew or learned of his Careful habits in money matters in the Campaign of 1856 I am Entirely Confident that Every dollar and dime I ever gave him was Carefully and faithfully applied to the uses and purposes for which it was given   This I think Covers your main question   There are Several other things which I think Germane to the general subject which I intended submitting to your judgment but Circumstances beyond my control prevents my doing so at this time

Sincerely Yours
A. Campbell

LC: HW4678–81

559. Luther B. Baker (statement)[1]

[1887–88]

Upon reaching Washington D.C. with the body of J. Wilks Booth, it was at once removed from the tug boat; to a gun-boat that lay at the dock at the Navy-yard, where it remained about: 36 hours. It was there examined by the Surgeon General and staff and other officers and identified by half a score of others who had known him well.

Toward evening of the second day Genl. L. C. Baker, then chief of the "detective bureau of the war department," recved. orders from sec. Stanton to dispose of the body. Stanton said "Put it where it will not be disturbed until Gabriel blows his last trumpet."

I was ordered to assist him. The body was then placed in a row-boat, and taking with us one trusty man to manage the boat, we quietly floated down the river

Crowds of people all along the shore were watching us. For a "blind" we took with us a heavy ball and chain and it was soon going from lip to lip that we were about to sink the body in the Potomac. Darkness soon came on completely concealing our movements, and under its cover we pulled slowly back to the old penitentiay which during the war was used as an Arsenal. The body was then lifted

---

1. AL to Judd, Nov. 16, 1858, *CW* 3:337.

---

1. This statement was written on the letterhead of the State of Michigan, Auditor General's Office, with a printed dateline "188_".

from the boat & carried through a door opening upon the river front. Under the stone floor of what had been a prison cell, a shallow grave was dug, and the body, with the U.S. blanket "for a winding sheet," was there interred, where it remained untill Booths accomplices were hanged. It was then taken up and burried with his companions in crime. I have since learned that the remains was again disinterred and given to his friends, and that they now rest in the family burial place in — Baltimore Md.

L. B. Baker
Lieut. & A.D.M.
1st D.C. Cav.

LC: HW5266–67

560. Thomas W. Dresser to JWW

Springfield Ill. Jan. 3rd 1889

Dear Sir

Your favor of Dec. 30th was duly received. I was rather surprised that you made no mention of having received the photograph of Mrs Lincoln that I took so much trouble to hunt up for you. It is probable that I will be unable to give you such sketch of Mrs Lincoln as you desire.

She died in this City July 16th 1882   In the late years of her life certain mental peculiarities were developed which finally culminated in a slight apoplexy, producing paralysis, of which she died. Among the peculiarities alluded to, one of the most singular was the habit she had during the last year or so of her life of immersing herself in a perfectly dark room, and for light using a small candle light, even when the sun was shining bright out of doors. No urging would induce her to go out into the fresh air. Another peculiarity was the accumulation of large quantities of silks and dress goods by the trunk and cart load, which she never used, and which accumulated until it was really feared that the floor of the store room would give way. She was bright and sparkling in conversation and her memory remained singularly good up to the very close of her life. Her face was animated and pleasing; and to me she was always an interesting woman; and while the whole world was finding fault with her temper and disposition, it was clear to me that the trouble was a cerebral disease.

You may elaborate this into a more extended sketch if you choose, but I am too much cramped for time to do more.

Yours truly
Thos. W. Dresser

P.S. It *was* my father[1] mentioned by Rev. Dr. Robinson. He graduated in '23.

LC: HW4682

---

1. Rev. Charles Dresser (1800–1865) married AL and Mary Todd in 1842.

561. James C. Conkling to JWW

Springfield, Ill., Jany 11 1889

Dear Sir

I now enclose you a copy of the letter dated August 26 1863 by Mr Lincoln to me.[1] It has been carefully compared with the original and is a correct copy, except the words commencing "I know as fully as one can know &c" to the words "You say you will not fight to free negroes", were not included in the original, but were telegraphed the next day with instructions to insert.

I have no copy of the invitation extended to Mr Lincoln to attend the mass meeting

I will remark that Mr Bancroft, the historian in commenting on this letter, considers it addressed to me as one who was criticizing Mr Lincoln's policy. On the contrary, I was directed by a meeting of unconditional Union men, to invite Mr Lincoln to attend a mass meeting composed of such men, and he only took occasion to address his opponents through the medium of this letter

Yours truly
James C. Conkling

LC: HW4683

562. Charles Friend to WHH

Sonora Kentucky 17 July 1889

Dear Sir:

I would like to have a letter from you stating that I had assisted you in collecting the events of Pres — A Lincoln's early life, in Larue County, Ky. I was Post Master here and was kicked out by the Democrats when Pres Cleveland came into power. Made application and was indorsed by nearly all the Republicans here and in the District by the influential one. Was appointed 13 May, last and the Commission has been held up on account of a few lying Republicans and Democrats, I guess you have not forgotten me [My?] Uncle Dennis F. Hanks sent my letter to you and you wrote me, Uncle Dennis was a half brother of *A Lincoln* being a son of Nancy Hanks,[1] by Mr Grandfather Charles Friend, I know that you remember me after reading this, I think a word from you at this time would do me good and as I always responded to your calls you will help me.

---

1. *CW* 6:406–10.

---

1. Dennis Hanks was the son of Charles Friend and AL's mother's aunt, another Nancy Hanks.

What has become of Uncle Dennis, is he dead? or alive? If dead when did he die?

Yours Truly

Chas Friend[2]

LC: HW3565

---

563. *Charles Friend to WHH*

Sonora Ky 31 July 1889

While living in Hodgenville there came a man from Ill. who sayed that it was reported in that state that Abe Enlows was Abe Linco father. I heared the question put to "Old uncle" Abe Enlows by My Brother-Law Mr A. H. Redman   ther was another gentleman present — Dr W. H. Holt — Redman asked if it was true that he Abe Enlows was Abe's Father — the old man drew himself up to his full heigtht some 6 feet 3 in and stroked his long white beard and remarked that it was an honor to be proud of to even be thought to be father of a President and one that had risen by his own Merits to hold the proud position of President these United States. But said he I was only 15 years old when Abe was born — then sayed Redman you could not have been, being at that time only 14 years old when he was begotten. Now said Uncle Abe not too fast Al for I passed into puberty at 14 years and could have been his father at that age as easily as at any time from that until the present moment. Now to set that matter forever at rest I will say I never put my hand on her naked flesh or any part of her body save her hands, and never in life had Carnal intercourse with her. And further I believe that he was the son of Thomas Lincoln. I think all this grew out of his name being Abe the same of Mine, but I can account for that name; his grand Father was named Abraham Lincoln. the grandfather was killed by the Indians on Salt River not far from where now stands Shepherdsvile at an old salt works.[1] I will farther say that if he is not Thomas Lincolns son he was the son of Charles Friend this boys grand father — pointing at your Corespondent or William Cessna or George Brownfield his long

---

2. WHH note at the bottom of the page: *Weik I think that Friend is wrong in some of his statements, above as well his other statements which I sent you — 1st Because Dennis Hanks says that there were 2 Nancy Hanks — 2d Because Lincoln stated that __ was mistaken and his mother, implying that there were 2 Nancys & 3dly Helm says that the Hanks girls were good dancers; I do not say that this man is wrong in all that he says — This man is mistaken again when he says that one of the [Insons?] — as I remember not having the paper in my hand — is in your posession, married someone in Ky. We have it somewhere in our book that he is mistaken by stating facts differently in this too — see the beginning of our life of L. See also what Friend does say in a communication to me which I sent you —. Watch the corners. W. H Herndon.* Marginal note: *This man I take it is honest, but he jumps to conclusions too quick or does not remember things. On the other hand Why was Dennis Hanks taken away from his mother & always following Thos. Lincoln's mother words was Nancy Hanks the mother of Dennis & Abraham No doubt that Chas Friend was the father of Dennis. H.*

---

1. Marginal note in WHH's hand: *Old Abraham Lincoln, the Presidents grand father was killed on Salt Creek near [illegible] Shepherdsville Ky.*

bony body seems to point to the Brownfields more strongly as they were all long bony people oftan over 6½ feet in highth. The reason I think that he might be a son of Charles Friend is that Nancy Hanks Abes mother's first child Dennis F was by Charles Friend, but his shape does not point to that family as they was a short thick heavy set People and the Cessnas are of the same shape being closely related to the Friends.

You ask me a question was he Thomas Lincoln Castrated. I heard a Cousin of my fathers Judge Jonathan Friend Cessna say that his father Wm Cessna say that Thomas Lincoln could not have been Abes Father for one of Thomas' testacles was not larger than a pea or perhaps both of them wer no larger than peas, and "uncle Billie" Cessna sayed he believed that Abe was my uncle and based this reason the fact that Nancy Hanks first child Denis was Chas Friends boy. Be that as it may let it go. Now whose son was Denis Friend Hanks. There never was but one Hanks family in this County (Hardin) and they was all sisters   Mary or "Pollie" who married Thomas Sparrow Elizabeth or "Betsey" who Jesse Friend Nancy who Married Thomas Lincoln. Whe Charles Friend married my Grad Mother Sallie Huss he told he that he had a son by Nancy Hanks and she told him to get the boy word So and Dennis stayed with his father until Sparrow and the other families left her for Ind and Ill. Uncle Dennis aske grand father if he might go with him and Tom Spery and the old people gave him their consent. My Grand Mother told me the facts

Chas Friend

LC: HW3567

564. Charles Friend to WHH

Sonora Ky 20 Aug 1889

Dear Sir:

Your of 10 Inst received 10 Oclk this morning. Where could have been? There never wer but One family of Hanks in this County that I ever hear of. And they wer all women. I never heard any thing against the women except Nancy. Judge J. F. Cessna Cousin of my father told me that Uncle Isaac Friend was once in love with her and at a party at night after a log rolling in the day he (Isaac) was laying with his head in her lap and swore that he feld the Child kick in her belly when talking to the boys about this matter Later he learned that his brother Charles Friend had done the work for her, Dennis Friend Hanks was the boy that did the kicking, which kicked Uncle Isaac out of marrying her, I hav written Uncle Dennis several time and asked him what relations he bore to President Lincoln and he will never answer it. The first letter he ever wrote me he sayed   "My mother was a Hanks she sayes your Grand father was my father this don't doubt," Evry old person that I ever talked to on the subject agree by saying that Nancy Hanks Denis' Mother was A Lincoln's mother.

<table>
<tr><td></td><td>Married</td></tr>
<tr><td>Nancy Hanks</td><td>Thomas Lincoln</td></tr>
<tr><td>Betsey   "</td><td>Thomas Sparrow</td></tr>
<tr><td>Pollie   "</td><td>Jessey Friend</td></tr>
<tr><td>   "</td><td>Livi Hall[1]</td></tr>
</table>

These women wer all Sisters   Uncle Jessey Friend moved from here to Paris Ill and died there one of his daughters married a Mr Hatfield and returned to K

    Thomas Sparrow raised Uncle Dennis

    A Lincoln calling Dennis Cousin can be accounted for easy enough, In this County all bastard Children are taught to call their mothers Aunt, and of course he would naturally call Lincoln Cousin, I have asked Denis if his mother was not a Sister to Betsey Sparrow if they wer there would have, to be 2 Nancy's sister in one family which I cannot believe, Know I am right I heard my brother-in-law A. H. Redman of Glendale Ky. ask Old Uncle Abe Enlows if he was A. Lincolns father, there was present New Dr. Holt Mr W. H. Holt and myself. The old man drew himself up to full height over 6 feet and stroked his long white beard and sayed it was an honor to be thought to be father of President, but sayed he I never touch more than her hand in my life never had carnal knowledge of her or intercourse with her in my life. She was older than I, I was only 15 years old when Lincoln was born, Redman spoke up and said you mean to say you could not have been. No sir dont be too fast I could have been his father as well then I as at any time since up to the present time", I believe that he was the son of Thomas Lincoln, and this whole matter grew out of the name being the same as mine, But he was named after his grand father Abraham Lincoln who was killed by the Indians not far from where now stands Shepherdsville at the old Salt mills on Salt River. Though if he was an ilgitimate child he was one of 3 mens son George Brownfield Wm Cessna or Charles Friend. Certin Circumstances would point to Charles Friend that boys grand father (pointing at your correspond) was the father of her first child Dennis F Hanks, but the Friend are of a low heavy set people and so are the Cessna's both being of the same Pennsylvania stock. His shape features & likeness point to the Brownfields."

    I will say here I saw the remains of President Lincoln "in state" at Indianapolis and if any one had have taken me to the coffin and sayed there lies Your friend Geo. Brownfield Jr. I would have sworn before any Jury that it was he. If I had not known better, The resemblance was that close. Judge Jonathan Friend Cessna told that his father Wm Cessna told him that one if not both of Thomas Lincolns testicles we not larger than a pea. He Wm Cessna also sayed that Chas Friend was father of Denis a half if not whole brother of A Lincoln but did not believe it possible that Thomas could have been his father.

----

1. WHH's marginal note: *Lucy Hanks, Nancy's mother married Henry Sparrow as said / Who did Levi Hall marry* —.

During the war Larue County sent Dr J. H. Rodman to Washington to see the President to have the number of men corrected that was called for from the County under the draft. He sent up his Card and Mr. Lincoln sent word to Dr Rodman that he would see him. Rodman sayed that there was men there waiting to see the Pres' that had been there for weeks but could not get a glance, In Course of the coversation, Dr Rodman told him that the County had sent him a nice cane from near where he was born and that he would send it up as soon as the Silversmith put a gold head on it. Lincoln sayed how will I know who gave it to me, Dr Says the names of the Donars will be imposed on it to the President A. Lincoln, "Abe sayed what a fool, I am like the Irishman that went to the Post Office when the Post master asked his name sayed faith and my name on the letter" of Course my name will be on the cane, President asked Dr. Rodman about the Cessnas Brownfields Friends Ashcrafts Kirkpatricks & at last sayed where is my old friend and playmate Austin Golliher, Sayd Abe I would rather see Golliher than any man living, he played me a dirty trick once and I want to pay him up, One Sunday Golliher and another boy and myself wer out in the woods on knob Creek playing and hunting around for young squirels when I climed up a tree and left Austin and the other boy on the grown [shortly?]   Golliher shut his eyes like he was asleep I noticed his hat sat straight with the reverse side up I thought I would shit in his hat   Gollier was watching and when I let the load drop he swaped hats and my hat caught the whole Charge. At this recital the President laughed heartily." Dr J H Rodman sayed he seemed to know more about the general topography of the County than any person he ever say discribed ery house and farm hill Creek and family that lived here when he was a boy. He (Lincoln) asked about an old Stone house that stands on Nolynn Creek about 1½ miles east of Hodgensville near a fine spring where the young people used to hold there dances. Rev John Duncan a Baptist preacher told me that he and Abe used to go hunting both night and day and at one time they worked all one day trying to dig som kind of a "varment" out of the ground.[2] I guess the man you allude to is Abes old friend Austin Golliher of Larue County he lives about 20 miles from here. He is the only person now living that knows anything abot Lincoln or the Hanks. I could go and see him some day if it was not for the expense of going. I would visit him and get all he knows. He is very old and what is done must be done quickly as his days are few.

Yours Truly
Chas Friend

Could you send me any of A. Lincolns writing or his signature. CF[3]

LC: HW3575, HW3576r, HW3577, HW3576v, HW3578

---

2. See §439.

3. Marginal note: *If you write a history dont you think you ought to give me a copy.*

565. Edward L. Pierce to WHH

Milton (Mass)   15 Sept '89

Dear Sir

I have just finished reading, though too hastily, your most interesting life of Mr Lincoln.

I lived in Chicago from Jan '56 to July '57 and heard him speak in the canvass of John Wentworth for the mayoralty. I had not heard of him before and was greatly impressed with his logical and reflective style, so different from what was common in the West at the time. The next day I was introduced to him in the Tribune office by Dr Ray or Medill.[1] I remember one sentence of Wentworth at the meeting "I'll tell you why they hate me: It is because they know I shall leave No stone unturned to place that man, (pointing to Lincoln) in the seat now disgraced by Stephen A Douglass."

I was a Mass delegate (Gov Claflin[2] my colleague,) to the National Convention of 1860 and was a friend of Mr Lincoln from the start — tho' in order to keep company with my delegation voting for Mr Seward on the 1st two ballots. I was the guest of Dr Ray — and had corresponded with him about Lincoln before going to the convention.

Too much weight has been given to possible or probable bargains on Mr Lincolns account. Our delegation and all I met were governed by no such considerations. He was nominated because his debates with Douglass & his Cooper Institute Speech showed him to be sound, and because he was the only candidate truly reliable who would not, like Seward & Chase, encounter conservative prejudices. He would have been the candidate if no bargains had been made with Penn delegation. I remember well a talk with Carter.[3] He did not care for Cameron,[4] but said only (urging thus) that they could not elect Seward. I was satisfied before reaching Chicago on the Saturday before, when meeting the Indiana delegation at Michigan City, that Lincoln would be nominated. That made two of the 4 northern states which were lost in '56 for him, and the same considerations would carry Penn & New Jersey

I met Mr Lincoln twice at Washington, once when a private soldier in '61 when taken to him by my friend, Mr Chase, & a year later when I had charge of freedmen at Port Royal. Mr Chase sent me to him about them, but he did not behave well. He talked about "the itching to get niggers into our lines"   His son was very ill, and quite likely that had something to do with his temper at the time. I never met him again, and as I remember, did not care to. I was appointed by him without my knowledge, at Mr Chase's request, Collector of Int Rev for Boston when I was taking care of freedmen in South Carolina.

---

1. Dr. Charles H. Ray (1821–70) was editor-in-chief and Joseph Medill (1823–99) was managing editor of the Chicago *Tribune*.

2. William Claflin (1818–1905), governor of Massachusetts from 1869 to 1871.

3. David K. Cartter (1812–87), Ohio delegate to the 1860 Republican convention.

4. Simon Cameron (1799–1889), U.S. senator from Pennsylvania and AL's first secretary of war.

I had some correspondence with yourself in '60–'61 when I was anxious that Mr Lincoln should stand firm and I feared that he would come too much under the compromising influence of Mr. Seward.

You may perhaps recal my name in connection with a law book on railways and Mr Sumner's Memoirs[5]

I have said to Mr Hay[6] that biographers of Mr Lincoln avoid the subject of Mr Lincoln's great unpopularity with Congress in 1863 or about that period. I was myself at the time greatly disgusted with his scheme for the transporting the negro population out of the country — which was the subject of the *Ile À Vache* expedition under Senator Pomeroys patronage[7]   He was at the time as strong with the people as ever, but few MC's spoke well of him. Mr Blaine in his history[8] touches upon one cause — his treatment of the reconstruction bill. His retention of Seward had probably something to do with it — and there was also a feeling growing out of Mr Lincolns manner and style of conversation that he was not profoundly in earnest. This last feeling passed away with the Gettysburg speech.[9]

LC: HW3582–83

566. LeGrand B. Cannon to WHH

Near Burlington, Vt. Oct 7 *[1889]*

My Dear Sir

My friend Jno. Wilson by your permission sends me your letters to him in responce to his enquirys; for which consent I am grateful & will observe its confidences.

I was charmed with your Life of Lincoln[1]   its the only one attempted which I believe to be *truthful* & therefore instructive & satisfactory.

The facts which you make public in no measure detract, but on the contrary add luster to his great life. With his low breeding and surroundings, his small opportunity for education & culture, — the infalicity of his married life, & limitations overcoming & bearing all by his virtues & instinct for truth, is simply a marvel.

Your book further suggests to my mind, that that in seeking relief from the discords of his house, brought out his great quality to the Public had it been otherwise I doubt if he would have had the opportunity made a conspicuous record in history, & in this aspect his success, was an accident of life.

---

5. *A Treatise on American Railroad Law* (New York, 1857); *Memoir and Letters of Charles Sumner,* 4 vols. (Boston, 1877, 1893).

6. John Hay.

7. This sentence was written in the margin.

8. James G. Blaine, *Twenty Years of Congress: From Lincoln to Garfield,* 2 vols. (Norwich, Conn., 1884–86).

9. In a letter to WHH dated September 27, 1889 (LC: HW3598–99), Pierce apologized for not signing his name to this letter.

---

1. H&W (1889).

It was my great good fortune to know something of Lincoln distinct from his official life. It is the outcome of [it?].

Intensely in earnest, I entered the service at the opening of the Rebellion as a Staff officer in the Regular Army and was assigned to the Department of Virginia with Head Quarters at Fort Monroe, Maj Genr Wool in command of the Dept. & I was honored by him as his Chief of Staff & enjoyed his entire confidence. it was the only Gate open for communication with the Rebel Govt. & Genl Wool was the Agent for much intercourse.

In the early stages of the war there was a want of harmony between the Army & Navy about us, which seriously embarrased Military Operations resulting in the President & Sect'y — Chase & Stanton coming to Fort Monroe to adjust Matters.

Domestic comforts were limited at Head Quarters & the President occupied my room & I was (in accordance with Military etiquett) assigned to him as "Aid in waiting" & Scty. Altho I had frequently Met the Pres. as "Bearer of Dispatches" I was not a little prejudiced & a good deal irritated at the levity which he was charged with indulgence in. In grave matters jesting & [frolicking?] seemed to me shocking, with such Vital Matters to settle & I confess to thinking of Nero.

But all this Changed when I came to know Lincoln & I very soon discerned that he had a Sad Nature & that it was a terrable burden & that his saddness did not originate in his great official responsibility. I had heard that his house was not pleasant, but did not know that their was More beyond it.

The day after Lincoln came to us. He said to me I suppose you have neither a Bible or a copy of Shakespeare here. I replyed that I had a Bible & the Genl. Shakespear & that he never missed a night without reading it. The Prest. asked wont he lend it to me, which of course I obtained.

The day following he read by himself in one of my offices some two hours, or more, entirely [alone?]   I being engaged in a connecting room on duty. He interrupted & wished me to rest, & he would read to me. He read from MacBeth Lear & finally King John, & in reading the passage where Constance bewails the loss of her child to the King.[2] I noticed that he was deeply move, his voice trembled, laying the Book on the table, he said, did you ever dream of a lost friend & feel that you were haveing a direct communion with that friend & yet a conciousness that it was not a reality. My reply was, yes I think all may have had such an experience. He repleyd so do I dream of my Boy Willey. He was utterly overcome. His great frame shook & Bowing down on the table he wept as only such a man in the breaking down of a great sorrow could weep.

It is needless to say that — I wept in sympathy, & quitly left the Room, that he might recover without restraint.

Lincoln never again referred to his boy, but he made me feel that he had given me a sacred confidence & he ever after treated me with a tenderness, regard & confidence, that won my love, & I became to him & his memory almost an idoliter.

---

2. King John 3:3, 93–105.

Again, some days after I had been absent in a Reconnaisance, & returned just before dinner & was in the Room dressing for Dinner which was a formal Affair. As *[illegible]* the Administration we had almost daily Distinguished Forigners to dine.

The Prest. came in & seeing me in full uniform, said why Col, your fixing up mighty fine & if you lend me your brush & comb, I brush up to. handg him the things, he toyed with the comb. & said why this wont comb my hair if you have such a thing as they comb a Horses tail with, I can do it: & laughed in his merry way. by the way he said I will tell you a story about my hair when I was nominated at Chicago an enterprising fellow thought that every would like to see how Abe Lincoln looked, & as I had not very long before set for a Photograph in Chicago & this fellow had seen it, he *[illegible]* & bought the negative & got out no end of woodcuts & so active was the circulation that very soon after the news reached Springfield a Boy ran throught the Street crying out "buy a likeness of Abe Lincoln price two shillings, look a great deal better when he gets his hair combed"

I give you these tid bits as they may interest you for I know you loved him & nothing he said or did failed to interest me, & I feel it must you.

With a full appreciation of your work, & a lasting regard for, Lincolns memory. I shall persuade all my friends to read your Book with a confidence that they will be instructed & entertained & come to feel as I do that his position in the history of all great human characters will be no less unique than Superior.

I wish I could condence as you do & have written you hastily without review. So excuse everything except. the overestimate of Lincoln.

Yours Very Resp.
Le G B Cannon

LC: HW3602–8

567. Edward L. Pierce to WHH[1]

[ca. October 15, 1889]

Lincolns visit to Mass in 1848 is made too little of in the biographies of him. His first speech — made at the Whig convention at Worcester, was quite fully reported in the Boston Advertiser, with a sketch of his person and manner. He spoke also at Dedham (day time) Cambridge, Chelsea & Dorchester. — also twice in Boston — once at Faneuil Hall with Seward. A single passage — that he had thought out some things at home and wished to compare notes & — makes me think that he was conscious of his powers and wanted to try them on a different theatre — that is, before more cultivated audiences He was greatly liked. It was a style new to our people — and there was a general call for him as a speaker. His speech at Dorchester was in our own village — and I have talked with several who heard him.

At Worcester he gave offence by saying "I have heard you have abolitionists

---

1. This leaf may be a fragment or it may have been sent to WHH without salutation. The dating is conjectural, based on the internal evidence.

here. We have a few in Illinois, and we shot one the other day. The Free Soil papers criticised the passage and he did not repeat it. He had a humorous passage in his Worcester speech with reference to the Free Soilers as having one doctrine only. their platform reminding him of a tailor who advertised a pair of trousers as large enough for any man and small enough for any boy.

I have wondered how Mr Lincoln happened to come in '48. Mr Winthrop to whom I spoke on the subject does not remember, but thinks Mr Charles Hudson MC may have asked him. Mr Lincoln in Congress did not make much impression on Mr Winthrop.

I sent you the other day a paper of mine on the Convention of '60[2]

I have written *currente calamo* and in haste — simply to indicate points.

Yours truly
Edward L Pierce[3]

LC: HW4744

568. Edward L. Pierce to WHH

Milton Mass   27 Oct/89

My dear Sir.

Yours of 22 Oct is received.

I shall be happy to comply with your request.

Will you kindly return me my letter which will be my guide in rewriting — and you can mark with comments any points you wish more developed. I wrote it quite hastily, but suppose it covered most points.

My own *guess,* which perhaps I said before, is that he took the eastern trip with the consciousness of powers which he wished to try before a different audience — one as he thought more educated. I have thought this might be so when reading the opening passage at Worcester where he spoke.

Mr Winthrop[1] does not recal why he came — thinks Mr Hudson[2] of Mass M.C may have arranged for him. Mr L did not make much of an impression of Mr Winthrop [and?] the House.

I think I wrote you of Mr Lincolns speech for Wentworth for mayor at Chicago in Dec 1856.[3] The Chicago Tribune probably reports it in part. Joseph Medill of Chicago — also probably Horace White of Evening Post New York would remember about it.

Yours very Truly
Edward L Pierce

---

2. Apparently the article, not identified, referred to in §571.
3. At the bottom of the page, in WHH's hand: *written by Edward L Pierce   See his letter saying he wrote it   W.H.H.*

---

1. Robert C. Winthrop (1809–94), Speaker of the U.S. House of Representatives when AL was in Congress and later U.S. senator from Massachusetts.
2. Charles Hudson (1795–1881) had served with AL in Congress.
3. See §565.

P.S. I have since receiving yours found some notes I made two years ago about Mr L's visit to Mass. in 1848. our Mass Club (Republican) commemorated Mr L at one meeting — & I took that visit for my subject. John Conness, once senator from Cal — now a neighbor of mine spoke also on the same occasion. How soon do you contemplate a new edition!

   LC: HW3620–21

569. Edward L. Pierce to WHH

Milton Mass   23 Dec 1889

My dear Sir.

   I send you by this mail a parcel in large envelope containing my notes on Mr Lincoln's visit to Mass in 1848 — and other matters — this being in accordance with your request.[1] I also as you desired, return you the letters I send you some weeks since but as they are fully covered by the better prepared M.S.S. which I now send, it may be as well to destroy them to simplify matters.

   Please let me know that the M.S.S have reached you safely.

   In case you do not ever use the material I send, I would like the MSS on the visit of 1848 returned — as it might be of interest to have printed here.

   What I send is entirely at your disposal — to do as you like with — using in whole or in part.

Yours truly
Edward L Pierce

[Enclosure A]

570. Edward L. Pierce (statement for WHH)

[December 1889]

From Edward L Pierce. Milton, Mass[1]

   The first time I saw Mr Lincoln was in Chicago late in 1856 or early in 1857   at the time John Wentworth was a candidate for Mayor of that city. As

---

1. Because the contents of Pierce's large envelope are no longer intact, what is offered here is the editors' attempt to reconstruct the contents from the scattered materials in HW. On October 27, Pierce responded to a request from WHH to write something for the new edition of his biography on the topics Pierce had mentioned in his letter of September 15: (1) meeting AL in Chicago in 1856; (2) attending the 1860 nominating convention; (3) his encounter with AL as president; and (4) corresponding with WHH in 1860–61 about AL. These are the topics treated in enclosures A–D. Pierce's account of AL's giving Chase credit for the closing of the Emancipation Proclamation constitutes enclosure E. Pierce says he also included some notes on AL's visit to Massachusetts in 1848. These apparently included the extracts from the Worcester *Spy* supplied by Bartlett, enclosure F, and a notice of the Whig rally at Lowell from the Lowell *Journal and Courier,* Sept. 18, 1848, enclosure G. The original of Pierce's narrative does not seem to be in HW, but a version of it was included in the revised 1892 edition of WHH and JWW's biography. A fragment in Pierce's hand that may represent an omitted opening is printed as enclosure H. The portion that appeared in the 1892 edition is reproduced as enclosure I.

---

1. Docketing in Pierce's hand: *Various Points about Mr Lincoln from Edward L Pierce Milton.*

this was before his debate with Douglass he was not yet distinguished; and I only knew of him by his reputation as a leader of the Springfield bar. He spoke all evening with Mr Wentworth in what was then the large hall of the city. I remember nothing that he said, but I well remember that I was impressed with his logical and reflective power, and the absence of all attempt throughout his speech to produce a sensational effect: and his speaking seemed in these respects to differ from the style then prevalent at the West. His topics were national, while those of Mr Wentworth were local and personal. The latter said in the course of his remarks which were in style and manner the opposite of Mr Lincoln's. "Do you wish to know why I am hated by some men. I will tell you. It is because they know that I shall leave no stone unturned to put that man (pointing to Mr Lincoln in the seat which Stephen A. Douglass now disgraces" The next morning I was introduced to Mr Lincoln in the *Tribune* office"[2]

[Enclosure B]

571. Edward L. Pierce (statement for WHH)

[December 1889]

By Edward L Pierce
    Milton Mass.

National Convention of 1860

I cannot add anything about this convention to what I have written in the papers sent you published in "The State"[1]

This is certain — that Mr Lincoln's nomination was perfectly assured without *bargains* — and if *any* were made, they were made in face of an inevitable result, to gain points after the election

Seward or any Republican might have been elected as the event proved.; but this did not appear so when the convention met. There was a fair chance then that the Democrats would rally and unite.

The problem was — what candidate, reliable & true, would carry the four free states lost in 1856. Pennsylvania, New Jersey, Indiana and Illinois. It was honestly felt that it was hazardous to present to them Seward or even Chase. The names left for a choice were Judge McLean, Bates[2] and Lincoln. Illinois, Penn & N.J. three of the four had "favorite sons", Lincoln, Cameron & Dayton.[3] Cameron's nomination was out of the question

The unanimous support of one of the four Indiana which had no "favorite son", put Lincoln altogether ahead of Mc Lean and Bates; and besides strong anti-slavery men had prejudices against McLean and a distrust of Bates which was not felt

---

2. Marginal note: *(Joseph Medill of Chicago and Horace White of NY (the Evening Post) doubtless remember the meeting — The Chicago Tribune would show date and probably give some report of what Mr Lincoln said.)*

---

1. Not identified.
2. Edward Bates (1793–1869).
3. William L. Dayton (1807–64), former U.S. senator from New Jersey.

about Lincoln. When I met the Indiana delegation, or a part of it at Michigan City *en route,* for Chicago three days before the convention met and found them for Lincoln. I came to the conclusion that his nomination was the most probable outcome of the convention — and so wrote home to friends. Later before the convention, as I have elsewhere stated, on the request of the Massachusetts delegation to have different candidates who could carry each one of the doubtful states. Pennsylvania responded, naming three in this order 1 Cameron 2 McLean 3 Lincoln. Here were three states admitting that they could give their electoral votes for Lincoln — and the 4th New Jersey was subject to the same considerations as Pennsylvania. I do not see how the convention after this could avoid nominating Lincoln — who was a true man, obnoxious to no section — and according to testimony from the four free states lost in 1856, altogether likely to carry them.

No bargain was necessary to secure his nomination and none had any effect if it was made, to secure it. Doubtless after the election, persons who wanted to have positions and influence, did what they could to magnify them by claiming that they, for a few considerations promised gave essential support, and were now entitled to payment.

I was for Mr Lincolns nomination from my first arrival in Chicago the Saturday before the convention, acting from the considerations of policy growing out of the condition of the four states named, and believed that others who favored Mr Lincoln were governed in large numbers by the same considerations which governed myself.

"Bargain and Sale" are favorite terms among a certain order of politicians who often resort to them for explanations of results where better motives controled.

I give this summary — but I have stated the same more in detail in the papers referred to.[4]

[Enclosure C]

572. Edward L. Pierce (statement for WHH)

[December 1889]

I had an interview with Mr Lincoln Feb 15. 1862 just after my return from Beaufort S.C. whither I had been sent Mr Chase, the Secretary of the Treasury, to inspect and report as to the condition and needs of the freedmen recently brought within our lines by the capture of Hilton Head. and the Sea Islands. on my arrival at Washington I delivered to Mr Chase a full report which appeared shortly in the N.Y. Tribune and later in the Rebellion Record. Mr Chase wished to interest Mr Lincoln in the colored people and desired me to call on him, giving me a note of introduction which stated my errand. When I called Mr Lincoln had only one or two people with him, and did not seem to be busy; but he was evidently not happy. There was sickness in his family which proved fatal. When my turn came, I

---

4. Marginal note: *Convention of 1860 from Edward L Pierce Milton Mass.*

began my account of the negroes at Port Royal but he soon cut me short, saying that he ought not be troubled with such details: that there seemed to be a great itching to get negroes within our lines and that the Senate the other day hesitated to confirm General Halleck because he had excluded them. Observing his impatience, I attempted a shorter account than I had first intended, but he soon cut me short again by repeating what he had said before. I replied that these negroes were at Port Royal by no one's invitation, being domiciled there before our occupation; and unless something was done to organize and protect them, there would be a spectacle there which it would not be pleasant to contemplate. Not liking my reception, I rose, and backing towards the door, said "Mr Lincoln, I did not come to you of my own motion, and certainly not for any office or job, but only at the Secretary's request, to tell you about these people". He saw I was not pleased, and as I reached the door called me back, saying "I did not suppose you were a beggar, wait a moment"   He then took a card from a pile at his desk, and wrote on one, which I still have, as follows "I shall be obliged if the Sec. of the Treasury will, in his discretion, give Mr. Pierce such instructions in regard to Port Royal contrabands, as may seem judicious

                                    A. Lincoln
Feb 15. 1862"
    I mentioned the interview in an article for the Atlantic Monthly Sept 1863 p 296 entitled "The Freedmen at Port Royal"   The Secretary gave full instructions two weeks later and I sailed for March 3. 1862 with a colony of superintendents and teachers.
    The President approached the great question slowly and reluctantly and he little dreamed in February 1862 of the Proclamation he was to issue in the September and January following. He did not seem to have any faith that the two races could live together peaceably in a condition of civil equality and, perhaps influenced in part by the Blair's, adopted the solution of separation by colonizing the colored people. In 1863, calling to his assistance, Senator Pomeroy he sent a colony to *Ile A 'Vache* but it proved disastrous; and no further attempt in that direction was made.

[Enclosure D]

573. Edward L. Pierce (statement for WHH)

                                                    [December 1889]
    Mr Herndon wrote Feb 18. 1861 and March 4. 1861 letters to E. L. Pierce letters affirming his entire confidence that Mr Lincoln would prove faithful to his pledges against all schemes of compromise in that first letter Mr Herndon wrote "The very last words he said to me when I took leave of him were in substance "I am decided; my course is fixed; my path is blazed; the union and the Constitution shall be preserved, and the laws enforced at every and at all hazards   I expect the people to sustain me. They have never yet forsaken any true man"

[Enclosure E]

574. Edward L. Pierce (statement for WHH)

[December 1889]

From Edward L Pierce Milton Mass

The closing passage of Mr. Lincoln's proclamation of Emancipation was from Mr Chase. I first learned this from L. Miller Mc Kim, a Philadelphia abolitionist. He was calling one day with others on the President in relation to some plan concerning the freedmen. Mr Lincoln after awhile diverted the conversation by saying that he wished to read them the most eloquent passage he had ever seen, and taking from his pocket book a newspaper clipping proceeded to read the final passage of one of John Brights speeches, probably the one made Dec. 18. 1862 at Birmingham in which he predicted a grand future for our country. Mr McKim when he had finished said "that is indeed an eloquent passage, Mr President, but I know one more eloquent"   "What is it," inquired Mr Lincoln. "It is" said Mr McKim, the closing passage of your Proclamation in which you wrote "the considerate judgement of mankind and the gracious favor of Almighty God"   "Do you like that" said Mr Lincoln   "Yes, very much" said Mr McKim. "Well" said Mr Lincoln "Chase wrote that". I think that later Carpenter in his "Six Months at the White House"[1] gives an account of the circumstances at the time when Mr Chase suggested that there should be a different ending and Mr Lincoln asked him to draw one.

In the summer of 1863 I was with Mr Chase at the White Mountains. He had just left his place as head of the Treasury, and was very sore about Mr Lincoln. I told him this story as it had been recently given to me by Mr McKim and he said quietly and thoughtfully, "Well Mr Lincoln does do justice to others for what they do"

[Enclosure F]

575. [Fred?] H. Bartlett to Edward L. Pierce (letter and extracts)

Worcester, Mass., Nov — 5th 1889

Dear Sir —

Having been directed by His Hon. Mayor Winslow, I have examined the files of the "Spy" with reference to Mr. Lincolns address in Worcester, at the time of the Whig convention in 1848. I am afraid that I do not find anything that will be satisfactory to you. Enclosed you will find Extracts from the "Spy" of Sept 14 & 16 — 1848. —

Respectfully
[Fred?] H Bartlett
Clerk for the Mayor —

---

1. Carpenter.

P.S. I shall be willing to look further if you desire.[1]

"Spy" — Sept 14 — 184[8]
Extract

"Yesterday" — At about 9 o'clock the Taylor Club. to the number of some 50 or 60 proceeded by the Worcester Brass Band, proceeded from their head quarters to the railroad Depot. where they met a portion of the Boston Delegation. from which they escorted them through one or two streets back to the depot — where the citizens, numbering, we should say, some seven or eight hundred, were addressed by His Honor — the Judge of Probate of Worcester Co. by His Honor the Mayor of Worcester, by Mr. Taylor, Senator from Granby — almost a *fac smile* of Old Zach himself — by a Mr Woodman of Boston, and by Mr Abraham Lincoln, the recently defeated Taylor candidate in the *7th* district in Illinois for re-election to Congress — These gentlemen all said some things that were rather witty, though truth, and reason and argument were treated as out of the question — as unnecessary and not to be expected.

(Here follows the doings of the convention) The article closes by saying "That the conventional was addressed by Messrs Choate, Winthrop and Hudson, but we have neither time nor space for Comment"

"Spy" — Sept 16 1848

"The Organ, (referring to the "True Whig") complains of our suggestion that Abraham Lincoln was a *defeated* candidate. We know that a Cass man had been elected in his district and hence inferred Erroneously, as it appears, that Mr. Lincoln was the defeated candidate. It turns out, however, that it was *another Taylor candidate who was defeated,* Mr Lincoln, foreseeing the danger, having, prudently withdrawn himself."

[Enclosure G]

576. Extract from the Lowell Journal and Courier[1]

Sept. 18. 1848.

The Whig Rally

The City Hall was filled to its utmost capacity again, on Saturday night — Homer Bartlett, Esq., presiding, and Alfred Gilman acting, as secretary. The meeting was graced by the presence of many fair ladies — all true whigs. The chairman made a short, stirring address, and then introduced Geo. Woodman, Esq., of

---

1. Bottom margin: *Excuse sending in pencil.* On the verso: *Enclosures: Extracts, "Spy," Sept. 14, 1848; Sept. 16, 1848.*

---

1. Note at the top (brackets in the original): *[From Lowell Journal and Courier Sept. 18. 1848.]* Note next to the title: *(Editorial).* These notes are in a different hand from the text. This would appear to be the news story, as compared to the "editorial" from the same paper, given on pp. 91–92.

Boston, who made a very capital speech. Hon. Abram Lincoln, of Illinois, then addressed the assembly in a most able speech, going over the whole subject in a masterly, and convincing manner, and showing, beyond a peradventure, that it is the first duty of the whigs to stand united, and labor with devotion to secure the defeat of that party which has already done so much mischief to the country. He was frequently interrupted by bursts of warm applause. After the distinguished speaker closed, the Secretary read the letter from Gen. Taylor, which we give to day, and which was received with tremendous applause. The meeting then adjourned with cheer after cheer for Taylor and Fillmore. It was emphatically a whig meeting — not a word of trouble, or dissension, or doubt, coming up there.

[Enclosure H]

577. Edward L. Pierce (fragment of statement)

[1887?]

Late in the Summer of 1848 the Whigs of Massachusetts held their State Convention at Worcester for the nomination of Presidential Electors and a State Ticket. It was a period of Sanguine hope — they had succeeded the first time for sixteen years in choosing their presidential candidate in 1840 but the early death of Harrison deprived them of much of the fruit of their victory. Again in 1844 nothing but John Slidells atrocious Plaquimine fraud just defeated their candidate Henry Clay. Now, the democrats were divided the larger section nominating Lewis Cass — the Smaller Van Buren, while Zach. Taylor was the Whig nominee.

Nearly all the prominent Whigs of Masstts, (Save Danl Webster) were present. — Among them may be mentioned Edward Everett, Robt C. Winthrop, Rufus Choate, Geo Ashman, both the Hoars, Geo S Hillard, & Alex. H Bullock.[1] — There was present also Abraham Lincoln the sole Whig Representative in Congress from the distant State of Illinois. —

[Enclosure I]

578. Edward L. Pierce (statement for WHH)

[1887?]

It is not known at whose instance Mr. Lincoln made his visits to Massachusetts in 1848. The Whigs of the State were hard pressed at the time by a formidable secession growing out of General Taylor's nomination, and led by Henry Wilson, Charles Francis Adams, Charles Allen, Charles Sumner, Stephen C. Phillips, John G. Palfrey, E. Rockwood Hoar, Richard H. Dana, Jr., Anson Burlingame, John A. Andrew, and other leaders who had great weight with the people and were all effective public speakers. The Whig State Convention met at Worcester, September 13th. The Free-Soil secession was greater here than in any part of the State.

---

1. The document is written in ink but a few editorial marks appear in pencil: underlining *Edward Everett* (with a question mark in the margin) and striking through *both the Hoars*. On blue paper, numbered 1.

It was led by Judge Charles Allen, who was elected to Congress from the district. There was a meeting of the Whigs at the City Hall on the evening before the convention. Ensign Kellogg presided and except for his introductory remarks, Mr. Lincoln's speech, which lasted one and a half or two hours, was the only one. The Boston *Advertiser's* report was nearly a column in length. It said: "Mr. Lincoln has a very tall and thin figure, with an intellectual face, showing a searching mind and a cool judgment. He spoke in a clear and cool and very eloquent manner, carrying the audience with him in his able arguments and brilliant illustrations, only interrupted by warm and frequent applause. He began by expressing a real feeling of modesty in addressing an audience 'this side of the mountains,' a part of the country where, in the opinion of the people of his section, everybody was supposed to be instructed and wise. But he had devoted his attention to the question of the coming presidential election, and was not unwilling to exhange with all whom he might meet the ideas to which he had arrived." This passage gives some reason to suppose that, conscious of his powers, he was disposed to try them before audiences somewhat different from those to which he had been accustomed, and therefore he had come to New England. The first part of his speech was a reply, at some length, to the charge that General Taylor had no political principles; and he maintained that the General stood on the true Whig principle, that the will of the people should prevail against executive influence or the veto power of the President. He justifed the Whigs for omitting to put a national platform before the people, and, according to a Free-Soil report, said that a political platform should be frowned down whenever and wherever presented. But the stress of his speech was against the Free-Soilers, whose position as to the exclusion of slavery from the territories, he claimed, to be that of the Whigs; while the former were subject to the further criticism that they had but one principle, reminding him of the Yankee peddler, who, in offering for sale a pair of pantaloons, described them as "large enough for any man, and small enough for any boy." He condemned the Free-Soilers as helping to elect Cass, who was less likely to promote freedom in the territories than Taylor and passed judgment on them as having less principle than any party. To their defence of their right and duty to act independently, "leaving consequences to God," he replied, that "when divine or human law does not clearly point out what is our duty, it must be found out by an intelligent judgment, which takes in the results of action." The Free-Soilers were much offended by a passage which does not appear in the Whig report. Referring to the anti-slavery men, he said they were better treated in Massachusetts than in the West, and, turning to William S. Lincoln, of Worcester, who had lived in Illinois, he remarked that in that State they had recently killed one of them. This allusion to Lovejoy's murder at Alton, was thought by the Free-Soilers to be heartless, and it was noted that Mr. Lincoln did not repeat it in other speeches. It was probably a casual remark, which came into his mind at the moment, and meant but little, if anything. Cheers were given at the end of the speech for the eloquent Whig member from Illinois. The Whig reports spoke of the speech as "masterly and convincing" and "one of the best ever made in Worcester;" while the Free-Soil report describes it as "a pretty tedious affair." The next morning he spoke at an open-air meeting, following Benjamin F. Thomas and Ex-Governor Levi Lincoln, but his speech was cut short by the arrival by train of the delegates from Boston, who, with the speakers, proceeded at once to the hall. The convention listened to a long address to the people, reported by a committee, and then to a brilliant speech from Rufus Choate, followed by others from Robert C. Winthrop, the Whig Speaker of the House of Representatives, Charles Hudson, M.C., and Benjamin F. Thomas. Mr. Lincoln listened to these, but was not himself called out.

Mr. Lincoln spoke at Washingtonian Hall, Bromfield street, Boston, on the 15th, his address lasting an hour and a half, and, according to the report, "seldom equaled for sound reasoning, cogent argument and keen satire." Three cheers were given for "the Lone Star of Illinois," on account of his being the only Whig member from the State. He spoke at Lowell on the 16th, and at the Lower Mills, Dorchester, now a part of Boston, on Monday, the 18th. At this last place the meeting was held in Richmond Hall, and the chairman was N. F. Safford, living till 1891,[1] who introduced him as one of the Lincolns of Hingham, and a descendant of Gen. Benjamin Lincoln. Mr. Lincoln, as he began, disclaimed descent from the Revolutionary officer, but said, playfully, that he had endeavored in Illinois to introduce the principles of the Lincolns of Massachusetts. A few of his audience are still living. They were struck with his height, as he arose in the low-studded hall. He spoke at Chelsea on the 19th, and a report states that his speech "for aptness of illustration, solidity of argument, and genuine eloquence, was hard to beat." Charles Sumner had defended the Free-Soil cause at the same place the evening before. Mr. Lincoln spoke at Dedham, in Temperance Hall, on the 20th, in the daytime. Two Whig nominating conventions met there the same day, at one of which Horace Mann was nominated for a second term in Congress. A report states that he "spoke in an agreeable and entertaining way." He left abruptly to take a train in order to meet another engagement, and was escorted to the station by the Dorchester band. The same evening he spoke at Cambridge. The report describes him as "a capital specimen of a Sucker Whig, six feet at least in his stockings." Of his speech, it was said that "it was plain, direct, to the point, powerful and convincing, and telling with capital effect upon the immense audience. It was a model speech for the campaign." His last speech was on 22d, at Tremont Temple, with George Lunt presiding, in company with William H. Seward, whom he followed, ending at 10.30 P.M. The Whig newspaper, the *Atlas,* the next morning gave more than a column to Mr. Seward's speech, but stated that it had no room for the notes which had been taken of Mr. Lincoln's, describing it, however, as "powerful and convincing, and cheered to the echo." The Free-Soil paper (Henry Wilson's) refers to the meeting, mentioning Mr. Seward but not Mr. Lincoln. The next day Mr. Lincoln left Boston for Illinois. The *Atlas* on Monday contained this paragraph: "In answer to the many applications which we daily receive from different parts of the State for this gentleman to speak, we have to say that he left Boston on Saturday morning on his way home to Illinois."

---

1. A clear instance of later editing.

It is evident from all the contemporaneous reports, that Mr. Lincoln made a marked impression on all hs audiences. Their attention was drawn at once to his striking figure; they enjoyed his quaintness and humor; and they recognized his logical power and his novel way of putting things. Still, so far as his points are given in the public journals, he did not rise at any time above partisanship, and he gave no sign of the great future which awaited him as a political antagonist, a master of language, and a leader of men. But it should be noted, in connection with this estimate, that the Whig case, as put in that campaign, was chiefly one of personalities, and was limited to the qualities and career of Taylor as a soldier, and to ridicule of his opponent, General Cass. Mr. Lincoln, like the other Whig speakers, labored to prove that Taylor was a Whig.

Seward's speech at Tremont Temple, to which Lincoln listened, seems to have started a more serious vein of thought on slavery in the mind of the future President. That evening, when they were together as fellow-lodgers at a hotel, Lincoln said: "Governor Seward, I have been thinking about what you said in your speech. I reckon you are right. We have got to deal with this slavery question, and got to give much more attention to it hereafter than we have been doing."[2]

It is curious to recall how little support, in the grave moments of his national career which came twelve years later, Mr. Lincoln received from the Whigs of Massachusetts, then conspicuous in public life, whom he met on his visit. Mr. Lunt, who presided at Faneuil Hall, was to the end of his life a pro-slavery conserative. Judge Thomas, in Congress, during the early part of the civil war, was obstructive to the President's policy. Mr. Winthrop voted against Lincoln in 1860 and 1864. Mr. Choate died in 1859, but judged by his latest utterances, his marvelous eloquence would have been no patriotic inspiration if he had outlived the national stuggle. On the other hand, the Free-Soilers of Massachusetts, whom Mr. Lincoln came here to discredit, became to a man, his supporters; and on many of their leaders he relied as his support in the great conflict. Sumner was chairman of the Senate Committee on Foreign Affairs during the war; Wilson was chairman of the Committee on Military Affairs; Adams was Minister to England; and Andrew War-Governor of the State. These, as well as Palfrey, Burlingame and Dana, who, in 1848, almost every evening addressed audiences against both Taylor and Cass, while Mr. Lincoln was here, were earnest and steadfast in their devotion to the Government during the civil war; and the last three received important appointments from him. How the press treated Mr. Lincoln may be learned from the following editorial in the Lowell *Journal and Courier,* in its issue of September 18, 1848:

WHIG MEETING.
The sterling Whigs of Lowell came together last Saturday evening, at the City Hall. The meeting was called to order by the Chairman of the Whig

---

2. This quotation footnoted *Seward's Life, vol. ii, p. 80* and may have been the addition referred to in Pierce's letter of June 8, 1891. See p. 701.

Central Committee, Hon. Linus Child. Homer Bartlett, Esq., was chosen chairman, and A. Gilman, secretary. After a few animating remarks from the Chairman, he introduced George Woodman, Esq., of Boston, who made a very pertinent and witty off-hand speech, which was frequently interrupted by the spontaneous plaudits of the audience. At the close of his speech Mr. Woodman introduced the Hon. Abraham Lincoln, of Illinois. It would be doing injustice to his speech to endeavor to give a sketch of it. It was replete with good sense, sound reasoning, and irresistable argument, and spoken with that perfect command of manner and matter which so eminently distinguishes the Western orators. He disabused the public of the erroneous suppositions that Taylor was not a Whig; that Van Buren was anything more than a thorough Loco-foco on all subjects other than Free Territory, and hardly safe on that; and showed up, in a masterly manner, the inconsistency and folly of those Whigs, who, being drawn off from the true and oldest free-soil organization known among the parties of the Union, would now lend their influence and votes to help Mr. Van Buren into the presidential chair. His speech was interrupted by frequent cheers of the audience. At the close the secretary, by request, read the letter of General Taylor to Captain Alison, which had just been received, in which he says: "From the beginning till now, I have declared myself to be a Whig, on all proper occasions."

LC: HW3634–35 (cover letter), HW3592 (enclosure A), HW3589–90 (enclosure B), HW3584–86 (enclosure C), HW3591 (enclosure D), HW3587–88 (enclosure E), HW4687 (Bartlett letter), HW4354–55 ("Spy" extracts) (enclosure F), HW4356–59 ("Journal and Courier" extracts) (enclosure G), HW5366 (enclosure H); H&W (1892), 1:281–89 (enclosure I)

579. Jesse K. Dubois (JWW interview)

[1883–89]

J K Dubois — was admin. of L's estate[1] — went to N.Y. arranged $64,000 clm agst estate for Jewelry bought by Mrs L of Ball Black & Co of N.Y. without L's knowledge.

One day J K Dubois came to Ls office and found him going home with piece of meat for breakfast. D. accompanied him to house — Ms L. had some aristocratic company frm Ky and met L & D. as they came in the door. Upon opening the paper of meat she became enraged at the Kind L had bought. She abused L. outrageously and finally was so mad she struck him in the face. Rubbing the blood off his face L. told D. to accompany and both left the house and went down without breakfast &c.

ISHL: Weik Papers, "Real Lincoln" notes folder

---

1. Dubois may have acted as an agent in this transaction for David Davis, who was AL's executor.

580. John J. Hall (JWW interview)

[1883–89]

Jno J Hall born Apr 12 1829 Spencer Co Ind. lives on Thos L. old place is son of
Matilda Johnson Abe Ls step sister — bought farm, 20 acres in 1859 — Ths L
died in house now owned by H. showed Thos L. family Bible dated 1799. bound
by Ths L. in sheepskin. latter first belonged to Baptist — at time of death Campbellite[1]

L. came to Farmington where his step mother was after election and the mare
story[2] took place — H calls him Uncle Abe. — *[illegible]* — Very Kind to his step
mother who embraced and cried over him.

ISHL: Weik Papers, box 2, Memorandum Book 1

581. Emilie T. Helm (statement for WHH)

[post–July 1871–89]

The Paternal Grandfather of Mrs Lincol. Genl Levi Todd was born 1756 —
educated in Virgina & studied law in the office of Genl Lewis of Virgina came to
Kentucky 1776 — (You have his subsequent History)   He succeeded Danl Boone
as Col — became Major Genl — & one of the first settlers of Lexington Ky —
was married in Logans Port 25 Feb 1779 — to Jane Briggs neice of Col Ben &
John Logan. (Virginians)

The 7 child of Genl Levi Todd was Robert S Todd born Feb 25 1791 and died
16 July 1849 — His first wife was his Cousin Anni Eliza Parker, by whom he had
6 children — Was married to her about *1813 or 1814.* —
The children were
Elizabeth married to Hon N W Edwards of Springfield Ill
Francis married Dr Wm Wallace of Springfield Ill
Mary married to Abraham Lincoln of Springfield Ill
Ann Maria married to C M Smith of Springfield Ill
Levi died in 1865 at Lexington Ky
Geogr Rogers Clark Todd — living in North Carolina
(The three sisters are living at Springfield Ill).

Mary Lincoln had four children — sons — all of whom died in their Minority except Robt Lincoln of Chicago

The maternal Great Grandfather of Mrs Lincoln was General Andrew Porter
of the Revolutionary Army Of Pennsylvania born 24 sept 1743, (succeeded Genl
Peter Muhlenberg as Major General of the Pennsylvania Militia

His second wife the Great Grand Mother of Mrs Lincoln was Elizabeth Parker *(her Mother Elizabeth Todd)* —

---

1. Marginal note: *L placed stone over father's grave last visit to Farmintion.*
2. See §479.

Mrs Lincolns Maternal Grand Mother *Elizabeth Porter* born 27 sept 1769. married to Robert Parker of Lexington Ky 1790, where she died in 1851 —

Mrs Lincoln's great Uncles on Maternal side were Gov George B Porter — Governor of Michigan & James Madison Porter secretary of War under President Tyler & David Rittenhouse Porter who was twice Governor of Pennsylvania.

Mrs Lincoln was born in Lexington Ky, & was educated there was a fine french scholar & considered bright & witty by her friends. Was fond of reading all her life — Went out on a visit to Mrs N W Edwards her sister at Springfield Ill & there married Abraham Lincoln —

LC: HW3068–69

582. Emilie Todd Helm to JWW?[1]

Elizabethtown Ky. *[1887–89?]*

Dr Sir

I belive I have given you all the information you ask for — I think you could perhaps get an autograph from Mrs Edwards[2] — I cannot consent to part with mine — If there is any other information you desire that I can give you of course it will give me pleasure to give it to you — Enclosed you will find some printed matter[3] that you can perhaps use — Please return it to me as I have taken them from the book I am making for my Son & would not like to lose them —

Very Respectfully
E T Helm

[Enclosure?][1]

583. Emilie Todd Helm (statement)

[undated]

Robert S Todd (the Father of Mrs Lincoln) lost his first wife in 1824 (I think). He Married Elizabeth Humphreys in Nov 1826 — By his last Marriage he had eight children — two of whom are living — Mrs C H Kellogg of Cincinnati Ohio — and Mrs Genl. Ben Hardin Helm of Elizabethtown Ky — His three sons by the last Marrige entered the Confederate Army — one fell at the *battle of Shiloh (Corinth)* one fell at Baton Rouge & the third wounded by a bullet in his lungs,

---

1. The recipient is postulated on the basis of the request for an autograph, something unlikely for WHH but quite likely for JWW. Written in the top margin in Helm's hand: *Genl. Ben. Hardin Helm was Killed at the Battle of Chicamauga — Sept 1863 —.*

2. Elizabeth Todd Edwards, wife of Ninian W. Edwards.

3. Not present.

---

1. This may have been included in an earlier letter.

lingered for a few years and died after the close of the war — The three daughters who are dead were, Mrs C B White of Selma Ala — Mrs Wallace Herr of Ky & Mrs N H R [Danson?] of Alabama (Col [Danson?] is now at Washington as Supt of Bureau of Education).

Elizabeth Humphreys was a daughter of Dr Alexander Humphreys of Staunton Virginia & a grand daghter of Rev John Brown of Va a famous presbyterian clergyman of that day

LC: HW3918 (letter), HW3919 (enclosure)

584. Emilie Todd Helm (statement for WHH)[1]

[post–1866–89]

David Todd the Great Grandfather of Mrs Lincoln was of Scotch Irish Ancestry was born in 1723 — Part of His family settled in Montgomery Co Pa the rest going on into Virginia — In 1749 David Todd Was Married in Montgomery Co Pa to Hannah Owen. whose family were Quakers of Wales. Her Ancestor Robert Owen was one of the first Quakers in Wales and died in Montgomery Co Pa 1697. Mr John Biddle 230 South 3rd St a lineal descendant of the Owen family has in his possession papers which claim to trace the family to the 6th Century.

The Paternal Grand Father of Mrs Lincoln was the 4th child of David Todd   came to Kentucky at an early day — was lieutenant in the Campaign Conducted by Gen Geo Rogers Clarke & was engaged in several expeditions against the Indians NW of the Ohio River & commanded a battalion in the Battle of Blue Licks where his brother Col John Todd was Killed Genl Levi Todd succeeded Daniel Boone as Col & afterwards became Major General   was Maried 1779 to Jane Briggs neice of Col Ben Logan — Their son Robert S Todd of Lexington Ky was the Father of Mary wife of Abraham Lincoln   Her Mother was a relative of her Father Eliza Parker whose Grand Father was Genl Andrew Porter of Pennsylvania a Major General in the Revolutionary Army.

Robert S Todd was a Member of the senate of Ky 1845–1849 & was a candidate for reelection when he died — had been representative from Fayette Co Ky & had been over 20 years President of the Branch Bank of Kentucky of Lexington Ky

There are three generations of the Todd family buried in the Providence Presbyterian Grave yard 4 Miles S of Trappe Montgomery Co Pa David Todd — Genl Levi Todd   Robert S Todd & their descendants are buried in the Cemetery at Lexington Ky.

LC: HW5355, HW5289

---

1. Written on this document in blue pencil, probably by JWW: *Mrs. Emily Helm, Elizabethtown, Ky.*

585. *Edward L. Pierce to WHH*

Milton Mass 28 Jan '90

My dear Sir.

Yours is received

I am happy to say that I shall not disturb you in the possession of the M.S.S concerning Mr Lincoln which I sent you. — while you need them. Perhaps you might let me see *proof* of such parts as you may use — to avoid errors.

You will see in the "Nation" of this or next week a brief statement "Mr. Lincoln as a Colonizationalist" signed by a star which I contributed.[1] The dates & references may serve you.

Yours truly
Edward L Pierce

You might return me my M.S.S after you have used it.

LC: HW3647

586. *Horace White to JWW*

Feb 11, 1890.

My dear Sir:

I will undertake to write a chapter for you on the Lincoln-Douglas campaign of 1858, but I cannot say, just now how long a time will be required. I must look over my materials first. If I could detach myself from other occupations I could do it in short order. The Chapter would not take the place of the one you already have, but would be additional to it. The Matter you already have is first class as far as it goes.

Yours truly
Horace White

P.S.

I noticed one error in your present Chapter — not very important. It says that Douglas returned to Chicago from Washington & remained several days before delivering his first speech at the Tremont House. The fact is that he came directly from the cars to the balcony, with a tremendous procession & amid the booming of cannon & the blaze of fire works. It was a great *coup de theatre* carefully arranged weeks beforehand.

LC: HW4694–95

---

1. "President Lincoln as a Colonizationist," *Nation* 50 (Jan. 30, 1890): 91–92.

587. Edward L. Pierce to JWW

Milton Mass 12 Feb 90

Dear Sir

Yours is received. I think you would have done well to have stopped your 2d edition till you had made your additions.[1] I make my publishers mind me instead of minding them. An author likes to feel that the greater portion of his volumes in circulation are his *complete* work.

On Saturday last the Massachusetts Club — an old Republican Club which has dined every Saturday for 30 years — commemorated Lincoln on Saturday.

I enclose a report — but it is not correct enough to follow.[2] Governor Claflin stated that after the election of '64 Lincoln said he should change his Secretary of State soon.[3] Claflin was on the National Committee & a member of its Executive Committee.

Henry J Gardner who was Governor in 1855–6–7, gave reminiscences of Lincoln on his visit in '48 It seems he (Gardner) dined at Ex Gov Levi Lincoln's at Worcester the day before the Whig Convention, and your Mr Lincoln was there at the dinner. Years after when the latter was President, Gardner met L at Washington in the war — and L recalling his visit in 48 said "I went with hay seed in my hair to learn deportment in the most cultivated State in the Union — and I have never seen such a beautiful table and such fine arrangements as at Governor Lincoln's"[4]   Gov Gardner gives names of the guests at table as Rufus Choate, Geo Ashmun, Geo L Holland. Emory Washburn, A. H. Bullock, Charles L. Putnam, and Stephen Salisbury. Of these Washburn & Bullock as well as Gardner were afterwards governors.

I doubt if Gov Gardner can at this date remember names of persons at the table with certainty — and if Choate was present. The dinner is more likely to have been on the day of the Convention than the day before.

Gardner represents Mr Lincoln's address as most effective. I have asked him to write out his recollections so that I can send them to you.[5]

Yours truly
Edward L. Pierce

LC: HW4696–97

---

1. JWW had apparently informed Pierce that the publisher's schedule for the second printing of *Herndon's Lincoln* would not permit the inclusion of the additional material Pierce had provided (see Donald, 337). This material eventually formed chapter 10 in volume 1 of the revised edition (1892).

2. Not present.

3. Cf. testimony of MTL, §254.

4. Marginal note in WHH's hand: *Copy this sentence Weik & put it in our book.*

5. See §590.

588. Horace White to JWW

Mch 7, 1890.

My dear Sir:

I have returned the MS today, having kept it only two hours. Please acknowledge receipt when you get it.

The photo of Lincoln is good in one sense & bad in another. It represents him with no more expression than a post & yet it is just as he would look when sitting for a photo & putting on his most serious look, as though he had been just sentenced to death. The trouble was that this photographer did not have the *gumption* to stir him up & make him look animated. There was more difference between Lincoln dull & Lincoln animated, in facial expressions, than I ever saw *in any other human being.* I wish I had thought to put this into my "chapter."

Yours truly

Horace White

LC: HW4707

589. Edward L. Pierce to WHH

Milton Mass   27 May 90

Dear Sir

Yours of Feb 24 was duly received

I had mislaid Gov. Gardner's paper and so delayed my answer.[1]

In general Gov. G. is probably correct tho' perhaps faulty in details after so long an interval.

No doubt that was the dinner at Gov Lincolns[2] — but surely ER & Geo H Hoar were not present as they were out-and-out Free Soilers and very hostile to both host and guests

I do not think Everett[3] was there — as he did not speak at the Convention. If on the ground he would certainly have been in the programme.

Yours truly

Edward L Pierce

[Enclosure]

590. Governor Henry J. Gardner (statement for Edward L. Pierce)

[February–May 1890]

Gov. Levi Lincoln, the oldest living Ex-Governor of Massachusetts, resided in Worcester. He was a man of culture and wealth; lived in one of the finest houses

---

1. The original of Gov. Henry J. Gardner's memoir has not been located. A portion of the memoir, almost certainly edited according to Pierce's stated reservations, appeared in the 1892 edition of H&W (1:289–91) and is reproduced as an enclosure (§590).

2. Levi Lincoln (1782–1868), former governor of Massachusetts.

3. Edward Everett (1794–1865), former congressman, senator, governor of Massachusetts, cabinet officer, educator, and diplomat.

in that town, and was a fine specimen of a gentleman of the old school. It was his custom to give a dinner party when any distinguished assemblage took place in Worcester, and to invite its prominent participants. He invited to dine, on this occasion, a company of gentlemen, among them myself, who was a delegate from Boston. The dining-room and table arrangements were superb, the dinner exquisite, the wines abundant, rare, and of the first quality.

I well remember the jokes between Governor Lincoln and Abraham Lincoln as to their presumed relationship. At last the latter said: "I *hope* we both belong, as the Scotch say, to the same clan; but I *know* one thing, and that is, that we are both good Whigs."

That evening there was held in Mechanics' Hall (an immense building) a mass-meeting of delegates and others, and Lincoln was announced to speak. No one there had ever heard him on the stump, and in fact knew anything about him. When he was announced, his tall, angular, bent form, and his manifest awkward-ness and low tone of voice, promised nothing interesting. But he soon warmed to his work. His style and manner of speaking were novelties in the East. He repeat-ed anecdotes, told stories admirable in humor and in point, interspersed with bursts of true eloquence, which constantly brought down the house. His sarcasm of Cass, Van Buren and the Democratic party was inimitable, and whenever he attempted to stop, the shouts of "Go on! go on!" were deafening. He probably spoke over an hour, but so great was the enthusiasm time could not be measured. It was doubt-less one of the best efforts of his life. He spoke a day or two afterward in Faneuil Hall, with William H. Seward, but I did not hear him.

In 1860 business called me to Washington, and I paid my respects to the Pres-ident at the White House. He came forward smiling and with extended hand, saying: "You and I are no strangers; we dined together at Governor Lincoln's in 1848." When one remembers the increased burden on the President's mind at this trying time, the anxieties of the war, the army, the currency, and the rehabilitat-ing the civil officers of the country, it seemed astonishing to me to hear him con-tinue: "Sit down. Yes, I had been chosen to Congress then from the wild West, and with hayseed in my hair I went to Massachusetts, the most cultured State in the Union, to take a few lessons in deportment. That was a grand dinner — a superb dinner; by far the finest I ever saw in my life. And the great men who were there, too! Why, I can tell you just how they were arranged at table." He began at one end, and mentioned the names in order, and, I verily believe, without the omis-sion of a single one.

LC: HW3664 (letter); H&W (1892), 289–91

591. *Franklin T. King to WHH*

Kumler Ills Sept 12/90

Dear Sir

Allow me as an old acquaintance and Friend to make a few inquiries in regard to what took place many years since. I would like to learn what majority Mr Lincoln had when he was a candidate for Congress at the time Peter Cartwright ran as the democratic candidate in opposition to Mr Lincoln. Also what effect in your opinion the Free Soil vote had in the Springfield Congressional district had in securing Mr Lincoln's election

I took some considerable interest in said election in behalf of Mr Lincoln   Mr Thomas Alsop & myself were appointed a committee by a meeting of the "Free Soil" and anti-slavery people held in Springfield to wait on Mr. Lincoln & get his views on the subject of Slavery. We called on him and were so well pleased with what he said on the subject that we advised that our anti-slavery friend through-out the district should cast their vote for Mr. Lincoln: which was genirally done.

As you are aware Mr L. was elected, I would also like to know the counties that made up aforsaid Congressional districk. You are no doubt aware that it was through the influence of Mr. Lincoln that my brother T. R. King got the appoint-ment of Register of the Land Office at Springfield.[1] Hence it is that I would like to know the things I of which I have herein made inquirey. To be a little more pointed I will say that I have thought and still think that the course I took then may have had something to do in my brothers appointment as Register of land office. Anything bearing on the subject as above presented will be received with many thanks by your old friend. In conclusion allow me to congratulate you on your long, prominet, & successful life.

Most Respectfully Yours
Franklin T. King

P.S. Hope you will not think that I have presumed too much on your generosity and if you are too busy or think it will take too much of your time you need not trouble yourself to look up the records for I do not feel able to pay attorneys fees — the subject will not justify me to do so.

Yours &c Fr. T. King

LC: HW3686–87

592. Horace White to WHH

New York, Jan 26, 1891.

Dear Mr Herndon:

Your letter of the 23d is received.

Mr. Villard[1] has returned from Europe. His address at present is: Plaza Hotel, New York City.

Mr Hermann Kreismann, whom you will undoubtedly remember, came to this country with Mr. V. but he has gone back to Berlin, where he now resides. He has a fund of Lincoln reminiscences which it would be worth your while to tap. One

---

1. See §353.

---

1. Henry Villard (1835–1900), journalist and financier.

of them is to this effect; That after L's election as President, but before he had left Springfield Judd[2] & Kreismann went to Springfield on an important political errand & made an appointment to meet L, but he did not come & Kreismann was despatched to his house in quest of him. Arrived at the house he was ushered into a room where both Mr. & Mrs. L. were. The latter was on the floor in a sort of hysterical fit, caused by L's refusal to promise the position of Naval officer of the N.Y. Custom House to Isaac Henderson, who had sent a diamond brooch to a Springfield jeweller to be given to Mrs. L. in case she could secure the promise of this office. The fit continued until the promise was obtained. Henderson was, in fact, appointed. He was afterwards indicted by the Grand Jury for defrauding, the Government, & tried before Judge Nelson, but was saved from conviction by some technicality.[3]

You must not use this on my narration. Indeed it would be best not to use it at all. Kreismann has other reminiscences, but I don't know whether he could be prevailed on to write them out. Mr. Villard can give you his address. You remember he (K.) was appointed Sec'y of Legation at Berlin when Judd was appointed Minister.

Mr. Villard accompanied L. on his journey from Springfield to Washington in the spring of 1861 — i.e. in February, when he went to assume the office of President. He had also seen a good deal of L. in the campaign of 1858.

With cordial good wishes
Ever your friend
Horace White

LC: HW3719–20

593. Edward L. Pierce to JWW

Milton, Mass 8 June 91

Dear Sir,

I enclose you the addition to be inserted at the proper place in the reference to Mr Lincoln's visit to Mass in 1848 where mention is made of Mr Ls speaking in Boston with Mr Seward.

By the way I hope I made no blunder in speaking of the place where the meeting was held. It was at Tremont Temple — not Faneuil Hall. Please look and see.

Yours was duly received.

Yours truly
Edward L Pierce

---

2. Norman B. Judd.

3. Isaac Henderson, part-owner of the New York *Evening Post,* at first sought (unsuccessfully) appointment as naval officer at New York. Later he received an appointment from AL as naval agent in New York. In 1864 he was dismissed from the post on the grounds that he had accepted commissions from contracts let for government work.

[Enclosure]

594. Edward L. Pierce (addendum to statement)

The Whig meeting at the Tremont Temple is mentioned in Mr Seward's Memoir[1] where it is stated that as lodgers at the same hotel Mr Seward and Mr Lincoln engaged in conversation, the latter saying "Governor Seward, I have been thinking about what you said in your speech. I reckon you are right. We have got to deal with this slavery question, and got to give much more attention to it hereafter than we have been doing." This was their first meeting, and when they met again in 1860, Mr Lincoln recalling it remarked that it "had probably made a stronger impression on his memory than it had on Governor Seward's."[2]

Pierce

LC: HW4743 (letter), HW4745 (enclosure)

595. John P. C. Shanks (JWW interview)

Portland, Ind. Sep 19 1891

Mr. Shanks: On cars to accompany Lincoln to Wash. At Indps with Gen Tom. Nelson meets L at dinner — Bates House — never saw L. before   Shanks has unfortunate red nose to which L. calls attention at table. L. is worried over it. When the cars reach Cincinnati Nelson & Shanks go to drug store near Burnet House and see old druggist who suggests tipping the nose during the night with slight touches of acetic acid on pieces of cotton. This is done frequently during night. Next morning on looking into mirror Shanks in dressing discovers that too much acid is used and nose is bleached & shrivelled like wash-womans finger. Shanks is afraid to go into breakfast but his place at table being vacant L. will not meal to begin till Shanks comes in. When he does all laugh. L. asks Shanks why his nose is like blackslider. No answer. "Because" says L. "the last state of that nose is worse than the first."

ISHL: Weik Papers, box 1

596. Alexander Campbell to JWW

La Salle Dec 14th 1891

Dear Sir

I have been so afflicted with Rheumatisms and neuralgia for about three years as in a great measure unfit me for business of any Kind. It has however some what improved for the past month or so and I have been looking at my papers and letters which had long been neglected   I find a letter from you Dated Dec 1888. & which you say you have taken the liberty of furnishing to the publishers of

---

1. At the botton of the page: *note vol II pp 79.80.* See Frederick W. Seward, *Seward at Washington, as Senator and Secretary of State: A Memoir of His Life, with Selections from His Letters, 1846–1861,* 3 vols. (New York, 1891), 2:79–80.

2. Cf. with the text from H&W (1892), reproduced on p. 691.

Herndon's Memoirs of Lincoln my photo. And Excellent engraving therefrom has been made and will appear in the book. Also asking whether I had complied with Mr Lincoln request June 1858 for an advancement of $500.*00* to pay Campaign Expenses   As you have a copy of Lincolns of June 1858, you will see that it was an acknowledgement the Authority I gave him to draw on me for $500.*00* for Campaign Expenses for the Campaign Expenses of 1856 and asking for assistance for Expenses of in the Campaign of 1858 I gave him Money on two and probably occasions during that Campaign the Amounts I do not remember but I Know that they were comparitivly small with what I gave him in 1856. If my memory is not at fault I think I refered you Mr Herndon for information on that point. You ask whether Mr Lincoln Ever gave me a note or returned any of the money I ever gave him   I will say that never a note or one Cent of the money from him and further that I never Expected to receive any nor had Mr Lincoln reason to believe that he was any obligation that was under any obligation to make payment of any part of it   Inclosed please find ten dollars for which please send me a copy the Memoirs by *Express* if the have been published and retain the balance to pay you for the trouble in procuring my Engraving   If the work has not been published you can retain Enclosed Amount or such part thereof as you may think proper   The only apolog I have for writing with pencil is that my Rhumatism &c Makes it Extremely difficult to write with pen and ink.

Sincerely Yours
A Campbell

PS There is two or three parties to whom I may want to send copies if you should have them to spare   Let me Know at your Earliest Convenience and I will send you the names as want them [directly?] from. I will also remit the cost AC

ISHL: Weik Papers, box 1

597. James Harriott (WHH interview)

[undated]

Judge Harriott

Says that Mr Lincoln told him that Mrs Armstrong[1] first Saw and spoke to Mr Lincoln: he Said that L told him that when he L Came to Salem that the Clary boys intended to whip L & run him off— [can him?] &c — he threw Jack Armstrong —: L came to Beardstown and defended the Prisoner chgd nothing — had an old almanac — L did not Know it — no one noticed it — L. believed that the principle witness was true — moon theory[2] Saved the boy — There was no Excitement — no furror — no Enthusiasm: it was a Common trial — Generally the article[3] from beginning to End is a humbug —

Metzker[4] was the killed. One man[5] was Sent to the Penitentiary for the Same

---

1. Hannah Armstrong.

2. WHH has penciled in *didnt* between *theory* and *Saved*. The "moon theory" refers to the almanac evidence introduced by AL to show that the moon could not have illuminated the crime scene as testified.

offense 5 ys —: This man Struck Metzker with what was Called a neck yoke — Year 1858 — Armstrong tried — Armstrong got a Change of venue — Lincolns Theory was that the neck yoke killed Metz and that it cracked the Skull in front — where Armstrong is supposed to have struck — The Almanac may have cut a figure — but it was Doct Parkers[6] testimony Confirming Lincolns theory — the Court Saw this —

LC: HW3915

598. James H. Matheny (verses supplied to WHH)[1]

[undated]

And When we came, to Salem Dam,
Up we went, against it jam
We tried to cross, with all our might,
But found we could'nt, and staid all night

LC: HW4667

599. Wendell Phillips to WHH[1]

[undated]

Dear Sir
I said Lincoln voluntarily added to the domain of the Slave Act of '50 territory which had inadvertently been omitted — (I believe that Terr'y was the D.C.) — & on that account I called him "the Slave Hound of Illinois" — [Gay?] tried to wriddle their candidate out of the "sin —
I never charged A.L. with insincerity hypocracy or that sort of thing — Said that, heedlessly for party ends — to conciliate &c.&c. he volunteered to *extend* that odious fraud

Y

W. Phillips

I think now exactly as I did then — A.L. had merits but he had spots & large ones on his disk.

LC: HW3965

---

3. Not identified.
4. James P. Metzker.
5. James Norris.
6. Dr. Charles Parker.

---

1. Note in WHH's hand: *Words by J. H. Matheny.*

---

1. This is a copy of the original letter provided by F. M. Bristol, who bought the original from WHH.

600. John Q. Spears (WHH interview)

[undated]

A. Q. Spears[1] — Menard — Says — I Knew Mr. Lincoln from the time I was 4 years old — he used to Come out to my grand Mothers — the Doct — who was taken by the Indans in Tennessee — and liberated at Detroit — Mr. Lincoln used to talk to her instead of talking to Men: She was an intellectual woman. L said that if she had an Education she would have been Equal to any woman — Grand Mother and Mrs. Wm Green, among the women, were the first to bring Lincoln out to public view or notice. My grand Mother Said — "There is a great promise — a great possibility in Lincoln. Mary Spears was my grand Mothers name. Mrs. Green's name was Elizabeth.

LC: HW2586

601. Charles S. Zane (WHH interview)

[undated]

Chas. S. Zane

I heard Lincoln say about 1858 — say in October, that the Know-nothings — their ideas & platform wanted to circumscribe the Election franchise — universal Suffrage. That he was opposed to it — That he wanted to lift men up & give 'Em a chance. Lincoln said that he loved Joseph Gallespie — respected him highly &c — but he (L) Could not Endure to talk to J on that ground — that he (L) got Excited — So did Judge — and the best way was to quit

I know of a case in the Supm Court about 1849. or 1850. in which I (Herndon) wanted Lincoln to assist me to argue a question that involved the law of the Extension or contraction —, lessening & narrowing the right of Suffrage, it being a City Case & I being Mr L's partner as well as city attorney and he would not help me — Saying — "I am opposed to the limitation — the lessening of the right of suffrage — am in favor of its Extension — Enlargement — want to lift men up and broaden them — don't intend by no act of mine to Crush or Contract."

LC: HW4004

602. Charles S. Zane (WHH interview)

[undated]

Chas. S. Zane

Says that Julian of Indiana[1] as well as others in Washington in the last of Feby or the 1st day of Mch 1861. told him that Seward tried his best — brought to

---

1. Study of the Spears family and the details of this testimony indicate that this informant must be John Q. Spears, though both this notation and the docketing give the first initial as "A."

---

1. George W. Julian (1817–99), a member of Congress from Indiana.

bear on Lincoln all his tact — skill & power to get Mr Lincoln to modiy — or take out that Expression in his 1st inaugural wherein he L said that he would re-take forts &c — L. did not do it.

Sewards friends tried to make L not make Chase one of his Secry's and Chases men tried the same. Much opposition was made against Cameron — all to no purpose.

Lincoln often modified or changed his policy — those policies which acted as means — though he never changed his policy — his purpose of saving the Union — never dodged that —

LC: HW4007

603. Charles S. Zane (statement for WHH)

[undated]

In the prosecution of the war Mr Lincoln used such measures as he believed would be most likely to accomplish the paramount object, which was the preser-vation of the Union, and refused to use those which he believed would not be likely to aid in its preservation — He said in his letter to Mr Greely that "he would try to correct errors when shown to be errors and would adopt new views so fast as they should appear to be true views."

That which was necessary to accomplish his purpose was power; which con-sisted in the Confidence and Support of the people; when he believed another policy than the one he was using would give the people greater Confidence and bring more Support he would adopt the new policy. — He never Changed the paramount object of the war though he did change his war measures and policies.

LC: HW4016

PART 2

Informant Testimony Reported in Herndon's
Lincoln: The True Story of a Great Life *(1889)*

The following letters, interviews, and statement are taken from the first edition of Herndon and Weik's biography. They appear to be based on existing documents, the originals of which have not been located.

604. William L. Wilson to WHH[1]

February 3, 1882

I have during that time had much fun with the afterwards President of the United States, Abraham Lincoln. I remember one time of wrestling with him, two best in three, and ditched him. He was not satisfied, and we tried it in a foot-race for a five-dollar bill. I won the money, and 'tis spent long ago. And many more reminiscences could I give, but am of the Quaker persuasion, and not much given to writing.

H&W (1889), 97n

605. George W. Minier (statement)[1]

Apr. 10, 1882.

In the spring term of the Tazewell County Court in 1847, which at that time was held in the village of Tremont, I was detained as a witness an entire week. Lincoln was employed in several suits, and among them was one of Case *vs.* Snow Bros. The Snow Bros., as appeared in evidence (who were both minors), had purchased from an old Mr. Case what was then called a "prairie team," consisting of

---

1. A portion of a letter, prefaced in the biography: "William L. Wilson, a survivor of the [Black Hawk] war, in a letter under date of February 3, 1882, after detailing reminiscences of Stillman's defeat, says. . . ." No original has been found.

---

1. This was printed in the appendix with the heading "AN INCIDENT ON THE CIRCUIT." It may have been borrowed from Oldroyd, where it appears with only minor differences (187–89), but the presence of a date in H&W (1889) (absent in Oldroyd) suggests it may have been supplied independently to WHH.

two or three yoke of oxen and prairie plow, giving therefore their joint note for some two hundred dollars; but when pay-day came refused to pay, pleading the minor act. The note was placed in Lincoln's hands for collection. The suit was called and a jury impanelled. The Snow Bros. did not deny the note, but pleaded through their counsel that they were minors, and that Mr. Case knew they were at the time of the contract and conveyance. All this was admitted by Mr. Lincoln, with his peculiar phrase, "Yes, gentlemen, I reckon that's so." The minor act was read and its validity admitted in the same manner. The counsel of the defendants were permitted without question to state all these things to the jury, and to show by the statute that these minors could not be held responsible for their contract. By this time you may well suppose that I began to be uneasy. "What!" thought I, "this good old man, who confided in these boys, to be wronged in this way, and even his counsel, Mr. Lincoln, to submit in silence!" I looked at the court, Judge Treat, but could read nothing in his calm and dignified demeanor. Just then, Mr. Lincoln slowly got up, and in his strange, half-erect attitude and clear, quiet accent began: "*Gentlemen of the Jury*, are you willing to allow these boys to begin life with this shame and disgrace attached to their character? If you are, *I* am not. The best judge of human character that ever wrote has left these immortal words for all of us to ponder:

"Good name in man or woman, dear my lord,
Is the immediate jewel of their souls:
Who steals my purse steals trash; 'tis something, nothing:
'Twas mine, 'tis his, and has been slave to thousands:
But he that filches from me my good name
Robs me of that which not enriches him
And makes me poor indeed."

Then rising to his full height, and looking upon the defendants with the compassion of a brother, his long right arm extended towards the opposing counsel, he continued: "Gentlemen of the jury, these poor innocent boys would never have attempted this low villany had it not been for the advice of these lawyers." Then for a few minutes he showed how even the noble science of law may be prostituted. With a scathing rebuke to those who thus belittle their profession, he concluded: "And now, gentlemen, you have it in *your* power to set these boys right before the world." He plead for the young men only; I think he did not mention his client's name. The jury, without leaving their seats, decided that the defendants must pay the debt; and the latter, after hearing Lincoln, were as willing to pay it as the jury were determined they should. I think the entire argument lasted not above five minutes.

H&W (1889), 619–20

606. Thomas Mather (JWW interview)[1]

[ca. 1883]

"Entering the room," related Mather in later years, "I found the old warrior,[2] grizzly and wrinkled, propped up in the bed by an embankment of pillows behind his back. His hair and beard were considerably disordered, the flesh seemed to lay in rolls across the warty face and neck, and his breathing was not without great labor. In his hand he still held Lincoln's letter. He was weak from long-continued illness, and trembled very perceptibly. It was evident that the message from Lincoln had wrought up the old veteran's feelings. 'General Mather,' he said to me, in great agitation, 'present my compliments to Mr. Lincoln when you return to Springfield, and tell him I expect him to come on to Washington as soon as he is ready. Say to him that I'll look after those Maryland and Virginia rangers[3] myself; I'll plant cannon at both ends of Pennsylvania avenue, and if any of them show their heads or raise a finger I'll blow them to hell.' On my return to Springfield," concludes Mather, "I hastened to assure Mr. Lincoln that, if Scott were alive on the day of the inauguration, there need be no alarm lest the performance be interrupted by any one. I felt certain the hero of Lundy's Lane would give the matter the care and attention it deserved."

H&W (1889), 492–93

607. Leonard Swett to WHH[1]

CHICAGO, ILL., August 29, 1887.

My Dear Sir:—

Your inquiry in reference to the circumstances of the appointment of David Davis as one of the Justices of the Supreme Court reached me last evening. In reply I beg leave to recall the fact, that in 1860 the politicians of Illinois were divided into three divisions, which were represented in the Decatur convention by the votes on the nomination for Governor. The largest vote was for Norman B. Judd, of Chicago, his strength in the main being the northern part of the State. I was next in order of strength, and Richard Yates the third, but the divisions were not materially unequal. The result was Yates was nominated, his strength being about Springfield and Jacksonville, extending to Quincy on the west, and mine was at Bloomington and vicinity and south and southeast.

---

1. JWW wrote in *The Real Lincoln:* "I knew General Mather well, and when I was in Springfield often heard him relate the incidents of his trip to Washington [in 1861]" (1922:304). The account given there (304–6) conveys the same anecdote but in entirely different words. As no original has been found, the text given here is from H&W (1889) as being closer to the time of JWW's interviews with Mather in the 1880s.

2. Gen. Winfield Scott.

3. Threats to AL's inaugural had been made by secessionist sympathizers in Maryland and Virginia.

---

1. No original for this letter has been found, though it is referred to in Swett's letter of August 30, 1887, §523.

These divisions were kept up awhile after Mr. Lincoln's election, and were considered in the distribution of Federal patronage. A vacancy in the United States Senate occurred early in 1861 by the death of Stephen A. Douglas, and Governor Yates appointed Oliver H. Browning,[2] of Quincy, to fill the vacancy. There was also a vacancy upon the Supreme Bench of the United States to be filled from this general vicinity by Mr. Lincoln in the early part of his administration, and Judge Davis, of Bloomington, and Mr. Browning, of Quincy, were aspirants for the position. Mr. Browning had the advantage that Lincoln was new in his seat, and Senators were august personages; and, being in the Senate and a most courteous and able gentleman, Mr. Browning succeeded in securing nearly all the senatorial strength, and Mr. Lincoln was nearly swept off his feet by the current of influence. Davis' supporters were the circuit lawyers mainly in the eastern and central part of the State. These lawyers were at home, and their presence was not a living force felt constantly by the President at Washington.

I was then living at Bloomington, and met Judge Davis every day. As months elapsed we used to get word from Washington in reference to the condition of things; finally, one day the word came that Lincoln had said, "I do not know what I may do when the time comes, but there has never been a day when if I had to act I should not have appointed Browning." Judge Davis, General Orme,[3] and myself held a consultation in my law-office at Bloomington. We decided that the remark was too Lincolnian to be mistaken and no man but he could have put the situation so quaintly. We decided also that the appointment was gone, and sat there glum over the situation. I finally broke the silence, saying in substance, "The appointment is gone and I am going to pack my carpet-sack for Washington." "No, you are not," said Davis. "Yes, I am," was my reply. "Lincoln is being swept off his feet by the influence of these Senators, and I will have the luxury of one more talk with him before he acts."

I did go home, and two days thereafter, in the morning about seven o'clock — for I knew Mr. Lincoln's habits well — was at the White House and spent most of the forenoon with him. I tried to impress upon him that he had been brought into prominence by the Circuit Court lawyers of the old eighth Circuit, headed by Judge Davis. "If," I said, "Judge Davis, with his tact and force, had not lived, and all other things had been as they were, I believe you would not now be sitting where you are." He replied gravely, "Yes, that is so." "Now it is a common law of mankind," said I, "that one raised into prominence is expected to recognize the force that lifts him, or, if from a pinch, the force that lets him out. The Czar Nicholas was once attacked by an assassin; a kindly hand warded off the blow and saved his life.[4] The Czar hunted out the owner of that hand and strewed his pathway with flowers through life. The Emperor Napoleon III. has hunted out everybody

---

2. A mistake for Orville H. Browning.

3. William W. Orme of Bloomington.

4. Apparently an anachronistic reference to Czar Alexander II of Russia, who in 1866 was saved from an assassin's bullet by a peasant named Osip Komissarov.

who even tossed him a biscuit in his prison at Ham and has made him rich.[5] Here is Judge Davis, whom you know to be in every respect qualified for this position, and you ought in justice to yourself and public expectation to give him this place." We had an earnest pleasant forenoon, and I though I had the best of the argument, and I think he thought so too.

I left him and went to Willard's Hotel to think over the interview, and there a new thought struck me. I therefore wrote a letter to Mr. Lincoln and returned to the White House. Getting in, I read it to him and left it with him. It was, in substance, that he might think if he gave Davis this place the latter when he got to Washington would not give him any peace until he gave me a place equally as good; that I recognized the fact that he could not give this place to Davis, which would be charged to the Bloomington faction in our State politics, and then give me anything I would have and be just to the party there; that this appointment, if made, should kill "two birds with one stone;" that I would accept it as one-half for me and one-half for the Judge; and that thereafter, if I or any of my friends ever troubled him, he could draw that letter as a plea in bar on that subject. As I read it Lincoln said "If you mean that among friends as it reads I will take it and make the appointment." He at once did as he said.

He then made a request of the Judge after his appointment in reference to a clerk in his circuit, and wrote him a notice of the appointment, which Davis received the same afternoon I returned to Bloomington.

Judge Davis was about fifteen years my senior. I had come to his circuit at the age of twenty-four, and between him and Lincoln I had grown up leaning in hours of weakness on their own great arms for support. I was glad of the opportunity to put in the mite of my claims upon Lincoln and give it to Davis, and have been glad I did it every day since.

An unknown number of people have almost every week since, speaking perhaps extravagantly, asked me in a quasi-confidential manner, "How was it that you and Lincoln were so intimate and he never gave you anything?" I have generally said, "It seems to me that is my question, and so long as I don't complain I do not see why you should." I may be pardoned also for saying that I have not considered every man not holding an office out of place in life. I got my eyes open on this subject before I got an office, and as in Washington I saw the Congressman in decline I prayed that my latter end might not be like his.

Yours truly,
LEONARD SWETT.

H&W (1889), 502–5

---

5. After an abortive attempt to seize power in France in 1840, Louis Napoleon was confined in the Fortress of Ham in eastern France.

608. *Elizabeth Sawyer to JWW[1]*

CHICAGO, Oct. 12th, 1888.

Dear Sir:

My father was born in Keene, N.H., in 1790, entered Williams College, 1807, and removed to Chicago in 1835. After the re-accession of the Whigs to power he was on the 21st of June in 1849 appointed Commissioner of the Land Office by President Taylor. A competitor for the position at that time was Abraham Lincoln, who was beaten, it was said, by "the superior dispatch of Butterfield in reaching Washington by the Northern route," but more correctly by the paramount influence of his friend Daniel Webster.

He held the position of Land Commissioner until disabled by paralysis in 1852. After lingering for three years in a disabled and enfeebled condition. he died at his home in Chicago, October 23d, 1855, in his sixty-third year.

Very respectfully,
ELIZABETH SAWYER.

H&W (1889), 301n

---

1. Printed as a footnote, this letter is prefaced: "The following letter by Butterfield's daughter is not without interest," referring to Illinois politician Justin Butterfield. No manuscript of this letter has been found.

PART 3

Informant Testimony Reported in
William H. Herndon's Letters to Jesse W. Weik

Some of the following entries have been extracted from letters, for which the date is given, and some were apparently written out separately and included in letters. The reader should note that while some of these entries report recent conversations, others appear to be recollections of something related at a much earlier time, and that all were written more than twenty years after the death of AL.

609. James H. Matheny (WHH interview)

Jany 87

Judge Matheny tells me this story of Mr. & Mrs. Lincoln: the story was told him by one of the parties to it. About the year 1850 there lived in this city a man by the name of Tiger,[1] who was a personal friend of Lincoln: he was a kind but a powerful man physically. Tiger heard that Mrs. Lincoln was without help and Knowing that Mrs. Lincoln was a tigress and Could not for any length of time Keep a girl, thought that he had a niece, who was a fine girl, industrious, neat, saving, and rather handsome, who could satisfy any body on earth. So he sent the girl down to see Mrs Lincoln: she, Mrs L, was anxious to get a girl and arrangements were made between the two that Sarah[2] — the girls name, should stay and help Mrs L. Everything went on well for sometime, Mrs L bragging on her Sarah all the while to her neighbors & visitors. Sarah herself was no Common hired girl, but a fine woman and rather intelligent, pleasant, and social. Mrs. Lincoln at last got on one of her insane mad spells, insulted and actually slapt the girl, who could and would not stand it —: So she quit Mrs Lincoln — went home to her uncle Tiger's and told her story weeping and crying all the while. Tiger felt bad about the matter, but knowing that all quarrels generally have two sides to them, he was determined to find out the truth of the matter — So he went down to Lincoln's and when he got there he saw that Mrs. Lincoln had thrown the girls trunk and clothes out of the house and on the pavement in the street. On approaching the

---

1. Jacob Taggart, according to JWW's notes on this story. See §555, note 1.
2. A Sarah E. Taggart married Upton Crow in Sangamon County in 1850. See Power, 236.

house he saw the things; and just in the yard stood Mrs Lincoln ready for a fight. Tiger advanced and spoke to Mrs. Lincoln in a kind and gentlemanly way — said he came to see her and find out who was in fault, and what was the matter — all about it. Mrs L at once blazed away with her sharp and sarcastic tongue, having her insane mad spell on her — abused Tiger shamefully, calling him a dirty villain — a vile creature & the like. Tiger stood still, waiting for an opportunity to pitch in a word of peace and reconciliation, but to no purpose. Mrs. Lincoln got madder & madder — boiled over with her insane rage and at last struck Tiger with the broom two or 3 times. Tiger now got mad, but said nothing to Mrs. Lincoln — not a word — stood the licking as best he could Tiger at last gathered up the clothes of the girl and being a strong man threw the trunk on his shoulder and carried it and the girls clothes home to his niece. The older the thing — his licking by Mrs L, got the madder Tiger got, and so he swore to himself that no man's wife should thus treat him and go free from a whipping or at least the husband should humiliatingly apologise for the wrong done him by his wife. The longer the thing stood in Tigers mind the more furious Tiger got, and so he went down into the city in search of Lincoln, in order to make him correct the thing or to whip him — to apologise or to stand a thumping — licking — a severe whipping: he after some considerable search found Lincoln in Edwards' store recling on the Counter telling one of his best stories. Tiger caught part of the story that tickled him very much. However Tiger, being a man of *will,* called Lincoln out of the store and told him the facts of the fight between the women, and his licking by Mrs Lincoln; and said to Lincoln that he must *punish* Mrs. Lincoln and apologise to him — Tiger or — — — and just here Lincoln Caught what was coming — looked up to Tiger, having held his head down with shame as Tiger told the story of his wrongs, done him by Mrs L & said calmly — kindly — and in a very friendly way, mingled with shame and sadness — "*friend* Tiger, can't you endure this one wrong done you by a mad woman without much complaint for old friendship's sake while I have had to bear it without complaint and without a murmur for lo these last fifteen years" — Lincoln said what he did so kindly — so peacefully — so friendly — so feelingly so apologetically in manner and tone and so sadly that it quickly and totally disarmed Tiger who said to Lincoln — "Friend give me your hand. I'll bear what has been done me by Mrs. Lincoln on *your* account and *your* account alone. I'll say no more about the matter, and now; Lincoln, let us be forever what we have been — friends". Lincoln instantly took and grasped, warmly grasped Tigers hand and shook it in a real friendly, western Style — saying — "Agreed, friend Tiger, and so let us be what we have always been, warm personal friends" and they ever were afterwards.

LC: HW3342–44

610. John Moore Fisk (WHH interview)

Feby 18th '87

On Saturday Evening I was called out to write the will of Benj Bancroft[1] and at the house of Bancroft I found an old friend of Lincoln, whose name is Fisk: he told me the following story which is correct. A man by the name of Pollard Simmons was a good friend of Lincoln in 1834–6.[2] Jno Calhoun was the surveyor of Sangamon County — was "The Candle box Calhoun"[3] — and a democrat in 1834–6. Simmons loved Lincoln, who was very poor at that time, and he tried to get Lincoln in some business: he applied to Calhoun as the friend of Lincoln to give him a deputyship in the Surveying business. Calhoun as Simmons remembers it gave Lincoln a deputyship. Simmons got on his horse and went on the hunt of Lincoln whom he found in the woods mauling rails. Simmons Said "Lincoln I've got you a job" and to which Lincoln replied — "Pollard, I thank you for your trouble, but now let me ask you a question — Do I have to give up any of my principles for this job. If I have to surrender any thought or principle to get it I wouldn't touch it with a ten foot pole?" "No, you do not Lincoln," said Pollard Simmons, and to which Lincoln replied — "Ill accept the office and now I thank you and my superior for it"

LC: HW3357

611. Richard M. Lawrence (WHH interview)

June 23d 88

Mr. Lawrence, a merchant of Williamsville in this County gives me this incident of Lincoln. Lawrence was at the lecture and heard it and saw and heard Lincoln. About the year 1857 an accomplished lady came to this city to lecture — to read and to receite fine things from best authors. She was a fine reader &c. At Myers hall on the north side of the square this woman was to Lecture — or recite or whatever you call it: her subject — one of them was the recital of the piece — "Nothing to Wear".[1] She was reading finely and all was attention and silence in the hall. Lincoln seemed wrapt up in the piece — was all attention. In some turn of the piece when all was dead silence Lincoln burst out with a loud "ha ha" — a kind of deep satisfaction expressed in the ha ha — a kind of heavenly feeling at the turn of something in the piece. Lincoln felt glorious and forgot for the moment in his deep feeling where he was and what he was doing. The "ha ha" was the deep and honest Expression of an honest soul fired by the triumph of the right.[2] The audience was large & was at the time wrapt up in the piece and when Lin-

---

1. Benjamin Bancroft, a neighbor of WHH.
2. Pollard Simmons lived in New Salem and was later a miller in Mason County.
3. A reference to an electoral fraud in Kansas Territory.

---

1. See William Allen Butler, *Nothing to Wear* (New York, 1857).
2. Marginal note: *an honest & sincere Expression of joy at the victory of the good.*

coln burst out with his ha ha the scene was too much for them and so Lincolns ha
ha was met with a round of deep and thorough applause. The Lady was caught
up in the same cloud and was Compelled to join in the applause: she could not
restrain herself at the time. Lincoln's ha ha and the storm of applause at the ha ha
upset the Lady and it was some time before she could put on her gravity. Lincoln
during all this time seemed unconscious — was abstracted, — felt glorious over
the turn of affairs. Lincoln was solemn — honest — Earnest: it was the good approving the good — by the burst of the ha ha. After a few moments all was again
silence and the woman resumed the recital &c. &c. This ha has under the Circumstances was just like Lincoln: he forgot himself and where he was and his nature — his love for the good — and just Expressed itself in the ha ha.[3]

LC: HW3456–57

612. James Miles (WHH interview)

July 16th '88

James Miles tells me this — Mr Lincoln made a Speech in Petersburg during
the Douglas & Lincoln Campaign in 1858.[1] Lincoln did his best near his old home
— New Salem in Menard County. Lincon Spoke for about two hours in his very
best way. The speech was a fine one and claimed the attention of Every one Democrat as well as the Republicans, but what thrilled the audience was his apostroph
to Liberty, Concluding with the Expression "God gave me these hands (holding
them up to the vast audience) to feed this mouth (putting his hands to his mouth).[2]
This expression contained in the apostroph was more than Convincing: it literally Electrified them and Carried the Crowd with him as if the people were Caught
up in a Cyclone. This Expression was used by the Republicans as a Convincer
during the Canvass of '58. Others have told me this substantially, though with more
immagination &c &c.

LC: HW3462

613. Milton Hay and David Littler (WHH interview)

Octr 25th '88

I was in Hay's office on Tuesday and he said that Lincoln always spoke with
profound reverence of Bolin Green. He further said that it was reputed that Lincoln made his own stories — jokes or what not and that it was a mistake — that

---

3. Marginal note: *You had better get the poem "Nothing to wear" and read it for yourself. Lincoln may have
given out his ha ha for the Contrast of the Classes or for some ridiculous ideas, though Lawrence says it was an
Earnest & a sincere &c. It evidently pleased L for some reason.*

---

1. Possibly a speech delivered on October 29. *CW* 3:333.
2. Marginal note: *L's hands were Eloquent raised up high above his head: they spoke.*

Lincoln heard his stories; jokes &c. and never forgot them and that the secret of L's success in this line was in the active — personified telling of them (Lincoln always told his stories &c, acting a part of them in looks — jestures — acts &c Lincoln & his story were in harmony — were one & identical. I add the last idea as my own.)

Littler at the same time and place told me that Lovejoy,[1] about the year 56 or '58 at the fair grounds near this city was making one of his most Eloquent speeches in behalf of Liberty the world over and Especially the Colored Slaves of America. The Speech was pathos — fire — rhetoric set on flame by feelings. Ben. S. Edwards[2] was present and became Emotionally Excited and sprang up, saying to the vast crowd this — "I would shake hands with the very devil on this question" at the same time grasping Lovejoy's hands in his own. The difficulty with Ben was that before this scene of which he was apart he was frightened by the word abolition, but was willing now to accept the opprobrious term. Lincoln sat by — heard the speech and when B. S. Edwards did what he did, Lincoln wept like a child and burst into tears and as Littler said — "He (Lincoln) broke Completely down," I suppose from the fact that L intended to make a speech or had Commenced one and then broke down — will see Littler again & correct if I am mistaken about L's pupposed attempt to speak.[3]

LC: HW3493

614. David Littler (WHH interview)

Nov. 22d '88

I saw Littler on Saturday last: he says that Lincoln did not make nor attempt to make a speech at that moment of time spoken of when Ben Edwards said, "I would rather shake hand with the devil than to shake hands with Douglas on this question" or as some put it "I would shake hand with the devil on this question". Littler said that Lincoln made a speech — a glorious, grand one on the same evening in the Hall of the House of Representatives eclipsing all others — Trumbull's — Lovejoy's et al. The speeches, except Lincoln's were made in Wrights grove west of the city about one mile and near the Fair grounds —[1]

* * * * *

Dave Littler tells me this additional story. During some of the political Canvasses the people in Logan Co Ills — just north of this County & adjoining it — had determined to have a large meeting — a grand rally and had appointed the day & the hour. When the day & hour arrived the heavens opend with a terrific

1. Owen Lovejoy, an abolitionist minister and Illinois congressman.
2. A Springfield lawyer and the brother of Ninian W. Edwards.
3. For a clarifying interview, see §614.

1. Marginal note: *The speeches &c were made in the fall of 1858. Littler says that Lincoln wept like a child at that moment of time — scene &c.*

storm: it blew in hurricanes & rained in torrents. Only about 20 persons appeared. Lincoln had felt the sting of disappointment and therefore he did not wish others to be disappointed. After some reflection he said — "Boys the day is bad, too bad for many people to appear here to hear me speak, but as you have dared the storm to hear a speech you shall not be disappointed — Come let's us go over to Armingtons Hall & I'll give you a talk, such as I have". The 20 went over to the hall in Atlanta and Littler said to me — "For a Calm — Cool — profound speech I never heard so great, so learned, in the Liberty line, — so dispassionate a speech in my life". "I learned," — said Littler to me — "more of the ideas in the two hours speech of Republicanism then and there than I ever knew before. Why — the speeches of other men sounded dull & dead to me after that." Lincoln must have done his best on this occasion, because Littler felt what he said and did not seem to color his story.[2]

LC: HW3504–5

615. Jesse K. Dubois (WHH interview)

Decr. 1st '88

Thomas Lincoln with his family started to go from Ind to Ills in March '30. The weather was rough and cold. When Lincoln got somewhere near the line that divides Ind from Ills; after traveling several days, the family Came to one of those long loggy corduroi bridges laid over a wide swamp. The water was over the logs and a thin sheet of ice bridged the water. Now & then there were posts along the bridge to direct the traveller. The family came to the edge of the swamp. Abrm drove the Oxen, two yoke, but when he attempted to go into the swamp & on the bridge he could not make the oxen break the ice, without apparent cruelty. Abm coaxed and threatened by turns, but the oxen would not go on the ice; and at last Abrm saw that force must be applied — so he swung his long oxe lash around and around over the oxen high in the air and brought the lash down Cutting open the hide. The oxen at last went on the thin ice — broke their way &c. When about half way over Abe heard his poor dog bring a kind of despairing howl: he stopt the oxen, pulled off his shoes — rolled up his pants — got out of the wagon — jumped into the Cold water, the sheets of ice hitting his shins. He got to the dog — took him, frightened nearly to death, in his long & strong arms, Carried him to the wagon — put him in it, the dog cruching close to Mrs Lincolns feet, scared half out of his wits. The oxen were soon told to go on and *on* they went through the ice. After the family had crossed and got on dry land Abe found difficulty in getting the dog out of the wagon — at last he had to haul him out by force. When the dog was out and on dry land he cut up such antics as no dog Ever did before: he ran round and round Abe & laid down at his feet — got up and ran round and round again and again: he seemed — was grateful to Abe, his benefactor. Lincoln

---

2. Marginal note: *The place — village at which the speech was made was Atlanta, Logan Co Ills. H.*

said to Dubois after telling him the story — "Well, Jesse, I guess that I felt about as glad as the dog". This story I got from Dubois, he getting it from L many — many years ago when the two were young men.

LC: HW3515–16

616. Joshua F. Speed (WHH interview)

Jany 5th '89

Mr. Speed told me this story of Lincoln. Speed about 1839–'40 was keeping a pretty woman in this City and Lincoln desirous to have *a little* said to Speed — "Speed, do you know where I can get *some;* and in reply Speed said — "Yes I do, & if you will wait a moment or so I'll send you to the place with a note. You cant get *it* without a note or by my appearance". Speed wrote the note and Lincoln took it and went to see the girl — handed her the note after a short "how do you do &c.", Lincoln told his business and the girl, after some protestations, agreed to satisfy him. Things went on right — Lincoln and the girl stript off and went to bed. Before any thing was done Lincoln said to the girl — "How much do you charge". "Five dollars, Mr. Lincoln". Mr. Lincoln said — "I've only got $3.". Well said the girl — "I'll trust you, Mr Lincoln, for $2.. Lincoln thought a moment or so and said — "I do not wish to go on credit — I'm poor & I don't know where my next dollar will come from and I cannot afford to Cheat you." Lincoln after some words of encouragement from the girl got up out of bed, — buttoned up his pants and offered the girl the $3.00, which she would not take, saying — Mr Lincoln — "You are the most Conscientious man I ever saw.". Lincoln went out of the house, bidding the girl good evening and went to the store of Speed, saying nothing. Speed asked no questions and so the matter rested a day or so. Speed had occasion to go and see the girl in a few days, and she told him just what was said and done between herself & Lincoln and Speed told me the story and I have no doubt of its truthfulness.

LC: HW3531

617. Charles Chandler (WHH interview)

[1885–89]

An other good Story

Mr Chandler of Chandlerville in Menard County[1] about 1880–2 told me this story: he is a gentleman, and is the proprietor of the town of Chandlerville, about 34 miles North West of this City & 12 miles west or north West of Petersburg. The original pioner to this section of the world was at the beginning of things very

---

1. Chandlerville is now in Cass County and was never part of Menard County; Chandler was probably a resident of Morgan County at the time of this incident.

poor, but ambitious of wealth and distinction: they generally owned or had pre-empted a 40 acre tract of land; and it was the generous and manly custom among us that no neighbor should interfere with his neighbor in the matter of land that *immediately* joined his farm; and which he from necessity or convenience wanted or should have. To violate this rule was robbery & consigned a man *to felony* in the opinions of his neighbors. Mr. Chandler had a small farm and wanted — need-ed — Must have from necessity an 80 acre tract adjoining his 40.: he had no money but was honest and his credit good among all his neighbors. This I know — have known him for many years — possibly 40, if no more. A man who had money and who did not live very far from Chandler, wished the same piece of land and put his eye and his heart on it, though he did not need the land and was not of the Chandler neighborhood, exactly: he knew that he was violating — if not de-fying custom. One morning he arose Early — put $100. in his saddle bags and started on a fine swift horse for Springfield in order to enter the 80 ac which Chan-dler ought to have by custom and its rights. This man Confided the purposes of his trip to Springfield to one or two men in the neighborhood: They no sooner saw the man off on his trip than they saddled up horses and ran over to Chandler and told him what was up in the air. Chandler had no money, but the men, his good neighbors who notified him of the intended wrong, thought that Chandler had not so much money by him as he needed, had taken the precaution to take with them to Chandler's more than the hundred dollars. These men told Chan-dler that the man had gone to Springfield to enter the wanted 80   Chandler was thunder struck at the news, and the meanness of the man — said he had no mon-ey, and that it now was too late to collect or borrow any from neighbors or friends. The men who had the kindness to tell him the story of the contemplated wrong said to Chandler, "Come there is no time to talk now — go saddle old "Bess" — your swiftest and best animal — here is the money — a cool hundred — use it as you please — buy a horse on the road if you must, but by all means beat the vil-lain to Springfield and get your land." There was no time for thanks and Expres-sions of gratitude. Chandler only prayed to himself — Caught and Quickly bri-dled old "Bess —" took the hundred, & $80 of his own and was off for Springfield like an arrow, going under whip and spur. The man had some two hours start of Chandler. However Chandler knew the woods and pathes and Struck straight through the Country for Springfield. The man rode leisurely along, not thinking that Chandler knew anything about the matter. Chandler rode swiftly from his farm to Salisbury 14 miles north west of Springfield, having ridden under whip — Spur and gallop some 20 miles, when he overtook two men going to Spring-field — one of whom was — Abraham Lincoln on horseback. "Bess" was nearly out of wind and covered with lather — foam from head to foot. Lincoln asked Chandler — a stranger to him Except by reputation — what was the cause of his great hurry. Chandler told his story quickly — his wants & his needs — the cus-tom of the Country — the man's meanness. &c. Lincoln heard his story and quickly sprang from his own horse — and said to Chandler —. "There is no time to be lost — here's my horse — quickly mount him and go quickly. My horse is quick

— has wind and grit: he'l take you to Springfield in quick time — put him up at Herndon's Tavern[2] and he'l be well attended to. This Coming from a mere stranger except by reputation made Chandler think that there was a providence at last in all things. Chandler thanked Lincoln and got on the horse and was off again: he put whip and spur too to the horse: it was a noble one. Chandler soon struck the village of Springfield — hitched the horse to the rack in front of the Register's office — ran in and Said — "Here Mr. Register — I want to enter this piece of land," Explaining by numbers — section — township and range & its location — "Well," said the Register, "Your turn will soon come —. Mr Clerk take a note of the land and the Man's name," which was done, and Chandler was a happy man — for he was first on time and on demand: he Counted off his hundred dollars and handed it to the Register of the land office, who gave him his Certificate of Entry. Chandler now was fixed — glad — happy. Just about this time in Came the man and to his utter astonishment he saw Chandler there with a grin on his face and the Certificate of the entry of the land in his hand: he knew that the fates had beaten him: he took it and a good "Cussing" from Chandler as well as he could — quit the office and started back for home a whipt man. Chandler did put up Lincoln's horse at Herndon's tavern, and did hire a man to rub him dry and to blanket him. In some two or three hours after the entry of the land Lincoln landed in the village and quickly asked — Chandler — "How did you succeed;" and to which Chandler replied — "All's well — got my land — see here," Showing his certificate of entry. Chandler and Lincoln were strangers no more but were ever afterwards firm personal and political friends. Chandler thanked Lincoln a thousand times for his kindness. Lincoln subsequently surveyed off the land for Chandler — such were the "barbarian" — "Savages" of Illinois in 1832–40.

LC: HW3781–83

618. Clarissa Tuft Van Nattan (WHH interview)[1]

[1885–89]

Two young girls by the name of Tuft[2] lived about 1855 in Springfield near Mr Lincoln's home: the girls were aged 13 & 15 respectively. One of these girls is now my neighbor & has been for near 20 years. She is respected & truthful and tells the following facts to me — She and her younger sister was sent out in the praire to drive up the Cows. They got the cow & were Coming home with her and as they came into the outskirts of the City they were running & romping as young girls do. The younger sister got on the pavement & was running backwards as fast as she could run. Lincoln's face was towards her back & her back towards Lincolns

2. The Indian Queen, run by Archer G. Herndon, WHH's father.

1. Marginal note: *One of these girls the older was Married Some 20 years ago & is now my neighbor — Her name now is Mrs Norman Vannattin.*
2. The Tufts lived on Eighth Street at Madison, three blocks north of the Lincolns.

face As she was running with her back toward Lincoln, he going East and she going west her foot caught in the pavement somehow & was about to receive a terrible fall, when Lincoln stretched out his long arms and Caught her and saved her from a hard fall on the bricks.

Lincoln looked down into the girls face while he held her in his arms with one of his kind, tender, and sympathetic looks and instantly thereby assured the girl that she was safe in his great arms. The little girl looked up and smiled, and thanked Lincoln for what he did. Lincoln put the girl on he feet, Saying to her — "Now my little daughter you can say that you have been in Abrahams bosom". The girl laughed most heartily at Lincoln's off hand hit.

LC: HW3763

619. Stephen Whitehurst (WHH interview)

[1885–89]

Mrs Lincoln & Lincoln — "a fuss"

Stephen Whitehurst, Editor of the Conservative[1] & brother in law to Judge Matheny,[2] told me that one day in 1856 or 7 a man by the name of Barrett[3] was passing by Lincoln's house and saw a woman chasing a man with a table knife or butcher knife in her hand: they ran down through the Lincoln garden going from the west to the East and towards Whitehurst's house. Barrett did not pay much attention to the parties, thinking that what he saw was sport or fun. Just as the man & woman were running down the Garden walk going East some men & women were in the street going from East to West, so that all were meeting face to face. Mr Whitehurst's back yard & Lincoln's back yard looked onto each other — ie one in Lincoln's back yard Could see into Whitehursts & vice a versa. Whitehurst on that hour & moment saw what was going on between the man & woman. Lincoln, for it was he, saw the men & women in the street Coming from the East going west meeting Lincoln & wife nearly face to face & he knew that he & wife had been or would be discovered, turned suddenly around, caught his wife by the shoulder with one hand & with the other caught his wife at the heavy End — her hips if you please and quickly hustled her to the back door of his house and forced — pushed her in, at the same time, as it were, spanking her heavy end, saying to her at the same moment — "There d—n it, now Stay in the house and don't disgrace us before the Eyes of the world." Whitehurst saw & heard all this & when the affair was quite over Barrett told Whitehurst what he saw just a moment before & a part of what Whitehurst had seen. Whitehurst & Barrett are men

---

1. A paper begun in 1856 to support the Whig party, opposed to AL and the new Republican party.
2. James H. Matheny.
3. Possibly W. T. Barrett, Sangamon County assessor and treasurer, or J. H. Barrett, his deputy.

of truth, if I have the right Barrett in my mind. Whitehurst is at all Events. This story was told to me in 1867.

W. H. H

I recorded these facts the hour they were told me and put them in a little book which I loaned to Lamon. This is my recollection / H

LC: HW3771

620. Norman B. Judd (WHH interview)

Octr 2d '90

I wish to relate to you an important fact. Soon after the assassination of Mr. Lincoln I interviewed Mr Judd, two or three times, in relation to his knowledge of Lincoln *generally* and particularly about what L said in reference to the questions he intended to ask Douglas at Freeport. Turn to our life of L. 410. Douglas put 7 questions to L. at Ottawa. Lincoln went to Chicago and had a meeting of his friends and told them that he intended to put 4 questions to Douglas at Freeport and among those questions was the 2d one which was substantially this "Can a territory exclude slavery from its limits while in a territorial condition or state". At the meeting of Lincoln's friends at Dixon or Chicago were Peck — Judd — Ray Et al.[1] All of them, after Lincoln had read the 4 questions to be put to Douglas at Freeport, objected to them and said in substance that Douglas would not positively answer the question directly and that if he did it would be in the affirmative and that would Elect him to the Senate again. "It is none of your business Mr Lincoln particularly to put the question because you are the Candidate for the U.S. Senate and that is your particular business" said Lincoln's friends. Lincoln replied "Douglas will answer the question as soon as asked & if he does not I will push him to the wall at every joint debate or wherever I shall speak other wise than in joint debate; and the sooner Douglas answers the better for him. The people demand a direct answer". "Douglas will answer in some glittering generalities and Evade the question" said Peck — Ray Et al. "Yes, he will answer directly" said Lincoln; and to which Lincoln's friends said, "To put the question is none of your business Mr. Lincoln and to which Mr Lincoln said — "Yes it is my business, and if Douglas answers the question, which he will, Either way he is a dead cock in the pit." Mr. Lincoln here went into a kind of argument to Convince his friends that he was right and conluded by saying — "I am after larger game. The battle of 1860 is worth a hundred of this —" . . . Lincoln evidently wanted to kill Douglas politically and did it effectively. I say that Judd told me what Lincoln said in the meeting of friends at Dixon or Chicago, I think Chicago, though White says that

---

1. Ebenezer Peck, a Chicago lawyer and politician; Charles H. Ray, editor-in-chief of the Republican newspaper, the Chicago *Press and Tribune*.

the meeting was at Dixon. Probably he is correct. Though Peck — Ray — Judd
Et all say that Lincoln uttered the above words still I doubt the *Exact words.*, because, as you well know, Mr. Lincoln was one of the most secretive men that ever
lived. The expression means that, "I am a candidate for the Presidency of the U.S.
of America. That is what I am fighting for". I do not think that Mr Lincoln ever
uttered the words as stated, though he looked at the time for the office. I think at
most that the words as above are inferences, legitimate ones. Lincoln never told
mortal man his purposes and plans — Never. Evidently L beat around the bush.

    LC: HW3691–92

621. James H. Matheny (WHH interview)

                                                Decr. 4th '90
    I wish now to make an other statement. If you remember you once asked me if
the text in Lamon's life of Lincoln was Correct — page 396, as I remember it, and
in answer to which question I said "It was substantially Correct" & I say so now.[1]
Our Judge J. H. Matheny said to me, only a month or so before he died which was
some two months since, that he heard Lincoln say in substance: "If Douglas can draw
off such & such men from the cause of republicanism and be made to support him,
who says he does not care wheteher slavery is vted up or voted down — if he can get
strong & influential leading republican papers to laud him — & if he can attack
and partly crush Buchanna's administration & can get in Illinois so many votes to
Buchannans none, then he will play the *devil* at Charleston.

    LC: HW3708

---

    1. Refers to a passage in Lamon reporting a statement by AL, concluding: "A man that can bring such
influence to bear with his own exertions may play the devil at Charleston" (396). Lamon's anonymous informant may well have been WHH himself.

PART 4

Informant Testimony Reported in Jesse W. Weik's
The Real Lincoln *(1922)*

The following entries report the text of one letter and the substance of several interviews conducted by JWW with Lincoln informants prior to the publication of *Herndon's Lincoln* (1889). The letter and Weik's notes for these interviews, if any, have not been located, and the texts are given as they appear in the narrative of *The Real Lincoln*.

622. Samuel H. Treat (JWW interview)

[1883]

In the winter of 1883 I spent a good portion of one afternoon with a gentleman who was present and heard Lincoln's first oral argument before the Supreme Court of Illinois. It was Samuel H. Treat, who had himself been on the Supreme bench and at the time of my visit was serving as Judge of the United States District Court. His recollection of the political campaign of 1846, when Lincoln defeated the redoubtable Peter Cartwright for Congress, was to me an especially interesting chapter. He said he admired Lincoln and he entertained me with several vivid and characteristic episodes in which the latter figured. I tried to draw out his opinion of Mrs. Lincoln, but with poor sucess, for, beyond the simple admission that he was acquainted with her coupled with the names of three or four other persons who, he claimed, could adequately describe her "if they dared to," he declined to commit himself.

On the afternoon just mentioned when I visited him Judge Treat told me, among other things, that one morning Lincoln came to his office and joined him in a game of chess. The two were enthusiastic chess-players and when the opportunity offered indulged in the game. On the occasion named they were soon deeply absorbed, nor did they realize how near it was to the noon hour until one of Lincoln's boys came running with a message from his mother announcing dinner at the Lincoln home, a few steps away. Lincoln promised to come at once and the boy left; but the game was not entirely out; yet so near the end the players, confident that they would finish in a few moments, lingered a while. Meanwhile almost a half an hour had passed. Presently the boy returned with a second and more urgent call for dinner; but so deeply engrossed in the game were the two players they apparently failed to notice his arrival. This was more than the little fellow could stand; so that, angered at their inattention, he moved nearer, lifted his foot, and deliberately kicked board, chessmen, and all into the air. "It was one of the most abrupt, if not brazen, things I ever saw," said Treat, "but the surprising thing was its effect on Lincoln. Instead of the animated scene between an irate father and an impudent youth which I expected, Mr. Lincoln without a word of reproof calmly arose, took the boy by the hand, and started for dinner. Reaching the door he turned, smiled good-naturedly, and exclaimed, 'Well, Judge, I reckon we'll have to finish this game some other time,' and passed out. Of course I refrained from any comment," continued Treat, who, by the way, was old and had never been blessed with a child, "but I can assure you of one thing: if that little rascal had been a boy of mine he never would have applied his boots to another chessboard."

    Weik, 102–3

623. Dennis F. Hanks (JWW interview)

                         Charleston, Illinois, Oct. 28, 1886
"They told me the Lincolns had a baby at thur house," he related to the writer at Charleston, Illinois, Oct. 28, 1886, "and so I jest run all the way down thar. I guess I was on hand purty early, fur I rickolect when I held the little feller in my arms his mother said, 'Be keerful with him, Dennis, fur you air the fust boy he's ever seen.' I sort o' swung him back and forth; a little to peart, I reckon, fur with the talkin' and the shakin' he soon begun to cry and then I handed him over to my Aunt Polly[1] who wuz standin' close by. 'Aunt,' sez I, 'take him; he'll never come to much,' fur I'll tell you he wuz the puniest, cryin'est little younster I ever saw."

    Weik, 44

624. Jonathan Birch (JWW interview)[1]

                                    [1887?]
"At the appointed time," said Mr. Birch when he related the incident, "I knocked at the door of his room and was admitted. Motioning me to be seated he began his interrogatories at once without looking at me a second time to be sure of the identity of his caller. 'How long have you been studying?' he asked. 'Almost two years,' was my response. 'By this time it seems to me,' he said laughingly, 'you ought to be able to determine whether you have in you the stuff out of which a good lawyer can be made.' Then he asked me in a desultory way the definition of a con-

---

1. Apparently Mary Hanks, who married Jesse Friend.

---

1. JWW wrote that Birch, who was his neighbor and legal adviser in Greencastle, Indiana, had studied law in Bloomington, Illinois.

tract and two or three other fundamental questions, all of which I answered readily and, as I thought, correctly. Beyond these meager inquiries, as I now recall the incident, he asked nothing more. Meanwhile, sitting on the edge of the bed he began to entertain me with recollections—many of them characteristically vivid and racy—of his own practice and the various incidents and adventures that attended his start in the profession. The whole proceeding was interesting and yet so unusual, if not grotesque, I was at a loss to determine whether I was really being examined or not. In due time we went downstairs and over to the clerk's office in the court-house, where he wrote a few lines on a sheet of paper which he enclosed in an envelope and directed me to report to Judge Stephen T. Logan, the other member of the examining committee at Springfield. The next day I went to Springfield where I delivered the note as directed. On reading it Judge Logan smiled and, much to my surprise, gave me the required certificate or license without asking a question beyond my age, residence and the correct way of spelling my name. The note from Lincoln read:

MY DEAR JUDGE —
The bearer of this is a young man who thinks he can be a lawyer. Examine him if you want to. I have done so and am satisfied. He's a good deal smarter than he looks to be.
Yours
LINCOLN

Weik, 133–34

625. *Jonathan Birch (JWW interview)*[1]

[1887?]

"Having no office of his own, Mr. Lincoln, when not engaged in court, spent a good deal of his time in the clerk's office. Very often he could be seen there surrounded by a group of lawyers and such persons as are usually found about a court-house, some standing, others seated on chairs or tables, listening intently to one of his characteristic and inimitable stories. His eyes would sparkle with fun, and when he had reached the point in his narrative which invariably evoked the laughter of the crowd, nobody's enjoyment was greater than his. An hour later he might be seen in the same place or in some law office near by, but, alas, how different! His chair, no longer in the center of the room, would be leaning back against the wall; his feet drawn up and resting on the front rounds so that his knees and chair were about on a level; his hat tipped slightly forward as if to shield his face; his eyes no

---

1. For JWW's personal relation to Birch, see §624, note 1. JWW says that Birch met with WHH when the latter came to Greencastle, Indiana, in 1887 to collaborate with JWW on their biography and that "what Birch, who was the embodiment of truthful and conscientious statement, said about Lincoln was verified by Herndon" (Weik, 198). This appears to be excerpted from a statement published after Birch's death in *The Outlook,* Feb. 11, 1911, reprinted in Rufus Rockwell Wilson, ed., *Intimate Memories of Lincoln* (Elmira, N.Y.: Primavera Press, 1945), 104–8.

longer sparkling with fun or merriment, but sad and downcast and his hands clasped around his knees. There, drawn up within himself as it were, he would sit, the very picture of dejection and gloom. Thus absorbed have I seen him sit for hours at a time defying the interruption of even his closest friends. No one ever thought of breaking the spell by speech; for by his moody silence and abstraction he had thrown about him a barrier so dense and impenetrable no one dared to break through. It was a strange picture and one I have never forgotten.

"In his physical make-up Mr. Lincoln could not be said to be a man of prepossessing personal appearance; but his splendid head and intellectual face made up in a large measure for all his physical defects, if such they might be called. When intellectually aroused he forgot his embarrassment, his eyes kindled, and even in his manner he was irresistible. It is well known that he was more or less careless of his personal attire, and that he usually wore in his great canvass with Douglas a linen coat, generally without any vest, a hat much the worse for wear, and carried with him a faded cotton umbrella which became almost as famous in the canvass as Lincoln himself. Late one afternoon during this canvass I boarded the train at Bloomington, soon after which Mr. Lincoln himself entered the same car in which I was seated, wearing this same linen coat and carrying the inevitable umbrella. On his arm was the cloak that he was said to have worn when he was in Congress nine years before. He greeted and talked freely with me and several other persons whom he happened to know, but as night drew on he withdrew to another part of the car where he could occupy a seat by himself. Presently he arose, spread the cloak over the seat, lay down, somehow folded himself up till his long legs and arms were no longer in view, then drew the cloak about him and went to sleep. Beyond what I have mentioned he had no baggage, no secretary, no companion even. At the same time his opponent, Judge Douglas, was traveling over the State in his private car surrounded by a retinue of followers and enjoying all the luxuries of the period.

"It was during this canvass, with every fiber of his being tremulous with emotion, I heard him, in one of his speeches denouncing the extension of slavery, passionately exclaim: 'That is the issue that will continue in this country when these poor tongues of Judge Douglas and myself shall be silent. It is the eternal struggle between these two principles—right and wrong—throughout the world. They are the two principles that have stood face to face from the beginning of time; and will ever continue to struggle. The one is the common right of humanity and the other the divine right of kings. It is the same principle in whatever shape it develops itself. It is the same spirit that says "You toil and work and earn bread and I'll eat it." No matter in what shape it comes, whether from the mouth of a king who seeks to bestride the people of his own nation and live by the fruit of their labor, or from one race of men as an apology for enslaving another race, it is the same tyrannical principle.'[2] The melting pathos with which Mr. Lincoln said this and its effect on his audience cannot be described."

Weik, 198–201

---

2. This is from AL's speech in the last joint debate with Douglas at Alton, October 15, 1858, *CW* 3:315.

626. Milton Hay (JWW interview)

[ca. 1883–88]

Speaking of Lincoln and his wife Milton Hay, the uncle of John Hay, said: "If he had married a woman of more angelic temperament and less social ambition, he, doubtless, would have remained at home more and been less inclined to mingle with the people outside. She had a very extreme temper and made things at home more or less disagreeable. This probably encouraged Mr. Lincoln to seek entertainment elsewhere. Mentally she was a bright woman with decided aristocratic pretensions, but she was of very saving habits. In dealing with others she was very determined; not easily moved or thoughtful about what she should say or do."

Weik, 91

627. James H. Matheny (JWW interview)

[ca. 1883–88]

Judge Matheney agreed with Davis and Hay. He told me also that although in worldly matters Lincoln was a prudent and careful as the average man, yet he never succeeded in acquiring very much property. Compared to his second partner, Stephen T. Logan, David Davis, and a few other associates of like standing at the bar, he was poor. At the time of his election in 1860 the house in which he lived was the only real extate he possessed and his personal accumulations did not exceed ten thousand dollars. His tastes were proverbially simple; he indulged in no excesses and his expenditures were kept at the minimum. His wife, on the other hand, had a weakness for certain luxuries, but they were modest and only few in number. She loved fine clothes, but in other respects she was close and in no sense extravagant.

Weik, 91

628. John S. Bradford (JWW interview)[1]

[1883–89]

Some years ago when I had invested in my first carriage I invited Mrs. Lincoln to accompany me and my family in a drive to the country. We drove to the Lincoln residence, and when the madame came down the front steps to join us in the carriage, she appeared to be very nervous and more or less wrought up. What had caused her agitation she failed to disclose. We suspected that there had been a collision or disagreement of some kind with her servant, for, just as she settled back in her seat, she exclaimed with a sigh: "Well, one thing is certain; if Mr. Lincoln should happen to die, his spirit will never find me living outside the boundaries of a slave State."

Weik, 99

---

1. This incident is told in abbreviated form in H&W (1889), 424n. In *The Real Lincoln,* JWW prefaces this quotation as follows: "John S. Bradford, at one time State Printer, told me this incident in his office in Springfield and I made a note of it at the time" (99).

629. Louisa Hosey? (JWW interview)[1]

[1883–89]

At first, when I sought to interrogate her, she was somewhat reticent if not really unresponsive, but when I explained that Mr. Herndon had sent me to see her with the assurance that her name should not be used, she gradually relented and eventually answered all my questions. She admitted that she had employed Lincoln and Herndon to look after her interests when her case came up in court. The first thing done was to ask for a change of venue, which, having been granted, she and the witnesses, some of whom were female inmates of her own household, others sundry gentlemen of gay and sportive tendency, were obliged to travel a short distance over the country to another court. "There was a good crowd of us," she related, "and a livelier delegation never drove over the prairies. As to the behavior and actions of Mr. Lincoln, I must say it was in every respect correct so that I can recall nothing improper or out of place about it. Of course he talked to me a good deal, and for that matter to the other ladies too."

"Where and when was it he talked to you?" I asked.

"Sometimes in the office, sometimes in the court-house, and sometimes elsewhere."

"Did he ever talk with you alone?"

"Yes, I have frequently been in his office and spoken to him when no one else was there."

"What did he talk about?"

"Usually about business; also many other things that suggested themselves. The truth is he was an interesting talker on all subjects."

"How did he conduct himself? Was he agreeable?"

"To me he seemed always a gentleman. I could see nothing wrong or unpleasant about him."

"Did you ever hear him tell stories?"

"Yes; a good many."

"Were any of these stories told when you and he were alone?"

"Yes; and I remember that he told some when one or more of the ladies who accompanied me were present."

"What kind of stories were they?"

"Various kinds. Of course I can't describe them now, but I remember that they were all very much alike in one particular and that is that they were usually funny."

"Were any of them suggestive or objectionable?"

"No, I do not think they were."

---

1. This interview appears in JWW's account of being sent by WHH to question a former client about AL's professional behavior and his "demeanor and conduct toward the fair sex." The client was a woman who, "handicapped by a shady reputation, had landed in court charged with keeping a house of ill-repute or some like offense." The case occurred "at an early day," according to WHH, and the woman is said to be reformed and "leading a correct and becoming life" (Weik, 82–83). A search of the records compiled by the Lincoln Legal Papers Project indicates that *People v. Joseph Klein and Louisa Hosey* is the only case that seems to fit this description. A charge of fornication and adultery was brought in Sangamon County in 1843, which, after a change of venue to Menard County, was dismissed by the prosecution in June 1845.

"Then what would you say about their propriety; that is, would you consider what he said unfit to be told in polite society or in the company of ladies?"

The last question was evidently more or less of a tax on the old woman's memory or perhaps her conception of propriety; for she hesitated a few moments, as if buried in thought, before she answered; but she soon rallied and then responded:

"No, although some of the things he said were very amusing and made me as well as the others laugh, I do not think it would be fair to call them improper; in fact, I believe they could with safety have been told in the presence of ladies anywhere." At this point the witness halted again, but only an instant; for she promptly recovered her equanimity and concluded her testimony with the following emphatic and sententious declaration which I have never forgotten: "But that is more than I can say for Bill Herndon."

Weik, 83–85

630. Clifton H. Moore (JWW interview)[1]

[1883–89]

"In the summer of 1858," said Mr. Moore to me, "Douglas made a speech at Pontiac during the course of which he venture to quote from Holland's 'Life of Van Buren.' A day or so later Lincoln passed through here and among other things told me that Douglas in his speech at Pontiac had seriously misquoted Holland, a fact he could easily establish if he only had Holland's book; but unfortunately not a copy was to be found in Clinton. The next morning he pushed on to Bloomington. He was still so wrought up over Douglas's misrepresentation that David Davis was finally induced to send a man on horseback to Springfield with a note from Lincoln asking for the book. In due time the messenger returned with the desired volume which he turned over to Lincoln, who took it with him, threatening to confront Douglas with it at the earliest opportunity."

As indicative of Lincoln's real opinion of Douglas, Mr. Moore related this circumstance which so deeply impressed me that I made a note of it at the time: "On the day Mr. Lincoln delivered his speech at Clinton during the campaign of 1858 he was in my office; and I shall always remember with regret one thing he said about Douglas, which was this: 'Douglas will tell a lie to ten thousand people one day, even though he knows he may have to deny it to five thousand the next.'"

Weik, 230–31

631. Leonard Swett (JWW interview)

[ca. 1887–89]

"I shall never forget," Mr. Swett once told me, "the first time I saw Mr. Lincoln. I had expected to encounter him at Springfield, but he was absent from home, nor

---

1. JWW says he visited the informant in Clinton, Illinois, and heard this story.

did our meeting occur till later. It was at the town of Danville. When I called at the hotel it was after dark, and I was told that he was upstairs in Judge Davis's room. In the region where I had been brought up, the judge of the court was usually a man of more or less gravity so that he could not be approached save with some degree of deference. I was not a little abashed, therefore, after I had climbed the unbanistered stairway, to find myself so near the presence and dignity of Judge Davis in whose room I was told I could find Mr. Lincoln. In response to my timid knock two voices responded almost simultaneously, 'Come in.' Imagine my surprise when the door opened to find two men undressed, or rather dressed for bed, engaged in a lively battle with pillows, tossing them at each other's heads. One, a low, heavy-set man who leaned against the foot of the bed and puffed like a lizard, answered to the description of Judge Davis. The other was a man of tremendous stature; compared to Davis he looked as if he were eight feet tall. He was encased in a long, indescribable garment, yellow as saffron, which reached to his heels, and from beneath which protruded two of the largest feet I had, up to that time, been in the habit of seeing. This immense shirt, for shirt it must have been, looked as if it had been literally carved out of the original bolt of flannel of which it was made and the pieces joined together without reference to measurement or capacity. The only thing that kept it from slipping off the tall and angular frame it covered was the single button at the throat; and I confess to a succession of shudders when I thought of what might happen should that button by any mischance lose its hold. I cannot describe my sensations as this apparition, with modest announcement, 'My name is Lincoln,' strode across the room to shake my trembling hand. I will not say he reminded me of Satan, but he was certainly the ungodliest figure I had ever seen."

Weik, 192–93

632. Henry C. Whitney (JWW interview)[1]

[1887–89]

"Mr. Lincoln would advise with perfect frankness about a potential case," he once said, "but when it was *in esse,* then he wanted to win as badly as any lawyer; but unlike lawyers of a certain type he would not do anything mean, or which savored of sharp practice, or which required absolute sophistry or chicanery in order to succeed. In a clear case of dishonesty he would hedge in some way so as not himself to partake of the dishonesty. In a doubtful case of dishonesty, he would give his client the benefit of the doubt, and in an ordinary case he would try the case so far as he could like any other lawyer except that he absolutely abjured technicality and went for justice and victory denuded of every integument.

---

1. JWW explained: "After Lincoln became President, Mr. Whitney removed to Chicago, where, in the eighties, I spent a good deal of time with him" (Weik, 193).

"As attorney for the Illinois Central Railroad I had authority to employ additional counsel whenever I chose to do so, and in Judge Davis's circuit I frequently applied to Lincoln when I needed aid. I never found him unwilling to appear in behalf of a great 'soulless corporation.' In such cases he always stood by me, and I always, of course, tried to win. There was nothing of the milksop about him, nor did he peer unnecessarily into a case to find some reason to act out of the usual line; but he had the same animus ordinarily as any other lawyer. I remember a murder trial in which he was joined with Leonard Swett and myself for the defense.[2] Swett was a most effective advocate, and when he closed in the afternoon I was full of faith that our client would be acquitted. Lincoln followed the next morning, and while he made some good points the honesty of his mental processes forced him into a line of argument and admission that was very damaging. We all felt that he had hurt our case. In point of fact our client was convicted and sent to the penitentiary for three years. Lincoln, whose merciless logic drove him into the belief that the culprit was guilty of murder, had his humanity so wrought upon that he induced the Governor to pardon him after he had served one year."

Weik, 194–95

633. Henry C. Whitney (JWW interview)[1]

[1887–89]

"Judge Davis," said Whitney, "held court, and Lincoln, who had two or three cases to try, was there also. At the judge's request I secured a room for him, also for Lincoln and myself, at the American House, a primitive hostelry kept by one John Dunaway. The building had three front entrances from the street, but not a single hall downstairs; one of these entrances led directly into the ladies' parlor, and from it an entrance was obtained to the dining-room and from another corner a flight of stairs conducted us to our room. Close by the front and dining-room doors hung a gong which our vulgar boniface, standing in the doorway immediately beneath our windows, was in the habit of beating vigorously as a prelude to our meals. It was frequently very annoying, and so often disturbed our slumbers in the early dawn that we decided one morning it must be removed or forever silenced. By a majority vote Lincoln was chosen to carry out the decree. Accordingly, shortly before noon, he left the court-room, hastened to the hotel, passed through the dining-room, and, in a mischievous prank, took the offensive and noisy instrument from the place where it hung and quietly secreted it between the top and false bottom of a center table where no one would have thought of looking for it. In a short time I encountered Dunaway, our host, coming down from our

---

2. Probably refers to the Patterson case, described by Whitney for WHH in §521.

---

1. This anecdote, according to JWW, is one that Whitney "told me once" (Weik, 209). Cf. §298.

room, where he had been and still was searching anxiously for the gong which some ruthless hand had, alas, abstracted. I passed on, and when I reached our room I realized I was in the presence of the culprit, for there sat Lincoln in a chair tilted awkwardly against the wall after his fashion, looking amused, sheepish, and guilty, as if he had done something ridiculous as well as reprehensible. The truth is we all enjoyed the landlord's discomfiture, and even Judge Davis, who urged Lincoln to restore the gong, was amused. Presently, however, Lincoln and I repaired to the dining-room, and while I held the two contiguous doors fast Lincoln restored the gong to its accustomed place, after which he bounded up the stairs two steps at a time, I following. The next day when the Chicago paper came in—it usually arrived about noon—it brought the news that Lincoln had received 110 votes for Vice-President at the Philadelphia Convention the day before.[2] The announcement created something of a stir. Lincoln and Davis had left the court-room and had gone down to the hotel, where I joined them a few minutes later, bringing with me Judge Cunningham's[3] copy of the 'Chicago Press' which I read to them. Of course Davis and I were more or less jubilant. Alluding to Lincoln's rude and undignified prank with the hotel gong, Davis laughed and with harmless irony admonished him: 'Great business for a man who aspires to be Vice-President of the United States.' But the news of the honor shown him at the Philadelphia Convention made but slight impression on Lincoln. Apparently he was unmoved, if not indifferent, his only response being: 'I reckon it's not me. There's another Lincoln down in Massachusetts. I've an idea he's the one.'

"The term of court that week at Urbana was decidedly prosaic, and the cases tried, usually by the court without aid of a jury, were meager both in amount and incident. In due time Lincoln was ready to return home. He had collected twenty-five or thirty dollars for that term's business, and one of our clients owed him ten dollars which he felt disappointed at not being able to collect; so I gave him a check for that amount and went with him to the bank to get it cashed. T. S. Hubbard was the cashier who waited on us. I never saw Lincoln happier than when he gathered his little earnings together, being, as I now recollect it, less than forty dollars, and had his carpet-bag packed ready to start home."

Weik, 209–11

634. Henry C. Whitney (JWW interview)[1]

[1887–89]

"Very soon thereafter," he once said to me, "I became acquainted with Lincoln. It was about the time of my first appearance at the bar. I did not feel the slight-

---

2. AL received these votes at the Philadelphia convention on June 19, 1856.

3. J. O. Cunningham, editor of the Urbana *Union* in 1856, later became a judge.

---

1. Whitney's first acquaintance with AL was in 1854. Cf. §534.

est delicacy in approaching him for assistance; for it seemed as if he invited me to familiarity if not close intimacy at once; and this from no selfish motive at all— nothing but pure philanthropy and goodness of heart to a young lawyer just beginning his career. He sat on the bench for the judge a while that term; and my first motion in court was made before him. The next day he made some arrangements for his horse and buggy and took the train to fill an appointment farther north.

"I saw him start for the train. He was obliged to ride over two miles in an old dilapidated omnibus, and being the sole occupant of the conveyance had somewhere procured and held in his hand a small French harp with which he was making the most execrable music. I rallied him on this, to which, stopping his concert, he replied: 'This is my band; Douglas had a brass band at Peoria, but this will do me.' He resumed his uncouth solo as the vehicle drove off, and the primitive strains, somewhat shaken up by the jolting conveyance, floated out upon the air till distance intervened."

Weik, 212

Register of Informants

The brief biographical data given below represent an attempt to afford the reader some indication of who William H. Herndon's informants were and to suggest the kind of relationship, if any, each may have had with Abraham Lincoln. In consulting these entries, the reader is cautioned to bear in mind certain considerations. First, as most of these informants are not historic figures in the ordinary sense, basic information about them is generally hard to come by and has frequently proved unobtainable. In some cases it has not even been possible to ascertain birth and death dates. By contrast, the lives of some otherwise very obscure informants, thanks to genealogists and family historians, are reasonably well documented. Thus the information available to the editors has been highly uneven, and this circumstance is necessarily reflected in the entries.

Second, while the editors have endeavored to indicate possible sources of prejudice, the biases of Herndon's informants, like those of people in general, are often submerged and difficult to gauge. Politics is an obvious example. Many of the informants from Menard County, for instance, were Democrats and politically opposed to Lincoln for much of his career. Yet they often seem to be personally well disposed toward the man himself, who in turn was known for his ability to get along well with his political adversaries. Nor were political allegiances always static and straightforward. For example, to the intensely political men in Lincoln's circle who had to find their way past the wreckage of the Whig party in the 1850s, it mattered greatly whether one found refuge in the traditional Democratic party, took up with the nativist American party, or made common cause with the abolitionists by joining the Republican party. While these differences might be the source of bitter resentments and hard feelings, they were not always or equally so, and it is probably fair to say that most of the informants who disagreed with Lincoln's political course still liked him personally.

Third, in the absence of more pertinent information about the informants' character and credibility, circumstances showing their status or standing in their community are frequently cited, though it is duly acknowledged that these are no guarantors of integrity or reliability where personal testimony is concerned. Thus, gaining the limelight by election or appointment to office, while possibly indicative of public favor, is not here equated with honesty or candor. Nonetheless, such circumstances are offered to help identify the informants and to indicate their backgrounds and distinctions.

Full citations for the sources given in abbreviated form can be found in the Short Citations and Abbreviations section on pages xxix–xxxii. The letters cited as sources were solicited by the editors and are on file at the Knox College Library, Galesburg, Illinois.

ABELL, ELIZABETH (CA. 1804–?)

The wife of Dr. Bennett Abell and the sister of Mary Owens, Elizabeth Abell was described by AL's close friend William Butler as "a cultivated woman—very superior to the common run of women" in frontier Illinois. AL lived for a time with the Abells, and Butler believed that it was "from Mrs. Able *[sic]* he first got his ideas of a higher plane of life—that it was she who gave him the notion that he might improve himself by reading &c." In 1836 she promoted a courtship between AL and her sister. (Reep; *Federal Census of Menard County,* 1880; Burlingame)

ARMSTRONG, HANNAH (1811–90)

Hannah Armstrong's husband, Jack, leader of the notorious Clary's Grove boys, became a close friend of AL after their famous wrestling match. Thereafter, AL was a familiar presence in the Armstrong home, where Hannah Armstrong laundered and mended his clothes. After her husband died, she appealed twice to AL for help, and he responded by defending her son William "Duff" Armstrong, who was accused of murder, and later ordering his discharge from the Union army. *(CG)*

ARMSTRONG, JOHN (1814–77)

Postmaster of Springfield under AL's administration, Armstrong was a respected Sangamon County contractor and builder. In 1859 he was on the executive committee of the Republican party in Springfield, of which AL was also a member. (*CW; ISJ,* December 24, 1877)

ARNOLD, ISAAC NEWTON (1815–84)

A Chicago attorney and officeholder who became acquainted with AL at the bar and in Illinois politics, Arnold wrote two of the earliest biographies of AL: *History of Abraham Lincoln and the Overthrow of Slavery* (Chicago, 1866); and *The Life of Abraham Lincoln* (Chicago, 1885). *(ALE)*

ASHLEY, JAMES MITCHELL (1824–96)

An abolitionist lawyer and editor from Toledo, Ohio, Ashley was elected to Congress in 1858. He introduced in 1863 the constitutional amendment abolishing slavery. *(BDATG)*

BAKER, EDWARD L. (1829–97)

The son of David J. Baker, a prominent Illinois attorney and short-term U.S. senator. In 1855 Baker and a partner purchased the *Illinois State Journal,* the Springfield newspaper with which AL was strongly identified. *(HEI)*

BAKER, GEORGE E.

An associate of William H. Seward, Baker edited Seward's *Works* before the Civil

War and served as a clerk in the State Department during Seward's tenure there. (Glyndon G. Van Deusen, *William Henry Seward* [New York, 1967])

BAKER, LUTHER BYRON (1830–96)

During the Civil War Baker was a first lieutenant and regimental quartermaster of the First District of Columbia Cavalry. For helping to capture John Wilkes Booth, Baker received a $3,000 share of the government reward. (William Hanchett, *The Lincoln Murder Conspiracies* [Urbana, Ill., 1983]; pension files, National Archives, Washington, D.C.)

BALCH, GEORGE B. (1828–86)

A farmer who also served as postmaster and railroad agent in Coles County, Illinois, Balch initiated the movement to mark Thomas Lincoln's grave. (*HCC;* Coleman)

BALE, ESTHER SUMMERS (1821–72)

Bale came to New Salem with her parents from Green County, Kentucky. In 1839 she married Hardin Bale, operator of a woolen mill there and later in Petersburg, Ill. (Hurdle)

BALE, HARDIN (1816–79)

Born in Green County, Kentucky, Bale came to Illinois with his parents in 1830. He learned the milling business from his father and built a carding mill at New Salem in 1836–37. In 1839 Bale moved the establishment to Petersburg and began a partnership with Samuel Hill. (Hurdle; Miller)

BARNET, JAMES

Barnet was living in Camden, Oldham County, Kentucky, in 1867.

BARRET, RICHARD FERREL (1821–1908)

The husband of Sarah Rickard, Barret was a veteran of the Mexican War from Sangamon County and later practiced medicine in St. Louis and Kansas City. (*ISJ,* December 11, 1908; Power)

BARRET, SARAH RICKARD (1824–1911)

Sarah Rickard's sister Elizabeth was married to AL's close friend William Butler, a Whig politician and officeholder in Springfield. While boarding with the Butlers in the late 1830s, AL met Sarah and later proposed marriage. (*ISJ,* October 28, 1911; Power)

BARRETT, GEORGE J. (1818–77)

A Methodist minister of New York birth, Barrett was a missionary to the Chippewa before serving in several other locations in Illinois. He was the father of Oliver R. Barrett, the Lincoln collector. (*Minutes of the 54th Session of the Illinois Annual*

Conference of the Methodist Episcopal Church [1877]; *Minutes of the 94th Session of the Illinois Annual Conference of the Methodist Episcopal Church* [1917])

BARRETT, JOSEPH H. (1824–1910)

A Cincinnati Republican journalist and politician, Barrett penned one of the first Lincoln biographies, *Life of Abraham Lincoln* (New York, 1865). *(NCAB)*

BARTLETT, FRED H.

Bartlett was a clerk employed by the mayor of Worcester, Massachusetts, in 1889.

BATEMAN, NEWTON (1822–97)

Between AL's election and his removal to Washington, D.C., Bateman, who was the state superintendent of public instruction, occupied an office adjacent to that of the president-elect in the Illinois State Capitol. Later Bateman was president of Knox College in Galesburg and editor in chief of the *Historical Encyclopedia of Illinois. (DAB; HEI)*

BEDELL, GRACE (1848–1936)

The little girl who suggested to the president-elect that he grow his beard. She was born in Westfield, New York, the daughter of a Republican stove and carriage maker. *(ALE)*

BELL, ELIZABETH HERNDON GRAHAM (1833–88)

A daughter of the New Salem schoolmaster, Mentor Graham, "Lizzie" Herndon Graham Bell was born in New Salem. After her marriage to Abram Bell, she lived in Petersburg, where she was a leader in the temperance cause. (Walsh)

BENNETT, JOHN (1805–85)

A Petersburg, Illinois, storekeeper, Bennett knew AL before he moved to Springfield and served with him as a fellow Whig in the Illinois House of Representatives in 1840–41. (Wayne C. Temple, "Lincoln and Bennett: Story of a Store Account," *Lincoln Herald* (Fall 1967); *IAMM*)

BENNETT, WILLIAM

This shadowy informant may have been a brickmaker in Petersburg, Illinois. *(HMMC;* Onstot)

BIRCH, JONATHAN (CA. 1834–1906)

After examination by AL at Bloomington and subsequent admission to the Illinois bar, Birch moved to Covington, Indiana, and then to Greencastle to practice law. *(Federal Census, Fountain County, Indiana, 1860; IDRPC)*

BLACK, CHAUNCEY FORWARD (1839–1904)

The ghostwriter of Ward Hill Lamon's 1872 Lincoln biography, Black was the son of Jeremiah Black, a stalwart of President Buchanan's cabinet. He became the law partner of Lamon after the Civil War and a Democratic politician in his own right. (*NYT,* December 3, 1904)

BLISS, JOHN SPOOR (1832–91)

Bliss was a Wisconsin journalist who interviewed AL shortly after his nomination to the presidency. (*USBD* [Wisconsin]; *Janesville Gazette,* May 14, 1891)

BOAL, ROBERT (1806–1903)

Boal was a medical doctor who served three terms in the Illinois legislature as a Whig and as a Republican. (*TISHS* [1904]; *BEI)*

BRADFORD, JOHN S. (1815–92)

A veteran of the Mormon War, the Mexican War, and the California gold rush, Bradford held a number of offices in Springfield and Sangamon County and was said by JWW to have openly disliked AL. (*HEI/Sangamon; ISJ,* January 24, 1892; Weik)

BRANSON, NATHANIEL WILLIAM (1837–1907)

Branson was a Petersburg, Illinois, lawyer who dabbled in Republican politics. His wife, Fannie, was the daughter of Dr. Francis Regnier of New Salem. *(BEI)*

BRINKERHOFF, GEORGE MADOC (1839–1928)

A disbursing clerk in the office of the Illinois state auditor during the Civil War, Brinkerhoff was comptroller of the city of Springfield from 1865 to 1870. (*HEI/ Sangamon; HSC; JISHS* 21:3 [1928])

BROOKS, SAMUEL S. (1801–65)

Brooks was an early Illinois Democratic newspaper editor who began his career in Edwardsville in 1832 and was later associated with newspapers in eight other Illinois communities. (Franklin Scott, comp., *Newspapers and Periodicals of Illinois, 1814–1879,* Collections of the ISHL. No. 6., 1910; "Woodland Cemetery Records," Quincy, Ill.)

BROWN, ALFRED MACKENZIE (1811–1903)

Born, like AL, near Hodgenville, Kentucky, Brown lived most of his life in Elizabethtown, where as a young man he entered the store of John B. Helm as an apprentice and eventually became a partner. He was a strong Confederate sympathizer. *(WWWHC)*

BROWN, CHRISTOPHER C. (1834–1904)

Brown studied law at Transylvania University and was admitted to the Illinois bar in Springfield in 1856 after being examined by AL and WHH. In 1859 he married "Bettie" Stuart, the daughter of John T. Stuart, and entered the law firm of

Stuart and Edwards. (Wayne C. Temple, ed., *Lincoln as Seen by C. C. Brown* [Prairie Village, Kans., 1963])

BRYANT, JOHN HOWARD (1807–1902)

A brother of the poet William Cullen Bryant, John Bryant lived in Bureau County, Illinois, and was a founder of the state's Republican party. He was appointed a collector of internal revenue by AL in 1862. *(HEI)*

BURBA, ERASTUS R. (1815–93)

Born in New York, Burba came to Hodgenville, Kentucky, in 1843 and in 1862 was elected county clerk of LaRue County. (*Federal Census, LaRue County,* 1850; Benningfield)

CAMPBELL, ALEXANDER (1814–98)

Campbell moved to LaSalle, Illinois, in 1850 to become involved in coal mining and in Whig and Republican politics. During the campaigns of 1856 and 1858, he loaned AL money for incidental campaign expenses. In 1858 he was elected to the Illinois House. (*BDAC;* Irwin Unger, *The Greenback Era* [Princeton, N.J., 1964])

CANNON, LEGRAND B. (1815–1906)

A New York banker and outspoken advocate of the Union, Cannon organized pro-Union activities in New York City, including a mass meeting in Union Square. Given an army commission, he served on the staff of Major General John E. Wool at Fortress Monroe, where he met AL. (*NYT,* November 4, 1906)

CARMAN, CALEB (1805–88)

Born in Canada in 1805, Carman came to Illinois about 1820 with his father, who ran a saw and grist mill at Sangamo Town on the Sangamon River. Carman first knew AL in 1831, when AL was helping to build a flatboat near Sangamo Town, and later at New Salem, where Carman worked as a carder and shoemaker and took in AL as a boarder. (Onstot; McKenzie)

CARPENTER, FRANCIS B. (1830–1900)

In 1864 Carpenter spent six months in the White House working on a portrait of AL, his "First Reading of the Emancipation Proclamation of President Lincoln." Carpenter's memoir of this experience, *Six Months at the White House with Abraham Lincoln* (1866), is a much-cited source of Lincoln anecdotes. *(DAB; ALE)*

CASSIDY, MICHAEL MARION (1825–1905)

Cassidy was a farmer, lawyer, judge, and coal mine developer in Mt. Sterling, Kentucky. (Samuel M. Cassidy, *The Cassidy Family and Related Lines* [Lexington, Ky., 1985]; William DePrez Inlow, *In Old Kentucky: The Story of My Forbears* [Shelbyville, Ky., 1950])

CHANDLER, CHARLES (1806–79)

The founder of the town of Chandlerville, Illinois, was born in Connecticut and moved to Illinois in 1831. *(HEI/Cass)*

CHAPMAN, AUGUSTUS H. (1822–98)

Chapman married Harriet A. Hanks, daughter of AL's second cousin, Dennis F. Hanks, and Sarah Elizabeth Johnston Hanks, AL's stepsister. After serving as an officer in the war, Chapman was appointed agent for the Flathead Indians in Montana by President Johnson in 1865. (*Charleston Courier,* September 15, 1898; Coleman)

CHAPMAN, HARRIET HANKS (1826–1915)

The daughter of AL's stepsister Sarah Elizabeth Johnston Hanks and his second cousin, Dennis F. Hanks. Harriet Hanks grew up near, and continued to live close by her grandmother, Sarah Bush Johnston and her grandmother's second husband, Thomas Lincoln, AL's father. In the mid-1840s she lived for a year and a half with AL's family in Springfield. (Coleman)

CLAGETT, WILLIAM T.

Clagett's testimony indicates that he was raised in Grayson County, Kentucky.

CLARK, HENRY (1805–87)

Clark came to Illinois in 1826 from Barren County, Kentucky. A neighbor and friend of AL and fellow soldier in the Black Hawk War, Clark chose AL as his second in a fistfight. (*Petersburg Observer,* July 18, 1887; Reep; letter from Lola B. Clark, April 29, 1992)

CLARY, ROYAL A. (1813–74)

After emigrating from Tennessee, Clary's family helped establish the Clary's Grove settlement near the future site of New Salem. In 1832 Clary served with AL's company in the Black Hawk War. When almost fifty years of age, Clary enlisted in the Union army. (Onstot; Whitney; *CG*)

COGDAL, ISAAC (1812–87)

A native of Kentucky, Isaac Cogdal was a farmer and stone mason who operated a quarry in Menard County and provided material for many buildings in the region. An active Whig and later Republican, Cogdal eventually was admitted to the Illinois bar in 1860, having been encouraged in the law by his old New Salem friend, AL. (Onstot; *HEI/Sangamon*)

COLLINS, RICHARD H. (1824–89)

Collins, a graduate of Centre College and Transylvania Law School, worked as an editor and historian, an attorney, and a judge. *(Lawyers and Lawmakers of Kentucky* [Chicago, 1897]; *BEK)*

CONKLING, EDGAR

A brother of AL's friend James C. Conkling and a former resident of Springfield, Edgar Conkling was a successful manufacturer and railroad promoter in Cincinnati. (Charles Cist, *Sketches and Statistics of Cincinnati in 1851* [Cincinnati, 1851]; letter from Anne B. Shepherd, August 23, 1994)

CONKLING, JAMES COOK (1816–99)

Conkling came to Springfield in 1838 and developed a close personal and professional relationship with AL. He served on the Republican State Central Committee and was a presidential elector in 1860 and 1864. Through Conkling, AL defended his positions on emancipation and the use of blacks in the military in a letter to a Springfield Union meeting in August 1863. *(ALE)*

CRAWFORD, ELIZABETH (1806–92)

With her husband, Josiah, Elizabeth Crawford came in 1826 from Kentucky to Spencer County, Indiana, where they were near neighbors to AL's family. AL and his father were both employed at various times by Josiah Crawford, who supported AL's presidential campaigns and his course during the Civil War. (Adams; *Spencer County [Ind.] Cemetery Inscriptions* [Rockport, Ind., 1987])

CRAWFORD, SAMUEL A. (CA. 1826–1900)

A lifelong resident of Spencer County, Indiana, Samuel Crawford was the son of AL's neighbors Josiah and Elizabeth Crawford and the husband of Nancy Ann Grigsby. (*IPW,* September 28, 1889; Adams; Crawford file, LBNM)

CREAL, RICHARD A. (1801–81)

Creal was a farmer in LaRue County, Kentucky, who lived on the Lincoln birthplace farm in 1866. (*Federal Census, Larue County,* 1850, 1880; Edward Benningfield, comp., *LaRue County, Kentucky, Cemetery Records* [Owensboro, Ky., 1982])

CULLOM, SHELBY MOORE (1829–1914)

At AL's suggestion Cullom studied law with John T. Stuart and was admitted to the Illinois bar in 1855. A Republican, he served as Speaker of the Illinois House, U.S. congressman, governor of Illinois, and was a longtime member of the U.S. Senate. (*DAB;* Howard)

DAVIS, DAVID (1815–86)

Born in Maryland and educated at Kenyon College, Davis came to Illinois in the 1830s to practice law, eventually settling in Bloomington. Elected as a Whig to the state legislature in 1844, he attended the state constitutional convention of 1847, devoting special attention to the judiciary. For fourteen years (1848–62) he presided over the Eighth Judicial Circuit in Illinois. AL practiced before him for over ten years and at times presided over Davis's court when the judge had other business. At the Republican convention in Chicago in 1860, Davis managed AL's nomination effort, and in February 1861 he accompanied AL to Washington, D.C., for the inauguration. In 1862 AL appointed Davis to the U.S. Supreme Court. At AL's death, Davis was executor of his estate. *(DAB; NCAB)*

DAVIS, JAMES (CA. 1807–?)

An acquaintance of AL in New Salem, Davis was at various times a farmer, teamster, and "grocery clerk" in Petersburg and Menard County. *(Federal Census, Menard County,* 1850, 1860, 1880)

DEFREES, JOHN D. (1810–82)

An Indianapolis lawyer, editor, and politician, DeFrees managed Edward Bates's 1860 campaign in Indiana. A former chairman of the Whig and Republican parties in his home state, he was appointed government printer by AL, an office he held until 1869. (William Wesley Woollen, *Biographical and Historical Sketches of Early Indiana* [Indianapolis, 1883])

DICKEY, THEOPHILUS LYLE (1811–85)

A Kentuckian who settled and practiced law in western Illinois, Dickey was elected judge of the Ninth Circuit in 1848, an office he held for four years. A delegate to the first Republican convention in Illinois in 1854, he ran for Congress as an Independent in 1856 and supported Douglas in 1858 and 1860. *(DAB)*

DICKSON, WILLIAM M. (1827–89)

A graduate of Miami University, Dickson practiced law in Kentucky and then in Cincinnati, where in 1852 he married a cousin of MTL. A friend of AL, during the Civil War he spent much time in Washington, D.C. (George Irving Reed, comp., *The Bench and Bar of Ohio: A Compendium of History and Biography* [Chicago, 1897])

DONNOHUE, DILLARD C. (CA. 1815–98)

A member of the Putnam County, Indiana, bar, Donnohue also served as mayor of Greencastle. (Jesse Weik, *Weik's History of Putnam County, Indiana* [Indianapolis, 1910]; *Federal Census, Putnam County,* 1860; *IDRPC)*

DOUGHERTY, JOHN R. (1824–1904)

Born in Spencer County, Indiana, Dougherty began flatboating between Rockport, Indiana, and New Orleans at the age of sixteen. In 1849 he became owner and manager of a wharf boat in Rockport, shipping grain and produce. He was active in local politics. *(HWSP; Rockport [Ind.] Journal Weekly,* September 2, 1904)

DRESSER, THOMAS W. (1837–1907)

Dresser's father, Charles, married AL and Mary Todd in 1842. At the outbreak of the Civil War the Virginia-born Dresser volunteered to serve the Confederacy. He was captured and in December 1862 returned to Springfield, where he had been raised. Completing a medical degree in New York, he began a practice in Springfield in 1864 and attended MTL in her final illness. (Wallace; *HSC; ISJ,* April 28, 1907)

DUBOIS, JESSE K. (1811–76)

Born in Lawrence County, Illinois, Dubois attended college at Bloomington, Indiana. In 1834 he was elected to the Illinois General Assembly with AL and was re-elected for three more terms. At the first Republican state convention in 1856 he was nominated for state auditor on AL's recommendation and served two terms. He remained active in Republican politics, and though a disappointed federal officeseeker, he was an early supporter of AL's re-election in 1864. *(HEI)*

DUMMER, HENRY ENOCH (1808–78)

Dummer emigrated from New England to Springfield, where from 1833 to 1837 he preceded AL as the partner of John T. Stuart. During this partnership, AL borrowed law books from the firm's library. (*HEI/Sangamon* 1:606; Paul M. Angle, "The Record of a Friendship: A Series of Letters from Lincoln to Henry E. Dummer," *JISHS* 31 [1938])

DUNCAN, JASON (1799–1885)

A native of Vermont, Duncan moved west in the 1820s, receiving his medical degree in Missouri. He arrived in New Salem about the same time as AL and lived at James Rutledge's tavern, where he set up his medical practice. Duncan left in 1834 and a short time later married a New Salem girl, Nancy Burner. (*Knox County Republican,* September 20, 1885)

DUNCAN, JOHN (1804–?)

Duncan was a minister in LaRue County, Kentucky, in the 1860s. (Louis A. Warren, *Lincoln's Parentage and Childhood* [New York, 1926])

EASTMAN, ZEBINA (1815–83)

In 1839 Eastman joined Benjamin Lundy at Hennepin, Illinois, in publishing the antislavery newspaper *Genius of Universal Emancipation.* In 1840, with Hooper Warren, he began publication of *The Genius of Liberty,* moving that paper to Chicago in 1842, where it ultimately merged with the *Chicago Tribune.* In 1861 Eastman was appointed by AL as U.S. consul at Bristol, England. *(BEI; HEI)*

EDDY, FRANCIS MARSHALL (1842–1909)

The son of Henry Eddy, a longtime lawyer and editor in Shawneetown, Illinois, Eddy lived most of his life in Gallatin County. (Glen Miner, comp., *Gallatin County, Illinois, Cemeteries* [Thomson, Ill., 1973])

EDWARDS, ELIZABETH TODD (1813–88)

Elizabeth Todd was born into a wealthy and aristocratic Kentucky family and, in 1832, married into another. In 1835 she and her husband, Ninian W. Edwards, moved to Springfield, and in 1839 she invited her younger sister Mary to live with her. Cultured and charming, Elizabeth Edwards was Springfield's leading hostess whose home was the resort of the city's socially and politically ambitious young men. There AL and Mary Todd met and courted, and there, in spite of the Edwards's active discouragement of the match, they were married on November 4, 1842. Elizabeth Edwards visited the Lincolns in the White House, where MTL became resentful toward her and actively sought her husband's dismissal from his federal post. In her later years, MTL sought refuge in her sister's Springfield home, and it was there that she died in 1882. (*ISJ,* February 23, 1888; *DAB; ALE;* O. H. Browning to N. W. Edwards, May 26, 1865, CHS)

EDWARDS, NINIAN WIRT (1809–89)

The son of the Illinois territorial governor Ninian Edwards and brother-in-law of MTL, Edwards graduated from the law department of Transylvania University. He served briefly as Illinois attorney general in 1834, later becoming a Springfield merchant. He also served with AL in the Illinois General Assembly (1836–40). In 1839 Mary Todd came to live in the Edwards's Springfield home, where she met and eventually married AL. In 1852 Edwards, to the mortification of AL, left the Whig party to become a Democrat, and during AL's campaigns of 1858 and 1860 was a supporter of Stephen A. Douglas. As Illinois's first superintendent of public instruction, he secured passage of a school law that laid the foundation for the state school system. Though politically at odds with his brother-in-law, Edwards prevailed upon AL in 1861 to give him a lucrative federal office—captain and commissary of subsistence—but pressure from critics and the connivance of MTL led to his removal two years later. (*DAB; ALE;* O. H. Browning to N. W. Edwards, May 26, 1865, CHS)

EISENMAYER, GEORGE C. (1820–93)

Eisenmayer was a Bavarian immigrant to St. Clair County, Illinois, who farmed near Mascoutah and was an early vintner there. (letter from Mary McMillon Sauerhage, July 27, 1994; letter from Elfred M. Worms, August 24, 1994; *History of St. Clair County* [Philadelphia, 1881])

ELLIOTT, WESLEY (1822–97)

The son of a pioneer Springfield tavernkeeper, Elliot farmed in Menard County, then participated in the Pike's Peak gold rush and remained in the Far West for several years. (Power; *ISJ,* January 24, 1897)

ELLIS, ABNER Y. (1807–78)

Ellis moved from Kentucky to Sangamon County in 1825 and had a long involvement in the mercantile business in New Salem and Springfield. Ellis's father was in business with WHH's father, Archer G. Herndon, and Ellis himself was at one time associated in merchandising with AL's closest Springfield friend, Joshua F. Speed. In 1849 Ellis was appointed postmaster at Springfield. (Power; letter from Marie T. Eberle, August 25, 1993; letter from Deanna Kohlburn, September 8, 1993)

ELMORE, HARDIN H. (1813–1902)

Born in Cumberland County, Kentucky, Elmore settled in Sangamon County in September 1834, in what later became Loami Township. (Power; *ISJ*, September 20, 1902)

ELMORE, TRAVIS (1820–88)

Travis Elmore knew AL at New Salem and his father served in AL's company in the Black Hawk War. (Whitney; *Federal Census, Menard County,* 1850; tombstone at Oakland Cemetery, Petersburg, Ill.)

EMERSON, IRA (1823–98)

A pioneer preacher, Emerson was the Methodist minister in charge at Pleasant Plains, Illinois, in 1866 when he was approached by Ben Irwin in WHH's behalf. (*ISJ*, May 5, 1898)

ENGLE, WILLIAM (1801–70)

A native of Virginia, Engle came to Illinois in 1823 and was a farmer, merchant, and politician. He represented Menard County in the General Assembly but was best known locally as a storyteller. (Onstot; letters from James E. Remer, March 3 and December 1, 1992)

ENOS, PASCAL P., JR. (1816–67)

Educated in St. Louis and Jacksonville, Enos began his business career as a clerk in Springfield. Politically active as a Whig and then a Republican, he was elected to the State legislature and later was appointed clerk of the U.S. Circuit Court by Justices John McLean and David Davis. (Wallace; *HEI*)

FELL, JESSE W. (1808–87)

Pennsylvania-born Fell was the first lawyer in Bloomington, Illinois. In the winter of 1834–35 he began a long political association with AL. He worked hard in 1860 to gain the Republican presidential nomination for AL, having previously solicited a brief autobiography from AL and circulated it among Eastern voters. (*ALE*)

FICKLIN, ORLANDO BELL (1808–86)

Ficklin was born in Kentucky, studied law in Missouri, and settled in Illinois in 1830, first in Mount Carmel and later in Charleston. He served with AL in both the Illinois and U.S. House of Representatives. A Whig turned Democrat, Ficklin was often associated with AL in the trial of cases in the Illinois circuit courts. *(ALE)*

FISK, JOHN MOORE (1822–1918)

Fisk was a neighbor of WHH when the latter was farming north of Springfield after the Civil War. (*HSC;* Floyd S. Barringer, comp., *Sangamon County Cemeteries,* vol. 2 [Springfield, Ill., 1971])

FRANCIS, ELIZA RUMSEY (1793–1893)

Francis moved in 1831 with her husband, Simeon, to Springfield, where he published the *Sangamo Journal,* a Whig paper. Simeon Francis was closely associated with AL in politics, and Eliza Francis is said to have encouraged the reconciliation between AL and Mary Todd. (*Portland Oregonian,* May 1, 1893; letter from Sandy McGuire, June 26, 1994)

FRIEND, CHARLES (1841–1922)

Friend was supposedly the grandson of Dennis Hanks's father and the postmaster at Sonora, Kentucky. (Daniel E. McClure, Jr., *Two Centuries in Elizabethtown and Hardin County, Kentucky* [Elizabethtown, 1979]; James Allison Jones and Mary Josephine Jones, comps., *Cemetery Inscriptions, Hardin County, Kentucky* [Owensboro, Ky., 1987])

GENTRY, ANNA CAROLINE ROBY (1807–83)

Anna Gentry was the daughter of Absalom Roby and the wife of Allen Gentry, with whom AL made his 1828 flatboat trip from Rockport, Indiana, to New Orleans. (*HWSP; Rockport [Ind.] Journal,* January 28, 1970; Gentry file, LBNM)

GILLESPIE, JOSEPH (1809–85)

A special legal and political friend of AL whose acquaintance dated from the Black Hawk War, Gillespie observed AL for more than thirty years and served with him in a variety of capacities. A protégé of Cyrus Edwards in Edwardsville, he attended Transylvania University at Edwards's urging and studied law with him before his admission to the Illinois bar in 1836. Gillespie served in the General Assembly in 1840–41 and 1846–58, practiced law in Madison County, and between 1861 and 1873 was judge of the Twenty-fourth Circuit. Gillespie and AL were associated professionally through their Supreme Court practice, and they were both involved in the promotion of the Republican party in Illinois. His political pilgrimage from Whig to Republican, aside from his Know-Nothing interlude in the mid-1850s, was very similar to AL's. Gillespie was of particular service to AL in the senatorial campaign of 1858, and AL attested that their relationship was one of complete trust. (Frederic B. Crossley, *Courts and Lawyers of Illinois* [Chicago, 1916]; *HEI)*

GODBEY, RUSSELL (1800–88)

Godbey came to Menard County from Virginia in 1830 and shortly thereafter employed AL to resurvey his lands. Though an active supporter of the Democratic party, during the Civil War he was strongly in favor of the maintenance of the Union. *(IAMM)*

GOODPASTURE, ABRAHAM H. (1812–85)

A native of Tennessee and a minister for a half century, Goodpasture was licensed to preach in 1835. Moving to Illinois sometime before 1850, he became a member of the Sangamon Presbytery and pastor at Concord Cumberland Presbyterian Church near Petersburg in Menard County. (letters from Mrs. Burl E. [Genevieve] Goodpasture, August 8 and 15, 1992)

GOODRICH, GRANT (1811–89)

Born and raised in New York State, Goodrich studied law there and in 1834 moved to Chicago, where he was associated with AL in practice before the federal courts. *(Chicago Tribune,* March 16, 1889; *HEI; BEI)*

GOURLEY, JAMES (CA. 1810–76)

A native of Pennsylvania and a boot- and shoemaker who had known AL from the 1830s, Gourley was for many years a near neighbor of the Lincolns in Springfield, living one block east of them. Gourley served as deputy sheriff of Sangamon County and was also a deputy U.S. marshal. *(Federal Census, Sangamon County,* 1850, 1860; *HSC;* A. S. Edwards to Jesse Weik, June 15, 1915, Weik Papers, ISHL; *Spgfld 55–56)*

GRAHAM, WILLIAM MENTOR (1800–1886)

Graham was born in Kentucky but moved to Illinois in 1826, where he lived and taught school near New Salem. He attracted attention by claiming after AL's death that AL had been one of his pupils. This was disputed by some former residents and appears doubtful, though there is testimony that he helped AL in studying grammar and surveying. During the Civil War, Graham, a converted Democrat, was a sturdy supporter of the Union cause. *(ALE)*

GREENE, JOHNSON GAINES (1820–85)

Greene, a younger brother of Lynn McNulty ("Nult") Greene and William Graham ("Bill") Greene, was one year old when his family migrated to Illinois from Tennessee. An adolescent during AL's stay at New Salem, he later became a successful Menard County farmer and livestock dealer. *(CG; IAMM;* Onstot)

GREENE, LYNN MCNULTY (1814–82)

The brother of William Graham and Johnson Gaines Greene, "Nult" Greene attended Illinois College at Jacksonville in the 1830s. In 1840 he married Nancy

Owens Abell, the daughter of Bennett and Elizabeth Abell and the niece of Mary Owens Vineyard. (*CG;* Walsh; Onstot)

GREENE, WILLIAM GRAHAM (1812–94)

Greene's family moved from Tennessee to what became Menard County, Illinois, when he was nine. In 1831 he was AL's helper in Denton Offutt's store at New Salem, marking the beginning of a lifelong friendship. "Bill" Greene was a member of the volunteer militia that chose AL as their captain for the Black Hawk War. He attended Illinois College at Jacksonville from 1833 to 1836. After college Greene left Illinois to teach briefly in Kentucky and Tennessee and to pursue business ventures in Mississippi and Memphis. Returning to Illinois in 1845, he engaged in farming, stock dealing, banking, and railroad development, earning the reputation for sharp business practices and becoming one of the wealthiest men in the area. During his presidency, AL appointed Greene collector of internal revenue in his district. WHH suspected Greene of exaggerating his knowledge of AL. *(CG; BEI; HMMC)*

GRIGSBY, NATHANIEL (1811–90)

Grigsby's family moved from Kentucky to Spencer County, Indiana, just before the Lincolns and were their close neighbors. AL and Nathaniel Grigsby grew up and went to school together, and Grigsby's brother Aaron married AL's sister Sarah. Grigsby remained in touch with AL long after the latter left Indiana. An early Republican and a AL supporter in 1860, Grigsby enlisted with four of his sons in the Tenth Indiana Cavalry in 1863. (Grigsby biography, Grigsby Vertical File, and Family Tree Information, Grigsby's Declaration for Original Invalid Pension, LBNM; Elizabeth N. Nicholson, ed., *Memorabilia: The Grigsby Family, 1779–1979* [Chestnut Hill, Mass., 1979])

GRIMES, JAMES WILSON (1816–72)

One of Iowa's premier politicians for more than thirty years, Grimes served in the territorial and state legislatures of Iowa and was its governor from 1854 to 1858. He also served in the U.S. Senate for ten years (1859–69) and was one of the seven Republican senators who voted "not guilty" at the impeachment trial of President Andrew Johnson in 1868. *(DAB; BDAC)*

GRIMSHAW, JACKSON (1820–75)

A Quincy attorney, Grimshaw was a delegate to the Republican convention in Bloomington in 1856. An unsuccessful candidate for Congress in 1856 and 1858, he was appointed in 1865 by AL as collector of internal revenue for the Quincy District. *(HEI)*

HALL, JAMES (1802–89)

Hall, a physician born and educated in New England, later relocated to Baltimore and became deeply involved in the colonization of blacks to Africa. Before the Civil

War he was an agent of the Maryland State Colonization Society and a director of the American Colonization Society. (*Baltimore Sun,* September 4, 1889)

HALL, JOHN JOHNSTON (1829–1909)

Hall was the son of Matilda Johnston and Squire Hall, his mother being AL's step-sister. After the death of Thomas Lincoln in 1851, Hall purchased the Lincoln property, where he and his family resided with Lincoln's widow. (Coleman; *PBRCC*)

HANKS, DENNIS F. (1799–1893)

A first cousin of AL's mother (see the appendix) and ten years AL's senior, Hanks was a close friend during AL's boyhood in Kentucky and Indiana. When AL's mother and Hanks's foster parents died of "milk sickness" in 1818, he joined the Lincoln household in Spencer County, Indiana, and lived there until his marriage to Sarah Elizabeth Johnston, daughter of Thomas Lincoln's second wife, in 1821. Hanks continued to live in the Lincoln neighborhood until the two families re-moved to Illinois in 1830. His daughter Harriet lived with AL's family in Spring-field in the 1840s to better her education. After the 1864 draft riot at Charleston, Illinois, Hanks was sent to Washington, D.C., on behalf of some of the arrested rioters. Though sixty-six when WHH began to question him, and suspected of exaggerating his role in AL's life, Hanks had closer sustained personal contact with AL during his formative years than any other informant. *(HEI; ALE)*

HANKS, JOHN (1802–89)

Hanks was born in Nelson County, Kentucky, and was a first cousin of AL's mother, Nancy Hanks (see the appendix). He lived for four years with the Lincoln family in the 1820s in Spencer County, Indiana, where he worked with AL on Thomas Lincoln's farm. Hanks later moved to Macon County, Illinois, and partly on his advice Thomas Lincoln moved there with his family in March 1830. Hanks was involved with AL in Denton Offutt's flatboat expedition to New Orleans in 1831, and the next year he was in the Black Hawk War. Thereafter, he farmed in Macon County, mined in California for three years after 1850, and, though almost sixty at the outbreak of the Civil War, enlisted in the Twenty-first Illinois Regiment. His identification in 1860 of some rails split by AL led to the latter's being called "the railsplitter" in the presidential campaign. WHH believed that AL had a high re-gard for this member of his family. *(Decatur Republican,* July 2, 1889; *ALE)*

HANNA, WILLIAM H. (1823–70)

Born in Indiana and trained as a lawyer there, Hanna came to Illinois in 1849 and established a law practice in Bloomington, where he had frequent contact with AL. ("Wm. H. Hanna Bulletin, March 25, 1906," Dwight E. Frink Collection, McLean County Historical Society, Bloomington, Ill.)

HARDING, JACOB (1802–83)

A native of Virginia, Harding lived in Tennessee for several years before moving to Paris, Illinois, in about 1837. There he established the *Prairie Beacon* in 1848 and served as editor until shortly before 1861. (letter from Terence A. Tanner, January 6, 1992; inventory of Jacob Harding Papers, ISHL)

HARRIOTT, JAMES (1810–69)

A New Jersey native, Harriott served in the Illinois House of Representatives from 1844 to 1846. After moving to Pekin, he was elected judge of the Twenty-first Judicial Circuit and presided at the 1858 murder trial of William "Duff" Armstrong. (letters from Loree Bergerhouse, July 11 and August 30, 1993)

HARRIS, JOHN THOMAS (1823–99)

An attorney in Harrisonburg, Virginia, Harris held county offices and served as a Democratic presidential elector in 1856 and a member of Congress in 1859–61 and 1871–81. *(BDAC)*

HARRISON, GEORGE M. (1813–73)

Born in Rockingham County, Virginia, Harrison came to Sangamon County with his parents in 1822. During the Black Hawk War he served with AL in a spy company and made the journey home to Sangamon County with him. Harrison later studied medicine in Springfield under Dr. Jacob M. Early and graduated in April 1840 from Rush Medical College in Pennsylvania, the second graduate of a medical college from Sangamon County. *(HSC;* Power; *ISJ,* September 3, 1873)

HART, CHARLES HENRY (1847–1918)

A young Philadelphia law student, Hart was an AL enthusiast and WHH correspondent whose parents had visited AL in the White House. *(DAB)*

HAY, JOHN MILTON (1838–1905)

AL's secretary and biographer, Hay was raised in Warsaw, Illinois, and studied at Brown University. In Springfield to read law with his uncle, Milton Hay, he renewed an earlier friendship with John G. Nicolay and first met AL. When Nicolay was chosen the president-elect's secretary, Hay was named his assistant. In the White House, Hay screened visitors, read mail, prepared a daily news summary, and acted as a messenger. He also kept a diary, now an important source on the workings of AL's administration. In March 1865 Hay was appointed secretary of legation in Paris, later serving in various foreign posts. In the early 1870s, with the blessing and cooperation of Robert Todd Lincoln, Hay and Nicolay began collaborating on a massive biography of AL. *(ALE; DAB)*

HAY, MILTON (1817–93)

Hay was a law student of John T. Stuart and AL in Springfield and later practiced with Stephen T. Logan, who became his father-in-law. AL secretary and biographer John Hay was his nephew. *(HEI)*

HAYCRAFT, PRESLEY NEVIL (1797–1884)

The brother of the Kentucky informant and local historian Samuel Haycraft, Presley Nevil Haycraft knew AL's parents as a child. (*The Jess M. Thompson Pike County History* [Pittsfield, Ill., 1951])

HAYCRAFT, SAMUEL (1795–1878)

A native of Hardin County and Elizabethtown, Kentucky, Haycraft began his public career at the age of fourteen in the office of the county and circuit clerk. In 1816 he was appointed clerk of the circuit and county courts and held this office until 1851. Thereafter he alternated between the practice of law and the holding of county and state offices. As a youth he had known Thomas Lincoln in Hardin County, and on the strength of this connection and his standing as a local historian, Haycraft corresponded with AL about his family in 1860. Though Kentucky was bitterly divided during the Civil War, Haycraft remained a loyal supporter of the Union. *(BEK)*

HELM, EMILIE TODD (1836–1930)

Emilie Helm, a half-sister of MTL, was the daughter of Robert S. Todd and his second wife, Elizabeth Humphreys. She married Ben Hardin Helm, who became acquainted with AL and was later a Confederate general. She remained a Southern sympathizer, though she visited her half-sister in the White House after her husband's death at Chickamauga in 1863. (R. Gerald McMurtry, *Ben Hardin Helm* [Chicago, 1943]; Jean H. Baker, *Mary Todd Lincoln* [New York, 1987])

HELM, JOHN B. (1797–1872)

Helm was born in Kentucky, where he studied law and operated a store in Elizabethtown. Later he practiced law and held appointive offices, being politically a states' rights Democrat. In 1852 he moved to Hannibal, Missouri, where he became interested in real estate development, practiced law, and was elected judge of the Court of Common Pleas. (*History of Marion County, Missouri* [Belmont, Calif., 1979])

HERNDON, ANNA MILES (1836–93)

Anna Miles was the daughter of G. U. Miles, a Menard County pioneer and early political associate of AL. The second wife of WHH, she was the mother of two of his children. (*ISJ,* January 8, 1893)

HERNDON, ARCHER GRAY (1795–1867)

The father of WHH, Archer Herndon was an early settler in Sangamon County, arriving in 1821 and afterward becoming a successful merchant and tavernkeeper in Springfield. He served in the state senate 1834–42 and was, with AL, one of the famous "Long Nine" from Sangamon County. (*HEI;* Power)

HERNDON, ELLIOT B. (1820–95)

Brother to WHH and son of Archer Herndon, Elliot Herndon was a Democrat and lawyer who served as Springfield city attorney, Sangamon County attorney, and U.S. district attorney under President Buchanan. He also edited the *Illinois State Democrat* in Springfield during the Buchanan administration. (*HSC*; Power)

HERNDON, JAMES A. (1813–?)

A cousin of WHH, James Herndon knew AL in New Salem, where he kept store briefly in 1832 with his brother J. Rowan Herndon. James Herndon later moved to Columbus in Adams County and still later to Quincy, working as a painter, butcher, and harnessmaker. (Reep, 117; *Federal Census, Adams County,* 1850, 1860; *Quincy;* letter from Wayne Temple, September 6, 1994)

HERNDON, JOHN ROWAN (CA. 1806–?)

"Row" Herndon was a brother of James A. Herndon and a cousin of WHH. With his brother he operated a general store in New Salem in 1832 before selling his interest to AL. Herndon left New Salem in 1833 following the death of his first wife, who was killed by a gun he accidentally discharged. He moved first to Island Grove in Sangamon County; by 1840 he was living in Adams County, Illinois, at Columbus, where he was a butcher, operated a small farm, and apparently also served as a constable. (Benjamin P. Thomas, *Lincoln's New Salem* [Springfield, Ill., 1934]; *Federal Census, Adams County,* 1840, 1850, 1860; *Quincy;* letter from Wayne Temple, September 6, 1994)

HERNDON, REBECCA DAY JOHNSON (1790–1875)

A native of Virginia, the mother of WHH was a young widow when she married Archer Herndon in Kentucky in 1816. Four years later she accompanied him with their growing family to Illinois. (Power; burial record card, Oak Ridge Cemetery, Springfield, Ill.)

HEWITT, VIRGIL (1840–98)

A Confederate veteran, Hewitt was elected county clerk of Hardin County, Kentucky, in 1866. (H. A. Sommers, *History of Elizabethtown, 1869–1921* [Owensboro, Ky., 1981])

HICKOX, VIRGIL (1806–81)

Longtime chairman of the Illinois Democratic Central Committee, Hickox was a personal and political friend of Stephen A. Douglas. In 1851 he and a group of businessmen undertook the construction of a railroad from Alton to Springfield, later promoting its Chicago extension. (Power; Wallace)

HILL, JOHN (1839–98)

Hill was born in New Salem, the son of Parthena Nance and Samuel Hill, the leading New Salem merchant and a close friend of AL. As editor of a Democratic Petersburg newspaper, John Hill vigorously supported Douglas in the 1858 senatorial and the 1860 presidential campaigns. During the Civil War he was the commissioner from the Illinois state government to Illinois regiments. Later he was elected to the General Assembly, and in 1872 he moved to Georgia. (letter from Rosella H. Rogers, February 28, 1991; *NMB;* Onstot)

HILL, PARTHENA NANCE (1816–98)

Parthena Nance came to Illinois with her parents from Green County, Kentucky, in 1832 and settled near New Salem. In 1835 she married Samuel Hill, a New Salem storekeeper and friend of AL. The Hills moved from the dying New Salem in 1839 to Petersburg, where Samuel died in 1857. (*NMB;* Family Notes by Parthena Nance Hill, October 1895, Nance Collaterals Papers, Lincoln Library, Springfield, Ill.)

HOAGLAND, H. H. (1839–1905)

Hoagland was born in Morgan County and moved to Petersburg in 1857. He attended Jubilee and Lombard Colleges. In 1871 he was admitted to the Illinois bar and practiced law until 1882, when he was elected county judge. (*Petersburg Observer,* May 20, 1905)

HOHIMER, HENRY (1805–89)

Hohimer's family lived in the New Salem area, and his brother served under AL in the Black Hawk War. (letters from Margaret Hohimer, April 30 and May 15, 1991)

HOLLAND, JOSIAH GILBERT (1819–81)

Holland practiced medicine briefly and taught school but finally settled on literary pursuits. From 1850 to 1866 he was associated with the *Springfield* (Mass.) *Republican.* In 1869 Holland helped to establish *Scribner's Monthly* (later renamed *Century Magazine*), which he edited until his death. His admiring biography of AL, the first to be substantially researched, was published in 1866. *(DAB)*

HOUGHLAND, JOHN S. (CA. 1825–72)

Houghland was a physician who practiced in Spencer County, Indiana, and the surrounding counties. (*Rockport [Ind.] Democrat,* October 12, 1872)

HOWARD, JACOB MERRITT (1805–71)

A leading Michigan politician for more than three decades, Howard was one of the prime movers in organizing the Republican party. He was elected to the U.S. Senate in 1862, and as a Radical leader he played a prime role in drafting the Thirteenth Amendment and other significant pieces of Reconstruction legislation. *(DAB)*

ILES, ELIJAH (1796–1883)

Iles was one of Springfield's earliest pioneers and the proprietor of its first store in 1821. A shrewd and highly successful businessman, he profited from extensive early land acquisitions. He served in both the Winnebago War of 1827 and the Black Hawk War of 1832. (Power; *HEI*)

IRWIN, BENJAMIN F. (1822–1902)

Irwin, a Republican and minor public official living at Pleasant Plains, helped WHH identify and locate Lincoln-era informants in Sangamon and Menard Counties. (Power; *Federal Census, Sangamon County,* 1850, 1870; Walsh; letter from Mark D. Irwin, July 15, 1992)

JAYNE, WILLIAM (1826–1916)

Jayne was the son of Springfield's first physician, Gershom Jayne, and the younger brother of Mary Todd's close friend Julia Jayne. He was born in Springfield, educated at Illinois College, then received his medical degree from the Medical College of the University of Missouri in 1849. He returned to Springfield to practice, serving as AL's family physician. A Free-Soil Whig who turned Republican, Jayne was elected mayor of Springfield in 1859 and to the Illinois Senate a year later. AL appointed Jayne to be the first governor of Dakota Territory in 1861, and Jayne later won a contested election to represent Dakota in Congress as its territorial delegate. He returned to his Springfield medical practice in 1864. (Power; *BDATG*)

JENKINS, JOHN T. (1818–83)

A Maryland native, Jenkins served several terms as county clerk of Logan County, Illinois, between 1850 and 1883. (*History of Logan County, Illinois* [Chicago, 1886]; Logan County Cemetery inscriptions)

JOHNSON, [?]

This unidentified informant from "Egypt" was apparently a delegate from southern Illinois to the Illinois Republican state convention in 1860. Neither of the Johnsons listed at the convention, from Clark and Henry Counties, would appear to be this Johnson. (*ISJ,* May 12, 1860)

JOHNSON, S. T. (CA. 1831–?)

A resident of Spencer County, Indiana, in 1865.

JOHNSTON, THOMAS LINCOLN DAVIS (1837–?)

A son of AL's stepbrother John D. Johnston and a grandson of Sarah Bush Lincoln, Johnston was frequently in trouble with the law. In 1856 and 1857 AL assisted him when he was charged with petty larceny. Johnston's legal difficulties continued after the Civil War. (Coleman)

JONAS, ANNIE E. (1842–1926)

Jonas was originally from Quincy, Illinois, where her father, Abraham Jonas, was AL's friend. She later married an Episcopal clergyman and moved to Minneapolis. (City of Minneapolis, Division of Public Health—Vital Statistics, death certificate; *Minneapolis Journal,* February 20, 1896)

JONES, JOHN A. (1815–99)

"Fiddler" Jones was the brother of Hannah Armstrong. He served with AL in the Black Hawk War, later moving to Madison County, Iowa. (Walsh; letter from Lorraine Kile, August 11, 1994)

JUDD, NORMAN B. (1815–78)

A close political associate of AL, Judd used his position on the Republican National Committee to bring to Chicago the convention that nominated AL for president in 1860. He traveled to Washington, D.C., with AL in February 1861 and was appointed minister to Prussia, where he served for four years. He later served two terms in Congress. *(ALE; DAB)*

KELLY, JOSEPH J. (1826–1904)

A lawyer in DeWitt County, Illinois, Kelly served from 1860 to 1868 as clerk of the DeWitt County Circuit Court. (*History of DeWitt County, Illinois* [Chicago, 1910]; pension files, National Archives, Washington, D.C.)

KERCHEVAL, SAMUEL EDWARD (1847–1910)

Kercheval was a longtime politician in Spencer County, Indiana. (*American Biographical History of Eminent and Self-Made Men of the State of Indiana* [Cincinnati, 1880]; *Rockport [Ind.] Journal,* December 23, 1910)

KEYES, JAMES W. (CA. 1806–88)

Keyes, who came to Illinois from Virginia, was a tailor in Springfield in 1850 and later a Sangamon County farmer. (*Federal Census, Sangamon County,* 1850, 1860, 1870; *ISJ,* May 20, 1888)

KING, FRANKLIN T.

A merchant and physician in Springfield and later McLean, Illinois, King was a brother of Turner R. King, another WHH informant. (Bailey and Hair, comps., *A Gazetteer of McLean County* [Chicago, 1866])

KING, TURNER R. (1812–88)

Born in Sutton, Massachusetts, King came to Springfield in 1840. At Congressman Lincoln's urging, King was appointed register of the Springfield Land Office by President Zachary Taylor, and in 1862 AL appointed him U.S. collector for the Eighth Congressional District. (Power; letter from Joy Craig, October 23, 1993)

KIRK, ANDREW ST. CLAIR (1822–99)

Kirk was a Kentuckian who was raised in Sangamon County, Illinois, and spent most of his life farming near Athens in Menard County. (Power; *IAMM; Illinois State Register,* January 15, 1899)

KLEIN, JOHN

A John Kline served in Captain Levi Goodan's company of General Samuel Whiteside's brigade of mounted volunteers during the Black Hawk War, enlisting at Springfield. (Whitney)

KYLE, JOHN GLOVER (1840–87)

Kyle, who was educated at Centre College, Transylvania University, and the Louisville Law School, practiced in Harrodsburg, Kentucky. (Perrin; *BEK; Cemetery Records, Mercer County, Kentucky, 1969–89* [Harrodsburg, Ky., 1989])

LAMAR, JOHN WESLEY (1822–1903)

Born in Spencer County, Indiana, Lamar received his education in the same log schoolhouse AL once attended. A farmer and political officeholder, he was a member of the Fifty-third Indiana Volunteer Infantry during the Civil War. (letter from Jean Stevens Wiggin, March 25, 1992)

LAMON, WARD HILL (1828–93)

A Danville attorney and an associate of AL on the Eighth Circuit, Lamon was called by AL "my particular friend." He accompanied the president-elect to Washington, D.C., in 1861 and was appointed U.S. marshal for the District of Columbia. Though much criticized for his conduct, he was a trusted member of AL's inner circle. In 1872, together with Chauncey F. Black, Lamon published a controversial biography of AL based on research material collected by and purchased from WHH. *(ALE; DAB)*

LAWRENCE, RICHARD M. (1827–?)

Of Tennessee birth and a Democrat, Lawrence conducted a general merchandise business in Williamsville, Illinois, in Sangamon County. He also served as postmaster of that town. *(HSC)*

LIGHTFOOT, JOHN A. (1814–?)

Lightfoot was born in Kentucky and moved with his parents to Sangamon County in 1830. After the Civil War he was employed in the U.S. Custom House in New Orleans. (Power)

LINCOLN, MARY TODD (1818–82)

Born in Lexington, Kentucky, of an aristocratic family and well educated, Mary Todd left home in 1839 to live in Springfield with her sister Elizabeth (Mrs. Nin-

ian W. Edwards). After a troubled engagement that was interrupted for a year and
a half, she married AL on November 4, 1842. Though a devoted wife and mother, MTL had a volatile personality and a hot temper. Many of AL's friends, including
WHH, considered AL's domestic life unhappy, but WHH also insisted that he
sympathized with MTL because, as he told his collaborator, the "domestic hell of
Lincoln's life is not all on one side." MTL's undisguised ambition for her husband
was credited by some of these same friends as an important ingredient in his political success. During AL's presidency, MTL gave special attention to White House
social affairs but was widely resented for her extravagance, her Southern back-
ground, and for meddling in affairs of state. Divided loyalties within her own family
and particularly the death of her son Willie contributed to her emotional insta-
bility, which, following AL's assassination, became pronounced. In 1875 she was
judged incompetent and briefly committed to a sanitarium in Batavia, Illinois. She
died in Springfield at the home of her sister Elizabeth. (*DAB;* WHH to JWW,
January 9, 1886, in Hertz)

LINCOLN, ROBERT TODD (1843–1926)

The eldest child of AL and MTL, Robert Lincoln graduated from Harvard in 1864,
studied law briefly, and then served on the staff of General Ulysses S. Grant. In
1867 he was admitted to the bar in Illinois, and in 1868 he married Mary Harlan, the daughter of U.S. Senator James Harlan from Iowa. Robert disliked and
distrusted WHH and disapproved of his biographical project, particularly WHH's
probing of AL's rude beginnings and his private life. Secretary of war under Presidents Garfield and Arthur and minister to England under Benjamin Harrison,
he became wealthy in later life as president and then chairman of the board of the
Pullman Company. *(DAB)*

LINCOLN, SARAH BUSH JOHNSTON (1788–1869)

Sarah Bush had three children by her first husband, Daniel Johnston: Sarah Elizabeth, who married Dennis Hanks; Matilda, who married Squire Hall and later
Reuben Moore; and John Davis Johnston. After the death of AL's mother, Thomas Lincoln returned to Kentucky in 1819 and proposed to the widowed Sarah
Johnston. After paying her debts, he married her and brought her to Indiana, where
she reformed the Lincoln household and proved a kind and affectionate stepmother
to the Lincoln children. AL seems to have been genuinely attached to her from
the beginning and was more solicitous for her welfare than for that of his father.
After Thomas Lincoln's death, Sarah Bush Lincoln lived with relatives, finally residing at the home of her daughter Matilda Moore in Coles County, where AL
paid his last visit to her in 1861. *(ALE)*

LINDER, USHER F. (1809–76)

Born in Kentucky, ten miles from the birthplace of AL, Linder came to Illinois in
1835. A lawyer, he served in the General Assembly with AL, as attorney general,

and as a delegate to the Democratic National Convention in 1860. He wrote a colorful memoir, *Reminiscences of the Early Bench and Bar of Illinois,* which was published after his death. *(HEI)*

LITTLEFIELD, JOHN HARRISON (1835–1902)

Littlefield entered the Lincoln-Herndon law office in 1858 as a student and campaigned for his mentor in 1860. In 1862 he was appointed to a clerkship in the Treasury Department in Washington, D.C. After the war his painting of AL's deathbed scene and his later Lincoln portrait were widely circulated. (Daniel Trowbridge Mallett, comp., *Mallett's Index of Artists* [New York, 1948]; Harold Holzer, et al., *The Lincoln Image* [New York, 1984]; letter from Brian A. Williams, April 14, 1992)

LITTLER, DAVID T. (1836–1902)

Littler studied law in Lincoln, Illinois, and was admitted to the bar in Logan County, on the Eighth Judicial Circuit. Later he moved to Springfield and became a law partner of Milton Hay. *(HEI)*

LLOYD, BUNBRY B. (1816–76)

A prominent dentist in Springfield, Lloyd was born in Kentucky, removing to the Illinois capital in 1847 and residing there until shortly before his death. *(ISJ,* July 18, 1876; *Spgfld 55–56)*

LOGAN, STEPHEN TRIGG (1800–1880)

Logan was educated in Kentucky and was not yet twenty-one when he was admitted to the practice of law there. Before moving to Springfield in 1832 he was a deputy circuit clerk and prosecuting attorney. In Illinois his talents were quickly recognized; he was elected circuit judge in 1835 and again in 1839 and also served four terms in the Illinois House. He was best known as a lawyer, however, enjoying an extensive trial and appellate practice and being an acknowledged leader of the Springfield bar. His law partnership with AL lasted from 1841 to 1844 and was apparently dissolved on friendly terms. Logan served as a delegate to the 1860 Republican convention that nominated AL; a year later he was a member of the Washington Peace Convention that met in an attempt to avoid the war. WHH had a poor opinion of Logan, who was apparently quite wary of WHH as a biographer of AL and told him surprisingly little. *(ALE; DAB)*

LONG, JAMES G. (1824–?)

A son of Kentucky immigrants to Illinois, Long served as sheriff of Menard County from 1848 to 1852 and held a clerkship in the Pension Office in Washington, D.C., when he responded to WHH's queries about government records. (Power)

LORD, A. F.

Lord was a citizen of Springfield and a client of AL and Herndon in 1859 or 1860.

MATHENY, JAMES H. (1818–90)

Matheny grew up in Springfield, where his father held the important position of county clerk. At the age of fifteen he worked as a clerk in the Post Office and the office of the recorder, later serving as a court clerk. Matheny was one of the young men of the town who attached themselves to AL when he first came to Springfield and was a groomsman at AL's wedding in 1842. Like AL, he was an ardent Whig and an enthusiastic admirer of Henry Clay, even leading an expedition to Kentucky in 1840 to hear the great man speak. Admitted to the Illinois bar as a young man, Matheny was active in the courts of Sangamon and adjoining counties. Douglas charged in the 1858 debates that Matheny had acknowledged in a speech that AL and Trumbull conspired to "abolitionize" Illinois Whigs and Democrats, a charge that AL denied. In 1872 Matheny embarrassed WHH by publicly recanting, under pressure, some things he had once told WHH about AL's early religious beliefs. In 1873 he was elected county judge. (Power; *HSC; ALE;* Donald)

MATHER, THOMAS SCOTT (1829–90)

Born in Connecticut, Mather served as adjutant general of Illinois from 1858 to 1861. During the Civil War he served as colonel of the Second Illinois Light Artillery, as chief of staff to General John A. McClernand, and as acting assistant inspector general of the Department of the Susquehanna. In 1865 he was breveted brigadier general. (Roger D. Hunt and Jack R. Brown, *Brevet Brigadier Generals in Blue* [Gaithersburg, Md., 1990])

MCDONALD, JOSEPH EWING (1819–91)

McDonald was a Democratic Indiana lawyer who occasionally practiced along with AL and other Eighth Circuit attorneys at Danville, Illinois. He also served as attorney general of Indiana and in the U.S. House and Senate. *(DAB)*

MCHENRY, HENRY (1802–81)

McHenry came to the area of New Salem from Kentucky between 1825 and 1830 and married the sister of Jack Armstrong. He was a resident of Clary's Grove when AL first came to New Salem and may have been one of the Clary's Grove boys. He moved to Cass County and later to Petersburg, where he eventually became the owner of a hotel. AL appointed him provost marshal during the Civil War, in which role he earned a reputation for fearlessness in the unenviable job of apprehending army deserters in an area with strong Southern sympathies. (Power; *HMMC; IAMM; CG;* Reep)

MCNAMAR, JOHN (1801–79)

John McNamar, using the alias McNeil, was one of the first merchants at New Salem, engaging in a partnership with Samuel Hill in 1830. He sold out in 1832 to return to New York with the intention of bringing his parents to Illinois. McNamar and Ann Rutledge were engaged to be married, but in part because of his long delay in returning, Rutledge became engaged to AL. While living with her parents on a farm owned by McNamar, Ann Rutledge died shortly before his return from the East in 1835. McNamar was married by 1840 and lived in the area of New Salem for the rest of his life. (*Federal Census, Menard County,* 1840, 1850, 1860; *IAMM; HMMC;* Walsh)

MCNEELY, ROBERT T. (1805–86)

McNeely lived in New Salem and then in rural Morgan and Menard Counties before moving to Petersburg to engage in the mercantile business. (*HMMC;* Miller; tombstone at Rose Hill Cemetery, Petersburg, Ill.)

MCNEELY, THOMPSON WARE (1835–1921)

A Petersburg lawyer, Menard County politician, and congressman, McNeely questioned some older Menard County residents, including his father, Robert T. McNeely, on WHH's behalf. *(BDAC)*

MCPHERSON, EDWARD (1830–95)

A Pennsylvania newspaper editor, McPherson served two terms in Congress after 1859 and then was clerk of the U.S. House of Representatives until 1875. *(BDAC)*

MELVIN, SAMUEL H. (1829–98)

At various times a druggist, banker, and railroad promoter in Springfield, Melvin also seems to have been involved in the 1873 controversy between WHH and Reverend James Reed over AL's religion. (*USBD* [Illinois]; *ISJ,* February 12, 1898)

MILES, GEORGE URIAH (1796–1882)

Originally from Maryland, G. U. Miles came to Illinois Territory in 1816 and resided in several places before finally settling in Sangamon County in 1836. His daughter Anna became the second wife of WHH in 1862. Miles served as an agent for WHH in Menard County during 1865 and 1866, interviewing residents who had known AL and reporting his findings to WHH. (Miller; *HMMC; IAMM*)

MILES, JAMES (1822–1913)

Miles was born in White County, Illinois, the son of George Uriah and Jane Miles. In 1840 he settled in Menard County where he engaged in farming and became friends with AL. Miles was a brother-in-law of WHH and a lifelong Democrat. (*Petersburg Democrat,* February 15, 1913; Miller; tombstone at Oakland Cemetery, Petersburg, Ill.)

MILES, JOHN

Possibly a relative of WHH's second wife, John Miles interviewed John Hanks for WHH. He was quartermaster of the Thirty-fifth Illinois Infantry during the Civil War. (*History of Macon County from Its Organization to 1876* [Springfield, Ill., 1876])

MILLER, WILLIAM

A William Miller of Sangamon County commanded a battallion of the Fourth Regiment of the Third Brigade of Mounted Volunteers during the Black Hawk War. (Whitney)

MINER, ORLIN H. (1825–79)

Shortly after moving to Illinois in the mid-1850s, Miner was appointed chief clerk in the state auditor's office by Auditor Jesse Dubois. He held this position until 1864, when he was elected to succeed Dubois. *(HEI; HSC)*

MINIER, GEORGE W. (1813–1902)

A minister in the Christian Church, Minier served churches in and around the Eighth Judicial Circuit in central Illinois. (*Portrait and Biographical Record of Tazewell and Mason Counties* [Chicago, 1894]; *Tazewell County, Illinois Cemeteries,* (Pekin, Ill., 1982)

MONFORT, JOSEPH G. (1810–1906)

After teaching in Ohio and attending Miami University, Monfort became a Presbyterian minister, serving in Ohio and Indiana. He also edited the *Cincinnati Herald and Presbyter* for nearly a half century. (*History of Cincinnati and Hamilton County, Ohio* [Cincinnati, 1894]; *Who Was Who in America*)

MOORE, CLIFTON H. (1817–86)

A DeWitt County lawyer, Moore was associated with AL on the Eighth Judicial Circuit and was a partner of Judge David Davis in real estate transactions. (John M. Palmer, *The Bench and Bar of Illinois* [Chicago, 1899]; *HEI*)

MOORE, ISAAC S. (1831–87)

One of the foremost lawyers of his time in southern Indiana, Moore went on to serve as a judge in Boonville, where he lived for the last twenty-five years of his life. (*Dale [Ind.] Reporter,* May 27, 1887; letter from Jean Stevens Wiggin, March 25, 1992)

MOORE, MATILDA JOHNSTON HALL (1809–78)

Matilda Johnston was AL's stepsister and nearly his age. They lived in the same family circle from 1819 until her marriage to Squire Hall, a half-brother of Dennis Hanks, in 1826. After her husband's death she married Reuben Moore. She was living with her mother, Sarah Bush Lincoln, in Coles County, Illinois, at the time of AL's last visit in 1861. (Coleman; *HCC*)

MOSELY, ROBERT (1815–86)

Mosely moved to Illinois from Kentucky in 1838. He maintained a mercantile business in Coles and Edgar Counties and was a Republican member of the Illinois House of Representatives from 1858 to 1860. (*History of Edgar County, Illi-*

nois [Chicago, 1879]; Philip L. Shutt, comp., *Edgar County, Illinois, Deaths and Some Burials* [Paris, Ill., 1970])

MURPHY, LIZZIE

No information was found on this informant.

NEEDHAM, TIM (1842–1918)

Needham reversed the usual immigrant path and moved with his parents from his Illinois birthplace to Hardin County, Kentucky, at an early age. He studied law in Elizabethtown and Louisville, began his practice in Elizabethtown, and later pursued careers in banking and journalism. (Perrin; E. Polk Johnson, *History of Kentucky and Kentuckians* [Chicago, 1912])

NELSON, THOMAS HENRY (1824–96)

Nelson was born in Kentucky and moved to Rockville, Indiana, where he commenced the study of law. First meeting AL in 1849, he relocated to Terre Haute in 1850 and established a successful law practice that sometimes brought him into contact with AL in eastern Illinois. As president, AL appointed Nelson minister to Chile. *(DAB)*

NICOLAY, JOHN G. (1832–1901)

Bavarian-born Nicolay left a Pittsfield, Illinois, newspaper in 1856 to work in Springfield in the office of the secretary of state. There he met AL and was appointed his private secretary after AL received the presidential nomination. After the war Nicolay served as consul in Paris and as marshal of the U.S. Supreme Court. He collaborated with John Hay on a ten-volume biography of AL. *(DAB; ALE)*

OGLESBY, RICHARD JAMES (1825–99)

Oglesby practiced law in Sullivan, Illinois, and went to the Illinois Senate as a Republican in 1860, resigning at the outbreak of the Civil War, from which he returned a wounded hero. In 1864 he was elected to his first term as governor of Illinois, during which Illinois ratified the Thirteenth and Fourteenth Amendments and repealed its "Black Laws." Oglesby was elected governor twice more and also served in the U.S. Senate. *(DAB; ALE)*

ORENDORFF, ALFRED (1845–1909)

An Illinois native, Orendorff served in the last year of the Civil War and in 1867 joined the law firm of Herndon and Zane. He continued in the firm after Zane and Herndon left. (*JISHS* 2–3 [1909]; *TISHS* [1910])

OSKINS, JOHN (1820–70)

Oskins lived in Spencer County, Indiana, when AL did, and later in Perry County. Though younger than AL, Oskins professed to have attended school with him. (Oskins file, LBNM)

PALMER, JOHN MCAULEY (1817–1900)

Originally a Douglas Democrat, Palmer broke with his party over the Kansas issue and became a Republican in 1856, presiding at the party's founding convention that year in Bloomington. He served in the Union army and later was an Illinois governor and U.S. senator. (Howard)

PANTIER, DAVID M. (1808–89)

Born in Ohio, Pantier moved with his family to Shawneetown, Illinois, in 1815 and then to what is now Menard County in 1826. He served in the Black Hawk War as a private in AL's company. *(HMMC)*

PARKS, SAMUEL C. (1812–1917)

Parks was born in Vermont and educated in Indiana. In the spring of 1840 he moved to Springfield, where he read law and became a friend of AL. After moving again to Lincoln, Illinois, he was associated with AL in many Logan County cases on the Eighth Judicial Circuit. Parks worked for AL's nomination at the Chicago convention in 1860, and in 1863 AL appointed him an associate justice of the supreme court of Idaho Territory. He is best remembered for his copy of Howells's campaign biography, in which AL marked certain errors in the margin. (Lawrence B. Stringer, *History of Logan County, Ill.* [Chicago, 1911]; William Dean Howells, *Life of Abraham Lincoln* [1860; rpt., Bloomington, Ind., 1960])

PHILLIPS, WENDELL (1811–84)

Phillips joined the Massachusetts Anti-Slavery Society in 1837 and became a leading advocate of abolition. During the Civil War he was often severely critical of AL's administration, though approving the Emancipation Proclamation. *(DAB)*

PIERCE, EDWARD L. (1829–97)

Pierce graduated from Brown University and Harvard Law School. He practiced briefly in Cincinnati in the office of Salmon P. Chase, whom he later served as secretary in Washington, D.C. He was a Massachusetts member of the Republican National Convention that nominated AL. In 1863, at Chase's request, AL appointed Pierce collector of internal revenue at Boston. After the Civil War Pierce was a political officeholder in Massachusetts and authored the official biography of Charles Sumner. *(DAB)*

PINKERTON, ALLAN (1819–84)

Pinkerton was a Chartist refugee from Scotland who began his American police work as a sheriff's deputy in Cook and Kane Counties, Illinois, and as the first detective in Chicago's newly organized police force. He established a private detective agency in 1850, one of the first of its kind in the country, the success of which brought it (and him) a national reputation. In addition to thwarting an early attempt on AL's life, Pinkerton directed important counterespionage activities for the Union army. *(DAB)*

PIRTLE, HENRY (1798–1880)

A prominent Kentucky lawyer and jurist, Pirtle was a partner of James Speed, who served in AL's cabinet, and whose brother, Joshua Fry Speed, was perhaps AL's closest friend. *(NCAB; BEK)*

PITCHER, JOHN (1794–1892)

After graduating from Yale and studying law, Pitcher traveled West, finally settling in southern Indiana, where he practiced law until after the Civil War. An itinerant lawyer, Pitcher practiced in Spencer County at the time AL lived there. (statement of Kate Pitcher Whitworth, n.d., HW)

PORTER, JASPER W. (1841–1921)

Porter was Champaign County circuit clerk from 1876 to 1888 and again from 1896 to 1912. (*Champaign News Gazette,* June 4, 1921; *History of Champaign County* [Philadelphia, 1878])

POWELL, ELIHU NEWPORT (1809–71)

Powell came from Ohio in 1836 to Peoria, where he practiced law and was involved in local politics. In 1856 he was elected judge of the Sixteenth Circuit to fill a vacancy, returning to private practice at the end of his term. (*Peoria Transcript,* July 17, 1871; *History of Peoria County* [Chicago, 1880])

RARDIN, JAMES K. (1851–1912)

A Coles County, Illinois, native who entered the newspaper business in Charleston in 1880, Rardin moved to Chicago in 1887 to edit a Democratic campaign sheet and later returned to Charleston to establish another Democratic paper. (*HEI/ Coles; PBRCC; Charleston Courier,* December 14, 1912; letter from Paul H. Verduin, September 21, 1994)

RAY, CHARLES HENRY (1821–70)

A New Yorker who moved west in 1843, Ray met AL in 1845 while editing a temperance paper in Springfield. After a stint editing the Democratic *Galena Jeffersonian,* Ray took a strong stand against the Kansas-Nebraska Act. In 1855 he purchased an interest in the *Chicago Tribune* and became its editor in chief. He was a founder of the Republican party in Illinois. *(NCAB; HEI; ALE)*

RICHARDSON, JOSEPH C. (1816–92)

Richardson grew up in the same neighborhood as AL in Spencer County, Indiana. Later in life he became active in Republican party politics. (*Evansville Journal,* August 6, 1892; Richardson file, LBNM)

RICHARDSON, NANCY CASTLEMAN (1783–1868)

Nancy Richardson and her husband, John, moved to Spencer County, Indiana, from Kentucky in 1817 and were early neighbors of the Lincoln family. Silas and

Joseph Richardson, both WHH informants, were her children. (Richardson file, LBNM; Nila Michel Papers, LBNM)

RICHARDSON, SILAS (1812–84)

Richardson lived on Thomas Lincoln's land in Spencer County after the Lincolns left Indiana for Illinois. He was a brother-in-law of WHH informants David Turnham and John S. Houghland. (*IPW,* February 2, 1884; *Federal Census, Spencer County, Ind.,* 1880; Richardson file, LBNM)

RIGGIN, AUGUSTUS KERR (1822–1903)

Riggin was a prosperous landowner in Menard County, the son of an early settler and founder of the town of Athens. He was an active Democrat until 1860. (James T. Hickey, "Three R's in Lincoln Education: Rogers, Riggin and Rankin," *JISHS* 52 [1959])

ROBY, ABSOLOM (CA. 1784–1870)

Of Maryland birth, Roby was living in Spencer County, Indiana, by 1828 and was a neighbor of the Lincolns. (*Spencer County [Ind.] Cemetery Inscriptions* [Rockport, Ind., 1987])

RODMAN, JESSE H. (1815–75)

Rodman, whose grandfather performed the marriage ceremony for AL's parents, lived in LaRue County, Kentucky, from 1838 until his death and called on AL during the Civil War to have his county's draft quota reduced. (Bessie Miller Elliott, *History of LaRue County, Kentucky* [N.p., n.d.]; Benningfield, 30)

ROE, EDWARD REYNOLDS (1813–93)

Roe was a physician and an early faculty member at Illinois Wesleyan University. Wounded in the Civil War, he returned to Bloomington in 1863, where he was elected circuit clerk in McLean County. *(HEI)*

ROMINE, JOHN (1806–88)

A near neighbor of the Lincolns in Spencer County, Indiana, Romine was a member of Little Pigeon Baptist Church and the son-in-law of the area's leading citizen, James Gentry of Gentryville. (*IPW,* March 24, 1888; Romine file, LBNM)

ROWBOTHAM, JOHN B.

Rowbotham was the illustrator of Barrett's *Life of Abraham Lincoln* and apparently a resident of Cincinnati.

RUTLEDGE, JAMES MCGRADY (1814–99)

Rutledge was a cousin of Ann Rutledge and said by family members to be her confidante when she was engaged to AL. He knew AL at New Salem and carried chain for him when he was surveying. For many years he evaded WHH's attempts to interview him about his cousin's love affair with AL. (Miller; Fern Nance Pond, ed., "The Memoirs of James McGrady Rutledge," *JISHS* 29 [1936])

RUTLEDGE, JASPER NEWTON (1837–1919)

A Menard County farmer and Republican officeholder, Rutledge was a first cousin of Ann Rutledge and the brother of James McGrady Rutledge. Born two years after his cousin's death, his knowledge of her love affair and engagement with AL came from his brother and others. (Miller; tombstone at Oakland Cemetery, Petersburg, Ill.)

RUTLEDGE, JOHN MILLER (1810–79)

The second child of Mary Ann and James Rutledge, one of the founders of New Salem, and the brother of Ann Rutledge. John Rutledge was living in New Salem in 1829 and during the Black Hawk War served as a private in AL's company. After the deaths of his father and sister in 1835, he and his family moved to Fulton County, Illinois, and later to Van Buren County, Iowa. (*CWTC;* Walsh; Whitney)

RUTLEDGE, ROBERT BRANNON (1819–81)

A younger brother of John and Ann Rutledge, he grew up in New Salem and knew AL there. Rutledge came into possession of the copy of Kirkham's *Grammar* that AL and Ann Rutledge were said to have used. In 1863 he was appointed federal provost marshal for Iowa and later became WHH's source for the Rutledge family's views and recollections. (*CWTC;* Walsh)

RYAN, MARGARET

A former domestic servant in the Lincoln home, Ryan was interviewed by JWW in Springfield. According to JWW she called on AL in the White House, but nothing further has been definitely learned about her. If she is the same person whose obituary appeared in *ISJ,* March 29, 1915, she was an Irish immigrant who was born about 1839.

SAWYER, ELIZABETH BUTTERFIELD (1827–1904)

Sawyer's father was Justin Butterfield, a Whig associate and sometime political rival of AL. She was the wife of Sidney Sawyer, a successful Chicago druggist. (*Federal Census, Cook County,* 1860; "Graceland Cemetery Records," Chicago)

SCOTT, JOHN MILTON (1832–98)

Scott practiced law in Bloomington and held local political offices in McLean County. He replaced David Davis on the bench of the Eighth Circuit in 1862 and in 1870 was elevated to the Illinois Supreme Court. (*NCAB; BEI*)

SCRIPPS, JOHN L. (1818–66)

In 1848 Scripps purchased an interest in the *Chicago Tribune,* becoming its principal editor. Upon selling his interest to a Whig group, he began publishing the

Daily Democratic Press in 1852. When the *Chicago Press and Tribune* was formed in 1858, Scripps again served as its senior editor. He composed a brief campaign biography of AL in 1860, for which AL answered questions about his early life and wrote out a biographical statement. AL appointed him Chicago postmaster in 1861. *(NCAB; ALE)*

SCROGGS, JOHN W. (1817–74)

Scroggs purchased the *Central Illinois Gazette* of Champaign in 1858 and was an early presidential supporter of AL. He was elected to the Illinois legislature in 1868 and served as a trustee of the University of Illinois from 1867 to 1869. (*University of Illinois Alumni Record* [1918]; Burt E. Powell, *Semi-Centennial History of the University of Illinois* [Urbana, Ill., 1918])

SELBY, PAUL (1825–1913)

While editor of the *Morgan Journal* in Jacksonville, Selby was active in organizing the Republican party of Illinois. He was a member of the Anti-Nebraska state convention that met in Springfield in 1854 and the Anti-Nebraska editorial convention that met in Decatur in 1856 to appoint the first Republican State Central Committee. *(HEI)*

SHANKS, JOHN PETER CLEAVER (1826–1901)

Shanks was elected to Congress in 1860 and served one term before volunteering for the Union army, after which he served a second term. (Rebecca A. Shepherd, Charles W. Calhoun, Elizabeth Shanahan-Shoemaker and Alan F. January, comps., *Biographical Directory of the Indiana General Assembly* [Indianapolis, 1980])

SHAW, J. HENRY (1825–85)

Shaw came to Illinois from Massachusetts in 1836 and eventually established a law practice at Beardstown. A talented writer and orator who later served in the Illinois House of Representatives, he appeared for the prosecution in the William "Duff" Armstrong murder case in 1858, the famous "almanac" case in which AL played the decisive role in gaining an acquittal for the son of his old friends Jack and Hannah Armstrong. (William Henry Perrin, ed., *History of Cass County, Ill.* [Chicago, 1880]; *Virginia [Ill.] Gazette,* August 17, 1885)

SHORT, JAMES (1807–74)

James Short's family settled very early in the New Salem area, and Short became one of AL's best friends. In bidding in AL's surveying equipment when it was auctioned off for debt and returning it to him, Short proved himself an important benefactor. Like AL, Short was a Whig in an area that was predominantly Democratic. When AL was elected president, he appointed Short agent for the Round Valley Indian Reservation in California. (*Petersburg Democrat,* February 21, 1874; Josephine Lynch Short, comp., *Short: An Early Virginia Family* [N.p., n.d.])

SHUTT, GEORGE (CA. 1832–93)

After moving to Springfield from Virginia, Shutt became a lawyer and involved in railroad development in Illinois. He was a neighbor of the Lincolns. (*ISJ,* October 4, 1893; *Leesburg [Va.] Mirror,* October 5, 1893)

SMITH, JAMES (1801–71)

A native of Glasgow, Scotland, Smith came to Springfield in 1849 to become pastor of the Second Presbyterian Church, where he served until 1856. He became acquainted with AL in 1850 when he conducted the funeral of AL's son Edward. Two years later MTL joined Smith's church. In 1863 Smith secured an appointment as U.S. consul at Dundee, Scotland, by appealing directly to MTL, who intervened on his behalf. (Albert Post, "Lincoln and the Reverend James Smith," *JISHS* 35 [1942]; Edgar DeWitt Jones, *Lincoln and the Preachers* [New York, 1948])

SMOOT, COLEMAN (1791 OR 1794–1876)

Smoot came to Sangamon County, Illinois, from Kentucky, settling in Indian Creek Precinct, where he became a successful farmer and stockraiser and served as its first justice of the peace. (Onstot; *HMMC;* letter from James P. Jones, March 13, 1993)

SPEARS, GEORGE (1805–92)

Spears was the son of a Kentucky slaveholder. After marrying in 1824, he migrated to Illinois with his wife, parents, and two former slaves. They settled in Clary's Grove, near what would later become the town of Tallula, and built one of the earliest brick homes in the region. (McKenzie; *HMMC*)

SPEARS, JOHN QUINCY (1828–1911)

Spears, a son of George Spears, farmed in Menard County, Illinois, and became a major landowner and merchant. (*HMMC; Petersburg Observer,* April 7, 1911)

SPEED, JOSHUA FRY (1814–82)

Speed has been called "Lincoln's only intimate friend." He was born of a prominent family near Louisville, Kentucky, and attended college for a year before moving to Springfield, Illinois, in 1835. He was a partner in a general store when AL moved to Springfield from New Salem in 1837 and began to share his lodgings over the store. Speed's store became a popular evening gathering place for the young men of the town, with AL often at the center of attention. Speed accompanied his socially awkward friend on visits to the Edwards home on "Quality Hill," where they met the Springfield belles of the day. Sharing similar temperaments and anxieties about women and marriage, Speed and AL's intense friendship survived a brief rivalry for the hand of Matilda Edwards before Speed returned to Kentucky in 1841. Speed helped AL through a period of suicidal depression following his breakup with Mary Todd in the winter of 1840–41, and AL returned the favor when Speed became apprehensive about his own forthcoming marriage in 1842. Speed made a fortune in the Louisville area in real estate and business and, though disturbed by the Emancipation Proclamation, remained loyal to the Lincoln administration during the Civil War. Speed's older brother, James, served as AL's second attorney general, from 1864 to 1865. (*ALE; BEK;* Douglas L. Wilson, "Abraham Lincoln and 'that fatal first of January,'" *Civil War History* 38:2 [June 1992])

STUART, JOHN TODD (1807–85)

Perhaps the person most responsible for AL's choice of law as a career, Stuart was born near Lexington, Kentucky, and was related to both Mary Todd and Stephen T. Logan. After graduation from Centre College and law study, Stuart moved to Springfield, Illinois, in 1828. He met AL in the Black Hawk War of 1832 and encouraged his political ambitions. When AL began his first term in the Illinois General Assembly in 1834, Stuart, then in his second term, served as AL's legislative mentor and encouraged him to study law. In 1837 AL moved from New Salem to Springfield to become Stuart's law partner and ran the firm single-handedly while Stuart was in Congress. Their partnership was dissolved amicably in 1841. Though both were strong Whigs and close political allies for many years, with the breakup of the Whig party in the 1850s AL and Stuart diverged. He declined to support AL either for the senate or the presidency and successfully ran for Congress as a Democrat in 1862. During the Civil War he supported the Union, though he was unsympathetic to emancipation. After the Civil War he was for years a director of the National Lincoln Monument Association. (*ALE; DAB*)

SUMNER, CHARLES (1811–74)

An outspoken senatorial advocate of equal rights for blacks and whites and a critic of AL's apparent tardiness in acting against slavery, Sumner nonetheless remained on friendly terms with the president. (*DAB; ALE*)

SWETT, LEONARD (1825–89)

A Maine native, Swett briefly attended Waterville (now Colby) College, leaving that institution to read law. After serving in the Mexican War he settled in Bloomington, Illinois, where in 1849 he met AL on the Eighth Judicial Circuit. Rising to become one of the most astute and sought-after lawyers in the state, Swett was at the same time a close legal and political associate of AL. He worked hard in 1860 and 1864 on behalf of AL's presidential nomination and renomination, and he also pressed David Davis's case for a seat on the U.S. Supreme Court. Although effective in promoting the political interests of others, Swett was awarded no political office of his own. He moved to Chicago in 1865, where he earned a reputation as a successful criminal lawyer. In 1875 he represented Robert Todd Lincoln in the latter's suit to have his mother declared insane. (*ALE; HEI*)

TAYLOR, GREEN B. (CA. 1819–?)

Taylor was the son of James Taylor, for whom AL reportedly worked as a farm hand and operator of a ferry across Anderson River, near its junction with the Ohio, in

1825. (Louis A. Warren, *Lincoln's Youth: Indiana Years, Seven to Twenty-One, 1816–1830* [Indianapolis, 1959])

TAYLOR, JAMES (1814–73)

Taylor was born in Christian County, Kentucky, and raised in Springfield, Illinois. Successively a resident of Petersburg, Springfield, and Beardstown, he served in the Black Hawk War and later as sheriff of Cass County, from 1850 to 1859. (Power; letter from Frances M. Winston, October 7, 1991)

TERRY, OLIVER C. (1834–1907)

Terry served as city treasurer and mayor of Mt. Vernon, Posey County, Indiana, where he interviewed Judge John Pitcher. (*History of Posey County, Ind.* [Chicago, 1886]; pension files, National Archives, Washington, D.C.)

THOMAS, WILLIAM (1802–89)

Thomas, a resident of Jacksonville, served in the Illinois Senate, the House, and as a circuit judge. (John F. Snyder, headnote to William Thomas, "The Winnebago War of 1827," *TISHS* [1907]; *BEI*)

THOMPSON, ELLA ARMSTRONG (CA. 1841–97)

The wife of Reverend E. J. Thompson, Ella Thompson served as scribe for Eliza Rumsey Francis in her abbreviated correspondence with WHH and JWW. (letter from Sandy McGuire, June 26, 1994)

TREAT, SAMUEL HUBBEL (1811–87)

Treat moved from New York to Springfield, where his success at the Sangamon County bar was so rapid that by 1839 he had been appointed to the bench of the Eighth Circuit. In 1841 he was appointed to the Illinois Supreme Court, where he sat until 1855, when he was appointed judge of the new federal district of southern Illinois. (*DAB*)

TURNEY, WILLIAM A.

Turney was clerk of the Second Grand Division of the Illinois Supreme Court from 1855 to 1870. (*Blue Book of Illinois* [Springfield, Ill., 1931])

TURNHAM, DAVID (1803–84)

A near neighbor and friend of AL in Indiana, Turnham claimed to have lent him books, including *Revised Statutes of Indiana*. First a farmer and later a merchant, he helped build the Little Pigeon Baptist Church, where AL's family worshiped. (letter from Barbara Hevron, January 25, 1992; Turnham file, LBNM)

ULRICH, BARLOW A. (1840–1930)

Ulrich was born in New York and raised in Springfield, Illinois. He received a law degree from the University of Michigan in 1864 and began practicing in Chicago, where he also engaged in the real estate business. (*NCAB*)

VAN BERGEN, PETER (1800–1879)

Considered one of Springfield's most prominent and influential citizens in its early days, Van Bergen came to Illinois in 1830 and dealt extensively in real estate in and around Springfield. A staunch Republican, he was once a demanding creditor but later a personal friend of AL. (Wallace)

VAN NATTAN, CLARISSA TUFT (1847–1929)

The Tuft family lived near the Lincolns in Springfield. Clarissa Tuft married Norman A. Van Nattan, a Civil War veteran and a farmer. (*HEI/Sangamon; ISJ*, January 6, 1929)

VINEYARD, BENJAMIN R. (1842–1905)

Vineyard's mother was Mary Owens Vineyard, the woman AL courted while at New Salem. He was also the nephew of another of WHH's informants, Elizabeth Abell, the sister of Mary Owens. Vineyard was an attorney in St. Joseph, Missouri, after the Civil War. (*Bench and Bar of St. Louis, Kansas City, Jefferson City, and Other Missouri Cities* [St. Louis and Chicago, 1887]; A. J. D. Stewart, ed., *The History of the Bench and Bar of Missouri* [St. Louis, 1898]; letter from Sue Horvath, August 11, 1994)

VINEYARD, MARY OWENS (1808–77)

Born in Green County, Mary Owens was a well-educated member of a wealthy Kentucky family. In 1833, while visiting her sister Elizabeth (Mrs. Bennett Abell), in New Salem, she first met AL. Three years later she renewed her acquaintance with AL, who had engaged with her sister to court Mary. In spite of disputes and differences, AL proposed marriage in the fall of 1837, but she rejected him, remarking later that "Mr. Lincoln was deficient in those little links which make up the great chain of woman[']s happiness." WHH heard of this courtship from other informants and persuaded Mary Owens Vineyard to share both her story and AL's letters to her. (*ALE;* R. Gerald McMurtry, appendix to McMurtry and Olive Carruthers, *Lincoln's Other Mary* [Chicago and New York, 1946])

VINEYARD, NANCY GRAHAM OWENS (?–1888)

Another sister of Mary Owens Vineyard, the two married brothers. (*The History of Refugio County, Texas, 1836–1986* [Dallas, 1985])

WALKER, WILLIAM F. (1820–98)

AL's co-counsel in the murder trial of William "Duff" Armstrong at Beardstown in 1858, Walker was a successful attorney in Havana, Illinois. The alleged murder took place in Mason County, where Havana is located, but the trial was moved to Beardstown in Cass County on a change of venue. (Helena Worner, *Walker's Grove* [N.p., 1965]; letter from William Reese Walker, January 15, 1993)

WALLACE, FRANCES TODD (1817–99)

Frances Todd, an older sister of MTL, came to Springfield from Kentucky to live with another sister, Elizabeth Edwards. Her marriage to Dr. William S. Wallace, a leading Springfield physician, in 1839 made room in the Edwards household for the younger sister, Mary. The Wallaces were present at the wedding of AL and Mary Todd at the Edwards home on November 4, 1842. (Wayne C. Temple, ed., *Mrs. Frances Jane Wallace Describes Lincoln's Wedding* [Harrowgate, Tenn., 1960]; *ISJ,* August 16, 1899)

WARNER, STEPHEN M. (1831–96)

A native of New England, Warner, along with Ferdinand Kohl of St. Louis, established the Centralia Iron and Nail Works in Centralia, Illinois. (*Centralia Sentinel,* April 16, 1896)

WARTMANN, JAMES W. (1832–1917)

Virginia-born Wartmann attended school in Cincinnati before moving to Spencer County, Indiana, where he practiced law in Rockport. In 1864 he moved to Evansville to serve as provost marshal and then commissioner of the board of enrollment. Though Wartmann apparently met AL in Washington, D.C., while on official business, he became WHH's first contact in Spencer County, Indiana, by being handed a letter that WHH had sent to Rockport addressed simply "Some Good Union Lawyer." (*Evansville Courier,* April 16, 1915; *Evansville Journal-News,* July 2 and 3, 1917)

WEBER, JOHN B. (1810–89)

Originally a cabinetmaker by trade, Weber was appointed copyist of the land records of Illinois in 1841, following a disabling accident. Like his brother George R. Weber, an editor of the *Illinois State Register* in Springfield, John B. Weber began political life as a Democrat but converted to Republicanism following the Kansas-Nebraska Act. (Power; *HSC;* burial record card, Oak Ridge Cemetery, Springfield, Ill.)

WELDON, LAWRENCE (1829–1905)

In 1854 Weldon moved to Clinton, Illinois, and thereafter practiced law on the Eighth Judicial Circuit with AL. In 1861 AL appointed him U.S. district attorney for the Southern District of Illinois. Later he practiced in Bloomington and served as associate justice of the U.S. Court of Claims. (*HEI; New York Times,* April 11, 1905)

WENTWORTH, JOHN (1815–88)

After arriving in Chicago in 1836, "Long John" Wentworth became editor and then proprietor of the *Chicago Democrat.* A Democratic congressman in 1843–51 and 1853–55, he bolted from the party after the repeal of the Missouri Compromise and joined the Republicans. Elected mayor of Chicago in 1857 and again in 1860, he aggressively supported AL's administration during the Civil War, even though relations between the two men were never cordial. *(HEI; DAB)*

WHITE, HORACE (1834–1916)

Born in New Hampshire, White moved with his family to Beloit, Wisconsin, in 1838 after his father founded the town. He graduated from Beloit College in 1853 and moved to Chicago, where he began a long journalistic career. In 1858 he reported the Lincoln-Douglas debates for the partisan Republican newspaper *Chicago Press and Tribune,* and during the Civil War he served as the paper's Washington, D.C., correspondent. After the war he bought an interest in the *Tribune,* serving as its editor in chief from 1865 to 1874. In 1884 he purchased an interest in the *New York Evening Post,* becoming its chief editor in 1899. He was instrumental in finding a publisher for the second edition (1892) of WHH's and JWW's biography of AL and contributed a chapter on the debates. *(NCAB; DAB)*

WHITEHURST, STEPHEN S. (1828–75)

In 1848 Whitehurst became editor of a Springfield temperance paper, the *Illinois Organ.* The next year he married Maria C. Matheny, the sister of AL's friend James Matheny. Later he served as deputy circuit clerk in Sangamon County and in the 1860s as circuit clerk. (Power; *HSC;* letter from Terence A. Tanner, January 6, 1993)

WHITNEY, HENRY CLAY (1831–1905)

Whitney came to Urbana, Illinois, in 1854 and practiced law with AL on the Eighth Judicial Circuit for the next seven years. Shortly after his inauguration AL appointed Whitney a paymaster of volunteers, a position he held until March 1865. After the war Whitney practiced law in Kansas and then moved to Chicago, where he was associated with Walter B. Scates, former justice of the Illinois Supreme Court. In 1892 he published a memoir, *Life on the Circuit with Lincoln.* (Paul M. Angle, "Introduction," in Henry Clay Whitney, *Life on the Circuit with Lincoln* [1892; rpt., Caldwell, Idaho, 1940]; Francis B. Heitman, *Historical Register and Dictionary of the United States Army* [Washington, D.C., 1903])

WICKIZER, JOHN H. (1821–89)

A Pennsylvania-born legal colleague of AL on the Eighth Judicial Circuit, Wickizer came to Bloomington in 1847, where he served as mayor and represented McLean County in the Illinois legislature for several terms. During and after the Civil War he held a variety of federal appointments under Republican administrations. (*Transactions of the McLean County Historical Society* 2 [1903]; *The History of McLean County, Ill.* [Chicago, 1879])

WILDER, DANIEL WEBSTER (1832–1911)

Born and raised in Massachusetts, Wilder graduated from Harvard in 1856, studied law at Harvard Law School, and was admitted to the bar in Boston in 1857. He then went west, editing outspoken Republican newspapers in Kansas and Missouri. In 1863 AL appointed him surveyor-general of Kansas and Nebraska. (*NCAB;* William E. Connelley, "Daniel W. Wilder, the Father of Kansas History and Literature," *Collections of the Kansas State Historical Society* 16 [1923–25])

WILSON, HENRY (1812–75)

A Massachusetts politician who nourished a hatred of slavery, Wilson left the Whigs to help found the Free-Soil party in 1848. As a member of the American (Know-Nothing) party in 1854, he again led a revolt over an evasive stand on slavery. Wilson was elected in 1855 to the U.S. Senate, where he chaired its Committee on Military Affairs during the Civil War and constantly urged AL to proclaim emancipation. He was vice president of the United States under Ulysses S. Grant from 1873 to 1875, when he died in office. *(DAB)*

WILSON, JOSEPH S.

Wilson was commissioner of the General Land Office in 1860–61 and again in 1866–71, serving as chief clerk in the interim. (Vernon Carstensen, *The Public Lands: Studies in the History of the Public Domain* [Madison, Wis., 1963])

WILSON, ROBERT L. (1805–80)

Of Pennsylvania birth, Wilson graduated from Franklin College in Ohio and moved to Sangamon County, Illinois, in 1833. In 1836 he was elected from Sangamon County to the Illinois House of Representatives where, with AL, he was one of the celebrated "Long Nine" who successfully brought the Illinois capital to Springfield. In 1840 Wilson moved to Whiteside County, Illinois, where he was appointed clerk of the circuit court, a position he held for twenty years. During the Civil War he was appointed a paymaster by AL. (*The Biographical Record of Whiteside County, Ill.* [Chicago, 1900])

WILSON, WILLIAM L.

A William Wilson served in the Black Hawk War in a Schuyler County company that belonged to the same regiment as the company AL commanded. (Whitney)

WINTERSMITH, ROBERT LAWRENCE (1816–90)

A rare Kentucky Republican, Wintersmith was in the mercantile business in Elizabethtown and Louisville, as well as in New Albany, Indiana. *(BEK; WWWHC)*

WOOD, WILLIAM (1784–1867)

After migrating from Maryland by way of Kentucky, Wood settled in Indiana territory by 1812. As occupant of a farm a mile and a half north of the Lincoln farm, Wood was a relatively close neighbor. (*Spencer County Census,* 1850; Nila Michel Papers, cemetery inscriptions, Wood file, LBNM)

WORTHAM, H. C.

Wortham was clerk of the Coles County Circuit Court in 1864–72. *(HCC)*

WRIGHT, ASA D. (1811–71)

Wright was a New Yorker who came to Menard County, Illinois, in the early 1830s. He served in the Mexican War and was involved in civic and business affairs in and around Petersburg. (*IAMM;* Miller; pension files, National Archives, Washington, D.C.)

ZANE, CHARLES SHUSTER (1831–1915)

New Jersey–born Zane moved to Sangamon County during his youth. He attended McKendree College in Lebanon, Illinois, from 1852 to 1855 and in 1856 began to study law with James C. Conkling. He was admitted to the Illinois bar the next year and in 1861 began practicing with WHH when AL left for Washington, D.C. After leaving WHH's office, Zane served as register of the Springfield Land Office, was the partner of Shelby Cullom (1870–73), and later served as chief justice of Utah Territory. He was married to Margaret Maxcy, a niece of WHH. *(DAB; NCAB)*

Appendix:
Brief Outline of the Joseph Hanks Family*

Paul H. Verduin

JOSEPH HANKS (1725–1793), a great-grandfather of President Lincoln, lived in Richmond County, Virginia, where he was a plantation overseer and tenant farmer. Migrated to Mercer County, Kentucky 1784, to Nelson County 1787. Children with his wife Ann "Nanny" Lee (c.1742–c.1794):

A. THOMAS HANKS (c.1759–c.1835).

B. JOSHUA HANKS (c.1762–c.1835).

C. WILLIAM HANKS (c.1765–1851/52). Moved to Spencer County, Indiana, c.1825–26, where he was a neighbor of young Lincoln for a year or two. To Sangamon County, Illinois c.1827; to Macon County c.1829. Neighbor of Abraham Lincoln's there 1830–31.

Children with wife Elizabeth Hall, sister of Levi Hall:

1. Nancy Hanks.

2. James Hanks.

3. William Hanks, Jr.

4. CHARLES HANKS (c.1798–c.1865). Published anti-Lincoln article in *Decatur* (Ill.) *Magnet* during the 1860 campaign.

5. Elizabeth Hanks. Her first husband Reason Ray settled in Sangamon County 1823. After his 1833 death married 1837 Samuel Dillon.

6. JOHN HANKS (1802–1889). Born in Kentucky, but resided intermittently in Indiana household of President Lincoln's father c.1822–26. Married 1826 Susan Malinda Wilson (1804–1863) in Kentucky. To Macon County, Illinois in 1828. Split rails with Lincoln there 1830, built a flatboat with him in Sangamon County 1831, had occasional personal, legal, and political contact with him until inauguration in 1861.

7. Sarah Hanks.

8. Joseph Hanks.

9. Lucinda Hanks.

---

*The editors believe that Mr. Verduin's account of the elusive Hanks family is the best available and are grateful to him for permitting a brief outline of his findings to be published here.

10. Celia Hanks.

11. Andrew Jackson Hanks (1815–1889).

D. *LUCEY HANKS* (c.1767–c.1833?). President Lincoln's maternal grandmother. Born Richmond County, Virginia. According to Herndon, Lincoln said Lucey became pregnant in Virginia by someone Herndon called
a "nobleman of Virginia," or "well-bred Virginia planter," an account both
credited and challenged by various Lincoln biographers. The child, born
about 1783–84, was President Lincoln's mother.

 Lucey Hanks presumably migrated to Kentucky with parents 1784. She
was accused by a Mercer County grand jury of "fornication," 1789. Case
discontinued when Henry Sparrow obtained marriage license, 1790. They
were married by Baptist elder 1791. Resided near Mitchellsburg, Kentucky,
in part of Mercer County that in 1841 became Boyle County. According
to Dennis Hanks, Lucey died "in 1833, as well as I Recollect—Not positive," an estimate supported by census data. Henry Sparrow obtained a
Revolutionary War pension, died in 1841.

Lucey's child, according to Herndon by a "nobleman of Virginia":

1. *NANCY HANKS* (c.1783–1818), married June 12, 1806 Thomas
    Lincoln (c.1776–1851) in Washington County, Kentucky.
    Children born in Hardin County, Kentucky:
    a. SARAH LINCOLN (Feb. 10, 1807–Jan. 20, 1828). Married
        Aug. 2, 1826 Aaron Grigsby in Spencer County, Indiana.
        Died in childbirth.
    b. ABRAHAM LINCOLN (1809–1865). Sixteenth President
        of the U. S.
    c. Thomas Lincoln. Died in early infancy, c.1811–12.

Lucey's child with an unknown man in Kentucky:

2. Sarah Hanks (c.1787–c.1854).
    Sarah's Kentucky-born illegitimate children were:
    a. Sophia Hanks (1809–1893). Until 1818 she lived with Eliz-
        abeth and Thomas Sparrow, her mother's aunt and uncle.
        After their death, resided in Spencer County, Indiana with
        Abraham Lincoln in Thomas Lincoln household.
    b. Greenberry Hanks (c.1812–1842).
    c. Creed Harris Hanks (c.1816–185?).
    d. Samuel Haden Hanks (1820–1898).
    e. Margaret Hanks (c.1823–c.1877). Married Jackson Legrand
        of Dubois County, Indiana.
    f. James Anderson Hanks (c.1825–1862).

Lucey Hanks' children with Henry Sparrow—all lived in Kentucky:

3. Polly Sparrow.
4. Rev. James Sparrow.
5. Betsy Sparrow.

6. Peggy Sparrow.
7. Thomas Sparrow.
8. Rev. Henry Sparrow.
9. George Sparrow.
10. Lucindy Sparrow.

E. CHARLES HANKS (c.1770–c.1828).

F. ELIZABETH HANKS (1771–1818). Married 1796 Mercer County, Kentucky, Thomas Sparrow (c.1770–1818), brother of her sister Lucey's husband. Resided in Mercer and Hardin Counties, Kentucky. Since they were childless, they acted as foster parents at various times for three illegitimate children in the Hanks clan: Nancy Hanks (President Lincoln's mother), Dennis Hanks, and Sophia Hanks. In 1817 followed Lincolns to Spencer County, Indiana. Elizabeth and her husband died of the milk-sickness, as did President Lincoln's mother, in 1818.

G. MARY (POLLY) HANKS (c.1773–c.1821). Married 1795 Jesse Friend in Hardin County, Kentucky. He was a brother of Charles Friend, the natural father of Dennis Hanks.

H. NANCY HANKS (c.1780–c.1829). Since this Nancy Hanks—Dennis Hanks's mother—was perhaps only four years older than her namesake niece, President Lincoln's mother, the two were often confused in later family traditions. After having Dennis Hanks out of wedlock, Nancy married in 1802 in Green County Levi Hall, brother of William Hanks's wife Elizabeth. Resided in the counties of Hardin, Green, and Grayson. About 1825 accompanied William Hanks's family to Spencer County, Indiana, where young Abraham Lincoln and her natural son Dennis Hanks were living. About 1829, both Nancy Hanks Hall and her husband Levi died of the milk-sickness, the disease that killed President Lincoln's mother and Elizabeth and Thomas Sparrow eleven years earlier.

Nancy Hanks Hall's child with Charles Friend:

1. DENNIS HANKS (1799–1892). President Lincoln's cousin-once-removed, foster brother, and step-brother-in-law. Born in Hardin County, Kentucky, and raised there by Elizabeth and Thomas Sparrow, his aunt and uncle. Acquainted with President Lincoln all of Lincoln's life, he lived in the Thomas Lincoln household with him 1818–21. A farmer in Indiana, he accompanied Thomas Lincoln in his migrations to Macon County and Coles County, Illinois. In the mid-1830's moved to Charleston in Coles County, where he became a shoemaker and resided most of the rest of his life. He married 1821 in Indiana Sarah Elizabeth Johnston (1807–1864), President Lincoln's step-sister, the oldest daughter of Daniel Johnston and his wife Sarah Bush, who in 1818 became the second wife of Thomas Lincoln. Their children who survived childhood were:

    a.   Sarah Jane Hanks (1822–1907).

    b.   John Talbot Hanks (1823–1915). Settled in California, then Oregon.

    c.   Nancy Hanks (1824–?).

    d.   HARRIET HANKS (1826–1915). Resided in the Abraham Lincoln household in Springfield, Illinois in 1844–46, while attending school. Married 1847 Col. Augustus H. Chapman of Coles County.

    e.   Amanda Hanks (1833–?).

    f.   Mary Hanks.

    g.   Charles Hanks (1841–1870).

    h.   Theophilus Hanks (1849–?).

Children of Nancy Hanks Hall with her husband, Levi Hall:

  2. William Hall.

  3. SQUIRE HALL (c.1805–1851). Married Matilda Johnston (b.1809), step-sister of President Lincoln and younger daughter of Daniel Johnston and his wife Sarah Bush, who became the second wife of Thomas Lincoln. In 1856, after Squire Hall died, Matilda married Reuben Moore. The children of Squire Hall and Matilda Johnston were:

    a.   John Johnston Hall (1829–1909).

    b.   Nancy Ann Hall (1832–?).

    c.   Elizabeth Jane Hall (1837–?).

    d.   Alfred L. Hall (1839–?).

    e.   Sarah Louisa Hall (1841–1935).

    f.   Joseph A. Hall.

    g.   Amanda Hall.

    h.   Harriet Hall.

  4. Lydia Hall. Deceased by 1858.

  5. Alfred G. Hall.

  6. Joseph Hall (1814–186_). Chose brother Squire Hall as his guardian in Coles County, Illinois court, Sept. 29, 1831. Squire Hall was appointed guardian of the children below:

  7. Mahala Hall (b.1817).

  8. Letitia Hall (b.1819).

I. JOSEPH HANKS, JR. (c.1784–1856). According to a daughter-in-law and a grandson, after his mother's death about 1794 he was returned from Kentucky to Hardy County (now in West Virginia), where he was raised by one of his two much-older brothers, either Thomas Hanks or Joshua Hanks. He returned to Kentucky about 1798, and according to these same sources and Dennis Hanks, was employed in the same carpentry shop in Elizabethtown, Kentucky where Thomas Lincoln worked. Resided in Hardin County 1805–14. In 1810 married Mary Young (1793–1872). In 1815 migrated to Crawford County, Indiana, and in 1825 to Sangamon

County, Illinois. In 1828, three years before young Abraham Lincoln arrived in that place, he moved to Adams County, Illinois, and with his wife spent his remaining years there.

The children of Joseph Hanks, Jr. and his wife Mary Young were:

1. Jacob Vertrees Hanks (1812–1894).
2. Elizabeth Hanks (1813–1830).
3. Susanna Hanks (1816–before 1826).
4. Nancy Hanks (1818–1890).
5. John Henry Hanks (1822–after 1894).
6. Joseph Hanks (1825–after 1894).
7. Mary Ann Hanks (1827–after 1894).
8. Amaltha Jane Hanks (1830–1891).
9. Isabelle Hanks (1833–after 1894).
10. Caroline Hanks (1836–after 1894).

Compiled January 1995

Index

AL = Abraham Lincoln
MTL = Mary Todd Lincoln

WHH = William H. Herndon

Note: Only those members of AL's mother's family referred to by WHH's informants are included here; others are listed in the appendix (pp. 779–83).

DOUGLAS L. WILSON, formerly George A. Lawrence Professor of English at Knox College, is Saunders Director of the International Center for Jefferson Studies at Monticello and the author of *Lincoln before Washington: New Perspectives on the Illinois Years* (1997).

RODNEY O. DAVIS, Szold Distinguished Service Professor of History and chairman of the American studies program at Knox College, is the editor of Thomas Ford's *History of Illinois* (1995).

TERRY WILSON, Assistant in Reference and Special Collections, Knox College Library, is the author of papers on the early legal history of Illinois.

PAUL H. VERDUIN is an independent scholar who has been researching for a decade the social history of Abraham Lincoln's immediate forebears. His findings will appear in *Blood of the Lash, Blood of the Sword* (forthcoming).